"The best all-around guide for North America, hands down."

Covering almost every resort in North America, this book is the most comprehensive out there. (Seven pages devoted to Ski Santa Fe?) Long on restaurant and hotel suggestions, it's also useful for getting off the beaten path. You may have skied Lake Tahoe many times, but only a local would send you over to Diamond Peak for tree skiing in Solitude Canyon. The best all-around guide for North America, hands down.

—*Ski Magazine*

"For anyone wanting to find out about and explore the full variety of North American skiing, ... SkiSnowboard America is better. As a reader, I like a book I can use while traveling, for booking a room or dinner. Is this too much to ask? Charles Leocha puts his readers first. Other guides would be better if they followed his example."

—*The Sunday Telegraph*

"...a no-holds-barred look at ski resorts. Unlike snazzy brochures that claim their respective resorts are perfect for everyone, this guide offers the lowdown on which places are better for families, singles, honeymooners, beginners and experts."

—*The Gannett Newspapers*

"Ski vacationers will want to look at Ski Snowboard America and Ski Snowboard Europe."

—*Consumer Reports Travel Letter*

"...a personal-experience feel, with insider tips."

—*USA Today*

"...convenient, indepth and portable...provides the down and dirty basics on major resorts."

—*Skiing Magazine*

"Up-to-the-minute info, so accurate that even ski resort personnel peruse these pages. Th only guidebook you'll ever need. The latest edition is packed chockablock with detailed information about the ski experience at every major resort in the United States and Canada."

—*Robb Report*

"Charlie Leocha is first a skier, then a writer. He shuns the party line of the big ski corporations, preferring instead to talk to locals. *Ski Snowboard America*'s perspective is direct, credible, and no-holds-barred."

—*Daily Record, NJ*

"The flavor, feel and personality of each resort."

—*The Boston Globe*

Thanks

No project as complex as this can be completed by
a single person or team without help from others.

•

Thank you to the public relations personnel at each of the ski resorts
reviewed in these pages: they carefully check facts,
phone numbers, prices and programs
even though they don't always agree with our reviews.

•

Thank you to Auto Europe for arranging automobile rentals
for the Ski Snowboard America and Canada and Ski Snowboard Europe staff
whenever they travel to Canada or Europe.
If you are planning to rent a car abroad,
this company is a secret all travelers
should know about — 800-223-5555.

•

And thank you to Travel Alberta International and Banff Lake Louise Tourism,
Sunshine Village, Ski Banff@Norquay and Lake Louise Ski Area
for hosting our January 2008 editorial conference.

SKI SNOWBOARD AMERICA

by Charles A. Leocha

Steve Giordano, Editor

Mitch Kaplan, Eastern Editor

Lynn Rosen, Western Editor

with

Peggy McKay Shinn, Karen Cummings

Claudia Carbone, Hilary Nangle,

Roger Lohr, Tom Patterson, Phil Johnson, Iseult Devlin

Bill Novak, Vicki Andersen, Diane Scholfield, Vanessa Reese

James Kitfield , Andrew Bill, Chris Elliott, Kari Haugeto

WORLD LEISURE CORPORATION

Hampstead, NH

Help us do a better job

Research for this book is an ongoing process. We have been at it for almost two decades. Each year we revisit many of these resorts, and every winter we speak with locals from every resort.

If you find a new restaurant, hotel, bar or dance club that you feel we should include, please let us know. If you find anything in these pages that is misleading or has changed, please let us know. If we use your suggestion, we will send you a copy of next year's edition.

Send your suggestions and comments to:

Steve Giordano, Editor *Ski Snowboard America*

World Leisure Corporation

Box 160, Hampstead NH 03841, USA

or send e-mail to

steve@skisnowboard.com

Distributed to the trade in the U.S.A. by
Midpoint Trade Books, Inc., 27 W. 20th Street, Suite 1102,
New York, NY 10011, Tel. (212) 727-0190, fax (212) 727-0195.
Internet: www.midpointtradebooks.com; E-mail sales: midpointny@aol.com

Distributed to the trade in the U.K. by
Portfolio Books Ltd: Suite 3 & 4 Great West House, Great West Road,
Brentford, Middlesex, TW8 9DF
Tel. 0208 326 5620 Fax. 0208 326 5621.
Internet: www.portfoliobooks.com

Mail Order, Catalog, other International sales and rights, and Special Sales by
World Leisure Corporation, PO Box 160, Hampstead, NH 03841.
Tel. (617) 569-1966, fax (419) 828-0119.
E-mail: admin@worldleisure.com; Internet: www.skisnowboard.com

Contents
by geographical regions

Western U.S. Resorts

Contributors

Charlie Leocha has skied virtually every major international resort. He writes about travel and skiing for magazines, newspapers and the Internet. Charlie is a black-diamond skier, but a double-diamond apres-skier. The rest of us bow to his energy and dancing ability. He's also the only staffer who knows which resorts have the best wine lists *and* the best bacon-and-eggs breakfasts. He is a member of the North American Snowsports Journalists Association (NASJA).

Steve Giordano is a veteran ski and travel journalist whose work has appeared in newspapers, magazines, books, radio and television. He used to be a ski patroller, but switched to ski journalism after pulling one too many drunks out of snowy creeks. A skier for more than 20 years, he switched to snowboarding long after reaching adulthood. He is a member of NASJA and SATW. He's also married to Lynn Rosen, and together they make sure our Northwest entries are up to date.

Lynn Rosen, an Emmy award-winning television and radio broadcaster, producer and director, is on the Journalism faculty at Western Washington University in Bellingham. She's also a theater critic and travel writer. Mountain scenery is quite dramatic, so it's fitting that Lynn belongs to the American Theater Critics Association as well as NASJA. She is one of the staff champion shoppers, an advocate for unique jewelry, shoes and clothing.

Mitch Kaplan took up the pen to support his inexhaustible ski habit and has been covering skiing, adventure and family travel ever since. He holds the unofficial New Jersey state record for the most consecutive days spent dreaming about playing in the snow. The author of several books and a member of NASJA, SATW and ASJA, he writes a ski column for *The Record*, New Jersey's second-largest daily. Mitch lives with his non-skiing wife, Penny, and two college-age children who won't empty the nest.

Claudia Carbone lives in Denver in her native state of Colorado. For her, a great day is dancing through knee-deep powder. Claudia writes for many publications. Her groundbreaking book, *WomenSki*, established her as an authority on women's skiing. Claudia is a founder of Snow Sports Association for Women and is the recipient of the Lowell Thomas Award from Colorado Ski Country and NASJA's Excellence in Snowsports Journalism–Writing award. She also is past president of NASJA.

Hilary Nangle realized early in life that work didn't have to be drudgery. Much to her parents' dismay, she spent years working for whitewater rafting companies and ski resorts, before finally landing a real job as a journalist. She now freelances for travel and ski publications and appears as a TV travel expert. She's a member of NASJA (and has won its Excellence in Snowsports Journalism award), and the Society of American Travel Writers (SATW). Hilary lives in Maine with her husband, Tom, a photographer.

Peggy McKay Shinn, a Westerner at heart, is now a resident Vermonter. She has skied at most major U.S. resorts, where she seeks out terrain that makes the rest of us grow weak in the knees. A NASJA member, she cast aside a graduate degree in environmental engineering to write full time. She gives us the real scoop on child-care and nursery facilities. Much to her mother's dismay, motherhood has not slowed Peggy down.

Karen Cummings has been writing about skiing for more than a decade. She lives life, balanced between Boston, Kentucky and Maine, with a smile. Karen began skiing at the tender age of 25 and immediately discovered apres-ski—her specialty. These days her nightlife forays are "research." Karen is an expert shopper and has bought something at every resort she visits. She is also our cross-country aficionado who loves a workout with skating skis and a new expert on skiing with her grandson.

Bill Novak, our snowboarding expert, is originally from Pennsylvania. He moved to Utah in search of deep powder and big mountains. Since the mid '90s, he has been spending the off seasons snowboarding, surfing, and globe trotting. This passion for snow and surf is what guided Bill's career direction. He teaches and guides skiers and riders almost every day during the season. His focus the snowboarding terrain, terrain parks and halfpipes at what ever resort he visits.

Tom Patterson spends equal time on his board, skis and skinny skis, the latter usually with daughter Ella in a baby carrier. He is a NASJA member and skis all over northern New England and Quebec. He spends his days in the exciting world of student loans, but his passion includes regular snowsports contributions to weekly and monthly publications near his home in Portland, Maine.

Vicki Andersen is a native Oregonian residing in Portland, and admits to first strapping on skis at age 2. By high school graduation she had been a regional correspondent for *SKI Magazine* and written a weekly newspaper ski column. She has been ski editor-*Northwest Sports Report*, contributing editor-*Texas Skis*, regional editor-*Pacific Skier,* associate editor-*Northwest Skiing* and staff writer-*Ski Oregon*, as well as producing countless articles for other publications. Vicki is a member of NASJA, SATW, and NOWA (Northwest Outdoor Writers Assn).

Roger Lohr, our cross-country skiing guru, lives in New Hampshire. His claim to fame: He's traveled and been on the snow either cross-country skiing, telemarking or snowboarding in 27 different states or provinces in North America. He edits our sister website, XCSkiResorts.com, which provides information about where to go cross-country skiing, Top 10 lists and promotional news for cross-country ski resorts and product suppliers. He also conducts the industry statistics for the Cross Country Ski Areas Association; and writes for *Ski Area Management, Nordic Network* and many regional magazines.

Vanessa Reese considers herself to be the world's first "black-diamond virtual skier." She works on *Ski Snowboard America and Canada* and *Ski Europe* and helped develop our website. Until a few years ago, the closest this Harvard graduate had ever come to a ski slope was Boston's blizzard of '78. Now she's visited several Western resorts, taken her first halting glides on cross-country skis, and discovered snow tubing and dogsledding.

Laurie Fullerton is a journalist specializing in skiing and yatching — nice combination. She has edited magazines and newspapers and authored three guidebooks covering the Canadian Maritimes, New Caledonia and the Philipines. Her byline has appeared in the *South China Morning Post, New York Times, Miami Herald, Yatching Magazine, Sailing Magazine, Torronto Globe and Post* and others.

Phil Johnson is an ex-president of NASJA, lives in upstate New York and has written travel, outdoor and ski columns for the regional papers for years.

Iseult Devlin, a former editor at *Skiing Magazine* and *Skiing Trade News*, is now a freelance writer. She has written about winter sports and gear for *Sports Illustrated for Women, Outside, Skiing for Women, Ski, Skiing* and other publications. Devlin is also the author of, *Winter Sports, A Ragged Mountain Press Woman's Guide* and raced on her college ski team.

Andy Bill has been fighting with, and losing to, his inner nomad for at least 25 years—working as a journalist on three continents. Along the way he has contributed to America's leading travel publications. Recent exploits include becoming the 12,161st member of the Sourtoe Cocktail Club (an august, if unsavory, society based out of Dawson City in the Yukon), surviving another ski season, and picking up a Northern Lights award. As an avid, if erratic skier, he has left his mark on many a tree.

James Kitfield is an expert apres-skier who first met Charlie dancing in a conga line through a bar in Verbier, Switzerland. Life has been downhill since, at least as often as he can manage trips to the mountains. On the slopes he points his skis down double diamonds. Amazingly, he has a serious side. He has been awarded the Gerald R. Ford prize twice for distinguished defense reporting, and the Jesse H. Neal award for excellence in reporting.

Kari Haugeto and **Christopher Elliott** live in Florida, but spend all winter dreaming about powder days in the mountains. Kari writes about apres-ski and nightlife activities as the editor of Cocktail. com. And Christopher, who writes about consumer and business travel issues for publications such as *The New York Times, National Geographic Traveler* and *Forbes*, covers mountain activities.

Both **Susan Staples** and **Diane Scholfield** the ex-editors and proof readers, have their fingerprints and commas all over this book.

Plan your winter vacation
with Ski Snowboard America

Here's a book to help you branch out and to find the perfect ski resort (plus accommodations, restaurants and nightlife) to match your ability, your pocketbook and your interests. For over-seas skiers, *Ski Snowboard America* offers insights to help you locate the resort that matches your dream of a North American ski vacation.

Not surprisingly, people take ski vacations for different reasons—for a romantic getaway, to have quality time with the family, to ski all-out with buddies, to ski a little and maybe shop a lot. And what happens when a hotshot skier travels with a first-timer or beginner? The average ski resort's brochure indicates that their resort is all things to all skiers—this is definitely not the case.

Ski Snowboard America is as straightforward and honest a guide to North America's top resorts as you can buy. Our goal is to match you with the right vacation spot. Our staff includes experts and intermediates (including some who learned as adults), Generation Xers and Baby Boomers, skiers and snowboarders, eggs-and-bacon breakfast eaters and gourmet-coffee-and-bagel fans. Each skier and snowboarder has various likes and dislikes, and resorts have different personalities. We recognize this—that's why we include our opinions and personal observations. We detail the personality of each resort: where we found the best skiing and snowboarding, where we liked to eat and where we enjoyed the liveliest off-slope fun. And we give you the facts and current prices, plus hotel and restaurant descriptions, lift ticket and lesson prices, children's programs, nightlife hot spots, and where to call, e-mail or write for more information.

What's new in this edition

Of course, prices, programs, lessons and facilities have been updated to provide the most ac-curate information available at press time about each resort. Some resorts have been completely transformed through new developments and new hotels.

The Alberta, Canada, chapters were completely rewritten after our staff held its annual editorial meeting in the Banff/Lake Louise region this past winter. We skied, stayed and dined

---

A note about prices and older editions of this book

We make every attempt to include prices for the current ski season. Unfortunately, as of late August many resorts had not announced their new prices. Current prices have the 2008/09 notation. Where there is no notation, assume prices are from last season (2007/08). The text will normally specify which season. In recent years, ski resorts have created lift ticket prices for every occasion: prices for various age groups, various days, various times of the season, supermarket discounts, ad infinitum. It's getting to be just as complicated to purchase lift tickets as it is to buy your airline tickets.

Prices in this guidebook are in no way official and are subject to change at any time. In fact, prices do change with different seasons; and resorts sometimes announce one price in July, change it by November, and change prices again during the season. Check our website, *www.skisnowboard.com* for the latest prices.

Ski Snowboard America is published every fall, but sometimes bookstores have older copies in their inventory. If you are reading this book in Fall 2009 or after, get the latest edition. It can be found in most major bookstores or order it through www.amazon.com or www.barnesandnoble.com.

---

at all resorts and visited local area museums, lodgings, bistros, restaurants and nightspots and individually fanned out to many of the rest. During the rest of winter, staff visited more than two dozen other resorts and updated and rewrote those chapters accordingly.

Keeping up with area code, resort, hotel, restaurant and price changes always keeps us busy. There are literally thousands of changes to the book each year.

Using the Internet–SkiSnowboard.com & XCSkiResorts.com

The development of the Internet has significantly changed the way people research and make reservations at ski resorts. Every world-class resort now has a website with basic information including statistics, lift tickets, ski school prices, and how to contact them. You even can book online on some of the more savvy resort sites.

We have gathered more information than we can possibly stuff into this guidebook, so if you want to know more about any of the resorts we review here, visit our websites, SkiSnowboard.com and XCSkiResorts.com. There you'll find additional facts, advice and words of wisdom; often you'll find out more about a resort than at the resort's own site. Indeed, few resorts work to promote the surrounding areas, but SkiSnowboard.com offers details about the surrounding areas as well as much more economical lodging and dining options. As prices change at each resort, we'll post that information.

We have included the Web addresses for every resort listed in this book. Use them as well as SkiSnowboard.com and XCSkiResorts.com to get the information you need.

Chapter organization

Each resort chapter has several sections. We begin by sketching the personality of the place—is it old and quaint, or modern and high-rise? Clustered at the base of the slopes, or a few miles down the road? Remote and isolated, or freeway-close? Family-oriented or catering to singles? Filled with friendly faces or an aloof herd of "beautiful" skiers?

The basic statistics of each resort include **addresses and phone numbers:** postal, e-mail, Internet, snow phones, toll-free—all of them that we could find.

The **base and summit altitudes** are important for those with altitude-related medical difficulties or for sea-level dwellers who plan to hit the slopes the same day they arrive. **Vertical drop, skiable acreage** and **number and types of lifts** provide a good idea of the resort's size.

Our terrain stats reflect *lift-served* terrain. Examples: Keystone, Colo., lists its vertical as 3,128 feet; we list it as 2,630. If you want that maximum vertical, you must take a snowcat or hike the extra 498 feet to the in-bounds summit. Grand Targhee has two mountains totaling 3,000 acres, but 1,000 of that acreage is reserved for snowcat skiing and snowboarding. Exceptions like these are explained where they occur.

Uphill lift capacity is the number of riders the lift system can carry each hour. **Bed base** is the approximate number of people who can be accommodated overnight near the resort. If the uphill capacity is much bigger than the bed base, the result is usually shorter lift lines. (Resorts with great uphill capacity/bed base ratios may still have long weekend lines if they are near major cities—we try to identify these.)

We tell you how close the **nearest lodging** is, if the resort has **child care** and the youngest age accepted, and the number of **terrain parks and pipes.** The **lift ticket** price in the fact box tells the per-day range of the adult lift ticket. The lower price usually is the per-day cost of the adult five-day ticket, or it is the midweek price. The higher price is the weekend walk-up-to-the-window cost. Ticket prices in the stat box are intended as an approximation; look in the chapter for more details.

Finally, **we rate the slopes** (based on five ability levels), the **dining**, the **nightlife** and the **other activities**. One star means it's poor, two is OK, three is good, four is very good and five is outstanding. Ratings are quite subjective, but they are a general consensus of the *Ski Snowboard America and Canada* staff. We are simply trying to point you in the right direction.

Following the fact box is a detailed description of the mountain. **Mountain layout** describes various sections of the mountain best for skiers at each of five ability levels. The Ride Guide at the end of this section tells riders where to go and where the flats are. **Parks and pipes** gives you the inside scoop on terrain parks, snowcross courses, jib parks, rail parks, superpipes, halfpipes, minipipes and quarterpipes so you know which resorts are the most fun for skiers and riders who like to play on manmade terrain. We also point you in the direction of natural terrain features that will make your day on the mountain complete.

Cross-country and snowshoeing information will tell you which resorts have Nordic trails, as well as significant cross-country and backcountry skiing opportunities nearby, and snowshoe rental and tour information.

Lessons details instructional programs for adults, including any special programs and recreational racing. "First-timer package" refers to a package with a half-day or full-day first-time lesson, a lift ticket (often just for the beginner lift) and use of rental equipment.

Children's Programs covers non-skiing nursery and day-care programs, children's ski and snowboard lesson programs, and special supervised activities available after the lifts close.

Lift tickets are listed using the age categories resorts use, such as adults, seniors, teens, juniors and children. We've organized them in a chart with one-day, three-day and five-day prices, followed by "Who skis free" and "Who skis at a discount" listed in paragraph form. Where prices are from last season, assume an increase of a couple of dollars.

Under **Accommodations** we list both the most luxurious places and many of the budget lodges, including features such as slopeside location, pools and hot tubs, health clubs and intra-resort transportation. We also suggest lodging that is particularly suited to families, and our favorite B&Bs and inns.

Dining always includes the gourmet restaurants, but we don't leave out affordable places where a hungry family or a snowboarder on a budget can chow down and relax. We have compiled these suggestions from dozens of interviews with locals and tourists, plus our own dining experiences.

Apres-ski/nightlife notes places to go when the lifts close, and where to find entertainment later in the evening. We tell you which bars are loud, which are quiet, the kind of music they play and whether they have live music.

Other activities covers off-slope activities—such as dogsledding, snowmobiling, ice skating, sleigh rides, shopping, fitness clubs and spas.

Getting there and getting around tells you how to get to the resort by air and car (and sometimes by train or bus), and whether a car is optional or necessary at the resort.

Types of accommodations

A **hotel** is relatively large, with 25 rooms or more, and comes without meals. If hotel rates include any meals, that is noted.

A **mountain inn** usually has fewer rooms than a hotel. Many have packages that include breakfast and dinner.

A **bed & breakfast (B&B)** tends to be even smaller, with just a few rooms. Most B&Bs have private baths now, so if guests must share a bath, we say so. Breakfast is included and some B&Bs also offer dinner.

Motels don't have the amenities of a hotel or the ambiance of a B&B, and often are farther from the slopes. Motels are good for families and budget-minded skiers.

Condominiums are the most affordable group lodging at North American ski resorts. They usually have a central check-in facility, and most have daily maid service for everything but the kitchen.

When you call the resort's central reservations number, ask for suggestions. Most of the staff have been on lodging tours and can make honest recommendations based on your needs. In the Canadian chapters, we note that prices are in Canadian currency, so take into account the exchange rate. Many higher-end accommodations and restaurants in Canada may actually be affordable for budget-conscious visitors from the U.S. and Europe.

Where you find $$$ signs, refer to this legend (also found on the bottom of pages in each chapter):

Dining: $$$$–Entrees $30+; $$$–$20–$30; $$–$10–$20; $–less than $10.
Accommodations: (double room) $$$$–$200+; $$$–$141–$200; $$–$81–$140; $–$80 & less.

Regional resorts

Throughout the book you'll find coverage of regional resorts too. These resorts are best for weekend or short midweek visits by skiers and snowboarders who live in that region. When a regional resort can be a side trip from a destination resort, we have included the description within that chapter. Regional resorts that are not near a large destination resort are in separate mini-chapters throughout the book.

These ski areas all have the following common features, *unless otherwise noted:*

• lodging within a 20-mile radius (Note: Some of the phone numbers listed for lodging are reservations services; others just provide information about lodging in the area. If no phone number is listed for lodging, call the ski area.)

• a day lodge with food service

• adult and child ski and snowboard lessons (children usually start at age 4)

• equipment rentals

We list toll-free phone numbers where available, plus the resort's recorded information line and website address. If you can't get a live voice from the info line, try the ski area's office number. (The toll-free numbers may not be applicable nationwide, since these resorts draw visitors primarily from the nearest urban areas.)

Ability levels

These are the terms we use in the "Mountain layout" and other sections:

● **First-timers** are just what the name implies. We apply the term to novices during their first couple of days on skis or a snowboard.

●● **Beginners** can turn and stop (more or less) when they choose, but still rely on snowplow turns if on skis and sideslipping if on a snowboard. This group feels most comfortable on wide, fairly flat terrain.

■ **Intermediates** generally head for blue trails and parallel ski or link snowboard turns (more or less) on the smooth stuff. They return to survival technique on advanced trails, and struggle in heavy powder and crud.

◆**Advanced** skiers and boarders can descend virtually any trail with carved turns, but are still intimidated by deep powder, crud and super steeps. Advanced terrain by our definition includes moguls and glade skiing.

◆◆**Experts** favor chutes, tight trees on steep slopes, deep-powder bowls and off-piste exploration. True experts are few and far between.

Skiing at altitude

People who visit resorts at higher elevations should be aware of health symptoms specific to altitude and preventative measures that can make acclimating more tolerable. The reduced oxygen at altitude may cause shortness of breath, a rapid pulse, increased blood pressure, and foot and ankle swelling. Dehydration is also an issue, since humidity is low. Dehydration can sap energy, cause headaches and affect athletic performance. Drink enough water to cause urination at least every three hours.

The effects of alcohol and other drugs are dramatically increased at altitude. At 6,200 feet, the effect of alcohol doubles for those living at sea level. Hangovers also will be worse at altitude. Avoid alcohol for at least the first 24 hours.

Acute Mountain Sickness (AMS) ranges from mild headaches to incapacitating illness. Although it generally occurs when sleeping above 8,000 feet, some will develop symptoms at lower elevations. Symptoms include headache, nausea, insomnia, fatigue, lack of appetite and light-headedness. Symptoms should improve with a lower elevation, rest and fluids over 24 to 48 hours. A prescription called Diamox, if taken prior to arrival at elevation, might help prevent AMS. Alcohol, tranquilizers, sleep medications and antihistamines may make AMS worse. AMS can progress to a much more serious illness known as High Altitude Cerebral Edema (HACE). This medical emergency presents incapacitating headaches, neurological symptoms such as a "drunken" gait, and may proceed to a coma. Prompt emergency help is critical.

Altitude sickness is quite common among children during the first few days, especially for those who live at sea level. Be sure to have lots of water available and be sensitive to a child's complaints of discomfort.

Because there's less atmosphere to filter out ultraviolet rays, high altitude predisposes people to sunburn and snow blindness (sunburn of the eyes). Sun block is imperative, even if it's not a blue-sky day. Don't forget to protect ears and scalp. Use UV-filtering sunglasses.

Nosebleeds occur more frequently at high altitude due to the dry air, particularly in the early morning. Humidifiers and petroleum jelly usually help prevent this problem. Pinching the nose for five to 10 minutes should stop the bleeding.

Sugarloaf
Maine

Summit: 4,237 feet
Vertical: 2,820 feet
Base: 1,417 feet

Address: 5092 Access Road, Carrabassett Valley, ME 04947
Telephone (main): 207-237-2000
Snow Report Number: 207-237-6808
Toll-free reservations: 800-843-5623 or 800-843-2732
E-mail: info@sugarloaf.com
Internet: www.sugarloaf.com
Expert:★★★★★
Advanced:★★★★★
Intermediate:★★★★
Beginner:★★★
First-timer:★★

Lifts: 15—2 high-speed quads, 2 quads, 1 triple, 8 doubles, 2 surface lifts
Skiable acreage: 1,400
Snowmaking: 94 percent
Uphill capacity: 21,810
Parks & pipes: 3 parks, 3 pipes
Bed base: 5,400
Nearest lodging: Slopeside, condos and hotel
Child care: Yes, 10 weeks to 5 years
Adult ticket, per day: $72 (07/08 price)
Dining:★★★
Apres-ski/nightlife:★★
Other activities:★★

Sugarloaf is unpretentious, genuinely friendly and as unaffected as an L.L. Bean boot. It delivers the best alpine skiing and riding in New England. Just ask Turnio Olympians—snowboard cross gold medalist Seth Wescott and alpine skiers Bode Miller and Kirsten Clark—who trained here as students at Carrabassett Valley Academy.

It would be hard to find another ski area in North America with such presence. It commands the landscape, a perfect white-capped pyramid piercing the sky and laced with ribbons of trails. Sugarloaf is an oasis in the wilderness. While there are the requisite condominiums and a growing number of trophy homes, the compact base village and handful of restaurants and stores clustered near the access road and along Route 27 are about it for shopping and dining. But, because most restaurants are independently owned, the food is very good.

Sugarloaf's renowned for the only lift-serviced, above-treeline terrain in the East. Don't let that scare you away. It has well-rounded, boundary-to-boundary skiing and riding. With 1,400 acres, it's the largest resort in the East, with the exception of Killington. Better yet: all that terrain is on one peak. Like other northern New England resorts, the weather can be brutally cold, especially if the wind is honking. And January days seem almost cruelly short. But when the sun peaks over the mountaintop and things warm up, there's no better place to ski or party. The annual Reggae Weekend in April always sells out.

With its 2007 sale to Boyne, the 'Loaf is finally getting some much-needed attention. Base buildings received sprucing up, Snowmaking and grooming have improved. For 08/09, Boyne is investing $5 million in water-pumping capacity and snow guns, permitting snowmaking earlier in the season and when temperatures are marginal. Although some of the lifts need updating, on all but the most crowded days, you can find lifts with short or no lines.

Mountain layout

The key to enjoying the 'Loaf is knowing how to move around the mountain without descending to the base. To do that, use the cross-cuts, which run more horizontally than vertically. Key cross-cut trails are Spillway, running east and west from the Spillway East chair apex; Peavy, which cuts across the mountain's midsection, running east, from Tote Road to Whiffletree; Mid-station, which cuts from Sluice, at the mountain's core, to Ramdown, connecting to King Pine area; and Lombard, which connects the top of Whiffletree with the base of Spillway. There are others, but locating these on your trail map will make navigating easier. Then there are the goat paths, which bisect glades and woods. If you want to avoid the occasional lift lines, use the Whiffletree and Bucksaw chairs and work your way over to the mid-mountain lifts that take you up higher.

◆◆**Expert,** ◆**Advanced:** This is a good all-around mountain for any level of skier, but what sets it apart is that it has enough steep and challenging runs to keep experts happy all day. In addition to more than 500 acres of classic wooded New England ski trails, Sugarloaf also has 80 to 100 acres of treeless snowfields at the summit, where experts can experience western-style, open-bowl skiing. Powder collects on the Backside, but the Front Face has some of the steepest terrain in New England; White Nitro literally falls away beneath you, and Gondi Line is a favorite for its consistent fall line. The downside: only one lift, a fixed-grip quad, services the summit, and it shuts down on occasion due to high winds.

Experts can easily figure out where to ski. Double-diamond on the trail map is the truth. Steep black runs beckon from the summit, and most also can be accessed from the East Spillway double chair. Bubble Cuffer, Winter's Way and Ripsaw are rarely touched by a grooming machine, dependent upon natural snow and littered with moguls and natural obstacles. The aptly named Misery Whip is an old, narrow T-bar line, cut straight and steep and rarely groomed. For serious bumps, head to Skidder or try Bubble Cuffer and Winter's Way.

Sugarloaf has glades, too, though they are yet to be discovered by the masses—perhaps because there are few signs—and chances are you'll have them to yourself. These glades include some of the biggest cliff drops on the East Coast, but don't waste your time looking for them on a map. For marked challenges, try Cant Dog or Stump Shot. Kick Back glade, between Hayburner and Skidder, still has some stumps settling in, so be alert. On the other side of Hayburner, Swedish Fiddle Glade has great lines that dump into some unofficial woods.

Given the abundance of steeps and the infamous snowfields, the real challenge for experts is what to do during the off-chance that you are here when the snowfields are closed or everything is just plain icy. That's when you want to head into the woods and find sheltered trails. The mountain holds lots of hidden challenges, the trick is to find them.

For advanced skiers, the blacks down to the King Pine quad are all sweet and steep. Bump monkeys should head for Choker, a natural snow trail on this side of the mountain. Widowmaker to Flume is usually groomed, but best early in the day. Narrow Gauge is perhaps the 'Loaf's most famous trail. It's the only trail in the East that's FIS approved for all four World Cup alpine ski disciplines. Usually groomed, but seldom seeing high traffic, are Lower Gondi Line and Lower Wedge.

■ **Intermediate:** Advanced-intermediates will find that in favorable conditions, they can handle some of the single-diamond blacks on this mountain. With a few exceptions, the western half of the mountain is an intermediate playground. Tote Road and Timberline to Scoot are long (Tote Road is 3.5 miles) and wide cruisers that wind from the summit to the base—skiers can be on these trails for a half hour, notes one regular. Hayburner and King's Landing both swoop down a continuous fall line, making them ideal for cruising. Ramdown, off the King Pine chair, has an often nasty first 25 yards, but work through it and be rewarded with a lovely cruise no matter which direction you choose. Ditto for Boomauger, when groomed.

Blueberry's Grove, between Cruiser and Whiffletree, and Ram Pasture Glade, off the lower part of Tote Road, are good introductions to tree skiing. Adventurous kids and playful adults duck off Lombard Cross-cut into Rookie River, where you work your way down a small frozen waterfall before following a winding riverbed. Just for kids is Moose Alley, a wiggle-woods off Cruiser. Be sure to look for Pierre the lumberjack, Blueberry Bear and Amos Moose.

●● **Beginner,** ● **First-timer:** At the base of the mountain, beginners will find the very broad and gentle Boardwalk run. Those looking for a little more challenge graduate to Lower Winter's Way (secluded with little traffic), off the Double Runner chairs, and from there to the Whiffletree quad. When you're comfortable on the Whiffletree trails, head for the summit and take a leisurely run down Timberline, a wide scenic trail that eases down the mountain's western edge before it connects with Tote Road. Be forewarned: The Chicken Pitch section of Tote Road is a notorious trouble spot; later in the day, it becomes a body slalom.

Terrain off the pokey Bucksaw chair offers a bit more challenge: a steeper pitch or narrower trails. The plus here is that these trails get very little traffic.

First-timers start on the long, gentle Birches slope, served by two chairlifts, Snubber and Sawduster. This is a great learning slope with only one caveat: It also is the access slope for a lot of slopeside lodging, so first-timers should quit a little early.

Snowboarding

SuperQuad area: Double Bitter or Wedge are winding and narrow, with natural bank turns and drop-offs. Skidder has a natural quarterpipe, riders' right. King's Landing and Hayburner have natural knolls. West Mountain trail also has some nice banks on riders' left, but beware of the clearance underneath the double chair and be sure to cut right toward Windrow near the end of the steeps to avoid the flats.

King Pine area: Misery Whip is at most 9 feet wide and usually ungroomed and full of huge whale-size bumps of stored-up snow. Take Boomauger to gain speed and lay down huge carves. Try to avoid returning to the base via Cross Haul from here. Some sections are pretty flat. Best choice: ride the lift up and work your way back towards the middle of the mountain.

Parks and pipes

The Yard is a 400-foot-wide, half-mile-long, expert terrain park, which cuts from the Peavy X-Cut down to Lower Narrow Gauge. Rails, a hip, three sets of jumps, including one that towers more than 50 feet, and other features are all strategically placed in view of the Super-Quad. At the base of Lower Winter's Way, accessible via Double Runner East (short side) is Sugarloaf's competition superpipe, **Pipe Dreams**, which is more than 400 feet long with 16-foot walls and a consistent 22-degree pitch.

Beginning and lower-intermediate freeriders can perfect their moves in The Stomping Grounds, with terrain elements and a minipipe. Also nearly 400 feet long, the 10-foot walls are more forgiving. The Stomping Grounds and learning pipe are on Lower Double Bitter, accessible via either the Sugarloaf SuperQuad or the Double Runner West (Long Side) chairlift.

Cross-country & snowshoeing (see also xcskiresorts.com)

The Sugarloaf/USA Outdoor Center (207-237-6830) is the largest and most complete in Maine, with 105 km. of trails groomed with double tracks and lanes for skating. Most of the trails are well suited for beginners and intermediates. The center is off Rte. 27, south of the resort access road. Three trails reach it from the resort's lodging facilities and the village area. The center also has a lit Olympic-sized outdoor skating rink, and a large lodge with a giant fireplace, deck and the Bull Moose Cafe, a locals' favorite.

Group and private lessons are available, as are equipment rentals. Multiday ticket holders can exchange a day of downhill for a day of cross-country, including trail fee, lesson and equipment. Exchange tickets at the guest services desk in the base lodge.

Snowshoeing: Snowshoers can use the machine-packed portion of all the cross-country trails, as well as access backcountry trails. Snowshoe programs include the guided Snowshoe Safari, Women's Stew & Shoe Tour and moonlight tours. Snowshoe rentals are available.

Lessons (07/08 prices)

Group lessons: The ski school uses the Perfect Turn® program, which has 10 levels of clinics. For lower-intermediates and above, ages 15 and older, the clinics last 90 minutes with a maximum of 11 clients. Enrollees watch a short video that demonstrates ability levels, eliminating the "ski-off," which can take up 40 minutes. Clinics meet twice daily; cost, $30. Two clinics the same day cost $45.

First-timer package: Perfect Turn clinics for ski or snowboard first-timers to beginners are 2 to 2.5 hours for day 1, 90 minutes each for day 2 and 3. Reservations are requested. The $80 Level 1 package includes the clinic, equipment, and a lift ticket for learning lifts. The resort guarantees Level 1 skiers that they will be able to ride a lift, turn and stop by the end of the clinic, or they can repeat it free or get their money back. Levels 2-3 cost $85 per clinic; a 2-day package is $130; a 3-day is $180.

Private lessons: $115 for 90 minutes, plus $50 each additional person; two hours $140, plus $100; three hours, $210, plus $150, with discounts for multiple hours.

Special programs: The Women's Turn program offers three-day programs with at least five instruction hours on the snow and after-ski activities. The cost is $325, which includes clinics, video analysis, equipment demos, lunch and apres-ski seminars. Reservations required.

Children's Programs (07/08 prices)

Child care: The center takes children ages 10 weeks to 5 years. A full day costs $60, a half day is $40 (a.m.) and $35 (p.m.); full day with skiing is $73, half day with skiing is $57. Reservations are required; call 207-237-6959.

At the 'Loaf it's obvious that a positive experience for visiting families is the number-one priority. The child care center is conveniently located trailside in Gondola Village, adjacent to the Base Lodge and on the primary on-mountain shuttle route. The facility is sizable, accommodating as many as 82 children, including up to 12 infants and 15 toddlers. Staff members are seasoned, averaging more than 10 years at Sugarloaf. Many seasonal employees are early childhood education students at the University of Maine in Farmington. The center is licensed and maintains more staff than required by state law—one care provider for every three infants or four toddlers. Some vacationers come here specifically because the child care is so good.

Children's lessons: Available for ages 3-14. Mountain Magic (ages 3-6): lessons, lift tickets and lunch for $73; a half day without lunch, $57. Rentals extra. Mountain Adventure (ages 7-14): $65 for a full-day lesson and lunch, and $52 for a half day without lunch; lift tickets and rentals are extra. Reservations are required at least 48 hours in advance. Teens ages 15-18 join the Mountain Experience clinic or take adult lessons. Moose Alley is a special kids-and-instructors-only section of the mountain where kids can do some controlled tree skiing.

Mooseketeers creates a fun-filled, positive first ski experience. Willing 3-year-olds are introduced to skiing through special games and personalized instruction in a 45-minute, private coaching session (first timers and less experienced skiers), or by joining Mountain Magic for a 1- to 2-hour morning group session (toilet trained three year olds who have skied before). Lunch, snacks, lift ticket, and ski rental equipment are included. Full day $73; half-day $57.

Special activities: Younger children will be thrilled to see one of four mascots in the child care center or skiing with them on-mountain. Amos the Moose, Pierre the Lumberjack, Blueberry the Bear and Lemon the Yellow-Nosed Vole all have fascinating stories behind them. The mountain provides age-appropriate programmed activities almost every night for children ages 5 to 12. Older kids enjoy tubing, snowshoeing or the Antigravity complex, while game, movie and pizza nights appeal to all ages.

 # Lift tickets (07/08 prices)

	Adult	Junior (6-12)
One day	$72	$49.
Three days:	$195	$129
Five days:	$305	$205 Early and late season prices are lower.

Who skis free: Children ages 5 and younger.

Who skis at a discount: Young Adults (13-18) pay $61 for a single day, $171 for three days, and $275 for five days. Seniors 65 and older pay junior prices. Purchase tickets online more than 7 days in advance and receive a 10-percent discount. Members of the military with ID card ski or ride for $39.

 # Accommodations

Packages at the Grand Summit include adult group lessons and use of its private health spa; condo and Sugarloaf Inn packages include adult group lessons and use of the Sugarloaf Sports & Fitness Club. Make reservations by calling either 800-843-5623 or 800-843-2732. The **Grand Summit Resort Hotel** ($$-$$$$) is the centerpiece of the Alpine village. It has a small health club with indoor pool, restaurant and lounge. The slopeside **Sugarloaf Inn** ($$-$$$) has a New England inn ambiance.

Condominiums: The resort has more than 900 condo units, all designed so skiers and snowboarders can slide back to their lodging. (Not all have lift access, but a shuttle runs from the lodging to the lifts.) Families like **Gondola Village** because it's close to the state-licensed child-care facility, and the Whiffletree quad, servicing designated family skiing trails, is outside the door. **The Bigelow**, **Snowflower** and **Commons** are more luxurious. **Sugartree** offers easy access to the health club, and **Snowbrook** has an indoor pool. **Timberwind** has rather small units, but has an outdoor hot tub, is just across the street from the fitness club and sits right next to the midstation loading of the Snubber chairlift.

For more affordable lodging, try Kingfield, 15 miles south, or Stratton, 7 miles north. **Three Stanley Avenue Bed & Breakfast** (207-265-5541; $), in Kingfield, is a Victorian-style B&B, where six rooms have private or shared bath. In Stratton, the **Spillover Motel** (207-246-6571; $) has clean rooms at reasonable rates, and the **Mountain View Motel** (207-246-2033; $) has eight pine-paneled units with nice views, two with full kitchens; pets allowed.

 # Dining

Sugarloaf has a full range of dining options. Many spots offer ski-in/ski-out lunches, a big plus for those who dislike crowded base lodges. For dinner, reservations are essential on weekends, holidays and special events. If you're visiting Sunday

Dining: $$$$–Entrees $30+; $$$–$20–$30; $$–$10–$20; $–less than $10.
Accommodations: (double room) $$$$–$200+; $$$–$141–$200; $$–$81–$140; $–$80 and less.

through Thursday, ask where the two-for-one specials are that night.

Sugarloaf's on-mountain restaurant, **Bullwinkle's** (207-237-6939; $–$$), was expanded and renovated in 2007 making it quicker to get food; better yet is the addition of a sit-down restaurant and full bar. On Saturday nights (more often, peak season and holidays), it transforms into an almost-elegant retreat for snowcat ride four-course candlelight dinners ($$$$).

While food in the **base lodge** is pretty good, it adds up very quickly. The independent restaurants located in the base village provide more bang for the buck. Both **Gepetto's** (207-237-2192; $-$$) and **The Bag** (207-237-2451; $-$$) are perennial favorites for lunch and dinner. Gepetto's has the more varied menu, with soups, salads, sandwiches and entrees served in a light- and plant-filled atrium, by the bar and upstairs. The Bag, a brewpub, is *the* place for soups, burgers and pizzas, although there's plenty more on the menu.

The **Double Diamond Steakhouse** (207-237-222; $$$$) in the Grand Summit Resort Hotel serves steaks, fresh fish and pasta dishes and has an excellent wine list. **D'Ellie's** (207-237-2490; $), a small, mostly take-out bakery/deli, serves excellent homemade soups, huge sandwiches (on homemade bread), good salads and the best full breakfast on the mountain. Avoid lunch crowds by ordering in the morning for later pick-up at the Express Lane.

Black Diamond Burritos ($) is a quick-serve, made-to-order spot adjacent to the Sugarloaf Board Room. Pizza is the specialty at **The Shipyard Brew Haus** (207-237-6837; $-$$), which, of course, serves Shipyard brews; and here's a hint: it's rarely busy at lunch. For dinner, it's wise to stick with the simpler offerings. Open for three meals daily; on-mountain pizza delivery from 5 p.m. to midnight (207-237-2395); free hors d'oeuvres Mon.-Thurs. from 3-6 p.m.; evening entertainment Wed.-Fri. For the region's best cuppa Joe and a bagel, head to **Java Joes** (207-237-3330; $).

If any place gives meaning to the phrase "don't judge a restaurant by its exterior," it's **Hug's** (207-237-2392; $-$$), an extremely popular hole-in-the-wall about 2 miles from the access road. Go for northern Italian food, accompanied by betcha-can't-eat-just-one-piece pesto bread and a family-style salad. **Tufulio's** (207-235-2010; $-$$), in Carrabassett Valley, is another Italian-accented locals' favorite, thanks to its wide-ranging menu, huge portions, family friendly atmosphere and two-for-one Sunday night specials. The **Carrabassett Inn** (207-235-3888; $-$$) is good for burgers and pizza, or passable Mexican fare on Mondays.

In Kingfield, **One Stanley Avenue** (207-265-5541; $$$) offers the area's only true fine dining; it's worth the drive. A good bet is fireside dining at **Julia's** (207-265-5421; $$), in The Inn on Winter's Hill; ask about wine tastings. Less fancy is **Longfellow's Restaurant & Riverside Pub** (207-265-4394, $-$$), a locals' favorite for its wide-ranging menu and good, filling food. **The Orange Cat** (207-265-2860; $) serves tasty homemade soups, creative sandwiches and baked goods. It opens at 7 a.m.; have breakfast and take sandwiches for later. **The Kingfield Woodsman** (207-265-2561; $) starts serving trucker-friendly portions at 5 a.m.

In Eustis, **The Porter House** (207-246-7932; $$) draws diners from Rangeley to Quebec. Downstairs is a casual/fine-dining restaurant, serving excellent fare with a creative touch. Just about everything is fabulous. Upstairs, the Heron Pub serves lighter fare and the full menu. Tuesday night features two-fer $25 entree choices. Make reservations on weekends, holidays and Tuesdays. In Stratton, the $7.95 Friday night Fish Fry at the **White Wolf Restaurant** (207-246-2922, $-$$) satisfies those on a lean budget; good burgers and exotic meats, too.

If you're planning on preparing your own meals, **Hannaford's** in Farmington has the best groceries selection and prices. **Tranten's**, in Kingfield, is a small grocery store with an o.k. meat and deli department. Buy extras three smaller stores: **Sugarloaf Groceries** in the base village, **Mountainside Grocers** at the base of the access road, and **Ayotte's**, down valley.

Apres-ski/nightlife

On sunny days, apres-skiers crowd the decks of **The Beach**, in front of the base lodge. **Gepetto's Side Bar** and **The Bag** are also lively on weekends; The Bag has live blues on Monday nights. The hot spot for live music—usually Boston bands, ocassionally nationally known acts—and dancing at night is the **Widowmaker Lounge**. For a more subdued atmosphere, try the Sugarloaf Inn, home of the **Shipyard Brewhouse** or **The Double Diamond Steakhouse and Pub** in the Grand Summit Resort Hotel. Just down the road, **The Rack** has a strong local following. **Judson's**, on Rte. 27, is a favorite with locals and UMaine and Colby College students. **Tufulio's** has a popular happy hour, as does **Carrabassett Inn**, especially on Mondays when the accent is Mexican. Ole! For preteens, **Pinocchio's**, downstairs from Gepetto's, has video games, pinball and board games.

 ## Other activities

Sugarloaf has a Turbo Tubing Park with its own lift and four 1,000-foot chutes. The park is open various days depending on the season, with one session midweek and two on weekends. The fee is $12 per session.

The Anti-Gravity Complex (AGC), at the base of the access road, has one of the highest **indoor climbing walls** in New England as well as an **indoor skating park, basketball court, track, weight room, trampolines, aerobic programs** and more.

The Sugarloaf Sports & Fitness Club, free to on-mountain guests, has an **indoor pool, indoor and outdoor hot tubs, steam room, sauna, weight room, racquetball courts, indoor climbing wall, Internet cafe** and **massage** services. On busy weekends and days with inclement weather, the fitness club can be crowded with screaming kids, so couples may want to stay in condos that have hot tubs.

Dogsledding, horse-drawn sleigh rides, snowmobiling, ice fishing and skating are among the activities that Sugarloaf Guest Services can arrange (207-237-2000).

Special events: Sugarloaf rolls back prices during **White White World Week**, held in late January. The annual **Reggae Weekend**, usually in mid-April, is a two-day bash with indoor and outdoor reggae bands. Book well in advance, as it usually sells out.

While there are few **shops**, that's not why folks come here. Kingfield has a handful of shops and galleries; Farmington and Rangeley, each about 45 minutes away, have more choices.

Getting there and getting around

By air: The closest commercial airport is the Portland International Jetport. There's also a small regional airport in Augusta. Bangor International Airport is another access point. Guests who fly into Bangor or Portland and who reserve lodging-and-lift packages through Sugarloaf/USA reservations can reserve transportation at the time of booking. There is an airstrip for private planes in Carrabassett Valley.

By car: Take I-95 north to Augusta, Rte. 27 north through Farmington and Kingfield. Or take the Maine Turnpike to the Auburn exit, Rte. 4 to Farmington and Rte. 27 through Kingfield. The drive is about 2.5 hours from Portland.

Getting Around: A car is optional—nearly everything in the resort is within walking distance. A free on-mountain shuttle runs on weekends and during holiday periods and is on call during the week. To do anything away from the resort complex, you will need a car.

Dining: $$$$–Entrees $30+; $$$–$20–$30; $$–$10–$20; $–less than $10.
Accommodations: (double room) $$$$–$200+; $$$–$141–$200; $$–$81–$140; $–$80 and less.

Nearby resort

Saddleback, Rangeley, Maine; 207-864-5671

Internet: www.saddlebackmaine.com; 5 lifts: 1 quad, 2 doubles, 2 tows; 58 trails; 400 acres; 2,000 vertical feet; 1 park, 1 pipe

What a sleeper! Underdeveloped, uncrowded, untamed are the words most often used to describe this area just 45 minutes from Sugarloaf, but that's changing. Since purchasing the resort in 2003, the Berry family, longtime Saddlebackers and area residents, have been infusing much-needed cash into improvements, upgrades and expansion.

For starters, rates were lowered and trail names reverted to their original ones, honoring fly-fishing lures. The past seasons saw a new quad servicing a new beginner area, the much-needed renovation and expansion of the base lodge (now with espresso bar and humongous stone fireplace), improved snowmaking and grooming, a halfpipe, paving of the access road (yippee!), new intermediate and expert trails and kiddie and expert glades.

Still, Saddleback remains an old-fashioned, family area, where it seems everyone knows just about everyone else. The base lodge is filled with brown-bags at lunch, and this isn't discouraged. Smiles are genuine; greetings warm.

Even in a bad snow year, Saddleback is blessed with an abundance of snow, an average of 200 inches each year. You can find powder stashes here long after they've been exhausted at nearby Sugarloaf or Sunday River.

In general, trails get progressively more difficult as you progress from east to west, with the most expert terrain, including some serious glades, on the top third of the mountain. Most trails are narrow, winding through birches and hardwoods and offering views of Saddleback Lake and the surrounding wilderness. From the summit (accessed via T-bar), you can gaze over the wind-stunted trees across the Rangeley Lakes to the Presidential Range and Mt. Washington. The middle chunk of the mountain is ideal for intermediates.

The lower third, especially the new terrain below the base lodge, is designed for beginners. The gentle learning area with its own chairlift and choice of trails attracts young families, first-timers and the not-yet confident.

The drawback to Saddleback is the lift system. The double chair serving the main core of the mountain is aged and slow. The only way to the summit is a T-bar, with a steep, often-icy track with no escape hatches. What is planned is an expansion of intermediate terrain and the eventual addition of another quad chair servicing it from a new base.

Saddleback has on-mountain condominium lodging, but you'll have to make your own entertainment here when the lifts close. Rangeley, 7 miles from the base, is a good-sized town with at least a dozen restaurants and a good range of lodging. There's an excellent Thai restaurant at the base of the Access Road.

Child care is available for children ages 8 weeks to 8 years.

Lift tickets (07/08): Adults, $40; ages 13–18 and college students, $32; ages 7–12, $30. Seniors 70 and older and children 6 and younger, free. Half-day tickets are available.

Distance from Boston: About 5-plus hours. Take I-95 North to the Maine Turnpike, get off at Exit 12 and follow Rte. 4 north through Farmington to Rangeley.

Lodging information: For the limited number of condos on the mountain (400 trailside), call the ski area number, 207-864-5671. To reach the Rangeley Chamber of Commerce, call 800-685-2537.

Sunday River
Maine

Summit: 3,140 feet
Vertical: 2,340 feet
Base: 800 feet

Address: P.O. Box 450,
Bethel, ME 04217
Telephone (main): 207-824-3000
Snow Report Number: 207-824-5200
Toll-free reservations: 800-543-2754
E-mail: info@sundayriver.com
Internet: www.sundayriver.com

Expert:★★
Advanced:★★★
Intermediate:★★★★
Beginner:★★★★★
First-timer:★★★★★

Lifts: 19—1 chondula, 4 high-speed quads, 5 quads, 4 triples, 2 doubles, 3 surface lifts
Skiable acreage: 667
Snowmaking: 92 percent
Uphill capacity: 32,000
Parks & pipes: 4 parks, 2 pipes
Bed base: 6,000 on-mountain; 2,000 nearby
Nearest lodging: Slopeside
Child care: Yes, 6 weeks to 6 years
Adult ticket, per day: $72 (07/08)
Dining:★★
Apres-ski/nightlife:★★
Other activities:★★

The "Rivah" sprawls across eight connected mountains in the Sunday River Valley. For all its vertical, Sunday River is very horizontal, spreading more than 3.5 miles across those peaks. The Resort lacks a true center. It has three separate base lodges: South Ridge, Barker Mountain and White Cap and the on-mountain North Peak Lodge. Those unfamiliar with the terrain can feel as if they're spending more time getting from one place to another than skiing. Keep a trail map handy, because you're going to need it.

Sunday River can suffer from its own popularity. Its trails can be crowded, and the frequent intersections are accidents waiting to happen. Hint: To avoid crowds, consider starting the day at Jordan Bowl and working back across the general flow of traffic (an ideal scenario for those staying at the Jordan Grand Hotel). Still, the plusses far outweigh the drawbacks. Sunday River's impressive size yields plentiful and varied terrain; its efficient lift system makes it pretty easy to get around; and its stellar snowmaking and grooming make skiing and riding here a delight.

New for 08/09 is a chondula, a high-speed six-person chairlift with gondola cabins interspersed amidst the chairs, from South Ridge base to North Peak, providing access to all peaks with one lift ride.

Six miles south is the antidote to the on-mountain modernity, the lovely town of Bethel, with its white-steepled churches and Victorian homes. Classic country inns and historical houses-turned-B&Bs provide lodging for those seeking New England charm. Bethel has a surprising variety of restaurants, from Korean to Texas-style barbecue. The free Mountain Explorer shuttle bus operates between village and mountain, and a free, on-mountain trolley connects base lodges and hotels.

Mountain layout

Sunday River defines sprawl. It spreads over eight connected peaks, each webbed with trails, cat tracks and lifts. Keep a trail map handy; you're going to need. Thanks to its horizontal vertical, it can feel as if you're spending more time getting from one place to another rather than skiing. The best antidote to that is to resist the urge to conquer it all and instead concentrate your efforts peak by peak. Sunday River's powerful snowmaking system provides reliable snow from November into April. Overall, the Rivah provides a bit of something for everyone, although real experts will find little that arouses intense excitement (unless they befriend a local and head out of bounds).

◆◆**Expert,** ◆**Advanced:** Oz is a playground for high-level sliders. Served by a fixed-grip quad, it features straight, fall-line, tree-studded drops. Aurora Peak, served by a fixed quad chair and a triple chair, is the spot to find tough skiing. Northern Lights, rated blue on the map, provides an easier way down the mountain, though it's no stroll through the park. Celestial, reached from Lights Out, is one of the nicest gladed trails. It starts out steep and wide, but mellows and narrows as you descend.

From the top of Barker Mountain, a steep trio—Right Stuff, Top Gun and Agony—provide advanced skiers long, sustained pitches. Agony and Top Gun are premier bump runs. Right Stuff is a cruiser after it's been groomed, but normally develops moguls by afternoon. Tree-skiing fans like Last Tango glade between Right Stuff and Risky Business, the gentlest and most spacious of the resort's nine mapped glades. Though it's not particularly steep, it's tight. A work road about two-thirds of the way down allows skiers to bail out onto Right Stuff. Those who continue through the trees will find the terrain getting steeper and narrower. If you're less than an expert, you won't have much fun on Last Tango's lower third.

From the top of Locke Mountain, T2 plunges down the tracks of an old T-bar providing a spectacular view of Bethel, the valley and Mt. Washington. On White Cap, White Heat is a wide swath straight down. Double-diamond Shockwave, considered by many as tougher than White Heat, offers 975 vertical feet of big bumps and steep pitches. Two gladed areas, Hardball (skier right) and Chutzpah (skier left), start out deceptively mellow and open-spaced, but watch out. Technically, they are the most demanding on the mountain.

■ **Intermediate:** Advanced intermediates are at home at Sunday River. The top of North Peak has the largest concentration of blue runs, though there's an intermediate way down from the top of every peak, mostly wide, undulating trails, such as Obsession off White Cap. Jordan Bowl provides some of New England's the best blue-square cruising on Excalibur and Rogue Angel, with the wide-open Blind Ambition glade accessed by the mellow Lollapalooza. Monday Mourning starts out steep and wide but mellows near the end.

Lower intermediates can head to the White Cap quad (far left on the map) and enjoy the relatively mellow Moonstruck, Starburst and Starlight runs. Off Barker Mountain, Lazy River is narrow by Sunday River standards and a fun cruise, but it can be strewn with people during busy times as it's the main route to adjoining Spruce Peak.

●●**Beginner,** ●**First-timer:** Once a skier is past basic snowplow and into easy turns, much of Sunday River beckons. The North Peak triple chair reaches long practice runs like Dream Maker. Lollapalooza, the green-circle trail in Jordan Bowl, is long and wide with great views, but not a trail that beginners should start out on; the upper part bumps up on busy days, and probably should have a blue rating. Farther down it's quite mellow. First-timers start on Sundance and have the entire South Ridge area to practice. Twelve South Ridge beginner runs have three chairs and a surface lift. This area can be crazy, though, as it's the resort's hub.

Snowboarding

Some favorite riders' trails are on Jordan Bowl, which is a pain in the glutes, calves and feet to get back from. You either have to hike to the #13 lift, which brings you to a somewhat maneuverable pitch, or chance the possibility of having to unstrap and skate your way over the dreaded Kansas trail, a long and almost uphill traverse. Other flat spots to avoid at all costs are Three Mile Trail, Southway and Easy Street.

Parks and pipes

Sunday River's commitment to terrain playgrounds is strong, as evidenced by a full-time parks and pipes manager on the operations staff. The resort consistently responds to its freeriders with innovative park designs and new or larger elements. The park plan mirrors the trail plan with something for every rider, in four parks spread across different mountain peaks.

Whoville on South Ridge is designed for kids with many snow features like bank turns, a 10-foot jump, a couple of rollers and some small rails. The South Ridge Jib Park, on Express Lane near the minipipe, is still perfect for novices, but offers slightly bigger rails.

The premier expert park is Rocking Chair Park, directly beneath the Barker quad and in plain view of thousands. The park features a bit of everything; the Red Bull element is hard to miss, with it's double take off. The park also features 40-foot jumps, hips, a stairset rail, 24-foot connectable boxes, saddle boxes, 30-foot flat-down boxes, rainbow and battleship rails, and a wall ride. It finishes with a nice quarterpipe. All features are changed frequently.

The superpipe is near the Locke Mountain triple chair. The Starlight Park at White Cap is a boardercross course.

The parks and pipes benefit from state-of-the-art maintenance equipment and the mountain's legendary snowmaking system. Sunday River commits snowmaking to opening parks as early as possible, usually its superpipe and a couple of parks by Christmas.

Cross-country & snowshoeing (see also xcskiresorts.com)

Sunday River does not have a dedicated cross-country center, but this part of Maine is known for some of the best Nordic skiing and snowshoeing options in New England, all within an hour's drive.

Sunday River's White Cap Base Lodge houses the **White Cap Fun Center** for families. Activities here include **guided snowshoe tours**. Snowshoe rentals are available.

Golf course skiing, with some wooded trails, is available at the **Bethel Inn Cross-Country Ski Center** (207-824-2175). The center has 40 km. of marked and groomed trials, 30 of which are groomed for both diagonal and skate skiing. It has rentals, lessons, evening sleigh rides and telemark instruction. This is a great place to learn. Midweek, the trail fee is also good for entrance to the outdoor heated pool, sauna and fitness center until 4 p.m.

Closest to the slopes, the **Sunday River Ski Touring Center** (207-824-2410) is run by the Sunday River Inn, on the Sunday River access road. It has 40 km. of groomed and tracked trails, as well as 2 km. lit for night skiing. It's family oriented, with warming shelters, an overnight yurt, a groomed dog trail, a downhill practice area and instruction. Ice skating, snowshoeing, sleigh rides and an outdoor hot tub and sauna round out the amenities.

Owned by a former cross-country ski racer, **Carter's Cross-Country Ski Center** (207-539-4848) has two locations. One, on Intervale Road, is just five miles from Sunday River, and has great views of the downhill area. It has 60 km. of trails for all levels (half groomed) and has a back-country experience with rustic get-away cabins. Carter's Cross-Country Center in Oxford, off Rte. 26, provides another alternative for skinny skis, with 25 km. of tracks.

Forty-five minutes from Bethel is the Jackson Ski Touring Center in New Hampshire's Mt. Washington Valley. See Attitash for details of the ski touring programs. **Bethel Outdoor Adventures** (207-824-4224) offers snowshoeing tours.

Lessons 07/08 prices

Group lessons: The Sunday River Ski and Snowboard School created the innovative teaching program called Perfect Turn®. It combines state-of-the-art ski technique with state-of-the-art educational theory. The Sprint Perfect Turn Discovery Center offers one-stop shopping for lift tickets, lessons and rental equipment.

Perfect Turn has eight levels. For lower intermediates and higher, the clinics normally last 90 minutes with a maximum of six skiers. Skiers watch a short video that demonstrates various levels of skiing ability. The video eliminates the "ski-off," which usually takes up about 40 minutes of lesson. Clinics are offered twice daily and cost $35.

First-timer package: The Learn-to-Ski-and-Ride packages include the clinic, equipment rental and a lift ticket for the South Ridge and North Peak. It costs $80. Sunday River guarantees Level 1 skiers will be able to ride a lift, turn and stop by the end of the clinic, or they can either repeat it free or get their money back. A three-day clinic costs $180.

Private lessons: $80-$95 for one hour; $200-$226 for a half day; $417 for a full day. Discounts available for second person in lesson.

Children's Programs (07/08 prices)

Child care: Available for children 6 weeks to 6 years. All-day programs are $60, including lunch; half-day programs are $40. Bring diapers, formula and food for infants. Reservations are required; call 207-824-5083. The main child care facility is at South Ridge (207-824-5083). Child care, day and evening, also at Grand Summit Resort Hotel (207-824-5889) and Jordan Grand Resort Hotel (207-824-5314).

Children's lessons: Sunday River's children's programs are among the best-organized and smoothest-running at any resort. The flow from equipment rental to classes is outstanding and all facilities are separate, which makes dealing with youngsters much easier. Resrvations are required for all children's lessons. Tiny Turns is a one-hour private lesson for 3-year-olds that's part of a half- or full-day session in day care. Cost is $65 for a half day; $85 for a full day.

Mogul Munchkins is for ages 3-6 (skiing only). A full-day clinic with lunch costs $85 for a full day. Lift tickets are included. Mogul Meisters is for ages 7-14 (skiing or snowboarding). Full-day costs $72; $87 with rentals. Half-day, $55; $70 with rentals. Lift tickets are extra.

Lift tickets (07/08 prices)

	Adult	Junior (6-12)
One day	$72	$49
Three days	$192	$129
Five days	$305	$205

Note: Regular Season prices; value Season tickets are less expensive.

Who skis free: Children ages 5 and younger ski free with parent.

Who skis at a discount: Ages 13-18 pay $61 for one day; $171 for three days; $275 for five days. Ages 65 and older pay junior rates.

Accommodations

The Summit hotels and condominiums are the most convenient to the slopes. But Bethel also has a group of excellent B&Bs and old country inns. Call **central reservations** (800-543-2754) or the Bethel Area Chamber of Commerce (207-824-3585) for **other lodging**.

Jordan Grand Resort Hotel and Conference Center ($$-$$$$) is slopeside to Jordan Bowl, but miles by car or shuttle to the rest of the resort. Enjoy whirlpool spa, indoor/out-door pool, full-service health club, restaurants, child care. Be forewarned: the walls are not well soundproofed. The **Grand Summit Resort Hotel and Conference Center** ($$-$$$$) is trailside with a 25-meter heated out-door pool, athletic club and one of the resort's better restaurants. The **Snow Cap Inn** is a short walk from the slopes, and the **Snow Cap Ski Dorm** next door offers affordable digs. All but the dorm offer packages with lift tickets.

Sunday River has nine condominium complexes throughout the resort; all are convenient to the slopes and have trolley service. **Locke Mountain Townhouses** are the most upscale, but hard to get, with the ideally located **Merrill Brook** condominiums not far behind.

Less than a mile from the area, the **Sunday River Inn** (207-824-2410; $-$$$) is a traditional lodge with large living room with fireplace. Family-style breakfast and dinner are included. There is Nordic skiing, ice skating, ski-jouring (harnessed dogs pull a person on skinny skis), plus a wood-fired hot tub and sauna. Choose from dorm rooms, rooms with shared or private baths. Shuttles take guests to Sunday River.

In Bethel, the **Bethel Inn and Country Club** (207-824-2175; $-$$$) has old-style atmosphere. Renovated rooms are first rate; others barely make the grade. The rates include breakfast and dinner. The inn also has a cross-country center, health club with outdoor heated pool and a shuttle to the ski area.

The **Sudbury Inn** (207-824-2174; $$-$$$), one of our favorites, has comfy rooms, one of the best restaurants in town and Sud's Pub, a popular watering hole; a few rooms are pet-friendly. **The Gideon Hastings House** (207-824-3496; $$-$$$) has four rooms as well as two suites with whirlpool tubs and a casual restaurant downstairs.

Just east of Bethel, on the road to the mountain, the **Briar Lea** (877-311-1299; 207-824-4714; $$) is an unstuffy B&B with an English accent and six guest rooms decorated with floral wallpapers and antique furnishings. All have TV/DVD and wifi. Some can be connected as suites for families. Well-behaved dogs and children are welcome. Rates include an English-style breakfast. The inn also has a good, authentic, English pub-style restaurant.

A Prodigal Inn and Gallery (800-320-9201; 207-824-8884; $$$) is a bit more upscale than other Bethel-area B&Bs. Bronze sculptures by innkeeper Tom White accent the public spaces, including a TV room with video/DVD library and fridge and a living room with fireplace. Some guest rooms have Jacuzzi tubs; all have CD players. Breakfasts are elegant, delicious and huge. Marcy White also prepares delicious afternoon snacks.

Crocker Pond House (207-836-2027, $$) is an elegant retreat in a woodsy location just outside town. The loft rooms are especially good for families. No TV, but many other com-forts, including classical music, afternoon refreshments, free wifi and in-room phones. Want the privacy of a motel with the charm of a B&B? Try **The Inn at the Rostay** (207-824-3111 or 888-754-0072, $-$$). Motel-style rooms ooze charm, with homemade quilts and country themes. All have TV, VCR and phone; some have refrigerators and microwaves. Free wifi, outdoor hot tub, afternoon snacks and a reasonably priced hot breakfast are provided.

 # Dining

Sunday River continues to strive to improve its dining and, although still no culinary capital, the options for good food are improving.

The **Phoenix House** (207-824-2222; $$$), opposite South Ridge Base Lodge, adds a sig-nificant contribution to that effort with truly fine dining in an expansive arts-and-crafts setting highlighted by floor-to-ceiling windows looking onto the ski hill. It specializes in fresh pastas

Dining: $$$$–Entrees $30+; $$$–$20–$30; $$–$10–$20; $–less than $10.
Accommodations: (double room) $$$$–$200+; $$$–$141–$200; $$–$81–$140; $–$80 and less.

and handcut steaks, and superb New Zealand rack of lamb. Create your own pasta dish from an extensive selection of pastas, sauces and ingredients. If your budget doesn't allow these prices, try eating downstairs at **The Well** (207-824-2222; $-$$), where you'll find a pub menu that includes soups, salads, various stews and grill items including a tuna burger.

Legends (207-824-3500, ext. 5858; $$$), in the Summit Hotel, ranks next in the mountain's fine-food realm. **Shipyard BrewHaus Restaurant** (207-824-5269; $$-$$$), in the White Cap Lodge, run by the Portland-based brewery, serves an upscale pub menu that includes cedarplank salmon, sesame tuna and lamb kabob. Warm up with some chili, made with Shipyard Beer. For dessert try the Stout Brownie Fudge Sundae. There's a good kids' menu, too.

Foggy Goggle ($-$$), in the South Ridge base, is packed for lunch, with good reason. The **Peak Lodge and Skiing Center** ($-$$), at North Peak summit, is popular for lunch with a giant deck. The Jordan Grand Hotel's **Sliders** ($$) is good for sunny day deck dining lunch.

In the Fall Line Condominiums is **Gringo Harry's** (207-824-4000, $$), which earns high marks from locals for its upscale Tex-Mex fare. The **Matterhorn/Great Grizzly American Steakhouse** (207-824-6836) occupies a large, memento-filled barn on the access road. It's great for all ages, serving everything from brick-oven-baked pizza and fresh pasta to steak (of course). Tuesday - Friday and Sunday nights, get your skis tuned while you eat. On weekend nights, there's family entertainment that switches to rock bands around 9:30 p.m. Go early to avoid waiting; this is one very popular spot, and it doesn't take reservations.

At the base of the access road, the **Moose's Tale** (207-824-3541; $-$$), in the Sunday River Brewing Company, serves okay pub grub and excellent on-premise-brewed ales.

For fine dining, it's a toss-up between **Sudbury Inn** (207-824-6558; $$-$$$$) and the **Bethel Inn** (207-824-2175; $$-$$$) for region's best. The Sudbury usually gets the nod. It recently was recognized by *Bon Appetit* for its roast duckling with maple syrup and wild blueberry glaze; the rack of lamb and cioppino are excellent, too. Both inns have white-tablecloth dining rooms, but neither is pretentious. Well-behaved children, welcome; reservations essential.

Relaxed dining, good food and service and a kids' menu have made chef-owned **S.S.Milton** (207-824-2589; $$-$$$) a local favorite. Settle in for some "gentle dining," at **Cafe DiCocoa** (207-824-5282; $–$$). On Saturday nights, it serves authentic, multi-course, fixed-price ethnic—usually Mediterranean—dinners; call for the menu and reservations. **Cafe DiCocoa's Marketplace** ($) makes a good breakfast or lunch choice. It's also a fabulous bakery and a gourmet store with prepared meals. Also good for prepared foods to go, natural and gourmet groceries, and—get this—super barbecue, is the **Good Food Store** (207-824-3754).

The Jolly Drayman at the Briar Lea (877-311-1299 or 207-824-4714; $-$$) is an authentic English pub and restaurant owners modeled on one in England, serving a good selection of brews on tap, single malts and a jolly-good pub-style menu. Larger and more lively is **Suds Pub** (207-824-6558, $–$$) in the Sudbury Inn, offering family-style pub fare plus pizzas, burgers, sandwiches, steaks and 29 beers on tap, served in a family-friendly atmosphere.

Even vegans have a choice in Bethel. Everything served at **Taste of Eden** (207-824-8939, $) is made from scratch from whole foods. Terrific and inexpensive, it's closed Fridays and Saturdays. For fabulous Korean and Japanese food and sushi, head to **Cho-Sun** (207-824-7370; $$-$$$). Reservations are a must weekends/holidays. Cheap eats and hearty breakfasts keep **Crossroads Diner & Deli** (207-824-3673, $) hopping.

There's a **small grocery store** on-mountain, but it's best to stock up before arriving. The **Foodliner** on Main Street is a good option; it has a surprisingly nice wine selection.

Apres-ski/nightlife

The real fun heats up on weekends. Immediate apres-ski is at the base of the slopes. **Foggy Goggle**, in the South Ridge base area, is the liveliest mountain spot. Also try the **Barker Pub** in the Barker Mountain base area or **Pugsley's Pub** at the White Cap Base Lodge. **The Well**, opposite the South Ridge Base Lodge, provides great slope views, big-screen TVs, and live entertainment on Saturdays and occasionally during the week.

Off-mountain, head to the **Sunday River Brewery**, on the access road. **Matterhorn** has 48-ounce Glacier Big Bowl drinks and extensive beer choices. **Suds Pub** in town has 29 beers on tap, bands on weekends and open-mike Hoot Nite on Thursdays.

The **Matterhorn** rocks until the wee hours of the morning, with great bands; if you've been seated for dinner, you don't pay the cover. The **Sunday River Brewery** has live music and excellent homemade brew. Downtown, the **Funky Red Barn** has town's only pool tables.

A sedate crowd fills **Legends** at the Summit Hotel for its acoustic music. It has family entertainment every Saturday. **Thumper's** is an on-mountain nightclub run by Shipyard BrewHaus that is open only during the Budweiser Rocks the River Concert Series.

Other activities

Swimming pools and **saunas** are in virtually every resort condominium complex. Guests staying at the few condos that don't have them get privileges at nearby complexes. The ski dorm has **video games** and **pool tables**.

The White Cap Fun Center activities include an **arcade, a lighted tubing park** and **skating rink**, and **fireworks** every Thursday and Saturday evening. Skate rentals are available. Bethel Station, about 4 miles from Sunday River, has a four-screen **movie theater**.

Arrange **snowmobile rentals and tours** through Sun Valley Sports (207-824-7533) or Bethel Outdoor Adventures (207-824-4224), which also offers **snowshoeing tours**. **Indoor laser tag, miniature golf** and **rock climbing** are available at B.I.G. Adventure Center (207-824-0929). For one-day or multiday fully-outfitted **dogsledding trips**, call Mahoosuc Guide Service (207-824-2073) in Grafton Notch.

Bethel has unusual **shops**. Bonnema Potters sells pottery depicting the Maine landscapes; Mt. Mann native gemstones; and Samuel Timberlake reproduction Shaker-style furniture.

Getting there and getting around

By air: The most convenient commercial airport is Portland International Jetport, 75 miles from Sunday River. Private pilots can land in Bethel. Bethel Express Corporation will pick up from either airport by reservation (207-824-4646).

By car: Sunday River is in western Maine, an hour and a half from Portland and three-and-a-half hours (with no traffic) from Boston. Take I-95 north to the Maine Turnpike, Rte. 26 to Bethel, then Rte. 2 east for six miles to Sunday River's access road.

RV parking, no hookups, is allowed in designated parking areas at the resort. An RV park is also at White Birch Camping, in Shelburne on Rte. 2.

Getting around: During the main part of the season, on-mountain transportation between the base areas is quite good on shuttle busses that look like old trolley cars. The shuttle loop expands to include the condos at night. In shoulder season, the mountain shuttles are by request only. Several off-mountain properties, such as the Sunday River Inn and the Bethel Inn, have shuttle service to and from the slopes. Midwinter, you can get along without a car, but they're nice to have, especially if you want to go to Bethel. Early or late season, you'll need one.

Dining: $$$$–Entrees $30+; $$$–$20–$30; $$–$10–$20; $–less than $10.
Accommodations: (double room) $$$$–$200+; $$$–$141–$200; $$–$81–$140; $–$80 and less.

Mt. Washington Valley

New Hampshire
Attitash, Cranmore and Wildcat and five touring centers
Also: Black, King Pine and Shawnee Peak

Mt. Washington Valley Facts

Address: Chamber of Commerce
P.O. Box 2300, N. Conway, NH 03860
Toll-free information: (800) 367-3364
Dining:★★★★★
Apres-ski/nightlife:★★★★
Other activities:★★★★★

Phone: 603-356-5701
Fax: 603-356-7069
E-mail: info@mtwashingtonvalley.org
Internet: www.mtwashingtonvalley.org
Bed base: 7,500+

Variety — that's what the skiing region of Mt. Washington Valley is known for, as skiers and riders can choose from the intimate feel of Mt. Cranmore to the splendid isolation of Wildcat with something in between for everyone. The Valley, as locals call it, has many bests. These include spectacular scenery, a long history of hospitality, extensive shopping, diverse nightlife and plentiful choices in skiing, dining, lodging and fun things to do.

Home to the main ski areas of Cranmore, Attitash and Wildcat, the Valley also has the smaller, but great beginner/family resorts of King Pine and Black Mountain within its confines. On a clear day, all but King Pine offer spectacular views of the Northeast's highest peak, the 6,288-foot Mt. Washington, and the surrounding Presidentials. And, if you need more skiing choices, just an hour's ride reaches Bretton Woods and Sunday River, while Shawnee Peak is located a half-hour drive east from North Conway. As if these choices weren't enough, some of the Northeast's best cross-country ski centers are here.

The few remaining grand old hotels attest to the fact that Mt. Washington Valley was a destination resort long before anyone came here to ski. In the 1930s, the variety of terrain in what was then called the Eastern Slope Region was a magnet to early skiers. Depression-era work crews cut trails (the Wildcat Trail was one of the first), and enterprising young men started ski schools bringing Austrian instructors and the famous Arlberg method.

If this ski history means nothing to you, no matter, Mt. Washington Valley has the best of now, too. Wide fall-line cruisers complement the classic, narrow winding trails of yesteryear. Modern condos, motels and hotels mix with country inns and B&Bs throughout the region, which encompasses the Conways, Bartlett, Jackson and extends through Pinkham Notch. Outlying towns, from Gorham to Snowville, N.H., to Bridgton, Maine, figure in the mix.

Some of the region's New England charm has been lost over the years as retail outlets and development moved in. However, shoppers flock here because of that evolution. Locals and longtime visitors know that the commercialization is condensed to the North Conway strip. They head to the villages outside the hub of North Conway for the quiet, and then come to the village and the strip for its many good bargains, pubs and restaurants.

 # Attitash

Mountain layout

Just west of Glen on Rte. 302 in Bartlett, Attitash is an all-around, two-mountain resort with a few expert touches. On the Attitash side is a warren of narrow New England trails and the newer Bear Peak trails provide great cruising terrain.

Ptarmigan, on Attitash, is one of the steepest trails in New England, but it is manageable for good intermediates, too. The rest of the mountain will keep 80 percent of skiers satisfied with Northwest Passage to Cathedral and Saco to Ammonoosuc providing inspired cruising, while Idiot's Option and Grandstand are favorites for their bump runs. The Attitash side of the mountain lacks a high-speed, base-to-summit lift but on the Bear Peak side there's a high-speed quad backed by several other chairlifts. Bear Peak features Illusion, Avenger, Kachina and Myth Maker: a foursome of cruising delights. Seeking more challenge? Jump into the Peak's ever-expanding glades.

The Attitash base has the primary lodge where you'll find the Adventure Center, the Learn to Ski and Ride programs and children's programs. Lessons, rentals and child care are all under one roof, and just outside, beginners have a "Snowbelt" lift. First-timers graduate from that to the adjacent learning slope served by a triple chair. From there, they move on to beginner trails around the nearby Double-Double lifts.

Snowboarding

When riding from Attitash to Bear Peak, avoid Bearback and ride the Abenaki quad instead. From Bear Peak to Attitash, avoid Bear Right to Stonybrook. Instead, when you see the bridge, take Bear Notch Pass to Stonybrook Bypass. Here, it's worth it to unstrap and walk the 50 feet to the top of the bypass. From there on, it's all downhill.

Parks and pipes

The ATP Freeride program includes: ATP Fly Zone Terrain Park on Thad's Choice; ATP Training Ground, an introductory Park on Far Out; ATP Stunt Ditch Superpipe; and ATP Freeride Series. ATP brings snowboarding to the forefront of Attitash's marketing strategy.

 ## Lessons (07/08 prices)

Group lessons: $30 per 90-minute session for levels 2-8.
First Timer Package: The 3-hour Guaranteed Learn to Ski and Learn to Ride package includes rentals, lifts and lessons for $155.
Private lessons: $69 per hour for one student. Bbefore 9 a.m. or after 2 p.m. is $55.

 ## Children's Programs (07/08 prices)

Child care: Available for ages 6 months to 6 years for $65 per day, including lunch, or $40 half day. Tiny Turns, an intro-to-skiing program for kids ages 3-5, costs $74/hour, $50 for children enrolled in child care. Reservations recommended, call 603-374-2368.

Children's lessons: ages 4-6, $79 full day (with lunch), $59 half day; includes lessons, and lift ticket; rentals cost $15.

Lift tickets (07/08 prices)

One day*: adult $65, young adult (13-18) $51, child (6-12) $45. Three days: $165/$129/$93. Five days: $255/$195/$145.

*Note: One-day tickets cost more on Saturdays and holidays.

Who skis at a discount: Students with college ID ski for same price as Young Adults. Seniors (65+) pay children's prices. Multi day E-tickets and midweek tickets purchased online at www.attitash.com at least seven days in advance offer an additional 10 percent off the already discounted multi day price.

Cranmore Mountain Resort

Mountain layout–skiing & snowboarding

Cranmore is one of the oldest ski resorts in the nation. The good, balanced terrain, modest size (yet with an extensive trail system) and convenient location make it an ideal mountain for families. The sunbathed slopes (predominantly south facing) and lower elevation means it's the warmest of all the valley resorts. Cranmore skis larger than it is, and has both open slopes (don't miss the back, or east, side of the mountain) as well as classic, narrower trails. This is a resort for beginners and intermediates. Experts and advanced skiers can have a good time, but they shouldn't expect anything too challenging. A Burton Progression Park debuts in 2007-2008.

A favorite is the old Rattlesnake Trail, to the skier's right off the summit. The Ledges and Koessler trails down the center and to the skier's left offer some challenge, as do the tight, but not too steep, Black Forest and Tree Meister glades from Rattlesnake and Kandahar.

In addition to the standard skiing and snowboarding, Cranmore offers night skiing on weekends, and Cranapalooza on Saturday nights—a family-oriented event featuring fireworks, torchlight parades, jugglers, clowns, and fire eaters. Cranmore also offers snow toys, and lift-serviced tubing on eight groomed lanes Fridays, Saturdays and during holiday weeks.

Pipes and parks

The Darkside Terrain Park has rails, jibs, jumps and boxes designed by the same folks who make the parks for the U.S. Open. The Darkside is home to the Jib Saw Massacre, a series of three snowboard competitions and one skiing competition. The Other Side Progression Park on South Slope has small rails and boxes to ease newbies into the terrain park scene.

Lessons (07/08 prices)

Group lessons: 90-minute group lesson, $39; $99 with lifts, and equipment .
First-timer package: Adult two-hour Getting Started lesson, with lift ticket and rental equipment, is $79 first day; and $60 for days two and three.

Private lessons: $85 for 90 minutes; $150 for a half day.

Children's Programs (07/08 prices)

Child Care: Cranmore's Penguin Park Day Care provides care for children ages 3 months to 6 years. There are indoor and outdoor creative play areas and nap areas. The cost is $40 for a half day, $65 for a full day or $15 per hour. Introductory ski and snow play programs are available. Reservations are recommended, call (800) 786-6754, ext. 8541 or 8542.

Children's lessons: "I Wanna Ski" intro to skiing, a 60-minute lesson for 3-year-olds,

Cranmore Facts

Summit elevation:	**1,700 feet**
Vertical drop:	**1,200 feet**
Base elevation:	**500 feet**

Expert:★ Advanced:★★
Intermediate:★★★★
Beginner:★★★★
First-timer:★★★
Address: 1 Skimobile Road
N. Conway, NH 03860
Ski area phone: 603-356-5544
Snow report: 603-356-7070
Toll-free reservations: 800-786-6754

Internet: www.cranmore.com
Number and types of lifts: 12—1 high-speed quad, 1 triple, 3 doubles, 5 surface lifts, 2 moving carpets
Skiable acreage: 192 acres
Snowmaking: 100 percent
Uphill capacity: 7,500 skiers per hour
Parks & pipe: 3 terrain parks
Bed base: 250
Nearest lodging: Slopeside
Resort child care: Yes, 6 months and older
Adult ticket, per day: $59 (08/09)

costs $65, including equipment and lift ticket. "I Wanna Snowboard" for ages 5-7, 60 minutes: $65. Penguin Camp, for ages 4–7, is a full-day ski program including lift ticket, lesson and equipment for $95; snowboarding available for age 8 and up. Helmet rental for all is $10. Adventure Camp for skiers and snowboarders ages 8–14 includes lift ticket, lesson and equipment. A full day is $95, with lunch.

Private instruction for children is $85 for 90 minutes; $150 for three hours; lift ticket and equipment required.

Lift tickets (08/09 prices)

One day: adult $49, teens (13–18) $38, kids (6–12) and seniors (65+), $28. Age 5 and younger ski free. Night skiing, $19. These prices are good any day of the season. Save up to 30 percent on your second day of skiing when you redeem your lift ticket at the ticket office by 4 p.m

Wildcat Mountain

Wildcat Mountain features back-to-basics skiing with old-style trails that ebb and flow with the mountain's contours. It's a true skiers' mountain with no residential development allowed in the protected wilderness area. Skiers and riders who frequent this mountain are fiercely loyal and the varied and challenging terrain give Wildcat a true heart and soul, and through investments in snowmaking, grooming equipment, a high-speed lift and trail widening, Wildcat has made major progress in the past few years.

Wildcat sits across a narrow ribbon of highway from Mt. Washington, home to some of the highest recorded winds in the world. While Mt. Washington's summit, at 6,288 feet, is higher than Wildcat's, at 4,062, and the mountain can be windy and cold. However, the location and elevation does have a silver lining: the scenery is consistently voted the best in the East by a major ski magazine and snow is plentiful—an average year yields at least 15 feet—that comes early and stays late, often well into May. Spring skiing at Wildcat is an event and every skier in the Valley looks forward to it.

Wildcat Facts

Summit elevation: 4,062 feet
Vertical drop: 2,112 feet
Base elevation: 1,950 feet
Expert:★★★
Advanced:★★★★
Intermediate:★★★★
Beginner:★★★
First-timer:★★★
Address: Rte. 16, Pinkham Notch
Jackson, NH 03846
Ski area phone: 800-255-6439; 603-466-3326
Snow report: 888-754-9453
E-mail: through website
Internet: www.skiwildcat.com
Number and types of lifts: 4—1 high-speed quad, 3 triples
Skiable acreage: 225 acres
Snowmaking: 90 percent
Uphill capacity: 6,700 per hour
Bed base: None at the area
Nearest lodging: About a quarter-mile
Resort child care: Yes, 2 months and up
Adult ticket, per day: $59 (08/09)

Attitash Facts

Summit elevation: 2,350 feet
Vertical drop: 1,750 feet
Base elevation: 600 feet
Expert:★★
Advanced:★★★
Intermediate:★★★★
Beginner:★★★★★
First-timer:★★★★★
Address: P.O. Box 308, Barlett, NH 03812
Ski area phone: 603-374-2368
Snow report: 877-677-SNOW
Toll-free reservations: 800-223-7669
E-mail: info@attitash.com
Internet: www.attitash.com
Number and types of lifts: 12—2 high-speed quads, 1 quad, 3 triples, 3 doubles, 3 surface lifts
Skiable acreage: 280 acres
Snowmaking: 97 percent
Uphill capacity: 14,385 per hour
Parks & pipes: 2 parks; 1 pipe
Bed base: 1,600 Nearest lodging: Slopeside
Resort child care: Yes, 6 months and up
Adult ticket, per day: $65 (08/09)

Mountain layout–skiing & snowboarding

Wildcat deserves its reputation as an experts' mountain. Upper Wildcat, to the left and Top Cat and Lift Lion in the middle can get your heart pounding. Bigger and better gladed runs, new in 06-07, create a change of pace from the huge vertical steeps and cruisers.

Beginners are not forgotten. The Snowcat area, with its own triple chair, is an ideal place for first-timers, and the 2.75-mile cruise down Polecat from the summit gives advanced beginners an authentic Alpine experience. Another favorite for those who want a nice glide in the woods is the Wild Kitten off the Bobcat triple. Intermediates have plenty to play on, too. The Tomcat triple reaches about two-thirds of the way up the mountain and is a good retreat when the wind blows hard on the summit quad. The Bobcat triple reaches a little below mid-mountain and provides access to the narrow trails at Wildcat's core, two glades and the Bobcat slope and the Cheetah slope, which is often used for races.

For a religious experience, try Lynx from top to bottom: it might just convince you that Wildcat is God's chosen mountain. Lynx has long been the 'Cat's most popular trail. It plays with you, dropping quickly at the summit, then rolling around a few bends before dropping and rolling again. When taken from summit to base, there are few trails in New England that can compare for range of terrain and the sheer joy of skiing. Wildcat has no terrain parks.

Lessons (07/08 prices)

Group lessons: $35 per session.
First-timer packages: $65, including rentals, lifts and lessons. Extra days $75, including lift ticket. **The First Impressions Program,** limited to five students, includes an all-day lesson, lift ticket, rentals, plus lunch and apres-ski hot chocolate with your instructor for $90; reservations required.

Private lessons: $62 for one hour; up to five people can share a private lesson, with each additional person paying $42.

Children's Programs (07/08 prices)

Child Care: Available for ages 2 months to 5 years old. Cost is $59 for a full day (with lunch); $39 for a half day (without lunch). The Cubs Nursery & Snowplay program is a combination of child care and snow play instruction for ages 3 to 5 (must be toilet-trained). Cost is $99 for a full day (with lunch); $69 for a half day (without lunch). Reservations are recommended on weekends and required midweek, and are required for children 18 months and younger; call 888-754-9453.

Children's lessons: Ski lessons are for ages 5–12, snowboard lessons are for ages 8–12. Program including lessons, lift ticket and rentals costs $89 for a full day (includes lunch); $99 with equipment rental; $59/$69 for a half day.

One hour private snowboard lessons are offered for 5-7 year olds snowboarders (based on availability) for $69 with rental. Reservations strongly suggested for all kids' programs.

Lift tickets (08/09 prices)

One day: adult $59, teen (13-17) $49, junior (6-12)/sr.65+ $29. Add-a-Day: $29 for all.

Who skis free: Children age 5 and younger with a ticket-holding parent. Anyone on his or her birthday, with valid ID.

Who skis at a discount: College students ski for teen prices. Everyone on Sunday afternoons: noon to close is $20. Two ski for $59 on non-holiday Wednesdays. Ages 50+ get a lift ticket and 10 a.m. lesson on non-holiday Tuesdays. Ladies get a lift ticket and 10 a.m. ski lesson on non-holiday Thursdays, plus a 10% discount on the children's programs (reservations required). Add any number of consecutive days for $29 per day for anyone.

Mt. Washington

A trip to Tuckerman Ravine on the east side of Mt. Washington is a rite of spring for New England's skiers and riders. Called the birthplace of extreme skiing, skiers have hiked into this snow-filled glacial cirque since 1914, and in the 1930s, races were held here. In fact, the first giant slalom in the United States was held at Tuckerman, as was the American Inferno, which started at the very summit of Mt. Washington and ended 4,200 feet lower at Pinkham Notch. Today the Tuckerman Inferno Pentathlon, staged every April, continues as a fund-raiser for the non-profit Friends of Tuckerman organization.

To reach the ravine from the Pinkham Notch Visitor's Center, hike a wide trail two miles to HoJo's shelter. From here, the floor of the Ravine is reached via a steep hike.

Although skiing Tuck's is only for experts, less experienced folks still make the trek to watch, or to ski and snow tube the shallower terrain close to the ravine floor. Most spectators of this unique spring scene head straight for Lunch Rocks, an outcropping on the right as you hike into the ravine. From here, you can rest and then kick step into the snow and hike up any of the gullies or the famous headwall. At day's end, you either ski down the Sherburne Trail or, if snow is thin, hike down. For weather and trail info, call 603-466-2721.

Cross-country & snowshoeing (see also xcskiresorts.com)

Jackson Ski Touring Foundation (603-383-9355 or 800-927-6697), on Rte. 16A in Jackson Village, is a mecca for Nordic skiers with more than 150 km. of trails (93 km. are groomed, 80 km. are skate groomed). It has lessons, rentals and snowshoeing.

Mt. Washington Valley Ski Touring and Snowshoe Center (603- 356-3042) has 65 km. of inn-to-inn trails (60 km. tracked, 20 km. skate groomed), plus ski school and rentals. It offers guided star-gazing tours and animal-tracking clinics.

The Appalachian Mountain Club (603-466-2721) maintains a network of touring trails radiating from the AMC Camp at Pinkham Notch. About 7 km. are rated Easiest or More Difficult (requiring skills up to a strong snowplow and step-turn), but about 40 km. are rated Most Difficult, with long challenging hills and narrow trails. **Great Glen Trails** (603-466-2333) has 40 km. of cross-country skiing (14 km. tracked, 20 km. skate groomed) and snowshoeing trails at the base of Mt. Washington, which translates into jaw-dropping scenery all around you. Telemarkers, cross-country skiers and snowshoers can take a snowcat partly up the Mt. Washington Auto Road, then ski down; sightseers also are welcome. It also has a snowtubing park.

Bear Notch Ski Touring Center (603-374-2277) is one of the Valley's best kept secrets. With a truly beautiful setting just north of Bartlett Village (Rte. 302), the 70 km. (60 km. tracked and skate groomed) of trails offer uncrowded, wooded scenery. **The Nestlenook Recreation Center** (603-383-9443), also in Jackson, has 35 km. of touring tracks that wind through its 65-acre farm. **Purity Spring Resort** (800-373-3754 or 603-367-8896), near Madison, has 15 km. of groomed and tracked trails. Rentals and lessons are available. **Purity Spring Resort** (603-367-8896 or 800-373-3754), near Madison, has 15 km. of groomed and tracked trails. Rentals and lessons are available.

Accommodations

If you like romantic country inns and B&Bs, you're in the right spot. The Valley also has plenty of moderately priced motels suitable for families.

For condominiums, chalets and motel suites, call **Top Notch Vacation Rentals** (800-762-6636; 603-383-4133; $–$$$$), which works with properties all up and down the Valley. **Luxury Mountain Getaways** (800-472-5207; 603-383-9101; $$–$$$$) has everything from one-bedroom condos to luxury villas. **Attitash Mountain Village** (800-862-1600; 603-374-6500; $–$$$$), across the road from the ski area, has inexpensive to upscale packages. For lodging information (but no reservations), call the **Mt. Washington Valley Chamber of Commerce** at 800-367-3364 or visit its website. Lodgings are listed by region:

Bartlett (Attitash Resort): Right at the base of Bear Peak, the ski-in/ski-out **Grand Summit Resort Hotel** (800-223-7669; $$–$$$$) provides all amenities from saunas and hot tubs to fitness rooms and restaurants. A visit to the **Covered Bridge House** (800-232-9109; 603-383-9109; $–$$) resembles a visit to Grandma's. Bed-cover quilts , braided rugs and stenciling characterize the decor. A family suite is available; rates include breakfast and use of the outdoor hot tub.

Active folks who don't need fancy digs appreciate **The Bartlett Inn** (800-292-2353; 603-

374-2353; $–$$$). Choose from shared-bath rooms in the main inn or cottages with private baths, some with fireplaces and kitchenettes. In the same room with two adults, kids younger than 12 stay free, teenagers stay for $19. Cross-country trails are out the back door.

Gorham (Wildcat): If you are skiing at Wildcat, this town, just to the north of the Valley, is where to stay. The **Royalty Inn** (800-437-3529; 603-466-3312; $–$$) has 90 rooms that are all spacious and well kept. Kitchenettes (stove tops, no ovens) are available. The family-owned **Town & Country Motor Inn** (800-325-4386; 603-466-3315; $) is a bit simpler, with recently upgraded rooms. Families will want to stay in the same building that houses the pool, video games and sauna. Children ages 13 and younger stay free. Dorm-style accommodations start at $15 per person.

Pinkham Notch (Wildcat): To be really close to Wildcat or to get a head start if you're climbing, skiing, or using Mt. Washington's cross-country trails, try the **Joe Dodge Lodge** (603-466-2727; $) at Pinkham Notch, run by the Appalachian Mountain Club. The two-, four- and five-bunk rooms are simple, and rates include either one or two meals. Three public rooms have fireplaces; one has a well-used piano, another is stocked with games and activities for children and the third has a library.

Jackson Village: This town is home to a collection of old-time mansions, hotels, farms and houses that have grown into upscale B&Bs. Many offer dining on premises. **Luxury Mountain Getaways/Nestlenook Farm on the River** (603-383-9443; $$$–$$$$) is an elegant Victorian fantasy land, with pastel colors and gingerbread trim. A full breakfast and snacks mean you never go hungry. The extensive grounds are peppered with ornate bridges and fanciful gazebos. Ask about add-on fees—they're steep.

The Inn at Thorn Hill (800-289-8990; 603-383-4242; $$$–$$$$), with views of Mt. Washington, is rebuilt in the style of Stanford White following a fire. Now offering spa services, the inn gets top ratings from both travel and dining publications. Rates include breakfast and a three-course dinner. Practically next door is a more affordable choice, **The Inn at Jackson** (800-289-8600; 603-383-4321; $–$$), a gem. It's an easy walk to Jackson's restaurants and shops. The **Ellis River House** (800-233-8309; 603-383-9339; $$–$$$$) is an elegant, country retreat furnished with antiques; many rooms have fireplaces and whirlpool baths. Unlike many B&Bs, each room has TV and phone. A gourmet breakfast is included. **Wildcat Inn & Tavern** (603-383-4245 or 800-228-4245 $-$$), under new ownership in 2007, is an old-time favorite with restaurant and a favorite local tavern in the adjacent building.

The Wentworth Resort Hotel (800-637-0013; 603-383-9700; $$$–$$$$) is an historic hotel and one of the area's best values. It has spacious rooms with big hot tubs, as well as a top-notch dining room and a nice lounge. Rates include a full breakfast and a multi-course dinner. The nearby **Snowflake Inn** (888-383-1020; 603-383-8259; $$$) includes king-size beds and two-person jetted tubs, Internet access and flat screen TVs with DVDs. Afternoon refreshments and a continental breakfast are included in the rate.

The **Eagle Mountain House** (800-966-5779; 603-383-9111; $–$$$) is a restored, rambling 19th-century resort hotel that welcomes families. Children age 17 and younger stay free if sleeping in existing beds. **The Christmas Farm Inn & Spa** (800-443-5837; 603-383-4313; $$–$$$), added a full-service spa in 2004. The rate includes breakfast, but a 15-percent service charge and taxes will be added to your bill. **Whitneys' Inn** (800-677-5737; 603-383-8916; $$–$$$), a restored 1840s farmhouse at Black Mountain, has Alpine and Nordic skiing from the door. Children may eat early at the kids' table with supervised activities following.

Intervale: **The 1785 Inn** (800-421-1785; 603-356-9025; $–$$$) is a country inn with perhaps the best view of the Valley and an extensive wine list. You can cross-country ski or

Dining: $$$$–Entrees $30+; $$$–$20–$30; $$–$10–$20; $–less than $10.
Accommodations: (double room) $$$$–$200+; $$$–$141–$200; $$–$81–$140; $–$80 and less.

snowshoe right out the back door of **The Forest Inn** (800-448-3534; 603-356-9772; $$), a cozy B&B on Rte. 16A, and **The New England Inn** (800-826-3466; 603-356-5541; $$–$$$$), has everything from inn rooms to romantic cabins and a deluxe lodge, plus a lively pub.

North Conway: With a few exceptions, North Conway's lodging is more motels and hotels, including national chains. **Stonehurst Manor** (800-525-9100; 603-356-3113; $$–$$$), in a turn-of-the-century mansion has the setting, rooms and restaurant that are pure elegance. Breakfast and dinner meal plans are optional. **North Conway Grand Hotel** (800-648-4397; 603-356-9300; $$–$$$) has many creature comforts and 200 deluxe guest rooms.

A minute from Main Street, **The Kearsarge Inn** (800-637-0087; 603-356-8700; $$–$$$) has in-room hot tubs, fireplaces, TV and suites designed for families with children. Continental or American meal plan and ski and stay packages are available. The **Wildflowers Inn** (866-945-3357; 603-356-7567; $–$$$$) is a Victorian showplace with to-die-for views of the Presidential Range, comfy public rooms and spacious guest rooms and suites, all with fireplace. Suites have private hot tubs, but there's a communal one on the deck. Rates include a full country breakfast.

Adventure Suites (888-626-6929; $$$–$$$$) is themed resort with suites for every guest type, from Motorcycle Madness to the Love Shack. Extensive amenities include in-room Jacuzzi, free movies, billiards, video games and fireplaces. Includes a substantial continental breakfast bar. The **Buttonwood Inn** (800-258-2625; 603-356-2625; $$–$$$) is tucked in the woods with cross-country skiing from the back door. Ask about the family suites. Rates include a full breakfast and afternoon snacks. **The Eastman Inn** (800-626-5855; 603-356-6707; $–$$) delivers warm hospitality with a Southern accent. Breakfast with waffle irons almost at your table is superb.

White Mountain Hotel and Resort (800-533-6301; 603-356-7100; $-$$) is at the foot of Whitehorse Ledge (the enormous, sculptured, granite cliffs you see from all North Conway). The views back across the Valley toward Cranmore are unmatched. Don't miss the lavish Friday seafood buffet. **The Eastern Slope Inn Resort** (800-862-1600; 603-356-6321; $$), in the heart of North Conway, is a classic New England inn with an indoor pool. **The Green Granite Inn** (800-468-3666; 603-356-6901; $-$$) is on Rte. 16 on the mile-and-a-half shopping strip. It has an indoor pool and a hot tub, and evening movies and children's programs are offered during weekends and vacation periods.

Mt. Washington Valley Motor Lodge (800-634-2382; 603-356-5486; $$) is a pleasant surprise for families, with clean basic rooms and a swimming pool. **Red Jacket Mountain View** (800-752-2538; 603-356-5411; $$–$$$$), is a rambling building and some loft rooms and townhouses, both good for families. It has a panoramic view of the Moat Range and an indoor pool and hot tub and an indoor water park. **The Briarcliff** (800-338-4291; 603-356-5584; $-$$), updated from a classic 1950s motel, is affordable and convenient.

For rock-bottom prices, head to **Hostelling International-White Mountains** in Conway (603-447-1001; $).

 Dining

The **Rare Bear Bistro** and **Black Bear Pub** at The Bernerhof (603-383-4414; $$–$$$), in Bartlett on Rte. 302 has its own nationally famous cooking school. **Stonehurst** (356-3113; $$) and **The 1785 Inn**, in North Conway (603-356-9025; $$–$$$), have excellent cuisine. In Jackson, **The Christmas Farm Inn** (383-4313; $$–$$$), **The Inn at Thorn Hill** (383-4242; $$$), **Wentworth Resort Hotel** (603-383-9700; $$–$$$), and **Thompson House Eatery (T.H.E.)** (603-383-9341; $$$) are all fairly expensive but renowned for their fine dining.

For more down-to-earth meals, in Glen, try the **Red Parka Pub** (603-383-4344; $$), for great barbecued spare ribs and prime rib. They don't take reservations; come early or expect up to an hour wait on Saturday nights.

In North Conway, **Moat Mountain Smoke House & Brewing Co.** (356-6381, $$), is a family favorite for wood-grilled or smoked entrees as well as lighter fare such as pizza and quesadillas. It brews its own beer on premises. Try either Irish or American comfort food—such as shepherd's pie or baby back ribs—at **May Kelly's Cottage** (603-356-7005; $$-$$$) just north of the village. New to the scene is the **Tack Room Restaurant & Tavern** (603-356-0077; $-$$) with simple, tasty fare and extensive beer selections located in the old Bigelow stables on Route 16. Horsefeathers (603-356-2687; $-$$) is perhaps the most popular spot in town. For a good time and plenty to eat, it's hard to beat, but it you're looking for gourmet, pass this one up, the menu promises more than it can deliver. **The Flatbread Company** (603-356-6321, $-$$), in the Eastern Slope Inn, offers casual dining in a sun room.

Delaney's Hole-in-the-Wall (356-7776; $-$$), a locals' haunt, inexplicably has South-western flair. **Maestro's Cafe and Deli** (356-8790; $-$$) offers pasta specialties. **Decades** (603-356-7080; $$-$$$), is a standard fare steakhouse with a large draft beer selection and a decent wine list. On the Rte. 16 strip, the **Red Jacket Mountain View** (603-356-5411; $-$$) serves very good food. The Muddy Moose (603-356-7696; $$) has affordable prices as well as some exotic choices, such as Wild Boar Marsala or Venison Pasta.

Ethnic fare is plentiful. Head to the **Shannon Door Pub** (603-383-4211; $), in Jackson, for Irish entertainment and good thin-crust pizzas. Pizza, from thin-crust to deep-dish, is found at **Elvio's** (603-356-3208; $) in North Conway. For Mexican, locals head to **Margarita Grille** (383-6556; $-$$), formerly Margaritaville, just beyond the Red Parka, on Rte. 302, in Glen, or to **Cafe Noche** (603-447-5050; $), in a brightly colored building on Main Street, Conway.

On particularly crowded weekends in the Valley, head to the spacious quarters of the **Red Fox Pub & Restaurant** (603-383-6659; $$), just south of the covered bridge in Jackson. With seating for 200, chances are you won't have to wait. The Sunday Jazz Brunch here is a locals' favorite and a bargain at $5.95 per person. Or try the Western-themed **White Horse Saloon** (603-356-9745; $$) on West Side Road for great ribs and wild game at reasonable prices.

For breakfast, head to **Peaches** (603-356-5860; $) on the main drag in North Conway. In Jackson, we recommend **Yesterday's** (603-383-4457; $) or the **Wentworth Resort Hotel** (603-383-9700), which serves an exceptionally good breakfast for $8, or for lighter fare, stop by the **Jackson Bistro**. This is a good place to pick up fat sandwiches and fancy confections to stash for lunch.

In Gorham, **Welsh's** (603-466-2206; $) is a family restaurant that serves hearty break-fasts and lunches. The oversized muffins and charbroiled burgers are especially delicious. Next to the Royalty Inn, try the family-style **Crabby Jack's** (603-466-3312; $-$$) Mexican restaurant **Libby's Bistro** (603-466-5330; $$), on Exchange Street, earns high marks for its ever-changing menu of creative entrees such as duck au poivre with a balsamic rhubarb sauce and strawberry rhubarb chutney. For down-to-earth fare, you can't beat **Wilfred's** (603-466-2380; $-$$), where turkey is a specialty.

At the Appalachian Mountain Club (603-466-2727; $$), meals are served family-style: a great way to meet some new friends

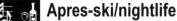

 ## Apres-ski/nightlife

The legendary **Red Parka Pub** offers lively après-ski and then nightlife activity into the wee hours. Something is happening every night, and its informal style runs to beer served in Mason jars to vintage skis and creative license plates covering the walls. Live music, live comedy or a movie is often featured; Open Mic Nights on Mondays.

In Jackson the **Wildcat Tavern** hops on weekends, or stop by **Shannon Door**.

For a mellow time and sipping a few beers, **Tuckerman's** at the New England Inn, on Rte. 16A in Intervale, is gaining in popularity, as is the **Moat Mountain Smokehouse and Brewery** on Rte. 16 on the northern edge of North Conway. On Friday and Saturday nights, **Horsefeathers**, in the center of North Conway, is standing-room only, and the **Up Country Saloon** and Red Jacket have live dance music. Locals hang out in **Hooligans, Horsefeathers** and **Delaney's Hole-in-the-Wall,** all in North Conway.

 ## Other activities

The Cranmore Sports Center (603-356-6301), at Cranmore base, is a huge all-season facility, with **indoor and outdoor tennis courts, pool, aerobics classes, steamroom** and **sauna**. It is also home to a huge (30 by 40 feet) **indoor climbing wall**. Classes are available through International Mountain Climbing School (603-356-6316). The owner, Rick Wilcox, has climbed Mt. Everest. Eastern Mountain Sports (603-356-5433) is in the Eastern Slope Inn. Both schools offer a range of **winter climbing and hiking programs**, including ice-climbing instruction, ascents of Mt. Washington and traverses of the Presidential Range.

The Appalachian Mountain Club (603-466-2721) has an active schedule of courses and workshops on **ski touring, snowshoeing, avalanches** and more. Take a **sleigh ride** in the Valley. Try Nestlenook's horse-drawn sleigh (603-383-0845) or The Stables at the Farm off West Side Road (603-356-6640). Sleigh rides can be combined with dinner at the Darby Field Inn (800-426-4147 or 603-383-2181), in Conway. Cranmore, Black Mountain, King Pine and Shawnee Peak have active **tubing hills**.

The Ham Arena (603-447-5886), in Conway, has **indoor ice skating**. Two-hour skating lessons start at $4 for children and $5 for adults. Call ahead for public skating hours. You can **ice skate** in Jackson, North Conway and at King Pine's covered ice arena (free with a lift ticket).

At the **Weather Discovery Center** (603-356-2137) experience what it felt like to be atop Mt. Washington in high winds or practice being a weather reporter and see yourself on TV.

Mt. Washington Valley may have the ski resort best **shopping** in the nation, with more than 100 factory outlets and no sales tax. The area also has many unusual boutiques with creative gift items. For a chance to meet local authors, stop by White Birch Books. The Chamber of Commerce in North Conway has Visitor Guides; as well as a map and guide to shopping.

Getting there and getting around

By air: Portland, Maine, less than 90 minutes from North Conway, is the closest major airport. Manchester, N.H., airport is about two hours by car.

By car: The Mt. Washington Valley is 140 miles north of Boston. Take I-95 to Rte. 16, then north on 16/302. An alternate route is I-93 north to Rte. 104 to Rte. 25 to Rte. 16 and on to North Conway. From Portland, follow Rte. 302.

North Conway has been notorious for its weekend traffic jams going through town. The new North-South connector road has taken some of the pressure off and is a good alternate route for those coming from the north or the south, but it's not well marked. Find it from the south by heading straight at all lights through Conway, turning left onto Route 302 about a mile out of town, and then turning right at the Wal-Mart (there's a light here, too).

It leaves you out right in the middle of North Conway, practically on Cranmore's doorstep. If you are driving from the Jackson/Wildcat/Attitash Bear Peak end of town to the south, the West Side Road lets you avoid most of the shopping traffic and the North Conway crowds. In any case, be patient if you're behind the wheel at 4 p.m., when the lifts close.

Getting around: Bring a car.

Other Mount Washington Valley Resorts

Black Mountain, Jackson, NH
800-698-4490; 603-383-4490; Internet: www.blackmt.com
4 lifts: 1 triple, 1 double, 2 surface lifts; 140 trail acres; 1,100 vertical feet

Black Mountain, a compact ski area at the top of Jackson Village on Rte. 16B, may be the best place in the valley for beginner lessons and family skiing. Wide-open Whitneys' Hill was the site of the first ski lessons in the Valley in 1936. Black is still an ideal place to take your first turns or have your children take theirs. The best beginner trails down the mountain are Sugarbush and Black Beauty, while Upper Galloping Goose and Mr. Rew offer some short expert fun. Upper-intermediate or expert skiers can play in the glades.

On the Jackson Ski Touring trail system, Black has more than its share of telemark skiers, both beginner and experts; with its top-to-bottom Skinny Ski Inferno, a classic event. Additionally, Black Mountain's southern exposure provides a warmer place to ski when it's just too cold at other Valley areas.

Lift tickets (07/08 prices): Adults, $39 weekends, $29 midweek; juniors (17 and younger) and seniors (65+), $25 weekends, $20 midweek; ages 5 and younger, free. The Passport, a day ticket valid for two adults and two juniors, is $99 weekends/holidays and $79 midweek.

Lessons: Group lessons cost $30 for a one-hour session. Learn to Ski or Ride is $59. Price includes rentals, lifts and lessons. Private lessons cost $45 per hour for one student.

Lodging information: 800-698-4490.

Purity Spring Resort/King Pine Ski Area, East Madison, NH;
800-373-3754; 603-367-8896; Internet: www.kingpine.com
5 lifts: 2 triples, 1 double, 2 surface lifts; 350 vertical feet; 60 skiable acres

King Pine is a little resort ideally suited for larger family gatherings of mixed skier (or rider) abilities. Some 80% of the terrain is designed for novice and intermediate skiers and riders, and wide, beginner-friendly trails take the intimidation factor out of learning for kids, as well as any first-timers. Along with night skiing Tuesdays, weekends and holidays, the resort rounds out the family recreational opportunities with snow tubing, snowshoeing, a beautiful 15-kilometer Nordic network and well-manicured ice rink.

Cozy bunkhouse-style rooms in the King Pine Lodge, and 70 other rooms at the Purity Spring Resort offer a range of lodging options, including cottages and condos. American Plan (AP) and Modified American Plan (MAP) accommodations are available. Midweek, the MAP includes lodging, alpine and XC skiing, breakfast and dinner, evening recreation, pool and ice skating. Weekend AP packages include lodging and six meals beginning with dinner on Friday night, ice skating and pool. Lift tickets are not included in weekend packages.

Lift tickets (08/09 prices): A wide variety of ticket options can be purchased a la carte or all-inclusive, and for a variety of time periods, including twilight, night and day/night. Adults, $42; kids (6–12) and seniors (65-69), $28; kids 5 and younger, free. You save 10% when purchasing consecutive-day, multi-day lift tickets. Night skiing is available. Tubing is $14 for two hours. **Lessons:** Group lesson cost $28 for 90 minutes. Private lessons cost $68 per hour. A First Time package is $66 adult/$53 junior (6-12)/$37 junior (4-5) for skiing or snowboarding; and first-tme junior snowboarders must be at least 8 years old. Package includes beginner lift ticket, rentals and lesson.

Shawnee Peak, Bridgton, Maine

207-647-8444; Internet: www.shawneepeak.com
5 lifts; 40 trails; 239 acres; 1,300 vertical feet; 2 terrain parks; 1 halfpipe

About a 30-minute drive from North Conway via Rte. 302, this family resort offers fantastic views across Maine's flatlands and lakes to the White Mountains. It has excellent snowmaking and a twice-a-day grooming program that allows for "first tracks" twice daily, if you're lucky. Its terrain offers a bit of something for everyone, and it's very popular with families. The toughest runs are at the top and left side of the mountain as you look at the trail map, and wide-open beginner slopes are to the right (or west).

Excellent, tight, gladed areas are nestled between the two sides of the mountain. Most of the trails to the left are New England-narrow. Upper/Lower Appalachian is a great steep cruiser with fabulous views that uses almost all of the mountain's vertical. Shawnee has the most extensive night skiing in New England with a lighted drop of 1,300 feet encompassing 17 trails. It also has a 68,000-square-foot learning area, a terrain park, a beginner terrain park and a 400-foot-long halfpipe.

Lift tickets (07/08 prices): Adults, $49 weekends/holidays and $34 midweek; ages 6–12 and 65 and older, $34 on weekends/holidays and $23 midweek; ages 5 and younger ski free when accompanied by a paying adult. Night skiing also is available until 9 p.m. Mon-Thurs and 10 p.m. Friday and Saturday; Monday night tickets cost $10 for everyone.

Lessons (07/08 prices): 3-2-1-Snow Fun, for first-time skiers or riders ages 8 and older, costs $189. It includes three days of lessons, lifts and rental equipment. For $319, you get a free season pass upon graduation. Individually, GET Skiing or Riding I offers two hours for $65; A one-hour private is $75. Children's lessons for all ages and abilities.

Children's Programs: State-licensed child care for children aged three months to six years. All-day programs are $60, including lunch; half-day programs are $40. Reservations using a credit card are required; call 207-824-5959. Lessons: Two First Timer Packages are offered for ages 8 and up. GET Skiing I is a 1.5 to 2-hour program, with rentals, lesson and beginner chair lift ticket; $65. GET Skiing II, also 1.5 to 2 hours, is for folks who skied a long time ago or first timers who are athletically inclined. Cost is $79 , including rentals, lesson and Pine Quad lift ticket. Helmets cost $10 extra. GET Snowboarding I and II are comparable. SKI-wee lessons for ages 4-5 on weekends/holidays are $70. For skiers 6-12, Junior Mountaineers offera half- and full-day lessons for $75/$95. Mini Riders for snowboarders aged 7-12 costa the same. Equipment rentals for these three programs are $15; helmet rentals $10.

Lodging information: For the limited number of condos on the mountain, call the ski area, 207-647-8444. For lodging in North Conway, call the Mt. Washington Valley Chamber of Commerce, 800-367-3364. The **Shawnee Peak House** (207-647-8444; $), an affordable 10-bedroom guesthouse, can handle up to 44 people and is ideal for families or groups.

Bretton Woods
New Hampshire

Summit:		**3,100**
Vertical:		**1,500**
Base:		**1,600**

Address: Route 302, Bretton Woods, NH 03575
Telephone (main): 603-278-3320
Snow Report Number: 603-278-3333
Toll-free reservations: 800-258-0330
E-mail: skiinfo@brettonwoods.com
Internet: www.brettonwoods.com
Expert: ★
Advanced: ★
Intermediate: ★ ★ ★
Beginner: ★ ★ ★ ★
First-timer: ★ ★ ★ ★ ★

Lifts: 9—4 high-speed quads, 1 quad, 1 triple, 1 double, 2 surface lifts
Skiable acreage: 434
Snowmaking: 92 percent
Uphill capacity: 14,000
Parks & pipes: 1 park, 1 pipe
Bed base: 3,400+
Nearest lodging: Slopeside
Child care: Yes, 2 months and older
Adult ticket, per day: $69 (08-09 prices)
Dining: ★★★★★
Apres-ski/nightlife: ★★
Other activities: ★★★

Great "family" skiing and absolute "hero" skiing are the two best ways to describe the ski experience at Bretton Woods. Challenge is not part of the equation here—it's really about getting the feeling that "boy, can I ski!" This goes for fledgling intermediates as well as 4-year-old beginners. Plus, you can't beat the views of New Hampshire's Presidential Range.

First opened in 1973, Bretton Woods stands in close proximity to the famed Mount Washington Hotel, that giant ark of a hotel. The ski area and the hotel, plus the Bretton Arms Inn, The Lodge, the Nordic center, and more than 900 surrounding acres comprise what is now known as Mount Washington Resort.

Bretton Woods' expansion into West Mountain and Rosebrook Canyon over the past 10 years has made it New Hampshire's largest ski area in terms of acreage, with four high-speed quads accessing the terrain. Long a destination for beginner and intermediate skiers, or those just looking for a relaxing day on the slopes, the mountain's gentle pitch and mostly wide-open terrain makes it a perfect place for all of the skiers in a family, from the youngest to the oldest.

With one base area, it's difficult to get lost, although at times, skiing the winding trails in the deep woods, you might feel lost. The free Learning Center quad serves a dedicated slope that allows beginners to easily link turns without knee-shaking fear.

The renovated base lodge is expansive. The children's center is convenient and well-equipped. And the staff, from parking attendants to cashiers, are genuinely happy to help.

With a little bit of pitch on the upper reaches of the newer slopes and the addition of glades—from wide-open gentle tree runs to gnarly stump- and tree-ridden precipices—there are now some thrills to be found for upper intermediate and expert skiers.

When the nearby Mount Washington Hotel began welcoming winter guests in late 1999, Bretton Woods became more than a regional ski area. It became a grand resort. The colossal turn-of-the-20th-century, Spanish Renaissance structure, with its Tiffany glass, one-sixth-mile-long wrap-around verandah, and plasterwork sculpted by Italian craftsmen has been updated and enhanced over the past year and a half, and look for the new 25,000-square-foot Spa at

Mount Washington Resort to open in December, 2008. Many celebrities —even presidents—have slept here. And, oh yes, there was that monetary conference in 1944.

Bretton Woods not only touts itself as a family ski resort, it really is. However, skiing isn't the only activity at Bretton Woods. The Mount Washington Hotel has a list of daily activities reminiscent of a cruise ship: morning fitness sessions, culinary demonstrations, martini tasting and bead workshops, just to name a few. Or hit the hotel during one of its many theme weekends, such as the Food & Wine Festival or Mardi Gras.

Night Skiing at Bretton Woods . When darkness falls, skiing continues. The Bethlehem Express high-speed detachable quad accesses the Bigger Ben, Big Ben and Bretton's Wood trails. The Lumber Yard Terrain Park hosts a "freestyle frenzy" informal jam session every Friday night. The Learning Center Quad is a four-person, user-friendly lift that services the lighted Rosebrook Meadow trail, ideal for the first-time skier or snowboarder. The Food Court, now serving Starbucks coffee, and Nash's General Store are open during night-skiing hours.

 ## Mountain layout–skiing & snowboarding

This is a mountain that was designed for beginners and intermediates but now has a growing assortment of glades and short steeps to provide thrills. The traditional Bretton Woods trails such as Sawyer's Swoop, Big Ben and Range View have been joined with an excellent series of expert glades in the newly developed West Mountain and Rosebrook Canyon. The trail names sound more sinister than they really are, however they do offer a quantum leap in difficulty over previous Bretton Woods trails.

Snowboarders, when riding back from West Mountain to the main base area, can avoid the Crawford Ridge, where its difficult to maintain momentum (and impossible for inexperienced snowboarders). About two-thirds of the way down Avalon, before a big rock on the right, turn right into the woods and cross over to Aggassiz. Then take the Coos Connector to the right and Coos Caper. To get to West Mountain off of Fabyan's Triple chair, speed and momentum are necessary to make it to the top of Avalon, so take off with keep-your-speed intentions.

◆◆**Expert, ◆Advanced:** Glades, glades, glades. Head to West Mountain and warm up on Peppersass or Cherry Mountain Slide, wide-open glades that aren't steep. The double-diamond glades on West Mountain have short steep pitches with varying density of trees. The most challenging terrain is now Rosebrook Canyon, an almost entirely gladed area on the resort's eastern side. With such thick, dark woods, this canyon feels like a backcountry experience. Only extreme-skiing junkies will be out of place and probably won't be found here unless they are skiing the trees out of bounds.

■ **Intermediate:** Cruising is ideal here. Coos Caper, Herb's Secret, Granny's Grit and Crawford's Blaze are great for just rolling those edges side-to-side. Strong intermediates won't feel over their heads on any of the single-black diamond trails such as MacIntire's Ride or Bode's Run. To sample glade skiing, try Peppersass, Cherry Mountain Slide or Millennium Maze on West Mountain. You can pop out on easier trails if the trees seem daunting.

●● **Beginner, ● First-timer:** The Zephyr and Bethlehem express quads serve long beginner runs perhaps the longest beginner runs you'll find anywhere. The traditional Bretton Woods trails, such as Sawyer's Swoop, Big Ben and Range View, are ideal for cruising on =autopilot. This is a good place for strong beginners to test their skills on blue runs such as Coos Caper and Granny's Grit. For first-timers, the Learning Center quad serves Rosebrook Meadow and Rosebrook Lane, both dedicated learning slopes.

Parks and pipes

Experienced riders might find the Accelerator Halfpipe and Terrain Park a bit of a yawn, but it suits the intermediates who favor this resort. Lit for night riding, they're professionally groomed by a Pipe Magician from Piston Bully, the manufacturer of groomers that are the demand for worldwide FIS and World Cup events.

Cross-country & snowshoeing (see also xcskiresorts.com)

This area averages 200 inches of snow every year. The 100 km. of cross-country and snowshoeing trails are on the grounds of the Mount Washington Hotel, and they offer 1,700 acres of spectacular scenery. The trail system is dotted with a series of restaurants and lounges. Intrepid cross-country skiers can glide from the top of the Bretton Woods ski area back to the hotel. Snowshoers who purchase a trail pass can use the skate lanes of the cross-country trails. Complimentary guided 90-minute ski tours through the Ammonoosuc Valley are available. They leave from the Nordic Center daily.

The variety and extent of trails rivals that of the nearby Jackson Ski Touring and Vermont's Stowe system. Trail fees are $17 for adults (ages 13-64) and $10 for juniors (ages 6-12) and seniors (ages 65 and older). Children 5 and younger ski free. Cross-country gear, snowshoes and pulks can be rented. There is a cross-country ski school and a telemark ski school, as well.

Lessons (08/09 prices)

Group lessons: $35 for 90 minutes.
First-timer package: The Red Carpet Learn-to-Ski, includes equipment, all-day lessons and a limited lift ticket for $69 per day.
Private lessons: $85 for one hour; $250 for a half day; $275 for a full day. Discounts available for additional students in a lesson.

Special programs: A Demo & Lesson package is a private lesson using the resort's demo fleet of skis, $95. Quick tips are a one-run lesson with a pro for $35.

Children's Programs (07/08 prices)

Child care: The Babes in the Woods program, with stories, crafts and games for ages 2 months to 5 years, is $85 for a full day (8 a.m.–4:30 p.m.) with lunch; $55 for a half day, morning or afternoon. Hourly prices are $15 with a two-hour minimum. Ski and Snow Play Program, a gentle introduction to skiing for children ages 3-5, is $115 for a full day (8 a.m.–4:30 p.m.) with lunch or $85 for the morning only. Reservations are required; call 603-278-3325.

Children's lessons: The Hobbit Ski and Snowboard School has ski (ages 4-12) and snowboard (ages 6-12) lessons with lunch and rentals for $115 full day; $85 half day. Reservations are required for snowboard programs; call 800-278-3345.

Lift tickets (08/09 prices)

One day, weekend/holiday: adults $69 ($59 for resorts guests), junior (5-12) $41 ($35). Three days: adults $164, juniors $100. Five days: $239/$147. One day midweek: adults $59 ($50), junior $25. Three days: $121/$82.

Who skis free: Age 4 and younger. The Learning Center Quad chair is free for all.

Who skis at a discount: Teens 13-17 pay $55 ($47 resort guest) for one day (weekend/holiday); $47 ($40) for one day (midweek non-holiday); $100 for three days (midweek non-holiday); and $156 for five days (midweek non-holiday). Seniors 65-plus pay $69 ($59 resort guest) for one day weekend/holiday, $25 midweek, non-holiday; $48 for three days, and $80 for five days midweek non-holiday. The Family Interchangeable Ticket allows parents to trade the ticket between each other; $69.

On non-holiday Wednesdays, two adults ski/ride for $59. On non-holiday Thursdays, seniors pay $45 for a lift ticket and 1.5-hour group lesson. On non-holdiay Tuesdays, $115 buys mothers (or grandmothers) a lift ticket and a child's all-day Hobbit Ski or Snowboard program.

Night skiing: Offered Friday and Saturday, from Dec. 26, 2008, through early March, and nightly during holiday weeks. A twilight ticket, valid 2 to 9 p.m., is $43 for all ages except juniors, who pay $34; a night ticket, valid 4 to 9 p.m., is $23 for all ages.

Accommodations

Accommodations at the resort: All Bretton Woods properties can be reached through 877-873-0626 or 603-278-1000. In winter, a complimentary shuttle operates to and from the slopes. Be sure to ask about packages, as Bretton Woods offers plenty, including themed weekends, such as food-and-wine, Mardi Gras, etc.

At first sight of the **Mount Washington Hotel** ($$$-$$$$) children will gasp, "It's a castle!" And it is. Flags fly from the two octagonal towers that anchor New England's largest wooden structure. From the expansive lobby defined by rows of square Corinthian columns to the classic operator-run elevator, the hotel defines Old World Charm, a step back in time, with excellent service and a touch of class: an orchestra plays on weekends in the dining room, and guests are asked to dress appropriately (that means jackets for gentlemen) in the dining room after 6 p.m. Shops and a great bar line the lower level, while the first floor has sitting areas in the main lobby and several private rooms for smaller functions or quiet reading. A new spa opens in December, 2008. The cross-country center, indoor and outdoor heated pools, ice skating and tubing hill are all at hand; the Alpine area is across the street.

The restored 1896 **Bretton Arms Inn** ($$-$$$) is more intimate. It has spacious rooms, old-fashioned charm, an excellent dining room, and guests may use all resort facilities. **The Lodge** ($-$$) caters to those on a budget. Rooms are nice, but not fancy; there's an indoor pool; and guests may use all Bretton Woods facilities, including the shuttlebus and the sports center. Bretton Woods also has **The Townhomes**, a group of 70 condominiums.

The **Notchland Inn** (800-866-6131; 603-374-6131; $$-$$$$), in Hart's Location, has 13 rooms, all with fireplaces. It has a hot tub, skating, and cross-country skiing from the door. **The Mulburn Inn** (800-457-9440; 603-869-3389; $$-$$$) in Bethlehem is an elegant Tudor-style B&B. At the **Appalachian Mountain Club's Highland Center** (603-466-2727; $-$$) at Crawford Notch rates include a hot buffet breakfast and a multi-course, all-you-can-eat supper. The lodge has 45 rooms, including private and family rooms (with private baths), and shared rooms/baths. Environmental educational programs are offered.

Dining

Unless noted, the phone number for all restaurants listed is **603-278-1000**.

The opulent **Dining Room at the Mount Washington Hotel** ($$-$$$) provides a unique and grand setting for any meal complete with serenading orchestra, daily menus, an extensive wine list and meals of extraordinary quality. Proper attire is required in the evenings (gentlemen, that means jackets). For a more intimate, atmosphere, try the **Bretton Arms Dining Room** ($$-$$$), recommended for its superb cuisine. For casual dining, head to **Stickney's** ($$) on the first floor of the Hotel.

Locals recommend the fine dining at **Notchland Inn** (800-866-6131; 603-374-6131; $$-$$$) in Hart's Location. Near the slopes, try **Darby's Tavern** ($-$$) for pizza and subs. **Fabyans Station** ($-$$) is a good eatery in an old railroad station. For cheap eats, the **AMC's Highland Center** (603-278-HIKE; $-$$) serves a hot buffet breakfast, lunch and a multi-course all-you-can-eat dinner, family style.

On the mountain, the **Top O' the Quad Restaurant** ($$) serves casual lunches daily. On West Mountain, stop by the railway car at the top for BBQ ($). In the base lodge, there's the **Slopeside Restaurant and Lounge** ($-$$) and **Lucy Crawford's Food Court** ($-$$).

Apres-ski/nightlife
Bretton Woods is not known for wild nightlife and apres-ski, still there's enough to keep most guests happy. You can dance to a dinner orchestra or head down into the stone depths of the Mount Washington Hotel to the **Cave Lounge**.

Other activities
The Mount Washington Hotel's activities include **horse-drawn sleigh rides, dogsledding, skating rink** and an **indoor pool** and **outdoor heated pool**. Don't miss the **historic hotel tour** offered daily. The resort also has **snow tubing,** and a separate sports center with **indoor pool, racquetball courts, exercise** and **weight rooms, hot tubs** and **sauna**. A new, full-service spa opens in December, 2008.

The historic steam-driven **Cog Railway**, is a "don't miss" activity, taking passengers one mile up (1,100 vertical feet) the flanks of Mt. Washington, New England's highest peak. It may sound intimidating, but its not. Wear an old jacket though. Soot from the coal-fired engine can be nasty. The train runs twice a day on weekends and during holiday weeks. Fare is $31 adults, $26 children; call 800-922-8825 for information.

Nearby, Cannon is home to the **New England Ski Museum**, a collection of ski memorabilia well worth a brief visit. **Cannon's tram** is open for non-skiing sightseers too.

The Rocks Estate in Bethlehem (800-639-5373) has **sleigh rides** and offers some **forestry-related activities**, as it's owned by the Society For The Protection of New Hampshire Forests. Nearby, Twin Mountain is one of New England's top **snowmobiling** areas, and the Mt. Washington Hotel offers its own snowmobiling program.

The AMC's Highland Center (603-466-2727) offers a full-range of **outdoor and educational programs, including rock climbing, snowshoeing, slide shows** and **natural history programs**. For a **shopping** spree, the factory outlet bonanza of North Conway is 30 miles southeast of Bretton Woods. No sales tax makes buying all the sweeter.

Getting there and getting around
By air: Boston's Logan Airport is 150 miles from the area. Manchester Airport, 100 miles south, is serviced by most major carriers and Southwest.

By car: From I-93 heading north, Bretton Woods is on Rte. 302: take Exit 35 to Rte. 3, which meets Rte. 302 at Twin Mountain.

Getting around: A car is a necessity to reach the resort conveniently, but a shuttle bus operates throughout the resort.

Dining: $$$$–Entrees $30+; $$$–$20–$30; $$–$10–$20; $–less than $10.
Accommodations: (double room) $$$$–$200+; $$$–$141–$200; $$–$81–$140; $–$80 and less.

Cannon Mountain
New Hampshire

Summit:	**4,146**
Vertical:	**2,146**
Base:	**2,000**

Address: Franconia Notch State Park
Franconia, NH 03580
Telephone (main): 603-823-8800
Snow Report Number: 603-823-7771
E-mail: info@cannonmt.com
Internet: www.cannonmt.com

Expert: ★ ★
Advanced: ★ ★ ★
Intermediate: ★ ★ ★ ★
Beginner: ★ ★ ★
First-timer: ★ ★ ★

Lifts: 9 — 1 70-personl tram, 1 high-speed quad, 2 quads, 3 triples, 1 surface lift, 1 moving carpet
Skiable acreage: 165
Snowmaking: 97 percent
Uphill capacity: 11,000
Parks & pipes: 1 terrain park
Bed base: 13,000 nearby
Nearest lodging: about 1/2 mile
Child care: Yes, 6 weeks and older
Adult ticket, per day: $60 (08/09 price)
Dining: ★ ★
Apres-ski/nightlife: ★
Other activities: ★ ★

World Cup ski racing phenom Bode Miller grew up skiing here. As a daring youngster, Miller honed his skills with free rein on the classic, narrow trails and the intimidating Front Five, which can be seen from I-93 and are as steep as you'll find in the East.

In the early 1930s, people came to Franconia Notch in winter for one reason: to ski Cannon Mountain on trails had been cut by the legendary CCC crews. More than 70 years later, people are still coming to ski, and now to snowboard, too. Like other historic ski areas, Cannon offers trails that wind their way down the mountain—for those not afraid to pick up some speed, it's possible to turn with the trail like it's a natural giant slalom course—as the trails make narrow, sinuous turns through the pine forest.

But that's not to say that beginners and intermediates should head elsewhere. As much hard-corps terrain as there is at Cannon, there are even more intermediate and beginner trails. More than two-thirds of the trails off the summit are smooth, wide, blue runs with stunning views. From the top, skiers can see the Presidential Range of the White Mountains and no signs of civilization except for the highway and base lodges.

Cannon embraces its history. The mountain is home to the New England Ski Museum, located adjacent to the Tram base, It's well worth a visit. The Taft Slalom is part of the first racing trail in North America, cut in 1933. And when the original 1938 aerial tramway was replaced in 1980, Cannon didn't tear down the base or summit stations.

On a quiet day, you half-expect the ghost-of-skiing-past to fly out of the woods, but it's more likely to be the next Bode-Miller-in-training. Cannon is indeed a favorite for families with skiers and riders of all levels. The summit building is recently renovated, making it easier to access it and the trails from the tram summit. And the Tuckerbrook quad area, which is a completely separate beginner area with its own lower priced lift ticket, is a perfect place for families with young children or beginners practicing their first turns.

Mountain layout– skiing and snowboarding

Cannon underwent a major expansion and renovation in 1999, but to those who love New England skiing, the Cannon of old is still recognizable. Long-known by experts as one of the most challenging mountains in the East, Cannon now has much more beginner and intermediate terrain.

◆◆ **Expert,** ◆**Advanced:** True experts will want to try the extreme terrain on Tramline Trail, and we're not misusing the word "extreme." The narrow trail is a series of cliff steps.

One of the longest glades in the East is Kinsman Glade, on skier's right of the tramline. The Front Five, as known to locals, are the intimidating-looking trails that appear to plunge into Echo Lake. These are accessed via Paulie's Extension or Lower Cannon. Three of them, Avalanche, Paulie's Folly and Zoomer, are marked black and rightfully so. The other two, Rocket and Gary's, have less pitch and no bumps.

For a backcountry experience, take Taft Slalom straight across the ridge, then hike the remaining few yards to Mittersill, Cannon's defunct neighbor. Skiers and riders can use Mittersill's trails on a don't-ask, don't-tell basis, but it's unpatrolled; you're on your own there.

From the summit, advanced skiers can experience New England skiing the way it used to be by winding down Upper Cannon, Skylight or Upper Ravine. To test your mettle on the Front Five, start on skier's left (Gary's) and work right until you feel you've hit your limit.

■ **Intermediate:** Although touted as an expert's mountain, intermediates will find plenty of terrain to suit their skills. From the summit, you can take Vista Way, Tramway or Upper Cannon, which swoops down through the forest. These feed into a collection of intermediate runs, including Middle Cannon and Middle Ravine. Or from the top of the Cannonball Express Quad, treat yourself to Upper Ravine, another swooping trail.

Intermediates wishing to return to the tram without scaring themselves on the Front Five can follow the Tram Cutback from Gary's, the easiest of the Front Five.

● ● **Beginner,** ● **First-timer:** The Tuckerbrook quad chair serves beginner trails—Bear Paw, Deer Run, Fleitman and Coyote Crossing—that are segregated from the upper mountain. From the Peabody Base Area, take Brookside to the Tuckerbrook area. The bottom half of Cannon has four long runs that suit beginners: Lower Cannon, Parkway, Gremlin and Turnpike; but, be forewarned that a slew of intermediate runs feed into them. The Eagle Triple Chair, from the Peabody Base Area, is the best way to access this terrain. More daring beginners can take the Peabody Express Quad.

The Brookside learning area adjacent to the Peabody Base Area is ideal for first-timers. The area is segregated from the rest of the mountain (so experts won't zoom through). It is serviced by its own triple chairlift as well as two surface lifts. First-timers can then progress to the short beginner trails off the Tuckerbrook quad chair

Parks and pipes

Cannon's terrain park is on the lower section of Toss-Up. Cannon is committed to a snowboarder-designed park. It encourages user-feedback. Both have greatly enhanced the experience.

Cross-country & snowshoeing (see also xcskiresorts.com)

The Franconia Village X-C Ski Center (800-473-5299) has 105 km. of trails, 65 km. groomed and tracked; 5 km. skate groomed. Ski-stay-sleigh packages are available through the Franconia Inn; same phone number.

Lessons (07/08 prices)

Group lessons: $36 per session.

First-timer package: The all-day learn-to-ski or -ride program costs $54 and includes lessons, rentals and a Brookside lift ticket.

Private lessons: One hour, $56; two hours, $81; three hours, $126; full day, $196.

Special programs: A ski guide for up to five people is $295 for a full day; $150 half day. Three workshops are available at 1:30 p.m. on weekends and holidays: mastering bumps, mastering Cannon's famous Front Five, and women's groups.

Children's Programs (07/08 prices)

Child care: For ages 6 weeks and older. For ages 12 months and older, $11 per hour; $36 for a half day; $77 for a half day with skiing; $61 for full day with lunch; $87 for full day with lunch and skiing. Hourly rates require two-hour minimum. Reservations advised; call 603-823-7722 ext 724.

Children's lessons: Cannon Kids is for skiers ages 4–7. Mountain Explorers is for skiers and riders ages 8–12. A half day lesson is $61; half day with rentals, $76; full day, $81; full day with rentals, $96.

Lift tickets (08/09 prices)

One day: Adult $60, Teen (13-19) $42, Child (6-12)/Seniors65+ $32

Who skis free: Ages 5 and younger when with a ticketed adult.

Who skis at a discount: On non-holiday Tuesdays and Thursdays, two people can ski for $60. The Tuckerbrook area is $30 any time. The Brookside beginner lift is free any time. Ages 65 and older pay junior rates. College students with ID pay teen rates.

Accommodations

Cannon has no slopeside lodging, but nearby Lincoln and Woodstock (about 15 minutes south) and Franconia (about 5 minutes north) have accommodations to suit just about any need. Plus, Bretton Woods is within striking distance. See Loon for recommended accommodations in the Lincoln/Woodstock area, or call Lincoln/Woodstock Central Reservations at 603-745-6221.

Long known as a ski town, Franconia has several quaint New England Inns, the nicest being the **Sunset Hill House** (800-786-4455; 603-823-5522; $-$$) and the **Franconia Inn** (800-473-5299; 603-823-5542; $$-$$$). Just outside Franconia on historic Sugar Hill (the site of the first ski school in North America), the **Sunset Hill House** is a restored farmhouse built in 1789 that has wonderful views of the Presidentials and the Green Mountains. **The Franconia Inn** is a lovely turn-of-the-century inn with hand-hewn beams in the cozy lobby and a sunny dining room. Some of the rooms have been renovated recently; others still have quaint old bathrooms with claw-foot tubs.

The Inn at Forest Hills (603-823-9550; $-$$) is a beautifully restored, English Tudor-style B&B built into a house that was once part of the grand Forest Hills Hotel. It's just about a mile from the village of Franconia, on Rte. 142, heading toward Bethlehem. The modern **Franconia Village Hotel** (888-669-6777; 603-823-7422; $$) has an indoor heated pool, fitness and games rooms, and a full-service restaurant.

Among the inexpensive lodgings are the **Hillwinds Lodge** (800-473-5299; 603-823-5551; $); the **Cannon Mountain View Inn** (800-823-9577; 603-823-9577; $), with rooms renovated in early 2004; and **The Eastgate Motor Inn** (866-640-3561; 603-444-3971; $) just off I-93. **The Kinsman Lodge** (866-546-7626; 603-823-5686; $) is a casual and affordable B&B.

About 30 minutes north is the newly renovated and reopened **Mountain View Grand** (866-484-3843; 603-837-2100; $$-$$$$). This sprawling historical hotel now houses a European-style spa on the fourth floor, and has a fitness center, indoor pool and steamroom.

 ## Dining

For elegant dining the **Sunset Hill House** (603-823-5522; $$) with views of the Franconia Range, and the **Franconia Inn** (603-823-5542; $$-$$$) are the best. Both establishments require reservations, even if you're a guest.

The **Pub with Mexican Grub** ($-$$) recently opened in the Franconia Hotel. For more traditional fare, head to the **Village House** (603-823-5405; $-$$) in downtown Franconia, where prime rib is the Saturday-night special, or The **Eastgate Restaurant** (603-444-3971; $-$$), considered one of the better local restaurants.

For breakfast, a drive of a few miles up I-93 to Littleton takes you to the **Littleton Diner** (603-444-3994; $), a traditional old diner car where you can get a great breakfast.

See **Loon Mountain** for more dining recommendations in the area.

 ## Apres-ski/nightlife

With no restaurants nearby, Cannon is not exactly bustling with apres-ski activities, but on cold days and immediately after skiing, **The Lift Pub** in the Peabody Base Lodge at the mountain is usually quite busy. The bar at the **Cannon Mountain View Inn** gets a lot of action, while down the road in Franconia, the **Village House** is a comfortable lounge with a lot of classic ski history and an evening entertainer. Or head back down I-93 and catch up with Loon skiers partying at **Woodstock Station** or the **Indian Head Resort**, where there are live bands Wednesday through Sunday.

 ## Other activities

The **New England Ski Museum** sits adjacent to Cannon's Tramway Base Station and has a collection of ski memorabilia well worth a visit. The museum is open noon-5 p.m. Friday-Monday, and admission is free. Cannon's tram is open for non-skiing sightseers for $10 a ride. **Snowtubing** at Cannon's tubing park on weekends and holidays costs $10 per session.

The Rocks Estate (800-639-5373) in Bethlehem, on a hilltop about 10 miles from Cannon, has **sleigh rides** and offers some **forestry-related activities**, since it's owned by the Society For The Protection of New Hampshire Forests.

The Franconia Inn (800-473-5299; 603-823-5542) has an **ice skating pond, sledding hill, winter horseback riding,** and **sleigh rides** and equipment rentals.

 ## Getting there and getting around

By air: Boston's Logan Airport is about 145 miles away from Cannon and the Franconia area. Manchester Airport is 85 miles south.

By car: From I-93 heading north, Cannon is visible from I-93 just north of Franconia Notch State Park. Take Exit 34B for the Tramway Base Station, Exit 34C for the Peabody Base Area.

Getting around: There is no on-mountain lodging; a car is a necessity.

Dining: $$$$–Entrees $30+; $$$–$20–$30; $$–$10–$20; $–less than $10.
Accommodations: (double room) $$$$–$200+; $$$–$141–$200; $$–$81–$140; $–$80 and less.

Loon Mountain
New Hampshire

Summit:	3,050 feet
Vertical:	2,100 feet
Base:	950 feet

Address: RR1, Box 41,
Lincoln, NH 03251
Telephone (main): 603-745-8111
Snow Report Number: 603-745-8100
Toll-free reservations: 800-229-5666
E-mail: info@loonmtn.com
Internet: www.loonmtn.com

Expert: ★
Advanced: ★ ★
Intermediate: ★ ★ ★ ★
Beginner: ★ ★ ★ ★
First-timer: ★ ★ ★

Lifts: 12—1 gondola, 3 high-speed quads, 1 quad, 1 triple, 3 doubles
Skiable acreage: 324
Snowmaking: 96 percent
Uphill capacity: 11,865
Parks & pipes: 6 parks, 2 pipes
Bed base: 13,000
Nearest lodging: Slopeside
Child care: Yes, 6 weeks and older
Adult ticket, per day: $69 (07/08 prices)
Dining: ★ ★ ★
Apres-ski/nightlife: ★ ★ ★
Other activities: ★ ★ ★

Loon switched ownership from Booth Creek to Boyne early in the 2007-08 season and many clients didn't take notice. They should this year. Along with fellow Boyners, Sugarloaf and Sunday River in Maine, Loon will offer the New England Pass for all three, plus a free "Boyne" points program. Still, the biggest difference here for fans is not ownership but expansion.

Last year Loon's faithful got just a peek at the long awaited South Peak. Now, there's more to see on and off the steadily expanding trail system. This year's major addition to the trails is Rip Saw, Loon's first double black diamond. It connects the top section of Boom Run to the lower section of Cruiser. The other new trail, Escape Route looks like a run to nowhere, dumping downhillers in the parking lot away from the current base facility. It's no joke. It's a portent of things to come as +Loon looks to start South Peak's base facilities in the next few years including a hotel/guest center.

The bulk of Loon's trails remain on the main mountain and provide decent vertical and plenty of choices. Many of the runs maintain their pitch from top to bottom (unlike some resorts, where most of the runs wash out to beginner terrain near the base). The mountain's black-diamond terrain will keep experts entertained, but, for the most part, Loon is an intermediate's mountain. The blue-square runs are true-blue friends for intermediates; beginners who venture onto them may find their limits tested.

The resort has some of the friendliest staff around, which keeps skiers and riders coming back. It also offers plenty of family-friendly activities, including snow tubing (both day and night), a climbing wall, and an ice skating rink. The two base areas are separated by a parking lot, but connected by a steam train that shuttles skiers and riders back and forth, a real hit with children. A shuttle bus connects South Peak to the Governor's and Octagon Lodges.

When it comes to lodging, the resort is a behemoth. It's one of the few resorts where the bed base is larger than the lift capacity. Combined with easy access off I-93 from Boston and other points south, this can create crowded conditions at times. Fortunately, Loon has made a number of improvements during the past few years. Among these are trail work to relieve congestion in high-traffic stretches, new lifts to get people up the mountain faster, the Burton Progression Terrain Park, more snowmaking coverage and a dedicated learning area.

Visitors to Loon in 08/09 will notice a new building near the base. It houses the White Mountain Adaptive Snowsports Program. The expanded space will allow the staff and volunteers working in this program to better enable physically and mentally challenged people to experience the beauty, challenges and community that attracts so many to Loon Mountain.

You can reserve tickets and/or lodging packages with a major credit card ahead of time on the resort's website or by calling 800-229-5666. The Unconditional Satisfaction Guarantee ensures you'll like the conditions, or you'll ski or ride free on your next visit.

Mountain layout–skiing & snowboarding

◆◆**Expert,** ◆**Advanced:** North Peak runs are challenging and well removed from lower-intermediate traffic. The steeps are there, but half the bumps are groomed out. To reach North Peak, take the gondola, then ski down Big Dipper, Triple Trouble or Angel Street to the North Peak Triple Chair. In fresh snow, experts will like the three tree-skiing areas: one is accessed off Upper Flying Fox, another off Angel Street and the third off Haulback, between Lower Flume and Lower Walking Boss. The steady steep pitch of Rip Saw should give experts a reason to spend some time at South Peak this season.

■ **Intermediate:** The intermediate runs are good and solid, with no expert surprises around the next clump of trees. The upper trails are a bit twisted, narrow and seemingly undirected, but they open onto a series of wide intermediate pistes. Flying Fox is a delightful cruise, with old-fashioned twists and turns through the trees and granite boulders. Depending on snow conditions, skiers can link up with the West Side trails via Upper Speakeasy, or they can drop down to the parking lot on many wide cruising runs (Rumrunner is a good choice, if there's no race on it), and ride the steam train the 100 yards to the adjacent base area and the gondola.

The sweetest, longest cruise is the perimeter-hugging Sunset to Bear Claw Extension to Upper Speakeasy to Lower Speakeasy, from the North Peak summit to the Governor's base.

●● **Beginner:** The center of the mountain, serviced by the Seven Brothers triple chair, has good intermediate trails that advanced beginners can handle. The east side of the chair has beginner runs such as Grand Junction, The Link, Brookway, and Lower Bear Claw.

● **First-timer:** There's a nice learning area next to the Governor Adams Base Lodge, , and a new magic carpet lift there gives first-timers an easy lift up the smooth Sarsaparilla slope.

Parks and pipes

The Kanc Quad and the Seven Brothers lift provide easiest access to the Loon Mountain Park between Lower Picked Rock and Picaroon. The gondola is also an option. Jumps range from little ones for newbies to hit-it-for-all-you're-worth-and-hope-you-make-it-to-the-landing kickers. Features include rails, a doghouse box, a rollercoaster rail and a 16-foot wall ride. We found good transitions and smooth landings, but the superpipe could use more grooming.

Loon has three Pocket Parks: Lower Picked Rock (with tabletops and a rail) and Bear Island Bypass (with berms and rollers) are designed for beginners. Little Sister is a boardercross with berms and rollers. The Burton Progression Park is perfect for novices.

Cross-country & snowshoeing (see also xcskiresorts.com)

The **Loon Mountain Cross-Country Center** (603-745-8111, ext. 5568) has 25km. of groomed and tracked trails that wind along the scenic Pemigewasset River. Children ages 5 and younger and seniors 70 and older ski free.

Lessons (07/08 prices)

Group lessons: $59 for three hours in the morning; $55 for the two hour afternoon session.

First-timer package: For skiers or riders, this includes equipment, two-hour lessons and lift ticket; cost $109. You can purchase two more days for the same price at any time during the season. Purchase three days and get a free pass for the remainder of the season.

Private lessons: For one person, $199 for three hours.

Racing: A race course is served by the Seven Brothers lift.

Children's Programs (07/08 prices)

Child care: Loon has a spacious Children's Center near the Governor Adams Lodge. Child care is available for ages 6 weeks to 6 years. Hours are 8 a.m. to 4 p.m. weekends and 9 a.m. to 4 p.m. midweek. A full day is $65. Reservations are required; call 603-745-8111.

Children's lessons: P.K. Boo Bear Ski Camp is a 3 year-old-only ski camp for beginner to novice ability, including full-day lift access, snacks, age-appropriate games, and up to two hours of on-snow instruction. Full-day, 9 a.m. to 3:30 p.m. with lunch costs $99. Half-day camps are available. KinderBear Camps for ages 4–6 of beginner to intermediate ability costs $99 full day with lunch and $74 half-day.

Beginner Discover Camp for ages 7-12 includes equipment and instruction; all day with lunch costs $99, half-day (no lunch) costs $80. Discovery Camp for experienced skiers costs $99 full day or $80 half-day, both including lunch. All children's lessons are run out of the Children's Center, which also houses a rental shop. Reservations are required for all programs; call 603-745-6281, ext. 5160 or 5162.

For novice snowboarders, Loon is a Burton Learn-To-Ride (LTR) Center.

Special activities: Teen skiers and riders join Sno Jam on weekends and holidays, all-day clinics for intermediates and above. The resort also offers teen Twilight Parties, with snow tubing, snowshoeing, ice skating, the climbing wall and a pizza party for ages 13-17 year-from 4:00-5:30 p.m. on select dates at Wanigan's Deli.

Lift tickets (07/08 prices)

	Adult	Child (6-12)
One day	$69	$49.
Three days	$189	$129.

Who skis free: Children ages 5 and younger, and seniors 80 and older.

Who skis at a discount: Young adults (13-18) pay $59 for one day; $159 for three days. Ages 65 -79 pay Young Adult rates.

Note: To reserve tickets, parking or rentals in advance, call 800-229-5666 or visit www.loonmtn.com.

Accommodations

The Mountain Club on Loon (800-229-7829; 603-745-2244) is a ski-in/ski-out property with everything under one roof, from parking to swimming pool, fitness club to restaurants, including a full-service spa. Note: Many of its rooms have a double Murphy bed with two small day beds along the windows. This arrangement is fine for couples, or for a family with young children, but it is awkward for two adults who don't want to sleep in the same bed. Instead, request two rooms that, when adjoined, make a suite. Loon also has condominiums. Make reservations through the Mountain Club.

The **Comfort Inn** (800-228-5150; 603-745-6700; $$) is right off I-93 at Hobo Railroad. It has both regular hotel rooms and one-bedroom suites with kitchenettes. Two prominent properties on the Kancamagus Highway (Main Street) in Lincoln are **The Mill House Inn** (800-654-6183; 603-745-6261; $-$$$) at The Mill and the **Nordic Inn Condominium Resort** (866-734-2164; 603-745-2230; $-$$), which offers condominiums (studios to three bedrooms). The **Rivergreen Resort Hotel** (800-654-6183; 603-745-2450; $$-$$$), owned by the same group that owns The Mill House Inn, is another condominium hotel. The last in a trio of "Mill" properties is **The Lodge at Lincoln Station** (800-654-6188; 603-745-3441; $$-$$$), a hotel along the Pemigewasset River. Accommodations are studios to one-bedroom suites. All of these properties are about one mile west of Loon.

Another couple miles away from Loon is **The Woodstock Inn B&B** (800-321-3985; 603-745-3951; $-$$), a typical New England lodge. The main building is more than 100 years old, and no two rooms are alike. You'll find the rooms tucked under the rafters, some with private bath, or shared bath, all with casual charm. Some rooms have hot tubs. The restaurant in the front of the inn is one of North Woodstock's most elegant; the one in the station at the rear is one of the town's liveliest. **Wilderness Inn B&B** (603-745-3890; $-$$) welcomes families with youngsters. Parents note: this place has laundry facilities. The B&B is only steps from the center of North Woodstock, which is filled with shops and restaurants.

Three motel-ish properties along Rte. 3 one exit up I-93 from Loon, have similar accommodations and prices, but different amenities. **Indian Head Motel Resort** (800-343-8000; 603-745-8000; $$) is a center of apres-ski action, with live bands, plus ice skating and Nordic skiing. **The Beacon** (800-258-8934; 603-745-8118; $-$$$) has indoor tennis and large indoor pools, but attracts the bus-tour crowd. **Woodward's Motor Inn** (800-635-8968; 603-745-8141; $-$$) is the most family oriented. It has the area's only racquetball court and best steaks. Another reasonably priced motel here is the **Drummer Boy Motor Inn** (800-762-7275; 603-745-3661; $-$$$), with an indoor pool, guest laundry and free continental breakfast.

 # Dining

The most elegant dining experience in the area is found at the **Woodstock Inn's Clement Room Grille** (603-745-3951; $$-$$$), which locals like for its informal dining with style, a great daily breakfast and   fabulous weekend brunch.

The Common Man (603-745-3463; $$-$$$) serves excellent food, with a menu ranging from lobster-corn chowder and rock-crab cakes to double-thick pork chops.

Locals claim the **Open Hearth Steak House** (603-745-8141; $$), at Woodward's Motor Inn, has the best steaks. The menu at **Gordi's Fish and Steak House** (603-745-6635; $-$$) ranges to steaks, Maine lobster, chicken, pasta and fish; a pub menu serves lighter fare.

Truant's Tavern (603-745-2239; $-$$) serves clever dinner entrees in a mock schoolhouse atmosphere; drinking in class was never so much fun. The bar hops on weekends. For a reasonably priced meal, head to **Woodstock Station** (603-745-3951; $-$$) in an old train station on Main Street. Options range from meatloaf to Mexican fare, and the restaurant brews its own beer. Locals agree that the best pizza in town is found at **Elvio's Pizzeria** (603-745-8817; $). The **Gypsy Cafe** (603-745-4395; $), on the Kancamagus Highway, across the street from The Mill is a good choice for either lunch or dinner, and don't miss the margaritas.

For convenient, on-mountain dining, there are two choices: the **Mountain Club on Loon**

Dining: $$$$–Entrees $30+; $$$–$20–$30; $$–$10–$20; $–less than $10.
Accommodations: (double room) $$$$–$200+; $$$–$141–$200; $$–$81–$140; $–$80 and less.

(603-745-2244; $$) and **The Black Diamond Bar** ($-$$), both at the Mountain Club. If you're off-mountain for lunch, **KimberLee's Deli** (603-745-3354; $), in Depot Plaza near the Loon entrance, has a good choice of sandwiches, soups, salads or breakfast bagel-wiches. In the Kancamagus Motor Lodge, **Brittany's Cafe** (603-745-3365; $-$$) is a good choice for either breakfast or dinner. **CJ's Penalty Box** (603-745-4899; $-$$) is a sports pub with light fare.

Winners for breakfast include the **Sunny Day Diner** (603-745-4833; $) and **Peg's Family Restaurant** (603-745-2740; $) in North Woodstock. Sunny Day also serves inexpensive homestyle dinners, such as salisbury steak and fried chicken. Or, try **King's Corner Cafe** (603-745-3802; $) in Depot Plaza for a full breakfast menu and deli sandwiches.

Apres-ski/nightlife

After skiing at Loon, head to the **Black Diamond Bar** in the Mountain Club for good weekend entertainment and a quiet apres-ski spot. The **Paul Bunyan Lounge** at the Octagon base has a young, rowdy crowd and really rocks. Or head to **Babe's** at the Governor Adams Lodge.

Off-mountain, those with romance on their minds head to the fireplace at the **Common Man**. Otherwise, **Gordi's Fish and Steak** has great munchies. Across the street, **CJ's Penalty Box Sports Bar and Pub** is usually hopping. Down Main Street, the **Olde Timbermill** in Millfront Marketplace has good singles action, with bands on weekends. From Wednesday through Sunday, live bands rock the **Indian Head Resort** The **Tavern Sports Bar** is low-key, with darts, video games and pool. Locals party at **Truant's Tavern** and **Woodstock Station**.

Other activities

Loon Mountain has **ice skating**, **tubing** (10 a.m. to 10 p.m. daily on Little Sister Trail on the Octagon side of the mountain), and **apres-ski entertainment for families**, with a separate **apres program for teens** during holiday periods and some weekends.

Profile Mountaineering, in Lincoln, offers introductory **ice climbing and winter mountaineering**. Alpine Village has a **rock-climbing wall**, as does the Pemi Valley Rock Gym (603-745-9800) in Woodstock. Alpine Adventures (603-745-9911) in Lincoln offers **guided snowmobile tours**. Creations in The Depot has **make-your-own pottery**. Lincoln also has a **movie theater** with four screens, several **specialty shops** worth a look, and some **factory outlets**. Factory outlet bonanza, North Conway, is 35 miles east, an hour's drive in winter.

Getting there and getting around

By air: Boston's Logan Airport is 140 miles from Loon. Manchester Airport (603-624-6556; www.flymanchester.com), 80 miles south, is served by Southwest and most major carriers.

By car: From I-93 heading north, Loon Mountain is about 2 miles east on the Kancamagus Highway (Route 112) from Exit 32 (Lincoln).

Getting around: Lincoln-Woodstock has a shuttle service and taxi, available anytime. Otherwise, a car is necessary.

Waterville Valley
New Hampshire

Summit: 4,004 feet
Vertical: 2,020 feet
Base: 1,984 feet

Address: One Ski Area Rd.,
Waterville Valley, NH 03215
Telephone (main): 603-236-8311
Snow Report Number: 603-236-4144
Toll-free reservations: 800-468-2553
E-mail: info@waterville.com
Internet: www.waterville.com

Expert:★
Advanced:★★
Intermediate:★★★
Beginner:★★★
First-timer:★★★

Lifts: 11—2 high-speed quads, 2 triples,
3 doubles,
Skiable acreage: 259
Snowmaking: 100 percent
Uphill capacity: 14,867
Parks & pipes: 5 parks, 2 pipes
Bed base: 2,500
Nearest lodging: Quarter-mile
Child care: Yes, 6 months-4 years
Adult ticket, per day: $61 (08/09 prices)
Dining:★★★★
Apres-ski/nightlife:★★
Other activities:★★

Since Waterville Valley is the first "big" resort on the way north on I-93, it's one of the most popular in New Hampshire. Its relatively low ticket prices add to its appeal. The resort built its reputation by staging 10+ World Cup ski races, but the emphasis now is on family. That has resulted in it becoming a more well-rounded area, as seen by its bountiful terrain parks.

A planned community/resort, Waterville Valley is sufficiently self-contained. The slopes are a short shuttle bus ride from the lodging and Town Square's shops, restaurants and bars. Most off-slope activities are in Town Square, including cross-country skiing, sleigh rides, ice skating, and a sports complex with pools, tennis, squash and racquetball courts and indoor track. Visitors can join family-oriented recreation programs, such as ice cream socials.

The mountain's single base area is ideal for families. Two high-speed quads start outside the base lodge, one being Quadzilla. Despite its scary name, the lift is decorated like a happy dog wearing a whirly-bird beanie. The propeller's speed shows wind speed. The other quad, White Peak Express, reaches almost to the summit. The High Country Double services the three uppermost intermediate slopes. Waterville enjoys significant vertical for an Eastern resort, although it's predominantly an intermediate's mountain. Almost all trails follow the fall line, top to bottom.

Mountain layout–skiing & snowboarding

Those without young children might find Waterville a bit limiting for a week's vacation, but fun for an extended weekend. There's a little bit of something for everyone. The emphasis is on "little bit" if you are an accomplished skier. That said, the black diamonds are really black diamonds and the blue squares are true intermediate runs, making them challenging for beginners. Waterville feels bigger than it is.

◆◆**Expert,** ◆**Advanced:** One of the toughest runs, True Grit, develops big moguls and drops down the Sunnyside face. With several tough rollers and steep pitches, the World Cup Slalom Hill is a good for testing experts' carving skills. There's a tree skiing area off Lower Bobby's Run about halfway down the trail on the left. Bobby's Run was named after the late

Senator Robert Kennedy, who frequented the resort after it opened in 1966.

■ **Intermediate:** Waterville's trails are not New England's typical steep and narrow pistes. Most are wide swaths with elbow room. Two former tough mogul runs, Ciao and Gema, are now groomed daily. Such trails as White Caps, Sel's Choice, Old Tecumseh and Tippecanoe are intermediate and advanced playthings. Upper Bobby's Run is a great intermediate trail, but if you don't want to find yourself on a black diamond or double-diamond mogul trail (Lower Bobby's), make sure you take a strong left to Terry's Trail or Old Tecumseh.

For a taste of tree skiing, Old T Trees is 4.5 acres of mixed hardwoods and evergreens for intermediates, located between the Old Tecumseh trail, Terry's trail, Tyler and Siegel Street. Something more resorts should do: Waterville has a designated "easier mogul field." For those wanting to move to the next level, this is great practice.

●●**Beginner,** ●**First-timer:** Beginner terrain at Waterville is limited, and beginners who have skied blue runs elsewhere might find Waterville's intermediate terrain challenging. But the Valley Run is a beginner/lower intermediate heaven with enough width to allow a couple days' skiing on different sections. This run is served by the Quadzilla high-speed quad.

Novices have a small area with a separate lift. Children have their own learn-to-ski area that's protected from other skiers and riders.

Parks and pipes

Waterville Valley has five terrain parks, including one for younger aficionados, a Boarder Cross that's open to the public, and a 400-foot-long superpipe. Waterville Valley also has a Burton progression park and is a Burton Learn to Ride Center.

The Exhibition Terrain Park & Halfpipe, located right above the base area, has a 16-foot superpipe, rails, tabletops, hips, trannies and kickers. The signature rail is a shaped C that's 22 feet long. The Hubba Street Course includes elements such as stairs and is at the base of Exhibition. While Exhibition has its own surface lift, if you access the top of the park from Psyched, you'll gain extra hits. There's a yurt at the park's summit where you can get warm. Younger kids can train for the big stuff in their own terrain park, Little Slammer, with minipipe, smaller tables, rails and boxes. Waterville also has a dedicated snowskate park next to the Quadzilla lift and an indoor skate ramp at the base lodge, tucked under the heated deck, with five-foot miniramp and lighted night sessions.

Cross-country & snowshoeing (see also xcskiresorts.com)

There are 76 km. of classic and skating trails with some of the best grooming in New England, as well as more than 35 km. of backcountry trails. The center has a couch, tables and a fireplace, and a full retail shop. Rentals and lessons are available, as are guided cross-country and snowshoe tours for all levels and ages. Call 603-236-4666 for more information.

Lessons (07/08 prices)

Group lessons: $37 for two hours. Multiple, transferable group lessons are available at five for $150 and ten for $270.

First-timer package: Learn to Ski/Ride costs $75 for lower mountain lift ticket (includes J-bar, Lower Meadows and Valley Run J-lift), a two-hour lesson and rental equipment. Snowboard lessons are through the Burton Learn To Ride Program. The Learn to Ski/Ride Passport program provides discounts for two more days. When you complete the third lesson, you'll receive a free season pass.

Private lessons: One person, one hour $95; $160 for two hours; $225 for three hours. Off-peak private lessons are available before 10 a.m. and after noon for $79 for one hour; $134 for two hours; $189 for three hours. Reservations required.

Special programs: Three-day Women's Retreats include lessons, video analysis, apres-ski parties and other special events. Call for dates and prices.

Racing: A course on Utter Abandon has races Wednesdays and Friday to Sundays.

Children's Programs (07/08 prices)

Child care: Waterville has two nurseries at its base area. Child care is available for ages 6 months to 4 years. All day is $72, with multiday discounts. Half day is $55, hourly is $20. Lunch is available for $7, or children may bring their own. Reservations required to ensure a space. Call 603-236-8311, ext. 3136.

Children's lessons: Mogul Mites, for 3-year-olds, Explorers, for ages 4-6, and Scouts, for ages 7-12, all cost $82 for a full day (with lunch). Ages 7 and older must buy lift tickets. Rental equipment is extra; rental helmets are available.

Lift tickets (08/09 prices)

One day: adult $61, teens (13-18)$51, youth (6-12) $37. Add-a- Day (per-day, any days) $51/$41/$27.

Who skis free: Children ages 5 and younger.

Who skis at a discount: Seniors 65 and older pay youth prices. College students with valid ID pay teen prices. The Parent Predicament ticket allows parents to use the same ticket so they can share baby sitting duties. Purchase tickets 48 hours in advance online and save $10 per day.

Note: Waterville charges one price for weekdays, weekends and holidays. New for 2008/09, Bretton Woods, Cranmore and Waterville Valley offer an anytime use pass, $849.

Accommodations

Waterville Valley has 2,500 beds in its Village, about 1.5 miles from the slopes. To make reservations at any Waterville Valley accommodations listed below, call 800-468-2553 or 603-236-8311. The "Winter Unlimited" package is all inclusive, offering all of Waterville's winter activities plus lodging for one price.

The **Golden Eagle Lodge**, with condominium suites, features a distinctive design reminiscent of the turn-of-the-century grand hotels. Additionally, Waterville has three hotel properties and four groups of condominiums, all in the valley. The **Valley Inn and Tavern** operates as a country inn with rates that can include meals, and the **Black Bear Lodge** is more hotel-like. All are in the same price range. The **Best Western/Silver Fox** offers continental breakfast and is the most economical place to stay. Condominiums also are available.

Dining

The most elegant dining is the **William Tell** (603-726-3618; $$-$$$) on Rte. 49 just down the valley from the resort. It has a strong Swiss-German accent with excellent wines. On Saturday nights, take a 30-minute snowcat ride up the slopes to the **Schwendi Hutte** (603-236-8311, ext. 3000). The food is some of the best in the valley, as is the ambiance. Reservations are required, and the snowcat ride and meal cost $65/person. Schwendi Hutte also has the best on-mountain lunch. Here you can slip off your boots and warm your tootsies in the slippers provided.

Dining: $$$$–Entrees $30+; $$$–$20–$30; $$–$10–$20; $–less than $10.
Accommodations: (double room) $$$$–$200+; $$$–$141–$200; $$–$81–$140; $–$80 and less.

The **Wild Coyote Grill** (603-236-4919; $-$$) in the White Mountain Athletic Club, offers nouveau cuisine with a Southwestern flair; calamari is a specialty. For moderately priced, Italian family fare, try **Aglio** (603-236-3676; $-$$) or call **Olde Waterville Valley Pizza Co.** (603-236-3663; $). **Diamond Edge North** (603-236-2006; $$), also in Town Square, offers classier meals with nicer presentations.

On warm days, head for barbecue on the deck of **Sunnyside Up** on Valley Run. The base area has a cafeteria, pizza corner and T-Bars. The food at **T-Bars** is nothing to write home about, but the ski memorabilia lining the walls is interesting. For breakfast, get coffee and pastries at **Waterville Coffee Emporium** (603-236-4021; $) or **Jugtown Sandwich Shop** (603-236-3669; $). The **Coffee Emporium** also cooks omelets, eggs, French toast and waffles.

Apres-ski/nightlife

Waterville now has a collection of bars in Town Square, each with slightly different apres-ski. They are all within a few steps of each other. **1291, Latitudes** and **Diamond's Edge** serve a good time, and later in the evening they stand in the same order, ranging from loud disco and rock to quieter music. **T- Bars**, at the mountain, has the normal collection of skiers for apres-ski until 5:30 p.m.

Just down the road from Waterville, on the way back to the interstate, try the **William Tell** for a cozy quiet apres-ski, or the **Mad River Tavern**, for a more raucous setting. Both have popular dinner menus.

Other activities

Waterville Valley has **sleigh rides** and an indoor fitness center with **pool, track, weight rooms and more**, as well as a covered ice arena for **skating**.

The resort also offers a **full recreation program** that includes activities for toddlers, youngsters and teens such as **ice cream socials, basketball** and **dances**.

Waterville Valley's Town Square has several specialty **shops** selling books, souvenirs, gifts, clothing and jewelry. Free **Internet access** is available at the check-in office.

Getting there and getting around

By air: Boston's Logan Airport is 130 miles south of Waterville Valley. Manchester Airport is 70 miles south.

By car: From I-93 heading north take Exit 28. The go 11 miles up Rte. 49.

Getting around: Waterville Valley offers a shuttle from the village to the slopes. It's wise to take the shuttle, since parking at the ski area can be a nightmare, although valet parking is available for $15. If you plan to venture away from the village or want to try to Loon, Cannon and Bretton Woods farther north, a car is a necessity.

New Hampshire Regional Resorts

The Balsams Wilderness, Dixville Notch, NH

(603) 255-3400; 800-255-0800 within NH; 800-255-0600 outside NH

Internet: www.thebalsams.com

4 lifts; 87 acres; 1,000 vertical feet; 1 terrain park

When you need to be pampered, owe your loved one a romantic weekend or want a family vacation without hassle, The Balsams Wilderness delivers. This remote resort, situated on a private, 15,000-acre estate in far northern New Hampshire, easily earns its four-star rating. This is not, however, a ski resort. Rather, it's a resort where skiing is just one of many amenities. The mountain is small, but crowds here are rare.

The Balsams Wilderness is one of New Hampshire's surviving Grand Resort Hotels and the first to be winterized. It resembles a Disney Castle, with turrets and towers, porches and balconies, and huge public rooms rambling from one to another. It's also the site of the first-in-the-nation primary, and the Ballot Room is a history lesson in itself. Guestrooms are mostly understated with an old-fashioned charm complemented with some amenities. Only a few rooms have televisions, but there is a big screen in the TV room.

In a break with the original Balsams tradition, rooms are available with only breakfast and with limited activities for those who do not want to participate in skiing and snowboarding. Award-winning chefs prepare a full breakfast buffet (or you can order from the menu) and five-course dinner daily. You can put your car keys away once you check in and you don't even need to carry your wallet. Children's programs include meals as well as skiing The hotel offers movies in a full-size theater, dancing and entertainment nightly in two lounges and often in the ballroom.

The Wilderness Alpine trails are varied, the people are very friendly and the area gets lots—and we mean lots—of snow. A triple chair accesses the summit. The terrain is primarily intermediate, but these long winding trails—up to 2 miles in length—just invite leisurely cruising. Expert skiers will not be tested at the Balsams but will enjoy the narrow twisting Notch and mountain's five gladed areas. Another triple serves the sunbathed beginner slope that is completely separate from the main mountain and has a perfect learning grade with a continuous slope. There's also a terrain park.

The Balsams has 95 km. of cross-country trails. One circuit has a vertical drop of 1,000 feet on trails 20 and 19. There are less daunting loops on the golf course. Trails are 12 feet wide and have two diagonal lanes and one skate lane. The resort also has a topographical trail map so you can avoid that big drop if you want. An ice-skating rink, 30 km. of designated snowshoeing trails, horse-drawn sleigh rides and a natural-history program with guided tours round out the outdoor experience. If you still have energy to burn, there's a small fitness center, and the hotel usually offers a morning exercise program and limited spa treatments.

Lift tickets (07/08): $38 for adults (older than 14) weekends/holidays, $33 midweek; $28 for ages 5–14 weekends/holidays, $23 midweek; seniors 70+ pay youth rates. (Skiing is complimentary for hotel guests.)

Distance from Boston: About 220 miles north via I-93 (to Exit 35) then Rte. 3 to Colebrook and Rte. 26 to Dixville Notch.

Lodging information: (800) 255-0800 within NH; (800) 255-0600, U.S. and Canada.

Ragged Mountain, Danbury, NH; 603-768-3475 or 603-768-3600

Internet: www.raggedmountainresort.com

9 lifts; 1,250 vertical feet; 220 skiable acres; 1 terrain park; 1 snowcross course

Ragged will be under new ownership for the 2007-08 season, but it remains an affordable resort experience for families that provides an excellent value with varied terrain on seven peaks. Ragged boasts New Hampshire's only high-speed, six-passenger chairlift, which takes skiers and riders from base to summit in just five minutes.

Spooks Gorge, on Ragged Mountain, provides advanced skiers with an extensive gladed area with trails long enough to leave skiers and riders huffing and puffing by the time they get out of the trees and bumps. For more glades, the Devil's Den on Spear Mountain give more challenge.

Intermediate cruisers head to Upper and Lower Exhibition, the widest and longest non-beginner run at Ragged. Sweepstakes or Birches are tighter and winding. The Glades run, reached by the Northeast Peak double chair, is a good choice.

Beginners will enjoy Juniper Meadows, a separate learning area, with seven gentle trails and four lifts, adjacent to the base area. There's no cross traffic from more advanced skiers and riders, which means less congestion and safer conditions for first timers. The runs are flat and the lifts are appropriately slow and easily boarded.

Ragged has traditionally provided one of the only consistently open boarder/skiercross courses in New Hampshire and a terrain park with 28 elements, including a halfpipe. The park is more than half a mile long, with no cross-traffic or intersections to break the flow. It's served by the six-pack lift and by its own triple. Snowboarders should be wary of the perimeter beginner runs (Easy Winder, Cardigan Turnpike) as these are generally flat.

The resort has two New England colonial-style base lodges with a small resort feel. The food is basic ski area fare with burgers, fries, soups and soft drinks. There is a bar and more seating on the upper floor. Tubing, ski school, equipment rentals and child care are available.

On-mountain lodging includes new, two-bedroom condos, as well as the Ridgeline Cabin that tops Northeast Peak. This rustic rental cabin ($750 per night) accommodates up to 30 people and has a wood stove, bunks, TV/VCR, cooking facilities, full bath, an outhouse and a wraparound deck with panoramic views of the White Mountains. Area lodging is limited to a few bed & breakfast inns and small lodges.

Lift tickets (08/09): Adults, $56 weekends/holidays and $46 midweek; teens (13–18), $46 weekends/holidays and $36 midweek; juniors (6–12) and seniors (65–71), $36 weekends/holidays and $26 midweek; seniors 75 and older, $26 weekends/holidays and $16 midweek. Ages 5 and younger ski free.

Distance from Boston: About 100 miles via I-93 to Exit 17/Rte. 4 West to 104 East.

Lodging information: (800) 887-5464; Ragged Mountain condos: (800) 400-3911.

Mount Sunapee, Newbury, NH; 603-763-2356

Internet: www.mountsunapee.com

10 lifts; 61 trails; 1,510 vertical feet; 220 skiable acres; 2 terrain parks; 1 superpipe

Offering views over the lake of the same name, Mount Sunapee has a loyal following of skiers who like its New England feel and close proximity to Boston (just 90 minutes for a Massachusetts-style driver). This mountain has seen a real renaissance since 1999 when the state of New Hampshire, which had run the mountain as part of its parks system, transferred operations and development responsibilities to the same family that owns and operates Okemo Mountain in Vermont.

This new management brought a proven recipe of maximum snowmaking, new lifts, new base lodge and a focus on family amenities to Mount Sunapee. Added snowmaking on Elliot Slope and Portage in 2006-2007 season has also helped .

Today Mount Sunapee has been ranked as the second most popular ski and snowboard resort in New Hampshire and has also received high grades in the East for snow quality, grooming, family programs, weather (while no one really has control over Mother Nature, the orientation of many of the slopes helps skiers find the sun), and accessibility.

The mountain is not giant when compared with some of its brethren, however, it makes the most of its size. The trails are cut to use as much of the mountain as possible, and from top to bottom, skiers and snowboarders can drop more than 1,500 feet and enjoy runs more than a mile long. Its 2 terrain parks and, perhaps surpirsingly, superpipe, illustrate the commitment to all comers.

Most of Mount Sunapee's skiers are day trippers due to its proximity to several of the Northeast's largest cities, but the nearby small towns of Charlestown, Bradford, New London, and North Sutton offer interesting dining. Lodging options are also growing.

Sunapee has long been the base for the New England Handicapped Sports Association (NEHSA), which provides programs for skiers with physical and mental challenges.

Lift tickets (07/08): Adults, $64 weekend/holiday and $60 midweek; young adult (13–18) and senior (65–69), $53 weekend and $45 weekday; junior (6–12) and super senior (70+), $40 weekend and $36 weekday. Children 5 and younger ski free with a ticketed adult. A day ticket for the South Peak Beginner Area is $6 for ages 6 and older. Everyone skis Mondays for $39.

Distance from Boston: About 90 miles northwest via I-93, I-89 and Rte. 103.

Lodging information: A selection of B&Bs, inns, hotels/motels and condos is available through the Mount Sunapee website and on skisnowboard.com/sunnapee/index.html.

Gunstock, Gilford, NH; 800-486-7802 or 603-293-4341

Internet: www.gunstock.com

7 lifts; 220 acres; 1,400 vertical feet; 1 terrain park with wall ride; 2 tubing tows

Gunstock is a family-friendly resort with an excellent learn-to-ski program, great cruising trails and plentiful winter sports, day and night. With the Panorama High Speed quad, you have access from the base to the summit in 6 minutes. Other recent improvements include snowmaking enhancements, increasing the size of the terrain park and new lighting that now means a total of 21 night skiing/riding trails served by 5 lifts.

The trails are kept in good condition thanks to Gunstock's Groom On Demand program: when the mountain needs attention, the cats go out. Advanced skiers can ski through glades on Middle Trigger and find bumps on Red Hat or Flintlock Extension. Intermediate glades can be found on Middle Recoil. Beginners have their own separate area at the Ski Learning Center, with handletow, conveyor lift and the Gunshy chairlift. The Gunstock Freestyle Academy offers Freestyle Ski or Snowboard camp sessions where you can learn to ride the Park and the Pipe with some of the best freestyle riders in the Lakes Region. These coaches design, build, and maintain the Gunstock Park, giving them home court advantage. Two terrain parks, including a progression park, serve all abilities, and Friday night rail jams are staged. Snow tubing is available day and night. Snowshoers and cross-country skiers can enjoy 52 km. of trails for hiking, skating and gliding. The surrounding N.H. Lakes Region has ample accommodation and plenty of restaurants, as well as other activities such as **ice fishing** and **snowmobiling**.

Lift tickets: Adults, $56 weekend and $48 weekday; teens (13–18), $46 weekend and $38 midweek; Child (6–12), $36 weekend and $28 weekday; seniors (69+), $46 weekend and $28 midweek. Night tickets are available. Skiers and riders ages 5 and younger and 70 and older ski free. Gunstock also has a Flex half-day ticket.

Distance from Boston: About 90 miles north via I-93 and Rtes. 3 and 11A.

Lodging information: (603) 293-4341 or (800) 754-7819.

Lake Placid/Whiteface

New York

Summit:	4,386 feet
Vertical:	3,166 feet
Base:	1,220 feet

Address: ORDA, Olympic Center, Lake Placid, NY 12946
Telephone (main): 518-946-2223
Snow Report Number: 518-946-7171
Toll-free reservations: 800-447-5224
E-mail: info@orda.org
Internet: www.whitefacelakeplacid.com

Expert: ★★★★
Advanced: ★★★
Intermediate: ★★★★
Beginner: ★★★★
First-timer: ★★★★★

Lifts: 11—1 eight-passenger gondola, 1 high-speed quad, 1 quad, 2 triple, 5 doubles, 1 surface lift
Skiable acreage: 250
Snowmaking: 98 percent
Uphill capacity: 14,000
Parks & pipes: 2 parks, 1 pipe
Bed base: 5,000
Nearest lodging: 1/2 mile in Wilmington, about 9 miles in Lake Placid
Child care: Yes, 12 months and older
Adult ticket, per day: $67 (07/08 prices)
Dining: ★★★★
Apres-ski/nightlife: ★★★★★
Other activities: ★★★★★

Strictly in terms of skiable terrain, Whiteface would fall somewhere in the middle of the pack of northeast resorts. But, it more than compensates with its dramatic 3,100-foot-plus vertical drop, the biggest in the East. There is plenty here to keep the heart rate, and the fun rate up there with the best.

Almost 30 years after it last hosted the Olympics, Lake Placid is still all about winter games. Race down the ice chute feet first on a luge sled and try not to stretch your toes to save that extra .001 of a second on the clock...try not to push just a little harder as you ski into the cross country finish stadium...try not to put a little extra lean into the scoreboard turn under the lights at the speedskating oval...look down the in-run of the 120-meter ski jump and...well, let's not go overboard here! You get the picture. This is not your average ski town.

Lake Placid, a surprisingly unspoiled, quiet village, hosted two Winter Olympics, (1932, 1980), and the 2000 Winter Goodwill Games. The memories these stir, combined with a plethora of ongoing outdoor activities and events, make Lake Placid a winter sports Mecca.

The Olympic Regional Development Authority (ORDA) operates the multi-facility recreational area. More world-class winter sports athletes train and compete here than anywhere else in North America. The facilities attract competitions in all of the Olympic winter sports, so athletes of all ages, nationalities and abilities fill the town throughout the season, constantly refreshing the village's Olympic atmosphere.

Even in non-Olympic years, there is always lots of top level competition in Lake Placid. These events are a great opportunity to see Olympic level competitors, up close, in interrnational competition, at neighborhood prices. An Olympic Sites passport will gain you access to venues and activities at a reduced cost.

The town of Lake Placid, situated between two Adirondack lakes, is home to the ice arena where America watched its Cinderella hockey team enter the history books with the "Do you believe in miracles?" victory over the heavily favored Russian team in 1980. The Mt. VanHoevenberg Sports Complex, six miles to the southeast, has the bobsled, luge and skeleton runs, as well as 50 km. of cross-country ski trails and the biathlon stadium. The Olympic Jumping Complex, where jumping and freestyle aerials take place, is on the edge of town.

The Alpine trails are 9 miles to the northeast, at Whiteface Mountain, officially in the town of Wilmington. Whiteface is one of those rare ski areas that has more to offer experts and beginners, but it still has plenty for intermediates. Experts find the upper half of the mountain challenging. Beginners find almost everything accessed by the Face Lift much to their liking. Intermediates find sufficient cruising and opportunities to advance their skills from the top of the mountain. New in 2008-09 is the Lookout Mountain terrain with its own triple chair and featuring a two mile blue-square run. The trails, for the most part, are nice and wide, which makes some of the black-rated steep runs manageable for solid intermediates.

Lake Placid's Main Street, with its mix of retail shops and restaurants, makes up in charm and bustle what it lacks in quaintness. Daytime or evening, many people find both relaxation and exercise on the Olympic oval (where Eric Heiden won five gold medals), on a dogsled ride across Mirror Lake, or via a three-mile walk around it. Another favorite is the floodlit, nighttime toboggan slide onto the frozen lake darkness. A word of caution: Wear old clothes!

Mountain layout

Whiteface has the biggest lift served vertical drop in the East at 3,166; 3,430 feet if you count hiking to the nearby Slides. Its position makes for spectacular views, but winter winds regularly whip across the valley and up the walls of Whiteface. Veteran eastern skiers do complain that Whiteface is often windblown, cold and icy. But, you can't fault an area for bad weather, and the addition of the Cloudsplitter gondola does provide relief, as well as comfort. On an ideal day, Whiteface is as good as it gets in the East, and spring here can be particularly good.

◆◆**Expert, ◆Advanced:** For some of the best expert skiing in the East, take the Summit Quad and test your legs on Cloudspin and Skyward, where the Olympic downhill races started. For true experts who don't mind a hike, the Slides is the real deal when conditions permit.

The black-diamond trails off Little Whiteface Approach, Upper Northway, Empire and Essex are often left to bump up, providing great terrain for advanced skiers. Whiteface has serious tree skiing, too: 13 acres of black/double-black glades are off Little Whiteface Mountain.

■ **Intermediate:** Take the Cloudsplitter gondola from the base or the Little Whiteface double from the midstation to the top of Little Whiteface. An observation platform, off to the left at the top, gives you an unparalleled view of the lakes and valley. Then try the snaking down Excelsior run, which twists to the midstation. You can cut the rounded corners of this baby like a bobsled, choosing your own pace. After that warm-up, tackle Paron's Run or The Follies from the top of the Summit Quad. Virtually the entire lower half of this mountain is a delight for intermediates. High-speed lifts have eliminated the old bottlenecks.

●● **Beginner, ●First-timer:** These levels have two secluded areas, the Mixing Bowl to the left and Kids Kampus at Easy Acres to the right. The Mixing Bowl allows adult beginners to progress out of the way of more accomplished skiers using Bear lift. Novices and families will enjoy Easy Acres, below the midstation lodge, with its own secluded lift and a series of beginner glades. Boreen is also a good choice for beginners.

Snowboarding

On Excelsior, keep your speed on the eighth and ninth corners to cross the short flat.

Parks and pipes

Terrain parks are located on Brookside, Lower Thruway and portions of Lower Valley and Bronze. There's a superpipe on Bear trail that has hosted events like the Winter Goodwill Games and the Paul Mitchell Board Frenzy Tour. The resort will offer World Cup snowboarding in March, 2009, with events in superpipe and snowboardcross.

Cross-country & snowshoeing (see also xcskiresorts.com)

Lake Placid stands as a major cross-country destination with 455 km. of trails. Foremost is the **Mt. VanHoevenberg Sports Complex** (518-523-2811), site of the 1980 Olympics Nordic and biathlon races. It has cross-country skiing you are unlikely to find elsewhere: 50 km. of marked trails that average 15 ft. wide, regularly groomed and patrolled; bridges built especially for cross-country skiers, so you don't have to worry about traffic; snowmaking (5 km.); and emergency phones. The complex has 10 marked loops: one expert, six intermediate and three novice, with additional expert skiing on the Porter Mountain racing loops. The stadium finish area has a fully equipped rental and retail shop along with food service. Snowshoeing is allowed.

The **Lake Placid Resort** (518-523-2556) has 25 km. of trails and connects with the more secluded **Jackrabbit Trail** (ski conditions: 518-523-1365), 50 km. that run from Keene through Lake Placid and Saranac Lake.

Snowshoeing trails crisscross the entire **High Peaks Wilderness** area; get maps and advice at Eastern Mountain Sports on Lake Placid's Main Street. **Dewey Mt. Ski Center** has snowshoe trails in addition to cross-country skiing. For a more controlled snowshoe experience, complete with bonfires for roasting marshmallows and educational stops on the trail, stop at the **High Falls Gorge** center (518-946-2278). Here you can follow a marked trek around the Ausable River gorge and be welcomed back with free hot chocolate or coffee. Reservations are recommended on weekends. For a full moon cross country experience, check with **Cascade Cross Country Ski Center** (518-523-9605) on Route 73 near Mt. VanHoevenberg.

Lessons (07/08 prices)

Group lessons: $30 for two hours; $80 for three sessions.
First-timer package: Ski School Director Ed Kreil's trademarked Parallel from the Start group lesson program with pass and equipment rental is $99 for skiers or riders for one day, $186 for two days and $256 for five days. It uses Snowblades and guarantees that in five days you'll be able to ski from the top of Little Whiteface.

The Burton Learn to Ride program includes lift ticket, two-hour lessson each day and rental equipment; cost is $99 for one day, $186 for two days and $256 for three days. The Ski/Ride to Perfection program includes rentals, lifts and lessons; cost is $90 for one day, $179 for two days, and $79 for each additional day.

Private lessons: $80 an hour, with $40 for an additional person. Full day (five hours) costs $350 for one person, or $475 for two to five people.

Children's Programs (07/08 prices)

Child care: The Bear's Den Nursery accepts children ages 1–6 years for $40 per half day or $65 per day, with lunch included in the full-day price. Reservations are recommended; call 518-946-2223.

The recently expanded Kids Kampus at Easy Acres (518-946-2223) has its own parking area, base lodge, lifts (including a Magic Carpet surface lift) and trails, and it is completely separate from the main ski trails of Whiteface while still connected with the lift and trail network, allowing parents to ski or ride to and from it.

Children's lessons: Play 'n Ski is for children ages 4–6. It includes ski lessons, lift ticket and indoor activities and costs $105 for a full day (with lunch), $70 for a half day. Ski or snowboard lessons with lift ticket for ages 7–12 are $90 for a full day (with lunch), $60 for a half day. Rentals are extra. Reservations required during holidays for all children's programs.

Lift tickets (07/08 prices)

	Adult	Child (7-12)
One weekday	$67	$40
Three weekdays	$185	$110
Five weekdays	$303	$184

Who skis free: Children ages 6 and younger, accompanied by an adult; ages 70-plus.

Who skis at a discount: Teens (13-19) and seniors (64-69) pay $56 for one day; $158 for three days; $260 for five days. Active military pay $38 any day.

Any three or more day lift ticket is the Ultimate Winter Passport and includes a free class lesson, free NASTAR run, an afternoon trail pass at the VanHoevenberg Cross Country Center, admission to the Olympic Ski Jumps and Mt VanHoevenberg Sports Complex sliding tracks, ice skating on the Olympic Speed Skating Oval and discounts on other activities.

Note: Holiday pricing is about $5/day higher. There are programs available on the Internet that offer additional savings for lift tickets purchased in advance.

Accommodations

Some of the larger hotels centered around the town of Lake Placid tend to be of the modern franchise variety. An important exception is the **Mirror Lake Inn & Spa** (518-523-2544; $$-$$$$), a traditional lodge right on the lake shore, and probably the finest overnight in the area. The New England-style exterior continues inside with antiques, chandeliers and mahogany walls. The inn has an indoor pool, whirlpool, sauna, health spa and game room. The two restaurants include one of the best in town, with candlelight dining overlooking the lake.

The new guy in town is **The Whiteface Lodge** (800-523-3387, 518-523-3400; $$$$), an elegant inn on Saranac Avenue built to replicate the classic Adirondack style. It features rooms and suites, an indoor/outdoor pool, spa, movie theater, ice skating rink, and fine dining in the vaulted ceiling, beam-butressed Great Room. It offers shuttle service to downtown and to Whiteface. The **Marriott Courtyard** (518-523-2900; $$-$$$) is on Route 73, about two miles from Main Street. If snowshoeing or cross-country is main interest, or to experience traditional Adirondack Lodge atmosphere, try the **Lake Placid Lodge** (518-523-2700; $$$$).

The **Lake Placid Crowne Plaza** (800-874-1980; 518-523-2556; $-$$), in town center, is Lake Placid's largest hotel (209 rooms). All rooms have refrigerators and microwaves; some have a Jacuzzi tub and fireplace. It has a large indoor pool, whirlpool, sauna, complete health club, 20 km. of cross-country trails and two restaurants. The **Golden Arrow Lakeside Resort** (800-582-5540; 518-523-3353; $-$$$) has spectacular lake views, an indoor pool, hot tub, sauna, weight room, and racquetball courts. It's the only certified "green resort" in town.

The **High Peaks Resort** (800-755-5598; 518-523-4411; $$-$$$) is the new name for the former the Lake Placid Hilton . Renovated, it features two indoor pools and private balconies for each lake view room, and a popular B&B package. There is also an excellent **Comfort Inn**

(800-858-4656; 518-523-9555; $$-$$$), formerly the Howard Johnson Resort Inn, in town.

Skiers on a budget should try **The Alpine Cellar** (518-523-2180 $$), **Art Devlin's Motor Inn** (518-523-3700; $-$$), **Town House Motor Inn** (523-2532; $-$$), **Alpine Air Motel** (518-523-9261; $-$$$), **Placid Bay Inn** (518-523-2001; $$), **Econo Lodge** (523-2817; $-$$), and **Wildwood on the Lake** (518-523-2624; $).

For lodging right by Whiteface, try the **Ledgerock** (800-336-4754; 518-946-2379; $-$$), a family-owned 19-unit motel, opposite the ski area entrance in Wilmington. The view from the spacious rooms looks just like the trail map. **The Hungry Trout** (518-946-2217; $$-$$$) and **Huntington's** (518-946-2332; $-$$), opposite the mountain's entrance, are good, as well.

Dining

The newest fine dining spot in town is **Kanu** at **The Whiteface Lodge** (518-523-0510; $$$$) where the menu is impressive and so is the setting. Across the street, **The Caffe Rustica** (518-523-3400; $$$) has earned a loyal following in just the past few years.

The Mirror Lake Inn's **The View Restaurant** (518-523-2544; $$$-$$$$), has fine dining in an elegant atmosphere. For less formality, **Taste** next door shares the same kitchen. Just around the corner, **The Interlaken** (518-523-3180 $$$) also features both fine dining and a pub menu. For those who have heard rave reviews about the **Lake Placid Lodge**, it re-opens in the fall after a three year rebuilding project following a fire in 2005.

Elsewhere in town, **The Brown Dog** (518-523-3036; $-$$$) is a deli by day but offers fine dining with wine by night. **The Great Adirondack Steak and Seafood Company** (518-523-0233; $$) serves beer brewed on premises and hearty food. **The Cottage** (518-523-2544; $$-$$$), associated with the Mirror Lake Inn, delivers good burgers and pub fare at the water's edge. Locals swear by the **Caribbean Cowboy** (518-523-3836; $-$$).

The Charcoal Pit (518-523-3050; $$-$$$) has been charbroiling steaks and chops for more than 25 years. **Veranda** (518-523-3339; $$), next to the Crowne Plaza, has a great view to go with fine food. **Charlie's** (518-523-9886; $$) on Main Street is operated by long time area chef Charlie Levitz. Try **Desperados** (518-523-1507; $-$$) for Mexican food. **The Fireside Steakhouse** (518-523-2682 $$) serves a great filet. **Mykonos'** (518-523-1164; $$-$$$) has good Greek fare.

On the village edge on Rte. 73 are two good spots—The **Downhill Grill** (518-523-9510; $-$$), and locals' favorite **Lisa G's** (518-523-2093, $-$$) , solid choices for lunch or an informal evening meal. **Simply Gourmet** (518-523-3111) on Saranac Avenue offers 46 deli style sandwich choices on-site or as take-out, and the same plus crepes on Main Street under the name **Big Mountain Deli** (518-523-3222). **Mr. Mike's Pizza** (518-523-9770; $) feeds the craving for inexpensive Italian. For sushi lovers, it's **Aki Sushi** (518-523-5826, $$-$$$).

For a hearty breakfast (all $-$$), head to the **Downtown Diner** (518-523-3709) on lower Main Street. **Soulshine** (518-523-9772) is the place for bagels, while **The New Leaf** (518-523-1847), on Saranac Avenue, is fine for coffee and a muffin. **HoJo's** (518-523-2241) on Saranac Avenue offers a popular buffet. On Sundays, **The High Peaks Resort** (518-523-4411) serves an excellent brunch (reservations required in holiday periods). En route to Intervale or Mt. VanHoevenberg, try **Chair 6** (518-523-3630) on Route 73.

In Wilmington, the upscale and excellent **Hungry Trout** (518-946-2217; $$) specializes in, you guessed it, fish. In the same neighborhood is the **Wilderness Inn** (518-946-2391; $$-$$$), where steak lovers will want to try the sandwich on the bar menu.

Dining: $$$$–Entrees $30+; $$$–$20–$30; $$–$10–$20; $–less than $10.
Accommodations: (double room) $$$$–$200+; $$$–$141–$200; $$–$81–$140; $–$80 and less.

Apres-ski/nightlife

Because Whiteface is separated from the town, however, most of the apres-ski action is in the base lodge. **Steinhoff's** and **R.F. McDougall's**, at the Hungry Trout, just down the road from Whiteface are also good for an apres-ski drink.

In town, **Wise Guys**, next to the speed skating oval, is a sports bar upstairs, a dance club downstairs, and serves pub grub into the wee hours. Most of the other nightlife action centers around the main hotels. **Roomers**, next to the Golden Arrow, the **Dancing Bears Lounge** at the Hilton and **Zig Zag's** are popular spots along Main Street. The **Lake Placid Pub and Brewery**, with its downstairs companion **P.J. O'Neils**, is on Mirror Lake Drive, and offers outstanding pub fare to go with its award-winning Ubu Ale. For a quieter, more mature nightspot, stop by **The Cottage**, across the street from the Mirror Lake Inn. The fire is always lit and the sunset view of the lake and mountains is postcard perfect. It also serves good burgers.

 ## Other activities

Lake Placid offers a fantastic array of winter activities. The half-mile **bobsled rides** at Mt. Vanhoevenberg Sports Complex are $75/person with souvenir photo and pin and a must for any Lake Placid visit. Rides are by reservation only (518-523-4436). While there, try the Luge Rocket.

Tours of the MacKenzie-Intervale Ski Jumping Complex, with chairlift and elevator ride, cost $9 for adults, $5 for children and seniors. Hours are 9 a.m. to 4 p.m.

The Olympic Speed Skating Oval is open daily for public **skating** 7-9 p.m., and 1-3 p.m. Saturdays and Sundays (518-523-1655). The cost is $5 for adults and $3 for juniors.

Operating hours for the **toboggan run** on Mirror Lake are Wednesday, 7-9 p.m.; Friday, 7-10 p.m.; Saturday, noon-4 p.m.,7-10 p.m.; Sunday, noon-4 p.m. The charge is $3 for adults, $2 for children, and $3 for the toboggan rental.

The **Olympic Winter Passport**, $29, includes a day of **cross-country** or **snowshoeing**; admission to the **jumping complex, museums** and **public skating**; a $10 discount on the half-mile **bobsled ride** and a 10% discount at the ORDA Store. The Ultimate Winter Passport package for $185 ($202 on holidays) adds lift tickets at Whiteface and Mt. VanHoevenberg.

Get into the real spirit of things by visiting the **Lake Placid Winter Olympic Museum**. This is a can't miss spot on the ground floor of the Olympic Arena with displays from the 1932 and 1980 Winter Olympics held at Lake Placid. It's open daily. Admission is $4 for adults, $3 for seniors and $2 for juniors. Call 518-523-1655, ext. 226 for more information. The **Olympic Arena** often has a **hockey** game or a **skating exhibition** free for the watching.

 ## Getting there and getting around

By air: Nearest airports are Burlington, Vt., and Albany, N.Y. Transportation from the airports is sporadic. Rent a car.

By train: Trains stop at Westport on the New York City-Montreal line. Ask the Lake Placid Visitors Bureau (800-447-5224) about shuttles. Amtrak (800-872-7245) has ski packages.

By car: From the south: N.Y. Thruway (I-87) Exit 24; I-87 (Northway) to Exit 30; follow Rte. 9 north two miles to Rte. 73; continue 28 miles to Lake Placid. From the west: I-90 (N.Y. Thruway) to Exit 36; I-81 north to Watertown; Rte. 3 east to Saranac Lake; Rte. 86 east.

Getting around: It's about 9 miles' drive to Whiteface and 6 miles to Mt. Van Hoevenberg from Lake Placid. A free shuttle service that connects the town with Whiteface from Christmas to April 1, but having a car makes getting around more convenient.

Jay Peak
Vermont

Summit:	**3,968 feet**
Vertical:	**2,153 feet**
Base:	**1,815 feet**

Address: 4850 VT Route 242, Jay, VT 05859
Telephone: 802-988-2611
Snow Report Number: 802-988-9601
Toll-free reservations: 800-451-4449 (outside Vermont)
E-mail: info@jaypeakresort.com
Internet: www.jaypeakresort.com

Expert: ★ ★ ★ ★
Advanced: ★ ★ ★
Intermediate: ★ ★
Beginner: ★ ★
First-timer: ★ ★

Lifts: 8—1 60-passenger aerial tramway, 1 high-speed quad, 2 quads, 1 triple, 1 double, 1 T-bar,1 moving carpet
Skiable acreage: 385
Snowmaking: 85 percent
Uphill capacity: 12,175
Parks & pipes: 4 parks
Bed base: 1,300 slopeside; 1,800 in area
Nearest lodging: Slopeside
Child care: Yes, 2-7 years; infant care for on-property guests available
Adult ticket, per day: $62 (07/08 prices)
Dining: ★ ★
Apres-ski/nightlife: ★
Other activities: ★

They call it the "Jay Peak Cloud." It hovers over the mountain, and dumps a foot or more of snow on days when skies are clear just five miles away. Jay averages 355 inches of snow a year and that's at least 100 inches more than others in the region. Some years, more snow falls here than anywhere east of the Sierras. One year, 571 inches blanketed the mountain. Even in a "poor" snow year, Jay receives several feet more than other resorts in the Green Mountains. If you're looking for (almost) guaranteed snow, Jay is your safest bet.

While it's a bit of a trek to get to here, it's well worth the effort. Most of the time, you will have the mountain—and the prodigious snowpack—practically to yourself. Even on powder days, you can find untracked snow all day long. During holiday weekends, you'll wonder why you ever went anywhere else.

People come to Jay for more than just the snow though. Many of the trails—particularly the glades—hold more challenge than you'll find at most Eastern resorts. Long before it was popular for Eastern resorts to cut glades, Jay's locals were sneaking into the woods to cut their own lines. After the resort president's son was caught skiing out of bounds, management cut some glades and opened them to the public, making tree skiing legit. Since 1987, the resort has cut 21 glades and two extreme chutes.

The focus here is the outdoors and all it has to offer, for better or worse. Come if you want to ski or ride your legs off, sink into a hot tub as the sun sets, then go to sleep early to get up early in the morning and do it all over again.

If you're here for a week, you might want to consider taking a day or two to ski Quebec's Eastern Townships resorts, especially Mont Orford and Mont Sutton.

Mountain layout

Since trails and glades are spread across two mountain peaks, there are two "sides" to the resort. Tramside has, obviously, the Tram, Hotel Jay, the main base lodge, customer service, and a rental shop. Stateside has a base lodge, ski patrol headquarters, and the "blue" and "red" chairs serving the left side of the mountain.

The biggest drawback to Jay's layout is that there are only three ways to work your way between the two peaks—Northway, Goat Run and Vermonter. These can get crowded, and the snow gets skied off, especially later in the day. Locals refer to the Green Mountain Flyer chair as the Green Mountain Freezer: you'll understand once you crest the ridge and get a full blast of the wind off the lake. It's best to avoid this lift if you're prone to getting cold quickly.

◆◆**Expert,** ◆**Advanced:** Experts who have never been here may very well quake in their boots when they see what Jay considers single-diamond terrain. The Face, The Saddle and Tuckermans Chutes are rock-and-tree-stub strewn, forcing you to pick your way over some gnarly stuff to get to the goods. All this in full view of the folks riding up the Tram.

However, the real challenge is in the woods. Warm up in Hell's Woods, Buckaroo Bonzai, Everglade and Beaver Pond Glade, then head to Timbuktu and Valhalla. Locals groaned loudly when Jay officially opened Beyond Beaver Pond Glade because it was just about the only piece of "unofficial woods" left on the mountain, but it is still pretty much untouched.

Kitzbuehl is a tight bumped run that'll leave you huffing and puffing. River Quai and Green Beret (when it's open) are both truly hairy trails. The monster moguls and double fall line on Powerline will give you a run for your money.

Advanced skiers ready to push themselves should take a glade technique lesson and head into the woods. For starters, try the "kiddie" glades, Kokomo, Moon Walk and Bushwacker.

Jay also has vast amounts (by Eastern standards) of backcountry terrain. But don't venture here alone or without a guide who knows the area well.

■ **Intermediate:** Most intermediate trails here would be rated advanced elsewhere. Warm up on Ullr's Dream (slip into the trees of Kokomo if you want to avoid the long flat at the end) or Northway to Angel's Wiggle. To test your ability in the trees, slip into Kokomo, Moon Walk or Bushwacker. To take in the amazing views at the top to Mt. Mansfield, Quebec's Eastern Townships, Lake Champlain, Mt. Washington and Montreal, ride the tram and ski Vermonter. Goat Run is also another fun trail, but the top gets icy and moguled on heavy-traffic days.

Most advanced-intermediates will enjoy the groomed black-diamond trails off the Jet Triple Chair, once you make it past the somewhat-steep top sections. A favorite is Derick Hot Shot, a narrow winding trail that gets moderate bumps on high-traffic days. If you're looking to make sweeping arcs, head to wide-open Jet and Haynes. If the top of Jet looks too steep, take Montrealer to Angel's Wiggle, then Wiggle all the way down; or choose from some wonderful intermediate terrain like Lower Milk Run, Paradise Meadows and Hell's Crossing.

● ● **Beginner,** ● **First-timer:** All of the beginner terrain is at the bottom of the mountain. A quad chair replaced the Metro T-bar, completely transforming the beginner experience. All the beginner trails are now connected, making it easier to move around the mountain.

A fabulous beginner run that doesn't get much traffic is Deer Run, a short traverse across the mountain to the right as you get off the lift. It's also fun to cut over to Queen's Highway. Bushwacker and Moon Walk Woods are great easy glades, with Moon Walk being open enough to groom. Or try Racoon Run, which accesses the newer condos and has its own chair.

Higher-level skiers and riders use some of the beginner trails to reach the Tram and Green Mountain Flyer, so keep an eye out for them.

If you're adventurous and want to try the intermediate terrain at the top of the mountain, it's wise to return to the base by mid-afternoon, before the snow on the major trails is skied off.

There is a dedicated learning center with a moving carpet at the base of Tramside, giving first-timers their very own piece of the mountain.

Parks and pipes

Jay's freestyle scene continues to evolve, with a big boost came with the decision to hire a park manager who treats the parks as a labor of love. You'll see him and his crew out hand-sculpting features to perfection. Jay now has four terrain parks and hosts several freestyle events.

The terrain park for experienced riders, called The Park, is on Lower Can Am. Features change throughout the season, but on any given day, you'll find rails (including a rainbow rail, an "S" rail and a rollercoaster rail), boxes (including a straight box and a "C" box), tabletops and step-ups. The Progression Park is on Rabbit Trail (rider's left of Lower Can Am). Tabletops range in size from small ones for beginners to huge hits for experts, allowing riders to practice new moves before heading to the main park.

Tramside has the two other parks. The Rail Garden is next to the moving carpet near the base lodge. Six to 10 rails, smaller versions than in The Park, help you learn the basics and improve your moves. Barrels, picnic tables, chairs and other random features mix it up for some extra fun. It's lighted for night riding after the lifts close. The Grom Park is on Harmony Lane and accessed by the Metro Quad. Small features are perfect for learning park moves.

Snowboarding

Ullr's Dream is a great warm-up run, but duck into Kokomo to avoid the lo-o-ong flat at the bottom. Riders coming out of Beaver Pond Glade and Beyond Beaver Pond Glade hook back up to Ullr's, so you'll also want to heed that warning (plus Beyond has its own unavoidable flat that will have you hoofing back to the trails). For sweeping arcs, head to wide-open Jet and Haynes. If they're too steep, take Montrealer to Angel's Wiggle, then take the Wiggle all the way down ,or choose from Lower Milk Run and Hell's Crossing to Paradise Meadows.

Cross-country & snowshoeing (see also xcskiresorts.com)

Jay Peak has 20 km.of cross-country skiing that networks into 200 km. of touring trails in the area. Instruction and rentals are available. Included in the Nordic trail system are more than 5 km. of snowshoe trails. Naturalist-led tours on snowshoes are scheduled Tuesdays, Wednesdays and Saturdays from 4:30 - 6:30 p.m. and cost $15. Check with the Ski School Desk to register. Extended or group tours can be arranged. For unguided snowshoers, rentals are available anytime through the rental shop.

Hazen's Notch Cross-Country Ski & Snowshoe Center (802-326-4799), about 10 miles away, is operated by the nonprofit Hazen's Notch Association. 64 km. of groomed and back-country trails, with fantastic views, include 16 km. of snowshoe-only trails. Ski and snowshoe rentals, instruction by appointment, and guided and full-moon snowshoe tours are offered.

Lessons (07/08 prices)

Group lessons: Two-hour lesson, $35. The Learn to Ski/Ride program includes a two-hour ski or snowboard lesson with rental and use of beginner lifts for $62. Multiday packages available.

Private lessons: $65 per hour, $25 for each additional person.

Special programs: Glade and powder clinics, two-hour sessions offered during prime conditions for advanced skiers and riders only, $39 per person, minimum three people per group. A one-day women-only clinic in mid-February is $229. Call 802-327-2186 for information.

Racing: Racing Camps feature gate running and on-hill training. NASTAR races at 1 p.m. on Thursday, Friday and Saturday. Special NASTAR Clinic available.

Children's Programs (07/08 prices)

Child care: Ages 2 to 7 years old. All ski and stay packages at Jay include free day care from 9 a.m.-9 p.m. Pre-registration is advised. Call 802-988-2611. Those staying off-resort can put their children in Jay's day care on a first come, first served basis only. Cost is $45 all day ($6 extra for lunch); $25 half day. Infant care for on-property guests is available on a fee basis with advanced reservations.

Children's lessons: Kinderski is for ages 3–5 and costs $45 for a half-day, $90 for a full day (includes lift ticket but not rentals). Lunch costs $6. Mini-Learn-to-Ride is the same program for snowboarders ages 5–6 and costs the same. Pre-registration is required for both.

Jay Explorers, a full-day program for ages 6–10, costs $62 (lift tickets, rentals and lunch, extra). Half-day costs $35. Miniriders is the same program for snowboarders ages 7-10.

Mountain Adventures is a full-day program for ages 10 and older who want to not only ski and snowboard, but try alternatives such as freeriding, telemarking and getting First Tracks before the resort opens to the public in the morning. Cost is $62 for a full day, $35 for a half day (lift tickets, rentals and lunch are extra).

Special activities: There is nightly supervised dining in Hotel Jay for ages 2-7; sign up by 2 p.m. There's also an activity room with ping pong, video games and pool table in the hotel. Movies are shown nightly at 7 p.m. (for kids) and 9 p.m. (for adults) on all on-property TVs, as well as in the family room of the Hotel Jay.

Lift tickets (08/09 prices)

One day: adults $65, junior (6-18), $45, toddler (6 and younger), $10. Three days: adult $153, junior $111, toddler $30. Five days: adult $216, junior $161, toddler $50.

Who skis at a discount: Seniors 65 and older pay $21 per day. College students with an ID pay $45 per day. A Beginner Zone ticket is $29 adult, $19 junior. Vermont and Clinton County, NY, residents with ID, and other mountain pass holders, pay $45 adult and $35 junior.

Notes: When staying for more than one day, it's to buy a lodging package that includes tickets. During non-holiday weeks, children 14 and younger stay and ski free, and teens 15-18 stay and ski for a reduced rate when sharing the same room or condo with their parents (meals are extra). Children 6 and younger always stay and ski free (and eat free in the Hotel Jay).

Canadian cash accepted at par for Canadian residents with proof of residency. All credit cards are processed in US funds only.

Accommodations

Jay Peak Resort assists guests in arranging lodging, air travel, train travel, shuttle van service to the airport and train station and rental cars. Jay Peak is overall a bargain. The best deal is to stay in the slopeside hotel or condos. During non-holiday weeks, children 14 and younger stay and ski free, and teens 15-18 stay and ski for $50 per day, when sharing the same room or condo with their parents (meals are extra). Children 6 and younger always stay and ski free (and eat free in the Hotel Jay). If you have kids ages 2-7, stay at Hotel Jay or the on-mountain condos, and you'll receive complimentary child care from 9 a.m. to 9 p.m., including a supervised dinner. Five-day stays and longer include a half-day complimentary lift ticket beginning at 12:30 p.m. on the day of arrival.

Hotel Jay (800-451-4449 or 802-988-9601; $$-$$$) offers a sauna, family room with fireplace and game room. Five-day packages for a family with two adults start at $649 per adult (includes meals for adults).

Slopeside condos range from luxury to economy. Five-day packages, including lodging and lift tickets, range from $479 to $869 per adult (prime time and holiday prices are higher). Meal plans are available. The ski-in/ski-out **Village Townhouses** have two to four bedrooms, are wonderfully spacious and provide all the amenities of home. Some units have a steam bath and sauna. What the resort calls "deluxe" accommodations can be found at the older **Mountainside, Trailside** and **Slopeside** condos. Many units in Slopeside are ski-in/ski-out, though some require a short walk, so make sure to get what you really want, especially if you have young kids. Value priced, they have kitchenettes, not full kitchens. **Stoney Path**, the economy condo lodging, is a five-minute walk to the lifts.

There is also a variety of chalets, cabins, motels, hotels, inns and B&Bs in the area. Jay Peak Resort can assist you, or call the **Jay Peak Area Association** at 800-882-7460. Remember to ask about ski-and-stay packages.

The 27-room**The Lodge at Jay** (800-204-7039; 802-988-4459; $-$$$$) was refurbished with warm Southwestern hues and handcrafted Vermont-made furniture. Rooms range from economy to family suites. A restaurant, steam room, sauna, fitness facilities, spa services, movie room and fireside lounges are on site. Breakfast is included; kids younger than 14 stay free.

The European-influenced **Inglenook Lodge** (800-331-4346; 802-988-2880; $$-$$$$) is a bit worn but owned by a friendly couple who welcome families and kids. Amenities include an indoor pool, hot tub, sauna, game room, restaurant and lounge. Prices include breakfast and dinner. Children 6 and younger stay free; kids 7-16 have reduced rates. The **Black Lantern Inn** (800-255-8661; 802-326-4507; $$-$$$$), about 20 minutes away in Montgomery, is a beautifully restored stagecoach stop circa 1803 and listed on the National Register of Historic Places. The inn has eight rooms and seven suites, all with private baths and decorated with Vermont antiques, some with gas fireplace stoves and jetted tubs. An outdoor hot tub, a sitting room warmed by a wood stove, and a bountiful breakfast add extra creature comforts.

Two Victorian inns can be found a bit closer in Montgomery Center. **Phineas Swann Bed & Breakfast** (802-326-4306; $$-$$$) has three bedrooms in the main house and four suites in its carriage house with fireplaces, jetted tubs en suite, and four-poster queen-size beds. An annex has one-bedroom apartments. Guests also enjoy a gourmet breakfast and afternoon tea. The **Inn on Trout River** (800-338-7049; 802-326-4391; $-$$) pampers guests with queen-size beds covered with down quilts, feather pillows and flannel sheets. A fancy breakfast is served. The main dining room and sitting room have fireplaces, and a Montgomery Soapstone Stove warms the split-level living room and library.

 # Dining

Each base lodge has a **cafeteria** that serves breakfast and lunch, and the food is quite good. For hearty sit-down meals, **Hotel Jay's Alpine Room Restaurant** ($$) serves breakfast and dinner. Although the atmosphere is rustic, the food is not. Entrees such as grilled maple mesquite pork loin and tequila roast duckling fill the menu.

For condo, townhouse or vacation home dwellers, **My Chef at Jay** (802-988-4137), run by Marcie Kaufman, a classically trained chef from the New England Culinary Institute, delivers meals. Order 24 hours in advance for delivery on Monday - Friday from 3 p.m. - 6 p.m., 9 a.m. - noon on Saturdays. three-course supper: $36/person; two-course, $22.

Two local inns are renowned for their fine dining. Top dog is **The Black Lantern Inn** (802-326-4507; $$), where candlelight sets the mood and the menu changes frequently. The elegant cuisine, cozy atmosphere and wallet-friendly prices here rival any you'll find across

Dining: $$$$–Entrees $30+; $$$–$20–$30; $$–$10–$20; $–less than $10.
Accommodations: (double room) $$$$–$200+; $$$–$141–$200; $$–$81–$140; $–$80 and less.

the border in Quebec. **Lemoine's**, at The Inn on Trout River (802-326-4391; $$), is an intimate restaurant with a country Victorian theme. Try the raviolini stuffed with Vermont cheddar cheese and walnuts topped with pesto, or the medallions of pork tenderloin in a maple syrup demi-glaze sauce. For simpler fare, consider the pub menu at **Hobo's Cafe** (802-326-4391; $$), also at The Inn on Trout River.

Ask at your hotel about French cuisine in nearby Quebec.

 ## Apres-ski/nightlife

The **Golden Eagle Sports Bar** and the **International Bar**, both in the Tram base lodge, and the **Sport Lounge at Hotel Jay** are the on-mountain places to head for when you quit the slopes. We recommend taste-testing the Vermont microbrews. Live entertainment, Karaoke nights and theme parties are frequently scheduled. **The Belfry**, just down the mountain road toward Montgomery Center, has a good selection of beers and local microbrews on tap and in the bottle.

 ## Other activities

The idea here is to enjoy the great outdoors. The **ice skating rink** is sometimes the site of impromptu ice hockey games. But you'll need to bring your own skates. The region is well known for its **snowmobiling**; rent a snowmobile and book a guided tour through the Jay Village Inn (802-988-2306). Try **night sledding** behind Hotel Jay; ask the front desk for sleds. For **sleighrides**, call Phil & Karen's Sleighrides (802-744-9928) in Westfield.

Hotel Jay runs **movies** nightly on channel 8 on all hotel TVs for kids at 7 p.m. and for adults at 9 p.m. (No, not those kind of "for adults" movies!) Waterfront Lanes (802-334-8144) in nearby Newport has **bowling**. Jay has a few **shops** worth visiting, including The Snow Job (the best tunes around) and the Jay Country Store. But, for a **shopping excursion**, head to Burlington, Montreal or Magog. In the spring, visit one of the nearby **maple sugar shacks**.

Getting there and getting around

By air: Burlington International Airport is served by Continental, JetBlue, United and USAirways. It takes 1.5 hours to drive from the airport to the mountain.

By car: Jay Peak Resort is on Route 242 in northern-central Vermont, just below the Canadian border, about equidistant between I-91 and I-89. Sample driving times: Boston, 3.5 hours; Albany, 4.5 hours; New York City, 6.5 hours; Toronto, 7 hours; Montreal, 1.5 hours.

By bus: Vermont Transit serves nearby Newport from all major New England points. Ground transportation is available.

By train: AMTRAK Vermonter to St. Albans, 45 minutes away. Ground transfers available to Jay Peak.

Getting around: Bring a car if you want to venture off mountain.

Killington
Vermont

Summit: 4,215 feet
Vertical: 3,050 feet
Base: 1,165 feet

Address: Killington Road, Killington, VT 05751
Telephone (main): 802-422-3333
Snow Report Number: 802-422-3261
Toll-free reservations: 800-621-6867
E-mail: info@killington.com
Internet: www.killington.com

Expert:★ ★
Advanced:★ ★ ★ ★
Intermediate: ★ ★ ★★
Beginner: ★ ★ ★
First-timer: ★ ★ ★

Lifts: 32—3 gondolas, 6 high-speed quads, 6 quads, 6 triples, 4 doubles, 7 surface lifts
Skiable acreage: 1,209
Snowmaking: 70 percent
Uphill capacity: 52,973
Parks & pipes: 3 parks, 1 pipes
Bed base: 5,500 at the base; 18,000 in the region
Nearest lodging: Walking distance
Child care: Yes, 6 weeks to 6 years
Adult ticket, per day: $79 (07/08 prices)

Dining:★ ★ ★
Apres-ski/nightlife: ★ ★ ★ ★
Other activities: ★ ★ ★

Tucked beneath Vermont's second-highest peak, the Killington Basin is a natural place for a ski resort. The K-1 gondola carries skiers and riders to the highest lift-served skiing in the state. The resort is huge, by Eastern standards, and truly has terrain for all abilities, including some super bumps, nice glades, old-time narrow trails and plenty of blue squares. Since the resort no longer offering super-inexpensive season passes, it's less crowded than it used to be.

The basin receives, on average, 250 inches of snow each year. If the snow doesn't fall from the sky, Killington/Pico makes it fall from its guns. With one of the world's largest snowmaking systems, the resort literally blankets its seven mountains in white.

Although Killington has consistent snow most of the winter, spring is probably the best time to ski or ride at Killington/Pico. Crowds gather on the deck of the Bear Mountain Lodge, hooting and hollering as up-and-coming bump skiers rip it up—or flail—on the legendary Outer Limits trail, the longest, steepest mogul slope in the East. The smell of burgers on the grill wafts into the air, beer is plentiful (for age 21-plus), and everyone is having a good time.

Killington, though, is not all things to all people. Its sheer size can be intimidating and navigating from one mountain to the next has left more than one skier or rider wishing they had their own GPS system. To add to the confusion, Killington has five base areas (six, if you count Pico's). Killington provides shuttle service at day's end for those who have taken a wrong turn and ended up at a base different from where they parked in the morning. Be sure to read the signs at each trail junction.

Only about 1,500 feet of Killington's 3,050-foot vertical drop is working vertical, and only three trails, mostly beginner, meander the last 1,500 feet down to the true base on Rte. 4. People looking to avoid the more crowded parking lots at higher up often park here, take the Skyeship gondola to the mountain(s) proper, then take the long run back at day's end.

Or you can ski Pico, a physically separate mountain from Killington's other six. Even though it's 10 minutes away by car, Pico is still worth visiting. Considered by many locals as a feather in the Mother Ship's cap, Pico has 2,000 feet of vertical, 48 trails and some very interesting "old fashion" terrain. Pico is open Thursdays through Mondays.

Mountain layout–skiing & snowboarding

Killington's five base areas (six, with Pico) disperse skier and riders across the seven peaks rather quickly, even on the busiest days. Three are clustered close together on Killington Road—Snowshed and Rams Head are across the street from one another; Killington base is just up the road. Bear Mountain, home of the famed Outer Limits bump run, is on Bear Mountain Road off Rte. 4. Also off Rte. 4 is the Skyeship Base Station, a good choice for those who don't want the hassle of the Access Road.

This is quite a confusing mountain for first-time visitors. Half of our snowboard writer's day was spent stopped and studying the trail map, trying to figure out where she was and how she got there, when she wanted to be two peaks over. To make the most of your time, either take a free "Meet the Mountains" tour or befriend a local. Be aware that some roped-off trails are not visibly marked until it's too late—around a bend or over a knoll—which means snowboarders have to hike a few feet back to the open trail. If it's the end of the day, consult your map frequently to make sure you'll end up at the same base area as your car.

◆◆ **Expert,** ◆ **Advanced:** Some of the toughest terrain is between Snowdon Mountain and Killington Peak. The Canyon quad chair services this area for access to double-diamond Cascade, Downdraft, Double Dipper and Big Dipper Glade.

Skye Peak is one of the most popular sections. Skyelark and Bittersweet are fairly easy expert trails, while Superstar and Ovation—the resort's steepest trail—will test any expert's legs. With plenty of machine-made snow, Superstar is often the last trail to close in spring.

Bear Mountain is another popular haven for experts, with double-diamond drops such as Devil's Fiddle and the infamous Outer Limits, where bumps are the name of the game. If you ski it on one of the rare days it's groomed, and if you fall, you may slide all the way to the bottom, much to the amusement of the crowd watching from the base and the chairlift.

After a good snowfall, head to Pico and get fresh tracks down the gnarly Giant Killer or Upper Pike. Upper KA and Sunset 71, narrow trails reminiscent of the early days of New England skiing, wind down from the top of Pico and offer interesting knolls, twists and turns.

■ **Intermediate:** The Rams Head high-speed quad is a good place for beginners and intermediates to start. Caper is a good warm-up cruiser. The Snowdon area is another mellow delight. It's served by two chairs from the base area and a mid-mountain Poma lift on Bunny Buster. Highline and Conclusion are good advanced cruising runs with excellent pitch. Bunny Buster and Chute have less of a grade.

Needle's Eye often has some of the best snow at the resort. The wide run drops beneath the second leg of the Skyeship gondola. Another cruiser in this area is the aptly named Cruise Control. A trip back up the Needle's Eye Express quad will put you back on Bittersweet for wide turns to the Killington Base Lodge or Snowshed.

Pico is home to 49-ner, a cruiser that offers superb views from the top of Pico. Nervous intermediates will find the top part of this blue square challenging, though.

● **Beginner,** ● ● **First-timer:** Green trails lead from all six interconnected peaks, which allows beginners panoramic vistas and thrill of skiing from the summit. But, beginners beware: it's easy to get lost at Killington on these meandering trails.

Killington, in theory, has a perfect learning area: Snowshed. Served by three chairlifts, this gentle slope is a segregated beginning area. But the top of the trail is accessible from the upper part of the mountain, which can make Snowshed crowded—and not just with other beginners. Experts often fly down the slope. Consider learning at another resort or head to Pico, where beginners learn at the more isolated Bonanza area.

Parks and pipes

Killington's signature terrain park on Bear Mountain has a 425-foot long superpipe featuring 18-foot walls cut by a Silver Zaugg, a boardercross course, and numerous hits, rails and boxes on Bear Trap and Wildfire. There's a good chance you'll see Killington's Park and Pipe crew, who are serious riders and hardcore jibbers, buttering up the transitions between jumps and hand-grooming park features or testing the product. Many park features have two differently sized approaches, one for the intermediate jumpers and one for advanced. The park has six rails, eight jumps, a quarterpipe and other features. Transitions between jumps are smooth, and the crew works harder on the landings than average.

Cross-country & snowshoeing (see also xcskiresorts.com)

At the base of the Killington Road, behind Base Camp Outfitters, **Mountain Meadows Cross-Country Ski Resort** (802-775-7077) has 57 km. of trails meandering across Kent Lake and through surrounding forests. **Mountain Top Cross-Country Ski Resort** (802-483-2311), in Chittenden, has 110 km. of trails, 40 km. of dual-set tracks and 0.5 km. of trails with snowmaking. Both have rentals, lessons, ski shops and warming huts; Mountain Top has sledding and horse-drawn sleigh rides. Woodstock's the **Ski Touring Center** (802-457-2114) has 75 km. of trails, lessons and rentals.

Lessons (07/08 prices)

Group lessons: A two-hour group lesson costs $49 ($52 holidays). Morning sessions run from 9:45 a.m. to noon; afternoon from 12:45 p.m. to 3 p.m. **First-timer package:** The Learn-to-Ski programs are based at Snowshed. A two-hour lesson with ticket and rentals costs $99 ($104 on holidays).

Private lessons: A one-hour clinic is $99 for one person, $170 for two people. A two-hour lesson is $170 for one person, $290 for two people. Three- and six-hour clinics also are available for $240 and $426, respectively, for one person; $410 (3-hour) and $594 (6-hour) for two people. Rates are higher during holidays.

Racing: Killington offers a weekend and week-long race program for those 18 and older in early December. The two-day program costs $255. The five-day clinic is $490. For information and reservations, call 800-923-9444.

Children's Programs (08/09 prices)

Child care: The Friendly Penguin Day Care is in the Rams Head Family Center and provides care for ages 12 weeks to 6 years. Cost is $130 per day and pre-paid reservations are required; call 800-923-9444. Frequent Kids Discount Cards, good for 11 or more days, provide a 15 to 30 percent discount.

Children's lessons: First Tracks is a combination of day care and lessons for ages 2–6 that includes lessons with no more than 3 kids per instructor, lift tickets and equipment. Cost is $180 for a full day (8 a.m.-4 p.m.) and pre-paid reservations are required.

MiniStars/Lowriders for ages 4–6 teaches children to enjoy the sport of skiing and snowboarding with no more than 5 kids per instructor. The all-day programs balance lessons and play and cost $180 for a full day (8:30 a.m.-3 p.m.) and includes lunch, lift ticket, and equipment. Pre-paid reservations are required.

Superstar programs for ages 7–12 cost $180 for a full day (9 a.m.-3 p.m.) and includes lunch, lift ticket, and equipment; $135 for a half-day (9 a.m.-noon, lunch not included). Lessons have no more than 5 kids per instructor. Snowzone Programs and Camp Freeride for teens 13–18 offer skiing or snowboarding for the same price as the Superstar programs.

Lift tickets (07/08 prices)

One day: adult $79*/$76, teen (13-18) $65*/$61, child (7-12) $55*/$53. Three days: adult $216, teen $174, child $150. Five days: adult $335, teen $265, child $230. *Saturday & holiday price.

Who skis free: Ages 5 and younger. Children ages 12 and younger ski free when accompanied by an adult who pre-purchases at least a five-day ticket (one child per adult).

Who skis at a discount: Ages 65-69 pay same price as teens, seniors age 70+ pay junior rate. Killington tickets are valid at Pico, but if you plan to ski just Pico, you can buy a Pico-only pass that's about $30 cheaper than the full pass. Public transportation between the two is on The Bus ($2); it stops along the Access Road. Catch it at the Snowshed Base Lodge.

Accommodations

Killington has very little slopeside lodging and no real ski-in/ski-out options; on-mountain condos are ski-in, but not ski-out. To make reservations for the **Killington Grand Resort Hotel, Killington Resort Villages** and most properties, call the **Killington Lodging Bureau** (800-621-6867).

The **Killington Resort Villages** has good values and the best location, with nearby athletic club facilities, some nightlife and an excellent shuttle bus system. Of the condo complexes here, **Highridge** units are by far the most desirable. **Sunrise**, at the base of Bear Mountain, is another good choice. Other condos include **The Woods at Killington**, which boasts hot tubs and saunas and a complete spa, and **Mountain Inn** and the **Cascades Lodge**, which are very convenient but basic. The Cascades has a nice indoor pool, and the **Mountain Inn** has some of the best nightlife, when the bar is hopping. The **Killington Grand Resort Hotel** ($$-$$$$), near the base of Snowshed, has 200 units from hotel rooms to penthouses, renovated in 2007, a full-service restaurant, outdoor heated swimming pool, health club, full-service spa and a "slopeside" location (you must walk across a pond on a long pedestrian bridge to reach the slopes). When reserving a room, ask for a "hotel room" or "suite." Most of the "studio" rooms only have sofas or Murphy beds. What you're paying for here is the location.

Also large is **The Inn of the Six Mountains** (800-228-4676; 802-422-4302; $$-$$$), with a 65-foot indoor lap pool, exercise room and frequent shuttles to the slopes. Rates include breakfast. Also on the Access Road, **The Birch Ridge Inn** (802-422-4293; $$$-$$$$) was created from a former executive retreat. The A-frame design gives it a 1960s flair, and the cuisine gets high marks. Near the base of the Access Road, the **North Star Lodge** (802-422-4040; $-$$) has a pool, shuttle service and is surrounded by good restaurants.

On Route 4 west of Killington, is **The Inn at Long Trail** (800-325-2540; 802-775-7181; $-$$). One of Vermont's first ski lodges, the inn still maintains its cozy, rustic feel. The 19 rooms are small, but the inn has a devoted following. Rates include breakfast and dinner. **The Vermont Inn** (800-541-7795; 802-775-0708; $$-$$$$), with 18 rooms, fireside dining, and everything homemade, is a charming New England country inn. Breakfast and dinner are included in the rates, and the food is excellent. The inn is about 1 mile west of Pico on Rte. 4.

The Mountain Top Inn & Resort (800-445-2100; 802-483-2311; $$$-$$$$) is 11 miles from Killington, has awesome views, and a cross-country center. **The Grey Bonnet** (802-775-2537; $-$$) on Rte. 100 North, has a nice indoor pool, sauna and pub. Rates include breakfast and dinner. You'll need a car to get to the ski area.

What a find! If you pine for the camaraderie of an old-fashioned ski lodge, with equally old-fashioned prices, check into the **Turn of River Lodge** (800-782-9867; 802-422-3766; $-$$), near the Skyeship base and just 3 miles from the access road. Relax by the huge stone hearth in the great room, play board games, watch TV, bring your wifi-equipped laptop or just lounge and chat with other guests. Private rooms have TV, phone and private or shared baths. There are also dorm beds. Discount lift tickets are available. A light Continental breakfast is included, and guests have the use of a refrigerator and microwave.

The **Woodstock Inn and Resort** (800-448-7900; $$$-$$$$), about 17 miles east of Killington, where rooms were renovated in 2006, has an air of sophistication, with particular attention paid to the bed linens. The resort houses an excellent fitness center with large indoor pool, two indoor tennis courts, paddle tennis courts, squash and racquetball courts, and a weight/cardio room. The dining room wine list has 184 selections. Midweek, the inn has a very attractive package with free downhill skiing (yes, free) at nearby Suicide Six or cross-country skiing at the Woodstock Ski Touring Center, run out of the resort's country club.

Dining

The Killington area has more than 100 restaurants and bars. The best is **Hemingway's** (802-422-3886; $$$$), one of only two four-star restaurants in Vermont. The fixed-price, four-course menu ranges from $55-$65.

Our other favorites are **Maxwell's Restaurant at The Summit** (802-422-3535; $$$$), award-winning but casual, with a menu that changes nightly and a great wine list; and the top-rated **The Vermont Inn** (800-541-7795; 802-775-0708; $$$$), with fine formal dining.

The **Birch Ridge Inn** (802-422-4293; $$$) has a small, but highly acclaimed restaurant. **McGrath's Irish Pub** (802-775-7181; $$), at **The Inn at Long Trail**, serves Guinness stew and shepherd's pie in its funky pub and restaurant built into a cliff. At **Charity's** (802-422-3800; $$), the bar is cozy and welcoming, and the portions healthy on a menu of steaks, barbecue and Italian dishes. **Casey's Caboose** (802-422-3795; $$-$$$), in a restored circa-1900 railroad car, is a good choice for steaks, seafood and pasta. The lunch and bar menus ($) offer hearty, cheaper alternatives. Check out the toy train running around the track along the ceiling. The rambling **Grist Mill Restaurant** (802-422-3970; $$) sits beside a tranquil pond and the rustic interior is comfortable and casual. Food (traditional New England fare) and service are average.

For restaurants a bit kinder to the budget: The **Wobbly Barn Steakhouse** (802-422-3392; $$) is known for steaks and a great salad bar (no reservations). **Mrs. Brady's** (802-422-2020; $-$$) serves the "basics" (salads, burgers, roast turkey and monster sandwiches). **Pizza Jerks** (802-422-4111; $) and **Outback Pizza** (802-422-9885; $), both on the Killington Road, serve decent pizza. **Sushi Yoshi and Hibachi Steakhouse** (802-422-4241; $-$$$) has the best—and only—Japanese and Chinese food on the mountain, including a sushi bar.

For breakfast, locals head to **Wally's All American Diner** ($), formerly Peppers, at the nightspot Outback. Portions are massive, and it caters to the hung-over. **Johnny Boys Pancake House** ($), on the Killington Road in front of the Comfort Inn, serves regular homestyle before-noon fare. For good coffee or quick breakfast, try **Sun-up Bakery** ($), but be forewarned: if there's 10 inches of fresh snow, the staff often shuts the doors and skis for a few runs.

Dining: $$$$–Entrees $30+; $$$–$20–$30; $$–$10–$20; $–less than $10.
Accommodations: (double room) $$$$–$200+; $$$–$141–$200; $$–$81–$140; $–$80 and less.

Apres-ski/nightlife

Killington's apres-ski scene, strung out along the Killington Road, is often voted number one in the nation, with the atmosphere generally raucous and young, and festivities often driven by excellent bands, some nationally known

Apres-ski at the mountain includes the **Mahogany Ridge at the Killington Base Lodge**, the **Long Trail Brew Pub** at Snowshed and the **Bear Mountain Lounge** at the Bear Mountain Base Lodge. On the Killington Road, apres-ski action is found in the **Lookout Bar & Grille**, or **Charity's**. **Outback Pizza** is a locals' favorite recommended for happy hour on weekdays, with $5 all-you-can-eat pizza on Monday nights; weekend entertainment and dancing extend into the evening. **Casey's Caboose** serves killer spicy buffalo wings free during happy hour. For rowdy apres-ski and then dancing to loud music, head to the **Wobbly Barn Steakhouse**. Big name bands often lead the line-up at **The Pickle Barrel**, a favorite among the young college crowd.

An older, quieter set meets at the **Summit** for happy hour. **The Garlic** has tapas and a martini menu. The Grist Mill restaurant/bar has earned a reputation in recent years as the place for slightly "more mature" skiers, but don't let that fool you: the place rocks on weekends, when live music and dancing are featured, and its circular bar and layout are perfect for checking out the action and people-watching. Plus, the **Grist Mill** makes toe-curling Goombays, a local concoction of fruit juices and various flavors of rum. Two Goombays and you'll understand why this rates as the unofficial drink of the official apres-ski/nightlife capital of the East.

From Pico, head a few yards up Rte. 4 to The Inn at Long Trail, where **McGrath's Irish Pub** serves Guinness tap; live weekend entertainment, performs on a stage built into a cliff.

 ## Other activities

An **outdoor skating rink** can be found below the Summit Lodge on Grist Mill Pond. For **snowmobiling** information call Killington Snowmobile Tours (802-422-2121).

The Spa at The Woods (802-422-3139) is a full-service European spa at The Woods Resort & Spa. Treatments include hot stone therapy, citrus body polish and seaweed body mask. **The Killington Grand Spa** (802-422-1050) is a full-service spa that opened at the Killington Grand Resort Hotel in 2006.

Shopping is plentiful, but as spread out as the resort. The Killington Shops at the Shack, several outlet-style stores, are at the intersection of Rte. 4 and the Access Road. Woodstock, about 17 miles east of Killington on Rte. 4, is one of Vermont's most beautiful villages and is packed with art galleries and shops. Even farther east on Rte. 4 in Quechee is the Simon Pearce glass-blowing workshop and store.

Rutland has a few chain and big-box stores, an unnoteworthy mall south of town, plus a handful of interesting shops in its old downtown section. Behind the mall is the Rutland Fieldhouse with **indoor ice skating** (802-775-3100). For **indoor rock climbing**, try the Green Mountain Rock Climbing Center (802-773-3343) on Rte. 4 on the way into Rutland from Killington. Rutland also has the Paramount Theatre (802-775-0570) that opened in 1914. It was recently restored and has been visited by music greats such as Arlo Guthrie and Alison Krauss, as well as several theater productions. Check paramountvt.org for programs.

 ## Getting there and getting around

By air: Major airports are in Burlington, Vt., Albany, N.Y., and Manchester, N.H. Burlington is about a 90-minute drive from Killington, while Albany

and Manchester are each about two hours. Green Mountain Limousine Service (802-773-1313) runs transfers from the Burlington airport. Thrifty Rental Cars has an office at the Inn of the Six Mountains. Major car rental companies are also available at the airports. Cape Air, partnered with JetBlue, has daily service from Boston into the Rutland State Airport, about a 20-minute drive from Killington, with rental cars available at the airport.

By car: Killington is at the intersection of Rtes. 4 and 100 in central Vermont, about three hours from Boston. Pico is located about 3 miles west of the Killington Road on Rte. 4.

By train: Daily service is available on Amtrak's Ethan Allen Express from New York City to Rutland, with bus service or car rental to Killington. Call 800-872-7245 for train information, or Killington Central Reservations (800-621-6867) for package information.

Getting around: Bring or rent a car or use the Killington Shuttle bus service. Though you might not use your car to move between your lodging and the slopes, Killington is very spread out, and you may want to visit the attractions nearby.

Nearby Resort
Suicide Six Ski Area, Woodstock, VT; 802-457-6661
Internet: www.woodstockinn.com/vermont-ski-resort.php.
3 lifts; 23 trails; 650 vertical feet.
In 1934, Bunny Bertram rigged up the first rope tow in America in a pasture north of Woodstock. Three years later, Suicide Six opened just over the ridge from Bertram's first tow. The little ski area has been in operation ever since. It's now owned by the Woodstock Inn & Resort. A shuttle runs from the hotel to the ski area. The ski area remains open to the public, as well.

From the road, you see just one trail: The Face, an intimidating precipice dropping under the chairlift. But there are 22 friendlier trails ranging from novice to expert, a halfpipe, two double chairlifts, and a J-bar on the Beginners' Slope. The base lodge, with 40-foot tall windows, has a cafeteria, a bar/restaurant, a ski shop and a ski school staffed by certified instructors.

The **Woodstock Ski Touring Center**, operating just south of the Village, has 60 km. of trails that extend around the Village and into the surrounding hills. Inn guests are also allowed to ski on the trail network in the **Marsh-Billings-Rockefeller National Historic Park**.

Suicide Six has no child care, but the ski school does offer children's lessons. If you are staying at the **Woodstock Inn & Resort**, ask for babysitting referrals.

Lift tickets (2007/08 prices): Adults, $55 weekend/holiday, $36 midweek; juniors/seniors, $40/$30. Lower rates early and late season. Guests at the Woodstock Inn & Resort ski for free on non-holiday midweek days.

Lodging: The elegant **Woodstock Inn** (800-448-7900; 457-1100; $$$$), in downtown Woodstock, is *the* place to stay. Tickets and equipment rentals are free for inn guests during midweek and non-holiday periods. The inn has an excellent indoor sports facility, a well-respected dining room and a more casual restaurant. Woodstock's other lodging includes a nice choice of small inns and B&Bs. These include the **Ardmore Inn** (800-497-9652; 457-3887; $$-$$), a lovely in-town B&B; The **Village Inn of Woodstock** (800-722-4571; $$-$$$) on the eastern edge of town; and the **Jackson House Inn and Restaurant** (800-448-1890; 457-2065; $$$$), heading west toward Killington, with its renowned dining room (reservations essential).

Getting there: Woodstock is 10 miles off I-89 on Rte. 4; 17 miles east of Killington.

Dining: $$$$–Entrees $30+; $$$–$20–$30; $$–$10–$20; $–less than $10.
Accommodations: (double room) $$$$–$200+; $$$–$141–$200; $$–$81–$140; $–$80 and less.

Mad River Valley

Sugarbush & Mad River Glen

Waitsfield/Warren Region Vermont

Dining:★★★★
Apres-ski/nightlife:★★
Other activities:★★
Toll free reservations: 800- 828-4748
Internet: www.madrivervalley.com

Sugarbush

Summit elevation:	4,083 feet
Vertical drop:	2,600 feet
Base elevation:	1,483 feet

Address: 1840 Sugarbush Access Road Warren, VT 05674-9572
Ski area phone: 802-583-6300
Snow report: 802-583-SNOW
Toll-free reservations: 800-537-8427
Fax: 802-583-6803
Internet: www.sugarbush.com
Number and types of lifts: 16—5 high-speed quads, 2 quad chairs, 2 triples, 4 double chairs, 3 surface lifts
Skiable acreage: 508 acres
Snowmaking: 78 percent
Uphill capacity: 25,463 per hour
Parks & pipes: 9 parks; 1 pipe
Bed base: 6,600 (2,200 on mountain)
Nearest lodging: Slopeside
Resort child care: Yes, 6 weeks and older
Adult ticket per day:$71 (7/08)

Expert: ★★
Advanced: ★★★
Intermediate:★★★★
Beginner: ★★★★
First-timer:★★★★

Mad River Glen

Summit elevation:	3,637 feet
Vertical drop:	2,037 feet
Base elevation:	1,600 feet

Address: PO Box 1089 Waitsfield, VT 05673
Ski area phone: 802-496-3551
Snow report: 802-496-3551
Toll-free information: 800-850-6742 (area Chamber)
Fax: 802-496-3562
E-mail: ski@madriverglen.com
Internet: www.madriverglen.com
Number and types of lifts: 5—3 double chairs, 1 single chair, 1 surface lift
Skiable acreage: about 115 acres
Snowmaking: 15 percent
Uphill capacity: 3,000 per hour
Snowboarding: Not allowed
Bed base: 6,600
Nearest lodging: About a quarter-mile
Resort child care: Yes, 6 weeks to 6 years
Adult ticket, per day: $56 (07/08 prices)

Expert: ★★★★
Advanced: ★★★★
Intermediate:★★★
Beginner: ★★
First-timer: ★

Conjure up a Hollywood-influenced image of Vermont, and chances are you'll picture the Mad River Valley. It's equal parts Bing Crosby's White Christmas and the Bob Newhart Show. The rolling, pastoral countryside is dotted with clapboard farmhouses, restored barns, restored inns and those iconic Vermont cows. The mountains rise sharply, and sideroads to ski areas wind through ledges cutting the landscape.

Once the playground for the well-to-do, the out-of-the-way Mad River Valley gradually fell out of favor with the "in" crowd and became the place that time forgot. This is a good thing. The valley remains free of large chain hotels, fast-food restaurants and other sprawl. Two small towns, Waitsfield and Warren, provide everything a visitor might need, and do so in that oh-so-Vermont, New York-accented, country-store fashion. You may be rusticating, but you needn't do without a fine wine and a fancy meal.

Sugarbush and Mad River are the yin and yang of the Alpine world. They balance each other and manage to entertain everyone from just-happy-to-be-together families to death-defying extreme skiers. Sugarbush has lots of snowmaking, the new base area Lincoln Peak Village, plenty of condos and, from an Eastern point of view, relatively wide trails.

Mad River Glen is the way skiing used to be, because, well, little has changed here over the years. Home to one of the few single chairs left in the country, Mad River has almost no snowmaking and no condos. Narrow trails that cut down the thickly wooded mountain are merely suggestions of where to ski. Diehards ski all over Mad River Glen, through trees, over frozen waterfalls and down cliffs. Its terrain attracts such a devoted following that Mad River is America's only skier-owned, nonprofit cooperative.

Sugarbush

 ## Mountain layout

Sugarbush is divided into two separate areas, Lincoln Peak and Mt. Ellen, connected by a 10-minute ride on rollercoaster-like, high-speed quad chairlift. Each of these mountains has sub-areas with its own distinct flavors, with more than 4,000 acres spilling from a five-mile wide ridgeline. Lincoln Peak Village, new in 2006-07, has been the most ambitious project in the resort's almost 50-year history. It features three facilities, including Clay Brook, the cornerstone of the revitalization, and the Gate House lodge, double the size of the old building from 11,000 square feet to 23,000 square feet.

◆◆**Expert** ◆**Advanced:** At Lincoln Peak, the runs served by the Castlerock lift are serious blacks and no place for the timid. The entire Castlerock area offers narrow New England-style steeps; but, if you're lucky, the Castlerock run will occasionally be groomed, making for a heavenly smooth steep. The Castlerock double chair is popular with those in this ability level, so be aware that sometimes there is a wait, albeit usually not more than eight to 10 minutes. The benefit is that these narrow trails do not fill up with yahoo skiers. You have to *want* to be there to end up at Castlerock.

From the summit of Lincoln Peak and the top of the Heaven's Gate triple, experts can drop down Ripcord or Paradise, two double-black-diamond runs that frequently bump up. The more wide-open Organgrinder (the old gondola lift line), which we dubbed "Organ Donor," is a wide, steep run that dares you to ski fast. Stein's Run, accessible by either the Super Bravo Express or the Valley House Double chairlifts, is another long, steep, mogul run. Egan's Woods, to skier's left of Stein's Run, is no doubt where extreme skier John Egan plays.

Mt. Ellen is primarily an intermediate playground, though the double blacks at the top—

F.I.S., Black Diamond, Exterminator and Bravo (the latter a single diamond)—are among the toughest in New England. The Green Mountain Express high-speed quad from the base connects to the Summit Quad, allowing easy access to the top.

■ **Intermediate:** Intermediates should start at the Super Bravo chair on Lincoln Peak, then traverse to the Heaven's Gate triple. Once at the summit, take Upper Jester, a run full of fun switchbacks that take you back to the top of the Super Bravo lift. From here, choose from Downspout, Domino, Snowball, Murphy's Glades or Lower Jester. On a busy day, these runs are crowded with skiers. Intermediates also tend to flock to the North Lynx triple on the upper part of North Lynx Peak. Here, the views are good, and the runs sometimes bump up.

The slopes tend to be less crowded on the lower part of North Lynx Peak and parts of Gadd Peak. Eden, a tree-skiing area on Gadd Peak, is the place to learn to navigate glades. Spring Fling is wide-open, attracts few skiers and is great for long, fast turns.

Mt. Ellen has wide-open cruising runs. On the map, the intermediate runs from the top of the Summit quad chair seem relatively short, but the map is misleading. The Rim Run, connecting to Upper Lookin' Good, Lower Rim Run, Cruiser and Straight Shot, is a classic cruising trail. The other intermediate section is Inverness, served by a quad chair.

●● **Beginner:** North Lynx Peak, on the far right side of the Lincoln Peak, is a good place for beginners. Start on Pushover and Easy Rider and then graduate to Slowpoke and Sleeper. At Mt. Ellen, Walt's Trail is a long green run from the top of the Inverness chair.

● **First-timer:** Lincoln Peak has Easy Rider, a gentle slope served by a double chair. Mt. Ellen has Graduation, Riemergasse and Sugar Run, also served by a double chair.

Parks and pipes

Sugarbush's terrain park and superpipe are on Mt. Ellen and have a dedicated chair. Getting there from Lincoln Peak requires a rollercoaster ride on the Slide Brook Express or taking the base-to-base trolley. Features in the park change throughout the season, but expect rails, jumps, hips, wedges, boxes, uptown-downtown buses and a double-barrel shotgun. All of Sugarbush's park rangers are professionally trained coaches. Tunes crank every weekend and the resort will even play tunes submitted by guests.

Snowboarding

The only trail that will leave you hiking here is Lower FIS; even if you hold speed you'll be booting out and kicking. It's worth it on a powder day, because this is a quiet trail that holds freshies late, but you will have to hike out. There are a few traverses where you'll need to keep up speed: Bailout from Castlerock Run to Heaven's Gate is not all that bad, a little speed will get the job done. The Northway, from Exterminator to the Inverness lift at Mt. Ellen, is long and somewhat flat as well, but speed should carry you, provided the surface is groomed; otherwise, you'll hike. Reverse Traverse, from the top of Stein's Run over to Murphy's Glades, is tough because you really can't get a lot of speed to go the distance. Instead, head down Snowball to Spring Fling.

Lessons (07/08 prices)

Group lessons: $45 for all levels except first-timers.

First-timer package: Learn-to-Ski or Ride clinics include lesson, lifts and rentals and cost $70. A three-day "Zero to Hero" package costs $210, usable any time during the season. Call 888-651-4827 for details.

Private lessons: $95 an hour; $75 each added hour; $25 for each additional person.

Special programs: The Sugarbush Ski & Ride School offers multi day clinics for snowboarders, women and expert skiers or riders, and specialty classes (powder, bumps, etc.) in private lessons. Outback Tours take advanced skiers/riders off-piste into Lincoln Peak's Slide Brook Wilderness area for 2.5 hours at 10 a.m. and 1 p.m. on Saturday, Sunday, and holidays when the natural snow coverage allows. Book through the Guest Service desk at Lincoln Peak. Cost: $45. Call 888-651-4827 for reservations.

Children's Programs (07/08 prices)

Child care: Available for ages 6 weeks to 6 years in Sugarbush Village, a group of condos to the far right past the main parking lot at Lincoln Peak. Day Care Cubs (6 weeks–6 years) get a non-ski program for $80 full day, $55 half day. Multiday pricing is available. Reservations required; call 802-583-6717.

Note: You can park at Sugarbush Village and buy lift tickets at the day school. Access the slopes by skiing or walking or taking the shuttlebus.

Children's lessons: Microbears for 3-year-olds combines day care with ski play: $104 full day, $75 half day. Minibears (ages 4-7) and Sugarbears (ages 7-12) combines lessons with snow fun: $104 full day, $75 half day. Equipment rentals: $20.

Full-day children's programs include lunch and lift tickets. Equipment is extra. Reservations required; call 888-651-4827.

Lift tickets (07/08 prices)

One day: adult $73 (weekend/holiday), $69 (midweek); child (7-12) $65/$59; senior (70+) $50/$46. Three days $156 (non-holiday)/$105/$127. Five days $260 (non-holiday)/$175/$209 ($55/day)

Who skis free: Children ages 6 and younger.

Who skis at a discount: Sugarbush lowers ticket prices during value season (opening through mid-December and in April). Sugarbush also offers a Mt. Ellen-only ticket for $59 (weekend/holiday) $52 (midweek) for adults, $42/$35 for seniors and $51/$43 for children, a smart buy for terrain park enthusiasts.

Notes: Holiday prices are higher. The Ski the Valley, a joint ticket for Mad River Glen and Sugarbush, is available when skiers purchase accommodation for three nights or more in the valley. The joint lift ticket allows skiers to choose where they want to ski in the valley each day. Make sure to ask about this special lift ticket when you make reservations.

Mad River Glen

Mad River Glen is a throwback to earlier ski days, and as one of our contributors put it, "It's the type of skiing that made my mother give up the sport." The ski area prides itself on being tough, and the bumper sticker, "Mad River Glen: Ski It If You Can," is all too true. Trail ratings are not inflated. Even the beginner trails here might be graded intermediate elsewhere. But MRG fans love this area and have shown their devotion by buying shares of this now skier-owned resort. And yes, we mean *ski* resort; *snowboards are not allowed*. MRG is traditional (it's one of two areas in the nation with a single chairlift), natural (little snowmaking, and lots of tight tree skiing), hard-corps (the ski shop at the base sells T-shirts with the slogan, "Friends don't let friends get first tracks") and homey (serious skiers have got to love a cafeteria with peanut-butter-and-jelly sandwiches to go). It's not for poseurs. Leave your Bogner suit home and don some wool pants. You'll fit right in. Free guided mountain tours are offered on weekends and holidays at 10 a.m. and 1 p.m.

Mountain layout

◆◆**Expert** ◆**Advanced:** Experts will be happy anywhere at Mad River Glen, especially after a snowstorm. All expert trails are natural-snow trails. (when it falls); they bump up nicely and don't get as icy as the East's other resorts.

While the line for the single chair is usually about 10 minutes long, it can approach 45 minutes on peak holidays and good powder days. Experts happily wait. From the top of this lift, then can immediately drop down the Chute under the lift or traverse to Catamount Bowl, one of the most wide-open runs on the mountain. For more of a challenge, find a guide or hook up with a local and venture into the area called Paradise, entered by dropping down a five-foot waterfall. Ask around for Octopus's Garden and the 19th and 20th Holes. At the single chair's midstation, tree skiing beckons through the Glades to the right as you ski off the chair.

■ **Intermediate:** Mad River Glen is not known for its cruiser runs. From the top of the single chair, intermediates have only one route, upper Antelope, which splits into Catamount after a few turns. Both runs are quite narrow and, beware: halfway down, Antelope veers into the woods, gets steeper, and, hard to believe, even narrower. Unless you're up for a challenge, follow Broadway under the lift, and head to the other side of the mountain.

Intermediates find better terrain selection off the Sunnyside Chair. Quacky to Porcupine is a nice run. Bunny will also take you from Quacky to the base. To the right of the chair is a series of expert trails, Panther, Partridge, Slalom Hill and Gazelle, most of which empty into Birdland. Confident intermediates will find these runs challenging, if not downright scary. A missed turn may mean you have to sideslip into a trail.

If you feel like you're ready to tackle MRG's classic terrain (i.e., the woods), give yourself a sampler. From the top of the Sunnyside chair, take Fox to the big intersection and traverse straight into the woods. The trees soon open up into the Glades. If this trail seems fun, congratulations! You're ready for the tough stuff. If you're intimidated, bail out on Bunny.

●● **Beginner,** ●**First-timer:** Birdland is ostensibly the beginner area, but to get there, you have to have good route-finding skills. Otherwise, you'll find yourself at the top of an overly-moguled expert pitch vowing to give up the sport. Take the Sunnyside chair to the top, then follow Fox to Snail, catwalks that will take you to the land of green circles. Granted, Duck, Lark, Robin, Wren and Loon are for beginners. Learn to ski here, and little will daunt you elsewhere. But be aware that the Birdland Chair runs only on weekends and holidays. During those times, however, a novice-level skier can spend an entire day here, dine at the Birdcage lodge at the bottom of Birdland, and avoid the sometimes long base-area lift lines. Mad River's old-fashioned lifts also mean less on-trail skier traffic that beginners will welcome.

For first-timers, Callie's Corner rope tow is isolated and provides an easy intro.

Snowboarding, parks and pipes

Snowboarding is not permitted at Mad River Glen. Snowboard at nearby Sugarbush Resort. Mad River has no terrain parks or halfpipes. Its natural terrain offers more than enough thrills.

Lessons (07/08 prices)

Mad River Glen has a ski school that, like the area, marches to its own drummer.

Group lessons: The Create Your Own Group is $125 for a one-hour lesson. A second two-hour Create Your Own Group on the same day is $100.

First-timer package: The Beginner "You Can" Learn to Ski Package, including lifts, two-hour lesson and rentals, is $70 for either Alpine or telemark. A follow-up two-hour lesson on the same day costs $50. A nice touch for beginners—so few come here to learn that classes almost always end up being private lessons.

Private lessons: Cost is $65 for an hour, plus $25 per additional person; $100 for two hours, plus $54 per extra person. The "I Can" card delivers three one-hour private lessons for $150

Special programs: Free Heel Fridays is a two-hour telemark lesson, at either 10 a.m. or 1 p.m., for $40.

 ## Children's Programs (07/08 prices)

Child care: The Cricket Club Nursery (802-496-3551 ext. 20) offers infant care for children 6 weeks to 18 months for $60 for a full day, $45 for a half day, $115 for two days. Child care for children ages 18 months to 6 years costs $55 for a full day and $40 for a half day, $105 for two days. The Ski and Play introduction to skiing program is $70 for a full day with lunch and two lessons, $135 for two days. A half day with one ski lesson is $50, $100 for two days. Children ready for more advanced skiing should register in the regular lesson programs . The nursery takes no reservations, but if you check your child into the nursery on Friday and pay for two days, you're guaranteed a spot on Saturday. Or, if you call at 8:15 a.m. and say you're coming, they'll hold a spot for your kid.

Lessons: Programs run from 10 a.m. to 3 p.m. A full day is $80 with lunch, half-day is $50, without lunch. Mad River offers a number of options for kids and teens: Rockin' Robins is for kids ages 4-12 who are learning to ski for the first time; class size is limited to three. Chipmunks is for ages 4-7 who have had some ski experience and are able to ride lifts. Kids 7 and older can chose from Panthers, Development Team, Freestyle Team, Telemark Team and Junior Race Program.

Private lessons: for kids 3–12 cost $40 per hour, $25 for each additional child; $70 for two hours, $35 for each additional child. Weekdays, the lack of volume means that kids' groups lessons are offered as privates at weekend junior group rates.

Lift tickets (08/09 prices)

One day holiday: adult $64, junior (6-17) $41. Three days holiday: adult $183, junior, 123. Five days adult, $295, junior, $195.

Who skis free: Ages 70 and older ski free five midweek days per season. Children 5 and younger are issued a free ticket when skiing with a paying adult.

Who skis at a discount: Seniors 65-69 pay junior prices. Mad River offers a number of deals, check its website for details and coupons.

Notes: Tickets are cheaper during non-holidays. One-day non-holiday tickets are $60/$44/; three-day, $117/$85. Midweek, non-holiday: $39 for everyone. Mad River Glen offers multiple and frequently changing promotional programs that cater to different skier types. Updated promotions can be found on their web site or by subscribing to their e-mail listserv.

Note: Ski the Valley is a joint ticket for Mad River Glen and Sugarbush available when skiers purchase accommodation for at least three nights over a weekend or two nights mid-week in the valley.

Cross-country & snowshoeing (see also xcskiresorts.com)

The **Blueberry Lake Cross-Country Ski Center** (802-496-6687) has 23 km. of trails, beginner to expert, groomed for skate skiing and classic. Dogs are permitted. **Ole's Cross-Country Center** (802-496-3430; near the airport) has 50 km. of groomed trails on rolling terrain. Ole's also has snowshoeing and a Rossignol demo center. The **Inn at the Round Barn Farm** (802-496-2276) cross-country area, with 15 km. of groomed trails, is linked with Ole's.

Snowshoe treks (802-583-6537) are available in Sugarbush's **Slidebrook Wilderness Area**, a remote 2,000-acre wilderness between Mt. Ellen and Lincoln Peak. **Mad River Glen** (802-496-3551) has nearly 5 miles of snowshoe trails on the mountain, which connect with Vermont's famed Long Trail. Guided naturalist programs are offered every weekend. These include full-moon snowshoe treks, an evening naturalist series, slide shows and other events. You can arrange snowshoe treks through **Clearwater Sports** (802-496-2708). Carol Thompson of **Out Back Tracks** (802-496-3153) tells how to recognize animal tracks and interpret animal behaviors on personalized, guided snowshoe expeditions. Snowshoers who want to strike out on their own can take advantage of a variety of backcountry trails in the region. A trail map is available from the Sugarbush Chamber of Commerce.

Accommodations

Excellent country inns and B&Bs can all be booked through **Sugarbush Chamber of Commerce** (800-828-4748 or www.madrivervalley.com), **Sugarbush Central Reservations** (800-537-8427) or call the inns directly. The chamber Web site offers info on current availability and online reservations for 23 properties.

It is easy to be spoiled at **The Pitcher Inn** (802-496-6350; 888-867-4824; $$$$), a Relais and Chateau member property in Warren. We especially liked the Mad River, Mountain and Trout rooms. Many rooms have fireplaces, whirlpool tubs and steam rooms. Full breakfasts are served in the light-filled dining room, where gourmet meals are served at night. Afternoon tea and treats are served in the library. Drinks are served in the comfy downstairs lounge and adjacent games room. Owners Win and Margaret Smith are also part owners of Sugarbush.

The Inn at the Round Barn Farm (802-496-2276; $$-$$$$), a mile from Rte. 100, across the covered bridge on East Warren Road is one of the country's best B&Bs. The farmhouse has been turned into an elegant, spacious, peaceful 11-room bed-and-breakfast with children discouraged. The Richardson Room with Vermont-made canopied bed, skylights, gas fireplace, oversized jetted tub and steam shower is tops. Out back are 30 km. of Nordic tracks.

Tucker Hill Inn (802-496-3983; 800-543-7841; $-$$), two miles from the lifts, has 18 rooms and a steakhouse restaurant. **The Waitsfield Inn** (802-496-3979 or 800-758-3801; $-$$), in the center of Waitsfield Village, started life in the 1820s as a parsonage, was a sleeping-bag dorm for young skiers in the '60s and '70s and is now a quaintly elegant 14-bedroom B&B.

The **Sugartree Inn** (802-583-3211; $$) has award-winning breakfasts and a collection of rooms, ranging from large with canopied beds and/or fireplace to small; all are most pleasant. The inn is only a quarter mile from Sugarbush's slopes. The **Featherbed Inn** (802-496-7151;

$$), on Rte. 100 only a stone's throw from the resort access road, is a restored 1806 house and cottage with nine spacious individually decorated guest rooms, all with private baths and luxurious featherbeds, plenty of space to spread out and to-die-for gourmet breakfasts.

West Hill House B&B (802-496-7162; $$-$$$) is an 1850s farmhouse with eight guest rooms, all with private baths—most with jetted tubs—fireplaces and DSL Internet access. **Beaver Pond Farm Inn** (802-583-2861; $-$$) is right on the cross-country trails of the Sugarbush golf course. The **1824 House Inn** (802-496-7555; $) has eight rooms just north of town, with featherbeds and an outdoor hot tub. It's chef-owned and offers intimate, gourmet dinners, by reservation only, to both lodgers and the public.

The nicest full-service hotel property is the **Sugarbush Inn** (802-583-6114; 800-537-8427; $$) on the access road. The inn and its 42 rooms are well-kept but nondescript. Closer to Sugarbush resort you'll find **Sugar Lodge at Sugarbush** (800-982-3465; $-$$), only a half mile from Lincoln Peak. It parallels good-quality chain lodging with a hot tub and lounge. The **Weathertop Lodge** (800-800-3625; 802-496-4909; $-$$), on Rte. 17 between town and Mad River Glen, is an affordable B&B.

The Inn at The Mad River Barn 802-(496-3310; $-$$) has rustic but spacious rooms and some of the best lodging food in the valley (both in quantity and quality). To stay here is to step into a wonderful 1940s ski lodge. Families, and the budget-minded, will want to check into John Egan's **Big World** on Rte. 100 (802-496-5557; $-$$) or the **Hyde Away Inn and Restaurant** (802-496-2322; $-$$) on Rte. 17. Both are great spots for children and close to the slopes.

Of the condominiums in the **Village at Sugarbush**, the most luxurious are the **South-face Condominiums** with hot tubs in each unit and a shuttlebus ride from the slopes. The **Snow Creek** condos are ski-in/ski-out, but plagued by the noise of snow guns out the back window. **Paradise** condos are newer but a good walk from the slopes; however, they have a free shuttle service. The **Summit** units are roomy, and **Castle Rock** condos are close to the slopes. **Trailside** looks like boxes stacked on one another, and the **North Lynx** condos are 10 minutes from the lifts. Rates range from $145 for a one-bedroom in value season to $635 for a four-bedroom during holidays. Guests may use the indoor pool, tennis, racquetball, squash courts, aerobics, whirlpool tubs, steam room and Nautilus equipment at the Sugarbush Health and Racquet Club for an additional fee.

The Bridges Resort and Racquet Club (800-453-2922; 802-583-2922 ; $$-$$$$), with tennis courts and an indoor pool, is across the street from the Sugarbush ski area parking lot. These units are quieter than the mountain units and have wonderful amenities as well as a regular shuttle. Skiers heading for Mad River Glen should check into the unfortunately named **Battleground** condos on Rte. 17 (800-248-2102; 802-496-2288).

Dining

The Mad River Valley has more than 40 restaurants, many offering excellent food. Most require reservations, so call before venturing out. Valley residents are quite proud of having no fast-food chain restaurants. At Sugarbush, great food, light and wide open spaces are some of the features in the new Gate House Food Court in Lincoln Peak featuring a revamped Castlerock Pub. It will be the apres-ski place to be in Lincoln Peak Village

The top of the line is **Chez Henri** (802-583-2600; $$-$$$), in Sugarbush Village at the base area of Lincoln Peak. The oldest restaurant in the valley, it captures a true French bistro feeling, with low ceilings and a flickering fire. The owner, Henri Borel, personally greets

Dining: $$$$–Entrees $30+; $$$–$20–$30; $$–$10–$20; $–less than $10.
Accommodations: (double room) $$$$–$200+; $$$–$141–$200; $$–$81–$140; $–$80 and less.

guests and makes them feel at home. He also supervises the excellent wine selection. Chez Henri features lunch, fondue in the late afternoon, then dinner until 10 p.m.

The **Pitcher Inn Restaurant** (802-496-6350; $$$$) serves contemporary American fare with a New England accent. The understated dining room has a huge fireplace and windows overlooking the Mad River. Or, reserve an intimate dinner table in the wine cellar. The **Spotted Cow** (802-496-5151; $$-$$$$) has gained a reputation for some of the best food in the valley. Pricey to be sure. Don't miss the Bermuda fish chowder; it's worth the trip to Waitsfield.

John Egan's Big World Pub & Grill (802-496-3033; $$) serves excellent food and is a great place to bring the family. There's something to please everyone, from innovative to basic. It's owned by extreme skier John Egan, so take time to look at all the ski paraphernalia. Look for it at a new location at the junction of Rtes. 100 and 17. **The Common Man** (802-583-2800; $$-$$$) attracts a faithful clientele and has a reputation for good food. But, for the money, it's not quite as "common" as the name implies. The atmosphere might be called a New England Baroque barn with crystal chandeliers. The **Warren House** (802-583-2421; $$), down a driveway to the left as you approach the Sugarbush parking lot, has developed lots of fans and offers an eclectic menu rivaling any in the area, along with a good wine list.

Michael's Good to Go (802-496-3832; $$), at the Village Square Shopping Center, has gourmet dinners to go such as Ants Climbing a Tree (organic pork and thin noodles stir-fry) and Jamaican Jerk Chicken. The **Steak Place at Tucker Hill** (802-496-3025; $$) serves beef before a flickering fireplace under a beamed ceiling, and has light apres-ski and late-night fare.

Millbrook Country Inn (802-496-2405; $$), on Rte. 17, has a small dining room with a fireplace, original art and antiques. The meals are prepared from local organic produce. **Rosita's** (802-583-3858; $-$$) serves "honest and good" (and plentiful and affordable) Mexican food. It's normally packed. **Mad River Barn Restaurant** ($) has a popular Saturday buffet and serves dinner Sunday through Friday from 6:30 to 8 p.m. Worth the effort is the clay-oven wood-fired, organic flatbread pizza at **American Flatbread** (802-496-8856; $), open only on weekends, at the Lareau Farm Country Inn. A toasty bonfire is a nice distraction during the long wait (anywhere from 30 to 90 minutes).

To stretch the budget and still get good wholesome food, try the **Hyde Away** (802-496-2322; $-$$), on Rte. 17. **BonGiorno's** (802-496-6265; $), also on Rte. 17, is the place pizza and affordable pasta, with delivery as well. For simple quick food, try **The Den** (802-496-8880; $-$$), on Waitsfield's main street. **Jay's** (802-496-8282; $) doesn't claim to be anything fancy but it's good for family fare. The **Easy Street Cafe and Market** (802-496-7234; $-$$), on Rte. 100 north of the Sugarbush Access Road, an eat-in/take-out gourmet deli serving breakfast and lunch, plus frozen dinners, prepares excellent homemade soups, hot dishes, salads and sandwiches. The **Valley Pizzeria** (802-496-9200; $) makes real brick-oven, hand-thrown pizza. It's as close to Jersey pizza as you'll ever find in Vermont, one local tells us.

For breakfast, locals tell us **Easy Street** is far and away the breakfast place in town, and that the **Warren Store** makes great breakfast burritos. Also try the **Hyde Away** or **Pepper's Restaurant** (802-583-2202; $) at Pepper's Lodge. The **Mad River Barn** lays out excellent homemade muffins and jams and serves only real maple syrup. At **Pete's Eats**, you can get breakfast while having your skis tuned at the shop next door.

For condos, pick up basics, dinners-to-go, beer and wine at the **Paradise Deli & Market** (802-583-2757) on the access road, or at the **Warren Store** (802-496-3864). There are two supermarkets in town: Shaw's and Mehuron's Market. Shaw's has the better produce. **Mehuron's** is the locals' choice; the bonuses here are the butcher and fish departments.

Apres-ski/nightlife

Après-ski starts at the base lodges that do booming business at the bar as the lifts close. At Sugarbush's Lincoln Peak, the Castlerock Pub, remodeled for 2007, should be quite lively. **Chez Henri's Back Room** is the on-mountain apres-ski hangout and can rock all evening. **The Hyde Away** is where you will find the locals; the **Blue Tooth** on the access road is most popular with tourists. On weekends try the **Sugarbush Inn** for a more upscale, older crowd. The base area bar at Mad River Glen, **General Stark's Pub**, follows the area's retro atmosphere with plenty of fun in an old-time bar. After leaving Mad River Glen, the next place to stop is the **Mad River Barn**. The bar there looks like an old Vermont bar should look: moose head hanging over the fireplace, hunting scenes on every wall, big couches and stuffed chairs, wood paneling and bumper pool or shuffleboard. **Local Folk Smokehouse** is a great bbq, tex mex and family friendly bar. **The Purple Moon Pub**, next door to the Easy Street Café, is a non-smoking spot for live music and apres-ski snacking.

 ## Other activities

Sleigh rides and skijoring (802-496-7141) can be arranged at the Vermont Icelandic Horse Farm in Waitsfield. (Skijoring involves being pulled on skis by a horse.) Find sleigh rides, too, at the Mountain Valley Farm (802-496-9255). There's **ice skating** at the Mad River Skatium, next to Shaw's Supermarket in Waitsfield. The Big Picture Theater & Cafe (802-496-8994), in Waitsfield, has **first-run movies and live concerts**, plus an Internet cafe serving whole foods.

The Alta Day Spa (802-496-2582) is an Aveda **concept day spa** in Warren, provides massages, exfoliations, wraps, masques and facials. Signature treatment is the Dead Sea Full-Body Masque, $110 for 1.5 hours. Massage rates begin at $65 for one hour; stone massage is $115 for 1.5 hours. **Salon services, manicures and pedicures** also are available. Mad River Massage (802-496-5638) on Rte. 100 just south of Rte. 17, in Waitsfield, offers nine different 60-minute massages, including relaxation, shiatsu, reflexology, sea salt and Reiki, at $55-$65.

The Sugarbush Sports Center and the Bridges Resort and Racquet Club have various **sports and exercise facilities**.

Waitsfield and Warren have **art galleries, country stores and antique and collectible shops** that are fun for browsing and buying. Most shops in tiny Warren Village are within easy walking-distance of each other.

 ## Getting there and around

Getting there: Sugarbush is off Rte. 100, about 20 miles south of Waterbury. Burlington airport is about a 45-minute drive. Amtrak offers train-ski-lodging packages, with daily service from New York, Philadelphia and Washington, D.C.; call 800-237-5547; 800-872-7245 for train only.

Getting around: The Mad Cab (802-793-2320) offers airport pickups and transportation throughout the valley. The Mad Bus (802-496-7433) provides free, round-trip travel between designated stops in Warren and Waitsfield, including the Sugarbush base areas and Mad River Glen (weekends and holidays only). Two buses leave Lincoln Peak consecutively, on the hour and half hour. Schedules can be obtained from your lodging or online at www.madrivervalley.com/transportation. For a one-time visit to town it's OK, but for more frequent visits, drive or rent a car. Valley Rent-All (802-496-5440) rents cars locally.

Dining: $$$$–Entrees $30+; $$$–$20–$30; $$–$10–$20; $–less than $10.
Accommodations: (double room) $$$$–$200+; $$$–$141–$200; $$–$81–$140; $–$80 and less.

Mount Snow
Vermont

Summit: 3,600 feet
Vertical: 1,700 feet
Base: 1,900 feet

Address: 39 Mount Snow Road
Mount Snow, VT 05356
Telephone (main): 802-464-3333
Snow Report Number: 802-464-2151
Toll-free reservations: 800-245-7669
E-mail: info@mountsnow.com
Internet: www.mountsnow.com

Expert:★★ **Advanced:**★★
Intermediate:★★★★
Beginner:★★★★
First-timer:★★

Lifts: 19—3 high-speed quads,
Skiable acreage: 590
Snowmaking: 80 percent
Uphill capacity: 30,370
Parks & pipes: 12 parks, 2 pipe
Bed base: 10,000
Nearest lodging: Base area, condos, hotel
Child care: Yes, 6 weeks to 6 years old
Adult ticket, per day: $68 (07/08 price)
Dining:★★★★
Apres-ski/nightlife:★★
Other activities:★★

For those living in the Northeast's major metropolitan areas such as New York, Albany and Hartford, Mount Snow, in southern Vermont, with a summit elevation of 3,600 feet, is renowned as the closest big-mountain resort.

Thanks in part to local gal Kelly Clark winning gold in the halfpipe at the 2002 Olympics, Mount Snow is attracting the hip—the freeriders who want to see action and be part of it. Beginning in 2008-09, the entire Carinthia area has been given over to freestylers adding seven new parks and one pipe to an already impressive array of dedicated terrain. Events like a snowcross (snowmobile motocross races) and ridercross series bring thrills and spills to the resolute. While snowcross is all about spectating, anyone—skiers, snowboarders and skiboarders—can enter the NASTAR races. Big Air and freeskiing competitions—with names such as Mother Hucker and Anti-Gravity Grail—also dot the winter calendar.

Along with the free-spirited crowd, Mount Snow is a big draw for families for both the terrain and the price. The mountain's ego-boosting trails are long, undulating cruiser runs, where kids can learn and parents can enjoy their turns. The nine sections of gladed terrain—regularly thinned and pruned—mean even intermediates can feel "extreme."

New ownership in 2007-08 has meant a new commitment to snowmaking throughout the resort.

Mountain layout–skiing & snowboarding

◆◆**Expert,** ◆**Advanced:** Aggressive skiers and snowboarders looking for a shot of adrenaline should head straight for the North Face, a group of isolated steeper runs, such as Ripcord, with a 37-degree pitch. On the opposite side of Mount Snow, Beartrap is a haven for bump skiers, in part because of its sunny face and snowmaking coverage. Beartrap has its own double lift. Along the trail, the resort pumps out loud music from 900-watt speakers to get you in the spirit.

■ **Intermediate:** Other than the North Face, the rest of Mount Snow is cruising paradise. You can carve hero turns down just about any trail on the mountain. Be sure not to miss Snowdance, a trail as wide as a football field is long, off the Canyon Express chair lift. The Sunbrook area, off the south side of the summit, is an ideal spot for lower-intermediates. Beware, the Sunbrook quad is s-l-o-w.

Although the resort's glades are all marked with black diamonds, they're an unintimidating place to practice in the trees.

●●**Beginner, ●First-timer:** From the summit, beginners will feel comfortable on Deer Run and Long John, two trails that make 2.5-mile-wide traverses of the mountain. At the south end of the resort is Carinthia, which offers long mellow runs for advanced-beginners, lower-intermediates and anyone else who wants to have a playful cruise. There are enough zigs, zags and small drops to keep you awake. Beware, though: terrain park athletes flock to this area and can fly by slower skiers, unnerving those who are still learning the sport.

First-timers can start at the Launch Pad area outside the Perfect Turn® Discovery Center on the right side (looking up the mountain) of the main base area. This well-staffed area is segregated and has its own lifts: two moving carpets, a rope tow and a triple chair.

Parks and pipes

Always a top spot for freestyle devotees, Mt Snow has really upped its commitment in 2008-09 by converting its entire Carinthia area into a massive, 95 acre park system. The new layout includes some 125 freestyle features across 12 full terrain parks to serve newbies through grizzled veterans. There are glades, a superpipe with 18' walls, and a mini pipe, too. Focusing all the freestyle activity to Carinthia creates the largest park area in the East.

Carinthia has its own high speed quad lift and a double chair. And at break time, there is a remodeled base lodge with an outdoor deck and free wireless internet.

Cross-country & snowshoeing (see also xcskiresorts.com)

The Mount Snow Valley has three major ski touring centers. **The Hermitage:** (802-464-3511), a nearby country inn has an excellent cross-country system. Located right across from the main entrance to Mount Snow and serviced by a shuttle bus, **Timber Creek Cross-Country Ski Center:** (802-464-0999) offers x-country and snowshoe trails, rentals and instruction. Trails meander through pine woods and climb hills with great views of Mount Snow.

The **White House Cross-Country Touring Center:** (802-464-2135) offers 12 km. of groomed trails for cross-country and snowshoeing. Trails for everyone traverse through high meadows and forested valleys, past beaver ponds and marshes into virgin forests. After skiing, the White House Inn is a great spot to unwind and have a drink or dinner.

The **Mount Snow Grand Summit Resort Hotel:** offers Tubbs Snowshoe rentals.

Lessons (2007/08 prices)

Group clinics are offered in skiing and snowboarding, for adults and children, from first-timers through lower intermediates. Private clinics are available for all levels, from beginners through experts. The Mount Snow Adaptive program gets handicapped and mentally challenged individuals to experience the thrill of skiing—many of them for the first time.

Adult group clinics, offered several times a day, are $43 for two hours.

First-timer package: Learn-to-ski or snowboard is a half-day program using the Guaranteed Learning Method. The day begins in the Discovery Center, with an introductory video while their teaching pro brings in the rental equipment. The outdoor experience lasts for several hours and includes a break for hot cocoa. In the afternoon, practice centers around the Launch Pad learning area with its two magic carpets and triple chair.

Private Lessons: Private clinics are available by appointment for all ages and ability levels, lasting 1-6 hours for up to four people.

Special Programs: An adaptive program, family ski/snowboard clinics, and advanced clinics for skiers and riders are available.

Children's Programs (2007/08 prices)

Child care: Open 8 a.m. to 4:30 p.m. daily for children ages 6 weeks to 6 years. The cost is $75 for a full day with lunch. **Cub Camp**, an introductory one-hour ski program for 3-year-olds, costs $95 and includes equipment during the session and full day child care. Reservations required; call 800-889-4411 or 802-464-4152. **Mount Snow Child Care** has babysitter referral service. Sitters will come to your vacation home, condo or hotel room. Cost is $12/hour for one child, $1/hour for each additional child (rates do not apply New Year's Eve). Call 800-889-4411 or 802-464-4152. This is a first come, first served service so advanced reservations are suggested.

Children's lessons: Programs are available for ages 4–14. Kids 4–6 enroll in **Snow Camp**, $97 for a full day or $177 for two days, including lift ticket, clinic and lunch. Rental equipment is available at an additional charge. Half-day costs $67 or $119 for two half-days.

Ages 7–14 enroll in **Mountain Camp** or **Mountain Riders**, $83 for full day and $148 for two days with clinic and lunch. A lift ticket is required, but not included, and rental equipment is extra. A half-day clinic is $48 ($85 for two half days) for Mountain Camp or Mountain Riders, including a snack.

Lift tickets (2007/08 prices)

One day: adult $72 (weekend/holiday), $63 (midweek); young adult (13-18) $60 (weekend/holiday), $52 (midweek); child (6-12)/Seniors (65+) $48 (weekend/holiday) $42 (midweek). Three days*: adult $192, young adult $162, child/senior, $126. Five days*: adult $305, young adult $250, child/senior $190 ($38/day).

*Note: Multiday prices are for stays that include weekends and are rounded to the nearest dollar to include the 7 percent Vermont sales tax. Weekday multiday tickets cost less; holiday prices are higher. Purchase tickets online at least 72 hours in advance and save 10 percent.

Who skis free: Children ages 5 and younger. Children 12 and younger ski free when their parent buys a three- to five-day midweek, non-holiday lift-and-lodging package.

Who skis at a discount: Ages 65 and older pay junior prices. Check the website for occasional deals.

Accommodations

Condominiums and several lodges at the base area have shuttle service to the slopes. Most of the other lodging lines Rte. 100 between the slopes and Wilmington, with some tucked on side roads back into the foothills.

Per-person rates are a bargain. A one-night package combines one hotel night with a day of skiing starting at $79 a day. Sunday through Thursday packages are very attractive. For a vacation planner, call 800-245-7669.

Condominiums rates are based on the size of the unit and number of bathrooms. They start at about $305 on the weekends; half that midweek. **The Seasons, Snow Tree, Snow-mountain and Deer Creek Condominiums.** (800-451-4211; 802-464-7788; $$$-$$$$) are at the base of the lifts, but only the Seasons complex is actually ski-in/ski-out. Seasons' condos are the most highly recommended with an athletic center, indoor pools, saunas and hot tubs. Two-bedroom/two-bath units cost around $900 for a weekend.

Timber Creek Townhomes. (800-982-8922; 802-464-1222; $$$$) are luxury condos across Rte. 100 from the ski area. They have a fitness center and 18 km. of cross-country trails. Shuttle buses run to the ski area. **Greenspring at Mount Snow** (800-247-7833; 802-464-7111; $$$-$$$$) are upscale condos a mile from the slopes. This complex has the best athletic center in the area.

The Mount Snow Grand Summit Resort Hotel & Conference Center (800-498-0479; $$$-$$$$) is a slopeside ski-in/ski-out, full-service resort hotel with 200 rooms, ranging from studios to 3-bedroom units. It has a heated outdoor pool and hot tubs, indoor sauna and steam room, fitness center, spa, restaurant, game room and wifi.

Snow Lake Lodge (800-451-4211; 802-464-7788; $$-$$$) is a sprawling 92-room mountain lodge near the base of Mount Snow. While fairly basic, the lodge does have a fitness center, sauna, indoor hot tub, outdoor hot tub and apres-ski entertainment. The Sundance base lodge is a 300-yard walk or a free shuttle ride away. The lodge is excellent with children.

The Inn at Sawmill Farm (802-464-8131; 802-464-8131; $$$$), a Relais and Chateaux propety, is one of the nation's top country inns. Secluded in a renovated dairy barn and out-buildings, the inn coddles guests with spacious rooms decorated in a country chic style. Fresh flowers, wood-burning fires, meticulous service and an excellent dining room complete the picture. The inn is not suitable for children, nor does it take credit cards.

The White House of Wilmington (802-464-2135; $$-$$$), Rte. 9, Wilmington, is an upscale, romantic 23-room inn serving breakfast and dinner. The inn has an indoor pool. Less than a quarter-mile from Mount Snow, the **Big Bear Lodge** (800-388-5591; 802-464-5591; $$$$) is family-friendly and comes highly recommended by the locals.

For the 'no-dogs-left-behind' crowd, **The Paw House Inn and Resort at Mt. Snow** (802-558-3426; $$$) is your place at the mountain. It features 18 "tail-proof" rooms plus many ameneties for both pet and petter. The restaurant on site is named "Fetch". **Nordic Hills Lodge** (800-326-5130; 802-464-5130; $$$$), 179 Coldbrook Rd. in Wilmington, is friendly and clean. Rates include breakfast and dinner.

Gray Ghost Inn (800-745-3615; 802-464-2474; $$-$$$), on Rte. 100, West Dover, is a large country inn operated by a British couple. Many rooms have smaller beds or bunk beds for children, and there is a game room. Rates include a continental breakfast. **Trail's End** (800-859-2585; 802-464-2727; $$-$$$), on Smith Road in Wilmington, has 15 country-style rooms. Meals are served family-style, so visitors will no doubt make new friends.

Old Red Mill (800-843-8483; 802-464-3700; $-$$), Rte. 100 in Wilmington, was created from a former sawmill and is one of the area's bargains. Rooms are small, but all have TV. Larger rooms are available for families. The common areas are rustic. **Horizon Inn** (800-336-5513; 802-464-2131; $-$$$), Rte. 9 in Wilmington and 13 miles from Mount Snow, has an indoor heated pool, whirlpool, sauna and game room.

Bed & Breakfasts. Mount Snow also has a group of charming and elegant B&Bs with rates starting at about $125 per night on weekends and $70 midweek. These B&Bs are small, with fewer than 15 rooms. Locals recommend **The Inn at Quail Run** (800-343-7227; 802-464-3362; $$$$), which welcomes children and pets. Its brunch is considered the valley's best.

In West Dover: **The Doveberry Inn** (800-722-3204; 802-464-5652; $$), on Rte. 100,

Dining: $$$$–Entrees $30+; $$$–$20–$30; $$–$10–$20; $–less than $10.
Accommodations: (double room) $$$$–$200+; $$$–$141–$200; $$–$81–$140; $–$80 and less.

is run by culinary-school-trained chefs Michael and Christine Fayette. It's not suitable for young children. Historic **West Dover Inn** (800-732-0745; 802-464-5207; $$), also on Rte. 100, built in 1846, has 12 elegant rooms furnished with antiques, hand-sewn quilts and color TVs, as well as two suites with fireplaces and jetted tubs. **Deerhill Inn** (800-464-3100; $$-$$$$), on Valley View Road, is a chef-owned romantic hillside inn with panoramic views of Mount Snow.

In Wilmington: The **Red Shutter Inn** (800-845-7548; 802-464-3768; $$-$$$), on Rte. 9, is a country home built in 1894 that has been converted into an elegant country inn with nine guest rooms. **The Nutmeg Inn** (802-464-3351; $$-$$$), on Rte. 9W, was built in the 1770s and has 10 rooms and three fireplace suites decorated with country accents and quilts.

Dining

The top dining experience (and the most expensive) is the **Inn at Sawmill Farm** (802-464-1130; $$$-$$$$), which holds a Wine Spectator Grand Award. Ask to see the wine cellar. The antique-decorated **Hermitage** (802-464-3511; $$-$$$) serves an eclectic menu with entrees such as angel hair and pesto topped with a red-wine roasted duck and shiitake mushrooms or hand-cut Black Angus steak.

Soft jazz and candlelight set the tone at **Le Petit Chef** (802-464-8437; $$-$$$), a chef-owned French bistro in a 19th-century farmhouse. Another fine dining choice is **Two Tannery Road** (802-464-2707; $$$). **Doveberry Restaurant** (802-464-5652; $$$) is small and intimate with a Northern Italian menu; the husband-and-wife chefs have worked in Nantucket and San Francisco. The **Deerhill Inn and Restaurant** (802-464-3100; $$$) in West Dover, has won awards for its American cuisine and boasts a strong wine list.

Locals head to **The Route 100 Steakhouse** (formerly Hennessey's) (802-464-9361; $$) for consistently good food at reasonable prices. **The White House** (802-464-2135; $$) with its 30-foot buffet table, is the choice for Sunday brunch, but the French-accented dinners are excellent, too. Locals tell us **The Inn at Quail Run** (802-464-3362; $$) serves the best brunch in the valley.

The Roadhouse (802-464-5017; $$) is normally packed. It serves large portions of steak, chicken, ribs, swordfish and trout. **Dot's of Dover** (802-464-6476; $) in the Mountain Park Plaza, serves breakfast, lunch and dinner daily, plus an excellent Sunday brunch. The chili has won awards. Also enjoy dinner daily at **Dot's Restaurant**, on Rte. 9 in Wilmington (802-464-7284; $). For economical eats, try **Poncho's Wreck** (802-464-9320; $$), a local institution with an eclectic dining room serving Mexican food, steaks, lobsters and fresh fish.

Anchor Seafood (802-464-5616; $$), specializes in surf and turf. **Cafe Tannery** (802-464-2078; $-$$) offers burgers, burritos and salads, and does take-out. **The Vermont House** (802-464-9360; $-$$) on Wilmington's main street, serves good food for cheap prices and is another of the locals' favorites. **TC's Family Restaurant** (802-464-9316; $-$$), owned by Olympic gold medalist Kelly Clark's parents, has inexpensive family fare. For groceries, head to **Shaw's** on Rte. 9 in Wilmington, east of Rte. 100.

Apres-ski/nightlife

The Snow Barn features live music most weekends, sometimes with up-and-coming national acts. It has a separate area for pool and other games, with a central stone fireplace and a pizza window. Both Snow Barn and **Deacon's Den** usually have cover charges.

Apres-ski at **Cuzzins** is a wild affair where the DJ gets folk up and dancing on the tables.

The line is long, but the fun is worth it. **Walt's Pub**, at the Snow Lake Lodge, has a quiet, family-style atmosphere with "unplugged" music on Saturday nights. There is also live jazz at **Harriman's Restaurant** in the Grand Summit Hotel on Fridays and Saturdays. The **Midstation Bar** has acoustic music.

One of the most popular nightspots, **The Silo**, is actually in a converted grain silo (in the Silo Family Restaurant on Rte. 100). It caters to a young crowd and has practically a monopoly on nightlife for the snowboarding set. Locals head to the Silo every evening for 10-cent wings from 4-6 p.m. Downstairs is a smoke-filled cigar bar for aficionados. The **Dover Bar & Grille**, across Rte. 100 from The Silo, is another local hangout.

Other activities

The Mount Snow Valley is reportedly the busiest area for snowmobiling in Vermont. Try **High Country Snowmobile Tours** (800-627-7533; 802-464-2108), which operates from the base of Mount Snow, **Wheeler Farm** snowmobile tours (802-464-5225) in Wilmington and Stizmark (802-464-3384). High Country has a supervised snowcross course called, Ski Doo Mini Z, for kids ages 6-10.

The **Adams Family Farm** (802-464-3762), 4 miles south on Higley Hill Rd. (off Rte. 100), has an indoor petting farm where kids help milk goats and find eggs to take home for breakfast. Sleigh rides are available. Open Wednesday, Friday, Saturday and Sunday, 10 a.m.-5 p.m. Mount Snow runs a lift-served **tubing hill** open Friday and Saturday evenings. Rates are $20 per four-hour session or $8 for a single ride.

A **movie theater**, in the Mountain Park Plaza on Rte. 100 in West Dover, shows first-run movies. The Grand Summit Resort Hotel now has a **spa** offering **massage therapy, facials** and **body treatments**. Reservations are required; call 802-464-6606. Wilmington Village has **boutiques, galleries** highlighting local and national artists and a few intriguing **shops**.

Getting there and getting around

By air: Airports are in Albany, N.Y. and Hartford, Ct., both less than a two-hour drive.

By car: Mount Snow is the closest major Vermont ski resort to New York and Boston. It is on Rte. 100, just 9 miles north of Wilmington.

By Train: Train service is available via The Amtrak Vermonter to Brattleboro, Vermont, and the new Ethan Allen Express to Rensselaer/Albany.

By Bus: Adventure Northeast Bus Service provides direct service from New York City www.AdventureNortheast.com or call 718-601-4707 or 802-464-2810. Vermont Transit (802)-254-6066 and Greyhound 800-231-2222 offer service to Brattleboro. Round-trip shuttles to Mount Snow are available on request.

Getting around: A car isn't necessary, but is convenient, especially at night. During the day, take shuttle buses to and from the lifts; at night, take the MOOver, a free shuttle that serves much of the Mount Snow Valley from the resort down into Wilmington. It runs late on weekends. You can't miss it: the buses are painted like Holstein cows.

Dining: $$$$–Entrees $30+; $$$–$20–$30; $$–$10–$20; $–less than $10.
Accommodations: (double room) $$$$–$200+; $$$–$141–$200; $$–$81–$140; $–$80 and less.

Okemo
Vermont

Summit: 3,344 feet
Vertical: 2,200 feet
Base: 1,194 feet

Address: 77 Okemo Ridge, Ludlow, VT 05149
Telephone (main): 802-228-4041
Snow Report Number: 802-228-5222
Toll-free reservations: 800-786-5366
E-mail: info@okemo.com
Internet: www.okemo.com

Expert:★
Advanced:★
Intermediate:★★★★★
Beginner:★★★
First-timer:★★

Lifts: 19—5 high-speed quads, 4 quads, 3 triples, 7 surface lifts
Skiable acreage: 624
Snowmaking: 97 percent
Uphill capacity: 32,050
Parks & pipes: 6 parks, 2 pipes
Bed base: 10,000
Nearest lodging: Slopeside
Child care: Yes, 6 weeks to 6 years
Adult ticket, per day: $77 (08/09)
Dining:★★★
Apres-ski/nightlife:★★
Other activities:★★

With five mountain areas, including Jackson Gore, the resort is one of the largest in New England. Rising more than 2,200 feet above the bustling village of Ludlow, Okemo's mostly intermediate trails run down the mountainside like ribbons of white flowing down the fall line.

More than just terrain, Okemo is about service and snow quality. The resort covers 95 percent of the terrain with machine-made snow, then grooms it to "hero snow" quality. A few laps off the Northstar Express Quad on blue runs such as World Cup, and you may start to feel as if you could, well, ski on the World Cup.

Okemo has been compared with Deer Valley in terms of service. Hands-on owners Tim and Diane Mueller can often be found loading lifts or busing trays in the cafeteria on busy weekends. Everyone smiles, says good morning, and asks how your day is going. Everyone, that is, except the grumpy guy who woke up late and had to park in a far-distant lower lot. Okemo's main base area has limited parking. Once on the mountain, you have to take one of two lifts to get to the more wide-open terrain on the mountain proper. On busy weekends, these two lifts are a bottleneck.

Jackson Gore presents a better option for day skiers—although reaching the base lodge from its parking lot also requires some hiking (or the shuttle). Still, Jackson Gore is much less crowded, easier to handle and radiates a more pleasant, less frenetic atmosphere. Anchored by a colossal neo-Colonial structure that's home to the 117-room Jackson Gore Inn, the area has the feel of a college campus. A few steps from the inn is the Spring House, a large fitness and aquatic center. Across the parking lot is the Ice House, home to a semi-enclosed skating rink.

Within the inn itself are a cafeteria and restaurant, day care center, ski school and shops, and amenities such as a full-service spa and indoor/outdoor swimming pool. Carrying skiers and snowboarders up the mountain are two high-speed quad chairlifts, two moving carpets servicing a new beginners' area (yeah!).

Mountain layout

The mellow skiing and much of the beginning ski school action take place on the gentle rise served by two sister lifts, South Ridge Quads A and B. These two quads also provide access to several clusters of slopeside condos and townhouses, as well as serving as the gateway to the rest of Okemo's lift system. There can be a logjam at these two lifts, but once up on the mountain you can choose from several chairs to get to the upper trails.

The Jackson Gore base area is a more laid-back alternative, and is less crowded on busy weekends. The Coleman Brook Express serves beginner terrain and accesses the Jackson Gore Express, which takes you to 2,725-foot Jackson Gore Peak. It also links you to the main mountain. The Northstar Express is always the most popular on weekends and holidays. To save time, take the Black Ridge Triple to the Green Ridge Triple. Both Green Ridge and Northstar unload by the Summit Lodge. Another well-kept secret: ride the Sachem Quad to the Glades Peak Quad and head to the South Face Area to enjoy the glades and long cruisers.

◆◆**Expert,** ◆**Advanced:** There are no true double-black trails on the mountain. Outrage and Double Black Diamond are both gladed and not particularly precipitous, but enjoyable and challenging with proper snow conditions. Black Hole, at the top of Jackson Gore, has tight trees and a healthy pitch. Quantum Leap and Vortex, on Jackson Gore, have a good pitch at the top but quickly mellow out. For 08/09, two new black trails have been cut on Jackson Gore.

The other challenge is Okemo's mogul runs. Wild Thing, Blind Faith and Punch Line are often left to bump up; when groomed, they are delightful cruising runs. Elsewhere on the mountain, you can often find manmade bumps on Sel's Choice and the Ledges.

■ **Intermediate:** Overall, the pitch on this mountain is so consistent and the trails are so similarly cut, a skier would be hard pressed to describe the difference between Dream Weaver at one side of the mountain and Sidewinder on the opposite side. This is not a negative, just a fact of life. Intermediates should choose their trails based on crowds. Our experience has been that while a cruise down Punch Line and Blind Faith may be crowded, wide arcing turns can be made down Upper and Lower Tomahawk and Screamin' Demon without another person in sight. As its name implies, the Solitude area is often the least crowded and has loads of intermediate terrain.

●●**Beginner,** ●**First-timer:** The 4.5-mile Upper and Lower Mountain Roads are the easiest route from the top. But beginners can ski virtually anywhere marked intermediate on this mountain. The Green Ridge triple and the Solitude Peak high-speed quad have many trails that are mellow enough to help you maintain control. On Jackson Gore Peak, try Tuckered Out for a long, winding slide punctuated by gentle undulations and fine views.

Jackson Gore, with its two moving carpets and high-speed quad serving gentle terrain, is tailor-made for novices and beginners. The rental shop, Learning Center and kids' programs are all in the same building too. Choose to start here, if possible.

That said, we'll tell you about the learning area near the original base lodge. It's served by two quads and two free surface lifts. Unfortunately, the first novice lessons take place in an area that is crisscrossed by more advanced skiers moving between lifts and condos. Fortunately, the children's learning area at Jackson Gore is tucked away from other skiers.

Snowboarding

If you're an expert or advanced rider, Okemo won't offer enough of a challenge unless you're happiest in the park and pipe. But the resort, home to 2006 Olympic halfpipe gold medalist

Hannah Teter, has a thriving community of riders not confined to the young and restless. Gray-haired ski patrollers and instructors foster a pro-boarding attitude.

Parks and pipes

Okemo's 500-foot-long, Zaugg-maintained, SoBe superpipe was one of the first earthen pipe built in Vermont. The walls are 18 feet high. For those seeking a bit less air, there's a minipipe at Hot Dog Hill.

Okemo has six terrain parks. Blind Faith Terrain Park, in the South Face area, has rollers, bank turns and tabletops. The Dew Zone is next to the superpipe. It's loaded with rails, including rainbows, Cs, rollercoasters, flat-to-down and flat stock rails. The Nor'Easter Terrain Park is the longest. It contains rails, step downs, spines, S-turns, tabletops, funboxes, hips, double tabletops, hit tables, rollers and pyramid jumps. Hot Dog Hill, below the Sugar House, is geared to beginners. Tomahawk is a "familycross" park. The constantly evolving parks are groomed nightly. They're designed by Park Rangers and have staggered take-offs to accommodate various abilities and comfort levels.

 ## Cross-country & snowshoeing (see also xcskiresorts.com)

The **Okemo Valley Nordic Center** (802-228-1396), set along the Black River a half-mile from Okemo Mountain, has fine facilities that include a rental and repair shop, a restaurant, and 26 km. of trails. Twenty are groomed for skate skiing. Instruction is available. It also has 10 km. of dedicated snowshoe trails. Changing rooms with showers are available. The center is open from 8 a.m.-4 p.m. on weekends and holidays; Monday through Friday, it opens at 9 a.m.

The Okemo Express Rental Shop (802-228-1780) at Okemo Mountain also rents snowshoes. Guided evening snowshoe tours are planned during the Christmas, Martin Luther King and Presidents Week holidays. Tours leave the Okemo base area at 7 p.m.

 ## Lessons (07/08 prices)

Group skiing and snowboard lessons: $47 for a two-hour beginner lesson. Beginners get free (yes, free!) lessons in the early season. The beginner package includes a lower-mountain lift ticket, a level 1 or 2 group lesson at 10 a.m. or 1 p.m. and rental equipment (skis, boots, poles, or boots and snowboard). This program is available for ages 7 and up, free before Christmas week..

First-timer package: For skiing or snowboarding, First Tracks packages include lesson, rentals and beginner lifts for $95; for juniors, $85. Double Tracks builds upon the skills learned in the first day by getting students back for a second straight day. It includes three lessons, two on the first day and one on the morning of the second day. The second day's lift ticket can be upgraded to a full-day, all-mountain lift ticket. Cost is $150 or $135 for juniors.

Private lessons: $95 for one hour; discounts available for additional hours and students. Early- and late-day privates are offered at 8:30 a.m. and 2:30 p.m. for $69. Parent and Tot private lessons, as well as adaptive private lessons, are also available.

Special programs: Women's Alpine Adventure Clinics are for women of all abilities. Cost: five-day program, three-day weekend , $649; $489; two-day midweek, $329.

Children's Programs (07/08 prices)

Child care: Ages 6 months to 6 years at the Penguin Playground Day Care Center. Parents can choose between Okemo base or Jackson Gore base facilities: $78 for a full day with lunch; $58 for a half day. Sunday morning, 8 a.m.–1 p.m., costs $65, with lunch. Mini Stars ski lessons for kids ages 3–4 cost $59 for 1-.5- hour session ($45 as an add-on to day care). Rentals are extra.

Children's lessons: Ages 4–7 (skiing) and 5–7 (snowboarding) enroll in Snow Stars at either base area: $98, full day with lunch; $72, half day; $80 for Sunday morning. Rentals are extra. Half-hour private "Starbooster" lessons are available for children ages 3-7 for $47.

Young Mountain Explorers and Young Riders, ages 7–14, have supervised lesson programs for $85 a day. A single 2-hour lesson is $47. A 2-hour intermediate/advanced Adventure Workshop is $60. Rentals and lift tickets are extra.

First Tracks for first-timers includes lesson, rentals and beginner lifts; cost: $85, ages 7–12; $95, ages 13–18. Double Tracks is a two-day first-timer package; cost: $135, ages 7–12 ;$150, ages 13–14.

Reservations required for all programs. Call 802-228-1780.

Special activities: Kids' Night Out, for ages 6 months to 12 years, includes evening care from 6–9:30 p.m. on Saturdays. Kids eat pizza, watch movies and play games. Call 802-228-1780 for price and reservations. Price is $30 per child.

Lift tickets (08/09 prices)

One Day (weekend/holiday): adult $77, young adult (13-18) $65, junior (7-12) $50. One Day (weekday): $72/$61/$47. Two days (weekday): $132/$110/$82. Five days (weekday): $280/$240/$180.

Two days (weekend/holiday): adult $144/$149, young adult $122/$127, Junior $94/$97. Five days (weekend/holiday): $276/$310 - $234/$265 - $179/$200.

Who skis free: Children ages 6 and younger.

Who skis at a discount: Age 65-69 pay young adult rates; 70-plus pay junior rates.

Sunday morning discount: The Sunday Solution is available every Sunday, as well as some Mondays in January. Ski 8 a.m.-1:30 p.m. for $68 adult; $58 young adult/seniors and $45 junior/super-senior (ages 70+) and hit the road before the rest of the traffic. Vermont and New Hampshire residents pay $35 (all ages) for the Sunday morning discount. Some Tuesdays in December, January and March, women ski for $39. Check the web site for other discounts.

Accommodations

First-class hotel amenities are available at the full-service, 117-room **Jackson Gore Inn** (800-786-5366; $$$-$$$$). Accommodations are high-quality and comfortable, ranging from standard hotel rooms to one- to three-bedroom units, with full kitchen and jetted tubs. There's an indoor-outdoor heated pool, restaurant and lounge, health club and underground parking. Okemo has many **slopeside condos and townhouses** (800-786-5366). Per-person rates vary widely depending on location and size; a five-night ski week range would be $375-$850 off-mountain to $450-$1,000+ slopeside. Kids ages 12 and younger stay free at Okemo condos. As always, ask about packages.

The Okemo/Ludlow area, including Chester, Springfield, Weston, Plymouth and Proctorsville, has more than 50 country inns, B&Bs and motels. **The Governor's Inn** (800-468-3766; 802-228-8830; $$-$$$$) is on Main Street and is one of Ludlow's nicest lodges. All rooms

Dining: $$$$–Entrees $30+; $$$–$20–$30; $$–$10–$20; $–less than $10.
Accommodations: (double room) $$$$–$200+; $$$–$141–$200; $$–$81–$140; $–$80 and less.

have private baths and are furnished in Victorian fashion, complete with puffy comforters. Rates include breakfast only or breakfast and six-course dinner. The **Andrie Rose Inn** (800-223-4846; 802-228-4846; $$$-$$$$), is a country inn tucked on a side street in Ludlow. Most rooms have jetted tubs, and the suites have fireplaces. The inn also has well-appointed condos, some that sleep as many as 12.

North of Ludlow on Route 100, **The Echo Lake Inn** (800-356-6844; 802-228-3075; $$-$$$$) is a rambling New England inn. It has been completely refurbished with an excellent dining room and cozy public rooms. Presidents Coolidge and McKinley slept here. Rates with breakfast only or with breakfast and dinner are available. **The Inn at Water's Edge** (802-228-8143; $$$-$$$$), on the shores of Echo Lake, is a refurbished 150-year-old Victorian home. It has a traditional English pub and 11 small, antique-furnished rooms. Rates include breakfast, dinner served fireside and afternoon tea. Of note, the inn caters to couples.

The **Hawk Inn and Mountain Resort** (800-685-4295; 802-672-3811; $$$$), 9 miles north of Okemo on Rte. 100, has luxury country inn and townhouse facilities. This complex features an indoor/outdoor pool, sauna, sleigh rides and fine dining. Rates include breakfast. **Castle Hill Resort & Spa** (800-438-7908; 802-226-7688; $$$$) is a gracious, turn-of-the-century former Governor's mansion. The owners have painstakingly preserved the old-world standard, furnishing the entire mansion with period furniture. The food is exceptional and the dining room extremely romantic. A full-service Aveda Fitness Center and Spa.

The **Cavendish Pointe Hotel** (800-438-7908; 802-226-7688; $$-$$$), 2 miles from Okemo on Route 103, is a 70-room country-style hotel, with restaurant, indoor pool, lounge and game room. The **Best Western Colonial Motel** (802-228-8188; $$-$$$) offers very affordable lodging within walking distance of Ludlow's shopping, nightlife and dining. **Happy Trails Motel** (800-228-9984; 228-8888; $$-$$$) in Ludlow offers great bargains with a good hot tub. **The Timber Inn Motel** (802-228-8666; $-$$) has the cheapest rates in town.

 # Dining

Coleman Brook Tavern (802-228-1435; $$$-$$$$), at Jackson Gore, is the resort's best restaurant and has full-service, all-day dining. It also has an adults-only wine room that allows quiet, sophisticated dining surrounded by wines that make up the most exclusive restaurant wine list in Vermont. Try the lamb lollipops and polenta.

Upstairs is **Siena's** ($$-$$$) is named for Italy's famous horse race, Palio di Siena. The restaurant serves stone-baked gourmet pizzas, artisan breads, and family-style salads. Pasta sautes are the chef's specialty. Siena's is only open on the weekends for dinner Friday and Saturday nights and lunch on Saturday and Sunday.

On mountain, don't miss **Epic** ($-$$), in the Solitude Day Lodge. This sit-down restaurant has a well-priced eclectic menu, with items such as a smoked salmon BLT, duck quesadilla, and delicious soup specials (apple butternut bisque). Epic is only open for lunch.

Other excellent dining choices are **Smokey Jo's** for fine prime rib sandwiches, **Jump** for Chinese food at the **Summit Cafe**, **Sitting Bull** for sit-down wraps, chicken tenders and fries and **Amigos** for Tex-Mex. **Vermont Pizza Company** in the Sugarhouse (mid-mountain) for wood-fired pizzas. Jackson Gore also has the **Roundhouse food court** with cafeteria fare.

Upscale restaurants serving dinner in the area include the **Echo Lake Inn** (802-228-8602; $$-$$$), 4 miles north of town, where Chef Kevin Barnes has been creating gourmet delicacies for more than a decade. It has excellent meals with a gourmet touch. Entrees include dishes such as ostrich medallions, angus sirloin, Vermont lamb loin and seared veal rack.

The River Tavern Restaurant (802-672-3811; $$-$$$), at the Hawk Inn and Mountain

Resort, serves delicious meals. The tortilla-crusted lamb chops with tart cherry chipotle sauce are wonderful. **Castle Hill** (802-226-7361; $$$-$$$$; above) offers refined dining in a most romantic setting at the junction of Rte. 103 and Rte. 131. Enjoy the Salmon Wellington. **The Inn at Water's Edge** (802-228-8143; $$$$) serves fixed-price dinners for $30/person evenings at 7 p.m. Make reservations and select your dinner by noon on the day of your reservation.

A must visit is the **Old Town Farm Inn** (888-232-1089, $-$$$), a charming, family friendly, restored 1861 Vermont farmhouse in Chester. What really makes this restaurant unique is the Japanese dinners prepared by owner, Chef Michiko, a sixth-generation chef. Everything is made to order, so be sure to allow plenty of time for a leisurely meal. Bring your own bottle.

The following restaurants are not as upper crust, but serve excellent affordable meals, perfect for families. **Willie Dunn's Grille** (802-228-1387; $$), at the Okemo Valley Golf & Nordic Center, offers superb affordable meals. **Sam's Steakhouse** (802-228-2087; $$), on Rte. 103, serves a filet mignon so tender it can be cut with a butter knife, as well as seafood, chicken, sinful desserts and an incredible salad bar; first come, first served. **D.J.'s Restaurant** (802-228-5374; $-$$) gets high marks from locals for its prime rib, steak, seafood, pasta and fabulous salad bar.

The Pot Belly Pub (802-228-8989; $$) has good old American food like meatloaf, pork ribs, steaks and salads. **The Killarney** (802-228-7797; $$), at the bottom of the Okemo access road, features classic Irish pub fare with a variety of draught beer selections. The menu features bangers and mash, shepherd's pie, corned beef and cabbage and traditional American fare. **Cappuccino's** (802-228-7566; $$-$$$) has a strong local following. The pastas and veal dishes are worth the visit. **The Combes Family Inn** (802-228-8799; $$$) serves a home-cooked single-entree dinner at 7 p.m. each evening. Call for the day's menu and reservations. **Java Baba's** (802-228-2326; $) at the base of the access road has over-stuffed chairs and couches, and serves fresh-baked muffins, pastries, homemade soups, sandwiches, salads, desserts and, of course, a variety of coffee drinks.

On Main Street in Ludlow, **Trappers Restaurant** (802-228-5477) and **The Hatchery** (802-228-2311) are the locals' recommendations for breakfast. **Wicked Good Pizza** (802-228-4131; $) has good pie (pizza pie, that is). **Chef Mei** (802-228-4355; $-$$) offers Chinese specialties, eat in or take out. North of Ludlow on Rte. 103 is **Harry's** (802-259-2996; $-$$), an understated place that has a high repeat business because of its moderate prices and international cuisine. In Chester, have a meal at **Williams River Cafe** 802-875-4486; $-$$). Breakfast and lunch are always good. Dinner is served Wednesday to Sunday. Or try **Fullerton Inn** (802-875-2444; $$$) for an elegant affair. **The Inn at Weathersfield** (802-263-9217; $$$$), in Perkinsville, has won the Wine Spectator Award and many other culinary awards.

Apres-ski/nightlife

The **Sitting Bull Bar & Restaurant** is the center of apres-ski at Okemo, with regularly scheduled parties, a wide-screen TV, $1 draft beer day on non-holiday Wednesdays and live music on weekends. Down the mountain, head to **Willie Dunn's Grille**, at the Okemo Valley Golf & Nordic Center, or **Archie's Steakhouse** for chicken wings and draft beer specials. **Coleman Brook Tavern**, in Jackson Gore, has comfy chairs and couches, a martini menu and a wide selection of exclusive wines and premium liquors.

Later in the evening, **The Pot Belly Pub** has country rock, 60s and 70s classics with a great bar and a big TV. Watch out when ordering their wines by the glass—they simply recork any leftover bottles each night and save them for the next day, so only order the wine if you

Dining: $$$$–Entrees $30+; $$$–$20–$30; $$–$10–$20; $–less than $10.
Accommodations: (double room) $$$$–$200+; $$$–$141–$200; $$–$81–$140; $–$80 and less.

can see them open a new bottle. **Christopher's** in the basement of the Old Mill, has bands. **The Loft** is a true locals' favorite where all the ski school instructors go for sizeable portions of apres munchies and full meals. **Killarney** traditional Irish pub and restaurant, with acoustic music on weekends, is another locals' favorite.

Other activities

The Spring House, a **fitness and aquatic center** at the Jackson Gore base area, features a **two-lane lap pool, small kids' pool with frog slide, 10-person hot tub, racquetball court, weight and cardio room, and aerobics** and yoga classroom. The Jackson Gore Inn has a **full-service spa**. Also at Jackson Gore is The Ice House, a **covered ice skating rink** with an adjacent warming hut, and a **tubing** hill with three lanes accessed by a 400-foot carpet lift. Tubing starts at 3 p.m. on weekends and during holidays. Snow tubes are available for rent at the Jackson Gore Mountain Services Center.

A few miles south on Route 103, the Castle Hill Resort has a wonderful full-service **Aveda spa** (802-226-7419) set in a former carriage house that's listed on the National Register of Historic Places. The spa has four cozy treatment rooms, a hair salon, and manicure/pedicure stations and a fitness center, plus an outdoor heated pool, hot tub, and solarium. Book ahead.

The **Okemo Valley Indoor Golf Training Center** (802-228-1396), at the country club, is a 6,000-square-foot facility with a nine-hole putting green, swing stations, and a full-swing golf simulator where golfers can tee up one some of the world's best courses.

The **Fletcher Farm School for the Arts and Crafts** (802-228-8770) offers classes in watercolor, funky felted hats, decoupage, rug hooking and more.

Ludlow also has a moderate array of specialty shops with clothing, antiques and gifts. **Chapter XIV** mixes books with women's clothing and jewelry, children's clothing and toys and other fun and artsy items. **Blue Sky Trading** has a nice selection of Vermont-made pottery and jewelry. **Noah's & Garden** has dried floral arrangements. **Chrisandra's Interiors** sells eclectic distressed furniture. **Hunter Lea** has fine art and prints.

One of the best browsing stores in the Northeast, the **Vermont Country Store** is in Weston. It's packed with clothing, housewares, funky specialty foods (sample everything) and things you never knew you wanted but, seeing them, now wonder how you've lived without them. A more genuine country store experience is had at **Singleton's**, about 3 miles south of the mountain in Proctorsville. You can purchase antique guns, some of the best bacon and ham we've ever tasted and, as for the cheese, Singleton's goes through four or five wheels a week!

Getting there and getting around

By air: The nearest major airports are Burlington, Vt.; Manchester, N.H.; or Hartford, Conn., all about two hours away. Regional service is available from Rutland (25 miles from Okemo) to Boston or from West Lebanon, N.H.

By car: Okemo is in south-central Vermont on Rte. 103 in Ludlow, about two hours from Albany, N.Y.; three hours from Boston; and 4.5 hours from New York City.

By train: Amtrak has service from New York's Penn Station to Rutland, 25 miles from Okemo. Thrifty operates a car rental office at the train station in Rutland.

Getting around: We recommend a car. Unless you are staying on-mountain, parking can be a bear. If you're staying in town, use the free Village Shuttle that operates four routes through Ludlow and Proctorsville on weekends and holidays, from 7:30 a.m.-5:30 p.m. An on-mountain shuttle runs daily mid-December through March, connecting all on-mountain properties with the base area and the Nordic Center.

Smugglers' Notch
Vermont

Summit: 3,640 feet
Vertical: 2,610 feet
Base: 1,030 feet

Address: 4323 Vermont Rte. 108 South Smugglers' Notch, VT 05464
Telephone (main): 802-644-8851
Snow Report Number: 802-644-1111
Toll-free reservations: 800-451-8752
UK 0800-169-8
E-mail: smuggs@smuggs.com
Internet: www.smuggs.com
Expert:★★★★
Advanced:★★★★
Intermediate:★★★ **Beginner:**★★★★
First-timer:★★★★★

Lifts: 8—6 double chairs, 2 surface lifts
Skiable acreage: 318
Snowmaking: 62 percent
Uphill capacity: 7,100
Parks & pipes: 3 parks, 1 pipe, 1 minipipe
Bed base: 2,800
Nearest lodging: Slopeside
Child care: Yes, 6 weeks to 3 years
Adult ticket, per day: $62 (08/09 prices)

Dining:★★
Apres-ski/nightlife:★★
Other activities:★★★★

Smugglers' Notch is one of the best family resorts in North America. Smuggs (as it's known) has taken home the prize for best family ski resort from scores of magazines and has won surveys for Best Family Programs in North America seven times.

Treasures, the resort's state-of-the-art child-care center, set alongside the bunny slope and surrounded by a 4,000-square-foot outdoor playground, is a beautiful facility. Staff is trained in first aid, CPR, child development and behavior management. Smuggs understands small children—and their parents—very well. Kid-level fish tanks, one-way viewing mirrors, radiant floor heating and remote-access cameras are just a few special touches here. Treasures joins a long list of family amenities, including a tubing hill, outdoor ice rink, indoor pool and hot tubs, aquatic center with kids' splash pool and more hot tubs, two teen activity centers and the FunZone, with indoor games and other attractions, and organized dances for teens—even a weekly study hall for kids who need to keep up with their schoolwork.

At Smuggs, "family fun" means fun for everyone. In fact, the resort guarantees it: If any family member fails to have fun in one of the resort's programs, Smuggs will refund the entire program portion of that family member's stay. They rarely have to make good on that deal.

There's plenty here for adults, too, starting with the resort's three mountains. The big one, Madonna, has a 2,610-foot vertical drop with glades, bumps and really steep steeps. (Anyone with the mistaken impression that Smuggs is just for kids needs only to peer over the ledge of the trail named F.I.S. and take in the 41-percent gradient.) To the west, Sterling Mountain offers a wide range of terrain for skiers of all levels, while Morse, to the east, is more friendly for first-timers and young children.

Some visitors may be discouraged to find that Smuggs uses slow double chairlifts. It's a tradeoff: There are occasionally long liftline waits on weekends and holidays, but trails are rarely crowded.

Mountain layout

Kids swarm over Morse Mountain, center of ski school classes, apres-ski bonfires and hot chocolate, making it a magnet for those who revel in a family atmosphere. Almost all the condos are located on or near Morse. Experts and advanced skiers head to Madonna Mountain. Intermediates cruise down Sterling.

If you're a day visitor of intermediate skiing ability or better, pass by the main village. Continue uphill to the top parking lot. You'll find fewer cars and a short walk to a point where you can ski to the Sterling and Madonna lifts. And, you can ski back to your car at day's end.

◆◆**Expert,** ◆**Advanced:** The real challenge is from the top of Madonna Mountain. Five double-black-diamond trails beckon. The Black Hole, which is between Liftline and Freefall, adds trees to the steeps. The icefalls, ledges and stumps on Upper Liftline will make even true experts hold their breath. Freefall is just that: The turns come quickly and you drop 10 to 15 feet with each turn. Upper F.I.S. sports a 41-percent gradient, and with the addition of top-to-bottom snowmaking it has become a tad more civilized than in the past.

If you're hooked on glades, you'll want to check out Doc Dempsey's. Another quick adrenaline rush is Highlander Glades on Sterling Mountain. Tree skiers will be awed by the amount of uncut terrain within the resort's boundaries: Keep an eye out for locals who might share their secret stashes. An unofficial easy glade that makes for a great first foray into the woods for kids is off the top of the Practice Slope Extension.

The best bump runs are F.I.S., the middle portion of Upper Liftline, Smugglers' Alley and Exhibition. The snow on Madonna Mountain takes longer to soften, so warm up on Sterling and head to the Madonna 1 chair after 11:30 a.m. or so.

■ **Intermediate:** Fifty-five percent of the trails are rated intermediate. Intermediate runs are concentrated on Madonna and Sterling peaks. Two favorite routes for lower intermediates who want big-mountain skiing are off Sterling: Upper Rumrunner to Lower Rumrunner, and Upper Rumrunner to Black Snake to the bottom of Treasure Run to Lower Exhibition. The views are spectacular both ways. For advanced-intermediates who want to test their mettle, try Chute on Sterling Mountain. It's a short run that's steep with some bumps and stumps, especially in the spring. But it's only 15 to 20 turns long, in case you decide you're in over your head.

●●**Beginner,** ●**First-timer:** The third mountain at Smugglers' is Morse, with 17 trails ranging from beginner to expert. It is the ski schooler's mountain. You won't find any hotshots here. Morse also is home to Mogul Mouse's Magic Lift, a half-speed double chair especially kind to beginners and young children. From the top of the lift begins the Magic Learning Trail, with nature stations, exploration paths and ski-through "caves."

Morse Bowl is served by the Highlands double chair and has five trails for beginners and advanced beginners, and a separate base lodge.

Snowboarding

One drawback for boarders is occasional difficulty riding back to Morse Mountain (and their condos) from Madonna and Sterling. Meadowlark trail from the upper base lodge back to the Village has a gentle grade. If the snow is fast, it's fine; if it's spring and the snow is sticky, take the shuttlebus. Same goes for visitors staying in the condos around Morse Highlands, whose ski-in/ski-out access is too flat for boarding home. Fortunately, the shuttlebus operation is excellent. Just make sure everyone keeps a map and schedule handy. (Smuggs runs a shuttlebus every 20 minutes between the resort village and the upper mountain. An on-demand shuttle is available within the village.)

Parks and pipes

Smuggs has three progression parks and a halfpipe. Beginners stick to the park on the Hibernator trail on Morse, and the minipipe on the Logjam trail in Morse Highlands, then graduate to

Birch Run Park on Sterling Mountain, which offers 1,000 feet of small thrills. Intermediates and experts head to the Zone on Sterling, with its rails, slopestyle hits and giant air ramps. The halfpipe is on Madonna. The Smuggs crew keeps the pipe, jumps, rails and jibs in top shape.

Smugglers' Night School of Boarding meets at Sir Henry's Hill & Fun Park at the base of Morse Mountain on Tuesdays and Wednesdays evenings. The three-hour sessions are for novices ages 6 and older; coaches are positioned strategically on the hill.

Cross-country & snowshoeing (see also xcskiresorts.com)

Smugglers' Notch has 34 km. of scenic, groomed and tracked, cross-country skiing trails, plus 24 km. of snowshoe trails. The **Nordic Ski and Snowshoe Adventure Center** offers rentals, lessons, backcountry and night tours, plus snowshoe rentals and tours, including kids' rentals, family tours and winter walking tours.

Lessons (08/09 prices)

Smuggs calls its ski school Snow Sport University, and its director, Peter Ingvoldstad, has been acclaimed as one of the most innovative teachers in the country. Lessons for beginning adults are included with the Club Smugglers' Advantage Package. Lesson registration is taken when you make your reservations. Lessons also can be purchased separately.

Group lessons: A 90-minute lesson costs $45. Telemark lessons cost the same. Max5 lessons: A 2.5-hr program from 9:45 a.m.-12:15 p.m., five people per class maximum, $75.

First-timer package: The First Timer One-Day Package is $99 and includes a 90-minute coaching session, rentals and lift ticket valid on Morse Mountain. Lessons on the second and third days cost $30 each.

Private lessons: $70-$85 per hour for the first person, $40-$50 for each additional; six-hour private instruction or guided tour cost $299 per person or $399 for up to five people. Lessons with Peter Ingvoldstad, $150 per hour.

Special programs: Classes on style, terrain park tactics, jibs & jumps, parents teaching children to ski, halfpipe tricks, night snowboarding and programs for skiers 55 and older. Boarding School is the snowboarding version of this same program.

Children's Programs (08/09 prices)

Child care: Ages 6 weeks to 3 years old. Children are separated into three age groups. Cost is $85 per day or $15/hour. The Treasures Child Care Center just puts this resort at the top of the child-care world. The state-of-the-art facility, fully licensed by the state of Vermont, is staffed by 20 professionals. Reservations are required; make them when you book your vacation. Given 24 hours notice and a $4 finders fee, Treasures also will arrange for an evening babysitter (cost $15/hour + $1/hour for each additional child, paid to the sitter).

Little Rascals on Snow, a skiing program for 2-1/2 to 3-year-olds, is run from Treasures. Ski time, quiet time, and play time are combined for a low pressure introduction to skiing and winter fun. The daily fee is $109.

Children's lessons: Kids and teens are divided into four age groups: 3–5 (4–5 for snowboarding), 6–10, 11–15 and 16–17. The teen programs allow kids to meet new friends with whom they can hang out at the supervised evening teen activities.

Full-day programs (9 a.m.–4 p.m. daily except Thursday, 9 a.m.–2:30 p.m.) can be purchased separately, for $109 per child per day, or can be included in one of several ski and lodging packages for considerably less. Programs include ski or boarding lessons, outdoor games, science discovery, hot lunch and indoor entertainment in the afternoon. Several 1.5-hour lesson programs are offered at $45 for kids ages 6-17 who don't want a full-day program.

Special programs: Mom & Me/Dad & Me program teaches parents how to teach their youngsters to ski or board for $70 per parent/child session. Scouts Honored allows scouts to earn snow sport merit badges. Other special programs include terrain park tactics, recreational racing and Night School for Boarding.

Special activities: Three nights a week (Wednesday, Thursday, and Saturday), Treasures hosts Kids' Night Out, with dinner and activities for ages 3–11, at $29 per child, so Mom and Dad can have some fun on their own. Given 24 hours notice and a $4 finders fee, Treasures will also arrange for a babysitter to come to your lodging.

Lift tickets (08/09 prices)

One day: adult $62, youth (6 to 18), $46. Multi-day (per each additional day): $48/$36.

Who skis free: Ages 5 and younger and 70 and older.

Who skis at a discount: Seniors 65 to 69 pay youth prices. Morning (8 a.m.-noon) and afternoon (noon-4 p.m.) half-day tickets available for $48.

* Notes: If you're staying for more than one day here, the wise move is to buy a lodging package that includes tickets and lessons. Holiday prices are higher. Early- and late-season prices are lower. Prices include 6 percent Vermont sales tax.

At Smugglers' Notch, the best way to save money on lift tickets is to buy a Bash Badge. This allows all holders to pay $25 any day, no restrictions, all season long. The Bash Badge also comes with other discounts such as 50 percent off equipment rentals, group lessons and cross-country trail fees, as well as 20% off at 3-Mountain Outfitters (the resort's sports shop), all children's ski and snowboard camps and the Treasures nursery. The Bash Badge costs $139 for adults, $119 for youth. But purchase in the early pre-season and save up to $40.

Smugglers also offers the Bash Badge Plus ($209 for adults, $189 for youth), which has the same benefits as the Bash Badge with the addition of free skiing or riding pre- and post-season.

Accommodations

To book lodging at Smugglers' Notch, call 800-451-8752. Accommodations in the Resort Village are condos and are a short walk to the lifts; other resort condos are either slopeside or a short shuttle-ride to the lifts.

Prices start at $99 per day per adult and $85 per day for youths 18 and under for the Club Smugglers' package, which includes lifts and lessons. Children ages 6 and younger ski and stay free. Free off-slope activities such as a welcome party, use of the pools and hot tub, family game nights, outdoor ice skating, family sledding parties, Showtime Theatre (the resort's variety show), nightly teen activities and entertainment, a weekly torchlight parade with fireworks finale and a party will keep most everyone entertained.

Condos at Smugglers' are spacious, clean and family-furnished. Condos closer to the Village tend to be older; condos up the road in the West Hill, Highlands Hill and North Hill communities are newer but less conveniently located. The on-demand shuttle is very convenient though. Kitchens in all units are well equipped, and the newer condos have some excellent amenities, including very good music and video systems. Daily housekeeping and Internet access through a local provider are both available for an extra fee.

Smugglers' central check-in area is designed around the concept that once you check in, you have everything you need—lift tickets, instruction vouchers, rentals and child-care arrangements. Computers at the front desk are tied to key areas such as the rental shop to make the resort very guest-friendly.

Dining

You never have to leave the Village to eat. For home-baked breakfast treats and giant cookies, try **The Green Mountain Deli** (802-644-8851; ext. 1141; $), with fresh-roasted coffee, espresso or cappuccino. Lunch favorites include chili in a bread bowl, spinach salads and made-to-order deli sandwiches. **Riga-Bello's Pizzeria** (602-644-8851;ext. 1142; $-$$) offers daily specials, pizza, salads, calzones and stuffed breads with meat and vegetable fillings—for eat-in, take out or condo delivery. The **Morse Mountain Grille** (802-644-8851;ext. 1247; $-$$) is open continuously for breakfast, lunch and dinner, including light fare. The Pub at the Mountain Grille offers cozy seating and light fare in front of a fieldstone fireplace. **Ben & Jerry's Scoop Shop**, in the Village Lodge, is open daily, serving more than 15 flavors of its famous ice cream, low-fat ice cream and sorbet.

The **Hearth and Candle** (802-644-8090 $-$$$) is a privately operated restaurant in the Village with a friendly, though more formal, atmosphere. Families are served in the cozy Hearth Room, and couples desiring a quiet atmosphere are escorted upstairs to the adults-only Birch Room. Entrees range from steak and pasta to exotic preparations of fish and game. The Tuesday-night **Snowshoe Adventure Dinner** takes adults to the top of Sterling Mountain for a gourmet meal in a cabin lit only by candles, then sends the whole crowd back downhill on snowshoes to work off the calories.

Restaurants dot the route between the resort and Jeffersonville, 5 miles away. Some examples: **Stella Notte Restaurant** (802-644-8884; $-$$), across the road from the resort entrance, offers authentic Italian cuisine with a country flair, antipasti, some favorite pastas, stuffed pork chops, grilled shrimp and children's tomatoey favorites. The **Three Mountain Lodge** (802-644-5736; $$) serves an eclectic menu in a classic log-lodge atmosphere.

Angelina's (802-644-2011; $-$$) in Cambridge has great pizza, with a thin crust that's crispy on the bottom, soft on the top and loaded with sauce. Our kids, who consider themselves pizza connoisseurs, gave it an 8 out of 10. **158 Main Restaurant and Bakery** (802-644-8100; $-$$) has brought nouveau cuisine to the valley. Tasty premise-baked breads surround favorite sandwich stuffings, as well as unexpected pairings of fresh vegetables and meats in hot and cold dishes for breakfast, lunch and dinner.

Apres-ski/nightlife

Smugglers' has lots to do once the slopes close down. It's family-oriented activity, but even our childless staffers have had more fun than they expected. See Other Activities for a description of off-slope family fun.

Recent efforts to entertain adults more fully have been very successful in the summer and have carried over to winter with well-attended events for those 21 and older in **Bootlegger's Lounge** in the village. The lounge has a full-service bar and serves a wide selection of beers, plus munchies. There's a big-screen TV and nightly entertainment includes live acoustic performances, local bands, a magic show, karaoke, a DJ video party, and dance party.

If you're coming right off the slopes of Madonna or Sterling, stop by the **Black Bear Lounge** on Friday and Saturday afternoons. Starting at 2 p.m., a DJ spins tunes, with trivia, prizes and drink specials. And there's shuttle service available back to the main village.

Dining: $$$$–Entrees $30+; $$$–$20–$30; $$–$10–$20; $–less than $10.
Accommodations: (double room) $$$$–$200+; $$$–$141–$200; $$–$81–$140; $–$80 and less.

Nearby, at **Brewski Bar**—a ski-bum fave—bands play music, the beer flows, the pool tables beckon and kids and family activities can be left behind. Across from the Smuggs entrance, **Stella Notte** often has local bands, as does the **Tavern at the Smugglers' Notch Inn** down in Jeffersonville.

Other activities

There are so many off-slope activities that it feels like a summer camp—or a cruise with snow. **Kids' parties, karaoke, snowshoeing, sledding, swimming pools (including a kids' splash pool), hot tubs, ice skating,** and **snowmobiling** keep kids off the couch (and sometimes even off the slopes) day and night. There's also **air boarding, dog sledding** and **tubing**.

The **FunZone** is filled with **a 22-foot giant inflatable double-lane slide, a very popular obstacle course, miniature golf, a bouncy house**, and **basketball hoops**. There is also a giant **Twister game and a kid-size climbing wall**. Wear warm socks (no shoes allowed).

The resort has **two teen centers**, and while both are supervised, there is a strict No Parents Allowed policy, which pleases the kids. Outer Limits Teen Center Teens is for 16-plus, with **music videos, Internet access, Xbox, DVDs, a pool table, ping-pong**, and the like. Ages 13-15 have Teen Alley, with similar amenities. Evening activities include a Saturday night dance and FunZone party just for teens. Thursdays at 9 p.m., teens age 16 and older get the FunZone to themselves; on Fridays at 9 p.m., it's reserved for ages 13-15.

Adults can sign up for a variety of workshops in the **Artists in the Mountains** program. Pick from **glass etching, fabric stenciling, digital photography, sculpting, painting**, or **beading**. The classes include materials and cost $10 - $48. The Mountain Massage Center not only offers **yoga classes** and **massages**, it holds a **massage class** to teach you the basics.

Don't miss a visit to the **Boyden Valley Winery**, 8 miles away. This fourth-generation Vermont farmer makes award-winning wines using Vermont apples and berries and his own grapes and maple syrup. The area also has **antique galleries, artisan galleries, art galleries** and **shops selling Vermont-made products**. The resort provides itineraries to those wishing to head out to local attractions.

Getting there and getting around

By air: Burlington International Airport is 40 minutes away. Shuttles are available (24-hour notice required; book it when you book lodging).

By car: Smugglers' Notch is on Rte. 108 near Jeffersonville in northwest Vermont. *Note: The stretch of Rte. 108 between Stowe and Smugglers' is closed in winter.*

Getting around: The resort has a free shuttle linking the mountain condos with the village center and the upper mountains. There are several older condo complexes within walking distance of the village. If you want to visit some of the restaurants in or on the way to Jeffersonville, you'll need a car. A local taxi service also is available.

Stowe
Vermont

Summit: 3,640 feet
Vertical: 2,360 feet
Base: 1,280 feet

Address: 5781 Mountain Rd.,
Stowe, VT 05672
Telephone (main): 802-253-3000
Snow Report Number: 802-253-3600
Toll-free reservations:
(800) 247-8693 for slopeside
E-mail: info@stowe.com
Internet: www.stowe.com

Expert:★★★★
Advanced:★★★★
Intermediate:★★★★
Beginner:★★★★
First-timer:★★★

Lifts: 13–1 eight-pax gondola, 1 10-pax cross-over gondola; 3 high-speed quads, 2 triples, 4 doubles, 2 surface lifts
Skiable acreage: 485
Snowmaking: 73 percent
Uphill capacity: 15,516
Parks & pipes: 3 parks, 1 pipe
Bed base: 5,000+
Nearest lodging: Slopeside, hotel
Child care: Yes, 3 months and older
Adult ticket, per day: $84 (07/08 prices)
Dining:★★★★
Apres-ski/nightlife:★★
Other activities:★★★

The first sight of towering Mt. Mansfield with its snow-capped summit is breathtaking. The mountain, Vermont's highest at 4,395 feet, is home to Stowe's famed ski resort. Site of Vermont's first racing trail—Nose Dive, cut in the early 1930s—Stowe Resort has retained its old-time New England feel. Its trails zigzag along forest contours or drop precipitously straight down the fall line. Across from Mt. Mansfield is Spruce Peak with kinder, gentler terrain and a sunnier exposure. Both Mansfield and Spruce are vintage Vermont.

But vintage doesn't mean stodgy and Stowe is on the move. When Spruce Peak at Stowe is finished, the resort will have a true base village. Spruce's improvements include three lifts with a high-speed 10-passenger cross-over gondola that carries guests between Spruce Peak and Mt. Mansfield. The upscale Stowe Mountain Lodge opened in spring, 2008.

But the mountain isn't the only Stowe experience. The Village of Stowe, with its white-steepled church and main street lined with historic buildings, is the epitome of how most folks picture Vermont. Between the village and the mountain are historic inns and swanky resorts, two world-class spas, and restaurants to serve every appetite and palate. There is no place like Stowe. With very little run-out at the bottom, the trails will keep you turning almost until the liftline. It's one of many reasons that the mountain has so many diehard fans.

 ## Mountain layout

The skiing at Stowe is on two sides of a valley, now connected by the 10-passenger high-speed cross-over gondola. On one side you'll find the famous "Front Four"—Goat, Starr, Liftline and National—as well as the long and gentle Toll Road trail, and other famous trails like Nose Dive and Hayride. The Gondola serves the Cliff House Restaurant and trails such as leg-burning Chin Clip and cruisers including Gondolier and Perry Merrill. On the other side of the valley, Spruce Peak rises to 3,390 feet. The site of Stowe's new mountain village, Spruce now has top-to-bottom snowmaking on several trails and great intermediate runs. The Spruce base is also home to the child care center.

◆◆**Expert,** ◆**Advanced:** Part of the legend of Stowe revolves around its Front Four, and the fact that it features some of the steepest and most difficult runs in skidom. Having descended the Front Four is a badge of honor for Northeast skiers and deservedly so. Besides being steep, the headwalls are frequently draped with New England hardpack, and the trails liberally moguled. Experts who are gunning for all four should begin with National and Lift-line. The resort's winch cats allow groomers to prepare these two from time to time. Starr is not groomed, and the view from the top, as it disappears in a 37-degree dive, is one you won't forget. If you haven't met your match by this time, then you're ready for Goat, a moguled gut-sucker no more than three to five large bumps wide, with a double fall line.

For off piste terrain, try the trees off Bypass. The pitch eases on Nose Dive, with more wide-open trees to skier's left off the main trail. Skiers are also known to hike The Chin—Mt. Mansfield's highest point at 4,395 feet—where there is intense out-of-bounds skiing and riding. But hook up with someone who's familiar with the area. The cliff bands and tight chutes are nasty, and you can easily wander to the backside with no clue how to return to civilization.

For advanced skiers, a very nice section of glade skiing through well-spaced trees is just off the top section of Nose Dive. Chin Clip from the top of the gondola is long, moguled, and moderately narrow, but it doesn't have quite the steep grade that the Front Four boast.

■ **Intermediate:** This group can enjoy nearly 60 percent of the trails, including much of Spruce Peak. At Mt. Mansfield, ski to the right or left of the Front Four. Advanced-intermediates will probably want to chance the tricky top part of Nose Dive for the pleasure of skiing the long, sweeping cruiser that beckons further down. Going left from the top of the FourRunner Quad, take Upper Lord until it leads you to a handful of long, excellent intermediate trails that run all the way to the bottom on Lower Lord, North Slope, Standard and Gulch.

From the quad, reaching the intermediate skiing under the gondola presents a problem, unless you're willing to take Nose Dive, rated double-black at its top. Otherwise, it's a hike from the quad area over to the gondola; or, you can take the green-circle Crossover trail toward the bottom of the mountain, which allows you to traverse directly across the Front Four to the gondola base. To work your way back from the gondola to the quad, take the Cliff Trail, which hooks up with Lower Nose Dive and dumps you at the base of the high-speed chair.

For a little elbow room, try Perry Merrill or Gondolier from the gondola, or cut wide turns down Main Street on Spruce Peak. Spruce Peak is a cruiser's delight, and a real treat on powder days. Intermediates may also enjoy Stowe's night skiing. The upper portion of Perry Merrill and about 85 percent of Gondolier are lit Thursday through Saturday until 9 p.m. The ride up is in the warm gondola.

●●**Beginner,** ●**First-timer:** There are very nice beginner trails off the lower lifts on Spruce Peak and off the Toll House chair on Mt. Mansfield. You won't find yourself worrying about faster skiers, so you'll be able to enjoy the experience.

One route we recommend to all levels is the 4-mile-long, green-circle Toll Road, which starts at the top of the FourRunner quad. This is a marvelous trail for lower-level skiers, but the more proficient probably will enjoy it, too, for its beauty. You pass through a canopy of trees, where you can hear only birds chirping or snow plopping from branches. A little later you find the small wood-and-stone Mountain Chapel, where on Sundays at 1 p.m. you can attend an informal church service. You just won't find this type of intimate ski trail out West.

First-timers should start at Spruce Peak base area. Once you're comfortable on the greens at Spruce Peak, move over to Mt. Mansfield and work up to the runs off the Toll House chair (Chair 5), then advance to the Mountain Triple (Chair 4).

Parks and pipes

At the mountain that Burton founder Jake Burton Carpenter now calls home, snowboarding is one of the top priorities. Tyro, the biggest of the resort's three terrain parks, attracts many Burton employees and features more than a dozen different elements, including boxes, rails, jibs, tabletops, rollers and a quarterpipe. Tyro's lower section has so many rails you can't hit them in one run. In the early season, when Tyro isn't yet open, Stowe sets up rails on lower North Slope, an area locals call Jib Nation.

Crossover accesses Stowe's superpipe, a competition-caliber pipe on North Slope. It and Tyro are best reached via the Mountain Triple. There is great freeriding to Tyro from the top of the Lookout Double or FourRunner Quad.

Stowe's two other terrain parks are designed for learners or less hardcore aerialists. The Midway Mini Park, near the Midway Lodge, features its own surface lift and hits that are out in the open for everyone to see. The Spruce Terrain Park. beneath the Alpine Double chairlift on Spruce Mountain, offers easy elements and fewer riders lined up to hit them.

Snowboarding

Freeriders will really like this mountain. Beginners should focus on Lower Spruce. Intermediates should head to Mt. Mansfield for long carving runs on Gondolier, Perry Merrill and Sunrise. You'll also enjoy the intermediate trails on Spruce, which are now covered with snowmaking and served by new lifts. As the day progresses, advanced riders should move from Liftline and Nose Dive to Hayride and Centerline, then North Slope. Nose Dive takes you into some nice tree riding. There's also good hikeable terrain off the gondola. Avoid the Toll Road, it's way too long and has too many flats (even for an expert).

Rimrock, which takes you from Nose Dive over to the trails off the gondola, requires you to carry speed (but don't miss those nice tree shots). Crossover, which takes you from the quad trails to the gondola trails, also has some pretty flat parts. And be ready for the flats coming from Tyro, site of the terrain park, and Standard back to the lifts.

Cross-country & snowshoeing (see also xcskiresorts.com)

Stowe has one of the best cross-country networks in the country. Four touring areas all interconnect to provide roughly 150 groomed km. of trails, an additional 110 km. in the backcountry, and a slew of trails for snowshoeing.

The **Trapp Family Lodge** (802-253-5719; 800-826-7000) organized America's first touring center and has 60 km. of groomed and machine-tracked trails that connect to another 100 km. in the Mt. Mansfield and Topnotch Resort networks. Trapp's also has 45 km. of backcountry trails. Rentals and instruction are available. The **Edson Hill Touring Center** (802-253-7371) has about 50 km. of trails with 25 km. of them groomed. Elevation varies from 1,400 to 2,100 feet. **Stowe Mountain Resort** (802-253-3000) has 80 km. of trails, 35 km. of which are groomed. The **Topnotch Resort** (802-253-8585) has 30 km. of trails, most of which are groomed and tracked.

Snowshoe rentals and guided tours are available at **Umiak Outdoor Outfitters** (802-253-2317).

Lessons (07/08 prices)

Group lessons: $48 for 90 minutes, $41 midweek.
First-timer package: Stowe for Starters includes up to two 90-minute group

lessons, rentals and a Spruce Mountain lift ticket for $100 weekends and holidays, $85 midweek. Stowe recommends that you learn on Spruce Peak until comfortable on all blue terrain before "graduating" to the more difficult terrain on Mt. Mansfield.

Private lessons: Multilingual, telemark, racing, pipe/park and adaptive-specific pros are available. One person, one-hour, $114; 2 hours, $200; half-day, $286; full day, $435. For 2-5 people: $172/$300/$428/$652. Midweek/non-holiday prices are lower, as are one-hour private lessons from 2:30-3:30 p.m.

Semi-private lessons: Levels 6-9 can take two-hour semi-privates for $82 (weekends and holidays). Prices drop a few dollars midweek.

Special programs: The Women in Motion three-day program for intermediates and better takes place on January, February and March dates. Lodging and lift ticket packages available; call for pricing.

Children's Programs (07/08 prices)

Child care: The center takes children ages 3 months through 3 years. Full day with lunch is $88 ($102 weekends/holidays). A full day with a morning ski session for 3-year-olds is $105 ($125 weekends/holidays). Parents must provide formula and food for infants. Toddlers are served lunch and offered snacks throughout the day. Reservations are required; call 802-253-3000, Ext. 3686.

The Cubs Infant Care Center, near the base of the Sunny Spruce quad chairlift, is state licensed and features a small, friendly staff that average a decade or more at Stowe.

Children's lessons: Headquartered at Spruce Peak, full-day programs for skiing and snowboarding ages 4-12 include lunch. Cost is $105 ($125 weekends/holidays). The Big Easy is a two-hour semi-private lesson with a maximum 3-to-1 student-teacher ratio for first-time skiers and snowboarders ages 4-12. Cost, including lift ticket, is $68 ($82 weekends/holidays). A program called 3 Ski is a two-hour lesson with lift ticket for 3-year-olds for the same price as the Big Easy.

Lift tickets (07/08 prices)

One day: adult, $84 (holiday) $79 (regular); junior (6-12), $60 (holiday) $58 (regular); senior (65+), $70 (holiday) $66 (regular).

Three days: $225/$210 - $123/ $114 - $150/ $132.

Five days: $325/ $310 - $205/ $175 - $245/$210.

Who skis free: Children ages 5 and younger with paid parent or guardian.

Night skiing: $27 adults, $24 seniors, $21 for children. Twilight ticket, valid from 1 to 9 p.m.: $65/ $60/ $55 (holiday prices higher).

The Vacation Rewards Program provides 15 percent off multi-day tickets when you make a minimum seven-day advance purchase. Call 888-253-4849.

Accommodations

When staying at least three days, ask about the Stowe Vacation Program. Extras include night skiing, extra half days, lessons, and more. Lift tickets will be waiting for you with your room key. Call 800-247-8693.

Opened in June, 2008, the luxury **Stowe Mountain Lodge** (802-253-3560; $$$$), has 139 rooms set at the base of Spruce Peak. The lodge has a spa and wellness center, meeting space, concierge service, and the restaurant Solstice, where Chef Sean Buchanan partners with the Vermont Fresh Network and Chefs Collaborative to create unique northern Vermont dining.

When the Trapp family's life was dramatized in "The Sound of Music," their everlasting fame was guaranteed. The **Trapp Family Lodge** (800-826-7000; 802-253-8511; $$$$), which they established near Stowe upon arriving in the United States, is a legend in its own right. It's a self-contained resort with an excellent cross-country center. The collection of restaurants is among the best in the area, and a modern pool and fitness center provide excellent amenities. Make reservations early because this lodge is normally full throughout the season (Christmas reservations should be made about a year in advance). Rates include breakfast and dinner.

Topnotch at Stowe Resort & Spa (800-451-8686; 802-253-8585; in Canada 800-228-8686; $$$$) is the area's top spa/fitness destination. Rooms range from doubles in the main hotel to condominiums. The experience is all about comfort and luxury, from the overstuffed chairs in the lobby to the amazingly comfortable bed pillows in the rooms. The spa is world-class, and the resort has the only indoor tennis courts in Stowe.

The Inn at the Mountain (800-253-4754; 802-253-3656; $$-$$$$), is part of Stowe Mountain Resort. The flavor is country New England. Stowe's best family accommodations are at the **Golden Eagle Resort** (800-626-1010; 802-253-4811; $$-$$$). This sprawling complex has more than a dozen buildings and facilities, from motel rooms with kitchenettes to apartments. The complex has one of the best fitness centers in town, which includes an indoor pool. It is all unpretentious and affordable. There are dozens of pricing options; contact the property and explain your needs.

The **Stoweflake Mountain Resort and Spa** (800-253-2232; 802-253-7355; $$$-$$$$), on the Mountain Road, has a trendy spa and sports club. This property has had continual upgrades over past years. Rates include breakfast and dinner. The Stoweflake also manages a nice group of townhouse condos with studio to three-bedroom units. **Ye Olde England Inne** (800-477-3771; 0800-962-684 toll-free from the U.K.; 802-253-7558; $$-$$$$) is also on the Mountain Road. Bigger than a country inn and smaller than a full-fledged hotel, it has an English country motif and lavish Laura Ashley touches. The Bluff House, perched on the hill behind the inn, has luxury suites with unobstructed valley views. Room rates include breakfast.

Stowe Inn (800-546-4030; 802-253-4030; $$-$$$) is a renovated 17th-century landmark on the Mountain Road. Some of the deluxe inn rooms in the main lodge feature four-poster sleigh or panel beds. Standard doubles in the carriage house are a good value yet well-adorned. Breakfast and afternoon snacks are included; Harrison's Tavern is downstairs for dinner. **Green Mountain Inn**(800-253-7302; 802-253-7301; $$-$$$$) on Main Street is a charming old inn in the middle of town. The wide-planked floors are pine, and the furniture is comfortable antiques. The hotel has an annex that is not quite so quaint but is off the main road. Rates include a huge breakfast buffet.

Ten Acres Lodge (800-327-7357; 802-253-7638; $$-$$$$), on Luce Hill Road, is a converted 1840s farm house. Rooms vary in size; the common areas are beautiful. Eight modern units, called the Hill House, are tucked into the woods behind the old farmhouse. These all have fireplaces in the rooms and share an outdoor hot tub. Rates include breakfast. **The Gables Inn** (800-422-5371; 802-253-7730; $$-$$$$), on Mountain Road, is a real lived-in house, which helps everyone have a good time. The breakfasts are among the best in Stowe. Rates include two meals. **Stone Hill Inn** (802-253-6282; $$$$) is exquisitely luxurious, designed for romance and comfort; no kids allowed. The nine rooms, each decorated differently, include a king-size bed, a cozy sitting area, a fireplace in the bedroom and in the bathroom, and a jetted tub for two. Prices include breakfast, evening hors d'oeuvres and unlimited soft drinks.

On the budget side, **The Stowe Motel & Snowdrift** (800-829-7629; 802-253-7629; $-$$) has clean, nicely-appointed motel rooms, some with fireplaces and kitchenettes.

Dining: $$$$–Entrees $30+; $$$–$20–$30; $$–$10–$20; $–less than $10.
Accommodations: (double room) $$$$–$200+; $$$–$141–$200; $$–$81–$140; $–$80 and less.

Dining

Stowe has long been famous for its cuisine. The **Blue Moon Cafe** (802-253-7006; $$-$$$) is considered tops for fine dining. **Norma's Restaurant** (802-253-9263; $$$-$$$$) is Topnotch Resort's newest dining experience. Breakfast, lunch and dinner are served in this bustling, bright restaurant with a panoramic view of Mt. Mansfield. Fresh, local ingredients are combined creatively.

Winfield's Bistro (802-253-7355; $$$), at the Stoweflake, serves nicely gussied-up American cooking with an international flair, and it has an excellent wine list. The **Trapp Family Lodge** (802-253-8511; $$$-$$$$) traditionally serves an excellent Austrian-style meal for a $42 fixed price. A la carte dining is also available. Diners choose from about a dozen entrees. Live harp music accompanies dinner. **Michael's on the Hill** (802-244-7476; $$-$$$), south of Stowe on Route 100, is a chef-owned restaurant in an 1820s farmhouse with spectacular mountain views. The European-influenced menu is sophisticated and changes seasonally. There's live piano music in the lounge on Friday and Saturday nights.

Harrison's Restaurant and Bar (802-253-7773; $$-$$$) is now on Main Street and features New American cuisine. The **Stowe Inn Tavern** (802-253-4030; $$-$$$) has a similar American menu; it overlooks Stowe Village. Sit near the bar, a mahogany masterpiece.

The **Whip Bar & Grill** (802-253-7301; $$), in the lower level of the Green Mountain Inn, is good for a light dinner or sandwiches. **The Shed** (802/253-4364; $-$$) has a microbrewery and is great for steaks and prime rib. **Foxfire** (802-253-4887; $$) has good Italian food, as does **Trattoria La Festa** (802-253-8480; $$). **Mr. Pickwicks** in the Ye Olde England Inne (802-253-7558; $$) serves excellent game. **Red Basil** (802-253-4478; $-$$) specializes in fantastic Thai food and has a great martini menu. There's a sushi bar too.

For alternatives that aren't budget-busters, try **Miguel's Stowe Away** (802-253-7574; $-$$) on the Mountain Road, or the **Cactus Cafe**(802-253-7770; $-$$) for Mexican food; **Restaurant Swisspot** (802-253-4622; $-$$) for fondues and decadent Swiss chocolate pie; The **Depot Street Malt Shoppe** (802-253-4269; $) for a 1950s-style fountain shop; and **Gracie's** (802-253-8741; $) on the Mountain Road for great burgers and meatloaf.

The country breakfasts at **The Gables** (802-253-7730; $) shouldn't be missed.

On-mountain, there are several choices for lunch and snacks. The **Fireside Tavern** (802-235-3000; $$) in the Inn at the Mountain at the base of the Toll House lift, serves hearty breakfasts and lunches. The **Midway Cafe** ($) in the Midway Lodge has good pizza and paninis. Or try **Jose's Cafe** ($), also in the Midway Lodge, for Mexican fare. The **Cliff House Restaurant** ($-$$) at the gondola top has a nice upscale atmosphere and great views. You can check your email at the **Octagon Web Cafe** ($), at the top of the Forerunner express quad.

Apres-ski/nightlife

The **Matterhorn Bar**, a raucous little roadhouse on the mountain road is packed and rollicking apres-ski. There's a dance floor, a disc jockey, loud music, pool tables, a big-screen TV and a sushi bar. A more low-key apres-ski at the mountain is in the **Fireside Tavern** at the Inn at the Mountain. The **Rusty Nail** is the "in" spot for dancing and live music, frequently blues. **The Shed** brews its own beer. **Mr. Pickwick's** at Ye Olde England Inne gets a good pub crowd with its 150-plus different beers, and the bar at **Miguel's Stowe Away** seems to be a singles meeting place. **The Back Yard** is small and normally has plenty of beer to drink around a fire.

Other activities

Stowe has two world-class **spas**: the Spa at Topnotch Resort (802-253-6463) and the Spa at Stoweflake Mountain Resort (802-253-7355). With booklets full of treatments, massaging waterfalls, and gender-specific hot tubs, saunas, and steamrooms, you could easily forget about skiing and spend the entire day at either spa.

Indoor tennis can be played at the Topnotch Tennis Center (802-253-9649) on the Mountain Road. The center has four indoor courts and Boomer, a computer-guided ball machine that let's you play actual matches. In the Village, Jackson Arena has an Olympic-size **ice skating** rink (802-253-6148). The Swimming Hole (802-253-9229) has a 25-meter **indoor pool, kids pool with waterslide, fitness classes** and **weight training equipment**.

Rent **snowmobiles** at Nichols Snowmobiles (802-253-7239) or from Farm Resort (802-888-3525). **Horse-drawn sleigh rides** take place at Edson Hill Manor (802-253-7371), Stowehof Inn (802-253-9722), Pristine Meadows (802-253-9901), Charlie Horse (802-253-2215), Stoweflake (802-253-7355), the Trapp Family Lodge (802-253-8511) and Topnotch (802-253-8585). Stowe also has **horseback riding** at Edson Hill Manor (802-253-7371) and Stowehof Inn (802-253-9722).

The **Vermont Ski Museum** is located on Main Street in Stowe Village. **Ben and Jerry's ice cream factory** (802-244-5641) is nearby in Waterbury, and has tours that include samples. Winter is a good time to visit. The **Cabot Cheese Factory** (802-563-2231) is also open.

Stowe has more than a hundred **shops** and **art galleries**, most in town. Shaw's General Store is a century old and was the town's first ski shop. Other unusual shops are Moriarty Hats & Sweaters, for knitted goods, and the Stowe Craft Gallery. At Waterbury's Cabot Annex, you can purchase Vermont specialty foods. The complex also is home to Lake Champlain Chocolates (Yum!), Vermont Teddy Bears and Mesa International, which sells home furnishings.

Getting there and getting around

By air: Burlington International Airport is 45 minutes away. Most hotels have a transfer service; or, rent a car. The Stowe Area Association provides discounts on flights and rental cars when you make your hotel reservations.

By train: Amtrak's Vermonter offers private berths, cocktail-bearing attendants and the chance to watching the moonlit landscape of New England whirl past your window to the lonely call of the train whistle. You arrive in Waterbury, 15 miles from Stowe, early in the morning (the Stowe trolley meets each daily arrival and departure). Reservations are required. The Stowe Area Association offers 10 percent off Amtrak tickets with no date restrictions.

By car: Distance from Boston is about 205 miles; from New York, 325 miles. The resort is a few miles north of Waterbury Exit 10 on I-89.

Getting around: You can manage without a car, but we recommend one. We realize that this will only contribute to increased street congestion, but the alternative is the Town Trolley, which runs between the village of Stowe and Mt. Mansfield. It provides, in the words of a British journalist who begged a ride back into town with us, "an epic voyage." The trolley. Makes. A lot. Of stops. Between town. And. The. Mountain. But it's free and runs from the village from 7:30 a.m. to 4:30 p.m., and from the mountain from 8 a.m. to 5 p.m. at 30-minute intervals.

Dining: $$$$–Entrees $30+; $$$–$20–$30; $$–$10–$20; $–less than $10.
Accommodations: (double room) $$$$–$200+; $$$–$141–$200; $$–$81–$140; $–$80 and less.

Stratton Mountain
and the Manchester area

Summit: 3,875 feet
Vertical: 2,003 feet
Base: 1,872 feet

Address: RR1 Box 145,
Stratton Mountain, VT 05155
Telephone (main): 802-297-2200
Snow Report Number: 802-297-4211
Toll-free reservations: 800-787-2886
E-mail: skistratton@intrawest.com
Internet: www.stratton.com
Expert: ★
Advanced: ★★★
Intermediate: ★★★★
Beginner: ★★★★
First-timer: ★★★★
Lifts: 16—1 12-passenger gondola, 4 high-speed six-packs, 4 quads, 1 triple, 1 double, 2

surface lifts, 3 moving carpets
Skiable acreage: 583
Snowmaking: 90 percent
Uphill capacity: 29,550
Parks & pipes: 4 parks, 2 pipes
Bed base: 8,000 in region
Nearest lodging: Slopeside
Child care: Yes, 6 weeks and older
Adult ticket, per day: $69/$78 (07/08 prices)

Manchester Region
Dining: ★★★★★
Apres-ski/nightlife: ★★★
Other activities: ★★★

Stratton seems to be moving in two distinct directions. On the one hand, the self-proclaimed "Snowboarding Capital of the East" offers truly inexpensive midweek deals. On the other hand, the resort has invested significant money in high-end lodging, built an exclusive members-only club and imposes one of the most expensive single-day lift tickets in the nation. Go figure. The bottom line, however, is this: Radical dudes, easy-going intermediates, professionals on hiatus and families can all find their place at Stratton.

Stratton's base area has always been a helter-skelter affair, with various lodgings and condo complexes scattered amidst private homes. The recent creation of a car-free base village has improved the ambiance. The village creates a centralized locale for swanky shops, restaurants, slopeside condos and even a Bavarian-style clock tower—all linked by a heated cobblestone walkway. At least the resort, like the Tin Man, has gotten a heart. Jitney service does connect the dots and, to some extent, getting around has improved. Still, due to poor signage and a snake-pit road layout, arriving—especially after dark—can be confusing.

Other base-area improvements include an expanded cafeteria that can now handle the weekend lunchtime crowds; a self-contained, slopeside kids' ski-snowboard school facility; and The Wreck, an under-21 club that's open weekends and holiday weeks.

Stratton was the first Eastern resort to permit snowboarding and few resorts equal Stratton's dedication to the sport, specifically their terrain parks. Parks serve every ability level and the resort pioneered a required certification program to ride its most advanced park. It also offers Burton Learn to Ride, the Cadillac of introductory snowboarding programs, and hosts the annual Burton U.S. Open Championships and winter-long, select Saturday night snowboard competition series. It matches its snowboarding commitment with freeskiing zeal.

Outside the parks, the full variety of downhill choices can be found on 94 trails and 600-plus skiable acres. A 12-passenger, high-speed gondola and four six-packs swiftly move onto the mountain. For a less frenetic ambiance, the Sun Bowl base lodge is more "small ski area" in ambiance. A smattering of excellent gladed runs completes the picture.

The resort is 20 miles outside Manchester and its twin, Manchester Center. The accessing highways, Rtes. 11 and 30, are lined with shops, accommodations and some pretty good restaurants. The non-ski and apres-ski crowd can visit numerous antique and craft shops as well as stores like Claire Murray Design, the Northshire independent book stores (ranked one of the best in the country) and factory outlet malls that include Tommy Hilfiger, Theory, Ralph Lauren and Armani. The nearby Orvis fly-fishing store and school offer fly-fishing lessons in season. The lavish Sunday brunch at the Equinox Hotel or a visit to the Southern Vermont Arts Center can gild a ski weekend or vacation.

Mountain layout

Excellent grooming on the mostly intermediate terrain makes Stratton one of America's best ego-inflating resorts. Experts can find some good challenges especially in the trees, but won't be pushed unless they venture into the trees or moguls. One should come here to be pampered and feel good about one's skiing. This mountain is also great for wide-open, top-to-bottom cruising.

◆◆**Expert, ◆Advanced**: The pitch for cruising is nice enough that no expert or advanced skier will complain. The more challenging terrain lies off the summit accessed by the gondola. Polar Bear, Grizzly Bear and Upper Tamarack are narrow runs in fine New England tradition with good vertical. The Ursa Express "six-pack" chair is great for continuous laps. Upper Kidderbrook to Freefall provides a good advanced cruiser on the Sun Bowl side. Upper Standard, under the gondola, starts steep but mellows. Upper Spruce is the easiest double-diamond, with tempting glades to the right. World Cup and Bear Down get bumped up; Upper Downeaster and World Cup have the mountain's steepest. Stratton has a large variety of tree skiing and the double-diamond glade runs are challenging with jumps, steeps and narrow passages.

■ **Intermediate**: The upper mountain has some steeps for advanced intermediates. Upper Lift Line to Lower Lift Line, the mountain's longest fall-line trail, is made for big giant-slalom turns. Upper Drifter to Lower Drifter is the same. North American is a black diamond and with its rollers gets steep in spots. The Sun Bowl chair has excellent cruisers down Rowley's Run and Sunriser. On the lower mountain, Yodeler is a good warm-up run.

●●**Beginner, ●First-timer**: Stratton has a Ski Learning Park with 10 gentle trails and its own lift. This park includes a terrain garden with sculpted bumps and rolls for practicing balance and independent leg action. It's a great environment for children. A long top-to-bottom trail, Mike's Way to West Meadow to Lower Wanderer, makes beginners feel like champs. They can also take in the views from the top. At Sun Bowl, head to Lower Middlebrook. The other beginner trails, 91, Big Ben and Main Line, are only accessible from intermediate trails.

First-timers should stick to the Teddy Bear, Club and Villager lifts on the far left of the base area. Stage I and Village Walk are friendly places to learn to ski or ride.

Parks and pipes

Stratton, demonstrates its commitment to the sport with four feature-filled terrain parks and by hosting the annual U.S. Open Snowboarding Championships in March. Indeed, no matter where you go here, there's bound to be a park nearby. The biggest is Suntanner Park which is based on Western-style terrain parks with more flow. Every season it has different features and jump lineups, the highest visibility and the most traffic. Old Smoothie has more technical features such as table tops and rails that are higher off the ground. Terrain park users must have a Safety Education System (SES) pass in all parks. This can be earned through a 20-minute class with a video presentation, question & answer period, park-and-pipe etiquette and safety tips.

Stratton also features park progression allowing beginner riders and skiers to start on the easy stuff and work their way up to the tough. The Burton Kids' Parkway was designed and created to teach little rippers about park features, etiquette and safety. It features a green-light/red-light stop-and-go system and is always staffed with park crew and instructors.

Another park, Tyrolienne, has mostly small terrain features like table-tops and butter boxes designed to help skiers and riders work on their skills. To reach East Meadow, a beginner freestyler's park, take the Janeway Junction, far rider's left. The upper section has a few rollers and a small spine; the lower section is set up boardercross style. A kids' learning park on Tyrolienne has small rollers, spines and a minipipe. Beeline has a box which is popular.

U.S. Open competitors trick off a park and pipe on Sunriser Supertrail. Built about a week before the Open, the huge 22-foot tall and 450-foot-long superpipe is open to the public for a week after the competition.

Snowboarding

Avoid cutting across the mountain via Black Bear and Old 8. It's better to just go straight down to the Sun Bowl and avoid the flats. Also avoid Old Log Rd. on the other side of the mountain, because you'll have to take off your board and hike it.

Cross-country & snowshoeing (see also xcskiresorts.com)

Viking Ski Touring Center (802-824-3933, www.vikingnordic.com) in Londonderry provides 30 km of groomed trails through woods and open fields, best suited for intermediates, but with some advanced trails. This is one of the oldest cross-country centers in North America.

The **Stratton Nordic Center** (802-297-4114) at the Sun Bowl has 20 km. of tracked cross-country trails and 50 km. of backcountry skiing. Skiers can use the Sun Bowl Lodge for rentals, dining and lounging. Lessons and guided tours are available. The **Stratton Mountain County Club** has terrain that is ideally suited for first timers and families. It is on the Stratton access road and has a retail shop and rental equipment for skiing and snowshoeing.

Equinox Resort (802-362-4700) in Manchester offers xc skiing on the Equinox golf course and on Equinox Mountain, scenic property in the Taconic Range above Manchester. **Hildene Ski Touring** (802-362-1788,) in Manchester Village has 15 km. of trails through the pine-covered estate of Robert Todd Lincoln. There is a warming hut in the carriage barn, with rentals, trail tickets and light refreshments. **Grafton Ponds XC Center** (802-843-2400) in Grafton is on Rte 121. It has 30 km. of groomed trails, lessons, rentals, sleigh rides, ice-skating and retail. The Nordic ski center is linked to the Old Tavern in Grafton (47 rooms and restaurant) where Emerson and Thoreau visited. **Wild Wings Ski Touring Center**(802-824-6793) in Peru, VT, is a family xc ski area with 20 km of groomed trails, rentals, lessons and hot refreshments and snacks.

Lessons (07/08 prices)

At the on-mountain Adventure Center you can try telemark skis, a snowboard, Snowblades or freeride skis designed for fun and tricks, especially in the halfpipe and terrain parks. Begin at Village Rentals in the Village Lodge in the Courtyard. Then, go on to the mountain to the rental tent to pick up equipment and finally up to the Ski & Snowboard School. Give yourself plenty of time or you'll miss your lesson.

Group lessons: $39 for 1.75 hours. Learn to Freestyle terrain park and halfpipe lessons for snowboarders are $45; $79 with rentals.

First-timer package: For skiers, $98 includes beginner lift ticket, two 1.75-hour lessons and rental equipment. Snowboarders take the Burton Learn to Ride program, also $98.

Private lessons: One hour: $105 holidays, $99 Saturdays, $95 Sunday mornings, $89 midweek. Half day: $315/$295/ $270/ $240. Full day: $540/$495/ $450/ $390.

Special programs: Stratton has women's ski and snowboard camps during the season designed to boost confidence and enhance strength, style and technique. Call for prices.

Children's Programs (07/08 prices)

Child care: Stratton's Childcare Center, in the Village Lodge, takes children from ages 6 weeks to 5 years and is open 8 a.m. to 5 p.m. Drop-off is under the upper parking deck. A full day with lunch and snack costs $95 midweek, $110 weekends, $115 holidays. A half-day morning costs $79 ($65 midweek); half-day afternoon costs $65. Reservations required; call 800-787-2886.

Children's lessons: An all-day Little Cub snow school program for ages 4 to 6 costs $110; half day costs $65. The Big Cub program for ages 7 to 12 is all day and costs $110; lift ticket is extra. A first-timer ski or snowboard package for ages 7 to 12, including beginner ticket, rentals and two 1.25-hour lessons costs $98.

Lift tickets (07/08 prices)

	Adult	Child (7–12)	13–17/65+
One day (holiday/weekend)	$78	$51	$66
One day (weekday)	$69	$55	$60
Three days (holiday/weekend)	$207/$176	$137/$126	$184/$149
Three days (weekday)	$155	$114	$134
Five days (holiday/weekend)	$280/$228	$180/$176	$242/$200
Five days (weekday)	$217	$174	$193

Who skis free: Children 6 and younger.

Who skis at a discount: Ages 65-69 pay the same as young adults. Ages 70 and older pay junior prices.

Accommodations

The town of Manchester is a tourism mecca with accommodations from giant resorts and B&Bs to a slew of lesser-priced roadside motels. The **Manchester and Mountains Chamber** (802-362-2100) and the **Londonderry Chamber** (802-824-8178) can help with arrangements. The hotels and B&Bs listed below are near the ski areas.

At Stratton: Lift and lodging packages (midweek, non-holiday) begin at $59 per person, per night, based on double occupancy. For reservations at any of Stratton's lodges, call 800-787-2886 (800-STRATTON). The **Long Trail House** units will comfortably house a family for an extended stay, with an outdoor heated pool, hot tubs and underground climate-controlled parking. The **Stratton Mountain Inn** is a full-service lodge that's also good for families. The **Liftline Lodge** provides Stratton's most economical lodging on the mountain and has many of the resort's restaurants. Stratton Reservations also has plenty of **condos** in the village and in the valley, all within easy reach of the slopes. Stratton Mountain packages offer great discounts. Children younger than age 6 stay and ski free anytime. Children 12 and younger stay free in the same room with their parents.

Nearby, in Jamaica (the town, not the Caribbean island), we highly recommend the elegant colonial **Three Mountain Inn** (800-532-9399; 802-874-4140; $$-$$$). On the Select Registry, it's cozy, elegant and the innkeepers strive to exceed your expectations. On Rte. 11, the **Swiss Inn** (800-847-9477; 802-824-3442; $-$$) has basic, clean rooms and a wonderful restaurant. For an upscale B&B, call The **Macartney House** (802-824-6444; $$-$$$). Near Bromley is the **Wiley Inn** (888-843-6600; 802-824-6600; $-$$), good for couples and families alike. The **Londonderry Inn** (802-824-5226; $$), on Rte. 100, has 25 individually decorated rooms.

These property management companies deal with condos throughout the area: Bondville Real Estate (888-U-love-VT; 297-3316) or Winhill Real Estate (800-214-5648; 297-1550).

Dining

At Stratton Mountain: **Verdé** (802-297-9200; $$-$$$) in the Landmark Hotel is the latest rave spot at Stratton. Entrees from the Mediterranean grill include wild mushroom crespelle and zarzuella, a Spanish fish stew.

Great Italian food is the main theme on the mountain, with **Mulberry Street** (802-297-3065; $$) serving basic pastas and pizzas. **Mulligan's** (802-297-9293; $$) serves moderately priced, basic American fare with a good kids' menu in a loud, TV-in-every-corner atmosphere. **Luna** (802-297-4032; $$-$$$) at the Stratton Mountain Club, is open to the public for dinner by reservation. The **Stone Chimney Grille** (802-297-2500) in the Stratton Mountain Inn specializes in family dining, with steaks, seafood and a salad bar.

At the **Soupman** (802-297-4376; $) there are several soups of the day along with sandwiches and salads. **Cafe on the Corner** (802-297-6020) is a good breakfast/brunch eatery. **Wired at the Copper Cup (802-856-1309)** is a good spot for lattes and the Internet. Newspapers are also sold here.

Off the mountain: At the base of the Stratton access road are several good restaurants. **Out Back at Winhall River** (802-297-3663; $$$), just south of the access road, has phenomenal lobster bisque along with other casual fare. It has live music on certain nights. The **Red Fox** (802-297-2488; $$-$$$) serves "Vermont" nouveau cuisine in a restored barn and has live music.

The award-winning **Three Clock Inn** (802-824-6327; $$$), in South Londonderry, brings a bit of authentic Provence to the hills of Vermont. An upscale favorite for Stratton regulars— many of whom owner/chef Serge Roche knows by name—the inn has a wine collection in keeping with its gourmet menu. Serge's **Pantry** in South Londonderry has delicious paninis and other sandwiches to go along with breakfast and a large variety of cooked dinner fare to take home. The **Three Mountain Inn** (800-532-9399 or 802-874-4140; $$$), in Jamaica, has an intimate and elegant dining room. The lobster with saffron-champagne butter and mushroom risotto is not to be missed.

The **Frog's Leap Inn** (802-824-3019; $$$) serves creative meals by candlelight. The **Garden Cafe** (802-824-9574; $$$) has been serving upscale meals for more than 15 years.

Jake's Cafe (802-824-6614; $) serves pizzas and sandwiches. **New American Grill** (802-824-9844; $-$$) has a great variety of entrees and casual dining at reasonable prices. **Johnny Seesaw's** (802-824-5533), just down the road from Bromley, offers high-end dining serving enormous portions and is a perfect family spot. Reserve well in advance.

Apres-ski/nightlife

At Stratton, apres-ski rocks on the deck of **Grizzly's** with delicious pizza and entertainment almost every weekend; in **Mulligan's** with its 50 different beers; or at the Stratton Mountain Inn's **Bear Bottom Pub**. Come evening, the on-mountain action continues in the **Green Door Pub** in Mulligan's, with live entertainment on Saturdays and big-screen football on Sundays, plus pool and foosball. The no-smoking bar has patio seating, daily drink specials and 10-cent wings on Fridays. The place is mobbed on weekends.

Off the mountain, try the locals' hangout, **Red Fox** in Bondville, for live music on weekends. If you're into the cigar and martini crazes, head to **Mulberry Street**. The **Perfect Wife**,in Manchester has live bands every weekend in season and live music four nights a week.

 ## Other activities

Phoenix, an under-21 club in Liftline, has **games, big-screen video, a DJ, snacks** and **smoothies**. It's open from 6 p.m. on weekends and holidays.

The Millhouse in the Commons area just behind the Long Trail and next to the Founders Lodge, Stratton's newest property has **ice skate rentals** and two skating ponds. Hours are 1-10 p.m. on Saturdays and holiday weeks, Sundays from 1-8 p.m.

Teens can go to the **Wreck** in the Stratton Sports Center. There are video games, a play-station, a climbing wall, courts for indoor soccer and an indoor skate park. A fixed-up **movie theater** in Manchester has two screens.

The **Riley Rink** (802-362-0150) in Manchester also has ice skating. The **Stratton Sports Center** (802-297-4230) has indoor tennis, racquetball, indoor pool, hot tubs, saunas, fitness center, tanning salons and massages.

There is **snowmobiling** at the resort and in the valley. **Sleigh rides** are offered by Horses for Hire (802-297-1468) in Rawsonville, just south of Bondville on Rte. 30, Karl Pfister's Sleigh Rides (802-824-4663) in Landgrove, near Bromley, Sun Bowl Ranch (802-297-5837) at Stratton and Taylor Farm Sleigh Rides (802-824-5690) in Londonderry.

Find **spa services** at the Avanyu Spa (800-362-4747), at the Equinox Resort in Manchester, which offers everything from Reiki to arnica sports massages to maple leaf scrubs. Or try The Spa at Stratton Mountain (802-297-3339), a full-service day spa open from 8 a.m.-9 p.m.

Shopping is a major non-ski activity in the Manchester region. About 40 factory outlet stores, including Coach, Brooks Brothers, Cole Hahn and Garnet Hill, are spread throughout Manchester, along with boutiques and shops with handcrafted regional gift items and unusual clothing. The mountain village has an assortment of shops ranging from apparel to crafts.

 ## Getting there and getting around

By air: Manchester is about 90 minutes from the Albany, N.Y. airport and requires a car for easy access.

By car: Manchester Center is at the intersection of Rtes. 7A and 30 in southwestern Vermont, about 140 miles from Boston and 235 miles from New York City. Stratton is on Rte. 30 about 20 miles east of Manchester. Look for the Stratton Mountain Road from Rte. 30. If you're heading straight for Stratton from I-91, take Exit 2 at Brattleboro, follow signs to Rte. 30, then drive 38 miles to Bondville and the Stratton Mountain Road. Bromley is six miles from Manchester traveling on Rte. 11, eight miles west of Londonderry.

Getting around: Bring a car.

Dining: $$$$–Entrees $30+; $$$–$20–$30; $$–$10–$20; $–less than $10.
Accommodations: (double room) $$$$–$200+; $$$–$141–$200; $$–$81–$140; $–$80 and less.

Nearby resorts

Bromley, Manchester Center, VT; 802-824-5522
Internet: www.bromley.com
9 lifts; 300 skiable acres; 1,334 vertical feet; 3 terrain parks; 1 halfpipe

Bromley, 6 miles east of Manchester, is a no-nonsense, function-over-fashion ski resort. Its base area consists of a lodge. Period. Slopeside are a hotel, some condos and a few private homes, but no stores or restaurants. People come to Bromley to ski, ride and hang out with their friends and families on its usually sun-drenched slopes. Although significantly smaller than Stratton, Bromley has trails for everyone, from gentle beginner runs that wind down the mountain through the woods to expert pistes with shots through the trees.

Lift tickets (07/08): One day for adults, $63/$66 weekend/holiday and $25 midweek; ages 7–12, $39/$42; ages 13–17, $55/$58.

Lodging: For slopeside lodging stay at **Bromley Sun Lodge** (800-722-2159; 824-6941; $-$$$). Condos and private homes (up to four bedrooms) are either slopeside or fed by a shuttle to the base lodge.

Distance from Boston: Manchester Center is at the intersection of Rtes. 7A and 30 in southwestern Vermont, about 140 miles from Boston and 235 miles from New York City. Bromley is 6 miles from Manchester traveling on Rte. 11, just 8 miles west of Londonderry.

Vermont Regional Resorts

Ascutney Mountain Resort, Brownsville, VT; 802-484-7711; 800-243-0011
Internet: www.ascutney.com
5 lifts; 55 trails; 1,800 vertical feet

Ascutney, off I-91 on the New Hampshire/Vermont border, is a mid-sized resort that appeals to young families with a variety of activities both on and off the hill, including tubing, ice skating, pizza parties, torchlight parades and a good children's ski school. Recent years have seen big improvements here, including a high-speed quad to a new summit, improved snowmaking and an enhanced children's learning area. Ascutney's terrain is a good mix for advanced and intermediate skiers and riders, with plenty of narrow, twisting old-style New England trails. There's a separate beginner area that's perfect for learning or for skiing with little ones. The base area is anchored by a 240-room ski-in/ski-out hotel.

Lift tickets (07/08): Adults, $60 weekend/holiday and $56 weekday; juniors (7–16) and seniors (65–65), $44 weekend/holiday. Those 6 and younger, and 70 and older, ski free.

Distance from Burlington: About 105 miles south I-89, I-91, Rte. 5 and Rte. 44. Ascutney is about 130 miles from Albany, NY, and about 130 miles from Boston or Hartford, Ct.

Lodging information/reservations: 800-243-0011.

Snowshoe
West Virginia

Summit: 4,800 feet
Vertical: 1,500 feet
Base: 3,200 feet

Address: 10 Snowshoe Drive, Snowshoe, WV 26209
Telephone (main): 877-441-4386
Snow Report Number: 304-572-4636
Toll-free reservations: 877-441-4386
E-mail: info@snowshoemtn.com
Internet: www.snowshoemtn.com

Expert: ★
Advanced: ★★
Intermediate: ★★★★★
Beginner: ★★★★★
First-timer: ★★★

Lifts: 14—3 high-speed quads, 2 quads, 6 triples, 2 surface lifts, 1 moving carpet
Skiable acreage: 244
Snowmaking: 100 percent
Uphill capacity: 22,900
Parks & pipes: 4 parks, 1 pipe
Bed base: 1,800 condo & lodge rooms
Nearest lodging: Slopeside
Child care: Yes, 12 weeks and older
Adult ticket, per day: $70 (08/09)
Dining: ★★★★
Apres-ski/nightlife: ★★
Other activities: ★★★

"Northern exposure with southern hospitality" is the way Snowshoe folks like to describe themselves. The ski area gets nearly 200 inches of annual snowfall, so you've got to admit they have a point. The vast majority of the nearly half million skiers who come here annually live well south of the Mason-Dixon line.

Snowshoe Resort is the closest "big mountain" skiing to be found in the South. It's the region's most elaborate and extensive, and it does very well by its core customers. It attracts a curious blend of D.C. bureaucrats, Nashville nurses and Atlanta attorneys. Most love to ski and come here because it's close and has great facilities. Some come just to experience snow, struggle through skiing and party up a storm. The terrain is approachable with superb snowmaking and grooming that allows low-intermediates and intermediates to have a good time. Pickings are slim for the true advanced and expert skier.

The resort comprises three areas: Snowshoe, Silver Creek and the Western Territory, each with its own personality. The Silver Creek section is excellent for families, especially those with younger children, with its combination of single-facility, ski-in/out lodging, night skiing, terrain park and snow tubing. It's also less crowded than the other areas, and the slopes are wider and better designed than at the Snowshoe area, but the skiing is less challenging.

This is an "upside down" resort: The base facilities are at the summit. A mountaintop village has been under construction for several years and a lodge, condominiums, restaurants, shops and a new conference hall have been and continue to be added, including Seneca Lodge, a 62-unit facility at the Village at Snowshoe. In the state-of-the-art rental shop, Expedition Rentals, 20 flat screen televisions display the latest resort and other information.

Three new slopes opened for the 2007-08 season, Sawmill Glades, Sawmill and Camp 99, all served by the Soaring Eagle Express high-speed quad chair. These runs now provide ski-in/out access for the new Sawmill Village, a gated community of eco-friendly, single family homes.

Mountain layout

Experts will find challenge on two trails in The Western Territory, which is across the street from the rest of the trails. This ensures that only skiers and riders who want to be here are here. The trails opened in 2007-08, Sawmill Glades, Sawmill and Camp 99, are also rated expert. The rest of the resort caters to intermediates and lower levels, with a nicely isolated area for first-timers and novices.

◆◆**Expert,**◆ **Advanced:** To reach The Western Territory, site of the expert terrain, you must cross the street. Literally. It's across the access road from Snowshoe; a shuttle bus transports skiers between Silver Creek and the Snowshoe/Western Territory areas. Given the predominance of once-a-year ski-weekers, this area is usually least crowded. It has just two runs, Cupp Run and Shay's Revenge, which take advantage of Snowshoe's total vertical drop. Both earn their black-diamond rating. At moments along Cupp's, nifty little places can be found to zip into the trees. The lower section of Shay's is significantly steep and often bumps up.

At Snowshoe, Sawmill Glades, Sawmill and Camp 99, are rated black.

Silver Creek holds two trails marked black, Flying Eagle and Bear Creek. While these have short sections that present some pitch, competent intermediates can handle them.

■ **Intermediate:** This is an intermediate skier's delight. More than one-third of the runs here are rated blue-square. At the Snowshoe area, the best runs are Ball Hooter and Skip Jack, which lead down to the Ball Hooter and Grabhammer chairs respectively. On packed weekends, traffic can be a problem here. Another interesting, less-traveled option is the Upper Flume/J Hook/Lower Widowmaker route, found to skier's far right off the Widowmaker chair. Even though the Northern Tract is rated beginner, it is a great place to find untracked powder after a storm.

At Silver Creek, Fox Chase-to-Laurel Run offers the most extended blue-rated run. Cascade and Slaymaker-to-Spur are also good cruisers, but none is particularly long. An intermediate will have a blast at Silver Creek amidst much smaller crowds compared to Snowshoe.

●●**Beginner,** ●**First-timer:** The resort caters to green-level skiers and riders. At the far left, off Snowshoe's top ridge, is the Northern Tract, a comfortably isolated group of a half dozen easy trails that gives green-trail skiers their own lift-served real estate off the Powderidge chair. These trails are wide enough to be reassuring, but meander a bit to lend texture.

Silver Creek's green-rated runs are generally short but very welcoming, presenting a good place for first-timers to begin the transition to more general terrain. Cubb Run gently hugs the far right edge of the area and allows access to three chairlifts.

The good news is that the Skidder area for first-timers is just a few steps from the Shavers Center, home to the ski school and rental shop. The bad news is that it's laid out laterally on the ridge top and can become a bit frenzied with skiers and riders passing through en route to other parts of the hill. The terrain itself is conducive to learning: short, wide and gentle.

Snowboarding

The resort's terrain is generally snowboarder-friendly, with a minimum of crossover trails and relatively few spots that require unstrapping and pushing. Riders can add some texture to the general cruising nature of the main mountain by taking the short detour onto the Knot Bumper/Glades combination off the Ball Hooter chair. The resort stages a variety of competitions and other events throughout the season, so keep an eye on the calendar.

Parks and pipes

The Super Park at Silver Creek is spread across seven trails: Timberjack, Mountaineer, Cascade, Fox Chase, Laurel Run, Bear Claw and Buck Saw. This park includes a variety of aerial features, rails and boxes. You'll also find a 400-foot halfpipe. A boardercross course on Slaymaker and Spur includes gates, berms and rollers.

On the Snowshoe side is the Spruce Glades Pro Park near the top of the Ballhooter lift. The Pro Park requires a $5 park pass that you receive after watching a safety video. The park has rails, spines and steps, plus tabletops and jumps that range from 35 to 50 feet.

The Spruce Glades Terrain Garden at Snowshoe, a beginner terrain park, has a few small rails, a funbox and small snow features for aerials. Silver Creek's Mountaineer Terrain Garden also provides an introduction to riding rails and getting air for the novice.

Cross-country & snowshoeing (see also xcskiresorts.com)

The resort's cross-country skiing operates out of the **Snowshoe Outdoor Adventure Center** (304-572-5477), between Snowshoe and Silver Creek. The trail system covers 40 km. along the Cheat Mountain Ridge Trail, as well as through the backcountry. The center is fully equipped with rentals and offers instruction.

The **Elk River Inn** (304-572-3771), in Slatyfork about 5 miles from the bottom of the Snowshoe access road, has a touring center and immediate access to 5 km. of adjacent groomed trails. Another 35 km. can be accessed nearby. Rentals and instruction by appointment.

Lessons (07/08 prices)

The Snowshoe Ski and Snowboard School is in the main resort complex's Shavers Center, and adjacent to Silver Creek's Silver Creek Lodge.

Group Lessons: Lessons for ages 13 and older (skiing or snowboarding) are 1.75 hours long. Cost is $54.

Private Lessons: A 5-hour lessons costs $399; 4-hour, 329; 3-hour, $249; 2-hour, $179; 1-hour session, $109. Additional people, $39/hour. Reservations advised; call 877-441-4386 or 304-572-1000.

Special programs: Snowshoe offers adaptive lessons and a variety of race programs.

Children's Programs (07/08 prices)

Child care: For ages 12 weeks to 12 years old. Ages 12 weeks up to 2 years old the cost is $80 all day with lunch; $45 half day without lunch; $15 per hour with a two-hour minimum. Ages 2–12 cost $70 all day with lunch; $40 half day without lunch; $12 per hour with two-hour minimum. Reservations required; call 877-441-4386 or 304-572-1000.

Children's lessons: Lessons for ages 4–12 have two groups: ages 4–6 (skiers only) and 7–12 (skiers and snowboarders), based also on ability level. The half-day sessions run from 9–11:45 a.m. and 1–3:45 p.m. Cost is $74. Rates do not include lift tickets, equipment rental or lunch. Reservations recommended.

Special activities: The Kids' Night Out program is offered Wednesdays, Fridays and Saturdays from 6 to 9 p.m. for ages 5–12. It costs $45 and includes arts and crafts, snowshoeing, bonfires, storytelling, and other indoor and outdoor activities. Reservations suggested.

Lift tickets (07/08 prices)

One day (weekends): adult $70, child (6-12) $55. Multi-day (per day/weekends): adult $69, child $54. One day weekday: adult $55, child $44.

Who skis free: Children 6 and younger.

Who skis at a discount: Students with ID and seniors (65+) pay $65 for one day (weekends); $64 per day for multi-day (weekends).

Who skis at a discount: Students with ID and seniors (65+) pay $50 weekdays. There are additional discounts for guests staying at resort lodging. Early/late-season prices are less.

Notes: Night skiing tickets, 4:30-10 p.m., and a Twilight Skiing pass valid 12:30-10 p.m are sold. A one-day ticket is valid from 8:30 a.m. to 10 p.m. Holiday prices are higher.

Accommodations

The resort is in the process of creating a signature base village (in this case, at the mountain's top) at Snowshoe. It holds a vast array of housing of all types, including some 1,500 condominium and lodge units and, at the base of the access road, a nice but basic motel. For **reservations**, call 877-441-4386 or 304-572-5262.

Allegheny Springs Lodge ($$-$$$$), near the Ballhooter lift, is the poshest lodging in the Village at Snowshoe. Studio, one-, two- and three-bedroom units are elegantly understated. The lodge also features a front desk with concierge and valet service, hearth room with two fireplaces and library, exercise room, a fresh-water thermal pool in the courtyard, hot tubs, a full-service restaurant and a day spa.

Sawmill Village is a gated community of eco-friendly single family homes, all outfitted with Energy Star appliances. **Rimfire Lodge** ($$-$$$$) is set in the heart of the pedestrian village. It has hotel rooms, plus studio, one- and two-bedroom units. Accommodations are comfortable, but smaller units can be a bit cramped. Most units have kitchens, all have gas-fired fireplaces, and guests get the advantage of underground parking. The intra-resort shuttle stops at the door. **Highland House** ($$-$$$$) overlooks the Ballhooter lift. Units run the gamut from hotel rooms and so-called deluxe hotel rooms to two-bedroom condos with a den.

Silver Creek Lodge ($$-$$$$) is the 240-unit, self-contained base facility at Silver Creek. Accommodations range from studios to four-bedroom condos, plus a penthouse. This is an ideal site for families with young children, as the tubing hill, night skiing, terrain park, kids' ski school, child care, rental shop, pool and other amenities are right there.

Expedition Station ($$-$$$) has 100 units set right in the heart of things—and at the top of the resort's main trails. Units run from studios to three-bedrooms, and feature all the expected amenities. **Soaring Eagle Lodge** ($$-$$$$); the first phase of this eventual 140-unit collection. It features luxury condos ranging from studios to three-bedrooms, with such amenities as flat screen televisions, high-speed Internet and direct access to the new high-speed Widowmaker quad lift. **Inn at Snowshoe** ($-$$) sits at the base of the access road six miles from the summit village. It has 150 rooms, including some one-bedroom suites.

Off the mountain, the area has a handful of nice B&B's. The **Elk River Inn** (304-572-3771; $-$$) is comprised of a 10-room inn, a five-room farmhouse with three shared baths and kitchen, and five kitchen-equipped cabins. It's 5 miles from the access road and offers breakfast, an excellent restaurant and on-site Nordic skiing, as well as its own snowboard shop.

The **Morning Glory Inn** (304-572-5000; $-$$$) is 3 miles from the access road. It has six large bedrooms with oversized jetted-tub bathrooms, a large, homey, public living room and a full breakfast that's substantial and homemade. The **Brazen Head Inn** (304-339-6917;

$-$$$), 7 miles north of the mountain on Rte. 219, offers comfortable B&B lodging and dining. The 20-room roadside lodge also has dining and features an Irish-style pub.

 ## Dining

This resort is a beacon of creative, gourmet dining in West Virginia. The **Foxfire Grill** (304-572-5555; $$-$$$) puts fun into the dining experience with a menu that's irreverent and hillbilly tasty. Make sure to try the southern barbecue, fried bologna sammich, the ribs and have a fried PB&J for dessert.

Modeled after the Harris Grille in Charlotte, North Carolina, **The Village Bistro** (304-572-2213; $$-$$$) prides itself on its "international cuisine with a southern-American flair" and features daily blue-plate specials. The large bar area has great views of Snowshoe Mountain. The decor at the **Junction Restaurant** (304-572-5800; $$) hearkens back to logging boom times and the heyday of Shay steam locomotives, with memorabilia from the nearby Cass Scenic Railroad. The food is classic American fare and reasonably good. **Hoot's Bar and Grill**, only steps from the Soaring Eagle Express lift, features appetizers, burgers, dogs and other munchies. **The Cheat Mountain Pizza Company** (304-572-5757; $-$$) serves uninspired pizza, as well as salads, calzones and other Italian fixins.

For a unique dinner adventure, head to the **Sunrise Back Country Hut** (304-572-5477; $$$$). After a two-mile ride on snowmobile or all-terrain vehicle, enjoy an elegant meal in a beautiful, isolated, rustic setting for $175 per couple. Also unique is **Red Rover** (304-572-4444; $-$$), a "hot-doggery" and wine bar, where dogs are paired with beers and wines.

The terrific waffle breakfast at **The Boathouse** (304-572-1000; $), a rustic day lodge at the base of the Ballhooter Lift, is a great way to start the day. Lunch is also available. At Silver Creek the **Black Run Sugar House** (304-572-5746; $) serves fine flapjacks slathered with West Virginia maple syrup. Also in the village are a **Starbucks** and **The Blue & Gray Cafe**, which serves panini sandwiches, soups, and salads. **Shavers Centre Food Court** has Burger Slope and Souper, offering burgers, homemade stews and salads, plus **Moonshine**, a bar.

The loss of one of the state's best restaurants, the Red Fox in 2006 is regrettable. But, **Ember**, (304-572-1111; $$-$$$) in the Soaring Eagle Lodge, compensates somewhat with items like fresh grilled fish, steaks, sushi and Thai specialties.

Off mountain, the **Restaurant at the Elk River Inn** (304-572-3771; $$$) serves a changing menu of truly gourmet regional and international dishes, superb desserts and a nice selection of local microbrews. Reservations are recommended.

Apres-ski/nightlife

A surprising amount of activity goes on here after dark, including night skiing. If you're looking for a bar scene or club, you can easily find it.

For immediate apres-ski head to **The Junction**, packed with tourists, or to **Foxfire Grill** and hang out with patrollers and instructors. Foxfire keeps heating up and the crowd stays late. **Yodeler's Pub** also draws a good bar crowd as the day skiing ends and then again late in the evening. **The Boiler Room**, a bit out of the way at the top of the Widowmaker lift, serves unremarkable burgers and Mexican fare, but somehow manages to have one fine bar. Gregarious bartenders, good brew and a friendly locals' atmosphere make it a good spot for a drink.

Later on Snowshoe keeps rocking. **The Connection** is the hottest spot on the mountain. Yes, it's in the Shavers Centre base facility, so there's nothing exotic about it, but the upstairs club scene really does rock. Live bands and a DJ are a regular feature, plus there's pool, foosball, some video games and a large-screen TV. The partying usually lasts well into the night.

Dining: $$$$–Entrees $30+; $$$–$20–$30; $$–$10–$20; $–less than $10.
Accommodations: (double room) $$$$–$200+; $$$–$141–$200; $$–$81–$140; $–$80 and less.

Comedy Cellar Bar (304-572-5440 for performance information) is squirreled away in the basement of the Mountain Lodge. The bar itself is small and intimate and open nightly Tuesdays - Saturdays at 9 p.m. Local Roy Riley shares the small stage with pros on the national circuit for an evening of stand-up comedy. It's adult entertainment, and it's lots of fun.

If you're staying over on the family-oriented Silver Creek side, you have two choices right in Silver Creek Lodge. **The Bear's Den** is a fine spot for a quiet beer or hot drink on a cold day. At **Misty's Sports Bar**, you can quench your thirst while playing billiards or foosball.

Other activities

The Big Top at Snowshoe Mountain, adjacent to the Shavers Centre base lodge, is a 15,000 square-foot family fun center. Indoors, it houses an arcade with 60-plus video games, table games, billiards and a video cafe. Outdoors, is a Eurobungy. And, there's a stage and performance area, as well. Snowshoe Resort offers **snowmobiling tours**. The cost for a one-hour tour is $100/person midweek and $125 on weekends/holidays; ages 6-15 ride for $45. Extended backcountry tours for experienced drivers cost $150. Reservations can be made at the Adventure Center in the base village.

The spectacular **Split Rock Pools**, just across from Allegheny Springs, has an exceptional **water slide** for the kids and **hot tubs** for the adults. Entrance is included with packages booked through Snowshoe Central Reservations. The tubing hill at **Ruckus Ridge Adventure Park** at Silver Creek costs $17 per person for two hours.

Spa Vantage (304-572-0804), at the Vantage, offers massages, manicures and pedicures, waxing, facials, hair salon, workout facility, men's and women's saunas and outdoor hot tubs. This is the only fitness center open to the public. Treatment prices range from $15 for waxing to $120 for an 80-minute Swedish massage or stone therapy.

Nobody is going to mistake this place for a shopper's paradise. The base village represents an attempt to lure some interesting **shops**, but it's minimal. We like The Chocolate Factory (304-572-1289) because, well, who doesn't love chocolate? Wildcat Provisions sells provisions for your condo, but beware the high-elevation prices. If you're heading to a condo, best to pack in supplies from your local supermarket, then add absolute necessities, or must-be-fresh stuff here. It also rents videos and VCRs, sells gas and makes some pretty good sandwiches.

Getting there and getting around

By air: Roanoke, Va., airport is about three hours from the resort. Yeager Airport in Charleston, W.V., is about 3.5 hours away. Greenbrier Valley Airport in Lewisburg, W.V., about 1.5 hours from Snowshoe, is only served by US Airways, but offers the Greenbrier Valley Airport Shuttle (304-536-1193) for those who choose not to drive.

By car: You're going to end up driving here, even if you fly, since the nearest sizable airport is nearly three hours away. The resort is on Rte. 66 off Rte. 219, about 45 miles south of Elkins, W.V. It's rather remote no matter from which direction you approach. From the south or the west, take I-64, exit at White Sulphur Springs, then take Hwy. 92 and 39 to Marlinton, until you see the Snowshoe signs. From the north, take I-79, exit at Weston (Highway 33 at exit 9), go to Elkins, then south on Hwy. 219. From the East, it's I-81 to Staunton, Rte. 42/39 west to Rte. 28 south; or, from Harrisonburg, Va., take Rte. 33 west to Rte. 28 south.

Getting around: As long as you're on the mountain, the shuttle bus will reliably get you where you need to go. If you want to go off-mountain, you're going to need that car. Parking is a bit chaotic; however, Rimfire Lodge has underground parking.

Alyeska
Alaska

Summit:	2,750 feet
Vertical:	2,500 feet
Base:	250

Address: P.O. Box 249, Girdwood, AK 99587
Telephone (main): 907-754-1111
Snow Report Number: 907-754-7669
Toll-free reservations: 800-880-3880
Reservations outside U.S.: 907-754-1111
E-mail: info@alyeskaresort.com
Internet: www.alyeskaresort.com

Expert:★★★
Advanced:★★
Intermediate:★★★★
Beginner:★★
First-timer:★★

Lifts: 9—1 60-passenger tram, 1 high-speed quad, 2 quads, 3 doubles, 2 surface lifts
Skiable acreage: 1,400
Snowmaking: 42 percent
Uphill capacity: 11,416
Parks & pipes: 2 parks, 1 pipe
Bed base: 533
Nearest lodging: Slopeside, hotel
Child care: Babysitting services
Adult ticket, per day: $55 (08/09)

Dining:★★★★
Apres-ski/nightlife:★★
Other activities:★★★

Alyeska offers convenient, big-mountain skiing without the threat of altitude sickness. It also boasts an average of more than 700 inches of snow.

Just 40 miles southeast of Anchorage, Alyeska offers convenient, big-mountain skiing without the threat of altitude sickness. A 60-passenger tram and the high-speed quad that services the summit mean lift lines are short on weekends, nonexistent midweek. Alyeska averages more than 700 inches of snow each season, and had a high of 1,116 inches a few years back.

The Hotel Alyeska provides luxurious accommodations at the tram base. The tram zips up 2,028 feet of Alyeska's 2,500-foot rise in just three-and-a-half minutes, rising over the forested lower half to the glaciers and open bowls near the summit and providing a birds-eye view of the mountain's two faces—the original main face and the newer North Face.

Contrary to popular opinion, the weather in this part of Alaska is quite tolerable in winter, with temperatures an average of 10 to 30 degrees Fahrenheit. What can make it seem colder here is the darkness that prevails during the heart of winter. By mid-February, however, Alyeska boasts more daylight hours than any other ski area in North America. And here's a real bonus for late-night revelers: Lifts don't even open until 10:30 a.m., meaning you can sleep in, have breakfast and get first tracks. Normal closing time is 5:30 p.m., but on Friday and Saturday nights from mid-December until mid-March, the lifts remain open to 9:30 p.m.

When Alyeska's skies are clear, the skiing is great. But the slopes sometimes are blanketed with severe whiteout or flat light conditions (we've checked with several ski journalists on this, and every one said this happened during part of their visit). Such conditions can be unnerving, especially above treeline, and can cause vertigo in susceptible skiers. Locals advise skiing at night (or late in the day) when visibility is better.

Mountain layout

Intermediates will have a field day here, especially with the wide-open bowls and spectacular views from the top of the Spirit quad. Experts have some good drops but the real challenge of Alyeska is the tremendous variety of terrain and snow conditions from top to bottom. Snow may be groomed, cut up or untouched. Sometimes it's powder at the top, moistening to mashed potatoes at the bottom. An extended snowmaking improvement will include coverage from the bottom of the mountain to the top of the tram. These upgrades were scheduled for the 2007-08 season allowing the entire mountain to open by Thanksgiving.

Expert, Advanced: The high-speed quad Spirit of Alyeska carries skiers 1,411 vertical feet to the top of the lift-serviced terrain, which is at the base of the Alyeska Glacier. Up here it's wide-open, above-treeline skiing. The entire 2,500 feet of ver-tical is skiable in one continuous run, with intermediate to super-expert pitch depending on your choice of route.

From the quad, experts can go right and drop down Gail's Gully or Prospector and take a gully left or right of Eagle Rock, then back to the quad. Experts willing to work can take the High Traverse from the quad, arcing through The Shadows between Mt. Alyeska and Max's Mountain, and dropping down through new snow and open steeps; or continue over the ridge to find good steeps and a short section of gladed skiing on Max's Mountain (when opened by the ski patrol).

The lower half of the steep North Face makes it possible to ski double-black terrain from the upper to the lower tram terminal. You can scout out this gnarly area while you ride up the tram. The upper part (called Tram Pocket) is above treeline; the lower part is heavily forested with two trails—Jim's Branch and Last Chance. Descend Tram Pocket, then cut over to the rest of Alyeska's runs to avoid the gladed area below.

Intermediate: Alyeska also has an unusual combination of open-bowl skiing and trails through the trees directly under Chairs 1 and 4. Intermediates can take the quad chair, drop into the bowl and ski whatever you can see. It doesn't take much judgment to figure out whether you are getting in over your head, and this bowl gives you plenty of room to traverse out of trouble. The bowl funnels into Waterfall and ends on Cabbage Patch before reaching the base area.

For intermediates taking the Spirit quad chair to the top of the resort, swing left when you get off the chair and follow the Mighty Mite. This takes you past the Glacier Express restaurant in the Glacier Tram Terminal, and back to the quad by three intermediate routes, or tip down South Face (very steep and ungroomed).

Beginner: Beginners should stick to the area served by Chairs 3 and 7. The area is pretty big, but unfortunately used by everyone on their way home. The terrain park has moved to Tanaka providing more beginnner terrain runs on Chairs 3 and 7. New magic carpets in this area will eliminate the tow type lift and make life for the beginner skier and snowboarder a bit easier.

First-timer: Don't make the long trip to Alyeska solely to learn to ski. Not a huge amount of easy terrain, plus the flat light problem, could put a serious crimp in those plans. If "the Alaska experience" (scenery, dogsledding in Iditarod country, being able to brag you "survived" Alaska in winter) is your main goal, then definitely make the trip. You can find some great things to do off the slopes while everyone else skis.

Parks and pipes

Alyeska's two machine-built terrain parks below Eagle Rock and at Tanaka have several tabletops, rails and quarterpipes. They're the best bets on icy days. Throughout the season, the resort builds one or two halfpipes near the base of Tanaka Hill that are well maintained with a halfpipe groomer.

Snowboarding

Because of Mt. Alyeska's natural topography—with its steep vertical and rocky slopes—the entire mountain becomes a natural terrain park under a blanket of snow.

Cat trails cut across several sections of the upper part of the mountain, creating a series of awesome cat-track jumps. You can catch great air coming off the cat track just above Gun Mount 2. Jumps in "The Fridays" on North Face are a snowboarder's dream, as are hits on Half Moon and Horseshoe off the Silvertip Run. Many aren't on the trail map, so ask the locals and they'll gladly share some secret spots. Heading down the mountain is Lolo's Leap, with 10- to 30-foot drops into the trees.

Keep your speed up going into Ego Flats in the bowl area and on the Prince Run heading back to the tram base and the Hotel Alyeska or you'll be walking.

In spring, wait until after noontime for the snow to soften for the best riding. The best-kept local's secret at Alyeska is anytime it's raining on the bottom, you can count on it dumping lots of fresh pow up top!

Cross-country & snowshoeing (see also xcskiresorts.com)

The 10-km. **Winner Creek trail** leaves from Alyeska's base and winds through woods, across meadows and up and down gentle hills. The trail is not groomed, and locals recommend it for snowshoeing.

Groomed and tracked trails are located in the nearby **Moose Meadow** area—locals will point you there. It's groomed and tracked by a volunteer trails committee. Rental equipment is available at the Hotel Alyeska's rental shop. In spring, you need to wait late enough into the morning for the ice cover to melt. Lessons are not regularly scheduled, so make advance reservations with the ski school by calling 907-754-2280.

If you are a serious cross-country enthusiast, Anchorage is the place to go. You can find nearly 115 km. of groomed cross-country trails in **Kincaid, Russian Jack** and **Far North Bicentennial** parks. Kincaid Park is the best developed with more than 1,500 acres covered by trails for all abilities. The Nordic Skiing Association of Anchorage (907-561-0949; grooming report, 907-248-6667) maintains the trails, all supported by donations and volunteer labor (Hint: If you use the trails, please make a donation.). NSAA puts out a great map of the trails, printed on a water-resistant paper.

Lessons (07/08prices)

Group lessons: Alyeska packages its ski and snowboard lessons, a real benefit for those traveling from the Lower 48. For example, adult intermediate and advanced skiers can get a lesson, lift ticket and rentals for $75, or the lesson alone for $40. (The snowboard price is $80 for the package, $40 for just the lesson.) Beginner skiers and snowboarders pay $60 for a package, $40 for just the lesson.

First-timer package: First-timers pay $60 for a lift ticket-lesson-rental package; for the lesson alone, $40.

Private lessons: Skiing, telemarking or snowboarding cost $60 for one hour, $30 for extra students. Telemarking lessons are not regularly scheduled, so make advance reservations with the ski school, 907-754-2280. If you're enrolled in a private lesson, ask about discounted lift and rental prices.

Special programs: The Challenge Alaska Adaptive Ski School, a chapter of Disabled Sports USA, provides skiing for the disabled: all disabilities, all ages, by reservation only. A skier with a disability and buddy, can buy discount lift tickets and rent adaptive ski equipment. Open daily, usually December 15 to April 15. The Hotel Alyeska and Tramway are fully wheelchair-accessible, and Challenge Alaska has material on other wheelchair-accessible accommodations and amenities. Challenge Alaska, 3350 Commercial Drive, Suite 208, Anchorage AK 99501; phone 907-783-2925.

Racing: A $1-per-run race course is open on selected dates.

Children's programs (08/09 prices)

Child care: Ages 6 months to 10 years. At **Little Bears Playhouse** in nearby Girdwood, children ages 6 to 14 months cost $40 for a half day and $55 for a full day. Kids 15 months to 35 months are $27 for a half day, $41 for a full day. For children ages 3 to 10, the cost is $35 for a half-day, $49 for a full day. An up-to-date immunization record and a complete physical exam signed by a doctor are required. Reservations are a must; call 907-783-2116 or ask when you reserve lodging. Little Bears is open 7 a.m. to 6 p.m. weekdays, 10 a.m. to 6 p.m. on Saturdays, through the ski season (closed on Sundays). Babysitting is no longer available at the resort.

Children's lessons: Cubs and Super-Cubs cater to ages 3–4 learning to ski; Mini-Riders is for ages 5–7 learning to snowboard. Cost is $50, including lift ticket, one-hour lesson and rental; available only on weekends, holidays and during Anchorage School District spring break. Group lessons for ages 5–13 for skiing and 8–13 for snowboarding are offered daily. A two-hour lesson, all-day lift ticket and rental package ranges from $55–$65, depending on ability level. If you don't need rentals, ask about discounted pricing.

Lift tickets (08/09 prices)

	Adult	Child (8-13)
One day	$55	$35
Three days*	$150 ($50/day)	$85 ($28/day)

* The best deal on multiday tickets comes with lodging-lift packages.

Who skis at a discount: Students with ID (14-17) and seniors (60-69) pay $40 for one day. Ages 70 and older pay $10 for one day. Children 7 and under ski free with a ticketed adult; otherwise they pay $10. A lift ticket for Chairs 3 and 7 only costs $25 for anybody.

Note: Keep in mind that Alaskan winter days are shorter than they are farther south. The lifts don't start running until mid-morning at 10:30 a.m., but the "ski day" ends at 5:30 p.m. (Daylight lingers for about 90 minutes after the sun sets in early February, and you can see very well.) Night skiing on 27 trails covering 2,000 vertical feet runs Fridays and Saturdays 4:00-9:00 p.m. mid-December through mid-March: Adults, juniors, seniors 60-69 and students cost $35; children $25; and seniors 70 and older, $10.

Accommodations

Because Alaska is quite a distance for most of Ski America & Canada's readers, air-lodging-lift packages are a good idea. **Daman-Nelson Travel**

(800-343-2626; www.daman-nelson.com) has great deals with round-trip air, lodging at the Hotel Alyeska, transfers and activity cards good for lift tickets, cross-country ski rentals or snowshoe rentals. Ask about packages that include the Iditarod and related festivities.

The **Hotel Alyeska** (800-880-3880; 907-754-1111; $$$-$$$$) is a self-contained resort which underwent major renovations for the 2007-08 season. Packages are the way to go, and package rates begin at $279 per room per night, single or double occupancy. This includes lodging, breakfast for two and two adult all-day lift tickets. That's an excellent deal for a hotel that has a $1,200-per-night Royal Suite. There is no charge for up to two children younger than 18 who are staying in the same room in existing bedding with a maximum of two adults. Though the hotel has 307 spacious rooms, several restaurants, shops and other guest facilities, it has a very intimate feel. Take the Alyeska Tramway right outside the door or ride Chair 7 to the lower-elevation terrain at the ski area's base.

Other than the hotel, lodging is in condos or bed-and-breakfast inns. **The Winner Creek Bed & Breakfast** (907-783-5501; $-$$) is a new log lodge owned by 30-year Alaska residents Victor and Kim Duncan. It's within walking distance of Alyeska. **Alyeska Accommodations** (907-783-2000) is a place to start, or get a list of B&Bs on the Girdwood community Web site, www.girdwoodalaska.com. B&B rates range from $45-$125 per night, based on double occupancy; condos range from $125-$250.

The larger bed base is in **Anchorage**, a 35- to 55-minute drive depending on weather:

Major hotels include the recently renovated **Anchorage Hilton** (800- HILTONS, 445-8667; 907-272-7411; $$$-$$$$), with views of the Chugach Mountains and Cook Inlet; **Holiday Inn** (800-HOLIDAY, 465-4329; 907-279-8671; $-$$); **Sheraton Anchorage** (800-478-8700; 907-276-8700; $$-$$$$); and **Westmark Anchorage** (800-544-0970; 907-276-7676; $-$$). The **Hotel Captain Cook** (800-843-1950; 907-276-6000; $$-$$$$), with its newly remodeled rooms and suits, has a great downtown location, very convenient to the Fur Rendezvous festivities, shopping and restaurants. It also has one of the best hotel health clubs we've come across. Another place we like downtown is the newly refurnished **Historic Anchorage Hotel** (800-544-0988; 907-272-4553; $$-$$$$). It's quietly elegant, with 10 suites (each different), 16 standard rooms and complimentary continental breakfast.

We've listed a small portion of the lodging that's available. We expected lodging prices to be rock bottom in winter, but Anchorage does a steady convention business then. Prices aren't as high as they are in summer, but most are in the $100 to $200 per night range. More options are listed in the excellent free Visitors Guide, available by writing to the **Anchorage Convention & Visitors Bureau**, 524 W. Fourth Ave., Anchorage, AK 99501-2212. Phone: 907-276-4118, fax 907-278-5559, Web site: www.anchorage.net.

Dining

In the Hotel Alyeska the **Pond Cafe** ($-$$) serves breakfast, lunch and dinner with a California-Alaskan menu—try the caribou stew with a big sourdough cheese roll and lots of vegetables. Elegant dinners are the Hotel's forté. We heartily recommend the **Katsura Teppanyaki** ($$$) open for dinner five nights a week. It seats about 20 diners around a U-shaped table facing the chefs who prepare the meals in front of you. Make plans for dinner at the four-diamond **Seven Glaciers Restaurant and Lounge** ($$$) on the second level of the Glacier Terminal at 2,300 feet. The view is beyond belief and the gourmet meals are excellent. You won't be desappointed. Call 907-754-2237 for reservations at all three. **The Bake Shop** (907-783-2831; $) in the ski area base lodge has superb soups, sandwiches and energy-filled, buttered sticky buns. Lots of locals, ski instructors and patrollers eat here.

Dining: $$$$–Entrees $30+; $$$–$20–$30; $$–$10–$20; $–less than $10.
Accommodations: (double room) $$$$–$200+; $$$–$141–$200; $$–$81–$140; $–$80 and less.

Alyeska vicinity:

Perhaps the best and most legendary restaurant in the area is the **Double Musky Inn** (907-783-2822; $$$), a mile from the lifts on Crow Creek Road. It's mind-boggling to find great Cajun food in Alaska (go for the French Pepper Steak). Service is excellent and the decor is a delight—Mardi Gras beads everywhere and posters on the ceiling. Busy nights may require a two-hour wait, but it's worth it. No reservations, opens at 5 p.m. Tuesday through Thursday, 4:30 p.m. Friday through Sunday; closed Mondays.

Chair Five (907-783-0933; $-$$) is casual and big on burgers and pizza, but also offers an interesting and changing menu of pasta, meats and fresh pasta. A favorite is pasta primavera with sundried tomatoes. It's in the Girdwood business district next to the Post Office. **Turnagain House** (907-653-7500; $$-$$$), a white-tablecloth restaurant looking out on Turnagain Arm halfway to Anchorage, has a reputation for fine seafood and excellent service.

Anchorage:

A special-occasion restaurant for local is **Simon & Seafort's Saloon & Grill** (907-274-3502; $$-$$$). It specializes in seafood and steak. Take a walk through the bar and try to find the on-purpose errors in the paintings. Ask for a table next to the large picture window and get there before dark so you can admire the view across Knik Arm. **Marx Brothers Cafe** (907-278-2133, reservations required; $$-$$$) is known for inventive continental cuisine, a notable wine list and impeccable service in a cozy frame-house setting that reminds us of a small New England inn. **Southside Bistro** (907-348-0888, reservations recommended; $$-$$$), with its highly inventive Italian and fusion cuisine, has frequent menu changes, a huge wine list, a bright and open atmosphere, excellent service and white tablecloths.

For great views, especially at cocktail time, try the top-floor **Crow's Nest** (907-276-6000; $$$) at the Hotel Captain Cook, or **Top of the World** (907-265-7111; $$$) in the Hilton. **Josephine's** (907-276-8700; $$$) in the Sheraton which also has a view, is a good choice for Sunday brunch. Make reservations if dining at any of these restaurants.

Many Japanese have settled in Anchorage, and restaurants such as **Akaihana** (907-276-2215; $$) and **Tempura Kitchen** (907-277-2741; $$) are among the Asian eateries. They offer tempura, sukiyaki and other cooked dishes as well as sushi and sashimi. Anchorage also has Thai, Chinese and Korean restaurants.

For moderately priced, delicious food—and great beer—head to **The Glacier Brew House Restaurant** (907-274-2739; $$) on Fifth Avenue.

Families should head to **Sourdough Mining Co.** (907-563-2272; $) for great ribs and corn fritters; **Hogg Brothers Cafe** (907-276-9649; $) for wow omelets; the **Royal Fork Buffet** (907 276-0089; $) or **Lucky Wishbone** (907-272-3454; $) for the best fried chicken. **Gwennie's Old Alaska Restaurant's** (907-243-2090; $) costumed staff serves big breakfasts and sandwiches midst historic photos.

 # Apres-ski/nightlife

The **Aurora Bar and Lounge** in the Hotel Alyeska has a somewhat lively atmosphere where skiers can watch sports on TV. Patrons may play the piano, sing, dance and make the evening as lively as they want. The lounge is quieter, with a stone fireplace, comfortable sofas and chairs. For apres-ski, head to the **Sitzmark Bar** at the base of Chair 3 for burgers and live bands on Friday and Saturday nights during ski season. The **Double Musky** and **Chair 5** also have taverns.

Anchorage has a highly developed nightlife and cultural scene, a legacy of pipeline days, long winter nights and generous doses of oil-patch money. The city reportedly had an orchestra before it had paved streets.

For loud rock and dancing try **Chilkoot Charlie's**, 2435 Spenard Rd., "where we cheat the other guy and pass the savings on to you." (They sell T-shirts with that slogan—it's a great souvenir.) Chilkoot's is huge—six bars with about 30 beers on tap, two stages. Generally, the ratio of men to women is about seven to one and any attire goes. .

Humpy's on Sixth Avenue has 36 beers on tap and occasional live entertainment. For quieter dancing and a slightly older clientele try **Legends** at the Sheraton, **Whale's Tail** at the Hotel Captain Cook, or the lounge at the **Golden Lion Best Western**. For country music, head to **Last Frontier Bar** or **Buckaroo Club**.

You may be surprised at the visiting artists and productions at the **Alaska Center for the Performing Arts** downtown. For recorded information, call 907-263-2901.

Other activities

The variety of winter activities is staggering. We list just a sampling. We encourage you to get the excellent free Visitors Guide from the **Anchorage Convention & Visitors Bureau**, 524 W. Fourth Ave., Anchorage, AK 99501-2212. Telephone: 907-276-4118; Web site: www.anchorage.net.

Think of Alaska in winter and you think of **dogsleds**. Call Chugach Dog Sled Tours in Girdwood near the ski area (907-783-2266) for reservations, Last-minute calls don't work. Or make reservations through the guest services desk at the Hotel Alyeska. If you're staying in Anchorage, drive about 20 minutes to the hamlet of Chugiak to Mush a Dog Team-Gold Rush Days (907-688-1391). As you travel the trail, you'll see a recreation of an Alaskan gold miner's camp. You'll be amazed at how cramped and cold those unheated tents must have been.

Dogsled races are a focal point of **Fur Rendezvous**, held annually in mid-February. The World Championship Sled Dog Race is the sprint (some sprint—25 miles a day for three days) counterpart to the more famous endurance race, The Iditarod, which is held after Fur Rondy on the first Saturday in March. Fur Rondy also has fireworks, a snow sculpture contest, a small carnival, a snowshoe softball tournament (hilarious for spectators) and the World Championship Dog Weight Pull, a contest detailed in Jack London's book, *Call of the Wild*. Alaskan Natives come from all parts of the state for Fur Rondy and many wear traditional fur parkas, stunning works of art with intricate patterns. By the way, if seeing people wearing fur offends you, don't come at this time. You'll only work yourself into a lather over something that has kept native Alaskans alive and warm for centuries. If you're a dog lover, don't miss the start of **The Iditarod**, when about 1,500 sled dogs are parked on main street in downtown Anchorage. Early in the morning, you can visit with the dogs and the mushers.

Several companies offer **flightseeing tours** via helicopter or fixed-wing planes. It is the best way to see Alaska's spectacular mountains and glaciers and well worth the cost. We flew with Era Helicopters (800-478-1947; 907-248-4422; www.eraaviation.com) into the rugged Chugach Mountains that border Anchorage. On an overcast day, you'll gain an appreciation for the arduous conditions that 19th-century mushers endured to bring supplies over mountain passes from Seward to Anchorage. On a clear day, you'll see Mt. McKinley off in the distance, its broad hulk standing apart from surrounding mountains. Alpine Air (907-783-2360) operates tours out of Girdwood. They will pick up at the Hotel Alyeska.

Alyeska offers **snowcat skiing** and **heli-skiing** with more than 750 square miles of back-country slopes. Chugach Powder Guides (907-783-4354) operates out of the Hotel Alyeska. A full-day heli-skiing package is $675, with a guarantee of 16,000-20,000 vertical. A full-day snowcat package is $150 standby, $195 by advance reservation. **Tandem paragliding** with

Dining: $$$$–Entrees $30+; $$$–$20–$30; $$–$10–$20; $–less than $10.
Accommodations: (double room) $$$$–$200+; $$$–$141–$200; $$–$81–$140; $–$80 and less.

a certified pilot 2,300 feet above the ski area is another thrill for visitors. Available daily in summer and by appointment in winter. Call Alyeska for more details, 907-754-2275.

Also operated out of the Alyeska Hotel are Alaska Heritage and Kenai Fjords Tours which offer **wildlife and glacier tours** of the local waters with the possibility of a visiting dinghy bearing oysters and lots of lore from a local oyster farmer. alaskaheritagetours.com, 907-276-6249; kenaifjords.com, 800-478-8068.

In Anchorage, the **Anchorage Museum of History and Art** (907-343-4326) is a must-see, with excellent displays that show 10,000 years of Alaskan civilization, from ancient days through the Gold Rush and the great earthquake of 1964. The **Alaska Native Heritage Center** (800-315-6608; 907-330-8000) provides an introduction to Alaska's native population. Although it's not fully open in winter, special events such as cultural gatherings and art shows are reason enough to visit.

In Seward, two hours' drive south of Alyeska Resort, you can visit the **Alaska SeaLife Center** (907-224-6300), funded by Exxon Valdez oil spill restoration funds and dedicated to understanding and maintaining the integrity of Alaska's marine ecosystem. It's a combination aquarium and museum, with interactive exhibits, displays and touch tanks for children.

Renown Charters and Tours (800-655-3806; 907-224-3806) offers an exciting wildlife cruise that circumnavigates Resurrection Bay and touches briefly into the Gulf of Alaska; transportation is available from the Hotel Alyeska.

The **Big Game Alaska Wildlife Center** (907-783-2025), just 10 miles south of Girdwood, is dedicated to the rehabilitation of orphaned and injured animals. Here you can get close enough to pet moose, Sitka deer, caribou and reindeer. Also on premises are birds of prey, buffalo and muskox. It's open daily, 10 a.m.-4 p.m.

If you need another reason to visit Alaska in the winter, the **Northern Lights** might be it. If you've ever seen photos of the aurora borealis, with its green, blue and red streaks of light across an ink-black sky, you have an inkling of how magnificent this phenomenon is. For forecasts on when to plan your trip to maximize the chances of seeing the Northern Lights, go to this Internet site: www.geo.mtu.edu/weather/aurora. The Hotel Alyeska has a unique Northern Lights wake-up service and a seven-minute electronic display of the aurora on the ceiling of the hotel's three-story lobby.

Getting there and getting around

By air: Anchorage International Airport is served by many major airlines. East Coast skiers who want to make the trek to Alyeska would be well advised to find a travel agent who specializes in Alaska in order to find the best airfares and packages.

By car: The Hotel Alyeska Resort is 45 miles south of downtown Anchorage. Get on Gambell Street south, which becomes the Seward Highway, Route 1, along Turnagain Arm, which has one of the highest tides in the world. The drive is quite scenic; try to alternate drivers so everyone can admire the view. Have your camera ready for the Dall sheep, moose and bald eagles often seen along the way. Turn left at the Girdwood/Alyeska highway turn-off. The resort is three miles up the road.

Getting around: If you stay in downtown Anchorage or at the Hotel Alyeska, you can get by without a car. Alaska Sightseeing or The Magic Bus (907-268-6311) can take you from the city to the resort with advance reservations. Ask at the hotel desk. Otherwise, you'll need a car. **Glacier Valley Stagecoach** offers a transportation loop that services 19 Girdwood areas including many stops in town and at The Alyeska Resort.

Reno/North Lake Tahoe Area

Alpine Meadows

Squaw Valley USA

Northstar-at-Tahoe

Diamond Peak

Mt. Rose

Sugar Bowl

with Reno, Nevada

Toll-free reservations:
(888) 434-1262, North Lake Tahoe
(800) 468-2463, Incline Village/Crystal Bay
(888) 448-7366, Reno
Internet: www.mytahoevacation.com (North Lake Tahoe)
www.renolaketahoe.com (Reno)
E-mail: info@mytahoevacation.com (North Lake Tahoe) or
info@renolaketahoe.com (Reno)
Dining:★★★
Apres-ski/nightlife:★★(near the lake) ★★★★(Reno)
Other activities:★★★

Few regions on the North American continent have the ski-resort diversity of the Reno/Lake Tahoe region. When you consider the elements of a perfect ski vacation—variety of terrain, good snow, comfortable lodging, beautiful scenery, a wide choice of restaurants and nightlife, myriad other activities, accessibility—Lake Tahoe would rank near the top in all but a couple of categories (and it would be above the median in those).

Lake Tahoe, one of the largest and most stunningly beautiful mountain lakes in the world, straddles the border of California and Nevada about 200 miles east of San Francisco. Tahoe has received accolades from travel writers for more than a century. Mark Twain was one of the first to note its beauty. In 1861, he wrote in "Roughing It," Tahoe was "the fairest picture the whole earth affords." Because the lake is so deep and doesn't freeze, it retains its sapphire-blue color throughout the winter. Its name comes from a Washoe Indian word meaning "lake in the sky." The lake is about 6,200 feet above sea level.

Tahoe is best divided into two regions for vacation purposes. Though you can run yourself ragged by trying to visit every major area in a week, it's better to concentrate on the North Shore or the South Shore. The two regions provide very different vacation experiences.

South Tahoe is densely developed, with high-rise casino-hotels hugging the state line, frequent big-name entertainment and non-stop, apres-ski activity. It has three ski/snowboard resorts, one of which overlooks the twin towns of Stateline and South Lake Tahoe. Speaking in general terms, South Shore tends to attract first-time visitors who live outside California and Nevada, while the North Shore attracts fewer first-time visitors, but loads of Californians.

Resort skiing in California started in the North Lake Tahoe region in the late 1930s, when a group of investors, including Walt Disney, started Sugar Bowl. The 1960 Winter Olympics were staged at another North Tahoe resort, Squaw Valley USA. North Tahoe isn't as densely developed as the South Shore, and it covers a lot more miles of the lakeshore. The North Tahoe region has 12 Alpine ski facilities (the lake is visible from five of them) and six cross-country areas. The five largest Alpine resorts are Squaw Valley USA, Alpine Meadows, Northstar-at-Tahoe, Diamond Peak, Mt. Rose and Sugar Bowl. More and more visitors are staying nearby in Reno. It is the air hub and has far more dining and lodging opportunities than the towns on the lake. However, Reno is a relatively long drive from these areas, except Mt. Rose, which is its neighborhood mountain.

Note: If you need child care for your infant, ski elsewhere. None of the North Lake Tahoe resorts offers child care for children younger than age 2. Resorts that accept children 2 and older require toddlers to be toilet-trained. They also require a birth certificate with proof of age.

Squaw Valley USA

The largest ski resort in North Lake Tahoe, Squaw Valley looks and feels like a ski area in Europe's Alps. The high alpine terrain is vast and the village—a mix of new development and 1960s Olympic architectural relics—is delightful.

Squaw Valley USA opened in 1949 but became part of skiing lore in 1960 when the resort hosted the Winter Olympics. Racing down steep, snow-filled gullies and around exposed cliff bands, with only a few pines dotting the landscape, the European racers must have felt right at home. With so many wide-open bowls and snowfields—4,000 acres of them—Squaw Valley has few named runs; the lifts have names, and skiers and riders pick their own routes down the mountain. What would be called a trail map at some resorts is referred to as a Mountain Guide at Squaw.

Access starts in the village with the 28-person Funitel or the 110-person cable car. Both lifts take skiers and riders to mid-mountain, where experts can go higher and intermediates and beginners can spend the day. Or start with Exhibition/Searchlight for a warm-up run, then move to higher terrain. Five separate peaks, each with every conceivable exposure, overlook Lake Tahoe.

Visitors who don't wish to ski can take the cable car to High Camp for lunch or to swim in the heated outdoor pool or ice skate in a spectacular rink overlooking the Olympic Valley.

In the evenings, the Village at Squaw Valley bustles with shoppers and folks walking to dinner. The European-style pedestrian village has a total of 286 slopeside condominiums, 17 boutique shops and seven restaurants.

 ## Mountain layout

Expert and Advanced: Serious skiers and riders visit from all parts of the globe to ride this amazing mountain—a must on any expert's check list. On a good powder day spectators can watch a number of California's best riders ski off 100-foot cliffs and ride down lines that seem inconceivable.

At the base of the mountain, the KT-22 quad climbs 2,000 vertical feet up some of the toughest pistes within the resort. If a look at the northside makes your throat tighten in fear, head to the saddle between KT-22 and Squaw Peak. It's not a gentle route, but it's not vertical either.

Half way up the mountain, the Cornice 2 and Headwall lifts lead up to Squaw Peak. Here giant cornices form from the high winds and the open bowls fill up with 15 feet of snow. On the average powder day, the ridge line off the lifts turns into a huck fest with hundreds of riders throwing themselves off the massive cornices into the powdery bowls below.

The Siberian quad is the lift that comes closest to Squaw Peak. From this lift the ridge line is hiked to the world famous Palisades. The Palisades are essentially sheer cliff bands that range between 10 and 120 feet, and they are doable, theoretically. On epic powder days, pro skiers and riders come out of the woodwork to throw themselves off these rocks in view of photographers who are there to document it all.

The Granite Chief triple lies on the far northern boundary of the resort and is a veritable playground of chutes, boulders and trees. Traverse far rider's right for an amazing granite boulder field where giant rocks are randomly scattered down a steep pitch. With a little creativity, double, triple and even quadruple cliff drops can be lined up.

Squaw Valley USA

Summit elevation:	9,050 feet
Vertical drop:	2,850 feet
Base elevation:	6,200 feet

Address: Box 2007, Olympic Valley CA 96146
Area code: 530
Ski area phone: 583-6985
Snow report: 583-6955
Toll-free reservations: (888) 766-9321
or (800) 545-4350
Fax: 581-7106
E-mail: squaw@squaw.com
Internet: www.squaw.com

Number of lifts: 34—1 cable car, 1 Funitel, 1 Pulse, 3 high-speed six-packs, 4 high-speed quads, 1 quad, 8 triples, 10 doubles, 3 surface lifts, 2 moving carpets
Snowmaking: 10 percent
Skiable acreage: 4,000 lift-served acres
Uphill capacity: 49,000 per hour
Parks & pipes: 3 terrain parks, 1 superpipe, 1 halfpipe
Bed base: 3,500 within 3 miles
Nearest lodging: Slopeside
Resort child care: Yes, 3 years and older
Adult ticket, per day: $73 (07/08 prices)

Expert:★★★★★
Advanced:★★★★★
Intermediate:★★★★
Beginner:★★★ **First-timer:**★★★

Intermediate: Intermediate terrain has challenge and variety—perhaps more challenge than most might expect or, perhaps, want. Just because a lift is colored blue doesn't mean that all terrain serviced by it is blue. Siberia Express accesses the largest intermediate bowl, advanced levels turn left getting off the lift, intermediates traverse to the right, which feeds into the Gold Coast terrain and other wide-open slopes. Newport, Gold Coast and Emigrant lifts offer acres of open-bowl intermediate terrain. The Shirley Lake Express, which accesses 375 acres of intermediate terrain, was upgraded to a detachable six-pack for the 2007-08 season. Shirley Lake gets high traffic; adjacent Solitude is much quieter. Careful though: Wander off the groomed runs in Solitude, and cliff signs are numerous. Or, ride the KT-22 chair, head west on the Saddle Traverse, then drop into the Saddle, which is groomed.

The Mountain Run is a crowded end-of-the-day three-mile cruise. If you're tired or don't like rush-hour traffic, consider downloading on the tram or gondola. Another great cruise is Home Run. Or give the Olympic High ski run a try. It follows the route of the original 1960 Olympic men's downhill. It begins above the bottom shack of Headwall and heads to the base.

Beginner and First-timer: Though Squaw Valley's well publicized steep terrain has given it a menacing reputation, it has a little-known surprise: This is a great spot for beginners. Squaw has a wide, gentle bowl at the top of the High Camp cable car and the Gold Coast Funitel known as Bailey's Beach, served by two slow-moving lifts. Best advice for beginners: Travel across the bowl from the top of the cable car or the Funitel from lift to lift - from Bailey's Beach, to Belmont to Riviera to East Broadway (or the reverse) and then head back for lunch at either Gold Coast or High Camp. Beginners can ride all the way to the High Camp summit at Squaw for the views, the gentle (always) groomed slopes, the great snow and lunch with fabulous views. They just hop the cable car or Funitel up to High Camp and Gold Coast (where they'll also find restaurants, shelter and an outdoor ice rink), and at the end of the day, ride the cable car or the Funitel back down. It's a friendly, well-groomed and easy beginner's area with spectacular views for those who are just starting their skiing careers.

The Papoose Learning Area is tucked away at the base area next to the tubing area on the lower mountain near the Far East lift and has two surface lifts for first-timers.

Parks and pipes

Let's just say that Squaw is monstrous, and so are its parks and pipes. In various locations you'll find a superpipe, halfpipes, quarterpipes, plus terrain features like tabletops, rails, rollers and volcanoes. All parks and pipes are cut daily and the Riviera halfpipe is cut twice, once for night sessions and again after night operations so the pipe is fresh in the morning. The pipe sessions can definitely get heated—prepare to be humbled by locals. There's a reason many pros call Tahoe home.

The Mainline Terrain Park is the home of Squaw's legendary Mainline Superpipe, a 550-plus-foot-long pipe with 17-foot walls that overlooks Lake Tahoe. You won't know whether you're catching your breath because of the exertion or the view. Just below the pipe are an assortment of rails—a 30-foot single-kink rail, a 40-foot S rail, a 52-foot S box, a 40-foot double-kink rail, and the massive 78-foot swirly rail-and a wide-open area of tabletops and jumps. Throughout the season, depending upon weather, additional features may include hips, rollers, a snowcross course and volcanoes. You can get here by taking the Gold Coast, Mainline or Siberia lifts.

Central Park in the Riviera area just below the top terminal of the Funitel is the heart of Squaw's intermediate parks and pipes. Intermediate riders and freeskiers will find a standard halfpipe, tables, jumps, rails, boxes, and whatever the park designers feel like putting in here, all accessed by a dedicated lift. You can reach it from the High Camp lift too. Riviera is lit until 9 p.m. and has a pumping sound system to keep you going.

Belmont Park is for kids and people new to parks and pipes. It has small berms, rolls, and bumps to help you get used to catching air. Take either the Belmont lift or the Links lift on the upper mountain to get here.

Snowboarding

If there was ever a resort that catered to every aspect of snowboarding, that resort would be Squaw Valley. From the massive parks and ridiculously steep lines and giant cliffs to the perfect long groomers, Squaw Valley should impress any rider from any continent.

Unfortunately, these features are not secrets, and it is clearly evident on a blue bird powder day when all 4,000 acres get tracked out in 2 hours. However, even when racing the thousands of other riders for the lines of the day, Squaw will be a memorable session and possibly serve up some runs of a lifetime.

The KT-22 quad is an amazing lift. The chair seems to go straight up as it climbs the 2,000 vertical feet. The front, or east, side of this has a number of open bowls, cliffs and little chutes. This is a sweet, long, steep run, and is the first to get tracked out on a powder day, so get in line early. On the north side of the KT-22, the Jonny Moseley's Run is even steeper and more technical. On hard pack icy days, make sure those edges are sharp and do not blow it. A fall at the top of Jonny Moseley's Run would not stop until 1,000 vertical feet below.

The 6-person Gold Coast Express lift is one of the main arteries on the upper part of the mountain. From the top of the Gold Coast Express Lift, all of the parks and the pipe can be lapped and tons of wide open intermediate and beginner groomers wind down the mountain.

In the far northern corner of Squaw, the Granite Chief triple is another gem of the resort. With mostly north facing shots, the snow quality lasts a little longer up here and the terrain is just as sick as it is on the rest of the mountain.

 ## Lessons (07/08 prices)

Group lessons: Beginner to intermediate skiers and snowboarders get instruction through a "Ski Your Pro" format, where instructors are assigned to training areas on the mountain, and skiers/riders can join in on the hour for $49. Higher-level skiers/riders get two-hour workshops on specific skills, such as moguls, powder, gate training, freeriding, halfpipe and terrain park, also for $49. A book of five two-hour lessons is $199.

First-timer package: A First Time Adventure Package that includes a beginner lift ticket, rentals and a two-hour lesson is $89 for skiing or snowboarding.

Private lessons: $109 for one hour; $319 for three hours; $529 for a full day; $169 for a two-hour early bird special that starts at 9 a.m.

Special programs: An intro to telemarking lesson includes beginner lift ticket, rentals and two-hour lesson for $89; reservations required, call (530) 581-7263. Squaw Valley also has a full-service adaptive ski school.

Racing: A coin-op course is at the top of the Shirley Lake Express.

Children's programs (07/08 prices)

Child care: Squaw Valley does not provide child-care services.

Other options: Baby's Away (800-446-9030; 530-544-2229) rents and will deliver baby items (cribs, strollers, toys, etc.) to your hotel or condo. For **babysitting referrals**, call North Lake Tahoe Resort Association (800-434-1262; 530-583-3494).

Children's lessons: A combination ski lesson and snowplay program is offered for ages 3–4; cost is $109 ($139 holidays). Ages 4–11 can take an all-day lesson, with lunch, lift ticket, activities and instruction for $109 ($139 holidays). The half-day price is $79 ($108 holidays) and includes a snack instead of lunch. Snowboard lessons start at age 8. Reservations strongly recommended; call (530) 581-7166.

Lift tickets (07/08 prices)

These are regular season prices, holiday prices are higher.

Adult one-day ticket $73; 3 days $181 ($60/day); 5 days $292 ($58+/day)

Youth age 13-18 $55

Child 12 and under $10; 3 days $30 ($10/day); 5 days $50 ($10/day)

Who skis free: Ages 76 and older. Those 85 and older are paid $5 in resort script good at the resort's restaurants and retail shops.

Who skis at a discount: Tickets for ages 65-75 are $45 and youth ages 13-18 are $55.

Full-day lift tickets include night skiing until 9 p.m. (mid-December through mid-March). Night skiing (after 4 p.m.) costs $20 for adults, $15 for youth, $12 for seniors and $5 for children. Non-skiers can ride the cable car and gondolas for $19 for adults, $15 for seniors and youth, $5 for children 4-12, and free for ages 3 and younger.

Accommodations–Squaw Valley

Olympic Valley (that's the name of the base-area town; Squaw Valley is the name of the resort) has several lodging choices. All have easy access to the slopes. If you're staying here, it is best to rent a car if you'd like to explore dining and nightlife in Truckee and Tahoe City. For central reservations at Squaw Valley call 800-545-4350.

The **Village at Squaw Valley** (866-818-6963; $$$$) has a brand new collection of luxury one-, two- and three-bedroom condominiums across from the lifts, each with kitchen, fireplace and balcony. Other amenities are laundry facilities and underground parking. Four outdoor hot tubs are reached by heated sidewalks.

The **PlumpJack Squaw Valley Inn** (800-323-7666; 530-583-1576; $$$-$$$$), with 61 rooms, originally housed delegates to the 1960 Winter Olympics, and is right across from the cable car building and has a European flare—from the boisterous bar to the stylishly remodeled rooms to service at a level on par with the grand Continental hotels. Rooms are outfitted with down comforters, hooded bathrobes, VCRs plus, alap pool and two hot tubs.

Resort at Squaw Creek (800-327-3353; 530-583-6300; $$$$) is a multistory luxury hotel that blends well with the valley. It connects with the ski area by its own lift, and is a self-contained resort, with five restaurants and three outdoor pools (one of which is open in winter), several hot tubs, health and fitness center, full-service spa, cross-country skiing and an ice-skating rink.

Squaw Valley Lodge (800-992-9920; in California, 800-922-9970; $$$-$$$$) is only a few yards' walk from the lifts. The lodge boasts a fully equipped health club, free covered parking and kitchenettes in the units. **The Olympic Village Inn** (800-845-5243; 530-583-1501; $$$-$$$$) has five hot tubs, and all units have kitchens. **Red Wolf Lodge** (800-791-0081; $$$$) at the base of Red Dog Chair next to the Children's Center has studio, one- and two-bedroom units with full kitchenettes.

Alpine Meadows

It's hard not to like Alpine Meadows Ski Resort. It has expert terrain, sweeping intermediate bowls, scenic trails and a good beginner area. And it's bigger than it looks from the base lodge. You'll see the terrain unfold beneath when you take the Summit Six (a six-seater) to the top. In the Lake Tahoe area, Alpine Meadows has traditionally been the ski area with the earliest and longest season (it's open well into May and some years, until July 4).

For beginners and intermediates, there's the Hot Wheels chair. This lift is also gives access to the back bowls. Scott Chair, which accesses expert terrain, was upgraded from a double to a triple. The added weight of the triple chairs allows the Scott Chair to run more often in bad weather, good news to experts who want to get to this area during a snowfall. It also speeds toward the Lakeview Chair, which has great views of Lake Tahoe from the top.

Here's a bit of local knowledge: If the wind is out of the southwest, Alpine Meadows is usually open, even when other areas are on wind hold. Better yet, the wind blows the snow into the bowls. On the other hand, when it blows out of the east...take heed.

Alpine Meadows Facts

Summit elevation:	**8,637 feet**
Vertical drop:	**1,802 feet**
Base elevation:	**6,835 feet**

Expert:★★★★
Advanced:★★★★★
Intermediate:★★★★
Beginner:★★★
First-timer:★★★

Address: Box 5279, Tahoe City CA 95730
Area code: 530
Ski area phone: 583-4232
Snow report: 581-8374
Toll-free information: (800) 441-4423

Fax: 583-0963
E-mail: info@skialpine.com
Internet: www.skialpine.com

Number of lifts: 13—1 high-speed six-pack, 2 high-speed quads, 3 triples, 5 doubles, 2 surface lifts
Snowmaking: 12 percent
Skiable acreage: 2,000 acres
Uphill capacity: 18,400 per hour
Parks & pipes: 1 park, 1 superpipe
Bed base: 10,000 (N. Lake Tahoe Area)
Nearest lodging: Tahoe City, 6 miles
Resort child care: None
Adult ticket, per day: $58-63 (07/08 prices)

The Ski Tahoe North Interchangeable ticket (877-949-3296) allows guests to ski/snowboard at Alpine Meadows, Diamond Peak, Homewood, Mt. Rose, Northstar, Squaw Valley and Sugar Bowl and accommodates those looking for the best conditions. There are wind holds on some mountains on some days and snow conditions vary from resort to resort. The ticket is $58 per person, per day for two-or-more-day tickets, is valid all season and doesn't need to be used on consecutive days. Tickets are two-for-one at Homewood and Diamond Peak.

 ## Mountain layout

Expert: Alpine Meadows has plenty of great bowl skiing and enough steeps to keep hearts in throats. Here's a route suggestion: Take the Summit Six and descend into the expert Wolverine Bowl, Beaver Bowl and Estelle Bowl (to the right as you ascend), then take the Summit Six again and cruise into the upper-blue territory of the Alpine Bowl. Finally, take the Alpine Bowl Chair and traverse to the Sherwood Bowls on the back side, or take the High Yellow Traverse to the Saddle Bowl. When you come up the Sherwood Chair, drop down Our Father, then head to Scott Chair and try out Scott Chute for a direct plunge, or take it easy on tree-lined roundabouts. The Promised Land has great tree skiing for top skiers.

Advanced: Take your warm-up in Alpine Bowl, staying to skier's right on Rock Garden and Yellow Trail as you cruise down to the Hot Wheels chair. Then head for the Back Bowls. If there's a line at Hot Wheels, you also can reach the bowls via the Scott Chair through the blue-square Lakeview area to Ray's Rut. Depending on your mood, you can stay on the groomed Sherwood run to check out the scene, or traverse to the steeper Sherwood Face or South Face. You may want to stay here all day—one of our staffers did.

Intermediate: Options exist off every chair, but the vast majority of intermediate terrain is off the Roundhouse, Lakeview and Yellow chairs. Lakeview, on the back side, is solid blue. When comfortable here, ride the Summit Six and descend Alpine Bowl. Be forewarned that on a stormy day, when whiteout conditions may occur, it's a bit of a challenge to find a marked intermediate run. Scott Ridge, off the Scott Chair is another good choice. Weasel Run, off the Hot Wheels Chair, is an intermediate family ski area.

Plenty of terrain for this level off these lifts: Alpine Bowl, Roundhouse and Lakeview. The terrain off the Kangaroo lift is a short intermediate run, but much of it is devoted to race programs and terrain parks. All this activity creates a narrow descent—a challenge for some intermediates.

Beginner: The Meadow and Subway chairs are dedicated to beginners.

First-timer: This level has a small but sheltered area close to the base lodge.

Parks and pipes

Riders and skiers will jump for joy when they see the nicely kept superpipe. It's together with the terrain park—Roo's Ride—and the boardercross course off the Kangaroo lift. The park includes rails, tabletops, funboxes and quarterpipes. The pipe and terrain park are open for night riding 5-9 p.m. nightly, complete with a speaker system for tunes.

Snowboarding

Even though Alpine Meadows is paying more attention to its manmade features, most riders agree that the natural terrain is the real reason to come here. If you like in-bounds hiking, this is the place for you. Unfortunately, you might be doing some hiking even if you're not looking for it: There are some flat spots and traverses that you might just find yourself cursing. The biggest beware is traveling back from the Lakeview and especially the Sherwood lifts to the front side.

Dining: $$$$–Entrees $30+; $$$–$20–$30; $$–$10–$20; $–less than $10.
Accommodations: (double room) $$$$–$200+; $$$–$141–$200; $$–$81–$140; $–$80 and less.

The Bowls are great powder runs—with special kudos to Upper Beaver and Estelle Bowl—and there are plenty of steeps, gullies and nutty drops if you go looking for them. Mix it up with some of the tree runs such as Hot Wheels Gully, you'll be happy you did. If you're there after a fresh dump, look for the wind lips—you'll find yourself airborne for days—and see if you can find Munchkins and Outer Outer.

If you favor groomers, don't panic. Alpine does a real nice job and there's plenty to choose from all over the mountain. Beginners will find very gentle terrain and the learning area is sheltered from the rest of the trails.

Lessons (07/08 prices)

Group lessons: $70 for 2.25 hours. Lessons on demo equipment are available. **First-timer package:** Includes beginner lifts, equipment and instruction for $119. Normal beginner lessons cost $125 for a full day and $99 for a half day.

Private lessons: For one person, $99 for one hour; $259 for three hours; $499 for all day. For two to four people, $149 for one hour; $299 for three hours; $599 for all day. Discounts are available for lessons taken in the afternoon on non-holiday days. Privates using demo equipment also are available.

Special programs: Tahoe Adaptive Ski School offers half-day adaptive lessons (includes beginner lift ticket and adaptive ski gear); reservations required, call 530-581-4161. Multiday clinics for women, men, experts only, and early-season warmup also are available. Call for details, dates and prices.

Racing: Daily race-training clinics are offered; one day costs $55 and a book of five sessions costs $235. There is a race every Thursday, with two runs for all abilities with special prizes. Call for details and prices. Alpine Meadows also has coin-op racing.

Children's programs (07/08 prices)

Child care: Alpine Meadows does not provide child-care services.

Other options: Baby's Away (800-446-9030; 530-544-2229) rents and will deliver baby items (cribs, strollers, toys, etc.) to your hotel or condo. For **babysitting referrals**, call North Lake Tahoe Resort Association (800-434-1262; 530-583-3494).

Children's lessons: Kids Camp for children ages 4- 6 costs $125 for a full day (including lunch, snack, equipment, lift ticket and two 2-hour lessons). A half day costs $99 . Reservations required, 530-581-8240. Private lessons are available and snowboard lessons for ages 4–6 are by private lesson only; call for reservations and prices.

Mountaineers is for children 7–12, skiing or snowboarding. A full-day program includes lunch, lift ticket, rentals and lessons, $125. A half day costs $99.

Lift tickets (07/08 prices)

Adult $58 ($63 holiday); **Junior** (5-12) $10 all days

Who skis free: Children ages 4 and younger.

Who skis at a discount: Ages 62-69 pay $39 and teens 13-18 pay $49 all the time; seniors 70 and older pay $15 all the time. Parents can get an interchangeable ticket that can be traded between them for $58 a day ($63 holidays).

Notes: The resort does not offer multiday discounts.

On holidays and midwinter weekends, the resort limits the number of tickets sold to keep the slopes from becoming too crowded. You can reserve lift tickets in advance. Holiday periods are Christmas/New Year's week, Martin Luther King, Jr. weekend, and Presidents' Day weekend.

Accommodations–Alpine Meadows

Alpine Meadows doesn't have accommodations at the base, but has lodging-lift packages in the region. Call **Alpine Meadows** at (800) 949-3296. A bed & breakfast package includes some two-dozen North Shore lodges, some starting at $59 per person, double occupancy, for lodging and a lift ticket.

Northstar-at-Tahoe Resort

From your car to the Big Springs Express Gondola, you'll walk through the pedestrian village lined with boutique shops, restaurants, outdoor fire pits, and an ice skating rink. Looking out over the village are 100 new luxury condominiums. And everything is designed to be as environmentally friendly as possible. On-mountain improvements include the Village Express quad chairlift, and more mountain improvements are scheduled. Still a family-oriented resort, kids will find the hidden Adventure Parks, kid-friendly menus in the on-slope restaurants and cafeterias, and non-skiing fun like snowtubing and the bungee trampoline.

Northstar is one of 14 Alpine resorts in the Lake Tahoe region. Unlike Squaw or Alpine, you won't find bowls and cornices at Northstar. Instead the skiing is all trail-cut with a bunch of awesome tree skiing. The tree skiing on Lookout Mountain rivals any found in the region. Combined with the widely spaced trees on the Backside, Northstar provides an excellent variety of tree skiing for everyone, from intermediates making their first forays into the woods to experts looking for the tightest glades they can ski. The Ski Tahoe North Interchangeable ticket (877-949-3296) allows guests to ski/snowboard at Alpine Meadows, Diamond Peak, Homewood, Mt. Rose, Northstar, Squaw Valley and Sugar Bowl and accommodates those looking for the best conditions. There are wind holds on some mountains on some days and snow conditions vary from resort to resort. The ticket is $58 per person, per day for two-or-more-day tickets, is valid all season and doesn't need to be used on consecutive days. Tickets are two-for-one at Homewood and Diamond Peak.

Northstar-at-Tahoe Facts

Summit elevation:	8,610 feet
Vertical drop:	2,280 feet
Base elevation:	6,330 feet

Expert:★★
Advanced:★★★★
Intermediate:★★★★★
Beginner:★★★★★
First-timer:★★★★
Address: Box 129, Truckee, CA 96160
Area code: 530
Ski area phone: 562-1010
Snow report: 562-1330
Toll-free reservations:
(800) 466-6784

E-mail: northstar@boothcreek.com
Internet: www.northstarattahoe.com
Number of lifts: 16—1 gondola, 7 high-speed quads, 1 triples, 2 doubles, 1 surface lift, 4 moving carpets
Snowmaking: 50% of developed acres
Total acreage: 2,420 acres
Uphill capacity: 21,800 per hour
Parks & pipes: 6 terrain parks, 2 pipes
Bed base: 5,500 at resort
Nearest lodging: Ski-in/ski-out, slopeside
Resort child care: Yes, 2 years and older (toilet-trained)
Adult ticket, per day: $74 (07/08)

Dining: $$$$–Entrees $30+; $$$–$20–$30; $$–$10–$20; $–less than $10.
Accommodations: (double room) $$$$–$200+; $$$–$141–$200; $$–$81–$140; $–$80 and less.

Mountain layout

Expert and Advanced: Experts who expect a real challenge should go elsewhere, you won't find any scare-the-pants-off-you terrain here.

Lookout Mountain, with 200 acres of terrain and a high-speed quad, finally gives Northstar some bite. Here you'll find steep runs, trees, and great views overlooking Truckee's Martis Valley and the surrounding mountain peaks. There are five steep drops named after the surrounding reservoirs: Prosser, Stampede, Gooseneck, Boca and Martis. The trails can be classified as advanced, but the trees are clearly expert. Stampede, Gooseneck and Boca are left to bump up while Prosser and Martis are groomed regularly. After a storm, Northstar is one of the prime areas where you can enjoy powder through the trees long after Alpine and Squaw's powder has been skied off. Plans to expand Northstar are in the works.

The Backside has nine moderately steep, sustained pitches off Northstar's back side. Advanced skiers or those aspiring to the upper levels of intermediate will find some challenge in the short drops off the East Ridge. Tonini's is the longest, but The Plunge is the steepest. Chute, Crosscut and Powder Bowl are also fun—short but sweet.

Intermediate: Excellent grooming and a commitment to families colors the majority of Northstar's front side Easy Rider Blue. Ride the Vista, Comstock or the six-passenger Tahoe Zephyr Express lifts, and choose your sweet poison, but try to avoid Main Street, which is more like an expressway during rush hour. This group will enjoy most of the mountain, particularly the smooth blues that descend from the two ridges into Main Street, an intermediate run that nearly every other run on the mountain feeds into. Avoid Main Street except when you need to get to a lift. Strong intermediates should try some of the black runs here, perhaps Burnout or Rail Splitter on the backside, if they're groomed. Be forewarned: Both are looonnggg, and neither has an escape hatch. They will provide a good challenge to an intermediate looking to improve.

Beginner and First-timer: Northstar is the best first-timer and beginner resort in the region because its gentlest terrain is below the gondola, while all other runs are above it. Better skiers leave this area to the learners except at day's end, when some of them use it to practice tucks. Luckily for everyone, it's fairly flat, so no one can keep up excessive speed.

Parks and pipes

If you like terrain parks and pipes, Northstar is right up your alley. You'll find six terrain parks (not counting the kids' Adventure Parks), a 420-foot superpipe and a halfpipe. Some of the parks have scaled-down features for beginners; Magic Moguls will remind you of a parking lot full of snow-covered VW bugs; another is a snake-run with high walls; and Sidewinder and Forerunner runs now host the Burton Progression Park with hits and rails made especially for those learning to ride in the park. The superpipe is on Pipeline. Get a good view of it from Chilly Peppers, a patio restaurant at the Big Springs Day Lodge, where parents can drink microbrews and watch their kids get serious airtime. As for Adventure Parks, they're adventure zones for kids—pint-size terrain parks scattered across the mountain that include bumps, jumps, hideaways and snow play areas.

Snowboarding

If you're craving serious steeps with sick air, you'll need to go somewhere else. Northstar is really geared more towards groomed cruising and woods riding with some good bumps through the center of Lookout Mountain.

On Lookout Mountain, riders claim Stampede, Gooseneck and Boca are divine. On the

Backside, stick to the right side of the area where the trails drop right to the Backside Express Chair. If riders swing to the left down Challenger, they will face a long runout at the bottom of the area. Jibboom and Powder Bowl are some other favorites.

Stay on the front side if you're like wide-open groomed runs for intermediates and beginners. The terrain here is mellow and will boost your ego.

Lessons (07/08 prices)

We provide prices for regular season. During peak/holiday periods, prices are higher.
Group lessons: Free 75-minute skill improvement clinics are held in the afternoons, Sunday-Friday, for intermediate and higher levels, skiing and snowboarding, ages 13 and older (not available during holiday/peak periods). Sign up at the summit of the Comstock Express chair, first-come/first-served. Other group lessons are $54 (regular season) and $65 (peak-season) for ages 13 and older.

First-timer package: First-time ski and snowboard students ages 13 and older get a 2.5-hour lesson, with beginner lift access and rental equipment, for $89 (regular season), $99 (peak season). A three-day package costs $175, and days do not have to be consecutive.

Private lessons: (Regular season prices) For ages 13 and older, $119 for one hour; $279 for a half day; $379 for a full day. Semi-private lessons (up to five people) cost $169 for one hour; $329 for a half day; $449 for a full day. Three- and six-hour privates include free use of demo equipment. Reservations are recommended.

Children's programs (07/08 prices)

Child care: Ages 2-6 years (toilet-trained). All day costs $99 with lunch and snacks ($109 in peak season) ; half day costs $79 ($89 in peak season). Activities include art, snow play, science, drama and language development. Reservations recommended; call (530) 562-2278. Hours are 8 a.m. to 4:30 p.m.

Other options: Baby's Away (800-446-9030; 530-544-2229) rents and will deliver baby items (cribs, strollers, toys, etc.) to your hotel or condo. For **babysitting referrals**, call North Lake Tahoe Resort Association (800-434-1262; 530-583-3494).

Children's lessons: All-day program for children ages 4–12 is $119 with lifts, lessons, equipment and lunch. A half-day program is $92 (without lunch). Lessons only cost $99 a day and $79 for a half day. Ages 4–6 get indoor activities as part of the program. Holiday rates are higher. Meet at Starkids Center at mid-mountain. Children 13 and older enroll in adult programs.

For children ages 3—4 and their parents, a 2 p.m. daily **Teach Your Tots** session is available for $119, or $129 during peak season. Phone 530.562.2470 for more information..

Here's something you shouldn't pass up: Northstar's instructors will teach parents how to teach their 3- and 4-year-olds in a free program called Mommy, Daddy & Me, offered Sunday through Friday (non-holidays) at 1:30 p.m. Meet at mid-mountain at the Ski & Snowboard School.

Lift tickets (07/08 prices)

Adult (23-64) $74 (regular season prices)
Child (5-12) $28
Who skis free: Children 4 and younger ski free with a paying adult.
Who skis at a discount: Young adults (13-22) pay $64 for one day and $52 per day for multiday tickets. Ages 65-69 pay young adult rates; ages 70 and older pay $28 for one day and $19 per day for multiday tickets. Unlimited gondola rides for non-skiers cost $17.

Note: Prices are higher during holiday periods. Northstar limits its daily ticket sales; cars will be turned away once sellout has occurred. There are bargains available from Safeway and partner shops that allow savings of about $11 per day on 2 of 3 day tickets, equipment and lunch. An afternoon-only program is $92 for ages 4–6 get indoor activities. Holiday rates are higher. Meet at the Children's Teaching Area at mid-mountain. Only for kids 12 and younger.

Here's something you shouldn't pass up: Northstar's instructors will teach parents how to teach their 3- and 4-year-olds in a free program called Mommy, Daddy & Me, offered Sunday through Friday (non-holidays) at 1:30 p.m. Meet at midmountain at the Ski & Snowboard School.

Diamond Peak Facts

Summit elevation:	8,540 feet
Vertical drop:	1,840 feet
Base elevation:	6,700 feet

Expert:★ Advanced:★★★
Intermediate:★★★★
Beginner:★★★
First-timer:★★★
Address: 1210 Ski Way, Incline Village, NV 89451
Ski area phone: 775-832-1177
Snow report: 775-831-3211
Toll-free reservations: (800) 468-2463

Fax: 775-832-1281
E-mail: info@diamondpeak.com
Internet: www.diamondpeak.com
Number of lifts: 6—1 high-speed quad, 2 quads, 3 doubles
Snowmaking: 75 percent
Skiable acreage: 655 acres
Uphill capacity: 9,800 per hour
Parks & pipes: 1 terrain park
Bed base: 6,000
Nearest lodging: About 1/4 mile away
Resort child care: Yes, 3 years and older (toilet-trained)
Adult ticket, per day: $48 (07/08 price)

Diamond Peak

Bigger is not always better, nor desirable. For skiers and snowboarders who don't want the expansive terrain of most Lake Tahoe resorts, let us recommend Diamond Peak Ski Resort, a medium-sized but exquisite jewel that destination vacationers too often overlook.

Diamond Peak often is less crowded than the other large Tahoe areas and perfect for families. Visitors repeatedly remark about that this is a very friendly area. Take a camera—the view is beautiful.

With runs knifing down through Ponderosa Pines along a long single ridge, Diamond Peak offers an excellent family mountain where all trails funnel to a single base area. The views down toward the lake are spectacular and the early-morning groomed corduroy alongside powder seems to drop right into the water.

The tougher trails drop from the crest of the ridge traced by Crystal Ridge and the intermediate trails are clustered within sight of the base lodge. Intermediates can't go too far wrong at this resort and advanced skiers will have a good time frolicking.

Diamond Peak is only 27 miles from Reno, Nev. This very upscale community is the closest Lake Tahoe ski area to the gambling center. A Hyatt Regency hotel anchors what for the most part makes up the "resort." In reality, this is a small bedroom community with a collection of condos and one casino hotel and a very good mid-sized ski area with great views.

Don't expect to find wild nightlife outside of the Hyatt Casino. The village highlight after the recreation center seems to be the bowling alley with a virtual golf course.

The Ski Tahoe North Interchangeable ticket (877-949-3296) allows guests to ski/snowboard at Alpine Meadows, Diamond Peak, Homewood, Mt. Rose, Northstar, Squaw Valley and Sugar Bowl and accommodates those looking for the best conditions. There are wind holds on some mountains on some days and snow conditions vary from resort to resort. The ticket is $58 per person, per day for two-or-more-day tickets, is valid all season and doesn't need to be used on consecutive days. Tickets are two-for-one at Homewood and Diamond Peak.

 ## Mountain layout

Diamond Peak was the first U.S. resort to install a "launch pad" loading system, a conveyor belt covered with a skiable felt surface. All of its quad chairs have this family-friendly loading system.

Expert and Advanced: Solitude Canyon has the most advanced terrain. The rest of the resort's terrain falls from a single ridge that starts at the summit and ends at the octagonal Snowflake Lodge overlooking Lake Ta-hoe. The canyons and gullies off Crystal Ridge (a long blue run) are labeled advanced, but strong intermediates will have a blast on them.

Intermediate: This is a wonderful area for intermediates, especially families who don't want to worry about the kids taking a wrong turn and getting lost. The aforementioned Crystal Ridge is a 2.5-mile-long blue from the summit, with a stunning view of the lake. The lower-mountain runs off Red Fox also have a nice intermediate pitch.

Beginner and First-timer: This is a great learner's mountain more because of its friendly atmosphere and manageable size rather than its terrain (unfortunately, the amount of beginner terrain is a bit limited). Diamond Peak employs about 100 instructors—equal to much larger areas—another indication that it's a good place to learn.

Parks and pipes

The terrain park at Diamond Peak is great for intermediate and novice riders. Nothing here is lethal, so parents can relax when the kids are out jibbing. The main park is on the Spillway. When lapping the Crystal Express, riders can get a good run through "The Glades" and finish it up in the Spillway Park. A few medium size kickers are lined up on one side of the run and a decent rail/box progression is on the other. The boxes and rails are pretty average, but are perfect for kids and rider's just learning how to jib. The Popular trail off of the Lakeview quad has a few little jumps and some ride-on features. This empties onto the Lodge Pole trail, which also has two ride-on boxes.

Snowboarding

The Crystal Express high speed quad is the lift of choice when looking for a long continuous run. This chair climbs a decent pitch and accesses a number of north facing runs. Fall line down from the top of the lift enters into "The Glades." This steep, consistent shot is a good first run on a powder day, as the trees are perfectly spaced all the way to the bottom. Riding down the Crystal Ridge, four black diamond runs are lined up on the rider's right. Most of these runs are pretty open and all of them are north facing. The "Diamond Black" run usually gets bumped out, but the trees on the side are a good place to look for hidden powder.

From the peak, a boot track traverses up and across to the rider's right. This short hike leads to Solitude Canyon and is well worth the few minutes of walking. When the rest of the resort is tracked, this secret powder stash will still have a few good lines to hit.

Lessons (07/08 prices)

Group lessons: Lessons are 105 minutes long. Cost is $24 (ski or snowboard); two sessions in the same day cost $37.

First-timer package: Learn-to-Ski/Snowboard including beginner lifts, rentals and 105-minute lesson is $62.

Private lessons: $60-$72 an hour, depending on the time you take your lesson, with multi-hour discounts. The Family & Friends Private Lessons is for two to five people in a lesson, with prices starting at $90 an hour. Reservations recommended, call 775-832-1135.

Children's programs (07/08 prices)

Child care: Ages 3 to 7 years (toilet-trained). Cost is $48 for a half day (10:30 a.m.–12:30 p.m. or 2–4 p.m.); $75 for all day. Diamond Peak's Bee Ferrato Child Ski Center is named for its director, a New Zealand native every kid will want to adopt as a grandmother. Reservations required; call (775) 832-1130.

Other options: Baby's Away (800-446-9030; 530-544-2229) rents and will deliver baby items (cribs, strollers, toys, etc.) to your hotel or condo. Away Wee Go Baby Equipment Rentals (775-690-3379) is another option. For babysitting referrals, call North Lake Tahoe Resort Association (800-434-1262; 530-583-3494).

Children's lessons: All-day group lesson, rentals, ticket and supervised lunch for children 7–12 costs $90. All-day group lesson with lunch for kids 4–7 costs $95 plus $20 for rentals. Children ages 3 and up can enroll in Diamond Pete's Special: two-hour private lesson, two-hours of child care, rentals, lift and lunch for $180. Three-year-olds can also take private lessons: $75 for one hour, $140 for two hours. Reservations are required for private lessons, call (775) 832-1298.

Lift tickets (07/08 prices)

Adult (18-59) $48

Child (7-12) $18

Who skis free: Ages 6 and younger, and 80 and older.

Who skis at a discount: Ages 13-17 pay $38; ages 60-79 pay $18. Parents can buy an interchangeable adult ticket for $48 that either of them can use—a good deal for those with toddlers.

If you are planning on skiing more than just one day, consider the Diamond Peak Mini Pass program, where you can buy tickets in combinations of two, three, five or seven days, starting at $85 for two days (tickets are valid any day of the season). Purchase tickets at any ticket window.

COSTCO DISCOUNTS: Diamond Peak Ski Resort is selling discount lift tickets at Costco. The tickets are available in two-packs for $69.99; that's $35 per day versus the regular rate of $48. Call the resort or look on its website for Costco locations that are participating in this special.

Accommodations–Diamond Peak

Incline Village has several hotels and condo complexes. It also has private homes that can easily sleep 12-16 people. For **Incline Village accommodations**, call 800-468-2463.

The **Hyatt Regency Lake Tahoe Resort, Spa and Casino** (888-591-1234; 775-832-1234; $$$$) is a four-star luxury hotel that resembles the grand homes built in the 1920s. The resort has just undergone a multi-million dollar renovation and the lobby and rooms are wonderful, with natural pine, leather furnishings and autumn colors. The **Cal-Neva Resort, Spa & Casino** (800-225-6382; 775-832-4000; $$-$$$$; right) is split by the state line and once was owned by Frank Sinatra and visited by Marilyn Monroe. Every room has a lake view, the best from the deluxe suites on the top three floors. There are also honeymoon bungalows with heart-shaped tubs, round beds and mirrored ceilings. The **Tahoe Biltmore Casino** (800-245-8667; 775-831-0660; $$) in Crystal Bay has midweek ski packages with Diamond Peak, including a lift ticket, lodging, a full breakfast and transportation to and from the slopes.

The **Inn at Incline Motor Lodge and Condominiums** (800-824-6391; $$) has more modest facilities but rooms are comfortable and there's an indoor pool and hot tub. Haus Bavaria (800-731-6222; $$-$$$$) is a European-style guest house with five rooms and **Crystal Bay Motel** (775-831-0287; $-$$) is an economy property near casinos.

Mt. Rose Facts

Summit elevation:	**9,700 feet**	**E-mail:** deepsnow@skirose.com
Vertical drop:	**1,800 feet**	**Internet:** www.skirose.com
Base elevation:	**8,260 feet**	**Number of lifts:** 7—2 high-speed 6-pax,
Address: 22222 Mt. Rose Hwy., Reno, NV 89511		2 quads, 2 triples, 1 surface lift
Ski area phone/reservations: 775-849-0704		**Snowmaking:** 28 percent
Snow report: (800) SKI-ROSE (754-7673)		**Skiable acreage:** 1,200 acres
		Uphill capacity: 13,400 per hour
Expert:★★★★★		**Parks & pipes:** 2 terrain parks
Advanced:★★★★★		**Bed base:** thousands in Reno
Intermediate:★★★★★		**Nearest lodging:** Reno, NV 25 miles
Beginner:★★★		**Resort child care:** No
First-timer:★★★		**Adult ticket, per day:** $64 (08/09 price)

Mt. Rose

At the top of the mountain along the road from Reno to Lake Tahoe, sits one of America's undiscovered gems, Mt. Rose. This area has long been the mountain of choice for Reno natives who can reach the slopes in about a half hour.

In the past, it was a collection of enjoyable cruising and beginner trails that caught the early-morning sun and then the last rays of the sun on the other side of the mountain. All of that still remains, but the super-steep north-facing chutes, which recently opened, have changed the reputation of this mountain. These chutes have put Mt. Rose on the map.

Today Mt. Rose now has perhaps the largest selection of lift-served steep terrain in the country. This is the real thing, but with an escape valve. There are few places in the ski world where these kinds of steeps are side-by-side with rolling cruisers. Just head up the Northwest Magnum six-pax and turn right or left.

The Ski Tahoe North Interchangeable ticket (877-949-3296) allows guests to ski/snowboard at Alpine Meadows, Diamond Peak, Homewood, Mt. Rose, Northstar, Squaw Valley and Sugar Bowl and accommodates those looking for the best conditions. There are wind holds on some mountains on some days and snow conditions vary from resort to resort. The ticket is $58 per person, per day for two-or-more-day tickets, is valid all season and doesn't need to be used on consecutive days. Tickets are two-for-one at Homewood and Diamond Peak.

Dining: $$$$–Entrees $30+; $$$–$20–$30; $$–$10–$20; $–less than $10.
Accommodations: (double room) $$$$–$200+; $$$–$141–$200; $$–$81–$140; $–$80 and less.

Mountain layout

Expert Advanced: The Chutes are long double-diamond steeps that are easily accessible. The 16 chutes all drop down to the Chuter quad, which then delivers skiers and riders to the the East Bowl where the Blazing Zephyr six-pax takes them back to the top to drop in again.

The Chutes basically are steepest on the eastern side of the Chutes. Start with Nightmare. If you can handle that move over to Chaos. El Cap and Jackpot are considered two of the toughest fall lines. If you ski the chutes when the gates are closed, you lose your ticket.

Intermediate: This is a wonderful area for intermediates. The Slide side (eastern side) of the mountain has delightfully long cruisers that inspires song. Though some of the trails are marked with diamonds, there is nothing here that will get any intermediate in trouble. Swing to the far eastern runs such as South Rim and Washoe Zephyr. Cruise down Big Bonanza and Bruce's. Bash you way straight down the face along Silver Dollar. No matter what route you ski or ride, it will be about 1,500 feet of non-stop vertical.

Later in the day after the sun has softened up the easters side, head to the west. Take the Kit Carson Traverse over to Ramsey's and the Kit Carson Bowl. Any confident intermediate can drop into one of a half-dozen black-diamond trails. When groomed, they are smooth and easy, when bumped up, it will take a little more time to get down, but none are dangerous.

Beginner & First-timer: Beginners have a secluded area to the far west section of the resort. Take the Ponderosa lift then the Galena lift to a web of trails that serve as great learning terrain. North Rim, Galena, Bronco, Mustang and Ski Off are all good beginner trails. Nearby there are runs that go through the trees.

Parks and pipes

There are two terrain parks. Double Down, a massive one on the east side under the Zephyr lift with more hits, spines and jumps than I could count riding over it. The second park, Badlands, is smaller on the Little Red Bowl off Fremont.

Snowboarding

The resort's terrain features attract boarders at every skill level, from first-timers to the most advanced. This is an excellent resort for riders who are ready to test themselves in the Chutes.

Lessons (08/09 prices)

Group lessons: Lessons are one hour and a half long. Cost is $39 (ski or snowboard). Sessions start at 10 a.m. and 2 p.m..

First-timer package: $59 includes equipment and lift ticket for the green runs. Lessons begin at 10 a.m., 12 p.m. and 2 p.m. Arrive a good hour early to gear up. The one-stop setup is located on the lower level of the Main Lodge.

Private lessons: $59-$69 an hour, depending on the time you take your lesson. Each additional person costs $59.

Children's programs (08/09 prices)

Child care: There is no nursery program.

Children's lessons: The Rosebuds Ski and Snowboard Camp teaches children how to turn the mountain into their playgrounds. Children ages 4–10 can take ski lessons and those ages 7–10 can take snowboard lessons.

A two-hour session costs $65 and a full day is $130. This includes lift ticket and rental equipment. Class levels range from turtles who have never skied or boarded, to squirrels who can stop, to foxes who can turn, to bears who are confident on all blue trails.

Private lessons cost $90 for an hour and $60 for each additional person or hour.

Lift tickets (08-09 prices):

Adult (18-59) $64; **Teen** (13-17) $44; **Child** (6-12) $17.
Who skis free: Ages 5 and younger.
Who skis at a discount: Seniors (60-74) pay $44; Super Seniors (75+) $17.

Sugar Bowl Facts

Summit elevation: 8,383 feet
Vertical drop: 1,500 feet
Base elevation: 6,883 feet
Address: P.O. Box 5, Norden, CA 95724
Area code: 530
Ski area phone/reservations: 426-9000
Snow report: 426-1111
Expert:★★
Advanced:★★★
Intermediate:★★★★★
Beginner:★★★★
First-timer:★★★

E-mail: info@sugarbowl.com
Internet: www.sugarbowl.com
Number of lifts: 14—1 gondola, 5 high-speed quads, 2 quads, 3 doubles, 3 surface lifts
Snowmaking: 25 percent
Skiable acreage: 1,500 acres
Uphill capacity: 13,755 per hour
Parks & pipes: 3 parks, 1 pipe
Bed base: 460
Nearest lodging: Slopeside
Resort child care: Yes, 3-5 years (toilet-trained)
Adult ticket, per day: $60 (07/08 prices)

Sugar Bowl

Founded by Walt Disney, Sugar Bowl is one of the oldest resorts in the Lake Tahoe region and the oldest chairlift-served resort in California.

Although it is keeping pace with the modern ski era—with high-speed lifts, excellent grooming, and a plethora of terrain parks and features—the resort is, ironically, not suffering from "Disneyfication." From the moment you step out of your car and board the gondola to ride down across a valley to the lifts, you feel like you're stepping back in time. The snowbound Village is a small collection of old ski chalets, the Inn at Sugar Bowl (which also serves as a base lodge), the child-care center, and a ski shop. Period. No Starbucks. No fancy truffle shop. You can feel your body clock slow as soon as you step off the gondola.

People come to Sugar Bowl only to ski and ride. And those who aren't spending the night at the Inn should park at the Mt. Judah parking area, thus avoiding the slow Village Gondola. From Mt. Judah, your mountain adventure begins quickly thanks to two high-speed quads. If you're looking for the classic Sugar Bowl experience, head to the top of Mt. Lincoln and ski Silver Belt to Steilhang. As you dive under the first cliff and into the natural gully, imagine yourself racing the infamous Silver Belt giant slalom, which attracted the world's best skiers from 1940-1975. In 2000, the race was revived as a very gnarly invitation-only skiercross event.

We recommend Sugar Bowl for a day's change of pace from the larger Tahoe resorts. However, remember that it's one of the first ski areas on the drive from San Francisco, Oakland and Sacramento and gets its big crowds on weekends.

Sugar Bowl has three peaks—Mt. Judah, with its own parking lot and base lodge; Mt. Lincoln; and Mt. Disney, reached initially by the Village Gondola. The three peaks are connected. This is one of the few ski areas where we agree with virtually all their trail ratings. Most of the lifts are high speed and a skier can pack in lots of vertical very quickly.

The Ski Tahoe North Interchangeable ticket (877-949-3296) allows guests to ski/snowboard at Alpine Meadows, Diamond Peak, Homewood, Mt. Rose, Northstar, Squaw Valley and Sugar Bowl and accommodates those looking for the best conditions. There are wind holds on some mountains on some days and snow conditions vary from resort to resort. The ticket is $58 per person, per day for two-or-more-day tickets, is valid all season and doesn't need to be used on consecutive days. Tickets are two-for-one at Homewood and Diamond Peak.

 # Mountain layout

Expert and Advanced: Mt. Disney, one of three peaks at Sugar Bowl, has advanced runs off either side of a ridge. Mt. Lincoln also has advanced terrain dropping directly beneath the lift. There's an expert very steep cliff area, The '58 and The Palisades, to the right of the Mt. Lincoln Express that's double diamond and comparable to the jumps at Squaw. There is some good tree skiing off Crow's Nest peak down the face or through Strawberry Fields.

Intermediate: From the top of the Disney Express head down the left side of the ridge along Crow's Traverse then drop down Pony Express, Montgomery and Upper Mac into Disney Meadows. Keep up your speed and stay high at the end of the run to avoid having to push to the lift. From the top of the Mt. Lincoln Express head to the right down Crowley's Run, Rahlves' Run and eventually head back top the base of the lift along Ridge Run or Silver Belt Finger. The entire area served by Mt. Judah Express and Jerome Hill Express is an intermediate paradise, perfect for long cruising with occasional short steeps.

Beginner and First-timer: Beginners have beautiful long runs off the Christmas Tree and Mt. Judah chairs. White Pine at Mt. Judah is an excellent teaching area, segregated from the main ski trails. Beginners staying at the Inn at Sugar Bowl can reach the Christmas Tree and Mt. Judah chairs via the Nob Hill chairlift.

Parks and pipes

Sugar Bowl has incredible natural hits and quarterpipes. Real experts should check out the 58's and Palisades off Mt. Lincoln, and the Sugar Bowl off the Disney Express. On Sunset (off the Mt. Judah Express lift), the resort takes advantage of the natural gully-like terrain with added banks, whoops, gullies and drops. If that isn't enough there are manmade terrain parks to suit every ability level. A joint sponsorship with SnowBomb means the parks are bigger with more terrain features for everyone. Sugar Bowl has two major parks, Golden Gate Terrain Park and The Switching Yard on Coldstream, both off the Mt. Judah Express lift. Expect to find tabletops, rainbow rails, step-ups, boxes, spines and hips. For beginners and children, a dedicated family park on Nob Hill is within eyesight of the Village Lodge deck. Skilled skiers and riders will find the superpipe near the base of the Mt. Lincoln Express.

Snowboarding

Strawberry Fields and Crow's Nest Face are not to be missed on powder days. The groomers off the Jerome Hill Express are great for high-speed arcs. Remember to keep your speed up for the flat between the Mid Mountain Lodge and Village Lodge and at the bottom of the runs down from Crow's Nest.

Lessons (07/08 prices)

The Mountain Sports Learning Center is at Mt. Judah, has designated parking and is a one-stop shop for rentals, lessons, lift tickets. It also has a basket check, bathrooms and a ski shop.

Group lessons: $45 for two hours.

First-timer package: Learn-to-Ski/Snowboard including beginner lifts, rentals and 2-hour lesson is $85 ($95 holiday).

Private lessons: $90-$130 an hour, depending on the time you take your lesson and if it's during a holiday season.

Children's programs (06/07 prices)

Child care: Ages 3-5 years (toilet-trained). All day costs $100; half day is $70 (no lunch). Sugar Bears Child Care is a licensed center with educational and recreational activities as well as skiing and quiet time. The program includes snacks, lunch, lessons and ski equipment. Reservations required; call (530) 426-6776 well in advance. The child-care center has two locations: The Village, reachable only via the gondola, and in the Learning Center at the Mt. Judah base area.

Other options: Baby's Away (800-446-9030; 530-544-2229) rents and will deliver baby items (cribs, strollers, toys, etc.) to your hotel or condo. For **babysitting referrals**, call North Lake Tahoe Resort Association (800-434-1262; 530-583-3494).

Children's lessons: Base Camp is a program for 4- to 6-year-olds and involves at least one hour on snow. Choose full day for $100 or a half day for $70. Summit Adventure Camp is for ages 6-12 (ski or snowboard). A full day costs $100 and includes lifts, equipment, lessons and lunch; half-day costs $70 (no lunch). The First Tracks package for teens who are first-timers includes lift ticket, two-hour lesson and rental (ski or snowboard) and costs $75. Lessons are out of the Mountain Sports Learning Center at the Mt. Judah base area.

Lift tickets (07-08 prices)

Adult (23-59) $60; **Child** (6-12) $15; **Young Adult** (13-22) $50.

Who skis free: Ages 5 and younger.

Who skis at a discount: Seniors (60-69) pay $38 and Super Seniors (70+) pay $5.

Accommodations–Sugar Bowl

The Inn at Sugar Bowl (530-426-6742; $$$$) was built at the base of Mt. Disney in 1939 and is one of the most unique ski lodges in North America. A seven-minute gondola ride from the Donner Pass Road (where you parked your car), the inn—and the gondola, for that matter—take you back to a time gone by. Lying in bed at this isolated inn, you only hear the wind in the treetops outside the snowbound three-story, shed-like building, a utilitarian structure constructed to withstand the heavy Sierra snows. The rooms are bright and comfortable, but except for a private bath and TV, there are no frills. You are paying for the location (slopeside) and intimacy. Breakfast and dinner (and lunch on the weekends) are served in the inn's small elegant dining room, and people often gather in the bar or comfortable lobby outside the dining room where it's easy to strike up conversations with fellow guests. The lobby and bar also are hotspots for the inn's wireless Internet connection.

Dining: $$$$–Entrees $30+; $$$–$20–$30; $$–$10–$20; $–less than $10.
Accommodations: (double room) $$$$–$200+; $$$–$141–$200; $$–$81–$140; $–$80 and less.

Cross-country & snowshoeing (see also xcskiresorts.com)

The Lake Tahoe region may have the greatest concentration of large cross-country ski areas in the U.S., with more than 800 km. of groomed trails. We have listed the bigger operations; local tourist offices can direct you to smaller and less expensive centers. Many of the ones we list here also have full-moon tours and snowshoe rentals and tours, so call for information.

The largest private trail system in North America is in California at **Royal Gorge** (800-500-3871, nationwide; 800-666-3871, Northern California only; 530-426-3871) just off I-80, west of Donner Summit at the Soda Springs exit. Royal Gorge has nearly 9,000 acres of terrain, and more than 300 km. of trails with a skating lane inside the tracks.

Royal Gorge has four surface lifts to help skiers up the tougher inclines. It is a full-service ski area, with rental equipment, ski school, ten warming huts, four cafes and a full-time ski patrol. Trailside lodging is at **Rainbow Lodge**, an historic 1920s B&B, or at **Wilderness Lodge**, a rustic retreat in the middle of the trail system. Book either through the ski area.

Northstar-at-Tahoe (530-562-2475) has 50 km. of groomed and marked trails. All are near the day lodge and downhill slopes. This is one of the gentler trail systems in the area—very good for families and those just learning. Lessons and rentals are available, as are snowshoe rentals.

The Tahoe Donner Cross-Country Area (530-587-9484) is off I-80 at Donner State Park exit. This area has 100 km. of trails, all double-tracked with wide skating lanes, and a day lodge with cafe. Tahoe Donner has California's only lighted night cross-country skiing, Wednesdays and Saturdays. Cross-country gear, snowshoes and pulk sleds are available for rental.

Squaw Creek Cross-Country Ski Center (530-583-6300) is a small area at the Resort at Squaw Creek, which has rentals and lessons. Trails cover 18 km., are groomed daily, and range from beginner to expert. Child care is available for kids ages 4 and older.

Tahoe Cross-Country Ski Area (530-583-5475), 2 miles east of Tahoe City, is now a non-profit ski foundation. It has 65 km. of groomed skating lanes and tracks, a day lodge, cafe, lessons and rentals. Call to inquire about bringing your dog. Snowshoes and pulk sleds also are available for rental.

Spooner Lake Cross-Country (775-887-8844, recording; 755-749-5349, live voice) on Hwy. 28, about a half-mile north of Hwy. 50, has more than 80 km. of trails, nearly all of which are machine groomed, with one 19-km. backcountry trail. Lessons and cross-country gear, snowshoe and pulk sled rentals are available; you also can rent a backcountry cabin.

Reno/Tahoe Accommodations
Downtown Reno

Reno offers big-time casino atmosphere closer to the North Shore and at lower prices than you'll find surrounding the lake. Reno also has a planetarium and two major museums, and is 30-45 minutes by car from the North Shore resorts. This is a good place to stay if you want to save some serious money and have a big enough group to split a rental car cost. Some hotels have ski shuttles, but most visitors here probably will want a car. Reno Central Reservations is at 888-448-7366.

Reno is no longer the half-awake cowboy gambler's town it used to be. It's also no longer considered as the quickie divorce capital of America, although you can still get a divorce here. During the 1990s, the city made renovations downtown to refurbish old buildings, add street artwork and develop recreational attractions and is still working on improvements. The town fathers took a train that went through the main section of downtown which stopped traffic causing long waits and put it under the streets. It has made a huge difference in traffic flow in the downtown sector.

During the winter, you can ice skate on a large outdoor rink, visit a world-class automobile museum and enjoy concerts and plays in a thriving arts community. Reno has chain motels, multistory casino-hotels and lots in between. Reno's airport has many nonstop and direct flights, and the city also is served by Amtrak's California Zephyr, which runs from the San Francisco Bay to Chicago.

Circus Circus (800-648-5010; 775-329-0711), **Silver Legacy** (800-687-8733; 775-325-7401) and **El Dorado** (800-6485966; 775-786-5700) are three casino resort hotels connected by an enclosed and connected shopping and restaurant mall. The mall forms a "T" shape, with Silver Legacy at the base of the T, Circus Circus to the left and El Dorado to the right. Any of these hotels is a good choice for a group that has some non-skiers, since there is so much to do without ever having to brave icy sidewalks. In the Silver Legacy's lobby, don't miss the ostentatious display of silver and crystal items once owned by Sam Fairchild, "the wealthiest silver baron Nevada has ever seen."

The **Grand Sierra Resort & Casino** (800-501-2651; 775-789-2000) used to be the Reno Hilton and is still so new, it retains some vestiges of the old hotel, such as the Reno Hilton evacuation notices on the backs of the doors and Hilton guest books on the coffee tables. The Grand Sierra is another great place to stay if not everyone in your group skis, because its enclosed shopping area has not only shops and eateries, but also a movie theater with four screens showing first-run movies, a bowling alley with 50 lanes, a ski shop, gym, spa and hair salon. The hotel has three outstanding fine-dining restaurants—the Steak House, Asiana and Dolce—as well as more casual places to grab a bite.

Inspired by the old Italian city in Tuscany, **Siena Hotel Spa Casino** (877-743-6233; 775-327-4362) sits along the Truckee River in downtown Reno, a tranquil setting in an otherwise busy city. Thanks to the owner's love of art, you'll find interesting pieces scattered throughout the property. Flags of the Contrada (regions in Tuscany that participate in the famous horse race Il Palio) fly in the casino and adorn the walls of the elegantly understated room decor. Siena has three restaurants—Lexie's on the River for fine dining, Contrada Cafe for casual fare, and Enoteca, a sexy wine bar with live jazz. The award-winning **Spa at Siena** (775-321-5868) offers customized treatments from 9 am to 9 pm every day.

Silver Legacy Resort Casino (800-687-8733; 775-325-7401) in the heart of downtown sports a lush Victorian theme. It has six restaurants of all levels and plenty of nightlife and entertainment as well.

John Ascuaga's **Nugget** (800-648-1177) in Sparks, sits off by itself, but features a wonderful Basque restaurant, Orozko, as well as Trader Dick's with a Polynesian theme.

Peppermill Casino (800-648-6992; 775-826-2121) is in the part of Reno closest to Mt. Rose and in the center of the city's shopping district. Starting as a coffee shop in 1971, it's now one of the largest family-owned hotel casinos in the country with more than 1,100 rooms and suites, eight restaurants, 14 themed bars and a waterfall pool.

Lake Tahoe's North Shore

The North Shore is relatively quiet. The North Shore has bed-and-breakfast inns, cabins on the lake, plush or spartan condominiums, and medium-sized casino hotels—a place for everyone. The best source for lodging-and-lift packages is **North Lake Tahoe Resort Association Lodging Information & Reservations,** 888-434-1262 or 530-583-3494; its web site is www.mytahoevacation.com. The agency also can suggest private homes and condos.

Incline Village has several hotels and condo complexes. It also has private homes that can

Dining: $$$$–Entrees $30+; $$$–$20–$30; $$–$10–$20; $–less than $10.
Accommodations: (double room) $$$$–$200+; $$$–$141–$200; $$–$81–$140; $–$80 and less.

easily sleep 12-16 people. For **Incline Village accommodations**, call 800-468-2463.

The **Hyatt Regency Lake Tahoe Resort, Spa and Casino** (888-591-1234; 775-832-1234; $$$$) is a four-star luxury hotel that resembles the grand homes built in the 1920s. The resort has just undergone a multi-million dollar renovation and the lobby and rooms are wonderful, with natural pine, leather furnishings and autumn colors. The **Cal-Neva Resort, Spa & Casino** (800-225-6382; 775-832-4000; $$-$$$$) is split by the state line and once was owned by Frank Sinatra and visited by Marilyn Monroe. Every room has a lake view, the best from the deluxe suites on the top three floors. There are also honeymoon bungalows with heart-shaped tubs, round beds and mirrored ceilings. The **Tahoe Biltmore Casino** (800-245-8667; 775-831-0660; $$) in Crystal Bay has midweek ski packages with Diamond Peak, including a lift ticket, lodging, a full breakfast and transportation to and from the slopes.

The **Inn at Incline Motor Lodge and Condominiums** (800-824-6391; $$) has more modest facilities but rooms are comfortable and there's an indoor pool and hot tub. Haus Bavaria (800-731-6222; $$-$$$$) is a European-style guest house with five rooms and **Crystal Bay Motel** (775-831-0287; $-$$) is an economy property near casinos.

The most upscale bed-and-breakfast is the **Rockwood Lodge** (800-538-2463; 530-525-5273; $$-$$$$), originally built in the mid-1930s. There are four rooms, two with private bath. It has antique furnishings, plush carpet, brass-and-porcelain bath fixtures, and down comforters on the beds. The lodge is next to the Ski Homewood Ski Area, on the west shore of Tahoe about 7 miles south of Tahoe City. This is a no-smoking inn and does not accept children.

The **Mayfield House** (530-583-1001; $$$), another B&B, was once a private residence in Tahoe City. The atmosphere is elegant and romantic, and full breakfasts come with the rate. Each of the rooms has a private bath.

Other B&Bs that are recommended are **The Cottage Inn** (800-581-4073; 530-581-4073; $$$) in Tahoe City; **The Shore House** (800-207-5160; 530-546-7270; $$$) in Tahoe Vista; or **Tahoma Meadows Bed & Breakfast** (530-525-1553; $$-$$$$) in Homewood.

Just south of Tahoe City is the **Sunnyside Lodge** (530-583-7200, or in California only, 800-822-2754; $$$), directly on the lake. There are 23 rooms, all with a lake view and a few rooms have fireplaces. Perhaps the most luxury for the money on the North Shore can be found in the **Tahoe Vista Inn & Marina** (530-546-7662; $$$) in Tahoe Vista. The six units here are spectacular and sited directly on the lake.

The **Cal-Neva Resort, Spa & Casino** (800-225-6382; 775-832-4000; $$-$$$$) is split by the state line and once was owned by Frank Sinatra and visited by Marilyn Monroe. Every room has a lake view, the best from the deluxe suites on the top three floors. There are also honeymoon bungalows with heart-shaped tubs, round beds and mirrored ceilings. The **Hyatt Regency Lake Tahoe Resort, Spa and Casino** (888-591-1234; 775-832-1234; $$$$) is a four-star luxury hotel that resembles the grand homes built in the 1920s. The resort has just undergone a multi-million dollar renovation and the lobby and rooms are wonderful, with natural pine, leather furnishings and autumn colors. The **Tahoe Biltmore Casino** (800-245-8667; 775-831-0660; $$) in **Crystal Bay** has midweek ski packages with Diamond Peak, including a lift ticket, lodging, a full breakfast and transportation to and from the slopes.

The **Granlibakken Resort & Conference Center** (800-543-3221; $$-$$$$) in Tahoe City is a great place to stay. Lodging is in 160 privately owned suites and townhouses and some feature a kitchen and fireplace. Sizes start at one bedroom and top out at a six-bedroom, six-bath townhouse. Two saunas and an outdoor spa are on site. The lovely complex sits on a hill among towering pines and red firs, next to the site of a former ski jump used for the 1932 Olympic tryouts. Two cross-country ski trails and a beginner's Alpine hill also can be found here.

For families or anyone looking for a great deal, **North Lake Lodge** (530-546-2731; $$), in Kings Beach only a few feet from the shore, is one of the oldest hotels but still in great shape. Continental breakfast is included and the shuttles stop just across the street.

River Ranch (530-583-4264; $$) on Hwy. 89 near Alpine Meadows is another moderately priced lodge. This historic ski lodge sits on the banks of the Truckee River and rooms are furnished with early American antiques. Continental breakfast is included, and the shuttles for Squaw Valley and Alpine Meadows are nearby. A rushing river lulls you to sleep.

Truckee

The town of Truckee is convenient to Northstar and Sugar Bowl. The **Richardson House** (888-229-0365; 530-587-5388; $$$), built in the 1880s as a private residence, has been restored as a comfortable Victorian B&B, furnished primarily with period oak pieces. Six of eight rooms have private baths; some with Victorian soaking tubs, others tiny shower baths. A full breakfast is served family style; tea and cookies are always available.

Industrial chic meets cool green in the **Cedar House Sport Hotel** (866-582-5655; $$$-$$$$), which opened in summer 2006. Purposefully designed and built from the ground up as a green hotel, the complex has 42 rooms or suites in four connected or adjacent timber buildings. Hospitality is European style, with bedding comprising puffy duvets and high-thread-count linens and an expanded continental breakfast with meats, cheeses, fruit, pastries and hard-boiled eggs.

For real western authenticity, try the **Truckee Hotel** (800-659-6921; 530-587-4444; $$), welcoming guests since 1873. Mostly it housed timber and railroad workers, but one of the residents was a madam who reportedly ran a little business on the side. It was renovated in 1992, but you'll still feel like you're sleeping in the Old West. Eight of the 37 rooms have private baths, including old-fashioned, claw-footed tubs. Some rooms are large enough to sleep six. Breakfast and afternoon tea served in the parlor are included with the B&B rates.

Dining

Dining is in the midst of a renaissance in North Lake Tahoe. The old Mom'n'Pop places are giving way to some upscale gourmet eateries. All restaurants are within a half-hour drive of each other. They are listed geographically—Very North Tahoe, Tahoe City, Truckee, Incline Village and Squaw Valley.

Very North Lake Tahoe (Carnelian Bay, Tahoe Vista, King's Beach, Crystal Bay)

Le Petit Pier (530-546-4464; $$$$) in Tahoe Vista presents up-scale French cuisine. Locals refer to this restaurant as "where to go on a very special date." Reservations needed.

In Spring 2003 the **Wild Goose** (530-546-3640; $$$-$$$$), named after one of Tahoe's double-ender launches, made its debut with an interior that's reminiscent of the lake cruisers of the 1920s, replete with mahogany, leather and polished steel, plus lake views. The Paris-educated chef, whose mantra is "nuances and simplicity," uses fresh seasonal and regional ingredients to create Contemporary American cuisine that showcases a sophisticated combination of flavors and textures.

Spindleshanks (530-546-2191; $$$), also in Tahoe Vista, has been awarded "Best Wine List" several years in a row. The food matches at somewhat reasonable prices. The place gets packed. Call for reservations or go early. On Wednesdays, when the appetizers are half price all evening at the bar, get a spot there and order a couple to make a nice light dinner.

The **Soule Domain** (530-546-7529; 775-833-0399; $$$) in Crystal Bay receives consistent raves from people at both ends of the lake. **Gar Woods Grill & Pier** (530-546-3366; $$-$$$) in Carnelian Bay serves a California grill menu.

Dining: $$$$–Entrees $30+; $$$–$20–$30; $$–$10–$20; $–less than $10.
Accommodations: (double room) $$$$–$200+; $$$–$141–$200; $$–$81–$140; $–$80 and less.

For sushi head to **Hiro Sushi** (530-546-4476; $$) in Kings Beach, where you should order the all-you-can-eat menu (you only have an hour to stuff it in). The caterpillar rolls, made with eel, look just like caterpillars down to the antenna. The best Mexican in the area is **La Mexicana** (530-546-0310; $$) in Kings Beach.

Lanza's (530-546-2434; $-$$), an institution in Kings Beach, also has excellent Italian fare at family prices. **Steamer's Beachside Bar and Oven** (530-546-2218; $-$$) has been voted best pizza on the North Shore. Other good places for pizza are **C.B's Pizza** (530-546-4738; $) in Kings Beach and **Jiffy's Pizza** (530-546-3244; $) in Tahoe Vista.

For breakfast try the **Old Post Office** (530-546-3205; $) at Carnelian Bay and order the deluxe French toast or create your own omelet. At the **Log Cabin** (530-546-7109; $$) in Kings Beach you can get lobster and shrimp scrambles, trout Benedict and fancy pancakes. The price bargain is breakfast at the Tahoe Biltmore ($) served 24/7.

Tahoe City and nearby

Wolfdales (530-583-5700; $$$$) with its frequently changing menu is superb. Claiming the food is "cuisine unique," it's essentially Asian and European with a taste of California mixed in. Reservations are suggested.

Christy Hill (530-583-8551; $$$$) is a real find. The menu, which changes several times each week, is loaded with the freshest fish and specialty produce. The restaurant is open for dinner only from Tuesday through Sunday. Call for reservations. **Truffula** (530-581-3362; $$$) in Tahoe City is a gourmet find. The tiny place serves "wild food from land and sea" in a modern atmosphere.

Swiss Lakewood Restaurant (530-525-5211; $$$) in Homewood is Lake Tahoe's oldest and one of its finest dining experiences with impeccable service. It is currently closed for the 07-08 season but plans to reopen in the summer of 2008. Cuisine is French-Swiss and classic continental. Closed Mondays, except holidays. **Sunnyside** (530-583-7201; $$$) has good meals and a great setting. The crab legs are wonderful and on Wednesdays fish tacos rule.

Yama Sushi and Robata Grill (530-583-9262; $$-$$$) in the Lighthouse Shopping Center is a classic sushi restaurant but also includes grilled meats, fish and vegetables. **Coyotes Mexican Grill** (530-583-6653; $$-$$$) is recommended by return visitors and locals alike.

River Ranch (530-583-4264; $$-$$$) at the access road to Alpine Meadows has been there for years and still gets great reviews. In the spring sitting by the river is a joy. Another Tahoe original is the **Old European Restaurant and Bar/Pfeifer House** (530-583-3102; $$), just north of Tahoe City on the road to Alpine and Squaw, with its tradition al German meals.

Fiamma (530-581-1416; $$), in the middle of town, has a wood-fired pizza oven. Also try **Lakehouse Pizza** (530-583-2222; $$) for a great lake view. **Za's** (530-583-1812; $$) serves moderately priced Italian.

For Mexican with a big dose of margaritas and a shoulder-to-shoulder crowd on weekends, a good choice is the **Hacienda del Lago** (530-583-0358; $) in the Boatworks Mall. If you want lots of good food at very reasonable prices, try **Bacchi's** (530-583-3324; $) for Italian or **Bridgetender** (530-583-3342; $) for great half-pound burgers and an extensive beer selection.

For breakfast head to **The Fire Sign** (530-583-0871; $), about 2 miles south of Tahoe City, where many believe the best breakfasts and lunches in the region are served, or go to **Rosie's Cafe** (530-583-8504; $), where breakfast is a locals' affair. Near Alpine Meadows, try the **Alpine Riverside Cafe** (530-583-6896; $-$$) for breakfast and lunch.

Truckee

One of Truckee's most highly recommended restaurants is **Dragonfly** (530-587-0557; $$$), which promises "dining on a higher level." That can be interpreted in several ways: location—it's upstairs; cuisine—the upscale, Asian-fusion menu may include such intriguing choices as ginger lacquered muscovy duck legs or Thai tamarind fishermen's stew; or commitment—it adds $1 to every bill to support the local land trust.

Farther east on the street is **Pianeta** (530-587-4694; $$$), an intimate restaurant with a combined nouveau and classic Italian menu: from olives and antipasto to mushroom dumplings, pasta with roasted eggplant to basic spaghetti. The same owners also run the **Pacific Crest** (530-587-2626; $-$$), attached to the Bar of America. This Victorian-styled restaurant has an international menu with dishes from several countries: Soba noodles with ginger stir-fry, lamb shank over couscous, risotto, paella, and more. **Moody's** (530-587-7619; $$$$) in the Truckee Hotel has a playful menu that will make gourmands smile: crispy pig trotters, poached duck egg, a foie gras "short stack," veal sweetbreads, and the like.

West of the walking district along the road to Donner Pass are more local favorites. Family owned and operated for more than 35 years, **El Toro Bravo** (530-587-3557; $) has an excellent reputation for Mexican cuisine, with fajitas topping the menu. **Java Sushi** (530-582-1144; $$) serves what its name implies. Try the Saturday Night Special served every night. They also serve tempura, teriyaki and broiled salmon.

Overlooking downtown is the perennially popular **Cottonwood** (530-587-5711; $$-$$$). Big windows in the main dining room frame downtown Truckee and historic photos and artifacts, from the building's first life as a ski lodge, fill the rooms. Menu ranges from cassoulet to Thai red-curry prawns.

Pick up dinner-to-go from the prepared foods at **Piper's Patisserie** (530-582-2256, $-$$), a gourmet deli and wine store with casual seating. Fabulous baked goods, creative dinner fare, salads, sandwiches and some of the fanciest ice cream we've ever seen.

For breakfast, go early to the **Squeeze In** (530-587-9814; $$), where the list of omelets requires a speed-reading course. The place has all the atmosphere you could want in a breakfast joint, built in a former alley and only 10 feet wide. On weekends, expect to wait a while.

Northstar-at-Tahoe Resort

Not content to rest on their laurels, the chefs at Northstar's restaurant, **True North Restaurant and Bar** (530-562-2250; $$$), decided to reinvent themselves with a new menu, new name and refurbished interior. Consistently one of Tahoe's best restaurants and recipient of the "Wine Spectator" Award of Excellence, it now showcases sustainable food choices using Niman Ranch all-natural beef and pork, fresh organic produce and Monterrey Bay Aquarium-approved seafood flown in daily from Honolulu.

Incline Village

On the northeastern side of the lake, in Incline Village, go to the **Lone Eagle Grille** at the Hyatt Regency (775-832-3250; $$$$) for some of the best food on the Nevada lakeshore. The soaring stone and timber and the massive fireplace blend with magnificent views across the lake at sunset, and the cuisine and wine list provide accomplished accompaniment.

Le Bistro (775-831-0800; $$$$), across the street from the Hyatt Regency, is considered the best restaurant on the lake by some locals. As the name implies, the focus is on French fare.

The Big Water Grille (775-833-0606; $$$), at the bottom of the hill at Diamond Peak, is another find. A Native American name for Lake Tahoe, the **Big Water** features an eclectic menu and spectacular lake views—the perfect setting for romantic dinners, apres-ski relaxation and group gatherings. The menu features American Contemporary cuisine with Mediterranean

Dining: $$$$–Entrees $30+; $$$–$20–$30; $$–$10–$20; $–less than $10.
Accommodations: (double room) $$$$–$200+; $$$–$141–$200; $$–$81–$140; $–$80 and less.

and Pacific-Rim influences.

Cafe 333 (775-832-7333; $$$), written up in Bon Appetite several times, is favored by Incline locals. It has French country decor and a moderately priced menu. The **Wild Alaskan Fish Company** (775-832-6777; $$) is one of the top spots for excellent seafood on the lake. It's just plain good.

Ciao Mein Trattoria (775-832-3275; $$) in the Hyatt has a menu that is half Italian and half Chinese. **Azzara's** (775-831-0346; $-$$) serves good, reasonable Italian food. **Austin's** (775-832-7778; $) gets raves for meatloaf and homemade soups. **T's Rotisserie** (775-831-2832; $-$$) gets the nod from knowledgeable locals for chicken and burritos. **Hacienda de La Sierra** (775-831-8300; $) is a top Mexican spot. **China Wok** (775-833-3633; $-$$) is the only true Chinese place in town.

Squaw Valley

With the new restaurants in Squaw Valley's pedestrian village added to the excellent upscale choices at the lodges here, you don't have to leave the resort to get a good meal.

PlumpJack Squaw Valley (530-583-1576; $$$$) is an extraordinary dining experience in a style that is as unique as the cuisine is delicious. The wine list is carefully selected and prices are very reasonable, given the high quality. Reservations suggested.

Plumpjack Balboa Cafe Squaw Valley (530-583-5850; $$$$) in the Village at Squaw Valley is an American bistro with San-Francisco-style dining. It's owned by the same team who own PlumpJack Squaw Valley (if you're familiar with San Francisco, you'll also be familiar with the fine reputation of their two restaurants there).

Glissandi (530-581-6621; $$$$) at the Resort at Squaw Creek brings New York and San Francisco style and service, all overlooking Squaw Valley. Reservations suggested. Also in the hotel, **Ristorante Montagna's** (530-581-6619) serves a California/Italian fusion cuisine. Try **Graham's** (530-581-0454; $$$) at the Christy Inn for gourmet southern European meals.

The sushi restaurant in the village, **Mamasake** (530-584-0110; $-$$$), has become a new hotspot. It could be just because the "Eat Raw at Squaw" proposition is hard to skip but it's more likely because the food here really is good. Other new village restaurants worth a visit are **High Sierra Grill** (530-584-6100; $-$$$) for steaks and other grilled items; **Tantara Bakery, Bistro and Beyond** ($-$$), which transforms itself from a bakery for breakfast to a deli and bistro for lunch and dinner; and the **Fireside Pizza Co.** (530-584-6150; $$) for fancy pizzas made with sourdough crust and farm-fresh ingredients.

Apres-ski/nightlife

River Ranch on the Alpine Meadows access road was voted to have the top apres-ski in North Lake Tahoe. If you're going by Squaw, the **Loft Bar** is the old-timer locals' hangout and the **Red Dog Bar & Grill** is a favorite with the Squaw Valley employees. **Bar One** has live music, dancing and pool tables, while the **Plaza Bar** is where sports fans go to see sporting events on the big screen TV. For a more intimate apres-ski, the bar at the **PlumpJack Squaw Valley Inn** has a cozy fireplace and an excellent selection of wine.

In **Tahoe City**, places to head include **Pete 'N Peters, Bridgetender, Rosie's Cafe, Pierce Street Annex** (behind Safeway near the Boatworks Mall, voted best pick-up place), or **Jake's on the Lake. Hacienda del Lago** in the Boatworks has nachos 'til 6 p.m. **Sunnyside**, just a couple of miles south of Tahoe City on the lake, has a lively bar. For the best live music, try **Sierra Vista**, adjacent to the Boatworks Mall.

In Truckee, you can find music at **Bar of America and the Pastime Club** on Commercial Row. The **Cottonwood Restaurant** overlooking Truckee on Hwy. 267 has jazz. **Trio** is

Truckee&Mac246's latest stylish watering hole, where the emphasis is on socializing over wine&Mac247; rather than merely tasting. A menu of light appetizers and desserts is available to accompany the three and six ounce pours of wine. Live music in the evenings is garnering Trio a reputation as a happening nightspot.

The casinos on North Lake Tahoe have entertainment every night. Sure bets are the **Cal-Neva Lodge** (775-832-4000), **The Crystal Bay Club** (775-831-0512), **Hyatt Lake Tahoe** and the **Tahoe Biltmore** (800-245-8667). Call to see what shows are currently performing.

Spindleshanks Bar in Tahoe Vista is a great apres-ski spot where drinks and appetizers are half price every day during happy hour. On Wednesdays the appetizers are half price all evening. The lakefront **Gar Woods Grill & Pier** in Cornelian Bay is worth an apres-ski visit not just for the view, but for the clever laugh-out-loud names and descriptions of the drinks.

Other activities

Squaw Valley's High Camp at the top of the cable car has ice skating, snow-tubing, dining and more. **Polaris Park**, located mid-mountain at Northstar, has lighted snow play areas for tubing, snowbiking and other activities. It is open weekends and holidays, 3 to 9 p.m. **Sleigh rides** are available at **Northstar-at-Tahoe**, 530- 562-2480, and in the **Squaw Valley Meadow**, 530-583-6300. The region also has **snowmobiling, scenic flights, hot-air balloon rides, horseback riding, sleigh rides, bowling, movies and health clubs. Snowfest** is North Tahoe's winter carnival, usually in late February/early March. Call 800-824-6348 or 530-83-3494 for a complete list of things to do.

At Diamond Peak, check out the **Incline Village Recreation Center**, which has aerobics, basketball court, weight room, European sauna and an indoor pool among its amenities. Another spot for family fun is **Bowl Incline** with more than bowling. You'll find pool tables, other pinball gizmos, video poker built into the bar and a golf simulator where you can play seven world-class courses. The **Incline Village Cinema** is an excellent movie theater.

There are also plenty of **casinos** on the north shore. The **Tahoe Biltmore** is a favorite of locals for slots and poker. The **Hyatt Regency Lake Tahoe** is also an excellent casino and has perhaps the best shows. The best shopping is in the **Boatworks Mall**.

National Automobile Museum: The Harrah Collection, 10 S. Lake St. in Reno, has more than 200 classic and antique automobiles. Admission is $9 for adults, $7 for ages 62 and older, $3 for ages 6 to 18, and free for ages 5 and younger.

Getting there and getting around

By air: Reno-Tahoe International Airport has more than 100 nonstop flights a day from various parts of the country. Allegiant Air has non-stop service between Bellingham, WA and Reno-Tahoe. The airport is 50 miles from Alpine Meadows.

The new North Lake Tahoe Express daily airport shuttle service is available to and from North Lake Tahoe and the Reno-Tahoe International Airport. The shuttle runs from 3:30 a.m. until 12 midnight. Fees are $35 per person, one-way, and $60 round trip. Discounts available for groups of two or more. Reservations are required and can be made four hours in advance.

By train: Amtrak (800-872-7245) serves Truckee and Reno on the California Zephyr line, running from Oakland to Chicago.

By bus: Shuttles run from almost every major hotel to each major ski resort. Check for schedules when you arrive.

Sierra Nevada Gray Lines (800-822-6009; 775-329-1147) operates a daily ski shuttle between Reno and Alpine Meadows as well as Northstar-at-Tahoe (except Saturdays). Squaw

Dining: $$$$–Entrees $30+; $$$–$20–$30; $$–$10–$20; $–less than $10.
Accommodations: (double room) $$$$–$200+; $$$–$141–$200; $$–$81–$140; $–$80 and less.

Valley USA (800-446-2928) operates a Reno/South Lake Tahoe Shuttle from mid-December through the end of March. Tahoe Casino Express (800-446-6128) runs between Reno airport and South Shore.

By car: Driving time from Reno is about an hour to any major North Shore resort. San Francisco is about four hours away via I-80 to the North Shore. During storms, the California Highway Patrol doesn't let drivers come up the mountains without chains or a four-wheel-drive vehicle, so be prepared. Alpine Meadows is on Hwy. 89 (runs between I-80 and Hwy. 28, which hugs the North Shore).

Getting around: As much as we hate to recommend adding more auto pollution to this pristine location, rent a car. If you stay near one of the ski resorts, your dining and evening options would be limited without one. Alpine Meadows, Squaw Valley, Sugar Bowl, Diamond Peak, Northstar and Homewood all have shuttles from North Tahoe towns.

North Lake Tahoe has launched a free, evening bus service from Squaw Valley to Tahoe City to Crystal Bay, Truckee and Tahoma. The service is from 7 p.m. to 12:30 a.m. and runs through April 8. Truckee has also launched a new, free nighttime downtown shuttle service that will run through April 8. Hours of operation are 6 p.m. until midnight, seven days a week.

Other Reno/North Lake Tahoe resorts
Homewood Mountain Resort, Homewood, CA; (530) 525-2992
Internet: www.skihomewood.com
8 lifts; 1,260 skiable acres; 1,650 vertical feet; 1 terrain park; 1 halfpipe

Homewood Mountain Resort, on the west shore of Lake Tahoe, is one of three Tahoe ski areas that can qualify for Best View Of The Lake honors. This area, though smallish by Tahoe standards, has more than 1,200 skiable acres accessible from either of two base areas called North Side and South Side.

Lift tickets (07/08): Adults, $53; junior (13–18), $35; seniors (70+), $15; $10; kids 5-12, $10; 4 and younger, free.

Distance from Reno: About 50 miles from Reno via I-80 west and Hwy. 89 south.

Distance from Sacramento: About 120 miles via I-80 east and Hwy. 89 south.

Lodging information: (877) 525-7669 or (800) 824-6348.

Boreal, Truckee, CA; (530) 426-3666
Internet: www.borealski.com
9 lifts; 380 skiable acres; 500 vertical feet; 7 terrain parks; 1 superpipe

Boreal is a wide ridge of fairly short ski trails right off I-80 on the Donner Pass. It's the closest resort to Sacramento and San Francisco. Boreal, purchased in 1995 by the company that owns Alpine Meadows, is very popular with riders, who like the short, straight runs off the summit and the eight Vans-sponsored terrain parks. Boreal also has runs down its back side.

Boreal has night skiing and a night halfpipe and terrain park. It is the home of the Western Ski Sport Museum, generally open during Boreal's ski hours.

Lift tickets (07/08): Adults, $44; juniors (13-18) $39; children (5–12), $12; seniors (60+), $25; children 4 and younger free.

Distance from Reno: About 45 miles west on I-80.

Distance from Sacramento: About 80 miles east on I-80.

Lodging information: (530) 426-1012.

South Lake Tahoe Area

Heavenly Mountain Resort
Kirkwood
Sierra-at-Tahoe

Toll-free reservations: (800) 288-2463
Internet: www.bluelaketahoe.com

Dining:★★★
Apres-ski/nightlife:★★★★★
Other activities:★★★

Few regions in the world have what South Lake Tahoe does: almost 10,000 acres of lift-served terrain that annually receives an average of 40 feet of snow, a stunning Alpine lake—72 miles of shoreline—that never freezes, and sunny skies for more than 300 days a year. Add to this live entertainment, 24-hour access to slot machines and casino table games and lots of great food. South Lake Tahoe is slightly more than an hour from a major international airport.

Better still, you can pick your style of vacation. Part of the town (South Lake Tahoe/ Stateline) lies in Nevada, so if you like to stay up late dancing and gambling, you can book a room at one of four giant, high-rise casino hotels. A few steps across the Nevada/California state line, which runs right through town, life is quieter. But the new gondola has stretched the modern part of the city about half a mile to the west. Here in Alpine-style Heavenly Village you can take a the gondola right to the top of the mountain, enjoy the hustle and bustle of the South Shore's casino nightlife, shop in one of the village's stores, or sit back and quietly soak in the area's innate beauty.

When you're ready for the slopes, you can pick from three resorts: Heavenly and Kirkwood, two of the largest Tahoe resorts, and Sierra-at-Tahoe, just 12 miles down the road. Heavenly is the most popular Tahoe resort with out-of-towners. Kirkwood has a well-deserved reputation for awesome terrain and massive amounts of snow. You also shouldn't miss Sierra-at-Tahoe, known for its tree skiing and incredible backcountry terrain.

Heavenly Mountain Resort

Heavenly is big. It's a top-ranked resort with some great expert terrain—Mott Canyon and Killebrew Canyon on the Nevada side; its famous face run, Gunbarrel, on the California side; and loads of tree skiing. The resort also has excellent intermediate and advanced skiing.

The gondola has changed this resort dramatically. Skiers and riders can be seen walking from the casinos and other hotels to the lifts that rise right from the center of the action.

Heavenly is also the only two-state mountain resort—you can start out from either California or Nevada. The gondola provides direct access from the center of the South Lake Tahoe/ Stateline district to the resort, and the 12-minute ride gives skiers and riders a killer view of the lake. There's a public parking garage at Heavenly Village, near the base of the gondola. More parking is available at the California base just up Ski Run Blvd. On busy weekends, skiers and snowboarders who are looking to avoid crowds can start from the Nevada side. Take Hwy. 207 (Kingsbury Grade) to either the Stagecoach or Boulder bases.

The most spectacular view of the Lake Tahoe area and the lake itself—perhaps the most awesome view from a ski area summit anywhere—is at the top of the Sky Express. From here on a sunny day just after a storm, the lake looks like a brilliant blue sapphire, nesting in soft folds of white velvet. Pack a camera or stop at one of the photographers lining Ridge Run.

Mountain layout

You can't ski down to Heavenly Village, and the gondola stops downloading people at 4 p.m., so be sure you wind your way back to the top of the gondola before then (via 49'er, Sam's Dream, Cascade, or the California Trail). Signage is good at Heavenly, so you shouldn't have trouble finding it.

Expert, Advanced: Heavenly's first trails, Gunbarrel and East Bowl, strike awe in all but the best skiers. From the top of the tram, they seem to drop 1,700 feet straight down into Lake Tahoe, pausing only briefly at Heavenly's small California base area. Mogul skiers learn the hard way here, and the bumps really are bigger than some cars.

Or you could head to Mott Canyon on the Nevada side. Off the Dipper Express, Mott Canyon is accessible from designated gates. Hully Gully and Pinenuts are double-diamond runs that allow you to do some reconnaissance on the canyon's north-facing chutes. But if you're already uncomfortable, don't try Bill's, Snakepit, or The Y—listed in order of difficulty and accessed via gate 1. They are three of the steepest lift-served runs in the West. Killebrew Canyon is even more treacherous. If the bumps on the California face look too menacing, head to the Sky Express chair, right off the gondola down Von Schmidt's Trail. From the top of the Sky Express, the best of the California side opens up. Drop down Ellie's if you are looking for bumps.

Then strike out for Nevada for the other half of Heavenly's terrain. It will take a few chairlift rides. The blue runs around the Dipper Express quad and Stagecoach Express are screamers. But beware, the Dipper gets jammed on busy days. North-facing Milky Way Bowl at the top of the Dipper can have some of the best snow at the resort.

Intermediate: On the Nevada side, Tamarack Express, Comet Express, Dipper Express, North Bowl, Olympic and the Stagecoach Express are all good choices. Tamarack, Dipper and Comet provide access to both sides of the resort.

On the California side, Ridge Run, off the Sky Express, swoops down the resort's western periphery. Offshoots include Liz's, Jackpot and Canyon. Round-A-Bout descends to the California Lodge, zig-zagging down to World Cup. To avoid that, download on the Gunbarrell Express, which ends steps from the bus depot. The tram docks at the other end of the parking area, which makes for an uncomfortable walk in or with gear to the bus depot.

For a looonnnngg run, hug the resort's eastern perimeter, taking Skyline Trail, from the summit of the Sky Express to Dipper Knob, to Big Dipper, to Perimeter, to the base of Galaxy.

If you want long smooth cruising, head to the right from the Sky Express when you get off the chair and steam down Liz's, Canyon, High Roller or Ridge Run. Just below the Sky Deck, you can drop into Maggie's Canyon.

Beginner, First-timer Heavenly's green terrain is smack in the middle of the boarding area for four lifts. People dart in every direction, making a most intimidating scene for many beginners.

However, the resort now has an isolated 15-acre learning area at the top of the gondola that has improved the learning experience here. The learning area is served by three lifts—a quad, a mighty might tow and a moving carpet. A ski school yurt and nearby food service cap if off.

Parks and pipes

The advanced park, High Roller California, is on the upper California side off the Canyon chair. The High Roller Superpipe is at the top of the Powderbowl chair on the California side. The resort purchased a 22-foot Zaugg pipecutter and plans to build Tahoe's largest pipe. The intermediate park, High Roller Stateline, is off the Tamarack chair on the California/Nevada border. The beginner park, Low Roller, is between Groove and Patsy's chairs on the California side.

Heavenly has South Lake Tahoe's only after-hours terrain park—with hits, rails and funboxes—lighted 5-9 p.m. every Thursday through Saturday. The High Roller Nightlife Park is off the World Cup chair next to Heavenly's California Lodge. The resort has frequent rail jam competitions and DJs spinning tunes.

Snowboarding

Riders flock to Heavenly for its steeps, powder-filled canyons and powder stashes in the woods. The biggest bummer is the terrain layout isn't exactly snowboarder-friendly—the traverses are flat, flat, flat and you have to do a lot of strapping and unstrapping to move around the mountain. But, all that work is worth it, especially after a powder dump.

General consensus among riders is the California side is too bumped up (stay away from Gunbarrel and East Bowl if you hate bumps like most riders do), so the Nevada side is the place to play. Mott Canyon and Killebrew Canyon have the steepest terrain at Heavenly. But beware: by steep, we mean way steep. For strictly trees, head to Dipper Knob Trees and the area known as the "western perimeter" (off Olympic Chair, ride the ridge to the trees, where you'll find natural hits, waves and lots of powder).

Other playgrounds include the numerous hits in Sand Dunes, the waterfall in North Bowl trees and the natural pipe left of Sky chair. Stick to Stagecoach and Olympic lifts if you want to carve your brains out. First-timers will find isolated learning terrain with its own lifts at the top of the gondola.

 ## Lessons (07/08 prices)

Group lessons: Levels 3-9 (skiers and snowboarders) choose from a 2.75-hour lesson for $85 or an all-day clinic with lift ticket and lesson for $135.

First-timer package: A 2.75-hour lesson, rentals and access to the

---

Heavenly Mountain Resort Facts

California Side—
Summit elevation: 10,067 feet
Vertical drop: 3,500 feet
Base elevation: 6,540 feet

Nevada Side—
Summit elevation: 10,067 feet
Vertical drop: 2,840 feet
Base elevation: 7,200 feet

Address: Box 2180, Stateline, NV 89449
Ski area phone: 775-586-7000
Snow report: 586-7000, press 1
Toll-free reservations: (800) 432-8365
E-mail: info@skiheavenly.com
Internet: www.skiheavenly.com

Number of lifts: 30—1 aerial tram, 1 gondola, 2 high-speed six-packs, 7 high-speed quads, 5 triples, 4 doubles, 6 surface lifts, 4 moving carpets
Snowmaking: 70 percent of trails
Total acreage: 4,800 patrolled acres (1,084 skiable trail acres)
Uphill capacity: 52,000 per hour
Parks & pipes: 4 parks, 1 pipe
Bed base: 22,000 in S. Lake Tahoe
Nearest lodging: At base of gondola
Resort child care: Yes, 6 weeks and older
Adult ticket, per day: $76 (07/08)

Expert: ★★★★
Advanced: ★★★★★
Intermediate: ★★★★
Beginner: ★★★
First-timer: ★★★

beginner lifts costs $128, ski or snowboard. Same offer applies to novices with some experience on snow. Ask about multiday savings.

Private lessons: $350 for three hours; $525 for all day (six hours). Additional people cost $50 each for any lesson shorter than six hours, but six-hour privates can have up to six people at no extra charge. Reservations suggested, call 800-HEAVENLY.

Special programs: Heavenly has adaptive clinics and clinics for women. First Tracks gets you on the mountain a half-hour before the lifts open and includes breakfast at Lakeview Lodge.

Racing: A coin-op course is on the Yahoo run on the California side.

Children's programs (07/08 prices)

Child care (California side only): Ages 6 weeks to 6 years. Full-day program costs $115 (booked in advance) or $140 (walk-in); half-day, morning or afternoon, costs $100 (booked n advance) or $125 (walk-in). Lunch included except in afternoon class. Ski instruction/day-care combo programs also are available for ages 3 and older. Reservations required; call 800-HEAVENLY one to two months in advance.

Other options: If you need non-skiing child care, Bright Beginnings (775-588-5437) is a state-licensed day-care center in Stateline for ages 6 weeks to 12 years. The center is open Monday–Saturday, 8:30 a.m.–4:30 p.m. Reservations are required. The child-care centers at Heavenly (775-586-7000) and Kirkwood (209-258-7274) both have a list of babysitters, but expect to pay $15/hour for a sitter. Baby's Away (800-446-9030; 530-544-2229) rents and will deliver baby items (cribs, strollers, toys, etc.) to your hotel or condo anywhere in the Lake Tahoe area.

Children's lessons: Full day for ages 4–13 costs $165, including instruction, rentals, helmet, lunch and lift access. Ages 7–13 can take snowboard lessons for the same price. Reservations for full-day programs are highly recommended; call 800-HEAVENLY. Children can get "private" (up to 6 people) clinics for $525 for a full day or $350 for a half day.

Lift tickets (07/08 prices)

(Based on Jan 6-Jan 18, 2008 prices; Resort has 11 pricing seasons.)

Adult (19-64) 2-day ticket $152; 3-day $222; 5-day $350

Child (5-12) 2-day ticket $74; 3-day $105; 5-day $ 155

Who skis free: Children ages 4 and younger ski free with a paying adult.

Who skis at a discount: Teens (ages 13-18) and Seniors pay $126 for 2 days.

A gondola ride for sightseers costs $24 for adults; $22 for teens and seniors; $15 for children; free for ages 4 and younger.

Kirkwood

Kirkwood has no bright lights, no ringing jackpots, no wide blue lake, no high-rise buildings and no urban noise. Instead, you have the feeling that you are entering a special secret place, known to a select few. Yet you're at one of Tahoe's "big six" resorts.

As you drive up the access road from Hwy. 88, it's easy to see why these giant bowls were chosen for a ski resort. Skiers and snowboarders leave tracks on every slope leading down to Kirkwood Village. No town existed before the resort came to fruition in 1972. Kirkwood sits in a natural basin with a base elevation of 7,800 feet—the highest in the Tahoe area. In a mountain range known for heavy powder (a.k.a. Sierra cement), Kirkwood's snow is often lighter and fluffier and more abundant than the other Tahoe resorts. Consequently, the resort frequently stays open into May with good late-season conditions.

Mountain layout

Kirkwood has both named and numbered its lifts. Locals and staff tend to use the numbers, so we list those in parentheses in the following terrain descriptions.

Expert, Advanced: Kirkwood locals know to follow the sun. And if the snow is fresh, head to the Sunrise chair (Chair 4). But beware, it can be heavy too, or sunbaked. To return to the front side, drop down to Thunder Saddle and pick one of four north-facing chutes to return to the frontside. Back at the main base area, pick from the Wagonwheel/The Wall (Chair 10) or Cornice (Chair 6) lifts. Both serve steep, wide-open bowls and white-knuckle chutes. For a real thrill, traverse from Chair 10 to the top of Notch Chute in The Sisters. The first "step" is the crux; make that, and the rest is easy. Relatively, that is. Cornice serves single-diamond runs that feel like double-diamonds (e.g., Lost Cabin). From the top of Cornice, you can also traverse right to Palisades Bowl for some good powder shots.

Intermediate: In general, intermediate trails progress in difficulty as you move from skiers' left to skiers' right on the mountain (from Chair 7/TC Express, to Chair 4/Sunrise). Intermediates can stay on the lower sections of the face, using TC Express (Chair 7) and Solitude (Chair 5), or work their way over Caples Crest (Chair 2) to the Sunrise section.

The entire lower mountain, with just a couple of exceptions, is perfectly suited for intermediates. When you're ready to test your black-diamond skills, try the groomed runs off Chair 11.

Beginner, First-timer: Beginners will find gentle trails served by Snowkirk Chair (Chair 1) to the east, and Bunny Chair (Chair 9) and TC Express (Chair 7) at the far west. First-timers should head straight for the Timber Creek Lodge, a right-hand turn before you reach the main parking lot (there's a sign). Here novices will find a rental shop and ticket window, plus Chairs 9 and 7 (Bunny and TC Express) that serve novice and low-intermediate terrain.

Experienced skiers should park in the main lot and get their tickets in the main lodge farther down the road, but if there's a novice in your group, you can get to the main area using Chair 7. Kirkwood has by far the best setup for novices in the South Tahoe region.

Parks and pipes

The parks and pipe at Kirkwood are just as impressive as the natural terrain that surrounds them. Directly above the Kirkwood Mountain Village, the superpipe is easily seen from below.

Kirkwood Facts

Summit elevation:	9,800 feet
Vertical drop:	2,000 feet
Base elevation:	7,800 feet

Address: Box 1, Kirkwood, CA 95646
Ski area phone: 209-258-6000
Snow report: (877) 547-5966
Toll-free reservations: (800) 967-7500
Fax: 258-8899
E-mail: info@kirkwood.com
Internet: www.kirkwood.com

Number of lifts: 12—2 quads, 7 triples, 1 double, 2 surface lifts
Snowmaking: 5 percent
Skiable acreage: 2,300 acres
Uphill capacity: 17,905 per hour
Parks & pipes: 3 parks, 2 pipes
Bed base: 2,000 in resort, 22,000 in S. Lake Tahoe
Nearest lodging: Slopeside, ski-in/ski-out
Resort child care: Yes, 2 years and older
Adult ticket, per day: $69 (07/08)
Expert: ★★★★★
Advanced: ★★★★★
Intermediate: ★★★★★
Beginner: ★★★★
First-timer: ★★★★★

The Solitude chair is the lift of choice for the Stomping Grounds Park. This is the "big-boy" park on the resort and most features are for advanced riders only. The park changes occasionally, but most of the time there are at least 5 table tops all with different sized lips. The largest ones have 40-50 foot gaps and are pretty serious. Next to the Stomping Grounds, the Mokelumne run usually has another park for intermediate riders. Here the features are not as severe, and it is a good place to warm up before hitting the Stomping Grounds.

The TC Express lift has another park more suited for intermediate and beginner riders. The "Playground's" rails and boxes are of low consequence and most of them have the ride-on option. This is the perfect spot for riders who want to practice jibbing without risking their lives.

Snowboarding

The Cornice Express offers advanced to expert terrain only. The groomed slopes under the lift are the easiest way down, and traversing to the rider's right leads to some steep, technical rocky sections with a few good chutes. If snow conditions are icy, make sure edges are sharp. A little bonus to this area is the natural halfpipe where all these runs drain. The "Drain" swerves and curves at a perfect pitch for about 700 vertical feet. The gully has an endless supply of wall hits and hips, and gets more fun with every run.

Traversing to the rider's left off of the Cornice Express accesses hundreds of acres of some sick riding. A couple hundred feet down the ridge line is the wide open Sentinel Bowl. Between the lift and Sentinel, a bunch of technical chutes drop off of the ridge line and are then followed by some rolling terrain to the bottom of the run. With a little exploration, tons of natural gaps and hips can be found. Traversing out further on the ridge line is the iconic Glove Rock. A little skating and booting around Glove Rock will be rewarded with some powder stashes in the Palisades' glades.

Traversing rider's left off of the Sunrise lift heads into some killer terrain on the other side of the ridge. This area leads back to the Caples Crest lift and to the base of the resort. From the ridge line a number of technical chutes and rock drops roll into the giant valley below. Riding down the ridge, the chutes tend to get more difficult and have greater consequences for blowing it. Riders really need to have it together before jumping into this super steep and rocky terrain. If not, prepare to be a pinball bouncing from rock to rock to the bottom.

Lessons

We provide regular season rates. Holiday rates are higher.
Group lessons: Two-hour lessons cost $40.
First-timer package: The learn-to-ski or -snowboard package including a two-hour lesson, beginner lift ticket and rental equipment costs $79. Snowboard lessons are through the Burton Learn To Ride program, which uses special snowboards to make learning easier.
Private lessons: For one person, $95 for one hour; $220 for three hours; $260 for four hours; $350 for all day. For up to five people, $145 for one hour; $300 for three hours; $450 for six hours. Ask about discounts for taking classes after 12:30 p.m. on non-holidays.
Special programs: Expedition: Kirkwood is a backcountry education program that offers a series of camps and clinics that cover all aspects of backcountry skiing and riding, from skiing steeps and variable snow conditions to safety and rescue. Other programs include clinics for women, the Women's Learn-to-Ride Center, the all-mountain day camps, parks and pipes, and tackling non-groomed terrain. Call for dates and prices.

Children's programs

Child care: Ages 2–6 years, toilet-trained. All day costs $100 including lunch, a half day costs $80. Kids ages 4–6 can combine day care and a ski lesson for $100. Holiday rates are $6 more. The child-care center is slope-side, across from Red Cliffs Lodge. Reservations recommended; call 209-258-7274. Licensed child care for infants can be arranged with an outside agency at 209-258-8783.

Other options: If you need non-skiing child care, **Bright Beginnings** (775-588-5437) is a state-licensed day-care center in Stateline (just north of the casinos) for ages 6 weeks to 12 years. The center is open Monday–Saturday, 8:30 a.m.–4:30 p.m., and the staff is very friendly. Reservations are required. The child-care centers at Heavenly (775-586-7000) and Kirkwood (209-258-7274) both have a list of **babysitters**. Expect to pay $15/hour. **Baby's Away** (800-446-9030; 530-544-2229) rents and will deliver baby items (cribs, strollers, toys, etc.) to your hotel or condo anywhere in the Lake Tahoe area.

Children's lessons: Ski lessons for ages 4–12 and snowboard lessons for ages 7–14 include rental equipment, lunch, lessons and lifts for $105 for a full day and $85 for a half day (no lunch). Multiday discounts are available. Holiday rates are higher. Helmets are encouraged for all children. Rentals are available. The children's ski and snowboard school is in the Timber Creek novice area, the first right-hand turn before you reach the main parking lot.

Lift tickets (07/08 prices)

Adult (19 and older) $69
Children (6-12) $14

Who skis free: On Sundays only, two free child (12 and under) tickets with any paid adult lift ticket or adult pass. Offer not valid 12/31, 1/14 and 2/18. Available at any ticket window.

Who skis at a discount: Ages 5 and younger pay $8; juniors 13-18, $56; ages 65-69, $38; seniors 70 and older, $15.

Note: Holiday rates are higher. ETickets cost less.

Accommodations–Kirkwood

The village has many recently built condos, shops, and services such as an ice rink and recreation center/swim complex. Phase One of the village is now complete and includes **Snowcrest Lodge**, **The Mountain Club** and the **Lodge at Kirkwood**. The **Meadow Stone Lodge** is just steps from the lifts. Perhaps the best part about the new village is that it's, well—new. Of the other condo-complexes on the Meadow Side, the top choice is **Sun Meadows**, which is across from the Solitude and Cornice chairs and about as centrally located as you can get in Kirkwood. The second choice is **The Meadows**, between Timber Creek and the Cornice Chair. Rates range from $160-$299 for a studio to $555-$699 for a three-bedroom condo. Packages—particularly midweek stays—bring down the cost. Reservations: 800-967-7500 or 209-258-7000.

Near the mountain: For a classic Sierra experience, book a cabin at **Sorensen's Resort** 800-423-9949; 530-694-2203; $$-$$$$. Nestled beneath a cliff in the Hope Valley 14 miles from Kirkwood, Sorensen's is a secluded, quiet camp bustling with winter activity, including cross-country skiing.

Dining: $$$$–Entrees $30+; $$$–$20–$30; $$–$10–$20; $–less than $10.
Accommodations: (double room) $$$$–$200+; $$$–$141–$200; $$–$81–$140; $–$80.

Sierra-at-Tahoe

Sierra-at-Tahoe is one of the South Shore's best-kept secrets: There's 2,000 acres of fun just waiting to be gobbled up.

There are 14 Alpine resorts in the Lake Tahoe region, which includes California and Nevada. With so many to choose from, you're certain to find at least one that's perfect for your needs.

Sierra-at-Tahoe often is overlooked by destination skiers to the South Shore. What a shame. Sierra-at-Tahoe has more than 2,000 vertical feet and 2,000 acres, and the tree skiing is some of the best in the country. Roughly 1,500 of the 2,000 acres are in the trees, old growth fir trees that, as one local put it, seem "strategically placed."

Just 12 miles south (about 30 minutes), this fun, big resort has an intimate feel. The resort has opted to invest its money into on-mountain upgrades; consequently you won't find any lodging or even a mountain village at its base. You will find a compact base area that's easy to get around, fabulous terrain, an efficient lift network, and great customer service, thank you very much.

 ## Mountain layout

Sierra-at-Tahoe spreads its terrain across two peaks. Sometimes it can be somewhat confusing trying to get back and forth, but you'll get used to it. If all else fails, both peaks funnel traffic back down to the base area.

Expert, Advanced: Not too much an advanced skier cant handle here, although its wise to ask about current conditions and be confident on inbounds, ungroomed blacks before heading to Huckleberry. On Huckleberry, ask for directions to the Golf Course, where the Upper and Lower Nines have well-spaced trees and a less-intimidating pitch.

In West Bowl, the trees between Horsetail and Clipper hold almost unlimited stashes. When you hit the lift line, don't bail. Head back into the trees on the other side for more untracked, creamy powder. The terrain around the Grandview Express gets tracked quickly, but you can still find fun in the trees between Preacher's Passion and the Tahoe King lift. It's steep and littered with giant boulders that, when covered with 10 feet of snow, resemble giant gnomes.

Five backcountry access gates were recently opened and this is still one of the resort's best-kept secrets. You can find fresh powder here a week after a storm. Access is free with the purchase of a lift ticket and guided tours are available daily.

For advanced skiers, Sierra-at-Tahoe has a good collection of bumped-up black-diamond trails off the Grand View Express. Eastabout, Castle, Preacher's Passion and Dynamite all cascade roughly 1,300 vertical feet. Also try Clipper and Horsetail in the West Bowl.

Intermediate: This is a wonderful area for intermediates. West Bowl will fast become the favorite area of the mountain for this level. Lower Main is a steep, groomed run that rises above the day lodge. It's gotta be the toughest blue run here.

Intermediates are in for a treat in West Bowl. Powderhorn is a leisurely carpet ride wrapping around the resort's periphery. Pyramid parallels it. Both are wide, with plenty of space to negotiate steeper sections. Dogwood to Beaver wraps around the east side of the bowl. If you're confident on these trails, consider Horsetail, if it's groomed. It has the same fall line, but is narrower.

Off Grandview, play on the trails in The Circuit—Coyote, mokey and Lobo, where most of the mountain's terrain parks are located, or drop down Upper Snowshoe to Lower

Snowshoe, Shortswing or Hemlock.

Beginner, First-timer: This is a great learner's mountain. Sierra-at-Tahoe has a super learning slope called Broadway, right at the day lodge and served by its own quad chair. Sugar 'n' Spice is a 2.5-mile, easy cruise from the summit. Ride the Grand View Express chair and take a moment to look at the view of the lake (much better on the roof deck of the Grand View Grill). As you descend Sugar 'n' Spice, stay a good distance from the snowbank on the left edge of the run, especially when it gets to be head-high. Hot shots like to shoot out of the trees between this run and Upper Snowshoe. Fortunately, Sugar 'n' Spice is plenty wide. Stay to the middle or the right and give the idiots some room.

Upper Snowshoe is another good beginner run, but be sure to turn right at Marten to meet up with Sugar 'n' Spice, or you'll be on Lower Snowshoe, a blue run. Another chair that serves good beginner terrain is Rock Garden.

Parks and pipes

Sierra-at-Tahoe has five terrain parks, all marked with icons on the trail map. One of the most well-known parks is on The Alley and has five rail slides, two hits, two tabletops (with multiple hits) and a sound system. Aspen West is home to the 17-foot superpipe, which attracts some incredible skiers and riders and is highly regarded. Advanced tricksters, hear this: Head to Sierra's super-sized terrain park on Bashful to test your mettle on the 40-foot Wall of Fortune. Intermediates should go to the park on Upper Main or Broadway, where you'll find rail gardens for jibbing, tables of all sizes and plenty of fun boxes. Beginners will find the Boardercross track on Smokey is the perfect place to test your speed on berms, rollers and banked turns.

Snowboarding

Like riding in the trees? About 1,500 of the 2,000 acres here are woods, and powder stashes often stay hidden in the old-growth forest for days after a storm. Ride the Grand View Express or West Bowl Express and just jump into the trees—anywhere. Five backcountry access gates were recently opened. Like chutes? Rock drops? Endless powder fields? You'll find it all here

Sierra-at-Tahoe Facts

Summit elevation:	**8,852 feet**	**Snowmaking:** 10 percent	
Vertical drop:	**2,212 feet**	**Skiable acreage:** 2,000 acres	
Base elevation:	**6,640 feet**	**Uphill capacity:** 14,921 per hour	
		Parks & pipes: 5 parks, 2 pipes	
Address: 1111 Sierra-at-Tahoe Rd.		**Bed base:** 22,000 in S. Lake Tahoe	
Twin Bridges, CA 95735		**Nearest lodging:** About 12 miles away	
Area code: 530		**Resort child care:** Yes, 18 months and older	
Ski area phone: 659-7453		**Adult ticket, per day:** $65 (07/08 price)	
Snow report: 659-7475			
Toll-free reservations: (800) 288-2463		**Expert:**★★	
Fax: 659-7749		**Advanced:**★★★★	
E-mail: sierra@boothcreek.com		**Intermediate:**★★★★	
Internet: www.sierratahoe.com		**Beginner:**★★★★	
Number of lifts: 12—3 high-speed quads,		**First-timer:**★★★★	
1 triple, 5 doubles, 2 moving carpet, tube tow			

in the mountain's all-natural terrain park. Access is free with the purchase of a lift ticket and guided tours are available daily.

Lower Main is a steep, groomed intermediate run that rises above the day lodge. Work on your high-speed carving technique here. West Bowl will fast become the fav area of the mountain for intermediates. The Backside is another good spot to test powder skills.

Lessons (07/08 prices)

Group lessons: Two-and-a-half-hour lessons for advanced-beginners through advanced skiers and snowboarders cost $48 for lessons only; $84 with lift ticket and rentals ($87 on holidays). A full-day program costs $99 with lifts and rentals ($103 holidays).

First-timer package: A First Time package including beginner lifts, rentals and a two-a-half-hour lesson is $84 (regular season) $87 (holidays) for skiers or snowboarders; all day costs $99 (regular season) $103 (holidays). A two-day lesson package with an all-mountain lift ticket, rentals and lesson costs $121 ($60 per day). A three-day Ride or Ski Guarantee includes three days of lessons, lifts and rentals, and a guarantee that you'll be able to ski/ride top-to-bottom on a beginner trail or a fourth lesson is free; cost is $147 ($49 per day).

Private lessons: $99 ($109 holiday) for an hour; $172 ($182 holiday) for two hours; $202 ($222 holiday) for three hours; $302 ($322 holiday) for all day. Semi-privates for up to five people are $220 ($230 holiday) for two hours; $250 ($260 holiday) for three hours; $450 ($460 holiday) for all day. A 9 a.m. one-hour private costs $64. Reservations required, call (530) 659-7453.

Children's programs (07/08 prices)

Child care: Ages 18 months to 5 years. Cost is $108 (regular season) and $114 (holidays) for full day (includes lunch); $87 for a half day. Multiday discounts available. Reservations recommended; call 530-659-7453.

Children's lessons: A special all-day program for kids 3–4 combines ski lessons and daycare, $108 (regular season) and $114 (holidays). It includes lunch, snacks, lift ticket, lessons and day care. An all-day ski program for ages 5–6 costs $127 (regular season) and $135 (holidays). An all-day snowboard program for ages 5–6 costs $115. All-day ski or snowboard instruction is $108 (regular season) and $114 (holidays) for ages 7–12. All programs include lessons, rentals, lifts and lunch; reservations are strongly recommended.

Lift tickets (07/08 prices)

	Adult (23-64)	Child (5-12)
One day	$65	$16
Three days	$135 ($46/day)	$48 ($16/day)

Who skis free: Ages 4 and younger.

Who skis at a discount: Young adults ages 13-22 pay $55 for one day; ages 65-69 pay $47; ages 70 and older pay $18.

Ages 13-64 can buy Sierra's 3-Pak of tickets, which are non-transferable but do not have to be used on consecutive days, for $135 ($46/day). No blackout dates. they can be purchased online. **Note:** Holiday rates are higher.

Cross-country & snowshoeing (see also xcskiresorts.com)

The Lake Tahoe region may have the greatest concentration of large cross-country ski areas in the U.S., with more than 800 km. of groomed trails. Most of that is on the north end of the lake, but South Shore has a good network of trails, too. Most also allow snowshoes.

Sierra-at-Tahoe (530-659-7453) has more than 3 miles of groomed snowshoe trails complete with interpretive trail signs. Daily snowshoe rentals and guided tours available. There are no cross-country trails or tours here, but telemark skiers can get tours either in-bounds or into the backcountry, at Sierra's new Telemark and Backcountry Center. Telemark gear is available for rental.

Spooner Lake Cross-Country (775-887-8844, recording; 775-749-5349, live voice) on Hwy. 28, about a half-mile north of Hwy. 50, has more than 80 km. of trails, nearly all of which are machine groomed, with one 19-km. backcountry trail. Lessons and cross-country gear, snowshoe and pulk sled rentals are available; you also can rent a backcountry cabin

Kirkwood Cross-Country (209-258-7248) has 80 km. of machine-groomed tracks, skating lanes and three interconnected trail systems with three warming huts, including the 1864 Kirkwood Inn, a trappers' log cabin full of nostalgia. Rental gear includes cross-country, telemark, snowshoes and pulk sleds. Lessons are also available.

Hope Valley Cross-Country Ski Center (530-694-2266) is near the junction of Hwy. 89 and 88. It has about 100 km. of marked trails, a quarter of which are groomed. Trail fees are by donation. Lessons and rentals are available. The trails at Sorensen's Resort (800-423-9949; 530-694-2203) hook into this system.

Camp Richardson Resort (530-541-1801 or 530-542-6584) in South Lake Tahoe has a cross-country ski center with lessons, rentals and 35 km. of groomed trails along the Lake Tahoe shoreline. There are additional marked trails venturing into Desolation Wilderness.

Heavenly's Adventure Peak (775-586-7000) at the top of the gondola includes a cross-country skiing and snowshoeing center. You'll find 5 km. of groomed trails that meander through the forest and provide awesome views from nearly 3,000 feet above Lake Tahoe.

Accommodations

South Shore accommodations divide into four categories: the multistory casinos hugging the Nevada border for great views and nonstop nightlife; the top of Kingsbury Grade, near the base of Heavenly's Nevada side, for upscale condominiums and top-quality hotels; along the California lake shore for moderately priced motels; and at Kirkwood to escape the hustle and bustle. Central Reservations for South Lake Tahoe is 800-288-2463.

If you plan to do all your skiing at Heavenly, **Heavenly Tahoe Vacations** (800-243-2836; 775-588-4584) can arrange an entire ski vacation including airfare, transfers, lessons, rentals, non-ski activities, skiing and lodging. If you can stay Sunday through Thursday nights, you can get extremely good deals. Lodging and lift packages can run as low as $69 per person, per night, double occupancy. If you're here Friday and Saturday, however, prices double or sometimes triple.

If you like to be in the middle of the action, try **Harveys Resort & Casino** (800-648-3361 from outside Nevada or 775-588-2411 from Nevada; $$-$$$) and **Harrah's Casino Hotel** (800-648-3353; 775-588-3515; $$-$$$$), which have everyone's highest ratings, from AAA to Mobil. Most rooms have lake views, although you may have to crane your neck to see it. Other casino-hotels within walking distance of the state line are the **Montbleu Resort**

Dining: $$$$–Entrees $30+; $$$–$20–$30; $$–$10–$20; $–less than $10.
Accommodations: (double room) $$$$–$200+; $$$–$141–$200; $$–$81–$140; $–$80.

Casino and Spa (888-829-7630; 775-588-3515; $$-$$$$) and the **Horizon Casino Resort** (800-648-3322; $$-$$$$). Ask for a lakeview room with a balcony at the Horizon.

On the California side, several beautiful hotels have been built in the past few years. **The Marriott Grand Residence Club** (866-204-7263; $$-$$$$) is in the Heavenly Village development at the base of Heavenly's gondola. It features in-suite kitchens, laundry service, a ski-check room, as well as a number of retail shops and the FiRE + iCE Restaurant (see Dining). It's also the closest hotel to Heavenly's gondola.

Also near the gondola is one of our favorite places, the **Embassy Suites Lake Tahoe Resort** (800-362-2779; 530-544-5400; $$-$$$). Just 50 feet from the nearest casino, it has an indoor atrium, indoor pool and hot tub, an exercise center, on-site restaurant and lounge.

Big timbers, a huge stone fireplace and a soaring great room welcome guests at **Black Bear Inn Bed & Breakfast** (877-232-7466 or 530-433-4451, $$$-$$$$). Five guestrooms in the main inn and three intimate cottages surrounding a lovely courtyard all have fireplaces, king beds and TV/VCR/DVDs; cabins also have kitchenettes. Rates include a full breakfast, afternoon refreshments and use of an outdoor hot tub; robes provided.

Next door is **The Deerfield Lodge at Heavenly** (888-757-3337, $$$-$$$$) a one-time motel that was renovated and reopened in 2006 and upgraded to boutique status, providing such amenities as concierge service, in-room fireplaces; slate baths with rain forest showers and Jacuzzis; and goose down comforters, pillowtop mattresses and pillows. A continental breakfast is provided.

Smack dab on the lake (but behind an unattractive shopping center), the **Lakeshore Lodge & Spa** (800-448-4577, 530-541-2180, $$-$$$) has rooms and suites, some with kitchens or kitchenettes, as well as condominiums. A continental breakfast is included; and there's a full-service day spa on the premises.

The California side of South Lake Tahoe has many hotels and motels lining Hwy. 50. Among the best are two Best Western properties—**The Timber Cove Lodge** (800-528-1234; 530-541-6722; $-$$$), on the beach; and **Station House Inn** (800-822-5953; 530-542-1101; $$-$$$), within walking distance of the casino area, on the California side of the border. **The Sunterra Lake Tahoe Vacation Resort** (530-541-3568; SS-$$$) right at the junction of Hwy. 50 and Ski Run Blvd. has condos right on the lake.

Two miles from the casinos, **Inn By The Lake** (800-877-1466; 530-542-0330; $-$$$) sits almost at the shore (although on the wrong side of Hwy 50). It has 100 guest rooms—including nine suites with kitchens, but many of the regular guest rooms are large and have refrigerators—plus a free continental breakfast with enough selections to keep you full until lunch, heated pool, and bi-level hot tub. It's also one of the stops on the free shuttle to the slopes.

For the rustic-minded, try the **Historic Camp Richardson Resort** (800-544-1801; $$-$$$). The cabins have large fireplaces, spacious living rooms and full kitchens. Perfect for couples traveling together or families who enjoy various outdoor sports. Onsite sledding, snowshoeing, cross-country trails and wilderness sleigh rides complete this seasonal resort. The historic hotel and beachside inn provide more "civilized" accommodations. A similar mountain paradise can be found on the Nevada side at **Zephyr Cove Resort** (775-588-6644; $$-$$$). The beachfront resort offers mountain cabins set amidst the pines, guided snowmobiling tours, cross-country skiing, plus it's the home of the M.S. Dixie II paddlewheeler, which operates year-round.

Adjacent to the Lakeside Beach is the funky **Royal Valhalla Motor Lodge** (800-999-4104; 530-544-2233; $-$$$), some rooms with kitchens and most with wonderful lake views. Just two blocks from the casinos, it sits in a quiet neighborhood.

Lakeland Village (800-822-5969; 530-544-1685; $$-$$$$) has a hotel and condominiums on the lake with shuttlebus service to Heavenly and Kirkwood. The units range from studios to a lakefront four-bedroom, three-bath unit. For those who want a room 150 yards from Heavenly's California base, the **Tahoe Seasons Resort**, with 160 suites, has received good reviews from everyone locally (530-541-6700; $$-$$$$). Another possibility is the **Holiday Inn Express** (800-544-5288; 530-544-5900; $$-$$$$).

One for couples only: **The Fantasy Inn** (800-367-7736; 530-541-4200; $$$-$$$$) has about 60 rooms designed for romance and a wedding chapel. Each room has one bed in a choice of several shapes (round, heart-shaped, water or regular mattress, king-size), a jetted tub for two, an in-room music system with 30 channels, adjustable peach-colored lighting and showers with double shower heads. Sixteen of the rooms have themes, such as Rain Forest (plants and rattan decor), Caesar's Indulgence (a sexy black decor), and Romeo and Juliet (the honeymoon suite). Theme suites are in the $245-$295 range. Ask about special ski and/or wedding package rates.

 # Dining

Evan's American Gourmet Cafe (530-542-1990; $$$) on Rte. 89 has become one of the best-liked restaurants on the South Shore. The chef prepares California Cuisine with an unusual flair. Expect to pay for his efforts, but they are well worth it.

For a superb meal, great wine list and attentive service—with a beautiful view—head to **Friday's Station** (775-588-6611; $$$) at the top of Harrah's casino-hotel.

Other recommendations are **Fresh Ketch** (530-541-5683; $$$) for fish; **Dory's Oar** (530-541-6603; $$$) for steaks and seafood; or **ECHO Restaurant & Lounge** (530-543-2140; $$-$$$) in the Embassy Suites hotel for its delicious American fusion cuisine.

Beacon (530-541-0630; $$-$$$) at Camp Richardson is known for its blackened prime rib. **Nephele's** (530-544-8130; $$) serves California cuisine in a cozy setting. Next door to Nephele's is an outstanding restaurant called **Cafe Fiori** (530-541-2908; $$). It doesn't seat many, so reservations are a must. The food and the wine list are superb.

Several new restaurants have opened in Heavenly Village. The energetic and fun **FiRE + iCE** (530-542-6650; $-$$) at Marriott's Timber Lodge next to the gondola is an improvisational grill where you choose the ingredients for the chef to grill. In April 2004 Sammy Hagar opened his second **Cabo Wabo Cantina** (775-588-2411; $$) in Harveys Resort Casino. Open for lunch and dinner, it specializes in authentic but creative Mexican dishes such as ahi tuna tacos and frozen margarita cake. When the clock strikes 10 p.m., it turns into a hopping nightclub.

Good reasonable restaurants include **The Cantina Bar and Grill** (530-544-1233; $) for Mexican; **Scusa** (530-542-0100; $$) for Italian (a local favorite); **Sato Japanese Restaurant** (530-544-0774 or 530-775-588-1914; $-$$) in the Horizon Casino for surprisingly good sushi specials; **Shoreline Cafe** (530-541-7858; $$) for good pasta specials and an extensive kids' menu; or **The Tudor Pub** (530-541-6603; $-$$), upstairs from Dory's Oar, for fish & chips and European beers on tap. And **Del Soul** (775-588-3515; $$) is a casual Mexican Grill.

Sprouts (530-541-6969; $) is another local favorite. The extensive menu includes rice bowls, hummus melts and lasagna. Don't miss the smoothies, especially if you're ailing after a long night. A shot of wheatgrass might cure all. A small eclectic cafe with an island atmosphere (check out the salt and pepper shakers on each table), **Freshies** (530-542-3630; $) is another good bet for fresh, healthy food. In keeping with the name, the cafe offers half off soups on powder days.

For great breakfasts head to the **Red Hut Waffle Shop** (530-541-9024; $), where you can pack into a small room and listen to the talk of the town. Another branch is on **Kingsbury Grade** (775-588-7488; $), handy for skiers heading to the Nevada side of Heavenly. At **Heidi's** (530-544-8113; $), get anything from dozens of types of Belgian waffles to chocolate pancakes.

Dining: $$$$–Entrees $30+; $$$–$20–$30; $$–$10–$20; $–less than $10.
Accommodations: (double room) $$$$–$200+; $$$–$141–$200; $$–$81–$140; $–$80

If you're in over the weekend you must go to **Llewellyn's** (775-588-2411; $$) at Harvey's Resort Hotel for Sunday brunch; food is flavorful and the view breathtaking. If you're a jetlagged easterner and wake up at 4 a.m., head to one of the casino's 24-hour restaurants. The Horizon's Four Seasons serves a basic breakfast, and you can pick up a latte at Starbucks in the hotel lobby.

And just in case you crave a malt "so thick it holds the straw up," go to the **Zephyr Cove Resort**. Try the banana-chocolate shake. **Alpen Sierra Coffee Roasting Company**, at Hwy. 50 and Pioneer, is considered one of the area's best coffeehouses and serves locally roasted mountain coffee.

On the mountains:

The best on-mountain lunch we had in South Lake Tahoe was at Sierra-at-Tahoe. We had a delicious Thai chicken wrap (kind of like a burrito), washed down with a Sierra Nevada Pale Ale at **The Sierra Pub** ($) in the day lodge. The pub serves several microbrews and wine by the glass, as well as nonalcoholic beverages. On weekends, there's live music on the sundeck. Another option is the **Grandview Bar & Grille** ($) at the summit, where you can chow down on Asian fare such as Kung Pao chicken and lettuce wraps while you drink in the views. Fresh-ground coffee and fresh-baked goods are sold in the day lodge ($).

 ## Apres-ski/nightlife

The gondola changed the apres-ski scene here at Heavenly. **Fire and Ice** right at the gondola base has fire pits to provide warmth on the deck spreading from the restaurant. The **Blue Angel Cafe** on Ski Run Blvd. has affordable bears and reasonable pizzas. **Blue Moon**, in front of the Tahoe Beach & Ski Club, also has good immediate apres-ski.

Mulligan's, a great Irish pub near the state line, has terrific live music (listenable rather than danceable), pool tables on the first floor, giant TV screens and is packed every night. **McP's** across from the gondola has great music as well seven nights a week.

Later in the evening, **blu** in the Montbleu Resort Casino and Spa is a spectacle of light, sights and sounds as their DJs provide the rhythm track for an evening of hip-swinging. **The Pub at Tahoe**, a great Irish pub near the state line, has terrific live music (listenable rather than danceable), pool tables on the first floor, and is packed every night.

If you've been to rocker Sammy Hagar's legendary **Cabo Wabo Cantina** in Cabo San Lucas, or always wished you could visit, you'll want to head to his Tahoe nightclub inside Harveys Resort Casino. Everyday drink specials make this a great gathering spot. It really starts rocking at 10 p.m. Live entertainment most nights sometimes means impromptu appearances from big-name musicians in the area to perform in concert at other venues.

Other spots recommended by locals are **Divided Sky** and **Hoss Hoggs**. Both have a loyal group of local bands that play most weekends. **Dixon's** features some good and not so good open mike nights plus the town's largest beer selection and happy hours from 3-6 p.m.

The bargain spot is the **Lakeside Inn and Casino** with $1 beers at happy hour and $2 beers the rest of the time. Food is also a grand bargain.

Mott Canyon Tavern & Grill (775-588-8989; $) has 13 beers on tap, late night food and a late night happy hour from 12 a.m. to 4 a.m.

And of course, the **casinos** have musical reviews that are extravaganzas of sight and sound. Some shows run through the season; others are top-name singers and comedians who do one or two shows. Check a local newspaper for up-to-date listings.

 ## Other activities

Gaming isn't the only game in South Tahoe. Beyond betting the farm or catching a show, the options are plentiful. Heavenly's **Adventure Peak**

Snow Park (775-586-7000), at the top of the 2.4-mile gondola, offers lift-accessed snow tubing, snow biking, sledding and snowshoeing. The 50-mph zipline ride from the top of the Tamarack Express lift to the top of the gondola has a vertical drop of 525 feet. In the Heavenly Village at the base of the gondola (in the center of town), an open-air ice rink is open every day (530-543-1423). Or you can ice skate at the **South Lake Tahoe Ice Arena** (530-542-6262), open every afternoon from 1-5 p.m. and some evenings and mornings. Skates are available for rent.

Call **Lake Tahoe Balloons** (530-544-1221) for balloon rides and **Lake Tahoe Adventures** (530-577-2940) for snowmobiling. The **Husky Express** (775-782-3047) takes people in the Hope Valley. **Camp Richardson** (530-541-3113) has sleigh rides through meadows; reservations required. When you're shopping in Heavenly Village, check out **Cowboys & Indians** (530-542-1018) across the street from Rayle's grocery store. If everything weren't for sale, you might think this was a museum. The owner, Gary Wyles, aka "Hoss the Boss," and his ever-present canine boxer, Sugar Ray, are always on site. Note: This is the place for local information and dirt.

Local and imported wines for sale by the bottle and wine tasting by the glass can be found at **Wines on the Lake** (530-544-3839). They also sell beers, ales and wine-related gifts.

The **South Lake Tahoe Ice Arena** (530-542-6262) is a 37,000-square-foot, indoor, official NHL ice arena, with daily public sessions and skate rentals. It's adjacent to the Recreation Center & Swim Pool Complex (530-542-6056), with indoor pool, weight room and gym.

Getting there and getting around

By air: Reno-Tahoe International Airport has more than 100 nonstop flights a day from various parts of the country. Allegiant Air has non-stop service between Bellingham, WA and Reno-Tahoe.The airport is 55 miles from South Lake Tahoe. The Lake Tahoe Airport, near South Lake Tahoe, has limited service from California. Buses and hotel shuttles take skiers to the resorts from both airports. Tahoe Casino Express (800-446-6128) runs 18 times daily between the Reno airport and South Shore.

By boat: The Tahoe Queen, an authentic Mississippi sternwheeler, double-decked and heated, takes South Shore skiers and snowboarders across Lake Tahoe to Squaw Valley (buses take skiers from the dock to the ski areas).

By bus: Free shuttles run from almost every major hotel to the resorts.

By car: Driving time from Reno to Heavenly is about 70 minutes. San Francisco is about four hours away on Hwy. 50. Sierra-at-Tahoe is 12 miles south of the lake on Hwy. 50. During storms, the California Highway Patrol doesn't let drivers come up the mountains without chains or a four-wheel-drive vehicle, so bring chains or be sure the car rental agency provides them.

Getting around: Bring a car if you intend to move frequently between the south and the north shores; otherwise, a car is optional. We'd say have one if you like to roam far afield at night. If not, you can walk to restaurants and nightspots near your hotel and use the ski shuttles during the day. Part of the redevelopment of South Tahoe also includes public transportation. BlueGo is a bi-state streamlined shuttle system intended to eliminate the need for private vehicles.

Dining: $$$$–Entrees $30+; $$$–$20–$30; $$–$10–$20; $–less than $10.
Accommodations: (double room) $$$$–$200+; $$$–$141–$200; $$–$81–$140; $–$80 and less.

Mammoth Mountain
June Mountain
California

Summit:	**11,053 feet**
Vertical:	**3,100 feet**
Base:	**7,953 feet**

Address: Box 24,
Mammoth Lakes, CA 93546
Telephone (main): 800-626-6684;
760-934-2571
Snow Report Number: 888-766-9778
Toll-free reservations: 800-626-6684;
888-466-2666
Reservations outside U.S.: 800-626-
6684; 760-934-2571
E-mail: info@mammoth-mtn.com
Internet: www.mammothmountain.com
Expert:★★★★★
Advanced:★★★★★
Intermediate:★★★★★
Beginner:★★★ **First-timer:**★★★
Lifts: 29—3 gondolas, 2 high-speed six-packs,
10 high-speed quads, 1 quad, 7 triples, 4 doubles,
2 surface lifts
Skiable acreage: 3,500+
Snowmaking: 33 percent

Uphill capacity: 59,000
Parks & pipes: 7 parks, 3 pipes
Bed base: 30,000
Nearest lodging: Slopeside
Child care: Yes, newborns and older
Adult ticket, per day: $83 (07/08 prices)
Dining:★★★
Apres-ski/nightlife:★★
Other activities:★★

June Mountain Facts
Summit elevation: 10,135 feet
Vertical drop: 2,590 feet
Base elevation: 7,545 feet
Number and types of lifts: 7—2 high-speed quads, 4 doubles, 1 surface-lift
Skiable acreage: 500+ acres
Parks & pipes: 1 park, 1 pipe
Uphill capacity: 10,000 per hour
Bed base: 2,000 local

No mountain is better named than Mammoth. When you stand at the base lodge and scan the mountain, you can't even see a quarter of the ski terrain. The encircling ridge, all above treeline, promises dramatic skiing, but what you can't see is even better. Lower peaks such as Lincoln Mountain, Gold Hill and Hemlock Ridge, all with groomed swaths and moguled canyons, stretch 6.5 miles in width. Mammoth is one of the nation's largest winter resorts in size, and at times it's the nation's busiest, with more than 14,000 skiers and riders swooping over its slopes on an average weekend. Chair 9 has been replaced with a high-speed six-pack chair and dubbed the Cloud 9 Express. The new lift (2007-08 season) carries skiers from the Eagle Lodge side of the mountain to 10,371 feet near Dragon's Back providing access to hundreds of acres of intermediate and advanced terrain.

Its season runs from early November through June—legitimately. Mammoth often relies on its 430 acres of snowmaking to be open by Thanksgiving, but snow often falls by early November. Skiing and riding here on the Fourth of July is a well-loved tradition among the diehards who haven't had enough.

Until recently, Mammoth was owned in part by Intrawest, a ski and golf resort company based in Vancouver. Intrawest's most visible involvement is a slopeside pedestrian village with 275 residential units and 140,000 square feet of retail space for shops, galleries, bars and restaurants that will be completed in five to 10 years. Visitors who stay in one of the three Village lodges, White Mountain Lodge, Lincoln House or Grand Sierra Lodge, can take advantage of the Mountain Center, a 17,000-square-foot skier services building in the center of the Village. It is connected to the Village Gondola, which whisks guests up to Canyon Lodge, eliminating the need for a car once you're in the town of Mammoth Lakes.

Up the road at the main base area, a labyrinthine base lodge houses the ski school, lift ticket windows, rental shops and hundreds of lockers for locals and visitors. The slopeside Mammoth Mountain Inn recently underwent a $1.5 million renovation, as did the third floor of the main lodge, where $4 million went into a compete cafeteria remodel including the addition of sky box-like lofts that overlook the slopes.

At the bottom of the mountain road lies the small but spread-out town of Mammoth Lakes. As the town grew to support the ski area's success, newcomers haphazardly transplanted Southern California sprawl and mini-malls to the mountains. Since the village was built two years ago, it has begun to establish the town center Mammoth has never really had.

If size intimidates you, Mammoth's little sister June Mountain, a half-hour drive from Mammoth Lakes, will appeal to you. Its Old World village atmosphere in a sheltered canyon is on a more human scale. That is not to say it's a puny resort: it has seven chairlifts and a 2,590-foot vertical rise (as opposed to 3,100 feet at Mammoth).

Mountain layout

This mountain is very, very large - with 157 named trails. No matter what your ability level, you won't be shortchanged. First-time visitors should pack a trail map. Seriously. Almost everything goes by number. The mountain is crisscrossed with a network of chairlifts numbered in the order they were built. It makes perfect sense to visitors who grew up with the mountain, but it's confusing to the first-time visitor who hears regulars planning their day football-quarterback style, "Take one to three, then back side to 23, down the ridge to 14, then to 13 and lateral to one." Now that the resort has installed several high-speed lifts and given them names, regulars still refer to the lifts by their former number, which makes it even more confusing for the first-time visitor. For the record, Chairs 1, 2, 3, 4, 6, 10, 11, 15, 16 and 17 all have names now, and exist only in the memories and automatic brain-recall of Mammoth regulars. Die-hards have been known to attempt a day of skiing the chairlifts in order—a hefty task that requires crisscrossing and careful planning, not to mention hiking.

If you're with a group, decide where to meet if you get separated. Pick a centrally located chair, rather than McCoy Station or the Main Lodge.

If you come on a weekend, avoid the Main Lodge at the top of the mountain road (unless you're staying at the slopeside Mammoth Mountain Inn). Tickets are sold (in order as you come up the road) at Little Eagle Lodge next to Juniper Springs Resort, Canyon Lodge, The Roller Coaster lift, Stump Alley Express and the Main Lodge. Little Eagle Lodge and the Canyon Lodge are actually off the main road to the ski area, so ask someone to direct you. To avoid weekend crowds, take Chairs 9, 25, 22, 21, 12, 13 and 14, listed from left to right on the trail map.

First-timers should go to Canyon Lodge or Main Lodge. Those with a little experience also can start at Little Eagle Lodge on the Eagle Express

Expert, Advanced: Expert yaa-hoo skiers will strike out for the ridge, reachable by the gondola or a series of chairs. From the ridge, any chute or path will open into a wide bowl.

Mammoth's signature run, a snarling lip of snow called Cornice Bowl, looms large in every expert's memory bank. Other runs dropping from the ridge are considered steeper and more treacherous. Reached from the gondola, Hangman's Hollow—Mammoth's toughest—is an hourglass-shaped chute hanging from the summit and bordered by wicked rocks. At its narrow part there's space for only one turn—a perfect one. Other expert shots are off Chair 22, and on powder days you can often find untracked or less-tracked snow on the far east Dragon's Back off Chair 9, or the far west (hiking access only) Hemlock Ridge above Chair 14.

One of the most popular advanced areas is the group of bowls available from Face Lift Express (formerly Chair 3). They're great warm-up runs for experts, but plan to get here early on weekends. The high-speed lift has helped lessen the formerly outrageous lines (that's our term; one of our favorite Mammoth employees describes it as "healthy"), but it is still busiest on weekend mornings around 9:30 a.m. Midweek, no problem.

A slightly less busy alternative is triple-Chair 5, the next chair to the left on the trail map, or Chair 14, to the far right on the map. Chairs 22 and 25, which provide access to Lincoln Mountain and its intermediate runs and advanced chutes, rarely have lines.

Intermediate: The middle part of the mountain is still above treeline, so those at this level have plenty of room to traverse on the single-black runs. Hidden canyons like Lower Dry Creek (off the Face Lift Express) are full of swoops and surprises, and require tighter turns. For long cruising, head to Eagle Express. Other intermediate playgrounds are served by the tree-lined runs from The Roller Coaster and Canyon express quads and Chairs 8, 20 and 21. At the other edge of the area is Chair 12 and the drop over to Chairs 13 and 14.

Beginner, First-timer: If you aren't a first-timer, but still practicing turns, the runs near Canyon Lodge are best. Trails such as Hansel and Gretel weave gently through evergreens, providing sheltered slopes for learning, away from the speed demons. When you're ready for the next step, Christmas Tree, a long run under Eagle Express, is pretty gentle. This part of the mountain gets soupy in the afternoon on warm days, however. If you're intimidated by crowds, and you're trying to step up to the intermediate level, avoid Stump Alley and Broadway, both usually packed with speeders.

For long mellow cruisers with a view, explore the backside off the Face Lift Express, wander through Dry Creek's canyon and natural gullies, or ride Ricochet's open glades.

The first-timer slopes are off the Discovery Chair at the Main Lodge and Chair 7 from the Canyon Lodge, separated from the hot shots.

Parks and pipes

Mammoth puts mammoth amounts of money—more than $1 million—into 90+ acres of parks and pipes. Main Park is arguably one of the best freestyle areas in North America. Due to its proximity to the Southern California world of skate and surf culture, Mammoth is an industry leader so progressive that each season's new park features are kept mum until opening day. A ride on Thunderbound Express is entertainment in its own right, as most freeskier and snowboarder pros pass though here—if they don't call it home. You'll find the 600-foot-long Super-Duper Pipe with walls that soar 18 feet high, and the Super Pipe with 15-foot walls, both sculpted every night. In addition to urban art-like features for top performance, including a 16-foot-by-32-foot wall ride, kinked boxes, c-boxes, hits and tables as big as 80 feet in length, Mammoth also has a fully developed park for the smaller skill set. Wonderland Park includes low-to-the-snow rails and the Wonderland Pipe with 5-foot walls. The intermediate-level South Park is located on Roller Coaster West, and Jibs Galore, on Carousel, has rails tucked among the trees. More possibilities include an X-Course, Forest Trail Park and Disco Park. One thing is for sure: With eight runs dedicated to parks, freeriders won't be bored.

Snowboarding

So you're a leap-of-faith kind of rider? The plunge off the summit ridge offers a slew of descents with one thing in common: All are so sickeningly steep you can easily reach out and touch the snow while turning. Want to test Newton's theory of gravity? Drop into the steeps of Climax, pop the cornice into Dave's Run, dance between the rocks in The Wipeout Chutes or jump into Hangman's Hollow. If you really want to shake up your innards, dart through the rocks at the top of Phillipe's and straight-shoot it all the way to the bottom.

Mammoth is definitely one of the carving capitals of the West, so check out the arcs and deep trenches below while riding up the chair, and then slice some yourself. St. Anton, Stump Alley and Gremlin's Gulch are just three of the carving runs to hit. Just make sure to get up early if you expect freshies or perfect corduroy. For long mellow cruisers with a view, explore the backside off the Face Lift Express, wander through Dry Creek's canyon and natural gullies, or ride Ricochet's open glades.

June Mountain

June Mountain doesn't have Mammoth's range of terrain, but most skiers and boarders will enjoy it. The pace at June is slower and the crowds considerably fewer. It is a very good choice for mid-winter Saturdays and holiday periods, as well as for families with young children who ski faster than their parents.

June Mountain has none of the high broad bowls that make Mammoth Mountain famous. The steepest terrain at June, The Face, is as steep as anything at Mammoth. Because it is on the lower mountain, it unfortunately doesn't keep the snow as long as the upper runs. Since June is more sheltered than Mammoth and none of its slopes is above treeline, June tends to hold powder longer than Mammoth's more exposed bowls and the snow doesn't crust up so quickly. There's a great view of June Lake from the upper runs.

Though June has a few expert drops, this level will be bored quickly. Intermediates will have a ball, however. Schatzi is a fantastic and long cruiser, and Matterhorn often is totally deserted. Beginners should stick to the mid-mountain, though Silverado is a gentle, long and uncrowded trail from the Rainbow Summit. June Mountain has two terrain parks covering 50 acres. For a small ski area, June is an impressively big player in terrain park innovation, with a top-notch superpipe that gets cut nightly, large jumps and tabletops, and rails of every variety.

 ## Cross-country & snowshoeing (see also xcskiresorts.com)

Nineteen miles of groomed trails, actually summer roads, wind around four of the dozen or more high Alpine lakes for which the town of Mammoth Lakes is named.

Tamarack Lodge (800-626-6684; 760-934-2442) maintains the trails. Rentals and lessons are available. Reserve on weekends. Cabins are available for rent.

The Lakes Basin includes many trailheads into the backcountry, where no fee is charged. Stop into the lobby, where mulled cider is on hand and historical vibes radiate from the gigantic old stone fireplace. Special nighttime ski and snowshoe tours are offered under full moons, but because that's only three days per month, they tend to fill up quickly.

 ## Lessons (07/08 prices)

Prices are for Saturdays and holidays; prices are somewhat lower Sunday through Friday. At Mammoth, lessons are available at the Main Lodge, the Canyon Lodge and Little Eagle Lodge. Reservations are strongly suggested. For Mammoth, call

800-626-6684. For June Mountain Ski and Snowboard School, call 760-648-7733.

Group lessons: All-day beginner and intermediate lessons cost $109. A 2 and one-half hour advanced lesson is $70,

First-timer package: Rentals, beginner lift ticket and three hours of lessons are $149 for skiers and snowboarders.

Private lessons: Up to 5 people, a one-hour lesson costs $150; three hours in the morning costs $410 or $375 in the afternoon; full day (6 hours) is $585.

Racing: Mammoth has a well-established racing heritage. It has hosted World Cup races, and several U.S. Ski Team coaches and executives call this resort home. Races occur almost every weekend, ranging from amateur ski club races to highly competitive events.

Children's programs (07/08 prices)

Child care: Ages newborn to 8. Cost is $95 for a full day. Fees include snacks and lunch, except for infants. Day care can be combined with ski and snowboard school for ages 3–8. They get supervised activities, plus a lesson and rentals, for $155 for a full day.

Reservations are strongly advised for all child-care programs, at least four to six weeks ahead; call 800-626-6684. Day care is located at both The Small World Day Care Center at Mammoth Mountain Inn, just across the street from the Main Lodge, and the child-care center at June Mountain. Open from 8:30 a.m. to 4:30 p.m. Parents also can arrange evening babysitting services through the Small World Day Care Center.

Children's lessons: The Woollywood Ski School teaches kids ages 3–12; snowboard lessons start at age 5. Full-day packages (lessons, lunch, lift ticket) for skiing or snowboarding cost $135. First-timers also can take a two-and-one-half hour lesson for $70. Helmets are required for all children in ski school lessons; rentals are available. Reservations for kids' lessons are strongly recommended; call 800-626-6684.

Lift tickets (07/08 prices)

Adult (19-64) $83; **Youth** (13-18) $62; **Child** (7-12) $41

Who skis free: Children ages 6 and younger and Seniors 80 and older, as do first-timers taking a ski school lesson.

Who skis at a discount: Seniors (65-79) pay $41. If you purchase a regularly-priced lift ticket at least 14 days in advance, you'll receive a 5% discount - even on holiday rates.

Note: Prices are regular season non-holiday; multi-day pricing is available. Mammoth lift tickets are valid at both Mammoth and June; however, June-only tickets are not valid at Mammoth.

Accommodations

Mammoth Mountain Inn (800-626-6684; 760-934-2581; $$-$$$$) at the main base is the most convenient to the mountain. The slopeside **Juniper Springs Lodge**, **Sunstone** and **Eagle Run** (800-626-6684; 760-924-1102; $$$-$$$$) feature deluxe condominium-style rooms with full kitchen, gas fireplaces and balconies, plus two heated outdoor pools, two hot tubs, a fitness center and underground parking.

Lincoln House, White Mountain Lodge and Grand Sierra Lodge (800-626-6684; 760-934-1982; $$$-$$$$) make up the Village at Mammoth. Choose from studio to three-bedroom luxury lodge condos. Amenities include gas fireplace, DVD player, daily housekeeping and nightly turndown service, fully equipped kitchens, slate floors and dining area. There are several restaurants on site and gondola access to Canyon Lodge.

Tamarack Lodge & Resort (760-934-2442; $$$-$$$$) has 34 cabins and about a dozen lodge rooms located on Twin Lakes, 2.5 miles from Mammoth.

We list just a few of the places to stay in town. As a starting point, call **Mammoth Lakes Visitors Bureau** (888-466-2666) for a reservation referral. Generally, condos start at about $100 per night, while hotel accommodations—we use the term loosely, as Mammoth currently has more motels than true hotels—can be found for less than $80 per night.

Mammoth Lakes has been called Condo City of the Sierras. Just beyond midtown, **Snowcreek** (800-544-6007; 760-934-3333; $$-$$$$) is its own wooded neighborhood. Units are spacious one-, two- and three-bedroom loft style condos.

Closer to the slopes, next to The Canyon Lodge, are many large condominium complexes with a range of units. Try **Mountainback** (934-5000) or **1849 Condominiums** (800-421-1849; 760-934-7525; $$$-$$$$).

In the middle of town, only a walk to restaurants and a shuttle to the lifts, **Sierra Nevada Rodeway Inn** (800-824-5132; 760-934-2515; $-$$$) has hotel rooms and chalet units. Check out **Alpenhof Lodge** (760-934-6330; $-$$$) or the **Snow Goose Inn** (800-874-7368; 760-934-2660; $-$$$), one of a few bed-and-breakfast inns in town, decorated with antiques, with breakfast served communally in a friendly atmosphere.

Mammoth has several inexpensive motels, including **Econo Lodge/Wildwood Inn** (800-845-8764; 760-934-6855; $-$$), **Motel 6** (800-466-8356; 760-934-6660; $-$$) and **Swiss Chalet** (800-937-9477; 760-934-2403; $-$$).

Lodging at June Mountain Double Eagle Resort & Spa (877-648-7004; 760-648-7004; $$$) in town has several two-bedroom cabins (all No Smoking), plus a restaurant called Eagle's Landing that serves delicious meals and has a magnificent view of the surrounding peaks.

June has two large condominium complexes, with prices starting at less than $100 midweek and $135-$150 weekends. **Interlaken** has studios to three-bedroom units. **Edgewater** only has units suitable for six to nine people. All other lodgings at June are small and quaint, even funky. Call **June Lake Properties Reservation** at at 800-648-5863 or 760-648-7705. **The Haven** (760-648-7524) has studios for about $70.

Also try **Fern Creek Lodge** (800-621-9146; $-$$$), **Whispering Pines** (800-648-7762; $-$$), or **Boulder Lodge** (760-648-7533; $-$$).

 # Dining

Mammoth Lakes has nearly 60 dining options, from gourmet French cuisine to delicatessen sandwiches and quick take-out.

The best gourmet menu is at **Skadi** (760-934-3902; $$$), with a romantic atmosphere and mountain views. Another choice for fine dining is **Cervino's** (760-934-4734; $$$), with a menu that leans toward Northern Italian cuisine.

Petra's (760-934-3500; $$) is a wine bar serving more than 28 wines by the glass along with an ever-changing menu of appetizers served "tapas" style.

For the most romantic (and expensive) dining, head out to **Lakefront Restaurant at Tamarack Lodge** (760-934-3534; $$$) where the menu is basic but the presentation excellent. Another top choice, with country French cuisine and one of the best wine lists in town, is **The Restaurant at Convict Lake** (760-934-3803; $$$), 4 miles south of Mammoth Lakes on Hwy. 395. Look for the Convict Lake turnoff just south of the airport.

Nevados (760-934-4466; $$-$$$) serves contemporary cuisine and has been one of Mammoth's top restaurants for more than 20 years. For steaks, prime rib and seafood, head

Dining: $$$$–Entrees $30+; $$$–$20–$30; $$–$10–$20; $–less than $10.

Accommodations: (double room) $$$$–$200+; $$$–$141–$200; $$–$81–$140; $–$80 and less.

to **Whiskey Creek** (760-934-2555; $$-$$$), The **Mogul Restaurant** (760-934-3039; $$) or the **Chart House** (760-934-4526; $$-$$$). **Mogul** has built its reputation as the best steak house, but we give it best marks for the grilled seafood as well.

Families (or anyone with limited funds) should stop in at **Berger's** (760-934-6622; $-$$) for big, big portions. The tuna salad is massive and you can have not only burgers but also chicken, salad or Canadian stew. Another family spot is **Angel's** (760-934-7427; $$) with great ribs, beans and barbecue.

Nik-N-Willie's Pizza (760-934-2012; $) has the best in town. Pizzas also are featured at **Giovanni's** (760-934-7563; $), **Perry's Italian Cafe** (760-934-6521; $), **5 Boroughs Pizza** (760-924-1045; $) in the village or **Tommy Ho's** (760-934-8140; $).

The best Mexican food is at **Roberto's** (760-934-3667; $) with homemade tortillas and big servings; or head to **Gomez's** (760-924-2693; $).

Grumpy's (760-934-8587; $) holds the distinction of the town's best fried chicken, also the best cole slaw, all presented in a big-screen TV, no-smoking, sports-bar atmosphere.

Sand Dollar Sushi (760-934-5282; $-$$) in the village has a good sushi bar and **Shogun** (760-934-3970; $) also has Japanese cuisine and sushi. Try **Matsu** (760-934-8277; $) for inexpensive Chinese-American and **Thai'd Up** (760-934-7355; $) for Thai cuisine.

Austria Hof (760-934-2764; $$-$$$) and **Alpenrose** (760-934-3077; $$) serve German and Austrian specialties.

The best breakfast in town is served at **Good Life Cafe** (760-934-1734; $), which has a very diverse early-morning menu, and also offers lunch-type meals. Locals also recommend **The Stove** (760-934-2821; $), with biscuits 3 or 4 inches high. Another restaurant with hearty breakfasts is **The Breakfast Club** (760-934-6944; $) at the intersection of Old Mammoth Road and Hwy. 203.

Coffee lovers, your choices are **Looney Bean** (760-934-1345; $) in the Rite Aid shopping center; **Stellar Brew** (760-924-3559; $) on Main Street next to the Chevron station; World Cup Coffee (760-924-3629; $) on Old Mammoth Road across from the movie theater; **Paul Schat's Bakery and Cafe** (760-934-6055; $) on Main Street; and the **Old New York Deli and Bagel Co.** (760-934-3354; $). All have good pastries as well.

On the Mountain

For full-service lunch or evening dining at the mountain, try the California cuisine at **Aalto** (formerly the Mountainside Grill, 760-934-0601; $$) in the Mammoth Mountain Inn. Other best bets for on-mountain lunch are the **Mill Cafe** ($) at the base of Stump Alley Express, serving sandwiches and garlic fries, **Canyon Lodge** ($) with its food court that solves any craving or **Parallax** ($$) in McCoy Station for fine luncheons highlighting Cal-Asian cuisine. **Tusk's Bar** in the Main Lodge ($) features a fireplace and a front-row view of antics in the Unbound Terrain Park.

June Lake The best dining is at the **Eagle's Landing Restaurant** (760-648-7897; $$-$$$) at the Double Eagle Resort and Spa. The **Tiger Bar and Cafe** (760-648-7551; $-$$) is good for burgers and chicken. What there is of June nightlife happens at the Tiger Bar, as does breakfast—go figure, June's a small town. The **Sierra Inn Restaurant** (760-648-7774; $$) has a slightly more upscale menu than The Tiger Bar. The best dining is still in Mammoth Lakes.

Apres-ski/nightlife

Lively apres-ski gets under way across the parking lot from the Main Lodge at the **Pizzeria Cervinia**. At the Canyon Lodge base area, try **Grizzly's** outdoor bar and babecue. **Roberto's** upstairs bar in town is a popular apres-ski hangout; enjoy cool margaritas and four-dollar tacos. At **Sherwin's**, at Sierra Meadows Ranch, there's live enter-tainment most weekends. Entertainment and a newly revamped menu is featured at Mammoth Mountain Inn's **Bacaro** (formerly Dry Creek Bar).

Mammoth's longtime meet market (you may meet someone whose parents used to party hardy here in their younger days) is **Whiskey Creek**, which serves six microbrews. There's plenty of nighttime hoopla at **Grumpy's**, with five giant-screen TVs, pool, foosball, inexpensive chili and burgers. Visiting Brits like this place, and also hang out at the **Clock Tower Cellar** at the Alpenhof Lodge. For casual beer and pool, try **The Tap** on Main Street.

Lakanuki is a tiki-style bar that gets everyone up dancing and **Henessey's** is an Irish bar with a nice outdoor patio. **Dublin's** is a happening Irish bar and next door **Fever** nightclub is the "see and be seen" place to be.

Other activities

Complimentary Naturalist Tours are available for skiers and snowboarders at 10:30 a.m. and 1:30 p.m. on Fridays, Saturdays and Sundays.

Snowmobiles can be rented from **Mammoth Snowmobile Adventures** (760-934-9645), **DJs Snowmobile Adventures** (760-935-4480) or **Mammoth Polaris** (760-924-3155). The area has about 300 miles of snowmobile trails, some signed and groomed, others not. Bobsledding or tubing down a designated track is available through **Sledz** (760-934-7533). Dogsled rides are offered by **Dog Sled Adventures** (760-934-6270).

Peruse local artisans' crafts, photography and artwork at **Edisto Gallery and Tea Room** on Old Mammoth Road, Mammoth Gallery or **Gallerie Barjur** (next door to one another in the Village). **Snowcreek Athletic Club** (760-934-8511) has a variety of indoor and outdoor facili-ties including an indoor swimming pool, tennis courts, daily yoga classes and racquetball.

Don't be fooled into thinking that the only shopping exists in the Village. Mammoth's shopping is oriented as much for the local population as for tourists. You won't find many trendy boutiques here, though there is a factory outlet center on Main Street, and many small shopping malls scattered throughout town.

Mammoth Lakes also has two movie theaters (one with two screens), **Minaret Cinemas** and **Plaza Theater** (both at 760-934-3131). The Mammoth Times, the local weekly newspaper, is a good source for special events listings.

Getting there and getting around

By air: Horizon Air daily service from Los Angeles to Mammoth Yosemite Airport starts on December 18th, 2008. The nearest major airport is Reno, 165 miles away. Rent a car for the drive south, because ground transportation is spotty, and you probably will want a car in Mammoth.

By car: Mammoth is 307 miles north of Los Angeles on Hwy. 395 and 165 miles south of Reno on the same highway. June Mountain is 20 miles north of Mammoth Lakes off Hwy. 395.

Getting around: The resort operates a free shuttle that runs throughout the town and to Mammoth's Main Lodge (4 miles out) and to the Canyon Lodge and Little Eagle Lodge. A Park and Ride lot is located on Old Mammoth Road across from the Chart House. A nightly shuttle makes loops around town until midnight during the week, 1 a.m. on Friday and Sat-urday nights, or call **Mammoth Shuttle** (760-934-3030) or **Sierra Express** (760-924-8294). Most visitors have a car.

Dining: $$$$–Entrees $30+; $$$–$20–$30; $$–$10–$20; $–less than $10.
Accommodations: (double room) $$$$–$200+; $$$–$141–$200; $$–$81–$140; $–$80 and less.

Aspen Snowmass

Colorado

Aspen Mountain
Buttermilk
Aspen Highlands
Snowmass

Address: Aspen Skiing Company, P.O. Box 1248, Aspen, CO 81612 or Snowmass Resort Association, P.O. Box 5566, Snowmass Village, CO 81615
Area code: 970
Ski area phone: 925-1220 or (800) 525-6200
Snow report: 925-1221 or (888) 277-3676
Toll-free reservations: (800) 262-7736 or 925-9000 (Aspen); (800) 760-9627 (Snowmass)
Fax: 925-9008
E-mail: info@aspensnowmass.com (resort) info@stayaspen.com (Aspen reservations) info@snowmassvillage.com (Snowmass)

Internet: www.aspensnowmass.com (ski area) www.stayaspensnowmass.com (lodging) www.aspenchamber.org (visitor information) www.snowmassvillage.com (Snowmass Village)
Bed base: 7,750; 14,303 within 10 miles (Aspen) 7,750 at base; 13,050 within 10 miles (Snowmass)
Nearest lodging: Slopeside, hotels, condos
Resort child care: 8 weeks and older
Adult ticket, per day: $87 (07/08)

Dining:★★★★★
Apres-ski/nightlife:★★★★★
Other activities:★★★★★

Ask a crowd of non-skiing Americans to name a ski resort, and you can bet a bundle that Aspen will be one of those, though they will probably know more about the rich and famous who frequent the resort than about its equally notable skiing. With four mountains within 12 miles of each other (one of those, Snowmass, is detailed separately), offering 46 lifts and 336 trails spread over 5,285 skiable acres, a trip to Aspen just for the skiing would be well worth it. But Aspen has much more—like amazing views for starters.

Don't head to Aspen purely to observe celebrities, however. You may not find any. They are most common during the Christmas-New Year holidays and March's sunshine days, but they are difficult to spot when in ski clothes. If you want to mix with the upscale crowd, stay close to the Aspen Mountain gondola base, where the fanciest hotels and shops are clustered. You'll find a mixed crowd here, which combines expensive and reasonably priced restaurants and bars. Beyond downtown, the outward signs of wealth disappear.

If all your information about Aspen comes from People magazine, you probably think you can't afford to ski here. True, lift tickets are among the priciest in America, but it's a little-known fact that lodging and restaurants have a wide price range, starting out with inexpensive dorm accommodations and topping out at stratospheric luxury suites.

Perhaps due to Aspen's glamorous reputation, its adventurous nature is sometimes overlooked. Aspen also draws skiers and snowboarders who couldn't care less about the off-mountain scene. They come for the slopes, which have received rave reviews for decades. Aspen Mountain challenges intermediate through expert skiers and snowboarders and boasts a green reputation. Among other efforts, Aspen has built the state's first wind-powered chair lift. Buttermilk is the perfect beginner and cruising mountain, plus it's home to the ESPN Winter X Games and the and the Crazy T'rain Terrain Park. Highlands is the most varied for its size, with terrain for experts and beginners, cruisers and bumpers.

If you're determined to see celebrities at Aspen, three sightings are guaranteed on Aspen Mountain. Look for shrines for Elvis Presley, Marilyn Monroe and Jerry Garcia. The Elvis shrine is in a grove of trees just below Back of Bell 3. Marilyn's shrine is on a cat track above the Elvis shrine and Jerry is memorialized in a grove of spruce trees to skiers' right on Ruthie's Run after you unload from the FIS chair. Ask an Aspen ambassador for directions and be sure to take your camera. For a little romance, check out the Valentine's shrine between Walsh's and Hyrup's on Aspen Mountain. Aspen Mountain is not recommended for beginners and first-timers.

Snowmass

Though it is lumped into the Aspen experience by geography, Snowmass stands on its own as a winter destination. Snowmass ranks among the top 10 resorts in America in size, and it's the second-largest in Colorado (after Vail). It covers more than 3,132 acres—more than Aspen Mountain, Buttermilk and Highlands combined. And thanks to a surface lift to the top of the Cirque (formerly reached by a hike or snowcat), Snowmass lays claim to the longest vertical drop in the United States, 4,406 feet. (Big Sky, MT, has a 4,180-foot vertical; Jackson Hole, WY, 4,139 feet. Now you have your apres-ski bar conversation opener.)

The Snowmass Village Mall seems to stretch forever uphill with shops, restaurants, bars and skier services, but all are handicap accessible and if you are so inclined you can use hotel and public elevators (at 8,104 feet, you'll soon know why we added this).

The resort has started construction on its new base village, due for completion in 2012. Improvements in 2005/06 added a six-pack—Village Express—to replace the old Fanny Hill chair. The new chair gets to Sam's Knob in nine minutes. Sky Cab takes passengers from the new base area to the mall in just two minutes. The new Elk Camp Gondola installed in '06 runs from the base of Fanny Hill to Elk Camp in eight minutes with a midway loading and unloading station. Hundreds of condos line the lower part of the resort, and about 95 percent of the lodging is ski-in/ski-out. It doesn't get much more convenient than this.

A note to those staying in a ski-in/ski-out condo: Make note of where you are before you head down to the lift for your first run. We had a heck of a time knowing where to cut off from the ski run to our unit in a sea of brown condos at the end of the day.

Tip: Day skiers who want to avoid crowds and parking hassles can drive or take the shuttle to Two Creeks base at the south end of Snowmass. Here parking costs $12, but it's well worth the convenience of a small base area. From here Two Creeks lift hooks up with the lift system.

Mountain layout

Aspen's four mountains are close to each other, but not interconnected. A free shuttle runs from base to base. ASC runs a very efficient equipment transfer program between its four mountains. For $5, you hand over your skis, poles or snowboard to an attendant in the base area at the end of the day, tell him/her where you're skiing the next day, and your gear will be waiting for you at that base area the next morning. It works very well.

◆◆**Expert: Highlands** is the best-balanced mountain of the three with slopes for every level, and it's the locals' favorite. The vertical rise is one of the highest in Colorado. Three high-speed quads whisk you to the summit so you're not wasting time on lifts.

From the top of Loge Peak, the run back to the base is an uneven series of steeps, cat tracks and gentle runouts. This mountain has some fantastic long cruises. The ridge, knifing directly to the summit, has thrilling pitches down both sides. Other than a few short blacks, such as Suzy Q and Limelight, the terrain makes a pronounced jump from intermediate to expert.

Experts should head for the steeps at the top of Loge Peak in the Steeplechase (sunny in the morning) and Olympic Bowl (sunny in the afternoon) areas. These are very steep with no

Aspen Mountain Facts
Summit elevation: 11,212 feet
Vertical drop: 3,267 feet
Base elevation: 7,945 feet
Number of lifts: 8—1 gondola, 1 high-speed quad, 1 high-speed double, 2 quads, 3 doubles
Snowmaking: 31 percent **Skiable acreage:** 673 acres
Uphill capacity: 10,775 per hour **Parks & pipes:** 1 park (open only in spring)
Expert:★★★★ Advanced:★★★★★
Intermediate:★★★★
Beginner/First-timer: Don't go here

Buttermilk Facts
Summit elevation: 9,900 feet
Vertical drop: 2,030 feet
Base elevation: 7,870 feet
Number of lifts: 9—2 high-speed quads, 3 doubles, 4 surface lift
Snowmaking: 25 percent **Skiable acreage:** 470 acres
Uphill capacity: 7,500 per hour **Parks & pipes:** 5 parks, 1 pipe
Expert:★ Advanced:★★ Intermediate:★★★★
Beginner:★★★★★ First-timer:★★★★★

Aspen Highlands Facts
Summit elevation: 11,675 feet
Vertical drop: 3,635 feet
Base elevation: 8,040 feet
Number of lifts: 5—3 high-speed quads, 2 triples
Snowmaking: 14 percent **Skiable acreage:** 1,010 acres
Uphill capacity: 6,500 per hour **Parks & pipes:** None
Expert:★★★★ Advanced:★★★★★ Intermediate:★★★★
Beginner:★★★ First-timer:★★

Snowmass Facts
Summit elevation: 12,510 feet
Vertical drop: 4,406 feet
Base elevation: 8,104 feet
Number of lifts: 24—2 gondolas, 1 cabriolet, 1 high-speed six-pack, 6 high-speed quads, 1 triple, 4 doubles, 4 surface lifts, 5 moving carpets
Snowmaking: 6 percent **Skiable acreage:** 3,125 acres
Uphill capacity: 31,080 per hour **Parks & pipes:** 3 parks, 2 pipes
Expert:★★★★ Advanced:★★★★ Intermediate:★★★★★
Beginner:★★★ First-timer:★★

bail-out areas, so be sure you want to be here. Both areas have long cat tracks back to lifts.

Some of Colorado's steepest slopes stand above Loge Peak in Highland Bowl. You can reach the tops of the 40- to 45-degree slopes by hiking up the ridge for 20–60 minutes; or, if you happen to be at Loge Meadow between 11 a.m. and 1 p.m., hop on a free snowcat for a ride to the first access gate. The gladed runs here will keep you on your toes. The Temerity triple means you can ski another 1,000 vertical feet down Highland Bowl and not hike out. The lift also accesses 180 acres of chutes and trees.

Also check out the lower mountain. The Thunderbowl chair will take you from the base to the top of Bob's Glades or Upper Stein, or you can drop into double-black territory at several points along blue-square Golden Horn.

The basic guideline for **Aspen Mountain** is that the intermediate terrain is on the top knob around the summit and in the gullies between the ridges. The expert stuff drops from the ridges into the gullies. Of the blacks, take your pick and be sure you're up to it. These runs are very black. For bumps and trees, Bell Mountain right under the gondola is a good choice. Watch for the ski patrol to open Walsh's after a storm. It can be powder heaven, a run you can brag about all week. Guided "Powder Tours" are offered on the back side of Aspen Mountain; call (800) 525-6200 for information.

At **Snowmass,** the most extreme terrain is in the Hanging Valley Glades, which for years management was not comfortable opening. Accessed by the High Alpine lift, an ancient double chair, the options are countless, including steep chutes Possible and Baby Ruth into Hanging Valley Glades, or straight over the headwall to at least a dozen drops into the Hanging Valley.

Another extreme playground is the Cirque, a scooped-out place between Sheer Bliss and High Alpine lifts. This is served by a wind-powered surface lift that gets very popular on powder days, at the top of which you'll find the "Rocky Mountain High" run, named in memory of the late singer John Denver. Don't try this area unless you're comfortable on Hanging Valley Wall. The right side holds almost as many chutes as the Wall, and you'll need to make tight, jump turns at the top of Rock Island and KT Gully. Even more challenging is AMF at the top. A local says it stands for "Adios, My Friend," but we think he gave us the "this-is-a-family-guidebook" version.

◆ **Advanced:** If you consider yourself a very confident advanced skier, read the expert section. If you feel you have recently reached advanced status, read the intermediate section. In our experience, there's a big jump from intermediate to expert terrain at **Highlands** and **Aspen Mountain. Buttermilk's** marked advanced terrain is really more advanced-intermediate.

At **Snowmass,** look skier's left for chutes and drops and to the lower right side of the Sheer Bliss run to get the feel of the famous Cirque terrain without the heart-gripping fear of knowing you are not ready for that stuff. Skiers ready to burn up steep-pitched cruising will think they've found nirvana when they make the first descent into the Campground area. Here is a wonderful long run: To come off the top of Big Burn on Sneaky's, tuck to avoid the uphill stretch at Sam's Knob, cut south around the Knob and head into the blacks of Bear Claw, Slot, Wildcat or Zugspitze to the base of the Campground lift. The Campground runs on a deep powder day can make you thankful the chair at the bottom is not high-speed.

■ **Intermediate:** If you'd like to say you skied a black run on **Aspen Mountain,** Upper Little Percy or Red's Run are occasionally groomed. The ticket office or the on-mountain Concierge Center at the summit has a grooming report (you can check this at all the mountains, by the way).

Unsure if you can handle the terrain? If you can ski blues at other areas, do this: Ride the gondola to the top and ski the gentlest terrain, at the summit—runs such as Dipsy Doodle, Pussyfoot and Silver Bell. Keep riding the Ajax Express and Gentlemen's Ridge lifts. If any of those blue runs presents a challenge, ride back down in the gondola. The alternative to riding down is Copper Bowl or Spar Gulch, two narrow gullies that get packed late in the day as skiers funnel into them toward the base. Both runs join at Kleenex Corner—a sharp, narrow turn—then dump into Little Nell, a steep blue just above the gondola base. It's known as "Little Hell" because at day's end, it's crowded, usually a little slick and/or moguled, and smack in view of everyone.

At **Buttermilk,** intermediates with confident turns will have fun on Jacob's Ladder and Bear, which drop from the Cliff House to the main area, but the real playground is under the Tiehack chair. Much of this area is colored black on the trail map, but don't get too excited—it's just the toughest stuff on *this* mountain. You'll discover good upper-intermediate trails that make inspiring cruisers. In one day you can ride the Upper Tiehack chair a dozen times, taking a different cruise on each 1,500 vertical-foot run. Javelin is the best of the lot—a couple of tree islands to keep you awake and a lot of good dips and rolls. Smile in the evening when you overhear others scoffing about what a waste Buttermilk is for real skiers, and savor memories of 15,000 feet of vertical in just one afternoon.

At **Highlands,** intermediates will want to take these lifts: Cloud Nine, Olympic and Loge Peak. (The easiest of the intermediates are off Cloud Nine.) Don't miss Golden Horn and Thunderbowl on the lower mountain, very wide cruisers.

At **Snowmass,** intermediate terrain is literally everywhere, including from the summit (Cirque) and even the never-ending Green Mile, an upper intermediate run from High Alpine. There's a half-day's worth of intermediate options on each of Sam's Knob, Elk Camp, Two Creeks and Alpine Springs. The Big Burn is legendary cruiser fun. It's an entire side of a mountain that was allegedly set aflame by Ute Indians in the 1880s as a warning to advancing white settlers. The pioneers settled anyway, but the trees never grew back thickly, so the run, dotted by a few spruces, is a mile wide and a mile-and-a-half long. Fanny Hill six-pack whisks you from the Mall area directly to the Burn summit in less than 10 minutes. For an intermediate uncomfortable around trees, the Powerline Glades are a great primer.

●● **Beginner: Aspen Mountain** may be the only mountain in America that has no designated green-circle runs. Don't try it if you're a beginner.

Buttermilk is all that Aspen Mountain isn't. Beginners can experience top-to-bottom runs as soon as they master snowplows. The beginner terrain concentrates under the Buttermilk West chair. Tom's Thumb, Red's Rover, Larkspur, Westward Ho and Blue Grouse will keep beginners improving. The Homestead Road turns back to the Savio chair and lazily winds its way to the Main Buttermilk area.

At **Highlands,** beginners are best served by the trails from the Exhibition chair—Prospector, Nugget, Exhibition, Red Onion and Apple Strudel.

At **Snowmass,** beginners have a wide gentle area parallel to the village. Fanny Hill eases down by the mall, Wood Run lift opens another easy glide around the Wood Road side of the village, and further to the left a long straightaway, Funnel, will give beginners the feeling they're really covering terrain. Beginners who want to see more of the mountain can head up to Sam's Knob and try the Top of the Knob, with its spectacular views and great menu, and head down a meandering trail bearing the names Max Park, Lunchline and Dawdler, which turns back to Fanny Hill. (Avoid the blue runs on the face of Sam's Knob because they are not for beginners.) The next step up would be Elk Camp, labeled blue but very gentle.

● **First-timer:** Take your first few lessons at **Buttermilk**. Of Aspen's four mountains, this is by far the best for a first day on skis or a snowboard. We would give the beginner terrain at **Snowmass** a higher rating but for one important fact: Many of the ski-in/ski-out condos are along the green runs, so at the beginning and end of the day, they often are used by skilled skiers and snowboarders in a hurry to get to either the lifts or the hot tub.

Snowboarding

At 673 acres, **Aspen Mountain** is not even one-fourth the size of Snowmass, but every acre is infinitely rideable. The mountain scenery is sublime—better, even, than Telluride or Crested Butte. This is a mountain for expert riders who respect and even revere a pristine Alpine playground. There are no beginner trails and scant few true intermediate runs. But if you have good skills, the mountain is replete with bumps, steeps and natural halfpipes.

If you measure the quality of your riding by the perfection of the "esses" and the depth of the trenches you leave behind, **Buttermilk** is the place for you. Buttermilk has numerous constant-pitch, top-to-bottom fall line, groomed runs ideal for laying out one perfect carve after another. Larkspur is one of the most fun carving runs on the mountain, but you'll go into the trees on either side if you don't keep your turns tight. The mountain gets interesting over on Racer's Edge and Javelin. These runs get groomed and they're steep enough to force even advanced riders to concentrate on working their edges. Cutting down from Tiehack Parkway are the Ptarmigan and Timber Doodle Glades. Here, intermediate boarders can learn to ride in the trees. The terrain is steep enough not to stall out, yet the trees are spaced far enough apart to learn.

Highlands attracts riders who are interested in riding blacks and double-blacks. While the resort's quick to point out they actually have more green and blue terrain than black, if intermediate cruisers or a great terrain park is what you're looking for, you'll be happier at Snowmass or Buttermilk. Highlands is where advanced and expert riders go to go steep on big powder days. Get ready for a spectacular descent in the 12,500-foot Highland Bowl, 100 or more turns in champagne powder up to your waist—or higher. Your best bet is to do it your first time with a guide who has ridden it several times before. The new Deep Temerity triple chairlift means no more heinous traverse back to the lift.

Snowmass is so huge there's excellent terrain for riders of all levels—and persuasions—and generally little walking if you stay alert. Some areas to prepare for: the approach to Campgrounds, Two Creeks, Funnel and Alpine Springs lifts; the entire basin near the future base village on the way to the Makaha Terrain Park; the runs over the Trestle to the Sheer Bliss chair; Turkey Trot over to Elk Camp; and even the ride out below the Cirque can stop you in your tracks on powder days. Expert riders should head to the legendary Cirque. And from the top of High Alpine, ambitious riders hike 10 minutes to get hang time on Hanging Valley Wall. Advanced riders can play anywhere else, especially on Sam's Knob and the less-tracked Campground, as well as the Burn and rider's left along Sheer Bliss. Intermediate boarders seeking to get away from crowds on Fanny Hill should head for Elk Camp, where you'll find groomed intermediate slopes and a high-speed quad that lets you rack up the vertical. From the top of the Elk Camp lift, a short 5- to10-minute hike takes you to Long Shot, a backcountry-like, ungroomed run that winds 3 miles through the National forest—getting you even further away from the bubbas. For some big whoops, the Naked Lady offers some fun rollers.

Parks and pipes

The wild side of **Buttermilk** is the top-to-bottom Playstation 2 Crazy T'rain Terrain Park. Nearly 2 miles long, it features 30 rails and the only 15-foot superpipe in the four Aspen mountains. It's geared toward intermediates and better. At the bottom of the park a gigantic kicker allows tricksters with huge, and we're talking *huge*, air skills to put on a show for everyone at the base area. Hopefully, there's an ambulance standing by. **Highlands** doesn't have a halfpipe or terrain park; however, Prospector Trail is known locally as Grommets Gulch and is a natural halfpipe. Just a few yards away from the Sundeck restaurant on **Aspen Mountain,** former competitive skateboarder and snowboarder Othello partners with Aspen Skiing Company to teach rail riding in Othello's Rail Riders. Camp attendees learn how to get on a rail properly, how to balance and land, what not to do, tricks and terrain park etiquette. The camp also has a hut with video games, music, records and DVDs. Reservations are required; call the ski and snowboard school. For a long cruiser that forms a wild natural halfpipe, there's Spar Gulch, which cuts a steep "V" down the heart of the mountain to the patio of The Little Nell.

Snowmass' three terrain parks, Little Makaha, Midway Intermediate and Pipeline, cover the gamut of freestyle abilities, from first-timer to advanced trickster. Little Makaha, under the Funnel chair, is designed expressly for beginners and those ready to go the next step, with medium-sized bumps, boxes, rails, rollers and banks. A beginner pipe is on lower Velvet. The Midway Park now benefits from snowmaking and bigger jumps, more challenging boxes and more elements than the Makaha. The place for serious freestyle terrain elements is Pipeline Park on Sam's Knob. This is a continuous line of elements starting on Banzai Ridge, continuing on Coney Glade and finishing with Doddler Bowl. With a quick ride on Sam's Knob Express, this is a hardcore lap of quality hits and features. The superpipe can be found opposite Doddler at the end of the Coney Glade section.

Cross-country & snowshoeing (also see xcskiresorts.com)

Aspen/Snowmass has the most extensive free Nordic trail system in America, more than 65 km. of groomed trails called "Aspen's fifth mountain." The **Aspen Nordic Council's** (800-525-6200; 923-3148) free system is accessible from Aspen or Snowmass and includes easy golf-course skiing as well as more difficult trails rising up to Snowmass.

In addition to the free trails provided by Aspen's Nordic Council, **Ashcroft Ski Touring Unlimited** (925-1971) has 42 km. of groomed and set trails, and backcountry skiers can use summer hiking trails. Lessons and rentals are available. Other centers are the **Aspen Cross Country Center** (544-9246) on the Aspen Golf Course off Hwy. 82; **Ute Mountaineer** (925-2849); **Braun Hut System** (925-6618), which has information on trails to Crested Butte; and **Snowmass Cross Country Center** (923-3148).

Hut systems connect Aspen with Vail on the Tenth Mountain Trail and with Crested Butte over the Pearl Pass. Guides are available and recommended. Call Tenth Mountain Trail Association for more information, 925-5775, or send e-mail to huts@huts.org.

Snowshoeing is quite popular in town, so ask about those programs at any of the cross-country centers mentioned here. In conjunction with the Aspen Center for Environmental Studies (ACES), **Aspen Skiing Company** has naturalist-guided tours on Aspen Mountain and Snowmass. Tours include lifts, equipment and a snack; call 925-1220 or ACES at 925-5756 for reservations. You also can snowshoe up Aspen Mountain or Buttermilk at certain times and on certain runs. The lift ride down is free. Ask an Aspen Skiing Company concierge about this.

Lessons (07/08 prices)

Aspen Snowmass guarantees its lessons. If you are not completely satisfied, get another lesson free or get a refund. For brochures and information, or to make reservations for ski and snowboard school programs, call (970) 923-1227 or (877) 282-7736, or visit the web site. We list programs for Snowmass separately.

Group lessons: Adult small group lessons for Level 5 and up cost $130 a day. They are offered at all the mountains, and are limited to three per class for all levels. Unlimited extensions are $114 per day.

First-timer package: Beginner's Magic is a lesson package for Levels 1-4 offered at Buttermilk. Three-day ski/snowboard packages (including lessons, lift tickets, rentals) run $352. One-day programs are $140. Unlimited extensions of either program are $119 per day.

Private lessons: $605 for a full day, $2,825 for five full days. Other options are available. Reservations are required. Lessons are offered in several languages, and include ski storage, lift line privileges, and demo discounts as well as an ebook on instruction written by longtime Aspen pro Weems Westfeldt. Offered every day on every mountain.

Special programs: These are numerous clinics, including clinics and/or ski and snowboard weeks for women, bumps, powder, off-piste, all-mountain, disabled skiers, video analysis, equipment assessment and many more.

Racing: NASTAR courses are on Silver Dip Swing at Aspen Mountain (daily) and Nugget at Highlands (Wednesday-Sunday). Clinics also are offered

Children's programs (07/08 prices)

Child care: Ages 8 weeks to 4 years. Cost is $135 for a full day. Reservations are required, call 970-923-1227. State-licensed daycare is now in the brand new 25,000 square-foot Treehouse Kids' Adventure Center at the new base village at Snowmass. The one-stop facility serves as ski school check-in, rental and retail shops and family fun center. Child care in Aspen is offered by Kids' Club in the Yellow Brick Building, 315 Garmisch St. The state-licensed program offers indoor and outdoor (non-skiing) activities.

Other options: Aspen Babysitting Company (948-6849) offers babysitting services at your hotel room or condo (insured and bonded). Little Red School House (923-3756) has licensed day care for ages 3–5. Baby's Away (800-948-9030; 970-920-1699) rents and will deliver baby needs to your lodge, such as crib, stroller, car seat and toys. Reservations are recommended for all of these services.

Children's lessons: Aspen Skiing Company has different children's programs, depending on the mountain. All kids 12 and younger *must* wear helmets while in ski and snowboard school. Helmets can be rented for $8 a day. Equipment rental is additional. Lift tickets are extra for kids 7 and older. All-day programs include lunch. For more information about lessons, call 970-923-1227 or (877) 282-7736.

Ages 3–6 (Level 1–4) ski at Buttermilk, ages 5–6 (Level 5 and higher) ski at Aspen Highlands. Cost is $135 for a full day; $90 for a half day. Reservations are strongly recommended; if space is available for walk-ins, prices are higher. Ages 7–12 skiing and ages 8–12 snowboarding pay $2 per day at Buttermilk or Aspen Highlands. Kids 7-12 who are first-timers can take a lesson package that includes lesson, rentals and lift ticket for $109 (must be 8 years old to snowboard).

Special activities: Children from 5th through 12th grade can mingle with local kids in the afternoons at the Aspen Youth Center (hotline with weekly activities information, 970-925-7091) in downtown Aspen. The center has **games, ping-pong, pool tables, movies** and a **dance room.** The center does special programs depending on the season. Admission is free.

Lift tickets (07/08 prices)

	Adult	Youth (13-17)	Child (7-12)
One day	$87	$79	$57
Four days*	$324 ($81/day)	$300 ($75/day)	$216 ($54/day)
Five days*	$395 ($79/day)	$355 ($71/day)	$245 ($49/day)
* out of 10			

Who skis free: Ages 6 and younger.

Who skis at a discount: Ages 65 to 69 pay youth rates; 70 years and older pay $74 at the window or can buy The Silver Pass for $239 for the season.

The best ticket prices are found by making a seven-day advance purchase of four or more days. To purchase tickets, call 877-282-7736 or buy online through the resort's web site. Also check lift/lodging packages.

Note: All tickets are valid at all four mountains. These are peak season prices.

Accommodations

Accommodations in Aspen range from luxurious and pricey to modest and inexpensive. **StayAspenSnowmass**, 800-262-7736 or 970-925-9000, can reserve nearly all properties listed here. Multi-day lift-and-lodging packages are the best deal. You also can log on to www.stayaspensnowmass.com and check out the "Virtual Hostel" for last-minute, discounted lodging packages.

Hotel Jerome (800-331-7213 or 970-920-1000; $$$$) on East Main Street reflects Aspen's glory days. On the National Register of Historic Places, The Jerome is a grand old hotel restored to more elegance than the silver barons ever knew. Even if you don't stay there, this Aspen landmark is worth a walk-through to view the antiques and old photos.

The Little Nell (888-843-6355 or 970-920-4600 ; $$$$) is just steps from the Silver Queen Gondola at the base of Aspen Mountain. It has received the highest rating (five on a 1-5 scale) from several rating services, such as AAA and Mobil. All rooms have fireplaces, sofas, oversized beds with comforters and marble bathrooms. There is a spa and a heated outdoor pool.

The St. Regis, Aspen (888-454-9005 or 970-920-3300; $$$$) is richly appointed, with a tasteful decor that brings to mind an exclusive hunting club. It has a fitness center and various ski packages. Its restaurants are top-flight. Though the red brick building is just a few years old, it looks like it belongs to historic Aspen.

The Residence (970-920-6532; $$$$) has world-class European suites in an historic downtown landmark building. Also luxurious are the **SKY Hotel** (970-925-6760 or 800-882-2582; $$$$) and the delightful award-winning **Hotel Lenado** (800-321-3457 or 970-925-6246; $$$$). The latter, another property of the Sardy House owners, may be small, but it's huge in amenities, personality and service. A delicious hot breakfast is included in the room price, which drops into the $$$ category during shoulder seasons.

One of our readers tells us **Hotel Durant** (877-438-7268; 970-925-8500; $$-$$$$) is one of his favorite "little hotels." Beautifully renovated in 1996, it's just two blocks from downtown and one-and-a-half blocks from lift 1-A.

Our favorite place in Aspen, a lodge of a kind that's disappearing all too fast, is **The Mountain Chalet** (800-321-7813 or 970-925-7797; $-$$$). This place is just plain friendly to everyone, including families. If you can't stand a 3-year-old crawling over a lounge chair in the lobby or families howling over a game of Monopoly, then don't stay here. Rates are reasonable and include a hearty breakfast served family-style. It's a few blocks from Aspen

Mountain's Silver Queen gondola, and across the street from the transportation center. Package deals for lodging, lift tickets and full breakfast are as low as $84 per person per day in a dorm bunk or a four-person room; about $94 per person per night for two to a room. To get these prices, call the chalet directly. In sharp contrast to the quintessential ski lodge Mountain Chalet, across the street is the brand new **Hyatt Grand Aspen**, a fractional ownership property (866-517-9715).

Other places that treat guests very well are the **Mountain House Lodge** (866-920-2550; 970-920-3440; $$), the **Hotel Aspen** (800-527-7369 or 970-925-3441; $$) and the **Molly Gibson Lodge** (800-356-6559 or 970-925-3434; $$). Also try **St. Moritz Lodge** (800-817-2069; 970-925-3220; $), a hostel only five blocks from the center of town. The historic **Christmas Inn** 232 W. Main St is now the **Annabelle Inn** (877-266-2466 or 970-925-3822; $$-$$$$). Each of its 35 rooms has been uniquely renovated and include flat-panel TVs and free high-speed internet access.

You can still find inexpensive rooms at the renovated **Innsbruck Inn** (970-925-2980; $$), **Ullr Lodge** (970-925-7696) and budget champion Tyrolean Lodge (888-220-3809 or 970-925-4595; $).

ResortQuest and **Frias** are the largest condo management companies in the area. Resort-Quest (800-GO-RELAX) has three check-in locations in town at 720 East Hyman, 747 So. Galena and 940 Waters Ave. It manages a slew of condos, townhomes and private homes as well as the Inn at Aspen. **Fasching Haus, Durant Condominiums, Fifth Avenue, Summit Place, Aspen International** and **Alpenblick** are within a short walk to the gondola. **Chateau Eau Claire** and **Chateau Roaring Fork** are two of their popular units. **Shadow Mountain** is not fancy but has a ski-in/ski-out location. ResortQuest categorizes its properties under a rating system. Ask about it when you book with them. All reservations include complimentary shuttles from the Aspen Airport. Tip: if you don't like the snow conditions when you get to a ResortQuest property, you can re-book with them within seven days at another resort in Colorado, Utah or Idaho. Ask about their Snow Guarantee.

Frias (877-636-4626) books for the new **Hyatt Grand Aspen** and **St. Regis Residence Club** and also manages a large portfolio of privately owned condos. For luxury, three-bedroom condos on the slopes, try **Mountain Queen Condominiums** (970-925-6366). **The Gant** (970-925-5000 or 800-345-1471) at the foot of Aspen Mountain is another choice.

Accommodations—Snowmass

Nearly half of the lodging at Snowmass is at hotels, and there are thousands of condominiums, 95 percent of which are slopeside ski-in/ski-out. For other recommendations and reservations, call **Stay Aspen Snowmass**(888-649-5985 or 970-925-9000) or go to www.snowmassvillage.com.

The Silvertree (877-766-1999; $$$$) is the biggest hotel (260 rooms) with a conference center and feels like it inside. But it sits conveniently above the Snowmass Village Mall where most of the activity takes place.

Stonebridge Inn (800-213-3214; $-$$$), in the center of the village recently was renovated with $1 million in upgrades and added meeting space and a deck.

Less expensive hotel or lodge accommodations include the **Pokolodi Lodge** (800-666-4556; $-$$$); **Snowmass Inn** (800-635-3758; $-$$$); **Snowmass Mountain Chalet** (800-843-1579; $-$$$), which includes a full breakfast, delicious soup lunch and slopeside convenience; or **Wildwood Lodge** (877-766-1999; $$-$$$$). Parking arrangements vary by property and can be inconvenient.

Dining: $$$$–Entrees-$30+$; $$$–$20-30; $$–$10–20; $–less than $10.
Accommodations: (double room) $$$$–$200+; $$$–$141–$200; $$–$81–$140; $–$80

The Crestwood Condominium Hotel (800-356-5949; $$$-$$$$) is comfortable and roomy, right next to the slopes and well-designed for groups. Units have fireplaces, a bathroom for every bedroom, laundry facilities, new swimming pools and exercise room and airport shuttle service.

The Sonnenblick (877-766-1999; $$$$) has only large units, three or five bedrooms. For more moderate condos, try **Terracehouse** (800-525-9402; $$$-$$$$), a short walk to the lifts, or **Lichenhearth** (800-525-9402; $$$-$$$$), adjacent to the Fanny Hill lift. **The Top of the Village** (800-982-1311; $$$-$$$$) and the **Timberline** (800-922-4001; $$-$$$$) condos are a good 5- to 10-minute climb above the village mall. For economy condos, we like **Willows** (800-525-9402; $$$), two levels below the village mall.

Woodrun Place Condos and Conference Center (800-668-0401; $$$$) has had an extensive face-lift on its exterior to the tune of $12 million. The 33 townhomes at **Woodrun V** (800-718-3694 ext. 8; $$$$) have new exteriors and heated walkways, a new business center and other upgrades. The condos are right next to the midway loading station for the new Elk Camp Gondola. **Chamonix** (800-365-0410; $$$$) is another upscale condo complex we like.

Dining

We can't possibly review all the restaurants in Aspen, because the region's packed with worthy places to eat, but this list will get you started. Don't even think of going anywhere without a reservation. Exotic ingredients and ethnic foods are definitely trendy in Aspen. This is a place where you can thoroughly enjoy the fine restaurants, knowing that the next day you'll ski off those calories. But be careful—most menu items are separately priced and the bill can add up.

If cost is what you're worried about, many restaurants in Aspen have a "bar" menu or "small plates" entrees. These menus are the locals' secrets to eating well, and they aren't your usual hot wings and nachos. They're culinary delights but in smaller portions than regular entrees, running $8-$15, such as roast sirloin steak with gourmet mashed potatoes at **Cache Cache**, spinach-and-ricotta-cheese ravioli in a light smoked-ricotta-and-sage sauce at **L'Hostaria** or the Sambal shrimp quesadilla at **Elevation**.

Montagna (675 E. Durant; 970-920-6313; $$$$) at the Little Nell specializes in contemporary American Alpine cuisine. Executive Chef Ryan Hardy delights with an intricate blend of flavors, textures and colors. Montagna is a Grand Award recipient, the highest achievement from *Wine Spectator*. Open for breakfast, lunch and dinner, as well as Sunday brunch.

Syzygy (520 E. Hyman Ave.; 970-925-3700, reservations required; $$$-$$$$) has a menu that combines French, Southwestern, Asian and Italian influences. Don't be put off by the hard-to-pronounce name (Siz-i-je) or the obscure explanation of its meaning on the menu. The food here is simply exquisite.

Sun-drenched flavors of the mediterranean describes the delicious dishes at **the wild fig** (970-925-5160; $$$$) on East Hyman across from the Wheeler Opera House.

Go to **Piñons** (second floor at 105 S. Mill; 970-920-2021; $$$$) to dine in what feels like a cozy Western ranch, with stucco walls, a leather bar and menus and huge brass bowls. All meats and fish are grilled over mesquite and cherry wood. Desserts vary daily.

If you think that at these prices, you should be entertained and have your apartment cleaned for a year, one man will at least do the former. Owner Mead Metcalf has been playing to **The Crystal Palace** sellout crowds each evening at 6:45 nightly for more than four decades (300 E. Hyman Ave.; 970-925-1455; $$$$, reservations may be necessary several weeks in advance). The Crystal Palace's talented staff not only cranks out a full dinner and bar service, but then belts out a cabaret revue spoofing the media's latest victims.

R Cuisine has replaced **Range**at 304 E. Hopkins. We haven't tried it yet, but longtime Aspen chef Barclay Dodge can't go wrong.

Cache Cache (lower level of the Mill St. Plaza; 970-925-3835; $$-$$$) gets a thumbs-up from locals for French provincial cuisine, especially the half-price early-bird specials. The polenta nicoise, wild mushroom cannelloni and perfectly grilled yellowtail are favorites. **Rustique** (216 S. Monarch; 970-920-2555; $$-$$$) serves a wonderful cassoulet Toulousain with duck confit and sausage. It also has a child-friendly menu with 25 classic French favorites called "Small Plates."

Kenichi (533 E. Hopkins; 970-920-2212; $$$) and **Takah Sushi** (320 So. Mill; 970-925-8588; $$-$$$) are the locals' favorite for Pan Asian cuisine and sushi. Always crowded, reservations are a must, especially on Friday and Saturday nights.

Matthew Zubrod, who used to be executive chef at the Ritz-Carlton, opened **DishAspen** (430 E. Hyman; 970-925-1421; $$$) in the former Mogador Restaurant space on the Hyman St. Mall in spring of 2006. He serves creative American comfort foods like lobster corn dogs, truffle mac 'n cheese and C.L.T. sandwiches made of crab, lettuce and tomato. And there's always a "dish" of the day.

An enormous crystal chandelier in the foyer of a Victorian home sets the tone for **LuLu Wilson** at 316 E. Hopkins. (970-920-1893; $$$-$$$$), the newest offering to Aspen's elite dining scene. The service matches the elegant decor with foreign-accented waiters carefully attending each table. Entrees include braised rabbit, wild sablefish, roasted Guinea Hen and winter vegetable risotto.

Outstanding gourmet Italian restaurants are **Campo de Fiori** (205 E. Mill; 970-920-7717; $$-$$$) and Campo's cousin (same owner) **Gusto Ristorante** (415 E. Main; 970-925-8222; $$-$$$). Gusto's contemporary cuisine is refreshingly different than the classic dishes of Campo de Fiori and a tad less expensive. **Mezzaluna** (970-925-5882; $$-$$$) serves popular choices of wood-fired pizzas, pasta and meat-chicken-fish entrees at reasonable prices. **Olives Aspen** (970-920-7356; $$$) at the St. Regis has a broad Mediterranean-based menu with subtle Cajun influences inspired by new chef Patrick Dahms who hails from New Orleans. Valet parking is complimentary.

Zocalito Bistro (970-920-1991; $$-$$$) serves Latin cuisine with wonderful sauces and spices. It's also a rum bar at 420 E. Hyman.

The contemporary and casual **Elevation** (304 E. Hopkins; 970-544-5166; $$-$$$) serves New American cuisine with Asian influences. **Genre** (316 E Hopkins; 970-925-1260; $$-$$$), an intimate French bistro owned by local ski competitor Vince Lahey, has a strong local following, serving authentic French cuisine at reasonable prices. **L'Hostaria** (620 E. Hyman; 970-925-9022; $$-$$$) showcases decor and recipes direct from Italy.

A chain eatery in Aspen? It's happened with the arrival of **Ruth's Chris Steakhouse** at 447 East Cooper Ave. (970-925-1167; $$$$). Seafood selections share the menu with its famous Midwestern beef choices.

For more affordable dining, try **Asie** ($$), the "hottest place in town" for Asian fare and **Blue Maize** (308 S. Hunter; 970-925-6698, $$) for Southwest and Latin American food. How about a bistro in a bookstore—Explore Bookstore's upper level graduates into a smart vegetarian bistro with summa cum laude desserts and aptly named **Explore Bistro** (221 E. Main; 970-925-5338; $$). **The Steak Pit** (corner of Hopkins and Monarch; 970-925-3459; $$) has been in business since 1960, serving some of the best steaks in Aspen along with a sumptuous all-you-can-eat salad bar. **Little Annie's** (970-925-1098; $-$$$) has an American

Dining: $$$$–Entrees $30+; $$$–$20–$30; $$–$10–$20; $–less than $10.
Accommodations: (double room) $$$$–$200+; $$$–$141–$200; $$–$81–$140; $–$80 and less.

menu and a rustic old Aspen atmosphere.

Little Ollie's (downstairs at 308 S. Hunter; 970-544-9888; $) has healthy Chinese food and offers take-out. **The Cantina** (corner of Mill and Main; 970-925-3663; $-$$) is a trendier Mexican alternative with the "best Mexican food north of San Antonio." **Taqueria Sayulita** is an affordable Mexican eatery at 415 East Hyman. For barbeque lovers, **Texas Red's B-B-Q** (970-920-7754; $$-$$$) won't disappoint. Homemade sauces and dry rubs ensure fork-tender meats and chicken.

The Big Wrap (520 E. Durant; 970-544-1700; $) features burrito-like wraps but with a variety of exotic fillings. **Boogie's Diner** (534 E. Cooper; 970-925-6610; $) is a real '50s diner with oldies music, blue plate specials and meatloaf (great milkshakes, too). **Brunelleschi's Dome Pizza** (970-544-4644), nicknamed "Bruno's," serves gourmet pizza and pasta for the family at 205 Mill St.

For a real adventure, head out to the **Pine Creek Cookhouse** (970-925-1044; $$$). At an elevation of 9,725 feet, the log cabin is in the midst of towering pines beneath Elk Mountain peaks some 12 miles up Castle Creek Road. It is accessible by a 1.5-mile snowshoe or cross-country trek or by a sleigh drawn by a team of Percheron horses. Views are outstanding. Reservations are essential (at times two to four weeks in advance), as the logistics of running a kitchen not reached by road in winter is no small matter. The Cookhouse feeds several hundred people each day, and all that food (wild game is its specialty) comes in by snowmobile.

Turning now to breakfast, **The Wienerstube**, a.k.a. "the Stube" (633 E. Hyman 970-925-3357; $) is *the* place. Come here for Eggs Benny, omelets, Austrian sausages and homemade Viennese pastries.

Believe it or not, **Hickory House** (730 W. Main St.; 970-925-2313; $), known for its baby-back ribs, serves one of the best breakfasts around. **Poppycock's** (609 E. Cooper; 970-925-1245; $), a contemporary cafe with fancy pancakes, crepes and eggs, is delightful.

Main Street Bakery Cafe (201 E. Main St.; 970-925-6446; $) has homemade baked goods, granola, fruit, eggs and great coffee. For the best coffee in town, head to **Bagel Bites** (300 Puppy Smith St in Clark's shopping center; 970-920-3489), or **Ink! Coffee** (inside the D&E Snowboard Shop in the Aspen Mountain Building).

Dining in Snowmass

If you are worried about staying in Snowmass and missing out on Aspen's fining dining atmosphere, do not fret. We found excellent dining options here. By the way, every restaurant in Snowmass has children's menus

Known for its dogsledding and kennels, **Krabloonik** (970-923-3953; $$$$) has an even bigger reputation for its restaurant's wild-game selection and extensive wine list. In a rustic log house at Snowmass, this venue is the one Snowmass option where you can ring up Aspen-level dinner tabs.

Many think **Artisan Restaurant** (970-923-2427; $$$) in the Stonebridge Inn serves the best meal in the valley from a superb handcrafted menu of seafood and vegetarian options. In a homey rustic setting, it also has more martini choices than any place else. The Snowmass Club bistro, **Sage** (970-923-0923; $$$), offers distinctive food with fixed-price options in a casual unpretentious atmosphere.

Most of the other eateries are in the Snowmass Village Mall (if we don't tell you, that's where you'll find them).

The Margarita Grill (970-923-6803; $$-$$$) serves southwestern cuisine influenced by Central America. **Il Poggio** (970-923-4292; $$-$$$) prepares classic Italian fare in two settings: an elegant experience complete with extensive wine choices, or casual with homemade pastas and hearth-baked pizzas. Service can be on the slow side in the more upscale dining room, where reservations are required.

Butch's Lobster Bar (970-923-4004; $$$), at the top of the village, is owned by a former lobsterman from Cape Cod; **Brothers' Grille** (970-923-8285; $-$$) in the Silvertree Hotel reportedly has the best hamburgers in the valley; and **Mountain Dragon** (970-923-3576; $-$$), owned by the town mayor, is one of the hottest spots for dinner or drinks. It serves Chinese, sushi and free appetizers during happy hour.

The Stew Pot (970-923-2263; $-$$) features soups, tasty and unusual stews and sandwiches. The **Paradise Bakery** ($) serves homemade baked goodies for breakfast and inexpensive lunch options for those on the run. For pizza, steaks or hoagies, try **Pastore's Taste of Philly** ($). The best place to get fueled for the day is at **Fuel** on the Main Mall level. **Brothers Grille** also has heaping helpings of morning food and **The Big Hoss Grill** (970-923-2597; $) serves everything from hearty "Hoss" breakfasts to barbeque-to-go.

Spend an evening at the **Burlingame Cabin** (970-923-0479; $$$) for family-style meals or the **Lynn Britt Cabin** (970-923-0479; $$$, fixed-price menu) for gourmet four-course affairs, both nestled in aspen groves on Snowmass Mountain. At both, a heated snowcat and well-blanketed open-air sleigh transports guests to a cabin with wood stove, bluegrass entertainment and sing-alongs.

Snowmass Village excels with mountaintop cookery. **Gwyn's High Alpine Restaurant** (970-923-5188, reservations are essential), at the top of Alpine Springs (Lift 8), is among the best food in the region, on or off mountain. You can hike up for breakfast before the lifts open. **Krabloonik** (970-923-3953), mentioned earlier as a dinner choice, is also open for lunch. It's at the base of Campground off the Dawdler Catwalk. Another on-mountain option is **Up 4 Pizza** (970-923-0464; $) at the top of the Big Burn in Snowmass. For quick "power food," head to one of the **yurts** near the snowboard halfpipes and the terrain park, or at the bottom of Assay Hill. At the Two Creeks base area, chorizo and egg burritos start the day at **Two Creeks Mexican Cafe** ($). Fajitas, taco salad and burritos are typical lunch fare. **The Cirque Bar & Grill** ($-$$), slopeside at the Snowmass Village Mall, has a buffet breakfast for a fast exit to the slopes in the morning, and a more leisurely sit-down lunch and dinner service.

Dining on the mountains

The crown jewel of Aspen's on-mountain dining is the **Sundeck Restaurant** (970-429-6971; $$), housed in a magnificent lodge that replaces the old Sundeck building at the top of the gondola. It's a favorite spot for spectacular views, people-watching and innovative cuisine served from individual food stations. Check out the priceless old ski photos.

The Tavern (970-920-9333; $$$) in **The Little Nell** at the base of Silver Queen Gondola, is open for lunch and apres ski only. Lunch is from a new bistro-style menu featuring fondue, lasagna, lamb Bolognese, a raw bar and the famous truffle fries. Outdoor seating makes primo people-watching.

Bump's (970-925-4027; $-$$), at the Buttermilk base area, features foods from a wood-fired rotisserie, brick ovens and a pit smoker, as well as huge salads, pastas and stews.

Bonnie's ($-$$), just above Lift 3 on Aspen Mountain, feeds some 1,500 hungry skiers per day between 9:30 a.m. and 2:30 p.m. Go before noon or after 2 p.m., unless you love lines. The double decks outside are the places to be during the day. Owner Bonnie Rayburn's gourmet pizza on freshly made crust is a huge crowd pleaser.

Other on-mountain options include the **Cliffhouse** ($) atop Buttermilk with an outdoor

Dining: $$$$–Entrees $30+; $$$–$20–$30; $$–$10–$20; $–less than $10.
Accommodations: (double room) $$$$–$200+; $$$–$141–$200; $$–$81–$140; $–$80 and less.

deck serving its famous custom-cooked Mongolian Barbecue. **Cloud Nine**, a European-style bistro with a fixed-price menu, is decorated in early evacuation gear since it shares space with the Aspen Highlands ski patrol. It has killer views of the Maroon Bells, Aspen's world-famous peaks. Snowcats can bring you there for evening dining; call 544-3063. **Merry-Go-Round** ($), mid-mountain at Highlands, serves grilled bratwursts, burgers and Mexican fare and is the location for the legendary jumping show on Freestyle Fridays.

The Village at Aspen Highlands is shaping up nicely, although it's a bit dark in color for our tastes and the buildings block the mountain view. Retail shops and restaurants are filling the empty spaces. We like **Willow Creek** at the Ritz Carlton Club and **ZG Grill** for lunch (great burgers) and dinner. A new gourmet pizza place called **Crust** ($) opened summer of '06 in the village.

 ## Apres-ski/nightlife

On low-season days when the slopes are virtually bare, it's surprising to see the hordes of people out at night. That confirms the truth that many visitors to Aspen don't ever go on the mountain. Slopeside, **The Tavern** is a big draw for catching afternoon rays as the lifts start to close. If you don't find what you want there, the crowd spreads out to **The Terrace Room Bar** at the Little Nell Hotel, **Mezzaluna, 39 Degrees** at the SKY Hotel, **Little Annie's, Cooper Street Pier** and the noisy and crowded **J-Bar**, (Jack Nicholson's hangout at the Jerome). Apres-ski comes in all varieties here, from **The Cantina**, with its very happy hour (have a margarita in the compadre size), to the quiet and genteel **Hotel Jerome Library Bar**.

At night, the music and dance beat begin to take over. Earlier in the evening, the high-energy place to find out who's in town is **Mezzaluna** with its brassy horseshoe-shaped bar. It's a good singles bar and gives you the best in upscale people-watching. **The Shadow Mountain Lounge** at the St. Regis has live music. **The Little Nell** bar and **Syzygy** have jazz. DJs rule at **Bar Aspen**.

Jimmy's, an American restaurant and bar, is where the swank dinner crowd hits the dance floor on Saturday night for its signature Salsa Night. You'll also find what they claim to be one of the largest tequila menus in the country (more than 65). **Club Chelsea** is the locals' favorite dance club for rap and hip-hop. is what becomes on Fridays—a huge dance floor and bar.

The Wine Spot at the Grand Hyatt is a civilized quiet place to enjoy a drink. The bar has a Cruvinet system of preserving and dispensing wine by the glass.

Eric's Bar, Cigar Bar and **Aspen Billiards** all attract singles and have lots of micro-brews on tap (great scotch, too). Another beer spot is **McStorlie's Pub**. A relatively mixed crowd congregates in **Little Annie's. Cooper Street Pier** is very much a local and college student hangout.

There are many other night spots in town; pick up a copy of *Aspen Magazine's Traveler's Guide* for a list, or check local papers, *The Aspen Times* and **The Aspen Daily News** for current happenings.

At Snowmass, you'll find most of the down-valley locals at the **Mountain Dragon** and **Butch's Lobster Bar** during apres-ski. **The Cirque Bar & Grill** has live music daily but tends to be crowded and somewhat rowdy. **Brothers' Grille** has five different draft beers and about a dozen hot drinks for quick warm-ups. **Zane's Tavern** is a sports bar with apres-ski drink specials. Renowned magician Doc Eason performs bar magic weekly at the **Stonebridge Inn** (970-923-2420). At night Snowmass Village is largely quiet.

Other activities

Sleigh rides take place at the **T-Lazy-7 Ranch** with **Maroon Bells Outfitters and Lodge** (970-920-4677). The T-Lazy-7 leads snowmobile tours around the Maroon Bells and through the ghost town of Independence. For winter fly-fishing trips call **Aspen Outfitting Co.** (970-925-3406), **Oxbow Outfitting Co.** (970-925-1505) or **Aspen Sports** (970-925-6332).

The 83,000-square-foot **Aspen Recreation Center** (970-544-4100) near the base of Aspen Highlands has an NHL-sized ice rink for public ice skating (skate rentals available), an aquatic area with a six-lane, 25-yard competitive swimming pool, a leisure pool with a two-story water slide, hot tubs, steam rooms, a 32-foot climbing tower, weight room, batting cages, locker rooms and a concession stand. You also can ice skate across from the transportation center at **Silver Circle Ice Rink** (970-925-6360) and indoors at **Aspen Ice Garden** (970-920-5141).

The **Aspen Center for Environmental Studies** 970-925-5756) is a non-profit organization that holds many interesting programs, including Naturalist Nights every Thursday evening and Potbelly Perspectives, tales of travels and adventures, every Wednesday. They also have snowshoe tours on top of Aspen Mountain and Snowmass.

Cooking School of Aspen offers classes from Aspen's finest chefs for adults and kids (970-920-1879). More winter cooking classes are given by the chef at **Olives Restaurant** in the St. Regis Hotel (920-7356).

The **Wheeler Opera House** (970-920-5770) hosts a variety of big-time entertainers throughout the season. Belly Up Aspen (450 So. Galena; 544-9800) is a live music venue for major attractions, such as Ben Harper, B.B. King, Joe Cocker, Jurassic 5

When you're in Aspen you expect the best, the most state-of-the-art, the highest quality and the trendiest. SpaAspen delivers all that and more. By purchasing a SpaAspen service at the 77,000-square-foot **Aspen Club & Spa** (970-952-8900 or 866-484-8245), you have access to The Aspen Club for the day, which encompasses a health and fitness center and the Aspen Club Sports Medicine Institute. The facilities include everything you'd expect and more: 34 treatment rooms, swimming, tennis, child care, relaxation lounges and healthful food at the Variety Cafe. Services include 17 types of massage, seven types of body treatments, numerous skin care programs and a full salon. Signature services are the high altitude and apres-ski massages (both $125 for 50 minutes), and the Alpine rejuvenator body treatment ($180 for 80 minutes).

Remède Spa at the St. Regis Resort Aspen (970-920-3300) is a 15,000-square-foot facility that includes a fitness center with on-staff certified trainers and nutritionists, full-service salon and full-service spa with 15 treatment rooms for massages, facials and body treatments.

Many winter visitors to Aspen never touch the slopes during their stay. This place is a shopper's paradise. It's Beverly Hills and New York City in the Rocky Mountains. Even if you can't afford the mostly high-end merchandise, browsing is part of the fun. High on the browsing scale is **Boogie's**, 534 E. Cooper St. for funky clothes, jeans and other stuff. Boogie Wienglass also owns **Tomorrow's Laundry** (303 So. Galena) filled with jeans and tops to go with them. **Les Chefs D'Aspen**, on the corner of Cooper and Hunter, sells imported kitchenware plus local gourmet foods and coffee. **Aspen Leaf Soap Factory** on the Hyman Mall makes all soaps, lotions and potions by hand. There's also **Aspen Potters** for ceramics; **A Great Find** for, well, great finds for the home; and **Daniels** for antiques.

Clothing and accessory stores are abundant and filled with unusual items. Some of our favorites: **Bandana Kids & Woman, Goldies and the Kids, D&E Women, Mark Richards, Pitkin County Dry Goods, Misstyx, Midland Clothing Co, Prada**, and **Aspen Sports**.

Don't miss a visit to **Explore Booksellers and Bistro**, 221 E. Main. It's a legend in Aspen. Here you can pick up your favorite novel or ski guidebook and have dinner too (see Dining).

Most of Aspen's 30 art galleries are within a four-by-three-block area between Spring and Monarch Streets and Hopkins Ave. and Durant St. Our favorites are **Omnibus Gallery** for vintage poster art; **Galerie Du Bois** for Impressionism; **Highline Gallery** for glass art; **Pam Driscol Gallery** for life-size bronze sculptures; and **Baldwin Gallery** for contemporary collections.

The Ultimate Taxi (970-927-9239) is a unique way to tour Aspen. This disco on wheels probably will top your list of Aspen memorable experiences.

Other activities—Snowmass

Explore the wilderness around Snowmass on a free leisurely guided 45-minute **Nature Tour** with an **Aspen Center for Environmental Studies** (970-925-5756) naturalist. Trips are daily 11 a.m.-1 p.m.

For a wilder time in the wilds of Snowmass, Maroon Bells or Independence Pass, go on a two- or four-hour guided **snowmobile tour**. Contact **Blazing Adventures** (970-923-4544), **Western Adventures** (970-923-3337) or **T-Lazy-Seven** (970-925-4614).

Krabloonik Kennels in Snowmass Village (970-923-4342) is known for its daily two-hour dogsledding tours through the Snowmass wilderness area, led by Iditarod-experienced huskies. Morning or afternoon rides include a four-course gourmet lunch at Krabloonik's restaurant.

Above It All Balloon (970-963-6148) and **Unicorn Balloon** (970-925-5752) are two Hot air balloon companies that can give you a bird's-eye view of the Elk Mountains and local wildlife year-round.

Pokolodi Lodge hosts **campfire sing-alongs** (Mondays) and **story-telling** (Wednesdays) complete with hot chocolate and marshmellows from 4-5 p.m. Free for all ages. Let your kids get creative at a free hour of **Kids Krafts** near the ticket pavilion in the Snowmass Mall from 4-5 p.m. Tuesdays and Thursdays while you enjoy apres-ski of a different kind. While you're there, ask where the best **sledding** slope is.

Snowmass has the only **Zipline** (970-925-1220) in the world that picks you up while skiing or boarding and takes you on an 800-foot drop down the mountain. So far, it's also the only winter zipline in Colorado.

Snowmass Recreation Center (970-922-2240) is a brand new facility with lap pool and fitness center. Cost is $15 a day for non-residents or less with punch passes. The **Aspen Rec Center** (970-544-4100) sits between the town of Aspen and Snowmass and has more activities for the whole family, including climbing wall, pools with slides and a hockey rink. The **Snowmass Club** (970-923-5600) has a full-service spa.

The Anderson Ranch Arts Center (970-923-3181) in Snowmass Village exhibits work by visiting and resident artists during the winter. The center also offers a series of workshops in ceramics, woodworking and photography from January through April. Call for current events. For more information about off-slope activities, see Aspen or contact Snowmass Village at 800-766-9627.

Getting there and getting around

By air: Aspen's Sardy Field, 3 miles from Aspen and 6 miles from Snowmass, is served by regular flights from six cities: Denver, Chicago, San Francisco and L.A. (United connections), Salt Lake City (Delta) and Phoenix (U.S. Airways).

Eagle County airport, about 70 miles away, is becoming the best-served airport for this resort. It hosts flights from Northwest, American, Continental, United, U.S. Airways and Delta. American has daily flights arriving from Dallas/Ft. Worth and Chicago and Saturday flights from New York and Miami. Continental has daily flights from Houston and nonstop service from Newark. Delta flies from Atlanta with Saturday nonstops from Cincinnati. Northwest flies from Minneapolis/St. Paul daily. United flies daily from Denver. U.S. Airways has weekend nonstop service from Charlotte and Philadelphia. Colorado Mountain Express (800-525-6363) shuttles skiers from Eagle to Aspen.

If you find yourself in Aspen without your gear or outdoor clothing, make sure to ask the airlines for a voucher to rent what you need until they show up with your luggage. All the airlines hand out coupons for equipment in case yours is delayed. These vouchers are accepted at virtually every sports shop in town.

If your luggage gets waylaid, call Lorenzo Semple at **Suit Yourself** (970-920-0295). He will be at your door with a van full of ski and snowboard clothing for you to rent during your stay. His wide inventory includes one-piece ski suits, jackets and pants, and accessories. He takes airline vouchers.

Regular ground transportation also leaves the Denver International Airport for Aspen, but it's about a five-hour drive on I-70, about 220 miles away. Rental cars and private limos are available at both Denver and Eagle County Airport.

By train: Amtrak has service to Glenwood Springs, where skiers can get ground transportation the rest of the way.

Getting around: Aspen has a free bus system, RFTA, with several routes in town and to Glenwood Springs. There also is a separate, free shuttle between the various ski mountains during the day; there is a small fee after 4 p.m. Downtown is enjoyably walkable. Thank goodness a car is unnecessary because parking is definitely a pain.

Nearby resorts

Sunlight Mountain Resort, Glenwood Springs, CO; (800) 445-7931

Internet: www.sunlightmtn.com

4 lifts; 470 acres; 2,010 vertical feet; 3 terrain parks

Not only is this a less pricey ski option if you're headed to nearby Aspen, but Glenwood Springs is the home of the world's largest hot springs pool, two blocks long and kept at a toasty 90 degrees. Most of Ski Sunlight is intermediate terrain, though the double-black-diamond Sunlight Extreme provides steep and gladed challenges for the best of skiers and riders.

Lift tickets (06/07 prices): Adults, $45; Junior (6-12) and Senior (60-69), $35; 70+ and younger than 6, $10.

Distance from Denver: About 222 miles west on I-70 and Hwy. 82. The closest airport is Vail/Eagle, about 30 miles east of Sunlight Mountain. Aspen is about 40 miles south. Glenwood Springs is a daily stop on Amtrak's California Zephyr route from San Francisco to Chicago.

Summit County
Colorado

Reservations: 800-530-3099 or 970-262-0817 (chamber)
E-mail: info@summitchamber.org
Internet: www.experiencethesummit.com (chamber)
www.townofdillon.com (Dillon)
www.townoffrisco.com (Frisco)
www.silverthorne.org (Silverthorne)
www.summitnet.com

Summit County Facts
Dining:★★★
Apres-ski/nightlife:★★★★
Other activities:★★★★

Within Summit County, a little more than an hour's drive from downtown Denver, are five of Colorado's top ski areas—Breckenridge, Copper Mountain, Keystone, Arapahoe Basin and Loveland. Each resort, except A-Basin and Loveland, has its own lodging, shopping and restaurants.

If you plan to do most of your skiing at just one area, stay at that resort. But if you want to experience them all (and you're not looking for much night life), then set up your base camp in Dillon, Frisco or Silverthorne, three small towns off I-70 that surround Lake Dillon. This tri-town area is in the center of the ski action—Breckenridge is about 9 miles south, Copper Mountain is 5 miles west, Keystone is 7 miles away in a third, and A-Basin just a little farther than Keystone.

Summit County is above 9,000 feet. If you like spring skiing, take note: High elevations mean a longer ski season. Each of these areas stays open until mid-April. Arapahoe Basin, with its base lodge above 10,000 feet, often stays open through June.

Vail Resorts owns Keystone and Breckenridge. It has an interchangeable lift ticket that includes Vail, Beaver Creek, Keystone and Breckenridge. Or buy a multiday ticket for just Keystone and Breckenridge for a little less. Your Keystone-Breckenridge ticket is also valid at Arapahoe Basin, and you can buy that ticket separately. A separate ticket is necessary to ski at Copper Mountain.

Accommodations
Frisco:

This is our first choice for a home base for several reasons. It's the closest town to Breckenridge and Copper Mountain and Keystone isn't far away. And since Frisco is a town without a ski mountain and Copper Mountain is a ski resort without a town (though it has a village), the two have partnered with lodging packages and a free direct shuttle between the two.

Hotel Frisco (800-262-1002; 970-668-5009; $-$$$) was completely remodeled a few years ago. The cozy ski lodge, at 308 Main St., has 16 lovely rooms, a huge river-rock fireplace in the lobby and an outdoor hot tub. Guests can access the Internet free via high-speed modems.

Frisco Lodge (800-279-6000; 970-668-0195; $$) at Fourth & Main has been hosting people since the 1800s when Frisco was a stagecoach stop. The staff members are long-time residents with insiders' knowledge of the area.

The Frisco River House(877-677-1458; 51 West Main; $$$$) is a gorgeous nine-bedroom amenity-loaded private home that's perfect for families or groups wanting to stay together. It's right in town and close to the bus stop.

Cross Creek Resort (800-748-1849; 970-468-6291; $$-$$$) has 17 condos perched streamside on Ten Mile Creek on the western edge of town.

Chain hotels include Best Western Lake Dillon Lodge (800-727-0607; $$), **Holiday Inn** (800-782-7669; $$) and **Ramada** (970-668-87830), all clustered around Summit Boulevard.

The budget motel **Alpine Inn** (800-314-3122; $) with continental **breakfast sits behind the Best Western on the shuttle route. Pet-friendly lodges are Best Western, Hotel Frisco, Ramada, Streamside House** (303-750-0353) and **Woods Inn** (877-664-3777)

Dillon/Silverthorne:

The **Best Western Ptarmigan Lodge** (800-842-5939; 970-468-2341; $$-$$$) in the Dillon town center is one of the best bargains, particularly during the early and late seasons and in January. Another moderately priced motel is the **Dillon Inn** (800-262-0801; 970-262-0801; $$-$$$) which has an indoor pool. **The Lodge at Carolina in the Pines** (262-7500; $$-$$$$) is a B&B with a serene setting that overlooks Lake Dillon.

Off the interstate in Silverthorne are side-by-side chain hotels: **La Quinta** (800-321-3509; 970-468-6200; $$-$$$) and **Days Inn** (800-329-7466; 970-468-8661; $$-$$$). The Summit Stage stops at their doors. **Comfort Suites** (970-513-0300; 276 Dillon Ridge Road; $$) is in the same **vicinity** off highway 9 in Dillon.

Budget travelers might want to try the **Super 8** (800-800-8000; 970-468-8888; $$-$$$) in Dillon, across from the Summit Place Shopping Center. Three of the best low-cost restaurants are in this center. Or try the **Alpen Hutte Lodge** (970-468-6336; $-$$), 471 Rainbow Dr. Both the Greyhound bus from Denver and the Summit County shuttle buses stop there. About $27 will get you a bed in an eight-person dorm room. There are also private rooms that sleep two and private family rooms that sleep four. The lodge has a nice kitchen, is clean and walking distance from restaurants (especially the brewery) and shopping.

The towns have many more B&Bs, chain hotels, private homes and condos. For reservations, call **Summit County Central Reservations**, (800) 365-6365, or **Reservations for the Summit** at (800) 999-9510, or the **Summit County Chamber**, (800) 530-3099 or locally, 970-668-2051.

Dining
Frisco:

Far and away, Frisco's best restaurant is **Samplings** (corner of 4th and Main, 970-668-8466; $$—$$$$). Dining here is like a wine tasting event. Choose gourmet dishes from six categories, all served on salad-size plates to taste and share (or not). Wines come from an impressive collection by the bottle, by the glass, or by the flight. A 20-foot-long community table adds to the fun and friendship that comes with sharing meals. There's conventional seating, of course, in the casual rustic digs. It opens at 2 p.m., just in time for the apres-ski crowd.

Blue Spruce Inn (20 Main St., 970-668-5900; $$-$$$) is in an historic log cabin. Entrees include such dishes as veal picatta, steak Diane, and lamb chops with pesto. Reservations recommended.

The '90s bistro atmosphere at **The Boatyard Pizzeria and Grill** (304 Main, 970-668-4728; $-$$) complements an extensive a la Carte menu that includes some of the best salad entrees in the county.

Silverheels at the Ore House (603 Main St., 970-668-0345; $$-$$$) is a century-old dance hall legend with a history. Lady Silverheels brought smiles and solace to many an early miner. This restaurant brings much of the same to its patrons with fine Southwestern fare in the form of steaks and chops, seafood and desserts like mud pie and Mexican caramel flan.

Dining: $$$$–Entrees $30+; $$$–$20–$30; $$–$10–$20; $–less than $10.
Accommodations: (double room) $$$$–$200+; $$$–$141–$200; $$–$81–$140; $–$80 and less.

Farley's Chophouse (423 Main St.; 970-668-3733; $$), named for a beloved dog at Copper Mountain, is famous for its prime rib and signature steak Filet Farley, but also serves chops, chicken and seafood.

With more and more Mexicans moving to the county, authentic Mexican restaurants are popping up and **Fiesta Jalisco** (450 W. Main, 970-668-5043; $$) is a good one; also in Dillon and Breckenridge. But the one locals are loving is **Carlos Miguel's** (720 N. Summit Blvd.; $-$$; 970-668-4900). It's fresh, fine Mexican food—tableside-prepared guacamole, ceviche de camaron, cochinita pibil—at affordable prices.

A great family food spot is **A-Train Bistro** and **Pizzeria** (970-668-4448; $-$$) one block off Main St. on Creekside Drive. There's also a nice selection of salads, pastas and meat and fish entrees. More family dining is at **Po' Boys Cajun Cookin' and Sports Bar** (620 Main St.; 970-668-2233; $-$$).

For good budget eats (Frisco has a lot of them), **Deli Belly's** (275 Main St.; $) has giant sandwiches. **Moosejaw** (208 Main St.; 970-668-3931; $) has been around since 1973, so it's gotta be good. If hot homemade soup sounds good after a cold day, take out a quart or three from **Mi Zuppa** in the Safeway shopping center on Summit Boulevard. In the same center, **Food Hedz World Cafe** (970-668-2000; $$) offers an excellent eclectic menu for the world's peoples.

Quite a few Internet Cafes are sprinkled around Summit County. **Frisco Internet Cafe** (319 Main St.; 970-668-0971) is a good one with camera card readers, CD burners and more.

Dillon & Silverthorne:

A good choice for finer dining is **Ristorante Al Lago** (240 Lake Dillon, 970-468-6111; $$). A large selection of range-fed veal shares the menu with imported pasta dishes, chicken entrees and seafood—all expertly prepared in Northern Italian style. Reliable food and service at the family-owned **Arapahoe Cafe and Pub** (626 Lake Dillon; 970-468-0873; $$) have made it a traditional favorite in Summit County since 1945.

For more casual dining in Dillon, try the **Dillon Dam Brewery** (970-262-7777;$-$$), which lives up to its slogan, "the best dam brewery in town." Get your name in early; the place jams on weekends. **Pug Ryan's** (Dillon town center, 970-468-2145; $-$$) is fantastic for steaks and microbrewed beer. **Wild Bill's Stone Oven Pizza** (Dillon town center, 970-468-2006; $) is a hit for—what else?—stone-oven pizzas. **Old Chicago Restaurant** (970-468-6200; $-$$) with 110 different beers and great happy hours is at Four Points by the Sheraton Hotel. **Jersey Boys** (149 Tenderfoot; 970-513-1087; $-$$) prepares "east-coast style" pizza and sandwiches to order, as well as other dinner dishes.

City Market serves as anchor for the Dillon Ridge Market Place. But a couple of good eateries here are worth trying. **Masato's** (970-262-6600; $-$$$) is an excellent Japanese restaurant and sushi bar (also in Avon, near Vail) and **Maxwell St. Grill & Pizzeria** (970-262-2020; $-$$), serving pizza, pasta and Chicago-style hot Italian sandwiches.

In Silverthorne, you can cook your own meat over an open grill at **The Historic Mint** (347 Blue River Pkwy., 970-468-5247; $$). Or enjoy Tex-Mex food at **Old Dillon Inn** (970-468-2791; $). **Ti Amo** ($-$$$), our fave for Italian, has moved way north in Silverthorne near Target on Hwy. 9. The Italian owners keep the food authentic and consistently good.

For budget diners, the Summit Place Shopping Center on Hwy. 6 on the Dillon-Silverthorne border has good restaurants, including **Sunshine Cafe** (970-468-6663; $), jammed with locals; and **Nick-N-Willy's** (970-262-1111; $) for very good bake-your-own take-out pizza.

Breakfast:

The Arapahoe Cafe (970-468-0873, $), is a huge favorite with locals. The service is great, the menu names are creative (Arapahuevos Rancheros, Hans and Franz Power Breakfast, etc.) and eavesdropping on the other tables will fill you in on local politics.

Definitely in the running for the Best Breakfast title are **Sunshine Cafe** (Summit Place Shopping Center, $) and **Log Cabin Cafe** (Main St., $) in Frisco.

For those who prefer a lighter breakfast, head for the **Butterhorn Bakery** (408 W. Main St.; $) in Frisco. Across the street is Pika Bagel Bakery ($) and Rocky Mountain Coffee Roasters at 2nd & Main, a very cool coffeehouse. In Silverthorne try **Blue Moon Baking Company** (Summit Place Shopping Center; $) or **Mountain Lyon Cafe** (Blue River Pkwy.; $).

 ## Apres-ski/nightlife

Mountain resorts and brew pubs seem to go hand in hand. Summit County has five, three in the tri-town area: **Backcountry Brewery** on the corner of Summit and Main in Frisco, **Pug Ryan's** and **The Dillon Dam Brewery**, both mentioned in Dining. (The others are in Breckenridge and Keystone.)

Pick up a Summit Daily News to find apres-ski specials and entertainment around the county. One you won't want to miss is the saloon at the **Blue Spruce Inn** in Frisco. The 1860s back bar is the centerpiece of a warm gathering place with half-priced appetizers and daily $2 drafts from 4-7.

The leading sports bar in Frisco is **High Mountain Billiards**, an upscale game room with pool tables, dart boards, shuffleboard, chess, checkers, backgammon and sports TV. This richly decorated bar in Dillon attracts a mostly over-30 clientele and is open till 2 a.m.

Old Dillon Inn in Silverthorne has live country & western music on weekends and the best margaritas in town. Also in this area is **Murphy's** (501 Blue River Parkway) for Irish specialties and The **Mint**, Summit County's oldest bar at 347 Blue River Parkway.

Another popular choice is the **Pub Down Under**, underneath the Arapahoe Cafe in Dillon. **The Cala Inn** in Summit Cove (between Dillon and Keystone) is a new Scottish/Irish bar with great drink specials and delicious food, including a Guinness Steak Pie.

 ## Other activities

Companies that offer **snowmobiling** and/or **sleigh and dogsled rides** are Tiger Run Tours, 970-453-2231; Good Times Adventures, 970-453-7604; High Country Tours, 970-668-9945 and Two Below Zero Dinner Sleigh Rides, 970-453-1520. Colorado Rocky **Ballooning** (970-468-9280) sails the Summit skies year-round weather permitting.

Summit Activities Center offers an **activity concierge service** at (888) 230-2844 or 970-547-1594.

Cross-country ski or **snowshoe** at the Frisco Nordic Center (970-668-0866) on Hwy. 9 about 1 mile out of town toward Breckenridge. Rentals and instruction are available. The Frisco Nordic Center is now tied into Breckenridge Nordic Center and Gold Run Nordic Center, providing more than 90 km. on one pass (see Breckenridge for details).

Pack an extra suitcase for **shopping**. Better yet, buy a bag at one of the luggage stores in the Silverthorne and Dillon Outlet Stores. Then fill it with bargains at nearly 80 brand-name stores. This is probably the largest **factory outlet center** in Western ski country.

Collectibles and antiques lovers will go bonkers at Junk-Tique, 313 Main St. in Frisco. Also on Frisco's Main St. are Todd Powell Photography Gallery for one-of-a-kind takes on local landscapes and Blue River Pottery Studio Gallery. Buffalo Mountain Gallery for **western art** is at 711 Granite St. Cigar lovers can stop by Antler's Liquor Store in front of Wal-Mart, which has what the owner claims is the largest **humidor room** in Colorado. Next door, Antler's Ski & Sport carries a large supply of everything for **outdoor sports** from shoes to sunglasses.

Dining: $$$$–Entrees $30+; $$$–$20–$30; $$–$10–$20; $–less than $10.
Accommodations: (double room) $$$$–$200+; $$$–$141–$200; $$–$81–$140; $–$80 and less.

 # Getting there and getting around

By air and car: Frisco, Dillon and Silverthorne are just off I-70, about 75 miles west of downtown Denver and 90 miles from Denver International Airport. **Colorado Mountain Express** vans (888-426-9523; 970-468-7600) transport from Denver International Airport, about two hours away.

Frisco is laid out nicely for walking along Main Street. Dillon Town Center is walkable, but the rest of Dillon and Silverthorne are too spread out for strolling around. A nice bike path connects the two. A car is the best way to get around quickly. Next is the Summit Stage, a free bus system that runs between the towns and the ski areas all day and into the night—until 1:30 a.m. But stops are on the hour and at peak times on the half-hour. You can pick up a schedule at any of the bus stations or information, or call 970-668-0999. If you really enjoy nightlife and want to do extensive exploration of the restaurants and bars, we recommend a car. There are several car rental agencies in Summit County. One is **Getting around:Hertz** based in Frisco, 970-668-1031. **Summit Taxi** (970-468-2266) provides transportation to the entire community.

Nearby resorts

Loveland Ski Area, Georgetown, CO; (800) 736-3754 or (303) 571-5580

Internet: www.skiloveland.com
11 lifts; 1,365 acres; 2,410 vertical feet; 1 terrain park

You see the area as you approach the Eisenhower Tunnel along I-70 west from Denver. It looms into the distance right up to the Continental Divide, and spreads out on both sides of the interstate. A ski area in two parts, Loveland Basin and Loveland Valley are connected by a lift and a shuttle service. Loveland Valley, on the left as you approach the tunnel, is great for beginners, intermediates and anyone who wants to hide from the stiff winds that sometimes plague Loveland Basin. The Basin is a real stash, jammed with enough expert and advanced terrain to challenge the best and stuffed with intermediate runs and long cruisers, most of which you can't see from I-70.

The Ridge, with its 400 acres of wild terrain, tops out at 13,010 feet, and is an above-timberline Alpine garden of glades, chutes and bowls. A few seasons ago the area opened Chair 9, the highest four-passenger chair lift in the world, so you no longer have to hike up to get the goodies. Advanced skiers should head for Chair 1 for bumps and chutes. Avalanche Bowl is a nasty short and sweet drop and Busy Gully demands tight turns right under the chair. Chairs 4 and 8 access the far right, a mix of wilderness-type bowls at the top, narrowing into tree bashing in the East and West Ropes and at Fail Safe. Intermediates and beginners can handle everything else, particularly Chairs 2, 4 and 6. The resort and Airwalk created a terrain park together with rails and funboxes.

Child care starts at 12 months. Telemark Clinics are scheduled throughout the season.

Lift tickets (07/08 prices): Adults, $54; children (6–14), $24; seniors (60–69), $40; ages 5 and younger ski free. Lower rates early and late season. Skiers 70 and older can buy an unrestricted season pass for $69.

Distance from Denver: 56 miles west via I-70 (about 80 miles from Denver airport).

Lodging information: (800) 225-5683. Lodging can be found in Georgetown, Idaho Springs or Dillon, each within 15 miles.

Breckenridge
Colorado

Summit:	**12,840 feet**
Vertical:	**3,398 feet**
Base:	**9,600 feet**

Address: Box 1058, Breckenridge, Colorado 80424
Telephone (main): 800-789-7669
Snow Report Number: 970-453-6118
Toll-free reservations: 877-593-5260; UK: 0-800-89-7491
E-mail: breckinfo@vailresorts.com
Internet: http://www.breckenridge.com

Expert:★★★★★
Advanced:★★★★★
Intermediate:★★★★
Beginner:★★
First-timer:★★★

Lifts: 30—1 8-passenger gondola, 2 high-speed six-packs, 7 high-speed quads, 1 triple, 6 doubles, 4 surface lifts, 9 moving carpets
Skiable acreage: 2,358
Snowmaking: 24 percent
Uphill capacity: 37,880
Parks & pipes: 5 parks, 4 pipes
Bed base: 25,000
Nearest lodging: Slopeside
Child care: Yes, 2 months and older
Adult ticket, per day: $83 (07/08 price)
Dining:★★★★
Apres-ski/nightlife:★★★★★

Breckenridge is one of the most popular ski areas in Colorado and the most visited resort in North America.

With four mountains, steep treelined gullies, a third of the trails ranked intermediate, Alpine bowls that cap the mountain range and five terrain parks, Breck has something for everyone. With the addition of the Imperial Express in 2005, the resort now claims the highest high-speed quad chairlift in the world. This lift takes skiers and riders to the top of Peak 8 at nearly 13,000 feet and accesses 550 acres of steeps, chutes and glades that were previously hike-to and out-of-bounds terrain.

But it's the Town of Breckenridge that sets this destination resort apart. The 148-year-old town is richly colored by its gold mining history and still retains its Victorian charm and devil-may-care attitude of yesteryear. The streets of the authentic 19th-century town bustle with sightseers and shoppers checking out the shops and boutiques (203 at last count) and geographically significant museums, most housed in brightly-colored Victorian buildings. In fact, downtown Breckenridge is Colorado's largest historic district, with 249 vintage places of interest. In the evenings, locals and tourists congregate for happy hour, dinner, and maybe the theatre and late-night libations in the town's 76 restaurants and bars. If you take a day or two off from the slopes, you won't be bored here. As proof of this, more than 1.6 million skiers and riders come to Breckenridge each winter.

But popularity has its downsides, particularly in the early season when scores of skiing-starved Front Rangers—nhabitants of Denver and its suburbs—flock to the slopes. Even mid-winter, Breckenridge can get crowded. It's best enjoyed on non-holiday weekdays. Although tourism is the heart of Breckenridge, it's not its soul. More than 3,000 residents live in Breckenridge year-round, and they care deeply about the town from a civic standpoint, making it feel more down-to-earth than some of Colorado's more chi-chi resorts.

Many shops and restaurants tend to cater to the upscale crowd. With Vail's ownership, this trend probably will continue. Restaurant and ski-area workers remain as friendly as ever, though, and some long-time Breckenridge locals still retain much of the casual attitude of their 19th-century predecessors, which helps balance out any stuffiness that the tourists may bring.

With Vail Resorts ownership comes development. The company has begun construction on The Breckenridge Peaks, a modern master-planned ski-in/ski-out community to complement the historic town. The neighborhoods will be made up of a new village on Peak 7 and a redeveloped village at the base of Peak 8. Both will be connected by the 8-passenger Breck-Connect Gondola that loads from the transportation center close to Main Street. The joint city/resort gondola opened in December of 2006.

Breckenridge is part of Summit County. This county has four well-known ski areas—Breckenridge, Keystone, Arapahoe Basin and Copper Mountain—and more dining and lodging than most ski resorts on North America.

Mountain layout

Breckenridge's skiable terrain spans four interconnected mountains: Peaks 7, 8, 9 and 10 in the Ten Mile Range of Summit County. Skiers can load lifts from four base areas: The Village in town at the bottom of Peak 9; Beaver Run, also on Peak 9; the base of Peak 8 (this was the original ski area that opened in 1961); and the Snowflake base on Four O'Clock Road. While this sounds exhausting, it's just a matter of deciding from which base you want to start and then hop a free shuttle from your closest stop in town or from the free parking lots. (Note: close-in pay lots fill by 9:30 a.m. most days.) Even though the Peak 8 SuperConnect makes peak-to-peak skiing easy, get a map anyway. It can be daunting.

To help guests negotiate from peak to peak, free mountain tours are offered from the bases of Peaks 8 and 9 every morning. And now you can ski and ride straight to town from Peak 8 via a bridge called the **Skyway Skiway**, eliminating the need to ride a bus down. This and the new gondola are the resort's efforts to smoothly connect the dots from mountain to town.

Expert, Advanced: Breckenridge has a very high percentage of black-diamond terrain (55 percent overall) and some of the highest in-bounds skiing in North America. The high Alpine bowls of Peaks 7 and 8, the steep treed trails on the North Face of Peak 9, and the mogul runs spilling off the sides of Peak 10 make up most of the hundreds of acres of expert, steep terrain.

The new Imperial Express chairlift now carries skiers and riders to Imperial Bowl, crowning Peak 8 and topping out at nearly 13,000 feet. A previously out-of-bounds cache of 150 acres called Snow White is now open to experts from Imperial Express along with 400 acres of double-black terrain. This lift also dramatically shortens the hike to the top of Peak 7. If the lift is closed, you can still get to sensational snow on Peaks 7 and 8 via a long, curving T-bar. "Skiing the T-bar" all day is the expert's mantra during apres-ski.

The North Face on the back of Peak 9 also is expert territory. Powder builds up in the trees on its steep north side, and the 15-minute hike keeps it fresh. On Peak 10 you'll find Mustang, Dark Rider and Blackhawk sporting monstrous bumps.

Another good spot for bumps is off the E Chair on Peak 9. Peak 10 is evenly split between black and blue runs. Cimarron, marked black on the map, often is groomed because of race training that takes place here. The Burn, dropping to skier's left of the high-speed lift, offers short-but-sweet tree skiing and is great on a powder day.

Intermediate: The face of Peak 9 is ballroom skiing at its best. Consistently smooth grooming on perfectly pitched terrain makes it ideal for moderate ability levels on runs like

Cashier, Columbia and Sundown. Avoid Bonanza, a slow-skiing area packed with practicing skiers. Advanced-intermediates enjoy the blue/black terrain of American, Gold King, Peerless and Volunteer, which often sprout mild bumps.

A few nice intermediate runs spill down Peak 8—North Star, Duke's and Claimjumper. Right next door the trails on Peak 7 rock and roll for excellent cruising. For steeper cruising, head to Peak 10 and alternate between Centennial, Doublejack and Crystal. The pairing of a high-speed lift and mostly expert-marked terrain keeps crowds minimized here.

Beginner, First-timer: The beginner terrain on Peak 8 is shorter, but usually less crowded, than on Peak 9. The trails are away from traffic, offering a perfect place to practice turns and cruising. The only thing that might make you nervous are the snowboarders heading to the terrain parks. Peak 9 has the most terrain for beginners, but it can get very busy. The trails here are wide and gradual, especially Silverthorne. Watch out for fast skiers and boarders who cut through to get back to the base, especially at the end of the day. Stick to the Quicksilver lift and Chair A here; avoid the Beaver Run and Peak 8 SuperConnect lifts, they will take you higher to steeper terrain. Adventurous beginners might prefer to head to the blues on Peak 7. The trails are never crowded, loads of fun, and are served by a six-pack chair. Hint: snowcats freshen the snow about 11 a.m. on most of the runs here.

First-timers will want to practice on the moving carpets at either Peak 8 or 9 before tackling anything off the other beginner lifts. You'll find the first-timer area separate and roped off on Peak 9, immensely reducing the intimidation factor.

Parks and pipes

Three words for experts: Freeway Terrain Park. Peak 8's superpipe and terrain park have become legendary among snowboarders and freeskiers. Breckenridge was the first mountain in the country to build a superpipe—400 feet long with 18-foot walls—and the local talent shows it. The monster park is packed with rails, including rainbow rails and C rails, plus tabletops ranging from 35 to 62 feet, and a 55-foot stepup. On any given day, show up at the park and you'll quickly realize why you're not a pro rider. Breckenridge hosts the U.S. Snowboard Grand Prix the third weekend in December. This is the nation's first major snowboard competition of the season and world-class riders go head-to-head in the Freeway Park and superpipe.

If you're not ready for Freeway, then head to one of Breck's four other smaller parks and start practicing. The resort's smallest park and pipe—best for learning—are on Eldorado on Peak 9. The next step up is the park and pipe on Peak 8 on Trygves (near Freeway), with small and medium-sized features and a small pipe. Before trying out Freeway, it's a good idea to go to Peak 9's Country Boy Terrain Park, with its medium-to-large-sized features and medium pipe. Breck is making it incredibly easy for you to progress according to your abilities. With a world-class terrain park reputation at stake, expect each of these parks to meet Breckenridge's stringent design standards while providing a safe and fun introduction to freestyle terrain.

Snowboarding

For steeps and deeps, head to the Imperial Express chairlift. Once hike-to terrain, it's where the locals head after a big dump. Some of the their favorites are the Lake Chutes, the Windows/Peak 9 Chutes and Imperial Bowl. Peak 10's got a few high-speed cruisers that will let you open up your board too.

For intermediates, practically the whole mountain is your canvas. Stay away from the mogul runs and you'll be smiling ear to ear. Breck beginners have the most beginner terrain in Summit County at your disposal. Peak 9 is the best for a first snowboarding day. The resort has a snowboard-specific learning area on Eldorado, served by two conveyor belts. There's a learning terrain park here too.

Cross-country & snowshoeing (see also xcskiresorts.com)

Breckenridge Nordic Center, Gold Run Nordic Center and Frisco Nordic Center are operated as a cooperative system, providing about 100 km. of trails on one pass.

Breckenridge Nordic Ski Center (970-453-6855), near Peak 8 base on Ski Hill Road and on the free town bus route, has 30 km. of groomed skating and classic skiing, including 20 km. of snowshoe trails in a beautiful forest setting. Equipment rentals, lessons, waxing services and guided backcountry tours are available.

Gold Run Nordic Center (970-547-7889), off Tiger Run Road at the Breckenridge Golf Club, grooms 20 km. of trails for beginner through advanced skating and classic skiers, as well as snowshoe and dog-friendly trails. There's also equipment rentals (including snowshoes), lessons, guided backcountry tours, and horse-drawn sleigh rides, plus a restaurant for evening dining.

Frisco Nordic Center (970-668-0866), down the road off Hwy. 9, has 46 km. of groomed classic and freestyle trails and 14 km. of snowshoe trails that traverse the peninsula of Lake Dillon. Rentals and instruction are available.

Lessons (07/08 prices)

Lesson packages for all abilities encourage spreading out learning: Start with the Option Pack—one full-day lesson and two half-day lessons any time during your vacation ($190). We provide prices for regular season; rates are a bit lower during the value season.

Group lessons: $95 for a full day (five hours); half day costs $80.

First-timer package: First-time Discovery Series for three full-day lessons with ticket and rentals costs $245. Instructors meet you in the rental shop to guide you through the process.

Snowboarders take a full-day class through the Burton Learn-to-Ride program, which offers lessons, lunch, ticket and Burton equipment designed to "fast track" the learning curve for $216; reservations required.

Private lessons: $390 for three hours; $560 for a full day. Reservations are recommended.

Special programs: There are many daily and multiday programs, including racing, telemark, bumps, Big Mountain Adventure (for the chutes, cornices and steeps off Imperial Chair), parks and pipes, and lessons for disabled skiers. Women's camps (skiing, snowboarding, telemarking and backcountry) include lunch, video analysis and updates on new women-specific gear. A two-day Prime Time seminar (50-plus age group) includes lift tickets, instruction, video analysis and a group dinner. For more information and rates, call 888-576-2754.

Racing: NASTAR and self-timed courses are set up on Lower American on Peak 9.

Children's programs (06/07 prices)

Child care: Ages 2 months to 5 years. Cost is $105 a full day (regular season), including lunch. If you make a reservation 24 hours ahead, deduct $10 per day per child.

Breckenridge has two children's centers: the Peak 9 center is in The Village complex, but if you're driving, use the Peak 8 center—it's larger and has more activities. At Peak 8, look for the center above the lift ticket windows; at Peak 9, it's in the lower level facing Maggie Pond.

Reservations required; call (800) 789-7669, Ext. 3258 or 7449, well in advance.

Other options: Another possibility for child care and instruction is **Kinderhut** (800-541-8779; 970-453-0379), a privately owned children's ski school and licensed day-care center. It accepts children 6 weeks to 6 years. Also see Summit County.

Children's lessons: Lessons are offered at the Peak 8 Kids' Castle and Peak 9 Village Center. Note: It's a short hike from the parking lot to the Kids' Castle, so allow extra time. An all-day program for ages 3–4 (must be toilet-trained) includes morning lessons, afternoon care, lunch and rentals for $119 (regular season). Children 5–13 get a full-day program with lift, lesson and lunch for $130. Multiday discounts are available for all programs; rentals are extra for kids 7 and older. Ages 14 and older take adult lessons.

Special activities: Kids Night Out is an evening of dinner and fun, while Kids Day Off includes lunch and activities. Call (970) 389-3211 for information and reservations.

 # Lift tickets (07/08 prices)

	Adult (13-64)	Child (5-12)
One day	$83	$43
Three of five days	$249 ($83/day)	$129 ($43/day)
Five of eight days	$415 ($83/day)	$215 ($43/day)

Who skis free: Ages 4 and younger.

Who skis at a discount: Seniors 65 and older pay $73 per day. These high-season rates are lower during early and late season.

Vail, which owns Breckenridge, offers PEAKS discounted tickets; the best discounts are when you make an online purchase of a three-day or more ticket at least seven days in advance. Membership in PEAKS is free.

Interchangeability: Multiday lift tickets of three or more days also are valid at sister resorts Vail, Beaver Creek and Keystone, and at nearby Arapahoe Basin.

 # Accommodations

Breckenridge offers a wide assortment of housing options, everything from fabulous private luxury homes to large hotels to a hostel. Many are within steps of a lift or right on the slopes for true ski-in/ski-out lodging. Those in town sit close to the free bus stops and not far from the BreckConnect Gondola that travels to the base of Peak 8. Early December, January and April-May are the most affordable times.

Breckenridge Central Reservations (877-593-5260) handles much of the resort's lodging, but numerous property management companies can help you find the best property and price for your needs as well. A few are **ResortQuest** (800-627-3766), **Ski Country Resorts & Sports** (800-633-8388), **and Great Western Lodging** (888-333-4535).

Four wonderful, upscale condo lodges are within steps of lifts and/or bus stops. They are **Grand Timber Lodge** (877-453-4440; $$$$), **Valdoro Mountain Lodge** (800-436-6780; 970-453-4880; $$$$), **Mountain Thunder Lodge** (800-800-7829; $$$$), a Vail Resorts property, and **The Hyatt at Main Street Station** (800-869-9172; 970-453-4000; $$$$). Main Street Station, with its open plaza, shops and restaurants, closes the gap between the town and the ski area in one of the best locations on the south end of town.

The Village at Breckenridge(888-346-5754; 970-453-2000; $$$-$$$$) wraps the Peak 9 base area and sits just below the Quicksilver Super Chair. The units are spacious and newly remodeled. Amenities include a health club, heated underground parking, restaurants and rooms that will accept your dog.

The Great Divide Lodge (888-346-5754; 970-453-4500; $$$$) recently remodeled each

Dining: $$$$–Entrees $30+; $$$–$20–$30; $$–$10–$20; $–less than $10.
Accommodations: (double room) $$$$–$200+; $$$–$141–$200; $$–$81–$140; $–$80 and less.

guestroom, the entire lobby and pool/hot tub area\; just across the road from the slopes.

The River Mountain Lodge(888-627-3766; 970-453-4711; $$-$$$$) is a group of studio to four-bedroom suites in the heart of town, a block from Main Street and steps from the free ski-bus stop. This is one of the town's most reasonable accommodations.

The Lodge and Spa at Breckenridge (800-736-1607; 970-453-9300; $$$-$$$$) perches on a cliff at 10,200 feet with a magnificent view of the Breckenridge mountain range. This intimate log inn houses a full-service spa and very good restaurant. They provide a free shuttle to the ski area and are on the bus route.

Skiway Lodge (800-472-1430; 970-453-7573; $$-$$$$) is a ski-in/ski-out B&B on Ski Hill Road and accessed right off the mountain via the Skiway bridge, hence its name. The decor in its eight elegant rooms (all with balconies, three with fireplaces) evokes various times and places in history.

Little Mountain Lodge (800-468-7707; 970-453-1969; $$$-$$$$) is anything but little. This white-washed log home has an intimate staying-at-a-friend's-home feeling. The innkeepers add nice touches, such as placing a silver tray of coffee and tea at each guestroom door (there are 10) a half-hour before breakfast.

Allaire Timbers Inn (800-624-4904 outside Colorado; 970-453-7530; $$$-$$$$), a contemporary log inn on the south end, has great views and hospitable hosts. Each of the 10 guestrooms—all named after Colorado mountain passes—have private decks, and two suites come with their own hot tubs and fireplaces for a touch of Rocky Mountain romance.

Several 19th-century homes in town have been converted into charming B&Bs, some of which are: **Abbett Placer Inn** (S. French St., 888-794-7750; 970-453-6489; $-$$); **Barn on the River** (800-795-2975; 453-2975; $$-$$$); Ridge Street Inn (800-452-4680; 970-453-4680; $$); and **Fireside Inn** (N. French St., 970-453-6456; $-$$). The Fireside Inn is also a hostel with gender-segregated dorm rooms for $30-$38 per night, with two sets of bunk beds per room and shared baths.

If you like peace and quiet after a hard day of skiing, you'll love the B&Bs secluded in the pine and aspen forests away from town (you'll need a vehicle). **Muggins Gulch Inn** (800-275-8304; 970-453-7414; $$-$$$$) is a post-and-beam home on 161 acres 8 miles from town. Many guests come just for cross-country skiing, snowshoeing and playing in the snow around the property. Elegant English-country style defines **Colorado Pines Inn** (970-453-3960; $$-$$$), whose Australian-born owner believes "a good mattress and good food are essential" for a bed and breakfast and adds extraordinary hospitality to the mix. **High Country Lodge** (800-497-0097; 970-453-9843; $$-$$$) is a rustic inn 5 miles from town at 10,000 feet with amazing views of the Continental Divide. With 12 rooms, it specializes in family reunions and groups.

One of Colorado's finest RV resorts is on Tiger Run Road. The five-star **Tiger Run RV Resort** (800-895-9594) has a beautiful clubhouse with indoor pool and hot tub.

Scores of hotels, inns, motels and B&Bs can be found in Summit County. Many of these lodging options make access to the other Summit County resorts easier and almost all offer a savings over accommodation at the resort itself.

 # Dining

Breckenridge has emerged from the dining doldrums. With the increase in upscale homes and overseas vacationers, we expect the trend to continue.

The Cellar (200 S. Ridge St., 970-453-4777; $$-$$$$) has the same unique dining concept as Samplings in Frisco (see the Summit County chapter), where small plates of gourmet foods are shared with your companion diners.

Relish (137 So. Main, 970-453-0989; $$$) has the town's best mountain views above the Riverwalk Center (in the space that used to be Pierre's). Chef/owner Matt Fackler has been cooking in Breck for 10 years.

A little bit of French heaven is found at **Le Petit Paris** (970-547-5335; $$-$$$) at 161 Adams Ave behind the post office. **Top of the World Restaurant** (970-453-9300; $$$) in the Lodge & Spa is somewhat pricey, but consider the panoramic view as part of the meal.

The Hearthstone (S. Ridge St., 970-453-1148; $$-$$$) is quintessential Breckenridge—a stunning blue-and-white century-old house that sits prominently on the hill at the corner of Ridge and Washington.

Modis (970-453-4330; $$-$$$) is Breck's newest eatery at 113 S, Main St. It's named for what the owner's toddler son says when he wants more food - "mo dis". You'll want "mo" too. All entrees come with two sides, and the menu has extensive soup, appetizer and salad choices.

Carnivores should check out **Spencer's** (620 Village Run, 970-453-8755; $$-$$$) at Beaver Run for all-you-can-eat prime rib; **Kenosha Steak House** (301 S. Main, 970-453-7313; $-$$$); or the **Steak & Rib** (N. Main St., 970-453-0063; $$-$$$). For burgers, **Empire Burger** in La Cima Mall (970-453-2329, $) builds 'em better than any place in town. The best part is the choice of 15 dipping sauces for fries.

For things that swim (and some that don't), try **South Ridge Seafood Grill** (215 So. Ridge, 970-547-0063; $$-$$$). Don't miss a fun experience with great down-home Bayou food at **Bubba Gump Shrimp Company** (231 Main St., 970-547-9000; $-$$.) If you like shrimp in all sizes, shapes and flavors served in a Forest Gump-themed atmosphere, it's the perfect evening for you and your family.

Blue River Bistro (N. Main St., 970-453-6974; $-$$$) has it all, and is likely the best place for vegetarians, though a nice London broil an meat lasagna are also on the extensive menu. Salads as entrees are huge, and the many pastas like Linguine Portofino are divine.

A fun place to eat is **The Motherloaded Tavern** at 103 S. Main (970-453-2572; $$). Owned by two local moms, it's all about motherhood and comfort food, good and bad. The good is chicken 'n dumplings and mac & cheese; the bad is deep fried Twinkies (but no trans fat).

For a Mexican meal, head to **Mi Casa** (Park Ave., 970-453-2071; $-$$), **Fiesta Jalisco** (224 S. Main, 970-547-3836; $-$$) or **Jalapenos** (110 S. Park Ave., 970-547-9297; $-$$). Other ethnic dining options are **Red Orchid** (206 N. Main, 970-453-1881; $-$$) for Chinese; **Mountain Flying Fish Sushi Bar and Asian Kitchen** (500 S. Main, 970-453-1502; $-$$$) and **Wasabi** (311 S. Main, 970-453-8311; $-$$) for Japanese. Also **Denzaemon Cafe** (216 So Main, 970-453-9809; $) serves noodle and rice bowl dishes with 540-year-old recipes from Japan.

Beer lovers should try **Breckenridge Brewery** (S. Main St., 970-453-1550; $) for typical brewhouse food, house-made beer on tap and lots of noise or **Burke & Riley's Pub** (upstairs at 500 S. Main, 970-547-2782; $-$$) for Irish specialties. **Rasta Pasta** (S. Main St., 970-453-7467; $) specializes in whimsical Jamaican-flavored pasta. **Angel's Hollow** (S. Ridge St., 970-453-8585; $) is great for big-as-your-head burritos and burgers. **Euro Deli** (Lincoln Ave., 970-453-4473; $) has fab fresh sandwiches.

A toss-up for the breakfast winner is among **The Prospector** on S. Main Street, where the huevos rancheros will test your facial sweat glands; **Blue Moose** on S. Main ($), with a huge selection of egg favorites. A pancake's width behind is **Columbine Cafe** on S. Main ($) known for its generous omelets, eggs Benedict and specialty coffees. At **Daylight Donuts** (N. Main St.; $), locals love the pancakes, two eggs and bacon for $3. For lighter fare and gourmet coffee, try **Clint's** on S. Main ($); **Cool River Cafe**, a few steps off Main in the 300

Dining: $$$$–Entrees $30+; $$$–$20–$30; $$–$10–$20; $–less than $10.
Accommodations: (double room) $$$$–$200+; $$$–$141–$200; $$–$81–$140; $–$80 and less.

block ($); and **The Crown Cafe & Tavern** upstairs at 215 S. Main ($).

For years Breckenridge has lacked a good bakery, and now it has not just a good one, but a *boulangerie and patisserie*, **La Francaise** (411 S. Main, 970-547-7173; $). Fabulous French pastries, crepes, quiches and breads are baked daily. They also serve sandwiches on half baguettes and salads, and will cater French specialties like a Boeuf Bourguignon dinner with 48-hour notice.

Apres-ski/nightlife

Nearly every restaurant offers Happy Hour with drink specials after the slopes close. Breckenridge's liveliest apres-ski bars are **Tiffany's** in Beaver Run, the **Breckenridge Brewery** for a great handcrafted brew, **Park Avenue Pub** in the Village, and **Mi Casa**, with thirst-quenching margaritas—or try their sangrias by the liter. **Bubba Gump's** has a heated outdoor deck with a smashing view of the mountain. **Fatty's** bar takes up the entire first floor and locals fill it to the brim.

If you're having trouble adjusting to the altitude, head over to the **O2 Lounge** in La Cima Mall, where you can enjoy an herbal martini and oxygen-enriched air in 10- 20- and 30-minute increments.

While **Tiffany's** rocks until the wee hours, after dinner most of the action moves into town. At **Eric's** you'll find a rowdy crowd on TV sports nights. **Sherpa and Yeti's** on Main Street is the hot spot for live music and dancing.

Salt Creek on East Lincoln has live music and a huge upstairs dance floor that brings in the younger crowd. Tuesday and Thursday are cheap-beer-and-wing nights. There's always a long wait line to get into the action. **The Dredge**, which is a replica of the dredge boats that churned the Blue River for gold in the early 1900s, has a classy bar.

Summit County's 9:1 male-to-female ratio dramatically improves at **The Quandary** on Monday nights when those with two X chromosomes get free beer.

You'll find live music Friday and Saturday nights at Motherloaded, and wear your costume on Saturday (call for the theme). At 20 minutes after the 4 and 5 o'clock hours, they serve free shots of Mod Dogg 20/20 every day.

Cecelia's Bar makes great martinis, and recently expanded to add a dance floor and space for a DJ. **Liquid Lounge**, near Cecelia's, is a sure bet for great drinks and there's usually a DJ spinning tunes on the weekends. **The Crown** has cozy couches that are perfect for intimate apres-ski or late-night drinks, desserts or coffee.

Nightlife ends with a visit to **Charlie Dog's** off Main Street at 111 Ski Hill Rd. When every other restaurant in town is closed, you can still satisfy your late-night cravings with a Chicago Dog or a sub.

If you're wondering what happened to Shamus O'Toole's Roadhouse Saloon, it's been converted to **Breckenridge Theatre for Performing Arts** where **The Backstage Theatre** (970-453-0199) runs a variety of live shows throughout the season.

Other activities

Exploring historic Breckenridge is great fun, either with a formal **historic tour** or on your own armed with a free guidesheet. Don't forget the **Edwin Carter Museum** with its collection of Rocky Mountain fauna, and the **Barney Ford House Museum** with a fascinating history of a former slave who became the town's first black businessman.

Part of that history is with the **Backstage Theatre** (970-453-0199), which has been performing award-winning live shows continuously since 1974.

Kids will get a kick out of the hands-on exhibits at **Mountain Top Children's Museum** (970-453-7878) in the village on Park Avenue.

Good Times Adventure Tours (970-453-7604) offers thrilling **dogsled tours** and **snow-mobile rides**. Good Times is very hands-on, letting customers run their own dogsled team or take their own snowmobile for a spin.

There are also **mine tours** and **hut trips**. For information, call the Activities Center (877-864-0868). **Breckenridge Dinner Sleigh Rides** (970-547-8383) fill up quickly, so call ahead. There are two **ice rinks**, one indoors, for drop-in hockey and free skating (970-547-9974). The **Breckenridge Recreation Center** (970-453-1734) on Airport Road north of town offers an array of indoor activities for non-ski days, such as **swimming, tennis, racquetball, wall climbing, fitness center** and **basketball**. They offer child care for ages 2 months to 5 year.

If you happen to be in Breckenridge in mid-January, **Ullr** Fest with its parade and festivities is a great big hoot. Locals dress up in Nordic costumes, make a parade down the main street complete with naked streakers in sub-zero temps, throw candy and treats from the floats and make a family-wide festival out of the whole town.

Another popular event is the **Budweiser International Snow Sculpture Championships** at the end of January each year. Teams from around the globe turn 20-ton blocks of snow into art.

Twenty years combined experience stand behind the owners of **Blue Sage Spa** on Main Street (970-453-7676), a small sensuous spa voted Best Day Spa by Summit Countians.

At the full-facility **Grand Victorian Day Spa & Salon** (970-547-3624) in the Grand Timber Lodge, you choose from a long list of head-to-toe therapies and services, scrubs, peels and polishes for men and women.

Downtown has scores of **boutiques**. Some of our favorites on Main Street: Tom Girl; Big City Blues, Canary in a Clothes Mine and Goods, for clothing; Milagros (a handcrafted soap boutique), Wildflower and Breckenridge Hat Company for fun gifts; and Cookin' Cowgirl for kitchenware. Check out Hamlet's Bookshoppe on Main Street for local interest books and best-sellers. Peek inside Creatures Great & Small and Breckenridge BARKery if you're an animal lover.

The developing Breckenridge Arts District is between the corner of Main and Ridge on Washington Street. On an off-ski day, you can take a **workshop** at the Robert Whyte House or watch a guest artist work at the Tin Shop. For **fine art galleries**, we recommend: Paint Horse Gallery for western art, Breckenridge Fine Art Gallery, Hibbard McGrath Gallery, and Highlands Gallery.

 ## Getting there and getting around

By air: Breckenridge is about 100 miles west of Denver International Airport. Colorado Mountain Express (800-525-6363) offers regular van shuttles connecting the resort with the airport, as does Lift Ticket Limo (866-488-5280; 970-668-4899). For personalized private charter limos, vans and suburbans, make reservations with VailCoach (877-554-7433).

By car: From Denver, take I-70 to Exit 203, then south on Hwy. 9.

Getting around: Nearly everything is within walking distance and free buses cruise the streets regularly. The Breckenridge Free Ride provides bus service throughout Breckenridge and some outlying areas. The Summit Stage provides free transportation between Dillon, Silverthorne, Keystone, Frisco, Breckenridge and Copper Mountain. Call 970-668-0999 for route information. Keystone and Breckenridge also operate a free inter-resort shuttle, the Ski KAB Express (496-4200), at varying times according to demand. Vail Resorts Express (970-453-5000) shuttles daily between Breck and Vail.

Dining: $$$$–Entrees $30+; $$$–$20–$30; $$–$10–$20; $–less than $10.
Accommodations: (double room) $$$$–$200+; $$$–$141–$200; $$–$81–$140; $–$80 and less.

Copper Mountain
Colorado

Summit: 12,313 feet
Vertical: 2,601 feet
Base: 9,712 feet

Address: P.O. Box 3001,
Copper Mountain, Colorado 80443
Telephone (main): 970-968-2882
Snow Report Number: 888-229-9475
Toll-free reservations: 888-219-2441
Reservations outside US: 970-968-2882
E-mail: contactcenter@coppercolorado.com
Internet: www.coppercolorado.com
Expert:★★★★
Advanced:★★★★★
Intermediate:★★★★
Beginner:★★★★
First-timer:★★★★

Lifts: 22—1 high-speed six-pack, 4 high-speed quads, 5 triples, 5 doubles, 2 surface lifts, 5 moving carpets
Skiable acreage: 2,450
Snowmaking: 16 percent
Uphill capacity: 32,324
Parks & pipes: 4 parks, 3 pipes
Bed base: 3,942
Nearest lodging: Walking distance
Child care: Yes, 6 weeks and older
Adult ticket, per day: $79 (07/08 price)
Dining:★★★★★
Apres-ski/nightlife:★★
Other activities:★★

Copper Mountain is a self-contained resort with a perfectly organized mountain. New base development makes this a convenient and fun mountain for a vacation.

Copper Mountain is right off I-70 from Denver. Thanks to the area's natural topography, most trails are neatly organized by level of difficulty. From east to west, you'll find black-diamond to blue-square to green-circle terrain. But beginners aren't relegated only to the lower slopes and, unlike many other areas, have an equal share of Copper's terrain.

The area is named after an old copper mine whose remnants remain in the Copper Bowl area (in summer the mine tailings are distinct). But rather than attempt to honor days of old, Copper Mountain is a paean to modern-day master planning. Born in 1972, the base area still has a few remnants of buildings that pay tribute to that decade of architectural aberrance. However, having taken an "if-you-build-it-they-will-come" attitude, resort developer and former owner Intrawest has completed its intensive $500-million village construction. Now Copper's base area includes all the "total resort" amenities that skiers and riders have come to expect from Intrawest-developed properties.

Copper Mountain is part of Summit County, Colorado. This county has four well-known ski areas—Copper Mountain, Breckenridge, Keystone and Arapahoe Basin—and more dining and lodging than most ski resorts on North America. Locals have voted Copper their favorite mountain in the county for five straight years in the Summit Daily newspaper readers' poll.

Mountain layout

While it doesn't take a lot of brain power to figure out the terrain layout, there is plenty of demanding skiing for those who want it. Experts head to the summit, where chutes, cornices and double-diamond slits are worth studying in Copper's upper bowls. And because the terrain is so evenly distributed among ability levels, those wanting to improve and graduate with honors just have to work their way towards the other side of the mountain. If you use lifts as meeting places, pay attention to the American

Eagle and American *Flyer* chairs. If you're meeting someone at the top of one of those chairs, be very specific: They start in the same general area but unload on different peaks.

Expert, Advanced: Copper's mountains are lofty with Union Peak reaching 12,313 feet, Tucker Mountain 12,337 feet and Copper Peak 12,441 feet. And there, in the high Alpine terrain, lie the double-black-diamond bowls. There's a lot to explore. We especially enjoyed the gnarly Tucker's hike-to glades and chutes and the Enchanted Forest's untouched powder. Extra added attraction: Tucker Mountain Snowcats stand by to give you rides to the top of Tucker for a sweet descent when snow is fresh. If the south-facing snow has been sun-baked, pass on the cat until it snows again.

If you survive Spaulding Bowl, you can choose from several very worthy runs to the bottom of the Resolution chair where there's seldom a wait. The consistently good snow in Union Bowl under the Sierra lift gets even better when you hike to the top of the cirque. Not always so with Copper Bowl on the backside of Union Peak. Its slopes are south-facing so ask around before you dive in. It could be either ugly or divine.

The Super Bee six-pack accesses all terrain on the East Village side, including the relentless bumps on Far East, Too Much and Triple Treat under the Alpine lift. From the top of Super Bee you can slide down any of three short-but-sweet runs that parallel the Excelerator quad.

Intermediate: Exit to the right of the American Flyer quad and zip down American Flyer, The Moz and Windsong, all wide groomed runs under the Timberline Express lift. After fresh snow, Copperfields gives a good challenge with perfectly placed, soft bumps. If you like trees, there are many places here to jump in, but be wary that some are thick. A stash of delightful unmarked woods under the American Flyer can be reached by taking High Point and bearing left before the steep pitch. It has nicely spaced trees all the way to Timberline Express.

Darting down any of the runs under the American Eagle quad will peg the fun meter, but beware that Main Vein and Bouncer seem to be the busiest. Off the Super Bee chair, try Andy's Encore, a worthy intermediate highway. Collage is also on this side of the mountain and has a few fun steep pitches. Or duck off Collage into 17 Glade—the farther right you go, the more open it gets. To avoid lifts at the area's base, take Excelerator on the upper mountain for a quick set of laps. Trails such as Ptarmigan are wide, consistent runs back to the chair.

Beginner, First-timer: From the Village hop on the high-speed American Flyer (don't confuse it with the American Eagle) and make your way over to the runs at Union Creek. Most of this whole side of the mountain consists of sweeping groomed runs, perfect for the experienced beginner. For long runs to the bottom, from the American Flyer take Coppertone, an easy cruise. From both American Flyer and the High Point lifts, work your way to the Timberline Express quad chair, ride to the top and ski the delightful Soliloquy to Roundabout to the bottom.

You also can take the Rendezvous lift up top and enjoy the views while cruising Wheeler Creek and Union Park. Picnic tables provide plenty of opportunities to rest and check out the scenery. Avoid the Sierra lift here—it serves only blacks and blues.

Copper Mountain is a first-timer's dream mountain, with learning and beginner terrain naturally separated from the gonzo's terrain on the other side. The Village at Copper and Union Creek both have areas served by moving carpets for those first few times on snow.

Parks and pipes

Copper is duly recognized as one of the top resorts for parks and pipes. The parks are groomed every night while the pipes are cut every other night. The 20-acre Catalyst Terrain Park (Copper's main park) is on the Loverly trail and has three lines, one for each ability level. No matter how skilled you are, you'll appreciate watching what everyone else has up their sleeves—thrills and spills are legion. Beginners have small kickers and rails here. Once you're confident in your landings, you'll find larger kickers and some jumps to up the challenge. As for the pros, go for as much air as you want on the shack jib, giant tabletops, hip features and an 8-foot wall ride set atop a 17-foot quarterpipe. The signature jump, The Shaft, is a 60-foot table. A section of rails includes a variety of flat, kinked and rainbow rails leading into the well-designed and maintained 430-foot-long superpipe with its 18-foot-high walls.

If you like showing off, Copper's Main Vein Superpipe sits just above the base of the American Eagle lift and within view of the deck at Jack's. You can also watch pipe competitions and events from that vantage point.

Playground Kidz Park is full of small kickers, rollers and tables that provide the perfect venue to master your skills before moving on to the larger beginner features in the Catalyst Terrain Park. The resort also has a 200-foot-long minipipe with 6-foot-high walls.

Snowboarding

Arrayed across the face of Copper Peak are trails that progress from easy to thrilling to terrifying. This natural segregation of trails keeps rank beginners out of the way of overconfident intermediates and impatient experts.

For those who prefer solitude, there are the famed Copper Bowls, which feature treacherous steeps and plenty of fresh pow. Copper Bowl is a true backcountry experience that's lift-served. And there's Tucker Mountain's snowcat for an even more backcountry feel. Then there's the Spaulding Bowl at the top of the Storm King Poma ground lift—provided you can deal with a Poma. The chutes here funnel down to the quad-exhausting bumps of Resolution Bowl (or "Rezo," as locals refer to it). Three runs and you'll be heading for a beer to chase away the lactic acid.

Cross-country & snowshoeing (see also xcskiresorts.com)

Snowshoers will find 24.5 km. of unmaintained and unpatrolled trails meandering through the woods at Union Creek. Another spectacular ungroomed option is the bike path that runs through Copper Village west to Vail Pass. Go to the golf course if you want groomed trails. No day pass is necessary for snowshoeing unless you use a ski lift to access trails or backcountry routes. A free daily snowshoe tour in the Union Creek area includes a guide, snowshoes and poles. Sign up at the Guest Services Desk in the Copper One Lodge in The Village at Copper. The trip leaves at 10 a.m. and returns by 12:30 p.m.

Lessons (07/08 prices)

We list regular-season prices; value-season prices are a bit less.

Group lessons: $79 for a half day; $90 for a full day, $162 for two days and $243 for three days. Call 866-549-9934.

First-timer A half-day lesson (1-3:30 p.m.) costs $75. First-time snowboarders take Burton Learn-To-Ride classes, with special equipment designed to help you learn more quickly. You can also reserve rental equipment online at rentskis.com that will be waiting for you when you arrive.

Private lessons: Friends and Family Privates are for 4-6 people: a half-day lesson costs $390; $510 for a full day (six hours). Signature Privates Experiences for one-on-one attention cost $360 for half-day; $490 for a full day. A two-hour afternoon lesson is $280. Reservations for all private lessons are recommended. Call 866-464-4432.

Special programs: Roxy's Women's Wednesdays, Bump Busters, and Masters All-Mountain highlight the list. Call 866-464-4462 for details and prices.

Children's programs (07/08 prices)

Ages 2 to 4 years. Full day with lunch costs $93; half day is $78 (morning only). Parents should provide diapers, a change of clothing, a blanket and a favorite toy. Reservations required; call (970) 968-2318, Ext. 38101; or (866) 841-2481.

Special activities: Kids' Night Out, a "kids only" night filled with fun and games, videos and pizza for children up to age 10. Participation is free to parents who spend $30 or more per child while they shop or dine at Copper Mountain.

Other options: Copper offers evening babysitting in a guest's accommodations; reservations required (866-841-2481; 968-2318, Ext. 38101). In-room babysitting services require 24-hour advance reservations or cancellations and cost $12 per hour plus $1 for each additional child. Also see Summit County child care.

Children's lessons: Full-day ski or snowboard programs (lunch, lesson, lifts) for kids ages 6-15 costs $104; a two day lesson is $187; and a three day lesson is $280. Kids ages 3–5 pay $123 for a one-day lesson, $221 for a two-day lesson and $332 for a three-day lesson. Rentals are extra.

Lift tickets (07/08 prices)

	Adult	Child (6-13)
One day	$79	$39
Three days	$237 ($79/day)	$117 ($39/day)
Five days	$395 ($79/day)	$195 ($39/day)

Who skis free: Ages 5 and younger.

Who skis at a discount: Seniors 65-69 pay $64; 70 and older pay $31. Beginners on green slopes pay only $10.Those who buy a Copper Four Pass for $84 ski for $21 a day for four days.

Prices are lower during early, pre-holiday and late season. For $20 you can upgrade to a BeeLine ticket for immediate access in designated lift lines.

The best deals are offered through lodging-lift ticket packages. Visit Copper's website for details and to purchase online.

Accommodations

Lodging through **Copper Mountain Reservations** (888-219-2441) includes hotels, condos and a few townhomes. Most of this is new construction and all is just steps from the slopes, bars, restaurants and shops. All Copper lift/lodging packages include the **Beeline Advantage Program** (ask about it). This designated lift access bypasses lines on major lifts plus gives you a 15-minute head start for first tracks off the American Eagle.

The Cirque is Copper's most luxurious accommodation and features gourmet kitchens, heated bathroom floors, washer/dryers, DVD player/64-inch plasma TV screen media rooms, a kids' play area, fitness room, saunas, hot tubs, wading and swimming pools and an underground heated garage.

Two other companies book accommodations: **Carbonate Property Management** (800-

Dining: $$$$–Entrees $30+; $$$–$20–$30; $$–$10–$20; $–less than $10.
Accommodations: (double room) $$$$–$200+; $$$–$141–$200; $$–$81–$140; $–$80 and less.

526-7737) and **Copper Vacations** (800-525-3887).

Scores of hotels, inns, motels and B&Bs can be found in **Frisco** (via a free direct shuttle) and other parts of Summit County. Many of these lodging options make access to the other Summit County resorts easier and almost all offer a savings over accommodation at the resort itself.

Dining

JJ's Rocky Mountain Tavern (970-968-2318; $-$$) in East Village's Copper Station day lodge, is named after J.J. Brown, husband of the Titanic's "Unsinkable" Molly Brown, a Colorado legend. It's reminiscent of an 1800s tavern and serves casual American fare; lunch, dinner and bar menus are available. If it's a nice day, sit on the deck at **McGillycuddy's** (970-968-1000; $-$$), where you'll chow on authentic Irish food and beverages while overlooking West Lake in the Village at Copper.

The Double Diamond Bar and Grill (970-968-2880; $-$$) in the Foxpine Inn serves up the best Colorado beef burgers around. Every Friday owner David Luthi hosts a Fish Fry for less than $10.

Popular for families staying in the Village is **Alpinista Mountain Bistro** (970-968-1144; $$) serving three squares a day of hearty bistro meals. Happy hour specials, a kids' menu, microbrews, wine-by-the-glass and a great patio make it perfect for every age and stage.

In The Village at Copper, **Endo's Adrenaline Cafe** (970-968-3070; $) in the Mountain Plaza building enjoys a strong following for great salads, burgers and fries. **Jack's Slopeside Grill** ($) at Copper One Lodge, is a market-style eatery serving a wide variety of food, including a deli, from 7 a.m. to 6 p.m. **Camp Hale Coffee** ($) is there when you need it, serving bean brews and pastries at wake-up call and throughout the day. Try **Salsa Mountain Cantina** (970-968-6300; $) for Mexican and **Imperial Palace** (970-968-6688; $-$$) for Taiwanese and Szechwan Chinese. One local who used to live in Asia raves about the authentic deep-fried chicken wings and the great service at this family-owned eatery. At **Tucker's Tavern** (970-968-2033; $-$$) families rule with nightly specials like all-you-can-eat-spaghetti.

Dinner sleigh rides (866-416-9872; $$$$, reservations required) make a memorable event. A horse-drawn sleigh takes diners through the woods to a heated miner's tent for live entertainment and a gourmet meal.

There's also an excellent selection of restaurants in surrounding Summit County.

Apres-ski/nightlife

JJ's Rocky Mountain Tavern, with its live entertainment and bar menu, is without question the hottest spot here. It's in the East Village. Moe Dixon, a longtime favorite entertainer, always gets people dancing on the tables. In fact, the owners had to reinforce the bar top, thanks to the hordes who refused to remove their ski boots when dancing on the bar. Ban dancing? *NEVER!* It's Grande Apres every day with a free supersize of all draft beer from 3-6 p.m.

Zizzo Ski Bar, offers a sophisticated apres ski scene with live entertainment, multiple 52" TV screens, a Chicago-style menu as well as dancing and an extensive wine bar with weekly tastings. A popular hangout is **Endo's Adrenaline Cafe** in The Village at Copper, where you'll find drink specials in a sport-oriented atmosphere.

Jack's Slopeside at Copper One Lodge has live entertainment Thursday to Saturday. Expect sing-alongs and more dancing on the bar. Jack's counterpart **Jill's Umbrella Bar** serves up Mojitos and Long Island Iced Tea among other thirst quenchers that you'll need for the Thursday afternoon Salsa dance lessons.

Storm King Lounge features scotch and signature martinis, sushi, Sapporo and sake. Play pool and poker here while you imbibe. Now that the Cold War is over, the Russian-themed vodka bar and red nightclub

Pravda seems popular. A DJ keeps you thirsting for more of the exclusive list of 30 vodkas, served ice cold. You'll find other nightlife options throughout Summit County.

Other activities

Through the activities center (866-416-9872), you can book other activities in and around the area that include ice skating, tubing on a dedicated hill, ice skating, sleigh rides, snowmobiling, snowshoe tours, dogsled rides and kite skiing/riding on Lake Dillon. There's also the sports of curling and broomball on the ice at West Lake. No signup or equipment required; just show up in your sneakers or snow boots.

Copper Mountain Athletic Club (970-968-2882, Ext. 83025) has an indoor pool, sauna, steam room, hot tubs, cardiovascular equipment, racquetball courts and spa. Use of the club is free to anyone staying at a Copper lodging property. For more indoor activities, head for Coppercade that houses mini golf, pool tables and pinball machines of every kind.

Make the rounds of the many shops at Copper Station, West Lake and The Village at Copper. Upper-end souvenirs, logo clothing and sports gear fill most of them. Also browse through the boutique shops on West Lake and Copper One Lodge.

For health issues, visit **St. Anthony's Copper Mountain Clinic** (970-968-2330) in the Bridge End Building in The Village at Copper. They're open seven days a week, 8:30 a.m.-4:30 p.m.

For more activities see Summit County or Vail. Copper is about 20 miles from Vail and about 10 miles from the tri-town area of Dillon, Frisco and Silverthorne.

Getting there and getting around

By air: Copper Mountain is 90 miles west of Denver International Airport on I-70. Several ground transportation companies run vans between the airport and your lodge with many daily departures. You can make arrangements when you reserve lodging **The Copper Call Center** (800-841-2481), which can book your flights, rental cars and **Colorado Mountain Express** shuttle. Or call CME (800-525-6363) or **Lift Ticket Limo** (866-488-5280; 970-668-4899). For personalized charter limos, vans and suburbans, make reservations with **VailCoach** (877-554-7433).

By car: Right off I-70 at Exit 195. You can see many of the trails from the freeway.

Getting around: If you plan to frequent trips to Vail or to the other Summit County areas, you'll probably want a car. Otherwise you don't need one. Copper Mountain's updated fleet of buses enhances an already superb (and free) shuttle service that run constantly between 8 a.m. and 11 p.m. Walking is also easy between the outlying condos and the village center.

Free Summit Stage buses serve the three nearby ski areas as well as the towns of Dillon, Silverthorne and Frisco. Warning: The buses make lots of stops so it can take up to 90 minutes to make it down the road to the next resort. An express bus runs from the Frisco transfer station to Copper every half-hour. A multi-stop bus also runs so you can get a ride to Copper every half-hour during the day and early evening.

If you are not staying at Copper, a warning about parking: All close-in parking lots charge about $15-$20 per day, except the outlying free Alpine lot near the highway.

Dining: $$$$–Entrees $30+; $$$–$20–$30; $$–$10–$20; $–less than $10.
Accommodations: (double room) $$$$–$200+; $$$–$141–$200; $$–$81–$140; $–$80 and less.

Keystone
Colorado

Summit:	**12,408 feet**
Vertical:	**3,128 feet**
Base:	**9,284 feet**

Address: Box 38,
Keystone, Colorado 80435
Telephone (main): 800-468-5004; 970-496-4000
Snow Report Number: 800-468-5004
Toll-free reservations: 800-468-5004
Reservations outside US: 970-496-4000
E-mail: keystoneinfo@vailresorts.com
Internet: www.keystoneresort.com

Expert:★★
Advanced:★★★
Intermediate:★★★★
Beginner:★★★★★
First-timer:★★★

Lifts: 20—2 gondolas, 1 high-speed six-pack, 5 high-speed quads, 1 quad, 1 triple, 3 doubles, 1 surface lift, 6 moving carpets
Skiable acreage: 2,870 plus 1,417 in-bounds hike-to and snowcat-served acres
Snowmaking: 37 percent
Uphill capacity: 33,564
Parks & pipes: 2 parks, 1 pipe
Bed base: 6,000
Nearest lodging: Slopeside, ski-in/ski-out
Child care: Yes, 2 months and older
Adult ticket, per day: $83 (07/08 price)
Dining:★★★★★
Apres-ski/nightlife:★★★
Other activities:★★★

Keystone is a big, purpose-built resort that is praised for its family-friendly atmosphere. It also has extensive night skiing for those who can't get enough during the daylight hours.

If you're looking for that quaint 19th-century Victorian mining-town charm for which Colorado's known, you won't find it at Keystone. But if you're looking for a smoothly humming resort with buses shuttling to every corner, a child-friendly atmosphere and one of the Rockies' largest snowmaking systems, you'll be pleased as pie.

Keystone is known as a superb intermediate playground, but it has decent terrain at either end of the ability scale. There aren't many surprises here and it's hard to get in over your head. Another attraction is Keystone's extensive night skiing, which means you don't have to get up early to get in a lot of vertical.

For skiers and riders who feel uncomfortable in ungroomed snow, Keystone makes concerted efforts to keep its slopes baby-butt smooth. Keystone often doesn't get the natural snow its neighboring resorts do, so snowmaking on its lowest peak is a real plus.

But lest you think Keystone is all groomers (see mountain layout), in 2007 it added Independence Bowl to its hike-to and snowcat-accessed terrain, making Keystone the largest guided snowcat skiing and riding operation in Colorado.

Because Keystone is owned by Vail Resorts, plenty of money is funneled into the amenities. The resort's largest base area is River Run, a pedestrian village that includes boutiques, coffee shops, restaurants and condos at the base of the River Run Gondola. Though Keystone was never known for its nightlife, it has jazzed that up quite a bit.

Keystone is part of Summit County. This county has four well-known ski areas—Breckenridge, Keystone, Arapahoe Basin and Copper Mountain—and more dining and lodging than most ski resorts on North America.

Mountain layout

Keystone has three peaks, one behind another. In front is Dercum Mountain, named to honor Max and Edna Dercum, who pioneered the resort's founding. Dercum is laced with beginner and intermediate terrain, plus some expert glades on its backside. In the middle is North Peak, and finally, The Outback. Other than one snaking green-circle trail, these latter peaks have only blue and black terrain. Here's a larger, more detailed trail map.

Expert, Advanced: You won't find any double-diamonds here. For the most challenge, head to The Outback—a mix of open bowls, trails and glades. The quartet of Timberwolf, Bushwacker, Badger and The Grizz allow tree fans to pick how tight they want their forest. They also get massive bumps. Reach the two short black-diamond bowls here with a 10-minute hike from the top of the Outback Express. (This in-bounds terrain tops out at 12,408 feet, more than what's listed in the stat box, where we list lift-served terrain.)

North Peak is generally tamer than The Outback and is a great spot for working on technique and steeps. Star Fire, though rated blue, is a superb steep, groomed run, and a good warm-up for this area. Then head to black-diamond bump runs such as Ambush, Powder Cap or Bullet. Break your own tracks through the trees directly beneath the Santiago Express or duck into Bullet Glades for an adrenaline rush. Another stash of trees, called The Windows, requires a short hike from the bottom of the Outpost Gondola (off Dercum's back side).

Don't like to hike but still want to get into the backcountry? Keystone Adventure Tours operates two snowcats (weather dependent) for a taste of a backcountry experience while staying in-bounds. Ski or ride with KAT guides in Independence Bowl starting at 12,614 feet, with a stop at a yurt for a gourmet lunch prepared by Alpenglow Stube's chefs. Or earn your turns by hiking 30-45 minutes to more than 1,000 acres of Keystone's "sidecountry" in Bergman, Erickson and Indie Bowls. Either way, this is about the most affordable cat skiing you can get (see Lift Tickets for prices). Keep in mind that snow conditions can change in a heartbeat and powder ski tours don't always yield powder. You should be a strong skier or rider and able to handle variable conditions. What makes it worthwhile is the lack of crowds, potentially finding some untracked snow and getting above treeline.

Intermediate: You have the run of the three mountains, with appropriate terrain on each. Dercum has runs such as Paymaster, Wild Irishman, Frenchman and Flying Dutchman that play with God-given terrain. The twists and natural steeps on these cruisers represent trails at their best—they obviously did not have their character bulldozed out of them. Snowmaking covers the majority of Dercum's trails and the grooming ranks among the best in the country.

The Mountain House base area has three chairlifts that take skiers up the mountain. The other base area, River Run, is the lower station of the River Run Gondola. The gondola serves the night-skiing area. The resort says it's the largest single-mountain night ski operation in the United States.

Intermediates also can head to North Peak down Mozart, a wide blue run. Its width is essential, because it's the main pathway to the two rear peaks and can get crowded. North Peak, Prospector and Last Alamo are the easiest of the blues, with Star Fire a good test for The Outback. If you think Star Fire is fun, not scary, head down Anticipation or Spillway to The Outback and play on the intermediate runs under the Outback Express chair. The advanced-intermediate glades to skier's left—Wolverine, Wildfire and Pika—are not as tough as the glades of the Black Forest but also not a spot for timid intermediates.

Beginner, First-timer: Stay on Dercum Mountain, where nearly a third of all beginner terrain lies. The best runs for beginners are the legendary and long Schoolmarm plus Silver-spoon and Spring Dipper. True beginners should beware of that first plunge off the top onto Spring Dipper-for a short pitch, it's blue, a bit steep and only for greenies graduating into their blue phase.

Confident beginners who want the experience of spectacular views and lunch at the on-mountain restaurant at Outpost Lodge can ski down afterwards via Prospector on North Peak. Prospector is blue, but about two-thirds of it are in a slow zone so it's not too intimidating. Prospector merges with the slow zone on Mozart, but this trail is often crowded, so be alert. If you don't want to try the blues here, take the Outpost Gondola back over to easier terrain.

Keystone has a learning center at the top of Dercum Mountain, with two learning runs and a triple chairlift. Instructors who teach first-timers highly recommend the Discovery Learning Area, home to a self-contained kids' ski school. It's a large, wide-open space protected from the wind and elements and is serviced by a chair and two moving carpets (a magic carpet recently replaced the T-bar). It's less crowded than the rest of the mountain and is completely closed off to all other skiers, so it's pretty darned safe.

Parks and pipes

Keystone is a heavyweight contender with a top-rated terrain park, a superpipe, various festive events and the only legal night-riding in Summit County. The terrain park—A51—is in Pack-saddle Bowl on Dercum Mountain, away from the mainstream runs with its own lift called—duh—A51 Lift. To encourage snowboarders and freeskiers to claim this side of the mountain, the base area and Mountain House directly below it are designed with Gen X in mind.

A51 has three separate areas for beginners, intermediates and pros. The park features an 18-foot superpipe in the pro area that's sure to challenge even the best riders. Keystone has really stepped up to the plate with its rails and funboxes. The resort tells us it's in the running for the most rails in the nation but not all 51 of them are set up at one time. Instead they're rotated to keep things entertaining. On any given day you might find a 150-foot-long rail plus signature rails like the rollercoaster rail and the pro-restricted flaming barbecue rail. Next to A51 is the A51 Incubator with smaller rails and features for those just learning to play in the park.

 Cross-country & snowshoeing (see also xcskiresorts.com)

Keystone has an extensive cross-country touring area with 16 km. of groomed trails around the resort and an additional 57 km. of ungroomed backcountry skiing trails to ghost mining towns in the Montezuma area and around the region. **The Keystone Nordic Center** (970-496-4275) is located at the River Course clubhouse off Hwy. 6. Lessons and rentals are available. Cross-country activities include cross-country ski workouts with a personal fitness trainer, guided moonlight tours and peak-to-peak snowshoe treks. Snowshoe rentals are also available. The center has trail maps for the region and their clubhouse offers food service with outdoor chairs and tables. Choose from fresh-baked breads, soups and beverages including wine or beer for lunch. For those who stay at Keystone Resort, the Adventure Passport in the lodging packet offers free trail access and discounts on rentals. For a door-to-door service ride, call the E.A.S.E. bus (970-496-4200).

See Breckenridge for other options, including the extensive network provided by Breck-enridge Nordic Center, Gold Run Nordic Center and Frisco Nordic Center.

Snowboarding

You won't find any double-diamonds here. For the most challenge, head to The Outback—a mix of open bowls, trails and glades. The quartet of Timberwolf, Bushwacker, Badger and The Grizz allow tree fans to pick how tight they want their forest. They also get massive bumps. Reach the two short black-diamond bowls here with a 10-minute hike from the top of the Outback Express. (This in-bounds terrain tops out at 12,408 feet, more than what's listed in the stat box, where we list lift-served terrain.)

Other than the Outback, Keystone's steeps are mainly moguled, a major drawback for many advanced snowboarders. North Peak is generally tamer than The Outback and is a great spot for working on technique and steeps. Star Fire, though rated blue, is a superb steep, groomed run and a good warm-up for this area. Break your own tracks through the trees directly beneath the Santiago Express or duck into Bullet Glades for an adrenaline rush.

Intermediates have the run of the three mountains, with appropriate terrain on each. However, riders find the cruisers rather crowded. Dercum has runs such as Paymaster, Wild Irishman, Frenchman and Flying Dutchman that play with God-given terrain. The twists and natural steps on these cruisers represent trails at their best—they obviously did not have their character bulldozed out of them. Intermediates also can head to North Peak down Mozart, a wide blue run. Its width is essential, because it's the main pathway to the two rear peaks and can get crowded. On North Peak, Prospector and Last Alamo are the easiest of the blues, with Star Fire a good test for The Outback. If you think Star Fire is fun, not scary, head down Anticipation or Spillway to The Outback and play on the intermediate runs under the Outback Express chair.

First-timers and beginners will be glad to know gentle terrain is served by moving carpets and chairlifts, making it easy to get up the hill. Beginners should stay on Dercum Mountain, where nearly a third of all beginner terrain lies. The best runs for beginners are the legendary and long Schoolmarm, plus Silverspoon and Spring Dipper. True beginners should beware of that first plunge off the top onto Spring Dipper—for a short pitch, it's blue, a bit steep and only for greenies graduating into their blue phase. Confident beginners who want the experience of spectacular views and lunch at the on-mountain restaurant at Outpost Lodge can head down afterwards via Prospector on North Peak. Prospector is blue, but about two-thirds of it are in a slow zone so it's not too intimidating.

Keystone has a learning center at the top of Dercum Mountain, with two learning runs and a triple chairlift. Instructors who teach first-timers highly recommend the Discovery Learning Area, home to a self-contained kids' ski and snowboard school. It's a large, wide-open space protected from the wind and elements and is serviced by a chair and two moving carpets. It's less crowded than the rest of the mountain and is completely closed off to all other skiers and riders, so it's pretty darned safe.

 ## Lessons (07/08 prices)

Keystone provides regular- and value-season prices. Keystone Ski and Ride School features the University Trail, a 1,640-foot-vertical intermediate run dedicated solely to students.

Group lessons: A half-day session, for skiers or snowboarders, costs $85 regular season; all day, $95. Discounts available for previous students.

Private lessons: $410 for three hours and $610 for six hours. Price per lesson is valid for up to six people.

Special programs: Clinics and camps are held for women (Betty Fest) and racing. Call for prices and details (800 255-3715 or 970-496-4170).

Racing: NASTAR racing, clinics and a self-timed course are on Dercum Mountain.

Children's Lessons: See Child care below.

Children's programs (06/07 prices)

Child care: Ages 2 months to 6 years. Cost is $95 for a full day with lunch, half-day (mornings + lunch) is $80. With morning snowplay for ages 3-6, all day costs $115. Babies 2-15 months can have a one-on-one Nanny all day for $280.

The Keystone Children's Center at River Run is in the Silver Mill Plaza at the east end of the village.

Reservations: (970) 496-4181 or (800) 255-3715, or make online reservations.

Children's lessons: Kids 3–4 years old can take a learn-to-ski program that includes lesson, lift ticket, lunch. Cost is $119 for a full day beginning promptly at 9 a.m. Reservations are required; call (800) 255-3715. The full-day ski or snowboard program for ages 5–15 includes lift ticket, lesson and lunch for $130. Rentals for all programs are an additional $16. Value-season prices are somewhat less. Helmets are recommended for all children enrolled in ski and snowboard programs; helmet rentals cost about $12. On-line rentals can also be made at rentskis.com and will be ready when you arrive.

A special one-hour lesson where parents can learn to teach their little ones is Mom, Dad & Me; cost is $90 and reservations are required.

Lift tickets (07/08 prices)

	Adult (13-64)	Child (5-12)
One day	$83	$43
Three days	$249 ($83/day)	$129 ($43/day)
Five days	$415 ($83/day)	$215 ($43/day)

Who skis free: Ages 4 and younger.

Who skis at a discount: Seniors 65 and older pay $73 per day. Prices are lower during early and late seasons. All-day guided **snowcat** skiing is $199 per person (includes lift ticket, powder ski rental and gourmet lunch); one-way rides to Outback Bowls are $5.

Vail, which owns Keystone, offers PEAKS discounted tickets. Best discount tip: Make an online purchase of a three-day or more ticket at least seven days in advance. Membership in PEAKS is free. Check the resort's website for more information.

Interchangeability: Multiday lift tickets of three or more days also are valid at sister resorts Vail, Beaver Creek and Breckenridge and at nearby Arapahoe Basin.

Accommodations

Keystone Central Reservations (800-427-8308) books lodging, air transportation, lift tickets and other needs. Keystone is mostly a condominium community but also has two hotels and a quaint bed and breakfast that formerly was a stagecoach stop in the 1800s. Room or condo rates start at about $120 per night. Kids ages 12 and younger stay free with their parents, provided minimum occupancy is met and maximum occupancy not exceeded. All room reservations come with the Adventure Passport, a booklet that gives entry to more than $300 worth of activities (see Other Activities).

The quaint **Ski Tip Lodge** ($-$$$$), which was a stagecoach stop in the late 1800s, is a near-perfect ski lodge. Rooms are rustic in the best sense of the word with true ski history, the dining room is elegant and the sitting room is warm and inviting.

Keystone divides its lodging into seven "neighborhoods" and villages with access to a swimming pool or hot tub and are serviced by an excellent shuttlebus system.

The main hub is the attractive **River Run area**, which is walking distance from the River Run Gondola. The condos are spacious and convenient to the slopes and surround the best shopping in Keystone. A variety of outdoor concerts and events rock the plaza in winter.

River Run is flanked by the neighborhoods of **East Keystone**, built around Ski Tip Lodge and **North Keystone**, where the Inn at Keystone is located. From this neighborhood in the center of the resort the views are spectacular. Slopeside condos are truly ski-in/ski-out in the **Mountain House Neighborhood**, the second base area. The **Chateaux d'Mont** condos here are magnificent, luxurious and worth every penny. We strongly recommend trying to reserve one of these units.

To the west is **Lakeside Village** where shops, restaurants and the upscale **Keystone Lodge** hug the shores of the small lake and ice rink that is the focal point. **West Keystone**, close to the Conference Center, is the gateway to Keystone, where townhouses, private homes and condos greet visitors. The beautiful **Ranch** neighborhood follows the Snake River up the mountain toward The Keystone Ranch (see Dining).

Keystone's platinum collection of lodging properties continues to define luxury. When guests stay at one of these upscale condos—**Chateaux d'Mont**, **The Timbers** or **Lone Eagle** —they receive free ski check, welcome gifts, fresh flowers, a complimentary bottle of wine, personal concierge and daily newspapers.

Scores of hotels, inns, motels and B&Bs can be found in Summit County. Many of these lodging options make access to the other Summit County resorts easier and almost all offer a savings over accommodation at the resort itself.

Dining

Keystone has gained a reputation for fine dining, thanks to the Colorado Mountain College Culinary Institute that is based there. Qualified students apprentice for three years in the resort's restaurants under world-renowned chefs before receiving degrees in culinary arts from the American Culinary Federation.

Keystone has three dining experiences not to be missed—**Alpenglow Stube**, perched at 11,444 feet on North Peak and the highest gourmet restaurant in the country; **Ski Tip Lodge**, the cozy inn where all of Keystone's history oozes from every log; and **Keystone Ranch**, named one of Colorado's Best Restaurants by the Zagat Survey.

Alpenglow Stube ($$$) in The Outpost features rough-hewn timbers, massive fireplaces, vaulted ceilings and expansive windows. The Stube serves what we rate as the best on-mountain dinner available in the U.S. The adventure begins two valleys away with a ride on two gondolas suspended over the lighted slopes of Dercum Mountain. The restaurant is a large but cozy room that looks as if Martha Stewart's Swiss cousin were the decorator. The menu features a six- to eight-course menu (for a fixed price of $95 per person) of such fare as wood-grilled salmon, grilled wild game and slow-roasted duck. Figure about another $40 a bottle for wine.

Renowned among discerning clientele in Summit County, **Ski Tip Lodge** ($$$) is a cozy and inviting place with a standard for service that all restaurants strive for yet not all achieve. It serves a fixed-price, four-course meal for adults and a three-course meal for children 12 and younger.

Keystone Ranch ($$$) is a restored log ranch house built in the 1930s as a wedding present to Bernardine Smith and Howard Reynolds. Reportedly, the only completely original part of the house is the fireplace, yet you feel as if you're dining at the home of an intimate

Dining: $$$$–Entrees $30+; $$$–$20–$30; $$–$10–$20; $–less than $10.
Accommodations: (double room) $$$$–$200+; $$$–$141–$200; $$–$81–$140; $–$80 and less.

friend. American regional cuisine is prepared with Rocky Mountain indigenous ingredients—such as piñon-encrusted lamb or elk with wild mushrooms.

You say your kids want to ride the gondolas for dinner too? Take the family to **Der Fondue Chessel** ($$$), also at The Outpost at the top of North Peak. Enjoy fondue, raclette and wine (not for the kids, of course) with music by a Bavarian band.

In Lakeside Village, Keystone Lodge's **Bighorn Steakhouse** ($$-$$$) is renowned for its cuts of tender prime rib and its 16-ounce Cowboy Rib Eye Steak, hand cut and served on the bone in barbecue butter. The atmosphere is casual and relaxed. The **Summit Seafood Company** ($$), in the Keystone Inn, specializes in—what else?—fresh seafood, including mahi mahi, swordfish and even local trout.

For truly casual dining, we got a tasty individual-sized pizza and a draft beer sitting at the bar in the **Snake River Saloon**. But there's a room in back with a more formal sit-down dinner if you want. In the Gateway building just down the road, **The Haywood Cafe** ($-$$) has 12 TVs on its walls and speakers on every table. Across Hwy. 6 in the Mountain View Plaza is **Dos Locos** (970-262-9185; $-$$), a Mexican restaurant that is especially popular during happy hour when the margaritas flow and karaoke goes wild.

At River Run, try **Kickapoo Tavern** ($-$$) for appetizers or light fare such as the turkey chili (a house specialty), burgers, soup or low-priced salads. **The Wolf Rock Brewery** ($$$) is anything but your ordinary tavern. The chefs are creative across the board. **Paisano's** ($-$$) is a family-friendly, casual Italian restaurant. Dinner favors pastas, pastas and more pastas. Breakfast here is known for building your own fritattas and Italian scrambles or a sinful breakfast of Italian toast stuffed with mascarpone. For a lighter breakfast pick up a wrap or bagel sandwich at **The Inxpot** ($).

There's also an excellent selection of restaurants ranging from gourmet to fast food in surrounding Summit County.

Apres-ski/nightlife

Keystone's apres-ski and nightlife has come to life in recent years. Be sure to check out happy hour and apres-ski at the Jimmy Buffet-style **Parrot Eyes** in River Run. Hang out on the deck, delve into burritos, tacos, nachos or tamales and wash it all down with margaritas. Live music five nights a week keeps the apres-ski lively.

Other places for apres-ski activity include **Last Lift Bar** in the Mountain House at Dercum Mountain base, or **Snake River Saloon**, one of Keystone's older establishments that rocks on weekends with live music for dancing. **Tenderfoot Lounge**, in Keystone Lodge, has comfy couches and chairs, piano entertainment and a 15-foot fireplace.

At River Run, **Kickapoo Tavern** draws a crowd on its patio on sunny days and inside on snowy ones. Don't miss the Kickapoo Mountain Joy Juice, a surprisingly potent blend of rums and fruit juices. **Wolf Rock Brewery** is Keystone's only brewery and chophouse. Its handcrafted brews make it another favorite apres-ski scene in River Run. **The Inxpot** brews specialty teas, gourmet coffees and offers a full-service bar. Part coffeehouse, part bar, part bookshop, it's the kind of place that makes you feel like a local.

A "don't miss" is the **Goat**. Here you can catch a game of foosball, grab a beer and soak up the local scene. Warning: The decor is something you'd find in the basement of a fraternity house or at a garage sale in the 1970s. Live music adds even more entertainment.

Sports fans will enjoy **Pizza on the Plaza** in Lakeside Village, where you'll find flat-screen TVs, HDTVs and a big plasma screen. You name the sport, surely it's playing on one of the screens. To dance till you drop, head to Keystone's only nightclub, **Green Light**, in River Run, where the day lodge morphs into a dance party. It's open every weekend until 2 a.m. You'll find other nightlife options throughout Summit County.

Other activities

The Adventure Passport is free with a stay at Keystone Resort's lodging properties. It gives you free activities on and off the mountain, which have included yoga, wine tastings, horse-drawn sleigh rides, ice skating, snowshoeing, cross-country skiing and more. Make sure to take advantage of it. All non-skiing activities are booked by calling the Adventure Center at 800-354-4386 or locally, 970-496-4386.

Adventure Point at the top of Dercum Mountain is the place to head for frighteningly fast tubing and snowbiking. Through the activity center 4Fun, you can book two-hour guided snowmobile tours through the National Forest. Take control and be the driver, or simply ride along as a passenger. Reservations are required at both places. Ice skating in the middle of Keystone Village is open every day and night. The outdoor lake is reportedly the largest Zamboni-maintained outdoor rink in North America. Skate rentals are available. The fitness center at Keystone Lodge features massages, steam room, outdoor heated pool, cardio and weight rooms, and a hot tub.

For warmth after the cold, head to the brand new spa at the Keystone Lodge & Spa (800-468-5004), now the largest spa in Summit County. Designed with lots of natural light, it features an aromatherapy infinity tub and a Vichy shower room. In the Gateway Building, a full-service day spa, **Serenity Spa & Salon** (970-513-9002), uses natural products from world-renowned Aveda. The spa menu also lists a full array of salon services, including manicures for men.

If you need medical care, the **Keystone Medical Center** (970-468-6677) is as good as it gets in Colorado. Operated by Vail Valley Medical Centers, this facility has a "level V" trauma center designation which means whatever you've got, they can fix. Altitude sickness, broken bones, gashes, sprung knees and beyond, these people are experts. Oxygen available; 1252 County Rd., call for hours.

Also check out surrounding Summit County for other activities.

Getting there and getting around

By air: Denver International Airport is 90 miles away via I-70. Book transportation between the airport and the resort with the central reservations number, 800-427-8308. Colorado Mountain Express (800-525-6363) has regular vans between the resort and airport. For personalized private charter limos, vans and suburbans, make reservations with VailCoach (877-554-7433).

By car: Take I-70 west from Denver, through the Eisenhower Tunnel, to Dillon at Exit 205. Head east for 6 miles on Hwy. 6.

Getting around: Within Keystone an excellent free shuttle system runs continuously starting at 7:30 a.m. In the evenings the shuttles run every 20 minutes until mid-night on weeknights and until 2 a.m. on Fridays and Saturdays. Bartenders and hotel doormen will call the shuttle to ensure pickup in the evenings and late night, 970-496-4200. If you're staying and skiing mostly at Keystone, you won't need a car. The Summit Stage provides free transportation between Dillon, Silverthorne, Frisco, Breckenridge and Copper Mountain. Call 970-668-0999 for route information.

Dining: $$$$–Entrees $30+; $$$–$20–$30; $$–$10–$20; $–less than $10.

Accommodations: (double room) $$$$–$200+; $$$–$141–$200; $$–$81–$140; $–$80 and less.

Nearby resorts

Arapahoe Basin, Arapahoe Basin, CO; 888-272-7246

Internet: www.arapahoebasin.com; 7 lifts; 900 acres; 2,270 vertical feet; 2 terrain parks

Arapahoe Basin—or A-Basin, as the locals call it—is legendary for many things. It has the highest skiable terrain in North America (the summit tops out at 13,050 feet). It has some of the steepest terrain inside a resort's boundaries. It has one of the longest ski seasons in North America (usually ending in June, sometimes July). It has a relaxed, no-frills attitude—the type of place where few strive to wear matching ski outfits. Regulars affectionately called it The Legend.

Two above-timberline bowls dominate the upper half of the mountain which tops out on the Continental Divide. On a clear day, the view is amazing. But the real gestalt of A-Basin lies to the right of the Pallavicini Lift. The super-steep "Pali" side of A-Basin is for the strong and hardy who brave rocks, bumps and gullies. Making it down Pali is a rite of passage.

Montezuma Bowl is a mix of intermediate, advanced and expert cornices, chutes, glades and bowls, and has backcountry areas for adventurers who like to hike. A few runs are groomed nightly, but for the most part the 36 trails remain as nature designed them.

For all its gnarly reputation, A-Basin has excellent intermediate and beginner terrain on its front side. With its central base area, kids can't get lost and stress is minimal because it's rarely crowded. The highest chairs serve a slew of delightful intermediate trails. The above-treeline slopes mean runs are wide open and you can let your skis choose your path. A-Basin does a great job of grooming, but there's plenty of ungroomed terrain for those who like it au natural. The beginner trails wind down from the Exhibition chairlift. Wrangler is a very wide, flat trail that builds confidence. Chisholm and Sundance are the next steps up.

Not surprisingly, this is a tele-skier's dream mountain. Perhaps it's the laid-back attitude, perhaps it's the proud touting of its purist roots, perhaps it's the terrain that mimics the nearby backcountry. Whatever the reason, 15 percent of A-Basin's guests are telemark skiers.

As for snowboarders: Forget spring break in Mexico. There's nothing like A-Basin's spring corn snow, with a frequent overnight dose of powder. Riding varies from cornice jumps off of the Norway Lift to sweeping beginner and intermediate runs. With a quick hike, the East Wall delivers treeless powder runs with an intermittent jump or two. Bigger air hits can be found in the Rock Garden off of the Pallavicini Lift along with some rowdy, tree-lined chutes. On the lower part of the mountain, North Fork's natural berms and bumps are also worth a diversion.

A-Basin's main park, Treeline Terrain Park has rails, tabletops, boxes and a Huckster Jump for catching big air. This park—the highest in North America—is usually open into June when it really rocks. Beginners should try High Divide, a new park built on Sundance last season.

A new 7,200-square-foot building houses the rental and repair shop. Look for a new restaurant atop Exhibition Lift.

Lift tickets (2007/08 prices): Adults, $58; youth (15-19) $47 and seniors (60-69), $48; child (6-14), $25; and 70 and older, $10; ages 5 and younger, free. One child skis free with a full-price adult lift ticket. Prices for adults and youth/seniors are lower during spring. Though Vail Resorts doesn't own A-Basin, it has arranged for Keystone/Breckenridge lift tickets to be valid at A-Basin too. To get there, drive west on I-70 from Denver International Airport. Exit at Silverthorne/Dillon (in Summit County), then go 12 miles east on U.S. 6, past Keystone. It's about a 96-mile total drive.

Lodging information: Summit County Chamber, (800) 530-3099 or (970) 262-0817.

Beaver Creek
Colorado

Summit:	11,440 feet
Vertical:	4,040 feet
Base:	8,100 feet

Address: P.O. Box 7, Vail, Colorado 81658
Telephone (main): 970-845-9090 or 800-404-3535
Snow Report Number: 800-404-3535
Toll-free reservations: 800-404-3535
Reservations outside U.S.: 800-404-3535
E-mail: bcinfo@vailresorts.com
Internet: www.beavercreek.com
Expert:★★★
Advanced:★★★★
Intermediate:★★★★
Beginner:★★★★
First-timer:★★★

Lifts: 16 total: 10 high-speed quads, 2 triples, 2 doubles, 1 surface lift, 1 kids' gondola
Skiable acreage: 1,805
Snowmaking: 35 percent
Uphill capacity: 30,739
Parks & pipes: 3 parks, 1 pipe
Bed base: 3,741 at resort; 4,000 in Avon
Nearest lodging: Slopeside, hotels and condos
Child care: Yes, 2 months and older
Adult ticket, per day: Variable
Dining:★★★★
Apres-ski/nightlife:★
Other activities:★★★

Beaver Creek is one of the top luxury resorts in the country. It has everything you need for a top-notch vacation, and it doesn't have to empty your bank account—but it can if you're not careful.

The gated lower entrance of Beaver Creek Resort sets the tone for the privileged environment you will experience higher up. Beyond the multi-million-dollar homes lining Village Road, the resort sits like a crown jewel topping the mountain chain eight miles west of Vail. The resort is made up of three villages—Bachelor Gulch, Arrowhead and Beaver Creek knit together with a series of ski trails, a unique concept in American ski country.

The central complex at Beaver Creek Village is pedestrian-only with snow-free walkways, and upscale shops and restaurants are scattered throughout. The Vilar Center for the Arts features top entertainment and it, along with the outdoor ice rink, is the centerpiece. Four sets of covered escalators whisk skiers and snowboarders from the base to the Centennial Express lift.

More luxurious than big sister Vail, the Beaver Creek experience is carefully scripted to appeal to A-list guests—and their children. Underscoring the resort's attention to the little people, it installed not just a lift, but a gondola just for kids.

Pretentiousness is wearing off as the resort comes of age, but evidence of its ambitious youth remains. No one will ask for a copy of last year's tax return to verify your earnings, of course. Yet it's clear that this isn't a place for penny-pinchers, or even the budget-conscious.

But you don't have to go broke to truly enjoy the Beaver Creek experience. Just don't stay in the village-- stay in a nearby town like Edwards or Avon. Avon has a good shuttle system and now the Riverfront Express Gondola (new in 07/08), a vehicle than runs between the town's transit center and Beaver Creek Landing. From here, two lifts deliver you in 14 minutes to the main mountain's advanced beginner (and above) trails.

Mountain layout

To ski at Beaver Creek is to ski on corduroy. If you're an expert or advanced skier, don't let this drive you away. Beaver Creek leaves much of your terrain alone, such as Stone Creek Chutes and the Talons' long and steep bump runs where you'll find plenty of challenge. Other distinguishing features: a conspicuous absence of lift lines and copious snowmaking abilities.

Expert, Advanced: When Beaver Creek opened in 1980, its first runs were mostly beginner and intermediate. Some still think of it—mistakenly—as a cruiser mountain. Not so: Advanced skiers and experts should spend at least a day here, maybe more. Our advice is to choose a weekend, when the lines can climb over the 15-20-minute barrier at Vail, yet are nonexistent here.

What's surprising is the amount of truly tough stuff. The Birds of Prey runs rival anything Vail offers--all long, steep and mogul-studded. If you want to feel like a world-class racer, the downhill course, one of the most difficult in the world, is groomed as often as possible for a long and super-fast double-diamond cruiser. While somewhat shorter, Ripsaw and Cataract in Rose Bowl, and Loco in Larkspur Bowl, are equally challenging. Stone Creek Chutes are short but steep pitches of up to 45 degrees. Grouse Mountain is strictly for black-diamond types, no matter what the trail map may suggest. Only in spring, when slushier snow slows skiers down, should such runs as Screech Owl, Falcon Park and Royal Elk Glades be attempted by thrill-seeking advanced skiers.

Intermediate: Beaver Creek is an excellent resort for intermediates at every level. For those intermediates bordering on advanced, the runs under the Centennial Express lift are long and have a moderately steep pitch—enough to be exciting, but not the kind to scare you out of your bindings. If you can catch these runs after a grooming, the black-diamond-designated sections are definitely within the abilities of upper-intermediates. Centennial, the main run in this area, is not the best choice for a warm-up if the resort hasn't had snow in a while. It's in the shade early in the morning, and everyone uses it, so the surface can get skied off and a bit slick (but it's a super run under good conditions). Don't miss Harrier, to the skier's left of Centennial, when it's been groomed. Another great intermediate route from Centennial Express is Redtail to the Larkspur Lift, then descend down Larkspur Bowl.

Early in the morning, the runs under the Strawberry Park lift are in the sun. We recommend Pitchfork for your warm-up, and a couple of the runs in the Bachelor Gulch area for a follow-up. Arrowhead is another good choice for intermediates, though its southerly exposure means thin snow at the tail end of dry spells.

Beginner, First-timer: The easiest runs are at the top, accessed by the Centennial Express and Birds of Prey Express lifts. Once you reach the top, head over to Red Buffalo, Mystic Island and the other runs in the Slow Zone. Ride the Drink of Water lift again and again, because this area has no intermediate or expert runs where faster skiers will zip past you at high speeds. Flattops, Piney and Powell, to the other side of the Birds of Prey lift, are wide and gentle. You get back to Beaver Creek Village on a long, clearly marked beginner run (it's really a cat track) called Cinch. The Arrowhead section also is good for beginners, with a winding run called Piece O' Cake.

For first-timers, Beaver Creek's learning area is at the base, served by two lifts.

Parks and pipes

Centennial brings you right to the Moonshine Terrain Park. With every type of rail imaginable, logslides, hips, spines and some nice-sized tabletops—plus a yurt with foosball, cable TV and beverages—Moonshine Terrain Park is great for everyone from the intermediate on up. The superpipe is at the top of the intermediate Latigo run. From the expert who's working on backside rodeos, to the advanced rider learning how to do frontside airs, it's the ideal pipe to perfect your style and to get away from the crowds that some of the other mountains draw.

Zoom Room is a progressive beginner to intermediate park. It begins with smaller introductory features--including rollers, small tables and small rails--and moves to progressively larger features and rails. Park 101 has rollers, dots and other terrain features that allow lower-level riders and skiers of all ages to learn weighting and unweighting of boards and skis.

Snowboarding

Riding at "The Beav" is an experience all its own. With so much grooming and round the clock snowmaking, the runs can have a consistency that's sometimes almost too perfect. Don't worry, though, because the natural deep powder can still be found almost all season--just look in the woods. The woods are actually Beaver Creek's No. 1 asset to snowboarders. Powder lines, world-class log slides that will make any skateboarder envious and cliff lines abound, making The Beav one of the favorites among Colorado locals in the know. Be sure to check the trail map for snowboard gladed zones.

Beginners should stay away from Cinch. It's a beginner's nightmare: Intermediate and advanced riders should have no problem maintaining their speed on this cat track, but to the first-time rider, it's literally a speed death-sentence.

Cross-country & snowshoeing (see also xcskiresorts.com)

For a truly different Nordic experience at an Alpine ski area, head to **McCoy Park** at the top of the Strawberry Park Express Lift. Instead of skiing on the flats (usually a golf course) at the base of a ski area, you'll be on a 32-km. system at the summit, 9,840 feet, with spectacular views in every direction.

Tours, lessons and rentals are available. The park also has snowshoe rentals and tours. One such full-day tour includes a gourmet lunch; snowshoe tours include rental equipment. For more information on Nordic activities, call the Beaver Creek Nordic Center at 970-845-5313.

Lessons (07/08 prices)

Lessons meet at the base area near the Centennial Express lift. Instruction is available in nearly 30 languages. Call the Beaver Creek Ski and Snowboard School at (800) 475-4543 or (970) 845-5300.

Group lessons: A full-day group is $130. A great deal, available only during select times, is the 3-Peat Series: three consecutive adult lessons of any ability level for $260.

First-time series package: This great deal for ages 15 and up offers three consecutive full days of group lessons with lift tickets for $200 (an additional $65 with rentals).

First-time snowboarders also can take a Burton Learn-to-Ride clinic that uses special Burton snowboards, bindings and boots designed to reduce the difficulty of learning to ride: $265 for the three-day lift/lesson/rental package.

Private lessons: $465 for a half-day, $665 for a full day (for one to six people). Lessons include video analysis. Reservations are highly recommended.

Racing: Two NASTAR courses and a coin-op course are next to the Centennial run.

Children's programs (07/08 prices)

Child care: Ages 2 months to 6 years. Full-day program costs $115 during regular season. Reservations required; call (970) 845-5325. Hours are 8 a.m. to 4:30 p.m.

With one main base area, Beaver Creek is a good place to bring kids. The ski school and child-care center are right in the base village, although the Small World Play School is a bit hard to find. After crossing the covered bridge that leads into the village, turn left and walk down the stairs until you see the sign to your right.

Other options: The Park Hyatt (970-949-1234) offers programs for children, as well as babysitting, days and evenings. Baby's Away (800-369-9030; 970-328-1285) rents and delivers baby needs, such as cribs, strollers, high chairs, car seats and toys.

Children's lessons: Lessons are available for children as young as 3 years old (toilet-trained). Ski lessons are offered for kids 3–14; snowboarding lessons are for ages 7–14. Cost is $165 during regular season and includes lesson, lift and lunch. Teens 15+ can take all-day lessons for $165 (lifts and rentals extra) with organized teen groups during the holidays.

Reservations are not required, except for kids ages 3–6. Register for all lessons at 8 a.m. or pre-register the day before; you also can register online at the website. Call (970) 845-5464 for information. Beaver Creek encourages kids younger than age 14 enrolled in ski and snow-board programs to wear helmets. Rentals are available; if you don't want your child to wear a helmet, you must decline in writing in order for your child to participate. The Children's Ski and Snowboard School is in Village Hall.

Skiing with your kids: Like Vail, Beaver Creek is sprinkled with Kids Adventure Zones. Kids can search out such haunts as the Tombstone Territory or the Hibernating Bear Cave. Most are located off Cinch near the top of the Centennial Lift.

Lift tickets (07/08 prices)

	Adult (13-64)	Child (5-12)
One day	$89	$54
Three of five days	$267 ($89/day)	$162 ($54/day)
Five of eight days	$445 ($89/day)	$270 ($54/day)

Who skis free: Ages 4 and younger.

Who skis at a discount: Ages 65+ pay $79 for one day; $237 for three days and $395 for five days.

Vail, which owns Beaver Creek, offers PEAKS discounted tickets if you pre-purchase online a three-day or more ticket at least seven days in advance (international guests must buy 14 days in advance). Membership in PEAKS is free and you are automatically enrolled when you make your early purchase. Vail has a handful of pricing periods, so check carefully to see what the prices are when you plan to visit. Some pricing periods look the same until you consider longer stays.

Interchangeability: All lift tickets also are valid at sister resorts Vail, Keystone and Breckenridge, as well as at nearby Arapahoe Basin.

Accommodations

Beaver Creek lodging is expensive. It's tough to find a room for less than $200 per night, unless you want to vacation pre-Christmas or in April.

Consistently rated among the top hotels in the world, the ski-in/ski-out **Park Hyatt Beaver Creek Resort & Spa** (800-233-1234; 970-949-1234; $$$$) recently completed $20 million in improvements and the expansion of Allegria spa to 30,000 square feet, making it one of the largest and innovative spas in the country. There's also a heated outdoor pool, whirlpools, fitness rooms and marvelous lobby lounge as well as concierge and ski attendant services. The five restaurants and lounges address all styles of dining.

Chateau Residence Club (970-949-1616; $$$$) offers private luxury hillside condos with all the amenities of a hotel: concierge, daily maid service, a great restaurant and lounge, etc. It echoes the castle-like elegance of the Banff Springs Hotel with suites starting at $750 per night with a three-night minimum. .

The Ritz-Carlton, Bachelor Gulch (800-241-3333; 970-748-6200; $$$$) is architecturally inspired by the grand lodges of Yellowstone, Grand Teton and Yosemite National Parks. It delivers, as promised, seclusion, luxury and excellence. All guestrooms have separate showers and marble bathtubs; Frette linens and feather beds with duvets and goose down and non-allergenic foam pillows; DVD players and other high-end amenities.

The Pines Lodge (800-859-8242; $$$$;), a RockResorts condo-hotel near the Strawberry Park lift, is a member of Preferred Hotels and Resorts Worldwide. Guests can enjoy a hot tub, heated outdoor pool, fitness room and massage therapy. It has an award-winning restaurant (see Dining).

The Inn at Beaver Creek (800-859-8242; $$-$$$$) ski-in/ski-out lodging on a far smaller scale than the Park Hyatt, has 37 rooms and eight suites with a free hot gourmet breakfast.

The Beaver Creek Lodge (800-525-7280; 970-845-9800; $$-$$$$) is the only all-suite resort in the Vail Valley. The 71 units have living rooms, fireplaces, and TVs with VCRs. Once guests find the lobby to check in, the rest is easy.

The Centennial Lodge (800-845-7060; $$$$) claims to have the best prices on the mountain, but doesn't provide full hotel service. It has underground parking and a pool. This lodge has some condos and three hotel rooms. Both the Centennial Lodge and **Creekside Lodge** (970-949-7071; $$$$) are in the village.

The Poste Montane (800-497-9238; 970-845-7500; $$-$$$$) has heated underground parking and is smack in the middle of Beaver Creek Village, as is **St. James Place** (800-859-8242; 970-845-9300; $$$$).

The Borders Lodge (800-846-0233; 970-926-2300; $$-$$$$) is a comfortable ski-in/ski-out condominium complex next to Chair 14, within easy walk of the village. Its condos range in size from one to three bedrooms and the list of facilities includes two outdoor hot tubs and year-round pool. Note that restrictions are more severe than for a hotel reservation. Hefty cancellation fees apply, so read the fine print before booking.

Book **Trappers Cabin**(970-845-9090; $$$$) for a high-end, first-class adventure. It's a plush, four-bedroom log chateau at 9,500 feet, one of the only overnight moutaintop lodgings at US ski resorts. Meals are prearranged and first tracks are right out your door.

Elkhorn Lodge (888-485-4317; 970-845-2270; $$$$) has studios and one- to four-bedroom condos and penthouses with ski-in/ski-out convenience adjacent to the Elkhorn Lift (Chair 14). Amenities include fully equipped kitchens, fireplaces, balconies, spa tubs in the bathrooms, two outdoor hot tubs and a fitness area.

The Charter (800-525-6660; 970-949-6660; $$-$$$$), an award-winning property, which bills itself as having "all of the conveniences of a condominium with all of the luxuries of a world-class hotel," gives guests more of the typical Beaver Creek amenities. One- through five-bedroom units are available. Two restaurants offer menus to suit anyone's tastes.

In the town of Avon, the valley's best condo deals at the **Christie Lodge** (800-551-4320; 970-949-7700; $$-$$$$). Or, you can stay in the town of Edwards, about 5 miles from Beaver Creek. One possibility there is **The Inn at Riverwalk** (888-926-0606; 970-926-0606; $$-$$$). **VailNet** (www.vail.net) has a very good lodging search feature that will suggest lodging according to location, amenities and price.

Dining

Beaver Creek is infatuated with the term "gourmet." Everything, right down to the garden-variety burger, is designated gourmet. Plus, these Colorado chefs do love their spices. The dishes we tried featured gratuitous amounts of onions, garlic

Dining: $$$$–Entrees $30+; $$$–$20–$30; $$–$10–$20; $–less than $10.
Accommodations: (double room) $$$$–$200+; $$$–$141–$200; $$–$81–$140; $–$80 and less.

and exotic flavors.

Splendido at The Chateau (970-845-8808; $$$$) is very popular for locals, especially for special occasions. Many regulars come for the piano player, Taylor Kundolf, but chef David Walford has a huge following for his succulent game and international finesse with offerings such as roasted Maine sea scallops and fried sweetbreads. The wine cellar is vast. .

Mirabelle (970-949-7728; $$$-$$$$), a longtime local favorite at the bottom of the resort access road in an old farmhouse, serves well-prepared Belgian-influenced nouvelle cuisine. Excellent wine list with selections in many prices.

SaddleRidge (970-845-5450; $$$-$$$$) showcases the country's largest private collection of Western artifacts outside of a museum. It's open for dinner with a game-dominated a la carte menu. After dessert take a look at the saddle with Buffalo Bill's sketch impressed into the leather--the image is his own handiwork.

Grouse Mountain Grill (970-949-0600; $$$$), adjacent to the Pines Lodge, serves Rocky Mountain cuisine, featuring Colorado lamb and pretzel-crusted pork chops. The elegant European interior is intimate, all the more so because of the nightly jazz pianist who performs during dinner.

In Market Square, follow your nose to **Toscanini** (970-845-5590; $$-$$$$), a busy Italian restaurant overlooking the outdoor ice rink and featuring excellent seafood and pasta dishes. Special children's menu selections are available.

Beaver Creek Chophouse (970-845-0555; $$$) serves certified Angus beef and live Maine lobster in a slopeside location with a fantastic view.

A fairly new addition to the village center is **Foxnut Asian Fusion & Sushi** (970-845-0700; $$$). Its trendy interior of bright pink walls hung with Asian magazine ads, chartreuse booths and hanging lanterns deviates from the elegant Beaver Creek norm, but sushi fans love it.

Rocks Modern Grill (970-845-1730; $$$) is in the newly remodeled Beaver Creek Lodge and serves classic American food for breakfast, lunch and dinner. Dinner in the private wine room can be set up with a reservation.

By Beaver Creek standards, **traMonti** (970-949-5552, $$-$$$$) is one of the more inexpensive places to eat, with meat entrees between $20 and $30, and pastas less than that. It's in the Charter at Beaver Creek Hotel and serves pastas and risottos, and Northern Italian-prepared veal, steak, chicken and seafood.

Chef Pascal at slopeside **Bivans** (970-949-1234; $$-$$$) in the Park Hyatt Beaver Creek created the family-friendly menu and free s'more-gasbord happy hour around the fire pits. Now he's come up with the best meal deal in Beaver Creek: the Park Burger—a 6-ounce tenderloin burger surrounded by Porcini mushrooms, potato rosti and salad, topped off with a 6-ounce cookie with homemade ice cream and a glass of wine—all for $25.

Besides moving to a new location in the Poste Montane and expanding its space, the **Blue Moose** (970-845-8666; $$-$) also expanded its menu from pizza to a wide variety of Italian dishes.

The Golden Eagle (970-949-1940; $$-$$$) is a less costly, though not less exotic, place to dine. With entrees such as medallions of Australian kangaroo and roast loin of elk on the menu, guests can take a culinary world tour without leaving their seats.

Wolfgang Puck opens **Spago** at the Ritz-Carlton in Bachelor Gulch in November '07. We haven't tried it yet, but we know it will be in keeping with his commitment to serving fresh organic food from local farmers. The 126-seat restaurant should be a winner.

In Avon try **The Vista Brasserie** (970-949-3366; $$) for good American fare and **Fiesta Jalisco** (970-845-8088; $$) for tasty Mexican meals. **Masato's Sushi Bar** (970-949-0330; $$-$$$), the Chapel Square complex, has great sushi chefs and reasonably priced Japanese food. **Ti**

Amo (970-845-8153; $$-$$$) is Avon's best for good-value Italian. Or try the town of Edwards, just west of Avon. The **Gore Range Brewery** has outrageous salads, wood-fired thin-crust pizza, and peel-and-eat shrimp. There's also a very hip sushi restaurant called **Sato's** (970-926-7684). At Arrowhead, you can plop down under a blanket on a beach chair next to the fire pit and scarf down a Blinky Burger made famous by Blinky Blunk, the burger maker at **Broken Arrow Cafe.**at the base of the lift. It's *the* spot for apres ski at this village until 6 p.m.

Don't miss a wonderfully memorable dining experience at **Beano's Cabin** (970-949-9090, book early; $$$$). Groups are bundled onto a 40-person sleigh and pulled up the mountain under the stars by a snow-cat. The cabin always has a roaring fire going and well-prepared cuisine that incorporates organic food. Choose from a four-course meal or a chef's five-course blind tasting menu (for the adventurous diner).

Equally delightful is **Zach's Cabin** (970-845-6575, book early; $$$-$$$$), the newest addition to fine dining in Beaver Creek up on the mountain between Arrowhead and Bachelor Gulch Villages. Similar in concept to Beano's Cabin, this 13,000-square-foot cabin is nestled in a grove of aspen trees and guests arrive on a snowcat-drawn sleigh. The Cabin is open to the public for a la carte dinner Wednesday through Saturday nights throughout the winter season, and is available for private functions throughout the year. Both of these outstanding restaurants hold "Best Of" Awards of Excellence from Wine Spectator.

The village doesn't have a lot of choices for your first meal of the day. **Bivans** ($$) at the Park Hyatt has full breakfast buffet, featuring omelets made-to-order. You can get eggs, pancakes and waffles at **McCoy's** ($), a cafeteria set-up at the base of the mountain. For muffin-and-coffee breakfast fans, **Starbucks** is one level down from the Centennial Express lift. **Beaver Creek Chophouse** in the Beaver Creek Lodge serves an American continental breakfast.

 ## Apres-ski/nightlife

Asked what nightlife was worth a look, one worker first told us, "There isn't anything," then after a bit of thinking, amended her response to, "Well, there are some meeting places." The first place to stop on the way back to town from the Larkspur Bowl is **The Talons Deck at Red Tail Camp**, where revelers gather to begin apres-ski. In the spring, the deck is packed and Sundays mean live entertainment al fresco.

The Coyote Cafe would surely qualify as a meeting place, particularly among locals like the Beaver Creek Ski Patrol, at the end of the day. This Mexican cantina/watering hole caters to locals, and with well-drink and draught-beer specials at the end of the day, its prices are reasonable. Don't plan on staying out late--it closes at 11 p.m. (as late as 1 a.m. on hopping nights). If you're young and looking for apres-ski, this is it.

McCoy's is the place to go for live apres-ski entertainment as soon as you leave the slopes. Also try the **Dusty Boot Saloon**, where you'll find 46-ounce margaritas and a comprehensive tequila list. **Blue Moose** has great pizza and a fun atmosphere, and the lowest prices in Beaver Creek Village.

The Park Hyatt's **Whiskey Elk** bar, which stays open until 2 a.m., features entertainment from local musicians and serves small batch bourbons, single malt scotch, ports and wine by the glass. The fire pits get stoked when dark falls, and the s'more-gasbord loaded with sweet makings for that old campfire standby is served free to hotel guests. Families love it.

The best deck in Beaver Creek might be at the **Chophouse** (970-845-0555). While you watch the sunset with drinks and occasional live music, a magician entertains kids and adults six afternoons a week.

Dining: $$$$–Entrees $30+; $$$–$20–$30; $$–$10–$20; $–less than $10.
Accommodations: (double room) $$$$–$200+; $$$–$141–$200; $$–$81–$140; $–$80 and less.

Other activities

The **Vilar Center for the Arts** (888-920-2787; 970-845-8497) is a 528-seat performing arts center snuggled under the ice rink in Beaver Creek. It's modeled after a turn-of-the-century theater in Munich and presents world-class entertainment four to six nights a week. The year-round outdoor **Black Family Ice Rink** is in the heart of Beaver Creek. Ice skating exhibitions are held here periodically in the winter.

If you need to restore mind and body (like those sore skiing legs), visit one of Beaver Creek's **spas**. Treat yourself to an afternoon at the **Allegria Spa** (970-748-7500) at the Park Hyatt Beaver Creek Resort (see lodging), where the Feng Shui design encourages relaxation. It has 23 treatment rooms, a quiet sanctuary room, and private whirlpool tubs in the locker rooms. Treatments include a variety of massages, scrubs, facials, innovative water therapies, hot oil wraps, hair services, manicures and pedicures and Feng Shui-inspired rituals for balance, peace and energy.

Every Thursday night, level-five and higher skiers are invited to join in on **Thursday Night Lights**, a ski-down with glow sticks followed by a huge fireworks show. Register at the Children's Ski and Snowboard School. The resort concierge (970-845-9090) can make reservations for other activities, such as **dogsledding, snowmobiling, snowshoeing, fly fishing, ice fishing** and **sleigh ride dinners**.

A fun free activity is the **Rail Jam** every Thursday from 4-5 p.m. in front of the kids' ski school. Kids and their parents can practice rail slides and get tips from instructors. Also kids' tubing takes place a few nights of the week. For teens, there's a video arcade.

Beautiful **boutiques** line the pedestrian walkway in the heart of the resort. A special stop on your list should be The Golden Bear, just west of the skating rink in Beaver Creek. It's owned by local women whose logo is the golden bear (it's Vail's logo too), which you can find in all forms of jewelry and art. Great stylish clothes and other special gifts tempt the wallet.

Getting there and getting around

By air: Flights land at the Vail/Eagle County airport, about 35 miles west of Vail, and the Denver International Airport, 110 miles east. Eagle County airport is served by American, Northwest, Delta, Continental, United Express and United with non-stop flights from 14 major U.S. cities.

Ground transportation between Denver and Vail is frequent and convenient. The trip to Vail takes about two-and-a-half hours. Contact Colorado Mountain Express (800-525-6363); Vail Valley Taxi (877-829-8294; 970-476-8294); or Airport Transportation Service (970-476-7576). For personalized private charter limos, vans and suburbans, make resrevations with VailCoach (877-554-7433). Though flights into Denver may be a bit less expensive than Eagle, also consider the cost of round-trip ground transportation, where per person rates from Denver are about double those from Eagle.

By car: Beaver Creek and Vail are right on I-70, 100 miles west of Denver and 140 miles east of Grand Junction. Beaver Creek is 10 miles west of Vail and just three miles up from Avon.

Getting around: Beaver Creek is very self-contained. There is a complimentary shuttle called Dial-a-Ride that takes you anywhere within the Beaver Creek Villages between 6 a.m. and 2 a.m. daily. The shuttle is like a taxi, so ask your concierge or restaurant hostess to call (970-949-1938), and allow 10-15 minutes for pickup. Shuttles between Beaver Creek and Vail cost $3. If you plan to commute frequently between Vail and Beaver Creek, or if you are staying in one of the outlying towns such as Edwards or Minturn, you may want to rent a car.

Crested Butte
Colorado

Summit (lift-served): 11,875 feet	
Vertical:	**2,775 feet**
Base (lowest lift):	**9,100 feet**

Address: P.O. Box 5700,
12 Snowmass Road,
Mt. Crested Butte, CO 81225
Telephone (main): 970-349-2222
Snow Report Number: 888-349-2323
Toll-free reservations: 800-810-7669
or 800-810-7669
Reservations outside US: 970-349-2222
E-mail: info@cbmr.com
Internet: www.skicb.com
Expert:★★★★★ **Advanced:**★★★
Intermediate:★★★★
Beginner:★★★★
First-timer:★★★★

Lifts: 15—4 high-speed quads, 2 quads, 2 triples, 2 doubles, 3 surface lifts, 2 moving carpets
Skiable acreage: 1,125
Snowmaking: 25 percent (282 acres)
Uphill capacity: 20,000
Parks & pipes: 2 parks, 2 pipes
Bed base: 5,550
Nearest lodging: Slopeside
Child care: Yes, 6 months and older
Adult ticket, per day: $82 (08/09 prices)
Dining:★★★★★
Apres-ski/nightlife:★★★★
Other activities:★★★

Crested Butte is one of those perfect all-around resorts. Terrain serves every level of skier well, facilities are top-notch and the historic mining town offers plenty of diversions.

While the mountain, it is a changin' under the new ownership of Tim and Diane Mueller, Crested Butte is still the "anti resort" of Colorado—that is, anti-glitz, yet with all the amenities and spectacular scenery for which the state is famous.

Funky, laid-back and friendly are oft-heard descriptions of the Crested Butte experience. When you walk into any restaurant or bar in town, it doesn't matter if you're a janitor or a Fortune 500 CEO, you'll be treated with the same warmth and respect—as long as you leave your "big-city" attitude outside. Award-winning wine bars mingle with cook-your-own hot dog stands. Five-star lodging overlooks local hangout shacks in the woods. The apres-ski scene is rich at the resort's base, especially in spring, when lounging is best on the numerous large, sunny decks. Just down the road, the National Historic District of the town of Crested Butte bursts with charm and authentic Wild West. All this is what sets Crested Butte apart from other resorts.

Extreme terrain is Crested Butte's signature and for good reason. With an expanse of more than 500 acres of double-blacks, it's a lift-served backcountry world. In fact, locals who have skied and snowboarded here for years claim to not have had enough time to fully explore the possible lines. That's not hard to believe. Some traverses require a lot of work and take you across exposed steeps. Since there are so many excellent choices for dropping in, it's easy to give up and leave the untouched bounty beyond for more patient—and perhaps intrepid—souls.

Beginners and intermediates can find plenty of fun as well. The mountain is laid out in such a way as to keep beginner and intermediate skiers and riders safely on easier runs. Recent development has, in fact, made us wish we were beginners all over again. Not only is the beginner terrain gentle and extensive, it has its own midmountain cabin with in-your-face views of the main mountain, plus food service and outdoor seating. From this same mid-mountain cabin, intermediates can access blue runs off the backside that are sure to bring grins, whether the preference might be groomers, rollicking wood shots or trails left au natural.

 ## Mountain layout

Our base elevation in the **stats box** is at the point of the lowest lift, East River. The base area where the facilities are located is about 200 feet higher, at 9,375 feet. Our stats reflect lift-served access—you can hike to the 12,162-foot summit for a 3,062-foot-vertical descent.

Be aware that the trail map warns of extreme terrain, marked "EX" on the mountain, but not labeled on the map itself. It is possible at any time while on double-blacks to come upon sections with EX trail signs. Anyone who plans to spend extensive time in the Extreme Limits should consider buying the Extreme Limits Ski Guide, a trail map that covers this territory in depth.

Free guided tours meet daily at 9:45 a.m. to help guests learn their way around the mountain.

Expert, Advanced: It's advisable to make friends with a local or a mountain guide before venturing off into Crested Butte's steeps. They are filled with cliff bands, so be sure to know your line before jumping in. The hardcore runs are the infamous Extreme Limits. Pitches average 39 to 44 degrees, and extreme terrain is described by the Ski Safety Act as "cliffs with a minimum 20 foot rise over a 15 foot run and slopes with a minimum 50 degree average pitch over a 100 foot run."

To test your mettle on something difficult, but not too hairy, try Peel (just off the Silver Queen lift). Anything in this vicinity offers the longest amount of vertical. For a chute that's wide enough for some error but sure to give you rubber legs because of its 2,000-foot descent, try the 40-plus-degree Banana and its sister chute Funnel. To find where the untracked snow stays longest, work your way out to the farthest reaches of Teocalli Bowl and Third Bowl. If the weather and snow conditions are right, consider hiking to the summit, taking in the view, and floating turns down The Peak or Hall of Fame.

Note: You can hire a mountain guide for the Extreme Limits for $30 per person, and that's a steal of a deal.

Crested Butte's single-blacks are long, bumpy and fun. The well-traveled ones are under the Silver Queen lift, but the Twister lift is the local secret. Try anything in that area. While it is in the middle of everything, it doesn't get the traffic you would expect. The Double-Top Glades served by the East River Lift are a nice test of your skills.

Crested Butte doesn't have many single-diamonds and the double-diamonds are demanding. If you're adventurous, try the double-blacks that are just off lifts, which will cut down on long and exposed traverses—Peel, The Glades, Rachel's, and Half Pipe Gully into Headwall are good choices. If you prefer groomed terrain, you'll be relegated mostly to the realm of the blue-square, which can give you a rush but won't be challenging.

Intermediate: Crested Butte has added intermediate terrain, all linked by conveniently placed lifts, making it easy to work your way across the mountain to get to increasingly more demanding runs. Warm up on the Gold Link and Prospect lifts, exclusively serving intermediates. From here, head to the Teocalli and East River lifts for yet more isolation from faster skiers.

When you're ready for a big-mountain experience, Paradise Bowl awaits, giving you a taste of powder on good days. Explore this area and find many hidden, yet non-intimidating, nooks and crannies. From this area, put it in auto-drive down lovely, long trails such as Treasury, Ruby Chief, Forest Queen, Bushwacker and Gallowich.

Advanced-intermediates can manage most of the runs down from the Silver Queen lift. The short and steep Twister and Crystal both have good bailout routes about halfway down. Lower-intermediates will enjoy the greens off the Red Lady Express.

Kids can find plenty of fun in the glades off the Gold Link, Prospect and Red Lady lifts—they're more like luge runs though the trees. Keep an eye out for the signs with cartoon characters.

Beginner, First-timer: Red Lady Express accesses a nice variety of beginner trails. Wide-open green-circles are plentiful here. For solid beginners and beginner-intermediates this is heaven—all fun runs with no chance of getting in over your head, and few encounters with yahoos going too fast. For a change of scenery, head up Painter Boy Lift and take Gunsight Pass around the back of the mountain to the Teocalli Lift, which drops you off at the top of the same area served by Red Lady Express. Be sure to stop by the midmountain cabin and outdoor seating at the top of the Painter Boy lift when you need a break.

If you have only been on skis a few times or are a timid beginner, you might find some of these runs are more turquoise—greens leaning into blues. In this case, however, you'll be safe if you stick to Houston as well as skiing off the Peachtree and Painter Boy lifts.

Confident beginners should try the wide-open intermediate cruisers off Gold Link.

The resort has a terrific learning setup. First-timers are separated into one area for adults and another for kids, each served by a moving carpet. Kids also have a small snow play zone where they can get used to moving around on skis. Practice for a day or two on the three trails off Peachtree Lift before attempting the Red Lady Express. When you're ready for Red Lady, try Houston first since it's the gentlest. Houston also takes you to Painter Boy Lift.

Parks and pipes

As if the steeps and cliffs aren't enough, Crested Butte has an awesome advanced park along the lower Canaan run. The Canaan Terrain Park, above the Paradise warming house, is long, with good sequences of tabletops, rails and kickers—including a 55-foot monster—that allow for creativity. The wall ride is where you'll really find out just how good you are. Because the park's beneath the Paradise lift, it's the perfect place to collect a bunch of cheers—or jeers—depending on your style.

Crested Butte's 420-foot-long superpipe is also off the Paradise chairlift on Forest Queen. The Zaugg cuts it to be 55 feet wide and 18 feet high with a slope of 17 degrees.

Painter Boy Park at the top of Painter Boy offers solace to those who aren't ready to jump in with the big contenders, -though you'll see some kid riders and skiers here who are pretty hot. Kids as well as adults come here to ride the smaller features and get a feel for tabletops, rail slides and the minipipe.

Snowboarding

Crested Butte as a town harbors no prejudice against those who approach the world a little differently—and that reflects in its attitude toward snowboarders. Welcome. Now strap in and go for a ride. Just make sure to read the notes about cliffs in the **mountain layout section**, and find a local or guide to take you into the Extreme Limits the first couple of times.

A great feature about Crested Butte is the humongous amount of big air you can find, if you're into it. Anywhere experts go off the T-bars is good. The farther out you traverse from the top of these lifts, the less likely you are to see people. The downside is that if you want to do laps all the way to the bottom, it'll take you three or four lifts (depending on your destination) to get back to the top. Of course, this also helps preserve untracked snow.

An excellent choice for true hardcores is the 40-degree Headwall. Once again, the farther you traverse, the less likely you are to cross tracks. But don't go out here if you are not really a seasoned expert. The 12-inch-by-12-inch sign that reads "Cliff Area" actually means that there is a 400-foot-long cliff band below you. If Teocalli Bowl is open, go there immediately.

Off of Silver Queen, traverse to the phenomenally good west-facing chutes. Banana, Peel and Sunset Ridge are the places to be on a spring day, when there's lots of sun and conditions are soft.

Silver Queen takes advanced riders to some of the steeper groomed black runs in the state. Intermediates will have a ball in Paradise Bowl and on the long cruisers that start at the top of Paradise Express and dump you out at the base of the East River Lift. Be ready to feel weak in the legs by the time you reach the bottom. Beginners also have a great selection of trails, most just off the Red Lady Express. But don't skip the midmountain cabin and runs off Painter Boy Lift.

Flats are unavoidable here, as they are most everywhere. The really annoying one, though, is returning to the Red Lady Express after riding Peak, Peel, Banana, Funnel and Forest. Keep your speed or you'll get stuck on a heinous flat. It's—yes—a quarter-mile long. You'll also have to hike out from the Extreme Limits and Teocalli Bowl.

Cross-country & snowshoeing (see also xcskiresorts.com)

Crested Butte is linked with one of the most extensive cross-country networks in Colorado. The **Crested Butte Nordic Center** (970-349-1707) is at the edge of town, on 2nd Street between Sopris and Whiterock Streets. About 70 km. of Nordic tracks begin a few yards from the Nordic Center. The center also has an outdoor rink and sledding hill for apres-Nordic activity. There are more than 100 miles of backcountry trails. Group lessons, half-day and all-day tours are scheduled several times each week, but private lessons and special tours must be requested two days in advance. Snowshoe activities are offered. Snowshoe and cross-country rentals are available. There are also hut-to-hut cross-country and snowshoe trips.

Snowshoe tours at Crested Butte Mountain Resort (800-444-9236; 970-349-2211) depart from the Crested Butte Mountain Schools desk at 9:45 a.m. and 1:15 p.m. daily. You'll ride the Red Lady Express lift up the mountain, and then make an easy loop that offers spectacular views. Tour takes about 2.5 hours and includes a snack break. Moonlight snowshoe tours (full moon nights only) are a fun evening activity for people of all ages and abilities. You'll ride in a snowcat to the top of the Red Lady Express lift and snowshoe the moonlit mountain trails back to the base area for hot cocoa and Ben & Jerry's ice cream.

Lessons (08/09 prices)

Registration and reservations for **all programs** are at the Ski and Snowboard Instruction desk in the Gothic building, 970-349-2252 or 800-444-9236. Most of Crested Butte's professional instructors have received the "New Skiers Retention Accreditation" from the Rocky Mountain Division of the PSIA. The knowledge and skills acquired through this certification enable instructors to deliver the best first-time lesson possible. You can also rent your skis or snowboards on line before you leave home at Rentskis.com. Your equipment will be waiting when you arrive.

Group lessons: Ski and snowboard lessons are for all ability levels and cost $110 for a 2.5-hour lesson, $120, all day. Higher levels take specialized workshops to address personal goals, such as turning fundamentals, parallel turns, all terrain, telemark, and racing; cost is

$89-99 for 2.5 hours with a four-person maximum.

First-timer package: A three-hour novice ski or snowboard lesson with lift ticket and rentals costs $107. An all-day lesson costs $127. Three-day Learn-to-Ski packages are also available.

Private lessons: $255 for two hours. Each additional person costs $45. A six-hour (all day) private for one to five people is $575.

Children's programs (08/09 prices)

Child care: Ages 6 months to 7 years. For ages 6–18 months, cost is $95 for a full day, or $15 per hour. For ages 19 months through 7 years, cost is $90 for a full day, or $14 per hour. The program includes crafts, games, snow play and other activities, but no ski lessons; toddlers have separate programs from the older children.

Reservations are strongly recommended; registration and information are in the Kid's Ski & Snowboard World in the Whetstone Building at the base of the Silver Queen Lift. Call 970-349-2259 or (800) 600-7349 for reservations or more information.

Children's lessons: Programs for ages 3–7 include ski rental and supervised day care after the lesson; $120 for a full day (with lunch) or $110 for half-day (no lunch). More experienced kids have classes separate from beginners. For ages 8–12, a full day for skiing or snowboarding is $110 (includes lunch); half-day are $97 (no lunch); these prices do not include lift tickets or rental equipment. The all-day Rip Session and Parks and Pipes Session are for ages 8–15, Level 8 and 9 skiers and snowboarders; cost is $175. Race workshops are offered for children.

Register at the Kid's Ski and Snowboard World desk. Helmets are required for all children ages 12 and younger who are enrolled in lessons; rentals available.

Lift tickets (08/09 prices)

	Adult	Child (7-12)
One day	$82	$41
Three days	$246 ($82/day)	$123 ($41/day)
Five days	$370 ($74/day)	$195 ($39/day)

Who skis free: Ages 6 and younger.

Who skis at a discount: Teens (13-17) $74/day; $222 three days; $350 five days. Seniors (65+) $61.59/day; $132.75 three days; $249.75 five days.

Accommodations

Most accommodations are clustered around the ski area in Mt. Crested Butte. This historic town has a handful of lodges and quaint B&Bs, but they aren't as convenient to the slopes. However, they are less expensive, closer to the nightlife and offer a taste of more rustic Western atmosphere. A free bus service takes you right to the slopes every 15 minutes, so the primary inconvenience of in-town lodging is the short bus ride. Make sure to ask about lodging packages that include lift tickets.

Crested Butte Vacations (800-810-7669) can take care of everything from your plane tickets to lodging, lift tickets and lessons with one phone call. It also offers some of the best packages available. Before you make any arrangements, call and ask for the best possible deal.

The Grand Lodge Crested Butte ($$$-$$$$) is located in the base village a short walk from the lifts. It's the only full-service hotel other The Elevation Hotel, and offers hotel rooms

Dining: $$$$–Entrees $30+; $$$–$20–$30; $$–$10–$20; $–less than $10.
Accommodations: (double room) $$$$–$200+; $$$–$141–$200; $$–$81–$140; $–$80 and less.

and condominium units. You'll find an indoor/outdoor swimming pool, hot tub, fitness room, concierge, room service, gift shop and business center here.

Black Bear Lodge ($$$$), the newest high-end property, features three-bedroom condominiums near the Peachtree lift. The custom condos are spacious and include a gourmet kitchen, fireplace, outdoor hot tub and covered parking.

The Plaza ($$$$), just steps from the Silver Queen Quad, features one of the most luxurious and roomy condominium units in Mt. Crested Butte. There are two hot tubs, a sauna and covered parking. There's also a great pizza joint and pub here, The Firehouse Grill. Kid's World is just 50 yards away. **Treasury Point** ($$$$) features premier three- and four-bedroom townhomes. They are spacious and beautifully furnished, and include a garage and a complex with an outdoor hot tub.

The Villas ($$$$), the most luxurious townhouses in Mt. Crested Butte, are just across the street from the lifts. The three- and four-bedroom units are tastefully decorated, and have private balconies and fabulous views of Mt. Crested Butte.

The Buttes ($$$-$$$$) are well-appointed condos close to the lifts. Rooms range in size from studios to two bedrooms. **The Gateway** ($$$-$$$$), across from the Peachtree lift and near the Silver Queen, may be the best luxury of any condo on the slopes when you trade price for space and amenities.

Wood Creek and **Mountain Edge** ($$-$$$$) are convenient to the lifts, and the **Columbine** is a more moderate ski-in/ski-out property. These three, together with nine others within shuttlebus distance of the lifts, are managed by several agencies, so it's best to book through Crested Butte Vacations (800-810-7669).

Elevation Hotel (800-258-2633; $$$-$$$$), formerly Club Med (and a Marriott prior to 2000), is the only true ski-in/out hotel at the resort. Rooms feature a mini-kitchenette, flat panel HD TVs, CD Players, high speed internet, spa quality bath amenities, and beds with pillow top mattress and down duvets.

In town:

The Crested Butte Club Boutique Inn & Spa (800-815-2582; 970-349-6655; $$$-$$$$), 512 Second St., is the upscale, Old-World elegance champion of the area. Though the lifts are a bit far, this place is worth the inconvenience. Rates include a breakfast buffet and evening beverages. This is a no-smoking property.

The Claim Jumper (970-349-6471; $$-$$$), 704 Whiterock St., is an historic log-home bed-and-breakfast and the class act in town. It's filled with a collection of memorable antiques. Bedrooms have themes and are furnished with brass or old iron beds. There are six rooms, all with private bath. Rates include a full breakfast.

The **Cristiana Guesthaus** (800-824-7899; 970-349-5326; $-$$), 621 Maroon Ave., is a block from the ski shuttle and a five-minute walk from downtown. The mountain inn atmosphere encourages guests to get to know one another. The rooms are small, but guests spend a good deal of time in the common areas which is the point! Rates include breakfast..

The **Elk Mountain Lodge** (970-349-7533; $$-$$$), 2nd Street and Gothic Avenue, has simple but comfortable rooms, all with private baths. Ask for Room 20 on the third floor with lots of space, a balcony and a great view. Continental breakfast is included.

Other recommended B&Bs in town, both of which serve hot gourmet breakfasts, are the flowery **Victorian Elizabeth Anne** (970-349-0147; 703 Maroon Ave.; $$$) and **The Ruby of Crested Butte** (800-390-1338; 624 Gothic Ave.; $$), newly opened and classy yet dog-friendly.

For something out of the ordinary, call **PR Property Management** (970-349-6281), which has rentals including private homes and condominiums.

Dining

The WoodStone Grille (970-349-8030; $$$) at The Grand Lodge Crested Butte serves contemporary cuisine for breakfast and dinner. For a quick lunch, **WoodStone Deli** ($) is good for soup, pizza and specialty sandwiches.

For a full-service lunch, you'll find first-rate Italian fare from soups to desserts at **Rustica Ristorante** (970-349-2274; $-$$) in the midmountain Paradise Warming House. Rustica also has the earliest happy hour, from 2:30 to 3:30 p.m. But remember, you have to ski down the rest of the way afterwards. For a special evening, make reservations for **Dinner @ 10,000 Feet** (970-349-2211). A snowcat pulls you in an open sleigh up the mountain for a four-course dinner at Rustica.

If you're looking for an on-mountain gourmet lunch experience, you'll be delighted by the creative culinary practices at the **Ice Bar and Restaurant** (970-349-2275; $$-$$$). As you bite into delicate seafood and out-of-the-ordinary meat dishes, remember that this was. Make reservations for **Last Tracks Dinners** here through Guest Services (970-349-2211).

The hopping, slopeside **Butte 66 Roadhouse BBQ** (970-349-2999; $-$$) showcases everything from auto grills to sporting gear and whacky signs. It serves breakfast, lunch and dinner.. **Atmospheres** ($) is another good lunch stop.

The Avalanche ($) is another good lunch stop, especially for burgers and grilled sandwiches, and has killer cookies. It also serves hearty breakfasts and some great dinner deals.

Camp 4 Coffee ($) is the locals' favorite hangout and serves the "Best Coffee in Town" with tasty breakfast items, from pastries to breakfast burritos. Find it in the mountain village or at the top of Painter Boy Lift, where it also sells lunch items.

Another option: Make reservations for a **First Tracks Breakfast** (970-349-2378), where you'll meet at 8:15 a.m. at the Red Lady Express lift for first tracks on the mountain and an all-you-can-eat breakfast buffet.

In town:

The Timberline Restaurant (970-349-9831; $$$) mixes a trendy bar downstairs with Mediterranean decor upstairs. Chef Tim Egelhoff combines seasonal products to create a Cafe French Cuisine, whose roots are classic French with a pinch of California and a dash of the Rockies. The menu changes often. The early bird menu, served nightly from 5:30 to 6 p.m., offers a $15 three-course meal. Open Mon-Sun from 5:30-10 p.m.

Soup's on Restaurant (970-349-5448; $$$) is hidden in the alley behind Kochevar's Bar. This log cabin started at half its current size in 1916 as a private residence. Reserve two to three days ahead for one of two seatings, 6 p.m. and 8:15 p.m.

Harry's Fine Dining (970-349-9699; $$-$$$), near the four-way stop at 435 Sixth St., 349-9699; $$-$$$), prepares a four-course menu each night as well as a limited a la carte menu. Make reservations—the place is tiny, but filled with atmosphere and one not to miss.

Le Bosquet (970-349-5808; $$$-$$$$) serves Colorado roast rack of lamb, hazelnut chicken, and portabello Wellington. This is possibly Crested Butte's finest for formal French cuisine. The early bird menu, served nightly from 5:30 to 6:30 p.m., offers a $20 three-course meal.

Calypso and Crested Butte Brewery (970-349-5026; $$-$$$) features tropical fusion cuisine with dishes such as Lemon Grass Skewered, Pomegranate Molasses Lamb or Jerk Spiced shrimp. Award-winning beers are brewed in-house. Brewery tours 2-5 p.m. daily

The Wooden Nickel (970-349-6350; $$-$$$$) serves the best steaks in town.

The chef-owned **Bacchanale** (970-349-5257; $$-$$$) creates delightful Northern Italian dishes. Desserts are fabulous, especially the homemade tiramisu. Locals say this it the place with the biggest bang for the dollar.

Dining: $$$$–Entrees $30+; $$$–$20–$30; $$–$10–$20; $–less than $10.
Accommodations: (double room) $$$$–$200+; $$$–$141–$200; $$–$81–$140; $–$80 and less.

Lobar (970-349-0480; $$), hidden away in a cellar, is a chic sushi and tapas lounge with cushy seating and a long bar that serves as a gathering point. Food is exquisitely prepared.

For hard-to-beat group and family comfort food, go to **Slogar's** (970-349-5765; $$).

For other substantial meals, head down Elk Avenue to **Donita's Cantina** (970-349-6674; $$), where the margaritas are giant and strong and Mexican food comes in heaping portions. Be early or be ready to wait. No reservations. For a quick meal, try **The Last Steep** (970-349-7007; $-$$), very popular with locals and known for everything from sandwiches to "BBQ Rib Night."

Pitas in Paradise (970-349-0897; $) is reminiscent of a sandwich shop, only it serves blues on the radio and Greek specialties such as gyros, falafel, wraps and baklava. It has a full coffee bar, wine and beer in addition to your standard drink options. Even after you add a side, you're still coming in under $10, and with huge portions, you won't leave hungry.

Ginger Cafe (970-349-7291;$$) is a tiny place just off Elk is an Asian dining experience from Thai cooking to Curries with lots of vegetarian options. **Crave** (970-349-0570;$$) is Crested Butte's Cajun spot run by a young couple from Baton Rouge, Louisiana, so they know something about Cajun cooking. **Gas Cafe** (970-349-9656; $) on the way out of town towards Mt. Crested Butte serves a mean burger.

The best hearty, traditional breakfast is found at the **Paradise Cafe** (970-349-6233; $).Try the Eggs Paradise or the Potatoes Paradise. **McGill's** (970-349-5240;$) on Elk also serves primo breakfasts. Sunshine Deli slathers their Huevos ranchero with very spicy red chili sauce. **Teocalis** also had excellent huevos rancheros. The best coffee is served at **Camp 4**, tucked in a tiny cabin just on 4th Street just off Elk Avenue across from the museum.

 ## Apres-ski/nightlife

The immediate apres-ski action is at the slopeside **Butte 66 Roadhouse BBQ** in the Treasury Building, with apres-ski drink specials and live entertainment. Some head to the **Plaza Bar** in the Plaza Building.

Then the action begins to move downtown to **The Wooden Nickel**, with some wild drinks, and **The El Dorado**, known around town as "The Eldo" and, according to one local, it has a "smokin' dance floor." The Eldo also has a brewery. **Talk of the Town** is a smoky locals' place with video games, shuffleboard and pool tables. **Kochevar's** is another local favorite where Butch Cassidy and the Sundance Kid used to saddle up to the bar. **The Crested Butte Brewery** is a microbrewery with live music and dancing on weekends. Cover charges are $5 to $10, depending on the talent.

Duck into the cellar entrance of **Lobar** and discover the uptown side of Crested Butte. Sample sushi and tapas while DJs and live music keep you entertained.

The Princess Wine Bar at 218 Elk Ave. is the place to finish your night on the town. This Wine Spectator award-winning establishment offers a limited menu of appetizers and tempting desserts.

 ## Other activities

A **tubing hill** at the base area is open daily after the lifts close. For information on resort activities, call 970-349-2211. **Other winter activities** include snowmobiling, dogsledding, winter fly fishing, ice skating and sledding. Also, there's winter **horseback riding** with Fantasy Ranch and sleigh rides (with and without dinners) through Just Horsin' Around. Call the **Crested Butte Chamber of Commerce** at 970-349-6438 for brochures and information.

Crested Butte Mountain Guides (877-455-2307; 970-349-5430) offers avalanche safety courses, backcountry guiding, ice climbing, and backcountry gear rentals (beacons, shovels, backpacks and more). Backcountry gear can also be rented at The Troutfitter (970-349-1323).

There are loads of great **shops and boutiques** at the resort and especially in town. Among them: Diamond Tanita Art Gallery for jewelry and art; Cookworks, Inc., a gourmet kitchen shop; The Blue Moon Book Store; and the Milky Way for unique women's apparel and lacy things. The Alpineer has outdoor gear plus guide services and rentals. Shaken Not Spurred, tucked behind the Post Office, has wonderful Western wear and a fine selection of cowboy boots. Finally, visit the General Store, a collection of smaller crafts shops.

. **The Center for the Arts** (970-349-7487) has presentations throughout the year. To take in a movie, check out The **Majestic Theatre**.

Getting there and getting around

By air: Despite its seemingly isolated location, it's actually quite easy to reach Crested Butte. The nearest airport is Gunnison/Crested Butte Airport, 30 miles from the resort. It services both jets and commuter planes.

Alpine Express (800-822-4844; 970-641-5074) meets every arriving flight and takes you directly to your hotel or condo. For reservations, call Crested Butte Vacations (800-810-7669) or the company directly. Hertz, Dollar and Avis operate at the Gunnison/Crested Butte Airport.

By car: Crested Butte is at the end of Hwy. 135, about 30 miles north of Gunnison. It's about 230 miles from Denver via Hwys. 285, 50 and 135. From Colorado Springs, take Hwys. 24 West, 285 South, 50 West, then 135 North to Crested Butte.

Getting around: No need for a car. Crested Butte's free town-resort shuttle, running every 15 minutes, is reliable and fun to ride, thanks to some free-spirited and friendly drivers. Town taxi for after-hours travel is available at 970-349-5543. If you have a car, you'll find limited parking in town, so it's best to use the shuttle.

Nearby resorts
Monarch, Monarch, CO; (888) 996-7669; (719) 530-5000.
Internet: www.skimonarch.com.
5 lifts; 670 acres; 1,170 vertical feet

Monarch,on the Continental Divide at a high altitude, is known for powder. It gets about 350 inches of snow a year, but only about 170,000 skier visits (many Colorado destination resorts get that in just a couple of weeks). That means a lot more untracked snow. The resort caters to families with groomed beginner and intermediate terrain for those who don't like the steep and deep. Experts can opt for snowcat skiing and riding on more than 900 acres of backcountry terrain. This area is fairly isolated and without many off-slope activities. Child care starts at 2 months.

Lift tickets (08/09 prices): Adults, $54; children (7–12), $20; seniors (62–69), $29. Children 6 and younger, and seniors 70 and older, free.

Distance from Denver: About 160 miles southwest via Hwys. 285 and 50.

Distance from Gunnison (closest airport): About 35 miles east on Hwy. 50.

Lodging information: (800) 332-3668. Monarch has an overnight lodge 3 miles away; other lodging is in Salida, 18 miles east.

Dining: $$$$–Entrees $30+; $$$–$20–$30; $$–$10–$20; $–less than $10.
Accommodations: (double room) $$$$–$200+; $$$–$141–$200; $$–$81–$140; $–$80 and less.

Purgatory at Durango Mountain Resort

Colorado

Summit:	**10,822 feet**
Vertical:	**2,029 feet**
Base:	**8,793 feet**

Address: One Skier Place, Durango, Colorado 81301
Telephone (main): 970-247-9000
Snow Report Number: 970-247-9000
Toll-free reservations: (800) 982-6102
Reservations outside US: 970-247-9000
E-mail: info@durangomountain.com
Internet: www.durangomountainresort.com
Expert:★
Advanced:★★★
Intermediate:★★★★★
Beginner:★★★★★
First-timer:★★★★★

Lifts: 10—1 high-speed six-pack, 1 high-speed quad, 4 triples, 3 doubles, 1 moving carpet
Skiable acreage: 1,200
Snowmaking: 21 percent
Uphill capacity: 15,050
Parks & pipes: 2 parks, 1 pipe
Bed base: 3,120 near resort; 7,000 in Durango
Nearest lodging: Slopeside
Child care: Yes, 2 months and older
Adult ticket, per day: $62 (08-09 prices)
Dining:★★★
Apres-ski/nightlife:★★★
Other activities:★★★★

Purgatory at Durango Mountain Resort is a hidden gem. It's tucked away in Southwest Colorado in the four corners area and draws skiers and riders from New Mexico, Arizona and Texas. Folks wearing jeans and cowboy hats, whooping and hollering their way down beginner runs aren't uncommon. The preponderance of intermediate skiers means Purgatory's advanced trails are sparsely skied, so fresh powder remains untracked even longer. Boarders will love the mountain's many terraced runs The mountain's only downside is that it's 25 miles north of town, which is where the action is.

Durango's historic downtown is full of great restaurants, brew pubs and galleries. It's a college town as well as a ski town. So if you and your group can't have fun in Durango, well, you'd better just stay home. Inexpensive motels line Main Avenue, and rates for a single can dip as low as $29 a night during the ski season.

Purgatory Mountain receives an average of 260 inches of snow per year. Early-season snowmaking efforts here focus on covering a few runs well rather than a large area. The best snow conditions are typically in February and March.

Mountain layout

Thousands of years ago glaciers scraped out the Animas Valley, leaving behind terraced mountainsides. The terraces mean several of Purgatory Mountain's runs plunge downward for a bit, then level off, then plunge, then level off—all the way to the bottom, no matter what ability level you are. The effect is like a roller coaster ride. The roller coaster effect lures those who love to catch air (yes, there are warnings all over the place, but who can resist?), and those who need a breather will appreciate the flat rest stops.

All the signs on the mountain refer to lifts by number, but the trail map provides names, and sometimes people use names too, so we'll give you some of both.

Expert, Advanced: The toughest trail on the mountain is Bull Run, a double-black route that starts off rather gently beneath Dante's restaurant, next to Lift #5 (Grizzly). Once you're on the lower part of it, there's no getting off. It has a tough pitch as well as funnels and moguls. Bottom's Chute is a nasty surprise on your way to Lift #8 (Legends). Adventure skiers can try the powder stashes between Peace and Boogie. On the front side of the mountain, tree fans will like the aspens between Pandemonium and Lower Hades. Only experts looking for extremes will be disappointed.

From the top of Lift #1 (Purgatory Village Express), what starts out as Paradise soon turns into Pandemonium, a black diamond that gets steeper and bumpier the further down you go. Likewise, Upper Hades also starts out mild, but turns hellacious once you drop over the headwall onto Lower Hades. Styx, next to the ski area boundary, can be heavenly after a fresh snowstorm. The short traverse to Styx from Lift #1's top station means you'll encounter fewer skiers than ever on this utterly fabulous run.

On the back side of the mountain, Snag, perhaps the most terraced run on the mountain, leads skiers to challenging chutes all leading back to Lift #3 (Hermosa Park). Bump fans should also consider Wapiti, a black run under Lift #5 (Grizzly) that grows igloo-sized bumps. Lift #8 (Legends) in the far back is the home of most of the black-diamond terrain. It's easy to do laps here, on mostly bumpy runs—without moguls, this would be strictly intermediate territory. Beware: The triple is a slow chair, so racking up vertical is an exercise in patience. Poet's Glade and Paul's Park offer nice glade skiing, Elliott's has a nice sustained pitch.

Intermediate: Despite the mountain's name, this is Intermediate Paradise—such are the variety and plenitude of trails. There are endless options for whoop-de-doing at high speeds. There are occasional frustrating flats—some folks call the resort "traversatory"—but for the most part you'll find plenty of fun.

Intermediates seem to prefer the terrain served by Lift #3 (Hermosa Park Express). Regularly groomed runs include Peace, Boogie, Where, Zinfandel, and Airmail. On days with fresh snow Harris Hill can provide a fun cut-off. Want to ratchet it up a notch? From the top of Lift #3 continue down Legends toward Dead Spike. Dead Spike is frequently split groomed, with good intermediate "starter bumps" on the ungroomed side. Still not challenged enough? Continue further down Legends to the mid-loading station on Lift #8 (Legends). From the top of this lift, check out either Sally's Run or Chet's.

Beginner, First-timer: After graduating from the bunny hill, beginning skiers can head for Lift #4 (Twilight). It serves terrain ideally suited for beginners and families with small children. You won't be endangered by a lot of advanced, fast skiers in this area. The easiest trail is Pinkerton Toll Road, a winding cat track. Divinity and Angel's Tread are wide runs. Columbine winds through several stands of trees, giving beginners the feeling of being deep in the woods.

If this terrain is simply too easy, you may want to cut over from the top of Lift #4 to Lift #3 (Hermosa Park) via Salvation, where you'll find groomed intermediate terrain.

First-timers have their own learning area, Columbine Beginner's Area, complete with its own lifts, ticket office and restaurant. It's directly across from the lower parking lots. After a couple of lessons on the terrain under the Columbine Lift, beginners can ride the Lift #7 (Graduate) back to the base area. The "Family Ski Zone" under Lift #4 (Twilight) would be the logical place for beginners to head next rather than taking Lift#1 (Purgatory Village Express) to the top of the mountain..

Parks and pipes

Paradise Freestyle Arena features 10 consecutive hits with a 50-foot Big Air competition jump, plus jibbing features with boxes, a rainbow rail, two street rails, a balance beam and "The Serpentine," a 45-foot S-rail. The park is on the front side of the mountain and runs parallel to the Purgatory Village Express chairlift, with plenty of opportunities to "wow" the crowd. The Pitchfork Terrain Garden, behind the Powderhouse near the Engineer lift, has hits and features for those just starting out or looking to refine their skills in the park. The halfpipe here is 400 feet long with 15-foot walls.

Snowboarding

The signature run is Snag, an exciting roller-coaster ride of steep, moderate steps—all the way down! Advanced riders can catch air off each of the steps. Intermediates can use the flats above each headwall to catch their breath. Rider-constructed hits can often be found here and at various locations beneath the Legends lift.

On days with freshies, locals head for the Legends lift. Powder hounds can head into the trees on Poet's Glade or Paul's Park. From Lift the Grizzly lift, a delightful powder stash can often be found hidden away on Cathedral Tree Way (rider's left off Bull Run). On the front side try Styx where you'll most likely find waist-deep powder. Upper Hades transitions into Lower Hades, a major steep mogul field that when covered with a foot or more of fresh powder, can be an absolutely amazing ride, along with Pandemonium and Catharsis.

You'll find flat traverses connecting the front and back sides. Getting to the back side requires carrying a lot of speed on Hermosa Parkway. Reaching the maze at the bottom of the Hermosa Park lift without having to unstrap and skate requires executing a kamikaze-style run. To return from the back side, avoid the much-too-flat BD&M Expressway. Instead, zigzag: Take Path to Peace, ride Hermosa Park back up the mountain, Silver Tip it to either black-diamond Cool It or blue-square The Bank, then continue on past the bottom of the Engineer lift to Demon. The right side of Demon is a gully that provides a natural halfpipe but be extremely careful of beginners finding their way home on Demon after lunch.

Beginners should take the Purgatory Village Express and head for Sa's Psyche, beneath the Engineer lift. It's nicely groomed, gentle-pitched terrain, with only one flat spot. Snowboarders generally avoid the Twilight lift because of lack of suitable terrain.

 ## Cross-country & snowshoeing (see also xcskiresorts.com)

The Nordic Center (970-247-6000 Ext. 114 or 385-2114), maintained by the Durango Nordic Ski Club, is just north of the Alpine ski area and across Highway 550. There are 16 km. of groomed trails for classic and skate skiing. Nordic skiers find the same undulating terrain as alpine skiers do, with appropriate terrain for various ability levels.

The center offers clinics, races, group and private lessons, rentals, children's programs, daytime and moonlight tours. As part of Purgatory's Total Adventure Ticket, one Alpine ski day can be exchanged for the Nordic package. There are also guided backcountry and full-moon snowshoe tours, which can be booked through Durango Mountain Resort Ski Concierge in the Purgatory Village Center.

Lessons (08/09 prices)

We provide regular-season rates where available; holiday rates are higher. **Group lessons:** $60 for a 2 hour lesson with lift ticket. Afternoon sessions are offered at select times.

First-timer package: First-time skiers and snowboarders can buy a package of lift tickert and lesson for $89. Snowboarders can join the all-day lift ticket/lesson and equipment package for $117.

Private lessons: Packages are also available for hourly and full day lessons. Call for specific prices and reservations which are recommended; 970-385-2169.

Special programs: The resort offers clinics for snowboarding, racing, telemark skiing and mogul techniques. Clinics and daily events are announced on the daily snow report and posted with the list of groomed trails throughout the resort and on shuttles.

The Adaptive Sports Association (970-385-2163, Nov.-April) runs one of the nation's leading adaptive skiing programs here. Programs include lift ticket, adaptive equipment and lessons for the visually, physically or mentally impaired.

Children's programs (07/08 prices)

We provide regular-season rates; holiday rates are higher.

Child care: Ages 2 months to 3 years. Cost is $78 for a full day with lunch and $63 for a half day. Toddlers (ages 2–3) get outdoor snow play, arts and crafts, games, movies and story time. Reservations required; call (970) 385-2144 or (800) 525-0892. If you're not sure whether to put your child in day care or lessons, Durango Mountain's Kids Central, on the second floor of the Village Center, will help assess your child's abilities and interests, then escort him or her to the appropriate spot. Staff can recommend a babysitter.

Children's lessons: Ski lessons are available for kids 3–12 years old, snowboarding lessons are for kids 8–12. The program for 3-year-olds includes lunch, indoor activity, and an introduction-to-ski lesson with special skis that attach to snowboots. A full day costs $89, a half day costs $69. Cost includes rentals, lift ticket and lesson; reservations are required.

The full-day programs for ages 4–12, including lift ticket and lunch, cost $89; half day with ticket, $69. Rentals are extra. Reservations required for all ages.

Special activities: The Snowcoaster Tubing hill is the place where kids congregate after skiing and riding, or check out one of the many Family Movie Nights in the Community Center.

Lift tickets (08/09 prices)

	Adult	Child(6-12)
One day	$62	$34
Three days	$171	$93
Five days	$285	$155

Who skis free: Ages 5 and younger.

Who skis at a discount: Students (13-18) and seniors (62-69) pay $49 for one day; $138 for three days; $220 for five days. Ages 70+ pay $22 per day. Skiers who book packages through the resort receive discounted lift tickets. There are early/late season discounts.

Note: Holiday day tickets cost $67 for adults; $53 for students and seniors; $36 for children; and $22 for ages 70+.

Accommodations

Durango Mountain Resort has three primary lodging areas. The condos at the base area are the most expensive. A limited number of resort hotels and condos within 10 miles of the ski area are slightly less. Motels in Durango can cost as little as $29 per night, but are 25 miles away. Except on holidays, motel reservations are seldom needed in town. All Durango and Durango Mountain Resort lodging can be booked through **Durango Mountain Resort Reservations**, (800) 525-0892, or the **Durango Area Reservations** 800-525-8855. When you book three nights and three days of lift tickets with DMR, they'll give you a fourth day and night free except during Christmas week and 3/15-3/23 (the same goes for rentals and lessons). Call 800-982-6103. Online, check lodgings at www.durango.org. Several Durango properties are listed at Vacation Rentals by Owner, www.vrbo.com.

Base-area lodging is available at the **Purgatory Village Condominium Hotel** (970-247-9000, ext.100; $$-$$$$), and the following condo complexes: **Angelhaus** (970-247-8090; $$-$$$$), **Brimstone** (970-259-1066; $$-$$$$), **East Rim** (970-385-2100; $$-$$$$). **Edelweiss, Graysill, Sitzmark** and **Twilight View** (all $$-$$$$). Condos are full-service units with kitchens, fireplaces, common-area hot tubs and laundry facilities.

Several other full-service resorts are within 10 miles of the ski area: **Cascade Village** (970-259-3500; $$-$$$$), **Silver Pick** (800-295-4820; $$-$$$$) and **Lodge at Tamarron** (970-259-2000; $$-$$$$). Most of these outlying complexes offer free shuttles to the ski area.

Comfortable in-town lodging can be found at the **Hampton Inn** (970-247-2600), the **Doubletree** (970-259-6580), which accepts pets, and the **Marriott Residence Inn** (970-259-6200).

A plethora of older, less-expensive motels line North Main Ave., including the **Day's End** (970-259-3311). **The Spanish Trails Inn** (970-247-4173) offers kitchenettes and is across the street from City Market. For fans of funky (but clean) little motels, consider the **Wapiti Lodge** (970-247-3961), which is walking distance to downtown.

Five historic lodging properties are worth mentioning. **The Strater Hotel** (800-247-4431; $$$) and the **General Palmer Hotel** (800-523-3358; $$-$$$) are multistory, updated brick hotels more than 100 years old. Both are in the heart of the walkable downtown area. The Strater has a great Victorian-style hot tub area that would be the envy of many larger, more sophisticated properties and its Diamond Belle Saloon is a classic that's now non-smoking.

Leland House Bed & Breakfast and **The Rochester Hotel**, (800-664-1920 for both; $$-$$$ for both) across the street from each other on East Second Ave., are historic lodges owned by the same family, located in the heart of the downtown historic district. The Rochester has two dog-friendly rooms. The Leland House has a Durango history theme, with the rooms named after local historic figures. The Rochester Hotel has a Hollywood theme, with each room named for a film shot at least in part in Durango. "Butch Cassidy and the Sundance Kid," "Around The World in 80 Days" and "City Slickers" were all filmed in this region. **Jarvis Suites** (800-824-1024; 970-259-6190; $$-$$$) at 10th and Main are newly redecorated with a killer view of the action on Main St. Built in 1888, the hotel is on the National Register of Historic Places.

Two B&B's between Durango and the ski area bear mention: **Apple Orchard Inn** (970-247-0751; $$), on CR203 near Trimble Hot Springs, and **Country Sunshine** (970-247-2853; $$), near where CR250 runs into CR550N. Staying at either would drastically reduce the amount of driving you do.

Dining

There are several options at the base area. **Purgy's Slopeside Bar and Grill** serves burgers, Mexican and pizza in a bar atmosphere. After a full morning of skiing you'll savor the hearty homemade soups and stews at the **Mountain Market Deli**, a local's favorite lunch spot. **Village Coffee Co**($) is the requisite coffeehouse and bakery. **Creekside Cafe** ($) serves up breakfast and lunch in a family-friendly atmosphere.

Dante's, at the Grizzly midway station, serves lunch. **The Powderhouse Restaurant** beneath the Hermosa Park quad serves lunch fare along Italian themes.

You can find several great dining spots along the highway between town and the area. For fresh fish and local game, try the **Cascade Grill** (970-259-3500; $$$), 2 miles north of the resort. It offers elegant dining in a rustic setting. The **Hamilton Chop House** (970-259-6636; $$$), 10 miles south of the resort in the Lodge at Tamarron, serves excellent wild game, prime beef and seafood. **The Sow's Ear** (970-247-3527; $$-$$$) at the Silverpick Lodge is famous for its large hand-cut steaks. The **Aspen Cafè** (970-259-8025, $-$$) in the Needles Country Square is small and casual, but the owner cooks up a fine dinner.

You'll find restaurants of almost every persuasion downtown. Most don't require, nor accept, reservations.

Chez Grand-mere (970-247-7979; $$$) is a delicious taste of award-winning, five-star France in the Colorado southwest. The little building near the train depot is hard to find, so look behind the Polo Store and the Gaslight Theatre. **Seasons** (764 Main Ave., 970-382-9790; $$$) features rotisserie-roasted dinners and fine wines by the glass. **Ken & Sue's** (636 Main Ave., 970-259-2616; $$) is a favorite among locals serving Continental fare with a homey twist. Sunday brunch is served until 2:30 p.m. **Ariano's** (150 East College Dr., 970-247-8146; $$-$$$) serves northern Italian cuisine. Swanky **Randy's** (970-247-9083; $$-$$$) next door serves the nicest prime rib in town. For more Italian, **Mutu's Italian Kitchen**(701 E. Second Ave.; 970-375-2701). One of Telluride's best fine-dining restaurants **Cosmopolitan**($$-$$$) has opened another place of the same name, menu and reputation at 919 Main Ave.

The Ore House (147 College Dr., 970-247-5707; $$-$$$) is an Old West steak house, rustic and casual. **The Red Snapper** (144 East 9th St., 970-259-3417; $$-$$$) has fresh seafood and a great salad bar. The **Cyprus Cafe** (725 E. Second, 970-385-6884; $$) offers delicious Mediterranean dishes at reasonable prices. Their lamb dishes are to die for. **Francisco's Restaurante Y Cantina** (619 Main Ave., 970-247-4098; $$) has been a Durango landmark since 1968. Hidden-away **Gazpacho** (431 E. Second Ave., 970-259-9494) rivals Francisco's with authentic New Mexican cuisine. **Tequilas** (948 Main, 970-259-7655; $$) is another locals' favorite and serves the finest margarita in town. **East by Southwest** (160 E. College, 970-247-5533; $$) has a full sushi bar and Pan Asian cuisine.

Olde Tymer's Cafe (1000 Main Ave., 970-259-2990; $-$$) is tops for a good hamburger. Monday is burger night, Friday is the taco special. **Christina's** (21382 US Highway 160 West, 970-382-3844; $$) offers very reasonably priced continental cuisine. **Carver's Brewing Co.** (1022 Main Ave., 970-259-2545; $$) is the best place in Durango for breakfast; muffins and bagels are baked fresh daily. Carver's has a nice children's menu—their meals are served on a Frisbee they get to keep. **College Drive Cafe** ($) bakes the best homemade cinnamon rolls (closed Monday and Tuesday). If you prefer the eggs-and-bacon-type breakfast, head for the **Durango Diner** (957 Main Ave., $). Sunday brunch at the **Doubletree Hotel** ($$) is outstanding. Or start the day off at the **Steamin' Bean** ($) on Main Street, a great hangout for coffee, chess and chai. **Oscar's** in the City Market South Center is famous for decadent French toast.

Dining: $$$$–Entrees $30+; $$$–$20–$30; $$–$10–$20; $–less than $10.
Accommodations: (double room) $$$$–$200+; $$$–$141–$200; $$–$81–$140; $–$80 and less.

Apres-ski/nightlife

After the lifts close, some people congregate at **Purgy's Slopeside Bar and Grill**, which sometimes has a band. **Shakers Martini Bar** on the 2nd floor at Purgy's, features top shelf liquors, jumbo shrimp and olive skewers. In general, however, apres-ski is found in town, not on the mountain.

Most ski areas have a "locals" spot, and here it's the **Schoolhouse Cafe**, a small and friendly hangout located two miles south of the resort. It's across the road from the Needles Country Store on U.S. Hwy. 550. This is where the lift ops, ski patrollers and other insiders fill up on beer and calzones the size of footballs. The music rocks, and the pool table is free.

A wa-aay popular apres-ski spot that's available on trade with your Total Adventure Ticket™ is **Trimble Hot Springs** (970-247-0111), 8 miles north of Durango on the way back from the ski area. Natural mineral springs bubble into two outdoor therapy pools, one heated to 90 degrees and the other to 105. A heated outdoor 50-meter pool awaits lap swimmers. Massages are available; call ahead.

If you really want to party, go to downtown Durango—depending on the time of year, it's either jumping or mildly hopping. Spring Break, which goes on for several weeks in March, packs 'em in and the bars schedule lots of entertainment.

Carver's Brewing Co. offers several beers brewed on-site along with a full dinner menu. **Steamworks,** a brew pub on the corner of 8th Street and East Second Ave., pours award-winning beer and serves moderately priced food in a party atmosphere. **Lady Falconburgh's Barley Exchange** has 20 microbrews on tap and more than 80 different bottled beers. Its long picnic benches attract large groups of students from nearby Fort Lewis College. Their Philly Cheese Steak is excellent. **El Rancho** is Durango's old standby. You've got to stop and have at least one drink there, along with a bowl of free popcorn. Other bars have come and gone but "The Ranch" has served liquid refreshment since the days when Jack Dempsey fought his first fight there, although historians now say the fight actually occurred across the street. A mural on the side of the old Central Hotel depicts Dempsey's first TKO.

Durango has quite a variety of musical entertainment. Flyers posted around town will tell you who's playing where. **The Wild Horse Saloon** at College St. and Second Ave. has dancing and live music. **Coloradaponga's** is a smokey pool hall. **Scoot'n Blues** dishes up soul, jazz, and, of course, blues, blues, blues.

Over at the **Diamond Belle Saloon** in the Strater Hotel, a ragtime piano player plunks out hit tunes from the Gay '90s — 1890s, that is. The Diamond Belle recently went non-smoking, and their waitresses wear vintage-era costumes that are worth the price of a drink to see! A new favorite is **The Office** at the Strater, where the three-martini apres-ski is de rigueur. Check out the $11,000 chandelier.

Other activities

Durango has two **snowcat operations**. The San Juan Ski Company (970-259-9671; closed Tuesdays) takes skiers and boarders to 35,000 acres of powder for about $185 (including lunch, guide, powder skis and avalanche beacon). Reservations strongly recommended. El Diablo (877-241-9643; 970-385-7288) provides tours in the San Juan Mountains, including Molas Pass, near Silverton, a quaint Victorian mining town. Cost is $125 (including lunch, guide and avalanche beacon).

If you haven't had enough on-slope time, the resort offers **tubing**. Book activities such as **winter fly-fishing, snowmobiling** and **dinner sleigh rides** through the Durango Mountain

Resort Ski Concierge in the Purgatory Village Center.

Durango has a couple of off-slope activities unique in the ski industry. One of America's finest national parks is nearby, **Mesa Verde**. Anasazi Indian (Ancestral Puebloans) cliff dwellings dating back more than 800 years have been preserved here. Plan an early start for a day trip to Mesa Verde; it's about an hour west of Durango but over a mountain pass.

Another unique activity is the **Durango & Silverton Narrow Gauge Railroad**.If you don't have time for a train ride, visit the **Railroad Museum**. Admission is $5

There are several other museums in Durango: The **Animas Museum** (970-259-2402), 31st St. & W. 2nd Ave., shows exhibits on area history and Indian cultures. **Children's Museum of Durango** (970-259-9234), 802 E. 2nd Ave. upstairs in the Durango Arts Center, has hands-on exhibits for kids ages 2-11. **Grand Motorcar & Piano Collection** (970-247-1250), 586 Animas View Dr., displays a variety of antique and classic automobiles and grand pianos.

The Sky Ute Lodge and Casino offers basic gambling and some 380 Vegas-style slots.

Durango's **shops** smack of shabby chic, Old West and unique custom designs. We like The Tulip Tree, a gift shop at 600 Main Ave., and Durango International Fine Arts Gallery on College Ave. for collectibles. The Bookcase, 601 E. Second Ave., offers a fine inventory of used and collector books. The Rocky Mountain Chocolate Factory, which has branches at every Colorado resort, started in this location at the south end of Main Ave. The O'Farrell Hat Company, on Main near the General Palmer Hotel, offers what are acknowledged as the world's finest cowboy hats. You'll have to dig deep in your pocketbook to put one of their hats on your head, though. Real deep.

The **art galleries** are first rate. Among our favorites: Sorrell Sky Gallery on Main (on the corner of 9th), Durango Arts Center Gallery Shop at 802 E. 2nd Ave. for local artistry, and Toh Atin Gallery at 145 W. 9th St. for Southwestern art.

 ## Getting there and getting around

By air: The Durango-La Plata County Airport is 40 miles south of Durango Mountain Resort and about 15 miles from downtown Durango.

By car: The resort is 25 miles from Durango, 350 miles southwest of Denver, 232 miles northwest of Albuquerque and 470 miles northeast of Phoenix. There are no major mountain passes from the south or west. Durango is a four-hour drive from Albuquerque; six-plus hours from Denver in the winter over numerous mountain passes, which frequently close when it snows. Chains or 4WD are occasionally required on Hwy. 550N to the resort.

If you don't need lessons or rentals, the bunny hill offers the fastest access onto the mountain. Either get off the shuttle at the bunny hill or park your car in one of the two lower lots. You can purchase your lift tickets here, and at the end of the day, ski back to your car. From the bunny hill ride the Graduate lift directly to the Purgatory Village Express. To access the upper parking lots requires either chains or 4WD, and you'll do a lot more schlepping in ski boots and waiting in line at the base village than if you park low.

Getting around: Visitors have several ground transportation options: If you **rent a car**, request front wheel drive. Some of the larger hotels offer **shuttle service** to and from the slopes. **Mountain TranSport** shuttles between town and the slopes. **Durango Transportation** (970-259-4818) provides taxi service and airport pick-ups. **The Durango Trolley** provides in-town service on Main Avenues. Locals **hitchhike**.If you do, ask if you can contribute gas money.

Dining: $$$$–Entrees $30+; $$$–$20–$30; $$–$10–$20; $–less than $10.
Accommodations: (double room) $$$$–$200+; $$$–$141–$200; $$–$81–$140; $–$80 and less.

Nearby resorts
Wolf Creek Ski Area, Pagosa Springs, CO; (970) 264-5639

Internet: www.wolfcreekski.com

7 lifts; 1,600 acres; 1,604 vertical feet; base elevation 10,300 feet; summit elevation 11,904 feet

Wolf Creek is the "non-resort" where skiers and riders go to drown themselves in fresh powder, explore the trees and launch off cliffs. This isn't a destination resort with endless groomers, cute shops and activities for non-skiers. It's a gateway to the backcountry.

Because of the tremendous amounts of snow, avalanche control is a big issue. There are gates to access the ridgeline between Treasure Chair and Boundary Bowl, the Waterfall area, Montezuma Bowl, the Knife Ridge Chutes and Horseshoe Bowls. Unlike bigger resorts, Wolf Creek doesn't go out of its way to dynamite every rock, pull every stump, or remove every downed tree, all of which actually improve the stability of the snow pack. They just let the snow bury it all.

The facilities at the base of family-owned Wolf Creek are limited: A ticket office, a cafeteria and bar, a restaurant, restrooms, a tiny ski shop and an even tinier rental shop. But Wolf Creek has a wonderful feel to it. In the friendly cafeteria enjoy real, homemade food.

Holy Moses, visible from the lift, gives advanced skiers and riders a taste of what's available. For an even bigger taste, try black diamonds Prospector and Glory Hole. To access the gates leading here, ride Treasure Chair, then follow Navajo Trail or shortcut down lower Glory Hole. Stay slightly skier's right to get to Alberta Lift, which serves only expert terrain off Knife Ridge, Horseshoe Bowl and the tumbling terrain of the Waterfall Area. Trees, open glades and tight forests dot the natural landscape with only a handful of discernible runs. High alpine routes topping out at 11,904 span one end of the rim to the other, leading to the steep bowls, chutes and glades of Alberta Peak and Knife Ridge.

Advanced-intermediates should head for Silver Streak, Treasure, Alberta and Tranquility off Treasure Chair. Lower-level intermediates will enjoy trails like Charisma, Powder Puff and Windjammer off Bonanza chair. Snowboarders: Don't bother looking for a halfpipe and terrain park; there are none. Take advantage of the natural terrain features instead. Beginners should stick to the Raven Chair, and either Bunny Hop or Kelly Boyce trails. First-timers have a moving carpet and beginner's lift in front of the lodge.

We suggest you stay in either South Fork or, preferably, Pagosa Springs (as in Pagosa Hot Springs). Once you get past the slight sulfur smell, Pagosa's 11 different pools, all at different temperatures, are about the finest apres-ski experience there is. They're on the river, should you desire an icy plunge. Pagosa Springs has an old-world charm that's hard to describe. And it's inexpensive compared to destination resorts.

Lift tickets (2007/08 prices): Adults, $48; children (6-12) and seniors (65-79, 80+ ski free), $26; kids 5 and younger, $5.

Lessons: Full day/adults, $55; kids 5-8, $55; 9-12, $57. Beginner ski package, $47; beginner snowboard package, $57.

Driving distances: From Durango, 72 miles east on Hwy. 160; from Pagosa Springs, 23 miles; from South Fork, 18 miles.

Lodging information: The resort does not have lodging and it doesn't handle lodging reservations, but you'll find a complete listing of nearby accommodations on the resort website. Other resources: Pagosa Springs Chamber, 800-252-2204 or www.pagosaspringschamber.com; South Fork Business Association, 800-571-0881 or www.southfork.org/lodging.

Steamboat
Colorado

Summit:	**10,568 feet**
Vertical:	**3,668 feet**
Base:	**6,900 feet**

Address: 2305 Mt. Werner Circle, Steamboat Springs, Colorado 80487
Telephone (main): 970-879-6111
Snow Report Number: 970-879-7300
Toll-free reservations: 800-922-2722
E-mail: info@steamboat.com
Internet: www.steamboat.com

Expert:★★★
Advanced:★★★★
Intermediate:★★★★★
Beginner:★★
First-timer:★★

Lifts: 23—1 8-passenger gondola, 1 high-speed six pack chairlift, 5 high-speed quads, 2 quads, 6 triples, 3 doubles, 5 surface lifts
Skiable acreage: 2,965
Snowmaking: 15 percent
Uphill capacity: 32,158
Parks & pipes: 2 parks, 3 pipes
Bed base: 18,917
Nearest lodging: Slopeside
Child care: Yes, 6 months and older
Adult ticket, per day: $91 (08/09)
Dining:★★★★
Apres-ski/nightlife:★★★
Other activities:★★★★★

Unlike other Colorado ski resorts, Steamboat's expansive terrain — 3,668 vertical feet covering almost 3,000 acres — is below timberline, meaning there are no take-your-breath-away bowls or steep rocky chutes to pump adrenaline. But groves of aspens beckon you in for some of the best tree skiing anywhere.

Steamboat's geographic location near the Wyoming border has several advantages. At the Western foot of Rabbit Ears Pass, the resort is a haul from Colorado's Front Range, so the day-trippers who crowd the Summit County resorts don't fill the lift lines here.

Then there's the snow. Lots and lots of snow. Over-the-fence-posts snow. Up-to-the-second-story-windows snow. When-will-these-snowbanks-ever-melt snow. Storms blow in from the high plains of Northwestern Colorado and dump their load here. Plan a trip here and you're almost guaranteed snow.

Although Steamboat's famous picture, the ski trails rising behind a brown barn, alludes to the town's cowboy heritage, the resort itself is sleek and modern. The gondola rises from the heart of Steamboat Mountain Village where you can browse art galleries, shop for a new ski outfit and sip a Starbucks latte. Adjacent to the village is a colossal Sheraton, designed to accommodate the masses, not to exude any geographic or historic pretension. The only cowboy that you might see graces the head of Steamboat's resident celebrity and director of skiing, Olympian Billy Kidd.

The resort invested $16 million in improvements for the 07-08 season, including a new high-speed six-pack chairlift that serves the beginner trails and terrain park on Christie Peak, and regrading of the learning terrain, oddly called the Headwall, that rises from the base village.

Venture into downtown Steamboat Springs—about five minutes by car and 15 minutes by a free shuttlebus from the mountain—and you may see cowboys sauntering down the main drag. Northwest Colorado still has cattle ranches, so they'll probably be the real thing. But the only horse you'll likely see is a life-sized statue that stands on the sidewalk outside F.M. Light & Sons, a clothing store that has been open (and in the same family) since 1905.

But the town is more than a kitschy Western tourist hub. The 93-year-old Steamboat Springs Winter Sports Club at Howelsen Hill, across the river from downtown, is home to world-class athletes who train on the Nordic trails, ski jumps, and Alpine pistes there. With only a 440-foot vertical rise, Howelsen Hill is the oldest ski area in continuous use in Colorado and has been the training ground for 69 Olympians, including Buddy Werner.

Steamboat is also a terrific place for people who don't ski or ride. In addition to great shopping, it has activities that go beyond the usual sleigh rides and snowmobile tours (see Other Activities).

 ## Mountain layout

Steamboat is a gigantic ski area with everything from wide-open, gentle learning slopes to steep, powder-filled tree stashes. It is a perfect mountain for anyone learning to ski powder or trees. The cruising runs are wide and wonderful.

Expert, Advanced: Expert descents here mean trees, bumps in trees and short, sweet bump runs. There are a handful of double-diamond tree runs off Mt. Werner, but they're short and, while a bit unnerving, totally do-able. Drop over Storm Peak to the Morningside lift to avoid hiking to this terrain. For classic Steamboat trees, look to skier's right off the Sundown Express chair. These aspen and pine groves have been expertly thinned, both by humans and Mother Nature. Sundown Liftline and Shadows seem never-ending.

Elsewhere on the mountain, don't be shy about ducking into the trees, like the space between Concentration and Vagabond on the lower part of the mountain or the "Twisticane" trees between Twister and Hurricane. Once you start looking, you'll see that the entire mountain is one big skiable forest.

The 260 acres that make up Pioneer Ridge off the Pony Express lift have gained a local fan club with long, winding runs. It's fun because Steamboat shied away from the straight-down cut and went with the terrain angles here.

Intermediate: Among the great cruisers are the blue trails from the Sunshine and Sundown Express lifts (locals call this area "Wally World"), Vagabond and Heavenly Daze off Thunderhead Express. The blue runs served by the Sunshine Express also have spots where beginning tree skiers can practice. If crowds build in any of those areas, move lower on the mountain and take laps on the intermediate runs reached by the Bashor and Christie chairs, which often are deserted.

Longhorn, off Pioneer Ridge, is a locals' favorite with unparalleled views of the Yampa Valley. Skiers and riders can duck in and out of the lodgepole pines that border both sides of this run.

On many of the black-diamond runs, although the terrain has steep spots and the moguls get pretty high, the trails are generally wide, allowing ample room for mistakes and recoveries. Westside, a black trail below Rendezvous Saddle, is steep but usually well groomed. It's a good starting point for intermediates who wonder if they can handle the other black runs.

Beginner, First-timer: With the exception of some gentle terrain served by the Bashor and the new Christie Peak Express six-pack chairlift, most of the green trails above the base area are cat tracks. Wally World, between the Sunshine and Sundown chairs, has gentle blue runs that often attract classes; you have to watch out for and forgive skiers and riders who can't turn and stop. Many of the green runs are narrow. Some intersect higher-ability runs where bombers sometimes use the intersection as a launching pad for the next section, and a few have slightly intimidating drop-offs on the downhill side. If beginners are part of your group, encourage them to enroll in a clinic so they will have a pleasant experience.

A successful first-time experience—especially for adults—depends on two things: great instruction and suitable, uncrowded terrain. In the past, we've said Steamboat rates highly on the former, but not on the latter. However, as part of the resort's $40 million investment in improvements, the inappropriately-named Headwall near the base area was regraded in summer 2007 to improve the learning experience. This learning terrain, at the base of the mountain is separated from other traffic and lets novices totally concentrate on the fun.

Parks and pipes

Steamboat is ranked in the Top 10 in the country for its parks and pipes by several ski and snowboard magazines. Even its "vibe" gets high ratings. The Bashor lift serves both the Mavericks Superpipe and the SoBe Terrain Park. Mavericks Superpipe is a big hit. It's one of the longest superpipes on the continent (650 feet long, 50 feet wide and 15-foot walls with 17-foot transitions). There's a mega music system and snowmaking. A 50-foot quarterpipe finishes off the superpipe ride. The SoBe Terrain Park is chock full of features for all ability levels. You'll find 11 jumps with different landings, hips, tables and mailboxes, 14 rails including a flat bar, flat-down, rainbow, S-rail and crazy double barrel. Mini-Mav is a 250-foot-long minipipe version of Mavericks with 10-foot walls for beginner riders. There's also a kids-only terrain park, the Beehive, at Rough Rider Basin.

Snowboarding

Steamboat's trademark Champagne Powder® snow, which seems to fall in well-timed weekly accumulations, makes this a tree boarder's paradise. Shadows, with its steady pitch and widely spaced aspen trees, is possibly the most perfect tree run in Colorado. And Pioneer Ridge, below Storm Peak, invites exploration, although the long run-out makes a little hiking likely. When the pow blows out (as if), enter The Twilight Zone between the Sunshine and Sundown lifts. It's a difficult gladed run studded with moguls.

If you're lucky, you might run into Banana George Blair, Steamboat's 90-something snowboard ambassador and barefoot water skier extraordinaire. Always clad in yellow, Banana was extreme before the term was coined; he learned to snowboard at age 75. He's cooler than you, so share the love.

For beginning snowboarders, a moving carpet serves the learning area. This section, at the base of the mountain is separated from other traffic so novices can focus on their fun.

Cross-country & snowshoeing (see also xcskiresorts.com)

The **Steamboat Ski Touring Center** (970-879-8180) at 2000 Clubhouse Drive boasts about 30 km. of groomed trails winding along Fish Creek and the surrounding housing developments. The touring center has group and private instruction, rentals, a restaurant and backcountry guided tours. Snowshoeing is available on 10 km. of trails.

Steamboat offers on-mountain snowshoe tours that meet each Monday through Saturday from the top of the Gondola and are guided by the Steamboat Ambassadors. Bring your own shoes or rent from Steamboat Ski Rentals (970-879-5444).Rentals are also available on-line before you go from rentskis.com.

Track skiing is available at **Howelsen Hill** in downtown Steamboat Springs (970-879-8499) and at **Vista Verde** (800-526-7433; 970-879-3858), **High Meadows Ranch** (970-736-8416; 800-457-4453) and **The Home Ranch** (970-879-1780). All guest ranches are 18-25 miles from Steamboat Springs. The latter three cater to overnight guests but also welcome day visitors. Vista Verde's 30-km. system is especially good for beginners—most of the terrain is quite gentle. High Meadows grooms about 12 km. with additional trails groomed as needed. The Home Ranch, which has 40 km. of groomed track, offers cross-country, backcountry and telemarking.

For a real thrill take a tour to **Rabbit Ears Pass** (guided tours available through Steamboat Touring Center and Ski Haus, 970-879-0385); you'll be skiing on the Continental Divide. The marked backcountry ski trails range from 1.7 to 7 miles, from relatively gentle slopes to steep and gnarly. On a clear day you can see forever. Call or visit the **U.S. Forest Service** (29587 W. US 40 in Steamboat Springs, 970-879-1722) to get current ski conditions and safety tips. Other popular backcountry areas are **Buffalo Pass, Pearl Lake State Park, Stagecoach State Recreation Area and Steamboat Lake State Park**.

Lessons (07/08 prices)

Group lessons: For intermediate and advanced skiers or snowboarders, lessons cost $94 for a full day and $81 for a half day during regular season; $87 for all day and $76 for a half day during value season. Beginners can choose from just a clinic ($39 for all day, $34 for half-day) or a package (see below).

First-timer package: For first-timers and beginners, an all-day lesson, lift and rental package for skiers and snowboarders costs $114 regular season; $95 value season. Half-day packages cost $5 less. The resort allows novices to repeat the first lesson at no charge until they've learned to descend from the Preview lift in a controlled manner.

Private lessons: Regular season, cost is $200 for a 90-minute Early Bird Special starting at 8:30 a.m., $325 for two hours, $340 for a half-day afternoon, $390 for a half-day morning, $595 for all day. Value season prices are $190 for Early Bird Special, $295 for two hours, $310 for half-day p.m., $360 for half-day a.m. and $560 for all day. Reservations required; call (800) 299-5017. Adaptive private lessons are $90 for three hours; additional hours cost $30 each.

Steamboat offers free guided skiing for anyone over age 50. Called the Over the Hill Gang, it's open to anyone who is an intermediate skier or better. Meet outside the Ski & Snowboard School Ticket Office at 9 a.m. any day of the week. Or join the group at the Thunderhead Cafeteria between 11:45 a.m. and 12:30 p.m. for an afternoon of camaraderie on the slopes. The Over the Hill Gang started in 1985 and now has more than 400 members.

Racing: Steamboat is home to 69 Olympians so it's a natural for racing and competition programs. The resort has one of the largest race facilities in the world with NASTAR racing open to the public from 10:30 a.m.-12:30 p.m., Wednesdays through Sundays in the Bashor Race Arena. A daily pass (unlimited runs) costs $10/day. Also in the race arena is a dual race-training course—fun if you've always told your buddies that you would dust them in a race. The course is open from 9:30 a.m. to 3:30 p.m. at $1 per run. In March 2007, Steamboat is hosting NASTAR Nationals.

Steamboat also has the Billy Kidd Performance Center which offers one-, two- and three-day camps on specific dates for adults who are at least of intermediate ability. The camps refine technique in the bumps, through race gates and on tough terrain. One-day camps (Monday) cost $225; three-day camps (Monday-Wednesday) $675.

Children's programs (08/09 prices)

Child care: Kiddie Corral is for ages 6 months to 6 years. Cost is $105 all day with lunch ($98 all day during value season). Parents must provide lunch for kids younger than 18 months. Prepaid reservations required for all care programs. Cancellations must be 24 hours in advance to avoid being charged. Call the Kids' Vacation Center, 871-5375 or (800) 299-5017. Steamboat's children's programs have been very highly rated over the years by various magazines.

Other options: Baby's Away (800-978-9030; 879-2354) rents and will deliver baby needs to your lodge, such as cribs, strollers, car seats and toys.

Children's lessons (07-08 prices): Ages 2–5 can opt for a one-hour private lesson and all-day child care for $260 including lunch ($245 value season). Ages 3½–4 who want more time on the snow can take all-day clinics that have two to four hours on snow plus playtime and lunch for $117 ($110 value season). Ages 4–kindergarten can get even more time on skis in either a half-day program at $87 ($83 value season) or full-day for $104 ($97 value season). No lift ticket is required for kids ages 5 and younger.

However, lift tickets are extra for all programs listed below. Ages first grade–15 pay $110 for an all-day lesson with lunch or $90 for a half-day afternoon lesson ($103 all day, $90 half day during value season). Kids 8 and older who are at least intermediate skiers and riders can take a half-day freestyle park and pipe clinic for $85. Ages 13-17 who are at the intermediate level or higher can join the "Steamboat Teen Challenge" an all-day program (with lunch) offered at select times. The cost is $105 per day ($98 during value season). Steamboat also has the Billy Kidd Performance Center for ages 8 and older who are at least of intermediate ability (see Adult Lessons).

Skiing with your children: Steamboat has four kids-only lifts and two special teaching areas with their own moving carpets. More advanced children have kids-only ski terrain at Rough Rider Basin with its own lift plus Indian teepees, a frontier-style fort and the Beehive kids' terrain park. One child 12 or younger rents gear free with each five-day parental adult rental; certain restrictions apply. Rentals are available at the Kids' Vacation Center. Helmet rentals also are available.

Lift tickets (07/08 prices)

	Adult (18-64)	Child (6-12)
One day	$91	$56
Three days	$273 ($91/day)	$168 ($56/day)
Five days	$455 ($91/day)	$280 ($56/day)

Who skis Free: Children 5 and under.

Who skis at a discount: Teens 13-17 ride lifts for $73 a day for up to five days; six or more days, teens pay $69 per day; ID required. Ages 65-69 pay $73 per day; ID required. Ages 70 and older pay $40; ID required.

Note: Early-, late-, and mid-season prices are lower; holiday rates are higher.

Accommodations

Staying in the Steamboat mountain village is generally more expensive than in town. Condos outnumber hotel and motel rooms. Rates vary throughout the season: Before mid-December and after March 31 are cheapest; January comes next, and Christmas and Presidents' Weekend are most expensive.

Dining: $$$$–Entrees $30+; $$$–$20–$30; $$–$10–$20; $–less than $10.
Accommodations: (double room) $$$$–$200+; $$$–$141–$200; $$–$81–$140; $–$80 and less.

Steamboat Central Reservations (800-922-2722) will make suggestions to match your needs and desires. Let the reservationist know the price range, location and room requirements (quiet location, good for families, kitchen, laundry or other special amenities).

The Sheraton Steamboat Resort and Conference Center (800-848-8878; 800-848-8877 in Colorado; 970-879-2220; $$-$$$), a full-service hotel, sits 60 feet from the Steamboat Gondola. The Morningside tower condominiums here have two- to four-bedroom units. We love the views and open design of the main living areas.

With spacious one, two- or three-room suites complete with full kitchen, the fairly new **Steamboat Grand Resort Hotel & Condominiums** (877-269-2628; 871-5500; $$$-$$$$) is a great bet for extended families. Traditional hotel rooms and bigger penthouses are also available. There is complimentary wireless Internet access. The Grand has restaurants, a game room, outdoor heated pool, complete fitness center and a full-service spa.

Nearly all the other lodging at the ski area is in condominiums—hundreds of them surround the base. **Torian Plum** (800-228-2458; 970-879-8811; $$$-$$$$) is one of the best, with spotless rooms and facilities, an extremely helpful staff, the ski area out one door and the top bars and restaurants out the other. These are among the nicest condos we've stayed in anywhere. Torian Plum's sister properties, **Bronze Tree** and Trappeur's Crossing, have similar prices. Bronze Tree has two- and three-bedroom units. **Trappeur's Crossing** is about two blocks from the lifts, but offers a free private shuttle from 7 a.m. to 11 p.m. **Timberline** at Trappeur's Crossing and **Creekside** at Torian Plum (800-228-2458; 970-879-8811) are fairly new. We were knocked out by the mountain-facing views, mountain-style furnishings and the ski-in/ski-out location at Creekside. Ditto (except for views) at Timberline, two blocks from the Gondola, with on-call shuttle service.

Prices are generally based on how close the property is to the lifts. Among those in the expensive category are the **Best Western Ptarmigan Inn** (800-538-7519; 970-879-1730; $$$) at the base of the Gondola, **Storm Meadows Townhomes** (800-262-5150; 970-879-5151; $$$), **Norwegian Log Condominiums** (800-525-2622; 970-879-3700; $$$) and **Thunderhead Lodge and Condominiums** (800-525-5502; 970-879-9000; $$$).

Others in this price category are **Timber Run Condominiums** (800-525-5502; 970-879-7000; $$$) with three outdoor hot tubs; **The Lodge at Steamboat** (800-525-5502; 879-6000; $$$); and **The Ranch at Steamboat** (800-525-2002; 970-879-3000; $$$) with great views of the ski hill and the broad Yampa Valley.

Moving Mountains Chalet (877-624-2538; 970-870-9359) has luxury chalets adjacent to the ski area for groups of up to 14 people. They will arrange all travel, lodging, dining and recreation details ahead of time including a personal chef and pre-programmed cell phones.

The Village at Steamboat (800-333-1962; $-$$) has studio, one- bedroom, and two-bedroom units. The common areas are shared and include a recreation building with racquetball, locker room, steam room, sauna, indoor spa and swimming pool, outdoor spa and seasonal swimming pool, multi-purpose room with kitchen, and a game room.

Economy lodging includes **Alpiner Lodge** (800-538-7519; 970-879-1430; $$) downtown which features in-room wireless Internet access and mini-fridges; **Shadow Run Condominiums** (800-525-2622; 970-879-3700), 500 yards from lifts; and **Alpine Vista Townhomes** (800-525-2622; 970-879-3700; $$) just a bit farther.

The Steamboat Bed and Breakfast (877-335-4321; 970-879-5724; $$$) just a few years old, is at 442 Pine St., 2 blocks from downtown. This B&B has rooms filled with antiques. Rates include breakfast. No children or pets allowed.

Travelers who enjoy remote rural elegance will be delighted by a stay at **The Home**

Ranch (970-879-1700; $$$$) in the town of Clark a 40-minute drive up the Elk River Valley north of Steamboat. This is one of a handful of Relais et Chateaux properties in the U.S. Eight wooden cabins in the aspens of the Elk River Valley have views of Hahn's Peak and the surrounding mountains. Each is distinctly decorated with an outdoor hot tub and an inside wood stove. The main lodge also has six guestrooms and a dining room for three daily gourmet meals. The dining room is exclusive to ranch guests. Rates also include lift tickets and a shuttle to the ski area, though many people will be happy exploring the cross-country and snowshoe trails at the ranch.

Between town and the mountain is the pleasant **Iron Horse Inn** (970-879-6505, fax 970-879-6129; $$) offering recently renovated suites with kitchenettes (small but functional) and a two-story building of clean and comfortable hotel rooms.

Some chain motels have shown up in the last couple of years. They're generally scattered in a row along Hwy. 40 just before the turnoff to the mountain. The newest is the **Marriott Fairfield Inn & Suites** (970-870-9000; $$). Sixty-five no-frills rooms are a half-mile from Gondola Square on the free bus route. Others include **Holiday Inn** (970-879-2250; $$), **Hampton Inn & Suites** (970-871-8900; $$), **Inn at Steamboat** (970-879-2600; $$), **Bunkhouse Lodge** (970-871-9121; $$), and **Super 8 Motel** (970-879-5230; $$). Or you can stay downtown in the **Rabbit Ears Motel** (800-828-7702; 970-879-1150; $$) across the street from the hot springs pools. Look for the neon lights in the shape of a bunny's head.

Another option out of town is **Strawberry Park Hot Springs Cabins** (970-879-0342; $), about 10 miles north of Steamboat at the mineral hot springs. Both covered wagons and rustic cabins are available for overnight stays. Lodging price includes a hot springs pass—lovely soaking outdoors on a winter night.

 # Dining

Steamboat has great variety: more than 100 restaurants and bars, including one or more Cajun, Chinese, Japanese, French, Italian and Scandinavian. Look for the Steamboat Dining Guide in your hotel or condo—it has menus and prices.

On mountain

Without a doubt, the most impressive evening in Steamboat starts at Gondola Square at the Gondola terminal. Here, you set off on a journey into the stars to **Hazie's** (970-871-5150; reservations required for dinner, available Friday through Sunday and holidays; $$$) at the top of Thunderhead. Hazie's serves a special continental dinner with unbeatable views. Cost is $70 for adults, $54 for teens 13-18, and $36 for children 6-12; not appropriate for children 5 and younger. Cost includes gondola ride. You can also have lunch (reservations recommended) daily from 11:30 a.m. to 2:30 p.m. Choose from an assortment of soups and salads, entrees and burgers.

For elegant dining, it's hard to beat **The Cabin** (970-871-5550; $$$) on the lobby level of the Steamboat Grand. It features contemporary Colorado cuisine for breakfast and dinner and specializes in native Colorado wild game and "jet-fresh" seafood.

Ragnar's (970-871-5150; reservations required for dinner and suggested for lunch; $$-$$$) at Rendezvous Saddle halfway down the High Noon ski run features Scandinavian and continental cuisine. Start with the gravlax with mustard dill sauce, the Norwegian salad with proscuitto or seafood chowder. Friday through Sunday, Ragnar's offers a fixed-price Scandinavian menu at $98 for adults, $86 for teens 13-18, and $62 for children 6-12; not appropriate for children 5 and younger. The evening starts at Gondola Square, but once off the gondola at the top of Thunderhead, you climb into a snowcat-drawn sleigh to continue your journey

Dining: $$$$–Entrees $30+; $$$–$20–$30; $$–$10–$20; $–less than $10.
Accommodations: (double room) $$$$–$200+; $$$–$141–$200; $$–$81–$140; $–$80 and less.

to Rendezvous Saddle. Price includes gondola and sleigh ride. We recommend a mug of hot spiced glugg before relaxing to music and enjoying your meal.

Western BBQ (970-871-5150; reservations required; $$$) Friday through Sunday, features live country-western entertainment, dancing, an all-you-can-eat buffet and a full cash bar, all on the third floor of the Thunderhead Building at the top of the gondola. Cost is $47 for adults, $35 for teens 13-18, $24 for children 6-12, and free for ages 5 and younger.

The **Rendezvous Saddle** building, halfway down the High Noon ski run, was newly renovated for the 2006/07 season and features an updated cafeteria. **Stoker Bar** (970-871-5150; $-$$) on the first floor of the Thunderhead Building (at the top of the Gondola) has full-service lunch of soups, chile, sandwiches, micro beers and specialty drinks. The **Bear River Bar & Grill**, at the base across from the Gondola bay entrance, is a very popular gathering spot. **Gondola Joe's** is a full-service coffee shop and cafe in Gondola Square.

Saketumi (970-870-1019), pronounced "sock-it-to-me," is a hip spot on the mountain for sushi and Asian fusion cuisine. Open for lunch and dinner.

In town

For Steamboat's pinnacle of French dining, try **Harwigs & L'Apogee** (911 Lincoln Ave., 970-879-1919; $$$). While the food cannot be too highly praised, it is the wine list that is truly impressive. There are more than 500 wines, ranging from $12 to $1,000 a bottle.

Another fine-dining choice is **Antares** (57-1/2 Eighth St., 970-879-9939; $$$). Serving new American cuisine, this restaurant is housed in the historic Rehder building built in the early 1900s. Open daily 5:30 p.m. to 10:30 p.m.

For more than Mex, don't miss **La Montana**, (970-879-5800, 2500 Village Dr.; $$-$$$). The menu goes way beyond tacos and fajitas. More than 20 varieties of margaritas.

Cottonwood Grill (701 Yampa Ave., 970-879-2229; $$-$$$) downtown on the Yampa River, blends American and Asian flavors with traditional favorites.

A popular seafood restaurant is the **Steamboat Yacht Club** (811 Yampa Ave., 970-879-4774; $$). Its menu is designed to mix and match fish, cooking techniques and sauces to suit your tastes. It's one of the best restaurants for the price in town.

The Steamboat Smokehouse (912 Lincoln Ave.; $-$$) has a no-credit card, no-reservations, no-nonsense atmosphere with some of Colorado's best Texas-style barbecue. Toss your peanut shells on the floor and choose from ten beer taps to fill iced mugs.

Dos Amigos (970-879-4270; $$) serves Tex-Mex food and sandwiches and is part of the infamous "Steamboat Triangle" apres-ski circuit along with **Tugboat Grill & Pub** ($-$$) and **Slopeside**. **Cafe Diva** (970-871-0508; $$) is a wine bar in the Torian Plum Plaza that serves eclectic cuisine.

Family recipes are shared at **Mambo Italiano** (970-870-0500; $$), an inexpensive but excellent family-style diner with 19 different pastas. **Johnny B. Good's Diner** (970-870-8400; $), a fifties-style soda fountain, is best known for its chocolate milkshakes and quick service. Also great for breakfast.

Old West Steakhouse (970-879-1441; $$) has packed in the crowds for years with its generous portions of steak and seafood. Make a meal out of the appetizers. **Giovanni's** (970-879-4141; $$) has not only Italian fare, but also what may be the largest collection of Brooklyn memorabilia this side of the borough. For upscale Italian, head to **Riggio's** (970-879-9010; $$) on Lincoln. Seafood and veal are especially good and be sure to leave room for their homemade desserts. **Mahogany Ridge Brewery & Grill** (970-879-3773; $-$$), Steamboat's only brew pub, has great brews and decent pub grub. But the wait can be long.

If you're in town for breakfast or lunch, try the **Creekside Cafe and Grill** (970-879-

4925; $). Homemade soup, sandwiches and salads are served along with soothing classical music. For some quiet-time and a light lunch head to **Off The Beaten Path** bookstore and coffeehouse (970-879-6830; $) across from the Harbor Hotel. We like the bookstore, the great gourmet coffees and the linger-as-long-as-you-want attitude.

Other good downtown breakfast spots are **Winona's**, (try the cinnamon buns!) or **The Shack Cafe**. **The Tugboat Grill & Pub** at the base area. There's a **Starbucks** in the Sheraton at the base. Avid skiers can board the gondola at 8 a.m. (as part of First Tracks) and have breakfast at **The Stoker** afterwards.

Apres-ski/nightlife

Dos Amigos, as noted in the Dining section, is one leg of the "Steamboat Triangle." Have margaritas and half-priced apps here, then head for **Slopeside** and **The Tugboat Grill & Pub** for beer or mixed drinks. **Chaps**, in the Steamboat Grand, is a Western-themed bar and grill with live entertainment most evenings throughout the winter. A quieter apres-ski on the mountain can be found at **3 Saddles** in the Sheraton. Downtown, the **Old Town Pub** and **Mahogany Ridge** have great apres-ski. All tapas and house brews are half-price from 4-6 p.m. at Mahogany Ridge.

Sandwiched between Dos Amigos and Tugboat is a three-tiered building that you never have to leave. The main floor houses **Wired**, an Internet cafe by day and a martini bar by night. After 5 p.m. you can slurp a Mango Tango Tini, Dreamsicle or Slippery Banana from an extensive menu. Jocks can hit the sports bar, **Lupo's**, on the second level.

Downtown, the lively spots include **The Tap House**, **Steamboat Smokehouse** and **The Old Town Pub**.

Other activities

Steamboat has so much to do off the mountain, it's tempting to skip the skiing. Here is a mere sampling:

Soak in the natural thermal waters at **Strawberry Park Hot Springs** (970-879-0342), about 10 miles north of the ski area. Unless you have four-wheel drive, spend extra for a tour that includes transportation—the road to the springs is narrow, slick, steep and winding and parking is extremely limited. It's open from 10 a.m. t 10 p.m. during the week and stays open a little later on weekends. Helpful info: After dark, many bathers go without suits (unless it's a moonlit night, you won't see much) and Wednesdays are often designated as "clothing optional" days/nights. The only place to change is an unheated teepee, so wear your swimsuit under your clothes. Many people bring a plastic bag to store their clothes; otherwise steam from the pools combined with the cold air may freeze them. Water shoes will protect your feet from the rocky entry. Beverages are OK but no glass containers.

Families might prefer the **Steamboat Health and Recreation Center** (970-879-1828) in downtown Steamboat with lockers, workout rooms, hot springs pools, lap pools and a huge water slide.

Day spas we recommend are **Rocky Mountain Spa** (970-870-9860) on Burgess Creek Rd. at the mountain; **Life Essentials** (970-871-9543) downtown; **Sol Day Spa** (970-871-9765) in the Sheraton Hotel; and **Bear River Therapists** (970-879-8282). The **Steamboat Grand** (970-871-5514) also has a full-service spa. Ask for their signature treatments and enjoy.

Learn to drive on slick roads at the **Bridgestone Winter Driving School** (800-949-7543; 970-879-6104). Half-day, full-day and multiday lessons on a specially constructed course are a unique experience, one that could save your life.

Dining: $$$$–Entrees $30+; $$$–$20–$30; $$–$10–$20; $–less than $10.
Accommodations: (double room) $$$$–$200+; $$$–$141–$200; $$–$81–$140; $–$80 and less.

Steamboat Powdercats (877-624-2538 or 970-870-9359) offers deep powder cat skiing and boarding in the Steamboat vicinity. Runs vary in length from 600 to 1,600 vertical feet and in steepness from 20 and 45 degrees.

Other activities include dogsled rides (970-879-4662), ice skating at Howelsen Ice Arena (970-879-0341), ice climbing (970-879-8440), indoor climbing (970-879-5421), indoor tennis (970-879-8400), snowmobile touring, tubing, horseback riding and hot-air ballooning. Several businesses offer these last two activities; ask when you get into town. There are far too many more to list. You can make reservations for activities through **Steamboat Central Reservations** (800-922-2722; 970-879-0740) or **Windwalker Premier Tours** (800-748-1642; 970-879-8065).

Shopping opportunities are many and varied, both in the village and downtown. The Sports Stalker (970-879-0371) at Gondola Square rents ski clothes, mainly courtesy of the airline that lost your luggage. Steamboat has a movie theater downtown and a six-plex opened in 2006 near the mountain village.

Getting there and getting around

By air: Travelers arriving by air will find the Yampa Valley Regional Airport significantly expanded and renovated. This airport at Hayden, 22 miles away, handles jets. American, Continental, Delta, United and Northwest have nonstop flights from eight U.S. cities plus one-stop connecting service from more than 150 other domestic and international cities. Special air fares may be available through Steamboat Central Reservations: 800-922-2722.

Two ground transportation companies provide service from the airport and from Denver International Airport—Alpine Taxi/Limo (970-879-2800) and Storm Mountain Express. Avis, Budget and Hertz have cars available at the Yampa Valley Airport.

By car: Steamboat is 157 miles northwest of Denver. Take I-70 west through the Eisenhower Tunnel to exit 205 at Silverthorne (allow extra time if you want to stop at Silverthorne's factory outlet mall), north on Hwy. 9 to Kremmling, then west on Hwy. 40 over Rabbit Ears Pass to the resort.

Getting around: A car is optional. Steamboat has an excellent free bus system between town and ski area running every 20 minutes from 7 a.m. to 1:45 a.m. Call 970-879-3717 for information.

Telluride
Colorado

Summit:	**13,150 feet**
Vertical:	**4,425 feet**
Base:	**8,750 feet**

Address: 565 Mountain Village Boulevard, Telluride, CO 81435
Telephone (main): 970-728-6900
Snow Report Number: 970-728-7425
Toll-free reservations: 800-778-8581 or 888-353-5473
E-mail: info@tellurideskiresort.com
Internet: www.tellurideskiresort.com
Expert:★★★★★
Advanced:★★★★★
Intermediate:★★★★
Beginner:★★★★★
First-timer:★★★★★

Lifts: 18—2 gondolas, 7 high-speed quads, 1 quad, 2 triples, 2 doubles, 4 surface
Skiable acreage: 2,000+
Snowmaking: 15 percent
Uphill capacity: 21,186
Parks & pipes: 3 parks, 1 pipe
Bed base: 5,000
Nearest lodging: Slopeside
Child care: Yes, 2 months and older
Adult ticket, per day: $92 (08-09 price)
Dining:★★★★★
Apres-ski/nightlife:★★★
Other activities:★★★★

Telluride is at the crossroads of colliding worlds. The bottom of the box canyon in which Telluride sits is red-rock desert, while the mountains tumbling into town are snowcapped and craggy Alpine granite. Then there's the contrast in architecture between the Old West town of Telluride and the contemporary Telluride Mountain Village. The town of Telluride is a pageantry of Victorian buildings wearing bright, bold colors.

Mountain Village, on the other hand, is carved out of rock and log dressed in muted earth tones. Mountain Village, partway up the mountain, is hunkered in at 9,540 feet above sea level, while the town of Telluride rests at the very bottom of the trails at 8,750 feet. If you're skiing down any of the front runs that drop into town, it feels as if you're going to land on someone's doorstep. Another novelty is the free 2.5-mile gondola that links the town of Telluride with Mountain Village, making it a cinch to go back and forth between the two for shopping or dining.

Telluride certainly is one of the most breathtaking environments for a ski resort. Be prepared for recreating at high altitude, with lifts dumping you off as high as 12,260 feet. Perhaps the most delightful surprise about Telluride is that it's one of the few North American resorts that can truly be a remarkable vacation for just about everyone, regardless of skill level.

From a copious amount of gentle learning terrain to ideal powder training grounds for intermediates, it seems downright greedy to ask for more. As for advanced skiers and riders, whether you get your thrills ripping down steep trails that spit you out into town, or you long for the solitude of high-mountain peaks with no hint of civilization, it's here waiting. Those venturing into the backcountry have much to choose from, including a couple of peaks topping 14,000 feet.

Revelation Bowl has been added for the 2008-09 winter season. This European-style terrain, located directly off the back side of Gold Hill and Chair 14, is served by a quad-lift. Situated above tree line, the natural, wide-open bowl offers advanced and expert skiing.

Everyone here is quick to tell about Telluride's fascinating history, from Butch Cassidy robbing the bank to the first miners who strapped on a pair of 7-foot-long skis to glide down the mountain. No need for yarn spinnin' about Telluride's past; it's all woven into the fabric of life and as authentic as it gets. Fortunately skiing replaced the ailing mining industry in the early 1970s, saving the small community from becoming a ghost town. It also saved its rich past, preserving the entire town in a National Historic District that's worth the visit alone.

Mountain layout

Telluride has a very user-friendly trail rating system: It's divided into six categories instead of three or four. One green circle is easiest, then double greens-a bit more challenging, then single blues, double blues, single black and double black.

Expert, Advanced: Ask locals where to head first and you'll get a split decision: Some recommend the front face that drops into town, which put Telluride on the skiers' map in the first place. Others steer you to Gold Hill and Prospect Bowl, newer terrain that guarantees hoots and hollers.. Wherever you start, you'll end up skiing it all and having a ball, so it really doesn't matter in the end.

If you start on the front face, The Plunge and Spiral Stairs will make you or break you. This duo is as challenging a combination of steep bumps as you can find anywhere. The best part is your audience on the chair above. The Plunge is normally split-groomed, creating one of the steepest and most daringly exciting snow highways. If your knees give out you can bail. Whatever you do, don't let the jaw-dropping view into town distract you. The face is swathed in other double- and single-diamond trails, most with VW-sized bumps, so, if you can, go ahead and give those knees a real workout.

If you prefer more of a backcountry experience, Gold Hill and Prospect Bowl will suit you just right. The 450 acres of glades and above-timberline skiing on Gold Hill are sure to please. Do laps on these double-diamond runs by riding the Gold Hill lift, which dumps you off at the 12,260-foot mark, Telluride's highest lift-served terrain. If it's a clear day take a moment and a picture to admire and remember the magnificent view before dropping in.

Located directly off the back side of Gold Hill and Chair 14 is Revelation Bowl, new for the 2008-09 winter season. Served by a new quad lift this is being toured as European-style terrain situated above tree line, with natural, wide-open bowl skiing/riding aimed at advanced sliders and experts.

In Prospect Bowl, the expert terrain is off Prospect Ridge and Bald Mountain, and it's all hike-to but within bounds. On a powder day, the blues back here are delightful even for more accomplished skiers and riders. Ducking in and out of trees alongside the runs is way fun play.

For those who are properly equipped with Pieps and other safety equipment, Telluride also has backcountry access points off the top of the Gold Hill and Prospect Bowl chairs.

Intermediate: There are several lifts that are pretty much dedicated to intermediate terrain. On a powder day, confident intermediates should make a beeline to Prospect Bowl. It's a lift-served backcountry experience including Sandia, Magnolia and Stella that will let you rock 'n roll down the middle of the bowl with sections of glorious glades to explore.

See Forever—Telluride's aptly named signature run—is a giddy glide down the mountain, almost 3 miles top to bottom. If you're tired, it seems like it takes forever, but there's plenty of superb spots to stop and enjoy the view. On a clear day you can even see the Utah mountains.

The terrain off the Palmyra and Village chairs can keep you happy all day long. With names like Peek-a-Boo, Misty Maiden and Butterfly, you've just gotta let 'em run!

If the single-diamonds on the front face have been groomed, they are acceptable for strong intermediates. If they haven't been groomed, the moguls make these steep runs really tough and you'll want to stick to the blues instead.

Beginner, First-timer: Telluride is one of the top spots on the continent for beginners. Ute Park—the learning area in Prospect Bowl—has trail names that tie into the resort's mining past, like Galloping Goose, May Girl, Nellie and Little Maude. The Sunshine chair serves terrain that's a great ego booster once you've learned to link your turns. The runs are long and very gentle, allowing you to meander back to the lift.

For first-timers, the Meadows is about as perfect a novice area as you can find. The lift here is a Chondola, a hybrid high-speed quad with gondola cars also on the cable.

Parks and pipes

Telluride's Air Garden Terrain Park, with three distinct lines for all ability levels, has more than 11 acres and 480 vertical feet of berms, banks, rails, funboxes, A-frames, tombstones and tabletops. There's also a superpipe with 18-foot walls. Get there by riding the Village lift or the gondola. The Air Garden Yurt is at the top of the superpipe and offers riders a crankin' stereo system and excellent views of the park while taking a break. Newbies might want to get their park baptism in a learning park with rollers and berms off the Ute Park lift.

If you want, you can skip the manmade and head to the Plunge lift. East and West Drains form two natural halfpipes that are 2,000-feet and 4,000-feet long respectively. In addition, there's a 1,200-foot natural quarterpipe on Bushwhacker.

Snowboarding

The Plunge lift provides more vertical than any other lift on the mountain, serving a multitude of runs including The Plunge, a run visible from town. If you don't like moguls, stay away from these single- and double-diamond trails unless you ride the ones that have been split-groomed. For advanced gladed areas, the Apex chair is your best bet. Check out the trees between Allais Alley and Silver Glade.

For riders who get their fix with bowl skiing and deep powder, Gold Hill and Prospect Bowl give you the ultimate in big-board freeriding. You'll have to hike to the expert shots in Prospect Bowl, but they're all in-bounds so they're avalanche controlled.

For big powder days intermediate boarders will want to head straight for Prospect Bowl. Stella, Magnolia and Sandia will give you a rollicking ride and you can mix it up with glades. Near the bottom, you'll want to carry your speed so you don't end up hoofing to the lift. Or enjoy short runs off the Palmyra chair including Dew Drop (look for hits), Ophir Loop and Silver Tip. Avoid Cake Walk when you're done riding this lift. Instead, ride it back to the top then stay rider's right and pick up the Apex chair. You can then ride See Forever back to the gondola or drop off the front into town.

Too-flat runs for snowboarders to avoid include Bridges and Galloping Goose off the Sunshine chair.

Cross-country & snowshoeing (see also xcskiresorts.com)

The spectacular scenery in Telluride makes cross-country skiing pure joy. For high-mesa cross-country skiing this area is tough to beat. The **Telluride Nordic Center** (970-728-1144) offers a 30-km. network of groomed trails around town and the ski area. Lessons, rentals and full-day backcountry tours are available.

If you'd like to ski the intermediate and advanced groomed Nordic trails at Magic Meadows at the top of the Sunshine chair, buy a ticket at the downhill ski area ticket windows.

The San Juan Mountains set the stage with spectacular scenery for guided tours of a five-hut, 68-mile net-work of intermediate and advanced trails. While the **San Juan Hut System** (970-728-6935) is recommended for intermediates, you should really be a strong intermediate in good physical shape. You can tour the entire route or make individual huts your destination. Huts, about 6 miles apart, are equipped with padded bunks, propane cooking appliances and big potbelly stoves. Skiable terrain around the huts ranges from bowls, chutes and trees to gentle slopes. Guides are available for groups, with a maximum of eight skiers.

Lessons (08/09 prices)

Telluride's school has a good reputation. A successful learning experience requires two things: good instruction and appropriate terrain. Telluride has both. Clinics operate out of the Mountain Village Activity Center, a one-stop facility that has lift tickets, lessons, full-service rental shop, overnight equipment storage, children's ski school and child care. Peak/holiday rates are higher. A computer system links Telluride Sports' six rental shops and stores client information permanently so future rentals can be paperwork-free and equipment can be returned to any shop. You can also rent equipment on line at rentskis.com and it will be there for you when you arrive.

Group lessons: All-day group lessons cost $125 during regular season; morning clinics are available for $60.

First-timer package: For skiers or snowboarders, includes a full day of lessons, lifts and rentals for $145 during regular season; three-day program costs $325 regular season. Prices are lower during value season. Nordic and telemark are offered only on certain days; call for specifics.

Private lessons: $285 in regular season for two-hour early bird or late riser; half day is $405 in regular season; full day is $625. Prices are lower in value season.

Special programs: Many, including a highly acclaimed Women's Week program that offers lifts, races, video analysis, seminars, parties and more. Call for dates and cost; reservations required. Adaptive and telemark clinics are also available; call for details.

Racing: Run the NASTAR course near the Smuggler Express lift. .

Children's programs (08/09 prices)

Child care: Ages 2 months to 3 years. Cost for infants 2-11 months, $125for a full day with lunch; $100 for a half day. For toddlers 1-3 years old, $125 for a full day with lunch; $100 for a half day. Reservations are required; call (970) 728-7531 or (800) 801-4832 at least 24 hours in advance or make reservations at telluridekids.com. Children's ski and day-care programs are in the Village Nursery and Children's Center in the Mountain Village Activity Center. There's one staff person to every two infants and one staff person to every five toddlers. The activity center's glass kiosk atop the nursery's central playroom allows parents to peer down at their little ones without being seen.

Other options: Travelin' Tots (970-728-6618) is a retail store that rents cribs, linens, toys, joggers and more to avoid vacation packing hassles. Evening child care referrals are available.

Children's lessons: The Children's Ski & Snowboard School teaches kids ages 3-12 (snowboard lessons are offered for kids 7-12). Lessons, lift and lunch are $124 during regular season and $105 during value season for a full day, with multiday discounts. With lessons, rentals cost an additional $20. Half-day lessons are available. Helmet rentals cost $7, but are included in the kids' rental package. Reservations are required for lessons; call (800) 801-4832 or make reservations at telluridekids.com.

Special activities: A supervised program called Afternoon Kids Club is available after ski school programs; it's free for those enrolled in ski school. It runs from 3-4 p.m. and reservations are required. Wildlife Day introduces kids to animals from the Rocky Mountain Ark, a wildlife rehabilitation facility and licensed non-profit organization. Kids are exposed to injured, rehabilitated wild animals in a safe, fun and informative environment. Houdini, a prairie dog, or Liberty, a bald eagle, are just a few of the creatures the children might encounter during lunch hour. Weekly and holiday story readings are held throughout the year at the Wilkinson Public Library. There are also computers with a selection of interactive CDs and Internet access (970-728-6613).

Lift tickets (08/09 prices)

	Adult	Child (6-12)
One day	$92	$56
Three days	$267	$162
Five days	$435	$260

Who skis free: Ages 5 and younger.

Who skis at a discount: To get greater discounts on multiday tickets, book them online at least seven days in advance.

Seniors (65+) pay $82 for a one-day ticket, $237 for three days and $385 for five days.

Note: Tickets cost less during early and bargain seasons.

Accommodations

In Telluride you can stay down in the historic town or in the Mountain Village. We start with some of our favorite spots in town. Lodging in the mountain village is listed afterwards. Both **Telluride Resort Reservations** (800-778-8581) and **Telluride Central Reservations** (888-353-5473) are good places to start if you're not sure where you want to stay. Make sure to ask about lodging packages and specials. The resort's website also carries lodging deals.

Franklin Manor (888-728-3351; 970-728-3001; $$$-$$$$) could say its middle name is romance. Named for artist Richard Franklin, the manor showcases his neoclassical works in a gallery and all five uniquely decorated bedrooms.

The San Sophia Inn & Condominiums (800-537-4781; 970-728-3001; $$$-$$$$) is near the gondola and the Oak Street lift. This cozy inn is considered one of Telluride's best, with exceptional service. A luxury spot to stay is **The Hotel Columbia** (800-201-9505; 970-728-0660; $$$-$$$$) right at the Telluride base of the gondola. The hotel was built to look historic, but with the addition of space and amenities of modern hotel rooms, such as fireplaces, big beds, a rooftop hot tub and luxurious bathrooms. The hotel has an office for guests' use equipped with fax, copier and computer.

Ice House Lodge & Condominiums (800-544-3436; 970-728-6300; $$$$), a block from the gondola, has custom furniture, antique Navajo rugs and 6-foot tubs. Adjacent condos have full kitchens and two or three bedrooms. Amenities include a continental breakfast, apres-ski goodies, outdoor heated pool, hot tub and steam room. In stark contrast to the town's prevalent Victorian theme, **Camel's Garden Resort Hotel & Condominiums** (888-772-2635; 970-728-9300; $$$$), in the gondola plaza, is a contemporary structure. The ski-in/ski-out luxury

Dining: $$$$–Entrees $30+; $$$–$20–$30; $$–$10–$20; $–less than $10.
Accommodations: (double room) $$$$–$200+; $$$–$141–$200; $$–$81–$140; $–$80 and less.

property achieves understated elegance with handcrafted furniture, Italian marble bathrooms, oversized tubs and fireplaces. Views from the outdoor 25-foot hot tub are spectacular. A day spa is on the lobby level (see Other Activities).

The elegant and intimate **Hotel Telluride** (866-468-3504; 970-369-1188; $$$-$$$$), on the western edge of town, opened in September 2001. Prepare to be pampered here, from the feather bed and down comforter for a peaceful night's sleep to the granite counter tops and Italian tile in the bathrooms. A spa is on the premises (see Other Activities) as well as a bistro.

A member of the National Trust for Historic Hotels of America, the **New Sheridan Hotel & Suites** (800-200-1891; 970-728-4351; $$-$$$$) was lovingly restored for its 100th birthday in 1995. Rich dark colors, period Victorian furniture and black-and-white pictures from Telluride's past make a visit here feel historic. Breakfast, an open pantry with snacks and drinks and free Internet access are included in the price. The restaurant and bar are very good (see Dining).

Bear Creek Inn (800-338-7064; 970-728-6681; $$-$$$$), in a brick building on Colorado Avenue, has 10 rooms with private bath and TV, roof deck, sauna and steam room. Continental breakfast is included.

The Victorian Inn (800-611-9893; 970-728-6601; $$-$$$$), one block from the gondola, recently remodeled 14 of its 32 rooms, some with kitchenettes. While clearly Victorian, the decor is understated. Amenities include a complimentary continental breakfast, outdoor hot tub and sauna.

If you like seclusion, the family-owned **Skyline Ranch** (888-754-1126; 970-728-3757; $$) is eight miles outside of Telluride. Choose between no-smoking lodge rooms and individual cabins. Chefs are culinary school grads, so the meals are outstanding. Hot full breakfast and apres-ski munchies are included in the price. Even if you don't stay here, come one night for a sleigh ride and dinner. It's a tradition. Transportation into Telluride is provided.

All the condos below are managed by **ResortQuest Telluride** (877-826-8043). The **Riverside Condos** ($$$-$$$$) are perhaps the nicest in town and near the base of the gondola. **Manitou Riverhouse** ($$$$) is just as close to the lifts, but be ready for lots of stairs if you rent here. Around the Coonskin Base check into **Viking Lodge** ($$$-$$$$), **Etta Place** ($$$-$$$$) and **Cimarron Lodge** ($$$$), where you can almost literally fall out of bed and onto the lifts.

In the Mountain Village

Everything in the Mountain Village is either new or recently built and luxury is a given.

Smartly showcasing its Southwestern flair, **The Peaks Resort & Golden Door Spa** (800-789-2220; 970-728-6800; $$$$) pampers with spacious rooms, down bedding, terrycloth robes and slippers, glass-enclosed showers, freestanding oversized tubs and marble double-sink vanities. The ski-in/ski-out resort hotel has an efficient ski-valet service and an on-property rental shop. It has one of the largest full-service spas in the country and guests have daily spa access (see Other Activities). Children 16 and younger stay free in their parents' room. Pets are permitted, and the spa has programs just for them.

The highly praised **Inn at Lost Creek** (888-601-5678; 970-728-5678; $$$$) is a beautifully rustic, yet classic, slopeside lodge with 32 uniquely decorated rooms that include fireplaces, jetted tubs and steam showers, plus two roof-top hot tubs, topnotch guest service and the 9545 restaurant (see Dining). The great room, crafted of native stone and weathered timber, is warmly inviting. Choose from studios to two-bedroom suites.

Good for families, **The Mountain Lodge at Telluride** (866-368-6867; $$$-$$$$) has slopeside condos and lodge rooms, as well as a large log-and-stone cabin with awesome views that sleeps 8-14 (the lodge rooms only sleep two). Furnished in an upscale Western motif, the condominiums and cabin have gas fireplaces. Kids like the outdoor heated pool and hot tub, and The Lodge caters to families with unique packages, such as the Wrangler package for winter 2006/07: four nights for a family of four includes a two-hour horseback ride, evening sleigh ride, and cowboy steak dinner for everyone, plus lift tickets for two days. Rates start at $768 per person based on quadruple occupancy. Also in 2006/07, The Mountain Lodge at Telluride has partnered with the non-profit organization One Warm Coat to provide warm coats to those in need. Donate a "gently used" coat upon check-in and receive five percent off the entire reservation. Donate a maximum of four jackets and receive 20 percent off.

Aspen Ridge Townhomes (888-707-4717; $$$$) feature three-bedroom units with saunas, steam showers, hot tubs and fireplaces. **Bear Creek Lodge** (866-538-7731; $$$$) looks like a high-alpine chalet crossed with a rustic mountain lodge with its peaked roofs mimicking the mountain peaks around it. Deluxe rooms and one- to four-bedroom condos come with impressive views. Each unit has a jetted tub, washer and dryer, and a gourmet kitchen. Plus there are two outdoor hot tubs and a heated pool, a fitness center and an indoor hot tub, steam room and sauna. The January Special makes the entire month attractively priced.

Mountain Village has many condos, some of which start at $200 per night (double that for the ones closest to the lifts) and top out around $800. Call **ResortQuest Telluride** (877-826-8043) for more information.

Regional Lodging Program

Telluride has a Regional Lodging Program with seven neighboring towns. If you stay in one of these spots, you can get discount lift tickets throughout the season, saving up to 41 percent. The towns, their distance from Telluride and the number to call are: Cortez/Dolores/Rico/Mancos, four towns 25-70 miles away, 800-253-1616; Montrose, 65 miles, 800-348-3495; Ouray, 47 miles, 800-228-1876; and Ridgway, 37 miles, 800-754-3103. Durango, which is nearer to Purgatory at Durango Mountain Resort, also is part of this program, 800-228-1876. Durango is 125 miles from Telluride and just 25 miles from Durango Mountain Resort. If you want to do both resorts on one trip, it might be worth a call to this program.

 # Dining

Dining in Telluride and the Mountain Village is as much of an inspiring experience as the skiing and riding. It's hard not to have a good meal here, even in the simpler restaurants and cafes. The fine restaurants here have raised the bar for Colorado mountain cuisine.

In town

An award-winning wine list, elegant surroundings and superb New American creations make **Harmons** (970-728-3773; $$$) in the old train depot a perennial favorite. The menu includes seared scallops, garlic spinach, sweet carrot sauce with polenta and mango Napoleon.

La Marmotte (970-728-6232; $$$) serves French cuisine, but with a modern twist. **221 S. Oak** (name and address; 970-728-9507; $$$)is subtly chic with regional American dishes that vary nightly according to the freshest ingredients available.

Chef-owner Chad Scothorn, known for making Beano's in Vail such a treasure, is at the helm of **The Cosmopolitan & Tasting Cellar** (970-728-1292; $$$). His eclectic American fare is influenced by French, Southwestern and Thai flavors. **Rustico Ristorante** (970-728-4046; $$-$$$) is run by Italian natives and has authentic food at good prices. Dine on seafood and steaks at **The Bluepoint Grill** (123 So. Oak St, 970-728-8862; $$), then go downstairs to

Dining: $$$$–Entrees $30+; $$$–$20–$30; $$–$10–$20; $–less than $10.
Accommodations: (double room) $$$$–$200+; $$$–$141–$200; $$–$81–$140; $–$80 and less.

The Noir Bar, a cozy lounge. At **New Sheridan Chop House** (970-728-9100; $$$) the beef, pork and lamb dishes are excellent. Seafood and wild game are just as tasty.

Excelsior Cafe (970-728-4250; $$) has good-value North Italian cuisine and a special late-night menu. **Sofio's** (970-728-4882; $$) is a long-time Mexican tradition, but be prepared for a wait. The only brewpub in town is **Smuggler's** (970-728-0919; $-$$) on the corner of San Juan and Pine, where pub grub is served in an historic mining warehouse. **Shanghai Palace** (970-728-0882; $$) has a huge Chinese menu.

Whether you're looking for French pastries, Belgian chocolates, homemade soups and sandwiches, or an apres-ski glass of wine, you'll find it at **Wildflour** (970-728-8887; $-$$), a gourmet bakery in Camel's Garden Resort Hotel by the gondola. **Baked in Telluride** (970-738-4775; $-$$)is great for pastries, bagels, deli sandwiches, handmade pasta and pizza.

Coffeehouses have hit Telluride bigtime: **The Steaming Bean, Maggie's,** and **Between the Covers Book Store** are all located on Colorado Avenue.

In the Mountain Village

Indulge in the exquisite cuisine at **Allred's** (970-728-7474; $$$) while you drink in the staggering views from 10,551 feet above sea level. The menu changes frequently, but expect inspirational dishes. The Inn at Lost Creek houses a restaurant named for Mountain Village's altitude, **9545** (970-728-6293; $$-$$$). It boasts the most extensive single-malt scotch selection in Telluride. **La Piazza del Villaggio** (970-728-8283; $$-$$$) is the sister to Rustico in town. Same family, same great food. **That Pizza Place** ($-$$) is a funky pizzeria at the base of the village gondola that serves Sicilian-style pizza. **Legends** ($-$$), in The Peaks, serves light fare

At **The Telluride Coffee Company** choose from tea, coffee, juice and fresh pastries. Their coffee cart in Heritage Plaza is open for a rich cup of joe on the go. **Skiers Union** at the bottom of the Village chair has great juices and coffee.

On-mountain

Gorrono Ranch, mid-mountain on Misty Maiden, is a restored Basque sheepherder's homestead with American favorites. **Giuseppe's**, at the top of the Plunge lift, is the place for Italian fare with killer views. **Big Billie's** at the base of the Chondola and Sunshine chairs, named after the town's madame who died in 1957, specializes in southwestern and barbecue

Apres-ski/nightlife

For immediate apres-ski, stop at **"the Beach"** at Gorrono Ranch, the mid-mountain spot for sun and microbrews. Or pop into **West End Tavern** near the Coonskin lift. For views of Wilson Peak at sunset, sink into an oversized couch and sip an apres-ski drink in the **Great Room at The Peaks Resort** in the Mountain Village. A bar menu is available. **Eagle's Bar and Grille** on Colorado Avenue has great happy-hour prices.

For live music and dancing go to the **Fly Me to the Moon Saloon**. **The Last Dollar Saloon** (known to locals as "The Buck") has the best selection of imported beer in Telluride, plus pool tables and dart boards. It's a bit of a manly-man beer bar—not many women hang out.

The old Victorian **New Sheridan Bar** is one of the "must sees" in Telluride to experience the essence of the Old West.

Other activities

The mountain offers **snowbiking, tubing** and **snowskating** (wheel-less skateboards designed for snow) at Thrill Hill, an outdoor activity center at the base of Lift 2. For indoor fun, go to Plaza Arcade for **video games, foosball, air hockey** and **pinball**, or the Xbox Arcade next to That Pizza Place to play **Xbox games**.

Go on **sleigh rides** at Skyline Guest Ranch (888-754-1126); **horseback riding** with Roudy at Telluride Horseback Adventures (970-728-9611); **winter fly fishing** with Telluride Outside (970-728-3895); **hot-air ballooning** with San Juan Balloon Adventures (970-626-5495); **dogsledding** with Winter Moon Sled Dog Adventures (970-729-0058); on **snowmobile tours** of Telluride's mining past with Telluride Snowmobile Adventures (970-728-4475) or Dave's Snowmobile Tours (970-728-7737); and **helicopter skiing** and riding with Telluride Helitrax (970-728-8377; 866-435-4754). There's a pond in Mountain Village and another in town for ice skating. It isn't every town that has a colorful past like Telluride's, so **Boling's Historical Tour of Telluride** (970-728-6639) is well worth the time

Non-skiers and those who need a break might enjoy stretching their creative muscles at the Ah Haa School for the Arts (970-728-3886), which offers weekly and daily classes in **painting, silk dyeing and more**. First-run **films** are shown nightly at the Nugget Theatre and sometimes at the Sheridan Opera House.

At the **Golden Door Spa** (800-772-5482; 970-728-2590) in The Peaks Resort, enjoy a wide variety of massage techniques, facials, body and signature treatments.

Telluride has great **shopping** in one-of-a-kind **boutiques** and more than a dozen **art galleries**. Some of our favorites, all on Colorado Avenue: Lizard Head Mining Co., for its **custom-made jewelry**; At Home in Telluride, with **housewares and gifts**; Picaya, with **inexpensive jewelry and clothing**; the Scott White Contemporary Art Gallery, showcasing **contemporary artists**; Overland Sheepskin & Leather for **clothing, footwear, accessories and home products**; and Telluride Antique Market. **Horny Toad Activewear**, a national outdoor clothing company, is headquartered here.

Getting there and getting around

By air: Telluride has a small, weather-plagued airport six miles from town, served by United Express from Denver and America West Express from Phoenix. Montrose, 65 miles away, is where most visitors arrive, either by plane or by a weather diversion from Telluride. If you fly into the Telluride airport, pack a carry-on with enough essentials to get you through 24 hours. Your bag may not be on the same plane. Ground transport is provided by Telluride Express (970-728-6000), Mountain Limo (970-728-9606) and Alpine Luxury Limo (970-728-8750). Call 24 hours in advance for Montrose airport pickups.

By car: Telluride is 335 miles from Denver via I-70 west, and Hwys. 50, 550, 62 and 145. From the southwest, it is 125 miles from Durango via Hwys. 160, 184 and 145. From the Montrose airport head south on Hwy. 550 to Ridgway, then take Hwys. 62 and 145 to Placerville and Telluride.

Getting around: A car is unnecessary. A free bus service runs in town and the free gondola makes the commute between town and the Mountain Village simple. If the gondola is not running, call Dial-A-Ride (970-728-8888) when you get to the base of the gondola in Mountain Village and a van will ferry you without charge to destinations in the Mountain Village.

Vail
Colorado

Summit:	**11,570**
Vertical:	**3,450**
Base:	**8,120**

Address: P.O. Box 7,
Vail, Colorado 81658
Telephone (main): 970-754-5601
Snow Report Number: 970-476-4888
Toll-free reservations: 800-404-3535
E-mail: vailinfo@vailresorts.com
Internet: www.vail.com
www.vailalways.com (VailValley)

Expert:★★★★★
Advanced:★★★★
Intermediate:★★★
Beginner:★★★★
First-timer:★★★★

Lifts: 32—1 12-person gondola, 16 high-speed quads, 1 quad, 2 triples, 3 doubles, 9 surface lifts
Skiable acreage: 5,289
Snowmaking: 10 percent
Uphill capacity: 57,000
Parks & pipes: 4 parks, 2 pipes
Bed base: 11,059 within 10 miles
Nearest lodging: Slopeside, condos & hotels
Child care: Yes, 2 months and older
Adult ticket, per day: $89 (07/08 price)

Dining:★★★★
Apres-ski/nightlife:★★★★★
Other activities:★★★★

Vail was conceived as an Austrian village with condominium convenience, energetic nightlife, quiet lounges, fine dining and pizzeria snacking. The resort opened on Dec. 15, 1962, with one gondola, two chairs, eight ski instructors and a $5 lift ticket. Today Vail is as complete as a ski resort can be. Its off-slope activities are unsurpassed—shopping, skating, movies, museums, galleries, performing arts, sleigh rides and so much more—everything money can buy. Bring lots of that money—temptations abound and bargains are few. But you can find great deals during non-peak periods (early season, January and April).

Village and expenses aside, there is above all Vail Mountain—a single, stoop-shouldered behemoth. Though it does not have ultra-steeps or deeps, what it does have is three distinct mountains: There's a huge front face of long and very smooth cruisers, an enormous back-bowl of wide-open adventure spread across six miles unlike anything this side of the Atlantic, and Blue Sky Basin with lift access to boundless natural gladed terrain with cliffs, cornices and gullies.

Vail is sort of "urban skiing," if you get my drift. This city-town just doesn't feel rural. It bustles with traffic—and people—jams in peak periods. You won't see too many stars at night in the village—too many streetlights. But for many of the urban guests, Vail is just rural enough to let them feel they are getting away from it all. They find the well-lit streets comforting. They want the amenities of big-city life and they don't mind paying for it. Vail is their kind of place.

The LionsHead area makes up the western end of the front side of Vail and is a good place to start if you're staying on that side of the village. The main access is the Eagle Bahn Gondola, but three more chairlifts also serve the trails here. Born Free Express, directly parallel to the gondola, is rarely crowded—that's where the ski school and locals start off to dodge the occasional hordes.

At Blue Sky Basin, skiers and snowboarders will find an experience unlike anything else at Vail—from the rustic character of the buildings to the views, the snow and the challenging glade skiing and steeps. When some of the trails are groomed, low-intermediates can ski this remote area, which is peaceful and secluded. If they are not groomed, you need to be a strong intermediate who can handle powder and dance through some trees. It's really quite exciting. The two main areas of Blue Sky Basin were named for Vail founders Pete Seibert and Earl Eaton (Pete's Bowl and Earl's Bowl). Blue Sky is to the south of Vail Mountain's Back Bowls, on the south side of Two Elk Creek.

 ## Mountain layout

If you're skiing with a group, arrange a meeting place in case you get separated. This is one big mountain. After about a week here, you'll still be discovering new pitches and trails. By the way—locals call the lifts by their numbers rather than their names. If you want to play with them, do the same..

Expert, Advanced: We give the expert and advanced terrain here a thumbs-up because of the "sheer volume" quotient. That is, advanced and better can comfortably spend a week working out kinks in trees and bumps, and if you luck into a powder day, doing laps on Genghis Kahn alone will test your mettle. Overall, nothing should scare the bejeebers out of you, but you will have to sweat.

On the front side, as you face the hill, check out the double-black diamonds named Blue Ox, Highline and Rogers Run. Don't let the double-diamonds fool you—this is advanced terrain, but nothing that's dangerous. The straight-down-the-lift, waist-high, mogul-masher Highline is the stiffest test of the three, its challenge upgraded by the fact that it spills right under the Highline lift (a.k.a. Chair 10, which is a new high-speed quad) where other talented skiers are free with their vocal evaluations of your work. Nearby Prima, off Northwoods Express, is tougher still, and the best skiers like to make the Prima-Pronto run their endurance test. Pronto drops right down to Northwoods Express and gets its share of oglers in line. The Prima Cornice can get you sucking air at the top, but it needs plenty of snow to open. The only authentic gut-suckers on the front face are the tops of South and North Rim off the Northwoods lift, leading to a tight but nice Gandy Dancer, and even those are short and sweet.

Solid skiers, of course, will also want to explore Vail's famous Back Bowls. Stretching 6 miles across, they provide more than 2,734 acres of choose-your-own-path skiing. On a sunny day, these bowls are about as good as skiing gets. Just about any skier will tell you there is no other place to be on a powder day. Skiers who have skied Vail for years say they now ski the front side only when they come down at the end of the day. The bowls also are an excellent way to escape crowds.

Intermediate: Intermediate skiers and boarders will run out of vacation time before they run out of trails to explore. Few other mountains offer such expansive intermediate terrain and near-countless trails. Especially worthy cruising areas include the long ride down the mountain under and to the right of the Eagle Bahn Gondola, almost any of the runs bordering the Avanti express chair, the Northstar and Northwoods runs and the relatively short but sweet trio of runs down to Game Creek Bowl. Our vote for best run on the mountain, and one available to advanced-intermediates (though parts are rated black), is the top-to-bottom swath named Riva Ridge.

LionsHead is all about intermediate skiing. The trails tend to roll from the top of the gondola down to the valley like ribbon candy—each trail has a steeper section followed by an easier stretch, and steep is a relative term. Simba is a long swooping run, good anytime, and often chosen as the last run. But beware, it can resemble a freeway of skiers "heading to the barn" for apres-ski. Born Free is another classic intermediate run that loops lazily to the valley floor.

In Blue Sky Basin, when some of the trails are groomed, low-intermediates can ski this remote area, which is peaceful and secluded. If they are not groomed, you need to be a strong intermediate who can handle powder and some trees. Pete's Express Lift runs up the eastern most point of Blue Sky Basin in Pete's Bowl to access more than 125 acres of intermediate terrain.

Beginner, First-timer: Best areas are at Golden Peak and the top of the gondola, and a group of short green runs under the Sourdough Lift (now a high-speed quad) on the top left of the trail map. Unfortunately, Vail doesn't have a large area of concentrated green runs. Most lifts on the front face have one or two green-designated trails, a bunch of blue trails and one or two blacks. Take a trail map and pay attention to the signs.

Vail is one of the few resorts with beginner terrain at the top of the mountain. Take the Eagle Bahn Gondola and at the top, the beginner area offers an inspiring 360-degree view. A group of short green runs are served by a chairlift to skier's right (east) of the gondola, and beginners can do laps on this chair. The best part is beginners are the only ones using the chair.

Beginners can follow a series of cat tracks with names like Cub's Way and Bwana Loop that crisscross the mountain. If cat tracks make you nervous, Vail's trail map marks them with dotted lines so you'll know where they are. However, it's tough to avoid them here, unless you ride the gondola back down.

For first-timers, there are small learning areas in the Golden Peak base area and the top of the Eagle Bahn Gondola at Adventure Ridge. From Adventure Ridge, you can return to the valley via the gondola.

Parks and pipes

Vail puts a lot of effort and commitment into its parks and superpipe. Spread out among its four parks, you'll find countless tabletops, rails and log rails. The superpipe is 425 feet long with 22-foot walls. The Golden Peak Terrain Park is sweetly set up, starting off with a nicely groomed superpipe so you can hit the massive pipe in succession with the tabletops in one run, rather than having to choose one or the other. Below the jumps is the rail park, with rails of varying sizes and shapes. There are lots of rails and jumps, mostly tabletops with two approaches, that let you decide if you want to go big or bigger. If you're not an experienced jumper, you will probably end up landing flat on the tabletops, since most of them require major distance to make the landing. All the rails are for more advanced rail riders too.

Bwana Park in LionsHead and Hunky Dory Park off Chair 3 in Mid-Vail has a variety of smaller jumps and low-to-the-ground rails to provide a progressive learning experience for those who are developing their skills. Kids, or kids at heart, will enjoy Chaos Canyon, a kid's adventure zone and terrain park. It's under Mid-Vail Lodge, off Lion's Way. There are some fun features here, starting out with a series of banked turns winding through the woods.

Snowboarding

Let's make it easy: If you're going to ride Vail, we mean really ride the mountain, it's time to ignore trail names. If you tried to remember every little run at Vail, not only would you go mad, but you'd also probably drop a few I.Q. points. Besides, what you want to do here is focus on the kind of terrain you want to ride, then stick to the chair that accesses it. This way you avoid always traversing the mountain. By the way, riding the trees is the most direct way to avoid taking cat tracks and multiple lifts.

For the front side of the mountain, experts are going to want to ride the Northwoods lift a lot. On a powder day this is a great place to hit—it teems with rocks, steep lines and cliff gaps—but once it's tracked, get out of there. Head rider's right of the Vista Bahn (on a good snow day), or to The Riva Bahn and Vail's world-class terrain park and superpipe. Advanced riders who prefer trees enjoy Riva Glade and Hairbag Alley.

The back side of the mountain is where Vail really shines. A good place to start is at the top of Game Creek Express, where you can access the cornice through a short five-minute walk. Drop in off the cornice, then head down to the motocross jumps, which are exactly that—three giant windlips that form natural tabletops perfect for throwing down new tricks.

Make sure you check out Blue Sky Basin. It's not to be missed. You'll find an experience unlike anything else at Vail—from the rustic character of the buildings to the views, the snow, and the challenging glades and steeps. This area is different from the rest of Vail in terms of terrain—in layman's terms, if it's a powder day get back here as soon as you can! This is lift-accessed backcountry riding like nothing you've ever found at Vail. Blue Sky Basin is a rider's paradise—and since it's very remote, you won't have to ride a sequence of chairs once you get here.

For experienced backcountry riders only, find a local to guide you, get your Pieps and shovel and check out East Vail for some adrealine-pumping backcountry riding. There are five backcountry access gates at Vail. As we repeatedly warn throughout this web site, do not go into the backcountry without a knowledgeable guide. Once you leave ski area boundaries, you are on your own.

Golden Peak is it for beginners and first-timers. Not only do you get to learn on variable pitches and cruise on a high-speed quad, but Vail also was nice enough to put their immense terrain park right next to the beginner runs. Sometimes seeing the best riders in the world destroying the park right next to you can be humbling for first-timers, but it can also inspire a beginner to greatness. Vail makes sure that beginners absolutely know what they are getting involved with when they first start out. Vail has an excellent beginner instruction program. It's highly recommended that beginners take lessons, not only for the valuable skills they can pick up, but also for the guide service that the instructors provide on the mountain.

Cross-country & snowshoeing (see also xcskiresorts.com)

Two cross-country centers serve Nordic skiers and snowshoers, one at **Golden Peak** and one at the **Vail Golf Course**. Both offer lessons, tours and rentals. Call the Golden Peak Center at 970-479-3210.

Vail has beefed up its Cross-Country, Telemark and Snowshoe Adventure Center at Golden Peak, where guided tours and instruction are available through the Vail Cross-Country Ski School. Instructors specialize in cross-country skiing, telemark skiing, snowshoeing and skate skiing.

Lessons (07/08 prices)

Vail Snowsports School has offices and meeting places at Vail Village near the base of the Vista Bahn Express, at LionsHead next to the gondola, at Golden Peak next to Chairs 6 and 12, at Mid-Vail next to Chairs 3 and 4, and at the top of the gondola. Private lessons meet at Vail Village. Lessons are taught in more than 30 languages. Call the ski school at 970-476-9090. Prices we provide are for regular season.

Group lessons: $125 for a full day, all ability levels, skiing or snowboarding. Vail offers a wide variety of lesson-lift-and/or-rental packages for skiers and snowboarders.

The First Time Series is three consecutive full days of lessons that cost $265 for lessons, lifts and rentals; $200 without rentals.

You can also rent your skis or snowboards on line before you leave home at Rentskis. com. Your equipment will be waiting when you arrive.

Private lessons: One to six people cost $465 for a half-day, and $665 for the day. One- and two-hour privates are on a walk-in basis only. To reserve a private lesson, call 800-475-4543.

There are many special workshops that focus on specific skills or snow conditions, such as parallel skiing or bumps. Call 970-754-4328 to find your focus group.

We've had first-hand experience at the "Her Turn" Workshops, and strongly recommend them. The three-day program puts you in classes with other women of the same ability. Breakthroughs are common in the supportive small-group atmosphere. Offered select dates. Call the resort for information and reservations.

Racing: Vail has quite a recreational racing complex near the bottom of the Avanti Express lift with two NASTAR courses, two coin-operated courses, two courses reserved for groups, a course for teaching clinics and a Sybervision area. A surface lift serves the courses.

Children's programs (07/08 prices)

Child Care: Ages 2 months to 6 years. Supervised playroom and non-skiing programs cost $105 regular season. Reservations required; call (970) 754-3285.

Small World Nursery is run by the ski school and is in the Golden Peak base area. It is open 8 a.m. to 4:30 p.m. Of note, Vail's child-care programs are licensed and state of the art.

Other options: For a list of babysitters, call the Small World Nursery (970) 754-3285. **Baby's Away** (800-369-9030; 970-328-1285) rents and delivers baby needs, such as cribs, strollers, car seats and toys to your lodge. The company is very attentive to detail.

Children's lessons: Lessons are available for children as young as 3 years old (toilet-trained). Ski lessons are offered for ages 3-15; snowboarding lessons are for ages 7-12. Cost is $132 during regular season and includes lesson, lift and lunch. Holiday Camps are offered during holidays for kids ages 7-12 who are intermediate skiers and better. Call for prices and details.

Teens 13-15 can take a group lesson for $110 (lift tickets and rentals extra).

Register for all lessons at 8 a.m. or pre-register the day before; you also can register online at the web site. Reservations are not required. Vail encourages kids younger than age 14 enrolled in ski and snowboard programs to wear helmets. Rentals are available; if you don't want your child to wear a helmet, you must decline in writing in order for your child to participate. Children's Ski and Snowboard Centers are located at both Lionshead and at Golden Peak. Both centers offer "one-stop shopping" for lessons and rentals. You can reach either facility via the town bus.

Skiing with your kids: The resort is sprinkled with Kids Adventure Zones. Chaos Canyon features weather-theme trails Ricochet Ridge, Tornado Alley and Thunder Lane. Thunder Cat Cave has a replica of a wildcat hovering over a cave entrance. Inside, kids will find ecological information about the Rocky Mountains' four-footed predators. A Kids Adventure Map highlights most of the zones so kids can find them, but some are left up to discovery. With the help of Vail mascots, Ranger Raccoon and Crazy Coyote, children also learn about SKE-Cology™, highlighting environmental awareness and responsibility on the mountain. Kids even have their own restaurant at Mid-Vail called Chaos Canyon Kids' Cafe.

Special activities: Night Owls is a supervised evening of dinner and activities at Adventure Ridge for kids ages 7-18. Meet at 4:15 p.m. to head up the mountain. Cost is $70 regular season for ages 7-12; $80 for ages 13-18. Reservations are made at the children's ski and snowboard school.

Lift tickets (07/08 prices)

	Adult (13-64)	Child (5-12) $ 54
One day	$89	$54
Three of five days	$267 ($89/day)	$162 ($54/day)
Five of eight days	$445 ($89/day)	$270 ($54/day)

Who skis free: Ages 4 and younger.

Who skis at a discount: Ages 65+ pay $79 for one day; $237 for three days and $395 for five days.

Vail offers PEAKS discounted tickets if you pre-purchase online a three-day or more ticket at least seven days in advance (international guests must buy 14 days in advance). Membership in PEAKS is free and you are automatically enrolled when you make your early purchase. Vail has a handful of pricing periods, so check carefully to see what the prices are when you plan to visit. Some pricing periods look the same until you consider longer stays.

Note: These window ticket prices are valid through April 13, 2008, except very early and late seasons and the Christmas holiday.

Interchangeability: All lift tickets also are valid at sister resorts Beaver Creek, Keystone and Breckenridge, as well as at nearby Arapahoe Basin.

 ## Accommodations

Vail's lodging choices are so vast we can't even begin to list them here. Before you call Central Reservations, know your price range, what amenities you need and which ones you want, how close you'd like to be to the lifts and how close you'll settle for if you find nothing in your budget within that distance. Prices dip from 25 to 40 percent before Christmas, early January and in April. This coincides with an early season winter fest called **Snow Daze**. To book it, call 800-525-2257.

Most of Vail's premier properties are clustered in Vail Village at the base of the Vista Bahn Express. The exception is

The Arrabelle at Vail Square in Lionshead. This luxury hotel of the RockResorts group spills over with amenities, such as valet parking, concierge and butler services, and a full-service spa and fitness center. It's the dazzling centerpiece of Vail Square, a village pod with an ice skating plaza, expensive restaurants and shops, skier and guest services and snow-free walkways.

The Lodge at Vail (800-331-5634; 970-476-5011; $$$$) is the original hotel in Vail Village around which the rest of the resort was built. It is only steps away from the lifts, ski school and main street action. The Lodge serves a great buffet breakfast.

Gasthof Gramshammer (970-476-5626; $$$$) is at the crossroads of Vail Village. Our favorite and the most economical of the high-end group of hotels is the **Christiania** (800-530-3999; 970-476-5641; $$$$). **Sonnenalp** Resort (800-654-8312; 970-476-5656; $$$$) is a complex of buildings that exude Alpine warmth and charm. This long-time Vail property recently poured $4 million into renovations that include 40 new units plus **shops**.

Vail Marriott Mountain Resort & Spa (800-648-0720; 970-476-4444; $$$-$$$$) is top-of-the-line and is only a three-minute walk from the gondola. It recently completed $32 million in renovations, including guest rooms. **Lion Square Lodge** (970-476-2281; $$$-$$$$) is steps from the Eagle Bahn gondola and Born Free express lift.

The slopeside **Vail Cascade Resort & Spa** (800-420-2424; 970-476-7111; $$$$) celebrates its 25th anniversary in 2007/08 by completing the first phase of a $30 million remodel.

Dining: $$$$–Entrees $30+; $$$–$20–$30; $$–$10–$20; $–less than $10.
Accommodations: (double room) $$$$–$200+; $$$–$141–$200; $$–$81–$140; $–$80 and less.

The multi-award-winning property includes the Aria Spa & Club — the Vail Valley's largest fitness facility— as well as two ski shops and its own chairlift accessing Vail's slopes.

Condominiums are plentiful in the Vail region. The most reasonable for those who want to be on the shuttlebus route are in LionsHead, clustered around the gondola, and in East Vail at the recently renovated **Vail Racquet Club** (800-428-4840; 970-476-4840; $$-$$$).

The **Vailglo Lodge** (970-476-5506; $$-$$$), in Lionshead, is a 34-room Best Western hotel that operates like an elegant B&B. It has easy access to the slopes and town. For other relatively more affordable lodging, try **Antlers** (476-2471; $$-$$$$) in LionsHead.

A great value can be found at **Holiday Inn Hotel & Suites-Apex Vail** (800-543-2814; 970-476-2739; $$) in West Vail. Rooms are a nice surprise, a hot tub and fitness center are on hand, plus you'll get a complimentary breakfast and ski shuttle. A recommended B&B is the **Savory Inn** (866-728-6794; 970-476-1304; $$$-$$$$), where you'll stay in a wonderfully elegant log cabin lodge along the Gore Creek that also offers cooking classes with world-class chefs of the Cooking School of Vail.

Dining

Eating out in Vail is as much of a tradition as skiing the Back Bowls. More than 80 bars and restaurants offer the spectrum of options from pizza to exquisite gourmet dining. Always make reservations. Walk-ins have a slim chance of being seated.

La Tour (970-476-4403; $$$-$$$$) and **The Left Bank** (970-476-3696; $$$-$$$$), both French, have long been considered Vail's best. Another standby, **Sweet Basil** (970-476-0125; $$$-$$$$), is consistently good with creative dishes. **Terra Bistro** (970-476-0700; $$$) is on the east end of the Vail Mountain Lodge. Although difficult to find (the sign is very small), this upscale, eclectic restaurant specializing in "fusion cuisine" is a local favorite.

Chap's Grill and Chophouse (970-476-7014; $$$-$$$$), in the Vail Cascade Resort & Spa, serves some of the best steaks, wild game and seafood in the Vail area. We like **Lancelot** (970-476-5828; $$-$$$) for prime rib, **Montauk** (970-476-2601; $$$) for seafood, **Alpenrose** (970-476-3194; $$$) for German and its wonderful breads and pastries, and **Wildflower** (970-476-5011; $$$-$$$$) in **The Lodge** for contemporary American and an excellent wine list.

Less expensive is the legendary **Pepi's** (970-476-5626; $$) for the best goulash and white veal bratwursts; and **Campo de Fiore** (970-476-8994; $$-$$$), with fine Italian fare, an extensive wine list and a friendly staff.

Cucina Rustica (970-476-5011; $$-$$$) serves Tuscan-style Italian in **The Lodge**. If you're willing to drive west to a locals' favorite in Eagle-Vail, **Ti Amo** (970-845-8153; $$-$$$) won't disappoint. **Sapphire Restaurant & Oyster Bar** (970-476-2828; $$$) Vail's only oyster bar, serves creative seafood and some meat and fowl specialties. **Billy's Island Grill** (970-476-8811; $$) in LionsHead is also a good bet for steaks, fish, the salad bar and its famous mango margaritas.

Those on a budget should try **Pazzo's** (970-476-9026; $), which offers pasta and create-your-own-pizza. **Bart and Yeti's** (970-476-2754; $$) in LionsHead is great for lunch or light dinner. **Moe's Barbecue** (970-479-7888; $-$$) in LionsHead is a local's favorite for pulled pork sandwiches, chicken and such.

On the mountain, we recommend lunch at the **Two Elk Restaurant** (970-479-4560; $-$$) above China Bowl, with its log lodge frame, Ute Indian motif and views of the Gore Range. Go early or late, because finding a seat at prime time is tough. Or try the sophisticated lunches at **Larkspur** (970-479-8050; $$-$$$) in the Golden Peak base lodge. It's also one of our top choices for dinner, where you're able to pair your French-influenced American seasonal cuisine with one of the 4,000 bottles of wine. **Mid-Vail's food** court has moderate (for Vail) prices—$10 buys a huge potato with toppings, a local beer and a piece of fruit, for example.

The Game Creek Restaurant (970-479-4275; $$$$), which got a recent facelift, is extremely exclusive with members like Ross Perot and Charles Schwab, for example. Lunch is for members only, but it's open to the public for dinner via snowcat from the top of the Eagle Bahn gondola. For about $90 per person, sans alcohol and gratuity but including transportation, you get a six-course gourmet meal.

For breakfast, the best deal in town is at **D.J. MacAdams** ($), in LionsHead's Concert Hall Plaza, a tiny diner where you'll watch cooks make heaping plates of omelets, scramblets (like an omelet only using scrambled eggs) and blintzes. Wash it down with a fruit smoothie. It's open 24 hours, except Mondays (reopening at 7 a.m. Tuesday). **West Side Cafe** ($) in West Vail is a favorite for coffee and bagels or breakfast burritos. If you're looking for a buffet breakfast (continental or hot) in a fine-dining atmosphere, head to **Chap's Grill** ($$) in the Vail Cascade Resort & Spa or the **Mountain Grille Restaurant** ($$) at the Marriott's Mountain Resort at Vail. You can also get a la carte items at both.

Down Valley

Visitors with a car should drive west to exit 171 and turn off at old town Minturn where the **Minturn Country Club** (970-827-4114; $$$) lets you grill your own meat or fish steak. Just across the street, the area's best Mexican food is dished out at the raucous **Saloon** (970-827-5954; $-$$)—a favorite of World Cup racers—or **Chili Willy's** (970-827-5887; $-$$). The **Turntable Restaurant** (970-827-4268; $-$$) wins accolades for its green chili.

At the Edwards exit, left off the highway, check out the valley's oldest restaurant and bar, **The Gashouse** (970-926-3613; $-$$). Seafood, homemade soups, steaks, wild game and award-winning chili are served in a rustic 50-year-old log cabin. Apres-ski it's good for lobster tails, little-neck clams and jumbo lump crab cakes. The best sports bar and grill could be **Paddy's** (970-949-6093; $-$$) on Hwy. 6. The house specialty prime rib is big and fat.

Edwards is fast becoming a dining mecca. Great eateries are popping up right and left. Look for the **Gore Range Brewery** (970-926-2739; $-$$) for typical pub fare. There's also Chinese, Thai, Japanese and Vietnamese cuisine all over the place. The margaritas at **Fiesta's Cafe & Cantina** (970-926-2121; $-$$) are yummy (20 tequilas to choose from) and the chicken enchiladas in white jalapeño sauce are the house specialty. At **Markos** (970-926-7003; $) in the Edwards Business Plaza, you'll find pastas, pizzas and Caesar salads at rock bottom prices. Stop by **Bonjour Bakery** (970-926-5539; $) to pick up several loaves of to-die-for bread, but call for winter hours before you make the trip. **Juniper Restaurant**(970-926-7001; $$) in the Riverwalk Center serves "Comfort Fusion" cuisine, some of the best in the valley. **Frites** (970-926-2151) is a French-inspired steakhouse serving those fabulous namesake potatoes with many of the entrees like steak and roasted herb-crusted chicken breast. We like to eat at the bar upstairs to take in the full Chicago bistro atmosphere. **dish** (970-926-3433) dishes out small-plate meals that are excellent, but the dim candlelight makes it hard to see the menu (or the food).

 # Apres-ski/nightlife

Apres-ski is centered in the Village or in LionsHead. The **Red Lion** has a deck, live music and great nachos. In the Village, try **Los Amigos** at the base of the Vista Bahn and join the viewers on the deck watching late-day skiers make their way down the steep Pepi's Face. **Vendetta's** in the Village is a locals' favorite. **Mickey's** at the Lodge at Vail has the top piano bar. Several restaurants have house entertainers who are long-time career musicians. In LionsHead, **Garfinkel's** has a great sunny deck overlooking the slopes. Gather

Dining: $$$$–Entrees $30+; $$$–$20–$30; $$–$10–$20; $–less than $10.
Accommodations: (double room) $$$$–$200+; $$$–$141–$200; $$–$81–$140; $–$80 and less.

your buddies and try their shot wheel. **Bart & Yeti's**, named after the owner's late dogs, is like a classic Western tavern, studded with rustic logs, wagon wheels, stuffed birds and photographs depicting the Wild West. It's a tried-and-true locals' hangout with little fanfare.

For later nightlife, **The Tap Room** on Bridge Street caters to a movin' and groovin' mature crowd, while a few doors away, **Samana** attracts a young crowd with loud rock'n'roll. **The Club** normally offers acoustic guitar music. **8150** has live alternative music.

Other activities

Adventure Ridge at Eagle's Nest is an on-mountain activity center, open from 2 p.m. to 10 p.m. Families and adrenaline junkies enjoy this addition in the Eagle's Nest area at the top of the gondola. It includes a kids' snowmobile track, a lift-served tubing hill, ski-biking, rebound trampolines and other activities. Some activities require reservations, so call in advance. Blue Moon Restaurant & Bar serves very affordable family dinners. The gondola cabins are heated and lighted.

Vail has a number of athletic clubs and spas. The Aria Spa & Club (spa 970-479-5942, club 970-476-7400) at the Vail Cascade Resort has 14 treatment rooms including a couple's spa suite. Treatments include massages, wraps, soaks, facials, manicures and pedicures. The athletic facilities are the best in Vail and include a pool, 48 pieces of cardio equipment; free weights; indoor running track; and basketball, volleyball, racquetball and squash courts. The Spa at Vail Mountain Lodge (970-476-7960) also has fitness facilities in Vail Village and the only climbing wall in the Vail Valley. The Vail Racquet Club (970-476-3267) in East Vail has indoor tennis, squash and racquetball courts, swimming pool and weight room.

Getting there and getting around

By air: Flights land at the Vail/Eagle County airport, about 35 miles west of Vail, and the Denver International Airport, 110 miles east. Eagle County airport is served by American, Northwest, Delta, Continental, United Express and United with non-stop flights from 14 major U.S. cities.

Ground transportation between Denver and Vail is frequent and convenient. The trip to Vail takes about two-and-a-half hours. Contact Colorado Mountain Express (800-525-6363); Vail Valley Taxi (877-829-8294; 970-476-8294); or Airport Transportation Service (970-476-7576). For personalized private charter limos, vans and suburbans, make reservations with VailCoach (877-554-7433). Though flights into Denver may be a bit less expensive than Eagle, also consider the cost of round-trip ground transportation, where per person rates from Denver are about double those from Eagle.

By car: Vail is in the central Rocky Mountains of Colorado, 100 miles west of Denver, 140 miles east of Grand Junction and 35 miles east of Eagle.

I-70 is a scenic and direct route into Vail from just about anywhere. Once in Vail, follow the signage to the Main Vail Exit (176) where most lodging, parking and access to the mountain can be found. East and West Vail can also be easily accessed by exits (180 and 173) just before and after the Main Vail Exit.

Getting around: Most parts of Vail are very self-contained, and the slick, reliable bus service—the largest free transportation system in the country—runs throughout town from East to West Vail. Visitors and locals ride the free bus because parking is very limited and expensive. Shuttles to Beaver Creek leave from the Transportation Center above the parking structure in Vail Village. There is a small cost.

Winter Park

Colorado

Summit:		12,060 feet
Vertical:		3,060 feet
Base:		9,000 feet

Address: P.O. Box 36, Winter Park, CO 80482
Telephone (main): 970-726-5514
Snow Report Number: 970-726-7669
Toll-free reservations: 800-729-5813
E-mail: wpinfo@skiwinterpark.com
Internet: www.skiwinterpark.com,
www.winterparkresort.com, www.ride-winterpark.com (ski area)
www.winterpark-info.com (town)

Expert:★★★★ **Advanced:**★★★★
Intermediate:★★★★
Beginner:★★★★
First-timer:★★★★★

Lifts: 25—2 high-speed six-packs, 7 high-speed quads, 4 triples, 6 doubles, 1 surface lift, 5 moving carpets
Skiable acreage: 3,078
Snowmaking: 10 percent
Uphill capacity: 38,370
Parks & pipes: 5 parks, 1 pipe
Bed base: 12,500
Nearest lodging: Slopeside
Child care: Yes, 2 months and older
Adult ticket, per day: $86 (07/08 price)
Dining:★★★
Apres-ski/nightlife:★★
Other activities:★★★

Winter Park is Denver's local ski area. The mountain has a bit of everything and the town is small, but the big time is coming,

In the early 1900s, when the Moffat Tunnel through the Rockies was completed, Denverites began to ride the train here. The shacks first built for the tunnel construction crews made perfect warming huts for hardy skiers who climbed the mountains and schussed down on 7-foot-long boards. The ski area is part of the Denver public parks system (owned by the city and county of Denver), which explains its name, but it's operated by ski industry giant Intrawest. Today, Winter Park ranks as one of the largest ski areas in Colorado.

This is a great mountain with a wonderfully easy-going atmosphere. The ski area and most of the lodging are tucked into the woods off the main highway. Winter Park also has several traditional mountain inns—the kind with large common rooms where people can read, talk or play board games.

But, with Intrawest on the scene, the times are changing. Installed for 2006-07, the Eagle Wind triple chair runs up the backside of Parsenn Bowl to 11,486 feet. New in 2007-08 was Panoramic Express on Parsenn Bowl to take skiers to 12,060 feet, making it the highest high-speed six-pack chairlift in North America. The Zephyr Mountain Lodge, with shops and a restaurant on the ground floor and condos above, brought upscale slopeside lodging, and a new base area "village" comes to life for 2008-09, with condos, a shopping area, more restaurants, a "cabriotel" lift running from the village's far end to the slopes, and a parking garage. For now, Winter Park is still charmingly funky, affordable and low-key, with lodging designed with families in mind and one of Colorado's most respected ski schools. The children's and disabled-skier programs are among the biggest, most advanced and most respected in the nation.

Although Winter Park maintains a great family reputation, it is also a good destination for singles. The town benefits from having only a few, but good, nightlife centers. Meaning that you get to meet most of the other skiers in town if that's what you want; and the mountain inn lodging gives singles a great opportunity to meet other vacationers over dinner and drinks, or while enjoying the hot tubs. If you're looking for a solid good time without the fanfare, Winter Park presents you with one of the best opportunities. Families also may be interested in visiting nearby SolVista Basin at Granby Ranch. Eldora Mountain Resort is fun for skiers and riders of all abilities.

 ## Mountain layout

Though the mountain is completely interconnected by lifts, it has separate base areas: Mary Jane and Winter Park. So in this section, "the Winter Park side" refers to the portion of the resort to the trail-map right of the Zephyr Express chairlift.

Expert, Advanced: Visitors who have read about Winter Park arrive expecting a good intermediate resort with plenty of lower-intermediate and beginner trails. Yes, that's all here. What is surprising is the amount of expert terrain. Vasquez Cirque has nearly 700 acres of steep chutes and gladed powder stashes accessed by a hike along the ridge from the six-passenger Panoramic Express which is now the way to access the expert terrain on Vasquez Cirque.

Use the Eagle Wind Chair, a triple, to ski Left Hand, Black Coal, Thunderbird and a few others on Vasquez Ridge that comprise a collection of shorter, nicely pitched and sometimes gladed black-rated runs. The chair also allows for an easier return to Mary Jane for those skiing Vasquez Cirque.

Mary Jane is where you'll find the famous bumps and super-steeps. Try the chutes accessible only through controlled gates: Hole in the Wall, Awe Chute, Baldy's Chute, Jeff's Chute and Runaway, all reached by the Challenger, Sunnyside, High Lonesome or Supergauge Express chairlifts.

For advanced skiers, the most popular lift on the Winter Park side is the Zephyr Express. It provides access to Mary Jane (via Outhouse), or the advanced runs on the Winter Park side—Bradley's Bash, Balch, Mulligan's Mile, Rhetta's Run, Outrigger and Hughes. From the top of Zephyr, Outhouse is now a split-groomed trail, offering fans of big bumps or steep groomers a route to the base of Mary Jane. At Mary Jane, head for the black runs off the Supergauge Express. If you're still standing, you're ready for the runs off the Challenger chair—all black diamond, all ungroomed with monstrous moguls, and all tough as a bag of nails.

Intermediate: Parsenn Bowl has more than 200 acres of open space. If you hit Parsenn on a good day, you're in for a treat. The upper part is above treeline, medium-steep with spectacular views, while the gladed bottom is a delight, especially if you're just learning to ski between trees. Though rated blue and blue-black on the trail map, wind and weather conditions can make the bowl a workout. Winds occasionally close the Panoramic Express lift, which provides the only access. From the Panoramic, you can also reach the excellent intermediate gladed cruising runs Perry's Peak and Forever Eva.

Vasquez Ridge on the Winter Park side has an excellent collection of cruising runs. The only drawback to Vasquez Ridge is a long runout down the Big Valley trail; the Buckaroo trail lets you avoid it. To change mountains, green-circle Gunbarrel takes skiers to the High Lonesome Express quad and the Mary Jane area.

The Sunnyside lift on the Mary Jane side has excellent runs for intermediates. If you can handle these with no trouble, try Sleeper, one of Winter Park's "blue-black" designated runs that help intermediates improve to advanced.

Beginner, First-timer: The Winter Park base area serves most of the beginner trails. Beginners can ride to the top of the mountain to Sunspot and then ski down March Hare, or they can ski all the way back to the base using the Cranmer Cutoff to Parkway. When these become easy, try Cranmer, Jabberwocky and White Rabbit.

Winter Park is one of the best ski areas in the nation for novices. Discovery Park is 26 acres of gentle, protected learning terrain served by a double, a triple and a high-speed quad, which slows down for loading and unloading. Another 5 acres of beginner/teaching terrain can be found next to the Gemini Lift. Two moving carpets and one surface lift allow children and adults to make repeated runs without getting on and off a chairlift.

Parks and pipes

For several years running, Winter Park's parks have received a top-10 ranking by the readers of *TransWorld SNOWboarding*, and the resort continues to feed the freeriding frenzy with a superpipe and five terrain parks. Rail Yard Terrain Park on Allan Phipps trail is the place for experts. It's packed with 25 rails—including a couple of 30-foot banked C rails and a 15-foot trapezoid—and 16 components such as kickers and spines. Dark Territory, Rail Yard's limited access area, is an ever-evolving site with unique features like two jump lines, a variety of rails, boxes and manmade jibs.

The 450-foot superpipe is 50 feet wide at the base and has 18-foot walls. From the outdoor decks of Snoasis, guests have a great view of skiers and snowboarders catching huge air on the bottom three jumps. The Starter Park, located below Snoasis, is designed for the beginner-jibber, featuring small boxes. Dog Patch, located on the east side of the Eskimo Express, is an intermediate park, which is excellent for building skills. Dog Patch East, located just east of the original Dog Patch, offers a variety of non-traditional jib features.

Snowboarding

While Mary Jane is famous for its bumps, it also boasts smooth glades and chutes off of the Summit Express and Challenger lifts. Catch them on a powder day and you'll feel like a hero. Overall, the Mary Jane terrain is ideal for experts and advanced-intermediates, plus it's easy to negotiate with no flat runouts.

A note of caution: While the Winter Park side is better suited for beginners, it can be a challenge for riders because it has some flats and runouts. Take the Zephyr Express and Eskimo Express lifts to avoid most of them. Although you have to endure some flats, the Pioneer Express lift also offers some interesting intermediate terrain for riders, notably Upper Sundance to Buckaroo. On the way back to the Winter Park base, just be sure to take Parkway Trail or Larry Sale to avoid Turnpike at all costs—ALL COSTS. It's longer and flatter than Kansas.

Cross-country & snowshoeing (see also xcskiresorts.com)

Devil's Thumb Cross-Country Center (970-726-8231) has great views of the mountains and 105 km. of trails groomed for both skating and gliding. National-level competitors race and train here. The center is near Tabernash on County Road 83. Rentals and private and group lessons are available. You'll also find 20 km. of marked, groomed snowshoe trails.

Snow Mountain Ranch (970-887-2152), 8 miles west of Winter Park on Highway 40, offers 100 km. of groomed trails through a variety of terrain—open, wooded, hilly and flat. The system includes a lighted 3-km. loop for night skiing. The instruction staff includes national-level coaches and racers. Ski lessons, rentals, lodging, dining and child care are available. Snow Mountain Ranch is also a YMCA with inexpensive dorm and cabin lodging.

Nearby **Arapahoe National Forest** contains more than 600 km. of backcountry Nordic and snowshoeing trails. The **Fraser Experimental Forest Ranger Station** is the take-off point for marked trails suitable for all skiing levels of skiers, with no trail fees, but also no facilities.

Rocky Mountain National Park (970-586-1206) has many miles of Nordic skiing, most of it not necessarily tracked, with a backcountry feel.

On-mountain snowshoe tours are offered several times daily from the base of Winter Park Resort. The two-hour guided tour includes a chairlift ride to the tour's starting point, rental snowshoes, and information about native plants and animals. Winter Park and the Fraser Valley's extensive mountain biking trails are used in winter for snowshoeing. The trails are easy to follow and often packed down by snowmobile riders.

Lessons (08/09 prices)

The Ski & Snowboard School desks are in Balcony House at the Winter Park base. "Guest centered teaching" is Winter Park's forte, so a large variety of clinics and lessons are offered. We provide regular-season prices; value-season prices are lower. You can save 10% on regular lessons (not special programs) if you book online or call 800-729-7907.

Group lessons: A half day costs $69, for all levels, skiers and snowboarders.

First-timer package: A full day package with lessons, lifts and rentals costs $132.

Private lessons: cost for up to three people in a lesson is $359 for a half day; $489 for a full day. A First Tracks private lesson gets you on the mountain before the lifts open to the public—lesson goes from 8-9:30 a.m.; cost is $150. Reservations are highly recommended.

Special programs: Many. Two multi-day examples: Women's Progressive Ski Clinics, $250; Women's Ski & Ride Weekend, $195. Also offered are multi-session telemark, moguls and parks & pipes clinics. Super Parallel ($119) uses Salomon 120 cm short skis to teach skiers to use their weight and their own physiques in harmony with today's advanced equipment.

Winter Park's National Sports Center for the Disabled, the world's leader in disabled ski instruction, has a full-time race-training program for disabled skiers. Instruction is available for all levels, and the race program is open to advanced intermediates or above.

Racing: NASTAR, daily on the Cranmer Trail above Snoasis Restaurant. It costs $5 for two runs for adults or $7 for all day, and $3 for two runs for kids (12 and under) or $5 all day. Drop-ins are welcome in the Masters (25 and older) race-training program.

Children's programs (08/09 prices)

Children's lessons: We provide regular season prices. You can save 10% if you book seven days in advance by calling 800-729-7907. All-day programs for children ages 3-17 years, including all-day lift ticket, complimentary use of a helmet, lunch, instruction and supervision, cost $130 with rentals. Snowboard lessons are available for ages 6-17 years. Multi-day packages are available. "Just Because I am Three" is a program for children at least three years old, toilet trained and who don't take naps, and who are skiing at Level 3 or below. A full day with lunch and rentals costs $118.

Reservations for add-on private lessons are recommended, especially on weekends.

A Family Private lesson allows a family with similar abilities to learn together. Up to seven people can be in the group and the instructor tailors the lesson to meet the family's needs. The cost is $399 for a half day and $529 for full day.

Child care: Ages 2 months through 6 years. We provide regular season prices. All day, including lunch, costs $95; half day is $75 (no lunch). Multi-day programs are available. Complimentary use of a beeper/pager is included. Reservations are required for child care and can be made by calling 800-420-8093. Reserve early, as Winter Park sometimes hits capacity in its child-care program.

For 2008-09, the resort is introducing Willie's Birthday Party, a three-hour private lesson for a total of seven people, lunch and cake with Winter Park Willie, the resort's moose mascot, who also delivers presents and has a gift for all participants.

Kids Night Out is for ages 5-13, and consists of special activities both indoors and out.

Note: Winter Park has always been a leader in creative children's ski programs. Its multi-story Kids Adventure Junction handles more than 600 children on some days and does it very well. The Center is open from 8 a.m. to 4 p.m.

Lift tickets (07/08 prices)

	Adult	Child (6-13)
One day	$86	$45
Three days*	$225 ($75/day)	$108 ($36/day)
Five days*	$345 ($69/day)	$180 ($36/day)

*on-line purchase only

Who skis free: Kids 5 and younger always ski free.

Who skis at a discount: Ages 65-69 ski for $72. Seniors 70+ pay $35. Half-day tickets are offered for mornings or afternoons. **Note:** These are on-line, pre-purchase, regular season. Tickets purchased at the ticket window cost more, and multiday tickets purchased at the ticket window receive no discount from the daily rate. Holiday prices are higher; early- and late-season prices are lower. Winter Park offers discounts of 12-20% available at Front Range King Soopers stores (the days aren't specified, so you can buy as many tickets for as many days as you plan to ski/ride).

Accommodations

Winter Park Central Reservations 800-729-5813, can book 150 different lodging properties, plus air transportation, lift tickets and special activities.

In the new base village, **Fraser Crossing** and **Founders Pointe** ($$-$$$$) has nearly 200 new lodging options located within a short walk of the slopes. Among the mountain inns, the most upscale is the **Gasthaus Eichler** (800-543-3899; 970-726-5133; $-$$$). Prices include breakfast and dinner. **Arapahoe Ski Lodge** (800-754-0094; 970-726-8222; $-$$$) is a mountain inn with private baths. Prices include breakfast, dinner and transport to the slopes.

The **Woodspur Lodge** (800-626-6562; 970-726-8417; $-$$$) has newly restored and old style rooms. Rates include breakfast and dinner.

The **Timber House Ski Lodge** (800-843-3502; 970-726-5477; $-$$$) has a private ski trail back to the lodge. Rates include breakfast and dinner.

The **Wild Horse Inn** (800-729-5813; $$-$$$) is the most elegant of the local B&Bs with private baths. **Whistle Stop Bed & Breakfast** (800-729-5813; 970-726-8767; $-$$) is a casual B&B a block from the train station in Fraser. Two rooms have private baths and two have shared baths. The hearty breakfasts have become one of their top enticements.

The **Outpost Inn** (800-430-4538; 970-726-5346; $-$$$), a B&B, is comfortable and homey. Rates include breakfast, but no dinner.

Winter Park also has many condo complexes. The most luxurious is the **Zephyr Mountain Lodge** (800-729-5813; 970-726-8400; $$$-$$$$). The **Iron Horse Resort Retreat** (800-621-8190; 970-726-8851; $$-$$$$) has a swimming pool and a fitness center. **Winter**

Dining: $$$$–Entrees $30+; $$$–$20–$30; $$–$10–$20; $–less than $10.

Accommodations: (double room) $$$$–$200+; $$$–$141–$200; $$–$81–$140; $–$80 and less.

Park Mountain Lodge (866-726-5473; 970-726-4211; $-$$$) is across from the ski resort and is part hotel, part ski lodge. It was remodeled in 1999 and is an attractive and affordable choice for those who want to be close to the slopes.

The Vintage (800-472-7017; 970-726-8801; $$-$$$$) is right next to the ski area. It features a restaurant, fitness room, swimming pool and good shuttle service into the town. One of the finer properties in Winter Park, the Vintage has studios and suites available.

For condominiums in town, try either **Snowblaze** (800-729-5813; 970-726-5701; $$$-$$$$) or **Crestview Place** (800-729-5813; 726-9421; $$$-$$$$). Both are across the street from Cooper Creek Square. One of the most popularly priced condominiums is the **Hi Country Haus** (800-729-5813; 970-726-9421; $$$-$$$$). These condos are spread out in a dozen buildings and share a recreation center.

A couple of unusual alternatives outside of town are especially good for Nordic skiers. **Devil's Thumb Ranch** (800-729-5813; 970-726-5632; $$-$$$) and **Snow Mountain Ranch** (970-887-215.

 # Dining

The **Ranch House Restaurant at Devil's Thumb** (970-726-5633; $$$) has rocketed to the top of the "must try" dining experiences in Winter Park. Tenderloin steaks, rack of lamb, and fresh seafood are prepared in this rustic dining room.

The **Gasthaus Eichler** (970-726-5133; $$-$$$) in the center of Winter Park has an Austrian/German-influenced menu. **Fontenot's Cajun Cafe** (970-726-4021; $$), features fish dishes prepared New Orleans style. **The Sushi Bar** (970-726-0447; $$) serves fine sushi, sashimi and other Asian specialities.

The Untamed Steakhouse at Wildcreek (970-726-1111; $$-$$$) serves Wood Fire Prime Rib and houses a microbrewery. The **Mirasol Cantina** (970-726-0280; $) serves gourmet style tacos and burritos.

Smokin' Moe's (970-726-4600; $$), in Cooper Creek Square has spicy barbecue and "Okie baloney." For Mexican fare try **Fiesta Jalisco** (970-726-4877; $$). **Deno's** (970-726-5332; $-$$), a locals' favorite, has several good pasta dishes.

In Fraser, **DeAntonio's** (970-726-9999; $) makes good pizza and take-out food. **Randi's Irish Saloon** (970-726-1172; $-$$$) in downtown Winter Park is a good family restaurant with plenty of traditional pub food served at lunch and dinner. You can get excellent take-out Thai food from **Timberline Thai** (970-726-9390; $) or eat-in at the tiny, two-table dining area.

Hernando's Pizza & Pasta Pub (970-726-5409; $-$$) Serves thick-and-chewy-crust pizza with unusual topping combinations. Try the **Winter Park Pub** (970-726-4929; $$), downtown on Hwy. 40, which offers traditional pub fare.

For the best eggs-and-bacon breakfast in town head to **The Mountain Rose** (970-726-9940; $). **Carver's Bakery & Cafe** (970-725-8202; $-$$) behind Cooper Creek Square serves breakfasts, amazing cinnamon rolls and superb sandwiches.

On the slopes, the best lunch is at the Mary Jane base area in the **Club Car** (970-726-1442; $). Be sure to save room for the mud pie. The **Lodge at Sunspot** (970-726-1446; $-$$) atop the mountain is a spectacular setting for a gourmet lunch. A **Safeway** (970-726-9484) in Fraser can be reached by the free shuttlebus.

 # Apres-ski/nightlife

After a remodeling, the slopeside **Derailer Bar** is the place to be for apres-ski. **The Pub** is best described as "hardcore local," while **Mirasol Cantina**, is a good happy hour locale with two-for-one drinks and $1.50 tacos from 4-6 p.m.

For sports events, go to **Deno's Mountain Bistro**. Do some deck dining and drinking at **Doc's Roadhouse,** a tavern/restaurant on the ground level of Zephyr Mountain Lodge.

The Untamed Steakhouse at Wildcreek has live music and pool tables. **Randi's Irish Saloon** also features live music that draws the dancing crowd after dinner.

For a quiet drink without the loud music, head to **Five Mountain Tavern** in the Vintage Hotel or **Eichler's**. **The Sushi Bar** offers two-for-one sushi roll specials during happy hour.

Diehards using public transportation, take note: After midnight, the free shuttle service is finished, but **Home James** (970-726-5060) has taxi service available until 2 a.m.

Other activities

Devil's Thumb Outfitters (970-726-1099) and Dashing Through the Snow (970-726-5376) have old-fashioned **sleigh rides** with a stop for refreshments around a roaring campfire. Devil's Thumb Ranch (970-726-8231) has **winter horseback riding, sleigh rides** (including a dinner ride) and **ice skating**.

Ice skating can also be done at Cooper Creek in downtown Winter Park and at the Fraser Sports Complex in Fraser (970-726-8968), as well as at Snow Mountain Ranch (970-887-2152).

Dog Sled Rides of Winter Park (970-726-8326) stages **dogsled rides** pulled by spirited Siberian huskies, go through miles of spectacular backcountry. At the ski hill, nighttime **snow cycle** excursions are available 6-9 p.m. Fridays and Saturdays.

Trailblazer (970-726-8452; 800-669-0134) or Grand Adventures (970-726-9247; 800-726-9257) offer **snowmobile tours**.

For **snow tubing**, go to the Fraser Valley Tubing Hill (970-726-5954) or Snow Mountain Ranch (970-887-2152). The Base Camp 9000 **Indoor Climbing Wall** is a 750 square-foot, state-of-the-art apparatus located in the base area's West Portal Station building.

For **spa services**, visit Bella Vista in Fraser's Fraser Valley Shopping Center (970-726-9505) or the Ranch Creek Spa at Devil's Thumb Ranch (970-726-5632).

Getting there and getting around

By air: Denver International Airport is a hub for several major airlines. Home James vans take skiers from the airport to Winter Park. The fare each way is about $41. Reserve through central reservations, or contact the van lines directly. Home James: (970-726-5060 in Colorado; or (800-729-5813).

By car: Winter Park is 85 miles northwest of Denver International Airport on Hwy. 40. Take I-70 west to Exit 232, then head toward Winter Park and Fraser on Hwy. 40. Warning: beware speed traps when driving through Empire on Route 40, the first town just after and/ or before the I-70 exit.

By train: Amtrak's California Zephyr, which runs between Chicago and San Francisco, makes a stop in Fraser, only a few miles from the ski area: Amtrak 800-872-7245.

The Ski Train from Denver is also an option. Round-trip rates are about $65 club and $40 coach: 303-296-4754.

Getting around: Rent a car only for any extensive restaurant or bar hopping. Taxi service: Valley Taxi (970-726-4940) for $2 per pick-up, $2 per person and $2 per mile.

Dining: $$$$–Entrees $30+; $$$–$20–$30; $$–$10–$20; $–less than $10.
Accommodations: (double room) $$$$–$200+; $$$–$141–$200; $$–$81–$140; $–$80 and less.

Nearby resorts

SolVista Basin at Granby Ranch, Granby, CO; (970) 887-3384; (888) 283-7458

Internet: www.granbyranch.com

5 lifts; 406 acres; 1,000 vertical feet

SolVista Basin caters to families and is well suited for them, with ski-in/ski-out condos, gentle terrain, one central base lodge and many off-slope activities (be aware that they do not have child care). SolVista's ski area is comprised of two interconnected mountains. East Mountain is primarily for beginners and intermediates, while West Mountain's terrain is mainly intermediate and advanced with limited beginner access. Bear Bahn Park is a separate learn-to-ski park. All lifts radiate from a central base lodge making it easy for families and groups to ski together. It's also a great place to learn. Groups can rent SolVista for private night-skiing parties. The resort also has 25 km. of groomed Nordic track adjacent to the base lodge.

Lift tickets (2007/08 prices, low and high season): Adults, $47–$49; Juniors (6-12), $22–$25; Seniors (61-69) $32–$34; 70+ and 5 and younger, free

Distance from Denver: About 80 miles west via I-70 and Hwy. 40. It's 15 miles north of Winter Park.

Lodging information: SolVista Reservation and Travel (888-283-7458; 887-3384) is the central booking agency for more than 20 properties that include condominiums, family-style mountain inns, hotels, bed and breakfasts, motels, and property management companies.

Eldora Mountain Resort, Nederland, CO; (800) 444-0447; (303) 440-8700

Internet: www.eldora.com

12 lifts; 680 acres; 1,400 vertical feet; 4 terrain parks

Eldora's stats are misleading: This skis and rides like a bigger mountain and draws significant crowds from Denver, Boulder and the Midwest states. Actually four mountains, the area lays out nicely according to ability level. In the back, experts and advanced skiers head for Corona Bowl's black- and double-black-diamond terrain. Runs like the West Ridge are definitely challenging, and the chutes and glades are for experienced skiers only. Indian Peaks and Challenge Mountain are laced with wide-open cruisers such as everyone's favorite first run, Hornblower, while Little Hawk Mountain is the beginner and family skiing and riding zone. Tricksters can play in a terrain park with rails, rollers, table jumps and boxes.

Because this is the closest skiing to Denver, weekends can get crowded. But then, you won't have to drive crowded I-70 to get to Eldora—a fact that balances out the occasional lift lines. The resort has excellent kids' and family programs and the most popular Nordic trail system in the state. The 16,000-square-foot lodge, built of logs and natural indigenous rock, is centrally located and houses the rental shop, child care, ski school registration and dining services.

Lift tickets (2007/08 prices): Adult, $59; juniors (6-15), $37; seniors (65-74), $37; kids 5 and younger, and seniors 75 and older, $7.

Distance from Denver: Eldora is 65 miles from Denver International Airport, 45 miles from Denver via Hwys. 36 and 119, and 21 miles from Boulder. Eldora is the only ski resort with daily scheduled bus service via the Regional Transportation District, (303) 299-6002.

Lodging information: (800) 444-0447 (Boulder Convention and Visitors Bureau). Accommodations are in the historic mining town of Nederland, plus Boulder and Denver; www.eldora.com/mountaininfo/lodging.cfm.

Schweitzer Mountain Resort
and Silver Mountain, Idaho

Coeur d'Alene Region Facts	**Phone:** (208) 664-3194
	Toll-free information: (877) 782-9232
Dining:★★★	**Internet:** www.coeurdalene.org (visitors bureau)
Apres-ski/nightlife:★★★	**E-mail:** info@coeurdalene.org
Other activities:★★★	**Bed base:** 1,500 rooms

Families and friends who have gone to the Central Rockies for years for their annual ski vacations, in their quest for something new, are gravitating to the Selkirks at the western edge of the northern Rockies. That means the Idaho panhandle, snuggled between Montana and Washington, home to Schweitzer and Silver mountain resorts.

Schweitzer Mountain Resort is big—3,000 skiable acres—and it's coming on big in the minds of destination skiers. It's especially favorable to skiers who like a resort where one skier per acre is a crowded day. That makes it equally delightful for experts and beginners alike. Named for a Swiss hermit who once settled on the mountain, it's one of Idaho's largest resorts. It overlooks a huge lake, Lake Pend Orielle, and has an attractive mountain village at its base area.

As for Silver Mountain, well, in 1989, an Associated Press story announced the bad news: "Liability risks and increased costs of maintaining a dangerous mountain road have prompted Kellogg's City Council to close Silverhorn Ski Area this winter." It went on to announce the good news: "The hill will reopen next year under the new name of Silver Mountain and with a new $13 million gondola." The resort and its north-facing slopes went from zero in 1989 to Snow Country Magazine's Top 50 ski resorts in four years.

Both mountains are roughly equidistant from the lakeside city of Coeur d'Alene, a fun place to stay. It's thriving with plenty of dining, nightlife and shopping. The lake, one of 55 in the area, is more than 25 miles long. Near town are plenty of parks and hiking trails, and the Coeur d'Alene Resort has a floating boardwalk over the water that's almost a mile long.

Schweitzer Mountain Resort

Its acreage is the largest in Idaho and its vertical drop (2,400 feet) is second only to Sun Valley's 3,400 feet. It's been known to the region for nearly half a century as a true skiers' mountain, but now that the word is out nationally, things will certainly change.

A European-style village with shops, restaurants and lodging provides creature comforts, with more developments on the drawing board. However, many visitors stay in Sandpoint, 11 miles away on the shore of beautiful Lake Pend Oreille. This is the sort of place that people visit, then try to figure out a way to move here.

Schweitzer has mostly east-facing terrain. Compared to Rocky Mountain resorts, the elevation (6,400 feet) is not high, but it gets plenty of snow from its position in the Selkirks. When storms come from the north, the snow is dry and fluffy, but more often it's wet and dense. It's drier than the Cascade Concrete that falls on Washington and Oregon areas, but still wet enough to have earned the local term, Panhandle Premix.

Schweitzer cut its trails like Salt Lake City built its streets—wide enough to turn around a team of oxen. When the skies are clear, the vistas are outstanding: From the summit, skiers can look east into Montana's Cabinet Range and north to the Canadian Selkirks. And the view of big Lake Pend Oreille is stunning.

A surface lift provides access into a backcountry stash called "Little Blue." The area has five advanced runs and glades. The resort has a moving carpet in the learning area.

 ## Mountain layout

Schweitzer is spread across two bowls: Schweitzer Bowl and Outback Bowl.

Expert, Advanced: Schweitzer's runs and chutes are steepest at the top of its

Schweitzer Mountain Resort Facts

Summit elevation:	6,400 feet
Vertical drop:	2,400 feet
Base elevation:	4,700 feet

Address: 10,000 Mountain Road, Sandpoint, ID 83864
Ski area phone: 208-263-9555; (800) 831-8810
Snow report: 208-263-9562
Toll-free reservations: (800) 831-8810
E-mail: ski@schweitzer.com
Internet: www.schweitzer.com
Number of lifts: 9—1 high-speed six-pack, 1 quad, 4 doubles, 2 surface lifts, 1 moving carpet
Snowmaking: 47 acres
Skiable acreage: 3,000 acres
Uphill capacity: 9,267 per hour
Parks & pipes: 1 park, 1 pipe
Nearest lodging: Slopeside
Resort child care: Yes, 4 months and older
Adult ticket, per day: $55 (07/08 prices)

Expert:★★★
Advanced:★★★
Intermediate:★★★★
Beginner:★★ First-timer:★★★

Dining: ★★★
Apres-ski/nightlife: ★★
Other activities: ★★

Silver Mountain Facts

Summit elevation:	6,300 feet
Vertical drop:	2,200 feet
Base elevation:	4,100 feet

Address: 610 Bunker Ave., Kellogg, ID 83837
Ski area phone: 208-783-1111; (800) 204-6428
Snow report: 208-783-1111
Toll-free reservations: (866) 344-2675
E-mail: infosm@silvermt.com
Internet: www.silvermt.com
Number of lifts: 7—1 high-speed gondola, 1 quad, 2 triples, 2 doubles, 1 surface lift
Snowmaking: 35 acres
Skiable acreage: 1,590 acres (plus extensive off-piste)
Uphill capacity: 10,000 per hour
Parks & pipes: 1 park, 1 pipe
Nearest lodging: Gondola Base Village
Resort child care: Yes, 2 years and older
Adult ticket, per day: $46 (07/08)

Expert:★★★
Advanced:★★★
Intermediate:★★★★
Beginner:★★
First-timer:★★

Dining: ★★
Apres-ski/nightlife: ★
Other activities: ★★

two broad bowls, Schweitzer and Outback. The bowls are separated by the Great Divide, a long wide ridge that gives you a continuous option to drop into either bowl. Some double-black terrain tumbles off the Schweitzer Bowl rim, but most experts head up the Great Escape and turn right to Outback Bowl, where steeps are studded with cliff bands and trees.

A whole bowlful of chutes awaits advanced skiers in the Schweitzer Bowl. There are so many, they're lettered rather than named, as in A Chute, B Chute, and so forth. Upper Stiles and the adjacent Headwall Chutes are favored by those going for quick turnaround times. Off Stella The Six-Pack Chair are two adjacent single-black runs—No Joke and Revenge—that would be double-blacks anywhere else. They both are short thrills, but stay away on icy days. Make sure to check out the lift-served terrain in "Little Blue" with the longest run on the mountain - 1.7 miles.

Intermediate: You can wend your way down from the Schweitzer Bowl summit, but unload midway on the Snow Ghost chair for Outback Bowl because the upper terrain is tougher. Stella The Six-Pack Chair goes to the ridge of the Northwest Territory, where you'll find 150 acres of gladed and groomed terrain. Intermediate favorites here are Cathedral Aisle, Timber Cruiser and Zip Down.

Beginner, First-timer: No beginner runs come down from the top, but get a nice view by unloading midway up Chair One and heading down blue-square Gypsy. The Enchanted Forest and Happy Trails are perfect for children. Both run the length of the Musical Chairs chair, which goes right by the windows of the 40,000-square-foot Headquarters Day Lodge, so parents can check out their kids. The Enchanted Forest, with kid-high, widely spaced mounds that children can go over or around, is barred to adults and jealous snowboarders.

Parks and pipes

Stomping Grounds Terrain Park is accessed from the Chair One midstation. It's 50 acres of freeriders' fun, with beginner, intermediate and expert terrain featuring jumps, rails and tabletops. Weekly jam sessions and coaching events take place throughout the year. It's also open for night riding.

Snowboarding

Schweitzer is pretty much riders' heaven, even beyond the terrain park. The chutes and bowls are all blues and blacks with easy access and return. One exception is the "Cat Track to Village" that crosses under the Sunny Side lift—there's a bit of uphill toward the end. Ridge Run, left from the top of the Great Escape Quad, is very wide and gently sloped, so you might stall out in deep, ungroomed snow. Outback Bowl is choice for tree-running.

Cross-country & snowshoeing (see also xcskiresorts.com)

Schweitzer has more than 32 km. of trails, most groomed and track set. A snowshoe trail lets you explore Hermit's Hollow. Rentals and trail passes are available in the village at The Ski & Ride Center

Lessons (07/08 prices)

Group lessons: The Ski & RIde Center (800-831-8810) offers lessons for all abilities as well as daycare. Skis, snowboards and other snowsport equipment is available for rental. Custom group lessons are limited to three per class, so you'll get plenty of attention from the instructor. One- to 2-hour lessons cost $35 without gear rentals. A package including lessons, gear and lift ticket costs $85; a three-day package costs $210.

First-timer package: First-time skiers and riders get a lesson with beginner lift ticket and rentals for $65. A three-day package costs $119. Each lesson is between one and two hours long, depending upon number of students. After your lesson you can upgrade to an all-mountain lift ticket for $35.

Private lessons: $85 for one hour; $180 for a half day; $330 for a full day. First or last lesson of the day costs $65 ($95 for 2-5 people).

Racing: NASTAR races are held Friday through Sunday.

Children's programs (07/08 prices)

Child care: The Ski and Ride Center offers daycare. Ages 4 months to 12 years. For kids in diapers, cost is $55 for a full day; $44 for a half day. A hot lunch costs $5. Reservations strongly recommended; call 800- 831-8810, Ext. 2374.

Children's lessons: Kinder Kamp, for ages 4–6, includes a morning and afternoon lesson, rentals and an indoor recreation break and costs $85.

Mountain Riders, a ski and snowboard program for ages 7-12, costs $85 for all day, including lift ticket and lunch; with rentals the cost is $95.

Special activities: Ages 12–18 can hang out in the refuge and play foosball, Xbox, video games, and check out a bouldering cave. It's in the White Pine Lodge and is open Fridays thru Sundays, 2 to 8 pm. Sorry, no adults, so don't bother trying to sneak in.

Lift tickets (07/08 prices)

	Adult	Junior (7-172)
One day	$55	$40
Three days	$153	$111
Five days	$250	$180

Who skis free: Children 6 and under.

Who skis at a discount: College students and seniors 65 and older pay $45.

Accommodations

On the mountain, **Selkirk Lodge**, **White Pine Lodge** and **Schweitzer Resort Condos** (800-831-8810; $$$-$$$$) are all ski-in/ski-out properties with full amenities.

In downtown Sandpoint, lodging is inexpensive (many rooms less than $100 a night) and fairly basic. Try the four-room, lakeside **Coit House B&B** (866-265-2648; 208-265-4035; $$) for a romantic getaway that includes a hot breakfast. Right across the street, the same owners operate **K-2 Inn** (208-263-3441; $-$$), a no-smoking motel featuring rooms, suites and apartments with fridges and microwaves, plus a hot tub. **La Quinta Inn** (800-282-0660; 208-263-9581; $$) has 68 rooms, including three suites, serves a complimentary breakfast and welcomes pets.

Dining

Ivano's Ristorante (208-263-0211; $-$$$), a gracious Italian restaurant in Sandpoint, has been in business for more than 20 years and is one of the locals' favorites. An extensive entree selection includes pasta, fresh seafood, buffalo, beef, chicken, veal and vegetarian dishes.

Cafe Trinity (208-225-7558; $-$$$), one of Sandpoint's newest culinary additions, specializes in Creole cooking. Just two of many favorites are the spunky crawfish chowder and the pecan-crusted chicken salad. **Swan's Landing** (208-265-2000; $-$$$), a premiere steakhouse on the south end of the Long Bridge, pairs fabulous sunsets with Black Angus beef.

Chimney Rock Grill (208-255-3071; $$), in the Selkirk Lodge at the mountain, is known for its regional cuisine and serves an $18 seafood boil to die for. It includes three kinds of mussels, three kinds of clams, tiger shrimp, French bread, corn on the cob, potatoes, salad and is nicely finished off with huckleberry cheesecake.

For breakfast or lunch and great views, try **Cabinet Mountain Coffee** in the Lakeview Lodge. **Stella's Provisions** in the village is a one-stop, no frills sandwich shop with just what you need to keep you on the go.

Other activities

Sandpoint's **Winter Carnival**, usually held the third week in January, has snow sculpture extravaganzas, ice skating parties, a "Taste of Sandpoint" on the Cedar Street Bridge, a Parade of Lights and a host of special events on Schweitzer Mountain. For information, call the Greater Sandpoint Chamber of Commerce at 800-800-2106 or 208-263-2161. **Hermit's Hollow Tubing Center** operates Fridays through Sundays.

Train buffs, more properly called rail fans, consider Sandpoint to be a paradise. Railroad tracks here are called "The Funnel" because all 50 trains per day funnel onto the one track that goes through town. A good photo opportunity is the Pend d'Oreille transfer yard, which is used daily by Burlington Northern, Union Pacific and Montana Rail Link.

In the Selkirk Lodge on the mountain, **Heaven, the Spa** (208-263-8107) pampers guests with everything from hot rock treatments to Thai massage and more.

Shopping includes some culinary delights. **Coldwater Creek** (208-263-2265), in downtown Sandpoint in a beautiful facility on Cedar Street Bridge, is a huge signature store with a deli and wine bar. Don't miss the **Pend d'Oreille Winery** (208-265-8545), just a few blocks from Coldwater Creek. You can have four free tastings. Sandpoint is home to **Litehouse Bleu Cheese Factory** (208-263-2030), which has its full line and samples at its local retail store.

Silver Mountain

Silver Mountain's original name was Jackass Ski Bowl and it's been hard to market ever since. The name honored the discoverer of the metal that brought riches to the valley more than a century ago. Local legend says a donkey got away from its owner, scampered up a hill and was standing on a rock with a silvery glint when the owner caught up with it and found the precious metal. Bunker Hill Mine, which also took lead, zinc and copper from the hillsides, ran the ski area for employee recreation and changed the name to Silverhorn. But in the early 1980s silver prices plunged and Bunker Hill closed. What the company left behind was a white-knuckle road up to the ski area (later condemned by the city) and a Superfund cleanup site of astounding proportions. Kellogg took over what is now Silver Mountain and taxed itself $2 million to build the 45-tower, 3.1-mile gondola, the longest in the world. It rises out of the parking lot a quarter mile from I-90.

The gondola descends low over the houses and yards of the town of Wardner before climbing to Silver's "base area," called Mountain Haus, at 5,700 feet. A hefty portion of Silver's terrain is below the Mountain Haus, which gives the area its 2,200-foot vertical drop. There are no trails down to the base, though, so the gondola is the only way in and out.

This guarantee can't be beat: If snow conditions don't please you, return your lift ticket to the gondola base within an hour and a half and get a pass for another day. Or, for another $5, hit the snow tubing park for a couple of hours.

Dining: $$$$–Entrees $30+; $$$–$20–$30; $$–$10–$20; $–less than $10.
Accommodations: (double room) $$$$–$200+; $$$–$141–$200; $$–$81–$140; $–$80 and less.

Mountain layout

Silver has two connected peaks, Kellogg and Wardner. The gondola deposits skiers and snowboarders at Mountain Haus on Kellogg. Skiers and boarders fan out in several directions. Most stay on the Kellogg side, so to avoid even a mirage of crowds, head to the Wardner side.

Expert, Advanced: Experts come for the steep glades of giant Ponderosa pines and the open-boundary policy. Take the Wardner Peak Traverse to an inspirational knob with a stupendous view of the Silver Valley below. Some challenging black-diamond runs go back down to the Shaft and Chair 4. Terrible Edith, off Noah's and under Chair 5, is one of those runs that makes you feel like you're skiing down a globe. The farther down you go, the steeper it gets, until finally you see the cat track below—and that's only half-way down. For great thrills on the Wardner side, cut down anywhere from the early section of the Wardner Peak Traverse. The best skiing on powder days is off the scree slopes between the tops of Chairs 4 and 2. Pass Midway and keep going down through the Shaft to the Chair 4 base.

Intermediate: Silver Belt, from the triple Chair 2, is a wide and terrific intermediate warm-up run. At the Junction you can turn down Saddle Back for a bumpier ride or take a hard left on the Cross Over Run to the Midway load station on Chair 4 for a ride to Wardner Peak. From the top there are several trails back to Midway.

Beginner, First-timer: Beginner terrain has doubled in size affording more room to make pies and learn how to carve. There's an easy ride back up for the first-timers on the moving carpet lift. Chairs 1, 2, 3, and 5 at the Mountain Haus base area all serve beginner terrain. Below the lodge, Ross Run is a wide beginner favorite, allowing crossover to Noah's and back again, ending on Dawdler with a choice to return to Chair 5 or Chair 3.

Parks and pipes

Silver's terrain park on Lower Quicksilver has jumps, pools, wave walls and a halfpipe. Because the terrain park has been so popular with park junkies, extra real estate has been carved out and cleared of some tree islands.

Snowboarding

Experts come for the steep glades of giant Ponderosa pines and the open-boundary policy. Take the Wardner Peak Traverse to an inspirational knob with a stupendous view of the Silver Valley below. Some challenging black-diamond runs go back down to the Shaft and Chair 4. Terrible Edith, off Noah's and under Chair 5, is one of those runs that makes you feel like you're snowboarding down a globe. The farther down you go, the steeper it gets, until finally you see the cat track below—and that's only half-way down.

On fresh powder days, take Silver Belt to Rendezvous on the Kellogg side. For great thrills on the Wardner side, cut down anywhere from the early section of the Wardner Peak Traverse. The best riding on powder days is off the scree slopes between the tops of Chairs 4 and 2.

Silver Belt, from the triple Chair 2, is a wide and terrific intermediate warm-up run. At the Junction, riders who like bumps should turn down Saddle Back. To avoid the moguls, take a hard left on the Cross Over Run to the Midway load station on Chair 4 for a ride to Wardner Peak. From the top there are several trails back to Midway.

Chairs 1, 2, 3, and 5 at the Mountain Haus base area all serve beginner terrain. Below the lodge, Ross Run is a wide beginner favorite, allowing crossover to Noah's and back again, ending on Dawdler with a choice to return to Chair 5 or Chair 3.

Cross-country & snowshoeing (see also xcskiresorts.com)

Silver Mountain does not have any cross-country trails. However, it does have a scenic 5 km. snowshoe trail that's a nice break from skiing. Rent snowshoes at the resort's rental shop.

Lessons

Group lessons: 90-minute lessons cost $20; three-hour lessons, offered only on weekends and holidays, cost $39.

First-timer package: First-time skiers and riders get a 90-minute lesson with beginner lift ticket and rentals for $49. A three-day package costs $99.

Private lessons: $55 for one hour; $135 for three hours; $205 for a full day. Early-bird lesson starts at 9 a.m. and costs $40. Each additional person costs $10.

Children's programs (07/08 prices)

Child care: Ages 2 to 6. Cost is $39 for a full day; $25 for a half day; $8 per hour. Add a one-hour private lesson for $39. Private child care is available for younger children by special arrangement. The child-care center is in the Mountain Haus and is open 8:30 a.m. to 4 p.m. daily, plus during night-skiing hours on Friday and Saturday. Reservations strongly recommended; call 800-204-6428.

Children's lessons: All-day programs for ages 5–12 include lessons, rentals, lift ticket and lunch for $70; half day, $55 (without lunch). Snowboard lessons start at age 8.

Lift tickets (07/08 prices)

Adult (18-61) $46; **Child** (7-17) $31

Who skis free: Children 6 and younger.

Who skis at a discount: Seniors (62 and older) and college students with a valid ID pay $36 for one day.

Silver Mountain season passholders can ski 5 days free Mission Ridge and White Pass.

Note: Prices are higher for peak/holiday periods.

Accommodations

Morning Star Lodge (800-344-2675; $$-$$$) at the Gondola Base Village has recently-built condos with full amenities, spacious facilities and rooftop and ground level hot tubs.

The Mansion on the Hill (208-786-4455; $$$), a B&B in Kellogg that also owns **The Veranda** (see Dining), offers rooms, cottages and breakfast in a cozy setting. A day spa is on the premises.

The most affordable place to stay is at the base of the gondola at the **Baymont Inn**, formerly **Super 8 Motel** (800-785-5443; 783-1234; $-$$). It's next to the gondola base, extremely clean, with an indoor pool, hot tub and serves a continental breakfast in the lobby.

Silver Ridge Mountain Lodge ((800-435-2588) is close to the gondola village. **The Trail Motel** (208-784-1161; $-$$), clean and comfortable with restaurants nearby, is half a mile from the gondola village.

Silverhorn Motor Inn & Restaurant (208-738-1151; $-$$) located six blocks from the gondola village, has an indoor hot tub, restaurant, movie library and a free laundry.

Call toll free reservations (800-2204-6428) for many more vacations homes, condos and cabins.

Dining: $$$$–Entrees $30+; $$$–$20–$30; $$–$10–$20; $–less than $10.
Accommodations: (double room) $$$$–$200+; $$$–$141–$200; $$–$81–$140; $–$80 and less.

 Dining

Rumor has it that **The Veranda** (208-783-2625; $$), in a beautifully restored home with a country French theme, has the best dinner in Kellogg. About a 10-minute walk from the gondola base, it's owned by the Texan who also owns The Mansion on the Hill (see Lodging) and serves fine Pacific Northwest fare with microbrews and fine wines.

Silver's newest restaurants. **Noah's Canteen** and **Noah's Arcade**, are located in the gondola village. Listen for the historic Bunker Hill Mine whistle everyday at noon and four for lunch and happy hour respectively. The upstairs Arcade is perfect for families with kids while parents can settle in at Noah's Bar right downstairs for their favorite beverage before visiting the Canteen for a nice dinner.

Terrible Edith's ($-$$), named after a lady of the night from the mining-boom era, at the gondola base, features Italian food and microbrews. Edith's also serves a mean and reasonable breakfast. Locals say the best breakfast in town can be had at **Sam's** ($), across the highway from the gondola.

The Snack Shack at Midway 4, is open weekends and holidays, 11 am - 3:15 pm. Tell them what you'd like to see on the menu and they'll do their best to accommodate. **Mountain House Grill** at the Mountain Haus base area at the top of the gondola has great cafeteria-style chili, soup, pizza, burgers and quick snacks. On your way up, you might want to stop in at **Mountain Tapas Cafe** in the gondola village for espresso. Then stop in on your way down. They also serve tapas, fine wines and microbrews on tap.

CJ's Cafe in Kellogg, three minutes from the resort, serves breakfast and lunch. Bring your lift ticket for a free espresso. **The Enaville Resort** (208-682-3453; $-$$), off I-90 Exit 43A, is always a real treat for visitors new to the Kellogg area. Known locally as the **Snake Pit**, it's more of a destination dinery than a resort. Over its 125-year history, the Snake Pit accommodated a lot of people for a lot of purposes, but sleeping through the night was never one of them. Sorry, no overnighters these days. While you're wondering who those people dressed in camouflage are, enjoy an appetizer of Rocky Mountain oysters before moving on to buffalo burgers and barbecue.

 Other activities

Snowmobiling is very big in Wallace—where it's legal on city streets—10 miles east of Kellogg on I-90, and also at **Lookout Pass,** 10 miles past Wallace on the Montana border. Lookout has a snowmobile camp and access to 600 miles of snowmobile trails. Call 800-643-2386 for more information (Best Western Wallace Inn, a headquarters of sorts, for snowmobiling with free security snowmobile storage).

Peak Adventure Snowcat Skiing and Snowboarding (208-682-3200) gets you into the backcountry with Idaho powder, big air and soft landings. Silver's snow **tubing park** just got better with an additional 100 feet of fun on a new sixth lane. The park is open Fridays, weekends and holidays from 10 a.m. to 4 p.m., plus night tubing until 9 p.m. on Fridays and Saturdays. With a lift ticket, the cost is $5 for a two-hour session. Otherwise, adult tickets are $17 and all others pay $15.

Break out the water shorts 'cause Silver Rapids, the **indoor waterpark** is a giant facility with a surf wave, lazy river, family raft slide and altogether 20+ features. Check with them regarding prices and open-for-business times.

Silver Mountain's Mardi Gras party, normally the last Saturday in February, has a scavenger hunt for kids, face painting, children's snow castle and ice sculptures along with fun games. Later on it's time for the adults to cut loose with live music, drink specials, costume contest, a lot of crazy Mardi Gras attire and bead wear.

Perhaps symbolic of the new Kellogg spirit are the life-sized sculptures-from-scrap that are placed around downtown. They were made by Dave Dose, a high school teacher and county commissioner with a sense of humor. You'll find a variety of shops at the Gondola Base Village and in downtown Kellogg.

Coeur d'Alene

Coeur d'Alene, in the center of Northern Idaho, is a central base for exploring the area. It offers all the features of big-town life with a small-town ambience. The downtown area is alongside Lake Coeur d'Alene, which has 135 miles of shoreline. Many cruise boats offer lake trips to watch eagles, take in the scenery, eat dinner or visit the Famous Floating Golf Green and dozens of quiet coves. The cruises are on hiatus for most of the winter, but from Thanksgiving to New Year's, they tour around the area lakeside properties, which are festively lighted for the holiday season.

If you plan to ski at Silver Mountain or Schweitzer, make your base at the world-class **Coeur d'Alene Resort** (800-688-5253; 765-4000; $$–$$$$). The Resort is in the heart of downtown, on the lakeshore. It boasts a full-service spa, fitness center and four restaurants, including the newly renovated **Beverly's** ($$$–$$$$), an elegant, prize-winning, top-floor restaurant with spectacular views and a million-dollar wine inventory. Transportation is available to both mountains; an airport shuttle also is available.

Don't leave this city without a visit to **Hudson's Hamburgers** ($) for a "Huddy Burger." Just a block from the Coeur d'Alene Resort, it's an institution. Opened in 1907, the small diner-like restaurant with a simple, long counter lined by stools has been in the Hudson family for three generations. They offer three choices—hamburgers with pickles, onions and/or cheese—and each burger is made from scratch. They also offer three special sauces, which you can buy for a reasonable price (the hot spicy mustard is a treasure if you like hot and spicy).

The best breakfast around is at the Coeur d'Alene Resort at **Dockside** ($). It also has the best view. Everyone's favorite is the Sunday brunch at $25. Other great breakfasts can be had at **Michael D's** ($) at the end of Main Street and at **The Breakfast Nook** ($), known for crab omelets and hash browns.

 ## Getting there and getting around

By air: Spokane International Airport, in Spokane, Wash., is the nearest major airport. For ground transportation, call **Moose Express** (208-676-1561). Car rentals are available at the airport. The airport is 86 miles from Schweitzer, 75 miles from Silver Mountain and 40 miles from Coeur d'Alene.

By rail: Amtrak's **Empire Builder** stops in downtown Sandpoint, with connections to Seattle, Portland, St. Paul and Chicago. Car rentals are available in Sandpoint.

By car: Silver Mountain is in Kellogg, about 75 minutes from Spokane and right off I-90 east of Coeur d'Alene. Schweitzer is in Sandpoint, 90 minutes from Spokane. Take I-90 to Coeur d'Alene, then Hwy. 95 north to Sandpoint. The 9-mile access road to the ski area has six hairpin switchbacks and can be a bit hairy. If you make home base in Coeur d'Alene, Silver is 40 miles away and Schweitzer is 50 miles. Coeur d'Alene is off I-90, between Spokane and Kellogg.

Getting around: Plan on renting or driving your own car.

Dining: $$$$–Entrees $30+; $$$–$20–$30; $$–$10–$20; $–less than $10.
Accommodations: (double room) $$$$–$200+; $$$–$141–$200; $$–$81–$140; $–$80 and less.

Sun Valley
Idaho

Summit: 9,150 feet
Vertical: 3,400 feet
Base: 5,750 feet

Address: 1 Sun Valley Rd., Box 10, Sun Valley, ID 83353
Telephone (main): 800-635-4150
Snow Report Number: 800-635-4150
Toll-free reservations: 800-786-8259
Reservations outside US: 800-635-4150
E-mail: ski@sunvalley.com
Internet: www.sunvalley.com

Expert:★★★★
Advanced:★★★★★
Intermediate:★★★★★
Beginner:★★★
First-timer:★★★

Lifts: 21—7 high-speed quads, 5 triples, 5 doubles, 2 surface lifts, 2 moving carpets
Skiable acreage: 2,054
Snowmaking: 78 percent of groomed terrain
Uphill capacity: 26,780
Parks & pipes: 1 superpipe
Bed base: 4,500
Nearest lodging: Walking distance
Child care: Yes, 6 months and older
Adult ticket, per day: $80 (08/09)

Dining:★★★★★
Apres-ski/nightlife:★★★★
Other activities:★★★★

Sun Valley may provide America's perfect ski vacation. It has a European accent mixed with the Wild West. It is isolated, yet comfortable; rough in texture, but also refined; Austrian in tone, cowboy in spirit.

Ageless would be the one word to describe Sun Valley Village, America's first ski resort, built in 1936 by Union Pacific tycoon Averell Harriman. It exudes restrained elegance with the traditional Sun Valley Lodge, village, steeple, horse-drawn sleighs and steaming pools. Sun Valley does low-key with perfection. In contrast, the town of Ketchum is all-American West, a flash of red brick, a slab of prime rib, a rustic cluster of small restaurants, shops, homes, condos and lodges. It's the nearby town of Ketchum that actually curls around the broad-shouldered evergreen rise of Bald Mountain, known as Baldy to locals. Each snow ribbon dropping from the summit into the valley leads to the streets of Ketchum.

This is Hemingway country. When he wasn't hobnobbing with the glitterati of the day, he wrote most of *For Whom The Bell Tolls* in the Sun Valley Lodge, where the halls are covered with photos of Hollywood celebrities who first made the place famous. Sun Valley has developed many famous winter-sport athletes: The late Gretchen Fraser, who was the first American Olympic ski champion in 1948; Christin Cooper, a 1984 silver Olympic medalist; Picabo Street, who won a silver at the 1994 Olympics and a gold in the 1998 Olympics; and Muffy Davis, 2002 three-time Paralympic silver medalist and overall World Cup Champion..

It is the celebration of its history that makes Sun Valley stand out from the rest of America's ski areas. If you enjoy history, stay at the Sun Valley Lodge, a beautifully preserved property with a pronounced mid-20th-century feel. The elegance of a bygone era is encountered in the details: Uniformed doormen; a formal dining room; a large second-floor "drawing room" with the piano in the center, overstuffed chairs and sofas in the middle, and fireplaces at either end; and an immense "hot tub" swimming pool that dates to the early days of the resort. "Sun Valley Serenade," a 1941 movie starring Sonja Henie and John Payne, is as corny as can be when you see it at home but it's lots of fun to see it in Sun Valley, especially when you later try to track down the exact filming locations on the mountain and in the lodge.

 ## Mountain layout.

The main drawback to Sun Valley is the split in the ski areas. Bald Mountain (called "Baldy") is best suited for intermediate and advanced skiers, while beginners and first-timers should stick to Dollar/Elkhorn. Mixed-ability groups may not be thrilled. Dollar's base is a full 15-20-minute bus trip away.

Expert, Advanced: Baldy's terrain is best known for its long runs with a consistent pitch that keeps skiers concentrating on turns from top to bottom, rather than dozing off on a flat or bailing out on a cliff or wall. Mile-long ridge runs lead to a clutch of advanced and intermediate bowls.

Limelight is a long, excellent bump run for skiers with strong knees and elastic spinal columns. Of the other black-diamond descents, the Exhibition plunge is one of the best known. Fire Trail, on the ski area boundary, is a darting, tree-covered descent for those who can make quick, flowing turns. The Seattle Ridge trail with hypnotic views curves around the bowls. The bowl area below is a joy. The downhill skier's right is a little easier, skier's left a little tougher, and you can catch the sun throughout the day. There are sections to take 50-yard-wide turns, but there is no easy terrain where you can relax your quads. The only flats are on top.

Intermediate: Baldy is good for this level, too. Trails are not quite so wide as at other Rocky Mountain resorts, but are for the most part long, very long.

The best warm-ups are either the Upper and Lower College runs leading to the River Run area, or the Warm Springs run. Both descend from the top and head to the base (College takes a little jog and joins with River Run near the bottom). Warm Springs is labeled blue-square, while College is labeled green. but there's not much difference. Both are long, moderately steep, very well groomed and loads of fun.

Other good spots are Cozy, Hemingway and Greyhawk in the Warm Springs area. These are often less crowded because the trail map shows a black-diamond entry (there's an inter-mediate cat-track entrance a little farther down that isn't as obvious on the map) as well as the Seattle Ridge runs, marked green but definitely for intermediates.

Beginner, First-timer: Do not be fooled by the green-circle markings on the Baldy trail map. Beginners should not ski Baldy. The runs are seriously underrated for difficulty. Yes, yes, we're well aware that the green-blue-black ratings system reflects the relative difficulty of the trails at each individual resort. Sun Valley followed the rules and marked the "easiest" runs on Baldy with green circles. Compared to other resorts, however, these runs are blue-royal blue. If you are at all tentative about your skills, start out at Dollar/Elkhorn.

Skiing parents can enroll their children in ski school at the River Run Lodge and Skier Services building at the base of the River Run trail on Baldy. The ski school will transport children enrolled in novice lessons to Dollar. Adult first-timers should head directly to Dollar. The terrain here is perfect for learning and good for intermediates perfecting technique or starting out in powder.

Parks and pipes

A recently transformed 425-foot-long superpipe with 18-foot-high walls can be found in the Warm Springs area, to rider's left just below Race Arena. This state-of-the-art Pipe Monster-groomed terrain meets competition superpipe standards and heightens freestyle and snowboard fun.

Snowboarding

Baldy's terrain is best known for its long runs with a consistent pitch, great for turning perfect arcs. Be prepared for the mile-long ridge runs that lead to several advanced and intermediate bowls, but don't avoid them or you'll miss out on some prime terrain. If you're an intermediate planning to sample the Warm Springs terrain, just be aware that the intermediate entrance is a cat track. Novices and beginners will want to head to Dollar.

Cross-country & snowshoeing (see also xcskiresorts.com)

The Sun Valley/Ketchum area has about 210 km. of trails overall. The closest facilities are at the **Sun Valley Nordic Center** (208-622-2250 or 208-622-2251), within walking distance of the **Sun Valley Lodge**, where 41 km. of cross-country ski trails are groomed and marked for difficulty; 4 km. are dog friendly. Lessons are available. The **Atlas Snowshoe Center** rents snowshoes for the 6 km. of free designated snowshoe trails.

The Blaine County Recreation District grooms the **North Valley Trails**, which have more than 100 km. of groomed trails in the **Sawtooth National Recreation Area** supported by set trail fees or donations. Dogs are welcome to accompany you on 30 km. of designated groomed trails. The largest center is **Galena Lodge** (208-726-4010; grooming report, 208-726-6662) with 56 km. of trails, a full restaurant and a ski shop. It also has a 15- km. snowshoe trail and snowshoe rentals. Galena is 24 miles north of Ketchum on Hwy. 75. There is a bus that runs from Sun Valley North to Galena at 10 a.m. and then returns at 2 p.m., so there is no need to bring a car to access the North Valley Trails.

Wood River Trails features 30 km. of trails stretching north of Ketchum to Hailey and Bellevue. **Lake Creek** has 15.5 km. of trails, and three other areas have less than 10 km. each. The **Boulder Mountain Trail** stretches 30 km. from the Sawtooth National Recreation Area headquarters 8 miles north of Ketchum to Easley Hot Springs and Galena, and is groomed all winter, snow conditions permitting.

Avalanche and snow condition reports are available 24 hours a day from the Ketchum Ranger District (208-622-8027). **North Valley Trails** (208-726-6662) maintains a grooming hotline.

For backcountry tours through the largest wilderness area outside Alaska, contact either **Sun Valley Trekking** (208-788-1966) or **Sawtooth Mountain Guides** (208-774-3324). Both feature hut-to-hut skiing and the opportunity to stay in yurts as well

Lessons (08/09 prices)

Call the Sun Valley Ski School (208-622-2248 or 208-622-2231) for more information on any of these programs.

Group lessons: A two-hour lesson costs $75 for skiing and snowboarding; multiday discounts available.

First-timer package: A two-hour lesson, all-day rentals and lift ticket cost $120.

Private lessons: $225 for one person for two hours; all-day costs $520. Discounts are available for multiple hours (cheaper in the afternoon) and additional people in a lesson.

Special programs: A multiday women's clinic for upper intermediates and better is held at select times as are racing clinics. Call for dates, prices and reservations. There is also a Mountain Masters weeklong program to improve skiing and riding for $1,350.

Children's programs (08/09 prices)

Child care: Sun Valley's Playschool in the Sun Valley Village offers care for kids 3 months to 6 years, but the upper age limit is not strictly enforced, should you have a 7-year-old who doesn't ski or ride. Ages 3 months-2 years, cost is $110 full day. Reservations are required, and priority is given to guests in Sun Valley resort hotels and condos. Call 208-622-2135.

Other options: Super Sitters (208-788-5080) has screened sitters trained in CPR and first aid who do in-room babysitting. Babys Away (800-327-9030; 208-788-7582) rents and will deliver baby needs to your lodge, such as cribs, strollers, car seats and toys.

Children's lessons: An all-day program, including lunch, is $145 for kids 4-12 years old; snowboard lessons are for kids 7-12. Check pricing for tots, 3-4, and beginners, 4-5. Discounts are available for multiple days in all children's programs. Lift tickets are extra.

Intermediate to expert skiers and riders can join the All Mountain Team, which introduces kids to mountain safety, backcountry excursions and freeriding.

Special activities: Boulder Mountain Clayworks (208-726-4484) runs children's classes for throwing clay and painting pottery. A popular free activity is sledding down Penny Hill, across from the Sun Valley Barn.

Lift tickets (08/09 prices)

	Adult	Child (Up to 12)
One day	$80	$46
Three of four days	$231 ($77/day)	$129 ($43/day)
Five of six days	$380 ($76/day)	$210 ($42/day)

Note: These are prices for tickets at Baldy.

Who skis free: Children 15 and younger ski and stay free when they are with a parent (one child per parent) in a Sun Valley Resort hotel or condo. Call (800) 894-9931 for details.

Who skis at a discount: Ages 65 and older pay $55 per day. Prices for those who ski only at Dollar/Elkhorn are: adult $38, child $30. Sun Valley lowers ticket prices in early and late season.

Note: The Lift Exchange Program allows those with multiday tickets (three days or more) to exchange one day on the slopes for a choice of select events and activities.

Accommodations

For information or reservations for Sun Valley and Ketchum, call 800-634-3347; 800-786-8259.

The **Sun Valley Lodge & Sun Valley Resort** (800-786-8259; $$-$$$$;) is the heart of the resort, though it is not slopeside. You can relax on terraces and in grand sitting rooms beneath coppery chandeliers. Gleaming outside is a skating rink once ruled by ice queen Sonja Henie. The village is a 3,800-acre Alpine enclave of pedestrian walkways, wall paintings, snow sculptures and spruce foliage. Because the Lodge was built well before the time of group tourism, each room is unique. Pricing depends on room size and added factors such as view and balcony. The newly renovated **Sun Valley Inn** (800-786-8259; $$-$$$$), about a hundred yards from the Lodge, is a bit less expensive but shares most amenities.

Knob Hill Inn (800-526-8010; 208-726-8010; $$$-$$$$) is one of the Ketchum area's most luxurious, recently included in the exclusive Relais et Chateaux group. The building is so Austrian you feel as if you've stepped out of your car into the Tyrol. Though it looks old world on the outside, rooms are quite modern and spacious, especially the baths with Jacuzzi jets.

Dining: $$$$–Entrees $30+; $$$–$20–$30; $$–$10–$20; $–less than $10.
Accommodations: (double room) $$$$–$200+; $$$–$141–$200; $$–$81–$140; $–$80 and less.

Pennay's at River Run (800-736-7503; 208-726-9086; $$-$$$$) is a cluster of family-perfect condos within walking distance of River Run lifts. There is a big outdoor hot tub and units have VCRs. A snowmobile-drawn carriage carries guests to and from the River Run lifts.

Best Western Tyrolean Lodge (800-333-7912; 208-726-5336; $$), only 400 yards from the River Run lift, has an Alpine atmosphere with wood-paneled ceilings and downy comforters. A champagne continental breakfast is served. **Best Western Kentwood Lodge** (800-805-1001; 208-726-4114; $$) with an indoor pool is in the middle of town, convenient to everything. The rates here are a bit higher than at the Tyrolean.

Clarion Inn (800-262-4833; 208-726-5900; $-$$) is a hotel with a large outdoor Jacuzzi and continental breakfasts. Rooms open to outdoor walkways and the decor is simple. It can be quite rowdy during spring break and holidays.

Christophe Condo Hotel (800-521-2515; 208-726-5601; $-$$$$) has roomy condos with underground parking and heated pool. Make sure you know exactly how to get to your room; the outdoor walkways are somewhat confusing.

Tamarack Lodge (800-521-5379; 208-726-3344; $$) is in the middle of town with a hot tub and indoor pool. Good for families, the lodge is equipped with microwaves, refrigerators and coffee makers. It doesn't get any more convenient than this for nightlife and dining. Rooms with fireplaces cost more.

Povey Pensione (128 W. Bullion St., Hailey; 800-370-4682; 208-788-4682; $) is a century-old residence maintaining the original character of its builder, John Povey, a British carpenter, who built and lived in the house when Hailey was a mining town. Pastel wall coverings and antique furnishings give the three bedrooms an Old West character. This pensione is about 13 miles south of Ketchum and Sun Valley. If you stay here, rent a car. Children under 12 are not allowed.

Lift Tower Lodge (800-462-8646; 208-726-5163; $) gets its name from a section of an old ski lift and is very close to the River Run base. All rooms have refrigerators, TVs and phones. Complimentary breakfasts include bagels, coffee and orange juice. The free bus stops in front.

High Country Resort Properties (800-726-7076) has an extensive selection of homes, townhomes and condominiums for short- and long-term rentals in the greater Ketchum-Sun Valley area. Choices range from cozy cabins to luxury homes. Special services available include car rental, shuttle bus, airport pick-up, dinner reservations and activity booking.

Elkhorn Resort (800-333-1962; 208-265-8521; $$-$$$) has affordable condominiums on the bus route to the mountain and downtown. This place is close to Dollar Mountain, perfect for beginners.

For private home rentals, call **ResortQuest Sun Valley** (800-521-2515; 208-726-5601) or **Premier Resorts** (800-635-4444; 208-727-4000). Both have rentals near the lifts, downtown Ketchum, out at Elkhorn Village near the Dollar Mountain lifts, and homes that offer privacy and isolation.

Dining

On the mountain:

The **Warm Springs, Seattle Ridge** (208-622-6287), and **River Run** (208-622-2133), both great for apres-ski as well, day lodges have excellent restaurants. Skiers can settle down to a lunch of prime rib, salmon, stone-fired pizza and many other delights, all while enjoying panoramic views. Deli and gourmet cafeteria-style buffets are the latest in on-mountain dining and Sun Valley does it right. The **Roundhouse** (208-622-2371), built in 1939, is the first daylodge on Bald Mt. Midway up on the River Run side, this restaurant welcomes non-skiers as well who can buy a "foot traffic" pass and enjoy the food, friends and views—lunch only. Reservations recommended. The **Lookout Restaurant** (208-622-6261) is often hidden under a mound of snow, which keeps lunchtime crowds small, making it a good stop for quick burgers, sandwiches and salads The **Dollar Cabin** at the base of Dollar Mt., has recently been replaced with a new building.

In **Sun Valley Village:** The **Sun Valley Lodge Dining Room** (208-622-2150) has old-time elegance and is one of the only places in the area with live music and dinner dancing. Specialties include Steak Diane, Chateaubriand Béarnaise Bouquetière and fresh Idaho trout or poached salmon. The **Duchin Lounge**, (208-622-2145) named for Eddie Duchin by Averell Harriman, is just off the Sun Valley Lodge lobby and has grande apres-ski and dancing.

The **Ram** (208-622-2225; $$$), attached to the Sun Valley Inn, serves elegant European atmosphere with food ranging from fondues to grilled New York strip loin to fish and seafood. **Gretchen's** (208-622-2144; $$) in the Lodge has a fine dinner menu, including Idaho lamb and beef. Enjoy breakfast and lunch as well ($). Recent additions are **Bald Mountain Pizza and Pasta** (208-622-2143; $$) for dinner and the new **Inn Lobby Lounge** (208-622-2266; $$) in the Sun Valley Inn for a light meal. At **Sun Valley Deli** (208-622-2060) pick up sandwiches and quick snacks. The **Konditorei** (208-622-2235; $) has an Austrian flavor and excellent lunches, such as hearty soups served in a bread bowl next to a mountain of fruit. Follow up your meal with a stop at the **Chocolate Foundry** (208-622-2147; $) and take home something to satisfy your sweet cravings. The **Boiler Room** (208-622-2148) in the Village has great apres-ski along with comedy acts for the evening crowd.

In Ketchum:

Ketchum has some of the best restaurants in any ski resort in America. Anyone with fine dining on his or her mind will not be disappointed. The region's real gourmet action takes place here. The price ranges we give here are a rough guide.

These restaurants all vie for "best of Ketchum." **Michel's Christiania** (208-726-3388; $$$), run by Michel Rodigoz, serves fine French cuisine. **Felix's** (208-726-1166; $$$), which has moved to 380 1st Ave. North, offers a continental menu in a very international setting. **Evergreen Bistro** (208-726-3388; $$$) has an elegant atmosphere of wood, crystal and glass and quite possibly the town's best wine list. **Chandler's** (208-726-1776; $$$) serves gourmet meals in a series of tiny rooms. It's fun to sit near the fireplace if you are with a group. Their three-course fixed price meal is one of Ketchum's best bargains.

Bistro 44 (208-726-2040; $$$) serves authentic French cooking prepared by chef-owner Alain Gilot. It's open for lunch. Dinner is prepared in two seatings nightly, Monday through Saturday. Reservations are required for dinner. For trattoria-style cuisine and excellent fish specials at exceptional prices, head to the **Baci Italian Café and Wine Bar** (208-726-8384; $$). **Dean's Restaurant** (208-726-8911; $$), formerly the **Coyote Grill and Wine Bar** (same owners, same place, just a new name), has a very romantic setting. Filled with couches and overstuffed chairs snuggling tiny tables, the rooms accentuate the creative grill cuisine.

The **Pioneer Saloon** (208-726-3139; $$), a local hangout going back into Ketchum history, is known for its prime rib and baked potatoes. **Ketchum Grill** (208-726-4660; $$) has a daring, innovative menu with flavor mixtures that will keep your taste buds tingling. The restaurant participates in the Chef's Collective to buy only locally grown/hunted or organic produce. **Rico's Pizza and Pasta** (208-726-7426; $$) is the local's favorite spot for take-out Italian dishes.

Dining: $$$$–Entrees $30+; $$$–$20–$30; $$–$10–$20; $–less than $10.
Accommodations: (double room) $$$$–$200+; $$$–$141–$200; $$–$81–$140; $–$80 and less.

Sushi on Second (208-726-5181; $$) has Japanese fare. Locals say **Globus** (208-726-1301; $$) has good Chinese/Thai food. **Panda Chinese Restaurant** (208-726-3591; $) serves Chinese meals from several regions.

Warm Springs Ranch Restaurant (208-726-2609; $$) serves a wide-ranging menu including children's specials. Mountain trout swim in pools near the cozy cabin. The spots for excellent and inexpensive Mexican food are **Ketchum Kantina** (208-726-4213; $), on Main Street or **Desperado's** (208-726-3068; $) on Fourth Street. **Grumpy's** (no phone, we're told; $), on Warm Springs Road, is the locals' favorite for great burgers and beer.

Smoky Mountain Pizza & Pasta (208-622-5625; $) has great, very affordable Italian fare and massive salads. And the **Burger Grill** (208-726-7733; $$), another chain restaurant, serves up thick hamburgers, mounds of fries and frosty shakes.

Breakfast is important for most skiers. At the Sun Valley Lodge **Gretchen's** (208-622-2144; $) has plentiful fare with moderate prices and **Konditorei** (208-622-2235; $) in the Sun Valley Village has good breakfasts. The **Lodge Dining Room** (208-726-2150; $) serves an excellent Sunday brunch. The best breakfasts, however, are downtown in Ketchum. The **Kneadery** (208-726-9462; $) on Leadville Street has a cozy woodsy atmosphere. It's open for lunch as well. **Java on Fourth** (208-726-2882; $) has daily specials, excellent food and an unusual atmosphere. Outdoor seating is available. The **Rustic Moose** (208-727-9767; $) is a simple place with an extensive menu for breakfast or lunch.

Directly across the street from the Warm Springs Lodge at the base of Baldy is a Ketchum institution, **Irving's Red Hot** stand, where you can get great hot dogs. "The Works" (a dog smothered in fixings and chips) for only $2 is a lunch bargain that can't be beat.

One evening dining adventure that should not be missed is the horse-drawn sleigh ride dinner at **Trail Creek Cabin** (208-622-2135). The cozy rough-hewn cabin dates from 1937 and can be reached by sleigh, car or cross-country skis. For the sleigh ride, make reservations 72 hours in advance, but you can always check for open space. **Galena Lodge** (208-726-4010) also offers moonlight and star gazing dinners in the warmth of a rustic lodge.

Apres-ski/nightlife

If your skiing ends in Warm Springs, **Apples** is the spot for a mountainside debriefing. Overall, Warm Springs is the top base for slopeside revelry. Just remember not to take beverages on the bus; drivers are quick to enforce the rules.

The **Boiler Room** at Sun Valley has the Mike Murphy comedy show every afternoon at 5 p.m. for a moderate cover charge. The **Duchin Room** in the Lodge has music starting at 4 p.m. On Thursdays, head to **River Run Lodge** for musical entertainment.

At the western-bar-themed **Whiskey Jacques**, a favorite Hemingway haunt, patrons can listen to live music and dance inside an authentic log building. The **Pioneer Saloon** is famous for its steaks, prime rib, and decorations (mounted elk and moose). The saloon gets very crowded very early on weekends.

Another popular spot is **The Casino**, so named because there used to be slot machines where the tables now stand. Gambling is now illegal in this part of the country. It's something of a departure from the more intense nightclubs in the area with the dance floor replaced by pool tables.

The newest bar is **Cellar Pub**, an authentic Irish pub. It's a local's favorite that's smoke free and ambiance rich. You can get a hearty plate of fish & chips until 10 p.m.

The **Sun Valley Wine Company** has a wine cellar, reportedly the largest wine selection in Idaho, and offers a light lunch and dinner menu. It's above the Ketchum state liquor store on Leadville Street. Choose a bottle of wine from its large inventory, then enjoy it in a quiet, conversation-oriented environment next to a fireplace. It's open 10 a.m. through 10 p.m. weekdays but does close earlier if things are slow.

It's **Lefty's Bar & Grill** for locals, darts and draft beers. As the unofficial post-game headquarters of the Sun Valley Suns ice hockey team, this little hole in the wall really packs a crowd.

If you are staying in Sun Valley or Warm Springs and plan on partying in Ketchum, the KART bus system stops running at midnight, but A-1 Taxi (208-726-9351) is available until closing.

Other activities

Snowmobiling is available through **Smiley Creek Lodge** (208-774-3547). Ice skating is available year-round on the **Sun Valley Resort** outdoor rink. Ice hockey fans can catch home games of the Sun Valley Suns three times a month.

Sun Valley Heli-Ski (208-622-3108) offers backcountry ski adventures for all levels of skiers. Paragliding with **Fly Sun Valley** (208-726-3332) gets you floating over the mountains. Ice fishing/fly fishing is offered by **Silver Creek Outfitters** (208-726-5282) and **Lost River Outfitters** (208-726-1706).

There are also **horse-drawn sleigh rides and dog sled tours**.

The **Sun Valley Athletic Club** (208-726-3664) with daily and weekly rates is open to visitors with child care, massage, aerobics, weights and swimming. Also try **High Altitude Fitness** (208-726-1959). **Sacred Cow Yoga Studio** (208-726-7018), next to the Sun Valley Garden Center, offers a variety of yoga and meditation at varying levels throughout the week.

Shopping opportunities are extensive. The **Sun Valley Village** is full of boutiques and shops offering everything from Bogner and jewels to handmade chocolates. A few shops worth highlighting: **The Toy Store**, for unique and educational toys from around the globe; **Barry J. Peterson Jewelers**, for Limoges collectors' boxes, Lesäl ceramics and unique jewelry; **The Country Cousin** for low-priced accessories and gifts; and **T. D. Bambino**, where you can have fleece clothing custom-made. You can pick up some great bargains on secondhand items at the **Gold Mine Thrift Shop**, 331 Walnut Ave. Because this supports the The Community Library in Ketchum, residents give their (sometimes barely) used clothing and sporting goods to this store. By the way, the library is a gem. It has an amazing regional history section.

Sun Valley Center for the Arts has performances and showings during the ski season. For a schedule call 208-726-9491 or the **Chamber & Visitors Bureau**, 208-726-3423. Art galleries are another center of Ketchum and Sun Valley's cultural life. Sun Valley's Art Gallery in the Village and 12 galleries in Ketchum are members of the **Sun Valley Art Gallery Association** (208-726-8180). They provide a beautiful brochure with a map and offer guided evening gallery walks about a dozen times during the year.

Getting there and getting around

By air: The closest airport is Sun Valley Airport (Friedman Memorial, code SUN), 12 miles south in Hailey. Weather sometimes closes it in which case, the planes land in Twin Falls, about 90 minutes away and passengers are bussed at no charge. Boise airport, which provides the closest jet service, is about 155 miles and 2.5 hours away.

Several properties provide transportation, or you can use one of the following companies, most of which will pick you up in Hailey, Twin Falls or Boise: **Sun Valley Stages**, (800-574-8661); **Sun Valley Chauffeur**, (208-725-0880); **Sun Valley Express**, (800-622-8267; 208-342-7795).

By car: Sun Valley/Ketchum is 82 miles north of Twin Falls on Hwy. 75, and 152 miles from Boise. **Getting around:** You don't really need a car if you're staying in Sun Valley Village or near the KART bus routes, which link Sun Valley, Ketchum and Baldy and run about every 20 minutes. For schedule information, call 208-726-7140.

Dining: $$$$–Entrees $30+; $$$–$20–$30; $$–$10–$20; $–less than $10.
Accommodations: (double room) $$$$–$200+; $$$–$141–$200; $$–$81–$140; $–$80 and less.

Idaho Regional Resorts

Bogus Basin, Boise, ID (208) 332-5100; (800) 367-4397

Internet: www.bogusbasin.com

7 lifts; 2,600 skiable acres; 1,800 vertical feet; 3 terrain parks

Bogus Basin is much more than the day hill skiers would expect of a seven-chair mountain so close to a city (16 miles from Boise). Bogus is a community-owned, full-service destination resort. Boise's Amtrak station brings in the destination skiers and lodging both at the base and on the mountain keeps them on the slopes. Basically, Bogus is big.

Like British Columbia's Red Mountain, Bogus has 360-degree skiing around its highest peak. Shafer Butte, at 7,582 feet, is reached on the front side by the Superior lift, and on the back by Pine Creek lift. Don't miss the back side. It's like the front, only pumped up. The other peak, 7,070-foot Dear Point, is accessed by the Deer Point lift from Bogus Creek Lodge and via the Showcase lift.

What about the name Bogus Basin? Legend has it that fool's gold—iron pyrite—was mined there and marketed to gullible city folks as the real thing. There was real stuff in the area, however, and all the ski runs are named after legitimate mines. Bogus also has a complete Nordic program: 37km of groomed trails, rentals, lessons and a waxing bench all at the Nordic Center at Frontier Point Lodge, 208-332-5390.

The mountain also has two restaurants and the 70-unit, mid-mountain Pioneer Inn. Child care starts at 10 months.

Lift tickets (2007/08 prices): Adults, $46; children (7-11), $20; ages 6 and younger and ages 70 and older, free.

Distance from Boise: About 16 miles north. Coming east or west on I-84, take the City Center Connector to River Street exit, then 15th Street to Hill Road to Bogus Basin Road.

Lodging information: Pioneer Condominiums (800-367-4397; $-$) are on the mountain. In Boise, the elegant **Grove Hotel** (800-426-0670; $) is central to downtown.

Brundage Mountain, McCall, ID; 800-888-7544; 208-634-4151

Internet: www.brundage.com Snow report: 800-888-7544

5 lifts; 1,340 acres; 1,800 vertical feet; 1 terrain park

Brundage is definitely an underrated resort. The skiing is pleasant and uncrowded with occasional challenging drops but mostly cruisers. Intermediates find this mountain a real delight. Advanced and expert skiers and riders should head into the trees or chutes of the Hidden Valley area. Payette Lake, which Brundage overlooks, is beautiful and sparsely populated, with many outdoor activities. From the top of the mountain, you can see the Salmon River Mountains, Oregon's Eagle Cap Wilderness and the Seven Devils towering over Hells Canyon, America's deepest river gorge.

With the addition of two new fixed-grip triple chairs for 2007-08, Brundage doubled its uphill capacity to 6,700 per hour. One lift, the Lakeview, opens up 160 acres on the south side of the mountain for the first time. In a long-awaited land swap with the US Forest Service, Brundage gained 388 acres at the base area, making it possible to consider base development that for the first time includes lodging.

An espresso shack at the bottom of the Bluebird high-speed quad near the lodge will gas you up when you get tired. No Starbucks for the Potato State though—the coffee will be a special brew just for Brundage that's made by Idaho's own White Cloud Coffee. **The Bear's**

Den, a yurt at the top of the mountain serves snacks, hot drinks, beer, wine and spirits.

Brundage has a reputation for some of the lightest powder in the Pacific Northwest and one of the best snowcat skiing operations in the country. In a permit area of more than 19,000 acres in the Payette National Forest, the guided all-day tour costs $259 per person and includes lunch and snacks; half-day is $159 per person with just snacks.

Child care at **Bunny Hutch Daycare** starts at 6 weeks; reservations required: 208-634-4151, ext. 128.

Lift tickets (2007/08 prices): Adults, $48; junior (12-18) and senior (65+), $34; youth (7-11), $22; ages 6 and younger free.

Distance from Boise: About 110 miles north via Hwy. 55. The drive is quite scenic.

Lodging information: McCall Central Reservations 800-844-3246. Recommended: Luxury lodging, with individually decorated rooms, jetted tubs and bay windows, can be found at **The Ashley Inn** (866-382-5621; $-$) in Cascade on Hwy. 55, 23 miles south of McCall and 75 miles north of Boise. Or try the modern, comfortable **Hunt Lodge—**
Holiday Inn Express 800-465-4329; $-$) in McCall.

Tamarack Resort, Donnelly, ID; 208-325-1000; 877-826-7376

Internet: www.tamarackidaho.com
7 lifts; 1,100 skiable acres; 2,800 vertical feet; 2 terrain parks; 1 superpipe

Winter 2004/05 was the first lift-served ski season at Tamarack—the first four-season resort to be built in the U.S. in 22 years. Tamarack, which averages 300 inches of snow each year, is 90 miles north of Boise, west of the village of Donnelly and beside Cascade Lake in Idaho's gorgeous and largely untouched Payette River Mountains region.

Tamarack's original yurts that saw the resort through its first season have given way to Discovery Square, a group of temporary dome buildings that house necessary rental, retail and repair shops, eateries, skier services, children's center, food market and clinic. Its first hotel, The Lodge at Osprey Meadows, sits nearby with luxury rooms and condos, gourmet dining (Morels), hot tub and pools, fitness center and the full-service Sante Spa.

The summit of the 7,700-foot-high West Mountain is above treeline, but not by much. The top third is sparsely treed, but farther down the mountain, trails lace their way through the forest. Eventually the resort plans to have 11 lifts—seven of them high-speed—and 2,100 skiable acres. Tamarack has a 22-foot Olympic-sized SuperPipe. Grooming on the cruisers is impeccable, and improvements to snowmaking focus on high-traffic areas. The resort limits Alpine tickets to 2,000 people per day.

Five thousand acres of guided-only backcountry terrain is open to the north and south of the ski area boundaries. For expert skiers and riders only, the go-big-or-go-home features include cliffs, chutes and bowls.

The resort base sits at 4,900 feet where 25 km. of groomed trails for Nordic skiing and 15 km. of snowshoe trails are right outside the door of the lodge. Lessons and outings are available for both Nordic skiing and snowshoeing.

Lift tickets (2007/08 prices): Adults, $59; juniors (7-17), $30; seniors (65+), $41, ages 6 and younger, free.

Distance from Boise: 100 miles from Boise Airport on Hwy. 55. A shuttle between the airport and resort can be reserved by calling 208-325-1005 48 hours before pickup.

Lodging information: 877-826-7376 for Tamarack Resort Central Reservations.

Big Sky

Montana

Summit:	**11,166 feet**
Vertical:	**4,350 feet**
Base: 7,500 feet (Mountain Village)	

Address: P.O. Box 160001, 1 Lone Mountain Trail,
Big Sky, MT 59716
Telephone (main): 800-548-4486
Snow Report Number: 406-995-5001
Toll-free reservations: 800-548-4486
Reservations outside U.S.: 800-548-4486
Internet: www.bigskyresort.com

Expert:★★★★★
Advanced:★★★★
Intermediate:★★★★
Beginner:★★★
First-timer:★★

Lifts: 21—1 aerial tram, 4 high-speed quads, 1 quad, 5 triples, 5 doubles, 2 surface lifts, 3 moving carpets
Skiable acreage: 3,812-5,512
Snowmaking: 10 percent of trails
Uphill capacity: 23,000
Parks & pipes: 3 parks, 1 superpipe
Bed base: 4,250
Nearest lodging: Slopeside
Child care: Yes, 6 months and older
Adult ticket, per day: $78 (08/09 prices)

Dining:★★★
Apres-ski/nightlife:★★
Other activities:★★

From the moment you land at Bozeman's Gallatin Field, which feels more like a private rancher's massive lodge than an airport, you know you're in for a different kind of vacation. Here you can expect lots of friendly employees in cowboy hats holding open doors for you, a genuine laid-back atmosphere, spectacular scenery and plenty of challenging terrain.

Big Sky, with its impressive Matterhorn-shaped peak scraping the heavens at 11,166 feet, is a serious skier's mountain from the summit, yet it has excellent cruisers closer to the base. Indeed, the intermediate groomers are such a delight that experts who wear themselves out on the tougher terrain still have plenty to grin about as they swoop down the lower trails with friends and family.

An aerial tram with two 15-passenger cars whisks you up to the 11,150-foot mark on Lone Peak that gives you a stomach-in-your-throat close-up of the craggy mountain just before coming in for a landing. If you get to the top and find that the chutes, couloirs and steeps are more than you can handle, no problem—admire the views of the nearby Spanish Peaks Wilderness area and ride back down. Only 15 people per tram, so you'll have a marvelous feeling of privacy as you descend, either in the capsule or while attempting the steeps beneath it.

Big Sky attracts about 300,000 skier visits each season; however, they're all swallowed up by the 3,600-acre terrain. A big daily turnout is 4,000 people, meaning short lines for the lifts and roughly one skier per acre. With about 400 inches of snowfall, powder days are frequent and last much longer than the first run. Big Sky Resort and Moonlight Basin, which border each other on Lone Peak, offer the Lone Peak Pass, a joint lift ticket that allows guests access to 5,300 acres and a vertical drop of 4,350 feet. It's a serious thrill to ride Big Sky's tram to the top and ski down the chutes of Moonlight Basin on the other side. The only requirements are that you carry a transceiver and a shovel, and get the ski patrol's permission. Oh, you can't go it alone—you must ski with a buddy.

Mountain layout

Expert, Advanced: Most of the runs from the Lone Peak summit are rated double-black diamond—none are easier than a single diamond—and justifiably so.

Lone Peak and the immense bowl beneath it beckon skiers and snowboarders looking for powder, chutes, steep pitches and wide-open terrain. Take Lenin into wide-open Liberty Bowl to Dakota Gully to the trees of Bavarian Forest. This makes a long run with lots of challenges. Hippy Highway then funnels you back from the boundary edge to the Shedhorn lift.

You must register with the ski patrol to challenge the A-Z Chutes, the Pinnacles and Big Couloir, all formerly out of bounds on the Moonlight Basin side of Lone Peak. (The latter is 42 degrees steep and half-a-mile long). If you want to try this terrain, you have to take a transceiver, a shovel and a partner.

If the tram line is long, take Turkey Traverse and explore South Wall to your heart's content. The vast area on Lone Mountain's north side is where many locals play. The Challenger chair climbs 1,670 steep vertical feet to open hair-raising in-bounds terrain—some of the toughest in-bounds skiing in the country. Steep, long pitches drop down Big Rock Tongue, trees pepper narrow chutes on Little Tree and Zucchini Patch and untracked lines are often found as you traverse toward's Ray's Ridge and the boundary line.

Andesite Mountain is a gem of a secret for advanced and expert terrain. It's all below treeline, so you'll find glades like Rock Pocket, Snake Pit and Bear Lair, as well as some bump runs like Mad Wolf and Broken Arrow. For more trees, drop off Pacifier into The Congo, which eventually ends up on Safari.

Intermediate: Big Sky has two mountains, Lone Mountain and Andesite, that connect at the base. The blue-rated trails on both have a wide range in pitch and grooming. Not all the blue trails are groomed, and some have cat-track runouts or are short.

On Lone Mountain, try the groomed cruisers under the gondola and the Swift Current chair, such as Calamity Jane, Huntley Hollow and Lobo. If you want some bowl skiing, head to Upper Morningstar. For advanced-intermediates, trails off the Shedhorn lift are south-facing and get plenty of sun at times when the lower mountain is in the shade. On Andesite, skis run fast and long on Big Horn, Elk Park Ridge, Elk Park Meadows and Ambush. The manicured slopes of Tippy's Tumble and Silver Knife have some steep sections. During the spring, hit the trails off the Thunder Wolf quad early in the day before the sun has turned them into heavy mashed potatoes.

Beginner, First-timer: The south side of Andesite Mountain is great for beginners because of the wide, gentle slopes and because it gets a lot of sun. Enjoy runs such as Sacajawea, El Dorado and Ponderosa from the Southern Comfort chair. On the way back to the base village, the winding Pacifier lets you admire awesome views.

Though not physically isolated from the rest of the terrain, the learning area, at Lone Mountain's base, is away from high traffic until the end of the day. A moving carpet transports you up the slope to learn your first turns. For the youngest ones, a smaller moving carpet is in a fenced-off area in the base area used by children's ski school.

Parks and pipes

Big Sky has a well-kept halfpipe and terrain park on Andesite, near Ambush Meadows, reached by taking the Ramcharger quad and turning left. The halfpipe is just after the Ambush entrance and just before Tippy's Tumble.

After watching skilled riders in the park, newbies should head left of the pipe, for the beginner terrain park hits and a 6-inch-high rail slide. Intermediate and expert park riders will find the bulk of the terrain park and rail slides directly below the halfpipe. Several kickers range in difficulty depending on speed, the direction you go into the hit and land.

The rail slides, funboxes and wall ride here are all shapes and sizes. Several tabletops are near the bottom, with plenty of spectators watching from the base area and the lift, so don't blow it. On Lone Mountain, there's a natural halfpipe on Lower Morningstar and another on Buffalo Jump.

Snowboarding

For some ridge riding and above-treeline faces, continue up from the chairs via the adjacent Lone Peak Triple and the Lone Peak Tram to the top of Lone Mountain at 11,150 feet (if you want to reach the 11,166 summit, you'll have to hike it, enjoy the view and hike back down). Under the Lone Peak Tram, you'll find some serious descents. The most extreme—and narrow—run on the mountain is Big Couloir, just to the right of the tram. If it's open, watch some others pick their way down before you decide to try it. If you do, you are required to check in with the patrol and have a partner, beacon and shovel.

The South Face isn't as steep as the chutes under the tram, but you'll still find yourself leaning into the mountain when you're "taking a breather." Death slides are not uncommon here, so stay on the ball. If you like catching air time with the locals, there's often a group building jumps on Screaming Left, at the bottom of Liberty Bowl. If you prefer the woods, Bavarian Forest is a great romp. After the woods and runs below the face, try to stay central to avoid most of Cow Flats and Hippy Highway. Also try to avoid Middle Road when working your way back to the mountain village.

Cross-country & snowshoeing (see also xcskiresorts.com)

Nationally acclaimed **Lone Mountain Ranch** (800-514-4644; 406-995-4644) offers more than 65 km. of international-caliber Nordic skiing for all levels, with groomed and skating lanes. The trail system winds through open meadows and forested canyons. The Ranch teams with **Alpenguide Tours** of West Yellowstone to offer a variety of backcountry skiing, including snowcoach tours into the interior of Yellowstone to view its winter wonders. Deluxe, cozy cabins with fireplace and full bath can be rented for a week, including all meals, trail pass and evening programs. The Ranch has a Nordic shop with apparel, equipment and mementos. Lessons are available.

You can rent snowshoes from the Lone Mountain Ranch, **Grizzly Outfitters** (406-995-2939) and **Big Sky Ski Rental** (406-995-5841) in the Mountain Village Plaza's Snowcrest building. Big Sky has a marked and separated snowshoe trail up a portion of Lone Mountain called Moose Tracks—it starts at the base of Andesite and Lone Mountains.

Lessons (08/09 prices)

Group lessons: Half-day ski lessons cost $67, morning or afternoon. Snowboarding lessons also cost $67, morning or afternoon.

First-timer package: A half-day lesson with learning area ticket and rentals costs $115. Those who wish to ski the whole day can upgrade to a beginner chair ticket for an additional charge.

Private lessons: Two hours (up to three guests) cost $250 in the morning, $230 in the afternoon, $340 for a half-day afternoon, $360 for a half-day morning, $550 for a full day. Guide services cost the same. For a two-hour telemark lesson, $230, pre-register at 406 995-5743.

Special programs: Advanced clinics for Level 7 and higher concentrate on Lone Peak's steeps and tackle moguls, powder or other conditions du jour, $75.

Racing: Check in with the ski school daily for details.

Children's programs (08/09 prices)

Child care: Ages 6 months and older. For ages 6–23 months, cost is $90 for a full day, $65 for a half day. For 2–8 years old, $80 for a full day, $55 for a half day. Hours are 8:30 a.m. to 4:30 p.m. Immunization records are required. Reservations are also required for all child-care services and parents will need to bring some things, so call ahead, 995-5847. The bright, airy facility is at slopeside Snowcrest Lodge.

Children's lessons: Ages 3–4 can take a 45-minute introduction to skiing in the afternoon, $80 (day care and rentals extra). Mini Camp, for ages 4–6, is $142 and includes all-day ski lessons, activities and lunch. Mini Rider Camp, for ages 6–9, is $142 and Snowboard Camp, for ages 10–14, is $142. Snowboarders 15 and older can take a 2.5-hour lesson for $67. Prices do not include lift ticket and rentals for kids 11 and older. Helmets are available for rental. For information on lessons, call 995-5743.

Special activities: Kid's Club, based in the Huntley, is a very popular kids' program that's available from 3–5 p.m. Monday through Friday. The program is free, but advance registration is required because space is limited. A free fireworks show lights up the sky every Saturday at 8 p.m.

Lift tickets (08/09 prices)

	Adults	Juniors (14-21),
One day	$78	$58
Three days	$224 ($75/day)	$174 ($58/day)
Five days	$370 ($74/day)	$290 ($58/day)

Who skis free: Two children (up to age 10) ski free per paying adult, making skiing very affordable for families with several young children.
Who skis at a discount: Junior/College (11-17), $58. College students must have ID to get college rates. Seniors 70 and older, $68.

Accommodations

Big Sky is divided into three areas—the Mountain Village, the Meadow Village and the Canyon. These areas are serviced by a free shuttle system during the winter. A good starting point is **Big Sky Central Reservations**, 800-548-4486; 866-676-9977, which can book most of the lodging listed here.

In the Mountain Village:
The Summit at Big Sky ($$$-$$$$;) is a ski-in/ski-out condo-hotel with one- to three-bedroom units, plus eight penthouses, all with mountain views. The Summit has a sauna, steam room, pool-sized hot tub with views of the mountain, fitness facilities and day spa. **Alpenglow** ($$$$) is the newest condo complex with great views and contemporary western decor.

The ski-in/ski-out **Shoshone Condominium Hotel** ($$$$) has spacious condos with kitchens, fireplaces and jetted tubs, plus a lap pool, indoor hot tub, health club, steam bath and more. **The Huntley** ($$-$$$$), also ski-in/ski-out, includes a buffet breakfast and has an outdoor pool, two hot tubs, sauna, workout room and game room. Kids 10 and under stay free.

Mountain Village has many condo complexes, some of which are only a few years old.If you stay in condos, you have access to The Huntley's hot tubs and pool. **Lone Moose Meadows** ($$$$) is one of the newer slopeside complexes. If you want luxury, try **Snowcrest, Beaverhead** and **Arrowhead Condominiums** ($$$$) with two to four bedrooms. You'll find two- and three-bedroom units at **Skycrest** ($$$$), which also has underground parking, or try the more moderately priced **Stillwater** ($$-$$$$), which has studios and two-bedroom units.

Dining: $$$$–Entrees $30+; $$$–$20–$30; $$–$10–$20; $–less than $10.
Accommodations: (double room) $$$$–$200+; $$$–$141–$200; $$–$81–$140; $–$80 and less.

The slopeside **Mountain Inn** (877-995-7858; 406-995-7858; $$-$$$$) has 90 suites with fridges and microwaves that sleep up to six people. Amenities include an indoor pool, two hot tubs and an exercise room, plus a continental breakfast. Children 18 and younger stay free in their parents' room.

Condo and home rental agencies with Mountain Village properties include **ResortQuest of Big Sky** (800-548-4488; 406-995-4800) and **Big Sky Chalet Rentals** (800-845-4428; 406-995-2665).

In the Meadow Village (6 miles away

River Rock Lodge (800-995-9966; 406-995-2295; $$-$$$$) is a "boutique-style European hotel" built of stone and log with beautiful interior decor. Rates include continental breakfast.

East West Resorts (800-845-4428; 406-995-2665) manages several condo complexes here, including **Hidden Village** ($$$$), units are set in the forest with in-house hot tubs and garage, and Park ($$$-$$$$), with head-on views of Lone Peak. **ResortQuest of Big Sky** (800-548-4488; 406-995-4800) rents many condos on the cross-country trail system.

In the Canyon (3 miles from the Meadow Village, in the beautiful Gallatin River Canyon, 9 miles from the lifts, serviced by the shuttle):

Buck's T-4 Lodge (800-822-4484; 406-995-4111; $$$-$$$$) is not your ordinary Best Western. Despite extensive remodeling in the past few years, or perhaps because of it, the former hunting lodge retains its rustic appeal. Rates include a hot breakfast buffet. Free high-speed Internet access is available. Ski packages are offered with Big Sky and Moonlight Basin.

The Rainbow Ranch Lodge (800-937-4132; 406-995-4132; $$$-$$$$) is on the Gallatin River. A luxurious western-ranch lodge, it has 12 rooms with private baths, and an excellent bar and restaurant (see Dining). Ski packages are available.

The Comfort Inn (800-228-5150; 406-995-2333; $-$$$) is clean, though it has little charm. The nicest budget accommodations are at the **Corral Motel** (406-995-4249; $).

 # Dining

Big Sky is divided into three areas—the Mountain Village, the Meadow Village and the Canyon.

In the Mountain Village:

For a memorable meal, try **The Cabin Bar & Grill** (406-995-4244; $$-$$$), which specializes in regional cuisine. Leave the kids behind and enjoy an outstanding meal. **Peaks** (406-995-8000; $$$), in The Summit, showcases a menu of new Western cuisine in an elegant but casual setting. The pricey breakfast buffet is very good.

M.R. Hummers (406-995-4543; $$-$$$) aces its baby back ribs, prime rib and steaks, served in nice-sized portions by attentive staff. **Huntley Lodge** (406-995-5783; $$-$$$) is fine dining in a rustic lodge setting. It serves a very good, reasonably priced breakfast buffet.

Bambu Bar & Asian Bistro (406-995-4933; $$) gets crowded quickly with noisy patrons and serves average-quality Asian dishes, including sushi. **Dante's Inferno** (406-995-3999; $$-$$$) has slope views and Italian cuisine that's budget-busting for what you get. **Black Bear Bar 'n' Grill** (406-995-2845; $-$$) is a casual spot for breakfast or dinner. For a quick lunch, try **Mountain Top Pizza Pies** ($).

In the Meadow Village:

Lone Mountain Ranch Dining Room (406-995-2782; $$-$$$), in a stunning log lodge with elk antler chandeliers and a massive stone fireplace, serves first-rate American regional cuisine. Sleigh-ride dinners are offered; call ahead as space is limited.

La Luna (406-995-3280; $-$$) satisfies cravings for authentic Mexican food, from simple to fancy dishes. Guinness on tap and terrific pesto pizza can be found at **Uncle Milkies Pizza and Subs** (406-995-2900; $-$$). **Allgoods Bar & Grill** (406-995-2750; $-$$) serves hickory-smoked ribs, chicken, pork, homemade stews and burgers.

For hearty sandwiches, try **The Wrap Shack** (406-995-3099; $), **Slider's Deli** (406-995-2566; $), and the **Hungry Moose Market & Deli** (406-995-3045; $). For breakfast, stop in at the **Huckleberry Cafe** (406-995-3130; $), or the **Blue Moon Bakery** (406-995-2305; $).

In the Gallatin Canyon:

Just about the best resort dining in North America is hidden away in Montana at **Buck's T-4 Restaurant** (406-995-4111; $$$-$$$$). This rustic former hunting lodge plays funky folk or cool jazz while your taste buds bliss away on wild game, hand cut Montana beef, veal and seafood. **The Rainbow Ranch Lodge** (406-995-4132; $$$-$$$$) is known for elegant dining overlooking the Gallatin River.

Apres-ski/nightlife

The hub of night activity is the Mountain Village. Happy hour kicks off in **Chet's Bar** in the Huntley Lodge, with the Crazy Austrian show—just go see it. Chet's also has poker games which are legal in Montana. The **Carabiner** in the Summit is a wonderful place to relax with a drink in oversized chairs. Mellow live entertainment provides background music. **Black Bear Bar & Grill** and **Dante's Inferno** both rock hard and long. Other places to check out in the Mountain Village are **Alpine Lounge**, where the locals get wild, and **Bambu Bar**, where the 20-somethings gravitate for drinks. In the Meadow Village, it's quieter, but **Allgoods Bar & Grill** is likely to attract crowds at night. Allgoods also has a pool table, darts and poker. In the canyon, check out the **Buck's T-4** game room, with pool tables, foosball and video games. Locals like the **Corral** and the **Half Moon Saloon**, with darts and pool. Both are roadhouse-style Western bars.

Other activities

Yellowstone National Park is a big attraction and, although not all roads are plowed and open to vehicle traffic, the park is certainly open in winter. A 7:30 a.m. bus runs daily from Big Sky to West Yellowstone where snowcoaches pick up riders for guided tours of the park to see wildlife, thermal pools and Old Faithful. Expect to encounter buffalo, elk, bald eagles, trumpeter swans, wolfs and coyotes—many up close and personal. The family-owned Snowcoach Yellowstone (800-426-7669; 406-646-9564) has modern comfy snowcoaches and knowledgeable, engaging guides. West Yellowstone is Montana's west entrance to the park. For more information on the area's recreation, call the **West Yellowstone Chamber of Commerce** (406-646-7701) or check www.westyellowstonechamber.com.

Snowmobiling in Yellowstone National Park is extremely popular. Guides are required by law in the park, and most snowmobile shops offer a 10 percent discount with a Big Sky lift ticket and provide bus service from the resort and West Yellowstone. Try Rendezvous Snowmobile Rentals, (800-426-7669; 406-646-9564); Yellowstone Tour & Travel, (800-221-1151); or Two Top Snowmobile, (800-522-7802; 406-646-7802). You don't need a guide if you plan to snowmobile outside the park boundaries, where you'll find hundreds of miles of forest trails. To snowmobile closer to Big Sky call Canyon Rentals(406-995-4540) a half a mile south of the Big Sky entrance.

Dogsled rides rides are offered by Spirit of the North Dog Adventures (406-995-4644), Lone Mountain Ranch (406-995-2783) or 320 Ranch (406-995-4283). **Dinner sleigh rides** are also available.

Winter fly fishing on the Gallatin River can be booked through Gallatin Riverguides (406-995-

Dining: $$$$–Entrees $30+; $$$–$20–$30; $$–$10–$20; $–less than $10.
Accommodations: (double room) $$$$–$200+; $$$–$141–$200; $$–$81–$140; $–$80 and less.

2290) or East Slope Anglers (406-995-4369), who have licenses, equipment rentals and supplies.

Pamper yourself at the full-service Solace **Spa** at Big Sky (406-995-5803), in the Huntley/ Shoshone complex. With three treatment rooms in the Huntley and two in The Summit, the spa provides a full range of professional therapy including massage, body wraps, facials, beauty enhancements and aromatherapy. Poker is legal **gambling** in Montana and nightly games are available. The Huntley Lodge shows free **movies** in the amphitheater at night. If you have the opportunity to attend an **avalanche search and rescue demo** by the ski patrol and their dogs, don't miss it. Demonstrations are held every Saturday at 5 p.m. near the fire pit in the plaza area.

The Mountain Village and Meadow Village have many **shops and boutiques**, as well as **grocery stores**. If you're into Montana artists and jewelers, visit Painted Pony Gallery in Mountain Mall and Gallatin River Gallery in Meadow Village.

Getting there and getting around

By air: Bozeman Gallatin Field Airport is served by Horizon Air, United Express, Delta, Northwest and Big Sky Airlines. The resort is an hour from the airport. Car rentals are available at the airport. **Karst 4X4 Stage** (800-287-4759; 406-556-3540) shuttles passengers between the airport, the resort and West Yellowstone. If you're staying in a condo and don't plan to rent a car, call **Mountain Taxi** (800-423-4742), fax them your grocery list, and they'll do your shopping before you arrive, then transport you from the airport to your condo.

By car: The resort is 45 miles south of Bozeman (and 50 miles north of West Yellowstone) on Hwy. 191 along the Gallatin River.

Getting around: If you stay at the Mountain Village, a car is unnecessary unless you plan to do a lot of sightseeing. A free shuttlebus runs between the Big Sky villages 7a.m.-11 p.m.

Nearby resorts
Moonlight Basin, Big Sky, MT; 406-995-7600
Internet: www.moonlightbasin.com

7 lifts; 1,900 skiable acres; 2,720 vertical feet (lift-served); summit elevation of 11,150 feet

Moonlight Basin is on the north face of Lone Mountain and first opened in December 2003. Skiers and riders will find a vertical descent of 2,720 feet that's lift-served. With the Lone Peak Pass interconnect lift ticket with Big Sky Resort, skiers and riders have access to 5,512 acres— the most in the US with one ticket. Moonlight Basin's first terrain park, the Zero Gravity Park, is located on the Runaway trail and has over 30 features, including boxes, rails, berms, tables, rollers and small hits. The resort offers ski and snowboard lessons. Child care starts at age 6 months.

The resort's base area revolves around the very upscale **Moonlight Lodge and Spa**, which has four ski-in/ski-out luxury penthouse suites, and is home base to the two- and three-bedroom **Saddle Ridge Townhomes** and two-bedroom log cabins in **Cowboy Heaven**. **The Timbers** is the resort's slopeside restaurant. For apres-ski, **Timbers Bar & Lounge** has a great outside deck in addition to its beautiful rustic setting inside. The lodge has a full-service spa, shops and an outdoor ice rink too.

Moonlight Basin and Big Sky Resort, which share terrain on Lone Peak, offer the Lone Peak Pass, a joint lift ticket that allows guests access to 5,512 acres and a vertical drop of 4,350 feet.

Lift tickets (2007/08): Adults, $51; juniors (11-17), $39; students with college IDs/ seniors (70+), $46; kids 10 and younger ski free with paid adult.

Distance from Bozeman: The resort is 47 miles south of Bozeman (and about 50 miles north of West Yellowstone) on Hwy. 191 along the Gallatin River. It's 1.2 miles past Big Sky Resort.

Lodging information: Bookings are handled by East West Resorts, 866-212-0612.

Whitefish Mountain Resort

Montana

Summit:	**6,817 feet**
Vertical:	**2,353 feet**
Base:	**4,464 feet**

Address: 1894 Ambrosi Road
Whitefish, MT 59937
Telephone (main): 406 862-2900
Snow Report Number: 406 862-7669
Toll-free reservations: 800 858-4152
Reservations outside US: 406-862-2900
E-mail: info@skiwhitefish.com
Internet: www.skiwhitefish.com
Expert:★★★★
Advanced:★★★★
Intermediate:★★★★★
Beginner:★★
First-timer:★★★★

Lifts: 14 — 2-high-speed quads, 1 quad, 5 triples, 1 double, 4 surface, 1 moving carpet
Skiable acreage: 3,020
Snowmaking: 5%
Uphill capacity: 13,800
Parks & pipes: 1 park, 1 pipe
Bed base: 1,600 on mountain
Nearest lodging: Slopeside
Child care: Yes, 2 months and older
Adult ticket, per day: $56 (07/08 prices)

Dining:★★★
Apres-ski/nightlife:★★★
Other activities:★★★

Whitefish Mountain Resort, formerly Big Mountain, a comfortable and unpretentious resort in Montana, just up the hill from Whitefish, enjoys and suffers eclectic weather and snow conditions from fluff to fog to soup to cement. It's a mix of the western side of the Rockies and Pacific Northwest maritime, called "inland maritime," producing plenty of fluffy powder along with plenty of challenging conditions, depending on the weather.

The resort, in the far northwest corner of Montana near the Canadian border, is big, made bigger by its generous out-of-bounds policy. Every which way you look, Glacier National Park, the Bob Marshall Wilderness Area, the Flathead National Forest and the Canadian Rockies thrust jagged peaks into the sky, split by wide valleys filled with lakes and rivers.

The ski area base, Whitefish Mountain Resort Village, hosts a cluster of hotels and condo properties along with a number of restaurants and historic bars. This base area is currently under redevelopment and will offer extended facilities once their new Master Plan is put in place. Whitefish, a quaint historic railroad town just 8 miles down the mountain, is part of the Whitefish Mountain Resort experience.

The weather here is a mix of the western side of the Rockies and Pacific Northwest maritime, referred to as "inland maritime." Weather on the eastern side of the Rockies is reported on the Weather Channel—ignore it—where all the "...degrees below zero" occur. Toward the summit, spectacular "snow ghosts," are created—trees encased in many layers of frost and snow. The weather also produces plenty of fantastic powder, but without the sunshine you'll find in the southern Rockies.

A new, larger day lodge opened for the 2007-08 season on the site of the old Outpost Lodge, near the beginner area. The full-service lodge has ticket sales, rentals, the Kids' Center, the Snowsports Center and a cafeteria. A moving carpet for first-time skiers and riders has also made a debut.

Mountain layout

Whitefish Mountain Resort's Ambassador Program offers free tours of the mountain for intermediates and above at 10 a.m. and 1 p.m.

Expert, Advanced: Whitefish's generous out-of-bounds policy and the abundance of tree skiing make this resort a delight for expert and advanced skiers. Within the boundaries are 3,000 acres of sprawling terrain; another 1,000 acres are in the U.S. Forest Service permit area. Intermediate trails here follow the ridges and all advanced and expert lines drop off those ridges.

Most experts beeline to East Rim to tackle First Creek and North Bowl Chute (a.k.a. N.B.C.). This area has cliffs, but nothing you can't get around. You could easily spend all day here and not explore it all. Don's Descent, farther down off Russ's Street, is heavily treed. The other double-diamond area that's fun is Picture Chutes.

Throughout the entire Good Medicine, North Bowl and Hellroaring Basin areas you'll find fields of powder and thousands of trees. If you don't want to see any wide-open spaces, head to Stumptown, Window Pane or Teepee.

Intermediate: It's tough for intermediates not to have fun here. Half the mountain is rated just for you. Go straight off The Glacier Chaser for Chair 7 on the North Side, or make a U-turn to reach Toni Matt, The Big Ravine, Inspiration and MoeMentum (named for Olympic downhill champ Tommy Moe), all perfect for top-to-bottom power cruising with wide GS turns. Hellfire, the resort's longest trail at 3.3 miles, winds all the way around Hellroaring Basin for a real leg-burner.

If visibility is low at the summit, dip into the tree-lined 1,000 Turns, just off Toni Matt, which dumps you back onto the lower part of The Big Ravine. Lower-intermediates should take a few laps off Chair 2 or Heaven's T-bar before trying The Glacier Chaser. Chair 2's runs are equivalent in pitch to the blues off the front of the summit, but much shorter. The Bigfoot T-bar accesses three low-intermediate trails covering about 20 acres on the southern exposure above Russ's Street and the Evan's Heaven area. When you're ready for the summit, try the runs down the North Bowl first. The toughest part will be the upper part of MoeMentum, which can build formidable moguls by afternoon.

Beginner, First-timer: In 2006/07, Whitefish Mountain Resort made huge improvements to the beginner area, including a new day lodge—with the Kids' Center and Snowsports Center—a new lift and more terrain. The bulk of the beginner trails are here and under Chair 3, a bit higher on the mountain. The runs in the beginner area inspire confidence and smiles. If you're adventurous, work your way over to Chair 3, Easy Rider and Heaven's T-bar, where you'll also find the main base village. When you want to return to the day lodge, take the meandering Home Again run.

There is no beginner way down from the top of the mountain. If you want to go to the summit, Russ's Street is the easiest blue-square trail down—it has intermediate pitches at the top but turns into a beginner trail near the bottom. On the backside, Caribou is an easy run but also requires skiing part of the blue-rated MoeMentum (which is marked a slow zone on the part you'll have to ski to get to Caribou).

If you only want to use the bottom part of the mountain, buy the beginner lift ticket; it can be upgraded when you feel comfortable enough to go higher.

First-timers have an excellent learning area, separate from other skiers, on the gentle trails under Chair 6. A moving carpet makes it easy to get up the hill during the first few skiing adventures.

Parks and pipes

Whitefish Mountain Resort's Fishbowl Terrain Park is located on Hope Slope off Chair 3 on the front side of the mountain. It serves up tabletops, hits, gap jumps, rails, boxes and berms. The 450 feet long, 57 feet wide superpipe, above the park on the Ranger Trail headwall, has a 16 degree pitch and 18 foot high walls which are maintained with a Zaugg pipe grinder. The pipe is equipped with snowmaking, lights and a sound system to keep the blood flowing. The park also features lights to keep you on track.

Snowboarding

From the top of The Glacier Chaser, the hardest choice is deciding on which wide-open, rolling, impeccably groomed trail you should lay out a string of razor sharp, horizontal-flying Euro carves. A hint: There's no wrong answer, but just be sure to keep your speed on the cat track at the bottom. Whitefish Mountain Resort doesn't have scare-the-pants-off-you steeps, but it does offer exhilarating terrain and powder that stays long after a snowstorm. After a few warm-ups, duck into the bowls and trees almost anywhere across the mountain for some smooth powder turns, or head to the expansive out-of-bounds areas.

If you're working your way back from the part of the mountain served by Russ's Street, avoid long flats by dropping down Expressway and either taking Chair 4 or Chair 6 back up the mountain. Beginners will probably have problems carrying speed on the green-circle Home Again when trying to return to the beginner-area day lodge.

Cross-country & snowshoeing (see also xcskiresorts.com)

Whitefish Mountain Resort Nordic Center (406-862-2900) is adjacent to the Outpost Lodge (bottom of Chair 6) and has 16 km. of groomed trails for classic and skate skiing. Downhill ski pass holders can use the cross-country trails for free. Trail passes, maps and rentals are available at the Outpost Lodge or Whitefish Mountain Resort Sports in the base village. Snowshoers will find wooded terrain near the Nordic Center. A foot-passenger ticket can be bought for the chairlift to the summit where you can hike around in that area. Naturalist guides and snowshoe rentals are available.

Grouse Mountain Lodge (406-862-3000) in Whitefish has 10 km. of groomed cross-country trails and night skiing with 3.8 km. lighted.

The **Izaak Walton Inn** (888-5700), 62 miles east on Highway 2 (also an Amtrak flag stop), has 33 km. of groomed trails as well as guides who take skiers into the Glacier National Park wilderness. Guides for privates and groups are available.

Glacier National Park has natural cross-country and snowshoeing trails. Unplowed park roads and trails provide kilometer after kilometer of ungroomed passages. Check with the Communications Center (888-7800) or the park rangers for weather and snow conditions.

Lessons

Group lessons: Half day, $35; full day, $50.
First-timer package: Beginner lift ticket, rentals and two-hour lesson for skiing or snowboarding is $45; add $15 to upgrade to a full day.
Private lessons: One or two people, half day costs $160 ($50 for each additional person); full day costs $310 ($55 for each additional person). One-hour Quick Tips costs $80 (as available). Reservations are recommended.

Special programs: Whitefish Mountain Resort has two-hour clinics for bumps, steeps and powder for $35. Telemark workshops and Teen Camp are by appointment only, $45. Women-only and men-only workshops and advanced skiing seminars are taught at select times. Call the Snow Sports Center at (406) 862-2909 for dates and prices.

Racing: A NASTAR course is open off Chair 3 Thursdays through Sundays 11 a.m.–3 p.m. Cost is $5 for two runs and $1 for each additional run.

Children's programs (07/08 prices)

Child care: Ages 2 months to 12 years. Ages 2 months–15 months, full day $80; hourly rate, $12. Ages 16 months–3 years, full day $55; hourly rate, $9. Ages 4–12 years, full day $45; hourly rate, $7. Lunch an extra $5. Evening babysitter services are available.

The facility has room for just three infants at a time so reserve far in advance. Discounts available for families with multiple children. Reservations are required for infants and highly recommended for all others, (406) 862-1999.

Children's lessons: Skiers ages 4–5, and snowboarders ages 6–7, can take an all-day program with day care, rentals and lunch for $130; half day costs $70. No more than five kids per class.

Full day for kids ages 6–14 (skiing) and 8–14 (snowboarding) includes four hours of lessons (two sessions) for $50; half-day, $35. Lift tickets, rental gear and lunch are not included in the price.

Learn to Ski (ages 6–14) and Learn to Snowboard (8–14) is a half-day lesson, limited lift ticket and rentals for $45; add $15 to upgrade to full day.

Lift tickets (07/08 prices)

Adult one-day lift ticket is $56. Juniors (7–12) pay $30.

Who skis free: Kids 6 and younger; seniors 80 and older. Night skiing $15 for all. Beginner area $16.

Who skis at a discount: Ages 65–79 $46 for one day. College students $46.

Adult multiple-day tickets: Three days $156 ($52/day); Five days $260 ($52/day).

Accommodations

All lodging in Whitefish Mountain Village and Whitefish can be reserved by calling **Whitefish Mountain Reservations** at 800-858-4152 or the **Whitefish Chamber** at 877-862-3548. Rates are lower before Christmas, in January and in April; rates are higher during the Christmas/New Year and Presidents' Day holidays. Big Mountain guarantees that guests will get the best deal from the resort when booking through www.big-mountain.com.

The Kandahar Lodge at Whitefish Mountain (800-862-6094; 862-6098; $$-$$$$); evokes the golden years of skiing with giant log construction, historic photos of Whitefish Mountain's past and a massive fireplace in the lobby where guests gather round to share stories. The understated elegance is delightful, rooms are spacious with comfy beds and plenty of hooks for hanging damp skiwear, service is exceptional and meals are scrumptious. A gourmet breakfast is included. The Wellness Center has an outdoor hot tub, dry sauna and steam room; guests also can book spa services with Remedies Day Spa Express.

The simple but comfortable **Alpinglo Inn** (800-754-6760; 862-6966; $$) sits at the center of the village, with beautiful views from the restaurant and perhaps the most convenient location for skiers. Amenities include his-and-her saunas, two outdoor hot tubs overlooking the valley, laundry facilities and a gift shop.

The Hibernation House (800-858-4152; $$) is touted as the "friendliest lodge on the mountain." Whitefish Mountain's best lodging value, it is complete with a large indoor hot tub, ski storage, laundry room and buffet breakfast. Rooms have a queen bed, twin bunks and a private bath.

Morning Eagle (800-858-4152; $$$$) is the newest luxury ski-in/ski-out condominium development in the village. Studios and one- to three-bedroom units have full kitchens, washers and dryers, and complimentary high-speed Internet access in each living room.

Kintla Lodge (800-858-4152; 862-1960; $$$-$$$$) at the base of Chair 3 is a premier ski-in/ski-out condominium property with elevator access, underground parking, a lounge and large deck, ski lockers, outdoor hot tub, sauna, fireplaces in all living rooms and some master bedrooms, and complimentary high-speed Internet access.

The Edelweiss (800-858-4152; $$-$$$$) has studios, one- and two-bedroom condos, each with a fireplace (fire logs provided), full kitchen, and balcony or patio. Common areas and services include hot tub and sauna, use of the Swim Center, coin-operated laundry, and high-speed Internet access in the lobby (laptop and cable connection required).

In town:

The biggest and most convenient hotel is the **Grouse Mountain Lodge** (800-321-8822; 862-3000; $$-$$$; greets guests with a spacious lobby complete with floor-to-ceiling windows, fireplace, cozy chairs and couches for lounging. Service is excellent and the restaurant serves first-rate meals. It has an indoor pool, two outdoor spas and cross-country skiing is just out the back door.

The Pine Lodge (800-305-7463; 862-7600; $-$$$) boasts an indoor-outdoor pool with connecting swim channel, hot tub and free continental breakfast. The **Best Western-Rocky Mountain Lodge** (800-862-2569; $-$$$) includes a continental breakfast and features an outdoor heated pool and hot tub.

The Garden Wall Inn (888-530-1700; $$-$$$) is a meticulously renovated 1920s B&B with five guestrooms filled with period antiques. It's on the free SNOW bus route and within walking distance of downtown. Another B&B, **Good Medicine Lodge** (800-860-5488; $-$$) is built of cedar timbers with a Native American- and Western-influenced interior that's casual and invitingly rustic. **Hidden Moose Lodge** (888-733-6667; 862-6516; $$-$$$) showcases Montana-themed guestrooms with rich mountain colors and local art on the walls. Relax after skiing in the outdoor eight-person hot tub. The pet-friendly **Holiday Inn Express** (877-270-6405; 862-4020; $$-$$$) has an indoor pool with a 90-foot waterslide.

Dining

Summit House (406-862-1971; $) at the top of the mountain serves a variety of lunch options, including unusual choices such as a Cuban-style sandwich and a shredded beef burrito. It has a bar as well. It hosts **Moonlight Dine & Ski** ($$), with creative cuisine, throughout the winter; reservations required. The high-speed Glacier Chaser quad chairs are replaced by gondola cars to whisk evening diners up the mountain.

For a special evening and the best meal on the mountain, try **Cafe Kandahar** (406-862-6098; $-$$) in the base village. Chef Andy Blanton serves modern American cuisine with classical French and traditional Louisiana influences.

The Hellroaring Saloon (406-862-6364; $) retains its character as the original base lodge with its knotty-pine interior and skiing paraphernalia. Whether enjoying lunch or dinner, know that all food is homemade and tastes great. **Alpinglow Restaurant** (406-862-6966; $) has the best view of the Flathead Valley and serves a substantial breakfast as well as homemade soups for lunch. Dinner also is available.

Dining: $$$$–Entrees $30+; $$$–$20–$30; $$–$10–$20; $–less than $10.
Accommodations: (double room) $$$$–$200+; $$$–$141–$200; $$–$81–$140; $–$80 and less.

In the new base lodge, try **Mackenzie River Pizza Co.** and/or **Ed & Mully's** Memphis-style barbeque in the building that used to be home to **Moguls**. Ed and Mully's is named after two of the resort founders, Ed Schenck and Lloyd Muldown.

In the town of Whitefish: The finest dining in the area is at the **Whitefish Lake Restaurant** (406-862-5285; $–$$) in an historic log building built in the 1930s by the WPA at the golf course. **Grouse Mountain Lodge** (406-862-3000; $–$$) has two fabulous dining experiences. **The Grill**, dominated by a stone fireplace and mounted big game, specializes in creatively prepared entrees such as grilled venison chops with Duchesse parsnip and potato with stuffed Roma. **The Wine Room** has a temperature-controlled glass case displaying 700 bottles of the restaurant's 4,000-bottle inventory, which has earned it the Wine Spectator "Award of Excellence" for the past five years.

Pescado Blanco (406-862-3290; $–$$) creates an eclectic menu that is definitely not your typical Mexican fare. It's a unique Mexico-to-Montana fusion. Everything is handmade from the fresh salsas to the hand-pressed tortillas. The unusual creeps in with dishes like elk chorizo tacos, pheasant and Bison enchiladas and orange-ancho glazed duck. Seafood and steaks are also available along with soups, salads and a surprisingly extensive wine list. New Orleans-influenced **Tupelo Grille** (406-862-6136; $–$$) delights with selections such as crawfish cakes, ahi tuna, jumbo gulf shrimp and Creole chicken and dumplings. For first-rate sushi and inventive Asian grill dishes, head to **Wasabi Sushi Bar & Ginger Grill** (406-863-9283; $–$$). Wasabi has an extensive sake list and the wait staff makes great suggestions.

The family-run **Mambo Italiano** (406-863-9600; $–$$) is just plain fun. Portions are enormous, so expect leftovers to finish off another time.

McGarry's Roadhouse (406-862-6223; $–$$) has an open kitchen with a constantly changing menu of daily specials that reflect the flavors of the season. **Corner House Grille** (406-862-2323; $$) pairs French, Pan Pacific and New American foods with an extensive wine list. For local color, try **Truby's** (406-862-4979; $–$) for wood-fired pizza and great steaks. **Paddle & Axe Saloon** (406-862-7550; $–$) right across the street is a good place for steaks and pasta.

The Quickee Sandwich Shop ($–$) offers East Coast subs and great sandwiches. For breakfast, locals and tourists sip espresso at the **Montana Coffee Traders** or eat in "the Buff," at the **Buffalo Cafe** (406-862-2833; $). Try the Buffalo Pie — layers of hashbrowns, ham, cheese and poached eggs. It's open for lunch as well. **Baker Street Bistro** (406-862-6383; $), on the road out of town to the mountain, is an excellent breakfast spot with homemade bagels.

Apres-ski/nightlife

On the mountain, **The Hellroaring Saloon** serves some of the best apres-ski nachos anywhere. Best deal: If you buy a Hellroaring baseball cap you get your second beer free every day you wear it to the bar. **Moguls Village Pub** has nightly entertainment, as well as "Powder Hour" Mondays with instructors pouring free beer and yakking about skiing and the mountain during apres-ski. **The Bierstube** (a.k.a. "The Stube") offers free beer every Wednesday at 5:30 p.m. to celebrate the Frabert Clod of the Week Award, presented each week to the employee or visitor who commits the biggest goof-up.

In Whitefish, it's worth a visit to the **Palace Bar** on Central Avenue just to see its turn-of-the-century carved mahogany bar. **Great Northern Bar & Grille** on Central Avenue has live music from Thursday to Saturday and acoustic open-mic on Tuesday. Locals come for the burgers and wide selection of microbrewery beers and stay for the music and general debauchery. For free beer, stop by the **Great Northern Brewery**, home of Snow Ghost Winter Lager, with a friendly tasting room open to the public noon–8 p.m.

Another top spot is **Dire Wolf**, a favorite hangout for Big Mountain's boarders and teleskiers. It's just outside town on the road down from the ski area.

Having all the Central Avenue bars lined up makes it easy to check out the scene and decide where you want to set up camp. Choose from the no-smoking **Truby's**; **Casey's**, in the oldest building in town; and the no-smoking sports bar (high school sports, that is) **Bulldog Saloon**. Like martinis? Then head to **Paddle & Axe Saloon**, with a great dinner menu to boot. For a more mellow time, go to the lounge at The Grill in the Grouse Mountain Lodge.

For later night carousing, try the **Remington**, with gaming machines and poker, or the **Palace Bar**, both on Central Avenue. For a no-glitz, real cowboy evening—complete with live foot-stomping music and longneck beer bottles—head to the **Blue Moon Nite Club** in Columbia Falls at the intersection of Hwys. 2 and 40.

Other activities

Adrenaline junkies should try **snow cycles**, similar to full-suspension mountain bikes but with skis on the bike and mini-skis on your feet. A real blast! Lift-accessed **snow tubing** is offered along with a small **sledding hill**. **Snowcat skiing and riding** is offered in backcountry areas outside the resort's eastern boundary. Snowcat tours are four hours and cost $100 per person (that's on top of the regular lift ticket); call 406-862-2909 for information.

In Whitefish, **sleigh rides** leave the Grouse Mountain Lodge (406-862-3000) for a 20-minute ride to a camp near Lost Coon Lake. Guided **snowmobile** tours into the backcountry of the Whitefish Range are available from Whitefish Mountain's summit (862-2900). The Flathead Valley has more than 200 miles of groomed trails and nearly 2,000 miles of National Forest Service roads accessing ungroomed backcountry terrain. Contact the Flathead Convention and Visitor Bureau at 800-543-3105 for guide services and snowmobiling information.

Whitefish Mountain Village has a variety of specialty shops along the Kintla shopping pavilion and Morning Eagle boardwalk. Whitefish's Central Avenue has many art galleries and stores that stock Western clothing, jewelry and crafts. Montana Coffee Traders, on Hwy. 93 south of town, has many Montana food gift items.

Whitefish Mountain has a terrific Guest Services and Information center in the base village where you can find out more about other activities. Call 406-862-2900

Getting there and getting around

By air: Glacier Park International Airport in Kallispell, 19 miles south of the resort, is served by Skywest/Delta Connections, Horizon, Big Sky, Northwest and American West airlines. Call Flathead Glacier Transportation (406-892-3390) for ground transportation or check with your hotel for guest shuttle availability.

By car: Whitefish Mountain Resort is 8 miles from the town of Whitefish at the junction of Hwys. 2 and 93.

By train: Amtrak's Empire Builder stops in Whitefish daily from Seattle and Portland to the west and from Chicago and Minneapolis to the east. Kids ride free. Call 800-872-7245 for information.

Getting around: If you stay and play at the mountain, you won't need a car. The SNOW bus makes free daily runs between Whitefish and the mountain. The last run back up the mountain around 11 p.m. Wednesday through Saturday. However, most lodges have free shuttle service available for guests and taxi service also is available. A car is essential if you plan to explore.

Dining: $$$$–Entrees $30+; $$$–$20–$30; $$–$10–$20; $–less than $10.
Accommodations: (double room) $$$$–$200+; $$$–$141–$200; $$–$81–$140; $–$80 and less.

Ski Santa Fe
New Mexico

Summit:	12,075 feet
Vertical:	1,725 feet
Base:	10,350 feet

Address: 2209 Brothers Rd. #220, Santa Fe, NM 87505
Telephone (main): 505-982-4429
Snow Report Number: 505-983-9155
Toll-free reservations: 877-737-7366; 505-747-5557
E-mail: info@skisantafe.com
Internet: www.skisantafe.com

Expert:★★
Advanced:★★★
Intermediate:★★★
Beginner:★★★★
First-timer:★★★

Lifts: 7--1 quad, 2 triples, 2 doubles, 2 surface lifts
Skiable acreage: 660
Snowmaking: 50 percent
Uphill capacity: 7,800
Parks & pipes: None
Bed base: 5,500 in Santa Fe
Nearest lodging: About 15 miles away
Child care: Yes, 3 months to 3 years
Adult ticket, per day: $58 (08-09 prices)

Dining:★★★★★
Apres-ski/nightlife:★★
Other activities:★★★★

At Ski Santa Fe, snow-covered trails curl through towering Ponderosa pines in the Sangre de Cristo mountains, only 16 miles from the city of Santa Fe, the very heart of Southwestern style.

Take the bright sunlight of the high desert, fresh powder snow and a skier-friendly mountain, then add pre-Columbian Indian Pueblos, Spanish architecture, art galleries and top it with a renowned regional cuisine—you have the savory mix that makes up a unique ski vacation.

The town of Santa Fe (elevation 7,000 feet) offers numerous contradictions. It is old and new, high mountains and flat desert, with cool winters that surprise out-of-staters who think of New Mexico as hot and dry. Skiing in this state is unlike anywhere else on the continent. To get a more international ski vacation, you'd need a passport.

Some skiers think Taos Ski Valley is the only New Mexico ski area worth a long plane ride—not so. If your main interest is racking up vertical feet, then by all means head for Taos, but Santa Fe (just an hour north of Albuquerque) is a better destination for those who prefer a balanced ski-and-sightseeing vacation. Santa Fe is one of the most culturally fascinating cities in the United States. It is loaded with great restaurants, superior art galleries, a variety of activities and the ski area is a lot bigger than most people imagine. Though the mountain is known as a day-area destination for Santa Fe and Albuquerque skiers, out-of-town visitors will find a surprising amount of terrain.

Founded by Spanish conquistadors in 1607, more than a dozen years before the pilgrims landed in Plymouth, Santa Fe is North America's oldest capital city. It is rich in history and culture, but of a different kind from mining-town ski areas.

When the Spanish arrived, the area was already populated with 100,000 Native Americans who spoke nine languages and lived in some 70 multi-storied adobe pueblos, some still inhabited today. For the next 150 years Santa Fe grew as a frontier military base and trading center where Spanish soldiers and missionaries, Anglo mountain men and Native Americans mixed. In 1846, during the Mexican War, New Mexico was ceded to the United States. Santa Fe, at the end of the Santa Fe Trail, became a frontier town hosting the likes of Billy the Kid and Kit Carson.

In the early part of last century, Santa Fe took on a new flavor. It became a magnet for men and women of the arts and literature. D.H. Lawrence, Ezra Pound, Willa Cather, Jack London and H.L. Mencken either lived or vacationed here. Artists Edward Hopper and Marsden Hartley spent time here and Santa Fe was home to Robert Henri, George Bellows, Randall Davey, Georgia O'Keeffe and Aaron Copland. Today this city of 60,000 people is home to one of the world's premier art colonies.

The newly installed Millennium Chair serves a higher summit on the mountain, opening six new trails (two intermediate and four advanced) and raising the vertical drop at the area to 1,735 feet.

Ski Santa Fe has one of the highest lift-served elevations in the nation—12,075 feet on top, 10,350 feet at the base. If you're susceptible to altitude problems, take note. However, all lodging is in Santa Fe and some people are fine if they sleep at a lower elevation.

 ## Mountain layout Skiing/Snowboarding

Expert, Advanced: For the most part, the mountain's expert terrain is to the left of the Tesuque Peak chair. With fresh snow, locals go first to Columbine, Big Rocks and Wizard. These runs all check in as very steep and are for advanced skiers only. Roadrunner is the expert bump run directly under the Tesuque chair. Tequila Sunrise and Easter Bowl have the best glade skiing. ccccOn the far side of the mountain, reached by the Santa Fe Super Chief quad, Muerte and Desafio have isolated trail skiing for advanced skiers.

The Big Tesuque Bowl attracts the intrepid who enter this area via Cornice. (Once skiers leave Cornice, they are outside the ski area's permitted boundary.) Big Tesuque skiers find natural powder, bowl skiing and trees. The bowls empty onto the area's entrance road, three miles below the base area, leaving you to hitchhike back up. First-timers should go with a local who knows this area: It's genuine backcountry, it's big and people occasionally get lost.

Intermediate: On a fresh powder day (once a week on average), local intermediates and advanced skiers head straight for the Tesuque Peak triple chair, up to 12,000 feet and the top of the mountain. To the right of the lift (as the trail map reads) is Gayway, a glorious, groomed pitch with several spicy turns that gives new meaning to the term "spectacular scenery." On a clear day, you almost get the feeling of flying, thanks to the 150-mile vista as the trail drops away. Parachute, which parallels Gayway, is a groomed black diamond with a somewhat steeper pitch.

On the far side of the mountain, reached by the Santa Fe Super Chief quad, Middle and Lower Broadway have isolated trail skiing for intermediate skiers.

Beginner, First-timer: Beginners will be happiest on the lower part of the mountain on the wide boulevard of Easy Street. Advanced-beginners will find more challenges and a slightly steeper pitch on Open Slope and Upper and Lower Midland. If you're feeling adventurous, try Lower Burro for an exhilarating, winding trip through the trees on a mild pitch.

First-timers will find good terrain at the mountain's base served by the Pine Flats lift; It's protected by snow fences. For children Chipmunk Corner lift provides a tucked-away learning area .

Parks and pipes
Ski Santa Fe does not have any formal parks or pipes.

Cross-country & snowshoeing (see also xcskiresorts.com)

Santa Fe has no groomed or tracked trails. However, there are maintained backcountry trails in the **Santa Fe National Forest. Aspen Vista Road**, 2 miles below the ski area, is a popular and moderately difficult 7-mile trail. **Black Canyon Campground**, 8 miles up the ski road, is a popular area for beginners. Maps and information on conditions in the Santa Fe National Forest are available from the Santa Fe National Forest Service at 438-7840 (main supervisor's office) or 753-7331 (EspaÃ±ola Ranger District, which encompasses the Santa Fe area).

Lessons (08/09 prices)

Group lessons: Adult lessons cost $405. A second session on the same day costs an extra $20.

First-timer package: A full-day package of two group lessons, beginner lift and rentals cost $75 for skiers, $85 for snowboarders.

Private lessons: $750 for one hour; discounts available for multiple hours.

Special programs: Among them are a women's program, classes for ages 50 and older, mogul clinics, telemark lessons and powder workshops. Check with the ski school, 505-982-4429.

Racing: A coin-op race course is open Thursday through Sunday.

Children's programs (08/09 prices)

Child care: Ages 3 months to 3 years. All-day program costs $76; $60 half day. Ages 3 and 4 who are completely toilet-trained can register for Snowplay, a program that is "an introduction to the skiing environment." This program, which includes indoor and outdoor activities, is $80 all day and $64 half day. Reservations required; call (505) 988-9636. Only full-day packages for child care are sold during holiday periods.

Children's lessons: Ages 4–9, all day including lunch and lift ticket, $85 with rentals. Four-year-olds have a morning lesson with play activities in the afternoon; others have lessons in both morning and afternoon.

Lift tickets (08/09 prices)

	Adult (21-61)	Child (Up to 12) $40
One day	$58	$40
Three days	$161 ($54/day)	$112 ($37/day)
Five days	$258 ($52/day)	$178 ($36/day)

Who skis free: Skiers age 72 and older and kids who measure 46 inches or shorter in ski boots.

Who skis at a discount: Ages 62-71 pay the child rate. Teens (13-20) pay $46 for one day, $128 for three days and $205 for five. A ticket valid only on the beginner lift is $29 for all ages.

Note: Prices are rounded to the nearest dollar.

Accommodations

Ski Santa Fe has no base lodging, but even if it did, you'd want to be in Santa Fe for dining, shopping, the culture and the museums. Lift-and-lodging packages are the best deal; call **All Santa Fe Reservations** 877-737-7366 or the **Santa Fe Visitors Bureau**, 800-777-2489. Downtown is where the best restaurants, shopping and nightlife are concentrated, although we do recommend a few great dining options outside the Plaza area.

The Inn of The Five Graces (866-992-0957; 505-992-0957; $$$$ is one of America's most unusual and unique luxury hotels. It is a delightful compound of one- and two-story adobe and river-rock buildings. A walking tour of Santa Fe is given each afternoon at 4 p.m. and guests gather to enjoy wine and cheese between 5:30 and 7 p.m. There are no additional minibar fees; local calls, parking and breakfast are included and no tipping is allowed.

Inn of the Anasazi (800-688-8100; 505-988-3030; $$$-$$$$) is the politically correct place to stay. The hotel's restaurants use vegetables grown by local organic farmers. Leftovers are given to a homeless shelter and everything is recycled. **La Posada de Santa Fe Resort and Spa, a RockResort** (866-331-7625; 505-986-0000; $$-$$$) Afternoon cultural lectures, wine and cheese tastings and Native American flute concerts contribute to an experience that is so Santa Fe. Did we mention that it's a short walk to the Plaza?

La Fonda Hotel (800-523-5002; 505-982-5511; $$$-$$$$ is an historic place to stay. An inn of one sort or another has been on this site for 300 years (Billy the Kid worked in the kitchen here washing dishes). The current La Fonda incarnation was built in the 1920s. If you don't stay, at least stroll through and take a look.

Inn and Spa at Loretto (800-727-5531; 505-988-5531; $$$) is Santa Fe's ultimate pueblo-style hotel. Restored in 1998, its spacious rooms have traditional New Mexican decor with carved wood furnishings and authentic Native American art.

Eldorado (800-955-4455; 505-988-4455; $$-$$$$), the city's largest hotel, has just undergone an extensive renovation with a new spa and rates right up there with best in town.

The **Hotel Plaza Real** (877-901-7666; 505-988-4900; $$$) is convenient and comfortable. An ample continental breakfast is included and you can't beat its location in Old Santa Fe.

We also enjoyed the adobe **Inn on the Alameda** (888-984-2124; 505-984-2121; $$$) which is handy to Canyon Road and offers a continental breakfast. Excellent B&Bs are **Adobe Abode** (505-983-3133; $$$-$$$$), **Alexander's Inn** (888-321-5123; 505-986-1431; $$-$$$), the spacious **Dancing Ground of the Sun** (800-745-9910; 505-986-9797; $-$$$), the **Grant Corner Inn** (800-964-9003; 505-983-6678; $$) and the classy **Water Street Inn** (800-646-6752; 505-984-1193; $$-$$$).

Other accommodations to consider are the historic **Hotel St. Francis** (800-529-5700; 505-983-5700; $$), the **Hilton of Santa Fe** (800-336-3676; 505-988-2811; $$$) and the **Hotel Santa Fe** (800-825-9876; 505-982-1200; $-$$$) partly owned by the Picuris Pueblo.

Families should try the **El Rey Inn** (800-521-1349; 505-982-1931; $$-$$$), **Garrett's Desert Inn** (800-888-2145; 505-982-1851; $$), the **Campanilla Compound condominiums** (800-828-9700; 505-988-7585; $$$), and the **Otra Vez condos** (505-988-2244; $$-$$$).The closest Plaza area lodging to the ski area is **Fort Marcy Hotel Suites** (800-745-9910; $-$$).

Many of the chain hotels, such as **Comfort Inn** ($$), **Days Inn** ($), **Holiday Inn** ($$) and **Hampton Inn** ($) are less expensive and conveniently located on Cerrillos Road, which makes them handy for getting to the ski area, but out of walking range for downtown. **Santa Fe Sage Inn** (725 Cerrillos Road; 982-5952; $-$$) is an improved former Budget Inn.

 ## Dining

On the mountain, skiers have two choices. **La Casa Cafeteria** in the base lodge and **Totemoff's Bar and Grill** at the base of the Tesuque Peak Chair. La Casa offers a pasta bar and daily specials. Its breakfast burrito is wicked good, but only for brave palates. Totemoff's features burgers, salads, pasta, cocktails and a sun deck.

Back in the city, **Geronimo** (724 Canyon Rd., 505-982-1500; $$$$) is the spot for that spe-

Dining: $$$$–Entrees $30+; $$$–$20–$30; $$–$10–$20; $–less than $10.
Accommodations: (double room) $$$$–$200+; $$$–$141–$200; $$–$81–$140; $–$80 and less.

cial night out, with crisp linens, attentive staff and wonderfully prepared eclectic cuisine.

Santa Fe's favorite new eatery is **The Railyard Restaurant & Saloon** (505-989-3300; $$.This American steakhouse was created by the owner/chef of the award-winning **315 Restaurant and Wine Bar** (315 Old Santa Fe Trail; 505-986-9190; $$$) that offers French cuisine and excellent wines.

Four main hotel restaurants shouldn't be missed. We recommend the spectacular dining room at La Fonda, **La Plazuela** (505-992-5511; $$-$$$$). Breakfast lets you enjoy the colorful room for reasonable prices. **Baleen Santa Fe** (505-984-7915; $$$-$$$$) at the Inn and Spa at Loretto, is only steps from the Plaza. The food is inspired by New Mexican flavors. **Fuego** (505-986-0000; $$$$) at La Posada de Santa Fe has award-winning four-diamond fine dining. And the **Anasazi Restaurant** (505-988-3236; $$$-$$$$) at the Inn of the Anasazi serves a fabulous Sunday brunch and a signature dinner dish of grilled Colorado lamb.

The dining room at the **Coyote Cafe** (132 W. Water St.; 505-983-1615; $$$-$$$$) has a fixed-price menu and Southwestern cuisine. Those in the bar can order Ã la carte. **Pasqual's** (121 Don Gaspar; 505-983-9340; $$$) is great for breakfast but good anytime for New Mexican cuisine. Call for dinner reservations .**La Casa Sena** (125 East Palace Ave.; 505-988-9232; $$$-$$$$) is continental with a Mexican flair. Don't miss the adjacent **Cantina** ($$-$$$), where waiters and bartenders sing cabaret. At **Maria's New Mexican Kitchen** (555 W. Cordova Rd.; 505-983-7929; $), you'll probably meet the affable owner Al Lucero, who wrote Maria's Real Margarita Book featuring history and recipes of the more than 50 "real" margaritas served in the restaurant. Robert Redford, a frequent customer when he's in town, wrote the foreword. The food is also wonderful, especially the posole and green chile stew.

Locals flock to **The Shed** (113 Ã½ Palace Ave.; 505-982-9030; $$) and **La Choza** (905 Alarid St.; 505-982-0909; $$) but watch out for the green chile--it could burn a hole in your ski boots. If you dare to try the chile make sure you get lots of garlic bread to ease the pain. **Los Mayas** (409 West Water St.; 505-986-9930; $$) serves fresh Mayan food with guacamole prepared tableside.

The Pink Adobe (406 Old Santa Fe Trail; 505-983-7712; $$-$$$) is Santa Fe's oldest restaurant, a local favorite and sometimes difficult to even get reservations (which are necessary). They specialize in New Mexican and Creole foods. Next door, **The Dragon Room** is a favorite of locals and visitors alike for cocktails. **El Farol** (808 Canyon Rd.; 505-983-9912; $$$) is the oldest Spanish-food restaurant and dates back to just a few years after the Pink Adobe. Specialties include a variety of curry dishes, hot and cold tapas as well as one of the best selections of Spanish wines in the U.S.

For a romantic evening try **Andiamo** (322 Garfield St.; 505-995-9595; $$). It is a little off the beaten track but serves unique pasta dishes with candlelight ambiance. The president of Italy gave **Osteria D'Assisi** (58 So. Federal Place; 505-986-5858; $$) the "Ciao Italia Award" for authentic Italian cuisine. The locals' favorite for inexpensive authentic Italian food is **Il Piatto** (95 West Marcy St.; 505-984-1091; $$).

The Cowgirl (319 S. Guadalupe; 505-928-2565; $-$$) is what the name implies with authentic Texas-style barbecue, kid's menu and play area. Don't hesitate to join the tourists at **The Ore House** (upstairs at 50 Lincoln Ave.; 505-983-8687; $$) on the Plaza for free apres-ski snacks. On Canyon Road, **Celebrations** (613 Canyon Rd.; 505-989-8904; $$) is in the heart of gallery row and is jammed at lunchtime.

Tomasita's Cafe (500 S. Guadalupe; 505-983-5721; $) is fast food with a twist. Portions are large, service is friendly and it's a favorite of Santa Fe families, so be prepared to wait. It is inexpensive with some of the best New Mexican fare in town. **The Plaza Restaurant** (54

Lincoln; 505-982-1664; $) is a throwback to diner days; Regulars swear everything is good and very affordable. **Zia Diner** (326 South Guadalupe; 505-988-7008; $) is an easy 15-minute walk from the Plaza and features All-American favorites (New Mexican style, of course) such as meat loaf stuffed with piÃ±on npiuts, basic pastas and soups. Buzz in to **Bumble Bee's Baja Grill** (301 Jefferson & 3701 Cerrillos Rd.; 505-820-2862; $) where you'll find fresh fast food like fish tacos and homemade burritos.

If you want a break from Mexican food, **Atomic Grill** (103 E. Water St.; 505-820-2866; $) serves wood-fired pizza, pastas and hamburgers together with about 80 different bottled beers. There's take-out and delivery too. **Khonami** (next door to the Cowgirl Hall of Fame) serves Japanese. Locals love **Jinja Asia Cafe** in the North DeVargas Center (510 Guadalupe; 505-982-4321; $-$$) where they blend cooking styles of Vietnam, Thailand, Indonesia, Malaysia and Japan for American tastes. Katrina survivor Honey Howard opened **LeMoyne's Landing** (420 N. Guadalupe St.; 505-820-2268; $$) and cooks what she knows best - New Orleans comfort food.

For breakfast with the movers and shakers in downtown Santa Fe, head to **Tia Sophia** (210 W San Francisco St, 505-983-9880; $). **Tecolote Cafe** (1203 Cerrillos Rd.; 505-988-1362; $-$$) is the place for breakfast just like Mom used to make if your mother liked using spices.

Apres-ski/nightlife

Aside from dining out, Santa Fe's nightlife is dismal. This town is more about art, history and culture. For elegant apres-ski (you can go in ski clothes) head for the bars at **Inn of the Anasazi** or **La Posada** both close to the Plaza. A wonderful place to mix dinner with entertainment is at **La Cantina** (505-988-9232) in the historic Sena Plaza, a stately adobe built as a family home in the 1860s. The restaurant features New Mexican specialties and singing waiters and waitresses. For about $20, you can eat, drink and hear an exceptional dinner theater show belted out between courses. Children are welcome, reservations a must. **Los Mayas** (505-986-9930) often has Flamenco dinner shows.

The Cowgirl, **El Farol** and **Willee's Blues Bar** have music and lively scenes.

The Catamount Bar & Grill (125 E. Water St.; 988-7222) is a sports bar teeming with locals and tourists featuring big-screen TV, pool tables and specials like "Jägermeister Night."

Other activities

The **museums** in Santa Fe are first rate. Buy a four-day pass for $15 which will admit you to five of the best: The Museum of International Folk Art (strong in Spanish art of the area), the Palace of the Governors (for local history), the Museum of Indian Arts and Culture, the Museum of Fine Arts, and the Museum Of Spanish Colonial Art. The Georgia O'Keeffe Museum has its own entry fees.

You should consider **touring** the eight Indian pueblos near Santa Fe. The San Ildefonso Pueblo, famous for its distinctive pottery style, is the most scenic. Its annual festival to honor its patron saint is in late January and features traditional clothing and dances. If you have a car, and especially if you are driving north on U.S. Hwy. 84/285 to Taos, be sure and take the Hwy. 503 turnoff at Pojoaque and drive east to Chimayo, site of the Santuario de Chimayo, famous for its dirt thought to have healing powers. At the end of the church parking lot, you'll find Leona's, a funky little walk-up where the tamale pie and burritos are exceptional. On the way to Taos you wind through foothills and into high mountain Hispanic villages like Truchas and Las Trampas. For beautiful woven blankets, stop at Ortega's in Chimayo, where family members still practice a craft brought to New Mexico in the 1600s by their ancestors.

Dining: $$$$–Entrees $30+; $$$–$20–$30; $$–$10–$20; $–less than $10.
Accommodations: (double room) $$$$–$200+; $$$–$141–$200; $$–$81–$140; $–$80 and less.

An initial warning: It will be much cheaper to ski all day than venture into Santa Fe's many tempting **shops** and **galleries**. That warning given, more than 250 galleries feature Native American crafts and art, as well as fine art on a par with galleries in New York, Florence or Paris. In fact, Santa Fe is the second largest art market after New York. Local artisans sell their wares from blankets on the plaza in front of the 390-year-old Palace of the Governors, a long-standing Santa Fe shopping tradition.

Canyon Road is the world-famous strip of galleries featuring wonderful art of all styles for all tastes. The walk from the Plaza area is pleasant. The **Waxlander Gallery** features wonderful pastel still-life works of J. Alex Potter. Our favorite is **Nedra Matteucci's Fenn Galleries**, 1075 Paseo de Peralta, just south of Canyon Road. The day we visited, we counted four Zuniga sculptures starting at $80,000 each. Don't miss the garden.

Two stores we love are **Nicholas Potter Bookseller**, an old house at 211 E. Palace stuffed with used and rare books and **The Shop**, also on E. Palace brimming with Christmas stuff. **Tees & Skis** near the Plaza carries mostly soft goods like hats, goggles and long underwear. In a good snow year, they'll inventory parkas and sweaters.

When one of our writers was in desperate need of a body tune-up after a bad landing, **High Desert Healthcare & Massage** (505-984-8830) just off the Plaza, worked wonders. Rates for massage and bodywork begin at $42 for a half hour and increase by quarter-hour to $93 for one and a half hours.

Soak away your cares and get a massage at the Japanese-influenced **Ten Thousand Waves** (505-992-5025, 505-982-9304). Prices for massage begin at $89 for 55 minutes. **Santa Fe Massage**, a day spa with locations at La Fonda (505-982-5511) and Hotel Santa Fe (505-982-1200), delivers a multitude of services all beginning at $45 for 25 minutes. A humongous menu of services is available at **Sterling Institute** (505-594-3223). Basic massage is $70 for 50 minutes. **RockResorts Spa** at La Posada is as full-service as you can find. The signature treatment is a chocolate-chile wrap, 50 minutes for $125. **SpaTerre** (505-984-7997) at the Inn at Loretto is also a full-service spa. A 50-minute massage begins at $90.

Call the **Santa Fe Visitors Bureau** (800-777-2489; 505-955-6200) for more information.

Getting there and getting around

By air: Albuquerque has the nearest major airport, 60 miles away. Private pilots can use the Santa Fe Regional Airport. For shuttles from the airport in Albuquerque to Santa Fe, call 505-474-5696.

By car: Santa Fe is north of Albuquerque on I-25, an easy hour's drive. The ski area is 16 miles from town on Hwy. 475.

Getting around: Getting around Santa Fe and to and from the ski area is difficult without a car, though a shuttle service is available from the airport to major hotels. The airport in Albuquerque has the leading rental car agencies.

Taos
with Red River and
Angel Fire, New Mexico

Summit:	11,819 feet
Vertical:	2,612 feet
Base:	9,207 feet

Address: Box 90,
Taos Ski Valley, NM 87525
Telephone (main): 505-776-87525
Snow Report Number: 505-776-2916
Toll-free reservations: 866-250-7313
E-mail: tsv@skitaos.org
Internet: skitaos.org

Expert:★★★★★
Advanced:★★★★★
Intermediate:★★★★
Beginner:★★
First-timer:★★★★

Lifts: 12—4 quads, 1 triple, 5 doubles,
2 surface lifts
Skiable acreage: 1,294
Snowmaking: 46 percent
Uphill capacity: 15,000
Parks & pipes: 1 park, 1 pipe
Bed base: 3,705 at base and in town
Nearest lodging: Slopeside; hotels, condos
Child care: Yes, 6 weeks to 3 years
Adult ticket, per day: $66 (08-09)

Dining:★★★★
Apres-ski/nightlife:★★
Other activities:★★★★★

Northern New Mexico has some of the best skiing to be found in the United States, and Taos has long been legendary for its steeps and deep powder. Most of the information in this chapter concentrates on Taos, which is a true destination resort, but we'll also give you a flavor of Red River and Angel Fire (see *Nearby Resorts* at end of chapter).

Taos Ski Valley is a little piece of the Alps, founded by a Swiss native and surrounded by hotels and restaurants built by Frenchmen and Austrians. It's near the town of Taos, which is a rich mix of Spanish and Indian cultures, blended over the centuries to produce the Southwestern style. This style, in art, cuisine and architecture, isn't trendy here; it's the way things have always been.

Taos Ski Resort has and enjoys its tough "expert only" reputation. It advises visitors to meet the challenge by enrolling in Ski-Better-Week, a package of lessons, accommodations, meals and lift tickets. Just about everybody staying at the mountain enrolls in ski school. If you aren't part of a class, you feel like the kid who didn't get chosen for the baseball team.

Fifty-one percent of Taos' runs are rated expert, and half of the expert runs are double-black diamonds. Intermediates will have a field day with great steep cruising. Beginners are limited or challenged, depending on how one looks at the terrain. But first-timers have a surprisingly good isolated area to learn. If you normally ski blue runs at other resorts, you can ski Taos.

The town of Taos is 18 miles from Taos Ski Valley. Long a haven for artists, the town has galleries, shops, restaurants and hotels ranging from luxurious to pedestrian. Also visit nearby Red River and Angel Fire, which both offer excellent and different ski experiences.

Mountain layout — Skiing/Snowboarding

Taos now allows snowboarding so truly has something for everyone in the intermediate, advanced and expert levels.

Expert, Advanced: For tree skiers and sliders, Taos has a special challenge, the twin runs Castor and Pollux. They hardly look like runs, just steep wooded parts of the mountain, where some joker put a sign that looks just like a trail marker. The trees are 2 to 15 feet apart.

Powder skiing lasts on Highline Ridge and Kachina Peak for two reasons: They're double-black diamonds and Kachina Peak is reachable only after an hour-and-fifteen-minute hike from the top chair at 11,800 feet to the ridge at 12,500 feet. You can, however, ski off Highline Ridge and West Basin Ridge after only a 15-minute hike. Skiers are advised to go with an instructor or a patroller. At the very least, they must check in with the patrol at the top of Chair 6. The ski patrol will give you a rough screening to see if you can handle the double-diamond terrain. In any case you must ski the ridge with a partner.

Advanced skiers won't be disappointed. All of the tree skiing is an effort and the black-diamond trails are as advertised. Hunziker, isolated by a short climb, has good bumps that narrow about halfway down the trail. Or try some of the off-trail skiing dropping from the ridges.

Intermediate: Taos has a lot of terrain at this level. Smooth bowls are found off the Kachina quad chair. Other good intermediate terrain is under Chairs 7 and 8. Anything marked as a blue trail is a blast, with plenty of length for cruising. If you feel pushed here; ski the greens for warm-ups and have some fun.

Beginner, First-timer: Taos has some nice beginner terrain, such as Honeysuckle, which descends the skier's right side of the ridge. Bonanza and Bambi give beginners a way down on the other side of the ridge. The main problem is negotiating either White Feather or Rubezahl when they are crowded with skiers coming back into the village. Despite the slow-down efforts of ski hosts stationed every 20 feet or so, both runs resemble the Hollywood Freeway at rush hour, except that the faster skiers aren't stalled in traffic. They zip around the slower ones, who are gingerly making their way home. On busy days it's a mess. Timing is important: Come down early, or better yet, be one of the last to descend.

Only athletic novices should attempt to learn here. Despite the highly regarded ski school, the jump from the tiny learning area to the mountain is enormous. Better learning terrain is at nearby Angel Fire or Red River.

Parks and pipes

The Out to Launch Terrain Park features two huge airs, a hip, a quarterpipe, and rails. The park, on Maxie's run under Lift 7, is groomed nightly.

Cross-country & snowshoeing (see also xcskiresorts.com)

Personal fitness trainer Bonnie Golden runs **Taos Fitness Adventures** 505-751-5977 with guided cross-country skiing and snowshoeing in the winter, plus hiking and custom programs in warmer weather. **Southwest Nordic Center** 505-758-4761 has cross-country lessons, tours and yurt trips. **Enchanted Forest Cross-Country Ski Area** 505-754-2374 is 40 miles northeast of Taos by Hwys. 522 and 38. It has 34 km. of backcountry trails, some groomed. Trail rates are $10 for adults, with discounts for teens, seniors and children. At the Miller's Crossing headquarters in downtown Red River, you can rent equipment (including pulks) and pick up trail maps.

Lessons (08/09 prices)

Group lessons: Two hours, morning or afternoon, $51. Some lessons at Taos concentrate on specific skills, such as moguls or telemarking.

First-timer package: Novice lift ticket, 4.5-hour lesson and rentals for $88; two days cost $148. All two-day participants who complete the classes get a special guarantee: If you can't yet ski Whitefeather from the top of Lift #1, you can take as many free lessons as it takes to master this feat. Those who master the two-day class can take a lesson package with rentals and lift ticket for $96.

Private lessons: For up to four skiers, costs are $170 for one hour, $250 for two hours, $350 for a half day, and $550 for a full day.

Special programs: Ski Better Weeks are the core of the Taos ski experience, developed by former French Junior Alpine champion and ski school technical director Jean Mayer. Participants are matched for six mornings of intensive lessons, and they ski with the same instructor all week. Sixty-five percent of the participants are intermediate or higher. Ski Week costs $234 for six days (lift ticket extra). Many lodging properties offer the Ski Better Week as a package with meals and accommodations. There are Specialized Ski Week programs for women, teens and for ages 50 and older at select times during the season.

Super Weeks, offered on select dates, are intense courses for those who wish to focus seriously on improving their skills. Participants are analyzed, videotaped and put through what amounts to a camp every morning and afternoon for a total of four hours. This is not a program for the timid or late-night party types, but most will find their skills much improved by the end of the week. It's offered at select times. Lesson prices start at $234.

Children's programs (08/09 prices)

Child care: Ages 6 weeks to 3 years. A full-day program including lunch and snacks costs $80; a half-day costs $60; hourly rates are $26. Toddlers get indoor activities and snow play. Reservations required; call (505) 776-2291 or fill out an online form. There is one staffer for every two infants.

Children's lessons: The Kinderkäfig Children's Center is unfortunately an inconvenient distance from the main base area. A full-day program for ages 3-15, including lesson, lunch and afternoon supervised skiing, costs $110 a day. (Ages 3-5 get a program that combines lessons, snow play and indoor activities.) Reservations are recommended; call (505) 776-2291.

Lift tickets (08/09 prices)

	Adult	Child (7-12)
One day	$66	$40
Three days	$189 ($63/day)	$111 ($37/day)
Five days	$315 ($63/day)	$185$37/day)

Who skis free: Ages 80 and older. Any child 6 or younger skis free when an accompanying adult purchases a lift ticket.

Who skis at a discount: Ages 65-79 pay $50, but seniors 70 and older planning to ski here for more than two days should purchase a season pass, which costs $100. Ages 13-17 ski for $55 a single day; $43 multiday. 80 and over ski free. The beginner lift is $20 for everyone.

Taos reduces its ticket prices in the early and late seasons; prices are higher during holiday periods.

Dining: $$$$–Entrees $30+; $$$–$20–$30; $$–$10–$20; $–less than $10.
Accommodations: (double room) $$$$–$200+; $$$–$141–$200; $$–$81–$140; $–$80 and less.

Accommodations

Taos' **Ski-Better-Week** packages include up to seven nights lodging (Saturday to Saturday), six lift tickets and six morning lessons. In some cases, meals are included. Prices range from about $586 to about $1,600 per person, double occupancy. If price or specific amenities are concerns, call **Southern Rockies Reservations** (866-250-7313), Ski Central Reservations (800-238-2829; 505-776-9555) or **Stay Taos Rentals** (800-480-7150; 505-758-7150)

Hotel Edelweiss (800-458-8754; 505-776-2301; $$-$$$$) is right at the base of the village. The new hotel offers the Ski Week package, including meals. **Snakedance Condominium and Spa** (800-322-9815; 505-776-2277; $$$$) has ski-in/ski-out rooms, usual amenities, bar; and a restaurant serving continental cuisine. **The Bavarian Lodge** (505-770-0450; $$$$) reflects a German/Austrian aura. **Hotel St. Bernard** (505-776-2251; $$$) managed by Taos ski school technical director Jean Mayer, offers the flavor of a European retreat. The cuisine and ambiance are both legendary and French. This hotel also offers the Ski-Better-Week packages with meals.

The Powderhorn (800-776-2346; 505-776-2341 $$$) has bright, clean, spacious rooms steps from the lifts. **Sierra del Sol** (505-776-2981; $$) has studios and condos. The **Alpine Village Suites** (800-576-2666; $$-$$$$), one of the newer properties, has private balconies. **Austing Haus** (800-748-2932; 505-776-2649; $$), 1.5 miles from the base, is the tallest timber frame building in the United States. The food is very good. Next door, **The Columbine** (888-884-5723; 505-776-5723; $$) is a twin of the Austing Haus. Between the ski area and town is a bed-and-breakfast inn, the **Salsa del Salto** (505-776-2422; $$-$$$.) Formerly the residence of Hotel St. Bernard owner Jean Mayer, it's now run by Jean's brother, Dadou, a French-trained chef who cooks Salsa del Salto's gourmet breakfasts.

The town of Taos: **El Monte Sagrado** (800-828-TAOS; 505-758-3502; $$$$) is one of the Leading Small Hotels of the World. The **Fechin Inn** (800-911-2937; 505-751-1000; $$-$$$$) is the next most luxurious place to stay. The Historic **Taos Inn** (800-826-7466; $-$$$$) is the cultural center of Taos. Rooms feature adobe fireplaces, antiques and Taos-style furniture. The **Sagebrush Inn** (800-428-3626; 505-758-2254; $$$-$$$$) is an historic inn with some of the best nightlife in town.

At the lower end of the price range are **El Pueblo Lodge** (800-433-9612; $-$$$). **Indian Hills Inn** (800-444-2346; $), and often, rooms in the chain hotels, such as **Holiday Inn** or **Ramada**. The least expensive is the skiers' hostel, **The Abominable Snowmansion** (505-776-8298; $) in Arroyo Seco, 9 miles from the Village, where the rates are about $25-$60

Four other B&Bs in Taos: **Hacienda del Sol** (505-758-0287; $$) owned by John and Marcine Landon; the **Old Taos Guesthouse** (505-758-5448; $-$$) owned by Tim and Leslie Reeves; and **Inn on La Loma Plaza** (505-758-1717; $$-$$$$) owned by Peggy & JerryDavis (both former mayors of Vail and Avon, CO). **Alma del Monte** (505-776-2721; $$) is managed by Suzanne Head. Book B&Bs through the **Taos B&B Association** (800-876-7857)

The **Inger Jirby Guest Houses** (505-758-7333; $$$$), a creation of an artist from Sweden, are eclectically decorated, luxurious and only two blocks from the plaza.

Dining

The Bavarian (505-776-8020; $$-$$$), at the bottom of the Kachina Lift, is one of the best dining spots in the ski valley with some of the best German cooking this side of the Atlantic. For another excellent meal head to the **Hondo Restaurant**

($$-$$$) at The Inn at Snakedance, dinner only. **Rhoda's Restaurant** (505-776-2005; $$), serves lunch and dinner and an excellent skier's lunch. **Tim's Stray Dog Cantina** (505-776-2894; $$) serves breakfast ,lunch and dinner. Find good huevos rancheros. (Very spicy.)

Have lunch at the **St. Bernard** where you can get burgers and fries or daily specials. It is one of the best values on the mountain.**Hotel Edelweiss** ($$-$$$) serves three meals daily to the general public. About a mile-and-a-half down the road is **X-Treme Steaks** (505-776-2451; $$-$$) in the Amizette Lodge. On the road into the valley, **OBL (Old Blinking Light)** (505-776-8787; $-$$) is known for its steaks, chile and giant margaritas. **Sabroso** (505-776-3333; $$) in Arroyo Seco has great atmosphere with great food to match.

The town of Taos: **El Monte Sagrado, De la Tierra** (505-758-3502; $$$) has been named one of the best new restaurants in the country.**Joseph's Table** (505-751-4512; $$$) in the Hotel la Fonda de Taos is a special-occasion spot. **Lambert's** (505-758-1009, $$$) three blocks from the Plaza is another posh choice. **The Trading Post** (505-758-5089; $$) has Cajun, New Mexican, Italian and steaks. **Orlando's** is the place for New Mexican cooking. **The Garden Restaurant** (505-758-9483; $$-$$$) offers New Mexican as well as American, Italian and French entrees.

Find more good dining at the **Downtown Bistro** (505-737-5060; $$) south of town. For two colorful spots, head to **Ogelvies** (505-758-8866; $$) on the plaza and **Doc Martin's** in the Taos Inn (505-758-1977; $$). **Michael's Kitchen** (505-758-4178; $) has large and excellent breakfasts. Or head to **El Taoseño** (505-758-4142; $) for a great breakfast burrito.

In Taos Ski Valley try the **Blueberry Blue Corn Pancakes** or Tim's fine Breakfast Burrito at **Tim's Stray Dog Cantina** (505-776-2894; $$). Ski patrollers and mountain workers fill up before their day on the slopes at **Katie's** cafeteria.

 ## Apres-ski/nightlife

When lifts close head to the deck of the **Hotel St. Bernard**, the **Martini Tree Bar** at the Resort Center, the **Edelweiss Bar** and patio, or for German beer at **The Bavarian**. **Tim's Stray Dog Cantina** serves fiery chicken wings at 3 p.m. The place to be and be seen is the **Edelweiss Bar** where the margaritas are from scratch. The music ranges from bluegrass to Spanish. **The Inn at Snakedance** has entertainment nightly.

On the road back to the town of Taos, **OBL (Old Blinking Light)** serves the areas biggest margaritas and the **Anaconda Bar** at El Monte Sagrado has great apres-ski bar food.

It's livelier in Taos town, but not wild (unless you hit the **Alley Cantina** on a good night). Some nights the Alley Cantina has a live band and dirty dancing. The **Sagebrush Inn** has C&W dances. The Kachina Lodge's **Cabaret Room** has a dance floor and occasional acts such as Arlo Guthrie, and **Ogelvie's Bar and Grill** in Taos Plaza hops. For microbrew fans, **Eske's Brew Pub** off the Taos Plaza is the spot. Be sure to try the unique Green Chili Beer at least once. Skiers and local artists mix at the **Adobe Bar** of the Taos Inn, the living room for artsy locals. Order a margarita and watch the beautiful people.

Up at the Taos Pueblo there is gambling at the **Taos Mountain Casino**.

 ## Other activities

Many instructors will suggest you make a trip to **Boot Doctors** (505-776-2489) and upgrade your equipment. This shop is the premier ski boot fitter in the United States. If it's time to get new gear, have custom boot beds tailored to your foot shape and body balance while you're in town. It will have a profound effect on your skiing. You can return as many times as it takes to get the fit perfect.

For Taos history and art, visit The **Martinez Hacienda**, the **Millicent Rogers Museum**

Dining: $$$$–Entrees $30+; $$$–$20–$30; $$–$10–$20; $–less than $10.
Accommodations: (double room) $$$$–$200+; $$$–$141–$200; $$–$81–$140; $–$80 and less.

and the **Fechin Institute**. **Adventure Tours** in Taos (505-758-1167) has sleigh rides and snowmobile tours. For recreation, visit **Taos Ice Arena** (505-758-8234),**Los Rios Anglers** (505-758-2798), **BobCat Pass Adventures** (505-754-2769), Sled Shed (505-754-6370), Fast Eddie's (505-754-3103) and **Roadrunner Tours** (505-377-6416).

    Night Sky Adventure (505-754-2941)offers a telescopic universe tour. Visit the **Taos Pueblo**. For dates, call the **Taos Chamber of Commerce** (800-732-TAOS). Georgia O'Keeffe and R.C. Gorman have made Taos legendary with art lovers. Get a list of 80 galleries from **Taos Chamber of Commerce**, 505-758-3873 or 800-732-TAOS.

Getting there and getting around

    By air: Albuquerque is the nearest major airport, 135 miles south, where you'll find rental car agencies. For ground transportation, contact **Faust's Transportation**, 505-758-3410 in Taos, or 505-843-9042 in Albuquerque; or **Pride of Taos**, 505-758-8340.

    By car: I-25 north to Santa Fe, then Hwys. 285, 84 and 68 to Taos. Taos Ski Valley is 18 miles farther north on Hwy. 150. For Red River head north on Hwy. 522 and east on Hwy. 38. For Angel Fire go east on Hwy. 64.

    Getting around: If you stay in Taos Ski Valley village and have no desire to go into the town of Taos 18 miles away, you won't need a car. Otherwise you'll need one. In Red River you won't need a car, but you'll need one to get there. The same goes for Angel Fire.

Nearby Resorts

Angel Fire Resort, Angel Fire, NM; (800) 633-7463

Internet: www.angelfireresort.com

5 lifts; 450 skiable acres; 2,077 vertical feetParks & pipes: 2 terrain parks, 1 halfpipe

Angel Fire is a modern resort about a half-hour—22 miles—east of Taos. Accommodations are close to the slopes; the mountain has been created for families and mellow skiing with touches of challenge. This resort is especially good for beginners and intermediates. There is expert terrain, but it's tucked away.

Beginners will want to take Headin' Home from the top of the high-speed Chile Express quad, stay on the trail or drop down Bodacious back to the base area. Beginners can also experience the back bowl by winding down Highway, then dropping off Hallelujah or La Bajada to end up at the base of the Southwest Flyer, another high-speed quad. **Intermediates** will have fun on Fat City, Fire Escape, Mother Lode and Arriba in the back bowl. We recommend staying in the back bowl. On the front side you can cruise down some good intermediate trails such as I-25, Prospector and Jasper's, but all end in a long runout to the base area. **Advanced/Expert** levels will find meager offerings but they can be fun. A cluster of black runs under Lift 6 provides a challenge. To the far skier's right of the back bowl, a series of advanced runs were recently added to Detonator and Nitro. Enjoy about 9 acres of glades on the front side between I-25 and Prospector.

Angel Fire has become New Mexico's premier **snowboarding** destination. The Chile Express high-speed quad whisks boarders to the top of the 10,677-foot mountain. Sound systems pump out great tunes underneath the lifts. Angel Fire has a young feel to it.

Beginner boarders will appreciate both Dreamcatcher and Lift #2, servicing Exhibition and Valley. It's a bunny hill with two levels of difficulty.There's also beginner terrain at the top of the mountain, on either side of the NASTAR race area, served by a short lift. The Summit Haus, a yurt-style restaurant with a full-service bar at the peak, adds a nice touch. **Intermediate and advanced riders** will prefer the back side of the mountain, serviced by a high-speed quad. Hell's Bells is a favorite run amongst advanced boarders. Intermediates will enjoy Fire Escape and Hully Gully, shifting to front-side runs like I-25 and Prospector on days when the sun is hidden and snow is pounding. Unfortunately, front-side runs all end in a long runout to the base area. For **Expert** snowboarders, hiking-accessed trails in the Back Basin including Nitro, Detonator and Baa-da-bing offer some of the steepest terrain on the mountain.

Parks and pipes: The resort has two terrain parks. Liberation Park, for experienced riders, is at the top of the mountain and reached by its own chair, Lift #3. It has tabletops, spines, funboxes, rails and jumps. Lowrider Park, on the lower section of Headin' Home, is the learning park, with short rails, funboxes, small jumps and rollers. It's also the place to perfect park technique. Angel Fire has the only halfpipe in New Mexico. It's in Liberation Park.

Angel Fire has an excellent ski school that focuses on kids, beginner and intermediate skiers Their snowboarding instruction is highly rated too. The resort recently expanded its children's ski and snowboard school with a 6,000-square-foot building. Angel Fire Resort Day Care 800-633-7463, housed in a new state-of-the-art facility near the kids' ski school, is open 8 a.m. to 5 p.m. Full-and half-day programs provide activities for children ages 6 weeks through 10 years with costs ranging from $40 to $85 for day care and lessons.

Adventure Park, at the base, has a day tubing hill. At the summit are 22 km. of cross-country and snowshoe trails. Lessons and rentals are available.

Lift tickets (2007/08 prices): Adult, $48; youth (7-12), $33; multiday discounts apply. Ages 6 and younger and ages 70 and older ski free.

Dining: $$$$–Entrees $30+; $$$–$20–$30; $$–$10–$20; $–less than $10.
Accommodations: (double room) $$$$–$200+; $$$–$141–$200; $$–$81–$140; $–$80 and less.

Lodging: The Angel Fire Resort Hotel (800-633-7463; $$-$$$) has standard and deluxe rooms and suites. The resort has managed **condominiums** ($$-$$$) and has a full program of ski packages. The hotel is slopeside and the condos have a shuttlebus.

Dining/apres-ski/nightlife: Dining is a resort affair. There aren't many choices outside of the base area. The top spot is **Aldo's Cafe and Cantina** (505-377-6401; $$), with Italian bistro cuisine, right next to the Chile Express lift. **Branding Iron** (505-337-4201; $) serves breakfast and dinner in the resort hotel. **Jasper's Bar** ($) in the resort hotel has a bar menu. **Zebadiah's** (505-377-8005; $-$$) is off the resort with a good family restaurant. **The Roasted Clove** (505-337-0636; $$) cooks fine continental dishes but is difficult to find. Be sure to ask for directions. For pizza call the **Pizza Stop** (505-337-6340; $), just off the mountain, specializes in freshly made crust and sauces, **Beverly's** (505-377-2337; $) or **Grapevine Gourmet** (505-377-2884), both in town. For the best barbecue in town, try **Willy's Smokehouse** (505-377-2765). The **Bear's Den** (505-377-1113) at the entrance of the resort serves breakfast, lunch and dinner. On the mountain, go to the **Summit Haus** for brats and burgers and **Village Haus** on the base area deck for snacks and grilled items. Both have full-service bars. Angel Fire snoozes in the evenings, but **Village Haus** has live entertainment, 3 p.m.-7 p.m. every weekend. There is also a bit of an apres-ski buzz in **Jasper's**.

Other activities: After a long day on the slopes you may wish to recharge with a Leg Anti-Fatigue Treatment at **Sage Skin and Body Care** (505-377-5959). **Roadrunner Tours** (505-377-6416) offers **winter horse rides** and old-fashioned **sleigh rides**. Try your hand at **ice fishing** in nearby Eagle Nest through the **Eagle Nest Marina** (505-337-6941). For solitude and meditation visit the **Vietnam Veterans National Memorial** (505-337-6900), the first memorial built to honor the men and women serving in Vietnam.

Red River Ski Area, Red River, NM; 505-754-2223

Internet: www.redriverskiarea.com
7 lifts; 290 skiable acres; 1,600 vertical feetParks & pipes: 1 terrain park

Red River, about an hour drive—37 miles—north of Taos, has no pretensions about Indians or the Spanish. This once was a down-and-dirty mining town with saloons and bordellos lining the streets. Today, Red River is one of the prettiest ski towns in the U.S.

Two main lifts drop right into town and most hotels and condos are within walking distance of them. If you don't want to walk, take the town trolley that makes its rounds every 15 minutes.

Red Chair and Copper Chair reach the summit from different spots in town. This is not high-speed quad territory; all these lifts are fixed-grip. There's a **terrain park** for those who like tricks and air. From the highest point, Ski Tip, **beginners** can drop to the other side of the peak to test about a dozen easy runs served by a double chair. Beginners can also ski all the way back to the base area along Cowpoke Cruise, which meanders down the entire 1,600 feet of vertical. **Intermediates** have the entire skier's right of the mountain. **Advanced and expert** skiers head to skier's left from Ski Tip. Here, they find a mix of trees and black-diamonds.

Red River has an excellent ski school that focuses on beginner and intermediate skiers as well as children. Lesson packages include lift tickets and rentals: $45-85. Red River's Youth Center and Buckaroo Child Care is open from 8 a.m. to 4:30 p.m. Children from 6 months to 4 years are accepted for child care; $30 for half day, $48 for full day with lunch. Kids ages 4-10 have lessons and indoor activities. Costs range from $35 to $87.

Lift tickets (2007/08 prices): Adult, $55; teen (13-19), $49; juniors (4-12) and seniors, $40. Multiday discounts kick in with three or more days.

Accommodations: Almost all hotels are relatively close to the lifts and the town. For **lodging information,** call 800-331-7699 or 505-754-2366. **Lifts West Condo/Hotel** (800-221-1859; 505-754-2778; $-$$) has spacious rooms and a wild second-floor hot tub. For European charm, stay at the **Alpine Lodge** (800-252-2333; $$$) or **Edelweiss** (800-445-6077; $$-$$$) with its heated swimming pool. The **Auslander Condominiums** (800-753-2311; 505-754-2311; $$), **Black Mountain Lodge** (800-825-2469; 505-754-2469; $$), **Copper King Lodge** (800-727-6210; 754-6210; $-$$) and **The Riverside** (800-432-9999; 505-754-2252; $) are all almost ski-in/ski-out.

Groups and large families can find great deals on cabin and townhouse rentals through **Red River Real Estate** (800-453-3498; $$-$$$$) or **Bandanna Red River Properties** (800-521-4389; $$-$$$$).

Dining/apres-ski/nightlife: Don't come here looking for fancy gourmet fare. This town is focused on good down-home meals with quantity. That said, **Brett's** (505-654-6136; $$) has an elegant dining room and a menu where everything from seafood to lamb is spiced with gourmet phrases. **Texas Reds Steakhouse and Saloon** (505-754-2922; $$) is everything a cowboy steakhouse should be. From the newsprint menu to the charbroiled beef, this is a carnivore's paradise. The **Lodge at Red River** (505-754-6280; $$) has a good family restaurant with plenty of steaks, but you can find trout and shrimp as well. **Timbers** (505-754-3090; $$) is another western-style steakhouse. For Tex-Mex head to **Sundance** (505-754-6271; $) or to **Angelina's** (505-754-2211; $). The new **Roberto's** (505-754-6270) inside Lift's West specializes in highly recommendable Old Mexican food. For N.Y.-style pizza and other Italian meals try **Pappa's** (505-754-2951; $). For breakfast head to **Mountain Village Diner,** across from the Chamber of Commerce, for an all-you-can-eat feast, to the **Alpine Lodge** for their breakfast burritos, or to **Shotgun Willie's** for the "Mountain Man Breakfast."

Red River is the nightlife capital of the region. Head to the **Motherlode Saloon** for dancing to live music. The **Mineshaft Theater** has concerts. **Texas Reds** has singers in the bar. And the **Bull O'The Woods Saloon** has cowboy karaoke. The **Lonesome Pine Pub** serves New Mexico microbrews on tap. **Chubbies Tavern** rocks during apres-ski with the college crowd.

Residents of Red River have an excellent sense of humor—and mischief. In November it's BYOT (bring your own turkey) for the annual Turkey Toboggan, where competitors race down the slope seated on the frozen beasts. February brings fully costumed Mardi Gras celebrations with awards for best and most unique masks. St. Patrick's Day is celebrated with a big ol' party. From mid-March to the end of the season, spring break "Beach Days" is the biggest celebration of the year with beach music, hula hoop contests, the flashlight parade for kids 12 and younger, a sand volleyball court and events all up and down the main street. This is a good party town.

Dining: $$$$–Entrees $30+; $$$–$20–$30; $$–$10–$20; $–less than $10.
Accommodations: (double room) $$$$–$200+; $$$–$141–$200; $$–$81–$140; $–$80 and less.

Ski Apache, Ruidoso, NM, (505) 336-4356; (505) 257-9001 (snow report)

Internet: www.skiapache.com

11 lifts, 750 acres, 1,900 vertical feet, 1 terrain park

Ski Apache, where trails cruise through the pines of the Mescalero Apache Indian reservation, sits at the end of a dramatic access road high above the cowboy town of Ruidoso in south-central New Mexico. This is the southernmost major destination ski area in North America, only 120 miles north of the Mexican border.

The region with the town and the resort occupies an oasis of pine-covered mountains surrounded by the sprawling New Mexican desert. From the Lookout Snack Bar, at the top of the gondola, the panorama is one of the most expansive to be found at any ski resort in North America. The view takes in the White Sands National Monument, the site of the first atom bomb explosion, the forest where Smokey Bear was rescued and the Old West towns where Billy the Kid roamed.

Trail names echo the Apache heritage—Geronimo, Screaming Eagle, Chino and Ambush. Skiers from Texas, Germans from nearby Holloman Air Force Base, and Mexican visitors all mix with the Mescalero Indians who make the resort work. You'll find no condo developments and no ski-in/ski-out hotels at the ski area—this is a pure ski resort. The elevation between 9,600 and 11,500 feet guarantees snow and the location in southern New Mexico tempers the weather and favors plenty of sunny days.

This is an intermediate's playground, but advanced levels won't be disappointed. Beginners will be pushed for all they're worth—the shift from mellow terrain to more significant steeps is a big one. Sometimes it's hard to tell the blues from blacks. They're both tough.

Twelve miles from the snowfields of Ski Apache and about 3,000 feet below the sacred Sierra Blanca peak, the town of Ruidoso spreads along a valley floor surrounded by gentle pines. This town is mainly a summer resort with the focus on Ruidoso Downs—home of quarter-horse racing, five golf courses and a full May-to-October program of music and cultural events. This makes winter the bargain time for most B&Bs, motels and hotels.

Mountain layout: Bounded by two ridges, Ski Apache is divided roughly in half by a third center ridge that runs parallel to the boundary ridges. The area's gondola runs along the center ridge from the base to the summit. At the top of the area on trail-map left, expansive Apache Bowl has wide-open skiing from 11,500 feet with about 650 feet of vertical. Most of the rest of the slopes are off the center ridge, which has a long intermediate trail running along the crest with expert and intermediate trails dropping to trail-map right. The rest of the skiing is near the bottom of the left boundary ridge. Again, a blue cruiser snakes along the crest and black-diamond pitches fall toward the base area.

◆◆**Expert** ◆**Advanced:** Experts may want to head elsewhere for extreme terrain, but you can find some challenge in the steeps and glades. For advanced skiers, there are plenty of moguls and steep pitches on all of the north faces. Apache Bowl and The Face (which drops into the bowl from the center ridge) offer great powder skiing when the conditions cooperate. Those who want to stay in the bowl can upload using a triple chair that allows them to stay right in the bowl without working their way back down to the base.

■**Intermediate:** This is a great resort for intermediates looking to improve. The blues are mellow and the blacks reach some excellent pitches. For cruising, stick to the ridges, or take your first runs on Ambush, Chino or Meadows, to the right as you unload from the gondola. For showoff time, take a few zips along Capitan, the run that drops right to the base area.

●●**Beginner:** Beginners have their own area served by Chair 7. Those shifting from beginner to intermediate should try Lower Deep Freeze and Snowpark.

●**First-timer:** The learning area is off Chairs 3 and 5 at the base. This area is fenced off so those taking first-time lessons are not subjected to more advanced skiers and snowboarders zipping through their classes.

Ride Guide: Apache Bowl is a favorite spot when powder falls or is blown over the ridge. Do laps off the lift that exclusively serves the bowl, then toss in some variety by riding up The Face and dropping off the ridge trails. The terrain forms natural halfpipes known locally as "the fingers" in the center of Apache Bowl. Yee-haw, as the Texans would say!

Lift tickets (08/09 prices): Adults (18–60), $51; teens (13-18), $43; children (12 and younger), $32; seniors (61-69), $45; seniors 70 and older, free.

Distance from Ruidoso: About 16 miles on Mechem Drive and Ski Run Road.

Lodging information: There are more than 70 lodging properties in the Ruidoso area. For a complete listing, see ruidoso.net.

The Inn of the Mountain Gods (257-5141; 800-545-9011; $$), is a massive casino set on one of the Indians' sacred lakes with picture windows that open to reveal the ski area on their sacred mountain in the far distance.

For luxury amidst beautiful art, head to the **Hurd Gallery & Guest Homes** (800-658-6912; 653-4331; $$$$) in San Patricio near the junction of Hwys. 70 and 380, about 30 miles from Ruidoso. Spectacular lodging starts at $200 a night.

Hawthorn Suites (258-5500; 866-211-7727; $$) is Ruidoso's newest upscale choice in lodging. It features all suites with amenities including indoor pool, hot tub and massages.

Swiss Chalet Inn (258-3333; 800-477-9477; $-$$), perched above town, is one of the last lodges before the turnoff to the resort. Views from the restaurant are beautiful.

Enchantment Inn (378-4051; 800-435-0280; $) is a full-service hotel. **Shadow Mountain Lodge** (257-4886; 800-441-4331; $-$$) is designed for couples, with king-size beds, fireplaces and hot tubs. **Holiday Inn Express** (257-3736; 800-257-5477; $-$$) includes breakfast. **Sitzmark Chalet Motel** (257-4140; 800-658-9694; $) offers inexpensive packages including lift tickets.

Condotel (800-545-9017; 258-5200) offers a large selection of two- to six-bedroom condos, cabins and private homes. These lodging choices can be viewed and booked online at www.ruidosoreservations.com.

Dining: Try **Pasta Cafe** (257-6666; $-$$) for Italian specialties and **Le Bistro** (257-0132) for faux French. **The Cattle Baron** (257-9355; $$) is the place to head for steaks. **The Texas Club** (258-3325; $-$$) also serves great steaks and all-American fare.

Tinnies Silver Dollar (653-4425; $$) provides dining with a step back in time about 30 miles from Ruidoso toward Roswell. The yesteryear dining rooms are lined with paintings harking back to the Old West or showcasing the Hurd/Wyeth family art. **The Green House** (354-0373; $$), in nearby Capitan, serves good grub fresh from its own greenhouse. Both are worth the drive.

Cafe Rio (257-7746; $-$$) on downtown's main drag serves a curious Mediterranean mixture (Italian, Portuguese, Greek) of pizza, pasta, soups and seafood in diner-like surroundings. **Terraza Camanario Restaurant** (257-4227) and **Casa Blanca** (257-2495; $) offer Tex-Mex. **Farley's** (258-5676; $) has a good family atmosphere with fajitas and burgers.

Dining: $$$$–Entrees $30+; $$$–$20–$30; $$–$10–$20; $–less than $10.
Accommodations: (double room) $$$$–$200+; $$$–$141–$200; $$–$81–$140; $–$80 and less.

Oregon regional resorts

Timberline Lodge, Timberline, OR; 503-622-7979
Internet: www.timberlinelodge.com
7 lifts; 1,430 lift-served acres; 3,590 feet vertical; 2 terrain parks; 1 halfpipe

Timberline is known for its summer skiing and beautiful, historic lodge. Timberline was the continent's first ski area to offer lift-served summer skiing, and now more than 50,000 skiers come each summer. The Palmer Snowfield, at 8,500 feet above sea level, has a steady pitch at the advanced-intermediate level. It's challenging enough that you'll find World Cup ski racers from several countries practicing technique. A high-speed quad, Palmer Express, allows Timberline to keep the terrain open nearly the entire year, and gives the area the greatest vertical drop in the Northwest—3,590 feet. The deep snows of winter sometimes require cat drivers to dig out the lift, the upper terminal of which is inside the mountain. Spring skiing is incredible off this lift. Palmer runs through Labor Day every year, conditions permitting (and they usually do).

Half of Timberline skiing is still below treeline and the main lodge, but few experiences in the skiing world match a ride up the Magic Mile Super Express and the Palmer Express to the top of the Palmer Snowfield. The original Magic Mile lift was the second ski lift in the country, after Sun Valley's. Silcox Hut, which served as the original top terminus and warming hut, has been restored and is open to overnight groups. Below the Timberline Lodge are many blues and greens, with a few short blacks. The trail system between the trees makes each run feel like a wilderness excursion.

Timberline has two terrain parks to challenge everyone from the amateur to the professional level. The parks and halfpipe are accessed by the Stormin' Norman high-speed quad.

Lift tickets (07/08 prices): Adult day tickets, $49; children (7–12), $30; ages 6 and younger and 72 and older, free with ID.

Distance from Portland: 68 miles.

Lodging information: (800) 547-1406. Inquire about the historic slopeside **Timberline Lodge** ($–$$$) and the mountaintop **Silcox Hut** ($$).

Mt. Hood Meadows, OR; (503) 287-5438 in Portland or 503-337-2222 at mountain
Internet: www.skihood.com
14 lifts; 2,150 lift-served acres; 2,777 feet vertical; 3 terrain parks; 1 superpipe

Mt. Hood Meadows has by far the most varied terrain of the Mt. Hood ski areas and is as big as many Western destination resorts. The Vista Express quad lift gets you to terrain that is not much used. Slopes to skier's right off the lift are regularly groomed and are some of the best and most diverse terrain on the mountain. Perhaps the name should be changed from the Badlands to the Goodlands. It's full of expert powder caches, pitches, cruisers and some beginner runs. Freestylers can now get to the Vista Park plus South Park and the superpipe in one run.

Heather Canyon, when it is open, has always been the favorite for experts. Three of its entry runs—Twilight, Pluto and Moon Bowl—are winchcat-groomed, which means advanced and upper-intermediate skiers can go where they once had feared to tread. Snowcat skiing adds another 1,020 feet of vertical drop. To start way high with the runs into Super Bowl, you must take the Super Bowl Snow Cat from the top of Cascade Express. The ride costs $10 per trip.

www.skisnowboard.com has detailed writeups about these resorts
www.xcskiresorts.com has details about nearby cross-country trails

Meadows has a lot of what you'd have to call "free range" terrain. Most anywhere is good for riding and most of the mountain rides big. The east-facing runs between the Cascade Express and the boundary—more of a face actually—are all smoothies, good for swooping back and forth. Between the Cascade Express and the Mt. Hood Express are six little bowls and patches of trees—all single-black runs. For the real deal, head to the experts-only Heather Canyon. Absolute Magnitude is the best to jump into from the Shooting Star Ridge. For the upper canyon, you have to take Cascade Express and turn right. Things are steeper up here.

A favorite intermediate area is under the Hood River Express chair, called "Hurry" (for its initials—HRE). The entire HRE pod is designated slow speed for families and novice skiers and snowboarders. Beginners have the runs under the Daisy, Buttercup and Red chairs. Mitchell Creek Boulevard, reached from the Red chair, is particularly great for kids. Night skiers are served by four chairlifts near the lodge, one of them a high-speed quad.

Lift tickets per shift (07/08 prices): Adult tickets, $54; juniors (7–14) and seniors (65+), $32; ages 6 and younger, $6. (Shifts are 9 a.m.–4 p.m., 11 a.m.–7 p.m., and 1–10 p.m.)

Distance from Hood River: 35 miles.

Lodging information: (800) 754-4663.

Mt. Hood SkiBowl, OR; 503-272-3206

Internet: www.skibowl.com

9 lifts; 960 lift-served acres; 1,500 feet vertical; 1 terrain park; 1 halfpipe

Mt. Hood SkiBowl is gaining a reputation for challenging ski runs with the addition of its Outback area and 1,500 feet of vertical reached from Upper Bowl. The mountain is now rated at 60 percent expert, but the 65 runs have enough variety for all skills. Beginners have some nice terrain, although the unloading ramps on the Multorpor side can be steep and intimidating for those at this level. The Multorpor side and the Outback are favorites for snowboarders.

The Terrain Park, on Lower Surprise, features a halfpipe, hips, lips, rollers and spines. The Stump Garden is a boardercross course, accessible from the Cascade chair.

Mt. Hood SkiBowl is one of America's largest night-skiing areas. It illuminates 34 runs, including some truly steep black-diamond runs. It also emphasizes ski racing, with programs for a variety of age groups.

Lift tickets (07/08 prices): Adult day tickets, $39; children (7–12) and seniors (65+), $21; ages 6 and younger and seniors 72 and older, free.

Distance from Portland: 53 miles.

Lodging information: (800) 754-2695; or visit the resort's web site.

Mt. Bachelor, Bend, OR; (541) 382-2442

Internet: www.mtbachelor.com

13 lifts; 3,683 lift-served acres; 3,365 feet vertical; 2 terrain parks; 1 superpipe; 1 halfpipe

Mt. Bachelor is not your typical mountain. At other resorts, the highest point often is difficult to distinguish from neighboring summits, which may be just a few feet higher or lower. But Mt. Bachelor, a stately volcanic cone that is part of the Cascades mountain range, rises from Oregon's high desert and is visible for miles in every direction.

On the eastern side of the Cascades, where snow falls lighter and drier than at other Northwestern resorts, Mt. Bachelor has become a popular destination for Western skiers and snowboarders. Despite no on-mountain lodging and little nightlife, Mt. Bachelor attracts visitors with its dependable snowpack, clear dry air, average daytime winter temperatures of 26 degrees, and fine skiing and snowboarding from early November into July.

Dining: $$$$–Entrees $30+; $$$–$20–$30; $$–$10–$20; $–less than $10.

Accommodations: (double room) $$$$–$200+; $$$–$141–$200; $$–$81–$140; $–$80 and less.

Visitors should keep in mind that all that snow results from a lot of storms, and winds often close the Summit Express chair, a high-speed quad to the 9,065-foot treeless summit. An average stormy day brings winds of 60 to 70 miles per hour, which can kick up ground blizzards where the snow swirls into a whiteout six feet high. (Visibility is usually better lower on the mountain, where the ski trails are protected by trees.) But when the weather is clear and you're standing on top, you can see California's Mt. Shasta 180 miles to the south.

Between the Outback and Red chairs is an unusual geologic feature, a lone cinder cone. It's not lift-served, so powder lasts there until it's wind-packed. By getting up a head of steam from Leeway, skiers can swoop up nearly two-thirds of the way and climb the rest.

Mt. Bachelor's Northwest Express Quad serves 400 acres of tree skiing and open-bowl terrain in an area called the Northwest Territory. When the Summit Express is open, experts should head for it. The steepest descent is through The Pinnacles, a jagged rock formation reached by a 150-foot hike from the top of the lift, then across the broad, ungroomed expanse of Cirque Bowl. Next might be Cow's Face, far to the left of Summit Chair, steep but smooth. Because it's unknown to many skiers, it doesn't get carved into moguls, but wind packs it hard. You can find moguls on Grotto, Canyon and Coffee Run, off the Pine Marten chair.

This mountain is best suited to intermediates. The Outback Express, with a 1,780-foot vertical rise, serves excellent intermediate runs. From this chair, Boomerang is the only run rated black, and it parallels the lift. One blue run, Down Under, often is left ungroomed for mogul enthusiasts. Other popular chairs for intermediates are the Pine Marten Express and the Skyliner Express. Old Skyliner, off the Pine Marten chair, has marvelous dips and rolls—far more fun than the usual freeway design of many intermediate trails.

For beginners, green-circle trails descend from every lift except the Summit and Outback chairs. More difficult trails are on either side, funneling the faster skiers away from those still learning to control their turns. Novices have their own terrain at both base lodges. Adjacent to the West Village Day Lodge is a short high-speed quad chair, Sunshine Accelerator. The runs it serves are called Milky Way and Home Run, a clear giveaway of the terrain's gentleness. At the Sunrise Lodge the Carrousel Triple chair gets riders to the Carnival and Marshmallow runs.

The resort has a superpipe built to Olympic specifications, 400 feet long with 17-foot walls. You'll find it next to the Pine Marten lift. A superpipe cutter keeps it in tip-top shape. On the other side of the Pine Marten Express is the Mt. Bachelor Slopestyle Arena. The Air Chamber Terrain Park covers the entire DSQ run near the Skyliner Express and is about 6,300 feet long and spread across 20 acres. It includes jumps, quarterpipes, spines, hips, tabletops and Signature Rails by the Mt. B Freeride Team. Parks and pipes beginners will find both an appropriately sized park near the bottom of the Sunshine Accelerator as well as a minipipe.

Most freeriding takes place in the Outback, which is loaded with trees and fall-line runs. For your final run in the Outback, try to take the Outback Express back up to Pine Marten Lodge. If you take the Northwest Express Quad up, you have to traverse the Northwest Cross-over, and it's a bit flat. The New Summit Express gets you to the Peak of Mt. Bachelor, well above treeline. There are some good steeps in The Cirque. Everything else up there to the left of the Express is gentle terrain.

Lift tickets (06/07 prices): Adult day tickets, $56-66; children (6–12), $30; teens (13–18), $39; 5 and younger and 70+, free.

Distance from Portland: 162 miles. **Distance from Bend:** 21 miles.

Lodging information: (800) 829-2442.

www.skisnowboard.com has detailed writeups about these resorts
www.xcskiresorts.com has details about nearby cross-country trails

Utah skiing

and staying in Salt Lake City

Salt Lake City Facts
Dining: ★★★★
Apres-ski/nightlife: ★★★★
Other activities: ★★★★★

Bed base: 17,366
Area code: 801
Reservations: (800) 541-4955 or 521-2822 (Salt Lake Convention & Visitors Bureau)
E-mail: slcvb@saltlake.org
Internet: www.visitsaltlake.com (Salt Lake Convention & Visitors Bureau) and www.skiutah.com (Ski Utah)
Visitor Information Centers: Salt Palace Convention Center, 90 South West Temple, open daily
(main location); Salt Lake City International Airport, open daily

---

Cosmopolitan city or an outdoor recreation destination? Salt Lake City is both in one. Recently named as one of Outside magazine's "18 perfect towns that have it all," Salt Lake, with all its snowsports options, also has pro basketball plus a symphony, opera, dance companies and live theater, not to mention the Mormon Tabernacle Choir. The choices of what to do when not on the slopes or trails are almost endless and include gourmet dining, rollicking brew pubs, comedy clubs, shopping, art galleries, and did we mention stuff like bobsledding, Nordic jumping and speed skating? You'd better stay an extra week.

Hosting the 2002 Olympics helped to enhance and show off the city and the nearby canyons. The quantity and quality of the snow has to be experienced in person to be truly appreciated. Yes, they must have inclement days, but it certainly seems that the snow comes mostly at night, leaving skiers and riders with feathery powder on beautiful bluebird days. In fact, rumor has it that it snows at Big and Little Cottonwood Canyon resorts on average every third day.

With the Ski Salt Lake Super Pass, you can ski at a different resort every day for the best possible price. It provides access to 7,500 acres of skiable terrain and makes Alta, Brighton, Snowbird and Solitude more affordable and accessible. You must be staying at a participating hotel in Salt Lake City. The Pass also includes round-trip transportation from downtown and suburban Salt Lake City to the resorts. Find it at 877-752-4386 or www.ski-saltlake.com.

Salt Lake shouts wide open spaces and Western scope with its distinctive streets built wide enough for a wagon with a team of oxen to make a U-turn, yet it is connected by non-stop flights to more than 90 destinations. This means skiers and boarders can have breakfast at home and take advantage of free skiing at Alta from 3 to 4 p.m. that afternoon. The towering Rockies and fantastic skiing and boarding are a mere 35 minutes from downtown. (For in-depth information on getting around the region, see Getting there.)

While the altitude – as high as 11,000 feet at some of the resorts – means drink lots of water and get plenty of sleep, there are those who have enough energy to go out on the town after attacking the slopes all day. Drinking is allowed in Utah (see **Apres-ski**). Microbreweries are everywhere. and martini bars are springing up for those who want their alcohol high-test. Add in jazz clubs, country western hangouts, piano bars and live music and staying in Salt Lake means skiers and riders will have a well-rounded winter resort experience in the middle of a happening city.

Accommodations

Salt Lake City has about 100 lodging facilities, so we can't possibly list them all. However, this should give you a good start. Although rates are a little higher downtown than in outlying parts of the city, it is worth the extra few bucks to be close to Salt Lake City's major attractions. Make sure to ask about ski-and-stay packages. Most Salt Lake hotels also sell the Ski Salt Lake Super Pass—an interchangeable voucher good for day passes at Alta, Brighton, Solitude or Snowbird—for as little as $55 (2008-09 price).

The Grand America Hotel (800-621-4505; 258-6000; $$$$) is the most recent property of Earl Holding, who also owns Sun Valley Resort, Snowbasin Ski Resort and the Little America Hotel chain. Elegantly appointed with authentic antiques, paintings, sculptures and carpets, this hotel could be listed as a museum. Ask about arrangements for an art tour when you visit. There is a full-service spa on the premises as well as a pool and hot tub.

The **Hotel Monaco** (877-294-9710; 595-0000; $$–$$$), a glamorous boutique hotel, is in an historic bank building. Definitely not a cookie-cutter property, the Monaco will deliver a pet goldfish to your room at your request and serves up free back and neck massages during the complimentary evening wine reception. And don't be surprised if you see your favorite rock star or NBA team in the lobby. The upscale **Marriott Salt Lake City Downtown** (888-236-2427; 531-0800; $$–$$$) has spacious rooms that are tasteful and comfortable with an indoor pool, hot tub, sauna and health club on the premises. Parking costs $10 per day. **Marriott Salt Lake City Center** (866-961-8700; 961-8700; $$–$$$), adjacent to the Gallivan Plaza, showcases a great ice-skating rink and cultural events. It has the same amenities, and parking is $10 per day.

Hilton Salt Lake City Center (800-445-8667; 328-2000; $–$$$) is one block farther south on West Temple. The Hilton spent $12 million to renovate the hotel and give it a new look. The **Peery Hotel** (800-331-0073; 521-4300; $–$$$), historic, elegant, and once a bordello. Enjoy architecturally distinct rooms with pedestal sinks, marble, and period furniture.

The tasteful **Little America Hotel and Towers** (800-453-9450; 363-6781; $–$$$), a sister property to Grand America Hotel, has some of the largest rooms we've seen in a hotel—great for spreading out all the gear that skiers carry. **Embassy Suites Hotel** (359-7800; $–$$$) has two-room suites with a free cook-to-order breakfast, plus there's a hot tub, indoor pool and sauna. The **Marriott University Park Hotel** (581-1000; $–$$$) is near the University of Utah, farther from downtown but closer to the resorts. Downtown, **Red Lion Hotel Salt Lake Downtown** (800-733-5466; 521-7373; $–$$$) has nicely appointed deluxe rooms, an outdoor heated pool, exercise facilities and free parking. For budget lodging, try the **Salt Lake City Center Travelodge** (531-7100; $), **Travelodge Temple Square** (533-8200; $-$$), or **Deseret Inn** (532-2900; $).

Three B&Bs in historic buildings are clustered about seven blocks from Temple Square, each with wonderfully decorated rooms. **The Anniversary Inn** (800-324-4152; 363-4900; $$–$$$$) is as romantic as it sounds, with themed rooms that cover everything from a mansion suite to a jungle safari and a sultan's palace. **The Armstrong Mansion Bed &Breakfast** (800-708-1333; 531-1333; $$–$$$$), built by a mayor of Salt Lake City for his bride in 1893, is a Queen Anne-style mansion on the National Register. It's been restored to its original appearance and each room is romance-themed with luxurious bedding. Some rooms have jetted tubs. The **Anton Boxrud Bed & Breakfast** (363-8035; 800-524-5511; $–$$) is a small mansion resplendent with polished wood, beveled glass windows, antiques and hand-woven lace.

A good, cheap place to stay the night before you fly out, is the **Days Inn Airport** (800-329-7466; 539-8538; $–$$) includes continental breakfast with make-your-own Belgian waffles. It's just minutes away from the airport, too.

 **Dining**

Downtown Salt Lake City has restaurants in nearly every food category you can name, including Afghan, Peruvian and Thai.

Metropolitan (173 W. Broadway, 364-3472; $$$) is Utah's most-awarded restaurant and has world-class New American gourmet cuisine that rivals some of the best of any other major city. It also serves vegetarian entrees. There's live jazz here on Saturday evenings.

Bambara (202 S. Main St., 363-5454; $$$) specializes in fresh, seasonal foods with Italian, French and Asian influences in a nouveau bistro setting in the Hotel Monaco.

Casually elegant Italian dining can be found at **Baci'Trattoria** (134 W. Pierpont Ave., 328-1500; $$). **Xiao-Li** (307 W. 200 South, 328-8688; $$) in the warehouse district features award-winning authentic Mandarin and Szechuan dishes and has a low-key, elegant atmosphere, with Oriental screens, high-backed rosewood chairs, and Chinese prints and scrolls on the walls. **Mikado** (67 W. 100 South, 328-0929; $$) has fresh fish and sushi, and has been in business for four decades. **Golden Phoenix** (1084 S. State St., 539-1122; $$) has been recognized as one of the top Chinese restaurants.

There are a wealth of choices for steak and seafood. **New Yorker** (60 W. Market St., 363-0166; $$$) is elegant, though you'll see people dressed in just about anything, including jeans. American cuisine is beautifully presented and don't be surprised if you see the mayor here, since it's the "in" place to dine. The more casual **Market Street Grill** (322-4668; $$) and the colorful **Market Street Oyster Bar** (531-6044; $$) focus on fresh seafood, but also serve steaks and pastas. (Market Street Grill has great breakfasts, by the way.) For understated elegance, go to **Christopher's Seafood and Steakhouse** (100 W. Broadway, 519-8515; $$). Big appetites will love the **Rodizio Grill** (459 Trolley Square, 220-0500; $$), an authentic Brazilian-style steakhouse. Kids younger than 9 eat free. **Lamb's Grill Cafe** (169 S. Main, 364-7166; $$) is Utah's oldest restaurant, dating to 1919, plus it serves a great breakfast.

The Garden Cafe (555 S. Main, 258-6000; $$) at the Grand America Hotel serves Seasonal Cuisine using fresh produce, seafood and game. Sunday brunch here is acclaimed.

At the base of Little Cottonwood Canyon is **La Caille** (942-1751; $$$), which gets rave reviews for its French cuisine, serving staff and setting. It's built to look like a French chateau and surrounded by gardens filled with swans, peacocks, rabbits and other animals. Make reservations; this place is *tres chic*. There's a B&B on premises.

Red Iguana (736 W. North Temple, 322-1489; $-$$) gets lots of rave reviews from locals for the top Mexican featuring a half-dozen moles and a great chile verde. **Cafe Pierpont** (122 W. Pierpont Ave., 364-1222; $-$$) is a festive and noisy Mexican restaurant reminiscent of a town square with wandering Mexican guitar players and women making tortillas from scratch near the entrance. Portions are huge here. The crab enchiladas suiza are fabulous. **Rio Grande Cafe** (270 S. Rio Grande, 364-3302; $) in the historic Rio Grande Train Station is another of downtown's best bets for Mexican.

Salt Lake City has three brew pubs and they're all worth checking out. **Squatters Pub Brewery** (147 W. Broadway, 363-2739; $-$$) entices with a broad, eclectic menu and everything sounds delicious. We suggest you select one of their dishes with beer as an ingredient. You'll also find good pub fare and beer at the other brew pubs: **Desert Edge Brewery at the Pub** (273 Trolley Square, 521-8917; $), in an old trolley building, and **Red Rock Brewing Co.** (254 South 200 West, 521-7446; $-$$), in a converted warehouse with many meals cooked in a wood-fired oven.

Dining: $$$$–Entrees $30+; $$$–$20–$30; $$–$10–$20; $–less than $10.
Accommodations: (double room) $$$$–$200+; $$$–$141–$200; $$–$81–$140; $–$80 and less.

Apres-ski/nightlife

Utah's liquor laws: Baby-boomer skiers remember when getting a glass of wine meant a trip to the state liquor store before going to a restaurant, then paying a setup fee before you could consume your own brown-bagged bottle. Now it's much easier, but here are a few tips:

Restaurants that have liquor licenses (most do) can serve alcohol from noon to midnight "to customers intending to dine." Wine and liquor menus are delivered along with your dining menu, and many restaurants promote their drink specialties on table cardholders. Some restaurants are still designated as private clubs, which means you'll have to pay a small temporary membership fee to get in.

Bars don't exist in Utah, at least not by that name. If you are planning just to drink, not eat, you'll have to do so at a private club. Don't be deterred by restaurant or nightclub advertising that has phrasing like this: "A private club for the benefit of its members." You, too, can become a member. Utah residents buy an annual membership costing up to $35 for each club. Visitors pay $5 for a membership, valid for three weeks for the visitor and seven guests. Annual members can bring guests, too. Just think of it as a cover charge.

You can also purchase beer, wine and liquor very easily. Grocery and convenience stores sell beer. Sixteen state liquor stores in the Salt Lake area sell wine, spirits, and beer (closed on Sundays). Wine lovers will want to visit the Utah State Wine Store, 255 South 300 East, which has more than 3,000 different varieties of wine.

After a day of skiing at Alta or Snowbird, check out **Cafe Trio** (733-6600), on your left at the southeast end of the Salt Lake Valley at the bottom of the mountains, for high-end brew, pub food and great apres-ski atmosphere.

For an unusual happy hour, stop by the **Cotton Bottom Inn** (2820 E. 6200 South; 273-9830) at the base of Big and Little Cottonwood Canyons. This is a raucous, sawdust-on-the-floor tavern with great garlic burgers and an earthy crowd. It is just off of Exit 7 on Hwy. 215.

Green Street (in Trolley Square) is apparently favored by Salt Lake City's career crowd. The Olympics brought a host of dance clubs to Salt Lake including **Vortex** and the **W Lounge**, both within a one-block radius on West Temple Street, across from the venerable **Port o' Call Social Club** (400 East and West Temple). **The Red Door**, Salt Lake's most sophisticated martini bar, is next door to Bambara and the Hotel Monaco. If you want to visit an establishment that's surely making the local Mormon population a bit crazed, stop in at the **Crazy Goat Gentlemen's Club,** a Salt Lake euphemism for the gay crowd (Arrow Press Square, 119 S. West Temple, in the rear).

If you like movies and microbrews, head to **Brewvies** (677 South 200 West; 322-3891). This establishment combines second-run (movies that have been released but aren't yet on video/DVD), independent and classic films with a gourmet-pizza-and-beer restaurant. Many people come to eat or drink, then decide whether to hang around for the movies being shown on four screens. You must be 21 years old.

For a more complete list of nightlife, pick up a free copy of *This Week Salt Lake.*

 ## Other activities

Experienced skiers can ski to six different resorts via backcountry routes on the all-day **Interconnect Adventure Tour** (534-1907; reservations required).

Mountain guides lead three to 12 skiers and some traversing and walking are necessary, so you need to be a confident skier and in good physical condition. The four-area tour (Solitude, Brighton, Alta and Snowbird) is offered three days a week, while the six-area tour (those four plus Park City Mountain Resort and Deer Valley) goes the other four days. Each tour costs $195, including return transportation and lunch.

If your legs are beat from skiing and snowboarding in too much powder, take a day off to visit **Antelope Island State Park** (801-773-2941 for entrance gate or 725-9263 for visitor center). The island is home to free-roaming herds of bison, bighorn sheep, mule deer and antelope, as well as smaller animals such as bobcats and coyotes.

This isn't the typical ski-town nighttime activity, but classical music lovers shouldn't miss the free 8 p.m. Thursday night rehearsals of the **Mormon Tabernacle Choir** at Temple Square. You also can attend Sunday when the choir broadcasts live from 9:30 to 10 a.m. Seating ends at 9:15 a.m. and you must stay seated for the duration of the half-hour program.

You can check out your ancestors at the **Family Search Center** at the Mormon computer center inside the restored historic Hotel Utah (15 ES Temple St.). Be sure to bring a list of family ancestors, names and dates to make your free search worthwhile. You can also do a free search at the nearby Mormon **Family History Library** (35 NW Temple St.).

Some other unusual ski town activities include attending a **Utah Jazz** (355-3865) basketball game, or getting all dressed up for **theater, symphony, dance** or **opera** performances.

Shopping here is extensive. At Trolley Square, beautifully restored trolley barns contain shops, art galleries and restaurants, plus a movie theater. The Gateway Plaza is a two-story outdoor pedestrian mall that surrounds the restored Union Pacific Depot, originally built in 1908 and featuring French Renaissance architecture. This isn't your ordinary shopping mall. In addition to shops, restaurants and a movie theater, you'll also find a planetarium here. Two giant contemporary malls, Crossroads Plaza and ZCMI Center, are across from each other near Temple Square.

Utah is home to five spectacular **national parks,** all within about four hours of Salt Lake: Arches, Bryce Canyon, Canyonlands, Capitol Reef and Zion. A side trip is definitely worthwhile.

Getting there and getting around

By air: Salt Lake City is a major airline hub. Ground transportation is well organized. You can go directly to the shuttle desks in the airport.

By train: Amtrak's California Zephyr stops in Salt Lake City at 4 a.m. coming from the West Coast, but the fare is cheap. From Chicago, the train arrives at midnight. Call (800) 872-7245 or consult the Amtrak web site, www.amtrak.com.

Getting around: Rent a car if you want to cover a lot of ground in the evening; otherwise, use public transportation. Getting to the resorts is a snap: Several ground transportation companies operate shuttles to the ski areas from Salt Lake City. Ask your lodging about them.

You can take the Utah Transit Authority light rail (known as UTA TRAX) from downtown and transfer to a UTA ski bus to take you to any of the Cottonwood Canyon resorts. This is very convenient and affordable, and the rail cars and buses are remarkably clean. It costs $6 round trip for a Ski Pass. Plan for about an hour total travel time. The only drawback: On Sunday, TRAX doesn't run from downtown until after 10 a.m. If you want to get to the resorts early, you can call a cab (about $25 one way; still cheaper than renting a car) to take you to the ski bus stop. Ride the Utah Transit Authority ski buses for $3 round trip from the park-and-ride at the canyon's mouth to any of the Cottonwood Canyon resorts (exact fare is required).

UTA also has a free fare zone downtown, convenient for sightseeing and evening activities. Buses run at night downtown until about 11:30 p.m., but only about once per hour. Call 287-4636 for more info. There are several taxi companies available, too.

Dining: $$$$–Entrees $30+; $$$–$20–$30; $$–$10–$20; $–less than $10.
Accommodations: (double room) $$$$–$200+; $$$–$141–$200; $$–$81–$140; $–$80 and less.

Nearby resorts

Sundance, Sundance, UT; (801) 225-4107; (800) 892-1600

Internet: www.sundanceresort.com

43 lifts; 450 acres; 2,150 vertical feet

Though this ski area has been owned by actor-director Robert Redford for more than 30 years, it has never been highly marketed—and that's on purpose. Skiing and snowboarding are not the resort's main event. Rather Redford has achieved a balance between outdoor recreation of all kinds, the arts and an intimate environment. Set on the slopes of breathtaking 12,000-foot Mt. Timpanogos, Sundance is regarded as the most beautiful ski area in Utah. To experience the challenging and varied terrain, get there early because the ski area limits lift tickets to 1,200 per day. Locals comprise 80 percent of the skier/snowboarder visits. Even when the 105 guestrooms are full, there is never a crowd on the mountain. Lodging packages offer many different possibilities like free lift tickets and full breakfasts in the Foundry Grill.

The area has a full-service Nordic Center featuring 40 km. of groomed cross-country trails and 10 km. of snowshoe trails. You'll also find two excellent restaurants, an eco-friendly gift shop, the historic Owl Bar, and the Sundance Art Shack offering a full schedule of classes, retreats and workshops throughout the year. Guests also enjoy screenings of award-winning films from past and present Sundance Film Festivals. (This annual event, held in larger Park City during late January, celebrates the achievements of independent filmmakers.)

Lift tickets (08/09 prices): Adults, $45; children 12 and younger, $22; children 5 and younger, free; seniors 65 and older, $12.

Distance from Salt Lake City: About 50 miles south via I-15, east on Hwy. 52, north on Hwy. 189, then a short hop west on Hwy. 92.

Lodging information: 225-4107 or (800) 892-1600.

Brian Head, Brian Head, UT; (800) 272-7426; (435) 677-2035

Internet: www.brianhead.com

10 lifts; 500+ acres; 1,320 vertical feet; 3 terrain parks; 1 halfpipe

Brian Head, in Utah's southwest corner near Bryce and Zion national parks, holds two distinctions among Utah resorts: It is one of very few *not* within an hour of Salt Lake City airport, and it draws virtually all its customers from Southern California and Southern Nevada. For these skiers, Brian Head is very accessible (all freeway until the last 12 miles) and has an excellent variety of mostly intermediate terrain covered by that famous dry Utah powder.

Child care starts at 6 weeks, and the town has several condo complexes, restaurants and a hotel. A tubing hill is open daily, and also at night every Friday and Saturday, plus during holiday periods. Brian Head also has night skiing on weekends and holidays. However, this is a quiet area in the evenings.

Lift tickets (08/09 prices): Adults, M-F,$35;wknd., $42; holidays, $49; children (6-12) and seniors (65+), M-F,$25, wknd., $30; holidays, $35; ages 5 and younger, free with paying adult.

Distance from Las Vegas: About 200 miles north by I-15 and Hwy. 143.

Distance from Salt Lake City: About 4 hours south via I-15 and Hwy. 143.

Lodging information: (800) 677-2810; www.brianheadutah.com.

Alta
Utah

Summit:	**10,550 feet**
Vertical:	**2,020 feet**
Base:	**8,530 feet**

Address: P.O. Box 8007,
Alta, UT 84092
Telephone (main): 801-359-1078
Snow Report Number: 801-572-3939
Toll-free reservations: 888-782-9258;
801-742-0101
E-mail: info@alta.com
Internet: www.alta.com
Expert:★★★★★
Advanced:★★★★★
Intermediate:★★★★
Beginner:★★★★
First-timer:★★★

Lifts: 11—2 high-speed quads, 1 high-speed
triple, 1 triple, 3 doubles, 4 surface lifts
Skiable acreage: 2,200
Snowmaking: 3 percent (50 acres)
Uphill capacity: 11,284
Parks & pipes: None
Bed base: 1,136
Nearest lodging: Slopeside, inns
Child care: Yes, 6 weeks and older
Adult ticket, per day: $64 (08/09 price)
Dining:★★★
Apres-ski/nightlife:★★
Other activities:★★

Alta sits at the top of Little Cottonwood Canyon in a high-Alpine basin where the ski experience is much like it was in 1938. That year, Alta opened with one rickety chairlift—which actually didn't carry any skiers until January 15, 1939—and one not-quite-finished lodge to house overnight guests. A few modern conveniences have found their way into the basin since then—such as three high-speed chairlifts, lift tickets with radio frequency ID chips that open gates in lift lines and free wireless Internet access at most lodges. But the gestalt of the place has remained the same.

The fact that Alta calls itself a ski area, not a resort, is telling. Here, it's all about the skiing—and only skiing; snowboarding is still prohibited. Rates at the five lodges include breakfast and dinner because Alta guests are here to eat, sleep and ski, and not necessarily in that order. There are no trendy nightclubs, shops or restaurants in Alta, although the dining in the lodges is excellent—tasty and hearty. Skiers save their energy for the slopes. The Rustler Lodge even has stools in front of its bathroom sinks, lest a skier be too weary to brush his or her teeth.

For many, Alta is love at first sight and the ski area attracts an enormous repeat following. The lodges report that 70 to 80 percent of their guests return. And it's not just the old-fashioned ambiance that's the lure. The basin is blanketed on average with over 40 feet of dry Wasatch powder each year. Skiing in this much light, fluffy snow is not only intoxicating, it's addictive. The steep headwalls spill onto rolling alpine meadows that cascade to the canyon floor. This mixture of terrain keeps it interesting.

But Alta's reputation for steep-and-deep belies its gentler side. The ski area is as much gently rolling alpine meadow with wide groomed swaths as it is heart-stopping headwall with waist-deep snow. It has some of the best beginner terrain in Utah and its children's programs are excellent. Only 11 of 116 total named trails are rated for beginners, but they are long rolling slopes that drop over 800 vertical feet—far longer than the average learning piste.

A great option for anyone staying here for at least a week: Purchase an AltaSnowbird ticket and enjoy the two resorts' combined terrain (snowboarders must either don telemark or Alpine skis or stick to Snowbird, since snowboarding is not allowed at Alta). To reach Snowbird, look for the gate in the saddle off Alta's Sugarloaf chairlift. A gatekeeper won't let anyone pass who doesn't have a combined ticket. Drop down the beginner and intermediate trails of Mineral Basin, then either return to the saddle via the Baldy Express chairlift, or take the Mineral Basin quad to Snowbird's Hidden Peak.

Mountain layout

The ski area has front and back sides with two base stations. Wildcat base area is the first one you reach. It has basic facilities—ticket office, restaurants, restrooms and ski patrol.

The Albion base area houses the Children's Center, Ski School, restaurant, retail and rental operations. Albion is where you'll find beginner slopes, but it also has intermediate and expert terrain at higher elevations. Albion and Wildcat bases are connected by a long, horizontal, two-way transfer rope tow: Just grab the rope and let it pull you along.

Expert, Advanced: Alta's trail map shows no double black diamonds. That's your first clue to the local attitude. If you're good enough to ski challenging terrain, you shouldn't need differentiation between advanced and expert. Yes, there is double-diamond terrain; it's up to you to figure it out.

The ski area's rep is "powder heaven." It's well deserved. Sure, Alta receives bountiful amounts of snow, but it also retains it well, thanks to plentiful trees and numerous sheltered gullies. While most skiers are carving on groomed runs a couple of days after a storm, the Alta cognoscenti are secretly diving into snow pockets in side canyons and upper elevations..

At the Wildcat base, the Wildcat and Collins lifts serve intermediate and advanced runs—narrow trails, bump runs, open powder fields and many glades. Even on powder days, only one lift ride is required to reach the reward.

From the Collins lift, skiers can access an entirely different ridge, West Rustler. Off High Traverse, a dozen-plus blacks fall on both sides of the ridge. Eagle's Nest, North Rustler and High Rustler descend the ridge's front face back to the Collins lift. On the backside, the East Greeley area highlights a seemingly endless series of broad bowl routes, including Greeley Hill, High Greeley and Eddie's High Nowhere—all leading to the Sunnyside lift or the Transfer Tow that traverses the base area. Stay high from Collins along blue-rated Devil's Way to reach short, steep shots on Keyhole Gulch, Glory Hole and Yellow Tail, then ride the Sugarloaf lift.

Far to skier's right runs the Supreme lift, accessed via Supreme Access off Razor Back (this is flat, so carry your speed). On powder days, go to the Albion base instead of the Wildcat base and head up to the Supreme lift, which drops you off at 10,595 feet. Once off the lift, where all but three runs are black-rated, drop in wherever you want; you can't go wrong. Some of Alta's best tree skiing is off this lift. The terrain is steep, the snow holds for days and trees are more abundant than the map shows. Just beware of cliffs, especially in the trees off Challenger. Supreme Challenge and Sidewinder surely deserve double-diamond ratings.

Experts hunting a unique Alta experience should seek Alf's High Rustler, named after one of the founding fathers of Alta. Getting there is adventure enough for some. Ride the Collins lift and take the high traverse. Stay on the traverse as it crosses the ridge toward Greeley Bowl, and keep on traversing. The traverse becomes narrow, the drop-offs precipitous on each side. Eventually it spirals around the mountaintop knoll, and opens to High Rustler, a beautiful, steep run that is little skied, enjoys breathtaking views of the valley, and spills right out into the lodges at the bottom.

Intermediate: Intermediate skiers experience a certain special heaven at Alta—well-groomed trails, ungroomed powder fields and friendly pitches with wide-open and un-peopled runs. Not even any lift lines! And remember, no snowboarders.

Start on the Albion side where intermediates have the most extensive terrain under the Sugarloaf lift. Find groomed cruisers plus a few very gentle pitches off to one side that don't get groomed—a super place to take some powder turns. Devil's Elbow is a real hoot, as is Roller Coaster.

On the Wildcat side, intermediate trails take you from the top of both the Wildcat and Collins lifts. Mambo and Main Street are loads of fun. Just watch for the steep top of Main Street. If you want a delightful powder field, head to Ballroom. Don't traverse too far, as the terrain gets steeper the farther you go (don't worry, you can see when it gets steeper).

Beginner, First-timer: Although Alta is well-known for its extremely difficult terrain, it also boasts exquisite grooming of the best snow in the region. This may come as a surprise, but Alta has the best beginner terrain in all of Utah.

The best beginner and first-timer terrain is at the Albion base. If you're staying at the Wildcat Base, take the transfer tow over to the Albion Base for warm ups and confidence-builders. The Albion and Sunnyside lifts access gentle slopes. This first-timer area is fairly safe and protected from faster skiers, but watch out for speeders on Home Run as it crosses the beginner runs. .

To get higher on the mountain, work your way up from the top of the Sunnyside lift to the Cecret lift and cruise down the Rabbit and Sweet N' Easy runs. Take a break at the legendary Alf's Restaurant facility, which also houses the ski school and demo center.

Snowboarding
Snowboarding is not permitted. Head next door to Snowbird.

Parks and pipes
In 2007, Alta closed the terrain park at the top of the Sunnyside lift. The resort found that most skiers used the "natural terrain features on our 2,200 acres as their preferred 'park.'"

Cross-country & snowshoeing (see also xcskiresorts.com)
Alta (801-742-9722) has 5 km. of groomed track for skate and classic skiing near the transfer tow. The Alta Nordic center at the Wildcat Base offers gear rental, including snowshoes and telemark.

Lessons (08/09 prices)
Bearing the name of Alf Engen, the Norwegian ski jumper who came to Utah in 1930, the ski school is recognized in the industry for its founder and contributions to the development of professional ski instruction. Lower-level ski lessons meet at the base of the Albion lift, while upper skill levels meet at the Mid-Mountain Meeting Place. For all ski school programs call 801-359-1078.

Group lessons: Levels 1-5 take two-hour lessons, $48. Levels 6 and up get 2.5-hour workshops that focus on specific skills, $62.

Private lessons: A one-hour lesson costs $90; additional person, $27. An early-bird lesson from 8:30-9:30 a.m. costs $100; additional person, $100. Two hours, $180; additional person, $54. Three hours, $270; additional person costs $81. All day, $540; additional person, $81.

Special programs: A 2.5-hour **telemark workshop** is offered for $62. Diamond Challenge is a 2.5-hour afternoon workshop for Level 9 (true expert) skiers for $62. The instructor gives pointers, but mostly acts as a guide to Alta's steep powder secrets. Alta Lodge has a special

Dining: $$$$–Entrees $30+; $$$–$20–$30; $$–$10–$20; $–less than $10.
Accommodations: (double room) $$$$–$200+; $$$–$141–$200; $$–$81–$140; $–$80 and less.

Powder Tracks class January 6-11. Cost is $2,357 per person for double occupancy; standard room. The resort also has an excellent collection of **Women's Programs** offered at various times throughout the year.

Racing: Alta's race course is located at the Sunnyside lift, open Friday and Saturday from 11 a.m. to 3 p.m. Pay at the race arena or at the ticket office.

Children's programs (08/09 prices)

Child care: Ages 6 weeks to 9 years. All-day infant care by reservation only is $90. All-day child care (3 and older) with lunch is $85. Multiday discounts available. All-day child-care program that includes a two-hour ski lesson is available for skill levels 1–2 for $85 (includes lunch). Alta's child-care center is a state-licensed facility owned and operated by Redwood Preschool, Inc. Space is limited, so reservations are highly recommended; call 801-742-3042 or book online.

Children's lessons: For beginner and intermediate skiers (skill levels 1–6), ages 4–12: All Day Adventure for skill levels 1–2 is $118 (with lunch); for skill levels 3–6, it's $108 (including lunch and lift ticket). Half Day Adventure for levels 1–6 is $48. For advanced and expert skiers (skill levels 7–9), ages 7–teens: All Day Explorer costs $135 (with lunch and lift); Afternoon Explorer costs $58. All children's lessons meet at the Albion base. For ski school programs, call 801-359-1078. Private lessons cost $90 an hour and Parent/Tot Private lessons are $90 per hour.

Lift tickets (08/09 prices)

	Adult	Child (12 and younger)
One day	$64	$32
Three days	$170	$96
Five days	$255	$160

Alta uses the Alta Card, a plastic reusable card imbedded with an RFID chip (radio frequency ID). The card costs $5 and is added to the first day's ticket price. At the end of the day, log onto alta.com, enter your Web ID, and see a history of your ski day.

Who skis free: All surface lifts are free, any time, any day. After 3 p.m. every day, skiing is free on the Sunnyside lift.

Who skis at a discount: Skiers pay $30 and $25 (to upload more ski days to an Alta Card) to use the beginner lifts in the Albion area. The AltaSnowbird ticket that allows you to access both resorts' terrain costs $84 a day; multiday AltaSnowbird tickets cost $163 for two of three days, $350 for five days.

Accommodations

Alta is one of the few ski areas that still has traditional ski lodges where breakfast and dinner are included in the cost. This is a super way to meet new people, particularly if you are traveling alone. Most of these lodges also have either dorm rooms or single occupancy rates available. Ask whether your room has a private bath, since some rooms do not.

It doesn't get any better than the luxurious **Alta's Rustler Lodge** (888-532-2582; 801-742-2200; $$-$$$$). Prices include a sumptuous breakfast and a savory gourmet dinner accompanied by live dinner music. **The Alta Lodge** (800-707-2582, reservations only; 801-742-3500; $$-$$$) is a 57-room inn. By guest preference over the years, the lodge has only one television and a video/DVD library. Breakfast and a four-course dinner are included in the price.

The **Alta Peruvian** (800-453-8488; 801-742-3000; $-$$$) has an outdoor pool and hot tub. No TVs, radios and all that. Rates include lift passes, breakfast, lunch and dinner. Ski out the back door. It's a short walk from the Wildcat Base or take the lodge's free shuttle.

Goldminer's Daughter (800-453-4573, reservations only; 801-742-2300; $$-$$$), named after a huge mining claim, is closest to the Wildcat lift. Extensive renovations have revamped the facility.

Snowpine Lodge (801-742-2000; $$-$$$), Alta's oldest ski-in/ski-out lodge has both private and dorm-style rooms. Dinner is served in a group dining setting and there's a made-to-order breakfast, both included in the price.

Two large condominium complexes, **Hellgate** (801-742-2020; $$$-$$$$) and **Blackjack** (800-343-0347; 801-742-3200; $$-$$$$) are between Alta and Snowbird, with Blackjack better situated for skiing between the two resorts. Both have van service to the ski areas.

Canyon Services (800-862-2888) rents luxurious condos and homes with fully equipped kitchens, washers and dryers, and cable TV. .

Dining

For one of the best gourmet meals anywhere, go to **Alta's Rustler Lodge** (801-742-2200; $$$) and enjoy a four-course, fixed-price dinner. There's also a kid's meal for children 7 and younger. Reservations are required. You also can eat breakfast and lunch here ($). A close second is **Alta Lodge** (801-742-3500; 801-322-4631 from Salt Lake), 801-742-3500; 801-322-4631 from Salt Lake; $$$), with another restaurant that serves a four-course, fixed-price dinner. Sunday evening buffet and their kids' dinners are also popular. Reservations are required for dinner. Lunch is also available ($).

The award-winning **Shallow Shaft** (801-742-2177; $$$), a restaurant on Alta's main road, is open for dinner-only and has innovative Southwest cuisine that features wild game, seafood, steak, pasta and chicken entrees. Reservations required.

For a tasty sit-down lunch on the mountain, head to the **Collins Grill** ($-$$), in the newly-built mid-mountain Watson Shelter. Both were fabulous. There are three on-mountain cafeterias. The **Albion Grill** ($) at the Albion base is not your average resort cafeteria. You'll find a great salad bar, homemade soups, chili and baked goods. It also serves a mean Reuben with fries. Wash this all down with one of the microbrews. You can get hearty breakfasts here too. At the Wildcat base, everyone congregates for breakfast and lunch at the **Slopeside Cafe and Espresso Bar** ($) at Goldminer's Daughter Lodge.

Apres-ski/nightlife

Local lore has it that the bookshelves at the Alta Peruvian have been voted the best nightlife in Alta (films and slideshows are shown here too). It's not far from the truth. People cook up their own nightlife here or crawl under the covers to rest up for more skiing tomorrow. At the **Alta Peruvian Lodge bar**, guests and locals gather for drinks at the lively bistro or around the fire. The **Sitzmark Bar** at the Alta Lodge is also good for apres-ski story-swapping. **Goldminer's Daughter Alpine Lounge** hops after the lifts close and has a good selection of beers. The **Eagle's Nest Lounge** at Alta's Rustler Lodge is the most upscale lodge bar and has killer views of the sunset over the mountains.

Other activities

Alta offers **snowcat skiing/boarding** on 325 acres in Grizzly Gulch, adjacent to the ski area. Runs average 1,500 vertical feet, with the highest elevation at 10,500 feet. Cost includes an orientation, continental breakfast and guides.

Dining: $$$$–Entrees $30+; $$$–$20–$30; $$–$10–$20; $–less than $10.
Accommodations: (double room) $$$$–$200+; $$$–$141–$200; $$–$81–$140; $–$80 and less.

For reservations, call 801-359-1078, Ext. 271 or 801-742-3333, Ext. 271.

A 45-minute guided interpretive ski tour is given by a Wasatch-Cache National Forest ranger on weekends and holidays at 1:30 p.m. Meet at the sign at the bottom of Cecret lift. Little Cottonwood Canyon also has spectacular helicopter skiing and snowboarding available from **Wasatch Powderbird Guides** 800-974-4354; 801-742-2800, based between Snowbird and Alta.

Alta is the winter base of the **Alaska Mountain Guides & Climbing School** 800-766-3396; 801-742-0100, with an office under the Albion Grill. It uses Alta chairlifts for access to many of its guided climbing and backcountry skiing courses. No previous experience is required—in fact, that's the point, to teach backcountry skills. Trips depart daily.

To revitalize yourself after a day on the slopes, go to **Alta Day Spa** 801-742-2200 at Alta's Rustler Lodge or have a masseuse visit you from **Wasatch Mountain Massage** 801-742-3313.

A few shops in the Little Cottonwood Canyon area have local handicrafts, artwork and books, but skiers don't come to Alta for the shopping. .

Getting there and getting around

By air: Salt Lake City is a major airline hub so flights are numerous from every corner of the continent. When you make your lodging reservations, ask about ground transportation arrangements. Most properties will make them for you. You also can go directly to the shuttle desks in the airport.

By train: Amtrak's California Zephyr stops in Salt Lake City. It arrives at 4 a.m. coming from the West Coast, but the fare is cheap. From Chicago, the train arrives at midnight. Call 800-872-7245 or consult the Amtrak Web site at www.amtrak.com.

By car: Alta is 25 miles southeast of Salt Lake City in Little Cottonwood Canyon on Hwy. 210. The most direct route from downtown and the airport is east on I-80, south on I-215. Take 6200 South exit (turns into Wasatch Blvd.) then follow the signs to Alta and Snowbird.

Getting around: If you fly in, you might not need to rent a car. Most of Alta's lodges have free shuttles to get you to the slopes or to visit neighboring restaurants. Some of Alta's lodges have shuttles that will take you to Snowbird and free bus service links Alta and Snowbird.

If you plan to ski at a lot of other Utah areas, stay in Salt Lake City. If you do, you can take the Utah Transit Authority light rail (UTA TRAX) from downtown and transfer to a UTA ski bus which takes you to any of the Cottonwood Canyon resorts. Be prepared to make transfers. This is convenient and very affordable, but pay close attention to bus schedules associated with going up and down the canyon. The rail cars and buses are remarkably clean. It costs $6 round trip for a Ski Pass. Ski buses have different daily weekday and weekend schedules. They start at 6:53 a.m. and stop around the city at 10 different hotels. Plan about an hour for total travel time. The only drawback: On Sunday, TRAX doesn't run from downtown until after 10 a.m. If you want to get to the resorts early, you can call a cab (about $25 one way; still cheaper than renting a car) to take you to the ski bus stop. You also can ride the Utah Transit Authority ski buses for $3 round trip from the park-and-ride at the canyon's mouth to any of the Cottonwood Canyon resorts (exact fare is required).

Another transportation alternative to get to the resorts are the private transportation services such as Canyon Hop at 801-860-7544, which is $36 per person round trip from Park City to any of the four Cottonwood Canyon resorts. Canyon Transportation at 800-255-1841, offers a $56 per person round trip from Salt Lake City to the resorts.

Snowbird
Utah

Summit:	**11,000 feet**
Vertical:	**3,240 feet**
Base:	**7,760 feet**

Address: P.O. Box 929000, Snowbird, UT 84092
Telephone (main): 801-742-2222
Snow Report Number: 801-933-2100
Toll-free reservations: 800-453-3000
E-mail: info@snowbird.com
Internet: www.snowbird.com

Expert:★★★★★ **Advanced:**★★★★★
Intermediate:★★★
Beginner:★★★
First-timer:★★

Lifts: 13—1 aerial tram, 4 high-speed quads, 6 doubles, 2 surface lifts
Skiable acreage: 2,500+
Snowmaking: 800 acres
Uphill capacity: 17,400
Parks & pipes: 1 park, 1 superpipe
Bed base: 1,800+
Nearest lodging: Slopeside, hotel
Child care: Yes, 6 weeks and older
Adult ticket, per day: $59-$69 (07/08 prices)
Dining:★★★
Apres-ski/nightlife:★★
Other activities:★★

Snowbird is to skiing and snowboarding what Oahu's North Shore is to surfing. Snowsports lovers come to this hallowed canyon to push their limits and ride hard.

With almost 3,000 vertical feet of steep bowls and tree-lined chutes, all covered in almost 500 inches of light Wasatch powder each year, Snowbird is a "must experience" mountain for any expert.

You get the sense of what this mountain is all about from Snowbird Center, a narrow spot in Little Cottonwood Canyon where the 8-minute tram ride starts. The slopes rise straight up from the canyon floor to Hidden Peak at 11,000 feet. The view from the tram, as it travels above the canyon wall, then high above the Cirque, will make experts quiver in anticipation and everyone else quiver in fear. Everything within view is a potential line and the only easy way down is an exposed serpentine cat track.

Snowbird is certainly not an experts-only mountain. The Creekside Lodge, which opened in 2006, sits below a wide gulley of easier terrain. And Mineral Basin, accessible from Hidden Peak, as well as a tunnel off the new Peruvian Express high-speed quad, is tamer than Snowbird's front side. It gets the dawn's early rays, so many head there for the day's first turns. But Snowbird is still a challenging mountain and not for the faint of heart.

Snowbird used to be Alta's backcountry—the resorts share Mount Baldy's flanks. It was the brainchild of Alta Lodge worker Ted Johnson who bought a mining claim at what is now Snowbird's base. Johnson envisioned an entirely different resort than laid-back, retro Alta—one with modern conveniences like a tram and large hotel. He convinced Texas oilman and rancher Dick Bass to finance the project. Snowbird opened in December 1971 with the tram, three other lifts and the Lodge at Snowbird. Two years later, the first wing of the massive Cliff Lodge opened. With concrete as the primary building material, Snowbird's base area—it's a stretch to call it a village—feels almost industrial. But in an avalanche-prone canyon, the solid buildings provide guests a high level of safety and comfort.

Inside the concrete edifices are all the amenities of a world-class resort. The Cliff Lodge's 11-story atrium is adorned with massive oriental rugs hung by rock climbers. Some of the best dining in Utah is found here. The Cliff Spa, high atop the Cliff Lodge, has an outdoor hot tub and heated pool, a steam room and massage therapists waiting to rejuvenate sore muscles so you can enjoy another day of knee-deep powder or turns down the Gad Chutes.

A great option for anyone staying here at least a week: Purchase an Alta/Snowbird ticket and enjoy the two resorts' combined terrain (snowboarders must either don telemark or Alpine skis or stick to Snowbird, since snowboarding is not allowed at Alta). The two resorts are connected by a ridgetop trail between Snowbird's Mineral Basin and Alta's Albion Basin. The gate takes you into the beginner and intermediate trails of Mineral Basin, and the intermediate and advanced trails of Albion Basin. You also can take a free ski bus between the two resorts.

 ## Mountain layout

Snowbird is divided into three distinct areas: Peruvian Gulch, Gad Valley and Mineral Basin. A good suggestion: Warm up in Mineral Basin where the sun shines and softens the overnight hard-pack early in the day. After a couple of runs in the bowls, head over to Gad Valley for a leisurely 3,000-vertical-foot drop to the Gadzoom high-speed quad. A northeast exposure on the Peruvian Gulch side keeps The Cirque's steep runs good all day, a treat for the late morning or early afternoon once the legs are warmed up but not shot.

Snowbird is a very tough mountain. If you're unsure of your ability, read the descriptions for the level above you and below you and begin by taking the easier routes. The rating of a trail can vary greatly according to snow conditions. Be advised that most intermediate trails here would be rated advanced elsewhere. In fact, Mineral Basin is this mountain's saving grace for intermediates. The terrain there is aptly rated for them and provides the opportunity to improve skills without being scared stiff. The single diamonds here can also be confidently tackled by advanced intermediates. If you are in a group of adventurous intermediates or better, Chip's Run provides the perfect opportunity for you to stay together because off of Chip's there are short drops of single- and double-diamond trails.

Expert, Advanced: Unlike many mountains that are steep near their summits, then flatten into more gentle run-outs, Snowbird is palm-sweating steep from the first turns off 11,000-foot Hidden Peak to leg-aching steep about 3,000 vertical feet later when the base area finally comes into view, looking like buildings at the base of a cliff.

The 125-person tram is the most direct route to Hidden Peak. When the first tram arrives at the summit on powder days, there's a mad dash for the slopes. Skiers and snowboarders hurl their equipment and then themselves over the docking station's railings to make first tracks. If you're the first on the Cirque Traverse or Mineral Basin's Pathway to Paradise, a long traverse to the basin's steeper sections, be prepared for faster, hungrier powder hunters to mow you over. Join the race. Or wait until others have departed, then go where they don't.

If the bowls, chutes, and trees look intimidating, the easiest ways down from Hidden Peak are Chip's Run, a narrow zigzagging cat track that winds down Peruvian Gulch's headwall, then spills into the more forgiving bottom of the Gulch, or the airy Road to Provo into Gad Valley.

But most experts will want to test their legs in The Cirque, a wide-open plunge that tumbles into even steeper bowls and chutes. You can choose a run that's steep or steeper, some with chutes that hold only enough powder to slow your virtual freefall. Anyone who has dropped through the rock- and tree-lined chutes of Upper Silver Fox, Great Scott or Upper Cirque deserves to be treated with reverence—they're using up their extra lives.

From the tram ridge, Primrose Path is an unrelenting black diamond, normally the choice of those who think twice about diving into The Cirque. But this terrain isn't even the toughest at Snowbird. For that, look for Gad Chutes or Barry Barry Steep, to the left off the Cirque Traverse. If you like trees, head to the Gad 2 lift.

The Peruvian Express quad, new in 2006, has changed how experts ski and ride Snowbird. On a powder day, many still head for the tram. But the Peruvian quad takes you 2,600 vertical feet into Peruvian Gulch and is a good way up the mountain when the tram line is long. Although the Cirque's steeps aren't accessible from here, it's a quick four-minute trip through a tunnel to Mineral Basin. Or follow the traverse on skier's right to the gladed double-diamond chutes and trees on the west-facing wall of the Gulch.

Advanced skiers who choose routes thoughtfully can find plentiful challenges and thrills at the right ability level. Off the tram, Regulator Johnson, a wide-open snowfield, presents the most obvious choice. It can be skied repeatedly from the Little Cloud lift, but it's a crossroads for many other routes and tends to chop up quickly. Johnson is black-rated, but it does have a wide groomed swath down the center, and this descent can be easier than Chip's sharp and crowded switchbacks, even though Chip's is rated blue.

To skier's left of Johnson, descending routes to Little Cloud can be varied. Shireen and Last Choice, black-rated, and blue/black Mark Malu Fork offer character variations.

Going to skier's right from the tram, follow Primrose Path all the way down, or branch off onto Adager or lower Silver Fox, for an incredibly long top-to-bottom slide.

Nash Flora Lode and Silver Dipper, found about two-thirds of the way across Path to Paradise, create perhaps the best drop-in for advanced skiers; Junior's Powder Paradise offers a gentler blue/black descent. Mineral Basin's far side (skier's right) is strictly expert territory. Skiing to Mineral Basin in the opposite direction off the tram, along Chips Access, leads to Double Down and Chamonix Chutes, two good runs for advanced skiers.

Intermediate: Do not board the tram without a test run elsewhere. A good tryout run is Big Emma from the top of Mid-Gad. Big Emma is rated green on the trail map, but its difficulty can vary with conditions. Many a beginner has halted along its upper rim, asking passing skiers and boarders, "Is there an easier way down?"

If you can ski Emma with ease, you have several options for the next test. Any of the blue-square runs off the three Gad chairs will be fun. Bananas and Election off Gad 2 are as exhilarating as it gets on skis. If you can handle these, you should be ready to tackle the easiest runs off the tram. Adventurous intermediates should try some of the short ungroomed pitches off Chip's for some extra challenge.

For others, the Baby Thunder area helps to bridge the steepness gap between Snowbird's novice slope and Big Emma, so head here for easier terrain. You can also work on technique on the greens under the Wilbere chair.

Mineral Basin is a wide-open bowl with a backcountry feel to it. Wilderness and a peaceful quietness surround you here, don't miss it. Meander your way down via Lupine Loop (green on the map) to figure out your comfort zone here. The blues are aptly rated. If you're learning to ski powder, you'll find the edges of the greens off Baldy Express are just the right pitch to give you that floating sensation without making you feel as if you're going too fast. There are also some widely spaced trees here to boost your confidence. If you're feeling bold, take the Bench Traverse and try the bowl. You can also reach Mineral Basin via the Peruvian Express, then the tunnel from Peruvian Gulch, thereby eliminating the need to take the tram, which can feel airy to those not accustomed to such heights.

Beginner, First-timer: The beginners' ski school with rentals, lift tickets and instruction is at the Snowbird Center base area, below The Cliff Lodge. Just beside The Cliff Lodge is the best lift for first-timers and beginners. The Chickadee run, with a gentle pitch and friendly lift operators, is guaranteed to be smoothly groomed, even on mornings after a huge snowfall.

Note: Other runs on other lifts that are designated green may not be groomed and may not be suitable for some (perhaps many) beginners. It's best to check before venturing out. Snowbird is a challenging mountain, so please take heed and know that it's very easy to end up on so-called beginner terrain that is extremely difficult. We recommend lessons for beginners, if only to have a guide to keep you out of trouble.

After a bit of a hike—and there seem to be quite a few to get around Snowbird—daring beginners can ski down Ski School Lane to the Wilbere Lift. The Mountain School Learning Area is just off the top of the Wilbere Lift, so you know it's got to be beginner-friendly.

Big Emma is a favorite cruiser when it's groomed. It's a bit steep and can be crowded. You can venture farther to the Baby Thunder Lift and ski the green Easy Street run, but this is mainly a blue and black area, so be aware of both the difficult runs and the fast skiers in this area. The Mid-Gad Lift also accesses some green areas, but again, be aware of crowded and craggy conditions.

For a memorable experience beginners can't find at most mountains, take the tram up to Mineral Basin, where you can get a view of the backcountry. Lupine Loop, an airy path that winds down Mineral Basin, will take you to Baldy Express. This lift feeds runs marked green on the map, but keep in mind that they will challenge most beginners. When you want to return to the base lodge, simply take the tram back down (do not even think about skiing down the front side, there is no easy way down).

Parks and pipes

Snowbird's Snowbird's terrain park is near the middle of the Mid-Gad lift exit on the Big Emma run. Each year Snowbird's parks have been getting bigger and better. The area served by the Baby Thunder lift is dedicated to the **expert terrain park**. The Tiny Tiger trail has the biggest tabletops on the mountain. Most of these jumps have a few different lips which can throw riders 10 to 60 feet down to the transitions. Depending on snow conditions, it can be hard to make it to the tranny, so check it out first or let someone else be the guinea pig. Past the hits there are a few really fun boxes and a couple of decent rails. Another run off Baby Thunder is Alice's Avenue. This is the intermediate park where the consequences aren't as high. Small to mid-size tabletops are found here with a few rides on boxes and rails.

Upper Blue Bell is home to a boardercross course with a luge, an intermediate hip jump and a couple of intermediate tabletops. Lower Blue Bell has five large expert rails and fun-boxes. Snowbird's second boardercross course, with six intermediate jumps and tabletops, is on Tiny Tiger.

The Snowbird superpipe lives on the Big Emma run. The pipe is 400 feet long, 50 feet wide and has walls up to 17 feet. The super big transitions make this pipe pretty user-friendly. Next to the pipe there is a smaller beginner park with a few super-mellow jumps. With the resort's huge selection of tabletops, boxes, rails and the superpipe, there are perfect hits for everyone from beginners to pro riders.

Snowboarding.

When it comes to the ultimate freeriding resort in Utah, Snowbird is the place. With a vertical drop over 3,000 feet, Snowbird offers steep, long, gnarly lines that can push anybody to the next level.

Riding up the tram will immediately put the magnitude of this mountain into perspective. The lower half of the tramline highlights endless steep tree shots. The upper half gives a bird's-eye view of the famous Cirque. Take advantage of the ride up to check out some lines or cliffs that look good.

At the top of Hidden Peak the riding options are unlimited. To the east lies Mount Baldy, a 15-minute hike to giant chutes and cliffs. To the west is the treeless Little Cloud bowl. For an even more technical line cruise out the Cirque Traverse to Lone Pine. Here on rider's right are multiple chutes and cliffs. On rider's left are big shots with scattered trees and rocks. If you drop in here, you'll eventually end up at the Gad Valley and the Gadzoom quad. The Gad Valley is much mellower with wide-open groomers braiding all over the mountain. However, there are still some good steep chutes and drops right under the lift.

Runs to rider's left of Gadzoom leads to the Little Cloud double. This area is divided into five wide-open bowls. On a powder day, it's wise to head here first because at times it quickly gets tracked out. Another option is to ride down past Little Cloud toward the Gad 2 Lift. This double chair accesses steep, north-facing trees that have good snow all day. Runs on rider's left head toward the far west boundary of the resort and to the backcountry gates. When open, this area is where some of the best lines of the day can be found.

On the backside of the mountain is Mineral Basin, a massive, south-facing paradise. Vast bowls, all-sized cliffs and some smooth, rolling groomers are all waiting to be hit. This side of the mountain resembles a big, natural terrain park. There is even an unofficial jump run which has hips, rollers, and a few cat track gaps. Just follow some locals to figure out the drill. Another section worth checking is Powder Paradise. From the top stay high on the right traverse to the boundary gate and hike to the goods from there.

Cross-country & snowshoeing (see also xcskiresorts.com)

Snowbird does not offer cross-country skiing but does offer snowshoe tours and snowshoe rentals. Call 801-933-2147 for more information. .

Lessons (08/09 prices)

Snowbird Mountain School has four one-stop locations for ski and snowboard school registration and buying lift tickets (tickets are not included in the lesson price). The offices are on Level 1 of the Cliff Lodge, the Plaza Deck of the Snowbird Center, the Cottonwood Room on Level 2 of the Snowbird Center and in the new Day Lodge in Gad Valley. For more information or reservations, call 801-933-2170.

Group lessons: 2.5-hour morning or afternoon **Mountain Workshop** sessions are open to skiers and riders of all experience levels and cost $80 each. Experts can take an all-day (10 a.m. to 4 p.m.) Mountain Experience for $135.

First-timer package: First-time skiers and snowboarders get a 2.5-hour group lesson, lift ticket and rentals for $90. Two sessions on the same day cost $145.

Private lessons: A three-hour session is $375 for one person, $435 for 2-5 students; a six-hour session is $600 for one person, $700 for 2-5 students. Mountain guide services are available for the same costs as private lessons.

Special programs: Women's Ski & Women's Snowboard, Kristin Ulmer's Ski to Live, and Dean Cummings Big Mountain Skiing and Snowboarding are all multi-day camps

Children's programs (08/09 prices)

Child care: Ages 6 weeks to 12 years. **Camp Snowbird** is located on level I of the Cliff Lodge. These prices are for regular season; value season prices are lower. It costs $95 a day with lunch for ages 6 weeks to 3 years; $90 for ages 3 years (toilet-trained) to 12 years, half day is $75. Evening babysitting is $16 an hour (minimum 3 hours), $2 for each additional child (maximum 4 kids), but you must be staying in a Snowbird lodge to use this service; 48-hour advance reservation required, cancel by 2 p.m. or pay a $25 fee. Reservations suggested for all child care; reservations two weeks in advance are required for infants and toddlers. Call Camp Snowbird at (801) 933-2256, or reserve when you book your vacation. Child care for infants and toddlers must be made 2 weeks in advance and paid for at the time of booking with a credit card.

Children's lessons: A program for 3-year-olds includes a one-hour private lesson with a half-day session of child care for $125 (with lunch and rentals); a full day costs $195.

Kids 4–6 get a program that combines a morning and afternoon lesson with indoor activities for $175 (with lunch and rentals). This program meets on Level 2 of the Snowbird Center. For ages 7–15, a full-day program with lunch and lessons costs $150 and meets in the Chickadee Bowl in the Snowbird Center. Ability levels are separated. Reservations are required for all children.

Private lessons: $375 for a 3-hour lesson for one, $435 per hour for 2-5 people. Six-hour private lesson costs $600 for one, $700 for 2-5 people..

Special activities: Kids' Night Out is for ages 4–6 and includes crafts, movies, outdoor play and dinner. Adventures After Dark is for ages 7–15 and includes outdoor activities such as snowshoeing, tubing, movies and dinner. Both programs are offered Wednesday and Saturday from 6:30-10 p.m.; reservations required. Wednesday nights cost $50, with second child in same family for $45; Saturday nights cost $60, second child in same family, $55.

Lift tickets (07/08 prices)

	Adult	Junior (12 and younger)
One day	$69	$29 (chairs only)
Three days	$174 ($58/day)	
Five days	$257 ($53/day)	

Who skis free: Children under age 6 ski the chairs free. Tram upgrades are $15 per day. Children of lodging guests ski the entire mountain, including tram use, free. There's no limit on the number of children as long as they are Snowbird lodging guests. Children must accompany adult to ticket office for a "Kids Ski Free" ticket. "Ski Free" tickets are for Snowbird only.

Who skis at a discount: Children ages 7-12 ride the chairs for $29 and an all mountain pass with the tram is $39. Seniors 65 and older pay $56 all mountain pass with the tram and $49 for chairs only. A ticket for only the Chickadee chair is $19.

Note: These are the prices with tram access. For chairs only, the one-day prices are $59 for adults; $49 for seniors. Don't buy tram access if you don't plan to use it.

The Alta/Snowbird ticket that allows you to access both resorts' terrain costs $79 a day; multiday Alta/Snowbird tickets cost $74 per day for three to four days, $69 per day for five or more days.

Accommodations

Lodging at Snowbird, which is all within walking distance of the base lifts, can be reserved at **Snowbird Central Reservations** 800-453-3000.

The Cliff Lodge ($$$-$$$$) spreads like an eagle's wings at the base. It has a **renowned spa** (see **Other Activities**), a rooftop pool, hot tubs, and mountain-view rooms with windows from the showers that have a view into the sleeping area and out to the vista beyond (there's a shower curtain you can pull for modesty). As part of the 2006 renovation, rooms also have flat-screen TVs, new bedding, bath fixtures, and artwork. Spa-level rooms feature Tempur-Pedic beds. The Cliff Lodge also has suites. Children younger than 12 stay and ski free with adults.

The **Lodge at Snowbird** ($$-$$$$), **The Inn** ($$-$$$$), and the **Iron Blosam Lodge** ($$-$$$$) are three condominium complexes with similar layouts. They're not as elegant or as expensive as the Cliff Lodge but are well maintained, roomy and comfortable. Amenities include outdoor swimming pools, indoor hot tubs and saunas. Rates start at $125 for an efficiency or studio during value season and top out at $539-$819 for a one-bedroom with loft during winter season.

Dining

The **Aerie Restaurant** (801-933-2160, $$$; reservations recommended) on top of the Cliff Lodge, is considered one of Utah's best restaurants. The Asian decor is elegant and tasteful, the views from the large picture windows spectacular and the food and piano player excellent. The adjacent **Aerie Sushi Bar** ($-$$) serves fresh hand-rolled sushi. At ground level of the Cliff Lodge's atrium, the **Atrium Restaurant** ($-$$) is fine for baked goods and espresso, a lunch buffet or snacks. **El Chanate** ($-$$) on Level A of the Cliff Lodge is the place for Mexican fare.

At the Iron Blosam Lodge, **The Wildflower** (801-933-2230; $$; reservations recommended) features outstanding Mediterranean cuisine. **The Lodge Bistro** ($$-$$$) in the Lodge at Snowbird has a cozy atmosphere with an eclectic bistro menu. The **Steak Pit** ($$$) in the Snowbird Center at the base of the mountain specializes in steaks and seafood. The rest of the eateries in the Snowbird Center cater to the ski crowd, serving breakfast and lunch. For sit-down service, **The Forklift** ($) has great sandwiches and salads, plus a large fireplace. For the best lunch value, go to the pasta bar at **The Rendezvous** cafeteria for huge servings of made-to-order pasta for $7.95. There's also a well-stocked salad island and the usual cafeteria fare. **Pier 49 San Francisco Sourdough Pizza** has sourdough pizza with lots of toppings. **Birdfeeder** has gourmet coffee fare and light snacks.

At Snowbird Center you'll find a grocery and deli with a take-out breakfast and lunch counter. Its liquor store is closed on Sundays and holidays.

Apres-ski/nightlife

Snowbird's ski and snowboard resort's nightlife is very quiet. For the liveliest apres-ski parties, try **Tram Club** on the bottom floor of the Snowbird Center. It has retro decor and a picture-window view of the tram's huge operating gears. It's your best bet if you want to dance. Sporting events are showcased on about a dozen TVs. **The Wildflower Lounge** is mellow and has a good bar menu. **The Aerie** has a bar with live jazz several nights a week. There's the usual bar menu plus fresh sushi apres-ski specials. **The Aerie** serves $10 cheese fondue from 5-6 p.m. **El Chanate Cantina**, which specializes in margaritas, is also a great place for Utah microbrews. They also serve $1 tacos from 4-5 p.m.. Watch sports events on four TVs, listen to live acoustic music, or spin something on the jukebox.

Remember: The nightspots are "private clubs" that charge a $4 three-week membership fee. If you are staying at a Snowbird lodge, the membership is included with your accommodations; however, the Tram Club is owned separately and requires its own membership. At

Dining: $$$$–Entrees $30+; $$$–$20–$30; $$–$10–$20; $–less than $10.
Accommodations: (double room) $$$$–$200+; $$$–$141–$200; $$–$81–$140; $–$80 and less.

night, you can take the free Snowbird shuttle to and from the Snowbird Center and the various restaurants and nightspots at the lodges. If you're staying at the Cliff Lodge, you can walk down some stairs and across the Chickadee novice slope to get to the Snowbird Center. However, we recommend the shuttle, which runs until 11 p.m. (sometimes later). The walking route is slippery and you'll be dodging skiers, snowboarders and others who use that slope at night.

Other activities

Ice skating is available at the Cliff Lodge on an outdoor rink; skate rentals available. You can go night skiing for $7 on the Chickadee novice slope outside the Cliff Lodge on Wednesday, Friday, and Saturday until 8:30 p.m. Snowmobile tours zip you through the awesome backcountry of Mineral Basin. Snowbird also offers guided backcountry tours with the resort's ski patrollers. All tours are dependent upon weather conditions, ability level and time availability; reservations required.

Snowbird is promoting backcountry safety awareness: An **Avalanche Rescue Training Center**, which simulates finding buried avalanche victims, is free for anyone who wants to practice. Call **Wasatch Backcountry Rescue** (801-933-2156).

Little Cottonwood Canyon has spectacular helicopter skiing available from **Wasatch Powderbird Guides** (800-974-4354; 801-742-2800) based between Snowbird and Alta.

The 27,000-square-foot **Cliff Spa and Salon** (801-933-2225 for the spa, 801-933-2268 for the salon), on the top floor of the hotel has 23 treatment rooms and a variety of treatments for body, face, hair and nails. You'll also find an exercise facility, a rooftop pool and hot tub and extensive yoga classes.

There are also **backcountry tours, ice skating, snowshoeing, snowmobiling** and **$7 night skiing**. For information on entertainment, contact **Entertainment & Special Events** 801-933-2110. A champion shopper will finish off the dozen or so shops in half a day. However, the **Salt Lake Valley**, where you'll find more extensive shopping, is a short drive away.

Getting there and getting around

By air: Salt Lake City is a major airline hub, so flights are numerous. Many well-organized companies provide ground transportation. When you make lodging reservations, ask about ground transportation arrangements and most will make them for you. You also can go directly to the shuttle desks in the airport.

By train: Amtrak's California Zephyr stops in Salt Lake City (at 4 a.m. coming from the West Coast but the fare is most reasonable. From Chicago, the train arrives at midnight). Call 800-872-7245 or consult the Amtrak Web site at www.amtrak.com.

By car: Snowbird is 25 miles southeast of Salt Lake City in Little Cottonwood Canyon. The most di-rect route from downtown and the airport is east on I-80, south on I-215, take 6200 South exit (turns into Wasatch Blvd.) then follow the signs.

Getting around: If you fly in, don't bother renting a car—Snowbird is entirely walkable. A free Snowbird shuttle also will get you to various points within the resort complex. Free bus service links Alta and Snowbird. If you plan to ski a lot of other Utah areas, stay in Salt Lake City (see SLC chapter). Public transportation makes it easy to get from the city to the resorts.

Brighton
Utah

Summit:	**10,500 feet**
Vertical:	**1,745 feet**
Base:	**8,755 feet**

Address:
12601 Big Cottonwood Canyon Road,
Brighton, Utah 84121
Telephone (main): 801-532-4731
Snow Report Number: 801-532-4731
Toll-free reservations: 800-873-5512
E-mail: info@brightonresort.com
Internet: www.brightonresort.com

Expert:★★★
Advanced:★★★★
Intermediate:★★★★
Beginner:★★★★
First-timer:★★★★

Lifts: 7—4 high-speed quads, 1 triple, 1 magic carpet
Skiable acreage: 1,050
Snowmaking: 20 percent
Uphill capacity: 10,950
Parks & pipes: 3 parks, 1 pipe
Bed base: About 50 (resort); 17,336 (Salt Lake City)
Nearest lodging: Walking distance
Child care: No
Adult ticket, per day: $58 (08/09 price)
Dining:★★
Apres-ski/nightlife:★★
Other activities:★★

Brighton is a no-frills resort that got 600 inches of snow last season, which made local skiers and riders very happy campers.

Founded in 1936, Brighton is Utah's oldest resort. It still retains its old-time charm, even though there have been many modern updates. The people here are low-key and friendly and it just feels like home.

The resort's two "sides" offer distinctly different experiences. The Majestic side is a forest of evergreens with winding and twisting narrow trails. In fact, Brighton offers the most extensive tree skiing of the four Cottonwood Canyons resorts. You can spend all day in the woods, coming out only for meals and lift rides. The Millicent side is more like what you'd expect out West with bowls, cliffs and wide-open spaces. Brighton has wide forgiving intermediate runs, a fact that makes the mountain attractive to Utahans just learning to ski and snowboard.

Brighton has some true expert terrain that provides access via its open-boundary policy to some of the best backcountry terrain in Utah. If our expert rating included the out-of-bounds terrain, it would deserve at least four, if not five, stars. We recommend that out-of-staters head into the backcountry with a local guide. And always stop by the ski patrol shack to get the latest news on avalanche danger and words of wisdom for the conditions of the day.

Brighton was one of the first Utah resorts to embrace snowboarding and, as a result, snowboarders remain quite loyal. The combination of exciting terrain, fabulous terrain parks, lots of snow and low prices adds to the resort's popularity with riders.

The neighboring resort in Big Cottonwood Canyon is **Solitude**. Together, these two resorts offer an incredible variety and depth of terrain. Brighton and Solitude offer a joint lift ticket allowing you to ski/ride both mountains, so make sure to inquire if you are interested. Brighton also has night skiing and riding with 20 lighted runs that include the parks and pipes.

The huge Brighton Center houses lift ticket sales, rental and retail shops as well as restrooms and lockers. Its cleanly utilitarian, Western appearance is appealing—a cross between log cabin and military barracks. There is a new day lodge at the bottom of the Millicent high speed quad. There isn't much to do here once the lifts close, but Brighton regulars like it that way.

Vacationers who want to taste the region's wide variety of skiing, riding and off-mountain activities may want to consider staying in nearby Salt Lake City.

Mountain layout

Brighton regulars refer to the "Majestic" side, served by the Majestic and other chairs, and the "Millicent" side, served by the new high-speed quad Millicent chair. Keep in mind that most runs are marked easier than they actually are, compared to other ski areas you may be used to, and many of the runs are relatively short.

Expert, Advanced: Nearly forty percent of Brighton is rated advanced or expert. The major portions of that terrain are found on the far side of skier's right (Majestic) and skier's left (Millicent) at higher elevations.

Millicent has less intermediate-level skier/rider traffic. The area holds some terrific in-bounds bowl and cliff skiing, including some smaller natural features perfect for those who are not overly daring or who are new to backcountry-style sliding. Steep open lines are found on Scree Slope and Lone Pine. Precipitous pitches can also be found on Spaghetti, while Captain Hook presents sharp pitch amongst trees.

The Cliff Area offers genuine out-of-bounds territory that's readily accessed from Millicent. But, even though it's within eyeshot of the marked pistes, it pays to go in with someone who knows the territory.

The old Millicent chair once a high-adventure to ride and a challenge to anyone who suffered from vertigo has been replaced by a new high-speed quad, that will change how the mountain skies and rides allow skiers and riders to pack more vertical than ever into a day.

The Majestic side, too, offers excellent challenges, highlighted by a short, heart-stopping run called Hard Coin off the Snake Creek Express. The trees are sometimes so thick you can hardly pick a line. It's exhilarating. A bit of hiking leads to a nice reward at the gladed Snake Bowl.

From the Great Western Express quad, four sheer, open-sloped challenges can be accessed: Endless Winter, Rein's Run, Clark's Roost and True Grit; each is a bit shorter than the last, but all get the legs pumping.

Some tree-skier favorites: Sawbuck and the trees between it plus Doyle's Dive, both off the Snake Creek Express; from the Crest Express Chair, the trees off skier's left of Wren Hollow (don't go too low, or you'll have to hike out of Cliff Area) and off Pacific Highway, just past Tantamount; from the Great Western Express quad, the glades between trails (scope it out from the lift) and those just outside the boundary line (careful: cliffs).

Brighton maintains an open-boundaries policy, allowing experts to ski/ride the backcountry as they wish. Just don't go alone, carry the appropriate equipment (minimally a beacon, probe and shovel), ask about current avalanche conditions and make sure someone knows where you've gone.

Advanced sliders are well-served, too. The Millicent chair accesses fine adventures on Devil's Dip, Chute 2, Boll Weevil, Exhibition and a long gallivant down Evergreen. On the Majestic side, the Great Western quad accesses Elk Park, which connects to Aspen Glo, Golden Needles, Silver Spur Desperado and Elk Park Ride, creating long, delightfully textured scrambles that mostly finish with generous intermediate cruises to the bottom. For moguls, try Rockin'R.

Intermediate: Intermediates have the run of practically the whole area. The Majestic side has trails with gentler pitches while the Millicent side is a bit steeper and more wide-open.

On the Majestic side, Western Trail, off the Great Western quad, has fabulous views. Thor, off Snake Creek Express, is a rolling and rollicking trail that gets you whooping and hollering. Pioneer, off Snake Creek, is a great cruiser. The Elk Park Ridge run descends 1,745 feet, summit to base, from the Great Western chair. The lower section is single-diamond because once you reach the end of the ridge, you'll have ungroomed snow. If you don't like skiing the ungroomed, branch off at Golden Needle for the rest of the way down.

If you're interested in testing out the trees, try any of the woods near the bottom of the mountain such as those off Hawkeye and Scout. Once you get comfortable there, dip in and out of the woods wherever it looks fun.

Beginner, First-timer: From the Brighton Center base, good beginner runs like Mary Back and Lost Maid descend from the Majestic chair. From the top of the Majestic, make your way over to the Snake Creek Express which goes to the top of Preston Peak. Beginners should keep an eye out so they don't get onto an intermediate trail: Greens and blues do a lot of intertwining here. Grooming, which is usually seamless, can make all the difference.

Brighton has a stellar reputation as the place where Utah skiers learn. One of the reasons is that skiers 10 and younger ski free and Utah families tend to be large in number. The Explorer chair serves two trails on a gentle slope apart from general traffic and is a great area for first-timers and beginners as well. Best for beginners to stay away from the Great Western Express and Millicent chairs, as they serve mostly black and double blacks with no easy way down. There is a "magic carpet" lift for the ski school.

Parks and pipes

Brighton's parks and pipe have been going off for more than a decade. Years before most resorts even allowed snowboarding, Brighton was building and grooming tabletops and pipes for its riders.

Off the Majestic lift lives "Big Bertha," a 30- to 50-foot tabletop. On a typical sunny day many locals will be spinning 7s and rodeos while flying 50 feet through the air. After Bertha there usually is another tabletop that leads to the superpipe. The superpipe is about 500 feet long with walls up to 14 feet. As it runs due north, the sun hits it evenly through out the day and it doesn't warp the walls.

Another option after Bertha is to go rider's right toward a rail and box section. This area was designed and built by Jarred Winkler, the pipe and park creator. Winkler is responsible for making all the rails, boxes and walls at Brighton as well as for a lot of the other resorts in the West. The park is constantly evolving so, depending on the mood of the crew, the set up is always changing. There are usually 15 to 20 features on this run which can all get pretty gnarly.

Getting off the Crest Express, head toward the My-Oh-My park. Here there are three tabletops in a row, all with three different-sized lips. These lips range from a foot or two of air, to 15 to 25 feet. The My-Oh-My section drains out to "Candy Land." This spot houses 10 to 15 rails and boxes and is the area to fine tune technical jibbing skills.

Off the backside of the Majestic lift is the learner park where beginners can experience hitting jumps or rails for the first time. Easy, low-consequence boxes and rails are set up here and tiny tabletops are available to learn technique and style.

Snowboarding

Brighton was the first mountain in Utah to allow snowboarding, and thus bred some of the best riders in the sport. Brighton should be on every rider's list to check out at some point.

Seeing and riding the resort that helped spawn some of the roots of snowboarding is essential in everyone's snowboarding career. The terrain at this mountain has undoubtedly helped push the sport to where it is today and it still produces some of the best riders.

On the far north side of the resort lays the Millicent (a.k.a. Milly) and Evergreen lifts. Here, the layout resembles one big natural terrain park. It's easy to link up a cliff band, chute, gully, open bowl and a natural kicker all in the same run. As the Milly lift approaches the top it climbs over "Killer," which is a 20- to 45-foot drop off a shear cliff. It has won more battles than it has lost.

Riding south, the next lift is the Crest Express. This is the main lift used to access the parks and pipe. Along with man-made features, there are a lot of steep, short shots through the trees and some open groomers. Watch out for the flat spots because it's easy to get stuck on deep powder days. Hugging the rider's left boundary line via Wren's Hollow leads to the "Rock Garden" (huge drops out of bounds).

Staying rider's right goes to the My-Oh-My terrain park. There are about five runs total, all of which funnel down to the Snake Creek Express. This high-speed quad accesses mellow, but perfect, tree runs and wide-open intermediate groomers. The Sunshine trail is great for carving turns or cruising. Staying right off this trail traverses toward Thor and Thunderhead, which are open, ungroomed areas with some moguls and small rock drops.

On the far east end of the resort is the Great Western Lift (a.k.a. GW). This is the place to hit after a big snowfall. The most challenging terrain is reached from this lift. Riding out the Great Western Trail, the run traverses over unlimited lines down some of the steepest terrain this mountain has to offer. For a mellower route go out the Elk Park Ridge. Off this ridge it's possible to charge down perfectly spaced aspens or rip down Aspen Glow or Golden Needle—both wide-open groomers.

Cross-country & snowshoeing (see also xcskiresorts.com)

At 8,700 feet between Solitude and Brighton, the **Solitude Nordic Center's Silver Lake Day Lodge** (801-536-5774) is a spectacular setting for cross-country skiing and snowshoeing. It has 20 km. of prepared trails for both classic and skating styles, plus ski and snowshoe rentals, lessons, light snacks and guided backcountry tours.

Lessons 08/09 prices)

Group lessons: For skiers and snowboarders, $40 for two hours. Also offered on Thursday nights for $40 (includes lift ticket at night). "The Works" package includes a group lesson, all-day ticket and all-day rentals for $95.

First-timer package: Includes a full day of rentals, beginner lift ticket and a two-hour group lesson, skiing or snowboarding, for $75.

Private lessons: $85 for one hour with each additional person $25. A 2.5-hour lesson costs $185; additional person, $60. All-day with lift pass is $305; additional person, $75. Reservations recommended; call 801-532-4731.

Special programs: Includes clinics for women, Burton Method Center Learn-to-Ride, parks and pipe, telemark and adaptive. Inquire at the ski and snowboard school.

Children's programs (07/08 prices)

Child care: Brighton Ski Resort does not offer non-skiing child care. See below for children's lessons.

Children's lessons: A full-day program with lesson, lunch and lift ticket for ages 4–12 costs $100; half day with lunch, $65. Two-hour ski or snowboard lessons also are available for $40. Rentals are an additional $15.

Lift tickets (07/08 prices)
- Adult $58; Child (7-12) $25

Who skis free: Ages 6 and younger, two children per paying adult with no restrictions or blackout dates.

Who skis at a discount: Ages 70 and older pay $20. A beginner lift pass, good on two lifts, is $32. A single-ride ticket is $12. Night skiing and riding costs $32.

Accommodations

The **Brighton Lodge** (800-873-5512; 801-532-4731; $$-$$$) is small, cozy, has a hot tub and is at the base of the lifts. Continental breakfast is included. Kids 10 and younger stay and ski/ride free (limit two per adult). **Mt. Majestic Properties** (888-236-0667) rents a tremendous selection of cabins and chalets right on the Brighton Circle with the easiest access to the resort. **Silver Fork Lodge** (888-649-9551; 801-533-9977; $$-$$$) just down the road is a peaceful, rustic mountain retreat. There's a sauna, weight room, ping pong and foosball table and a common room with a TV.

Dining

The **Alpine Rose** ($) is the main slopeside cafeteria that serves big hearty breakfasts, lunch and dinner. Try the barbecue on the sundeck. The **Brighton Chalet** ($) at the base of Mt. Millicent, serves quick meals. The slopeside **Molly Green's** ($-$$) is the place for sit-down pub service and local brews. Locals like to head down the road to the **Silver Fork Lodge** (801-533-9977, $-$$$) for all their meals.

Apres-ski/nightlife

Head to the slopeside **Molly Green's**, a rustic A-frame filled with chatter, or go to **Solitude**. For more lively nightlife, make the trip to Salt Lake City.

Other activities

There's nothing available here at the mountain. However, Salt Lake City offers a myriad of activities.

Getting there and getting around

By air and train: Numerous flights and Amtrak both serve Salt Lake City. Many companies provide ground transportation. When you make lodging reservations, ask and most properties will make arrangements or go to airport shuttle desks.

By car: Brighton is about 25 miles southeast of Salt Lake City in Big Cottonwood Canyon on State Hwy. 190 (Big Cottonwood Canyon Rd.). The most direct route from downtown and the airport is east on I-80, south on I-215, take 6200 South exit (turns into Wasatch Blvd.), then follow the signs to Solitude and Brighton.

Getting around: If you want to explore or go back and forth to Salt Lake City, a car is your best bet.

Dining: $$$$–Entrees $30+; $$$–$20–$30; $$–$10–$20; $–less than $10.
Accommodations: (double room) $$$$–$200+; $$$–$141–$200; $$–$81–$140; $–$80 and less.

Solitude
Utah

Summit:	**10,035 feet**
Vertical:	**2,047 feet**
Base:	**7,988 feet**

Address: 12000 Big Cottonwood Canyon, Solitude, Utah 84121
Telephone (main): 801-534-1400
Snow Report Number: 801-536-5777
Toll-free reservations: 800-748-4754
E-mail: info@skisolitude.com
Internet: www.skisolitude.com

Expert:★★★★
Advanced:★★★★
Intermediate:★★★★
Beginner:★★★★
First-timer:★★★★

Lifts: 8—3 high-speed quads, 1 quad, 1 triples, 3 doubles
Skiable acreage: 1,200
Snowmaking: 175 acres
Uphill capacity: 14,450
Parks & pipes: 1 park
Bed base: 425 (resort); 17,366 (Salt Lake City)
Nearest lodging: Slopeside, condos & hotel
Child care: None; babysitting available
Adult ticket, per day: $61 (08/09 price)
Dining:★★★
Apres-ski/nightlife:★
Other activities:★

Solitude is aptly named. Tucked away in Big Cottonwood Canyon with neighboring Brighton, it doesn't get the attention of say Snowbird and Alta just one canyon over. There are only 425 beds at the base, so it hardly qualifies as a big resort. All of which is excellent news for those few visitors seeking the trademark solitude and excellent skiing spread over 12,000 acres. "Cozy" might be an over worked adjective, but it certainly applies here. Solitude is family-owned and it shows. Loyal guests come back here year after year and staff members demonstrate the same loyalty (the director of slope-side maintenance, for example, has worked here since 1986).

The base itself suggests an old European mountain town in miniature, complete with a Bavarian-style inn, central clock tower, low-rise condo blocks and stores. Despite its newness, there is an old-world feel. It's quiet during the day and even quieter in the evening when the guests—mostly families—leave the one apres-ski spot, the Thirsty Squirrel, and drift along the snow-banked lanes, first to the small selection of restaurants, and then to an early night in the luxurious condos. But don't be fooled by its size. Especially when combined with Brighton (both resorts are covered in a single lift ticket), Solitude offers a variety and depth of terrain. Solitude has recently opened the new 12,000-square-foot Moonbeam Day Lodge with restaurant, bar, fireside lounge and skier services near the day skiers' parking lot. Adjacent to it, a quad chairlift takes skiers and riders to mid-mountain in the middle of Solitude's best intermediate and beginner terrain.

Mountain layout

Big Cottonwood Canyon's Solitude has excellent terrain for all levels. Skiers and snowboarders easily can progress here. One disadvantage to the trail layout for some groups: If your group includes people at the opposite ends of the ability scale, you'll likely spend your day on different parts of the mountain, but you can always meet up for lunch.

To help new visitors get a better feel for the resort, Solitude's trail map has helpful yellow notes on it. Although the quips are a bit trite —"Honeycomb Canyon: Two words: True Solitude"—the notes really do help decipher the trail map.

Expert, Advanced: Solitude gets far less traffic than the Little Cottonwood Canyon resorts, so the dry Wasatch powder can stay untouched even two days after a storm. Experts should head straight to the Summit or Powderhorn chair. The double-diamonds are short, palm-sweating steeps through the trees and even the single-diamonds don't leave much room for error. For longer runs, hike the ridge above Honeycomb Canyon. But check conditions first and never hike alone. The tree runs off of Eagle Ridge—Navarone and Here Be Dragons—are steep, tight and sometimes set-up.

Honeycomb Canyon is a great place for advanced skiers to hone powder skills. From the traverse, drop in wherever the pitch and powder looks right. Advanced skiers will also enjoy the bowl-like runs from the top of the Powderhorn chair; Paradise, Vertigo and Paradise Lost are open, airy, and leg-screaming steep. For offpiste terrain enthusiasts, the Queen Bess area north of the Honeycomb lift offers great powder skiing.

For fast, steep corduroy—and it usually stays as untracked corduroy well into the day—head to the right off the Eagle Express, the first high-speed chairlift installed in Utah. Challenger is reportedly the steepest groomed run in Utah. Fast turns here are as close to freefalling as many of us want to get. Serenity/F.I.S. feels even steeper, with ungroomed moguls on one side to slow the freefalling feel.

Intermediate: Intermediates have wonderful terrain to choose from. The Powderhorn and Eagle Express chairs have no green runs, just blue and black. If you're at the high end of the intermediate level, you'll like this terrain. If you're new to the intermediate level, try the Sunrise or Apex chairs. Sunshine Bowl is wide open and groomed, so you'll be carving some huge arcs on this one. Other places to let 'em rip: Rumble, Grumble and Stumble. Gary's Glade is a great introduction to glade skiing. You can duck in and out of the trees here. A hidden jewel of glades: the unnamed trees under the Apex chair.

The Summit chair has upper-intermediate runs like Dynamite and Liberty. Eventually you'll meet the runs off the Sunrise chair, which head back to the base. Want a taste of the backcountry? Woodlawn is a marked run that follows the floor of Honeycomb Canyon. On the map it's rated black and blue. Check the grooming report before you head in: When groomed, it's a great advanced-intermediate run—otherwise, it's advanced all the way, with some hefty mogul fields and a short but extremely steep section that looks like it might be a small waterfall in the summer. It's thrilling to watch the higher-level skiers tackling the canyon sides.

Beginner, First-timer: Novices start on the Link chair, a slow-moving lift that serves a nearly flat, very wide, isolated run called Easy Street. This is at the base of the New Moonbeam Lodge and the Snowsports Academy ski school, where all facilities are convenient for beginners. Look for Solitude's Director of Skiing, veteran Olympian Leif Grevie. He's always on site in a handsome Norwegian sweater providing gracious and helpful tips.

Once you conquer the gentle Easy Street run off the Link chair, graduate to the Moonbeam chair, where Little Dollie, Pokey Pine and Same Street will easily take you back down to the base. The Sunrise chair, out of the Village at Solitude, has one green trail, North Star, surrounded by lots of gentle blues that afford variety. Don't worry about hotshots on your beginner trails. However, the green slopes tend to be crowded, so be aware of beginning skiers who might not always be in control. The Apex chair is a good place for advanced-beginners. All the trails are rated blue here, but they are gentle and some are wide open, so if grooming is good, advanced-beginners should have no trouble.

Snowboarding

To sum up Solitude Resort, it's all in the name—secluded, and all to yourself. This mountain has steeps, bowls, tight tree shots and backcountry access to some of the sickest lines around.

Starting on the west side of the resort off the Eagle Express quad there's a group of several wide intermediate groomers. Staying far rider's left hooks up with Challenger, one of the steepest groomed runs in Utah. Dropping the fall line off the quad runs into the Sunshine Bowl, which is probably the most open shot the mountain has.

After passing the Sunshine Grill restaurant, cruise through the flat area and onto Main Street, another super wide-open groomer that runs all the way to the bottom by the Powder Horn lift. Half way up the Powder Horn lift, some unbelievable lines start to come into view. Steep, perfectly spaced tree shots are right under the lift. As the lift approaches the top, another area comes into sight with about six black diamond runs off to the rider's left. On a powder day this is the spot to fly as fast as possible laying out a wide turn or two every hundred vertical feet or so.

Heading south or rider's right off Powder Horn are Solitude's steepest runs. The three double-black diamond runs are Parachute, Middle Slope and Milk Run. Most of these shots start off with a 40-degree angle or steeper pitch and run for hundreds of vertical feet. At the bottom of these runs, cliff bands start emerging with a few fun chutes. Eventually most of these runs funnel down to the Summit lift. The terrain off the Summit lift is unreal. On the left side of the chair is the Evergreen ridge hike that separates Solitude from Brighton Resort. The lines off this ridge are all north facing and consistently have the best snow on the mountain. Choose lines carefully because it is easy to get cliffed out.

At the midpoint of the Summit lift the views get intense. On the lift's left lies a good-size pitch of steep glades called the Headwall Forest—at the bottom of this shot, keep a lot of speed to make it through a long flat spot. However, if you don't make it, there is only about a one- to two-minute walk that is well worth the sick shot. Additionally, on the lift's right, giant cliff bands and a few chutes are visible and these are only a few minutes away.

Once the Summit lift ride is over, prepare to be blown away by the view into Honeycomb Canyon. Fantasy Ridge climbs up and down the far end of Honeycomb Canyon and is accessed from this point when open. This ridge hike is crazy. It is really exposed and hairball—a slip in the wrong section would definitely result in a run to the nearest hospital. However, after completing the hike the rewards are sweet. Cirque-sized chutes and bowls are everywhere. It would take years to explore all of the possibilities found in this area of the resort. Another option is to take the traverses left or right. The left traverse usually is not snowboard friendly, but the right traverse is a little better. With some skating, sidestepping and walking it is possible to reach the amazing lines of the Black Forest. This is another north-facing gem at Solitude and it contains some of the most perfectly spaced trees one could ask for. Dropping anywhere in this paradise will be killer and will eventually empty out at the Honeycomb quad. From here, the short lift ride reaches the ridge back to the front side of the resort. To hit this shot again it's mandatory to take the Powder Horn and Summit lifts to the top. This sequence is definitely a time-consuming lap, but it also helps to conserve the powder days after a storm. Figuring out how and where to ride this mountain is half the fun of the Solitude experience. Pay attention and follow some locals, and the payoffs will be good.

Parks and pipes

Solitude has an excellent beginner park. Almost all of the hits and features have low consequences and are perfect for novice freestylers and kids. There are a few little to mid-size tabletops and a few ride-on rails and boxes. If the park seems a little mellow just start exploring the natural terrain park, which is all over the mountain.

Cross-country & snowshoeing (see also xcskiresorts.com)

At 8,700 feet between Solitude and Brighton, the **Solitude Nordic Center's Silver Lake Day Lodge** (801-536-5774) is a spectacular setting for cross-country skiing and snowshoeing. It has 20 km. of prepared trails for both classic and skating styles, plus ski and snowshoe rentals, lessons, light snacks and guided backcountry tours. During full moons, you can do moonlight cross-country skiing.

Lessons (08/09 prices)

First-timer package: Rentals, beginner lift ticket and a half-day morning lesson costs $115.

Private lessons: One hour costs $110 and $25 per additional person. A two-hour lesson at 9 a.m. or 1 p.m. costs $200 plus $25 for each additional person. A three-hour lesson costs $255 plus $35 for each additional person. A six-hour lesson costs $425 plus $35 for each additional person.

Racing: Solitude has an electronically timed, side-by-side dual course on the Main Street trail, open every day, weather permitting.

Children's programs (07/08 prices)

Child care: Play Academy is available for 4 and younger, $85 for a full day, or $15 an hour. Children's Play N Ski programs for kids ages 2 – 4 from 9 a.m. until 4 p.m. cost $155 and include a minimum of two hours spent skiing. Participants should bring their own equipment and clothing. Lift and lunch is included.

Children's lessons: Because Solitude is so family-oriented, its Moonbeam Ski & Snowboard Academy is one of the resort's strengths. Everything required to get kids outfitted, out onto the slopes—and fed, too—is under one roof. Ski lessons are offered for kids ages 4–12; snowboard lessons are for ages 7–12. The full-day program with lift ticket and lunch is $105; a half day without lunch is $65. Multiday packages available. Rentals cost $15 per day. A learn-to-ski or -snowboard package includes all-day lesson, rentals, lift ticket and rentals for $120. Private one-hour ski lessons for kids ages 2–4 and private snowboard lessons for kids 4–7 cost $75; reservations required.

Other activities: Club Solitude keeps kids busy with an outdoor heated pool and hot tub, a movie room, billiard room and kids-only game room featuring X-boxes. The village center is anchored by a skating rink.

Lift tickets (08/9 prices)

Adult $61; **Child** (7-13) $39

Who skis free: Ages 6 and younger ski for free, but need to get a ticket.

Who skis at a discount: Ages 70+ pay $40.

Note: Solitude is ahead of other North American resorts in its ticketing system. It has a Ride Access Card, an electronic ticketing system that allows skiers to pay by the run. It's completely transferable, usable on any day during the season and better than purchasing a multiday ticket. It's great for parents with young children (because you can share the ticket and switch babysitting duties); destination guests who only want to ski or ride for a half day; and guests who plan to ski or ride till they drop. The reusable card allows you to pay for individual lift rides, sold in increments of 10. The maximum number of rides the system will take off in a day is 10. So, if you buy a 30-ride ticket, and then ride 30 lifts in one day, you only lose

10 rides and still have two days or 20 rides left. Ten rides (these are 08/09 prices) cost $63; 20 rides, $124; 30 rides, $186; 40 rides, $248; 50 rides, $310. Remember: Help keep ticket costs down by recycling your card when leaving the resort; drop it at any of the convenient locations resort-wide.

Accommodations

Solitude has beautiful Alpine-inspired, base-area lodging—just enough to be a full-service destination resort without the sprawl or crowds. Everything is slopeside, most are ski-in, but none are ski-out since you have to walk a few yards to the lifts. If you like to be first on the lifts, stay here. All on-mountain guests have access to Club Solitude, in Eagle Springs East. Lodging can be booked by calling 800-748-4754.

Eagle Springs West and **Eagle Springs East** ($$$-$$$$) both feature luxurious one- to three-bedroom condominiums with hand-finished furnishings, generous gourmet kitchens, comfortable living areas and balconies. Heated sidewalks surround a large outdoor heated swimming pool with a waterfall, plus a waterslide for kids of all ages. On each side of the pool are 18-person hot tubs.

The Inn at Solitude ($$$-$$$$) has 46 spacious rooms, most with two queen beds (though kings and suites are available). All have terry-cloth robes to wear to the outdoor pool and hot tub, hair dryers, mini-refrigerators, TV with VCR (tape rentals available), and daily newspaper delivery. The Inn also has a full-service spa.

Creekside at Solitude ($$$$) has 18 condos ranging in size from one to three bedrooms. The condos are spacious and well-appointed, and share an outdoor rooftop hot tub. Each unit has a private deck and fireplace, full kitchen and TV with VCR. The three-bedroom units have a jetted tub and four bathrooms, so the person sleeping on the living room sofa has a bathroom, too. **Powderhorn Lodge** ($$$-$$$$) has one-, two- and three-bedroom condos with gas fireplaces, full kitchens and laundry facilities. There's an outdoor hot tub and a pool table in the lobby.

Dining

St. Bernard's (801-536-5508; $$$; reservations) in the Inn is Solitude's fine-dining restaurant, where you'll enjoy fireside meals in an intimate setting. A new chef brings a changed menu with him. Classic American cuisine has an inspired blending of tastes that are guaranteed to make you say "delicious." It's a Wine Spectator's "Award of Excellence" recipient, so you'll find great wines to accompany your meal. It also serves the resort's only formal breakfast ($), with both a continental buffet and made-to-order specialties.

Creekside Restaurant (801-536-5785; $$-$$$), on the first floor of the Creekside condos, serves lunch and dinner. Here you'll find yet another new chef on hand to heighten the dining experience at the resort. We dined on appetizers to get a full sense of the menu. Everything is creative and tastes wonderful. The baked polenta with woodland mushrooms is absolutely out of this world. Entrees range from wood-fired pizzas to pasta, lamb and veal.

A popular option is the **Solitude Yurt** (801-536-5709). Twenty people cross-country ski or snowshoe for 30 minutes to a yurt for a five-course gourmet meal and then ski or snowshoe back (it's a beginner trail both ways and the equipment is included in the cost). Coffee and water are the only provided beverages, but guests may bring their own corked wine and other beverages. The cost is $95, and no children younger than 8 are allowed. Reservations are a must for this, and don't be too disappointed if you can't get in. Salt Lake City residents really enjoy it and hog many of the available spaces.

Solitude's Mexican-themed cafeteria, **Last Chance Mining Camp**, is on two levels and can seat about 400 people. **Sunshine Snacks** on mid-mountain is open for lunch and looks out over "the beach" —one of the best people-watching areas. The **Moonbeam Day Lodge** has a cafeteria-style menu and a roof-top deck. Another place for a quick bite is the **Stone Haus**, a grocery store in the village, or the **Thirsty Squirrel**, which serves items such as panini, nachos and pizza.

 ## Apres-ski/nightlife

The Thirsty Squirrel is the place to head to swap stories, eat, drink and be merry. There's a pool table, wide-screen TV and local beer sold by the pitcher. There's also a beer bar at the **Last Chance Mining Camp** and a bar in the new **Moonbeam Day Lodge**. The village's condo check in/reception building is a state liquor store too, if you want to stock up your condo.

Remember: The nightspots are "private clubs" that charge a $4 three-week membership fee. If you are staying at a Solitude lodge, the membership is included with your accommodations.

 ## Other activities

After the lifts close, it's very mellow here. You can go **ice skating** at an outdoor rink in the village center; skate rentals are available. Club Solitude in Eagle Springs East offers complimentary activities to all on-mountain guests that include a **large-screen movie** in the media room, a **fitness room, billiards**, an **outdoor hot tub and pool**, and a **kids' playroom with board games**, **X-Box, foosball table, and computers with games**. There's also a fireside lounge that's great for relaxing. **Essentials Spa** (801-535-4137 ext. 5510) in the Inn at Solitude is a full-service spa offering facials, body treatments and massages. There are also sessions in yoga, Pilates and Thai stretching.

Getting there and getting around

By air and train: Salt Lake City is a major transportation hub, so flights are numerous. Amtrak also serves the city. Many companies provide ground transportation and it is well organized. When you make your lodging reservations, ask about ground transportation arrangements and most will make them for you. You also can go directly to the shuttle desks in the airport.

By car: Solitude is about 25 miles southeast of Salt Lake City in Big Cottonwood Canyon on Hwy. 190 (Big Cottonwood Canyon Rd.). The most direct route from downtown and the airport is east on I-80, south on I-215, take 6200 South exit (turns into Wasatch Blvd.), then follow the signs to Solitude and Brighton.

Getting around: If you're staying at the resort, you can walk to everything within the village. If you want to really explore and go back and forth between Salt Lake City and the resort, a car is your best bet. the canyon.

If you stay in Salt Lake City, you can take the Utah Transit Authority light rail (UTA TRAX) from downtown and transfer to a UTA ski bus to take you to any of the Cottonwood Canyon resorts. Riders are, naturally, mostly local skiers and mountain employees. Be prepared to make transfers and pay close attention to bus schedules.

Dining: $$$$–Entrees $30+; $$$–$20–$30; $$–$10–$20; $–less than $10.
Accommodations: (double room) $$$$–$200+; $$$–$141–$200; $$–$81–$140; $–$80 and less.

Ogden Region
Snowbasin and Powder Mountain

Ogden Facts
Area information: (800) 255-8824
E-mail: info@ogden.travel
Internet: www.ogden.travel
and www.skiutah.com (Ski Utah)

Dining: ★★★
Apres-ski/nightlife: ★★
Other activities: ★★

About 40 miles north of Salt Lake City is the growing ski city of Ogden. It is becoming a center for the ski and snowboard industry and is the city host for two excellent ski areas.

Ogden, envisioned as a Mormon town, was eventually developed by workers for the railroad in 1869. It has one of America's most picturesque and storied main streets, "Historic 25th Street," plus several hotels and plenty of dining options. In addition, the town is a center for the arts with galleries, theater, opera and orchestra performances throughout the winter.

Above Ogden, Utah, lies Eden in a hidden mountain valley at the end of a spectacular narrow canyon bordered to the north and south by giant ski and snowboard areas blessed with what many call the world's best snow. They have what are among the world's best views too—from their tops you can see four states: Utah, Wyoming, Idaho and Nevada.

The thinly-settled Upper Ogden Valley gently spreads around the Pineview Reservoir with a smattering of less than a thousand condominiums and private homes with limited restaurants, hotels and almost no nightlife. Once a trading post for fur trappers and pioneers, the valley is slowly beginning its controlled development towards destination resort status.

Powder Mountain extends across the northern border of the local county into Cache County and to the south Snowbasin's shoulders drop into Morgan County. These mountains are expansive, uncrowded and have excellent powder. But that is where their likeness disappears.

Snowbasin, Huntsville, UT; (801) 3991135
Internet: www.snowbasin.com
11 lifts; 2,650 acres; 2,950 vertical feet; 2 terrain parks

Snowbasin, home to the men's and women's Olympic downhill, Super G and combined races in 2002, is new with a tram, two gondolas, a high-speed chairlift and a handful of fixed grip chairs. Groomed trails crisscross the area. Earl's Lodge at the base lodge and Needles and John Paul Lodge at the top of the high-speed lifts are spectacular, modern, massive log buildings. The resort also claims the largest and most modern automatic snowmaking system in the country.

Snowbasin stretches along the southern edge of Ogden Valley. The ski and snowboard area has three distinct sections.

The John Paul Express lift and the Mt. Allen Tram serve Allen's Peak and the No Name area. This sector is rugged with expert slopes dropping steeply through trees. Here is where the downhill courses raged down almost 3,000 unrelenting and twisting vertical feet of terrain.

The center of the resort and the original heart of the trail system traces the mountain from Needles through Middle Bowl and Wildcat Bowl. The Needles Express gondola whisks skiers and riders up 2,310 feet from the base lodge. The degree of steepness declines a touch from that found at Allen's Peak and trails are a bit wider.

The final sector is beneath Strawberry peak served by a gondola, where wide open 2,472 feet of vertical terrain presents expansive bowl skiing and riding.

Lift tickets (07/08 prices): Adults, $62; children (7–12), $39; senior (65–74), $50; $22; children 6 and younger and seniors 75+, free with paying adult.

Powder Mountain, UT; (801) 225-4107; (800) 892-1600

Internet: www.powdermountain.net
7 lifts; 5,500 acres; 2,522 vertical feet

Powder Mountain is a throwback to the way skiing used to be with four chairs and three surface lifts that serve more than 5,500 acres of terrain with most of the resort left untouched by grooming machines. The mountain is replacing their double Hidden Lake chairlift to the top with a detachable high-speed quad which will open for the 2006-07 season. The lodge is rustic, small and cozy with basic soups, salads, scones and burgers. And snowmaking? Forget about it. Nature provides plenty of the real stuff.

This is a massive resort that's bigger than Snowbird and Alta combined. The lifts are few (four chairlifts and three surface lifts) and far between, however they link well with each other. A shuttlebus picks up skiers who drop over the backside. There are only a couple of groomed trails dropping down from the top of each lift. But what you see, you can ski or ride. There is also night skiing at the Sundown Lift from 4 – 10 p.m.

Every morning at 10 a.m., complimentary guides leaving from the Timberline Sports Shop are available to take skiers and riders on tours of the mountain to give everyone an orientation to the massive mountain. These orientation groups are popular and many of the skiers and riders end up signing up for a guide to take them to the best powder at the resort.

Lift tickets (08/09 prices): Adults, $56; children (6-12), $31; seniors (62–69), $44; seniors (70+), $22; ages 5 and younger, free.

Acommodations

The real bed base for both of these mountains is Ogden, only about 20-30 minutes down the mountain through the Ogden Canyon or around Snowbasin looping to the south. All this is only a half-hour north of the Salt Lake City airport. There is a cluster of lodging options in the Upper Valley closer to the ski areas. We start with the Upper Valley. Call (800) 554-2741.

UPPER OGDEN VALLEY: Columbine Inn (801-745-3772 x146; $$), at the base area of Powder Mountain, has affordable rooms ranging from basic double rooms with pull-out couch to three-BR condos with fireplaces right at the base area.

PowMow Condos (801-458-9112),Powder Ridge Condos and Sundown Condos (801-745-3722) have condominiums at the base area as well.

Red Moose Inn (877-745-0333; $$) combines motel convenience, hotel-style amenities and B&B atmosphere. Built in the grand lodge style, even standard rooms are spacious. Most rooms have minimal cooking facilities, but some have full kitchenettes.

Moose Hollow Condominiums (877-745-0333) on the road to Powder Mountain and under the same ownership as Red Moose Lodge, are new and upscale, ranging in size from two to five bedrooms. All have free, high-speed Internet, satellite TV and gas fireplace.

Lakeside Village (800-939-2030), on the shores of Pineview Reservoir, is the collection of condominiums most convenient to Snowbasin that provide real luxury in the Upper Valley.

Dining: $$$$–Entrees $30+; $$$–$20–$30; $$–$10–$20; $–less than $10.
Accommodations: (double room) $$$$–$200+; $$$–$141–$200; $$–$81–$140; $–$80 and less.

Most units have large whirlpool tubs in the master bath and a large outdoor hot tub on the deck. All have extremely well-equipped kitchens (right down to coffee grinders) and washer/dryers; most have fireplaces, and many have garages.

Snowberry Inn (745-2634 or 801-745-2634; $$) is a comfy B&B just 15 minutes from either Snowbasin or Powder Mountain. All rooms (some are pretty small) have private baths; best value is the family suite with kitchen. A full breakfast and afternoon refreshments are included, and there's a billiards table, darts, TV and outdoor hot tub

Jackson Fork Inn (800-609-9466 or 745-0051; $-$$), in Huntsville, has seven knotty pine 2-story suites in a converted dairy barn with complimentary continental breakfast.

All rooms at the riverside **Alaskan Inn** (801-621-8600 or 621-8600; $$$-$$$$) have an Arctic theme. Rates include a full breakfast, delivered to the room or cabin.

OGDEN CITY DOWNTOWN:

Marriott Ogden (888-825-3163; 627-1190; $$) 292 rooms in the middle of the action in downtown Ogden on 24th Street, with high-speed internet access, pool and fitness center. It's the only full service hotel in the area with a restaurant and private club for apres-ski.

Hampton Inn & Suites (800-486-7866 or 394-9400) is built in an historic downtown building. Free high-speed internet and local phone calls, plus a hot tub and fitness room.

Best Western High Country Inn (800-594-8979 or 394-9474) sits at Exit 347 off I-15 at 12th Street. It's only 35 minutes to the SLC airport and also to the ski areas. The hotel has a heated outdoor pool and hot tub. **Comfort Suites** (800-462-9925 or 621-2545) off 21st Street is a well appointed place with 142 rooms with an indoor pool and hot tub. It is within 30 minutes of the airport and the major ski areas.

Also check out the **Historic Ben Lomond Hotel**, (877-627-1900) and **Holiday Inn Express** (800-465-4329) in the Ogden area.

Dining

Dining at Powder Mountain

Dining here is a throwback to the 1970s in both atmosphere (rustic is a kind description) and offerings. The **Powder Mountain Restaurant** at the Resort Center, the largest restaurant on the mountain, serves cafeteria style at the main base area. It's famous for its scones, soups and sandwiches, but don't look for anything green on the menu. Downstairs in the same building the **Powder Keg** is the local watering hole with a selection of draft beers, good burgers, grilled and fried chix sandwiches. **Hidden Lake Lodge**, at the top of the Hidden Lake lift, serves burgers, fries, chili and similar fare along with spectacular views. **Sundown Lodge**, at the base of the Sundown lift, serves a limited menu of cold and hot sandwiches, fries and snacks.

Dining at Snowbasin: Dining here is a cut above the normal mountain fare found at many American resorts. **Earl's Lodge** at the base is framed of Canadian spruce with spectacular views of the mountain. It serves a sit-down meal or upscale cafeteria food.

John Paul Lodge and the **Needles Lodge** on the mountain serve lunches from several self-service stations. Select from soups and sandwiches, pizza and pasta or a daily entree. The lodge is designed in an octagonal layout reminiscent of the Round House at Sun Valley.

Dining in Ogden

The **Roosters Brewing Company and Restaurant** (801-627-6171; $–$$) is one of the town's best places to for a casual meal at a great value. The local homebrews are excellent.

Everyone raves about **Tona Sushi Bar and Grill** (622-8662; $-$$) and are amazed to find a sushi place of this quality is in Ogden. Sushi fans visit numerous times over a visit.

Union Grill (621-2830) in Union Station under the same ownership as Roosters is another local hot spot. The menu is basic American with steaks, chops and soups.

Prairie Schooner (392-2712 or 621-5511; $$–$$$), downtown next to the Ogden Archway, serves steaks, prime rib and seafood in an atmosphere of mini-Conestoga wagons.

La Ferrovia (394-8628) serves good Italian meals right on 25th Street.

The Athenian Restaurant (621-4911) on 25th Street, is the place for Greek food in town with the added attraction of belly dancing Thursdays through Saturdays.

Two-bit Street Cafe (393-1225), started by a New York transplant, serves breakfast at its long bar. This is the only antique store/restaurant on 25th Street.

For breakfast in town head to **Jeremiah's** (394-3273), considered one of the best places in Ogden with wonderful pancakes and cinnamon rolls.

Dining in the Upper Valley

Wolf Creek Resort Restaurants (866-0111 or 745-3737) are on the road to Powder Mountain. **The Grille** provides fine dining and good wines. **The Rusty Cactus** serves basic and filling Tex-Mex meals. **Tracks** is the breakfast spot with huge breakfast burritos.

Gray Cliff Lodge (392-6775), halfway up the Ogden Canyon, is an Ogden institution serving excellent lamb and mountain trout as well as steaks and seafood.

The Oaks (394-2421) also sits in the Ogden Canyon, just above the rushing river. It has been in operation for more than 100 years. Must be some good cookin'.

Jackson Fork Inn (745-0051; $$) serves good brunch on Sundays and dinner during the week. The menu is basic American with a few Italian entrees.

Yukon Grille (745-9293), in Huntsville right on Trappers Village Square, serves meals in a "Western antiques" atmosphere. Breakfast is creative with a Martini Omelet or chicken fried steak and eggs. They also have good Mexican food.

Eats of Eden (745-8618) serves pasta, pizza and sandwiches.

No trip to Ogden's Upper Valley is complete without a visit to the **Shooting Star Saloon** (745-2002), the oldest, continuously running tavern in Utah. While here dare to try a Star Burger, a burger-and-sausage combo that screams heart attack, but they say is harmless. Go, if only to see the stuffed critters, including a jackalope and, yes, a St. Bernard, and the ceiling of $1 bills and to listen to crooners on the jukebox. It is closed on Mondays and Tuesdays.

Red Dog Grill (745-2400) on the road to Snowbasin, is a choice place for breakfast.

Alpine Pizza (745-1900), run by a Chicago native, serves prize-winning pies ranging from the basics to their award-winning Carbonara with Alfredo sauce. They deliver.

Nightlife/Apres-ski

The Shooting Star Saloon (745-2002) Utah's oldest, in the Upper Valley, is a place skiers must have at least one drink. Avoid snacking on a Star Burger if you are planning to dine later in the evening. Don't miss the St. Bernard trophy on the wall. You'll never see another like it.

At Powder Mountain head to the **Powder Keg** for a brew right after skiing or riding. The place will be packed with instructors and others talking about their secret runs.

In downtown Ogden on Historic 25th Street, **Roosters Brewing Company** is on one side of the main street at 253 and **Brewskis** is on the other at 244. **The Wine Cellar** (2550 Washington Blvd.; 399-3600) has jazz most nights. **The City Club** is on 25th Street. **Angelo's Tavern**, also on 25th Street, has live music and a beer garden. **Mojo's** fills with a young crowd for music on Friday and Saturday nights, but no drinking. **Kokomo Club** on 25th Street has pool tournaments and big-screen TV.

Dining: $$$$–Entrees $30+; $$$–$20–$30; $$–$10–$20; $–less than $10.
Accommodations: (double room) $$$$–$200+; $$$–$141–$200; $$–$81–$140; $–$80 and less.

Park City, Utah

Deer Valley

Park City Mountain Resort

The Canyons

Regional Facts
Toll-free information:
(800) 453-1360 (Park City Chamber)
Fax: 649-0532 (lodging)
Internet: www.parkcityinfo.com (town)
Dining:★★★★
Apres-ski/nightlife:★★★★
Other activities:★★★

Walk outside the No Name Saloon at dusk, just as the lights of Main Street begin to twinkle seductively and the sidewalks fill with apres-ski traffic, and you can almost hear the clank of spurs. Squint your eyes and the strolling figures become the miners and cowboys who roamed this same street a hundred years ago, swaggering through 30-odd saloons in what was once one of the country's largest silver mining towns. Soon the vision is gone, and the people are once again modern-day funseekers. Yet the flamboyant atmosphere of the silver rush remains.

Park City originally was founded by soldiers who had been sent west to discourage Brigham Young from ending the Utah Territory's association with the Union. Park City boomed during the mining era, then almost became a ghost town during the Depression and World War II. Now Park City can be counted among the world's top winter resorts. This is the most accessible destination resort of its caliber in the country, just 30 miles from Salt Lake City via a major freeway. Skiers and snowboarders from across the country can leave home in the morning and be making turns at one of the region's resorts that afternoon.

Three world-class resorts surround the mountain city. Each has its own personality and caters to different clientele. Deer Valley doesn't allow snowboarders and banks on exclusivity, perfect service and flawless grooming. Park City Mountain Resort, with lifts right into town, caters to more of the middle- to upper-middle-class intermediate crowd with long, wide cruising trails highlighted with pockets of expert terrain. And The Canyons has carved out a niche for wide-open slopes and good out-of-bounds skiing. They all share the Old West mining atmosphere of Park City and the fine Utah powder.

This chapter is organized with the three resort descriptions leading off, together with supporting mountain-related information such as lessons, lift tickets, child care, and so forth for each of the three mountains. The general Park City information follows, such as town dining, accommodations, apres-ski and other activities.

Park City interchangeable lift ticket (07/08 prices)

The Silver Passport gets you on the lifts at Deer Valley, Park City Mountain Resort and The Canyons. You must advance-book (by 2 weeks) at least three nights of lodging before mid-April, 2009 to purchase the pass. You can use the pass at one resort each day. Snowboarders may not use Deer Valley's lifts, and the pass is not valid the week between Christmas and New Year. Adults pay $237 for three days ($79/day), $316 for four days ($79/day), $395 for five days ($79/day); children ages 6-12 pay $141 for three days ($47/day), $188 for four days ($47/day), $235 for five days ($47/day). More information: Deer Valley Central Reservations, 800-558-3337, Park City Mountain Reservations, 800-222-7275 or The Canyons Reservations, 888-226-9667.

Deer Valley Resort Facts

Summit elevation:	**9,570 feet**
Vertical drop:	**3,000 feet**
Base elevation:	**6,570 feet**

Address: P.O. Box 1525, Park City, UT 84060
Area code: 435
Ski area phone: 649-1000
Snow report: 649-2000 **Fax:** 645-6939
Toll-free information: (800) 424-3337
Toll-free reservations: (800) 558-3337
Internet: www.deervalley.com

Expert:★★★★
Advanced:★★★★
Intermediate:★★★★
Beginner:★★ **First-timer:**★

Number of lifts: 21—1 gondola, 10 high-speed quads, 2 quads, 6 triples, 2 doubles
Snowmaking: 28 percent
Skiable acreage: 1,825 acres
Uphill capacity: 44,100 per hour
Snowboarding: Not allowed
Parks & pipes: 1 park (skiers only)
Nearest lodging: Slopeside
Resort child care: Yes, 3 months - 12 years
Adult ticket, per day: $79 (07/08 price)

Deer Valley Resort

Deer Valley is one of North America's most exclusive resorts. Everything is top notch from the manicured snow conditions to the gleaming brass and glass cafeterias and gourmet restaurants. Deer Valley is as upscale as it gets in America, but without any snobbery that might affect other expensive places in the country. Visitors can relax, enjoy and leave feeling like they have received great value for their dollar. No snowboards, please. This is one of four American resorts that is for skiers only. This noticeably affects the ambiance of the mountain.

The resort itself is just a couple of miles from the historic mining town of **Park City**. Deer Valley is a cluster of condominiums and lush hotels huddled around a spectacular ski area. You can lounge in luxury up on the mountainside or head downtown to have fun in one of America's best ski towns.

Deer Valley is renowned for pampering its guests with top-flight meals, palatial accommodations, attentive service and impeccable slopes. Some of the many amenities include guest service attendants who lift skis off car racks when you drive up to unload, tissues at every lift, restaurants to make a gourmet salivate, free ski corral service where you can safely leave your best equipment and grooming crews who comb the snow so pool-table smooth that everyone skis smoother and better.

Experts who might scoff at the daily slope manicure can ditch the main drag. Scoot directly to the chutes and bowls off Empire Canyon or bumps off the Sultan and Mayflower chairs for advanced terrain. Deer Valley fills a marvelous niche in the ski world, satisfying those who enjoy elegance and are willing to pay a little more for their privileges.

Mountain layout

Keep in mind that there are really six mountains and one canyon here, ranging from Bald Eagle at 8,400 feet to the top of Empire Canyon at 9,570 feet.

Deer Valley has a solid reputation for service, grooming and over-all class, but make no mistake - the skiing is also spectacular for all levels. Slopes include tough trails, challenging terrain as well as plenty of intermediate runs. Beginners and first-timers will enjoy the separate, protected area on Bald Eagle Mountain known as Wide West.

Expert, Advanced: Empire Canyon, topping out at 9,570 feet, is not only the highest point at Deer Valley, but also the gnarliest. The double-diamond Daly Chutes, the Daly Bowl and the Anchor Trees are short, steep and superbly challenging. Single-diamond terrain at Lady Morgan Bowl in Empire adds some nice vertical. The Empire Express accesses the 500 acres of eight chutes and three bowls.

Flagstaff Mountain, with both bump and cruising runs, is easy to navigate and a good rendezvous when several members of your group ski at different ability levels. Experts take a short traverse to the left near the top of the Ontario run to Ontario Bowl's double-diamond tree skiing.

For black diamond terrain, take the Mayflower Lift to the far left on the trail map. Moguls on Morning Star, Fortune Teller, Paradise and Narrow Gauge are a delight. The long trails are bordered by glades—great places to drop into and out of on a whim.

While Mayflower and its neighboring chair, Sultan, feature ungroomed runs, the bumps rarely get too big. Orient Express and Stein's Way are advanced cruisers with good pitch. Perseverance, coupled with the initial steeper sections of Thunderer, Blue Ledge and Grizzly, are all challenging. Also look for the glades at the bottom of the Empire Canyon and Flagstaff areas.

Intermediate: Deer Valley offers both intermediate and advanced-intermediate terrain, though you'll find that the two are quite similarly challenging. If you want to have plenty of company (lots of traffic here) and beautiful scenery, the best runs are Sunset, Birdseye (both on Bald Mountain) and Success (on Bald Eagle Mountain).

Areas with the most intermediate runs are served by the Wasatch Express and Sterling on Bald Mountain and Northside Express on Flagstaff Mountain. Run after run down trails such as Legal Tender, Wizard, Nabob, Sidewinder and Hawkeye are a blast. The runs under the Northside Express are especially cool because they're farther from the base areas so they're not as crowded as the Wasatch Express area.

The Empire Canyon and Deer Crest areas also have some fun slopes. Try the advanced-intermediate bowls Conviction, Solace and Orion. The view of the Jordanelle Reservoir from the Deer Crest area is fabulous. But be forewarned: The double-blue Jordanelle run has one wicked narrow part that might be difficult for newly intermediate skiers. If beginners are skiing this lift, they'd be more comfortable taking Deer Hollow down to the gondola base parking lot.

Other great areas are Flagstaff Mountain and Bald Eagle Mountain, known as the "lower mountain." Last Chance passes by a lot of spectacular homes. New intermediates might want to stick to Deer Valley's green-circle runs at first. The greens here are a bit turquoise, just a shade easier than the true blues.

Beginner, First-timer: Deer Valley's offerings at the beginner and first-timer levels have improved in past years. Best areas are the outside runs on Flagstaff Mountain, Ontario and Mountain Daisy/Banner. Beginners will enjoy ideal terrain and a protected area on Bald Eagle Mountain with access via the Burns and Snowflake lifts. If you're a brave soul who wants practice, cruise Sunset, a gentle, scenic route that descends from the top of Bald Mountain. There's also the Little Chief Family Ski Area in Empire Canyon. Be aware that the green run, Bandana, off the top of Flagstaff Mountain, is a fairly steep green and for expert beginners only.

Parks and pipes

Deer Valley built a skiers-only terrain park called Tricks 'N' Turns (TNT) Park. It's in the Empire Canyon area, off the Little Chief chair, and is geared toward intermediate-level, family-oriented fun. The Ore Cart Rails include funboxes, double barrels, single rails, a few small jumps and some surprises. The Ore Cart Rails are adjacent to the Skier Cross Course on Nugget. The Skier Cross Course is a timed course, $2 per run, with large banked turns, jumps and rolls.

Snowboarding

Deer Valley forbids snowboarding. Head to Park City Mountain Resort or The Canyons instead.

Lessons (07/08 prices)

Reservations are essential for all programs; call 888-754-8477 or 435-645-6648, or book online.

Semi-private lessons: Semi-private Max 4 lessons, limited to four students, have replaced group lessons. A semi-private (all levels) costs $125 and lasts three hours.

First-timer package: None. Take semi-private or private lessons.

Private lessons: Beginners get a one-hour lesson for $135 (up to two skiers). All other ability levels pay $150 for one hour, $415 for three hours, $640 all day (up to two skiers).

Special programs: Women and men have three-day clinics at certain times in the season for $650 (lift ticket included). Mahre Training Center Camps are three-day and five-day camps held in December and January. Camps are taught by Deer Valley instructors, with some coaching from Olympic racers Steve and Phil Mahre. Call the resort for details, prices and reservations.

Racing: A race program called Medalist Challenge is held on the Race Course above Silver Lake Lodge, reachable by the Sterling or Wasatch Lifts. The cost is $10 for two runs and the daily chance to earn a medal. About once a week, Deer Valley's Ambassador of Skiing, Heidi Voelker, a three-time Olympian and 12-year veteran of the U.S. Ski Team, runs the course so you can compare your time to hers.

Children's programs (07/08 prices)

Child care: Ages 3 months to 12 years. Full day for ages 2–12 years, with lunch, costs $96. Full-day infant care, ages 2 months–8 months, including lunch if appropriate, $96. Reservations are essential. Call 645-6648 or reserve when you book lodging. Half-day is sold on space-available basis.

Children's lessons: Full-day programs for ages 3–12 cost $160 for lessons, lift ticket and lunch. Four-year-olds (potty-trained) have the Bambi Program that is a combination of day care and a 2.5-hour ski lesson. Three-year-olds have the Fawn Program that is a combination of day care and a one-hour private lesson. The Reindeer Club is for children 5–6 years. Classes average 4–6 students and meet from 10 a.m. to 3:45 p.m. Cost is $160 for lunch. lessons and lift tickets. The Adventure Club has been **Child care:** Ages 3 months to 12 years. Full day for ages 2–12 years, with lunch, costs $96. Full-day infant care, ages 2 months–8 months, including lunch if appropriate, $96. Reservations are essential. Call 645-6648 or reserve when you book lodging. Half-day is sold on space-available basis.

Children's lessons: Full-day programs for ages 3–12 cost $160 for lessons, lift ticket and lunch. Four-year-olds (potty-trained) have the Bambi Program that is a combination of day care and a 2.5-hour ski lesson. Three-year-olds have the Fawn Program that is a combination of day care and a one-hour private lesson. The Reindeer Club is for children 5–6 years. Classes average 4–6 students and meet from 10 a.m. to 3:45 p.m. Cost is $160 for lunch. lessons and lift tickets. The Adventure Club has been created for children between 7 and 12 years. Groups are limited to 7–10 children. Cost is $160 and it includes lunch, lessons and lift tickets. Ski and boot rentals are offered at a discounted rate of $18 per day. Equipment must be picked up 60 minutes prior to the 9 a.m. program start time, or the afternoon or evening prior.

Reservations are essential for all programs; call (888) 754-8477 or (435) 645-6648, or book online. created for children between 7 and 12 years. Groups are limited to 7–10 children. Cost is $160 and it includes lunch, lessons and lift tickets. Ski and boot rentals are offered at a discounted rate of $18 per day. Equipment must be picked up 60 minutes prior to the 9 a.m. program start time, or the afternoon or evening prior.

Reservations are essential for all programs; call (888) 754-8477 or (435) 645-6648, or book online.

Lift tickets (07/08 prices)

Adult (13-64) $83; Child (4-12) $50
Who skis free: No one.

Who skis at a discount: (07/08 prices) Kids 3 and younger pay $20 per day. Skiers 65 and older pay $56 for a single day; $156 for three days; $250 for five days.

Note: Adults pay $81 during the holiday season. For seven or eight days between Christmas and New Year's, Deer Valley's multiday discounts are suspended. However, ticket sales are limited, so on holidays the extra few bucks to ski Deer Valley are worth it. You can make ticket reservations when you book your lodging. This is highly recommended during the Christmas period and the February Presidents' Day holiday week.

You can catch a morning flight from almost anywhere and and ski Park City slopes the same afternoon, for free! The Park City Quick START (Ski Today and Ride Today) Vacation lets you convert your airline boarding pass into a same-day lift ticket to the Park City resort of your choice: Park City Mountain Resort, Deer Valley Resort or The Canyons Resort. You will need to bring the completed, required online redemption voucher (http://www.parkcityinfo.com/quickstart/), along with your same-day boarding pass and out of state photo I.D., to the resort ticket window, to receive your same-day lift ticket.

Accommodations—Deer Valley Resort

At Deer Valley the lodging has a decidedly upscale style flavor—and tariffs to match. Even in the value season the least expensive starts at about $200 per night. Accommodations have the same high quality one finds at the resort itself. Much of it is slopeside. If it's in your budget, enjoy. If not, find less expensive lodging in Park City—only a short and frequent shuttlebus ride away.

Top dog is the **Stein Eriksen Lodge** (800-453-1302; 435-649-3700; $$$-$$$$). Think of any luxury or service and you will no doubt find it—heated sidewalks between buildings, fireplaces in the rooms, fresh terrycloth robes, floor-to-ceiling windows. The lodge also has a 4,340-square-foot, full-service spa that's open for both guests and the public.

Other places to stay on the mountain include the **Stag Lodge Condominiums, The Chateaux at Silver Lake, The Lodges at Deer Valley, Black Diamond Lodge, Trail's End Lodge, Silver Lake Village and Snow Park**, all with similar luxurious amenities and all bookable through the Deer Valley website ($$$$) Call reservations for individual property details. The **Goldener Hirsch Inn** (800-252-3373; 435-649-7770; $$$$) offers the elegance and service of a top Austrian hotel at midmountain in Deer Valley.

The **Pinnacle Condominiums** ($$$$) have spacious and well-appointed interiors located near the bus stop. Closer to the lifts—actually ski-in/ski-out properties—are the **Pine Inn** ($$$$) and **La Maconnerie** ($$$$). All units have private spas.

The most economical Deer Valley condos are the **Snow Park** ($$$) units, where a one-bedroom without hot tub is about $325 in the regular season.

For reservations in Deer Valley, call **Deer Valley Central Reservations**, (800-558-3337; 649-1000). which offers numerous lodges, condominiums and private homes in the Deer Valley and Park City area.

Dining—Deer Valley Resort

Deer Valley's dining mirrors the overall high quality (and cost) of the resort, but the variety of exquisite places to eat may make it difficult to figure out which will be the site for the special evening of your ski vacation. It's easy to get there from Park City.If you don't have a car, take the free Park City Transit buses which run until 10 p.m. To make advance dinner reservations (recommended) from anywhere in the United States, call 800-424-3337.

The **Mariposa** (435-645-6724; $$$$) at Silver Lake Lodge is the gourmets' top choice. Order off the extensive lunch and dinner menus or get the full "taste" of The Mariposa's treats. Experience a delightful venue for lunch and apres ski. For dinner, try either the Chef's Vegetarian Tasting or a Mariposa Tasting Menu, an expanded six-course variety of the chef's specialties offered in small portions which are carefully paired with wines.

The **Glitretind Restaurant** (435-649-3700; $$$-$$$$) at Stein Eriksen Lodge offers creative, American fare. Glitretind's all-you-can-eat skier's lunch buffet with made-to-order pasta dishes, a carving table, various salads, cold meats and delectable desserts is a quite reasonably priced feast.

The **Seafood Buffet** (435-645-6632) at Snow Park Lodge, served Monday- Saturday evenings, is magnificent. The extensive variety of seafoods offered at this all-you-can-eat buffet is extremely popular. Reservations are suggested. Sample the Dungeness crab and tiger shrimp as well as the delicious roast beef. Dinner (07/08 prices), $60 for adults, $32 for children younger than 12.

Treat yourselves to a three-course, three-fireplace meal served at the **Fireside Dinner at Empire Canyon Lodge** every Wednesday, Thursday and Friday evenings (435-645-6632; reservations suggested.) In front of the Empire Fireplace, make plates of warm raclette, steamed potatoes, pearl onions, cornichons, cured Italian and Swiss meats and fresh baguettes. By the North Fireplace, choose from veal and wild mushroom stew, beef bourguignonne or vegetarian stew, plus a salad with ciabatta. At the Ontario Fireplace, enjoy fruits, cinnamon pound cake, almond biscotti and chocolate fondue. Selected wines and beers are available. Dinner is $50 for adults and $26 for children younger than 12 (07/08 prices). **The Goldener Hirsch Inn** (435-649-7770; $$$) in Silver Lake Village serves breakfast, lunch and dinner in an Austrian setting. Traditionalists will find weinerschnitzel, handmade bratwurst and raclette.

Deer Valley's **Royal Street Cafe** (435-645-6724; $$-$$$), open for lunch and dinner, is a bistro located in the Silver Lake Lodge.

For a great breakfast value, head to the buffet at the Snow Park Restaurant. For lunch go to the Silver Lake Restaurant or Empire Canyon Grill. The food is laid out like a magazine photo. These cafeteria-style restaurants glisten with shiny brass and sparkling glass. Don't miss their delicious signature turkey chili. It's so famous, they package it for take-home. You can buy the dry ingredients in the gift shop to share with friends and family.

Dining: $$$$–Entrees $30+; $$$–$20–$30; $$–$10–$20; $–less than $10.
Accommodations: (double room) $$$$–$200+; $$$–$141–$200; $$–$81–$140; $–$80 and less.

Park City Mountain Resort Facts

Summit elevation:	**10,000 feet**
Vertical drop:	**3,100 feet**
Base elevation:	**6,900 feet**

Address: P.O. Box 39, Park City, UT 84060
Area code: 435
Ski area phone: 649-8111
Snow report: 647-5449 or (800) 222-7275
Toll-free information: (800) 222-7275 (resort)
Toll-free reservations: (800) 927-7694
(Park City Mountain Reservations)
Internet: www.parkcitymountain.com and pcride.com

Number of lifts: 16—4 high-speed six-packs, 2 high-speed quads, 6 triples, 4 doubles
Snowmaking: 14 percent
Skiing acreage: 3,300 acres
Uphill capacity: 27,200 per hour
Parks & pipes: 4 parks, 1 pipe
Bed base: 21,500 (town)
Nearest lodging: Slopeside, condos
Resort child care: None; lessons start at age 3½
Adult ticket, per day: Rates change daily; see Lift Ticket section
Expert:★★★★
Advanced:★★★★
Intermediate:★★★★
Beginner:★★★ **First-timer:** ★★★

Park City Mountain Resort

Park City Mountain Resort is one of three major resorts surrounding the old mining town of **Park City**. Park City's mining heritage is quite evident at the resort, where old mine ruins dot the slopes. The Park City Historical Society has put up signs describing each of the sites so skiers and boarders can get a sense of history as they enjoy the day.

Most reviews of Park City Mountain Resort characterize it as a cruisers' paradise. While it may not have as many steeps as Snowbird or Alta, its bowl skiing and chutes are serious. It doesn't have a huge amount of lower-end terrain, but beginners can get high enough to see the views, something they can't do at every resort. Park City veterans say that it takes three days to ski every run on the mountain, then you can start on the hundreds of unlisted lines.

The Town Bridge that links the ski hill to the heart of Park City allows skiers and riders direct on-snow access to the Main Street hub of Park City. This means you can ski or ride straight to Main Street, have a choice of some 100 restaurants and shops to visit during lunch, and then ride back up the mountain on the Town Lift.

Park City Mountain Resort hosts the winter sport training programs of the National Ability Center. Activities include alpine skiing, snowboarding, bobsled, sled hockey and much more for people of all abilities and their families. Lessons, equipment and accessible, affordable lodging are available. Information: www.parkcityinfo.com and www.discovernac. org/ or phone 435-649-3991.

Mountain layout

The Town Lift triple chair loads from the lower part of Park City's Main Street to the base of the Bonanza lift partway up the mountain. Even on holidays or peak periods, the Town Lift is often empty, so you may want to take the free shuttle here and avoid the crowds

If Payday has a line, try the Eagle chair (to the far right of the base area) and head down blue-square Temptation to the King Con chair.

Expert, Advanced: Start off with a trip to the top of Blueslip Bowl off the Pioneer Lift. Reportedly, when this was the boundary of the ski area, resort workers regularly slipped under the ropes, made tracks down the bowl and then skied back into the resort. The management passed out blue (you're fired) slips to anyone caught floating through this powder bowl.

Jupiter Bowl has every type of steep expert terrain. To reach the Jupiter lift, take the Jupiter access road from the top of the Pioneer or Thaynes lifts. It's a long, flat traverse, so don't lose your speed. To the left as you get off the Jupiter lift are wide-open faces, especially on the West Face, which is the easiest way down (a relative term).

The adventurous (and those with parachutes) will find definite thrills in McConkey's Bowl and Puma Bowl. McConkey's is served by McConkey's Hi-Speed Six-Pack. Puma still requires a long traverse across a ridge and some hiking from either the Jupiter or McConkey's lifts to reach its steep faces and chutes on the backside of Jupiter Peak.

Try the blacks off the Motherlode triple or the neighboring Thaynes double. Glory Hole and Double Jack offer a good challenge. Or, ski the front face on the runs off the Ski Team Lift. Most of the deliciously long trails here are left au naturel, but Willy's is on the occasional grooming list. Hit it on the right day, and it's fun.

Intermediate: Choices are mind-boggling. If you want to start with a worthy cruiser, take Payday from the top of the lift by the same name. The views are spectacular, and at night it becomes one of the longest lighted runs in the Rockies.

Probably most popular are the 11 trails served by King Consolidated (called "King Con" by just about everyone). These runs have a steep, wide, smooth pitch.

Both intermediates and advanced skiers will enjoy the runs under the Silverlode chair.

To avoid crowds, try the four blues under the Pioneer chair. Or, board McConkey's, enjoy the spectacular view, and take the intermediate ridge routes down from the top. If you want to test yourself, look for a grooming report to find out which black-diamond runs have been groomed. The Silver Star lift takes you to three intermediate runs.

Beginner, First-timer: Even those just getting into their snowplow turns can take the Payday and Bonanza chairs to the Summit House and descend the 3.5-mile-long, easy run appropriately named Homerun.

For an adventure and to see a different part of the mountain, take the Mid-Mountain Run to the Pioneer chair, where you can have lunch and watch experts head down Blueslip Bowl.

The only complaint about the beginner runs here is that everyone else uses them too. The upper parts of the green-circle trails are used as access routes, while the bottoms are the end runs for skiers coming off more advanced terrain. The greens here are wide and gentle, but they wind in and around tougher stuff.

For first-timers, the First Time high-speed quad, which slows down during loading and unloading to help ease apprehensions of getting on and off the lift, serves two nice and easy trails. The Three Kings chair takes you a bit higher to more good learning terrain.

Parks and pipes

Both the Town Lift and the Payday Hi-Speed Six-Pack deposit you above the huge terrain park on Payday. The park has a sound system and is lit for night riding. You'll also find a superpipe on Eagle, similar to the one used in the 2002 Winter Olympics. Three additional terrain parks spread out the tricksters on Pick N Shovel, Jonesy's and the King's Crown Superpark. If you're lucky, you'll see the Park City All-Star riders and skiers jibbing in the parks.

Snowboarding

Park City Mountain Resort has some long, nearly flat runs that snowboarders will want to avoid. The two worst ones are Jupiter Access and Thaynes Canyon, both of which are used primarily to reach other parts of the mountain. In particular, Jupiter Access road from the top of the Pioneer or Thaynes lifts is a long, flat traverse, so don't lose your speed. You can avoid the worst traverses with advance planning. However, snowboarders have a bit of an advantage in Park City's hike-to powder bowls, because they get to hike to the best stuff in soft boots.

The best all-around freeriding area is below Home Run between the Claim Jumper and Parley's Park runs. Three lifts can get you there: Silverlode Hi-Speed Six-Pack, Motherlode Lift and Bonanza Hi-Speed Six-Pack. There are some good cuts through the trees, plenty of bumps and some wide smoothies good for kicking up the speed.

Lessons (06/07 prices)

Prices below are for regular season. Value season has lower prices.

Group lessons: For beginners and intermediates, $75 for three hours (ski or snowboard). Intermediate and expert skiers choose from skill workshops such as fine-tuning parallel turns, black-diamond terrain, moguls and all-mountain skiing, $75 for three hours. Power clinics train technical skiers for $35. Advanced snowboarders and better can choose between freeriding or park and pipes workshops, $75 for three hours.

First-timer package: The Learn to Ski Preferred Experience uses specially designed skis and is limited to five students. The Learn to Snowboard Preferred experience uses specially designed snowboards and is limited to four students. These all-day programs cost $175 for lesson and rentals. Lift tickets are extra. Reservations required; call 800 222-7275. A three-hour group lesson is also available for $75 (beginner lift ticket included; rentals extra).

Private lessons: For one person: $120 for one hour, $240 for two hours; $530 for six hours. Discounts are available for up to six people.

Racing: NASTAR is on the Blanche trail Wednesday through Saturday. Two runs cost $6; each additional run is $1. Park City Dual Challenge is set up on Clementine nearly every day. The cost is $1 per run; $5 for seven runs.

Children's programs (08/09 prices)

Childcare: Park City Mountain Resort does not provide child-care services. The Park City Chamber of Commerce can refer visitors to **child-care facilities** or **babysitting services**. Call 800-453-1360 or 435-649-6100. The "angels" of **Guardian Angel Babysitting Service** 453-783-2662 guard in-room, plus rent baby gear and shop for your groceries. **The Clubhouse** at 780 Main Street offers drop-in childcare from the age of 3 months to 12 years (also in-room babysitting services). The Clubhouse is about 100 yards from the Town Lift at the Marriott Summit Watch Courtyard; (435)940-1607 or www.parkcityclubhouse.com. **Baby's Away** (800-379-9030; 435-645-8823) rents and will deliver baby needs to your lodge, such as cribs, strollers, car seats and toys.

Children's lessons: Prices are for regular season, which covers most of the season; prices during value season are lower. Ages 6–14, $210 for a full day including lift ticket and lunch. The Kid's Signature 5 Program guarantees there will be no more than 5 students per instructor. Snowboard lessons start at age 7. A parks and pipes program is available for advanced snowboarders for the same cost. Children ages 3–5 have a program that includes lesson, lift ticket, rentals, lunch and indoor activities for $145 (three kids per instructor). Discounts for multiday lessons are available.

A one-hour ski-only private lesson costs $120 and is available on the hour.

First-timers must take the Children's Learn to Ski/Snowboard Preferred Experience, a full-day group lesson that costs $175 with lift ticket and rental of specially designed gear to help them learn. This class is limited to five students and success is guaranteed; if your child isn't riding the chair and turning on the beginner runs by the end of the day, another lesson is free.

Reservations are required for all children's programs; call (800) 222-7275.

Lift tickets (07/08 prices)

Adult $79

Who skis free: Kids 6 and younger with paid adult.

Notes: Park City Mountain Resort uses a variable pricing structure depending upon conditions (snow, weather, crowds, etc.). This means if you buy tickets at the window, you will most likely pay a premium rate. The only way to get a guaranteed price is to purchase tickets at least seven days in advance; good on multiday tickets only. A good way to estimate what you might pay at the ticket window on any given day is to note the cost of a two-day advance-purchase ticket and expect to pay at least half that price, which would amount to $79 for a day ticket in the 2007-08 season. To purchase multiday tickets, call Guest Services at (800) 222-7275 or book online. Early-season and value-season prices are lower. The resort has night skiing and riding from 4-7:30 p.m. Call for prices.

Ski Today and Ride Today: You can catch a morning flight from almost anywhere and and ski Park City slopes the same afternoon, for free! The Park City Quick START (Ski Today and Ride Today) Vacation lets you convert your airline boarding pass into a same-day lift ticket to the Park City resort of your choice: Park City Mountain Resort, Deer Valley Resort or The Canyons Resort. You will need to bring the completed, required online redemption voucher (http://www.parkcityinfo.com/quickstart/), along with your same-day boarding pass and out of state photo I.D., to the resort ticket window, to receive your same-day lift ticket.

The Canyons

The Canyons Resort is just a few miles away from the historic downtown area of Park City and is connected by a free shuttle service. With eight mountain peaks, The Canyons Resort is now one of the nation's top five largest resorts.

The Grand Summit Resort Hotel is the focal point of the base development. This hotel is actually worthy of the adjective "grand." The circular base village with its arched entrance is warm and inviting which creates a cozy feel to an area that opens up to a humongous amount of terrain and awesome vistas.

The local motto is "If you can see it, you can ski it." Gates to out-of-bounds skiing have serious signs warning of avalanche danger. Lives have been lost in recent years by people who didn't heed the warnings. There is so much expert and advanced terrain within bounds at The Canyons that skiers can explore the mountain until they drop from exhaustion. Tree skiing here is challenging and huge fun.

Intermediates have plenty to choose from and this is a great mountain if you want to improve to the next level. Beginners and first-timers have seven acres set aside specifically for them. The quad DreamCatcher serves 200 acres of mostly upper intermediate and advanced

The Canyons Resort Facts

Summit elevation:	**9,990 feet**
Vertical drop:	**3,190 feet**
Base elevation:	**6,800 feet**

Address: 4000 The Canyons Resort Drive
Park City, UT 84060
Area code: 435
Ski area phone: 649-5400
Snow report phone: 615-3456
Toll-free information: (800) 754-1636
Toll-free reservations: (888) 226-9667
Fax: 649-7374
Internet: www.thecanyons.com

Expert:★★★★★
Advanced:★★★★★
Intermediate:★★★★
Beginner:★★ **First-timer:**★
Number of lifts: 17—2 gondolas, 1 six-pack, 5 high-speed quads, 3 quads, 2 triples, 2 doubles, 2 surface lifts
Snowmaking: 4+ percent (160 acres)
Skiable Acreage: 3,500 acres
Uphill capacity: 25,700+ per hour
Parks & pipes: 2 parks, 1 pipe
Bed base: 1,200+ slopeside, 21,500 (town)
Nearest lodging: Slopeside
Resort child care: Yes, 6 weeks ad older
Adult ticket, per day: $76 (07/08 price)

---

terrain. The Tombstone Express high-speed quad has been replaced by a six-pack and the Cabriolet from the main parking lot has 12 new cabins.

The Canyons is one of the trio of resorts that make up the Park City area's skiing. It shares the amenities of the old mining town with the other two: Park City Mountain Resort and Deer Valley. Plan to ski all three while you're here.

 Mountain layout

The skiing and riding at The Canyons is spread across eight mountain peaks.

Expert, Advanced: Most of The Canyons' terrain is not visible from the base area. What you can't see are chutes and gullies as extreme as any in Utah.

Some real expert terrain is in the trees off the Ninety Nine 90 Express, Tombstone Express and the Super Condor Express. These lifts follow ridges, with the trees and steep runs dropping away on either side. Ninety Nine 90 has heart-stopping chutes off to the right like Red Pine and Charlie Brown. Peak 5 terrain is touted as intermediate tree skiing, but the trees—lots and lots of trees—make this area more of an expert's playground. The Condor chair takes you to terrain that is very steep, such as the South Side Chutes or the dense glades of Canis Lupis. Head to the top of Murdock Peak for ungroomed bowl descents.

Intermediate: There are blue runs from every chair, but sometimes only one or two per chair. Check your trail maps or ask a guest guide.

The best trails are in the center of the resort, under the Saddleback Express (Snow Dancer is quite nice), The Snow Canyon Express (wide paths here) and the lower mountain.

The blue runs under the Condor and Tombstone chairs are fun intermediate challenges, especially the double-blues like Cloud 9 (running the length of the Tombstone Express) and Apex Ridge next to the Super Condor Express. Ski Aplande, which takes off from Apex Ridge, a few times and you may feel up to some black runs like Devil's Friend and Rendezvous Ridge.

Beginner, First-timer: The Canyons has seven acres of beginner terrain near the top of the Flight of The Canyons gondola. The area is set aside from skier traffic and is framed by trees that separate beginners from main trails. There are also beginner trails off the High Meadow and Saddleback lifts and in the Dreamscape area.

Parks and pipes

The Canyons' award-winning 18-acre terrain park, which caters to all abilities, is off Snow Canyon Express. The elevation is high here, so the park has pretty consistent natural snow coverage. You'll find more than 30 features, including boxes, rails and various hits, plus the halfpipe.

The Canyons also has six natural halfpipes. Nearest to the base area are two that can be reached via the Golden Eagle chair. The higher of the two, The Tube, runs off Broken Arrow next to Grizzly. The lower, The Black Hole, cuts off Super Fury and comes out on Flume, below the Snow Canyon Express. A long narrow creek bed/halfpipe runs next to Spider Monkey. It's a beginner's terror. Perhaps the most well-known natural pipe is adjacent to Upper Boa and called Canis Lupis. Two more natural halfpipes can be accessed via Saddleback Express: The first is part of Pine Draw, which is the beginner/intermediate terrain park, and the second is to rider's left of the dedicated snowboarder trail CIA, formerly Painted Horse but renamed by snowboarders as the Canyons International Airport. Then there's the steep drainage off Ninety Nine 90 in Talus Garden: The tight, windy pipe is a challenge several thousand feet long.

Snowboarding

Way back when The Canyons was ParkWest, it was the first Park City ski area to allow snowboarding. The policy never changed, even though the area's name did a few times. Utah boarders are loyal because of that support, plus they know incredible terrain when they ride it.

For riding in the trees, Peak 5 is a good option. Terrain off the Ninety Nine 90 Express chair is excellent for snowboarding. Much of it is wide open, and there are plenty of chutes, steeps and trees. A 20-minute hike from the top of Super Condor Express to Murdock Peaks' 9,602-foot summit will get you freshies in Murdock Bowl, The Saddle Chutes or One-Hundred Turns.

Cross-country & snowshoeing (see also xcskiresorts.com)

White Pine Touring 435-615-5858 offers 20 km. of track and skate skiing, plus track, skate and telemark lessons at the Park City golf course and an adjacent dairy farm. For those who want to get off the flats, half-day snowshoe (Wednesday and Sunday) and ski (Tuesday and Friday) tours in the Uinta Mountains are available. If you venture out on your own, this is a good stop for advice and maps of the local mountain bike trails that are perfect for snowshoeing (many are accessible from downtown Park City).

The Homestead Resort 800-327-7220; 435-654-1102), 14 miles southeast of Park City in Midway, has 12 km. of skiing at Homestead Golf Course and 18 km. at Wasatch Mountain State Park. Snowshoeing and snowmobiling also are available. Nearby **Soldier Hollow**, site of the 2002 Olympic cross-country competitions, offers 26 km. of both track and skate skiing for all levels.

Lessons (08/09 prices)

Group lessons: Clinics are 2.5 hours and cost $75; a full day costs $129.
First-timer package: First-timers get a full-day lesson, lift ticket and rentals for $99. Reservations are highly recommended.

Private lessons: For one or two people, $138 for one hour, $255 for two hours, and $633 for all day. For three to five people, $255 for two hours and $708 for all day.

Special programs: Women's Workshop, a three-day program with U.S. Olympian Holly Flanders, is offered several times during the season. Olympian Sean Smith teaches two-day Mogul Clinics. For both programs, call for details and required reservations, 435-615-3449.

Children's programs (08/09 prices)

Child care: The Little Adventures Children's Center takes ages 6 weeks to 6 years. Snowplay for ages 2-3, with lunch, cost $95; half day, $75 with lunch.

Canyon Cubs, day care with a one-hour private lesson costs an additional $95 (an additional $110 during holidays).

Full day for ages 6 weeks to 2 years old costs $95; half day, $75. Day care is offered 8:30 a.m.-4:30 p.m. No hourly rates are available.

For advance reservations, call 615-3402. For same-day reservations, call 435-615-8036.

Other options: The Park City Chamber of Commerce can refer visitors to child-care facilities or babysitting services. Call 800-453-1360; 435-649-6100. **Baby's Away** (800-379-9030; 435-645-8823) rents and will deliver baby needs to your lodge, such as cribs, strollers, car seats and toys. The **Day Care Center** keeps a list of independent babysitters.

Canyon Cats, for ages 4-6, skiing only, is the most-requested program. It is a full day that includes lunch, lift ticket and equipment, plus indoor play time for younger children. It costs $135 ($144 during holidays) for lifts, lessons and equipment. Children with equipment and lift tickets pay $124 ($132 holidays).

Canyon Carvers, ages 7-14, skiing or riding costs $153 ($164 holidays) for lessons, lifts and equipment. Children who do not need lifts and equipment pay $124 ($132). Reservations are highly recommended; call 435-615-3449. **Canyon Cubs**, ages 2-3, get full day care plus a one-hour private lesson for $205—reservations are required; call 435-615-8036.

Lift tickets (07/08 prices)

	Adult	Junior (7–12)
One day	$76	$44
Three days	$216 ($72/day)	$126 ($42/day)
Five days	$340 ($68/day)	$205 ($41/day)

Who skis free: Ages 6 and younger.

Who skis at a discount: Skiers 65 and older pay junior prices. Tickets are cheapest when bought online at least 14 days early.

Note: Early- and late-season prices are lower; peak prices are higher.

Accommodations – The Canyons

A few steps from the Flight of The Canyons gondola, **The Grand Summit Resort Hotel** (888-226-9667; 435-615-8040; $$$$) has luxurious pent-houses, one- to three-bedroom condos, studios and hotel rooms. Most of the 360 rooms have balconies, fireplaces, jetted tubs and full kitchens. The hotel also offers a full-service health club, including a heated outdoor pool with hot tubs, steamroom, sauna and massage. The hotel has an on-site restaurant, bistro and lounges.

The 150-room **Sundial Lodge** (888-226-9667; $$$$) is in the heart of The Canyons Resort Village. The condominium lodge offers guestrooms and one- and two-bedroom condominium-style accommodations with kitchens and jetted tubs. Most condominiums have fireplaces and balconies. Guests have access to a rooftop hot tub and plunge pool.

The 200-unit **Silverado Lodge**, is directly across from the Grand Summit.

Dining – The Canyons

The Canyons has two on-mountain lodges for dining: **Red Pine Cafe** ($), at the top of the Flight of The Canyons gondola, serves healthy grilled food, pizza and deli sandwiches. The award-winning **Lookout Cabin** ($$), at the top of the Golden Eagle and Lookout chairlifts, has a table-served luncheon menu of grilled fish, meats and salads and a full-service bar.

In the base area, **Smokie's Smokehouse** ($-$$) serves family-style barbecue and Cajun fare and has an unobstructed view of the terrain park. The award-winning **Cabin** at the Grand Summit Hotel features an eclectic western cuisine with an extensive wine list. Dinner at the **Viking Yurt** includes a sleigh ride or choose to ski-in & ski-out for lunch when advertised. Access off Saddleback and Tombstone lifts.

Children's programs – Park City Region

Other options: The Park City Chamber of Commerce can refer visitors to **child-care facilities** or **babysitting services**. Call (800) 453-1360 or locally, 649-6100. **Baby's Away** (800-379-9030; 645-8823) rents and will deliver baby needs to your lodge, such as crib, stroller, car seat and toys.

Accommodations – Park City

In and around Park City are bed-and-breakfasts, country inns, chain hotels and condominiums. Park City's lodging is roughly grouped either in the old town surrounding the Resort Center Complex or in the Prospector Square area. A wonderful newer part of town is Lower Main (also called South Main), which surrounds the base of the Town Lift. All areas are served by the free shuttlebus system.

In old Park City the best is the **Washington School Inn** (800-824-1672; 435-649-3800; $$-$$$$). This is a very elegant 15-room (including three suites) country inn built in a former schoolhouse.

Brand new in the historic Old Town, **The Sky Lodge** (435-658-3336; $$$$) has 22 "residences" and an opulent spa. It aims to be considered one of the finest boutique resort hotels in the world and we think they've made it. The concept is opulent New York City loft — the smallest room is 1,260 square feet.

The Blue Church Lodge & Townhouses (800-626-5467; 435-649-8009; $$-$$$$) are constructed around an old church a block from Main Street. Listed on the National Register of Historic Places, it is a grouping of seven condominiums ranging from one to four bedrooms in the church, with four additional townhouses across the street.

If the key to lodging, as in real estate, is location, location, location, then **Treasure Mountain Inn** (800-344-2460; $$-$$$$) at the top of Main Street is a winner. These are studio and one- and two-bedroom condos with kitchens.

Another spot on Main Street is the **1904 Imperial Hotel** (800-669-8824; 435-649-1904; $$$), a B&B in a historic old house. All rooms have their own bath, telephone and TV. There's a big hot tub for everyone to use. Lizzie, the hotel's ghost, turns lights on and off and rings bells to get attention (she never appears in person). Legend is that Lizzie was killed in the Mayflower Room by a jealous lover. The hotel's sister property, **The Old Miners' Lodge** (435-645-8068; $$-$$$) is two blocks from Main Street on Woodside Avenue.

The bargain spots are dormitory digs and rooms in the **Chateau Apres Lodge**, "A Skier's Ski Lodge" (800-357-3556; 435-649-9372; $-$$). The lodge has a retro circular fireplace

Dining: $$$$–Entrees $30+; $$$–$20–$30; $$–$10–$20; $–less than $10.
Accommodations: (double room) $$$$–$200+; $$$–$141–$200; $$–$81–$140; $–$80 and less.

in the center of its common lounge. Complimentary continental breakfast and hot cider for apres-ski are included.

The South Main area is a hot spot in town. The **Marriott Summit Watch** (800-845-5279; 435-647-4100; $$$-$$$$) is in the middle of this pedestrian complex with restaurants, shops and the Town Lift right outside the door. A draw is the Marriott's Aquacade, a pool and activities center built under old trestles. Every evening there's something scheduled for kids, such as crafts, movies or ice skating , ranging in cost from $15 to $30.

Snow Flower Condominiums (800-852-3101; 435-649-6400; $$-$$$$) is 100 feet from the beginner area and offers studios to five-bedroom units. Each unit has single-person jetted tubs and underground parking.

For more economical condos, try **Edelweiss Haus** (800-245-6417; 435-649-9342; $$-$$$$) across the street from the lifts and the Silver King Hotel. Extras include a heated outdoor pool and hot tub. Hotel rooms to two-bedroom condos are available.

Other locations in town:

The Inn at Prospector Square (888-870-4386; 435-649-7100; $$-$$$$) is a group of condos that includes use of its athletic club in the rates. **The Yarrow Resort Hotel** (800-927-7694; 435-649-7000; $$-$$$$) is considered good family lodging. Children under 12 stay free and the hotel, with a year-round heated outdoor pool, sits amid shopping, movies and restaurants. It is on the shuttlebus route, about a five-minute ride from Park City's Main Street.

The 199-room **Park City Marriott** (800-754-3279; 435-649-2900; $$-$$$$) features a wide range of amenities including refrigerators and coffee makers in every room, plus double phone lines and desks with built-in outlets for those who must combine work with pleasure.

Dining – Park City

Park City's restaurants get better every year—and more expensive. Pick up one of the two free dining-guide magazines to get menus, but be aware that not all the restaurants are listed. Main Street is where you'll find many of the best restaurants in town: The top four are **Grappa, Chimayo, Zoom and Riverhorse**.

If you can pay the freight, the Northern Italian menu, wine list and ambiance are outstanding at chef Bill White's **Grappa** (435-645-0636; $$$-$$$$). It's in a 100-year-old building; try and get a table by the fireplace. Many locals recommend **Chimayo** (435-649-6222; $$$-$$$$), also owned by chef Bill White, for its inventive Southwestern cuisine (don't miss the dark chocolate flan). **Zoom Roadhouse Grill** (435-649-9108; $$$) is housed in the old train depot. Owned by Robert Redford, whose Sundance Film Festival transforms the town each January, it serves "plain folks food." Finally, the **Riverhorse Cafe** (435-649-3536; $$$-$$$$) is a can't-miss choice for anyone who enjoys contemporary American continental food in a low-key, elegant atmosphere.

Off Main Street, one restaurant that vies for best-in-town honors is **Adolph's/** (435-649-7177; $$$) next to the U.S. Ski and Snowboard Team office on Kearns Boulevard. The Swiss chef-owner prepares European-inspired cuisine. Hidden on Park Avenue, **Chez Betty** (435-649-8181; $$$) in the Copperbottom Inn serves excellent American/French cuisine in a formal setting. Head to **Nacho Mama's** (435-645-8226; $-$$) for tasty Southwestern/Mexican food and margaritas that go down far too smoothly and **Baja Cantina** (435-649-2252; $-$$) at the Resort Plaza for a festive atmosphere, huge burritos and Tex-Mex made with fresh ingredients. The lowest-priced Mexican restaurant is **El Chubasco** (435-645-9114; $-$$), in Prospector Square, where you'll get real Mexican food with quick service but no atmosphere.

Foron-mountain lunch, apres ski and dinner, at Park City Mountain Resort, try **Legends**

Bar & Grill on the ground floor at Legacy Lodge, around the corner from the Payday Lift . They have liquor service.

The Eating Establishment (435-649-8284; $) is a locals' cheap-eats favorite for meals any time of day, as is **Main St. Pizza and Noodle** (435-645-8878; $). For breakfast, **The Eating Establishment** ($) on Main Street is the leader for hearty-meal fans. The menu includes some trendy selections, such as smoked salmon Eggs Benedict.

On-Mountain — The Canyons: The Canyons has two on-mountain lodges for dining: **Red Pine Cafe** ($), at the top of the Flight of The Canyons gondola, serves healthy grilled food, pizza and deli sandwiches. The award-winning **Lookout Cabin** ($$), at the top of the Golden Eagle and Lookout chairlifts, has a table-served luncheon menu of grilled fish, meats and salads and a full-service bar.

Apres-ski/nightlife – Park City

Park City has some of the best nightlife of any ski town.

Immediate slopeside apres-ski centers are Deer Valley's **The Lounge**, where the deck in spring gets packed and live entertainment performs on the weekends; **Legends Bar & Bistro** and **The Brew House**, both in the Legacy Lodge at Park City Mountain Resort base; and **The Forum** at The Canyons.

According to locals, **O'Shucks** is the place to be on Main Street for the younger folks (skiers and boarders). **Harry Os**, half way down Main, is a giant warehouse of a bar, complete with six pool tables, a big-screen TV and a boisterous younger crowd. **The No Name Saloon**, next door, is your basic bar with a shuffleboard table, loud juke music and louder conversation.

Mother Urban's, named after a famous bordello madam, is a cellar version of a knotty-pine mining shack that sells 101 beers and features live jazz Tuesdays, Thursdays and Fridays. Also try the **Wasatch Brew Pub** at the top of Main Street, where you can watch the brewing process even as you reap its yeasty rewards.

When the **Egyptian Theater** performs plays, as it often does during the winter, it makes a nice evening's entertainment. **The Eccles Center**, which opened in 1998, houses two live stages and is a year-round focal point for the performing arts in Park City. For weekly arts and entertainment events, call 435-647-9747 or 435-655-3114.

Other activities – Park City area

The Canyons Resort Village has a quality **spa, health club and some good shopping**. There is also a nice **Yurt dinner** served by a snowcat-drawn sleigh and an excellent **Western BBQ**. Visitors can also take **hot air balloon rides and guided snowshoe tours**.Park City offers some rare sports treats: ski jumping, luge and bobsled at the **Utah Olympic Park**(435-658-4200). The park hosted the 2002 Olympic competition in those events. Yes, you can fly off the end of a ramp just like the Olympians do (you'll be on much smaller ramps, but it will feel like the 120-meter jump, let us assure you). You can take jumping lessons (required rental helmets included), or ride on the Olympic luge/bobsled track in a neophyte-friendly luge "ice rocket" or as a passenger in a four-person bobsled. (They supply the driver.) The park is open daily.

Experienced skiers can ski to six different resorts via backcountry routes on the all-day **Interconnect Adventure Tour** (435-534-1907; reservations required). Mountain guides lead three to 12 skiers and both traversing and walking are necessary, so you need to be a confident skier in good physical condition. The six-area tour (Deer Valley, Park City Mountain Resort, Solitude, Brighton, Alta and Snowbird) costs $250 (08/09 price) including lunch and return transportation.

Dining: $$$$–Entrees $30+; $$$–$20–$30; $$–$10–$20; $–less than $10.
Accommodations: (double room) $$$$ $200+; $$$–$141–$200; $$–$81–$140; $–$80 and less.

Outdoor adventures include snowmobiling, dogsledding, snowshoeing, hot air ballooning and fly fishing. You can reserve these kinds of activities by calling one central number at **ABC Reservations Central**, 800-820-2223 or 435-649-2223.

Gorgoza Park, a former ski hill that is now a tubing park owned by Park City Mountain Resort, is about five minutes out of town off of I-80. You'll find family fun on eight lanes of tubing and mini-snowmobile rides.

Stop by the Church of Jesus Christ of Latter-Day Saints' **Family History Center** at 531 Main Street (Mormon church). Computers are available for genealogy checks for anyone free of charge. The excellent **Park City Museum** on Main Street details local history. Admission is by donation, and is open every day at varying times.

The 30,000-square-foot **Papillon the Spa**, at the Westgate Park City Resort & Spa (435-655-2266) at The Canyons Resort, has 17 treatment rooms (13 massage and facial, two wet rooms, a couples room and treatment suite); private men's and women's locker facilities with relaxation lounges, saunas, steamrooms, showers and a coed hot tub with cascading waterfall.

Canyons Grand Summit Resort Hotel, (435-615-8035) slopeside at The Canyons, also has **spa services** (435-615-8035) which include body massages, facials, wraps, manicures and pedicures.

The elegant Stein Eriksen Lodge at Deer Valley also offers **spa treatments** (435-645-6475) from massages, to vichy showers, facials, soothing stone treatments, facials, manicures and pedicures.

Align Spa (435-647-9300) is a full-service day spa on the lobby level of Shadow Ridge Hotel and Conference Center. Massages, facials and body treatments are available.

Park City has two popular shopping areas: Historic Main Street in downtown Park City and a factory outlet center on the edge of town. You can jump on a free shuttle or take a cab for $6 round trip per person. Park City's free shuttlebus system now operates in town and out to **Kimball Junction/Factory Outlet Mall** (including The Canyons Resort). Main Street has museums, art galleries and fine and funky shops.

Getting there and getting around

By air: The drive from the Salt Lake City International Airport to Park City takes 45 minutes. Ground transportation makes frequent trips between the airport and Park City. Providers include **Lewis Brothers Stages** (800-826-5844; 435-649-2256); **Park City Transportation** (800-637-3803; 649-8567); and **All Resort Express** (800-457-9457; 435-649-3999). If you arrive without reservations, go to the transportation counter at the airport and you'll ride on the next available van. Call 48 hours in advance for Park City-to-airport reservations.

By car: Park City is 36 miles east of Salt Lake City, by I-80 and Utah Hwy. 224.

Getting around: If you're staying close to the town center or near a stop on the free bus line, you can do without a rental car. The town bus system has five routes with service every 20 minutes, if not more frequently, from 7 a.m. to 1 a.m. If you take a side trip to one of the Cottonwood Canyons ski resorts, **Lewis Brothers Stages** and **Park City Transportation** have shuttles. Lewis Brothers offers a Canyon Jumper package to Solitude and Snowbird, including transportation and lift ticket. Prepay the evening before you wish to ski.

Crystal Mountain
Washington

Summit:	7,012 feet
Vertical:	3,100 feet
Base:	3,912 feet

Address: 33914 Crystal Mountain Blvd., Crystal Mountain, WA 98022
Telephone (main): 360-663-2265
Snow Report Number: 888-754-6199
Toll-free reservations: 800-277-6475
Reservations outside U.S.: 360-663-2265
E-mail: comments@skicrystal.com
Internet: www.skicrystal.com

Expert:★★★★
Advanced:★★★★
Intermediate:★★★★★
Beginner:★★★
First-timer:★★★★★

Lifts: 11—2 six-passenger high-speed chairs, 2 high-speed quads, 2 triples, 4 doubles, 1 surface lift
Skiable acreage: 2,600 plus out-of-bounds-backcountry
Snowmaking: 1.3 percent (35 acres)
Uphill capacity: 20,310
Parks & pipes: none
Bed base: 350
Nearest lodging: Slopeside, cabins
Child care: None
Adult ticket, per day: $58 (07/08 prices)
Dining:★★★
Apres-ski/nightlife:★★
Other activities:★

When the weather is right and the snow is deep, hardcore skiers from all over the West Coast beam themselves to Crystal for unparalleled skiing.

The terrain is steep and thrilling and there's enough of it to keep the adrenaline rushing all day. There's enough snow too, often 12 feet deep at the top. It snowed 65 inches one record-breaking day during a recent season. Their average annual snowfall is 350 inches.

It's Washington's only destination Alpine ski resort (sorry, no cross-country or snowshoe terrain), just a 90-minute drive from Seattle. The on-mountain condos, lodges and restaurants delight local skiers who would otherwise have to leave the state for a ski vacation.

 ## Mountain layout

Experts may only see one-third of the 50 named trails designated for them, but they'll find their real thrills in the back country terrain. Seven days a week, conditions permitting, a shuttle bus picks up at the Northway lift and returns every half hour. The longest run is Northway, at 2.5 miles. And there's something to be said for skiing and riding a mountain dwarfed by nearby 14,410-foot Mt. Rainier..

Expert, Advanced: Black-diamonds comprise 30 percent of the terrain, thanks to 1,300 skiable acres in the inbounds backcountry areas, 1,000 acres of which are accessible from the Northway chair. It's the kind of terrain that is out of bounds at most ski areas—woods, chutes and steep bowls.

Intermediate: Blue runs make up another 57 percent of Crystal's 2,600 acres. However, runs are fairly short, such as Lucky Shot, Little Shot and Gandy's Run, all from Summit House. For a longer run, ski Green Valley from the right of Summit House to the base of the Green Valley chair and continue to the base area on Kelly's Gap Road.

Beginner, First-timer: Beginners can have fun on Broadway and Skid Road, both served by the new base-area lift, The Chinook Express. First-timers have their own Meadow and Fairway runs served by Discovery chair. Child novices now have a "moving carpet" lift called the Kid Conveyor instead of a handle tow.

Snowboarding

Crystal has woods, ridges and carving slopes that keep freeriders coming back. A lot of inter-mediate and advanced riders enjoy the up-mountain area off Green Valley Chair, reached by taking Chinook and Rainier Express chairs.

Both the Rainier Express to Summit House and the Green Valley Chair to Grubstake Point will get you to the Northway Ridge and Northway Notch. From those you turn right to the double-black-diamond bowls of North Country. Crystal is purposefully keeping the traffic flow low for everybody's skiing pleasure. From the top, riders can choose Snorting Elk Bowl, Northway Bowl, Paradise Bowl and Bruce's Bowl, and follow Right Angle Ridge to a variety of expert glades and chutes or head farther north to drop into places like Morning Glory Bowl and Brand X. Several new trails feed into the bottom of the new lift.

Lessons (07/08 prices)

Group lessons: Ski or snowboard: $55 for a two-and-one-half-hour lesson, $65 for five hours. With all-mountain lift ticket and equipment rental it's $115 for two-and-one-half-hours, $130 for five hours.

First-timer package: Ski or snowboard: $75 for a two-and-one-half-hour lesson, beginner lift ticket and rental equipment, $90 for five hours.

Private lessons: For up to two people, one hour, $85; two hours, $145; three hours, $195; full day, $365.

Children's programs (07/08 prices)

Child care: The resort does not offer non-skiing child care.

Children's lessons: Package includes lift, lesson and supervision; lunch included in full-day session. Ages 4-6 Full Day $90, Half Day $70; Ages 7-10 Full Day $118, Half Day $98. With rental equipment (ski/snowboard and boots) add $15. Call 360-663-3035.

Lift tickets (08/09 prices)

Adult (18-69) $60, **Youth** (11-17) $55

Who skis free: Children 6 and under.

Who skis at a discount: Juniors (7-10) $30. Seniors 70+ $35. Beginner-only lift ticket (Discovery Chair) $35. Half-day ticket (12:30 p.m.-4:00 p.m.) $55/Adult, $50/Youth. Crystal Mountain does not sell multiday tickets, but a book of five adult all-day vouchers saves $5 per day. The vouchers can be used by anyone and are available on-line at Crystal Mountain's web site and at local retailers until Dec. 31, 2008.

Accommodations

Lodging is walking distance from the slopes. Three hotels and more than 100 condominiums are run by three operations.

For the three hotels—**Alpine Inn** ($-$$), **Quicksilver Lodge** ($-$$) and **Village Inn** ($)—call **Crystal Mountain Hotels** (888-754-36400; 360-663-2262). At the legendary **Alpine Inn**, units range from a small room for two with a shower down the hall to a deluxe with two double beds. Connecting rooms are available. The Alpine's lobby is a cozy gathering spot for both guests and restaurant patrons. All the rooms were recently renovated.

The **Quicksilver Lodge**, also recently renovated, is a comfortable Camay soap/plastic cup kind of lodging with no-smoking rooms and feather duvets. The large open lobby with a piano, games and comfy furniture makes it very popular with families. It's a five-minute walk to the base. The **Village Inn** has queen and twin rooms with fridges.

For chalet suites, call **Alta Crystal Resort** (800-277-6475; 360-663-2500; $$-$$). Amenities include an outdoor heated pool and hot tub. A honeymoon cabin is available. For condos, call **Crystal Mountain Lodging Suites** (888-668-4368; 360-663-2558; $$-$$). All units have kitchens, some have fireplaces. The lower parking lot has 42 **RV hookups**, first-come, first-served, $20 per night with electrical hookups or $10 without hookups.

 ## Dining

Restaurants cater to both the white-linen and take-out crowds, with rustic dining, a cafeteria and apres-ski lounges in between.

Summit House ($-$), a rustic dining lodge on the mountain, is at the top of the Rainier Express lift (6,872 feet). You'll find gourmet pizzas and pastas along with soups and salads, but the main attraction is the view of Mount Rainier, so close it looks as if you can touch it. The newer **Campbell Basin Lodge** ($), near the top of the Forest Queen Chairlift, has a nice food court with stations for pasta, soup, grilled sandwiches, burritos, wraps, gourmet pizza and stir-fry. The Base Lodge also offers cafeteria-style food in the **Cascade Grill** and the **Glacier Express** on a heated outdoor patio.

At the larger base area, the **Alpine Inn Restaurant**, (360-663-7727; $-$$), open for breakfast and dinner daily, is a Crystal legend serving fine foods and wines. It's across the wooden footbridge into the woods. The Alpine also serves a great breakfast with traditional eggs Benedict, florentine, rancheros and even a tofu scramble. **The Bullwheel Pub & Grill** ($-$), upstairs in the main base lodge, has full cocktail service, the tastiest burgers at Crystal and a great view of the slopes. The **Snorting Elk Cellar** ($) downstairs in the Alpine Inn is like a Bavarian Rathskeller. Find all your essential grocery, bakery, beer and wine needs at **The Market at Crystal Mountain**.
The **Bullwheel Pub & Grill** has full cocktail service and a great view of the slopes, as well as apres-ski entertainment from 4:00 p.m.—6:00 p.m. on Fridays and Saturdays. **The Snorting Elk Cellar** in the Alpine Inn is like a Bavarian Rathskeller. It's always the place to gather after a great day on the slopes and there's live entertainment most Friday and Saturday evenings. The Elk has a terrific selection of microbrews, full cocktail service and expanded food service to the bar from its own deli. If you want to make your own apres ski/nightlife scene, you can find beer, wine and party munchies at **The Market at Crystal Mountain**.

 ## Other activities

You'll find a hot tub, sauna, showers and game room at **East Peak Massage and Fitness** (360-663-2505), next to the village Inn above Parking Lot C.

With adaptive ski equipment, **SKIFORALL** offers training and fun on the snow for children and adults with disabilities. Call 206-838-6030 or email info@outdoorsforall.org.

Getting there and getting around

By air: Seattle-Tacoma airport is served by most major airlines.

By car: Crystal is 76 miles southeast of Seattle and a 64-mile drive from Sea-Tac Airport. Drive south on I-5 from Seattle, take Exit 142 east to Auburn, Hwy. 164 to Enumclaw, and Hwy. 410 east to Crystal Mountain Boulevard.

Dining: $$$$–Entrees $30+; $$$–$20–$30; $$–$10–$20; $–less than $10.
Accommodations: (double room) $$$$–$200+; $$$–$141–$200; $$–$81–$140; $–$80 and less.

Washington State Regional Resorts

Mt. Baker, Bellingham, WA; 360-671-0211; 360-671-0211 (snow reports)
Internet: www.mtbaker.us
9 lifts; 1,000 acres; 1,550 vertical feet; 1 terrain park; 1 halfpipe

Mountain resorts need snow, and this resort in northwest Washington State gets more of it than any other. This is not hype. Mt. Baker holds the world record, certified by the National Oceanic and Atmospheric Administration, for a winter season's snowfall of 1,140 inches.

In an era when smaller ski hills and non-destination resort ski areas are disappearing, Mt. Baker's success is an exception. Location, location and location—Baker draws skiers and snowboarders from both Vancouver, British Columbia, one hour north and Seattle, two-and-a-half hours south—has a lot to do with it, but the main ingredients are the average annual 645-inch snowfall and its "non-corporate" style of management. It's just funky.

Mt. Baker's improvements in the past few years include a second Cascadian-style day lodge, five more quad lifts and expansion of its intermediate terrain. Now, even on record days, lift lines never top five minutes. Mt. Baker's four-year upgrade plan to replace all double chairs is now in the last phase.

The mountain offers all-day possibilities to skiers and snowboarders alike, with plenty of faces and woods that bring out the pioneer spirit. This is truly snowboarder heaven, where the hardcore insist "snowboarding was born."

One drawback to the ski area's low elevation is that the freezing level can yo–yo, and marginally cold days can turn snow to rain without notice. Ski patrollers keep a few sets of dry clothes in their hut for themselves. Bring a change of clothes for yourself, it's good insurance.

The Pan Dome side, served by Chairs 1, 2, 3 and 6, is for the mogul bashers and chute shooters. Hot skiers can play here endlessly challenging the steep and deep. Every time experts take one run, they are sure to find another just as hairy. Shuksan has more wide-open, powder bowl type of terrain. Experts-only runs include Gabl's Run under Chair 5 and The Chute. The Chute, a horrific, straight-down run under Chair 1, is where a staff writer once ended up in a tree well after a body slam with an unknown opposite-sex skier. The folks on the lift were well entertained and it took some creative maneuvers for the victims to extricate themselves. Make sure there's enough snow before you try this one.

The out-of-bounds areas are extremely attractive at Mt. Baker and many pass the caution signs and do the hikes at the top of Chair 8. But avalanches are a problem out of bounds, and sometimes people die. You must have an avalanche transceiver and know how to use it. Plus, have a partner, a shovel, and know your route, the terrain, avalanche conditions and predictions.

Nearly 70 percent of Mt. Baker's terrain is labeled blue or green. On soft snow days, intermediates can go just about anywhere on the mountain with confidence, minus the chutes, of course. On icy days, however, definitely avoid Razor Hone Canyon. It becomes a long series of shelves. North Face and Honkers get unforgiving too, with their boulderish bumps. Probably the most fun for intermediates is the terrain off Chair 8, especially Oh Zone and Daytona.

The beginner terrain is all at the bottom of the mountain. Chair 7 expands the Shuksan possibilities, but not much. Beginners will probably want to avoid Chair 8 for the time being— its terrain is mostly intermediate.

On the Pan Dome side, beginners can easily get back to the lodge on the Austin and Blueberry runs, even though they are labeled intermediate. The signs are good, but don't follow tracks or other skiers if you don't know where they're going. You may end up on steep Pan Face or unmapped places called Rattrap and Gunbarrel. The ski patrol performs rescues on icy crags that are best avoided. The learning areas are near the Heather Meadows base lodge and the White Salmon Day Lodge. The greatest variety is found at the Heather Meadows side. The slopes are long and gentle, not sectioned off, but not used by more accomplished sliders. Snowboard novices—some of whom feel immortal rather than timid—use this area. Timid novices probably are better off learning elsewhere.

Ride guide: The entire mountain is challenging fun for snowboarders. There is not much in the way of flats. Without speed from the top of Chair 3 to load onto Chair 2, you might have a short walk. The only in-bounds climb, maybe 50 yards long, is from the ends of Chair 6 and Chair 7 if you're heading to the Austin run or the Blueberry Cat Track to return to the upper lodge, Heather Meadows Day Lodge. The Sticky Wicket woods give good ride until the snow is flatted out. From the woods there are a few choice access steeps into Razorhone Canyon. There are several good chutes, especially in the spring, from Gabl's run into the little valley under Chair 5.

Parks and pipes: The huge terrain park is under Chair 8. It's 600 feet long, 80 feet wide and has anywhere from six to 12 features, depending upon snowpack. The permanent halfpipe is just to rider's right of Chair 7 on the White Salmon side. There's still the natural halfpipe—starting from the top of Chair 5, it follows a creek bed for a few hundred yards and is normally buried under 20 feet of snow.

Lift tickets (08/09 prices): Weekend/Holiday: adults (16–59), $47; youth (7–15), $35; senior (60–69), $41. Weekday: adults (16–59), $39; youth (7–15), $30; senior (60–69), $36. Kids 6 and younger ski free & seniors 70+ pay $23 all season.

Distance: The Mt. Baker Ski Area is at the end of the Mt. Baker Hwy., 56 miles east of Bellingham, I-5, Exit 255. The drive from Bellingham takes about 90 minutes; from Seattle, allow three hours; and from Vancouver, B.C., two hours.

Lodging information: Mt. Baker Lodging (800-709-7669; 599-2453; $$–$$$$), in Glacier, rents vacation houses. **Absolute Heaven Chalet Rentals** (866-421-8495; $$$$) rents a log chalet that sleeps 6 inside the Mt. Baker Rim gated community near Glacier. The **Snowline Inn** (800-228-0119; 599-2788; $–$$) rents studio units and condo loft units. **Glacier Creek Lodge** (800-719-1414; 599-2991; $–$$$) has motel and cabin units.

There are a lot of small, charming B&Bs in the Glacier area with two or more rooms that are all in the same price range. The luxurious **Inn at Mt. Baker** (599-1776; $$), just east of Glacier, was specifically built in 2000 to be a bed & breakfast.

Stevens Pass, Skykomish, WA; 206-812-4510; 206-634-1645 (info line)

Internet: www.stevenspass.com
10 lifts; 1,125 acres; 1,800 vertical feet; 2 terrain parks; 1 superpipe

The snow here is tough to beat. Geographical elevation combined with dry wind from the east make the snow conditions at Stevens Pass nearly perfect throughout the winter season. Annual average snowfall is 450 inches, providing an average snowpack of 110 inches. The upper-front of Big Chief Mountain is steep and dense with Alpine conifers and a few skinny runs. It's the most challenging terrain at Stevens. The lower-front of Big Chief has one open intermediate run. The backside of Big Chief, called Mill Valley, faces south and has lots of wide open runs and is popular among Stevens die-hards.

On the front of Cowboy Mountain lie most of the intermediate runs and lit night-skiing terrain. From the top of Cowboy, amazing scenery and backcountry access is possible, as well as more challenging expert terrain. Beginner terrain and the tubing hill are located in the heart of the base area.

The night terrain offers something for everyone—two high-speed quads combined with four additional lifts offer access to 12 major runs through 400 acres. Night operations run seven nights a week from 4-10 p.m. Tube City is also lighted until 9 p.m.

There is child care for kids ages 3-12 (must be toilet trained).

The Stevens Pass Nordic Center, 5 miles from the resort on Hwy. 2, has 28 km. of cross-country and snowshoe trails.

Lift tickets (08/09 prices): Adults (13-61), $62; children (7-12), $35; senior (62-69), $36; seniors 70 and older, $13; ages 6 and younger, $7.

Distance from Seattle: About 78 miles northeast on Hwy. 2.

Lodging information: The closest is **SkyRiver Inn** (800-367-8194; 360-677-2261; $) in Skykomish. Leavenworth, a tourist town with an Alpine Bavarian theme, is 35 miles east of Stevens Pass. For lodging information in Leavenworth, call **Bavarian Bedfinders** (800-323-2920) or the **Leavenworth Chamber Of Commerce** (509-548-5807).

The Summit at Snoqualmie, WA; 425-434-7669; 206-236-1600 (info line)

Internet: www.summitatsnoqualmie.com

26 lifts; 1,916 acres; 2,310 vertical feet; 5 terrain parks; 1 superpipe

The Summit, a Boyne Resort, comprises four separate ski areas, all within a mile of each other on Snoqualmie Pass. Three are connected by trails, and the fourth, Alpental, is a mile away on another face. The four areas—Alpental, Summit West, Summit Central and Summit East—share an interchangeable lift ticket and offer a free shuttle so skiers can get from one to the others. Our stats reflect the combined lifts and acreage, while the vertical listed is for Alpental. The vertical drop at the other three areas varies from 900 to 1,080 feet.

Alpental has the most rugged terrain and thus, reputation. Summit West features gentle green and blue runs, plus it's home to two terrain parks and a snowdeck/snowskate park. Summit Central has mostly gentle terrain with a few serious black-diamond drops off the ridge, as well as the flagship terrain park and 400-foot-long superpipe with 17-foot-high walls. The pipe has a sound system and is lighted for night riding. Summit East has some great tree runs among its attractions. At least one of the areas is closed every weekday, sometimes two are, but the entire complex is open weekends and holidays (call or visit the web site for the specific current schedule as it changes throughout the season).

A variety of children's lessons is available. Night skiing operates until 10:30 p.m. (9 p.m. Sundays) on any mountain open that day. A Nordic ski area offers 50 km. of trails.

Lift tickets (08/09 prices): Adults (13-61), $56; youth (7-12)/senior (62-69), $37; children 6 and younger & super seniors 70+, $11.

Distance from Seattle: About 50 miles east on I-90.

Lodging information: Best Western Summit Inn (800-557-7829; 425-434-6300). Visit the resort's web site for a listing of other lodging and private homes available for rent.

Grand Targhee
Wyoming

Summit:	**10,000 feet**
Vertical:	**2,000 feet**
Base:	**8,000 feet**

Address: P.O. Box SKI, Alta, Wyoming 83414
Telephone (main): 307-353-2300
Snow Report Number: 800-827-4433
Toll-free reservations: 800-827-4433
E-mail: info@grandtarghee.com
Internet: www.grandtarghee.com

Expert:★★★
Advanced:★★★★
Intermediate:★★★★★
Beginner:★★★
First-timer:★★★★

Lifts: 4—1 high-speed quad, 1 quad, 1 double, 1 moving carpet
Skiable acreage: 2,000
Snowmaking: None
Parks & pipes: 3 parks
Bed base: 432
Nearest lodging: Slopeside, hotel and condos
Child care: Yes, 2 months and older
Adult ticket, per day: $59 (07/08)

Dining:★★★
Apres-ski/nightlife:★
Other activities:★

Grand Targhee is a hidden resort with some of the best powder to be found in America. Don't expect a wild time with non-snowsports activity—this place is built for skiers and riders.

Sitting as it does on the windward side of the Grand Tetons, Grand Targhee is much more than the perfect intermediate resort. Whenever it snows—which is often, about 500 inches of snow falls here each winter—it's not an intermediate resort at all. The seemingly boundless open terrain becomes one huge powder stash. And the groomers aren't keen on packing it down. No-sir-ee, this Shangri-La designates beginner, intermediate and advanced powder areas on its trail map, with fresh ungroomed snow left on the gentle rolling terrain where powder puppies can cut their first turns.

The Sacajawea high-speed quad takes you to 500 acres of terrain on Peaked Mountain that could previously only be reached by snowcat. About a third of this terrain is groomed, the rest is pristine glade skiing and open bowls that are left untouched for fresh tracks. Better yet, on adverse weather days, Peaked Mountain provides protection from the wind and low clouds. And if you're looking for an out-of-bounds peak called Mary's Nipple, well, just look for the signs pointing to Mary's. All written references to anatomical features were dropped in spring 2003 so as to not offend guests. Presumably, the potentially offended don't speak French ("Regardez, les montagnes ressemblent a des grands tetons!"). The best part of this powder paradise is you won't have to share it with the masses, because this resort is grandly isolated. Grand Targhee is in Wyoming, but the only way to get here is through Idaho. Its huge bowls of snow are on the western slope of the Tetons, which hug the border between the two states. Targhee usually gets double their famous neighbor Jackson Hole's amount in snowfall. And with days where there are maybe 800 people on the mountain, and two-plus feet of powder, it's worth every dime.

No ski area is perfect for everyone, however. If you go stir-crazy without a variety of restaurants and other things to do, we suggest you stay in Jackson and spend one day of your vacation here. But if you'd like to completely unwind, ski during the day, read a good book at night and head home new and invigorated, this is the place.

Mountain layout

Expert and Advanced: Grand Targhee does not have much for experts, but that doesn't necessarily mean you'll be bored here, especially if you hit it after a big dump when the entire mountain becomes one big powder puff. Experienced powderhounds will want to opt for snowcat skiing on Peaked Mountain. Ten skiers per snowcat, with two guides, head out to enjoy this snowy playground. The longest run is 3.2 miles and covers slightly more than 2,800 vertical.

If you can't afford the cat, don't stress over it. Head for the treed chutes off Rock Garden, which are short but loads of fun. If—and only if—there's no snowcat running, you can hike above the Sacajawea lift and access some gnarly unnamed cliffs that drop you off into the ever-so-long Teton Vista Traverse.

Fred's Mountain's best advanced runs are found skiers' right off Rock Garden in a series of treed chutes called The Good, The Bad, The Ugly and The East Woods, all leading into Chief Joseph Bowl. To skiers' left, Instructors Chute and Patrol Chute are rewarding, but require a long green-rated runout on Teton Vista Traverse. For fast groovin'-on-groomed, try The Face to Ladies Waist.

The Sacajawea lift takes you to 500 acres of glades, bowls and a few groomed runs on Peaked Mountain. Most terrain here is intermediate-rated, but the groomed runs Northern Lights and Shadow Woman (both rated blue/black) present some nice pitches.

Intermediate: Fred's Mountain offers boundary-to-boundary skiing and riding. On snowy days, which come often, its blue runs and the trees between them are perfect pitches for pillows of powder. Chief Joseph Bowl, Blackfoot Bowl and the runs under Dreamcatcher Chair are, well, dreamy. On non-powder days, you can fly on the screaming groomers. Since the locals usually show up only when there's freshies, you'll have unbroken corduroy to yourself all day. If you want to try going off-piste, leftovers that have softened in the sun are fun on fat skis. The gladed terrain on neighboring Peaked Mountain was snatched from the cat-skiing area, corralled in-bounds and designated for intermediates. You can do laps here since this secluded patch of paradise boasts its own lift, Sacajawea.

Beginner and First-timer: The completely separate beginner area makes Targhee a recommended learning resort. While the beginner terrain appears limited as you look at the trail map, the trails have glades and fun themes, plus rollers and wide-open cruisers. They offer surprising variety that can keep children and adult beginners both challenged and occupied until their skills increase. Conveniently located near the ski school office, the area is served by the Shoshone quad lift and, for first-timers, a moving carpet.

The only downside for beginners is that the rest of the mountain has just one green-circle trail, the very long Teton Vista Traverse. Upper-level beginners can give it a try from the top of the Dreamcatcher quad, but be prepared for some narrow turns and fast skiers blowing by as they merge from other trails and make their way to the base.

Parks and pipes

"Trick Town" terrain park—geared towards intermediates and advanced-intermediates—has 15 features, including eight rails, and has been a big hit with riders and freeskiers on those days when they aren't out chasing fresh tracks. The park is near the base area, on Big Scout just to the left of the Dreamcatcher quad, and is served by the Shoshone quad.

The "North Pole Park" is perfectly suited for youngsters, beginners, low-intermediates and families. It's in the "Fun Zone," also off the Shoshone quad. The resort does not have a halfpipe (unless you count the natural halfpipe under Dreamcatcher lift—it's called Ladies Waist).

Snowboarding

Where else can you ride where the grooming policy on a powder day is to plow three lanes down the mountain for people who get stuck to get out?

Targhee has two user-friendly mountains with Western tree riding, open glades, steeps and chutes. The traverse from Peaked Mountain to the main area may cause problems for riders who aren't skilled in carrying speed. Just stay aware. The Sacajawea area has groomed runs, bowls and plenty of off-piste action, including some cliff drops.

Experienced powder hounds will want to take advantage of the 1,000 acres of snowcat riding on Peaked Mountain. Ten riders per snowcat, with two guides, head out to enjoy this snowy playground. The longest run is 3.2 miles and covers slightly more than 2,800 vertical.

Intermediate riders will pretty much have the run of the mountain. Fred's Mountain offers boundary-to-boundary skiing and riding. On snowy days, which come often, its blue runs and the trees between them are perfect pitches for pillows of powder. Chief Joseph Bowl, Blackfoot Bowl and the runs under Dreamcatcher Chair are, well, dreamy. On non-powder days, you can fly on the screaming groomers. Since the locals usually show up only when there's freshies, you'll have unbroken corduroy to yourself all day. If you want to try going off-piste, leftovers that have softened in the sun are fun on fat skis. The gladed terrain on neighboring Peaked Mountain was snatched from the cat-skiing area, corralled in-bounds and designated for intermediates. You can do laps here since this secluded patch of paradise boasts its own lift, Sacajawea.

Cross-country & snowshoeing (see also xcskiresorts.com)

Grand Targhee Nordic Center (800-827-4433; 307-353-2300) has 15 km of track groomed for touring and skating. The trails wind through varied terrain, offering beautiful vistas of the Greater Yellowstone area as well as meadows and aspen glades. The system includes a beginner track called Hamster Loop. The sandwich board at the lift-ticket kiosk lists the grooming report for the Nordic area.

Snowshoe in the Caribou-Targhee National Forest with Resort Naturalist Andy Steele and learn about winter ecology, animal tracks and native vegetation. Tours start at 10:30 a.m. and 2:30 p.m., Thursday through Sunday. Each two-hour session has a three-person minimum. This tour is free, but all tips go to support a non-profit wilderness organization. Snowshoe rentals are available; wear your own boots.

Lessons (07/08 prices)

Many instructors have been with the Ski Training Center since its first season in 1969, so you're in good hands.

Group lessons: $49 for adults, at 10 a.m. and 1 p.m.

First-timer package: A two-hour lesson with beginner lift ticket and rentals costs $69.

Private lessons: $80 for one hour, $130 for two hours, $180 for three hours, $280 for five hours ($25 for each additional person).

Special programs: In-bounds Adventure for a tour of the mountain's hidden stashes and some coaching too. Cost: $120 for two hours. The resort has several special clinics such as Extreme Skiing, Women Ski The Tetons, snowboarding and telemark. Call for details and prices.

Children's programs

Child care: Ages 2 months to 5 years. Kids 2 months to 2 years cost $51 per day; $39 per half day. Ages 3 to 5 cost $46 per day; $34 per half day. The program includes two snacks and lunch for the full day; just a snack for a half day. Packages are available with one-hour private or group ski lessons.

The kid's clubhouse is near the beginner skiing terrain and moving carpet lift. It has a homey, log cabin feel with separate rooms for quiet movie watching and active playtime. Reservations required; call (800) 827-4433.

Babysitting services are available outside of regular day care; ask at the main lodge front desk.

Children's lessons: Ski programs for ages 4–5 cost $95 for a full day with lessons, lifts, lunch and day-care activities; $59 for a half day. Ages 6–16 cost $95 for a full day with lessons, lunch and lift ticket; $48 for a half day. Snowboarding lessons begin at age 8.

Lift tickets (07/08 prices)

	Adult	Child (6-14)
One day	$59	$36
Three days	$162 ($54/day)	$108 ($36/day)
Five days	$260 ($52/day)	$180 ($36/day)

Who skis free: Ages 5 and younger with paying adult.

Who skis at a discount: Ages 65 and older pay $38 for one day. Those who ski more than one day at Grand Targhee probably are staying here too. In those cases Targhee's lodging-lift packages are the most economical and practical. On all Targhee lodging packages, children ages 14 and younger stay and ski free, one child per paying adult.

Accommodations

The small village sleeps about 450 people at two hotel-type lodges and a 32-unit, multi-story condo building. All are within an easy walk to lifts and base facilities. Most units come packaged with lift tickets, but you can rent rooms and condos without buying lift tickets (though we have no idea why you'd want to). Try to stay at Targhee Lodge, Teewinot Lodge or the Sioux Lodge Apartments. Kids 14 and younger are always free on lodging packages.

Packages that include ski tickets and two group lessons are offered for seven nights and six days, five nights and four days, and three nights and three days. Value Season brings significant savings. If you book a package from opening day to mid-December, not only will you save on your lodging, tickets and lessons, you'll also get the free snowcat skiing described in the Lift Ticket section (conditions permitting).

Call 800-827-4433 for central reservations

Dining

Don't underestimate: There's not much variety in this small village, but there's a lot of quality.

The newly remodeled **Targhee Steakhouse** ($$-$$$) is Targhee's finest restaurant, with entrees such as rack of lamb, whiskey chicken, shrimp scampi and poached salmon. It also serves breakfast and lunch.

Snorkel's ($) is the spot for great gourmet pizza and pasta with fun and games for the family. Breakfast here features sinful pastries and espressos. **Wild Bill's Grille** ($) in the Rendezvous Lodge has breakfast, pizza, a soup and salad bar, sandwiches and Mexican food. **The Trap Bar** ($) serves a fine Idaho potato with all the trimmings, basic grilled sandwiches, burgers and chicken, plus apres-ski snacks.

Dinner sleigh rides cost $35 for adults and $15 for kids (14 and younger).

Apres-ski/nightlife

This is not Targhee's strong point, but you'll be too tired after a powder day to really care. **Snorkel's** has apres-ski with varietal wines by the glass, microbrew beers and upscale appetizers in a relaxed atmosphere. **The Trap Bar** is livelier, with live music, plus great apres-ski snacks like the spilling-over nachos basket. Don't miss their specialty Targhatini, made with local huckleberries and local vodka in a trendy sugared glass—sweet but refreshing.

Other activities

Outdoor activities include a **tubing park** and a free ice **skating rink** (rental skates are available). For some extra excitement, grab a pair of goggles and mush a **dogsled** through an hour-and-a-half backcountry trip that includes a trail snack and beverage. Or you can take a **sleigh ride** or go **snowmobiling**. You'll also find a heated swimming pool and hot tubs.

The Spa at Grand Targhee (307-353-2300 ext. 1358) is a cozy, three-treatment-room spa where you can indulge in massages, herbal and mud wraps, baths, a sauna and aromatherapy.

Shopping in this small village includes a smart boutique, a general store, a hard-goods shop, snowboard shop, rental and ski repair shop, and a ski clothing shop. Be sure to visit A Touch of the Tetons, a boutique that showcases a large selection of locally made jewelry, gifts and women's clothing.

Getting there and getting around

By air: Targhee is served by airports in Jackson, Wyo., and Idaho Falls, Idaho. Jets fly into both airports and resort shuttles pick up guests by reservation. Four major carriers now serve Jackson Hole with jets: American, United, Northwest and Delta. There's non-stop daily service from Salt Lake City, Denver, Chicago, Minneapolis and Houston, plus weekend non-stop service from Atlanta and Dallas. You can rent a car at either airport.

By car: Targhee is just inside the Wyoming border on the west side of the Tetons, accessible only from Idaho. From Jackson, follow signs to Wilson on Hwy. 22, then go north on Hwy. 33 at Victor, Idaho. Turn east at Driggs (the sign is on the roof of a building), and drive 12 miles to the ski area. About eight miles from Driggs, you'll start to suspect you're lost, but keep going—you can't make a wrong turn. Coming from Idaho Falls, take Hwy. 20 to Rexburg, and turn east on Hwy. 33 to Driggs. Grand Targhee is 42 miles northwest of Jackson, 87 miles northeast of Idaho Falls and 297 miles north of Salt Lake City. Be forewarned: Leave at primetime and you're in a parade of bumper-to-bumper traffic, both up and down the mountain.

Getting around: If you are spending your entire vacation at Grand Targhee, don't rent a car—there's nowhere to drive. If you stay in Jackson, we recommend you ride the Targhee Express bus that picks up in Jackson and at Teton Village. It's $71 for round trip and full-day lift pass; call (307) 733-3135. The highway between Jackson and Grand Targhee is steep going over Teton Pass (up to 10-percent grade). We caution against staying at Targhee and driving to Jackson for the nightlife—if you want Jackson's nightlife, stay there.

Dining: $$$$–Entrees $30+; $$$–$20–$30; $$–$10–$20; $–less than $10.
Accommodations: (double room) $$$$–$200+; $$$–$141–$200; $$–$81–$140; $–$80 and less.

Jackson Hole
Wyoming

Summit:	**10,450 feet**
Vertical:	**4,139 feet**
Base:	**6,311 feet**

Address: P.O. Box 290,
Teton Village, Wyoming 83025
Telephone (main): 307-733-2292
Snow Report Number: 888-333-7766
Toll-free reservations: 800-443-6931
E-mail: info@jacksonhole.com
Internet: www.jacksonhole.com

Expert:★★★★★
Advanced:★★★★★
Intermediate:★★★★
Beginner:★★
First-timer:★★★★

Lifts: 12—1 eight-person gondola, 2 high-speed quads, 4 quads, 2 triples, 2 doubles, 1 moving carpet
Skiable acreage: 2,500
Snowmaking: 160 acres
Uphill capacity: 12,000 per hour
Parks & pipes: 2 parks, 1 pipe
Bed base: 10,000 in valley; 2,500 at base
Nearest lodging: Slopeside
Child care: Yes, 6 months through 2
Adult ticket, per day: $77 (07/08)
Dining:★★★★★
Apres-ski/nightlife:★★★
Other activities:★★★★★

Jackson offers some of the toughest skiing in the U.S., but one of its secrets is that it also has great intermediate terrain and fine learning slopes.

Teton Village, at the base of the mountain, has grown up to be a respectable home base for your vacation. The village offers everything you need, including a grocery and liquor store. Lodging ranges from what must be the cheapest slopeside lodging in the states, at Hostel X, to several posh mountain retreats and a multitude of condos. Add restaurants serving everything from burgers to sushi to wild game, and a smattering of nightlife, and you could easily spend your vacation right here.

News for 2008/09: the old aerial tram was retired but 100% of the mountain is still accessible, thanks in part to the new East Ridge Chair rising from the top of Sublette to just below Corbet's Cabin on the summit. Capacity to the base of the upper mountain has been increased by adding 18 more cabins to the Bridger Gondola. Sixteen more chairs have been added to the Thunder Chair.

Mountain layout

No mistake about it. Jackson Hole is a skier's mountain, and it's not for the faint of heart or the weak of quads. It's steep, often deep, the trees are tight and most would have it no other way. The resort has two mountains—Apres Vous Mountain is best known for its groomed intermediate cruisers as well as the black Saratoga Bow, and Rendezvous Mountain has a handful of groomed runs. Most of the blues here would be blacks anywhere else.

If you've got a group of five or six, hire a guide, because few of the mountain's prizes appear on the trail map. For even more thrills, head out-of-bounds, but only with the proper equipment. Remember: The trail map is only a guide to what's available; don't expect to find trails such as Dog Leg or Elephant Tree or areas such as the Liquor Cabinet on it. If you rely on the map, you're going to be frustrated, and your skiing experience will be unfulfilled.

Expert, Advanced: If you're looking for steep (and often deep), Jackson is your mountain. Fully half of the resort's 2,700 acres is marked with one or two black diamonds, and you can now reach 3,000-plus backcountry acres from on-mountain access gates.

The East Ridge Chair rises 600 vertical feet from the top of the Sublette Chairlift to just below Corbet's Cabin. This temporary double chairlift takes skiers and snowboarders up Rendezvous Bowl. From the top, you have two choices. You could head down the ridge to the infamous Corbet's Couloir, a narrow, rocky chute that requires a 10- to 20-foot airborne entry. Or take the "easier" way down, Rendezvous Bowl. Conditions here can vary from mild to intimidating. Corbet's Cabin, at the Summit, provides a warm, dry place to make your decisions; snacks and restrooms are available.

Below Rendezvous, drop into Cheyenne Bowl. If it hasn't snowed in a couple of days, try the bumps and trees on the north side of the bowl near Bivouac. Then yo-yo on the Sublette Quad until you've made lines down the Alta Chutes—some of the steepest marked terrain at Jackson—and the Expert Chutes below Tensleep Bowl.

Intermediate: This is the kind of mountain that makes carrying a trail map, and consulting it regularly, a good idea. Having said that, 50 percent of its 2,700 acres is not black diamond and most of the tough stuff is completely separate from the easier runs, so intermediates seldom have to worry about getting in over their heads.

You will want to concentrate on the runs skier's left of the tram, using the gondola and the Apres Vous Quad to access the wide-open groomers like Gros Ventre, Werner and Moran. The shorter runs down Casper Bowl—like Sleeping Indian and Wide Open—provide plenty of opportunities to try your luck in the trees. You can follow the fast, yet meandering cat tracks down from the gondola summit. Follow the solid blue lines for groomed terrain and the broken blue lines for ungroomed powder or bumps. Complimentary orientation tours for intermediate-level skiers depart the Mountain Host building daily at 9:30 a.m.

Beginner, First-timer: Jackson Hole's easiest terrain is served by two dedicated lifts, the Eagle's Rest double and the Teewinot Quad. The green-rated runs are appropriately gentle, and some present interesting meanders among the trees. Kids will love the informal single-tracks that squiggle into the woods. But the number of beginner runs is limited, advanced-beginners will grow bored rather quickly, and it's a big step from those gently undulating slopes to Jackson Hole's blues.

Jackson Hole's excellent learning terrain surprises most people. At the base of Apres Vous mountain, along the Eagle's Rest trail, stands a fenced-in area that's served by a moving carpet. Faster skiers can't get in, so those just learning won't get nervous. The transition to the adjacent green runs is made easy by dedicated beginner lifts.

Parks and pipes

Apres Vous on it's own could hold itself as a very strong freeriding mountain, and this is where the **superpipe** is, along with various hits and kickers built by the locals. We don't recommend building your own kickers; if you're busted, they'll pull your ticket. Luckily there are natural booters and kickers all over the place; try following some local riders around for the inside line. And don't miss Upper Dick's Ditch, where you'll find a natural quarterpipe and halfpipe.

The superpipe has a surface lift, so it's easy to get back to the top. The **terrain park**, served by the Apres Vous Quad, is next to the superpipe and has 10 components including jumps, rails, bumps and a small quarterpipe. Just like Jackson Hole's natural terrain, the park features are intended for those with some experience and are not really designed for first-timers. Take care and pay attention to the signs. There is a dedicated park and pipe staff always on hand to give advice, so make sure to check out conditions with them before you launch any air.

Snowboarding

Fully half of Jackson Hole's 2,500 acres is marked with one or two black diamonds, and with the mountain's no-rope-out-of-bounds clause, you can add the best off-resort backcountry riding available anywhere in the continental U.S. The terrain out there is for real, and if you're not prepared, or experienced, there is an enormous probability of getting seriously hurt or killed, so be careful.

At Rendezvous Mountain, chutes, bowls and steeps await you, but there is often a groomed alternative way down. For jumpers, there's Corbet's Couloir, a narrow, rocky passage that requires a 5- to 20-foot airborne entry into a usually tracked, steep mogul field. No way? Then consider the even more infamous S & S Chute (check out the video, "Subjekt Haakenson," to see Terje drop this line) or take the "easier" way down—Rendezvous Bowl, a huge face littered with gigantic moguls, bushes, rocks and, if you're lucky, powder. Follow that down to the Sublette chair and continue on to Dick's Ditch, or go to The Hobacks, where the local throng chases powder after every snowstorm.

The mountain is swathed in traverses that allow a snowboarder with any momentum an easy way down. And riders have the advantage over skiers when it comes to hoofing up to the hike-to terrain. That said, in Saratoga Bowl veer rider's right as you head down or you'll have an awful traverse, perhaps even a hike, out.

Cross-country & snowshoeing (see also xcskiresorts.com)

Jackson Hole has some of the most beautiful natural surroundings in North America. Nordic skiers can strike out for marked trails in **Grand Teton** or **Yellowstone National Parks**, or try one of the three touring centers in the Jackson valley.

The Saddlehorn Activities Center (800-443-6139; 307-739-2629), also called the Jackson Hole Nordic Center, has 17 km. of groomed track in Teton Village, next to the Snake River Lodge. The South Meadow has 7 km. of trails where dogs are permitted. Rentals and lessons are available, as are guided excursions into **Grand Teton National Park**. You can exchange your Alpine lift ticket for a Nordic trail pass on the same day of purchase, so you can Alpine ski in the morning and cross-country or snowshoe in the afternoon.

Teton Pines Country Club (307-733-1005) has 14 km. of groomed skating and classic lanes on a gentle golf course with more ups and downs than you'd expect. The **town of Jackson** grooms about 30 km. each week in Game Creek Canyon, Cache Creek Canyon and the Snake River Dike. Call 307-739-6789 for the current grooming conditions. Also, Grand Teton National Park grooms a 32-km. trail between the Bradley-Taggart Lakes parking area and the Signal Mountain parking area once a week, usually on Thursdays. The **Nordic Center at Spring Creek Ranch** (307-733-8833) is another alternative.

The Hole Hiking Experience (307-690-4453) provides half-day and longer, naturalist- or wildlife-biologist-guided snowshoe tours in the Bridger-Teton National Forest or Grand Teton National Park. You'll be picked up at your lodging, and tours are planned based on your fitness level and desires.

Lessons (07/08 prices)

You can make reservations for any ski school program including mountain guides by calling 307-739-2779 or 800-450-0477.

Group lessons: Full-day lessons cost $90 for beginners and $100 for intermediates. A half-day lesson in the afternoon is $80 (beginner, with lift ticket) or $120 (intermediate, with lift ticket). Afternoon semi-private, three-person groups are $85. A class for advanced skiers and riders with a maximum of four students is $110.

First-timer package: Jackson Hole's **Learn to Turn** program is $90 and includes a guarantee that learners will be able to control speed and make turns after one day of lessons. Beginners can repeat these lessons for free until they "get it." For snowboarders, the resort offers Burton's innovative Learn-To-Ride program for $90.

Private lessons: Given most commonly in a three-hour morning lesson. Three morning hours cost $360 and three afternoon hours are $310 for up to five skiers. Early Tram Privates start at 8:30 a.m. with four hours costing $430; a full day is $545 (the same as hiring a backcountry guide). Reservations are recommended for all privates and a $25 per person reservation fee applies for the second through fifth person on all Early Tram Privates.

Special programs: There are many, such as **instruction for the disabled** (adaptive lessons questions are answered via a special adaptive hotline during the season), Steep & Deep ($890, four days, separate skiing, snowboarding and tele sessions), Backcountry Camp ($675, three-day program), and women ski and women snowboard programs ($890, four days). These **multi-day camps** include coaching, lifts, video, some meals and more.

Racing Programs: There's a NASTAR course off the Casper Bowl Triple Chair. A Ski & Race Camp is offered in December; call for details and prices.

 # Children's programs (07/08 prices)

Child care: The Kids Ranch Wranglers group is for ages 6 months to 2 years. Cost is $130 for a full day. The flexible program also has two half-day options, one in the morning from 8:30 a.m. through 12:30 p.m. for $110; the other, 12:30 p.m. through 4:30 p.m., for $100. Toddlers get lunch and a snack; parents must provide food for infants.

Reservations (307-739-2691) and a copy of your child's immunization records are required. Kids Ranch children's programs are based at the Cody House, just above the gondola base.

Other options: For babysitting at your hotel or condo, call **Babysitting Service of Jackson Hole** (800-253-9650; 307-733-0685) or **Childcare Services** (307-733-5178). These services have sitters trained in first aid and child CPR. Select caretakers at the Kids Ranch also may be available to sit in the evenings. When you make day-care reservations, ask for the resort's list of sitters. **Baby's Away** (888-616-8495; 307-733-0387) rents and will deliver baby needs to your lodge, such as crib, stroller, car seat and toys. Inquire with your host lodge before making arrangements. You can rent strollers, high chairs and backpacks from **Teton Kids** (307-739-2176).

Children's lessons: Rough Riders is for ages 3–6 (must be toilet-trained) and includes lift tickets and rentals. A full day with lunch is $130; half day in the afternoon is $110. Pioneers (ages 3–4, beginners only) get an all-day lesson and lunch for $130; PM half-day is $110. Little Rippers is a semi-private snowboard lesson for ages 5–6 and costs $195 for a full day (lift, lesson, rentals and lunch). Explorers (ages 7–14) is $150 for full day with lift ticket, rentals and lunch. Team Extreme (ages 12–17) is a three-day program for advanced skiers and riders offered at certain times of the year. It includes lift ticket, rentals and lunch for $465. Holiday Camp, (ages 12–17) costs $150.

Special activities: Kids Night Out is a supervised dinner followed by indoor games and movies. Call for times and cost; reservations required.

Lift tickets (07/08 prices)

	Adult	Young Adult (15-21)	Child (6-14)
One day	$77	$63	$39
Three days	$222 ($74/day)	$182 ($61/day)	$111 ($37/day)
Five days	$360 ($72/day)	$295 ($59/day)	$180 ($36/day)

Who skis free: Children 5 and younger.

Who skis at a discount: Ages 65 and older pay children's prices. Beginners pay a minimal ticket fee for the beginner lifts.

Notes: A photo ID is required to obtain young adult and senior rates. Christmas prices are higher; early-season prices are lower.

Accommodations

Choose from three locations: Teton Village at the base of the slopes, with fewer restaurants and nightlife options; the town of Jackson, with lots of eating, shopping and partying but 12 miles from skiing; or hotels, condos and some fine resorts between the two. Bus transportation between Jackson and the ski area is readily available.

We haven't listed all of the available lodging, so call **Jackson Hole Central Reservations** (800-443-6931) for more information.

Teton Village

The following properties in **Teton Village** are all within steps of the slopes and each other, so the choice is on facilities or price rather than location. Most of these properties have ski packages.

The luxurious, ski-in/ski-out **Four Seasons Resort Jackson Hole** (800-295-5281; 307-734-5040; $$$$) is a recent addition to base area lodging. Rooms and suites, with natural wood, stone and local art, reflect the region's Western and Native American influences and include fireplaces, private balconies, down duvets and pillows. Children younger than 18 stay free if they're in the same room with parents.

One hotel that has changed names seemingly every other year has been completely renovated and morphed into the luxurious **Snake River Lodge & Spa** (800-445-4655; $$$-$$$$). Just steps from the gondola, the lodge has double rooms to three-bedroom suites.

The Bavarian-style **Alpenhof** (800-732-3244; 307-733-3242; $$-$$$$) is the closest lodging to the lifts and a classic benchmark in Teton Village. It has an outstanding dining room (see Dining). The casual Bistro, open for lunch and dinner, is also popular for apres-ski; snag an outdoor table in spring.

Extreme skier Rob DesLauriers opened a swanky condo-hotel on the edge of Teton Village in 2002. **Teton Mountain Lodge** (800-801-6615; 307-734-7111; $$$$) is appointed in the classic Western style featuring stone fireplaces, elegant but chunky furniture, kitchens and jetted tubs. High-end amenities include indoor/outdoor pools, fitness facilities and spa, and a very good restaurant (see Dining).

Village Center Inn (800-443-8613; 307-733-3990; $$), next to the tram, has 16 one- and two-bedroom units, some with lofts. **Crystal Springs Lodge** (800-443-8613; $$$) is a newly remodeled luxury condo property in Teton Village just 50 yards from the gondola. Condos have master bedroom suites with jetted tubs, gourmet kitchens, fireplaces and washer/dryer.

The Hostel X (307-733-3415; $) is family-owned and -operated and has some of the most inexpensive slopeside lodging in the United States. Rooms are spartan, but have private baths and maid service; amenities include a large lounge, outdoor grill, ping pong and pool tables, game area and laundry facilities.

Condominiums and **private homes** are available through **Jackson Hole Resort Lodging** (800-443-8613) and Jackson Hole Central Reservations (800-443-6931; 307-733-4005). Rates are about $115-$850 per night.

In the town of Jackson

Many of these accommodations in the **town of Jackson** also offer ski packages. All listed here are within a block of the public bus service to Teton Village unless noted.

One of the best, with a great location just off the main square, is the **Wort Hotel** (800-322-2727; 307-733-2190; $$$-$$$$), an 1880s-style, 60-room, four-diamond AAA-rated hotel. Inside is the Silver Dollar Bar, with its curving bar inlaid with 2,032 uncirculated 1921 silver dollars.

The **Quality Inn 49er Inn and Suites** (307-733-7550; $$-$$$) is a three-building complex conveniently located at the edge of town and a stone's throw from an express bus stop. Suites are spacious and feature fireplaces, large bathrooms, excellent fitness facilities and a hot tub. At the **Parkway Inn** (307-733-3143; $$-$$$) bed & breakfast, the decor is decidedly Old World Victorian.

Teddy bears slumber on fluffy white duvets at the **Rusty Parrot Lodge and Spa** (800-458-2004; 307-733-2000; $$$$), a classy, in-town B&B with a renowned restaurant (see Dining) and spa (see Other Activities). Rates include a full breakfast, perhaps apricot-glazed Belgian waffles, and all-day refreshments served fireside.

At **The Grand Victorian Lodge** (800-584-0532; 307-739-2294; $$-$$$), you get breakfast in bed so you can laze away the morning (or gulp it down while you rush to get ready for a powder day).

The **Bunkhouse Hostel** (307-733-3668; $), a no-frills dorm in the basement of a motel, comprises one 25-bed room, a separate room with couches for lounging and a kitchen area with microwave and refrigerators. There are separate men's and women's lavatories, and a laundry is available. The rate is $25 per night, first-come/first-served.

Between downtown and the ski area

The **Wyoming Inn of Jackson** (800-844-0035; 307-734-0035; $$-$$$$) and The Best Western Lodge at Jackson Hole (800-458-3866; 307-739-9703; $-$$$) are across the street from one another on Broadway (Hwy. 89) heading toward Teton Village from downtown.

Spring Creek Ranch (800-443-6139; 307-733-8833; $$$-$$$$) is distinguished by jaw-dropping views, primo service, one of the area's best restaurants (see Dining) and a secluded location atop the East Gros Ventre butte. Choose from hotel rooms, condos and luxurious executive homes.

Next door is the ultra-exclusive **Amangani** (877-734-7666; 307-734-7333; $$$$). If you've got mega bucks, stay here; it has everything you could imagine wanting and then some, but if you have to ask, fuggedabowdit.

On Teton Village Road a few miles from the ski area and town is **Teton Pines Resort** (800-238-2223; 307-733-1005; $$$-$$$$). The amenities list goes on and on: free pickup from the airport, shuttle service to and from both Jackson and Teton Village, free indoor tennis, use of a neighboring athletic club, daily continental breakfast, an excellent gourmet restaurant, 14 km. of cross-country trails, pool and hot tub.

The **Jackson Hole Racquet Club** (800-443-8613; $$-$$$$) is a popular and relatively inexpensive condo cluster. It's just 4 miles to Teton Village, and there's a grocery store on the premises as well as a restaurant, bar and liquor store. The resort runs a free shuttle to the mountain.

Just below Teton Village is the log-cabin-style **Wildflower Inn Bed & Breakfast** (307-733-4710; $$-$$$$), with in-room fireplaces, a shared hot tub and fitness area, and fabulous breakfasts. Recognized as one of the top romantic inns in the nation, it's just five minutes from the ski area and Grand Teton National Park.

Dining: $$$$–Entrees $30+; $$$–$20–$30; $$–$10–$20; $–less than $10.
Accommodations: (double room) $$$$–$200+; $$$–$141–$200; $$–$81–$140; $–$80 and less.

Dining

We'll start with the selection at the ski area, and work our way toward town. If you're staying in Teton Village, be sure to spend at least one evening in town, if only to see the lighted elk-horn arches in the town square.

Teton Village

At the elegant end of the spectrum is **Alpenrose** at the Alpenhof Hotel (307-733-3462; $$$-$$$$), a quiet, genteel place. You might begin with seared St. Jacques scallops and move onto roasted baby pheasant or walleye with French cockles. **Dietrich's Bar & Bistro** (307-733-3242; $$), also at the Alpenhof, brings the price down a notch and specializes in Alpine favorites such as fondues, bratwurst, sauerbraten and wienerschnitzel. They also serve entrees such as wild game loaf, fish and chips, and lamb cassoulet in a casual setting.

Cascade Grill House & Spirits (307-732-6932; $$$-$$$$), with a menu of "new Western" cuisine and an atmosphere to match, is in the Teton Mountain Lodge.

The elegant Four Seasons Resort has a restaurant and two lounges. The open kitchen and wood-burning fireplace set the tone for the **Westbank Grill** (307-734-5040; $$-$$$), which focuses on flavors and ingredients of the American West. The **Lobby Lounge** and **The Peak** both serve light meals and refreshments that are quite affordable for lunchtime skiers.

For a truly unique dinner experience, make reservations well in advance for the **Solitude Cabin Dinner Sleighrides** (307-739-2603; $$$). The price is steep ($69.95 adults; $38.95 children younger than 10; $14.95 infants to 3 years), but it includes a sleigh ride to an on-mountain cabin, a four-course meal and tax; choose from roast prime rib or broiled salmon filet.

The Couloir, part of the new Bridger Restaurant (located at the top of the Bridger Gondola at 9,095 feet) will be open for dinner from mid-January onwards. After dinner in the rustic-elegant Couloir you take a star-lit ride back to the valley in the Gondola.

The very funky **Mangy Moose** (307-733-4913; $-$$), is a three-fold find. Head downstairs to The Rocky Mountain Oyster for cheap eats for breakfast or lunch; to the restaurant for steaks, chicken, game, fish and an excellent salad bar; and to the Saloon for pizza and burgers and apres-ski.

You can grab a breakfast or lunch bagel in the **Bridger Center** locker area. For heartier quick morning eats, try the tramline burrito at **The Village Cafe**. Eat upstairs for fast service, or head down for a more leisurely meal and choices for the health conscious. You'll find bagels, sandwiches and hot soup specials at **Bridger Bagels & Espresso** on the first level of Bridger Center. **Jackson Hole Sports** on the second level of Bridger Center is the place for coffee, espresso and Danish pastries.

Jackson

Soft lighting, a roaring fire, and an open kitchen accent the intimate **Wild Sage Restaurant** (307-744-0935; $$$) at the Rusty Parrot Lodge. Many consider it Jackson's finest restaurant.

Off Broadway Grille (307-733-9777; $$-$$$) features entrees such as lamb tenderloin with a Mediterranean black olive tapenade, Thai-steamed seafood with Asian flavors or sauteed sea scallops and leeks in a creamy tomato-saffron sauce. **The Blue Lion** (307-733-3912; $$-$$$), hidden away in a blue-clapboard house with several intimate dining rooms, is known for its roast rack of lamb, which we describe as cooked a la shake 'n' bake.

Ask locals to recommend their favorite restaurant, and it's a good chance they'll mention **Rendezvous Bistro** (307-739-1100; $-$$). The well-prepared homestyle menu defies the moderate prices. Salads and sandwiches satisfy lighter appetites, while entrees, such as a mouth-watering free-range half chicken, confit of duck, rustic lamb stew and curry vegetables with wonton strips, satisfy those who've worked up an appetite. Begin with oyster shooters at the bar, and don't forget to ask about the daily plates. The atmosphere can be boisterous—its name is certainly fitting.

Another that earns accolades from locals is **Koshu** (307-733-5283; $$), part of the Jackson Hole Wine Company. An Asian-inspired menu showcases such items as kumamoto oysters, ahi tartare, pad thai and Peking duck breast. The small but sophisticated **Nikai** (307-734-6490; $-$$), two blocks north of Town Square, is where the younger, smarter crowd goes for sushi and Asian cuisine.

If you can't decide what you're up for, head to the fancy diner setting of the **Cadillac Grille** and **Billy's Burgers** (307-733-3279; $$-$$$) right on the town square. The dining room menu is heavy on meat and game but also has eclectic entrees like goat cheese ravioli. Billy's Burgers serves, well, burgers—best in town, say the locals. And if you just want a drink, it's 2-for-1 every night, 5-7 p.m.

Tired of Western kitsch? Try the **Cyprus Restaurant** (307-733-8220; $$-$$$$) a block off the main street with Mediterranean dishes like lamb and cous cous and a signature dish the locals call lobster mac & cheese. Belly dancers entertain guests every Friday night.

For casual inexpensive dining, the Jackson Hole classic is **Bubba's** (307-733-2288; $-$$), featuring heaping plates of "bubbacued" ribs, chicken, beef and pork. Try the Mexican huevos for breakfast or sink your teeth into one of Bubba's oversized omelettes. No sense in giving you the phone number, because Bubba's doesn't take reservations (it's on the main drag at 515 W. Broadway). Be prepared to wait, and while you do, send a member of your party to the liquor store—Bubba's is BYOB and they encourage you to bring your own bottles.

Another casual place is **Mountain High Pizza Pie** (307-733-3646; $) and they deliver when you can't quite get it together to go out. **Nani's Genuine Pasta House** (307-733-3888; $$), two blocks north of Broadway, and **Anthony's** (307-733-3717; $$), near the Wort Hotel, get raves from locals for authentic Italian regional cooking. For Mexican, head to **The Merry Piglets** (307-733-2966; $-$$) near the town square; for Thai, it's **Thai Me Up** (307-733-0005; $-$$) a block from the town square.

The hearty-breakfast king is **Bubba's**. For tamer breakfast fare try **The Bunnery** (307-733-5474; $) with excellent omelets, whole-grain waffles and bakery items, and **Jedediah's Original House of Sourdough** (307-733-5671; $) for superb sourjack pancakes.

Between town and the ski area

Set high on a butte with a wall of windows framing the Tetons, the Granary at Spring Creek (307-733-8833; $$$-$$$$) lets you drink in the views along with your elk tenderloin or hazelnut-encrusted trout. Desert tones provide a neutral background for the top-notch food and views. You may want to take a sleigh ride before dinner (reservations required). Come early on Fridays for the jazz happy hour. Note: This is not a good choice for vegetarians.

Another top choice is **The Grille at Teton Pines** (307-733-1005, $$-$$$) at the Teton Pines Resort, with a beautiful dining room and extensive wine list. **Stiegler's** (307-733-1071; $$) has specialties from chef-owner Peter Stiegler's home in Austria.

The Mexican restaurant with the best reputation is **Vista Grande** (307-733-6964; $-$$). The fajitas are a must-have. For casual dining, try the **Calico Italian Restaurant & Bar** (307-733-2460; $$), halfway between Jackson and Teton Village at a bus stop on Village Road and very popular with the locals.

If you're headed to Grand Targhee, rustic **Nora's Fish Creek Inn** in Wilson (307-733-8288; $$ for dinner) is a local favorite for any meal, especially breakfast.

Dining: $$$$–Entrees $30+; $$$–$20–$30; $$–$10–$20; $–less than $10.
Accommodations: (double room) $$$$–$200+; $$$–$141–$200; $$–$81–$140; $–$80 and less.

Apres-ski/nightlife

The Mangy Moose is by far the rowdiest spot in Teton Village for apres-ski and nightlife. It's also one of the best spots in all of skidom. Big-name entertainers often provide an intimate concert here, so check the newspaper listings.

The **Village Cafe** near the base of the tram is crowded with locals at the end of the day. **Cascade Grill House & Spirits** in the Teton Mountain Lodge is a local favorite and delivers great apres-ski atmosphere. **Dietrich's Bar & Bistro** at the Alpenhof Lodge attracts a sedate group, as does the lobby bar in **Snake River Lodge**, where you can curl up in an oversized chair by the fire. **The Peak** in the Four Seasons is busy and a surprisingly good value—the perfect place to swap stories over table games and TVs broadcasting sporting-event coverage. There's also a slopeside outdoor deck here. Fine wine and cheeses from around the world set the tone for the ultra-modern setting at **Vertical**, in the Best Western Inn..

In town, **The Million Dollar Cowboy Bar** attracts tourists who love saddle bar stools and line-dancing to live country & western bands. Try it, corny as it sounds, though the crowd tends to be 40 and older. It's cash-only, so leave the credit card at home. **The Silver Dollar Bar**, at the Wort Hotel, is similar, with 2,032 uncirculated 1921 silver dollars embedded in the bar. It serves great buffalo burgers and Starbucks coffee plus, on Sunday nights, all-you-can-eat pizza.

Locals say the **Cadillac Grille** has the best happy hour in town-two-for-one drinks every night from 5-7 p.m. Try their "signature" cosmopolitan. At **Nikai**, the "in spot" for sushi lovers, a DJ turns Friday night into hip-hop night.

The young set that likes to party hard heads to the **Log Cabin Saloon** to shoot pool, play foosball and darts, and drink heavily. Another hot spot is the **Rancher**, where drafts are $1 and mixed drinks $2 during Tuesday night Town Meetings. **The Shady Lady Saloon** at the Snow King Resort has live entertainment several nights a week.

The local crowd heads to the **Snake River Brewing Co.** for award-winning, yet affordable, hand-crafted lagers and ales as well as sandwiches.

Another local hangout is the **Stagecoach**, in Wilson. The busiest times are Thursdays for disco night (honest!) and on Sundays, when the legendary house band performs its mix of country & western, bluegrass and swing.

The **Bull Moose Saloon** (877-498-7993), 35 miles south of Jackson in Alpine, has mechanical bull riding every Wednesday, Friday and Saturday night. Ladies ride free; men pay $3 per ride, $10 for the whole night. The saloon also brings in exotic dancers about once a month, $10 admission.

 ## Other activities

To book most off-slope activities, call Jackson Hole Reservations at 307-739-3076. Most guests make the time to visit nearby **Grand Teton** and **Yellowstone National Parks**. Several unusual activities center around Jackson's abundant wildlife. Plan to spend a half day at the **National Museum of Wildlife Art** (800-313-9553; 307-733-5771) combining a museum tour with lunch in the cafe. The museum houses the nation's premier collection of fine wildlife artwork in varied media. Permanent and rotating exhibits are displayed in 12 galleries, but everywhere you look there's art, from the pawprints on the floor to the sculptures in the reception area and on the grounds. Lunch is a treat. The semi-self-serve cafe, operated by Spring Creek Ranch, dishes delicious soups, salads, sandwiches and kids' favorites. The **National Elk Refuge** is home to as many as 10,000 elk during winter. You can take a horse-drawn sleigh ride, accompanied by a refuge biologist, out to the herd. The approximately one-hour trip provides an unrivaled opportunity to view wildlife in its natural setting. Sleighs depart from the Jackson Hole and Greater Yellowstone Visitor Center at the north end of town. Include time to wander through the interpretive displays at the visitor center. Sleigh rides are first-come, first-serve, but large groups should make reservations (800-772-5386).

An outstanding educational tour is offered through **Wildlife Expeditions of Teton Science School** (307-733-2623). On the school's wildlife spotting tours, you ride with a biologist to help note the location and numbers of various birds and animals. Half-day, full-day and multiday tours, some into Yellowstone National Park, are offered. We spotted bison, elk, eagles, moose, deer, bighorn sheep, trumpeter swans and pronghorn. Everyone gets to use binoculars and a powerful spotting scope for up-close viewing.

Horse-drawn **dinner sleigh rides** are offered by **Spring Creek Ranch** (307-733-8833) and **Solitude Cabin** (307-733-6657). Bar-T-Five (733-5386) operates the sleigh rides on the National Elk Refuge and also has a **winter dinner show** with a barbecue dinner and "yarn-spinnin' " leading the entertainment.

The Jackson Hole Nordic Center (800-443-6139;1 307-739-2629) has hour-long **dogsled tours**. Mush with Billy Snodgrass at Continental Divide Dogsled Adventures (800-531-6874), the main dogsled outfitter in the region. Territory covers some 400 miles of spectacular scenic trails in the Shoshoni, Teton and Targhee National Forests. Choose from half-day, full-day and multi-day trips that include going from Jackson Hole to Togwotee Mountain Lodge or Brooks Lake Lodge on the Continental Divide and from Grand Targhee Ski Resort into the backcountry. Eight-time Iditarod veteran Frank Teaslee operates Jackson Hole Iditarod Sled Dog Tours (307-733-7388) at the entrance to Granite Creek, with full- and half-day options. We recommend the full-day trip into Granite Creek Canyon, which includes a soak in the hot springs and lunch. One child weighing less than 50 pounds is free with every two paying adults, and round-trip transportation from your lodging is available.

The Snow King Center (800-522-5464; 307-733-5200) houses a regulation ice rink, open to the public, where the local hockey team plays regularly. The center also hosts regular concerts and shows by big-name entertainers. Check local papers for events.

Other activities include **snowmobile excursions** to Granite Hot Springs, Yellowstone and Old Faithful, Togwotee Pass, Grand Teton, Gros Ventre, Grey's River and the Continental Divide. Most outfitters, and there are many, provide transportation to and from your lodging. Llama Louie's Reservations (307-733-1617), conveniently in the Mangy Moose, arranges snowmobile trips without a charge.

High Mountain Heli-Skiing (307-733-3274) offers helicopter skiing on untracked powder in five mountain ranges surrounding Jackson Hole. These folks have been operating for more than 25 years. A day trip usually delivers six runs of 12,000-15,000 vertical feet, with one guide per five clients. Rendezvous Ski and Snowboard Tours gives daily backcountry tours in Grand Teton Park, Teton Pass and other locations, while Snow King Mountain Guides operates trips off the back of Snow King and Teton pass for Nordic and alpine skiers.

The small, but full-service **Wilderness Adventure Spa at Spring Creek Ranch** (307-733-8833) is designed to incorporate feng shui principles of harmony and balance as well as to reflect Native American influences. Facilities include women's and men's steam rooms and a co-ed hot tub overlooking the mountains. Plan an afternoon here, perhaps followed by a sleigh ride and/or dinner in the Granary Restaurant. A 60-minute massage is $100.

The full-service, five-story Avanyu Spa (800-445-4655; 307-732-6070) at the Snake River

Dining: $$$$–Entrees $30+; $$$–$20–$30; $$–$10–$20; $–less than $10.
Accommodations: (double room) $$$$–$200+; $$$–$141–$200; $$–$81–$140; $–$80 and less.

Lodge has a free-form indoor-outdoor heated pool with waterfall hot tub in addition to rain and Swiss showers, hot tub, sauna and steam room in the locker rooms. Locker room lounges are inviting, with large-screen TV in the men's and a fireplace in women's. A 50-minute massage begins at $120. A spa menu is available.

In town, **The Body Sage Day Spa** (307-733-4455) at the Rusty Parrot Lodge offers traditional spa therapies including massage, facials and scrubs and exclusive treatments integrating local ingredients, such as rose petals. A one-hour massage is $100.

Shopping is plentiful. You can easily while away an afternoon browsing the boutiques, factory outlets and art galleries in Jackson. As a general rule, you'll find the farther you get from Town Square, the less expensive the prices are. The covered wooden sidewalks encourage window shopping, even when it snows. There are far too many good shops to single out many of them, but you'll find art galleries, plenty of Western clothing and items made from elk antlers.

Don't miss Coldwater Creek, across the street from the famous antlered town square. This familiar catalogue retailer also sports a basement discount area with true bargains. Valley Bookstore is your best source for books in all of Wyoming. Also across the street from the town square, this independently owned bookstore is a good source for books on the area as well as best-sellers and obscure finds. Another "must" is Thomas Mangelsen's gallery (888-238-0177), a block from the town square. One of the world's best nature photographers, Mangelsen documents only what's captured in the wild and not in captive situations. Hard to believe, but he uses no computer manipulation.

If you're a fan of classical music, the **Grand Teton Music Festival** (307-733-1128) stages a monthly concert series in Walk Festival Hall in Teton Village.

You can pick up culture, shopping, dining or vacation-planning guides at the Wyoming information center on the north edge of town, or call the Jackson Hole Chamber of Commerce (307-733-3316).

Getting there and getting around

By air: Four major carriers now serve Jackson Hole with jets: American, United, Northwest and Delta. There's non-stop daily service from Salt Lake City, Denver, Chicago, and Minneapolis, four-times-a-week service from Dallas, plus weekend non-stop service from Atlanta and Cincinnati. Check with the resort central reservations for air bargains. This is a small airport, surrounded by towering mountains, with pretty good chances of delayed flights. It may be a wise idea to build an extra day into your schedule heading in and out, especially if your travel requires several plane changes. And if weather grounds you, remember to ask about distressed traveler rates at local lodgings.

By car: Jackson is on Hwys. 89, 26 and 191 in western Wyoming. The town is 10 miles south of the airport, and Teton Village is 12 miles farther by Hwys. 89, 22 and 390. Driving, Jackson Hole is about five hours from Salt Lake City and 10 hours from Denver.

To stem the tide of traffic into Teton Village, Jackson Hole has opened the Stillson Parking Lot, which offers free parking about 7 miles from the base area with free open-air shuttles to and fro. All other parking at the base area is paid, up to $10 per day, unless you are riding with at least four or more in your car—then it is free anywhere.

Getting around: The rule in the past was rent a car. But for visitors to Jackson Hole who are staying at the ski area and focused on skiing and snowboarding, the mountain village has everything you need to stay busy for a week. You can use the shuttlebus to get into town, and taxis between the village and town are only about $10. If you are staying in town, a car may be more convenient and will save lots of time. While buses run regularly, they can add up to

45 minutes to your commuting time during the busy apres-ski period, and at night, buses from town to Teton Village run only once an hour.

Unless you are used to driving steep Rocky Mountain passes, we recommend that you take the Targhee Express (307-733-3101) to Grand Targhee in snowy weather. It's $15 well spent.

Motorists, take note: Highway signs say little about the ski areas. From town, follow signs to Teton Village to get to Jackson Hole Mountain Resort, and to Wilson when driving to Grand Targhee.

START (Southern Teton Area Rapid Transit) buses run frequently between Jackson and Teton Village to 10 p.m. in ski season for a small fee. Study the bus schedule and get on an express bus if you want to minimize your commute. Another good deal: books of bus passes sold at most resorts. They can save you a few bucks off the published fare. Five companies provide taxi services and airport shuttles: Jackson Hole Transportation (307-733-3135), Gray Line (307-733-4325), Buckboard Cab (307-733-1112), All-Star Taxi (307-733-2888) and All Trans (307-733-1700). Check websites for discount coupons on airport shuttles.

Nearby resorts

Snow King Resort, Jackson Hole, WY; (800) 522-5464

Internet: www.snowking.com

4 lifts; 400 acres; 1,571 vertical feet; 1 terrain park; 1 halfpipe

Snow King, Wyoming's oldest ski area, is in downtown Jackson, about 12 miles from Jackson Hole Ski Resort. Despite its in-town location, crowds don't exist here except for special events. The north-facing slopes plunge 1,571 feet, with some trails literally dropping out from under you. The steep, consistent pitch makes it a favorite for European World Cup teams, who often train here before events at Park City, for visitors who like to open throttle on manicured groomers and for local powder pigs who head here instead of fighting the tram crowds at Jackson Hole. Sixty percent of the mountain's 400 acres is rated advanced, and that includes some bump runs and glades; Bearcat to Bearcat Glades is a corker. Beginners and lower intermediates have a few gentle runs on the lower mountain. Another plus: The "Wow!" views from the 7,808-foot summit.

The resort includes a hotel and condominiums (see *Accommodations* above*).* The Snow King Center houses a regulation ice rink where you can skate, watch semi-pro hockey and perhaps even take in a concert by luminaries such as B.B. King. Snow King also has a multilane tubing park open weekdays, 4 to 8 p.m., and weekends, noon to 8 p.m.

Lift tickets (08/09): $41 adult; $31 for ages 14 and younger and 60 and older. Note that lifts open at 10 a.m. If your flight lands early enough, consider warming up here with a two-hour ticket, $22 adult, $17 juniors/senior. Or, combine a two-hour ticket with Sunday Brunch at Rafferty's, the hotel restaurant. Night skiing Tuesday through Saturday costs $20 adults, $15 junior/senior.

Canadian Resorts

Canada is a prime destination for a ski or snowboard vacation. Generally, the giant mountains and vast snowfields are in the West, while the narrow trails and quaint ski towns are in the East, just as they are in the U.S. But a Canadian ski/snowboard vacation also has some very attractive differences. Some examples:

• Some of Canada's leading winter resorts are in national parks. Banff and Jasper National Parks have four ski areas within their boundaries. The scenery is magnificent and wild animal sightings are common.

• You can stay in an opulent, historic hotel, even if you're on a budget. The Fairmont chain includes several grand hotels built to accommodate late 19th- and early 20th-century luxury rail travel. In summer these castle-like hotels are jammed with tourists willing to pay premium rates, but in winter, prices plummet.

• In Quebec, the French influence provides a European flavor to a vacation. Yet, English also is spoken so Americans shouldn't feel too overwhelmed.

• We provide prices in Canadian dollars, which, at press time in September 2008, was about C$1.06 for each U.S. dollar and C$1.50 for each euro. Canada has a Goods and Services Tax (GST) of 6 percent, and we note whether it is included in listed prices, which are rounded up to the nearest dollar. Visitors to Canada can no longer get a GST refund for goods they take out of the country or on hotel rooms. The refund program was discontinued when the federal government lowered the GST from 7 percent to 5 percent.

Canada can be as cold as you've heard, or warmer than you imagined. We've skied in windbreakers in January, and huddled into fleece neck-warmers during a sudden April snowstorm. Our advice is to plan for everything.

Authorities in the U.S. and Canada require U.S. citizens to carry a passport as of January 23, 2008 for air travel and June 1, 2009 for land and water travel. A passport is always required for citizens of countries other than U.S. and Canada.

Single and divorced parents, take note: In an effort to prevent child stealing, Canadian immigration requires that any parent entering Canada alone with his/her child show proof of custody, such as a notarized letter from the other parent. Anyone traveling with someone else's child (grandparents, uncles and aunts, friends) must present a notarized letter signed by both of the child's parents. If you're driving with friends in separate cars, be sure kids are matched with parents when crossing the border. Sometimes you'll breeze through without being asked for proof, but it's best to be prepared.

Banff, Canada

Sunshine Village & Banff@Norquay

Banff Region Facts
Dining:★★★★
Apres-ski/nightlife:★★★★
Other activities:★★★★★

Internet: www.skibig3.com (tri-area skiing)
www.bannflakelouise.com (tourism bureau)
www.canadianrockies.net (townsite)
Bed Base: 10,000 in Banff

While flying into Calgary during the day provides awe-inspiring views of the Canadian Rocky Mountains, perhaps the best surprise is to arrive late at night, when everything is enveloped in pitch black, and make the hour-and-a-half-long drive to Banff. That way, the next morning when you draw back the curtains, the massive craggy mountains are suddenly right there, in your face. What a wake-up call!

Banff is home to three resorts—Sunshine Village, Ski Banff @ Norquay and Lake Louise. The three mountains provide very different ski experiences, just one of the reasons Banff makes a fabulous ski trip. For those who have never skied out West, it's easy to be overwhelmed by the massive amount of terrain and the steep craggy peaks. You can plan your vacation accordingly to start at the smallest of the resorts and work up to the larger and more difficult ones: Spend your first day at Ski Banff @ Norquay, the next at Sunshine Village, then head to Lake Louise. There is a sense of being swallowed up by the wilderness—embraced by Mother Nature and then gently released to be part of her bountiful gifts here. Wildlife is plentiful, sightings of elk herds in town are common. Mule deer and bighorn sheep live in the Bow Valley, and sometimes bears and wolves can be seen along less-traveled roads.

The completion of the coast-to-coast railway in 1885 made one of the most picturesque and remote pockets in the Rocky Mountains suddenly accessible. This virgin landscape—formerly known only to Canada's Aboriginal peoples, fur traders and explorers—was now open to tourists. That same year, Canada established its first national park, Banff. Later, four other national parks were created nearby: Yoho, Jasper, Kootenay and Glacier, which explains why much of the region's rugged beauty remains essentially unspoiled. The scenery is still as magnificent as it was to the train travelers of the late 1800s with snow-capped mountain ridges, cliff faces pocked by glaciers, mountain lakes and hot springs.

Contrast this with the beautifully designed, compact, yet very cosmopolitan town of Banff, filled with excellent restaurants, nightclubs, shops and lodging. The atmosphere is a uniquely Canadian blend of quaint and rustic, set amid some of the most rugged scenery in the Rockies.

Because summer is the high season in the park, crowds diminish in winter and lodging prices are rock bottom, even at the most luxurious hotels. The temperature can be numbingly cold, or pleasantly warm if a Chinook wind blows. Unlike the Canadian resorts closer to the Pacific Ocean, ski areas in Banff receive a dry, fluffy powder that is the best thing this side of Utah.

Tri-Area Lift Passes (08/09 prices, without tax)

The Banff/Lake Louise Region has an interchangeable lift ticket. It can be used at Sunshine, Ski Banff@Norquay and Lake Louise, and includes a free shuttle between most Banff/Lake Louise hotels and the ski areas. It also includes a free night-skiing ticket (Fridays only) when used at Ski Banff@Norquay to make up the price difference. It's easy and convenient. Prices are lower when purchased with a vacation package. (Prices rounded to nearest dollar.)

	Adults	Children (6–12)	Youth (13–17)/Seniors (65+)
Three of four days	C$240	C$113	C$215
Five of seven days	C$400	C$188	C$356
Seven of nine days	C$548	C$258	C$488

Sunshine Village Facts		Ski Banff@Norquay Facts	
Summit Elevation	8,954 feet	Summit Elevation	7,000 feet
Vertical	3,514 feet	Vertical	1,650 feet
Base	5,440 feet	Base Elevation	5,350 feet

Address: Box 1510,
Banff, Alberta, Canada T1L 1J5
Telephone (main): 403-762-6500
Snow Report Number: 403-760-7669
Toll-free reservations: 877-542-2633
Reservations: 403-762-6500
E-mail: reservations@skibanff.com
Internet: www.skibanff.com
Lifts: 12 total: 1 high-speed 8-passenger gondola, 5 high-speed quads, 2 quads, 1 triple, 1 double, 2 moving carpets
Skiable acreage: 3,358
Snowmaking: None
Uphill capacity: 20,000
Parks & pipes: 1 park, 1 pipe
Nearest lodging: Slopeside, hotel
Child care: Yes, 19 months and older
Adult ticket, per day: C$74 (w/o tax)

Dining:★★★★
Apres-ski/nightlife:★
Other activities:★

Expert:★★★★★
Advanced:★★★★★
Intermediate:★★★★
Beginner:★★★
First-timer:★★★

Address: P.O. Box 1520,
Banff, Alberta, Canada T1L 1B4
Telephone (main): 403-762-4421
Snow Report Number: 405-760-7704
Reservations: 403-762-4421
E-mail: info@banffnorquay.com
Internet: www.banffnorquay.com
Lifts: 5 total: 1 high-speed quad, 2 quads, 1 double, 1 moving carpet
Skiable acreage: 190
Snowmaking: 85 percent
Uphill capacity: 7000
Parks & pipes: 1 park, 1 pipe
Bed base: 10,000 in Banff
Nearest lodging: Base of access road — ski-in only
Child care: Yes, 19 months and older
Adult ticket, per day: $49 (08/09)

Dining:★★★★
Apres-ski/nightlife:★★★★
Other activities:★★★★★

Expert:★★★
Advanced:★★★★
Intermediate:★★★★
Beginner:★★
First-timer:★★

Sunshine Village

Sunshine Village has long been known for its winding 13-minute gondola ride (or six minutes to Goat's Eye mid-station) that carries you almost 1,650 vertical feet from the parking lot, along the walls of a valley and box canyon, to the village and the rest of the lifts.

Creekside Bar & Grill and a rental shop sit near the parking lot at the gondola base, but the real base area for Sunshine is at the top of the gondola at 7,082 feet, where you will find a small village with two lodges, a rental shop, general store, restaurants and the Sunshine Inn, the only slopeside lodging in the national parks. The Inn has been completely remodeled and upgraded, with an outdoor hot tub, fitness center and massage facility. Guests staying here get first tracks off the Standish Lift 30 minutes before everyone else.

Mountain layout

Slopes are spread over three mountains, mostly above treeline. The three-mile run at the end of the day on Banff Avenue—from the Village down to the parking lot—is a run marked green for beginners that will seem tame for many intermediates. An alternative way down is Canyon Trail, which starts out intermediate and turns into a single-black diamond. You catch it near the base of the Jack Rabbit Quad. You can also download on the gondola, which many people do. Local's tip: Goat's Eye in the morning, Park in the afternoon.

Expert, Advanced: Get off the gondola at the Goat's Eye mid-station and board the Goat's Eye Express which whisks you to the top of 9,200-foot Goat's Eye Mountain. Here, there is almost 2,000 vertical feet of fabulous glades and steep but wide-open cruisers. A classic run drops between the two large rock outcroppings, called Cleavage by the locals, then continues into the glades below.

The runs under the Angel Express Quad—especially Ecstasy—have good pitch. Heading right at the top of the Angel Express will take you into a fairly steep bowl. Shoot down to the Continental Divide High-Speed Quad. This lift takes you a soaring to the almost-summit of Lookout Mountain. At the top you cross the Continental Divide from Alberta to British Columbia. These descents are wide-open, consistent pitches, as if a flat world was upturned about 25 degrees. Or drop into Bye Bye Bowl. If you don't carry your speed at the bottom, you will go "bye-bye" and have to hike. For some of the toughest in-bounds extreme skiing in North America, hike a short distance to Delirium Dive from the top of the Continental Divide Quad.

Three rules are strictly enforced at the control gate: 1) All skiers/riders must wear an avalanche transceiver; 2) All must carry a rescue shovel; 3) All must ski or ride with a partner.

Below Delirium is Silver City, another assortment of extreme choices. The resort's other extreme terrain, The Wild West, is on Goat's Eye and has the same restrictions, with its runs named for early settlers in the area. You'll also find fun, steep, whoop-dee-dos to the left off the new Standish Express Chair, and into the Paris Basin and Birdcage off the Wawa quad.

Intermediate: There's terrain from every lift for intermediates; however, be sure you are confident at this ability level if you try the runs on Goat's Eye or the peak of Lookout Mountain.

Find lots of fun on the blues off the Strawberry Triple on Mt. Standish. The grade's just right on Boutry's Bowl for those learning to ski powder. Carry your speed and cut through the woods to get back to the chair.

You'll find some short black runs off the Wolverine Express and the Jackrabbit Quad, both down-mountain from the other lifts. You can enjoy this area any time of the day. Then either ride the gondola to the top from midstation or take Miss Gratz to the Tee Pee Town chair. Most people play here in the afternoon on their way back down to the bottom base.

Beginner, First-timer: First-timers learn near the base village, where a moving carpet carries beginners to the top of a short gentle slope that is off to one side. There's also a Ski School Tow near the daylodge. Off the Angel Express on Lookout Mountain a smooth green runs back to the village base and the Strawberry Triple Chair which also has wide, sweeping runs to the village.

The top of Strawberry accesses the Continental Divide Express which crosses into British Columbia and has a wide open green back to the base. The Wolverine Express high-speed quad below the village has gentle wide slopes good for those still perfecting their technique. Greens from there wind back to the bottom of the Strawberry Triple. Both the Strawberry Triple Chair and the Wolverine Express high-speed have gentle wide slopes.

Parks and pipes

The Angel or Continental Divide chairs can access the Roger's Terrain Park. This park is the best in the Banff area and is meticulously manicured. Three different lines run parallel to each other, and all have a number of tables, kickers, and rail/box features.

Snowboarding

With three different mountains, tons of vertical feet, and some of the steepest inbound slopes in North America, Sunshine resort should be on every rider's itinerary while in Alberta.

From the base, grab your gear and run to the high speed gondola. Don't waste time getting ready in the parking lot, do it in the comfort of the gondola. While enjoying the ride, look up to the left and check out the Wild West. Cliffs and tight chutes are the only way down once you enter this area. To get here, get out of the gondola at the first stop and keep an eye out for Goat's Eye. This high speed quad is the preferred lift on powder days for advanced to expert riders. If venturing to the Wild West, first see if it is open. If so, make sure you have an avalanche beacon, shovel, and probe. They are required to get into this restricted area.

If the Wild West seems a little too wild, go right off the Goat's Eye quad and look for Cleavage. The Cleavage chute is separated by two giant rocks. Once you get through the cleavage just keep going down and head for the small bushes.

The jewels of Sunshine are off the Continental Divide Express. After checking in with ski patrol and being equipped with a beacon, shovel, and probe, the Milky Way ridge climbs up to the left. The knife edge ridge leads to the Galaxy Chutes, Delirium Dive, and Silver City. The entrances to these chutes are in the 40- to 60-degree range and require expert riding skills.

The Strawberry triple Chair and the Wawa quad go to areas that access a lot of beginner and intermediate cruisers. Both these spots have wide open runs all the way to the base.

The Mount Standish Express (quad) hovers over rolling hills and a small cliff band that runs parallel to the lift. This region resembles one big natural terrain park with hips, cliffs, and rollers all in the same run.

 ## Cross-country & snowshoeing (see also xcskiresorts.com)

There are some scenic, easy loops along the Bow River. Take Banff Avenue to the end of Spray Avenue, or turn left and cross the river. Trails wind through the whole area. **Parks Canada** puts out a very informative booklet on the extensive Nordic skiing and snowshoeing in **Banff National Park**. You can get a copy for a small fee at the **Banff Information Centre**, 224 Banff Ave., 9 a.m. to 5 p.m.

Fairmont Banff Springs Golf Course Clubhouse offers ski and skate rentals, plus group and private lessons. Maps and information on trails are available at the Clubhouse.

Several sports shops rent snowshoes. Ask your lodging concierge.

White Mountain Adventures (403-678-4099) is just one of many outfitters that offers naturalist-guided snowshoe treks, backcountry and cross-country skiing tours.

Lessons (08/09 prices, with tax)

Group lessons: Daily Group Workshops are full-day programs available to all ability levels. Levels 1-3 pay C$138 and groups are limited to eight people. Levels 4-6 pay C$159 and groups are limited to six people.

First-timer package: A full-day program with lesson, rentals and lift ticket is C$160. A three-day package costs C$390.

Private lessons: For up to five people, C$355 for three hours; C$535 for a full day.

Special programs: Sunshine Village encourages the traditional Ski Week, a weeklong stay at the slopeside Sunshine Inn, by providing packages including classes with the same instructor. Groups can be divided by ability level or by family and include evening activities. Call for prices, which vary by season and size of room.

Children's programs (07/08 prices, with tax)

Child care: Ages 19 months to 6 years. Full day with lunch is C$60. Multiday discounts available. Reservations recommended; call (877) 542-2633.

Children's lessons: Ages 3-6 can get a combo ski-and-play program. A full day with lunch and lift ticket costs C$103. Ski rentals are extra. Reserve through day care.

Kids Kampus is an all-day program for kids ages 6-12, skiing or snowboarding. Cost for full day with lunch is C$106; multiday discounts available. Lift tickets and rentals are extra.

Sunshine Mountain Riders for kids 13-17 explores the entire mountain in skiing and riding groups. Cost is C$140 for a full day with lunch; three days, C$403; five days, C$636.

The three-day Club Junior offers three days of fun on three mountains for C$271.

Lift tickets (08/09 prices, without tax)

	Adult	Child (6-12)
One day	C$80	C$38
Three of four days	C$240 ($80/day)	C$113 ($38/day)
Five of seven days	C$400 ($80/day)	C$188 ($38/day)

Who skis free: Children ages 5 and younger.

Who skis at a discount: Students ages 13-17 pay C$55 for one day. Ages 65 and older pay C$63. Multiday discounts apply.

Notes: Prices have been rounded to the nearest dollar. Check out the Tri-Area Pass if you're staying in Banff. It is valid at Sunshine Village, Ski Banff@Norquay and Lake Louise and includes bus rides from hotels to the ski areas. The bus ride alone is about C$15 round-trip between Banff and Sunshine Village, so the Tri-Area Pass can be a good deal even if you use it at Sunshine most of the time (detailed above).

Ski Banff @ Norquay

Like most local hills, this small but challenging area is where families and racers spend their weekends, so mid-week here is the best time to visit on your Banff winter adventure. With virtually no lift lines, you can really rack up the vertical. In fact, you may have so much fun, you might want to return before leaving for home. Its reputation for challenge hits you as soon as you drive into the parking lot and see the steeps served by the original Norquay double chair. But if you're not an expert, don't turn around and go home. There are a few convenient, forgiving beginner and intermediate areas. See mountain layout.

Norquay, 10 minutes from Banff, and home to two-time World Cup GS Champ Thomas Grandi, claims some of the best grooming in Western Canada. It also threatens the thighs with some gnarly bump runs and hard-core dynamite double-black super-steeps, as demanding as any slopes in the Canadian Rockies.

The winding mountain road that takes you up to the base lodge can be a bit dicey, but the views are incredible as you climb above the town of Banff. Cascade Lodge at the base has an excellent restaurant, a bar, three large stone fireplaces and the other usual services.

Mountain layout

The resort is small, especially by Rocky Mountain resort standards, and the base lodge is right at the bottom of all the runs on the same side of the mountain, so there's no chance of getting lost as you explore.

Expert, Advanced: The North American chair, called The Big Chair by locals, takes you to those ribbons of bumps tumbling down the mountainside. It's an old slow chair that rarely has a line. Be positively sure you want to be here. This is very tough stuff with no blue or green runs down. That said, these are quite possibly the most fun bump runs in all of skidom. And they are long.

Not quite ready for the intimidating mogul-choked runs off North American? Work your way to the other side of the resort, taking Cascade, then Spirit chairs to the Mystic Express. Most of the blues here have enough sustained vertical and pitch to rank as black at other resorts, and the majority are meticulously groomed: perfect for screaming cruisers.

Intermediate: Two things intermediates should know: blue slopes here are "dark" blue and cats do not groom on snowy days (so locals can get in their powder turns). So if you are a low intermediate, you'll want to start out on the groomed, gentle warm up runs off the Cascade lift just outside the base lodge.

Watch out for novice skiers and riders getting their ski legs. This area is listed as green, but it's more like a short blue. The Spirit and Mystic chairs climb up ridges that serve the area's intermediate runs that are pretty steep by most standards—most would be black at other areas. Start out on Hoodoo and work your way up to the tougher trails.

Look at it this way: if you want to ratchet up your intermediate skills a notch, this is the place to do it. If you can ski the blue runs here comfortably, you'll be able to ski blacks at other resorts just fine.

Beginner, First-timer: The beginner, first-timer area is conveniently located next to the Snow Sports Center/Ski School just across from the base lodge. Although this is NOT a hill for beginners, this small area is an easily accessible place to learn. It has a gentle well-groomed slope served by a moving carpet, the Sundance Conveyor, with an enclosed, protected run, Shenanigan. Next door, the Cascade quad chair serves most of the sheltered beginner terrain. Beginners would be advised to stick to these areas as the other Norquay green runs are much more advanced and sometimes quite hard-packed and icy when they're covered with man-made snow.

Parks and pipes

The small terrain park is under the Cascade quad, and is lit for night skiing. Some decent kickers are lined up and random features are scattered throughout the area. The good size quarter-pipe with a box on the lip is a lot of fun, and the many boxes offer low-consequence jibs for those who are learning.

Snowboarding

Overlooking the town of Banff, Norquay is a decent resort for the intermediate rider. The North American double chair accesses some steep terrain, which also offers a good challenge of skill and endurance. The 1,300-vertical-foot runs are on a consistent pitch, but they are covered with moguls from top to bottom. It is rare to find snowboarders on this lift, because of the constant bumps.

On the other side of the mountain the Crystal Express (quad) offers up a number of intermediate and slightly advanced runs. The off-piste advanced runs of Sun Chutes and Sheep Chutes are fairly dense glade runs with more bumps. Most beginners start off on the Cascade quad, where five short green runs meander to the bottom. Next to Cascade, the Spirit quad has 3 short intermediate runs.

Cross-country & snowshoeing (see also xcskiresorts.com)

There are some scenic, easy loops along the Bow River. Take Banff Avenue to the end of Spray Avenue, or turn left and cross the river. Trails wind through the whole area. **Parks Canada** puts out a very informative booklet on the extensive Nordic skiing and snowshoeing in Banff National Park. You can get a copy for a small fee at the Banff Information Center, 224 Banff Ave., 9 a.m. to 5 p.m.

Fairmont Banff Springs Golf Course Clubhouse offers ski and skate rentals plus group and private lessons. Maps and information on trails are available at the Clubhouse.

Several sports shops rent snowshoes. Ask your lodging concierge. **White Mountain Adventures** (403-678-4099) is just one of many guide outfits that offers naturalist-guided snowshoe treks, guided backcountry tours and cross-country skiing tours.

Lessons (07/08 prices, plus tax)

Ski Banf@ Norquay offers a large menu of lesson options (403-760-7716) from a broad range of expert professional instructors. Except for their Discover programs, lessons do not include lift tickets or rentals. Before you visit, you can get rentals online at rentskis.com and they'll be waiting for you when you arrive.

Group Lessons: All ability levels pay C$80 for a half day skiing or snowboarding; C$110 for a full day.

First-timer package: C$59 for a two-hour group lesson, Magic Carpet Lift ticket and rental equipment for skiers or snowboarders. Additional two-hour lesson in the afternoon, C$30.

Private Lessons: C$99 for one hour; C$179 for two hours; C$339 for three hours; C$525 for a full day. Each additional person costs C$30 per hour.

Lift tickets (07/08 prices, plus tax)

Adult C$49; Child (6-12) C$17

Who skis free: Children 5 and younger ski free when an adult buys a lift ticket. Tickets for only the Sundance Carpet Lift are $13 for adults and $12 for everyone else.

Who skis at a discount: Youth ages 13-17 and seniors 65 and older pay C$39 for a full day; C$32 for an afternoon ticket (noon-4 p.m.); C$25 for two hours. Ski Banff@Norquay has the region's only night skiing. It's on Fridays (5:00 p.m. - 10:00 p.m.) and costs C$24 for adults, C$12 for children, C$22 for seniors and students with ID.

Although Ski Banff@Norquay also sells multiday tickets, we've given you the ticket prices we think destination visitors are most likely to use. The area sells hourly tickets for two to five hours, ranging in price from C$29 to C$47 for adults (discounts for kids, youth and seniors). Our recommendation: Use the Tri-Area Lift Pass at Lake Louise and Sunshine Village, and buy a two- or three-hour ticket here. If you want to ski here again after two hours (and you may—it's a small yet fun place), then use a day on your Tri-Area Pass (detailed above).

 ## Accommodations

Banff has accommodations to meet every taste and every budget. Rooms can be found for as little as $50 (Cdn$), and premier locations are within most budgets. In addition to the 5 percent GST, Alberta also has a 5 percent lodging tax, tacking on 10 percent to your cost. **Banff/Lake Louise Central Reservations** (800-661-1676) books lodging in Banff, Lake Louise and Jasper. **Ski Banff-Lake Louise-Sunshine Reservations** (877-754-7076) books ski packages including the tri-area lift tickets and lodging at more than 30 Banff and Lake Louise properties.

Decore Hotels purchased Norquay's funky Timberline Inn, renamed it **The Juniper** (877-762-2281; 403-762-2281; $$-$$$$) and recently completed extensive renovations. It's at the bottom of Norquay's access road, so technically it's Banff's only ski-in hotel. You can ski in along a 1.5-kilometer trail, but you'll need the hotel's shuttle to take you to the lifts. Small dogs are allowed. The hotel includes a restaurant.

The Sunshine Inn (403-762-6500; 800-661-1676; $$$), at 7,200 feet in the center of Sunshine's base village, is the only slopeside lodging in Banff National Park. Surrounded completely by snow, with not a car in sight, the 84-room inn is reached by riding the gondola up from the parking lot. Rooms were recently renovated, with slate tile in the bathrooms, flatscreen TVs, and comfortable, if simple, furnishings.

We strongly recommend the experience of staying at **The Fairmont Banff Springs** (800-441-1414 in the U.S. and Canada; 403-762-2211; $$$-$$$$) the Scottish-influenced castle perched on a hill, a 15-minute walk from downtown. You have likely seen this classic, rundle-rock monolith in many photos. Its public areas are expansive, designed for turn-of-the-20th Century mingling. The hotel has an Aveda spa with saunas, steam rooms and hot tubs as well as a fitness room, salons and treatment areas. There are also indoor and outdoor pools, shops, restaurants and activities.

The **Banff Caribou Lodge & Spa** (800-563-8764; 403-762-5887; $$-$$$), a 10-minute walk from downtown, has an on-site spa, hot tub, steam room, exercise room, lobby with massive fireplace, wi-fi, heated underground parking with ski lockers, and The Keg Steakhouse & Bar.

Brewster's Mountain Lodge (888-762-2900; 403-762-2900; $$-$$$) in downtown Banff is a rustic, family-owned lodge with hand-crafted log furniture, the friendliest, most helpful staff on the planet, free wifi in rooms, a public internet terminal in the lounge above the lobby and a free continental breakfast in their funky basement area. There's always a fire burning in the stone fireplace in the lobby which you can smell throughout most of the hotel. Amenities include shops, laundry, ski storage, sauna, whirlpool and a very upscale restaurant adjacent to the lobby (See dining).

"An enclave of civility" is how the **Rimrock Resort Hotel** (800-661-1587; 403-762-3356;

$$$$) accurately describes itself. It's posh, sophisticated, elegant and refined, with a full-service spa and fitness center, an excellent restaurant, comfortable lounge and views to match.

Families might want to stay at the **Douglas Fir Resort & Chalets** (800-661-9267; 403-762-5591; Calgary direct, 403-264-2563; $$-$$$$). These are condo-style units with wood-burning fireplaces and full kitchens, two- and three-bedroom chalets and a few suites. Enjoy the waterslide, indoor swimming pool, hot tub and saunas.

The Mount Royal Hotel (800-267-3035 Western Canada only; 403-762-3331; $$-$$$$) has a great location in downtown Banff—an excellent choice for those who enjoy nightlife, but it gets a fair amount of street noise from Banff Avenue. It has an exceptionally good restaurant. See dining. **The Inns of Banff** (800-661-1272; 403-762-4581; $$-$$$$), a modern, multi-level lodge with balconies in most rooms, is a 15-minute walk from downtown. **High Country Inn** (800-661-1244; 403-762-2236; $$-$$$) on Banff Avenue, two blocks from downtown, is one of the least expensive lodgings with a pool and an Italian/Swiss Restaurant.

Banff Alpine Centre-HI (866-762-4122; 403-762-4123; $) on Tunnel Mountain Road and part of Hostelling International, recently added a 66-bed wing with rooms that have two or four beds and private bathrooms. Showers are shared in the older rooms. Facilities include a laundry, kitchen and pub-style restaurant. **SameSun Backpacker Lodge** (403-762-5521; $) 449 Banff Avenue, sports a friendly, funky atmosphere. What used to be Global VIllage Banff, this newly renovated dotown lodging caters to hostelers. The lodge offers most amenities available in higher-priced hotel/motels: WiFi and web access with no curfew, no lockout, ski packages and ski shuttles right outside your door.

If your flight home is early in the morning, you can't beat the **Delta Calgary Airport Hotel** (800-268-1133 or 403-291-2600; $$$-$$$$). Roll out of bed, then walk out the front door of the hotel and into the terminal. It also has a pool and fitness center, lounge and two restaurants.

Other accommodations are available in nearby Lake Louise.

The Fairmont Chateau Lake Louise (800-441-1414; 403-522-3511; $$$-$$$$), on the shore of Lake Louise, has spectacular views of Victoria Glacier across the lake. This elegant old world hotel dates back to a log chalet built in 1890. It has many restaurants, shops, a Nordic ski center, masseuse, nearly 500 guest rooms, impeccable service and free ski shuttles. **The Inns of Banff** (800-661-1272; 403-762-4581; $$-$$$$), a modern, multi-level lodge with balconies in most rooms, is a 15-minute walk from downtown. **High Country Inn** (800-661-1244; 403-762-2236; $$-$$$) on Banff Avenue, two blocks from downtown, is one of the least expensive and has a pool and an Italian/Swiss Restaurant.

The Post Hotel (800-661-1586; 403-522-3989; $$$-$$$$) is a cozy, beautifully furnished, 93-room log lodge with great views on all sides. You'll want to dress for your divine evening meal. There is also a free ski shuttle. Stay here if you like lodging of a quieter, gentler era.

Deer Lodge (800-661-1595; 403-522-3747; $$$) just a few minutes walk down the hill from the Fairmont Lake Louise Chateau, will drop your blood pressure. Rooms have no television, and many have no phones. Instead, read by a roaring fireplace in the enormous common region.

Lake Louise Inn (800-661-9237; 403-522-3791; $$-$$$$) is a simply decorated hotel good for families. Rooms range in size from economy double (two double beds) to superior lofts that sleep six. Amenities include heated indoor pool, hot tub, steam room and arcade room.

The **Canadian Alpine Centre & International Hostel** (403-522-2200; $), on Village Road, is everything you never expect in a hostel. It's bright, spotless, modern and convenient, with two-, four- and five-bed rooms with private toilets and shared showers. There are also a laundry and two spacious, well-equipped self-service kitchens. The lounge, with stone fireplace, comfy chairs and Internet kiosks, provides an elegant atmosphere matched by many hotels. The upscale

Accommodations (Cdn$): (double room) $$$$-$200+; $$$-$141-$200; $$-$81-$140; $-$80 and less.
Dining (Cdn$): $$$-Entrees $20+; $$-$10-20; $-less than $10

cafe (see Dining) is open 7 a.m.-9 p.m. Best of all, nightly bed rates start at $23; three-day ski packages, including tickets at Lake Louise, shuttles and breakfast, begin at $185.

Num-Ti-Jah Lodge (403-522-2167; $$-$$$) is about a half-hour's drive from Lake Louise. This funky stone-and-log hotel has 25 simple rooms, most with private baths and the restaurant is quite good (see Dining). It sits on the shores of Bow Lake, and on clear days you can see the glaciers.

Dining

For those staying on mountain at Sunshine Village, the **Eagle's Nest Dining Room** ($$$-$$$$) in the Sunshine Inn offers fine dining with lobster and filet mignon. **Chimney Corner Lounge** ($$) the inn's fireplace lounge, serves a very good sit-down lunch. Try the barbecued beef and a local-brewed ale. Ask to sit in the sunroom so you can watch the skiers and riders on Lookout Mountain. The cafeteria has one of the best selections of food at any ski area in this region. **The Creekside Restaurant** ($) at the base of the gondola serves a hearty breakfast or choose a la carte. Flavored cappuccinos are also on the menu. Take time to look at pictures from Sunshine's past during the early glamorous days of skiing, as well as Native American relics and antique outdoor winter gear.

In the Town of Banff, diners have a tremendous choice of restaurants. You will find almost every variety of ethnic food, as well as the familiar steak-and-seafood restaurants. Restaurants here, especially those on Banff Avenue, often are on the second floor above the shops.

The Fairmont Banff Springs alone has 10 restaurants. **The Banffshire Club** (403-762-6860; $$$$), the Fairmont's premium dining experience, evokes the intimacy of a rich yet understated private club. Tapestries, wrought-iron light fixtures, vaulted ceilings, archways, leather, fine linens, bone china and crystal set the stage for exquisite cuisine. The menu has a French influence, with entrees changing by the season to make the best use of fresh regional specialties. Wine aficionados will appreciate the wine list representing more than 2,000 labels; Scotch fans have a list of 75 Scotches. **Castello Ristorante** (403-762-6860; $$) specializes in Italian dinners. The expansive Saturday lunch buffet at the **Bow Valley Grill** (403-762-2211, Ext. 6841; $$-$$$) is worth a visit. Choose from a wide selection of salads, soups, side dishes and entrees as well as stir-fry and pasta stations. A dessert buffet is available for C$5 more. Austrian, German and Swiss fare, including schnitzels and fondues, are the specialties at **Waldhous** (403-762-6860; $$), an Austrian escape within a former golf clubhouse. Rich woodwork, a huge fireplace and Bavarian accents complement the menu. **Grapes** (403-762-2211, Ext. 6660; $$) is the 21-seat wine bar. Light meals are also available.

Le Beaujolais (corner of Banff Avenue and Buffalo Street, 403-762-2712; $$$) receives high praise for its French cuisine. Meals can be ordered a la carte, but the restaurant specializes in fixed-price three- or five-course meals.

The dining room at **Buffalo Mountain Lodge** (Tunnel Mountain Road, 403-762-2400; $$$) offers relaxed elegance with hand-hewn beam construction and a massive fieldstone fireplace. Rocky Mountain cuisine is its specialty, with a variety of wild game and fish. The wine list was awarded Wine Spectator's "Award of Excellence" several years in a row.

For Banff's only live dinner show, head to **The Balkan** (120 Banff Ave, 403-762-3454; $$-$$$) for authentic Greek, steaks, seafood and pasta. Tuesdays and - in season - Thursdays you can enjoy a belly dancing show. They'll even give you a plate to smash, but only if you join in the Zorba-style dancing!

Tiki bar meets the Wild West at the smoky **Grizzly House Restaurant** (207 Banff Ave., 403-762-4055; $$-$$$$). Alberta beef and exotic game meats are the specialties, fondues and hot rocks are the preferred preparations. Take a walk on the wild side and stretch your wallet and taste buds by ordering the exotic fondue dinner with shark, alligator, rattlesnake, ostrich, frogs legs, buffalo and venison.

The Maple Leaf Grille & Spirits (137 Banff Ave. 403-760-7680; $$$-$$$$) is a rustic-chic restaurant specializing in the bison tenderloin and other Rocky Mountain game. Start your meal with a seafood tower of oysters, mussels, prawns, scallops, smoked salmon, squid, crab, and lobster (all flown in fresh four times per week), and end with a molten chocolate souffle.

For gourmet Italian, try **Giorgio's Trattoria** (219 Banff Ave. 403-762-5114; $$) which serves Northern Italian pastas, thin crust pizzas, fish, veal and Alberta beef tenderloin. Also enjoy the extensive wine list in this warm atmosphere of candlelight, rich mahogany tables and excellent service. **Guido's** (116 Banff Ave. above McDonald's, 403-762-4002; $$) features good American Italian food, such as spaghetti, lasagna and chicken parmigiana. **Ticino Swiss-Italian Restaurant** (415 Banff Ave., 403-762-3848; $$-$$$) specializes in dishes from the Italian part of Switzerland.

Bumper's The Beef House (603 Banff Ave., 403-762-2622; $$-$$$), with a cozy log interior, has been serving Alberta beef since 1975. Tender prime rib comes in four cuts, accompanied by a very hot horseradish sauce. The chicken cafoosalum has a tasty maple sugar-lime sauce. The meal comes with a good salad bar; try the mango jalapeno salad dressing or the creamy cucumber. There's a good kids' menu, plus from adult choices, they will make smaller portions for children 12 and younger.

Not surprisingly, steaks and chops dominate the menu at the second-floor **Saltlik, A Rare Steakhouse** (221 Bear St., 403-762-2467; $$), where tables surround a copper, central fireplace. Veggies and potatoes are priced separately and served as sides. For those who prefer other protein, chicken, salmon and tuna also are on the menu.

Typhoon (211 Caribou St., 403-762-2000; $$-$$$) is the place for eclectic Asian cuisine, served in a colorful dining room. Make a meal from the all-day appetizers or choose from entrees such as green Thai chicken curry, spicy tiger prawns and pork & beef satay. Each is listed with a wine recommendation. Or choose from more than a dozen beers, half from Asia.

Across the street and owned by the same folks is the intimate **Cafe Soleil** (208 Caribou St., 403-762-2090; $-$$$), a Mediterranean tapas and wine bar attached to Brewster's Mountain Lodge. Choose from an all-day tapas menu, with more than two dozen tantalizing, affordable choices, or a Big Tapas menu after 6 p.m. Evening dining offers half a dozen choices of more expensive delicacies such as lamb tahini, beef tenderloin and seared ahi tuna. Paninis, pizzas and pastas are also available.

The popular **Coyotes Deli & Grill** (206 Caribou St., 403-762-3963; $$-$$$) specializes in tasty Southwestern meals, including vegetarian and pasta dishes. Try the smoked chicken burrito or the roasted vegetable and shaved asiago pizza. Open for breakfast, lunch and dinner. A reservation for dinner is recommended and if you're 15 minutes late, you lose it. If you want a natural meal to complement all that natural beauty, head to the **Sunfood Cafe** (Sundance Mall at 215 Banff Ave., 403-760-3933; $) for vegetarian fare such as stir fry, Swiss cheese roesti, smoked tofu and zucchini pasta and portabello pasta.

Earl's (229 Banff Ave. at Wolf Street, 403-762-4414; $$) gets rave reviews for moderately priced Canadian beefsteak, fresh salmon, pasta and thin-crust pizza. **St. James Gate Olde Irish Pub** (205 Wolf St., 403-762-9355; $-$$) specializes in hearty Irish pub food that warms the heart on a cold winter day. **Wild Bill's Saloon** (201 Banff Ave., 403-762-0333; $$-$$$) is a big ol' saloon and dance hall that serves big ol' burgers made from beef, elk, buffalo and boar, as well as seafood, steaks and chicken.

Accommodations (Cdn$): (double room) $$$$-$200+; $$$-$141-$200; $$-$81-$140; $-$80 and less.
Dining (Cdn$): $$$-Entrees $20+; $$-$10-20; $-less than $10

Aardvark Pizza & Sub (304 Caribou St., 403-762-5500; $-$$), "the locals' choice in homemade pizza for over a decade," makes a great thick-crust pizza. One of the most fun places to eat breakfast, lunch or an informal supper is **Joe Btfsplk's Diner** (221 Banff Ave. 403-762-5529; $) is set in 1950s-style diner decor complete with jukebox and Elvis posters.

For gourmet coffee, the best hot chocolate in town, delicious pastries and darn good chicken sandwiches, visit **Evelyn's Coffee Bar** (210 Banff Ave.; $) and its sister shops **Evelyn's Too** (229 Bear St.; $) and **Evelyn's Three** (119 Banff Ave; $). **Second Cup** (Cascade Plaza Mall at 317 Banff Ave.; $) serves fine coffees, pastries and atmosphere.

Apres-ski/nightlife

Apres-ski is more quiet than rip-roaring in Banff, but things really start hopping at night. Younger crowds probably will enjoy Banff nightspots, while older skiers might be happier at The Fairmont Banff Springs Hotel's many bars and lounges. The Happy Bus shuttles skiers to nightspots around Banff until midnight for $2, or you can walk between most lodging and town.

Apres-ski, head to **The Paddock** at The Mt. Royal Hotel. Crowds also gather at **The Rose and Crown**, an English-style pub with draught ale, a fireplace, pool table, darts and live entertainment. **St. James Gate Olde Irish Pub**, built in Dublin and assembled in Banff, is a traditional Irish pub with 33 draught beers and more than 65 single malt scotches. Tommy's Neighbourhood Pub on Banff Ave. is popular with the locals. **Magpie & Stump** serves up great nachos and some of Banff's best apres-ski.

Retreat after skiing into the cozy and justifiably popular **Cafe Soleil**, a Mediterranean tapas and wine bar. Nibble on selections from the all-day tapas menu, with more than two dozen choices, each more enticing than the previous.

In The Fairmont Banff Springs, the **Rundle Lounge** has quiet music for hotel guests. At the **Waldhaus**, not far off the lobby, Happy Hans and Lauren, on accordion and trumpet, get everybody singing. At night, **Bumper's Loft Lounge** has a casual crowd, with live entertainment and ski movies.

The lively **Saltlik Lounge** is where you can often hear live blues and jazz or watch sporting events on six large-screen TVs. **Wild Bill's Legendary Saloon** on Banff Avenue has country & western bands and a huge dance floor. Locals flock to **Barbary Coast** on Banff Avenue for what is repeatedly hailed as the best live music, usually along the rock/blues lines.

The Aurora, in the basement of the Clocktower Mall, features a lounge, cigar bar and dance floor with DJs and bands. This is the dance bar where everyone goes after every place else in town closes. Finish off your night on the lower level at 110 Banff Ave.

Other activities

Sunshine Village offers **Snowbike** rentals. Light weight with full suspension, they'll have you grinning from ear to ear as you carve turns on the slopes and kick up roosts in the powder. Rentals include the snowbike, blades, ski boots and helmet if you need them, as well as an introductory lesson with a guide.

Banff is a playground of activities in both summer and winter. One of the most popular activities is an apres-ski soak in the **Banff Upper Hot Springs** (403-762-1515). Cost is C$7.30 for adults, C$6.30 for children and seniors. You can even rent a swimsuit for C$1.90. Winter hours are 10 a.m. - 10 p.m., Friday and Saturday until 11 p.m. There's also the full-service Pleiades Massage & Spa (403-760-2500 for **spa** reservations).

Kids will love the two giant indoor **waterslides, kiddy pool, hot tub, steam room, fitness room, arcade, pool tables, and indoor playground** at the Douglas Fir Resort & Chalets

(403-762-5591) in downtown Banff (see Lodging). Cost is C$8 per person for non-guests ages 4 and up; kids 3 and younger are free.

Another popular off-slope activity is the **Johnston Canyon Icewalk** (White Mountain Adventures, 403-678-4099). Steel boardwalks are anchored into the limestone walls, and pass through a natural rock canyon, which leads to 33-foot Lower Falls.

Try **dogsledding** (Howling Dog Tours, 403-678-9588), **ice fishing** (Banff Fishing Unlimited, 403-762-4936); **ice skating** behind on a rink behind the Fairmont Banff Springs hotel or on the Bow River; a **sleigh ride** (Warner Guiding & Outfitting, 403-762-4551); or an introductory course in **ice climbing** or **ski mountaineering** (Yamnuska Mountain Adventures; 403-678-4164).

One of the most famous **heli-skiing** companies, Canadian Mountain Holidays, is head-quartered here (403-762-7100). RK Heli-Ski also does day heli-ski trips from Banff (403-762-3771), with transportation to Panorama in British Columbia. Book a sightseeing flight with Alpine Helicopters (403-678-4802) to view the magnificent mountain peaks.

While you can't **snowmobile** inside Banff National Park, there is awesome terrain available just outside the Park. Banff Snowmobile Tours (888-293-8687) will pick you up in Banff and Lake Louise for half-day or full-day tours, including snowmobile, all necessary gear, and a hot lunch. Discover Banff Tours (403-763-7183) provides snowmobile, equipment, transportation, hot lunch and snack for their full day outings. Toby Creek Snowmobile Tours (866-416-2034) operates out of two British Columbia locations, with daily transportation from Banff.

Museums of note: Banff Park Museum for the story of early tourism and wildlife manage-ment, and a taxidermy collection of animals indigenous to the Park; Cave & Basin National Historic Site, where the hot springs were first discovered; Whyte Museum of the Canadian Rockies, for historic and contemporary art and historic homes; and the Buffalo Nations Luxton Museum, for Plains Indians history.

In the townsite, **shopping** is plentiful, with hundreds of shops lining Banff Avenue and its side streets.

For non-kitschy Canadian **souvenirs**: Orca Canada or Great Northern Trading Company (clothing, jewelry, knickknacks), Rocks and Gems (inexpensive jewelry made from native Canadian gemstones), and A Taste of the Rockies (smoked salmon, jams and honeys).

Getting there and getting around

By air: Calgary Airport is served by major airlines. Rocky Mountain Sky Shuttle (888-762-8754; 403-762-5200), Brewster Transportation (403-762-6767) Greyline Transportation (403-762-9102) and Banff Airporter (403-762-3330) will get you from the airport to Banff.

By car: Banff is 85 miles west of Calgary on the Trans-Canada Highway, a 90-minute drive. Ski Banff@Norquay is on Norquay Road, one exit past Banff. The Sunshine Village exit is 5 miles west of Banff; it's 5 more miles to the gondola base parking area. Free shuttles pick up skiers at 11 Banff hotels and the bus depot. Check the website for updates on pick-up sites, schedules and fares.

Getting around: It is possible to ski Banff and Lake Louise without a rental car by using free shuttlebuses offered with the Tri-Area Lift Ticket to the ski areas. The Happy Bus takes you within the town and region (noon to midnight only between Oct. 1 and April 30, C$2 a ride). Taxis are available too, but that can add up quickly. For spectacular sightseeing and exploring, it's best to have a car. Again, check the website for shuttle schedules and fares.

Accommodations (Cdn$): (double room) $$$$-$200+; $$$-$141-$200; $$-$81-$140; $-$80 and less.
Dining (Cdn$): $$$-Entrees $20+; $$-$10-20; $-less than $10

Lake Louise Mountain Resort
Banff Region
Alberta, Canada

Summit: 8,650 feet
Vertical: 3,250 feet
Base: 5,400 feet

Address: P.O. Box 5, Lake Louise, Alberta, Canada T0L 1E0
Telephone (main): 403-522-3555
Snow Report Number: 403-762-4766
Toll-free reservations: 800-258-7669
E-mail: info@skilouise.com
Internet: www.skibig3.com

Expert:★★★★
Advanced:★★★★
Intermediate:★★★★
Beginner:★★★★
First-timer:★★★★

Lifts: 9—1 high-speed 6-person gondola, 1 high-speed six-pack, 2 high-speed quads, 1 quad, 1 triple, 3 surface lifts
Skiable acreage: 4,200, also powder and bowls
Snowmaking: 40 percent
Uphill capacity: 15,240
Parks & pipes: 1 rail park
Bed base: 10,000
Nearest lodging: About 2 miles away
Child care: Yes, 3 weeks and older
Adult ticket, per day: C$72+tax (07/08)

Dining:★★★
Apres-ski/nightlife:★★
Other activities:★★★★★

Lake Louise Mountain Resort, Canada's second-largest ski area after Whistler Blackcomb in British Columbia, is one of three resorts in Banff National Park. It's difficult to say what makes it more memorable— its colossal terrain with incredible diversity or the truly jaw-dropping views. One visit is usually all it takes for Lake Louise to make virtually everyone's top 10 list of mountain resorts.

The resort doesn't have a glitzy persona. Instead, Lake Louise is down-home, warm and friendly. It's a wonderful destination for families and groups with different ability levels. Its vast terrain provides plenty of fun and challenge for everyone. Lake Louise has some truly steep terrain balanced nicely with groomed intermediate runs fun for experts. Top that off with some challenging beginner and first-timer terrain, and everyone's bound to be happy.

Beginner terrain is minimal here, but the learning area and ski school are conveniently located right at the base lodge.

Mountain layout

Lake Louise Mountain Resort is comprised of four mountain faces that create three distinct areas: the Front Face, the Back Bowls (with 2,500 acres) and the Larch Area. The Lake Louise trail map has an excellent synopsis of where different ability levels should head, so be sure to grab one. With 139 named bowls, chutes and trails, you'll find it indispensable.

The Top of the World Express lift is a high-speed six-passenger chair that tops out at the saddle of a wind-exposed ridge, so bundle up. If you want sun all day and want to ski the whole area, go to the Back Bowls in the morning, Larch midday and end up on the Front Face.

Expert, Advanced: Unless you want to warm-up on intermediate cruisers, avoid the gondola and head for the Glacier Express quad chairlift. The Men's Downhill trail, named after the World Cup race hosted here every November, will get your blood (and adrenaline) flowing. It's also the same route used for the World Cup ladies' downhill. Then take the Top of the World 6-pack and drop into the Back Bowls.

From the top of the Larch Chair, some powder hounds hike the 8,900-foot summit to leave tracks down Elevator Shaft, between two rock outcroppings. The chute is within the ski area boundaries. Try Rock Garden in the Larch area, a hidden playground of loops, swoops, moguls and Cadillac-sized rocks. There's great tree skiing on Lookout Chutes and Tower 12.

Intermediate: The Front Face has a good web of intermediate trails served by the Glacier Quad, Top of the World six-pack and Grizzly Express Gondola. Even the Summit Platter gets intermediates to some great terrain and gorgeous views in Boomerang Bowl.

From Top of the World chair, you can cruise back down the front face or hop over to the back side bowls and the Larch area for the best intermediate skiing accessed by a high-speed quad. Wolverine, Larch and Bobcat are all long cruisers. Lynx has a black-diamond moniker, but can be handled by most adventurous intermediates. Rock Garden is a fun run, and you can dip in and out of the trees here.

Beginner, First-timer: For novices and kids, the Minute Maid Wilderness Adventure Park is a fully enclosed learning area for riders and skiers. This area is serviced by a moving carpet lift and is conveniently located near the Daycare Center.

Those with a bit more experience can ride the Glacier Express quad and head down Wiwaxy, a 2.5-mile cruiser. Next step up is the Grizzly Express Gondola for Deer Run and Eagle Meadows. With more confidence come the Back Bowls off the Eagle Chair for a cruise down Pika on the back side of the mountain.

Beginners have a couple of nice runs in the Larch Area, Marmot and Lookout, but these also include some narrow and steep cat track terrain. At the top of the lift, make sure to check what runs have been groomed. It makes all the difference here.

Parks and pipes

Lake Louise has only a small rail park that sits at the bottom of the Glacier Express and has a few rails and boxes. To enter the park a "park pass" is required. The pass costs $5 for the season and is offered to anyone who reads and signs the lengthy waiver.

Snowboarding

The above tree-line bowls range from intermediate to "if you fall, you die," and the lower mountain holds an interesting blend of glade areas and crusie groomers. On a powder day, taking a few laps on the Summit Platter is a quick, easy way to get in a lot of turns. If you're looking for a steeper, more exhilarating run, hike up the ridge to Mount Whitehorn and the "Ultimate Steeps." These runs off the peak disappear as the slope rolls over into the 45-degree and steeper range. Scoping these lines first from other areas may be smart, as there is no turning back after the first few turns. Eight distinctive chutes meander down the north side of the ridge into a giant apron and a flat run-out. Riding these fresh would be as good as heli runs.

Down the ridge on the other side of the saddle, the Paradise triple chair leads to the other freeride challenge of Lake Louise. The "Wall" and Eagle Ridge (a.k.a ER chutes) has more double black diamond runs that empty out onto the Pika trail. The beginner-rated Saddleback trail has lured novice riders into an area that many would not call easy.

The Larch Express quad is a great option for all levels of riders. Two long beginner runs, a number of intermediate cruisers, and some advanced glade runs are hidden from the crowds on the front side. From here the "Ski Out" run wraps around the main mountain to the resort base area. This run is not suggested for snowboarders, since a large part of it is flat and requires skating or walking. Instead, take the Ptarmigan quad up and over to the front side.

Cross-country & snowshoeing (see also xcskiresorts.com)

The **Fairmont Chateau Lake Louise** (800-441-1414; 403-522-3511) has about 50 km. of groomed trails and access to hundreds of miles of backcountry trails, with stunning views of the lake and mountains. The ungroomed, well-marked trail to **Skoki Lodge**, a rustic log cabin (no electricity, no plumbing, wood-burning stove, great food), begins just above Temple Lodge at the ski area and heads up the valley and over Boulder Pass, 7 miles one way. Reservations are required. The **Shoreline Trail** starting in front of The Fairmont Chateau Lake Louise is an easy mile and a half one way.

A complex 20-km. network called **Pipestone Loops** starts 4 miles west of the Lake Louise 6ver-pass on the Trans-Canada Highway. Although all are marked beginner, some are suitable for the intermediate.

About 25 miles from Lake Louise, just over the border into British Columbia, is **Emerald Lake Lodge** (800-663-6336 or 403-343-6321). It has a 40-km. network of groomed trails with views of the Presidential Range, lodging in comfortable cabins and activities such as skating, snowshoeing and a games room. The lodge has a shuttle to the Lake Louise ski area..

Lessons (07/08 prices, without tax)

Group lessons: For skiers or snowboarders, levels 2-3, it costs C$89 for two hours or C$119 for an all-day lesson. Levels 4-6 pay C$109 for two hours; C$139 for an all-day lesson that includes video analysis.

First-timer package: C$89 includes a full-day lesson, equipment rental and beginner lift ticket for skiers or snowboarders. A three-day package including lessons, rentals and lift ticket costs C$359; program starts on Sunday or Thursday.

Private Lessons: For skiers and snowboarders, one hour costs C$149; two hours, C$229; two hours after 2 p.m., C$195; First Tracks (two hours starting at 8:30 a.m.), C$235; full day, C$525. Private lessons accommodate up to five people.

Special programs: Lake Louise has several special clinics, some for two hours, others for several days, including Performance Plus Workshops, women's camps and more. Call for all details and prices (403-522-1333) .

The **Club Ski and Club Snowboard** programs operate at Lake Louise, Sunshine Village and Ski Banff @ Norquay. Groups of similar interest and expertise ski or ride together with the same instructor for four hours a day at each of the three areas, then dine at an optional closing-night dinner with prizes. The program starts Sundays and Thursdays, and one benefit is lift-line priority. The three-day program costs C$234 (plus tax, lift tickets and rentals).

Racing: A dual-slalom course is available for group bookings.

Children's programs (07/08 prices, without tax)

Child care: Ages 3 weeks to 6 years. Toddlers have their own play area. A full day is C$59 for infants to 19 months. Ages 19 months to 36 months cost C$49 for a full day; C$29 for a half day. Ages 36 months and older cost C$47.50 for a full day; C$29 for a half day. Ask about discounts for multiple children. Free snacks are provided; lunch is available by request for C$8. Infants younger than 19 months require reservations; no reservations are taken for other ages. Call 403-522-3555.

Children's lessons: A program for ages 3–6 provides day care, ski lesson and indoor and outdoor play. Cost is C$20 for one lesson, C$29 for two one-hour lessons; must book through day care.

All-day ski programs for children ages 5–12 and snowboard programs for kids 7–12 cost C$92. Lift tickets are an additional $24; rentals C$18; lunch C$13. All children must wear helmets; rentals available for C$7. A half-day program in the morning costs C$59.

Club Junior, fashioned after the adult's Club Ski and Club Snowboard programs, is a three-day program featuring group lessons and skiing one day each at the three Banff resorts; cost is C$256 plus tax, lift tickets and rentals.

 Lift tickets (07/08 prices, without tax)

	Adult	Child(6-12)
One day	C$72	C $24
Three days	C$216($72/day)	C$72 ($24 per day)
Five days	C$360($72/day)	C$120 ($24 per day)

Who skis free: Children younger than 5.

Who skis at a discount: Youth ages 13-17 pay C$50 for one day and C$45 for half-day; ages 65 and older pay C$58 for one day and C$46 for half-day. .

Who skis at a discount: Youth (13-17) and Seniors 65+ pay C$182 for three days, C$304 for five days and C$425 for seven days.

Tri-Area Lift Passes for the entire Banff/Sunshine/Lake Louise area are available. See page 432 for details and prices.

Accommodations

Banff/Lake Louise Central Reservations (800-661-1676) books lodging in Banff, Lake Louise and Jasper. **Resorts of the Canadian Rockies Inc.** (800-258-7669), which owns Lake Louise, books ski packages and lodging for these Western Canada resorts: Lake Louise, Nakiska, and Kimberley. You also can book online at www.skilouise.com. **Ski Banff/Lake Louise-Sunshine Reservations** (877-754-7076) books ski packages including the tri-area lift tickets and lodging at more than 30 Banff and Lake Louise properties. Packages are customized and can include Club Ski, Club Snowboard and Club Junior lessons, rentals, air and other activities. Also visit online at www.skibig3.com.

The elegant **Fairmont Chateau Lake Louise** (800-441-1414; 403-522-3511; $$$-$$$$), on the shore of Lake Louise, has a spectacular view of Victoria Glacier across the lake. This hotel, which has recently completed a new wing with a new steak house (see dining), dates back to a log chalet built in 1890. It has restaurants, shops, Nordic ski center, nearly 500 guestrooms and free ski shuttles to the Lake Louise ski area.

The **Post Hotel** (800-661-1586; 403-522-3989; $$$-$$$$) is a cozy, beautifully furnished, 93-room log lodge with great views on all sides and fireplaces in 38 of the rooms. The buffet breakfast is a board of tasty delights and dinners are exquisite. There is also a free ski shuttle.

A five minute walk from the Chateau sits the **Deer Lodge** (800-661-1595; 403-522-3747; $$$). Mostly rustic, the lodge has elements of luxury. Rooms have no television and some still have no phones, while others have wireless Internet access. **Lake Louise Inn** (800-661-9237; 403-522-3791; $$-$$$$) is a simply decorated hotel good for families. Amenities include heated indoor pool, hot tub, steam room and arcade room.

The **Canadian Alpine Centre & International Hostel** (403-522-2200; $), on Village Road, is bright, spotless, modern and convenient. There are also a laundry and two spacious, well-equipped self-service kitchens. The lounge, with stone fireplace, comfy chairs and Internet kiosks, provides an elegant atmosphere. The upscale cafe (see Dining) is open 7 a.m.-9 p.m. Best of all, nightly bed rates start at $23; three-day ski packages, including tickets at Lake Louise, shuttles and breakfast, begin at $185.

If you've got a car and want a rustic lodge experience in a spectacular wilderness setting, check into the **Num-Ti-Jah Lodge** (403-522-2167; $$-$$$). It's in the middle of prime territory for backcountry skiing, about a half-hour's drive from Lake Louise. This funky stone-and-log hotel has 25 simple rooms, most with private baths and the restaurant is quite good (see Dining). It sits on the shores of Bow Lake, and on clear days you can see the glaciers.

Dining

For breakfast on the mountain, the **Great Bear Room** ($) in the Whiskeyjack Lodge serves a yummy and affordable breakfast buffet. Reasonably-priced on-mountain lunch options are **The Powder Keg Lounge** ($$) with nachos, sandwiches and pizza; the **Great Bear Rstaurant,** with hot and cold luncheon buffets; and **Sawyer's Nook Restaurant** ($$) in Temple Lodge.

For dinner in **The Fairmont Chateau Lake Louise** (403-522-3511 for reservations at all its restaurants), the most elegant dining room is the **Edelweiss** ($$$), serving entrees such as salmon and duckling. Their newest restaurant in the new wing, **The Fairview Dining Room** specializes in the best Alberta beef to be found in the province. Once you've savoured the tender filet (which they will serve rare), or other entrees on the extensive menu, repair to the Lakeside Bar for a small-portioned flight of incredibly delicious and varied deserts and after-dinner drinks. The Swiss **Walliser Stube Wine Bar** ($$-$$$) specializes in raclette and fondue. The **Poppy Room**, a family restaurant, and the 24-hour deli are the only facilities open for breakfast in winter. **Glacier Saloon** ($) has steak sandwiches, finger food and salads. The Chateau's **deli** is also a good choice for a quick breakfast or lunch.

The Post Hotel (403-522-3989; $$$) is recognized as serving the finest continental cuisine in Lake Louise. For a special occasion, this is a wonderful place. **Deer Lodge** (403-522-3747; $$$), originally a general store for provisioning hikers, has homemade breads, yummy full breakfasts as well as innovative dinner specials and in-house baked pastries.

Lake Louise Station (403-522-2600; $$-$$$) is a restored railway station with views of the mountains and freight trains that often rumble past. The extensive menu offers pastas, lamb, Alberta steaks and fresh salmon, among other dishes.

A half-hour drive up the Icefields Parkway you can enjoy the Rocky Mountain cuisine at the **Elkhorn Dining Room** (403-522-2167; $$$) at Simpson's Num-Ti-Jah Lodge.

What a find! **Bill Peyto's Cafe** (403-522-2200; $) at the Canadian Alpine Centre & International Hostel promises great food at affordable prices. Breakfast is served until 2 p.m.

Apres-ski/nightlife

The **Powder Keg Lounge** is the apres-ski spot at the mountain. It's in the Lodge of the Ten Peaks and has live entertainment on weekends. On sunny spring days, hang out on the deck of the **Kokanie Kabin** near the base lifts.

Also jump into apres-ski and nightlife in town center in the hotels. At The Fairmont Chateau Lake Louise, The **Glacier Saloon** has a lively atmosphere and dancing, while the **Walliser Stube** is a bit more subdued. For those who quit the slopes early, high tea (C$48 for two) in the Chateau's Lobby Bar or Lakeview Lounge is an experience that invites lingering.

Quiet conversation is possible at **The Explorer's Lounge** in the Lake Louise Inn and The Post Hotel's **Outpost**. Explorer's now offers DJ and Karaokee nights during the week.

Other activities

The Fairmont Chateau Lake Louise offers guests a full menu of winter activities: **ice skating** on the lake around a magnificent ice castle that is lit at night with areas also cleared for **ice hockey** and **broom ball**, **snowshoeing**, **cross-country skiing**, also on the lake, and **shopping**. The hotel's bottom floor features an Aveda **spa** with all treatments available, as well as chocolate, clothing, sports and jewelry shops, all with outstanding goodies and merchandise.

Kingmik Sled Dog Tours (877-919-7779; 403-763-8887), operating since 1982, offers **dogsledding** trips ranging from a 30-minute introduction to the two-hour Great Divide Experience to the Aberta/British Columbia Great Divide, during which participants get a chance to drive the team. Each sled holds up to two adults and one child and costs C$275.

While you can't **snowmobile** inside Banff National Park, there is awesome terrain available just outside the Park. Banff Snowmobile Tours (888-293-8687) will pick you up in Banff and Lake Louise for half-day or full-day tours, including snowmobile, all necessary gear, and a hot lunch. Discover Banff Tours (403-763-7183) provides snowmobile, equipment, transportation, hot lunch and snack for their full day outings. Toby Creek Snowmobile Tours (866-416-2034) operates out of two British Columbia locations, with daily transportation from Banff.

The Banff/Lake Louise area offers many more opportunities for other winter sports such as **skating, dogsledding, ice fishing, ice canyon crawls** (the famous Johnston Canyon Icewalk) and **ice climbing**. For more information, contact the Banff Information Centre or the Lake Louise Visitors Centre (403-762-8421). Also see Ski Banff at Norquay for more details.

Getting there and getting around

By air: Calgary Airport is served by major airlines, including Air Canada.

By ground shuttle: Rocky Mountain Sky Shuttle (888-762-8754; 403-762-5200), Brewster Transportation airport and resort shuttle and Sundog airport and shuttle service(1-800-760-6934; 403-760-6934), Greyline Transportation (403-762-9102) or Banff Airporter (403-762-3330) will get you from the airport to Banff or Lake Louise and provide local transportation as well.

By car: Lake Louise Village is 115 miles west of Calgary and 36 miles from Banff.

Getting around: Bus service is available from the airport directly to most hotels. The Lake Louise shuttlebus is free and operates from most hotels to the base of the ski lifts. Buy the Tri-Area ski pass and your bus transportation is included. Check the websites for shuttle schedules and fares. A car is recommended for extensive sightseeing.

Accommodations (Cdn$): (double room) $$$$-$200+; $$$-$141-$200; $$-$81-$140; $-$80 and less.
Dining (Cdn$): $$$-Entrees $20+; $$-$10-20; $-less than $10

Marmot Basin

Jasper, Alberta
Canada

Summit: 8,534 feet
Vertical: 3,000 feet
Base: 5,590 feet

Address: P.O. Box 1300,
Jasper, Alberta T0E 1E0
Telephone (main): 780-852-3816
Snow Report Number: 780-488-5909
Toll-free reservations: 877-902-9455
Reservations outside US: 780-852-3816
E-mail: info@skimarmot.com
Internet: www.skimarmot.com

Expert:★★★★
Advanced:★★★★
Intermediate:★★★
Beginner:★★★
First-timer:★★★

Lifts: 9 total: 1 high-speed quad, 1
quad, 1 triple, 3 doubles, 2 surface lifts,
1 moving carpet
Skiable acreage: 1,675
Snowmaking: 30 percent
Uphill capacity: 11,931
Parks & pipes: 2 parks
Bed base: 5,500
Nearest lodging: 11 miles away in Jasper
Child care: Yes, 19 months and older
Adult ticket, per day: C$70+tax (08/09)

Dining:★★★
Apres-ski/nightlife:★★
Other activities:★★★★

Far into the northland and separated from the busy bustle of Banff by a three-hour drive, Jasper is far enough north and far enough from a major airport (Edmonton: four hours) that people aren't here by mistake or on a whim. People come to Jasper National Park for the scenery, the remoteness, the wonder of a herd of elk outside their hotel and the call of Canadian geese swooping over Lac Beauvert in the spring while the ski area still has winter snow.

The town of Jasper sprang up from a tent city in 1911 when the Grand Trunk Pacific Railway was laying steel up the Athabasca River Valley toward Yellowhead Pass. Its growth was rather helter-skelter. Hugging the Athabasca River up against the train station, the town is relatively simple and charming, consisting of clapboard cottages, local shops, a steepled Lutheran church, stone houses and lodgings with a varied architectural scheme.

Marmot Basin's base lodge, Caribou Chalet, is a beautiful 32,000-square-foot building that blends in with its surroundings. Skiers and boarders of different levels can ride the same lifts which makes Marmot great for family and group vacations. The terrain is fairly evenly divided among ability levels so everyone can enjoy the mountain. If you're looking to improve your skills, Marmot is a perfect choice.

Mountain layout

The area's one high-speed quad, Eagle Express, serves as the primary chair to the upper-mountain lifts. It can get somewhat crowded sometimes, so don't come back to the base during peak loading times, such as mornings before 9:30. Instead, try Caribou Chair on the lower mountain, far to the right, where there's rarely a wait. It has terrain for all abilities and also will get you to the upper-mountain lifts, Paradise Chair, Kiefer T-Bar, Knob Chair and Eagle Ridge Quad. Novice, intermediate, advanced and expert trails can be found off all lifts with the exception of the Knob Chair which has no green runs.

Marmot has four distinct areas:

The Lower Area, accessed by the Eagle Express Chair, School House Platter—excellent for beginners—the Caribou Chair and a magic carpet in the learning area.

The Upper Area, serviced by the Paradise Chair and the Kiefer T-Bar to the top of Caribou Ridge is great for experts and intermediates.

The Knob Area, served by the Knob Chair, features advanced and expert terrain.

Eagle Ridge Area, the newest area at Marmot, is serviced by the Eagle Ridge Quad which accesses 20 expert, advanced and intermediate runs on Eagle Crest and Chalet Slope as well as one long novice run on Chalet. If you want to learn about the local history while you explore the mountain, join a mountain host for a complimentary tour.

Expert, Advanced: Marmot has tree-lined runs toward the bottom and wide-open bowls at the top. Generally, the higher you go, the tougher the skiing gets. The Knob Chair takes you to the highest lift-served terrain. From the top of that lift, the hardiest hike the last 600 feet up to Marmot Peak. (Our vertical-foot and summit stats reflect the lift-served terrain, while those advertised by the area include this hike.) It's all Alpine bowls up here, and they are really sweet.

There's fine powder in Dupres Chute dividing it from steep, double black Charlie's Bowl, named after Charlie Dupres, who died in an avalanche here many years ago. You may want to opt for the "easier" Dupres Chutes and Dupres Bowl. Another good choice for bowls and untracked powder is to stay high and to skier's right of The Knob.

There's excellent glade skiing off the Paradise Chair and Kiefer T-bar, both of which serve Caribou Ridge. Off to skier's right the trees in a black area are truly misnamed Milk Run. Outer Limits is an off-piste experience similar to Eagle East off the back of the Paradise Chair. Plan for at least 30 minutes to make your way out along the flat Whistler Creek Trail, which dumps you out next to the third parking lot below the Caribou Chair.

Intermediate: Every lift has an intermediate way down, even The Knob. Punch Bowl and Paradise are especially delightful runs. The Knob Traverse takes you high on the mountain where you'll have incredible views.

On blustery days, stay low on the mountain, where trees provide shelter from winds that sometimes block visibility on the naked summit. The intermediate runs on Chalet Slope off Eagle Ridge, which also hold snow longest, are excellent choices.

Beginner, First-timer: The three lifts at the base serve most of the lower-level terrain. Beginners have expansive mountain access, with 1,100 vertical feet on Eagle Express and Tranquilizer Chairs after you master terrain from the School House Platter and the Magic Carpet at their base. Old Road is a great run for novice skiers and can be accessed from either the Eagle Express or the Tranquilizer chairs.

You can even head up to Caribou Ridge for an above-treeline thrill where a wide trail, Basin Run, takes you safely back to the lower slopes. A novice run on Chalet Slope off Eagle Ridge provides gorgeous views from the top before you wind down the mountain.

Parks and pipes

The terrain park is on Marmot Run in the upper area of the mountain with tabletops, hips, spines, rails, rollers and a quarterpipe. There's also a natural quarterpipe on Marmot Run.

During early season, Marmot terrain park staff installs a smaller rail park on an old road, just above the loading station of the Eagle Ridge quad.

Snowboarding

Most riders come here for the freeriding. Off the Knob Chair, a 600-foot hike accesses freshies in Upper Basin. Or choose Peak Run to scoot over to the gully off High Traverse or Thunder Bowl (carry your speed on this traverse). Don't skip Charlie's Bowl—there are so many lines here, it's possible to spend all day. Again, carry your speed from the top of Knob Chair to the entrance of Charlie's Bowl. There's a rather flat runout at the bottom, so you might have to hoof it a bit on both ends.

Chalet Slope off the Eagle Ridge Chair is a vast area of glades that will keep you challenged—and grinning. Powder lasts the longest over here. The chutes, bowl and glades on Eagle East are a challenge with important warning signs. Off the back side, is true back-country terrain. The drop-ins to this area can be intimidating and often require vertigo-inducing traverses. Pay attention to boundary signs funneling you back toward the trails or you'll have a long hike out.

The Outer Limits area off the back of Paradise Chair, the Whistler Creek Trail is mainly flat, with some short uphill sections so be forewarned. An adventure in this area may be more strenuous in the hiking than the sliding.

Intermediates have great choices all over the mountain. There's very nice beginner terrain at the base of the mountain, served by a Platter lift which can be difficult for snowboarders. Head higher up the mountain via the Paradise and Kiefer chairs for the Marmot Terrain Park located on Marmot Run in the Upper Area.

Cross-country & snowshoeing (see also xcskiresorts.com)

This is prime ski touring and snowshoeing country with scenery guaranteed to delight. Stop by Jasper National Park's Information Center or call 780-852-6176.

Jasper Park Lodge trails, about 19 km., are unparalleled for beauty and variety. The gentle, groomed and easily accessible trails wind around lake shores, Alpine meadows and forests. The easiest is Cavell, a 5 km. loop with many elk sightings. The perimeter loop samples a little of everything that the Jasper Park Lodge trails offer.

Near Jasper Townsite, a good level, nighttime-lit beginner trail is 4.5km Whistlers Campground Loop, 4.5 km. Pyramid Bench Trail, 4.7 km. rated intermediate, overlooks the Athabasca River Valley. Patricia Lake Circle, 5.9 km. intermediate (follow the trail clockwise), provides stunning views of Mt. Edith Cavell, the region's most prominent and dramatically sloped peak. Most lodges have trail maps.

For **guided cross-country skiing, backcountry** and **snowshoeing tours**, contact Edge Control, 780-852-4945; Beyond the Beaten Path, 780-852-5650; Overlander Trekking & Tours, 852-4056 (snowshoe tours only); or Alpine Art, 780-852-3709.

A full day's ski over Maccarib Pass from the Marmot Basin Road on the north shore of Amethyst Lake leads to **Tonquin Valley Lodge**, hearty home-cooked meals and welcome beds. Contact **Tonquin Valley Ski Tours**, Box 550, Jasper, Alberta T0L 1E0; 780-852-3909.

Lessons (08/09 prices, without tax)

Group lessons: Adults, 13+ – C$56 for two hours.
First-timer package: Includes lift pass, two-hour lesson and ski or snowboard equipment for C$84.

Private lessons: C$99 for one hour; C$438 for a full day. Discounts for an extra person.

Special programs: Ski Week packages are for all ability levels and include three days of lift tickets, three two-hour sessions, three days of rentals plus video analysis; cost is C$168.

Children's programs (08/09 prices, without tax)

Child care: Ages 19 months to 6 years. All-day care costs C$45. Lunch is an additional C$6. Per hour rate is C$7; each additional child in family, C$6 per hour. For reservations, call (780) 852-3816.

Children's lessons: Ages 4–5, two-hour group lesson, lifts, tickets and rentals, includes nursery, C$99.

For ages 6–12, there are several options. A full-day program, ski or snowboard, costs C$82 (includes lunch). A two-hour group lesson, ski or snowboard, costs C$72. Learn-to-ski or snowboard lessons including lift ticket and rentals are C$72. One-hour private lessons are C$93. Ski & Snowboard Weeks include three days of lessons, lift tickets, rentals and video analysis for C$168.

Lift tickets (08/09 prices, without tax)

-	Adult	Junior (6-12)
One day	C$70	C$25
Three days	C$206	C$75
Five days	C$342	C$125

Who skis free: Children 5 and younger.

Who skis at a discount: Youth/student prices (13-25) and seniors (65+) are C$56 for one day, with multiday discounts; college-age students must be full time and present a valid student ID.

During the Jasper in January festival, everyone 13 and older pays C$42 per day, juniors pay C$21.

Note: Prices are rounded to the nearest dollar. Early season rates are lower.

Accommodations

The resort does not have mountainside lodging. Stay in nearby Jasper which offers a variety of accommodations from downtown rooms to family-style units with kitchens to private lakeshore cabins. Many of the lodges listed have ski packages, so be sure to ask.

Jasper Tourism and Commerce (Box 98, Jasper, Alberta, T0E 1E0; 780-852-3858) will send a ski vacation planner that includes rates. Call central reservations at 877-902-9455 for a wide selection of accommodations, activities, tours, transportation and ski packages. This number is good for most all of the Canadian Rockies. For the Jasper area in particular, call **Jasper Central Reservations** at 800-473-8135 October through April.

The four diamond **Fairmont Jasper Park Lodge** (800-441-1414; $$-$$$$) is located on 900 acres a few miles from downtown Jasper. A wonderful mix of traditional log cabins from the 1920s and cedar chalets with spacious modern suites, all are elegantly rustic and comfortable. The more modern accommodations are linked by pathways along Lac Beauvert to the elegant main lodge. You'll find the best restaurant and the best service in Jasper here.

Pyramid Lake Resort (888-852-4900; 780-852-4900; $$-$$$), just outside Jasper, which began its life as a local fishing village, offers skating and cross-country trails at your doorstep. Most of the modern chalet-style accommodations have lovely lake views, private whirlpools, kitchenettes and fireplaces. The resort has a spectacular restaurant (see Dining) and recently opened cabins. Their motto: "The only thing we overlook is the lake."

The upscale **Chateau Jasper** (800-661-9323 or 780-852-5644; $$-$$$$), formerly Royal Canadian Lodge-Jasper, is about a 15-minute walk from "downtown" Jasper and has an indoor

Accommodations (Cdn$): (double room) $$$$-$200+; $$$-$141-$200; $$-$81-$140; $-$80 and less.
Dining (Cdn$): $$$-Entrees $20+; $$-$10-20; $-less than $10

pool and whirlpool, Sorrentino's Bistro Bar (see Dining), and heated underground parking. The Chateau offers a shuttle to town and back.

In town, **Jasper Inn** (800-661-1933 or 780-852-4461; $-$$$$) has spacious standard rooms, suites, loft units and condo-style units. There's an indoor pool, steam room, sauna, Jacuzzi and coin laundry. Very good restaurant on premises (see Dining).

The beautifully renovated **Sawridge Hotel & Conference Center Jasper** (800-661-6427 or 780-852-5111; $$-$$$$) offers everything from deluxe standard rooms to luxury parlor suites that reflect a Canadian flair. Indoor pool, outdoor hot tubs, Finnish sauna and laundry facilities. The European Beauty & Wellness Center here is a full-service spa. Very good restaurant on premises (see Dining).

The Astoria (800-661-7343 or 780-852-3351; $$) is a small hotel with charmingly renovated guest rooms right in the center of Jasper. **Whistlers Inn** (800-282-9919 or 780-852-3361; $$), also centrally located, has nice standards, deluxes and suites, some recently renovated. Steam room, outdoor rooftop hot tub, two restaurants, pub and gift shops.

Marmot Lodge (888-852-7737 or 780-852-4471; $-$$$) has rooms with kitchens and fireplaces. Restaurant, indoor pool, sauna and whirlpool located on the premises. No charge for children under age 12. The **Athabasca Hotel** (877-542-8422 or 780-852-3386; $-$$), one of Jasper's original lodgings, a Heritage Landmark since 1929, is located in the center of Jasper close to the bus and VIA RAIL station.

Dining

On the mountain, Marmot Basin has six places to eat plus a **Starbucks** next to the ski rental shop. Upstairs in the Caribou Chalet, the **Caribou Bar & Grill** ($-$$) serves excellent sandwiches, burgers and salads. Sit by the windows for spectacular views of the Athabasca River Valley and the mountain. There's also a **cafeteria** ($) in the base lodge which serves breakfast and lunch. **Paradise Chalet** ($-$$) at mid-mountain has a **cafe** and lounge ($) as well as a nice deck. On busy days, eat lunch at their **Charlie's Lounge** before 11:45 or after 1:15. For more casual meals, visit **Paradise Cafeteria** ($-$$) for self-service sandwiches, salads and made-to-order hot foods. **Eagle Chalet** ($-$$) at mid-mountain is a cozy rustic restaurant with a fireplace. Or sit on its big outdoor deck and watch skiers and riders as you enjoy a hearty meal.

Jasper has some excellent and varied restaurants. Canadian, Chinese, French, Greek, Italian, Korean, Japanese, Mexican, continental and family-style dining are all available.

The lakeview **Edith Cavell Dining Room** (780-852-6052; $$$) in the Fairmont Jasper Park Lodge specializes in elegant informality. The menu includes game specialties and delicious desserts. For breakfast, **The Meadows** ($-$$), just downstairs in the main lodge, serves light and simple fare in a more casual setting. A lovely breakfast buffet and lunch are also served.

The Pines (780-852-4900; $$-$$$) at Pyramid Lake Resort has a huge stone fireplace, soaring ceilings and spectacular views over Pyramid Lake which set the stage for a wonderful meal. The menu includes appetizers such as Rocky Mountain mushroom bisque and entrees such as rack of lamb, smoked chicken and shrimp carbonnara.

In Jasper, **The Inn Restaurant** (780-852-4461; $$) at Jasper Inn offers a cozy, casual atmosphere. The creative menu includes such appetizers as citrus-marinated chicken brochettes, pernod-soaked scallops and various pasta entrees. Also choose from Alberta beef, salmon, fish and chicken.

Andy's Bistro (780-852-4559; $$), very popular, especially with locals, has a friendly, intimate setting in downtown Jasper. The moderately priced menu emphasizes Swiss and

Canadian cuisine. Locals recommend the mixed salad and the lamb shanks. A C$25 special some nights includes an appetizer, entree and dessert.

Walter's Dining Room (780-852-5111; $$) in the Sawridge Hotel specializes in tasty Canadian and continental dishes. **Tonquin Prime Rib** Village (780-852-4966; $$) serves steaks, prime rib, barbecued ribs, seafood and Italian dishes. It has a bar and a beautiful view. Make reservations. **Fiddle River Seafood Company** (780-852-3032; $$-$$$) an upscale upstairs bistro, gets raves for creative fresh fish cooking. **Embers Steakhouse** (780-852-4471; $$) serves light and healthy cuisine (beef, local fish) in a casually elegant restaurant. **Sorrentino's Bistro Bar** (780-852-5644; $$$) in the Chateau Jasper features authentic Italian fare.

L&W Restaurant (780-852-4114; $$) with an atrium setting and remarkably broad menu is a great family restaurant. It has very good Greek cuisine as well as steaks, seafood, pasta, pizza. The kids menu has prices from C$5-$7. **Something Else Restaurant** (780-852-3233; $$) is also a good choice for families with a combination of good Greek, Italian and Cajun foods.

Whistlestop Bar (780-852-3361; $) at Whistlers Inn serves a bar menu in a cozy atmosphere.

The area's best sushi is served at **Oka Sushi** (780-852-3301; $$) in the Fairmont Jasper Park Lodge. Also quite popular is **Denjiro** (780-852-3780; $$) in downtown Jasper featuring Japanese entrees and a sushi bar.

Miss Italia (780-852-4002; $$) is the spot for Italian cooking. **Mountain Foods Cafe** (780-852-4050; $), a sit-down or take-out restaurant, has affordable prices for its deli items. For espresso and pizza by the slice, head to **Truffles and Trout** (780-852-9676; $). Steaks, ribs, donair, poutine, pizza and Italian dishes are served at **Jasper Pizza Place** (780-852-3225; $).

The **Soft Rock Café** ($), with Internet service, serves the area's best breakfast which is served it all day. For breakfast, lunch and diner, don't miss **Papa George's Restaurant** (780-852-3351; $-$$) in the Astoria Hotel on the main drag. It has a rich, lengthy history in Jasper and serves some of the best Italian food in the Rockies. **Bear Paw's Bakery** (780-852-3233; $), a local favorite with a big reputation, sells freshly baked goods daily. **Coco's Cafe** (780-852-4550; $), downtown on Patricia Street has awesome little dishes, pastries and Jasper's best coffee. They cater to vegans, vegetarians and carnivores.

Apres-ski/nightlife

Jasper is not famous for rocking nightlife, but you can certainly find some action. The **Atha-B Club** in Athabasca Hotel has the liveliest dancing in town. The hotel also has **O'Shea's**, an Irish pub. **Whistle Stop** at Whistlers Inn is a good pub-type night spot with darts, pool and big-screen sports. **De'd Dog Pub** in the Astoria Hotel is a locals' hangout that draws folks of mixed ages; light food is available. **Fireside Lounge** in Marmot Lodge has nightly entertainment. **Pete's** attracts a younger crowd with disco and occasional live music. Downstream is a no-smoking bar with good chicken wings.

At Jasper Park Lodge, the **Emerald Lounge** has hearty Apres-Ski snacks, and **Tent City Sports Lounge** recalls the history of the lodge and has lively entertainment.

Other activities

Visitors come to Jasper National Park to ski but also to enjoy the pristine wilderness and wildlife. There are a variety of ways to do the latter. Here are just a few: **Jasper in January** is the area's annual winter festival. Lift tickets drop considerably, as do lodging rates. Activities include a mountain-to-valley relay race, ice and snow sculpting, tobogganing, taste of the town food sampler, ice rescue demonstrations and more.

The **Maligne Canyon Icewalk** is a guided tour through the deepest canyon in Jasper National Park. It's a mile hike through a 6- to 20-foot-wide gorge on the frozen river floor

Accommodations (Cdn$): (double room) $$$$-$200+; $$$-$141-$200; $$-$81-$140; $-$80 and less.
Dining (Cdn$): $$$-Entrees $20+; $$-$10-20; $-less than $10

past ice caves, frozen waterfalls, towering canyon walls, fossils locked in time, and colors frozen into the ice. Take the crawl during the day or at night. Tours last two to three hours and are usually available from December through March. Winter boots and crampon soles are provided. Call **Overlander Trekking & Tours** (780-852-4056). Cost is about C$50 per person. Tours also provided by **Beyond the Beaten Path** (780-852-5650), or **Jasper Adventure Center** (780-852-5595).

Ice skating on a lake and **sleigh rides** are available at Jasper Park Lodge. Go **dogsledding** with Overlander Trekking & Tours, 780-852-4056. **Heliskiing** in Valemount, British Columbia, 56 miles away along a scenic drive, is available mid-February to mid-April, Overlander Trekking & Tours, 780-852-4056. Also Robson HeliMagic, 780-566-4700. Snowfarmers (250-566-9161) in Valemont has **snowmobile-serviced skiing and riding**. Maximum six guests, C$250 per person. Snowfarmers also provides snowmobile touring.

Jasper Activity Centre (780-852-3381) on Pyramid Lake Road has **swimming, curling, squash, racquetball, a weight room** and **indoor skating**. Minor league **hockey games** are held on Saturdays and Sundays.

Wildlife spotters are likely to see mule deer, bighorn sheep, mountain goats, elk, moose, caribou, wolves and coyotes. The best places to see herds of bighorn sheep and mountain goats are on Highway 16, on the mountainside just out of town headed toward Edmonton and on Tangle Ridge near the Columbia Icefield. Elk wander into Jasper proper, so they're visible everywhere.

The **exhibits** at Jasper-Yellowhead Museum and Archives (780-852-3013) highlight Jasper's history and human heritage such as the early explorers, the fur trade, the railway and skiing.

The Outer Limits retail **shop** at Marmot Basin has the newest gear and clothing as well as a good selection of outerwear. Downtown Jasper has some great specialty shops like Freewheel, Gravity Gear and Jungle Wear, along with a variety of **souvenir shops**. A good selection of merchandise can also be found at the stores at the Fairmont Jasper Park Lodge.

Arts Jasper (852-3964) presents films, arts performances, dance, theatre and music. Pick up a free winter guide for a complete overview of activities and attractions in Jasper.

Getting there and getting around

By air: Calgary and Edmonton are the primary gateways to the Canadian Rockies. These International airports provide non-stop and direct flights and connectors. If you don't rent a car, Greyhound operates daily service from Edmonton and Vancouver; call 780-421-4211.

By car: From Edmonton, Jasper is 225 miles west on Hwy. 16. The ski area is 12 miles south of Jasper via Hwy. 93, 93A and Marmot Basin Road. Jasper is about 170 miles north of Banff.

By train: VIA RAIL (888-842-7245) operates service to Jasper from Edmonton, Toronto and Vancouver on its recently restored '50s-style art deco train, The Canadian. Also ask about the Snow Train to Jasper.

Getting around: A car is best here. The ski area is a few miles from the town and lodging. Brewster Transportation operates the Banff-Jasper shuttlebus and the Marmot Basin shuttle into the townsite; call 780-852-3332.

Big White Ski Resort and Silver Star Mountain Resort

British Columbia, Canada

From British Columbia's west coast, the mountain ranges roll east in ascending waves until they reach the Rocky Mountain peaks on the Continental Divide. The British Columbia highlands and plateaus take moisture from the Pacific storms that drop dryer snow in the Monashees, Selkirks, Kootenays and Purcells on their way to the Rockies. It's here that you'll find the resorts of Interior British Columbia. The skiing experience in western Canada has its own fingerprint, its own special flavor with an inviting appeal to skiers from eastern North America, Europe and Australia. Big White and Silver Star are under the same ownership and with one lift ticket, skiers and snowboarders have access to almost 6,000 acres of skiable terrain.

Big White Ski Resort

The Okanagan Valley in interior British Columbia is the hot winter destination in the West and many advise getting here soon while it's still relatively affordable. For Australians, Big White is the second-biggest destination ski resort in B.C., after Whistler/Blackcomb.

Big White says, "We use only dry, natural Okanagan Powder." The village sits at 5,706 feet (B.C.'s highest base area) and lifts carry skiers up to 7,606 feet. That's about the same elevation as Whistler/Blackcomb but conditions differ as the air and snow are considerably dryer this far inland. One of Big White's signature features is its tree skiing. Clouds and water vapor from nearby Okanagan Lake combine with copious snowfall to form the signature "snow ghosts"—snow-clad trees that look like abstract sculptures.

Night skiing with 1,600 vertical feet is open Tuesday through Saturday, the largest in the Canadian West. The terrain park is lighted as well. Big White and nearby Silver Star Mountain Resort are under the same ownership and with one lift ticket, skiers and snowboarders have access to almost 6,000 acres of skiable terrain.

Mountain layout

Expert/Advanced: Experts gravitate to the long and inviting Gem Lake Express runs who can tackle any of the runs off the Gem Lake Express with black diamonds on the sign. Goat's Kick, skier's right off the Ridge Rocket Express, is an especially fun challenge. Skier's left from the Alpine T-bar leads to Parachute Bowl. Don't miss Big White's Pegasus and the double-black extreme playground, The Cliff, off the same lift. Natural hits and drops fall off the side of Perfection, Falcon Glades and around Gem Lake. For bumps, Dragon's Tongue to skier's right of Ridge Rocket Express rules, and try any of the runs off the Powder Express. There are also good bump runs over on Gem Lake right underneath the chair line.

Intermediate: Good warm-up runs are the Sun Run from the top of the Alpine T-bar, Exhibition, Highway 33, Serwas and Sundance. There's also fine terrain off the Rocket and

Big White Ski Resort Facts

Address: 1894 Ambrosi Road
Kelowna, B.C., Canada V1X 4K5
Area code: 250
Ski area phone: 765-3101
Snow report: 765-7669
Fax: 765-1822
Toll-free reservations: (800) 663-2772
E-mail: bigwhite@bigwhite.com (information)
or cenres@bigwhite.com (reservations)
Internet: www.bigwhite.com
Expert:★★★
Advanced:★★★★
Intermediate:★★★★
Beginner:★★★★ **First-timer:**★★★

Summit elevation: 7,606 feet
Vertical drop: 2,550 feet
Base elevation: 5,706 feet (Village base);
4,950 feet (Gem Lake base)

Number of lifts: 17—1 8-passenger high-speed gondola, 1 high-speed 6-pack, 4 high-speed quads, 1 quad, 1 triple, 3 doubles, 1 T-bar, 2 moving carpets, 1 handle tow, 2 tube lifts
Snowmaking: Only in terrain park
Skiable acreage: 2,765 acres
Uphill capacity: 28,000 per hour
Parks & pipes: 2 parks, 2pipes
Bed base: 14,000
Nearest lodging: Slopeside lodging, all ski-in/ski-out
Resort child care: 18 months and older
Adult ticket, per day: C$71 (08/09, without tax)
Dining:★★★

Powder chairs. Roller Coaster, Blue Sapphire and Kalinas Rainbow are highly recommended for those blue cruisers. International is an intermediate bump run. The blue ratings in the Black Forest are low-end. An entire area off Gem Lake Express is dedicated solely to intermediate runs, making it worthwhile to venture to this out-of-the-way part of the mountain.

Beginner/First-timer: People grouping together for lessons meet just across from the Village Centre Mall or at the Kids' Centre. A private and secluded teaching area with Magic Carpets is at the base of the free Happy Valley gondola, a short ride down from the Village Plaza. Many lessons are taught on Hummingbird, served by the Plaza Chair. All lifts serve at least one green run – Easy Out, Serwa's and Kangaroo are among the best runs. Ogo Slow is a very long run that goes from the Ridge over to the Gem Lake Express, but the terrain serviced by that lift is not terribly beginner friendly unless it's a powder day. Black Forest is ideal for novices - Millie's Mile, named after the owner's granddaughter is a good one.

Parks and pipes

TELUS Park has an on-mountain lodge and chairlift, so it can be used as a training and competition facility for snowboarding and freeskiing. The 50-acre park area centralizes the terrain parks, rail garden, pipes, boardercross and family fun-race area. An Olympic-sized, 500-foot-long superpipe, with 17-foot transitional walls, meets World Cup FIS and X Games standards. If that's too intimidating, try the 400-foot-long halfpipe with 12-foot walls. Look for an intermediate terrain and rail park, an advanced terrain and rail park and a boardercross course capable of hosting Olympic FIS qualifying events. Within the terrain parks, you'll find assorted mailbox sliders, step-up jumps and hips. Rails include minis, flats, rainbows, kinks and wide rails. The park is lit Thursday through Saturday for night skiing and riding.

Snowboarding

Big White was one of the first resorts in North America to openly welcome snowboarders, and there are plenty of reasons why. The gladed terrain is outstanding, with plenty of natural hits and rollers. Riders have a good time most anywhere on the mountain. Particularly popular is the Sun-Rype Bowl and the adjacent Black Bear run, both reached by the Gem Lake Express. The bowl is a big gentle swoop of a run that can get you into some trees known as the Black Bear Glades. The only double-blacks are reached by the Alpine T-bar, which many snowboarders find difficult to ride. The double chair to The Cliff and East Peak areas also have some great runs. There are some gentle ways down from the top of the T-bar if you change your mind, but at least have a look on the way up to the right into Parachute Bowl. On skis or on a board, Powder Bowl (skiers' left off the T-bar) is an outstanding intermediate run that offers big-mountain style riding without feeling that you're about to hurt yourself.

Cross-country & snowshoeing (see also xcskiresorts.com)

Big White has 25 km. (15 mi.) of scenic cross-country trails. Skiers can choose from groomed and trackset trails or wilderness routes. The beginners' trail is a 4.3-km. loop from the Plaza Chair. Tickets and maps are available from any ticket window. Cross-country skiing is included free with lift tickets.

Lessons (07/08 prices, without tax)

For information and reservations, call 250-491-6101; 250-765-3101.
Group lessons: A two-hour lesson costs C$50; multiday rates are available.
First-timer package: A two-hour learn-to-ski or -snowboard lesson, including Plaza lift ticket and rentals, costs C$99. A three-day package costs C$188.

Private Lessons: For up to three people, all day costs C$399; half-day afternoon, C$249; half-day morning, C$249; two hours, C$199; a 1.5-hour early-bird private starting at 8:30 a.m. costs C$125. Add an additional person to a private for C$45. Reservations are recommended for all private lessons and are required for an all-day lesson.

Special programs: Ski/Board Weeks are four-day programs with 2.5-hour lessons, video analysis, fun race, souvenirs and a wrap-up luncheon (start in December on Mondays). Additional programs offered: Free Ride Weekend Camps, TELUS Park Flight School and Heavy Metal Shop.

Children's programs (07/08 prices, without tax)

Child care: Ages 18 months to 6 years. It costs C$69 for a full day (lunch included); C$39 for a half day. Multiday discounts are available. Hourly rate is C$16. Ages 3–4 can add a lesson to the child-care program; C$119, including child care.

The Kids Centre in the Village Plaza, recommends reservations (250-765-3101, ext. 233). Parents/guardians must provide proof of birth date (either birth certificate or passport), immunization history and health insurance number. The resort accommodates dietary needs based on allergies and also requests that no nut products are brought into the child-care center. Big White's award-winning child-care program is recognized world-wide as top-notch.

Children's programs: Ages 4–12, a full day costs C$89 and includes lunch; half day costs C$50. Program for kids ages 4–6 includes indoor play time; snowboard lessons start at age 7. Private lessons are available and range from C$99 to C$350, depending upon the length of time and number of children.

Dining: $$$$–Entrees C$30+; $$$–C$20–$30; $$–C$10–$20; $–less than C$10.
Accommodations: (double room) $$$$–C$200+; $$$–C$141–$200; $$–C$81–$140; $–C$80 and less.

Special activities: The Kids' Centre offers Kids After Dark, supervised evening programs including Pizza and Movie Night, Craft Night, Torchlight Parade, Carnival Night, and Skating and Tubing Parties. Bookings can be made at the Kids' Centre prior to 3 p.m. on the day offered.

Lift tickets (08/09 prices, without tax)

	Adult	Child (6-12)
One day	C$71	C$35
Three days	C$197 (C$66/day)	C$91 ($30/day)
Five days	C$323 (C$65/day)	C$147 ($29/day)

Who skis free: Children 5 and younger.

Who skis at a discount: Youth 13-18 pay C$59 for one day, C$163 for three, C$267 for five. Seniors 65+ pay C$59 and Canadian college students with ID pay youth prices.

Note: Prices are before GST taxes and rounded to the nearest dollar. Big White has night skiing, 5 p.m.-8 p.m., Tuesday to Saturday, from mid-December to end of March. Adult night skiing (3:30-8p.m.) costs C$27.

Accommodations

Lodging in the Big White mountain village ranges from hostels, hotels and condos to private chalets, all ski-in/ski-out. **Big White Central Reservations** (800-663-2772 in North America; 250-765-8888) is a one-stop shop for accommodation and package vacation needs. You can also visit the website for accommodation details.

Chateau Big White ($$-$$$$) is close to services in the Village Plaza. **The Inn at Big White** ($$-$$$$), across the street from the Chateau, has 100 rooms, an outdoor pool and hot tub, fitness room, restaurant and lounge. **White Crystal Inn** ($$-$$$$), is a European-style hotel in the heart of the village.

Condominiums and vacation homes range in size from one to four bedrooms and feature full bathrooms and kitchens. Some units have gas fireplaces, balconies and private hot tubs. Choose from **Stonebridge Lodge** ($$$-$$$$), **Trappers' Crossing** ($$$-$$$$), **Timber Ridge** ($$$-$$$$), **Tree Tops** ($$$-$$$$), **Black Bear** ($$$-$$$$), **Grizzly Lodge** ($$-$$$$) and **Blacksmith Lodge** ($$$-$$$$).

Chateau On The Ridge ($$-$$$) features condos with kitchens, gas fireplaces and outdoor common hot tubs. **Das Hofbrauhaus** ($-$$$) is slopeside with an indoor pool, hot tub and racquetball courts, a restaurant and lounge. **Eagles Resort** ($$-$$$) offers 20 three-bedroom condos with gas fireplaces and kitchens, and a large hot tub on the property. **Graystoke Inn** ($$) has one- and two-bedroom condos with an adjacent common outdoor hot tub.

The Monashee Inn ($$-$$$) gives an unsurpassed view of the Monashee Mountains. **The Ponderosa Inn** ($-$$$), on the Easy Street trail, is family-oriented and has a hot tub and sauna. In the heart of the village, **Whitefoot Lodge** ($-$$) features a hot tub, sauna with a cold plunge and a laundry. Some rooms have kitchenettes.

Ptarmigan Inn ($$-$$$) is next to the village and has hot tubs, a plunge pool and sauna. One- and two-bedroom units are available. **Snowpine Estates** ($$-$$$$) has big chalets, either single-family or duplex, all with ski-in/ski-out access.

The slopeside SameSun **Backpacker Ski Lodge** (877-562-2783; 250-545-8933; $) is a hostel with dorm rooms, private rooms and deluxe rooms.

Self-contained RV parking is allowed in the Happy Valley parking lot near the skating rink and Lara's Gondola. The charge is $10.50 per night. Tickets can be purchased at the lift ticket window.

Dining

Unlike most other ski resorts, you don't have to drive or even walk more than a block or so to find a great meal. All restaurants are in or near the village center and represent a swell variety of offerings.

Beano's (250-491-3558; $), in the middle of the main ticket/rental building, serves the best coffee, soup and sandwiches in the village.

Snowshoe Sam's (250-765-1416; $$-$$$) is a legend at Big White. It concentrates mainly on steaks and chops, although the seafood and pasta are quite good. You'll need dinner reservations, especially on the weekend when it gets packed. Their claim to fame is Gun Barrel Coffee.

The **Swiss Bear Dining Room** (250-491-7750; $$-$$$) in the Chateau Big White serves authentic Swiss cuisine and specializes in fabulous fondues. Reservations are recommended. **Carver's Restaurant** (250-491-0221, ext. 407; $-$$), in the Inn at Big White, is a great family restaurant that features Indo-Canadian fare.

Coltino's Ristorante (250-765-5611; $$), at **Das Hofbrauhaus**, serves Italian fare as well as Alberta beef in a friendly family environment. **Raakel's** next door has apres-ski where they serve some mean salads, burgers and pizzas. They also offer the usual pub fare of wings, fries, even poutine—the French Canadian dish of French fries topped with cheese curd and steaming hot gravy.

Pappas Roasters (250-765-7866; $$) in the Whitefoot Lodge features Greek food with roast chicken the speciality. Ride the gondola down to the **Kettle Valley Steakhouse** (250-491-0130; $$-$$$), where you'll find a stylish wine bar, comfy surroundings and a menu with lots of steak that will satisfy your red-meat craving after a day on the slopes.

Apres-ski/nightlife

Big White has seven lounges and bars where live bands perform on weekends.

Snowshoe Sam's is commonly thought of as the best ski bar in Canada and we agree. It has DJ entertainment, live bands and dancing, even on the tables (not for the faint of heart or prudish). Their legendary after-dinner "Gunbarrel Coffee" show is a must.

Raakel's Ridge Pub, in Das Hofbrauhaus, has dancing and a nightly party atmosphere. The **Loose Moose Bar**, just a gondola ride down from the village, parties with live DJs and theme nights. It's a great place for family groups and get-togethers.

In Whitefoot Lodge, there is a **market** (250-765-7666) with everything from liquor to video rentals.

Other activities

The Happy Valley Adventure Centre at the bottom of the gondola offers a number of exciting adventures including the Mega Snow Coaster **tube ride** with 10 lanes and two lifts, **snowmobile tours, sleigh rides, weekend dog sledding, ice skating** and **snowshoeing**. The Happy Valley area also features a large lodge with **live entertainment**. At Quickpics (250-491-6104) in the Village Centre Mall, helmet cameras are available for rent for $C60 (half day) or $C100 (full day). The camera can also be attached to a toque or your head. For more information or to book other activities, visit the Activities Desk in the Village Centre Mall or call 250-491-6111.

Weekly activities include A Taste of Big White **Welcome Party** every Monday, **Torchlight Parade and Fireworks**, **Carnival Night**, **Big White Idol Karaoke** and **Bingo Night**.

Dining: $$$$–Entrees C$30+; $$$–C$20–$30; $$–C$10–$20; $–less than C$10.
Accommodations: (double room) $$$$–C$200+; $$$–C$141–$200; $$–C$81–$140; $–C$80 and less.

Silver Star Mountain Resort

The mountain and its village are highly rated for family skiing and village living. It's the fourth-largest downhill ski resort in British Columbia, after Whistler Blackcomb, Sun Peaks and Panorama. The resort averages 23 feet of annual snowfall and it's usually the first British Columbia ski resort to open. The south-facing Vance Creek area consists of gentle slopes and nicely groomed cruisers, while the Putnam Creek face is renowned for its deep powder and challenging black and double-black diamond terrain. After dark, the Summit Chair is lighted top to bottom for night skiing. The town of Vernon sits at the mountain's base, 14 miles away.

Mountain layout

Silver Star's terrain covers two very different mountain faces. For families we recommend the Vance Creek area served by the Summit Chair and the Comet Six-Pack Express. For the more adventurous, the Putnam Creek area can be accessed by the Powder Gulch Express and the Summit Chair. The backside is steep and challenging; the front side is beginner-friendly. From the top of the Summit Chair and the Comet Express, you can see Sun Peaks and Big White. From here, it's a 5-mile run to the bottom of Aunt Gladys at the Putnam Creek station.

Expert, Advanced: Experts, don't delay—head straight to the Putnam Creek side and scout the Back Bowl. Look for Free Fall, Where's Bob, Black Pine and Kirkenheimer. Three Wise Men, White Elephant and Holy Smokes will smoke your thighs. Then work your way over to the other side of the Powder Gulch Express to 3 Wisemen, Headwall and Chute 5. There are plenty of single-blacks on both sides of the mountain.

Intermediate: Gypsy Queen, reached via Aunt Gladys from Paradise Camp, is the most popular blue run on the mountain. Another really great run on the opposite side of the Powder Gulch Express, is Sunny Ridge. It takes off to the left just before Paradise Camp. [TOP]

Beginner, First-timer: If you want to get high on the mountain, you can't go wrong taking the Powder Gulch Express. From the top, Bergerstrasse, which becomes Aunt Gladys, makes

Silver Star Mountain Resort Facts

Summit elevation: **6,280 feet**
Vertical Drop: **2,500 feet**
Base elevation: **5,280 feet**

Address: Box 3002,
Silver Star Mountain, B.C., Canada V1B 3M1
Area code: 250
Ski area phone: 542-0224
Snow report: 542-1745
Toll-free reservations: (800) 663-4431
Fax: 542-1236
E-mail: star@skisilverstar.com
Internet: www.skisilverstar.com
Expert:★★★★ **Advanced:**★★★
Intermediate:★★★★
Beginner:★★★ **First-timer:**★★★★

Number of lifts: 10—1 high-speed six-pack chair, 2 high-speed quads, 2 quads, 1 double, 2 T-bars, 2 moving carpets
Snowmaking: No
Skiable acreage: 3,065 acres
Uphill capacity: 14,700 per hour
Parks and pipes: 1 park, 1 pipe
Bed base: 3,500 on mountain; nearby RV camping
Nearest lodging: Slopeside, all ski-in/ski-out
Resort child care: Newborn and older
Adult ticket, per day: C$70 (08/09, without tax)

Dining:★★★
Apres-ski/nightlife:★★
Other activities:★★★

a nice long 5-mile green run. You can also grab the Home Run Tee from there and take the Main St. Skiway straight to the village. Discovery Park is served by the moving carpet and is fenced to keep out the speedy interlopers, so it's a good place to make those initial first-timer turns. Once confident, head to the Silver Queen Chair for longer beginner runs.

Parks and pipes

TELUS Park Silver Star is a halfpipe and terrain park on Big Dipper, reached by riding down Little Dipper, Middle Dipper or Whiskey Jack. TELUS Park has features for all riders and skiers, from small lanes with fat boxes to learn-to-slide and mini-hits to learn how to catch your first air, to a large park lane with kinked rails. For advanced riders, long boxes and killer s-rails are coupled with large hits for big air.

Snowboarding

On the Putnam side, watch out for the Bergerstrasse flats above Paradise Camp. Once beyond it though, there are plenty of single- and double-black runs that will keep your inner freerider happy. The runs all are served by the Powder Gulch Express. Just take Aunt Gladys to the left and pick your chute off to the left.

Cross-country & snowshoeing (see also xcskiresorts.com)

Part of the High Altitude Training Center, Silver Star's cross-country trails attract skiers from around the world. Many of them are Olympic athletes in training. The network of trails includes the adjoining Sovereign Lakes Cross Country system, for a total of 100 km of groomed and track-set skiing. Lessons are available daily and cross-country ski camps are held in November. The 38 miles of trails at the resort are skating and classic groomed, and 2.5 miles are lit for night skiing. Guided snowshoe tours also are available.

Lesson (07/08 prices, without tax)

To make inquiries or reservations, call 888-558 2112 or 250-558-6064.
Group lessons: A two-hour lesson, beginning at 10 a.m. or 1 p.m., C$52.
First-timer package: Discover Skiing and Discover Snowboarding include lift, two-hour lesson and rental, C$54. A three-day package costs C$199.

Private lessons: One-hour lesson, C$119; two and a half hour lesson, C$259; full day, C$409. Discounts are available for up to three additional people. Reservations are highly recommended.

Children's programs (07/08 prices, without tax)

Child care: Ages newborn to 6 years. For infants up to age 3, cost is C$76 for a full day; C$49 for a half day. For ages 3–6, a full day costs C$60; a half day costs C$39. Full days include lunch; half days have a C$12 lunch option. Multiday discounts available. Reservations required; call (250) 558-6028.

Children's programs: Ages 4–12 get a full-day program (with lunch) for C$89; half day, C$52. Snowboard lessons start at age 8. A full-day package for Adventure Week includes five four-hour lessons and lunches, C$319; a half-day program of five two-hour lessons, C$220.

Youth ages 13–18 have lessons tailored after adult programs: two-hour group lesson, C$52; Discover Skiing and Discover Snowboarding include lift, two-hour lesson and rentals, C$54; Ski Weeks include five two-hour group lessons, social events, a fun race and video analysis for C$199.

Reservations required for all programs. For kids 12 and younger, call (250) 558-6028; for kids 13 and older, call (250) 558-6065.

Special activities: "Kids Night Out" is a supervised evening at Tube Town. The program runs Thursday only from 5 p.m. to 7:30 p.m. For ages 6–12, it's tubing and dinner for C$21; ages 3–5 get a movie and dinner for C$18. Reservations are required; space subject to availability.

Lift tickets (08/09 prices, without tax)

	Adults	Children (6-12)
One day	C$70	C$34
Three days	C$194 ($65/day)	C$88 ($29/day)
Five days	C$318 ($64/day)	C$142 ($28/day)

Who skis free: Children 5 and younger.

Who skis at a discount: Youth 13-18 pay C$58 for one day, C$160 for three, C$262 for five. Seniors 65+ and Canadian college students with valid ID pay youth prices.

Note: Prices are rounded to the nearest dollar. Night skiing is available Thursdays, Fridays and Saturdays, 3:30-8 p.m., C$26 adults and youth; C$21 children.

Accommodations

All Silver Star hotels are centered around the main village. Lodging can be booked through **Silver Star Holidays**, 800-663-4431.

Lord Aberdeen Apartment Hotel (800-553-5885; 250-542-1992; $$$-$$$$) offers private-entrance, one- and two-bedroom apartments, each with a full kitchen. **Silver Lode Inn** (800-554-4881; 250-549-5105; $$-$$$) is a Swiss-style hotel with 38 rooms.

Silver Star Club Resort (800-610-0805; 250-549-5191; $$-$$$$) has three buildings with outdoor hot tubs and a variety of accommodations, from standard rooms to two-bedroom units with full kitchens and fireplaces. **The Pinnacles Suite Hotel** (800-551-7466; 250-542-4548; $$$$) sits on the edge of the ski runs and has units with up to four bedrooms.

Putnam Station Inn (800-489-0599; 250-542-2459; $$-$$$) features a unique railroad atmosphere, plus an outdoor hot tub under the water tower. These units can all be booked through **Silver Star Accommodation** (877-630-7827; 250-558-7825) or **Mountain Vacation Homes** (800-489-0599; 250-542-2459).

Creekside condominiums ($$$-$$$$) have one- and two-bedroom units, with kitchens, fireplace and an outdoor hot tub. **The Grandview** ($$$) condominium complex has 33 two-bedroom units, each with a view of the Monashee Mountains.

Samesun Ski Hostel (877-562-2783; 250-545-8933; $-$$) offers ski-in/ski-out accommodations with hot tubs, free breakfast and linen service. Private or family rooms are available.

Dining

The Bulldog Grand Cafe (250-542-2459; $-$$), formerly the Putnam Station Inn, is an extension of the Bulldog Amsterdam with the feel of an Austrian ski resort. The **Silver Lode Inn Dining Room** (250-549-5105; $-$$) features Swiss and international cuisine and a buffet dinner on Thursday evenings. In the Silver Star Club Resort you'll find the most upscale restaurant, **Clementine's Dining Room** (250-549-5191; $-$$), with special prime rib Thursdays and buffet Sundays.

The Italian Garden (250-558-1448; $-$), with pick-up and delivery; and the **Vance Creek Saloon** (250-503-1452; $-$) serve light meals and snacks until midnight. Don't miss the **Lord Aberdeen Bistro** (250-542-1992; $) where soups are a specialty and there's a wide variety of homemade fare. **Long John's Pub** (250-549-2992; $) at the Lord Aberdeen Hotel offers pub fare, lunch, dinner and drinks; families are welcome.

Paradise Camp (250-558-6087; $-$), at the Powder Gulch Express midstation, is good for an informal lunch or snacks. Some ski writers think it's the best place on the continent to enjoy a beer on the outdoor sundeck in the spring. In the Town Hall day lodge, the **Town Hall Eatery** (250-558-6024; $) is the locals' hangout featuring soups, sandwiches, burgers and more.

Apres-ski/nightlife

Be sure to check out the Weekly Events Calendar when you check in. It lists the special apres-ski activities that vary from week to week.

Head over to the **Vance Creek Saloon** where there's entertainment to be had Wednesday to Saturday. **Charlie's Bar** is quieter and cozier. It's off the Silver Lode Inn Dining Room. In the lower level of Putnam Station is a fantastic little **Wine Cellar** featuring various wines and meals. **Long John's** at the Lord Aberdeen Hotel has live entertainment four nights a week.

Other activities

Silver Star's Adventure Park has a lift-served **Tubetown, skating pond, Mini-Z snowmobile park for kids, horse-drawn sleigh rides, snowmobile tours** and **snowshoe excursions**.

Via Snowmobile Safaris, you can tour the resort perimeter. For juniors ages 7-12, there is a **motocross style course** for scaled down snowmobiles. Advanced bookings must be made through the Information Desk. Call 250-558-6019. Guided **snowmobile tours** are available.

The National Altitude Training Center has a **climbing wall** (lessons available), **wax rooms** and a **fitness center**. On Thursday nights in the auditorium, the locals and staff put on an extravaganza of music, comedy and entertainment called **Silver Star Snow Show.**

You can also take a ride through the village in a **horse-drawn carriage**. For **shopping**, the village has a liquor store, ski & snowboard shop, clothing & gift shops and a grocery store.

Getting there and getting around

By air: Kelowna International Airport is about an hour's drive from Big White and Silver Star, and less than an hour's flight from Vancouver, Calgary or Seattle. Non-stop flights from Toronto are also available. U.S. Customs is at the Kelowna Airport. Big White and Silver Star's airport shuttles serve the ski areas; seats must be reserved 72 hours in advance. For Silver Star Central Holidays, call (800) 663-4431. For Big White Central Reservations, call 800-663-2772. Big White has a Budget rental agency on the mountain. One-way rentals to and from the airport can be booked through Big White Central Reservations. Ski free at Silver Star or Big White when you arrive with WestJet. Show your boarding pass and photo ID at the ticket office the same day you fly.

By car: Silver Star and Big White are in the heart of the Okanagan Valley. Silver Star is 40 miles northeast of Kelowna, and Big White is 35 miles southeast of Kelowna. The two resorts are 59 miles apart. The resorts are about 4.5 to 5.5 hours from Vancouver and Spokane and six to seven hours from Seattle.

Getting around: No car is needed at Silver Star or Big White unless you plan to explore. At Silver Star, a taxi loops continuously throughout the resort until 10 p.m. daily. Inter-resort shuttles provide transfers between Silver Star and Big White so you can ski for a day or split your stay between the resorts.

Dining: $$$$–Entrees C$30+; $$$–C$20–$30; $$–C$10–$20; $–less than C$10.
Accommodations: (double room) $$$$–C$200+; $$$–C$141–$200; $$–C$81–$140; $–C$80 and less.

Fernie Alpine Resort
British Columbia

Summit:	6,316 feet
Vertical:	2,816 feet (lift-served)
Base:	3,500 feet

Address: 5339 Fernie Ski Hill Rd., Fernie, British Columbia V0B 1M6
Telephone (main): 250-423-4655
Snow Report Number: 800-258-7669
Toll-free reservations: 800-258-7669; 866-633-7643
Reservations outside U.S.: 250-423-4655
E-mail: info@skifernie.com
Internet: www.skifernie.com
Expert:★★★★★
Advanced:★★★★★
Intermediate:★★★★
Beginner:★★ **First-timer:**★

Lifts: 10—2 high-speed quads, 2 quads, 2 triples, 4 surface lifts
Skiable acreage: 2,404
Snowmaking: 5 percent (125 acres)
Uphill capacity: 13716
Parks & pipes: 1 park, 1 pipe
Bed base: 4,368 on mountain; 6,754 in town
Nearest lodging: Slopeside, ski-in/ski-out
Child care: Yes, newborn and older
Adult ticket, per day: C$77 (07/08 prices)

Dining:★★★
Apres-ski/nightlife:★★
Other activities:★★★

Fernie Alpine Resort is fast finding a following of adventurous skiers and riders. The ridges, bowls and trees get dumped on with light snow that will keep any powderhound happy.

You'll find some of the steepest terrain you'll ever see in-bounds, and what's out-of-bounds is free for the taking too. The snow is unbelievable—deep and light and almost magical. The terrain seems unlimited—if you see it, and can get to it, you can ski it. There are no crowds, so you have the mountain practically to yourself.

While every bowl has some groomed terrain, most terrain is left the way Mother Nature made it—and that's the way Fernie's fans want it to be. Fernie has some of the steepest in-bounds terrain you'll find at any resort in North America. Because of that, there are many in-bound areas prone to avalanches. These areas are well marked, but you should know what to look for. If you suddenly come upon warning signs, pay close attention. About 60 professional patrollers, all trained in avalanche safety and explosives, keep Fernie under watchful eye.

Fernie, tucked into the craggy Lizard Range of the Canadian Rockies, is several hours from civilization and caters to a casual crowd that comes here for one thing and one thing only: the allure of the mountain. Much of the mountainside village is new and includes lodging, restaurants, apres-ski bars, coffee shops and a grocery store. Fernie, owned by Resorts of the Canadian Rockies, has plans for expansion both in the slopeside village and on the mountain. Fortunately, there isn't a lot of room for village expansion, so this resort should stay as intimate and laid-back as it is right now.

The turn-of-the-century coal mining town of Fernie is just three miles away. The main street, 2nd Avenue, is actually parallel to the road you'll travel on into town. Fernie burned down twice during the early 1900s and when it was rebuilt in 1910 builders were required by code to use brick and stone. The result is a colorful blend of shops, restaurants, clubs and bars.

Fernie is ripe with legends, including the powder-making Griz, honored with an annual winter carnival, and the curse-bearing Ghostrider, who appears in the shadows of Mount Hosmer. Ask any local, they love to share their history.

Fernie has recently upgraded snowguns, created access to more steep terrain and added glades in Currie and Timber bowls. It also did some brush cutting throughout the resort, added a trail out of Currie Bowl and a trail to bypass the Falling Star switchback.

 ## Mountain layout

Fernie consists of five seemingly limitless bowls of pure delight that dump you into gut-wrenching steeps and chutes, gnarly trees, gentle glades and thrilling trails. All have terrain for all abilities, it's really a matter of taking the time to totally explore each and deciding on your favorite. It's easy to spend all day exploring one bowl. It's a good idea to take a complimentary mountain tour on your first day so you can become familiar with how to travel the mountain; meet at the carousel in front of Guest Services at 9:30 a.m. and 1 p.m. Here is a larger, more detailed trail map.

Expert, Advanced: What can we say? It doesn't get better than this! Explore to your heart's content. Some traverses cross very steep terrain and if you're prone to vertigo, be prepared, but it's worth getting over it.

Find the "idiot's traverse" in Timber Bowl and head to some sweet trees off Diamond Back and in Anaconda Glades and Gotta Go, or head to Cedar Bowl and jump into King Fir and Cedar Ridge. Bootleg Glades have a sphincter-tightening drop-in, but you'll enjoy the goods once you're in. Surprize got its name after an avalanche etched it into the mountain.

After a storm, take the Lizard Traverse at least halfway across before dropping into wide-open floatable powder. Siberia Bowl has some great powder stashes too. On clear days after a big snowfall, follow the "leaping lemmings" line out of Currie Bowl and up to Polar Peak. And for days after, when much of the mountain is skied off, don't despair, you'll still find powder in the trees off Decline, leading into Easter Bowl and Lizard Bowl.

Intermediates:

If you're an intermediate who loves long cruisers, you'll get bored rather quickly. But if you're ready to test your skills and move to the ungroomed and trees, this is the mountain for you. All of the bowls have very nice intermediate terrain, just search for what you want: Small bumps, ungroomed, semi-steep or trees. It's easy to dip in and out off the groomed trails as you gain confidence.

You'll have great fun on Currie Powder and Currie Glades, wandering farther afield as you get more adventurous. The trees in Timber Bowl and Currie Bowl are fabulous ego-boosters. Dancer, Cascade and Bow in Lizard Bowl are wide-open slopes perfect for learning powder.

Beginner, First-timer: While Fernie has excellent beginner terrain that's nicely separated from other ability levels, it's still adventurous by most standards. Your best bet is to join a ski week group, where instructors can help you overcome any trepidation you may have.

For first-timers, the word on the street is that if you learn to ski here, you'll advance more rapidly than at most other resorts. This is a very challenging mountain. First-timers should join a ski week program where instructors can give expert advice.

Parks and pipes

Fernie has eliminated its meticulously groomed halfpipe as a safety measure initiated by its parent company, Resorts of the Canadian Rockies. A terrain park with rails and hits is on Upper Falling Star and is accessible by the Timber Bowl Express Quad. But most skiers and riders come here for the natural terrain.

Snowboarding

Fernie's natural terrain is a big draw to snowboarders. However, you'll find Fernie a challenge simply because of all the traverses. To access the best-kept secrets, you'll have to follow some harrowing traverses that are lo-o-ong excursions. However, the great terrain is worth every bit of the agony it requires to get to it. Your best bet is to explore each bowl thoroughly before moving on to the next one so as to minimize some of the traversing (such as to get back from the Haul Back T-bar). You definitely want to avoid the very long run-out at the bottom of Falling Star, where you'll end up walking out—most riders only use it when they return from hiking in the backcountry on this side of the mountain.

Cross-country & snowshoeing (see also xcskiresorts.com)

Fernie Alpine Resort has 10 km. of trails in a figure-eight loop, good for both skating and classic. Trail usage is free. Lessons and guided cross-country tours are available. Fernie does not rent equipment, so bring your own. You also can cross-country ski at the **Fernie Golf & Country Club**, where trails are beginner to intermediate.

Guided snowshoe tours with a naturalist are a great aerobic workout, plus you'll be entertained with local legends and lore. The network of **mountain biking trails** found throughout Fernie are excellent for snowshoeing. Pick up a copy of the trail guide at local retailers.

Lessons (07/08 prices, without tax)

Group lessons: Skiers and snowboarders levels 1-6 pay C$89 for a half-day lesson; C$109 for a full day.

First-timer package: The package, which includes a beginner lift pass, rentals and half-day group lesson (skiing, telemarking or snowboarding), costs C$69; a full day costs C$89. Fernie has an excellent learn-to-ski or -snowboard week package that we recommend to help first-timers feel comfortable with this adventurous mountain: Three-day programs start on Sunday or Thursday and include rentals, full lift pass and Ski Week lessons (see Special Programs below) for C$359; youth (13-17) pay C$335.

Private lessons: Skiing, snowboarding or telemarking lessons (five people maximum) cost C$235 for two hours; C$335 for three hours; C$525 for six hours (all day). An early-bird lesson for 1.5 hours that starts at 9 a.m. costs C$135; a two-hour late-day lesson costs C$149.

Special Programs: Ski & Snowboard Weeks will help you rise to the challenge of the mountain and are highly recommended. The three-day program gives you the same instructor every day and includes a NASTAR race, video analysis and apres-ski reception. For ages 18 and older. Programs start Sunday and Thursday. A three-day program costs C$359.

Children's programs (07/08 prices, without tax)

Child care: Ages newborn to 6 years old. For infants up to 18 monthscall for more information. For ages 19 months up to 3 years, a full day is C$49; half day, C$29. For ages 3–6 years, a full day is C$48; half day is C$29. Ask about discounts for multiple children. Free snacks are provided; lunch is available by request for C$8. A late fee of C$10 is charged for every 15 minutes late. Kids 3–4 years old can take a two-hour group lesson, booked through day care, for C$45. Reservations are recommended, especially for infants, at least 24 hours in advance. Resort Kids Daycare is a safe, licensed facility for children and is in the Cornerstone Lodge. Please do not send nut products with your child.

Children's programs: Full-day programs (skiing and snowboarding) for ages 5–12 cost C$89; half-day morning, C$59 (three hours); half-day afternoon, C$39 (two hours). Supervised lunch, C$14. Rental gear is extra. All children in ski school programs are required to wear helmets; rentals available. The first-timer package, which includes a beginner lift pass, rentals and half-day group lesson, costs C$59; a full day costs C$79.

Kids Adventure Camps, for ages 5–12, are three-day programs that include a NASTAR race, video analysis and apres-ski party. Three full days cost C$239 (starts on Sunday and Thursday); three half days cost C$159. Supervised lunch is an additional C$14 per day.

Special activities: Kids Activity Night is a supervised evening of activities (6–9 p.m. Wednesdays and Saturdays) for ages 6–12. Register for specific activities—such as meeting the horses that pull sleighs—or join for a whole week of fun (arts and crafts, snow soccer, storytelling and more). Activities vary nightly. Child must be registered with ski school by 5 p.m. that day, C$35 per child.

Lift tickets (07/08 prices, without tax)

	Adult	Junior (6-12)
One day	C$77	C$24
Three days	C$207($69/day)	C$66 ($22/day)
Five days	C$345 ($69/day)	C$110 ($22/day)

Who skis free: Ages 5 and younger.

Who skis at a discount: Youth (13-17) pay C$55 and seniors (65 and older) pay C$63 for one day.

Accommodations

Fernie's **Central Reservations** (800-258-7669; 403-209-3321) creates custom packages including lodging, lift tickets, flights and car rentals.

The magnificent riverstone-and-log **Lizard Creek Lodge** (877-228-1948; 250-423-2057; $$$-$$$$) just steps away from the Elk Quad chairlift but secluded off to one side of the mountain, does a marvelous job of blending luxury with rustic splendor. Richly appointed condominium-style units, in the main lodge and in two nearby buildings, range in size from studio to two-bedroom with loft. Each unit has a fully equipped kitchen, fireplace and balcony. The complex has an outdoor heated pool, spa, fitness center, lounge and gourmet restaurant.

Cornerstone Lodge (800-258-7669; 250-423-4655; $$-$$$$), is in the middle of the slopeside village near the Deer Chair. You can enjoy the nighttime view of the halfpipe sculptor as he meticulously prepares it for the next day's riders. All rooms are comfortably furnished deluxe suites with gas fireplace, fully equipped kitchen, washer and dryer, and balcony. Amenities include indoor hot tub, exercise room and underground parking.

Kerrin Lee-Gartner's Snow Creek Lodge (800-667-9911; $$-$$$$) is another excellent mountainside choice, where you'll find studios and one- and two-bedroom suites built in the style of early Canadian architecture with stone and logs. Units have decks or balconies, full kitchen and gas fireplace. Guests have a heated outdoor swimming pool, two whirlpools and a fitness room. Barbecues are held on a sun deck where you can order a cappuccino or cold drink from the licensed bar overlooking the mountain.

Griz Inn (800-661-0118; 250-423-9221; $$-$$$$), built in 1982 as the second on-hill accommodation, has hotel rooms, studios, and one-, two- and three-bedroom suites with lofts.

Suites include full kitchens. Amenities include an indoor pool, outdoor hot tub and sauna.

If you're on a budget but want to stay on the mountain, book in at the older but comfortable **Wolf's Den Lodge** (800-258-7669; 250-423-4655; $$), where standard hotel rooms have coffee makers and small refrigerators. Guests can use two indoor hot tubs, an exercise room and a game room, as well as common laundry facilities.

Various **townhouse** and **chalet** options are also available, so be sure to inquire about them if you'd rather stay in lodging of this kind.

Rocky Mountain Vacations (877-423-7905; fax 250-423-7995; $$$-$$$$) manages many private luxury chalets and condominiums with amenities such as outdoor hot tubs, saunas, entertainment centers, river rock fireplaces, full laundry facilities, fully equipped kitchens and mountain views. You can choose from mountainside, in town and rural locations.

In town:

If you really enjoy nightlife and dining out, you may prefer to stay in town instead of at the mountain.

The upscale **Best Western Fernie Mountain Lodge** (250-423-5500; $$-$$$) has deluxe guest rooms, some with kitchenettes, as well as themed hot tub suites. Guests have access to an indoor pool, indoor and outdoor hot tubs, fitness center, common laundry facilities, restaurant and lounge.

You can choose from standard hotel and junior studio rooms at the stone-and-log **Park Place Lodge** (888-381-7275; 250-423-6871; $$-$$$). Some rooms have kitchenettes and mini-refrigerators. The lodge has an indoor pool and hot tub.

Riverside Mountain Hotel & Chalets (877-423-5600; $-$$$$) is a resort with a range of accommodations, from value-priced hotel rooms to luxury chalets. **Cedar Lodge** (800-977-2977; 250-423-4622; $$) is an older property with prices to reflect it. Rooms have a microwave and fridge. **Travelodge Three Sisters Motel** (877-326-8888; 250-423-4438; $-$$) gives a basic motel experience.

Fernie also has two hostels, **SameSun Hostel** (877-562-2783; 250-423-4492; $-$$), part of a chain that also packages guided tours and **The Raging Elk Hostel** (250-423-6811; $-$$). Seasoned hostelers told us SameSun has nicer beds but can be noisy, while Raging Elk is less polished but has a separate common area for people who party or just want to stay up late.

 # Dining

For such a remote and tiny town, you'll find a remarkable choice of good dining, both on the mountain and in town. We suspect that as Fernie becomes a bigger blip on the radar screen, more skilled chefs will find their way here.

On the mountain:

You'd be missing out on a special gourmet experience if you don't eat at **Lizard Creek Lodge** (250-423-2057); $$$; reservations recommended. Make sure to try one of the local Okanagan Valley wines to compliment your meal. The fondue lunch, served in the lounge, is said to be excellent. Located at the top of the Timber Express quad, the recently opened (2006-07 season) **Lost Boys Cafe** features baked potatoes, fresh baked goods, Starbucks coffee and other specialties as well as beer and wine in a beautiful setting with indoor and outdoor seating.

Another gourmet experience, **The Wood on the Hill** (250-423-4597; $$), with a lively jazz-and-blues-influenced ambiance, is located near the base of the Mighty Moose.

Gabriella's Little Italy Pasta Place (250-423-7388; $) serves sandwiches on focaccia and heaping plates of pasta. **Kelsey's Restaurant** (250-423-2444; $-$$), in Cornerstone Lodge, is a chain pub-style restaurant with a rustic interior and a broad menu.

Slopeside Coffee and Deli (250-423-2440; $), in Cornerstone Lodge, is the place to go for Starbucks coffee and pastries, as well as deli sandwiches, soups and salads. **The Griz Bar** ($) lays out a mean salad bar, plus a basic bar menu for lunch. Downstairs is the **cafeteria**. For a quick energy fix, check out **Spuds "eh,"** a meals-on-wheels food truck that drops anchor in front of the ticket window and serves handcut fries with several types of sauces. The **Yamagoya** (250-423-0090; $$) is decidedly Japanese with a full sushi bar, private tatami rooms and sake bar.

In town:

A real culinary surprise is **The Curry Bowl** (250-423-2695; $$), a tiny restaurant owned by a young couple. They specialize in "enlightened Asian cuisine" of Thailand, India and Japan. Their Vietnamese summer rolls are a fabulous—and perfect—blend of chicken and shrimp wrapped in rice paper with cucumbers, red peppers, bean sprouts and fresh mint served with a sweet chili sauce. They don't take reservations, so get there early; otherwise, expect at least an hour wait (it's worth it). Open daily at 5 p.m.

If you're interested in a rare dining environment, go to **The Old Elevator** (250-423-7115; $$$-$$$$; reservations recommended), a grain feed store and grain elevator built in 1908 that have been lovingly refurbished. The creative continental menu, which changes seasonally, includes beef, western game, seafood and pasta dishes. The restaurant has received the Wine Spectator Award of Excellence for the past three years.

Las Tres Hermanas (250-423-3215; $$) in the Northern Hotel is a festive Mexican restaurant specializing in authentic regional dishes and margaritas.

Locals recommend "Pasta Tuesdays" at **Boston Pizza** (250-423-2634; $-$$) in the Best Western Fernie Mountain Lodge, where you'll get heaping plates of pasta for less than C$10. **The Pub Bar & Grill** (250-423-6871; $) in the Park Place Lodge is the place for pub grub.

Relax with a cup of gourmet coffee, cappuccino or espresso at **Cappuccino Corner** on 2nd Avenue. The black raspberry mocha is a very nice surprise. Board games and six computers with Internet access make this more than a coffee shop.

Apres-ski/nightlife

Crowds start gathering at **The Grizzly Bar** even before the lifts shut down and it revs up to a loud hum with tall tales of the day's skiing and riding. There's live music and dancing on weekends from 3 - 6 p.m. plus Saturday nights 9 p.m. to midnight. **Kelsey's** is the other on-mountain destination for a lively crowd. A more sedate crowd heads to the **Lizard Creek Lodge Lounge**, with comfy leather chairs and couches. Watch night fall over the mountain or the latest sports event on the big-screen TV.

In town, play pool, foosball, ping pong or watch your favorite sports on TV screens scattered throughout the **Pub Bar & Grill** in the Park Place Lodge. **Eldorado Lounge** is the town's most aerobic nightclub, with a dance floor that's hopping every night but Sunday. Or head to **Eschwig's** at The Northern Hotel. For a quieter evening, there's a **movie theater**.

Fernie was well known for its beer brewing till 1960 and the new **Fernie Brewing Company** hopes to revive that history. Local restaurants and pubs serve the company's microbrews.

Other activities

You can book a slew of activities through the resort's Guest Services (250-423-4655): **horse-drawn sleigh rides, torchlight run & BBQ, snowmobiling tours, wildlife viewing, ice fishing, backcountry tours**, and **dogsledding**.

Accommodations (Cdn$): (double room) $$$$-$200+; $$$-$141-$200; $$-$81-$140; $-$80 and less.
Dining (Cdn$): $$$-Entrees $20+; $$-$10-20; $-less than $10

Choose from three **cat-skiing** operations: You probably won't be able to book a stay at the highly respected Island Lake Lodge (888-422-8754) because they only allow 36 guests per tour, but it's worth a try. Powder Cowboy Cat-Skiing Tours (888-422-8754 or 250-423-3700) is now owned by Island Lake Lodge and has its own Bull River Ranch, with terrain. Fernie Wilderness Adventures (250-423-6704) takes you to terrain that's great for first-time cat-skiers.

Unwind after a hard day on the slopes at the **Spa** at Lizard Creek Lodge (250-423-2057), with treatments including aromatherapy, hydrotherapy and massages. In town, choose from Fernie Mountain Massage Therapy Clinic (250-423-5522), Hydrotherapy Spa & Massage Therapy Clinic (250-423-7667) and Jade River Healing Center Chinese Medicine Clinic (250-423-7667). It's also comforting to know the town has a hospital (250-423-4453).

If you're interested in learning about Fernie's history, pick up a copy of the **Heritage Walking Tour** booklet from the Fernie Information Center in town. You'll also find enough **shops** along 2nd Avenue to spend an afternoon browsing. There are several Alpine sports stores, all worth checking out. If you're looking for unique gifts, we recommend Stephanie's Glass & Art Studio for custom-made stained glass and work by local artists, Ghostrider Trading Co. for handcrafted items by local artisans and mountain-lifestyle clothing, and Carosella Artworks for home decor and jewelry. They also have a shop in the mountain village.

Pick up a copy of the *Fernie Guide* for other activity suggestions.

Getting there and getting around

By air: Most people fly into Calgary International Airport because it's served by most major airlines. It's about a three-hour drive to Fernie, though weather can affect travel time. Cranbrook Airport, served by Air BC, is an hour away. You also can fly into Glacier International Airport in Kalispell, Mont., which is about two hours away.

If you use the Rocky Mountain Sky Shuttle (888-762-8754 in U.S. and Canada, or 403-762-5200) from Calgary, make sure to ask your driver for local lore and wild tales of living in the rugged British Columbia wilderness. Mountain Perks (250-423-4023) runs another Calgary-Fernie shuttle service.

By car: If you drive, be watchful for moose, deer, elk and bighorn sheep, which often wander into the road. From Calgary: South on Provincial Hwy. 2 to Crowsnest Hwy. 3, west on Hwy. 3 until you reach the town of Fernie. If the weather is nice, you can take a slightly shorter more scenic route: south on Hwy. 2 to Hwy. 7, west on Hwy. 7 to town of Black Diamond, south on Hwy. 22, west on Hwy. 3.

Getting around: Kootenay Taxi runs a ski shuttle between the mountain and town; a schedule is available from the resort Guest Services counter and local accommodations. A one-way trip costs C$3; four one-way rides, C$10; a Frequent Rider Card (10 rides), C$25. In the evening, a free shuttle runs between 6 p.m. and 12:42 a.m. We found the shuttle schedule to be somewhat inconvenient and ended up calling for a taxi (250-423-4408) to return to the mountain each time (about C$18 one way with tip). If you plan to do any kind of exploring, rent a car.

Kicking Horse Mtn. Resort

British Columbia, Canada

Summit: 8,033 feet
Vertical: 4,133 feet
Base: 3,900 feet

Address: Kicking Horse Mountain Resort, 1500 Kicking Horse Trail, Box 839, Golden, British Columbia, Canada V0A 1H0
Telephone (main): 250-439-5400
Snow Report Number: 250-439-5400
Toll-free reservations: 866-754-5425
Reservations outside US: 250-439-5400
E-mail: guestservices@kickinghorseresort.com
Internet: www.kickinghorseresort.com

Lifts: 5—1 8-person gondola, 2 quads, 1 double, 1 moving carpet
Skiable acreage: 2,750
Snowmaking: None
Uphill capacity: 14,000
Parks & pipes: None
Bed base: 314 slopeside; 1,100 in Golden
Nearest lodging: Ski-in/ski-out
Child care: Yes, 18 months and older
Adult ticket, per day: C$60 (07/08)

Expert:★★★★★
Advanced:★★★★★
Intermediate:★★★
Beginner:★★★ First-timer:★★

Dining:★★★
Apres-ski/nightlife:★★★
Other activities:★★★

Kicking Horse Mountain Resort in interior British Columbia is a jeweled crown in the making—a true work in progress. It's on Highway 1, just 48 miles west of Lake Louise between Kootenay and Glacier national parks in the town of Golden. The once locally owned day hill is undergoing a huge infusion of money from its new owners, the Netherlands-based construction giant Ballast Nedam International, a company that traditionally builds dams and bridges.

Originally run by local volunteers and known as Whitetooth, this potentially world-class ski area was renamed Kicking Horse by Ballast Nedam. The company transformed the site, adding two new lifts including a bottom-to-top gondola, two ski lodges, its first slopeside lodging and other amenities. Their goal is to make this resort one of the largest ski areas in North America. The name Kicking Horse has its origins in a near-fatal accident suffered in an 1858 expedition to discover a route through the mountains for the railroad. In an effort to retrieve a recalcitrant pack horse, Sir James Hector was kicked so severely that he was thought dead and almost buried by his guides. When he later discovered the desired pass through the mountains, the nearby river and pass were named after his kicking horse in his honor.

Kicking Horse Mountain Resort's peaks were once prime heliskiing terrain, a vast wilderness ripe with other peaks that are still used for heliskiing and snowcat skiing. What Mother Nature has provided in her "eagle eye" views from the top of the ski area combined with its natural ski terrain make it hard for skiers and riders to resist.

The resort is situated amongst three mountain ranges—the Purcells, the Selkirks and the Canadian Rockies, a region full of national parks in every direction—Banff, Jasper, Glacier, Kootenay, Yoho and Mt. Revelstoke.

The resort has a hard core reputation. As with many other resorts with steep terrain, the avalanche danger at Kicking Horse is ever present, so ski and ride with care and respect for the mountain. The resort benefits from its location by missing wetter weather that can plague its southern B.C. neighbors. It gets lots of snow, though it can be heavy powder.

Full build-out of the $300-million, 10-year development is planned for 2010. The resort has a 4,133-foot vertical drop, second in Canada only to Whistler Blackcomb. When its skiable acreage increases from 2,750 to 4,005 at build-out, Kicking Horse will join the ranks of Vail, Squaw Valley and Whistler Blackcomb, all monstrous when it comes to lift-accessed terrain. The resort also will soon reap the benefits of a government investment of $125 million in roadway improvements. The funding will be used to augment the highway to four lanes, improving access to the resort from the East.

Down the road, Golden is a logger's village in the throes of a failing timber industry that sits at the foot of a developing ski hill with a very bright future. The influx of outside private and local provincial money promises to change Golden's fortunes.

Beginner and lower-intermediate terrain is greatly improved by grooming and access. The addition of a midstation on the beginner Catamount chair accesses shorter runs. The first phase of a child-care facility offers a convenient guest service for those with kids. The resort continues its real estate development as well.

Kicking Horse Resort has extreme potential and its new owners have the vision to make it happen. The resort's reputation has a real skiers' mountain appeal for advanced and experts.

 ## Mountain layout

For the 20 years prior to the Golden Eagle Express Gondola, heliskiing was the main way to enjoy the higher reaches of the resort. Now, everyone can ski and ride the high Crystal Bowl. In springtime, check to see if Boo, the grizzly, is showing himself at the mid mountain bear refuge.

Expert, Advanced: Experts, advanced skiers and riders, this is your mountain. Even without riding the Golden Eagle Express Gondola to the 7,700-foot top of the main peak, there are black-diamond runs to the bottom. The Pioneer double chair, at the head of the parking lot, gets you to all the serious lower-mountain runs. A good warm-up is Race Place. It's the longest of the lower runs and is normally groomed. Bumpsters will want to drop into Pioneer right under the lift.

The trail map of the higher peaks can be misleading, since most of the terrain is unnamed. The marked trails are merely "suggestions" to guide you. Turn right or left as you get off the gondola and drop into whichever bowl beckons. These were heliskiing runs with steep headwalls before the gondola was built. To the left is Bowl Over, reached by tight trees off CPR Ridge, the Flying Dutchman, or by hiking up to Terminator Peak.

To the right of the gondola is Crystal Bowl. When heading to the bottom, steer skier's left of the chair to avoid It's a Ten cat track, hooking up instead with several single-diamond trails that drop you off right at the parking lot, or blue cruisers that dump out at the base lodge.

When heading to the hike-to terrain, check in with ski patrol, ask about conditions and tell them where you're going. Rescues off the higher peaks can be harrowing because of cliffs

Intermediates: Intermediates can take any lift to access good terrain. To get into Bowl Over, take Sluiceway from the top of the gondola. It veers left as you get off the lift, follows a gentle ridge and then descends into Bowl Over. Continuing past treeline, the run becomes Knee Deep, aiming back toward the gondola, eventually joining It's a Ten. As you glide along It's a Ten, you have a choice of four blue runs to the bottom, plus a few blacks and a few greens.

If you want to stay up on the higher mountain for several runs, enter Crystal Bowl from the top of the gondola. You can do laps in Crystal Bowl off the Stairway to Heaven lift.

Beginner, First-timer: Beginners have a way down from all of the lifts except Stairway to Heaven. You can get on the gentler part of It's a Ten from the top of the Catamount quad chair, or simply go down Big Ben, where you'll find a slew of green trails going in all directions. All the terrain off Catamount is gentle and delightful.

After some warm-up runs here, confident beginners can take the gondola to the top and ski down the longest run on the mountain—the 10-km.-long cat track It's a Ten. Check to see if it's been groomed before you go.

First-timers will *not* want to do that. Instead, stay on the Pony Express carpet until you're feeling comfortable enough to try some longer trails off the Catamount quad. The lift's new midstation makes it easier for novices to work their way up to longer trails.

Parks and pipes

Kicking Horse has no plans to add terrain parks or pipes, but who needs 'em when most of the resort has above-Alpine heliskiing-quality snow and terrain? If you must, have a ball in the woods between Bubbly and Euphoria, where you'll find a natural halfpipe and terrain park.

Snowboarding

The jump-offs into the bowls are gut-sucking even for skilled riders, and there are a lot of steep shots off the ridges. Many a rider has had to be rescued off cliff areas here because it's impossible to change directions, so be careful and pay attention to your route. Make sure to ride the Stairway to Heaven for access to the black-diamond My Blue Heaven area.

Intermediates also have great choices all over the mountain. The mid-bowls are comprised of blue and green runs and a ride out and down Terminator will peg your fun meter for sure.

The most thrilling trees are under the Stairway to Heaven lift, but the woods lower down the mountain are also big and thick.

Beginners will be comfortable in the Catamount lift region, where there are several green runs mixed with blues.

Cross-country & snowshoeing (see also xcskiresorts.com)

Dawn Mountain Nordic Ski Trails at the resort's base has 14 km. of classic track-set trails, including 1.5 km. of skating track. There are beginner loop trails, plus intermediate and expert trails. A trailside warming hut sits 1 km. into the course. A donation is suggested for use of the trails.

Cross-country equipment and snowshoes can be rented from the resort's rental shop, **Canyon Creek Outfitters**.

Lessons (07/08 prices, without tax)

Group lessons: Group lessons cost C$140 per person for a full day (10 a.m. to 3 p.m.) and include lunch in the plaza. Morning-only lessons cost C$89. The maximum size of the group is four skiers or riders.

First-timer package: First-timers are offered the Discover Program. Cost is C$149 for a full day from 9:30 a.m. to 3 p.m. Lesson, lunch, rentals and beginner lift ticket are included. Morning-only lessons cost C$109. The maximum group is four people.

Private lessons: Private lessons cost C$499 for a full day and C$299 for a half day. Lessons are for up to five participants, offer lift line priority and overnight ski storage for multi day lessons. Video analysis is included in a full-day private and costs an additional C$20 for a half day. Two-hour lessons in the afternoons are available on a space-available basis.

Fresh Tracks is available with instructors from 9-10 a.m., Over Lunch is from 12-1 p.m. and Last Call is at 3 p.m. These one-hour lessons each cost C$70, are limited to three people and offer lift line priority.

Special programs: Guides take groups on "Rips, Tips and Tours" of the mountain to help skiers and riders discover the mountain's secrets. A two-hour tour in the a.m. or p.m. costs C$40. Performance Camps prepare advanced and experts for big-mountain as well as snowcat skiing and heliskiing trips. Full-day camp with clinic, video analysis and lunch at Eagle's Eye Restaurant costs C$230; maximum of three students.

Children's programs (06/07 prices, without tax)

Child care: Ages 18 months to 5 years. A full day, including lunch and snacks, costs C$75. A half day (up to three hours, morning or afternoon) costs C$45 and includes a snack; add lunch for C$10. Pre-registration is required; (866-754-5425) or information can be found at Guest Services in the Day Lodge. The child-care center is in the Day Lodge and is open daily from 9 a.m. to 4:30 p.m.

Children's programs: For children 6–12, a full day with lunch costs C$89; half day costs C$60. Lift and rentals are extra; helmets are provided free. Kids are grouped according to ability levels.

Tiny Tykes, for ages 3–5, costs C$89 for a full day (with lunch); C$60 for a half day. Cost includes lift pass, helmet and tip clips for skis.

Special activities: Kid's Night Out, offered Friday and Saturday evenings, costs C$25 per hour with a minimum two-hour stay. Four hours costs C$45. A variety of activities keep kids busy while parents get some time out.

Lift tickets (07/08 prices, without tax)

	Adult	Junior (7-12)
One day	C$60	C$28
Three days	C$178 ($60/day)	C$78 ($26/day)
Five days	C$284 ($57/day)	C$120 ($24/day)

Who skis free: Kids 6 and younger.

Who skis at a discount: Youth (13-18) and seniors (65+) pay C$51 for one day; three days, C$144; five days, C$230.

Sightseers: For C$20, adults can ride the gondola for lunch or dinner, enjoy the food and the spectacular views. Children, C$13-17. Family C$45.

Accommodations

Kicking Horse Mountain Resort has a toll-free reservations number for most area properties, 866-754-5425. You can also pre-book tickets and transportation. Development of the mountain village is quite recent, so all lodging is new or like new. All the small lodges are owned by delightful couples who know how to make a vacation relaxing and special.

A luxurious 48-unit Palliser Lodge in Gondola Plaza added 50 units, retail and shopping, Cabins of Kicking Horse and other town homes and upscale homes.

Glacier Lodge (877-754-5486; 250-439-1160; $$-$$$$) is a ski-in/ski-out condo lodge with 56 units as large as three bedrooms with loft. Designed to blend into its Rocky Mountain surroundings with its stone and timber architecture, it's just steps from the gondola. Each unit has a full kitchen, washer/dryer, gas fireplace and mountain views. Other amenities include outdoor hot tub, sauna, steam room and fitness center. Friendly staff manage the front desk. The nearly identical **Mountaineer Lodge** has another 51 units, is owned by the same company and is right next door.

Copper Horse Lodge (877-544-7644; 250-344-7644; $$$), an intimate and classy 10-room inn, has all the modern conveniences in its spacious rooms: multi-jet spa showers, terry robes, featherbeds, Internet access, phones, bar fridges and flat-screen TVs with DVD players. The one deluxe room has a jetted tub. Other amenities include a common area with soaring fireplace and game table, an outdoor hot tub, a bar (bartender will deliver drinks to guests in the common areas), and a very good restaurant (see Dining). Prices include a full hot breakfast. It's a short walk to the lifts.

The rock-and-timber **Vagabond Lodge** (866-944-2622; 250-344-2622; $$$), with 10 suites and comfy common areas for guests to mingle, is stunning and inviting—like a fancy European pension. **Whispering Pines** (250-344-7188; $$-$$$) has luxurious three-bedroom townhouses providing ski-in/ski-out lodging just a few minutes' away from the day lodge and near the gondola. All units have kitchens, fireplaces, washers and dryers, outdoor hot tub and maid service. Depending on the unit, up to eight guests can be easily accommodated.

There is another option for staying (literally) on-mountain: The exclusive C$875 per room, per night "Winter Getaway" at **Eagle's Eye Suites** (866-754-5425; $$$$). Just upstairs above the Eagle's Eye Restaurant at 7,700 feet, two lovely two-person suites with private balconies overlook the Columbia Valley and three mountain ranges. Amenities include pretty much anything you'd expect for that price, including your own 24-hour valet/concierge service, personalized dining menus, lift tickets, guaranteed first tracks, private ski instructor, champagne, gift basket and other takeaways. The most exclusive part of this package is the VIP gondola cabin with leather seats, CD player and wine bucket for those 12-minute rides.

The town of Golden offers comfortable chain properties and a number of inns and B&Bs. Many Golden properties have shuttle service available to the ski area as needed for a small charge.

The Prestige Inn (866-754-5425; $$-$$$) has kitchenettes, fridges, an indoor pool and hot tub. A day spa and liquor store also are on the premises. **Best Western Mountainview Inn** (866-754-5425; $-$$) includes an indoor pool, coin laundry room and extra-large, family-sized rooms. **Ramada Limited** (800-593-0511; 250-439-1888; $-$$$) has an indoor pool, hot tub, coin laundry, business center with Internet access and kitchenette suites. Complimentary continental breakfast is included.

The **Golden Rim Motor Inn** (877-311-2216; $) is a real treasure, with thoughtful staff making the stay highly memorable. You'll find a waterslide, hot tub, indoor pool, saunas and recreation room.

Hillside Lodge & Chalets (250-344-7281; $$), owned and operated by the Baier family, is a B&B located about 15 minutes west of Golden, just north of Hwy. 1 on the Blaeberry River. Guestrooms have private baths; sumptuous breakfasts are included. Sonja and Hubert Baier also serve dinner. Five chalets each have twin or queen beds, private baths, handcrafted furnishings, wood stoves and fridges. Coffee and tea are provided.

Tschurtschenthaler Lodge (pronounced Church-en-Taller; 866-344-8184 or 250-344-7325; $$) is five minutes south of Golden. Guest rooms have private baths. Breakfast, a sauna hut and breathtaking views are all included. **Cedar House Cafe & Restaurant** (250-344-4679; $$), just 15 minutes from the resort, rents a cabin that sleeps four and includes laundry, kitchen and TV.

Alpine Meadows Lodge (250-344-5863; $$), on a scenic benchland just outside Golden,

Accommodations (Cdn$): (double room) $$$$-$200+; $$$-$141-$200; $$-$81-$140; $-$80 and less.
Dining (Cdn$): $$$-Entrees $20+; $$-$10-20; $-less than $10

has 10 guestrooms overlooking the great room and serves full hot breakfasts. **The Golden Kicking Horse Hostel** (250-344-5071; $) has beds for C$20 per night, full kitchen facilities, free parking, other amenities and no curfew.

Dining

Hands down, the most spectacular and elegant dining at Kicking Horse is at **Eagle's Eye Restaurant** (866-754-5425; $$$$ for dinner; $$ for lunch), just a gondola ride up to the 7,705-foot summit. Billed as "Canada's Most Elevated Dining Experience," it's the highest restaurant in Canada, equally fabulous for lunch and dinner. Ambitious entrees run the gamut from a vegetarian roasted pepper with polenta to fish, duck, buffalo and wild caribou. Begin the meal with sumptuous starters like lox, mussels, buffalo carpaccio and foie gras. The wine selection is quite varied and features many British Columbia labels. It's open for lunch every day, for dinner only on Friday and Saturday. The Cascadian architecture and the views are both breathtaking.

In the mountain village, **Corks Restaurant** (250-344-6201; $$$), at Copper Horse Lodge, serves contemporary mountain cuisine, such as maple-glazed wild coho salmon, in a bistro setting. A take-out menu highlights its gourmet pizzas. Our favorite is the bizzaro pizza with spicy sausage, spinach, chicken and mango chutney. **Sushi Kuma** ($-$$), at Glacier Lodge is tiny but the chefs create big tastes, whether you choose sushi, noodles, rice bowls or dinner boxes.

You can grab a quick bite to eat at **Heaven's Door Yurt** ($) at the base of the Stairway to Heaven lift in Crystal Bowl. The **cafeteria** ($) at the Day Lodge serves great made-to-order omelets for breakfast, and soups, salads, sandwiches and burgers for lunch.

Off the mountain in Golden, **Cedar House Cafe & Restaurant** (250-344-4679; $$-$$$$) has an open concept kitchen and features a vegetarian menu alongside the obligatory Alberta beef, pork, salmon and lamb. The chef uses wild, sustainable fish, free-range meats and organic produce.

Kicking Horse Grill (344-2330; $$-$$$), owned by two Dutch cousins, is in an old log cabin that belies its interior of burled logs, white tablecloths, candlelight and jazz playing in the background. The laid-back staff members, called "culinary tour guides," are knowledgeable and courteous. The delectable menu changes every three months to showcase international dishes.

Eleven22 (250-344-2443; $$-$$$) is a bright and cheerful bistro with several small rooms that create an intimate setting. It specializes in vegetarian Thai dishes, pastas and a variety of meats. Open nightly for dinner, Thursday through Saturday for lunch.

Apres-ski/nightlife

Apres-ski revs up at the **Day Lodge** every afternoon. On Fridays and Saturdays only, end up at the Eagle's Eye at the summit for drinks and starters, then ride the gondola back down. **Corks** at the Copper Horse Lodge gets chatty with local beers, wine and contemporary music playing in the background. Try some of the tasty appetizers to tide you over.

For some raucous nightlife, head into Golden to **The Lodge**. Locals refer to it as a "peeler" bar and tell us that "fresh meat" Mondays are the rowdiest since that's opening night on the circuit for the new "peeler" of the week (if you don't know what a "peeler" is, think "better than a wet T-shirt contest").

Mad Trapper is a pub with pool tables and lots of locals. **Packers**, a dance bar, spotlights live bands on weekends, djs on Thursdays and Fridays, playing danceable rock and Top 40 tunes. If you don't want to dance, vie for the pool tables. Otherwise, downtown Golden hasn't grown into its apres-ski and nightlife britches. Yet.

Other activities

This region is the destination for world-class **heliski** and **snowcat skiing** operators, as well as **backcountry guided tours**.

One you might not have heard of yet, but should consider, is Chatter Creek Mountain Lodges (250-344-7199), owned by two local loggers who also happen to be passionate about skiing and riding. The skilled staff is laid back and friendly, the lodges are simple but comfortable, and the emphasis is on great skiing and riding in a pristine and spectacular environment. The remote lodges are accessed solely by helicopter. All terrain is accessed via snowcat, but plans are to add heliski terrain, which ranges from a base of 4,900 feet to a summit of 9,600 feet, with some skiing and riding on glaciers.

Pure Travel Group (866-666-6068 from N. America; 250-439-1800 from other countries) offers full day excursions to Revelstoke Mountain Resort, Ski Lake Louise and Panarama & **Hot Springs**, both with **skiing** and **dogsledding** and a 1/2 day **snowmobile** tour with entry to **Radium Hot Springs**.

Guided snowmobile tours are available through SnowPeak Rentals & Tours (888-512-4222; 250-344-8385) and Kinbasket Adventures (250-344-6012). Cedar & Sage Spa (250-0018; 250-344-7990), a privately owned **day spa** in the Prestige Inn, offers wraps, massages, masks, facials, manicures, pedicures and hair care. Just-for-men treatments also are available. The scenery in the region is simply amazing, with frequent **wildlife sightings**. Places worth day visits include **Lake Louise, Radium Hot Springs, Revelstoke**, and the surrounding **six national parks**. Make sure to pick up free area road maps. Most accommodations have them on site. For **shopping**, you'll find a few shops in the mountain village and a few more downtown in Golden. Not surprisingly, emphasis is on outdoor recreational products.

Getting there and getting around

By air: Calgary International Airport is your gateway to Kicking Horse Mountain Resort, which is about 3 hours west along the Trans Canada Highway in Golden, B.C. The airport is served by all major airlines.

By shuttle: The airport shuttle is operated by Pure Travel Group which offers luxury service including leather seats, DVDs, complimentary soft drinks, pillows and blankets along with resort information such as trail maps and the local magazine for Kicking Horse. Call toll free from N. America 866-666-6086; from other countries 250-439-1800. www.puretravelgroup.com

By bus: A daily shuttle bus service goes from the Calgary Airport to Calgary's Greyhound depot, where you can catch a bus to Golden. Call 888-438-2992 for the airport shuttle details and schedules. The Powder Express bus (800-644-8888; 403-762-4554) goes from Banff and Lake Louise hotels to Kicking Horse for a day trip; cost includes bus ride and lift ticket.

By car: If you rent a car at the airport, life gets much easier. From Calgary, take the Trans Canada Highway and travel west, past Banff and Lake Louise to Golden, about a 3-hour drive along a scenic route. The pass through the Rockies can be treacherous in bad weather, so be sure to check road conditions. Follow signs to Golden Town Centre.

Getting around: Snow Shuttles run from Golden accommodations to the resort for C$6. A one-way taxi ride between Golden and the resort is costly.

Accommodations (Cdn$): (double room) $$$$-$200+; $$$-$141-$200; $$-$81-$140; $-$80 and less.
Dining (Cdn$): $$$-Entrees $20+; $$-$10-20; $-less than $10

Panorama Mountain Resort

British Columbia, Canada

Summit: 7,800 feet
Vertical: 4,000 feet
Base: 3,800 feet

Address: Panorama Mountain Village, Panorama, BC, Canada V0A 1T0
Telephone (main): 250-342-6941
Snow Report Number: 250-342-6941
Toll-free reservations: 800-663-2929
Reservations outside US: 250-342-6941
E-mail: paninfo@panoramaresort.com
Internet: www.panoramaresort.com

Expert:★★★
Advanced:★★★
Intermediate:★★★★
Beginner:★★★
First-timer:★★★

Lifts: 9—1 8-person village gondola, 2 high-speed quads, 1 quad, 1 triple, 1 double, 2 surface lifts, 1 moving carpet
Skiable acreage: 2,847
Snowmaking: 40 percent
Uphill capacity: 8,500
Parks & pipes: 2 parks, 1 pipe
Bed base: 3,500 at the base
Nearest lodging: Slopeside, ski-in/ski-out
Child care: Yes, 18 months and older
Adult ticket, per day: C$54 (07/08)
Dining:★★★
Apres-ski/nightlife:★★★
Other activities:★★★

Panorama Mountain Village is two hours south of Banff on the west side of the Continental Divide, which separates Alberta from British Columbia. Just think about the massive snowfall from clouds trying to rise over the Divide. British Columbians figure they get the best of the winter deal.

Panorama is now one of the Canadian Rockies' premier winter vacation destinations. With the addition of ski terrain, high-speed lifts, restaurants, giant slopeside hot pools, accommodations and a village gondola, life is looking pretty good on the western slope of the Rockies.

The resort has almost 3,000 patrolled acres, including bowls, backcountry terrain in Taynton Bowl, the gladed Extreme Dream Zone, terrain parks and an FIS-regulation halfpipe. Panorama is known for its high percentage of intermediate, advanced and expert runs and, since everything is below treeline, it has an abundance of glade skiing.

 ## Mountain layout

At the very top, the Summit Hut and Taynton Takeout wait for you to enjoy the "view of a thousand peaks." First-time visitors can learn their way around with a free guide service.

Expert/Advanced: The resort has almost 1,000 acres of backcountry-style terrain in Taynton Bowl. The bowl used to be strictly heliskiing territory and provides loads of wide-open and naturally gladed runs. The main chutes have more than 1,700 feet of vertical. Also head to Millennium (a fall-line run off the top of the Champagne Express), the gladed Extreme Dream Zone and the wide-open Sun Bowl.

Intermediate: Intermediates favor Alive Glades and Sun Bowl. Some may think the one blue-square run from the summit is appropriately named Getmedown. Most intermediates will want to stay below the Summit Quad. Adventurous intermediates should test themselves on the single-blacks lower on the mountain before heading to the top.

Beginner/First-timer: Beginners should stick to the learning area and the Mile 1 Quad

Express to get comfortable before trying any of the other chairlifts. The learning area, with a platter, moving carpet and a chair, is in the lowlands, away from the hubbub.

Parks and pipes

In the Showzone Terrain Park, experienced riders and skiers will find multiple tabletops, kickers, spines, rails, funboxes and an FIS-regulation halfpipe. Little rippers and freestyle newcomers will be happy in Blue Park, with its scaled-down versions of all the elements found in Showzone to ensure a safer, yet fun, experience for kids and intermediate snowboarders. Both terrain parks are lit for night sessions and piped-in DMX music adds to the ambience.

Snowboarding

While most riders give the manmade stuff a thumbs up, they really come here for the natural terrain. This resort is an excellent choice for intermediate, advanced and expert riders. Check out almost 1,000 acres of backcountry terrain in the Taynton Bowl: You'll find chutes, glades and wide-open runs here. Be forewarned: It's a long trudge out of the bowl.

Cross-country & snowshoeing (see also xcskiresorts.com)

The **Greywolf Nordic Centre** (250-342-6941 ext. 3840) offers 20.5 km. of groomed cross-country trails for classic and skate skiing, plus 6.6 km. for classic only. The Nordic clubhouse has rental equipment, waxing service, lessons and refreshments, plus changing rooms, lockers and showers. Trail fees are $10 adults, $7 teens, $6 juniors. The Hale Hut warming cabin, on the Delphine Loop, has bathrooms and a firepit with firewood for those who need to take a break.

Lessons (07/08 prices, without tax)

The Bilodeau School of Skiing and Snowboarding at Panorama is highly regarded. **Group lessons:** Diamond Cutters is a one-day clinic (four hours) for intermediate and advanced skiers that teaches route selection and advanced skills. Cost is C$89 and includes lunch at the Elkhorn Cabin.

Group lessons for beginner and intermediate skiers last 1.5 hours and cost C$59. Group lessons for beginner and intermediate snowboarders are 1.5 hours and cost C$59.

First-timer package: First-time skiers can take a MagicTrax Group Lesson with specially trained MagicTrax instructors and "shortcut" shaped skis. The three-day program includes a 3.5-hour lesson each day and costs C$199; includes gear rentals.

Private lessons: One-hour lessons cost C$89; 1.5 hours cost C$119.

Special programs: Confidence Club for skiers is a three-day group clinic designed to help master the blue runs. Cost is C$199 for 10.5 hours of instruction.

Children's programs (07/08 prices, without tax)

Child care: Ages 18 months through 5 years old. All-day for ages 18 months–3 years costs C$65; for ages 3–5 years, C$55. Cost for a half day for all ages is C$35. Lunch is an additional C$7. Book a full day at least two days in advance and get 10 percent off. Hourly rates are available. For Wee Wascals reservations, call 250-341-3041. Evening babysitters are available by arrangement.

Children's lessons: There are extensive lesson offerings for children. Register in advance with the ski school for all children's lessons, 888-767-7799 or 250-342-6941.

The Snowbirds program is an introduction to skiing for kids 3–4 years old. Lessons start at

9:15 a.m. or 3:15 p.m. and cost C$39; most children spend the rest of the day in child care.

The all-day Adventure Club (10:30 a.m. to 3 p.m.) is designed for skiers ages 5–14 and snowboarders ages 8–14. It costs C$89 (includes lunch) for one day; C$229 for three consecutive days; each additional day costs from C$50 – C$60 depending on the extra days..

First Run Snowboard for kids 8 and older teaches the basic skills of sliding, turning on an easy slope and lift-riding. The 1-1/2-hour lesson starts at 10 a.m. or 1 p.m. and costs C$69.

Skiing with kids: The "kids only zone" is just off the Mile One quad chair. The Secret Forest is a magical place including a mid-mountain wooden fort and park where kids can kick off their skis and play.

Special activities: Horse-drawn sleigh rides take you along Toby Creek to Trappers Cabin, an old-time ranch where there's a roaring fire, hot chocolate and s'mores. Winter Wonderland is the place to go every Saturday night for a kid's parade, story telling and the snow dance. "Kids Night Out" include indoor games, activities and crafts for children ages 5–12. Older kids can go to Teen Movie Night or the e-zone games arcade. The Glacier nightclub also hosts Teen Club Nights on Thursday and Sunday nights.

Lift tickets (08/09 prices, without tax)

	Adult	Junior (7-12)
One day	C$67	C$27
Three days	C$179 (C$60/day)	C$74 ($25/day)
Five days	C$274($55/day)	C$119 ($24/day)

Who skis free: Ages 6 and younger.

Who skis at a discount: Teens (13-18) pay C$56; three days, C$144; five days, C$224. Seniors 65 and older pay teen prices.

Note: Prices are rounded to the nearest dollar.

Accommodations

Panorama has more than 600 slopeside condos and townhomes, plus a 102-unit hotel. Call 800-663-2929 or book online at www.skipanorama.com.

Wolf Lake, Aurora, Riverbend and **Hearthstone Townhomes** ($$$-$$$$) feature superior ski-in/ski-out access. These one- to three-bedroom lodgings throughout the village have full kitchens, fireplaces and VCRs.

1,000 Peaks Lodge and Summit, Ski Tip Lodge, Tamarack Lodge, Panorama Springs Condo/Hotel and **Taynton Lodge** ($$-$$$) are condos. All were recently built slopeside in the heart of the upper village surrounding the hot pools.

Horsethief Lodge and **Toby Creek Lodge** ($$) are family-style studio condos with one to three bedrooms, some with lofts, in the lower village. Units have full kitchens, fireplaces, VCRs, underground parking and easy ski and upper village access.

The Pine Inn ($-$$) has budget hotel rooms with full bath, television and coffee maker. **The Elkhorn Cabin Bed & Breakfast** (888-767-7799; $$$$) overlooks Toby Creek valley and Mount Nelson. It's rustic, romantic and very comfortable.

Dining

Wildfire Grill ($$-$$$) in the village specializes in casual contemporary cuisine. Try the grilled maple-bourbon-glazed salmon. **Ferrari's on Toby Creek** ($$-$$$), underneath the grocery store and Toby Creek Lodge, serves tasty seafood, Alberta beef, wild game and very imaginative pastas. **Crazy Horse Saloon** ($$-$) in the

Pine Inn has good food and a fun apres ski atmosphere. **The PicNic Market Deli** ($$-$), also connected to the Pine Inn, will make your lunch or dinner ready to go. The restaurant at **Earl Grey Lodge** ($$-$$$) continues to receive high praise for its eclectic regional menu.

Mile High Pizza ($-$$) in The Great Hall at Ski Tip Lodge makes mouth-watering pizza to go or to stay. Or stop in at **Jackpine Pub** ($-$$) at the Core Arcade for traditional alpine fare. **Chopper's Landing** ($$-$$$), overlooking Panorama Mountain Village, offers a licensed fireside lounge and family dining. While you're on the mountain, stop in at **The Cappuccino Hut** ($-$$) at the top of the Champagne Chair and grab a latte with a feast of ribs or buffalo burgers, coleslaw and potatoes. At 7,800 feet up the mountain, **The Summit Hut** ($-$$) serves fabulous views along with cafe-style meals. Additions to the legendary **Elkhorn Cabin** have almost doubled its size, expanded the gourmet menu, the live music entertainment and surprise performances.

Apres-ski/nightlife

Outdoor **hot tubs** are available, plus the Panorama Springs giant slopeside **hot pools**. Inside fun is available at the **Crazy Horse Saloon, Jackpine Pub, T-Bar & Grill, Heli-Plex Bar & Grill** (try the jumbo heli wings and the heli soup) and the **Glacier Nite Club**.

Other activities

In Ski Tip Lodge, the Mountain Adventure Centre (250-342-6941 ext. 3440) is a complete information and booking service for activities and events, including **hot springs tours, dinner shuttle to Invermere restaurants, day trips to Lake Louise, Kimberley and Kicking Horse Mountain Resort, games arcade, sleigh rides, snowmobile tours, massage therapist** and more.

Adjacent to the ski area is R.K. Heli-Ski Panorama Inc. (250-342-3889 or 800-661-6060), offering one-day **heliskiing** packages from around C$600. The company has 2,000 square kilometers of runs that include glaciers and glades, all between 5,500 and 11,000 feet of elevation.

Toby Creek Adventures (888-357-4449 or 250-342-5047) offers **guided snowmobile tours** specializing in hourly and multiday guided tours in the Columbia Valley between Fairmont Hot Springs and Radium Hot Springs..

Getting there and getting around

By air: Calgary International Airport is the gateway to Panorama. The airport is 185 miles from Panorama and is served by all major airlines. There is daily shuttle service from both Calgary International Airport and Banff. Transfers must be pre-booked with accommodations. Cranbrook Airport, 75 miles north of Panorama, is served by regional air carriers.

By car: From Calgary, take TransCanada Highway 1 west through Banff to the Highway 93 junction with Kootenay Parkway (about 12 miles past Banff). Take Highway 93 south to Radium, BC (63 miles). From Radium, drive south about 8 miles on Highway 95 to the town of Invermere, then continue 11 miles from Invermere directly to Panorama Mountain Village.

Getting around: While a car is certainly not needed at Panorama, the reality is that most visitors arrive by car, and they're handy for getting into Invermere on your own schedule.

Accommodations (Cdn$): (double room) $$$$-$200+; $$$-$141-$200; $$-$81-$140; $-$80 and less.
Dining (Cdn$): $$$-Entrees $20+; $$-$10-20; $-less than $10

Red Mountain Resort,
British Columbia, Canada

Summit: 6,800 feet
Vertical: 2,909 feet
Base: 3,888 feet

Address: 4300 Red Mtn. Road, PO Box 670, Rossland, British Columbia, Canada V0G 1Y0
Telephone (main): 250-362-7384
Snow Report Number: 800-663-0105
Toll-free reservations: 877-969-7669 or 250-362-7013
Reservations outside U.S.: 250-362-5833
E-mail: info@redresort.com
Internet: www.redresort.com

Lifts: 6—1 quad, 2 triples, 1 double, 1 T-bar, 1 moving carpet
Skiable acreage: 1,585
Snowmaking: None
Uphill capacity: 7500
Parks & pipes: 1 park
Bed base: 400 rooms within 6 miles
Nearest lodging: Slopeside
Child care: Yes, 18 months and older
Adult ticket, per day: C$59 (08/09)

Expert:★★★★★
Advanced:★★★★★
Intermediate:★★★
Beginner:★★ **First-timer:**★★

Dining:★★★
Apres-ski/nightlife:★★
Other activities:★★

Red Mountain Resort is one of those hidden gems that attracts hardcore skiers and riders. The mountain is for adventurous souls who like to play hard.

By Western standards, Red Mountain Resort is rather small, only 1,686 acres. So how can you possibly get lost here? Who knows, but it happens.

The trail map is a moot point...until the end of the day. That's when you sit down with a cold beer and try to figure out just where you've been that day. Sure there are plenty of trails, but the reason to come here is for the phenomenal tree skiing and riding—deep and steep to wide and sweet. Trail signs? Not for most of Red's true gems, even if it's marked right there on the map. Ask locals and they'll tell you to look for the four-by-four post to your right off the cat track (Beer Belly) or the round red reflector nailed to a tree on your left at the top of the saddle (Short Squaw). That's why it's a genuine surprise to be gliding through a prime piece of woods you've stumbled upon and suddenly see a small sign in the middle of the glade that says "Powder Fields." OK, so you're not really lost after all. *Someone's been here before you.*

Although Red Mountain recently replaced an old triple lift with a new quad, its first new lift in 30 years, it will still take you back to the good ol' days when skiing was glamorous, romantic and adventurous. Red is known for its tree skiing, deep powder and universal appeal to all ability levels of riders, downhill and and cross-country skiers.

Rossland isn't your ordinary ski town. If you didn't see the full-on view of Red Mountain rising in the background, you might not even know you're at a resort. This small town of 4,000 residents has no traffic lights, making it hard to believe that back in 1897, when thousands came hoping to prosper from the gold mines, this was British Columbia's largest city. Now you'll find a simple mining town with a touch of class that is sure to catch the unsuspecting visitor by surprise.

Mountain layout

After thirty years, Red Mountain added a new chair, a Doppelmayr CTEC quad to replace the old Sliverlode triple.

The ski area consists of two mountains: Red Mountain, an extinct volcano and the original site of the ski area, and Granite Mountain, which includes the Paradise area and mid-mountain lodge. Both peaks offer 360 degrees of skiing terrain.

The ski area is exceptional for advanced-intermediates to experts. Red is, after all, where Olympic Gold Medallist Nancy Green and dozens of other Canadian Olympians did and still do their training. Solid intermediates will be pushed to their limits. Lower-intermediates and beginners may be discouraged by the lack of gentle slopes. Snow Hosts give free guided tours of the mountain every day at 9 a.m. and noon leaving from the Welcome Center.

Expert, Advanced: Tree skiing and riding is the big draw here. Be sure to travel in pairs through the woods.

Red has a few short and steep runs at the top. Don't forget to check out the gladed area of widely spaced trees between Sally's Alley and War Eagle. Experts will want to head to Granite for fabulous tree skiing, chutes, bowls, steeps and cliff bands. The tight and steep trees of both Short Squaw and Beer Belly dump into hidden steep bowls.

The Powder Fields spread across the front of the mountain, with ledges and cliffs.

For some unnamed woods that are probably known primarily by locals, try the trees off Ruby Tuesday, Gambler Towers, the lower part of Boardwalk near Paradise Lodge and anywhere off Southside Road before reaching the roped-off area at Ledges Traverse.

Bump enthusiasts can test skills on the long and unforgiving Slides, which soften up nicely in the sun but can be littered with boulders. Near the bottom of Buffalo Ridge, you'll need to tuck straight up the ridge ahead of you to get here. Centre Star is another favorite for moguls.

Intermediates: On Red, take in the views overlooking town as you wind down Sally's Alley or let 'em rip down Face of Red and Back Trail. This is a marvelous resort for learning to ski and ride in the woods. The trees are evergreens with plenty of space in between them.

On Granite, head to the Paradise Chair. Groomed runs such as Southern Belle, Southern Comfort, and Gambler—among others—let you cruise and take a dip into the trees. Mini Bowls and Meadows have widely spaced trees. Drop in anywhere after passing Southern Comfort.

Ruby Tuesday and Gambler Towers are single-black runs, but groomed, so advanced-intermediates should have no problem navigating down them. Maggie's Farm is the next step for tree skiers and riders after they've become comfortable in the woods.

Beginner, First-timer: The beginner area is nicely separated from the rest of the mountain. Stick to the T-bar or the Doppelmayr CTEC quad chair for good spots to practice the basics. Confident beginners should ride to the top of Granite and cruise the 4.5-mile Long Squaw, which winds around the mountain and affords staggering views. The beginner trails in the Paradise area are quite nice, but it's a long cat track returning to the base. Avoid Red, except to use the T-bar—there's no easy way down from the top of this peak. Terrain for those shifting from beginner to intermediate is limited. Plenty of skiers and riders learn here. A moving carpet at the base area near the T-bar serves the learning terrain. The area is fenced off from faster skiers and riders. Once you're comfortable linking turns, try the Silverlode triple and T-bar.

Parks and pipes

The resort built its terrain park on skier's left of the T-Bar, in full view of everyone sitting outside on the base lodge's deck. Jeff Patterson, a world-renowned terrain park designer, is the creative force behind it. It's designed for all ability levels, including a fenced-off beginner section, and includes 15 rails, funboxes and tabletops.

Snowboarding

The woods here are what appeal to freeriders. Caution: Many trails through the woods are unmarked, ungroomed and unpatrolled. Don't ride alone. This is one mountain where hiring a local guide can make a big difference in your vertical day.

On Granite, the tight and steep trees of both Short Squaw and Beer Belly open into hidden steep bowls. The Powder Fields spread across the front of the mountain with challenging ledges and cliffs.

Most of the goods are off cat tracks that require carrying speed, and even then, there may be some hiking. Of note: To get to anything around Powder Fields and The Orchards, shoot across Boardwalk at the top of Granite and carry speed along a ridge and most likely walk the last section because there's a short hill at the end. To get to The Slides, as you near the bottom of Buffalo Ridge, rip straight up the ridge ahead. Ridge Road, which gives access to the Paradise area, Beer Belly and Doug's Run, is a bit flat in parts. Beer Belly, The Slides, Short Squaw and the rest of the diamond-rated trails around them finish at the end of Long Squaw and Easy Street, which are pretty flat near the end. Coming back from the Paradise area on Southside Road requires paying attention to speed.

Groomed runs such as Southern Belle, Southern Comfort, and Gambler—among others—let you cruise and take a dip into the trees. For starters, try Meadows, Mini Bowls, and Inagadadavida. Mini Bowls and Meadows have widely spaced trees. Drop in anywhere after passing Southern Comfort. Maggie's Farm is considered advanced-intermediate because of the tricky tree riding.

Beginners should stay on the open slopes or practice off the T-bar. Beginners like Long Squaw, a 4.5-mile cruiser that wraps around Granite Mountain. The green trails in the Paradise area are friendly for beginners, but it's a long cat track returning to the base. You might want to end your day early to avoid the rush back when the lifts close.

Avoid Red, except to use the T-bar—there's no easy way down from the top of this peak. Terrain for those shifting from beginner to intermediate is limited.

A moving carpet at the base area near the T-bar serves the learning terrain. The area is fenced off from faster skiers and riders. Once you're comfortable linking turns, try the Silverlode triple and T-bar.

 ## Cross-country & snowshoeing (see also xcskiresorts.com)

Blackjack Cross Country Ski Club (250-362-7163), across the road, has 40 km. of trails. About 30 km. are groomed, both double-tracked and for skating. Trails pass through hemlocks and next to frozen beaver ponds. The network has three shelters, including toilets, a first aid station and a cabin at the trailhead. Rentals and instruction are available through **High Country Sports** at the base of Red Resort.

The Cross-Country and Snowshoe Loop, accessible from the base area, connects to the Centennial Trail which winds its way from the mountain to Rossland's city center. Tracks are also set after snowfalls and open to cross-country skiers and snowshoers. Rentals are available through Red Resort's rentals.

Free cross-country skiing on tracks set after every snowfall is available 28 km. north of Rossland (on Hwy. 3B) in the **Nancy Greene Provincial Park**. The 45 km. of trails are maintained by the Castlegar Nordic Ski Club.

Lessons (08/09 prices, without tax)

For lessons or guides call 800-663-0105 ext. 235.

Group lessons: C$54 for two hours, skiing or snowboarding.

First-timer package: C$59 for the first and second day of skiing or snow-boarding—includes beginner lift ticket, lesson and rentals. A Discovery Private, a two-hour lesson designed just for first-timers, costs C$139.

Private lessons: One hour, C$89; half day, C$199; full day is C$335.

A Super Saver Private lesson is available Monday through Friday from 1-3 p.m. for C$119.

Children's programs (08/09 prices, without tax)

Child care: Club Red is a licensed child-care facility for ages 18 months to 6 years. Full day costs C$51; half day (less than 4 hours), C$31. Most bring lunch, but lunch is available for an extra cost. Reservations required; call 800-663-0105 ext. 237. The child-care center also can provide a list of babysitters.

Children's programs: For ages 3–6, a three-hour morning or afternoon lesson with hot cocoa break is C$44. Two-hour group lessons are limited to eight kids and cost C$44; a four-pack costs C$159. Reservations are required for all kids' programs.

Skiing/Snowboarding Discovery is a two-hour lesson for first-timers that includes a beginner lift ticket and rentals for C$59. Lessons begin daily at 10 a.m. and 1 p.m.

Lift tickets (08/09 prices, without tax)

	Adult	Junior (7-12)
One day	C$59	C$30
Three days	C$171 ($57/day)	C$84 ($28/day)
Five days	C$275 ($55/day)	C$130 ($26/day)

Who skis free: Children ages 6 and younger; seniors ages 75 and older.

Who skis at a discount: Skiers age 65-74 pay C$38 for one day, C$108 for three days and C$170 for five days. Teens 13-18 pay C$47 for one day, C$135 for three days and C$215 for five days.

A beginner-lifts-only ticket (moving carpet, T-bar and Silverlode lifts) is C$25 for adults and teens, C$20 for juniors and seniors.

Accommodations

Red Resort Central Reservations can book all travel, lodging and ski packages. Its toll-free numbers are 877-969-7669, or 250-362-7013 if you are calling from another continent and can't access the toll-free number. We list a few choices, but there are others. Prices at Red Resort are very reasonable, generally less than C$100 per night.

Carolyn's Corner, The Lofts, Copper Chalets, Red Robs and **White Wolf Cabins** (866-475-4733; $$$-$$$$) are luxury condominiums with one to four bedrooms at the base of the mountain. The condos are ski-in with a short walk to the lifts (just on the other side of the parking lot). Red Robs sleep up to four; The Lofts sleep up to six; White Wolf Cabins sleep up to 10; and Carolyn's Corner condos and Copper Chalets sleep up to 12.

The **Ram's Head Inn** (877-267-4323; 250-362-9577; $$), artfully blending Scandinavian and Native American motifs, is a short walk from the base area. The sauna and outdoor teak hot tub provide the perfect wind-down at day's end or simply lounge by the stone fireplace.

The funky, Swiss-chalet-style **Red Shutter Inn** (250-362-5131; $-$$), right in the ski area parking lot, has six rooms, an outdoor hot tub and cedar sauna.

In town, the full-service **Prestige Mountain Resort** (877-737-8443; $$$-$$$$) has deluxe guestrooms, suites, kitchenettes and theme suites. The pet-friendly **Thriftlodge** (800-663-0203; 250-362-7364; $-$$$) is a bit out of the center of town, but has comfortable rooms, large outdoor hot tub, free shuttle to the mountain and free continental breakfast. The simple **Rossland Motel** (877-362-7218; 250-362-7218; $) has rooms with kitchens which are perfect for families.

Rossland also has a few B&Bs. Try **Angela's B&B Guesthouse** (250-362-7790; $-$$), with its witty and friendly hostess who is sometimes your personal mountain tour guide, or **Black Bear B&B** (877-362-3398; 250-362-3398; $$), one of Rossland's heritage homes with original rich woodwork and leaded stained-glass windows. The **Mountain Shadow Youth Hostel** (888-393-7160; 250-362-7160; $) has rooms for C$20 a night. Most rooms are shared with five others but there are a couple of private rooms. Kitchen facilities are open to all.

Dining

The finest cooking is found at **Gypsy at Red** (250-362-3347; $$-$$$), at the base of Red Resort in the Red Robs. It's best described as California bistro meets the British Columbia mountains. From creative entrees of seared Ahi tuna and braised lamb shank to a long and varied tapas menu, you can't go wrong.

Munro's Restaurant (250-362-7375; $$-$$$) at Prestige Mountain Resort promises "Excellence In Dining" with prime rib, seafood and pasta dishes.

Idgies Restaurant (250-362-0078; $$) specializes in food from around the world—curry, Creole and lots of garlic. The tiny restaurant is dressed in bright yellows and blues and filled with the buzz of happy clientele. Fresh fish and pastas dominate the menu.

The **Flying Steamshovel** (250-362-7323; $) is a lively pub and Mexican restaurant with great views. **Sunshine Cafe** (250-362-7630; $) has basic burgers and pasta in major portions. **Rock Cut Pub & Restaurant** ($-$$), between the mountain and town, serves average pub fare. Its breakfasts get a thumbs up.

Clansey's is the locals' hangout offering a full breakfast and lunch menu. **Alpine Grind Coffee House** dishes out hot and cold breakfasts to go with its gourmet coffees and teas. On weekends, try the awesome Belgian waffles. **Sourdough Alley** on level two of the base lodge, serves great soups, sandwiches, burgers and fries for lunch, has an espresso bar and is also a good stop for breakfast.

Apres-ski/nightlife

For immediate apres-ski, head to the retro **Rafter's Lounge** upstairs in the base lodge, originally an old mining building. From old-timers to young freeriders, everyone lines up for cold drafts and launches into the day's tall tales, all the while surrounded by historical ski paraphernalia. Or try the more refined **Gypsy at Red** in the Red Robs to indulge in some mouth-watering tapas and wash them down with the drink of your choice.

By 5 p.m., the action has headed to Rossland, and it's mostly where you and your friends get together. **Rock Cut Pub**, just down the road, is where all the locals go to get wild. Free appetizers every Friday from 4-6 p.m. Buy a jug of beer, get 10 free wings every day. Bands get the crowd rocking on weekends. **Buffalo Ridge Sports Bar & Lounge** at The Prestige Mountain Resort and **Flying Steamshovel** are other hot gathering spots.

Other activities

The Rossland Arena has **hockey games, curling matches** and public **ice skating**. Book a sheet at the **curling club** (minimum two sheets or 16 people); call The Hub at the mountain (ext. 233). High Mountain Adventures (250-362-5342) has **snowmobile tours** and rentals.

Snowwater Heli-Skiing and Snowcat-Skiing (866-722-7669), with 80,000 acres just outside of Nelson, specializes in multiday **heli- and cat-skiing** packages in a custom-built mountain lodge with fabulous gourmet meals. Single-day trips also are available. Big Red Cats (877-969-7669), a cat service ski area ten minutes from Red Resort led by ex-Australian ski team member Kieren Gaul, offers skiers access to some 18,000 acres of backcountry cat skiing terrain.

The guides at Rossland Mountain Adventures (877-550-6677) provide **backcountry tours** and **clinics**. They have a variety of tours to choose from: single day, yurt and lodge touring, women only, and custom packages, to name a few. They also teach **courses in orienteering, avalanche awareness** and **wilderness first aid**.

For on-mountain renting and shopping, Red Sports, formerly LeRois Sports, provides rental, retail and customer service at the base of Red.

Rossland has a small collection of **shops**. Browse through Mainstage Gallery for local art, Gold Rush Books & Espresso for reading and sipping, The Cellar for Canadian-made gifts and both the Legacy Gift Room and Feather Your Nest for unique home products.

The biggest party of the year is the **Winter Carnival** for three days near the end of January with a snow sculpture contest, dances and other festivities. For details, call 250-362-5399.

Getting there and getting around

By air: The airport in Castlegar, 20 miles north, has flights from Vancouver and Calgary. Hotel pickup and rental cars are available, or call Castlegar Taxi, 250-365-7222. The nearest airport with U.S.-carrier service is Spokane, 125 miles south. The Red Express shuttle offers round-trip ground transportation between Red Mountain Resort and Spokane Airport and other airports listed here. Call resort reservations at 877-969-7669. Red Mountain also partners with Dollar Rent-a-Car if you'd like to rent a vehicle. Kelowna Airport is a 3 to 3 1/2 hour drive and Trail Airport is a 15 minute drive.

By car: Red Mountain is 3 miles from the town of Rossland and only 10 miles from the Canada-U.S. border on Hwy. 3B. From Spokane, take Hwys. 395 and 25 north to Rossland for a 2 to 3 hour drive.

Getting around: We recommend a car for off-slope exploring. If you're staying up at the mountain and want to eat in town, you're out of luck without a car. The town bus and hotel shuttles only go to the mountain around 8:30-9:30 a.m. and have return pickups when the lifts close around 3:30 p.m.

Accommodations (Cdn$): (double room) $$$$-$200+; $$$-$141-$200; $$-$81-$140; $-$80 and less.
Dining (Cdn$): $$$-Entrees $20+; $$-$10-20; $-less than $10

Sun Peaks
British Columbia, Canada

Summit: 7,060 feet
Vertical: 2,891 feet
Base: 3,933 feet

Address: #50-3150 Creekside Way, Sun Peaks, B.C., Canada V0E 1Z1
Telephone (main): 250-578-7222
Snow Report Number: 250-578-7232
Toll-free reservations: 800-807-3257
Reservations outside US: 250-578-7222
E-mail: info@sunpeaksresort.com
Internet: www.sunpeaksresort.com
Expert:★★★
Advanced:★★★★
Intermediate:★★★★
Beginner:★★★
First-timer:★★★

Lifts: 12—3 high-speed quads, 2 quads, 1 triple, 6 surface lifts
Skiable acreage: 3,678
Snowmaking: 40 acres
Uphill capacity: 12,000
Parks & pipes: 2 parks, 1 pipe
Bed base: 5,000
Nearest lodging: Slopeside, ski-in/ski-out
Child care: 18 months and older
Adult ticket, per day: C$71 (08/09)
Dining:★★★★
Apres-ski/nightlife:★★★
Other activities:★★★★

Sun Peaks is a huge resort in the heart of heliskiing country that seems to have appeared out of nowhere, with rapid development in the past few years. Locals launched the ski area in 1961, with volunteers carving many of the runs that are still skied today. Its strides toward the future of skiing began with Nippon Cable's purchase of the former Tod Mountain in 1992. More than C$450 million has been invested.

With a recently built first-class hotel and a third mountain adding almost 1,000 acres, Sun Peaks has certainly joined the big leagues. The resort's slogan is "Three Mountains, One Village" and the third mountain has made all the difference. The resort is now ranked the largest ski area in the interior and the second largest in British Columbia behind Whistler.

Al Raine and his Olympic ski-champion wife, Nancy Greene Raine, who together helped build Whistler to the international destination it is today, now call Sun Peaks home. Nancy is both the director and ambassador of skiing.

Mountain layout

Just a warning: If you use lifts as meeting places, be aware that Sun*dance* and Sun*burst* chairs unload at different points.

Expert/Advanced: Head to the top for bowls, chutes and headwalls. Hat Trick, to the right of the Crystal triple chair, dumps you unceremoniously into the woods. Challenger and Expo runs on the lower Burfield area are thigh-burning mogul monsters. Note: There's sometimes a fog line you should keep your eye on. It's pretty dicey up top when the sock is in, so think about sticking near the trees down a bit lower when the air is thick.

The six runs to the right of the Sun*burst* Express are big favorites for advanced skiers, but you'll have a fine ol' time in the Burfield Quad region. Off Juniper Ridge to the left are several challenging runs and Spillway down the upper east face always holds great snow. If there are intermediates in your group, you can head with them to Mt. Morrisey and play on four short trails that dump off Delta's Return. Spin Cycle makes you feel like you'll land on the village roofs below.

The new quad chair from the bottom of Cariboo allows quicker return to the Crystal Chair with entree to popular runs like Chute, Spillway, Green Door and the Headwalls. A name for this new lift is still being sought so go to the website with your suggestions and you may win a season pass.

Intermediate: The Sun*dance* Express to the right gets you to the top of Sundance Ridge where three blue runs (Grannie Greene's, Sun Catcher and Sunrise) begin. If you take the Sun*burst* Express, you'll find four long, steep, cruising blue runs on the left. Higher up, in Crystal Bowl, there are lots of blue runs. The recently opened Mt. Morrisey is mostly easy intermediate terrain.

The new quad chair at the bottom of the Cariboo accesses blue runs Distributor and OSV as well as Cahilty and Crystal Lane, green runs down to the base. Four new intermediate runs on the lower part of Orient Ridge provide easier access to the East Village development.

Beginner: The beauty of Sun Peaks is that there are green runs descending from every lift, including the new quad. One of the most fun is the famous 4-mile run that starts at the top of the Burfield Quad and goes all the way down to the village. If you want to do it again, be sure to take the Burfield run-out to skier's right under the Sunburst Express and back to the bottom of the lift.

First-timer: The Village Platter area is right beside the village, yet out of the way of through traffic and it's all for fist-timers. Its Gentle Giant run is perfect for beginners. In fact, these three beginner runs—Sunbeam, Gentle Giant and Cowabunga—are all definitely smooth, safe and gentle, guaranteed. A new magic carpet lift and expansion of children's and beginner teaching terrain and facilities improve first-timer's experiences.

Parks and pipes

Sun Peaks is a popular stop on the FIS Grundig Snowboard World Cup, so they take their parks and pipes seriously. The 2,500-foot-long terrain park covers 30 acres just to the left of the Sundance Express. There's an excellent halfpipe right underneath the lift. It's 325 feet long with an average slope of 20 degrees. It's maintained with a HPG 12-foot radius grinder. A well-designed half-mile-long permanent boardercross course—with tabletops, spines and a variety of hits that are frequently changed and maintained—leads down from the halfpipe to the terrain park. Improvements to the terrain parks on Sundance Mountain include rails, jumps and fun boxes, an expanded green/blue terrain park and a new edge park bully grooming machine. There's also a cool mini-terrain park area for beginners.

Snowboarding

Snowboarders love Sun Peaks. There are virtually no traverses with the exception of the Mt. Morrisey Connector run. Freeriders can choose everything from long, fall-line groomers to an incredible number of gladed runs. Even a rookie powder boarder will enjoy the Cahilty Glades. If you're looking for excitement, do the Chute trees, the Pink Flamingos or hike into the Gils backcountry.

 Cross-country & snowshoeing (see also xcskiresorts.com)

Sun Peaks has 40 km. of cross-country trails—half wilderness trails and half track-set trails and skating lanes. Rentals and lessons are available. Snowshoeing trails—go alone or with a guide—follow dedicated routes with bird feeding stations, wildlife viewing and a snow cave. **Stake Lake Trails** (snow phone, 250-372-5514) is just 25 minutes from Kamloops with 45 km. of well-groomed classic and skating tracks.

Lessons (07/08 prices, without tax)

Reservations are recommended for all lessons, especially during holidays.
Group lessons: Explorer lessons for beginners and intermediates cost C$49 for two hours. Top of the World Clinics for advanced and expert skiers cost C$59 for two hours.

First-timer package: A two-hour lesson plus rentals and beginner lift ticket costs C$56.

Private Lessons: For a two-hour lesson, C$180; a half-day lesson, C$299; an all-day lesson, C$399. The school also offers all-day, cat-skiing for C$250.

Special programs: Thursday is Ladies Day, a fun-filled program with lunch and prizes that features the resort's top female instructors; cost is C$85 (includes lesson and lift ticket). A one-hour private lesson with Olympic-champion Nancy Greene costs C$175 (C$45 for an additional person). Kids Ranch animated theme park with dedicated terrain especially designed for children 3-12 years old is located at the top of the Village Platter beside the School House building. A carpet lift services the new learning area.

Children's programs (07/08 prices, without tax)

Child care: Ages 18 months to 5 years. Full day 8:30 a.m.-4 p.m. costs C$69 with lunch; half day is C$36 with snacks only. Reservations recommended; call 800-807-3257.

Children's programs: Reservations are recommended for all children's lesson programs, especially during holidays. Sun Kids lessons are for ages 6-12; snowboard lessons start at age 8. Full day with lunch, C$117; half day, C$88 for the morning session or C$50 for the afternoon session. Lift ticket and rentals are extra, but are discounted. Sun Tots, for ages 3-5, costs C$50 for a one-hour private lesson, or a one- or two-hour private may be added to day care. Lift tickets are included in the cost of Sun Tots programs.

Special activities: The resort also has a skating rink and a lift-served tubing park with two lanes.

Lift tickets (07/08 prices, without tax)

	Adult	Youth (13-18)	Child (6-12)
One day	C$71	C$57	C$36
Three days	C$204(C$68/day)	C$162(C$54/day)	C$99(C$33/day)

Who skis free: Children 5 and younger.
Who skis at a discount: Seniors 65 and older, C$57 for one day.

Accommodations

All hotels are ski-in/ski-out; many other properties are as well. Central Reservations (800-807-3257; 250-578-5594) can arrange lodging, activities, rentals, lift tickets and more.

Nancy Greene's Cahilty Lodge (800-244-8424; 250-578-7454; $$-$$$$), a full-service condo-hotel with studios and large family units, is practically on the slopes just steps away from all village activities. This is home to Olympic Ski champion, Nancy Greene and husband Al Raine. Nancy's gold and silver Olympic medals are displayed in the lobby.

The 226-room **Delta Sun Peak Resort** (866-552-5516; 250-578-6000; $$-$$$$) includes shops, a business center, laundry facilities, an indoor/outdoor pool, three hot tubs, fitness center, spa, steam room and sauna, babysitting, game rooms, gourmet restaurant and a nightclub.

The **Pinnacle Lodge & Spa** (866-578-7850; 250-578-7850), at the base of the Mt. Morissey slopes is a first class traditional Canadian lodge. Suites include TV, fireplaces, robes, wireless internet access and all high-end amenities.

Sundance Lodge (800-483-2888; 250-578-0200; $$-$$$$) sits right at the base of the beginner's platter lift a short walk to the Sundance Express. All of the western-styled units have kitchens, coffee makers and microwaves.

The **Hearthstone Lodge** (888-659-2211; 250-578-8588; $$-$$$) and **Fireside Lodge** (888-659-2211; 250-578-8588; $$-$$$), across from Cahilty Lodge are both ski-in/ski-out condominium hotels with deluxe studios and suites. All suites have kitchens or kitchenettes, fireplaces and high-speed cable access. Plus there are fitness centers, hot tubs and restaurants (see Dining). **The Heffley Inn** (866-812-8333; 250-578-8343; $$) is a 26-room, European-style boutique hotel in the center of the village with a hot tub, sauna and steam room.

The Sun Peaks International Hostel (250-578 0057; $), a large rustic lodge at the base of the Burfield lift, offers slopeside accommodation from C$20 per person. It's at the bottom of Tod Mountain, just over half a mile from the main village.

 ## Dining

Put **Mantles Restaurant & Bar** (250-578-6000; $$-$$$) in the Delta Sun Peaks Resort on your "must-visit" list for its full menu of Pacific Northwest cuisine, tasty appetizers, gas fired pizza, rotisserie and a wide selection of beers, wines and drinks.

A high-end European-style restaurant with sterling hospitality is **Powder Hounds** (578-0014; $$-$$$) in the Fireside Lodge. The Hearthstone Lodge is home to two fine dining venues: **Bella Italia** (578-8832; $$-$$$) in Hearthstone Lodge serves authentic Italian cuisine with daily fresh-made pasta, and **Servus on Creekside** (250-578-7383; $$-$$$) features a European flair in an intimate, romantic setting.

Toro's (250-578-7870; $$) in the Heffley Inn, specializes in Asian flavors, including Thai, Chinese and Japanese. Prices are reasonable and take out is available. **The Steakhouse at Sun Peaks Lodge** (250-578-7878) satisfies your craving for classic New York steak, sirloin, rib eye or prime rib. This friendly steakhouse also has a great kids menu. Reservations recommended. **Mackdaddy's the Club** (250-578-2582) is located in the Delta Sun Peaks. European influences highlight the atmosphere and the food. After dinner, have a fling on their dance floor.

Masa's Bar & Grill (250-578-5434; $-$$) slopeside in the Village Day Lodge by the Sunburst and Sundance chairlifts, is a casual pub and family restaurant featuring great service and outstanding burgers. **Bottom's Bar & Grill** (250-578-0013; $-$$) in Sundance Lodge is invitingly noisy with good food that hits the spot after a day on the mountain. You'll quickly learn to trust the local McDonnell brothers' eclectic fusion menu at **Macker's Bistro & Bar** (250-578-7894; $-$$) in Nancy Greene's Cahilty Lodge. This long-time local favorite features fusion cuisine with warm service in a casual and fun atmosphere.

Bento's Day Lodge ($), east of the Village Day Lodge, is a quick cafeteria stop in your busy ski day. You can eat "bring your own" meals here too. For the best coffee on the mountain, go to **Bolacco Caffe** (250-587-7588; $) in the Sundance Lodge in the village. **Cafe Soleil** (250-587-5534), a deli-style espresso bar in the Village Day Lodge, serves gourmet coffees, baked goods, soups and sandwiches. The mid-mountain **Sunburst Restaurant** (250-578-7222; $) is the only on-mountain cafeteria.

Bella Italia (250-578-7316) in the heart of the village offers fine Italian cuisine. Enjoy your meals in their patio when weather permits. **Mountain High Pizza** (250-5787272) invites a "grab a slice" kind of meal or a take-home pie for the whole family.

One last sinful stop is **Baggs Sweets**, a long-time favorite located in the Hearthstone Lodge. Indulge in thirst-quenching coffees, desserts and chocolates or enjoy a pannini and a great bowl of soup.

Dining: $$$$–Entrees C$30+; $$$–C$20–$30; $$–C$10–$20; $–less than C$10.
Accommodations: (double room) $$$$–C$200+; $$$–C$141–$200; $$–C$81–$140; $–C$80 and less.

Apres-ski/nightlife

It used to be kind of quiet here at the end of the day, but things have livened up quite a bit. Two apres-ski favorites are **Bottom's Bar & Grill** (250-578-0013) and **Masa's Bar & Grill** (250-578-5434) for a chatty pub-style atmosphere.

Or try the nightclub **Mackdaddy's** (250-578-2582), just around the corner and downstairs from the Delta Sun Peaks Resort entrance in the Delta building. There's a $10 cover, full bar and a large, busy dance floor. **Mantle's Bar** (250-578-6000) in the Delta Resort also sees an age range in customers, but it's a quieter ambiance (no dance floor) catering to an older crowd.

 ## Other activities

At Sun Peaks' Annual **Icewine Festival**, started in 1999 and held in January. Check their website for yearly dates which vary. Participants slip and stroll between village hotels and restaurants with glass in hand on a progressive wine-tasting adventure. At least 20 Okanagan Valley wineries are featured with more than 100 wines. Festival events include tastings, a gourmet winemasters' dinner, seminars and an awards presentation.

The resort offers daily **cat skiing and riding** tours from the summit that are quite popular, so book as early as possible. For another kind of adrenaline rush, try **snowbiking**. An Olympic-sized, flood-lit skating rink offers drop-in hockey, skate rentals, stick rentals and more. When you're done skating, relax at the nearby **Sports Centre** in the outdoor pool or hot tub.

Special activities that children will especially enjoy are mini-snowmobiles, a bungy trampoline, tobogganing and a lift access area for tubing, night skiing and boarding that's open until 8 p.m.

One-hour **dogsled rides** leave from the horse barn at the east end of the village. Tours are offered Tuesday to Sunday at 10 a.m., noon and 3 p.m. Visit the Resort Activity & Information Centre (250-578-5542) in the Village Day Lodge for tickets. Sleigh rides leave from the Village Day Lodge. Choose between valley tours or evening dessert rides.

Sun Peaks Adventure Tours (250-578-5542) supplies helmets with visors and all exterior snowmobile clothing (except gloves). Snowmobile drivers must have a driver's license; passengers need only be adults or have parental consent.

 ## Getting there and getting around

By air: Kamloops Airport is the nearest airport. For shuttle service from the Kamloops Airport to Sun Peaks, call 250-319-3539. Horizon Air starts its service between Seattle and Kamloops in mid-December and runs through early April. Visit www.horizonair.com for details.

By car: Sun Peaks is a 45-minute drive from Kamloops. From Kelowna it's 2.5 hours, from Vancouver, 4 hours, from Seattle, 5.5 hours, and from Banff, 6 hours.

Getting around: You don't need a car if you plan to spend all your time at the resort. Regular shuttles (Mondays, Wednesdays & Saturdays; 800-244-8424) provide transportation to and from Whistler. Shuttles also connect with the Kelowna Airport as well as other BC Ski Country resorts (800-807-3257).

Accommodations (Cdn$): (double room) $$$$-$200+; $$$-$141-$200; $$-$81-$140; $-$80 and less.
Dining (Cdn$): $$$-Entrees $20+; $$-$10-20; $-less than $10

Whistler Blackcomb
British Columbia, Canada

Whistler Blackcomb Resort Facts
Address: 4545 Blackcomb Way, Whistler, BC, Canada V0N 1B4 (resort)
4010 Whistler Way, Whistler, BC, Canada V0N 1B4 (Tourism Whistler)
Area code: 604 (Note: Use the prefix when dialing local telephone numbers within Whistler)
Ski area phone: 932-3434; (800) 766-0449 (within North America); 0800-587-1743 (from the UK)
Snow report: 932-4211 or (800) 766-0449
Reservations: (888) 284-9999 or (800) 944-7853 (within North America); 0800-731-5983 (from the UK)
Internet: www.whistlerblackcomb.com (resort) or www.tourismwhistler.com (Tourism Whistler)
Bed base: 5,418 Nearest lodging: Slopeside, hotel and condos
Resort child care: Yes, 3 months and older
Parks & pipes: 5 parks, 3 pipes
Adult ticket, per day: C$83 (07/08, without tax)

Dining: ★★★★★ **Apres-ski/nightlife:** ★★★★★ **Other activities:** ★★★★★

Whistler Mountain Facts
Base elevation:	2,140 feet (Creekside)
	2,214 feet (Village)
Summit elevation:	7,160 feet
Vertical drop:	5,020 feet

Number of lifts: 22—1 10-person high-speed gondola, 1 6-person high-speed gondola, 7 high-speed quads, 2 triples, 1 double, 5 surface lifts
Snowmaking: 4.5 percent
Skiable acreage: 4,757 acres
Uphill capacity: 29,895 per hour
Expert: ★★★★★
Advanced: ★★★★★
Intermediate: ★★★★★
Beginner: ★★★
First-timer: ★★★

Blackcomb Mountain Facts
Base elevation:	2,214 feet (Village)
Summit elevation:	8,000 feet
Vertical drop:	5,786 feet

Number of lifts: 17—1 eight-person high-speed gondola, 6 high-speed quads, 3 triples, 7 surface lifts
Snowmaking: 10 percent
Skiable acreage: 4,414 acres
Uphill capacity: 29,112 per hour

Expert: ★★★★★
Advanced: ★★★★★
Intermediate: ★★★★★
Beginner: ★★★★
First-timer: ★★

Whistler Blackcomb has consistently been rated in ski and travel magazine surveys as the most popular ski resort in North America.

There are several reasons for this: two mountains with the largest vertical drop on the continent, 5,280 feet; tremendous bowl skiing; and runs that wind down the mountain seemingly forever—the longest run on each mountain is 7 miles. To top it off, the town has a people-friendly, five-village base area with lodging, restaurants and nightclubs, much of which is within walking distance. The main areas of Whistler Village are designed for pedestrian-only traffic.

The resort is huge, and its myriad attractions, both on-slope and off, have helped it to become one of North America's favorite international ski spots. Visitors flock here from Australia, Asia, Europe and Latin America as well as North America.

The resort is in the process of linking its two mountain peaks with a Peak to Peak Gondola which is scheduled for completion in December of 2008. It will travel 2.7 miles from Whistler's Roundhouse Lodge to the Rendezvous Lodge on Blackcomb Mountain. The new gondola will transport winter and summer guests in 28 sky cabins, two with glass floors affording views of the Fitzimmons Creek and valley between the two mountains.

A second new gondola is planned for completion in 2009 to service an Intrawest ski-in/ski-out development, Kadenwood.

Whistler's population is about 10,000. But as resorts go, this one ranks among North America's largest. Built in a European style, it has more than 120 restaurants and bars, more than 200 shops, plus more than 100 condos, B&Bs, lodges and hotels offering more then 5,400 units. What began as a pedestrian-oriented base village has grown into a complex that often requires a bus or taxi ride to move from place to place or from condo to the slopes. A sometimes-confusing system of free and pay buses facilitates travel throughout most of the area.

The resort is comprised of five villages. Whistler Village is the closest neighborhood to the main lifts for both mountains. Stroll the cobblestone streets, window-shop or have a latte in one of the many outdoor patios along the way. Village North, set north (but downhill) of Whistler Village, is where the locals go for the essentials. It holds a section called Marketplace where, along with a host of goods and services, you'll also find the post office, a grocery store and a liquor store. Upper Village, the Blackcomb base, is a 10-minute walk east of the heart of Whistler Village. While it has its own public base lodge, ticket office, children's center and shops, it's smaller and far less active than Whistler Village.

Creekside, also known as Whistler Creek, is the original Whistler base on the south end of the valley. It has undergone a major rejuvenation and is home to the legendary, original Dusty's Bar & BBQ, as well as Legends and First Tracks Lodge, Whistler's premiere suite property. The Creekside base area was redesigned with families in mind; it's quiet at night, without the clubs and street noise of the Village. Creekside is a five-minute taxi ride south.

Now that the International Olympic Committee has chosen Whistler (and Vancouver) to host the 2010 Winter Olympics and Paralympics, their winding Sea to Ski Highway seems paved with gold. Major highway upgrades are now in progress to the tune of C$600 million, as well as improved marine, coach, air and train service. Whistler will host Alpine and Nordic skiing, ski jumping, biathlon, luge, skeleton, bobsled, sledge ice hockey and curling. Snowboarding, freestyle skiing and the opening and closing ceremonies will be celebrated in Vancouver.

 ## Mountain layout

Whistler Blackcomb doesn't give you just a trail map—they give you a trail atlas. Tips: There are more tree runs, more cut trails on Blackcomb Mountain. Whistler Mountain has more Alpine bowls.

Expert, Advanced: For Whistler, start at the Whistler Village Gondola and take a speedy ride up 3,800 vertical feet to the Roundhouse Lodge. Ascending over so much terrain, you'll think you're at the summit, but one glance out the gondola building reveals a series of six giant bowls above the treeline. These spread out from left to right: Symphony Bowl, Harmony Bowl, Flute Bowl, Glacier Bowl, Whistler Bowl and West Bowl (plus the unseen Bagel Bowl, far to the right edge of the ski boundary), all served by the Harmony Express, Peak Chair and the new Symphony Express lift which serves 1,000 acres of inbounds backcountry terrain now called

Symphony Amphitheatre. On busier days, take the Fitzsimmons quad out of the Village, then the Garbanzo Express to get up on the mountain. Ski the top, especially late morning. Stay in the Alpine to avoid the crowds and stop for a late or early lunch for the same reason.

Experts will pause just long enough to enjoy the view and then take the Peak Chair to the 7,160-foot summit, turning left along the ridge. Navigate the tricky entrances to The Cirque or The Couloir and you'll be on some of Whistler's steepest terrain. Or continue down the ridge and drop into Glacier Bowl via the Saddle which is often groomed. Or turn right off the chair and drop into Whistler Bowl. A groomed path rips down Whistler Bowl and Shale Slope to the bottom of the Peak Chair—the steepest winch-groomed terrain in North America. Don't miss the new high speed Symphony Express which accesses 1,000 acres of high alpine. This area can be reached from the top of the Peak chair or the top of Harmony Express.

Most of the expert playground is above treeline, but the lower mountain has a few advanced challenges, most notably the Dave Murray Downhill. It starts at the top of Garbanzo Express (and Orange Chair) and drops more than 3,300 vertical feet to the Whistler Creekside base.

But wait, there's more—another whole mountain. Blackcomb's gondola, Excalibur, is right next to the Whistler Village Gondola in the village. Take it to the Excelerator and Glacier Express high-speed quads. Now you're almost at the top. Take the Horstman T-bar to reach Blackcomb's outstanding 7th Heaven Zone. .

Or from the top of the Horstman T-bar, drop down onto Horstman Glacier on Blue Line. Keep to the left and peer over the cornice into the double-black-diamond chutes. Just seeing the abyss—or seeing someone hurl himself into it—gives quite a rush. The best known of these severe, narrow chutes is Couloir Extreme. The entry requires a leap of faith and skill. For chutes that will give you a thrill but not a heart attack, find Secret Chute or Pakalolo, which is narrow and steep with rock walls on either side.

Experts and advanced skiers won't want to miss the Blackcomb Glacier Zone, accessed from the Showcase T-bar. Drop into the Blowhole, a wind-carved halfpipe between the glacier and a rock wall. Or if this gives you weak knees, keep heading out to the glacier itself, rated blue, but stay high and skier's left under Blowhole to get to more challenging terrain. Beware the five-kilometer runout at the end. For Blackcomb's true extreme—considered some of the best expert skiing in North America—head to the bowls off Spanky's Ladder.

Intermediate: For intermediate skiers, the general rule of thumb is that Whistler Mountain caters to lower-intermediates while Blackcomb suits upper-intermediates. Therefore, the former ability group should begin its adventure on Whistler Mountain. Don't hesitate going straight to the peak at 7,160 feet or to Little Whistler Peak at 6,939. The high Alpine terrain looks daunting from the chairlifts, but this is where you'll find the best snow and some of the finest and most scenic blue runs.

Left off the Peak Chair is The Saddle, an ultra smooth ride on a glacier. Because glaciers keep the snow refrigerated, it stays cold and dry. To the right is Highway 86, a long ridgeline cruiser that takes you down to Big Red Express. This lift takes you to a slew of blue runs and to Harmony Express, which carries you to Harmony and Symphony Bowls, where you can happily play all day. Burnt Stew Trail skirts the upper boundary. Then sail down Harmony Ridge, and if you're feeling frisky, drop into Low Roll for some soft, sweet bumps that provide a nice change of pace.

The Symphony Express takes you to spectacular high alpine intermediate terrain. Access it from the top of the Peak chair or Harmony Express for wide-open bowls, high-intermediate gladed areas and two conventionally cut trails for low-intermediates.

When you're ready to ski to Creekside, take the famous Franz's Run, a 5-mile peak-to-creek cruiser that begins above timberline and ends in the village. It's one of the longest runs in North America. .

At Blackcomb for upper- intermediates, the same rule applies: Stay high. Three express lifts—7th Heaven, Jersey Cream and Solar Coaster—will keep you smiling on appropriately named runs like Cloud Nine, Southern Comfort and Panorama. The snow on Jersey Cream and Cougar Milk is as smooth as cream cheese and the pitch of Ross's Gold, Cruiser and Springboard is perfect for, well, cruising.

Catch the sun by heading over to the 7th Heaven Bowl (Glacier Express to the Horstman T-Bar). With options to pick the degree of steepness you want to tackle, 7th Heaven is a perfect place for a group with abilities from lower- to upper-intermediate to ski, all meeting at the 7th Heaven Express.

To get to the base, be sure to read the map and take the trails on skier's right to get to the Blackcomb side or skier's left to make your way to Whistler Village.

Beginner, First-timer: The good news on the Whistler side is that there's plenty of green-rated skiing higher up on the mountain. The bad news is that skiing back to the base at day's end can be a navigation and traffic nightmare. On a beginner's first day, it's best to start with Whistler's midmountain. Take the Whistler Village Gondola to its top at Roundhouse Lodge. Good routes can be found by following Ego Bowl under the Emerald Express lift to either Pig Alley or Lower Whiskey Jack, back to the Emerald Express chair. Ride the chair back up to Roundhouse Lodge.

You'll find green-circle routes to the base village from the Roundhouse. But pay close attention to signs, check the daily grooming report before you launch—and take a trail map. Once you're on an intermediate trail, there's usually no green escape.

Blackcomb offers several exhilarating runs for the experienced beginner.

For thrilling views, make your way to 7th Heaven and take the Green Line all the way down. If you need lots of room to play, ride the Solar Coaster Express lift and glide along the Expressway to Easy Out. This run ends at the top of the Wizard Express where you may pick up the tail end of Green Line to the base.

The Olympic Chair runs at an easy-to-use slow speed and serves only first-timer terrain. Whistler's nearby Family Zone on the Emerald Express offers great terrain for family members just starting out. Kids should check out the kids-only tree houses in the Emerald Forest.

Parks and pipes

Talk about making it simple: Whistler Blackcomb's park rating system runs S-M-L-XL. If you're just beginning on the freestyle terrain, start with the Terrain Garden on Blackcomb, rated S. Then try the Habitat Park on Whistler Mountain, rated S-M, M-L. The Nintendo Park—rated M, L—and the Highest Level Terrain Park—rated XL—are both on Blackcomb. If you're unsure of yourself in the halfpipe, try the Whistler halfpipe, rated M, before moving on to the superpipes on Blackcomb, both rated L.

If giant parks and pipes are what you're seeking, look no further than Blackcomb Mountain. The Nintendo Superpipe is near the Highest Level Terrain Park. The Super Night Pipe—meeting World Cup specifications at 490 feet long with 16-foot-high walls—is on Lower Cruiser in the Base II area, providing easy viewing for spectators. It's open during Whistler Blackcomb's Night Moves on Thursday, Friday and Saturday nights from 5-9 p.m. Access is from Blackcomb's Base II parking lot, or via the Magic Chair.

The huge Nintendo Terrain Park will satisfy the best freestyle riders and intermediate jibbers too. Just below and to rider's left of the Rendezvous Lodge—accessible from Jersey

Cream Express, Solar Coaster Express and Catskinner Chair—enter the gate into banked turns, boardercross style, that dump you to a line of different-sized rails. Here is where the separation begins. Those who want to go huge, stay to the left and go into the next gate labeled the Highest Level. You'll need a special Highest Level Pass and a helmet. You can obtain one of these C$15 passes, good for the season, at Guest Relations in the Whistler Village Gondola building. After entering the checkpoint you'll find yourself in a world of giants, with tabletops, ramp jumps and rails—all designed for very experienced riders.

If you are not quite up to pro status, stay to the right of Nintendo Terrain Park, where the special pass is not required. You'll find significantly large features including spines, jumps and rails of all sizes and widths plus a funbox. If you want to keep riding the park, take the Catskinner Chair, which runs the length of the park. Unfortunately, you can't hit the Nintendo Superpipe if you want to catch Catskinner back up. At the bottom of the terrain park to the right is the Nintendo Superpipe. This is the most immaculate pipe we have ever seen. There's also a snowcross course, designed for intermediate to expert riders. Beginners haven't been left out as the Big Easy Terrain Garden here will let you get a feel for catching air.

On Whistler Mountain, at the top of Emerald Express Chair, you'll find the Whistler Halfpipe. It has walls about 14 feet high and is nicely maintained. The intermediate Nintendo Habitat Terrain Park is just below the halfpipe. The 600-foot-vertical park is packed with at least 15 rails, including a wide rainbow rail and a wide stepdown rail, plus a long funbox, rollers, hip jumps and a jib-proof picnic table. A sound system keeps the beat to your tricks.

Snowboarding

Most riders, especially freeriders, prefer the Blackcomb side because of the preponderance of fall-line runs. The Whistler side was originally designed with the mountain's contours in mind, but a lot of fall-line runs have been added in recent years to even the score.

To get out of the crowds and up to the goods on Blackcomb, from the base take Excalibur Gondola or Wizard Express, depending on which is closer. From either, take Excelerator Chair. To access the real extremes above treeline, take the Glacier Express.

From top of 7th Heaven or Horstman T-bar you can drop down into Couloir Extreme, Big Bang, or Pakalolo, some of the more extreme chutes on this mountain. Secret Bowl is a nice open area to taste some extremes without having to navigate your turns through a tight rocky space. Also from Glacier Express you can do a short hike to Spanky's Ladder, which opens to the "Gem Bowls"—Garnet, Diamond, Ruby and Sapphire Bowls—all double-black-diamond bowls and very intense riding.

For more extremes and to get to Blackcomb Glacier, take the Showcase T-bar. This is the highest lift on Blackcomb and offers access to a whole wonderful world of riding on a section of the mountain you can't even see from the other lifts. Just a few steps will bring you to the Blowhole, a double-black-diamond wind channel with a very steep pitch. Stay to rider's left after you exit Blowhole and continue down some great steeps. Or skip Blowhole if you want to hike a bit more to Blackcomb Glacier. The glacier is designated a blue, but the snow alone is worth checking out.

If you want to do some terrain above treeline but aren't ready for the extremes, from Glacier Express ride the Horstman T-bar over to the 7th Heaven Zone, where you'll find an array of ways down. There is even a green trail down, although it may be a bit more difficult than the typical green trail. This section of the mountain gets a lot of sun, so even on non-powder days the snow is soft and edgeable.

Blackcomb cruising runs like those around the Jersey Cream Express chair and the Jersey

Cream Wall have some nice little jumps when the snow is fresh. Some flats to avoid, unless you just must go across to the 7th Heaven Express, are 7th Avenue and Expressway to rider's right of the Catskinner Chair.

From Whistler Village, you can ride Whistler Mountain by taking the gondola to the Roundhouse at 6,069 feet. This is just above treeline and to stay above it, head either left to the Harmony Express chair for intermediates and advanced riders, or right to the Peak Chair for experts. If you're an intermediate and have mastered T-barism, head right to the T-bars that run up between T-Bar Run and the Headwall. The big bowls are reached from the Harmony Express..

While beginners can take a green run down from any chairlift (do it for the views on a sunny day), you'll want to practice near the Olympic Chair. It can be reached via the Fitzsimmons Express from the Village. But you've got your own bowl riding too—Ego Bowl just below the Roundhouse, reached by the gondola.

 ## Cross-country & snowshoeing (see also xcskiresorts.com)

Nordic skiing is nearby and easily accessible on the municipal **Lost Lake Trails**, 32 km. of double-tracked trails with a skating lane. Trails are well marked and start right from Day Skier Lot 4A off Lorimer Road in Whistler Village. At night, a 4-km. stretch of trail is lit until 10 p.m. The log hut at Lost Lake is a great rest stop. For conditions or information, call Cross Country Connection at 604-905-0071, where you can also rent cross-country gear.

Another local trail network is at **Nicklaus North Golf Course Trails**, with 6 km. of easy trails at the foot of Old Mill Road. Trail tickets and rental equipment are available at the Meadow Park Sports Centre (604-935-7529), which is a full fitness facility just 4 miles north of the village off Hwy. 99. Your trail pass includes a hot tub soak, steam room, sauna or swim at the center.

Whistler Cross Country Ski & Coast Mountain Guides (604-932-7711), a local outfitter for lessons or guided cross-country ski tours at the golf course, operates out of Whistler Village and runs a shuttle back and forth.

Snowshoeing in Whistler can be done on any of the local hiking trails. More isolated and easy snowshoeing on your own can be done along the **Cheakamus River**, accessed at Function Junction on the west side of Hwy. 99. The 12-km. hiking trail along the river is quite scenic. **Cross Country Connection** (604-905-0071) rents snowshoes. It's on the Whistler trail network, which can be reached day or night right from the village. The **Lost Lake Loop** is a popular and gentle trail that takes about 45 minutes to snowshoe.

Outdoor Adventures at Whistler (604-932-0647) offers an introductory snowshoeing experience that travels from the Whistler Gondola midstation back to the gondola base, primarily following a trail used for mountain biking in summertime. There is also an evening fondue dinner tour.

 ## Lessons (07/08 prices, without tax)

Prices provided are for regular season and are lower for value periods. It's best to call ahead for information and to reserve a space in a class, 800-766-0449, or locally, 604-932-3434. Whistler Days offers 50% off including Supergroups for 11 weeks during the season. Check for details.

Group lessons: Supergroups, limited to three students, are for skiers and snowboarders of all ability levels. A full-day program for beginners costs C$229; intermediates and higher levels pay C$269, lift tickets and rentals extra. Half-day lessons are available. Wednesday and Friday ski sessions include video analysis.

First-timer package: The ski program is a full-day for C$119; three days, C$317. Snowboarding lessons for adult beginners C$119 for one day; C$317 for three days, lift tickets and rentals extra. Rentals are also available online at rentskis.com. where you can pre-order and have equipment waiting for you when you arrive.

Private lessons: Skiers and snowboarders pay C$419 for a half day in the morning and C$329 for a half day in the afternoon; C$599 for a full day.

Special programs: Single-day and multiday camps aim at women, skiers and riders wanting to reach a higher level, backcountry, racing, parks and pipes and other topics. Visit the resort's website for details and prices.

Racing: Whistler Mountain offers a free drop-in race course at the Pontiac Race Center under the Emerald Express chairlift.

 # Children's programs (07/08 prices, without tax)

Child care: Ages 3 months to 4 years. Cost for a full day is C$101 (includes lunch and snacks). Whistler Kids has three locations offering day care from 8 a.m. to 3 p.m. and provides parents with pagers—just in case. The center in Westin Resort at Whistler Village accepts children 18 months through 4 years; the center at the base of the Wizard Express (Upper Village Blackcomb) accepts ages 18 months through 3 years; and the center at Creekside accepts ages 3 months through 3 years. Unless you are staying in Creekside, you will need to take the bus or shuttle from Whistler Village to Creekside. Reservations are strongly encouraged; mandatory during holidays and special events. Call 800-766-0449 or 604-932-3434.

Other options: The Nanny Network (604-938-2823) and **Babysitting Whistler** (888-906-2229; 604-902-2229) both offer 24-hour service with a minimum three-hour sitting, C$15 per hour. Both groups have crib, highchair and stroller rentals, though some of these items may be available through your lodging. **Teddy Bear Daycare** (604-935-8415) at Maurice Young Millennium Place in Village North watches children 7 a.m. to 7 p.m. and offers full-day and half-day rates for toddlers 2½ years old through school age. Parents must provide lunch; snacks and juice are included. The **Whistler Activity Centre** (877-991-9988; 604-938-2769) can refer you to other babysitting services.

Children's lessons: Full-day programs are available for ages 3-12 years for skiing and ages 6-12 for snowboarding. The cost is C$115. Lunch is included, but rental equipment and lift tickets are extra. Children's rental package includes a helmet. A popular program for ages 3-12 is a five-day Adventure Camp that starts each Monday; call for prices (there are two-day Adventure Camps offered on weekends). Teen programs (ages 13-18) are offered daily, also C$115 for a full day including lunch (lift tickets and rentals extra). Five-day teen camps cost C$336 (lessons only). For reservations, call 800-766-0449 or 604-932-3434.

Special activities: Whistler Kids offers a Kids Night Out program 6-10 p.m. Saturdays for ages 5-12. Cost is C$45; reservations required.

 # Lift tickets (07/08 prices, without tax)

	Adult	Child (7-12)
One day	C$83	C$45
Three days	C$243 ($81/day)	C$126 ($42/day)
Five days	C$395 ($79/day)	C$205 ($45/day)

Who skis free: Children ages 6 and younger.

Who skis at a discount: Teens (13-18) and seniors 65 and older pay C$70 for one day, C$207 for three days, C$336 for five.

For the best ticket prices, Whistler Blackcomb encourages you to buy them through its website in conjunction with another product such as lodging, rentals or lessons.

Note: Tickets are good at either mountain. Prices are rounded to the nearest dollar and may be higher during holiday seasons.

 # Accommodations

Lodging varies from dorm bunks to European-style B&Bs to luxury hotels to condos. Keep in mind, there are only four properties in Whistler that are exclusively hotels—The Fairmont Chateau Whistler, Four Seasons Resort Whistler, Hilton Whistler Resort, and Summit Lodge. All other properties are owner-owned and managed by property management companies. Many guests stay in the central village condominiums, but, because of individual ownerships, accommodations can vary widely in amenities, access, parking facilities and distance from the nearest village, shuttle or lift. When making reservations, in order to avoid surprises later, assume nothing.

The best starting point is **Whistler Central Reservations**, 800-944-7853, or **Resort Reservations**, 888-284-9999. During holiday periods (generally late December), seven-night minimum stays are given priority. The online vacation planner allows guests to book all aspects of a vacation to Whistler, including air, lodging, car rentals, equipment rentals, lift tickets and lessons. For those of you traveling with Fido, check out Puppyzone.com, a listing of hotels that take dogs (you'll find quite a few).

In order to help you get oriented, we've separated accommodations into the five villages that comprise Whistler Blackcomb, starting with the southern-most Creekside and working our way north through Whistler Village, Village North, Upper Village and Blackcomb Benchlands.

Creekside

First Tracks Lodge at Whistler Creek (604-938-9999; $$$-$$$$), Whistler's most exclusive suite experience with a 24-hour concierge, is about 11 yards from the base of the Creekside Gondola to the back door.

Legends (604-938-9999; $$-$$$$) is about 30 yards from the gondola. Both are recently built, feature upscale ski-in/ski-out lodging, are right in the middle of the revamped Creekside development and are owner-owned. **Whistler Resort & Club** (604-932-5756; $$-$$$), an older property, has standard hotel rooms and suites. It's a five-minute walk across the main highway to the Creekside Gondola base. You can hop a municipal bus every 15 minutes from any of these lodgings to the central Whistler Village for C$1.50.

Whistler Village

The 419-unit, all-suite **Westin Resort & Spa** (888-634-5577; 604-905-5000; $$$-$$$$) is mountainside with ski-in/ski-out access to both mountains, a world-class spa and health club, an indoor-outdoor restaurant with a West Coast menu and a cozy lounge for apres-ski. This four-star/four-diamond property features a 24-hour front desk, concierge and is a 30-second walk to the Whistler Blackcomb gondola base.

When you're walking in ski boots, location is everything. That's why **Hilton Whistler Resort** (800-515-4050; 604-932-1982; $$$-$$$$), formerly the Whistler Village Resort, is an ideal lodging choice. This resort within a resort has its own ski storage, rentals and service, and health club, plus 24-hour front desk and concierge. It's a three-minute walk to the Whistler Blackcomb gondola base.

You can roll out of bed and practically onto either the Blackcomb or Whistler gondolas from the **Pan Pacific Lodge** (888-905-9995; 604-905-2999; $$$-$$$$). This chic hotel boasts one of the best locations for skiers and riders and we can't argue. Studios, one- and two-bedroom units all have full kitchens and fireplaces. Amenities include outdoor heated pool and hot tubs, exercise room, guest laundry, spa services, in-resort shuttle service and a pub restaurant (see Dining and Apres-Ski/Nightlife). Its new tower opened in July 2005.

Pan Pacific has recently opened a second Whistler property, **Pan Pacific Whistler Mountainside** (888-905-9995; $$$-$$$$), an 83-room, all-suite luxury boutique hotel. Located in the heart of Whistler Village, near the Pan Pacific Lodge, this property features fold-away tables, breakfast bars, kitchens and efficient use of space. Amenities are similar to the Pan Pacific Lodge and include a lap pool, hot tubs, spa, fitness room, complimentary breakfast and evening hors d'oeuvres.

The **Crystal Lodge** (800-667-3363; 604-932-2221; $$$-$$$$) added 22 rooms in an extensive renovation for a total of 159 rooms. Cozy common areas around the fireplaces give it a European atmosphere. This lodging in the center of the village has 24-hour front desk service, elevators and is a two-minute walk to the Whistler Blackcomb gondolas. Underground parking is C$12 per day.

Hearthstone Lodge (800 663-7711; 604 932-4161; $$-$$$$), **Best Western Listel Whistler Hotel** (800-663-5472; 604-932-1133; $$$-$$$$), and **Blackcomb Lodge** (888-621-1177; 604-932-4155; $$-$$$), which recently underwent a $5-million renovation, offer good accommodations with 24-hour front desk service, elevators and some walk-ups. All are within three minutes walking distance of the main village and the Whistler Blackcomb gondolas.

Holiday Inn SunSpree Resort (800-229-3188; 604-938-0878; $$$-$$$$) is in Whistler Village Centre. Its suite design is very imaginative and no cleaning sprays are used in certain "allergy-free" rooms.

One of the newer properties in the heart of Whistler Village is **Adara Hotel** (604-866-23272; $$$-$$$$) a 41-room boutique hotel at 4122 Village Green close to shopping, restaurants and nightlife.

The **Coast Whistler Hotel** (800-663-5644; 604-932-2522; $$$) is well placed, across the road from Whistler Village. The rooms are small, the staff friendly. The pool and hot tub are busy every night. Kids stay free. It seems to be popular with the younger set and is on the outskirts of the main village, about a five-minute walk from the Whistler Blackcomb gondola base.

If you don't mind a longer walk to the village center, the **Tantalus Lodge** (888-633-4046; 604-932-4146; $$$-$$$$) is a comfortable suite alternative to staying in the heart of the village. It offers a complimentary shuttle during ski hours to the Whistler Blackcomb gondola base or take about a seven-minute walk over a hill. All 76 units have two bedrooms, two baths, full kitchen, fireplace and balcony. Good for couples traveling together or families with teens.

Upper Village

Opened in June 2004, **Four Seasons Resort Whistler** (888-935-2460; 604-935-3400; $$$-$$$$) raised the elegance bar in Whistler. This premier resort hotel features 242 spacious guest rooms, suites and townhomes. All units are decorated in rich colors blended with wood accents and have gas fireplaces; most have balconies. Amenities include a spa featuring special therapies for men and unusual, local organic seaweed treatments; restaurant and bar.

The **Fairmont Chateau Whistler** (800-606-8244; 604-938-8000; $$$-$$$$) is another Whistler premier property. It has 550 rooms in 12 stories, two restaurants (see Dining), an expanded lounge off the lobby for great apres-ski, an extensive health club and renovated world-class Vida wellness spa and prime ski-in/ski-out access to Blackcomb.

Accommodations (Cdn$): (double room) $$$$-$200+; $$$-$141-$200; $$-$81-$140; $-$80 and less.
Dining (Cdn$): $$$-Entrees $20+; $$-$10-20; $-less than $10

The **Glacier Lodge** (888-898-9208; 604-905-0518; $$$-$$$$), centrally situated at the Blackcomb base across from The Fairmont Chateau Whistler, features suites with kitchens, gas fireplaces, balconies, living rooms, dataport telephones, duvets and all the usual high-end amenities. It's a two-minute walk from the base of the Blackcomb Wizard lift.

Le Chamois (888-560-9453; 604-932-8700; $$$-$$$$), just down the plaza from The Fairmont Chateau, is another upscale property with all the usual amenities. The European-style hotel houses a topnotch restaurant (see Dining), and is a brief walk to the base of the Blackcomb Wizard lift.

Village North

Delta Whistler Village Suites (800-268-1133; 604-905-3987; $$$-$$$$) includes amenities such as kitchen facilities, pool, indoor/outdoor hot tubs and workout room.

The **Summit Lodge** (888-913-8811; 604 932-2778; $$$-$$$$), in the center of Whistler's Marketplace and a 10-minute walk to either the Blackcomb or Whistler bases, is a quiet, luxurious boutique retreat with 81 fireplace suites, covered balconies, soaker tubs, kitchenettes, down duvets, terrycloth robes and dataport telephones.

Pinnacle International Resort (888-999-8986; 604-938-3218; $$$-$$$$), on Main Street in Village North Centre, bills itself as Whistler's first "boutique/romance hotel." It has 84 suites with queen beds and double hot tubs close to the fireplace.

Glacier's Reach (800-777-0185; 604-932-1154; $-$$$) condos are owner-owned and some of the better value properties in Whistler. Many have kitchens and private outdoor hot tubs—their big claim to fame. Underground parking is C$12 per day. There's no elevator but there is a pool and common hot tub. It's a 10-minute free village shuttle ride to and from either base.

Benchlands

Marriott-Residence Inn Whistler/Blackcomb (800-331-3131; 604-905-3400; $$$-$$$$), with 186 units, is secluded, up at the end of Painted Cliff Road on the Blackcomb side beside the Wizard Express lift and alongside the Lower Cruiser run. Ski out to the Wizard Express in the Upper Village and ski in back to the hotel. Good spring bear sightings in this neighborhood.

Accommodations Outside Main Villages

These lodgings are a bit less expensive than those nearer the village core. You can catch a shuttle, taxi or municipal bus into the core for a small fee.

Edgewater Lodge (888-870-9065; 604-932-0688; $$$-$$$$) is on a peninsula of Green Lake, bordering a golf course and the River of Golden Dreams—great for those who want luxury and no village bustle. It has 12 rooms, six are suites, a hot tub, award-winning dining room serving breakfast for guests and dinner for anyone with reservations (see Dining), cross-country skiing and snowshoeing. It's a 10-minute drive from the village base.

Two dormitory lodges and a youth hostel have beds for less than C$40 a night and private rooms for about C$80 a night.

Fireside Lodge (604-932-4545; $) is about 4 miles south of the main village, a five-minute walk to the bus stop and another five-minute bus ride to the Whistler Blackcomb main base. **AMS/UBC Whistler Lodge** (604-932-6604; $), about a mile from Creekside Village, is a "bring-your-own bedding" lodging (though you can also rent bedding). It has a hot tub, sauna, common kitchen and laundry areas and is a short municipal bus ride or 20-minute walk to the Creekside base. **Whistler Hostel** (604-932-5492; $) is about 6 miles west of Whistler Village. Its desk is open mornings and afternoon/evenings only.

Durlacher Hof (604-938-1924; $$$-$$$$) is the genuine B&B article for skiers wanting an Austrian lodging experience. At the door, you swap your boots for boiled-wool slippers.

Each of the eight rooms has its own bath and extra-long beds. Breakfasts are always spectacular and on occasion, visiting celebrity chefs prepare dinner on the weekends.

Dining

For years locals have recommended the **Rimrock Cafe and Oyster Bar** (604-932-5565; $$$-$$$$) in Highland Lodge as the best restaurant in town. It's at Whistler Creek, about a half-mile south of the village. Entrees like blue marlin and roasted northern musk ox loin grace the menu, complemented by an extensive wine list. **Le Gros** (604-932-4611; $$$; reservations) is another local favorite for the best in modern European fare with a decidedly French twist. It's about a mile south in Twin Lakes Village, serves dinner only (seven nights a week) and is not usually listed in restaurant guides.

Bearfoot Bistro (604-932-3433; $$$-$$$$), next to the Best Western Listel Whistler Hotel, is a high-end French restaurant offering a fixed-priced gourmet chef's menu that begins with 1,600 wines. There is no menu per se but trust the chef with a multicourse dinner of oysters with Nashi pear, bronzed sea scallops, black cod, Ontario squab, loin of wild Arctic caribou, sorbet and soups, petit fours, all courses accompanied by friendly wines from the huge cellar. Where else could you get Dom Perignon by the glass? There's a less formal (and less expensive) wine bar adjacent to the restaurant with the same kitchen and a simpler bistro menu.

Fifty Two 80 Bistro (604-935-3400; $$-$$$$) at the Four Seasons Resort Whistler specializes in seafood and fun comfort foods such as shapely potatoes and massaged chicken. Whether you're in the mood for the seafood bar or a delectable five-course meal, all are accompanied by exemplary service, an atmosphere of elegant informality and a very nice selection of local wines. The name signifies Blackcomb's vertical drop: 5,280 feet.

Aubergine Grill (604-935-4344; $$$) at The Westin features magnificent views and specialty seafood menus from their executive chef. If you're into beef, don't miss the classic **Hy's Steakhouse** (604-905-5555; $$-$$$; reservations recommended), on the corner of Village Gate and Northlands boulevards, near the entrance to the village off Hwy. 99. Its slogan is "tender steaks and stiff drinks" and they're not kidding. **Val d'Isere** (604-932-4666; $$-$$$), in the Town Plaza and open for dinner only, features fine French cuisine and has a strong local reputation.

Umberto Menghi, a flamboyant Italian chef whose TV cooking show is popular in Canada (locals call Umberto "our Emeril"), is well known for his restaurants in Vancouver and two in Whistler. **Trattoria Di Umberto** (604-932-5858; $$), inside the Mountainside Lodge, offers elegant and traditional Italian fare in a casual, relaxed atmosphere. **Il Caminetto Di Umberto** (604-932-4442; $$$), open for dinner only, features more formal Italian Tuscan cuisine.

Mario Enero, once Umberto's longtime head chef, owns **La Rua** (604-932-5011; $$$-$$$$; dinner only, reservations recommended: in Le Chamois Hotel, one of the top-rated spots in all of Whistler. This fine Italian restaurant features great food and elegant service. If you like extensive wine lists and a sommalier to make recommendations for each course, then you'll enjoy **Araxi Restaurant & Bar** (604-932-4540; $$$-$$$$; reservations recommended), which specializes in West Coast fare and serves creative fish, meat, vegetarian and pasta dishes.

Quattro at Whistler (604-905-4844; $$-$$$$), in the Pinnacle Hotel, is one of the most popular Italian/Mediterranean restaurants in Village North. Especially notable are the antipasti—which include sausage, prawns, and broiled wrapped cheese—and house-made pastas. **Edgewater Lodge** (604-932-0688; $$$) requires reservations for a high-end dining experience from escargot to schnitzel to lamb to venison and everything in between.

When eating at **Wildflower** (604-938-2033; $$$), in The Fairmont Chateau Whistler, start

Accommodations (Cdn$): (double room) $$$$-$200+; $$$-$141-$200; $$-$81-$140; $-$80 and less.
Dining (Cdn$): $$$-Entrees $20+; $$-$10-20; $-less than $10

with an icewine martini, then delve into the innovative regional cuisine that is the specialty of this award-winning restaurant. Don't forget to check out their wine room.

Get a taste of **Austria at Bavaria** (604-932-7518; $$$), where schnitzels and fondues rule. The menu is primarily German with a touch of French. The food is good, but not necessarily exceptional; selections include a full range of Schnitzels, Spaetzle, Prawns Savoyarele and Oscar Veal; the fondues are excellent. It's at **Alpenglow** across from 7-11 on Main Street.

Elements Tapas Lounge (604-932-5569; $$), attached to The Kimpton-owned Summit Lodge in Village North is an intimate 40-seat room with a warm atmosphere and the stunning culinary quality that a Kimpton property always provides. The tapas menu offers exotic cold and warm plates of salad, seafood, meats and veggies as well as sweets, all at reasonable prices.

Sushi Village (604-932-3330; $$-$$$) on the second floor of the Sundial Hotel at the Whistler Blackcomb gondola base is legion. A good introduction to sushi is the combo A plate, with salmon, cucumber and tuna maki rolls; split that and a bowl of noodle soup and you've got a meal for two for less than C$16. For steaks cooked Japanese steakhouse-style, it's **Teppan Village** (604-932-2223; $$-$$$) in the Delta Resort at the Whistler Blackcomb base or the very popular **Sushi-Ya** (604 905-0155; $$-$$$) in the Marketplace area above McDonald's. They do take-out as well. **Zen** (604-932-3667; $$$), in First Tracks Lodge at Creekside, serves sushi in a sleek, modern atmosphere.

For good food at a good price, head to **The Brew House** (604-905-2739; $$). Its signature is its wood-fired pizza oven and rotisserie, yet also delivers a surprisingly wide menu of other well-prepared foods.

At the streetside entrance to the Le Chamois Hotel is a locals' favorite Thai restaurant, **Thai One On** (604-932-4822; $$), featuring nicely priced dishes for eat-in or take-out. **Zeuski's Taverna** (604-932-6009; $$), in the Whistler Town Plaza, has moderately priced Greek food. They also do take-out.

On some travelers' top-10 list you'll find the **Splitz Grill** (604-938-9300; $$) in the Alpenglow Building. It features burgerzburgerzbergerz: chicken, salmon, Italian sausage, lentil, veggie, smokies and whatever else you can dream up.

Caramba Restaurant (604-938-1879; $-$$), in Town Plaza, is a favorite of our staff Whistler experts. It is "Mediterreaneanish," with a great putanesca pasta, wood-fired pizzas and a Caramba salad (chicken, butter lettuce, peanut sauce), all at very reasonable prices. Don't miss a visit to **Kypriaki Norte** (604-932-0600; $-$$) for traditional Greek food including moussaka, souvlaki, spanakopita and saganaki.

Cinnamon Bear Bar (604-966-5060; $), near the Hilton, serves typical bar fare, burgers, pizzas and salads from 11 a.m. to 1 a.m. **The Keg** (604-932-5151; $-$$) at Whistler Village Inns and Suites has good steaks, seafood and basic Canadian/American food. **Hoz's Pub & Sports Bar** (604-932-5940; $-$$), in Whistler Creekside, is big on the typical snacks, burgers and fish and chips.

Four' (N) Twenty (604-935-1743; $-$$), above the Royal Bank in the village, serves good value for the Whistler dollar. Known as the home of savory meat and veggie pies, soups and sweets, this Brit establishment offers comfort food for a reasonable price. **Portobello** (604-938-2040; $$,) on the ground floor of The Fairmont Hotel, has a la carte dining at tables where you order from a menu, but also has an extensive deli counter where you can eat-in or take-out.

Get great Kung Pao chicken at **Earl's** (604-935-3222; $-$$. The desserts are massive. **Milestones** (604-938-4648; $-$$) near the Delta Whistler Village Suites has a huge family- and casual-style menu, plus the **Palomino Bar** ($$).

In the Pan Pacific Mountainside Lodge, **Dubh Linn Gate Old Irish Pub** (604-905-4047; $$), an authentic Irish pub, has a country feel with offerings of stews, steak & kidney pie, fish

& chips and the best draft beer selection in Whistler. **Crêpe Montagne** (604-905-4444; $$) at Market Pavillion serves French everything: music, language and savory crepes. Fondue and raclette are also available. The **Amsterdam Cafe** (604-932-8334; $$) is a primo people-watching spot, facing Whistler Village Square, the heartbeat of Whistler.

Zogs Dogs (604-938-6644; $) is an outdoor fast food stand in Mountain Square in front of Showcase, the snowboard retail store. Zogs features chili and cheese hot dogs, various flavored Beavertails (a Canadian fried pastry) and French fries with gravy and other fixings.

Ric's Grill (604-932-7427; $) in the Crystal Lodge is one of Whistler's lower-priced restaurants that locals and families patronize. Fare includes ribs, salads, stir fry, and various barbeque specialties with steak fries or foot-high onion rings. Pizza is available in either Chicago deep dish or thin crust.

Auntie Em's Kitchen (604-932-1163; $) in the Village North Marketplace, is a way-above-average deli with a deep menu featuring monster vegetarian sandwiches, matzo-ball soup, breakfast all day, and good breads and sweets, especially the cranberry-date bar. For a simple, cozy meal, sneak into **Gone Bakery & Soup Co.** (604-905-4663; $), just off the main Village Square behind the best bookstore in the village (**Armchair Books**) and right on the square. It has a reader board of daily deli specials where you can order at the counter and either take out or park yourself in their comfy chairs. Moderate prices and great food.

Ciao-Thyme Bistro (604-932-7051; $), in the Upper Village across from The Fairmont Chateau is known for its decadent cinnamon pecan buns. The cafe is tiny so it's a good place to order a fabulous breakfast to go. Locals say this bistro is the best breakfast in Whistler. **Ingrid's Village Cafe** (604-932-7000; $) on Skier's Approach near Village Square, is a local legend in Whistler. Enjoy a huge, best-in-Whistler breakfast for cheap in their cozy deli. Open 7:30 a.m. to 6 p.m. so you can get more than breakfast. **Dubh Linn Gate** (604-905-4047; $-$$) serves large portions of pancakes, porridge, eggs and omelettes. Perfect, unless the thought of eating breakfast in a bar makes your head spin. **Evergreens** (604-932-7346; $-$$) in the Hilton Whistler Resort has a fine daily buffet breakfast for less than C$20.

Riverside Junction Cafe & Internet (604-905-1199; $), 2.5 km north of the village at the Riverside Campground, offers all-day breakfast or lunch for a great value. It's open 7 a.m.-9 p.m. with licensed premises and offers hard-wired and wireless Internet connection. Other Internet cafes in the village include Cyber Web Internet Cafe, Hot Box Coffee and Internet and The Hub.

Sleigh Ride Dining

Enjoy a sleigh ride under the evening stars and then a fondue dinner in **The Chalet** (604-932-0647) at The Fairmont Chateau Golf Club. Reservations required. **Whistler Outdoor Experience** (604-932-3389) offers a number of sleigh rides and dinner combinations in the Whistler area.

On-mountain Dining

There's good food on the mountains as well. Two unique dining experiences that shouldn't be missed: **Waffles** at The Crystal Hut on Blackcomb and ribs at **Dusty's Bar & BBQ** at Creekside. The **Crystal Hut** ($-$$) on Blackcomb Mountain is fit for a king—or at least a prince. England's Prince Charles brunched on its signature homemade waffles and so should you. It's on the ridge just above the Crystal Chair. **Canadian Snowmobile Adventures** offers a **Mountaintop Fondue Ride** to the Crystal Hut, where you'll indulge in a candlelit cheese and broth fondue, as well as refreshments, dessert and live entertainment. **Dusty's** (604-905-2171; $-$$), at Creekside, has awesome buckets of ribs and great apres-ski. Don't miss this legendary establishment.

For fine Alpine dining, stop for lunch at **Christine's** (604-938-7437; $$-$$$) in Rendezvous Lodge on Blackcomb. Choose from excellent salads and entrees including salmon and creative tapas. Reservations are a good idea.

At the Glacier Creek Lodge on Blackcomb, choose from market-style fare at the **International Plaza** ($-$$) or grab a taste of West Coast specialties at the **BC Eatery** ($-$$).

The **Roundhouse Lodge** at the almost-top of Whistler boasts four restaurants (all 604-905-2373) including **Pika's** ($-$$), perfect for families craving burgers and fries or gourmet baked potatoes and home-made soup. Try **Steeps Grill** ($-$$) for a simple menu of signature seafood chowder, salads and entrees. **Mountain Market** ($-$$) offers open market-style dining with your pick of Thai, wraps, fish & chips, salads and deli sandwiches. **Paloma's** ($-$$) features Italian fare including pastas and pizza.

For those with more adventurous tastes, the **Mountain Top Fondue Dinner** starts with an exhilarating snowmobile ride at 1,828 m (6,000 ft) on Blackcomb Mountain, followed by dinner and live entertainment at the cozy Crystal Hut.

Chic Pea ($) at the top of the Garbanzo Express on Whistler is a neat midmountain natural wood cabin where you can get creative pizzas whole or by the slice, scrumptious freshly made subs and ooey-gooey cinnamon buns.

Eager skiers and riders can board the Whistler Village Gondola at 7:15 a.m. for **Fresh Tracks** buffet breakfast ($$, lift ticket extra; through mid-April) at the Roundhouse Lodge and first rights to the runs. Locals hail this as the best breakfast in town, but we're not sure why since it's a basic buffet—what you're really getting is early access to the slopes.

Apres-ski/nightlife

Apres-ski spills out onto the snow from **Garibaldi Lift Co. Bar and Grill** at Whistler Village Gondola base and **Merlin's** at Blackcomb. Both are beer-and-nachos spots with lively music. The outdoor patio at **Longhorn Saloon & Grill**, in the Carleton Lodge at the base of the village gondolas, always seems to be jammin'. It's known for its 29 burgers. **Dubh Linn Gate Old Irish Pub**, an Irish pub in the Pan Pacific Mountainside Lodge, is another place for immediate fun when the lifts close. Enjoy a rousing atmosphere with Celtic music, 50 whiskies and 16 beers on tap. **Citta's**, in the center of Whistler Village, has an atrium and is another good apres-ski and people-watching spot.

Amsterdam Cafe in Village Square is Whistler's funkiest local hangout for nighttime mingling. Drop into a deep couch or pull up a bar stool beside a famous local athlete.

For dancing, **Tommy Africa's** is in the main Whistler Village, under the Rexall Drugstore and behind the zebra poles. It's a treasure hunt to find, but the music and atmosphere make the search worth it. It's the "best place to dance in Whistler" as voted by the locals—and our staff! **Buffalo Bill's**, for 16 years one of Whistler's favorite nightspots, has pool tables, video games and a crowded but friendly dance floor. It's just across from the conference center in the main village. The **Savage Beagle**, near the Village Center, is recently renovated. This doggie dancing heaven favors funk and acid jazz in a double-decker, double-loud lounge right in the middle of downtown Whistler. More people watch than dance, but it's the dancers who have all the fun. Open until 2 a.m. Search out the legendary **Garfinkel's**, pumping electronia for the younger crowd, in the Delta Whistler Village Suites.

Dusty's Bar & BBQ at Creekside is still the locals' choice for stellar live music.

For a more civilized apres-ski or evening drink, snuggle in at The Fairmont Chateau Whistler's **Mallard Bar** just off the hotel lobby with a view of Blackcomb Mountain. The Four Seasons' **Fifty Two 80 Bar** is a relaxing place for a specialty martini or glass of British Columbia wine. The **Firerock Lounge** at the Westin Resort & Spa in the heart of Whistler

Village is an intimate spot to have a brew and some Northwest cuisine. **Black's Pub** on the square in the Sundial Hotel is also in Whistler Village, just 20 yards from the gondola bases. You'll get 180-degree views and have your pick of 99 beers and 45 scotches.

 ## Other activities

Whistler Heli-Skiing (604-932-4105) and **Coast Range Heliskiing** (800-701-8744; 604-894-1144) in Pemberton are the local experts in heli-skiing. Venture beyond the ski area boundary for one or more days. Daily and multi-day backcountry ski and snowboard tours are available through **Whistler Alpine Guides** (604-938-9242) and **Callaghan Country Wilderness Adventures** (604-938-0616). Whether you're new to the sport or an experienced climber, ice climbing with **Whistler Alpine Guides** (604-938-9242) will provide a once-in-a-lifetime experience.

Hundreds of miles of logging roads are accessible for snowmobiling. **Cougar Mountain Wilderness Adventures** (604-932-4086) and **Blackcomb Snowmobiles Ltd.** (604-905-7002; 604-932-8484) have tours several times a day, plus evening rides. **Canadian Snowmobile Adventures** (604-938-1616) offers luxury evening dinner tours up Blackcomb Mountain. **Cougar Mountain Wilderness Adventures** (604-932-4086) also offers dogsledding. It's very popular and usually sells out, so make reservations as early as possible.

Whistler is in a Coastal Temperate Rainforest, so touring the forest on ziplines across Fitzsimmons Creek is a natural. **Ziptrek Ecotours** (866-935-0001; 604-935-0001) offers a 2.5-hour tour, year round, that sends you whizzing along a recently expanded adventure with ten ziplines at speeds up to 40+ miles/hour about 200 feet above the creek. Zipsters are attached by body harness and carabiner to a steel pulley system—very safe—and the trip is as fun as anything you'll do at Whistler. This company also operates **Treetrek**, another year-round adventure. A spectacular network of suspension bridges, boardwalks and trails takes you from the forest floor to the upper forest canopy with views 150' down to the white waters of Fitzsimmons Creek.

Whistler Bungee (604-938-9333) lets you take a 160-foot dive from a pedestrian bridge—and live to tell the tale. It's about a 10-minute van ride from Whistler and is accessible only by snowshoe or snowmobile during the winter. The recently opened 1,000 foot long **Tube Park** (800-766-0449; 604-932-3434) on Blackcomb Mountain is just a free Excalibur gondola ride up to the Base II Zone which is open daily from noon to 8 p.m. Served by a tube-friendly, carpet-style lift, ride lanes range from green to black and are perfect for all ages.

Covered tennis courts are located at the Delta Whistler Resort. Ice skating, swimming and drop-in hockey take place at **Meadow Park Sports Centre** (604-938-7529) a few miles north of the village. Sleigh rides are offered by Blackcomb Sleighrides (604-932-7631) and Whistler Outdoor Experience Co. (604-932-3389).

The Whistler Activity and Information Centre (604-932-2394) provides information and reservations for these and other activities. Or try **Explore Whistler Adventures** in the Westin Resort & Spa (604-935-3445; www.explorewhistleradventures.com). **Village Concierge** (604-938-0999) books everything. Drop by their store on the Village Stroll or at **Explore Whistler** in The Westin Resort.

If the weather's bad, or for apres-ski, visit the indoor **Great Wall Climbing and Guiding Centre** (604-905-7625) where you can literally climb the wall (in the Sundial Hotel, lower level).

The independent **Vida Wellness Spa** (800-401-4018; 604-938-2086) in The Fairmont Chateau Whistler shares the locker rooms and health club facilities, including indoor and outdoor pools, hot tubs, steamrooms, sauna and exercise equipment, with the hotel. A 60-minute Swedish massage begins at C$135.

Accommodations (Cdn$): (double room) $$$$-$200+; $$$-$141-$200; $$-$81-$140; $-$80 and less.
Dining (Cdn$): $$$-Entrees $20+; $$-$10-20; $-less than $10

The Spa (604-966-2620) at The Four Seasons Resort offers the ultimate experience with 15 treatment rooms, full-service health club, fitness studio, steam and sauna rooms and all five-star services.

Suzanne Johnston and her husband opened **Whistler Body Wrap**: The Spa (604-932-4710) in 1989. It's a small, affordable day spa offering massages, wraps, facials, and salon services. If you crave more space and have the budget to splurge, opt for the Johnston's more spacious and luxurious **Avello Spa** (604-935-3444) at the Westin Resort & Spa. Signature treatments include hot rock and Thai massages. An 80-minute massage begins at C$180.

At **Nibbana Healing Spa** (604-935-5772), statues of Buddha preside over each of nine treatment rooms along with symbols of earth, wind, air and fire. This "spa with a soul" is in the lower level of the Glacier Lodge across from The Fairmont Chateau. A 60-minute massage begins at C$115.

Taman Sari Royal Heritage Spa (604-938-5982), in Summit Lodge, features traditional Royal Javanese therapy treatments where "East meets West" in a Zen-like retreat. The usual offerings include exotic twists with Oriental, Javanese and Royal Pramesari massage, reflexology and many more spa packages. A 60-minute massage starts at C$115.

The full-service **Solarice Wellness Centre & Spa** (888-935-1222; 604-935-1222) is a day spa in Whistler Village behind the Blackcomb Lodge. Solarice offers traditional spa services and wellness therapies such as Chinese medicine, yoga, pilates, tai chi, nutritional consultation, personal training and physiotherapy. A 60-minute massage begins at C$75. A spa menu is available. Reserve treatments at least a week in advance.

Here's a find: **Maurice Young Millennium Place**, called **My Place** (4335 Blackcomb Way; 604-935-8410 administration, 604-935-8418 box office), is Whistler's non-profit arts and community center. Activities include exhibits, concerts, films and both fitness (Pilates, yoga, kickboxing, etc.) and educational classes and religious services; call or stop by for a schedule. The **Youth Centre** (C$5) has table and computer games, big-screen TV and a variety of classes and contests geared to teens.

Who needs an art museum when you have the quality and quantity of galleries available in Whistler? The **Whistler Art Tour** brochure is a guide to galleries, public art, businesses with art displays, as well as to local artists who will open their studios to the public. Pick up a copy at My Place or local galleries. A guided art tour is sometimes offered on Tuesdays; ask at the **Black Tusk Gallery**, at 4293 Mountain Square in the skier's plaza at the base of Whistler (604-905-5540). The **Path Gallery** (604-932-7570) at 122-4338 Main Street in Village North features fine and traditional artwork by First Nations artists including masks, totems, drums, jewelry and prints.

Shopping is plentiful and we could write an entire chapter! But just enjoy the thrill of discovery. Here are a couple of invaluable finds for those of you renting equipment or suffering boot pain: **Wild Willies Ski Club** (604-938-8036) has three locations in Whistler where you can find the best price points for renting equipment and some good buys. **McCoo's** (604-932-2842), near the gondolas in the main village, has a tiny work bench in the back and a treasure of a bootfitter named George, who works miracles on those pain-causing ski boots. **Skitch Knicknacks and Paddywacks**, 4222 Village Square, carries a funky and fun selection of Canadian-made crafts. At the Olympic-made-famous **Roots** in Whistler Village you just might find some merchandise for the upcoming 2010 Whistler Olympics. And if you're looking for that perfect outfit, don't miss **Open Country** in The Fairmont Chateau. They have what everyone in Canada is wearing—washable leather! Jeans, slacks, jackets. **Expressions** provides a great rainy day activity: If you're into authentic Northwest Coast art, the **Black Tusk Gallery**, at 4293 Mountain Square in the skier's plaza at the base of Whistler, is a must. A fine selection of artisan crafts is carried at **Mountain Craft Gallery**. Collectors of artist-made Teddy bears will want to visit **Bear Pause. Rogers' Chocolates** is a haven for chocoholics.

The local medical clinic at **Town Plaza** (604-905-7089) is open seven days a week. For serious emergencies (8 a.m.-10 p.m.) call the **Whistler Health Care Centre** (604-932-4911). **Whistler Dental** (604-932-3677) offers emergency services, as does **Creekside Dental** (604-938-1550).

 # Getting there and getting around

By air: Most major airlines fly to Vancouver. Allow plenty of time in the Vancouver Airport, both arriving and leaving, for customs declarations, security and currency exchange.

Helijet (800-665-4354; Vancouver, 604-273-1414) flies twice daily from the Vancouver airport to Whistler, a 35-minute trip. Flights leave the airport at 11:50 a.m. and 2:40 p.m. daily. Passengers can check two bags not exceeding a total of 50 lbs.

By Train: Whistler Mountaineer (800-687-7245; 604-606-8460) leaves from North Vancouver daily at 8:30 A.M. for a three-hour scenic journey along the Ski-to-Sky route. The train returns to Vancouver daily at 7:45 A.M. Reservations are required. Check out details at whistlermountaineer.com.

Perimeter's Whistler Express (877-317-7788; Whistler, 604-905-0041; Vancouver 604-266-5386) connects the Vancouver Airport to Whistler 9 times a day, with the last bus leaving at 11:30 p.m. Reservations are required by noon, one day prior. Note on ground transportation: The Perimeter bus drops off and picks up only at certain hotels. If you are staying somewhere that isn't on their list, you must get yourself and your bags to a pickup point on time. So keep that in mind as you make lodging reservations.

By bus: Greyhound Canada (800-661-8747; 604-932-5031) operates from the Vancouver bus depot at Main and Terminal.

By car: From Vancouver, follow Hwy. 99 north all the way to Whistler. For part of the trip, Hwy. 99 merges with Hwy.1 (Trans Canada Highway). Keep an eye out for Exit 2, where Hwy. 99 splits off to go to Whistler. Note: Because of construction work on the road to Whistler in preparation for the upcoming 2010 Olympics, delays may slow your travels.

Getting around: You don't need a car in Whistler. But unless you're staying in Whistler Village or Upper Village, you'll probably rely on the free shuttle (604-932-4020) to get around. Buses run throughout the resort town with the "primary" route looping from the Village to Marketplace (Village North) to the Upper Village and the Blackcomb Mountain base lodge from 6:15 a.m. until 1 a.m. But beware! If you're staying at Creekside or the Benchlands, you'll have to switch buses in order to get to the Village loop. For local cabs, call Whistler Taxi (604-32-3333). Many of the nicer hotels offer free shuttle service.

Quebec City, Canada

Mont-Sainte-Anne, Stoneham, Le Massif

Quebec City Facts

Address: Greater Quebec Area Tourism and Convention Bureau, 835, avenue Wilfrid-Laurier, Quebec (Quebec) G1R 2L3
Toll-free reservations: 877-783-1608
Dining:★★★★★
Apres-ski/nightlife:★★★★★
Other activities:★★★★★

Phone: 418-641-6290
Fax: 418-522-0830
E-mail: info@quebecregion.com
Internet: www.quebecregion.com
Bed base: 11,200

Quebec is a city that not only embraces winter, it celebrates it. Founded in 1608 by the French navigator, geographer and explorer Samuel de Champlain, Quebec is the only walled city in North America outside of Mexico. Perched atop a 350-foot-high cliff overlooking the St. Lawrence River, it immerses North American visitors in French history and culture, providing a taste of Europe without the jet lag.

Drive down Grande Allée, enter Old Quebec through Porte (gate) Saint-Louis and descend into the 18th century. The narrow streets are lined with stately old homes, many of them now gourmet restaurants and boutique hotels. You half-expect to see horse-drawn carriages clacketty-clacking along les rues. Don't worry if your French is rusty (or nonexistent); almost everyone on the front lines of tourism speaks at least some English. And here's a real plus:Winter is low season in Quebec City. With the exception of Winter Carnival weekends, lodging rates are at their lowest.

Although you may have the city to yourself in the low season, you'll feel a certain *joie de vivre*. Everywhere you turn there's an activity: Tobogganing, sleigh rides, ice skating, ice climbing, snow rafting, dogsledding, cross-country skiing, you name it. Quebec is also alive with culture. The calendar is punctuated with festivals and the city dotted with 27 museums. With more than 4,900 restaurants representing 85 different ethnic styles, the city is also renowned for its cuisine.

Beginning the last weekend in January, Winter Carnival is a 17-day party presided over by the jolly snowman ambassador, Bonhomme. Nearly everyone wears the colorful sash that is the signature of Quebec, and the city is full of dancers, singers, bands, ice sculptures and parades. Perhaps the craziest, but most hotly contested, event is the canoe race across the ice-choked St. Lawrence.

Don't miss Quebec's little Champs Elysees, Grande Allée, near the Parliament. Private homes once owned by judges and members of Parliament have been converted to discos, restaurants and other outlets for nightlife. Cartier Avenue is great for shopping, and Petit Champlain, one of North America's oldest shopping streets, is lined with boutiques and galleries and feels like pure Europe. It can be reached by the funicular, a cable car outside Fairmont Chateau Frontenac, for C$1.75 each way, or via the infamous Breakneck Stairs.

Mont-Sainte-Anne, the largest ski resort in eastern Quebec, and Stoneham are each about 30 minutes away, while Le Massif is a little shy of an hour-long drive. Each resort has its own

Mont-Sainte-Anne Facts

Summit elevation: 2,625 feet
Vertical drop: 2,050 feet
Base elevation: 575 feet

Address: 2000, Beau Pre
Beaupre (Quebec) Canada G0A 1E0
Ski area phone: 418-827-4561
Snow report: 888-827-4579; 418-827-4579
Fax: 418-827-3121
Toll-free reservations: 800-463-1568
E-mail: info@mont-sainte-anne.com
Internet: www.mont-sainte-anne.com

Number and types of lifts: 13—1 high-speed 8-passenger gondola, 2 high-speed quads, 1 quad, 1 triple, 2 doubles, 6 surface
Skiable acreage: 450 acres
Snowmaking: 80 percent
Uphill capacity: 18,560
Parks and pipes: 1 park, 1 learning park
Bed base: 2,000
Nearest lodging: Slopeside
Resort child care: Yes, 6 months and older
Adult ticket, per day: C$57 (07/08 without tax)
Expert: ★★★★
Advanced: ★★★★
Intermediate: ★★★★★
Beginner: ★★★
First-timer: ★★★★

nearby lodging, though without the big-city activities. Visitors staying in downtown hotels can use the shuttle buses, which provide round-trip service to Mont-Sainte-Anne and Stoneham. The on-call Winter Express shuttle also goes to the mountains for just a few dollars more.

Mont-Sainte-Anne

Drive east along the St. Lawrence and you'll soon reach Mont-Sainte-Anne. With 2,050 feet of vertical, it's impressive, big-mountain skiing with a lift system to match. Trails drop from summit to base at a near-constant pitch with only a short runout to the lift. Trail ratings aren't inflated here and experts won't get bored; eight of the mountain's trails are true double diamonds, some with challenging bumps and/or glades and 10 are FIS-approved race trails. But this isn't to say beginners and intermediates won't have fun. There are plenty of wide cruising runs and gentle beginner trails spread across the mountain's three faces. All that and an excellent terrain park make it a good choice for all ability levels. In general, the slopes increase in difficulty as you move from east to west.

The South Side faces the St. Lawrence River, where all base facilities are located. It also bakes under the sun, so the snow is often heavier here. The North Side, or the backside, has a high-speed quad and a small lodge. The West Side is dedicated to backcountry skiing and riding on natural snow.

Mont-Sainte-Anne's riverside location delivers plenty of snow, an average of 160 inches a year. When the wind whips up the river, though, it's a bone-chilling and damp cold, so go prepared.

This resort lets you get a good taste of winter Quebecois-style. Don't miss the sugarhouse on the La Pichard trail, where you can taste real maple sugar on snow. You can try paragliding, ice skating, snowshoeing or dogsledding, all served with a French accent. Mont-Sainte-Anne's cross-country center is the largest in Canada and second largest in North America.

Mountain layout–skiing & snowboarding

♦♦**Expert** ♦**Advanced**: West of the gondola on the South Face is an expert's playground, with serious single- and double-black trails and glades. This is steep terrain with a continuous fall line. La Super S is long and smooth and steep; its evil twin, La S, is the same but with bumps. For even more challenge, head into the woods on La Brunelle or try La Triumph in the Black Forest glade. Two lifts—La Trip and La Sainte-Paix—service this area, but it's faster to shoot to the base and take the gondola. The Beast, new in 07/08, is a short double-black run boasting a 65-degree pitch. For a backcountry experience, head to the West Side.

On the South Side, take La Crete to La Beauregard for a long, steep, fast cruise. These are two of the 10 FIS-certified race trails on the mountain. La Pionniere, just east of the gondola, has the feel of an old-style New England trail as it twists its way down the upper third of the mountain. On the North Side, L'Archipel and La Surprenante are good choices. To escape the crowds, take L'Amarok on the West Side, served only by a T-bar. If your passion is bumps, work those knees on La Gondoleuse under the L'Etoile-Filante gondola. For a backcountry experience, head to the West Side.

■ **Intermediate**: While experts and advanced skiers head west off the gondola, interme-diates should head east (on the South Side), or over the top to the North Side. Warm up on Le Gros Vallon or La Beaupre on the South Side. Be sure to take at least one run on La Pichard to stop by the sugar shack for a maple-syrup treat. On cold days, ride either the gondola, L'Etoile-Filante, or L'Express du Sud, a high-speed quad with a bubble cover to shield the wind. Don't miss the North Side's great cruising trails and the intermediate-level glades, La Vital-Roy and La Sidney-Dawes. The snow is often softer here.

●● **Beginner** ● **First-timer**: The eastern edge of the mountain on both the South and the North sides is where you'll find the easiest trails. Take the gondola up, then work your way down La Familale on the South Side, L'Escapade and La Ferreolaise on the North Side, then return to the South Side on Le Chemin Du Roy, which wraps slowly and gently from the North Side summit to the South Side base. La Foret Enchantee, off La Ferrelolaise, has enjoyable beginner trails through the trees. Choose from three free surface lifts in the ski school area at the mountain's base. After mastering these, take the gondola to the summit and meander down the mountain's longest trail, Le Chemin du Roy.

Parks and Pipes

Mont-Sainte-Anne's 282,500-square-foot, mountain-top terrain park, La Grande Allee, is perfectly situated under the La Tortue quad chair on the South Side. This is a fun park, with numerous jumps of varying types and difficulty, a few rails and a fun box. It's best to check the jumps before hitting them full speed; they are not what they first appear. The park has a fairly mellow pitch, so you'll want to maintain speed; expect to skip some hits if you fall, as you'll need time to build speed again. The park is open at night. A learning park is nearby.

Cross-country & snowshoeing (see also xcskiresorts.com)

Superlatives are all one hears for the **Mont-Sainte-Anne Cross-Country Centre**, located 7 km. from the downhill area. With 224 km. of trails through the Laurentian forest, this center is the largest in Canada, second only to California's Royal Gorge in North America, and not to be missed just for the *joie de ski* Canadians exude on cross-country trails.

The Mont-Sainte-Anne Cross-Country Centre has plenty of trails for all abilities. A choice of varying length trail loops makes it easy to adjust your outing to your ability and stamina. Skating skiers will find a whopping 135 km. of groomed trails.

The area's base lodge has an extensive ski school, a small cafeteria, a waxing room and a cross-country boutique with rentals, which include a baby glider to pull along your youngster, if you choose not to leave him or her at the Alpine area day care.

A day trip for the not-faint-of-heart is the trek along the powerline (Sentier du Versant Nord) to the base of the north side of Mont-Sainte-Anne Alpine area. Though it's about a 7 km. trek, *all uphill*, the reward is the superb scenery along the way and a nice lunch at the Chalet du Versant Nord. And then there's skiing downhill all the way back to the base lodge.

Mont-Sainte-Anne also has 55.9 km. of snowshoeing trails. Try the guided tours with a Swiss fondue dinner at the Summit Lodge, on Wednesday and Saturday nights.

Lodging at the cross-country area includes the unique **B&B, L'Auberge du Fondeur** (418-827-5281; 800-463-1568) right on the trails, or the Ruisseau Rouge and Le Chaudron shelters along the trails. These rustic shelters can each accommodate up to eight skiers and are equipped with a woodstove so skiers can cook their own meals. Reservations are required (418-827-4561, ext. 408), but there is no charge for their use with purchase of a two-day or more ski pass.

You can also cross-country ski and snowshoe in nearby Québec City.

Lessons (07/08 prices, without tax)

Group lessons: A 2.25-hour session is C$53 (mornings only). During holiday and school break periods, only Adult Ski Week is available at C$179 for four mornings (must pre-register seven days in advance). Ski Week includes lessons, fun races, video, cocktail parties and other activities.

First-timer package: Iniski and Inisurf is a three-step beginner program, with each lesson lasting two hours. Initiation is C$59 and includes equipment for the day and access to beginner slopes. Practice is a second lesson in the beginner area and costs C$59 with rentals. Discovery is C$85 and includes rentals and a full-mountain lift pass.

Private lessons: One person for two morning hours is C$120. First Tracks one-hour private clinics, offered for intermediate and advanced levels, cost C$66 for one or two people, and include access to the lift 15 minutes before it officially opens. Last Tracks one-hour private clinics are available after 3 p.m. for C$66 for one or two people. A Pro for the Day costs C$320 for up to three students. An afternoon semi-private is C$107 for two hours.

Children's Programs (07/08 prices, without tax)

Child care: Mont-Sainte-Anne's award-winning Children's Centre takes children ages 6 months to 14 years. It houses a nursery, day care, ski and snowboard lessons, Kinderski program, equipment rental, a trail reserved exclusively for children, indoor and outdoor playgrounds and a video and music hall. The fee is C$49 per day for the first child in a family (the cost decreases for each additional child from the same family). Hourly rate is C$10. Meals are C$7.

Child care is wisely split into two sections: The day-care center for ages 2–10 and the nursery for babies ages 6–24 months. Day care in the nursery without skiing is available for children 7 months–6 years. Open 9 a.m. (8:30 on weekends) to 4:15 p.m., the Children's Centre is in the same building as the Ski & Snowboard School (note: It is a bit of a climb for a little one). There is at least one caretaker for every three babies, who have their own nap, play and feeding area. The nursery can accommodate up to 12 children daily.

Children's lessons: Ages 4–14 take a program from 9:30 a.m. to noon for C$59. Adventure Week is a four-day camp with lessons, fun races, videos, parties and other activities for C$315; pre-register seven days in advance. All instructors speak both French and English. Note: All prices are rounded up to the nearest dollar.

Lift tickets (07/08 prices, without tax)

Weekend prices	Adult	Young Adult (14-22)
One day	C$57	C$31.
Three days:	C$168	C$90.
Five days:	C$265	C$140.

Who skis free: Children age 6 and younger. Beginners ski on three lifts at no charge.

Who skis at a discount: Disabled skiers and riders. Night skiing costs C$27 for adults, $24 for teens and seniors, and $15 for children.

Note: Ticket prices have been rounded to nearest dollar.

Dual-Area Lift Ticket: The Carte Blanche is a multiday lift ticket valid at Mont-Sainte-Ann and Stoneham. It includes several perks, such as night skiing at Mont-Sainte-Anne and Stoneham. Adults pay C$168 for three days, C$265 for five days; ages 65+ pay C$138 for three days, C$220 for five days; ages 13-17 pay C$129 for three days, C$205 for five days; ages 7-12 pay C$90 for three days, C$140 for five days.

Accommodations at the resort

The full-service, ski-in/ski-out **Chateau Mont-Sainte-Anne** (800-463-4467; 418-827-5211; $–$$$), next to the gondola base, renovated its hotel in 2005/06.

Rooms are spacious and all have balconies and kitchenettes; loft suites also have fireplaces. You'll find a health club, indoor pool, hot tub and sauna, restaurants and lounges as well. The ChateauClub offers activities for families.

The family-friendly **Hotel Val-des-Neiges** (888-222-3305; 418-827-5711: $–$$) is five minutes from the base lodge (shuttles available to Le Massif) and has an indoor pool, whirlpool and sauna, lounge with deli menu, dining room and full-service spa. The hotel has whirlpool baths in most of its 200+ rooms. Suites with fireplaces and condos are also available.

For condominium lodging, try **Chalets Mont-Sainte-Anne** (800-463-4395; 418- 827-5776; $–$$), next to the Chateau; the ski-in/ski-out **Village Touristique Mont-Sainte-Anne** (800-463-7775; $–$$); the Swiss-style **Chalets Montmorency** (800-463-2612; $–$$), 800 yards from the lifts and with a free shuttle; or the stone Quebecois-style **Chalets Village** (800-461-2030; $–$$), each chalet with fireplace, double hot tub or sauna and multiple bedrooms and bathrooms. If you have need to house a large party, The Manor has 28 rooms.

Dining

Snowshoe from the top of the gondola to **La Crete Lodge** (418- 827-4561, ext. 0; $$$) for Swiss fondue on Wednesday and Saturday nights. Ride the gondola to the summit, then snowshoe to the lodge for a fondue dinner. It's a great family activity.

Auberge Boudreault (418-826-1333; $$–$$$) serves regional fine cuisine, fresh pastas, veal and game. **BeauRegard** (418-827-5211; $$$$) has won awards for its food and wine selection. **Le Brez** ($–$$) in the base village serves fondues and grill items.

In Beaupre: **L'Aventure** (418-827-5748; $–$$) is a lively bar and restaurant with an excellent view of the mountain. It serves an eclectic selection including Mexican and Italian favorites. The menu at **Le Resto-Pub St-Bernard** (418-827-6668; $–$$) lists steaks, pizzas and pastas. **Auberge La Camarine** (800-567-3939 or 418-827-1958; $$$) serves progressive French cuisine.

Auberge Baker, about 20 minutes toward Quebec City in Château-Richer (418-824-4478; 866-824-4478; $$$), serves country style and traditional Quebec cuisine like elk medallion with North Shore logenberry sauce, and a spectacular 7-course breakfast.

Apres-ski/nightlife

At Mont-Sainte-Anne, the place to head immediately after skiing is the **Chou-ette Bar**, in the main lodge at the base of the mountain. It has pool tables, music and dancing to a disc jockey. The **T-Bar** in Chateau Mont-Sainte-Anne is a good spot to stop later on for a relaxing drink in a more genteel atmosphere. On Wednesday through Saturday nights, entertainment is provided by a singer or musician.

Other activities

Mont-Sainte-Anne has a **skating rink** at the base. **Skating, dogsledding, paragliding and sleigh rides** can be arranged at the area. **Snowmobiling** is available nearby. For information on all, call 418-827-4561.

The Charlevoix region has deep roots in its Catholic religious heritage. In every parish you can visit the church of each village, but don't miss a trip to the spectacular **Basilica Sainte-Anne-de-Beaupre** (418-827-3781) on your route between Quebec City and Mont-Sainte-Anne. It's one of 20 pilgrimage shrines in Quebec. The original burned to the ground in 1927. This replacement is magnificent, immense and there's a fair touch of whimsy in the floor tiles depicting the seven deadly sins.

Getting there

Take Rte. 138 from Quebec City to St.-Anne-de-Beaupre, then Rte. 360 to the resort.

Stoneham

Stoneham is just 20 minutes north of Québec City. As you near Stoneham, don't be fooled. The resort is much larger than the few trails you see directly ahead. Thirty-two trails stretch across three mountains. The emphasis here is not on how big the vertical drops are (they range from 1,140 to 1,380 feet), but on how much terrain the connected mountains deliver. Stoneham has terrain from double-diamond glades to leisurely cruisers. Advanced skiers on multiday vacations will soon want to escape to Mont-Sainte-Anne or Le Massif. Kids will find a lot of activities to keep them occupied. And terrain park addicts will have met their match.

Situated in a sun-filled, wind-protected horseshoe valley, Stoneham attracts locals when the temperatures drop or the wind howls. The emphasis here is on having fun, whether on the slopes or in the restaurants and bars. Don't let the very English sounding name of the mountain mislead you; Stoneham is *tres* French; many patrons speak only French (but, most mountain personnel are bilingual). But that's good news, because as one Stoneham regular puts it, "The French know about food and they know about fun."

Sixty percent of the mountain, including a halfpipe, is lit for night skiing. With its party reputation, nighttime skiing/post-ski refreshments here is a Quebec City region must.

Accommodations (Cdn$): (double room) $$$$-$200+; $$$-$141-$200; $$-$81-$140; $-$80 and less.
Dining (Cdn$): $$$-Entrees $20+; $$-$10-20; $-less than $10

Stoneham Facts

Summit elevation: 2,075 feet
Vertical drop: 1,380 feet
Base elevation: 695 feet
Address: 1420, Chemin du Hibou, Stoneham, PQ, Canada G0A 4P0
Ski area phone: 418-848-2411
Snow report: 418-848-2415
Toll-free reservations: 800-463-6888
Fax: 418-848-1133
Internet: www.ski-stoneham.com
Expert: ★
Advanced: ★
Intermediate: ★★★★
Beginner: ★★★★
First-timer: ★★★★

Number and types of lifts: 8–1 high-speed quad, 2 quads, 1 double, 3 surface lifts, 1 moving carpet
Skiable acreage: 326 (daytime); 184 (nighttime)
Snowmaking: 86 percent
Uphill capacity: 14,200 per hour
Parks and pipes: 4 parks, 1 superpipe
Bed base: 500 at base; 10,000 in Quebec City, 20 minutes away
Nearest lodging: Slopeside
Resort child care: Yes, 1 month and up
Adult ticket, per day: C$49-$52 (08/09 prices, without tax)

Mountain layout – skiing and snowboarding

♦♦**Expert** ♦**Advanced:** Experts will want to head straight for Peak Four. Little grooming is done here and the trails are steep, skinny and bumped. Well-named trails Le Zipper, Le Kamikaza and Le Monstre are legitimate double blacks. They are left *au natural*, so you want to be on the look out for stumps, rocks, cliffs and other such obstructions in lean snow years.

Stoneham is primarily a family mountain and even double-black-diamond trails La Panoramique and La Bomba, though steep, are maneuverable for upper-intermediate skiers. If you like glades, head for La Sapinere.

■ **Intermediate:** The entire mountain is an intermediate's playground. Even the bump runs, glades and, as mentioned earlier, the groomed double-black-diamond trails should be tried and enjoyed. Undulating terrain and wide-open trails call for lots of top-to-bottom giant-slalom runs. For challenging fun, try La Chute and Bossanova. Both are long with steep pitches that mellow then drop again for little adrenaline rushes.

●● **Beginner** ● **First-timer:** Although considered a family mountain, Stoneham is surprisingly lean on true beginner terrain. Peaks One and Two have a couple of top-to-bottom green-circle trails (La Randonnee off Peak 1; La Laurentienne off peak 2), but even these have places that may challenge real beginners. The wide-open area served by a quad and two Poma lifts right in front of the main base lodge is a comfortable place for beginners and first-timers.

Parks and pipes

Our riders loved Stoneham which has some of the best terrain features we've seen in the East. It boasts a huge, well maintained superpipe as well as numerous terrain parks. A beginner's terrain park, with super-easy rails and jumps, is on the edge of Les Cantons. For more advanced features, cut over to La Traverse and head down Les Merisiers to La Fabuleuse. For continuous fun, just do laps on the A quad and the superpipe, with 17-foot walls. A Kokanee bus is buried in the park. There's also a mile-long boardercross course on La Rock-n-Roll.

Even adults have fun in Casimir's Enchanted Journey, a children's terrain park with large wooden animal and character cut-outs in the trees off Le Petit Champlain. Sous Bois is a natural terrain park. This wide, long glade is full of little hits, chutes through the trees, rolling turns and a few gentle moguls.

Lessons (07/08 prices, without tax)

All lessons are by reservation only, call 418-848-2415, ext. 537.

Group lessons: The Head Tyrolia Snow Sports Academy provides focused sessions for intermediate and expert skiers 19 and older. Two-hour morning sessions are offered on Monday, Friday, Saturday and Sunday for C$41. The "As the Bell Tolls" program is a 1-hour session with a pro for experts on weekends; cost is C$23.

First-timer package: A private one-hour lesson with equipment rental and lift ticket is C$79 for skiers and snowboarders. A 1.5-hour group lesson is C$45 for skiers (C$35 for a night lesson), C$52 for snowboarders (C$36 for a night lesson). Intro lessons for snowblades are also available.

Private lessons: C$59 for one hour for one person, plus C$29 for each additional person; C$75 plus C$35 for a two-hour lesson; C$109 plus C$50 for a three-hour series; C$199 plus C$69 for a five-hour series.

Children's Programs (07/08 prices, without tax)

Child care: Ages 1 month–12 years. 19 months and older pay C$29 with lunch; 1-18 months, C$37. Second child from the same family costs C$22. The hourly rate is C$11 for infants 18 months and younger; C$8 for those older than 18 months.

Day care has bilingual caregivers, but most of the children on any given day speak only French. Open from 8:30 a.m.–5 p.m. (9 a.m. on weekdays), the center is just a few steps from the main base lodge, but the walk to the actual skiing can be a bit of a trek for little ones. It has a large game room and separate sleeping and eating rooms, as well as a nifty adjacent outdoor playground. For those with young children, the day-care center will arrange babysitting if you call ahead. Reservations are recommended.

Children's lessons: Kidz Island has programs designed for children ages 3–6. A full-day (8:30 a.m.–5 p.m.; beginning at 9 a.m. weekdays) with a four-hour lesson, rentals, two snacks, lunch and day care is C$58. An afternoon program costs C$47. Multiday rates are available. For children just starting out, the ratio is four to six children per instructor.

The Adventure Package is a five-hour program (10 am.–3 p.m.) for ages 7–17 that includes lessons and lunch for C$59 (C$73 with lift ticket). Three consecutive days costs C$159 (C$201 with lift ticket) and five consecutive days is C$249 (C$319 with lift ticket). Discounted rentals available. Limited to eight students per group.

Note: Prices rounded up to the nearest dollar.

Lift tickets (08/09 prices, without tax)

Weekend prices	Adult	Teen (13-17)	Senior 65+	Child (7-12)
One day	C$49	C$37	C$40	C$22
Three days	C$144	C$108	C$117	C$63
Night	C$28	C$25	C$25	C$16

Note: Holiday prices are higher. Because of night skiing, Stoneham offers a variety of tickets including the longer day ticket (9 a.m. to 6 p.m.), a day-to-evening ticket (12:30 p.m. to closing), a half day ticket (12:30 to 4:30) and an evening ticket (3 p.m. to closing). Consecutive multiday tickets include night skiing and may be bought to seven days.

Who skis free: Children ages 6 and younger.

Accommodations at or near the resort

The practical **Hotel Stoneham** ($–$$) is an anchor in the ski area's mini-village with 60 spacious rooms where children younger than age 18 stay for free when sharing a room with their parents. The ski area also rents out about 100 condos through Condominiums Stoneham; the **Condo du Village** are most convenient. These vary in size from studios to four bedrooms and are at the base of the slopes. Attractive ski-and-stay packages are available. For reservations, call (800) 463-6888 or 848-2411.

Le Manoir du Lac Delage (866-222-3810; 848-2551; $–$$) is 10 minutes from the slopes, yet feels a world away. It's a meticulously appointed country inn, with an excellent dining room overlooking the lake, a full spa and an indoor pool. A Ski Stoneham package is available.

The best alternative to slopeside is in Québec City, although the nearby town of Ste-Foy (25-30 minutes away) offers a **Holiday Inn** (800-463-5241; 418-653-4901), a **Comfort Inn** (800-463-5241; 418-653-4901) the **Hotel Plaza** (800-463-5777; 418-658-2727), **Hotel Québec** (800-463-5777; 418-658-5120), and **Hotel Universel** (800-463-4495; 418-653-5250).

Dining

The tiny outpost lodge at the base of Peak Four has crepes, soup and sandwiches. Lunch and light snacks are also available in **Le Bar Le 4 Foyers** (the bar of the four fireplaces) in the base lodge. **Le Pub Totof's** ($-$$) serves delicious smoked-meat sandwiches in an English pub atmosphere. The **Feu Follet** ($$), attached to the base lodge, is open for breakfast, lunch and dinner. Retreat to **Le Gourmet Champetre** (418-848-2551; $$$) at the Le Manoir du Lac Dulage for fine dining overlooking the lake. A four-course table d'hote is $32.95. **L'Incontournable** ($-$$), also at Le Manoir, is a bar with fireplace, TV and pool table. It serves a light menu. See Québec City dining for some of the best dining choices.

Apres-ski/nightlife

Because the base area is so small, it may be hard to believe that the Quebecois leave Quebec City and head here to have fun, but that's what they do. **Le Bar Le 4 Foyers**, a funky Irish pub, brings in a wide range of musical performers, including the requisite rock bands and a disco night on Thursdays. It serves basic pub fare and screens nonstop snowboard flicks on the TV. There's also a pool table in the back room. **Le Pub Totof's**, on the other end of the village (a three-minute walk), offers a little more mellow fare, with folk and oldies plus a wide selection of beers. Skiers will find that even with a language barrier—many of Stoneham's regular skiers speak no English—apres-ski conviviality prevails, and trying to make your French understood, especially after a few drinks, is actually fun.

Other activities

Stoneham has **ice skating** as well as an **indoor climbing wall**. For **snowmobiling**, go to Lac Beauport to Nord Tour (841-2810) for rentals.

The **Spa Le Manoir du Lac Delage** (800-463-2841 or 848-0691) offers body care, massages, skin care, facials, back treatments and programs for hands and feet. Massages are C$40 for 30 minutes, C$65 for 60 minutes and C$85 for 90 minutes. Indulge yourself with a Leisure Package including a health assessment; use of the indoor pool, sauna and whirlpool; relaxation massage; fresh juice or herb tea; therapeutic bath; and pressure therapy for C$90. A four-hour package adds a body wrap and facial to the mix for C$150. After your treatment, splurge on dinner here. Stonham's mini-village has two small **stores**: Boutique Sports Alpins offers gifts and interesting ski items, and La Shop is for snowboarders.

Getting there and getting around

Stoneham is 20 minutes from Quebec City via Rte. 73 North. Take the Stoneham exit.

Le Massif

Perched on the edge of the St. Lawrence River, Le Massif is one of eastern Canada's great secrets, but not for long. Once accessible only by school bus, Le Massif has transformed itself into one of eastern Canada's most eco-friendly resorts. With the addition of a second high-speed quad, 16 new trails, a new chalet and access road at the summit, Le Massif has become the site of Canada's national training center for downhill and Super G. And the changes keep coming. The new owner Daniel Gauthier has invested C$5 million in a new high-speed quad, new intermediate and advanced trails and glades and increased snowmaking capacity.

The spectacular summit lodge takes advantage of the endless St. Lawrence views. And the trails appear to just plunge 2,500 feet directly down into the ice-choked St. Lawrence, referred to as the sea, given its greater than 10-mile width here. As you descend La Petite-Riviere, a classic first-run trail, a fishing trawler or cargo ship might pass silently right beneath you. Little wonder that Le Massif and its surroundings are within a UNESCO World Biosphere Reserve. Le Massif's owners have honored this beauty by developing the area in harmony with nature. The lifts are, for the most part, hidden in the trees and the trails follow the natural fall lines of the three connected mountains. Le Massif has Canada's highest vertical drop east of the Canadian Rockies.

When you visit, don't pack a lunch. The cafeteria food here is among the best and the most reasonably priced we've seen. On a recent visit, we had escargot over angel-hair pasta, Charlevoix sausage with fresh local cheeses and samplings of Charlevoix-region gourmet products—all worth every cent. Two pubs, one at the summit, the other at the base, serve a good selection of beers and wines. In keeping with a fitness-minded clientele concerned aboout proper eating habits, all high sugar-content beverages have been eliminated from the ski area's food services.

The farther east you head from Quebec City, the less English you hear, but even that's changing as more locals adapt to English-speaking visitors. Still, a little bit of patience goes a long way. If you meet French-only locals at some of the inns and restaurants, don't let any language barrier deter you. The Charlevoix Region will likely steal your heart.

Mountain layout

◆◆**Expert** ◆**Advanced:** Off the La Maillard Express Chair, the trails drop with sustained pitch and quickly accelerate you to rocket speed toward the river. La "42," an ungroomed, natural-snow trail, snakes its way down the eastern edge of the mountain. It's punctuated with bumps, stumps, narrow chutes and steep drops, clinched with

Accommodations (Cdn$): (double room) $$$$-$200+; $$$-$141-$200; $$-$81-$140; $-$80 and less.
Dining (Cdn$): $$$-Entrees $20+; $$-$10-20; $-less than $10

Le Massif facts
Summit elevation: 2,645 feet
Vertical drop: 2,526 feet
Base elevation: 118 feet
Expert: ★★★**Advanced:** ★★★★
Intermediate: ★★★
Beginner: ★★ **First-timer:** ★
Address: 1350 Rue Principale, C.P. 47, Petite-Riviere-Saint-Francois, Quebec, Canada G0A 2L0
Ski area phone:418-632-5876; 877-536-2774
Snow report: 418-632-5876; 877- 536-2774
Toll-free reservations: 866-435-4160

E-mail: info@lemassif.com
Internet: www.lemassif.com
Number and types of lifts: 5—3 high-speed quads, 2 surface lifts
Skiable acreage: 410 acres
Snowmaking: 48 percent
Uphill capacity: 8,700 per hour
Parks & pipes: 1 terrain park
Bed base: 1,000
Nearest lodging: One-half mile
Resort child care: Yes, 2 years and older
Adult ticket, per day: $59 (08/09 without tax)

---

the area's trademark jaw-dropping St. Lawrence views. L'Artimon is one steep tree trail. For a short, steep thrill, take the plunge on La Pointue. The double-black Le Charlevoix is the FIS-rated race training trail. From the Campe-Boule chair, La Tremblay can be challenging since it's rarely groomed. La Dominque Malais is a cool glade and La Fortin bumps up nicely.

■ **Intermediate**: With nary a bump in sight, this mountain is nirvana for cruisers. The black diamond and blue square designations seem almost arbitrary. Three-fourths of the runs are meticulously groomed and only occasional steep pitches give pause to an intermediate skier. The runs are long (2.36 miles, the longest) so rest stops allow for spectacular views of the ice-capped St. Lawrence. Concentrate your efforts on Le Grande-Pointe Express quad chair for the best vertical and choice. La Petite-Riviere, a blue, is a sweet way to launch your day with spectacular drop-dead views of the river.

●● **Beginner** ● **First-timer:** Stick to the beginner trails off the Camp-Boule Express chair in the Camp-Boule sector. The leap from first-timer to intermediate is better than before thanks to new beginner trails that go all the way to the lift. First-timers have a rope tow just below the summit day lodge.

Snowboarding
Early in the season, the traverse to the Le Maillard high-speed quad is a miserable hike. Instead, ride down La Richard or L'Archipel to get to the Maillard Express mid-station.

Parks and pipes
A big-air park is in the area served by the Camp Boule Express. There is no halfpipe.

 ## Cross-country & snowshoeing (see also xcskiresorts.com)
Le Sentier des Caps is developing a 65-km. cross-country network at the top of the ridge, about a mile behind the new ski lodge with a base on the access road from Quebec City. Near Malbaie, 160 km. of cross-country and snowshoeing possibilities are extensive and well developed in the **Parc Regional du Mont Grand-Fonds**. Trails for every level loop around lakes and past four chalets where skiers can rest and imbibe. Canada's largest cross-country center is at nearby Mont-Sainte-Anne.

www.skisnowboard.com

Lessons (07/08 prices, without taxes)

Group lessons: Le Massif offers only private and semi-private lessons.
Private lessons: A one-hour private lesson costs C$57 for one person; C$46 per person for two people. Two hours cost C$99 for one person; C$75 per person for two people. A private first-timer lesson costs C$99 for one person for 2 hours; C$88 per person for two people for 2 hours.

Special programs: The ski school also offers a "ski clinic of the day," in which specialized lessons are offered that fit the day's conditions

Children's Programs (07/08 prices, without taxes)

Child care: Le Massif has a day-care center at its mountaintop lodge. It comprises one large room and can handle 21 children. Comfortable furniture is set about with a crib area cordoned off by curtains. Equipment rental is across the hall. Day care is available for ages 2–10 years. The full-day program with lunch runs from 8:30 a.m.–4:30 p.m. and costs C$35; half-day (8:30 a.m.–12:30 p.m., or 12:30 p.m.–4:30 p.m.) is C$28. Hourly day care is available for C$10; a separate lunch can be bought for C$7. Reservations are required; call 418-632-5876 or 877-536-2774.

Children's lessons: A one-hour semi-private lesson can be added to the day-care program—a package program costs $71. The resort has a beginner area that's convenient to the children's room. Kid's Camp, a group program for ages 7–16, is C$61. All include lesson, lift ticket and equipment rental for the day; program runs from 10 a.m. to 3 p.m. Half-day program also available for C$45; starts at 10 a.m. or 1 p.m. Discounts for multiple days.

Lift tickets (07/08 prices, without tax)

Weekend prices	Adult	Young adult (18-23)	Senior 65+	Junior (7-17)
One day	C$55	C$43	C$40	C$31
Two days	C$104	C$82	C$80	C$59
Three days	C$153	C$120	C$120	C$87

Who skis free: Children ages 6 and younger.
Note: Weekdays, ages 55+ pay senior rates. Rates are rounded up to the nearest dollar.

Accommodations near the resort

Le Massif offers skiing packages at B&Bs, inns and motels, as well as chalets and villas in nearby towns; most include dinner for guests and are also open to the public for dinner. Baie-Saint-Paul is the largest town and offers the best variety of dining, lodging and nightlife. For regional information, call 800-667-2276. **Maison Otis** (800-267-2254; 418-435-2255; $$–$$$) pampers guests with one of the region's best dining rooms, a full-service spa, a cozy lounge, a lively cafe and even a discoteque. It also has an indoor pool, saunas and whirlpool tub. Rooms vary greatly, from cozy to sprawling; some have fireplaces and hot tubs. Rates include a choice-of-menu breakfast and a four-course dinner. **Auberge La Grande Maison** (800-361-5575; 435-5575; $–$$) is housed in a charming turn-of-the-century Victorian. Its health center/spa has therapeutic bath treatments. **Auberge La Pignoronde** (888-554-6004; 418-435-5505; $–$$) overlooks the town and bay and is some of the closest lodging to Le Massif. It's a good choice for families. It has a good restaurant, with a variety of meal plans available, and an indoor pool. **Hotel Baie-Saint-Paul** (800-650-3683; 418-435-3683; $) has spacious, although basic, rooms, an indoor pool and a restaurant.

La Malbaie, 45 minutes east of Le Massif, has an excellent selection of chic lodging as

Accommodations (Cdn$): (double room) $$$$-$200+; $$$-$141-$200; $$-$81-$140; $-$80 and less.
Dining (Cdn$): $$$-Entrees $20+; $$-$10-20; $-less than $10

well as a small ski area, Le Grand Fonds. The grandest lodging is at **Le Manoir Richelieu** (800-257-7544; 418-665-3703; $$–$$$), a four-star, five-diamond Fairmont resort with all the expected amenities, plus a casino, indoor and outdoor pools and full spa. Other on-site activities include cross-country, snowmobile and snowshoe trails, a skating rink, sleigh rides and dogsledding. Many rooms have magnificent St. Lawrence Riverviews.

Auberge des 3 Canards (800-461-3761; 418-665-3761; $$$–$$$$) is just down the hill from the Manoir Richelieu. All rooms have spectacular views to the river and its acclaimed dining, prepared by long-time Chef Eric Betrand from Strasbourg, France, has won numerous awards. Deluxe rooms come with jetted tub for two and a fireplace. **L'Auberge des Peupliers** (888-282-3743; 418-665-4423; $$$–$$$$) sits high atop a hill overlooking the St. Lawrence River and is one of the oldest guesthouses in the region. Rooms are a pleasant mix of antique and rustic, but include all the modern amenities you're accustomed to. Sauna and indoor jetted tub, plus spa services are available upon request. Breakfast and a five-course regional dinner prepared by a renowned chef are included.

One of the best reasons to visit Canada in the winter is to get low-season rates at high-end resorts. One such place is the Relais & Chateaux property **La Pinsonniere** (800-387-4431; 418-665-4431; $$–$$$$), a country inn hugging the shore in La Malbaie. Impeccable service, fine cuisine and a flair for romance define its character. An impressive collection of regional artists' masterpieces hangs on the walls throughout the inn.

Dining

Auberge La Maison Otis (800-267-2254; 418-435-2255; $$$$) has one of the region's best dining rooms, serving a four-course dinner that blends Charlevoix regional produce and French inspiration. **Auberge La Pignoronde** (888-554-6004; 418-435-5505; $$$;) also has a fine four-course dinner featuring regional produce. The menu changes nightly. **Resaurant Au 51** (418-435-6469; $$–$$$) serves excellent French dishes with local flair and a delicious cheese cake dessert made with local migneron cheese. **Restaurant Le Marion Grill** (418-435-5575; $$$), located in the Auberge La Grande Maison, offers beautifully prepared Charlevoix cuisine in a white table cloth ambience, using regional ingredients whenever possible. **Le Saint-Pub Microbrasserie Charlevoix** (418-240-2332; $–$$) brews its own beers and serves pasta and seafood. Enjoy lunch at surprising **Joe's Deli Bar Smoked Meat** ($) where the sandwiches are massive and tasty (and Joe is friendly and speaks English). **Vice Café** (418-435-0006; $) is a combination creperie and Internet café, serving crepes and sandwiches with live music on Friday evenings.

If you're willing to drive a bit, La Malbaie, an hour east of Le Massif and 45 minutes from Baie-Saint-Paul, has an excellent selection of fine dining. **Le Manoir Richelieu** (800-257-7544; 418-665-3703; $$$$) has several restaurants. Fresh regional cuisine is the highlight of Le Charlevoix, the fine dining room, which also showcases antiques and local art created exclusively for the restaurant. Views of the St. Lawrence River are splendid.

Auberge des 3 Canards (800-461-3761; 418-665-3761; $$$$) rivals the Manoir Richelieu with its acclaimed dining. Prepared by renowned Chef Mario Chabot, the multi-course dinners here have won numerous awards. **L'Auberge des Peupliers** (888-282-3743; 418-665-4423; $$$–$$$$) serves five-course gourmet regional dinners by renowned chef, Dominique Truchon. **La Pinsonnière** (800-387-4431; 418-665-4431; $$$$), a charming country inn hugging the shore in La Malbaie, also serves an exquisite five-course dinner, accompanied by libations from the12,000-bottle wine cellar of mostly French wines.

See Québec City dining for more dining choices.

Other activities

The Charlevoix region abounds with outdoor activities. **Snowmobiling** is extremely popular here as is **dogsledding**. Your hotel should be able to make arrangements. The Fairmont Manoir Richelieu has a **casino.**

The **Centre Sante Beaute Francine Thibeault**, in Baie-Saint-Paul (418-435-6028), offers a full range of **spa and salon services.** Among the services at the **Amerispa** (800-699-7352; 418-665-2600) at the Fairmont Manoir Richelieu, are Vichy shower massage, body wraps and back treatment. Massage begins at C$95. Be forewarned, not a lot of English spoken here.

Take a **scenic drive** along the St. Lawrence River from Pointe-au-Pic to Baie-Saint-Paul, through St. Irenee, known for the famous music academy Le Domaine Forget, and its river beaches. A spectacular descent brings you to the tiny 200-person town of Saint-Joseph-de-la-Rive, where a free ferry plies the route to Isle-aux-Coudres. Try the pastries at Boulangerie Laurentide, visit the Maritime Museum and see handcrafted papermaking at Papeterie Saint-Gilles. In Baie Saint-Paul, stop at the La Laiterie Charlevoix (418-435-2184) and La Maison D'Affinage Maurice Dufour (418-435-5692), where you can see **cheesemaking** in process and purchase fresh cheese. A must-stop for chocoholics is the Chocolaterie Cynthia, on rue St. Jean-Baptiste (418-240-2304).

The Charlevoix region's scenery and intriguing light attracts many important painters. Dozens of **art galleries** dot the entire route from La Malbaie. Baie-Saint-Paul has 20 galleries, although not all are open in winter. Many artists are represented at Galerie d'Art Iris, 30 rue St. Jean-Baptiste. La Maison de Rene Richard is worth a visit to see the development of one of Canada's most renowned artists. Le Centre d'Art has changing exhibits. Guy Pacquet often opens his home studio to visitors; the views are breathtaking, the artwork spectacular.

Getting there

Le Massif is 45 miles east of Quebec City on Rte. 138. A free shuttle from Baie-Saint-Paul daily at 8 a.m. weekends, 8:30 weekdays; return, 3:45 p.m.

Accommodations—Quebec City

Fairmont Le Chateau Frontenac (800-441-1414; 418-692-3861; $$–$$$$), perched on the edge of the Cap Diamant promontory in Old Quebec's upper town, is the grande dame of Quebec City. It is historic, formal, elegant and full-service. Rooms vary greatly, from small to spacious, some offering magnificent views of the St. Lawrence. Most packages here include the hotel's bountiful buffet breakfast, enough to fuel you through most of the day. The hotel has a health club with indoor pool and a full-service spa. Also full service are the **Quebec Hilton** (800-445-8667; 418-647-2411; $$–$$$$), and **Hotel Loews Le Concorde** (800-235-6397; 647-2222; $$–$$$$), both in old Quebec, but outside the city walls.

Some of the top hotels in town are termed boutique hotels. The following five, all in the Vieux-Port area, are among the city's best places to stay.

Hotel Dominion 1912 (418-692-2224; $$–$$$), perhaps the best of the lot, is ultra-modern yet hidden in an old factory. Glass showers and sinks highlight the bathrooms and the beds are covered with mounds of down. The spacious rooms have Bose Wave Radios and 27-inch TVs. Breakfast is a non-stop continental affair. The intimate **Auberge Saint-Pierre** (888-268-1017; 418-694-7981; $–$$$) is a treat. Guest rooms range from the *petite economique* ones with barely enough room to set down a suitcase, to grand suites, with elaborate whirlpool tubs for

Accommodations (Cdn$): (double room) $$$$-$200+; $$$-$141-$200; $$-$81-$140; $-$80 and less.
Dining (Cdn$): $$$-Entrees $20+; $$-$10-20; $-less than $10

two. There's a nice bar and a quiet living room with fireplace.

The Auberge Saint-Antoine (888-692-2211; 418-692-2211; $–$$$) is a luxurious retreat in the heart of a lively, attractive, 18th-century neighborhood with museums, art galleries, antique shops, boutiques and restaurants. Rooms are spread out in 300-year-old buildings on an important archaeological site. Artfully displayed artifacts throughout the hotel provide a glimpse into the life of Quebec's first inhabitants. Some of the 95 rooms have St. Lawrence River views, others of Quebec's fortifications, and many have a terrace and/or fireplace.

Hotel Le Clos Saint-Louis (418-694-1311; $–$$) is a romantic 25-room hotel filled with period antiques. Rooms are spacious, each with private bath, and the hotel, built as a stately home in 1844, opens directly onto one of the old city's main streets. Hotel Le Priori (418-692-3992; $–$$) has small rooms but much larger suites.

Small hotels within the city walls: the Hotel Clarendon (888-554-6001; 418-692-2480), the Hotellerie Fleur-de-Lys (800-567-2106; 418-694-0106; $$–$$$) and the Manoir de l'Esplanade (694-0834). Hotel Acadia (800-463-0280; 418-694-0280; $–$$) serves a continental breakfast and also has packages with Mont-Sainte-Anne. The Hotel Manoir Victoria (800-463-6283; 692-1030; $–$$$), in the old city, is a good choice for families. Also popular with families is L'Hotel du Vieux-Quebec (800-361-7787; 692-1850; $–$$$). Auberge Louis-Hebert (418-525-7812; $), on the Grande Allee, the heart of Quebec City's nightlife, also has a good restaurant, and rates include breakfast. As is true of much of old Quebec, the comforts are modern within 17th-century walls. Small, affordable inns and bed & breakfasts near the Frontenac offer simple rooms, usually with breakfast. Try the Hotel Manoir de la Terrasse (418-694-1592; $), the Manoir Sainte-Genevieve (418-694-1666; $–$$) or the Chateau Bellevue (800-463-2716; 418-692-2573; $–$$)

Three hostels provide bottom-dollar lodging: Auberge International de Quebec (418-694-0755; $), a member of Hostelling International, has a cafeteria and 279 beds in various configurations, including private and family rooms; Auberge de la Paix (418-694-0735; $) has 14 rooms with two to eight beds, a kitchen and breakfast; or Association du YWCA de Quebec (418-683-2155; $) has shared bathrooms, swimming pool and self-service kitchen.

For something different, try a night at the Ice Hotel (www.icehotel-canada.com; $$$). Constructed and furnished completely of snow and ice, opens in January and closes when it melts. Sleeping bags are guaranteed to keep guests warm; it's like very fancy winter camping.

Dining—Quebec City

You have to work to get a bad meal in this city. Almost all restaurants post their menu outside the door, and most include a *Table d'hote*, or set menu, usually with appetizer, entree and dessert, for a fixed price.

For traditional Quebecois cooking like *grandmere* used to make—pea soup, onion soup, meat pies, fish and game dishes and for dessert, maple syrup pie—dine at Aux Anciens Canadiens (418-692-1627; $$$–$$$$). Five cozy dining rooms on two floors have been built in one of the oldest houses in the city, Maison Jacquet. The building was constructed between 1675-76 with thick stone walls, wainscoting and recessed cupboards. The lunch menu (normally less than C$15) is served from noon until 6 p.m., making for an affordable and hearty early supper for skiers returning from the slopes.

Next door, Restaurant Continental (418-694-9995; $$$–$$$$) prepares Quebec's only true upscale French cuisine with flambe tableside service. The other top spot in the upper old town is Le Saint-Amour (418-694-0667; $$$$). One of our favorite restaurants in Vieux-Quebec is Auberge du Tresor (418-694-1876; $$$) which serves mussels (*moules*) that were the best we've eaten this side of the Atlantic Ocean. **Au Parmesan** (418-692-0341; $$$), with an accordionist and lots of singing locals, serves homemade pasta. **Gambrinus** (418-692-5144; $$$), overlooking the Place d'Armes, is an excellent Italian restaurant with a French flair and good seafood. A strolling musician performs at night. At **47ieme Parallele Resto International** (418-692-1534; $$$), you'll find home-style European and exotic dish presentations.

There's no graffiti at **Graffiti**, (1191 Cartier Ave; 418-529-4949; $$$), but an eclectic array of art adorns the brick and warm wood walls. French and Italian cuisine make up the two menus—a la carte and table d'hote. Don't miss the apple tart with maple sauce. Brunch in the atrium room is a popular Sunday event. We're told this is one of the city's best.

Another good choice is **Initiale** (418-694-1818; $$$$) which serves fine French cuisine. **Laurie Raphael** (418-692-4555; $$) emphasizes fresh Quebecois-style cuisine. The more casual art deco **L'Echaude** (418-692-1299; $$$) serves a mix of traditional and nouvelle French cuisine. **Cafe du Monde** (418-692-4495; $$–$$$), with its bistro atmosphere and affordable wines, fills with locals each evening. **Piazzetta** (418-692-2962; $$), only steps away, is an inexpensive choice for creative focaccio and pizzas (we loved the apple-and-pork pizza).

Rue du Petit-Champlain has several good eateries. Stone walls and a fireplace create an intimate setting at **Marie-Clarisse** (418-692-0857; $$$$), at the base of the funicular and the bottom of the Breakneck Stairs. It serves excellent fish and seafood in two intimate dining rooms. **Cochon Dingue** ($$) offers a wide-ranging, bistro-style menu that's good for families and it serves excellent breakfasts. Kids younger than 10 pay C$5 for a complete meal. Three Cochon Dingue restaurants are at 46, boul. Champlain (692-2013); 46, Rene-Levesque O. (418-523-2013); and 1326, av. Maguire (418-684-2013). **Le Petit Cochon Dingue** (OK, Cochon Dingue means Crazy Pig; 418-694-0303) is a traditional pastry shop with a bakery, cafe and sandwich shop. The donuts are, well, old-fashioned, and you can't beat the raisin buns anywhere. **Le Lapin Saute** (418-692-5325; $$–$$$) is popular for breakfast, but avoid it for dinner.

In the old train station, **Gare du Palais**, **l'Aviatic Club** (418-522-3555; $$$–$$$$) looks like an officers' mess and serves specialty foods from five continents. Stay awhile and join the nightlife.

Along the Grande Allee, start the night with dinner at **Louis-Hebert** (418-525-7812; $$–$$$) and you'll be well situated to enjoy this street's hearty nightlife afterward. This is where the cognoscenti dine, such as the Members of Parliament and other creme de la creme. Allow a long evening for your dining experience and don't be afraid of asking for special plates. There is also a boutique hotel above the cookery. **Cosmos** (418-640-0606; $$), on the Grande Allee, is *the* place to see and be seen. It has a fantastic Quebecois menu at a reasonable price. It's a trendy bistro with a vast offering from around-the-world salads to great sandwiches, pastas, frites, poutine and a huge dessert menu.

Take in a view of the whole city from **L'Astral** (418-647-2222; $$–$$$$), the revolving restaurant atop Loews Le Concorde hotel. It takes about one hour for it to make a complete circle. A buffet is served Saturday night, and the Sunday brunch is in a class of its own. Reservations are a must. For a carbo feed, head to the **Place du Spaghetti** (418-694-9144).

For simple, Mediterranean-style fare, head to **Freres de la Cote** (418-692-5445; $$), a lively restaurant with an open kitchen and wood-burning ovens. The eclectic menu ranges from tenderloin horsemeat to sweetbread to European pizza to osso bucco. **Portofino Bistro Italiano** (418-692-8888; $–$$), in the center of Old Quebec, is a good choice for pizza. The Pizza Grizzly (with smoked salmon) is particularly tasty.

Accommodations (Cdn$): (double room) $$$$-$200+; $$$-$141-$200; $$-$81-$140; $-$80 and less.
Dining (Cdn$): $$$-Entrees $20+; $$-$10-20; $-less than $10

If you're a bit adventurous, visit a **sugar shack**: Follow signs for a *cabane a sucre*. Most open only when the sap is running. The fare usually includes crepes, eggs, meat pies, meats, toast, baked beans, all topped with maple syrup and flavored with music and dancing.

Apres-ski/nightlife—Quebec City

The **Grande Allée** is lined with bars and restaurants and is the number one choice for nightlife in the city. Next to the Lowes Le Concorde, at 575 Grande Allée, there is a complex of nightlife. The top floor has a lounge called **Charlotte**, the second floor is a disco called **Maurice**, the ground floor is a bar called **Cosmos**. They were all filled on the Friday night we visited. The bar at street level fills first, then Charlotte's Lounge starts up about 10 p.m. followed by Maurice around midnight. **The Clarendon Hotel** has good jazz music. **St. Jean Street** offers a number of bars with traditional French music including **La Playa** that serves 75 different martini drinks to accompany Mexican food (go figure). **Le Capitole** features a Las Vegas-style dinner show. Don't miss having a drink at the **Bar St-Laurent in Le Chateau Frontenac**. **Le Pape George** is a bistro with French singers. Down in the vieux-port district at 37 Quai Saint-André stop in at **L'Inox**, a large, smoky brew pub with pool tables and loud music that attracts a young crowd.

Other activities

Quebec City has so much to offer you could spend most of your ski vacation in the city without even venturing to the slopes. Here's a sampling.

On the Terrasse Dufferin there is a not-to-be-missed, exciting **toboggan** ride that is open most days from 11 a.m to 11 p.m. Cost is only C$2 per rider. You can **ice skate** for C$5 at a rink nearby. The **funicular** (418-692-1132) is the shortest link between Dufferin Terrace at the Chateau Frontenac and Quartier Petit Champlain. This landmark and unique transportation vehicle provides commanding views of the St. Lawrence River, well worth the small charge. It is wheelchair accessible. Take a **ferry ride** across the river for a spectacular perspective of the walled city. It leaves every half hour during the day and every hour at night (418-644-3704).

The frozen falls at **Montmorency Falls Park** (418-663-3330) are one-and-a-half times higher than Niagara Falls. **Cable cars, bridges lookouts and trails** make it possible to get close to the falls. For **ice climbing**, L'Ascensation (418-647-4422) rents equipment and provides guides. At Village Vacances Valcartier (418-844-2200), 20 minutes north of the city, go **snow rafting, sliding** and **tubing** on 38 slides; **skate** through a forest; **race go-karts** on an ice-covered track; **snowmobile, ride horseback, dogsled** or take a **sleigh ride**.

In the city, you can **cross-country ski** on the Plains of Abraham (418-649-6476, information; 418-648-4212, trail conditions) or **snowshoe** or **sleigh ride** (418-687-0707). Station Touristique Duchesnay, surrounding the Ice Hotel, 20 minutes north of Quebec, has 150 km. of cross-country trails that wind almost exclusively through evergreens. Side-by-side tracks make cross-country for couples enjoyable. In the spring a stop at the sugar house is a good time.

The Greater Quebec has 1,512 km. of **snowmobile trails**. For rentals and guided tours, try Laurentides Sports Service Inc. in Charlesbourg (418-849-2824); Location S.M. Sport in Loretteville (418-842-2703); or Dion Moto (418-337-2776).

The history and culture of the region is captured in many **museums and interpretation centers** throughout Old Quebec City. Begin with a three-site ticket (C$8.50) for the Musee de la civilisation (85 rue Dalhousie, 418-643-2158), Musee de l'Amerique francaise (2 cote de la Fabrique, 418-692-2843) and Centre d'interpretation de Place-Royale (27 rue Notre-Dame,

418-646-3167). You'll be swallowed up in human adventure, the origins of the French-speaking world and 400 years of Place-Royale—the first permanent French settlement in North America, established in 1608. (Winter hours: 10 a.m.–5 p.m. Tuesday–Sunday; admission is free every Tuesday). Also worth visiting: Musee national des beaux-arts du Quebec (418-643-2150), the national art gallery partly housed in a former prison annexed to the 1933 museum by a glassed-in space (Wednesday has evening hours); Musee du Fort (418-692-2175) with a sound-and-light show about the famous battles of the city; and Musee d'art Inuit Brousseau (418-694-1828), the first museum dedicated exclusively to Inuit art and culture. The Citadelle (418-694-2815) is the largest military fortification in North America still occupied by regular troops and is the official residence of Governor General of Canada. It was built in 1820-1832.

The narrow streets of Le Quartier Petit Champlain, in Vieux-Quebec, are lined with ancient stone buildings housing **boutiques** with traditional and contemporary Canadian artwork, crafts, clothing and more. Artists sell their work on the pedestrian alleyway, Rue du Tresor, off Place d'Armes. The Galeries de la Capitale not only has 250 shops, but an amusement center. Boutique Metiers d'art at 29, Notre-Dame, has a vast collection of local and regional art. Potenciel L'Art de la Table, 27 rue du Petite Champlain, is a cook's heaven of upscale tools, cookbooks and trinkets for the kitchen. Zazu Boutique, 31, rue du Petite Champlain, just down the narrow street, features one-of-a-kind Montreal and Quebec designer women's clothing, such as hand-stitched parkas and coats with fur hoods and fashionable outer clothing for the below-zero temperatures in Quebec.

Getting there and getting around

By air: Fly into Quebec City's Jean-Lesage International Airport. HiverExpress operates an airport-city shuttle for C$24.50 each way; or take a cab, call 418-525-5191; or rent a car.

By car: Stoneham is 20 minutes from Quebec City via Hwy. 73N, taking the Stoneham exit. To get to Mont-Sainte-Anne, take Rte. 138 from Quebec City to St.-Anne-de-Beaupre, then Rte. 360 to the resort. It's about a half hour away. Le Massif is 45 miles east of Quebec City. Take Route 138 to Petite-Riviere-Sainte-Francois, then follow signs to Le Massif.

Getting around: The HiverExpress (418-525-5191) runs shuttles from downtown hotels to Mont-Sainte-Anne, mid-November to April for about C$25 round trip or C$20 one way. Shuttles leave Quebec City at 8 a.m. and 10 a.m. ; return at 4:30 p.m. From the ski area, shuttles leave at 9 a.m.; return 3:30 p.m. Reservations are compulsory (before 7 a.m. on the day of the trip) and may be made through your hotel. Shuttles to Stoneham also are offered.

Accommodations (Cdn$): (double room) $$$$-$200+; $$$-$141-$200; $$-$81-$140; $-$80 and less.
Dining (Cdn$): $$$-Entrees $20+; $$-$10-20; $-less than $10

Tremblant
Quebec, Canada

Summit: 2,871 feet
Vertical: 2,116 feet
Base: 755 feet

Address: 1000 Chemin des Voyageurs
Mont-Tremblant, Quebec Canada J8E 1T1
Telephone (main): 819-681-2000
Snow Report Number: 514-333-8936
Toll-free reservations: 888-857-8043
E-mail: info_tremblant@intrawest.com
Internet: www.tremblant.ca

Expert:★★★
Advanced:★★★★
Intermediate:★★★★
Beginner:★★★★
First-timer:★★★★

Lifts: 13—1 high-speed, 8-person
gondola; 5 high-speed quads;1 quad; 2
triples; 3 moving carpets; 1 cabriolet
Skiable acreage: 628
Snowmaking: 75 percent
Uphill capacity: 27,230
Parks & pipes: 3 parks, 1 pipe
Bed base: 3,500 at resort base
Nearest lodging: Slopeside, hotel & condos
Child care: Yes, 12 months and older
Adult ticket, per day: C$64 (07/08 without tax)
Dining:★★★★
Apres-ski/nightlife:★★★★
Other activities:★★★★

Tremblant is the highest peak in the Laurentians. Slopeside, you'll find a European-style village that gives you everything you need while vacationing here. When the brightly colored tin roofs of the mountain village glisten in the sunlight, they look like a bag of Skittles spilled across the snow. If you've ever been to Quebec City, you'll be convinced it's been moved to the mountains. Village designers wanted to blend man-made structures with nature, to provide intimate surprises with every turn, and they succeeded. The landscape changes with virtually every step: Glimpses of the mountain, or the lake at the foot of the mountain, or welcoming courtyards overlooked by colorful balconies, or rows of roofs tumbling down the mountainside like dominos towards the lake.

Tremblant is now developing another pedestrian village at the foot of the Versant Soleil (south side). Condos and buildings are already popping up—the two resort villages will be linked by a panoramic lift.

For a resort with more than 70 years of ski history, Tremblant is remarkably modern. None of the ski facilities, lodging or retail properties is more than a dozen years old, as all of the current development began in 1995. The village layout, while sprawling along the gradual uphill trek from lake to lifts, is completely engineered to accommodate guest transport, including the cabriolet for people and valets for both skis and cars. The resort works well enough to accommodate up to 12,000 visitors on busy days without significant congestion.

The complete resort experience includes the old village of Mont-Tremblant and the picturesque town of St. Jovite, dripping with Quebecois culture and the French language. Though the employees speak English, the native language here is French, and you will earn big smiles from locals if you give it a try. You get all the fun and excitement of trying out a foreign language with none of the frustration of not being understood. The entire experience is steeped in romance, so you'll win extra brownie points if you bring your lover here. Plus, there's little or no jet lag for North Americans. Keep in mind though, that the summit consistently registers the coldest temperatures south of Hudson's Bay.

Mountain layout

Tremblant is a hulk of a mountain with skiing on four faces. The trail map proclaims "North" and "South" sides, but they'd be more accurately portrayed as Northeast and Southwest. It is easy for skiers to follow the sun: Simply ski on the North Side in the mornings and then move to the South Side for the afternoons. The true south face, Versant Soleil, has 15 intermediate and advanced trails and glades. Most trails are groomed daily. But, 60 percent of the area consists of glades. Most skiers/boarders start on the South Side, site of the base village. On crowded days, savvy locals drive 15 minutes to the North Side, where they can avoid the crowds and get first crack at skiing in the sun.

◆◆**Expert, ◆Advanced:** The most challenging sections of the mountain are in The Edge and Versant Soleil. The Edge is reached by the Letendre trail, which starts halfway down the North Side and brings skiers to the The Edge quad chair. This chair serves only expert and advanced terrain. Only one trail, Action, is cut; the other descents are through the trees. The glades in Reaction and Sensation are thinned enough for strong intermediates, but those dropping down Emotion will push the expert envelope. For bumps, try Dynamite (on Versant North), one of eastern Canada's steepest trails, and Expo, beneath the lift. The drop down Devil's River and into the woods at Boiling Kettle is a rush.

Versant Soleil, accessed by the Le Soleil lift, is 80-percent expert with the bonus of sunshine. Blacks and double-blacks take you through fall-line glades— snow conditions and weather permitting. We didn't find any truly tough glade skiing here, but it was all rollicking fun.

Mostly, the single blacks are excellent choices for advanced skiers/riders, or experts who want to carve steep, narrow pitches. We found quite a range among the single-black trails: Some challenge worthy of the rating, such as Banzai and Le Tunnel; others could have been rated blue cruisers, such as Geant; Dernier Cri, we thought barely deserved a blue rating.

Kandahar is a ripping groomed cruiser, as is Duncan Haut with is great fall line vertical. There are steep drops off the catwalk down Vertige (a double diamond) and Dunzee. Both get bumped in spring. Ryan is one of the original trails, narrow and twisting with short, very manageable stretches of steeps that earn its lower section a double diamond. If you think Ryan is too challenging at the top, bail out on blue-square Charron before the narrow part.

■ **Intermediate:** On the South Side, Grand Prix, Beauvallon and Alpine are great wide-open runs. Kandahar, though rated black, is groomed. It has one steep section, but is a good choice for upper-intermediates. At day's end, Johannsen—a blue stretch at the base that funnels everyone off the mountain—gets bumpy and/or mushy, depending on temperatures.

The North Side appears tough on the trail map, but is more intermediate than advanced. Stay far right or left. Geant, Coyote and Duncan Haut are fine for confident intermediates; in some ways, they're better than blue-rated but traffic-filled Beauchemin and Lowell Thomas.

Franc Sud and Toboggan are challenging runs that allow intermediates a frightening glimpse of some gnarly Versant Soleil terrain. Le Soleil high speed quad provides welcome relief back to the summit of the mountain.

●● **Beginner, ● First-timer:** Le P'tit Bonheur takes beginners from the top of the North Side to the easiest mid-mountain trails, but the going can be slow. Still, most will stick to the South Side. From the top of the Flying Mile lift, beginners head left to La Passe and Nansen bas or right down Standard and Biere-en-bas (named after a shortcut secretly cut by a racer when the staff would race down at the end of the day for beers; winner got to drink for free). Finally, step to the top of the mountain and head down La Crête and all of Nansen. This is a fantastic area to start, but stick to Nansen or Roy Scott at day's end to avoid the crowds.

Novices start on the free moving carpets near the bell (the ski school meeting place). After that, they advance to the Flying Mile lift and Nansen.

Snowboarding

Try to avoid Beauchemin, Geant (long runout) and Le P'tit Bonheur on the North Side. Even skiers need to pole and skate on these runs.

Parks and pipes

Tremblant has dedicated about 40 acres to its terrain parks and superpipe. The 420-foot super-pipe is on the North Side, as is North Park, which also is known as the Intermediate Park. The area is groomed by a state-of-the-art snowpark grooming machine and has rollers, tabletops, spines, bankturns and rails. The park and pipe are reached by, and run alongside of, the Lowell Thomas lift, putting you in full view of folks on the lift. Helmets are mandatory in the park.

The Adrenaline Park is the gated park located just off the South Side's Flying Mile lift. Get a Park Pass at Guest Services and wear a helmet. It has the longest rails and the biggest tabletops and jumps, along with music. Major competitions take place here since it's in full view of the base area. The Progression Park is to the left of Adreneline, off green-rated La Passe.

Cross-country & snowshoeing (see also xcskiresorts.com)

More than 260 km. of cross-country trails and 17 km. for snowshoeing are scattered in the region, most of which are found in **Parc National du Mont-Tremblant** (819-688-2281; park admittance fee). Trails wind through maple and birch forests and provide views of wildlife and lakes. This vast reserve has two reception centers, with ski and snowshoe rentals and 150 km. of trails, 49 km. of which are marked. Pack a lunch and ski to one of the heated huts. Choose among trail degrees of difficulty and length. If you're lucky, guides will stop by a hut to tell about the region's history and the wildlife.

The **Centre de Ski de Fond Mont Tremblant** (819-425-5588) owned by the town, offers more than 100 km. of trails, with 50 km. double-tracked and 12 km. skate-groomed. It's connected to the Multifunctional Trail, which leads to the resort by a bridge crossing over the Diable River. The undulating trails are known for magnificent vistas. But, the majority of the vista vantage points are on diamond and double-diamond trails. The La Diable network has nine trails totaling 49 km. with six heated huts along the way. The Jack Rabbit network has seven trails, 30 km. altogether, with two heated huts. Skis and snowshoes are available for rent, and you can also arrange a trip on marked but ungroomed trails to backcountry bunkhouses.

Choose in-village, inn-to-inn trails in the **Mont Tremblant/St. Jovite region**, a wilderness trek in Parc du Mont-Tremblant, or experience the 200-kilometer **"Le P'tit Train du Nord,"** that runs from St.-Jerome through Mont-Tremblant to Mont-Laurier. St.-Jerome to Ste. Agathe is for cross-country skiing, and Ste. Agathe to Mont-Laurier is for snowmobiling.

Snowshoeing trails on Tremblant's summit are accessed from the gondola. Three-hour guided tours depart Tuesday, Wednesday and Friday afternoons from the **Activity Centre**. Full-day trips are available. Full Moon Snowshoe Outings are offered monthly by **La Source** (819-681-3000, ext. 46533).

Lessons (07/08 prices, without taxes)

Group lessons: C$52-C57 for a 105-minute morning or afternoon session.
First-timer packages: The Learn to Ski/Ride programs are 105-minute lessons with lift ticket and rentals; C$75 at 9:15 a.m. or 11:45 a.m.; C$59 at

1:15 p.m.

Private lessons: A 105-minute private lesson from 10:00 a.m. to 11:45 a.m. costs C$189 for one person, C$359 for two; from 1:15 p.m. to 3:00 p.m., C$155/$300. One hour at 8:45 a.m. or 12 p.m. costs C$105/$189.

Special programs: Ski Week includes three-and-a-half hours of lessons daily, all with the same instructor. Adults and teens pay C$249 to C$273 for four days; children 3-12 pay C$383. The program includes priority access to lifts, a recreational race, farewell dinner, lunchbox and souvenir group picture. Call 866-661-1366.

First Tracks allows riding the Express gondola anytime after 7:15 a.m., for a buffet breakfast at the Grand Manitou summit chalet and skiing beginning at 8 a.m. for C$18 plus lift ticket.

Children's Programs (07/08 prices, without taxes)

Child care: The Kidz Club and day-care center is at the Sommet des Neiges and provides direct access to the Onesime Magic Carpet. It provides care for children ages 12 months to 6 years for C$52-C$68 for a half day, depending on age, morning or afternoon and with/without lunch. A full day with lunch is C$92-$99. For reservations, call 888-857-8043. Check with the concierge at your hotel or condo for babysitting services —the sitter comes to your room.

Children's lessons: Adventure Day is for children 5-12 (ski) and 7-12 (snowboard). Peewee is for ages 3-4. Cost is C$102-C$107 half day, C$109-C$119 full day. The full day includes lunch. A weekend package costs $C209-C$229.

First-timer packages: The Learn to Ski/Ride programs are 105-minute lessons that include lift ticket and rentals. Ages 3-12 pay C$75.

Notes: Get a discount by reserving at least seven days in advance. Call 888-857-8043.

Lift tickets (07/08 prices, without tax)

	Adult	Child (6-12)
One day	C$65	C$39
Three days	C$192	C$115
Five day	C$319	C$192

Who skis at a discount: Seniors (65+) pay: one day C$50, 3 days C$149, 5 days C$248. Youth (13-17) pay: one day C$43, 3 days C$126, 5 days C$210.

Notes: Early-season prices (until Dec. 21) are lower. Pre-purchase tickets with lodging online during special dates and receive one or more free days of skiing. Prices are rounded to the nearest Canadian dollar. Taxes are not included.

Accommodations

Central Reservations (866-783-5630) can book all lodging and has good travel, lodging and ski packages. We list lodging choices in the base village, but there are less expensive alternatives nearby.

At the upper end of the village, the luxurious **Fairmont Tremblant** (866-829-7722; 819-681-7000; $$$-$$$$) is a magnificent stone-and-timber structure with ski-in/walk-out access, shops, restaurants, and health club with indoor and outdoor heated pools. **Le Westin Resort & Spa** (866-783-5630; 819-681-8000; $$$$) is a high-end condo-hotel with ski-in/ski-out access, featuring 126 rooms, an outdoor saltwater pool, 24-hour room service and a world-class spa. The all-suite **Le Sommet des Neiges** (866-783-5630; 819-681-2000; $$$$) is 100 feet from the Express Gondola. Suites have one to three bedrooms and include fireplace, full kitchens, washer and dryer, plus an exercise room, outdoor hot tub and indoor parking.

Ermitage du Lac (819-681-2222, $$$$) is a boutique hotel near the base of the Cabriolet lift at the lower end of the original village. The rooms include a continental breakfast. Their hot tub in front of the hotel sees lots of spirited action. The **Marriott Residence Inn, Manoir Labelle** (866-829-7722; 819-681-4000; $$$-$$$$) is at the lower end of the village. Price includes a continental breakfast. **La Tour Des Voyageurs** (866-783-5630; 819-681-2000; $$$-$$$$) is a condo-hotel with ski-in/ski out access, a swimming pool and exercise room.

Le Country Inn & Suites by Carlson 866-783-5630; 819-681-2000; $$$-$$$$) has comfortably appointed rooms, most with fireplaces and full kitchens, plus a sauna, outdoor hot tub, exercise room and indoor parking. The slopeside **Lodge de la Montagne** (866-783-5630; 819-681-2000; $$$-$$$$) has country-style condominium units, many with gas fireplaces and full kitchens. It has a sauna, outdoor whirlpool, exercise room and indoor parking.

Lining the cobblestone street leading from the Fairmont to La Tour Des Voyageurs are three- to four-story buildings that house restaurants and shops on the ground floor and condos above. The **Saint Bernard (Homewood Suites by Hilton), Johannsen** and **Deslauriers** condos (866-783-5630; $$-$$$) are very roomy and beautifully furnished. Other condo complexes are within 2 miles and have shuttle service to the slopes. **Pinoteau Village** (800-667-2200; $$$-$$$$) and **Condotels du Village** (800-567-6724; $-$$) have kitchens, balconies and fireplaces. Pinoteau Village has cross-country trails outside its doors; Condotels has a clubhouse with a sauna, hot tub and exercise room and pool table.

Central Reservations can book **Club Tremblant** (800-567-8341; $$$-$$$$), where rates include breakfast, dinner and lifts; the luxurious **Intrawest Resort Club** (800-799-3258; $$-$$$$); or condos, inns, motels and historic lodges in Mont-Tremblant and St.-Jovite.

For budget travelers, the **Mont-Tremblant Youth Hostel** (819-425-6008; $) offers four- to 10-bed dorm rooms and private rooms, all with shared baths. The lodge is in the village, about 2 miles from the mountain, and a shuttle (fee charged) stops at the front door. A fully-equipped kitchen is available, but the hostel offers an inexpensive continental breakfast. Guests can relax in a common room with TV, a library and Internet access.

Dining

Dining spans the gamut of options from haut cuisine to **outdoor barbecue venues**, where you can get a hot dog with chips, hamburgers or chicken for less than C$5. Most restaurants on the Place St. Bernard have grills blazing on sunny days.

Near Place St. Bernard: Aux Truffles (819-681-4544; $$$$), is one of our top choices and the most likely Tremblant venue to log a celebrity sighting. The wine list is both extensive and expensive; the cuisine is quintessential French fare at its best. The **Cafe Johannsen** serves soups, bagels, salads, beers, coffee and muffins. **L'Oberoi** (819-681-4555; $-$$) is a deli offering cheeses, pates and cold cuts, sandwiches, fresh breads and other dishes. For the best coffee and good pastries, visit **Au Grain de Cafe** (819-681-4567; $) just off the plaza.

Fat Mardi's Restaurant (819-681-2439; $$-$$$) is a Cajun-style bistro serving some authentic Louisiana cooking to warm up a winter evening. **Le Shack** (819-681-4700; $-$$) has a breakfast buffet; it's *the* spot for people-watching during lunch or an after-ski beer.

In Vieux-Tremblant: La Quintessence Restaurant (819-426-3400; $$$$), located in the Quintessence Hotel on the lake, is hands down the best restaurant at Tremblant. A four diamond experience, La Quintessence combines outstanding gastronomical creations with a 5,000-bottle wine cellar to help steal the culinary show. The three owners of **Creperie Catherine** (819-681-4888; $) used to cook aboard ships. Now, they offer Bretonne-style crepes with any filling you could possibly dream up in a delightful indoor/outdoor building.

Microbrasserie La Diable (819-681-4546; $-$$) serves light meals of European sausages alongside its six unique craft beers brewed on the premises. The beer comes in various strengths—don't mistake a 4 percent Diable for an 8.5 percent Extreme Onction! **La Savoie** (819-681-4573; $$) serves traditional French Alps fare in a cozy French Alpine setting. Everything on the menu is "all-you-can-eat" and prices are per person. The communal dining experience is great. Sit next to the cheese warmer; you'll become an expert in preparing raclette.

La Grappe a Vin (819-681-4727; $$-$$$) is an intimate wine bar where you can order 40 wines by the glass and another 130 by the bottle. Or choose from 43 ports and madeiras, 50 scotches and 30 imported beers. In addition, an oyster bar, wild game pates, local cheeses, fresh soups and salads are available. It's fun apres-ski and perfect for a light dinner.

For a true high-end feast, **Restaurant Yamada** (819-681-4141; $$$-$$$$) in Le Westin Resort specializes in Japanese cuisine emphasizing uncommon flavors. Choose among filet mignon on hot stone, sashimi pizza or seafood delights. **Windigo** (819-681-7685; $$-$$$) at the Fairmont Tremblant lays out a sumptuous theme buffet Thursday through Saturday and also serves Sunday brunch. **Spag & Co.** (819-681-4444; $$) has a family-friendly array of pastas, steak and wines. **La Chouquetterie** (819-681-4509; $) serves drop-dead pastries; try the cream puff Tropez style. **Queues de Castor** (819-681-4678; $), a.k.a BeaverTails®, is a tiny take-out spot serving a traditional Canadian pastry similar to fried dough. It's called a Beavertail because that's exactly what it looks like. It's sinfully yummy.

The Italian gourmet **Coco Pazzo Deli** (819-681-4774; $) sells cheeses, salamis, prosciutto and dry pastas. Around the corner at its restaurant, **Coco Pazzo** ($$$$), the menu includes roasted rack of lamb, spice rubbed and grilled veal chop and herb-encrusted sea bass, plus an interesting variety of pastas. **Les Artistes** (819-681-4606; $-$$$$) is a traditional French bistro. Enjoy offerings at the wine bar or on the terrace overlooking Lake Miroir. Smoked meats are a specialty in the Laurentians; **Moe's** (819-425-9821; $-$$), in St. Jovite, has the the region's best.

On the hill: For lunch, the **Grand Manitou**, at 3,000 feet atop the the Laurentians' highest peak, features hot meals, for $7 to $10, plus sandwiches to order, pizza, fries and hot dogs.

 ## Apres-ski/nightlife

Since many of the hot spots also are restaurants, see Dining for more information.

On sunny days, the best apres-Ski is on the terraces of **Place St. Bernard**, where a stage often is set up with a live bands. People sit in chairs with brews, enjoy the sun, listen to the music and watch everyone coming off the slopes looking for their friends.

La Grappe a Vin is the place for fine wine or liquors and light fare. **Microbrasserie La Diable** has canned music, good sausages for late-night snacks and six beers brewed on-site. **Le Shack** is a bit louder and often has a live band on the weekends. The whimsical decor of trees and flying geese overhead makes you feel like you're outdoors. The dancing never stops here; be prepared for a lot of apres-ski exercise. Each Saturday has a different apres-ski theme.

Cafe d'Époque in Vieux Tremblant sports strobe lights, loud live music (also CDs) and lots of bodies pressed together on the crowded rustic wood dance floor. OK at night, but a bit of a pit when exposed to daylight. **P'tit Caribou** ,also in Vieux Tremblant, gets high ratings from Canadian magazines. Great loud music and bar-top dancing by go-go girl wannabes. The people and noise make a wild party ambience. Be ready to stay up far too late into the night.

Other activities

At Tremblant, you can take a **sleigh ride**, **ice skate** on Lac Miroir, go **dogsledding** (you can mush the dogs yourself) **horseback riding**, **ice climbing** or **snowmobiling**. There's a **tubing park** in St. Jovite.

For a true Nordic experience, visit Le Scandinave (819-425-5524) for the **Scandinavian baths**. Start in a Finnish sauna or steam bath, then plunge into cold water under a waterfall, in a pool or in the local river. Warm back up in the outdoor hot tub, the sauna or steam bath. Repeat! Two or three hours of this affordable indulgence leaves you thoroughly refreshed.

The Spa-sur-le-Lac at Club Tremblant (819-425-8341) offers a more traditional experience with 11 **body-care and aesthetic rooms** and a **beauty salon**. The Amerispa Le Westin Resort Tremblant (819-681-7080) and The Fairmont Tremblant (819-681-7680) offer **complete spa services** including facials, manicures and massages.

Aquaclub La Source (819-681-5668), billed as "A Lake in the Laurentians," lets guests escape winter. This **family-oriented spa** includes an **exercise room** and a **lake** created to evoke the Laurentian outdoors complete with **beach, waterfall** and Tarzan-style **rope swing**. Book treatments, such as **sauna, steam bath, outdoor hot tubs, massage and other services** for those age 18 and older, at the Activity Centre (819-681-4848).

The village has about 45 **shops**. Some of the fanciest are in the Fairmont Tremblant. Chocoholics will want to make fast tracks to the Rocky Mountain Chocolate Factory, where they'll find creamy fudge and crunchy toffee. The village also has a two-screen **movie theater**.

To book any activity, call the Activity Center, 88-TREMBLANT or 819-681-4848. For more information, you can reach the Mont-Tremblant Tourism Office at 819-425-2434.

Getting there and getting around

By air: The nearest major airport is Montreal, 75 miles away. Most major airlines serve this airport from the U.S. and elsewhere in Canada. From mid-December to mid-April, Continental offers daily service from Newark to Tremblant itself.

By car: From Montreal, take autoroute 15 north to Sainte-Agathe. Merge with 117. Continue on autoroute 117 north past St. Jovite. About two kilometers (a little more than a mile) past the town, take exit #119, onto Montée Ryan. Follow blue signs to Tremblant.

Getting around: Most visitors arrive by car, so rent one if you fly into Montreal. And then to get some use from the car, we suggest side trips to Mont Tremblant Village and St. Jovite, or even some of the smaller ski areas in the surrounding area.

Packing tip: Bring shoes with good traction. The cobblestone street is fairly steep. Though it has shallow steps built along each side, most people walk in the street (no vehicles are allowed). It can be slippery late at night and early in the morning after melted snow re-freezes.

Nearby skiing

Gray Rocks, Mont-Tremblant (Quebec)

819-425-2771; 800-567-6767 Internet: www.grayrocks.com.
5 lifts: 1 quad, 3 doubles, 1 surface lift;
22 trails; 620 vertical feet

Gray Rocks is a mouse compared to Tremblant. It's a well-kept secret of the people of Montréal. Located only a few miles from the hulking Tremblant, this diminutive ski resort is obsessed with instruction, taking great pride in time-tested programs to create new skiers and riders, to develop ski and snowboard racers and to fine tune the technique of everybody who visits this surprisingly busy place. The resort is designed around all-inclusive ski weeks, which have been promoted continuously since 1951. Very little is lacking in the Gray Rocks ski package, which encompasses lodging, lift tickets, superb instruction, video analysis, spa privileges, souvenir photo and entertainment. Even the tips are built in. Top it off with a picturesque lakeside resort hotel (got skates?), and pound for pound Gray Rocks packs a pretty powerful ski vacation into a seemingly small package.

Gray Rocks offers a mainly intermediate terrain that wrap most of the way around the mountain, using a lot of double fall lines, moguls and terrain features to add challenge to solidly blue square runs. Snowboarding is quite popular here, but the rider-specific terrain is limited to a medium size terrain park.

Part of the success is creating group camaraderie, on and off the slopes. Since people learn best when they are relaxed and having fun, Gray Rocks considers its off-slope program as important as the lessons on the hill. Nightly entertainment, oui. But après-ski also has such creative alternatives as a cooking course, French lessons, wine-and-cheese get-togethers, classical guitar concerts, sleigh rides, a spa and fitness center - the list goes on. Gray Rocks has a day care and "Ski'N'Play" program for children. It even has a pet kennel.

While it is possible to purchase a la carte, Gray Rocks puts enough value in the ski packages to require little analysis. As of the 2007-08 seasons, one-night packages start at C$109 and six-night packages range from C$1232 to C$1630 depending on time period and accommodations.

The Valley of Saint-Sauveur Resorts

Saint-Sauveur des Monts (Quebec); (450) 227-4671; (514) 871-0101
Internet: www.montsaintsauveur.com
(Note: Telephone numbers link a caller to anything from mountain information to lodging reservations. Although the message is in French, there is an option to choose English. It works.)

Mont Saint-Sauveur, rising from the village of Saint-Sauveur, is the anchor property in a group of five ski areas that make up the Saint-Sauveur Valley. Collectively, the area features more than 30 lifts and 100 ski runs, about half of which are found at Mont Saint-Sauveur and its smaller twin, Mont Avila. With common ownership and geography, advanced snowmaking and two thirds of the runs open at night, this valley packs of a lot of skiing and riding into each season.

The commonality of the village, the valley and their Laurentian culture is where the similarities end. Each of the areas maintains its own little base village and the hills all ski differently. Glades are abundant, as are snowboarding and freestyle elements, but with average vertical of 675 feet, most runs are quick, albeit sometimes steep. While Mont Saint-Sauveur is the largest area with the most advanced snowmaking, Ski Morin Heights is known as the expert area and Ski Mont Gabriel is considered the snowboarding Mecca. The fifth area, Mont Olympia, is tamer and caters to beginners and families.

Lodging, retail and dining options are considerable. From the Manoir Saint-Sauveur, a four star property in the heart of the village, to numerous condos and family-run B&Bs, the valley has a large stock of diverse lodging options. More than 60 restaurants meet every budget expectation and shopping keeps the off-slope hours enjoyable.

Mont Saint-Sauveur and Mont Avila
Mont Saint-Sauveur: 8 lifts; 38 trails; 142 acres; 699 vertical feet
Mont Avila: 3 lifts; 11 trails; 35 acres; 615 vertical feet

Mont Saint-Sauveur and Mont Avila are considered two separate resorts, but they are actually linked together across the face of three hills with only a property-line boundary. Mont Saint-Sauveur is the "in spot" of the Valley with the highest vertical and most skiable acres. It has the most advanced and intermediate trails of the five with snowmaking on all 142 acres, so if you like to cruise, this is for you. It holds the record for the longest ski season in Quebec with about 180 days thanks to high-tech snowmaking.

Mont Avila also has a snow park for snow tubing and snow rafting, as well as ice-skating and snowshoeing opportunities. Like many Laurentian ski resorts, this hill opens a window on the Quebequois culture, with the "Erabliere" sugar shack where the traditional maple syrup on snow is served. Mont Avila has a snow tubing park and snow rafting, ice skating and snowshoeing, and is within walking distance from the village of Saint-Sauveur.

Ski Morin Heights
6 lifts; 23 trails; 90 acres; 656 vertical feet

Ski Morin Heights is characterized as the best-kept secret in the Laurentians. The resort offers a mix of snowsport activities: Skiing, snowboarding, back-country telemarking, cross-country and snowshoeing. If you enjoy expert glade skiing, Kicking Horse (skier's right on the edge of the area) will keep you grinning. Or move over a bit to eight more expert runs right next door. Although it accommodates all levels, this is the hill for the advanced and expert skier. It has the most double-blacks/blacks in the five-resort area. The village of Morin-Heights is at the base adjacent to the largest cross-country ski facility in the area, with 175 km. of trails.

Mont Olympia

6 lifts; 23 trails; 140 acres; 656 vertical feet

Mont Olympia has the best selection of trails for beginners and youngsters. Most of the runs are greens and blues, but with three double-blacks and three blacks, experts will find challenging terrain, so it's a great family hill. Mont Olympia gets more sun than any of the other Valley resorts and is best known for its Snow School and Olympic skier Jean-Luc Brassard.

Ski Mont Gabriel

7 lifts; 18 trails; 80 acres; 656 vertical feet

Ski Mont Gabriel is the only resort in the Valley to reserve half the mountain for snowboarding. It has a terrain park and a jumping site served by a dedicated surface lift. This area has served as the official site of the Canadian Freestyle Championships and has superb learning programs. Split between Mountain 1 and Mountain 2, Mont Gabriel is a snowboarding haven with mostly cruisers and carving runs. The section between its two mountains (simply named Mountain 1 and Mountain 2) has a big green area for the first-timers and beginners. Mountain 2 is snowboarder's heaven, but there are also some blue runs down from the top. Temperature-wise, this is the warmest ski area of the five resorts.

Eastern Townships, Canada

Mont Orford, Mont Sutton, Owl's Head and Bromont

The Eastern Townships' marketing efforts would have you believe that the four ski areas in the region—Sutton, Orford, Bromont and Owl's Head—are right next door to each other, but in reality they are from 20 to 45 minutes away from each other on dry roads.

If you're planning to visit all the areas, consider the interchangeable Townships Ski Ticket. Reserve when booking your lodging or purchase at any of the participating resorts.

Mont Orford; (819) 843-6548; (866) 673-6731
Internet: www.orford.com
7—1 6-passenger hybrid gondola, 2 quads, 1 triple, 1 double, 2 surface; 244 skiable acres; 1,772 feet vertical drop.

Mont Orford is operated under a long-term lease on government land within Parc du Mont-Orford. The resort is spread across three separate mountain peaks and has fabulous terrain for all abilities. Adventurous skiers will be challenged here and you will be completely surprised because at first glance the mountain looks rather tame. The trails are long, giving skiers and riders maximum use of the vertical drop, and follow the contours of the mountain.

Triple-diamond labels are a bit hyped, but experts won't be disappointed either. If you're looking for woods, unload from Le Quad du Village and stay along the top of the headwall. A new experience for using the woods, you'll see signs for various woods shots off the trails. No matter which way you go, you won't be disappointed. If it's in-bounds, you may ski it.

For those who prefer trails to woods, don't worry, be happy. Trois-Ruisseaux and Maxi on Mont Orford are especially delightful and both are groomed in the middle of the day, which is a special treat since these are popular trails. Trois-Ruisseaux is a winding trail, narrow in spots with nice steep pitches. Maxi, on the other hand, is steep and goes straight down the mountain. Watch out, you'll pick up lots of speed before you know it.

The intermediate trails on Mont Alfred-Desrochers are winding and rolling, sometimes narrow, but with a steady pitch and no unexpected steeps. A wonderful experience! Because the chair is a bit out of the way, you'll find these trails relatively uncrowded.

Sutton My Mountain Resort!; (450) 538-2545; (866) 538-2545
Internet: www.mt-sutton.com
9 lifts—1 high-speed quad, 2 quads, 6 doubles; 174 skiable acres; 1,500 feet vertical drop.

A trip to Sutton is a step back in time. The resort made its debut in 1960 and still has some of its original chair lifts, which you board after working your way through a lift line of wooden fences and passing ticket-checker booths that look like little red-trimmed log cabins. All around you, skiers and riders decked out in the latest gear and apparel chatter away in French. Which reminds us to tell you that Sutton and the nearby town may just be one of the friendliest places we've ever visited. Everyone seems to know everyone, and if they don't know you, they act like they do. By the way, just say bonjour or merci and everyone happily switches to English (yes, your accent will give you away!).

At first glance, Sutton appears to be a small area, but it skis like a large resort. Trails and glades take you all over the mountain before reaching the bottom. Ability levels are generally separated from each other: Beginner terrain is on the far right; intermediate terrain is in the middle; expert terrain is to the far left. Two lifts in the middle of the mountain also serve beginner terrain.

Glades, or sous-bois, clearly set this mountain apart from others. They were cut in 1960, long before other resorts even thought of glades, and are thinned enough to groom—not often, because they're most fun in the powder. How to ski this mountain? Follow where your skis take you; you'll go a different way every run. Trails follow the true fall line. You're constantly winding your way down the mountain. Trails are also usually left au naturel—only 13 are groomed nightly, and fewer than that on a powder day. Are you getting the message yet? This charming retro resort gets a lot of powder and that's what the skiers here like, so the owners don't mess with it. Speaking of the owners, the same family that opened the resort still runs it, with great affection and respect for the mountain and its guests.

Ski Bromont; Bromont (Quebec); (450) 534-2200; 1-866 BROMONT (276-6668)

Internet: www.skibromont.com
7 lifts—2 high-speed quad, 4 quads, 1 surface lift; 250 skiable acres; 1,329 feet vertical drop.

Bromont, the Eastern Townships ski area closest to Montreal, can be a very busy place, particularly at night. Québécois love their night skiing and Bromont fills that fancy very well. About 75 percent of the terrain, including the terrain park, is lighted for the night skiing which goes till 10 p.m. Sunday through Thursday and 10:45 p.m. Friday and Saturday.

The close proximity to Montreal ensures steady business and a lively night life. Indeed, six times during the season the resort stages Nuit Blanche, or "white night," in which you can ski or ride from 7 p.m.– 3 a.m. for C$21.75 (plus tax). These events are extremely popular, especially with the college and 20-something set, with high-powered dancing and partying in the bar until the wee hours.

Although the trail map is dominated by diamonds, the trails are really intermediate. Experts and advanced skiers will find that the cruisers are a great way to give tired legs a break after skiing hard all week at Mont Orford or Mont Sutton. Grooming is meticulous, and on weekends trails are groomed three times a day. Most skiers will want to spend only a day here because of limited terrain, but the area's expansion onto its eastern face, in a section called Versant du Lac, helps to add texture and terrain.

The mountain has a lower elevation than other resorts in the area so it often rains here when it snows elsewhere. Bromont gives you 30 minutes to test conditions—if you're not pleased, exchange your ticket for a coupon to return at no extra charge.

Owl's Head; Mansonville (Quebec); (800) 363 3342 for lodging

Internet: www.owlshead.com or info@owlshead.com
8 lifts—3 high-speed quads, 1 quad, 4 doubles; 120 skiable acres; 14,400 skiers/hr uphill capacity; 1,772 feet vertical.

Owl's Head is named after the Abenaki Indian's greatest chief, Owl, whose spirit will live forever through the naming of the mountain in his honor. The minute you get off the lift, any lift, you'll be awestruck by the views. Lake Memphremagog is below the base, and you often feel as if you'll ski right off the edge of the mountain into the lake. No kidding: The magnificent views are comparable to skiing in the Tahoe region of California. This is a lovely mountain; perfect for families and groups that want gentle skiing and nicely groomed trails and a few glades. However, it is small and most will not want to ski here for an entire week unless you have young children.

Index
downhill and cross-country
resorts alphabetically